ACCOUNTING TODAY

ACCOUNTING TODAY

PRINCIPLES AND APPLICATIONS

MARK F. ASMAN, Ph.D., C.P.A., C.D.P.
Professor of Accounting and MIS
Bowling Green State University

SCOTT S. COWEN, D.B.A., C.M.A.
Dean and Professor of Accounting, Weatherhead School of Management
Case Western Reserve University

STEVEN L. MANDELL, D.B.A., J.D.
Associate Professor of Accounting and MIS
Bowling Green State University

WEST PUBLISHING COMPANY
St. Paul ■ New York ■ Los Angeles ■ San Francisco

COPY EDITOR: Deborah Smith
COMPOSITOR: Parkwood Composition Service
ARTWORK: John Foster
COVER ARTWORK: *#6, 1983* by Karl Benjamin. Reproduced with permission of the artist.

A study guide has been developed to assist you in mastering concepts presented in this text. The study guide is available from your local bookstore under the title *Study Guide to Accompany Accounting Today: Principles and Applications* prepared by John F. Wells, Larry Larson, and Arlene Mayzel.

Photo Credits

1 (top) courtesy of Ernst & Whinney; **1 (middle)** courtesy of Luis Castaneda, The Image Bank; **1 (bottom)** courtesy of Deloitte Haskins & Sells; **2** courtesy of Ernst & Whinney; **6** courtesy of Lou Jones, The Image Bank; **7** courtesy of Deloitte Haskins & Sells; **8** courtesy of Luis Castaneda, The Image Bank; **10** courtesy of Ernst & Whinney.

All photos appearing in the Application sections are courtesy of the featured companies.

50 West Kellogg Boulevard
P.O. Box 64526
St. Paul, MN 55164-1003

Printed in the United States of America

Library of Congress Cataloging-in-Publication Data

Asman, Mark F.
Accounting today.

Includes index.
1. Accounting. I. Cowen, Scott S. II. Mandell, Steven L. III. Title.
HF5635.A84 1986 657 85-29552
ISBN 0-314-69644-X
1st Reprint—1986

To my parents, Catherine and Lawrence
Mark F. Asman

To my students at the Weatherhead School of Management
Scott S. Cowen

To the students and faculty of Bowling Green State University
Steven L. Mandell

CONTENTS IN BRIEF

CONTENTS

CHAPTER 4
THE ACCOUNTING CYCLE CONCLUDED PREPARATION OF FINANCIAL STATEMENTS 107

APPENDIX A
COMPUTERS AND ACCOUNTING 153

PART 5 ■ COST SYSTEMS 617

CHAPTER 20
MANUFACTURING COST SYSTEMS 647

CHAPTER 21
STANDARD COSTS 677

CHAPTER 24 COST-VOLUME-PROFIT ANALYSIS 765

CHAPTER 25 DECISION MAKING WITH A LOOK AT THE IMPACT OF TAXES 793

APPENDIX F
INTERNATIONAL ACCOUNTING 865

APPENDIX G
ACCOUNTING FOR NON-PROFIT ORGANIZATIONS 877

PREFACE

Accounting Today: Principles and Applications is designed for a comprehensive first course in accounting for students with no prior exposure to either accounting or business. The text is designed to satisfy the needs of both majors and nonmajors, and is intended for use in either a two semester or two/three quarter sequence course in accounting.

The importance of producing a high quality, accurate principles of accounting text has been an overriding concern throughout the writing process of *Accounting Today*. The text has undergone five drafts, each painstakingly reviewed by numerous qualified accounting instructors. The fourth draft was thoroughly class tested in addition to being tested in an industrial training environment. Finally, after typesetting, the accounting firm of Arthur Young checked the accuracy of all examples, exercises, problems and solutions. Every effort has been made to ensure an accurate, reliable, well-written textbook.

A comprehensive set of supporting materials has been developed to assist students in their learning effort and instructors with their teaching responsibilities. Materials available to students include microcomputer software (spreadsheets and tutorials), a software manual, working papers, a study guide, three practice sets, and check figures for each problem. Instructor's materials include an instructor's resource manual, solutions manual, transparency sets, practice set solutions manual, a test bank (both manual and computerized versions), and preprinted examinations.

This text package has been designed to answer the challenge of the rapidly growing integration of microcomputers into the principles of accounting course. Following Chapter 4 is an Appendix entitled Computers and Accounting which explores the role of computers in the accounting field and explains some of the implications of the new technology on accounting methods. The supplemental package includes computer assisted instructional software (13 modules) which will greatly help students understand key concepts. Additionally two problems at the end of every chapter are identified with a microcomputer logo. These problems can be solved on a computer using either the Westcalc spreadsheet (provided to qualified adopters of this text) or LOTUS 1-2-3. Appropriate templates are also provided, and a workbook to guide students in using spreadsheets to solve accounting problems is available.

As expressed in the title of this book, it is important that students both understand accounting principles and be able to apply them in real world settings. Accounting principles and the conceptual reasons for handling a given transaction in a particular fashion are presented in a carefully balanced manner. Concepts are applied to transactions illustrating the accounting process and to development of accounting reports, both internal and external. For students completing their study of accounting with this text, a sound foundation is provided for using and understanding accounting reports in their business careers. For students continuing into more advanced accounting courses, the conceptual material and its application to transactions forms the basis for advanced understanding.

Accounting Today is a complete text covering first a thorough presentation of financial material followed by comprehensive coverage of managerial topics. Notice that we refer to managerial accounting rather than cost accounting. Although the basic cost accounting systems are presented, the managerial/cost section of the text emphasizes understanding cost accounting and its role in the decision making process. In this way both the non-accounting major and the prospective accounting major are served. The non-accounting major who understands the accounting data framework will be better equipped to make intelligent decisions when relying on reports drawn from the system. The accounting major who understands the needs of managers will be better equipped to provide necessary information.

Finally, this text will aid the student in becoming an active participant in the learning process. While the problem material is based on chapter presentations, solutions will require more than a simple mechanical approach. The explanations and illustrations in the text will aid students in understanding and applying the concepts.

FEATURES

Part Division

The book is divided into six parts following a logical sequence of material beginning with an introduction to the framework of accounting and ending with managerial planning, control, and decision making.

Marginal Glossary

Key accounting terms are highlighted and clearly defined in a marginal glossary within each chapter and in a comprehensive glossary at the end of the text. Unnecessary technical jargon is minimized and every effort is made to provide a reading level, writing style, and format to maximize student comprehension and enjoyment.

Chapter Objectives

Chapters open with a clear and concise statement of learning objectives. These objectives are stated in terms of what the student will learn as he or she proceeds through the material.

Concept Summaries

Each chapter contains one or more concept summaries, important concepts synthesized into chart or tabular form. Concept summaries are strategically placed for maximum benefit.

Highlights

Every chapter contains a highlight providing an interesting and informative discussion point and/or application of materials to the real world. These highlights serve to solidify concepts and provide practical, interesting examples of text materials.

Demonstration Problems

At the end of key chapters demonstration problems are included which walk the student through a problem situation applying the materials in the chapter. These problems are designed to help the student achieve success when working on the assigned homework.

Point-by-Point Summary

Each chapter ends with a concise summary. Summary points are short, to the point, and convey essential facts so that students can quickly review important chapter coverage.

Questions

At the end of each chapter are ten questions designed to focus student attention on the key conceptual points contained within the chapter.

Exercises

Each exercise focuses on one important concept to reinforce student understanding. There are seven exercises following each chapter and five exercises following every appendix.

Problem Sets

Two parallel problem sets (A and B) follow each chapter. The problems are all labeled and range from those focused exclusively on one point or concept to comprehensive problems that require substantial student integration of text materials. The problems included on the tutorial software and those workable on the spreadsheets are identified with distinctive logos.

Appendices for Extended Coverage

Recognizing that different educational settings have different coverage needs, a series of appendices are included that provide a broader range of topics than is typically found in many principles texts. Appendices are included for Accounting and Computers, Special Journals and Ledgers, Inflation Accounting, Present Value Concepts, Income Taxation, International Accounting, and Not-for-Profit Accounting. Each of these appendices is designed to provide the student with an overview of the topic covered.

Applications

One of the most difficult tasks facing accounting instructors in principles courses is relating classroom instruction to the real world. To assist instructors in this effort, we have placed application cases taken from real companies at the end of each of the six text parts. Each application shows how a corporation implements the concepts presented in the preceding part. Each application presents a short history of the company, a description of the company's activities or product line, and a presentation of material relevant to the text part just completed, followed by a short series of questions requiring the student to apply knowledge gained in the preceding section.

In addition, actual examples from real companies are used throughout the text to illustrate materials covered. These illustrations are drawn from the annual reports of the corporations themselves.

SUPPLEMENTAL MATERIALS

Most accounting instructors face a difficult task in finding the time to teach all of the varied topics required in an introductory accounting course. To ease the preparation and teaching burden of instructors and to aid the students in synthesizing and understanding the masses of material in introductory accounting, a comprehensive set of support materials is available.

Instructor's Manual

This manual provides direct classroom lecture support including lesson outline suggestions, alternate teaching examples, and assignment suggestions for each chapter and appendix in the test. Alternative course outlines for semester and quarter coverages of the text are included.

Solutions Manual

A complete solutions manual for all end of chapter questions, exercises, problem assignments, appendix exercises, and application case questions is provided. The manual also includes assignment suggestions and alternative course outlines for semester and quarter coverage of the text.

Transparencies

A complete set of transparencies for all problems, alternative lecture examples, and concept summaries is available. Special care has been exercised to ensure that the transparencies are made from large-print masters so that student visibility in large classrooms is enhanced.

Test Bank

A complete test bank is available in both manual and computerized (Westest and Microtest) versions. A comprehensive set of true-false, multiple choice, and short exercise problems has been prepared for each chapter.

Preprinted Tests

Preprinted tests are available, both achievement tests and comprehensive exams, drawn from the master test bank.

Check Figures

A list of check figures with one figure provided for each problem in the text is available.

Working Papers

A two volume set of working papers (Volume 1 covers chapters 1–18; Volume 2 covers chapters 15–26) is available for student purchase. Care was exercised in the preparation of these working papers so that students are provided guidance in assignment preparation but still must think through the process to maximize the learning benefits of problem assignments.

Practice Sets

Three practice sets (two financial and one managerial) are available for student purchase. Each of these practice sets has been carefully designed to reinforce materials in the text through simulation of a real business environment. The first financial practice set emphasizes understanding the accounting cycle. The second financial practice set and the managerial practice set are designed to integrate the full range of financial and managerial topics respectively.

Student Study Guide

A student study guide designed to assist students with each of the chapters and appendices in the text is available for student purchase. The study guide provides a review of important chapter points and a self-test for each chapter so that students can assess their own understanding of the text materials.

Microcomputer Tutorial Software

A set of 13 computer-based tutorial modules is available free to qualified adopters. Each tutorial module is designed to help the student understand key material in either financial accounting (9 modules) or managerial/cost accounting (4 modules). Each module is built around a problem from the end-of-chapter problem sets.

Each module begins with a restatement of the problem on the computer screen and then poses a series of questions to the student. Answering each question requires the student to analyze the problem fact pattern and key in a solution. Incorrect solutions are analyzed and hints and/or on-line tutorials and examples are provided as needed.

Use of the tutorial modules does not require any prior programming or computer knowledge. The system is implemented as a menu-driven system. Each module allows the student to learn the material at his/her own pace with as much or as little review and explanation as he/she requires.

Spreadsheet System

The Westcalc spreadsheet system along with two problem templates from each chapter are available free to qualified adopters. Problem templates can also be used with LOTUS 1-2-3 for those who wish to use that system. Each template is similar in format to a traditional working paper with appropriate headings and work space.

Students are required to key in numbers, formulas, or labels, as appropriate, to complete the problem solution. Each number, formula, or label required as student input has been selected to focus the student's attention on key concepts. While eliminating drudgery (the spreadsheet system automatically provides many totals where arithmetic is the only skill needed), the system design has been carefully thought out to reinforce accounting understanding, not simply act as an electronic replacement for pencil and paper.

While prior familiarity with computers and spreadsheets is helpful, all necessary instructions are supplied with the system and key commands are on the screen for easy reference.

Spreadsheet Manual/Workbook

Using Spreadsheets with *Accounting Today* is available for student purchase. The manual provides general guidance to students in using spreadsheets with Westcalc and LOTUS 1-2-3 with examples and exercises. The textbook template problems are repeated along with notes, procedures, check figures, and template layout forms.

ACKNOWLEDGMENTS

It is difficult to properly thank all who supported and worked with us during the last five years in developing and class testing *Accounting Today*. We are indebted to a large number of colleagues throughout the country as well as to our students for their constructive comments and suggestions that led to improvements in the manuscript culminating in this text. Over the five years that we worked on this text, literally hundreds of individuals were involved. Space considerations do not permit us to mention all of these support people without whose help we could not have succeeded.

Some of the reviewers whose impact can be found in this text are

C. Wayne Alderman
Auburn University
Alabama

Mary B. Alexander
Indiana University

Enzo Allegretti
Westchester Community College
New York

Robert Allen, Jr.
Cerritos College
California

Wilton T. Anderson
Oklahoma State University

Joseph P. Aubert
Bemidji State University
Minnesota

David Bayley
Santa Monica College
California

Gary P. Briggs
State University of New York at Brockport

Bruce O. Bublitz
University of Alabama

Thomas A. Buchman
University of Colorado

David Buehlmann
University of Nebraska, Omaha

Ruth H. Bullard
University of Texas, San Antonio

Raymond J. Castaldi
Towson State University
Maryland

Gyan Chandra
Miami University
Ohio

John K. Cheever
California State Polytechnic University, Pomona

Ronald C. Clute
Loyola University of Chicago
Illinois

Kenneth L. Coffey
Johnson County Community College
Kansas

Dennis Daily
University of Minnesota

Rosemary W. Damon
Canada College
California

Patricia E. Elliott
University of New Mexico

Kenneth Elvik
Iowa State University

Irvin Feldman
Jersey City College
New York

Michael Filippelli
Bryant College
Rhode Island

Paul S. Foote
New York University

Robert Garrett
American River College
California

Louis Geller
Queens College
New York

Dennis Gordon
University of Akron
Ohio

Betsy C. Goss
University of Massachusetts

Raymond Green
Texas Tech University

Jack O. Hall
Western Kentucky University

Nabil Hassan
Wright State University
Ohio

Richard L. Hodges
Western Michigan University

George C. Holdren
University of Nebraska, Lincoln

Cynthia Holloway
Tarrant County Jr. College, Northeast Campus
Texas

Raymond T. Holmes
Virginia Commonwealth University

Dick Howe
Orange Coast College
California

George Ihorn
El Paso Community College
Texas

Antoine G. Jabbour
California State Polytechnic University, Pomona

Elise G. Jancura
Cleveland State University
Ohio

Catherine T. Jeppson
California State University, Northridge

Edward H. Julius
California State University, Northridge

J. Roland Kelley
Tarrant County Junior College, Northeast Campus
Texas

Sam Kniffen
University of South Dakota

Lawrence L. Kogut
Hillsborough Community College
Florida

Charles A. Konkol
University of Wisconsin, Milwaukee

Geraldine Kruse
Eastern Michigan University

Gerald Ludwig
West Los Angeles College

James F. McKinnie
Tennessee Technological University

Leslie L. McNelis
University of Texas, San Antonio

Patti A. Mills
Indiana State University

Joseph L. Morris
Arkansas State University

Ronald Moseley
Chicago State University

Roger P. Murphy
Iowa State University

Jacob B. Paperman
Wright State University
Ohio

Ron Pawliczek
Boston College

Margaret C. Reap
North Harris County College
Texas

Richard L. Rogers
Indiana University

Victoria S. Rymer
American University
Washington, D.C.

John R. Simon
Northern Illinois University

H. Lee Schlorff
Bentley College
Massachusetts

David Schmedel
Amarillo College
Texas

Richard J. Schmidt
California Polytechnic State University, San Luis Obispo

Mary J. Swanson
Mankato State University
Minnesota

Kirk Lee Tennant
Southern Methodist University
Texas

Richard L. Townsend
University of Tennessee

James P. Trebby
Marquette University
Wisconsin

Russell G. Vermillion
Prince Georges Community College
Virginia

DuWayne A. Wacker
University of North Dakota

Jackie G. Williams
Virginia Commonwealth University

Lee C. Wilson
Mesa Community College
Arizona

Gil Zuckerman
North Carolina State University

The corporations featured in the Applications have provided invaluable assistance: to each we express appreciation. In particular, we would like to acknowledge the assistance of Albert J. Weatherhead, III and Curtis Brown, Weatherchem Corporation; the late Herbert Summers of American Metal Treating Company; and Frederick Downey, John Campi, and Harold Gueritey of Parker Hannifin Corporation. We also owe the management of Parker Hannifin gratitude for allowing us to pilot test sections of the book with their employees.

Thanks are also due to Donna Pulschen, Beth Quinn, Marcia Strachan, Wendy Grant, Robert Knight, Martin Logies, Lynn Carlson, Joe McAleese, Annette Tomal, and Jeanalice Brickman for their help in manuscript preparation, research, review and administrative support.

We are particularly indebted to Patricia E. Cooke of Bowling Green State University for her tireless work on our behalf throughout the entire five-year development cycle, and Marjorie Feldman for her effort in coordinating the administrative and technical aspects of the management accounting section of the book.

We appreciate the participation of Arthur Young and Company, who reviewed all examples, exercises, problems and their solutions to ascertain that we were accurate in our presentation of these materials.

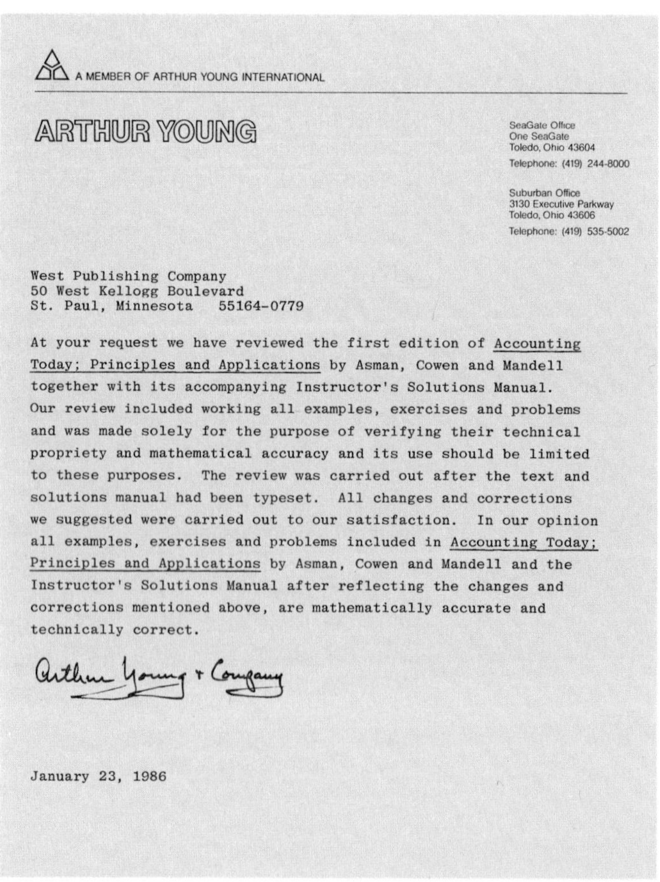

A MEMBER OF ARTHUR YOUNG INTERNATIONAL

ARTHUR YOUNG

SeaGate Office
One SeaGate
Toledo, Ohio 43604
Telephone: (419) 244-8000

Suburban Office
3130 Executive Parkway
Toledo, Ohio 43606
Telephone: (419) 535-5002

West Publishing Company
50 West Kellogg Boulevard
St. Paul, Minnesota 55164-0779

At your request we have reviewed the first edition of Accounting Today; Principles and Applications by Asman, Cowen and Mandell together with its accompanying Instructor's Solutions Manual. Our review included working all examples, exercises and problems and was made solely for the purpose of verifying their technical propriety and mathematical accuracy and its use should be limited to these purposes. The review was carried out after the text and solutions manual had been typeset. All changes and corrections we suggested were carried out to our satisfaction. In our opinion all examples, exercises and problems included in Accounting Today; Principles and Applications by Asman, Cowen and Mandell and the Instructor's Solutions Manual after reflecting the changes and corrections mentioned above, are mathematically accurate and technically correct.

Arthur Young + Company

January 23, 1986

AN INVITATION TO THE STUDY OF ACCOUNTING

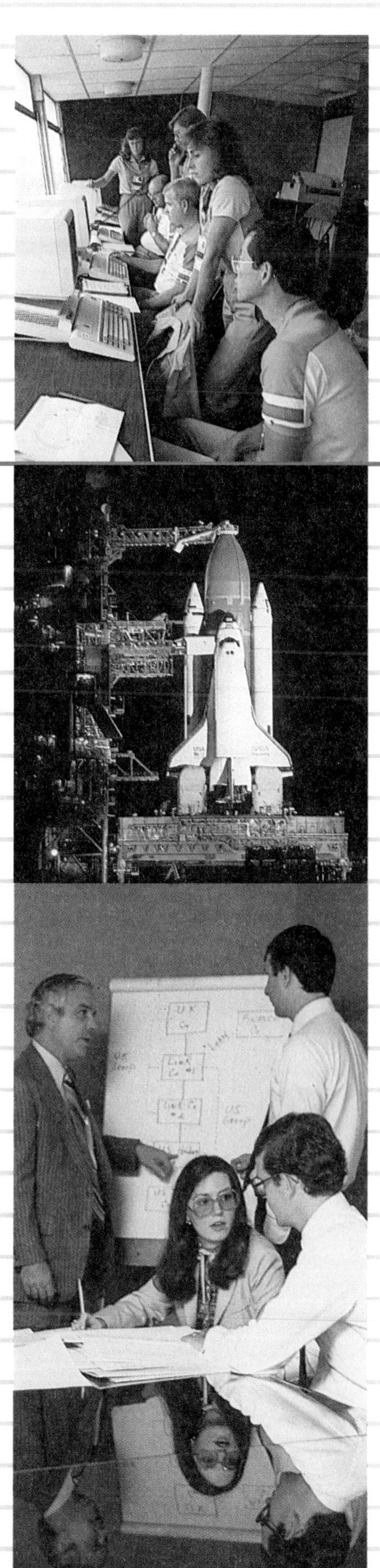

ACCOUNTING TODAY AND ITS USES

All businesses and investors in the United States—ranging from the 1984 Los Angeles Olympics to mental health services to the U.S. space program—benefit from the work of accountants. Accountants today are asked to apply their knowledge and skills in a host of ways that Bob Cratchit would find strange and exciting.

During the 1984 Olympics, a major accounting firm, Ernst & Whinney, was asked to apply its expertise to provide timely tabulation of the results of individual events. In 1983, accountants were asked to analyze the fiscal policy and practices with respect to delivery of mental health services in the state of New York and to make recommendations concerning funding and reporting policy. Accountants regularly provide the U.S. Congress and taxpayers with cost information on the space and other government programs so that legislative leaders and voters can assess the benefits received in comparison with the costs.

Indeed, accountants provide data on virtually every aspect of life where economic facts are needed. The goal of accounting today is to provide information to individuals to assist them in economic decision making. The world of accounting is broad and exciting. To fully appreciate the field of accounting, let's take a brief look at its origins.

A BRIEF HISTORY OF ACCOUNTING

Like French or Spanish, accounting is a language. It can be defined as the process of providing financial information to individuals who make economic decisions in

The Ernst & Whinney results team in action at track and field at the 1984 Olympics.

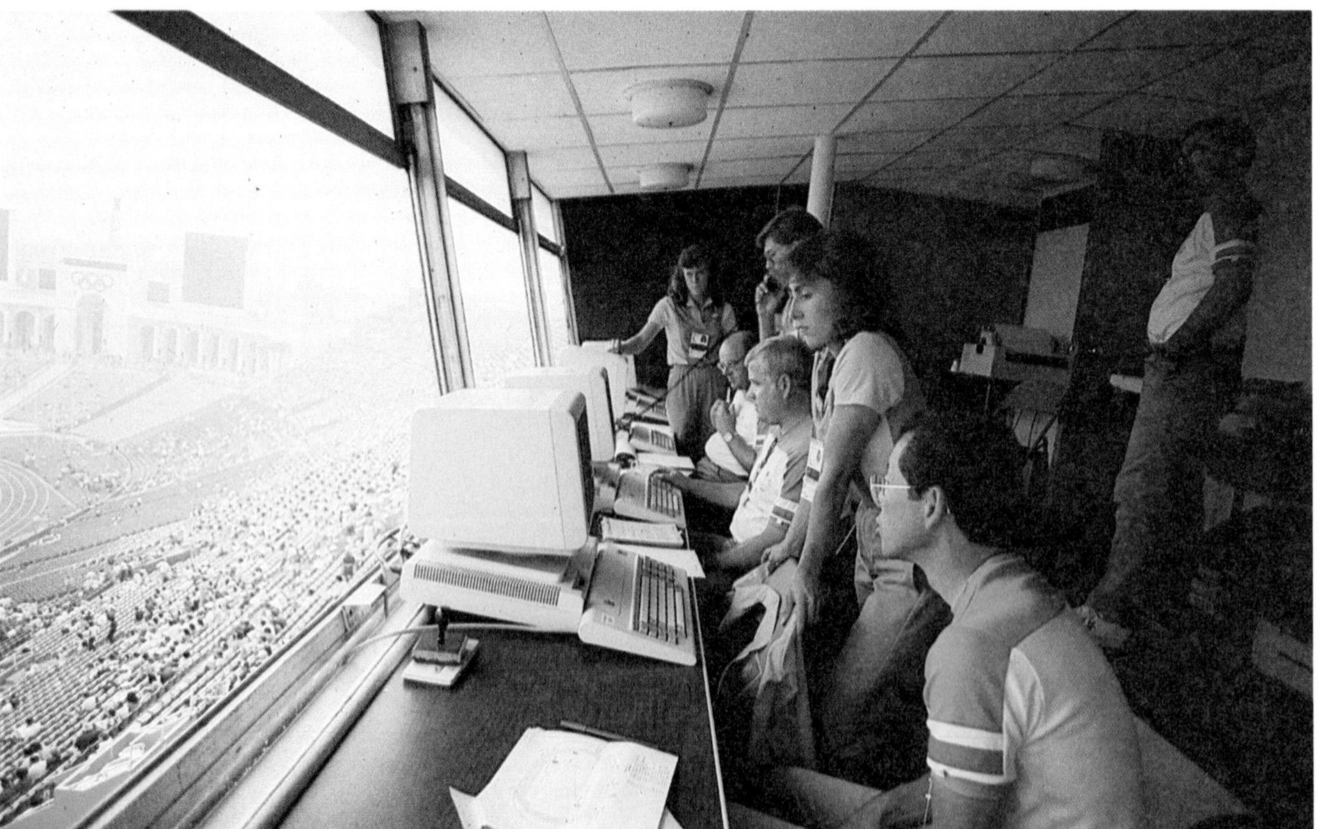

the context of specific organizations. Like other forms of communication, accounting has its own specialized vocabulary, principles, and concepts developed over the past 6,000 years. A brief look at the roots of modern accounting will help you to fully appreciate accounting practice in the microcomputer age.

In the Beginning

Among the oldest known documents in accounting are those of the Babylonians dating from 2500 B.C. Early accounting records have also been found in Egypt, China, Greece, and Rome. Because no set rules had yet evolved on how to do accounting, each system was specifically designed to meet the unique needs of a particular culture or organization.

The First Standardization

In 1494, A Franciscan monk, Luca Pacioli, published a book on double-entry accounting that has set the standard for accounting for the past 500 years. Before Pacioli's treatise, records were maintained in single-entry systems where only one side of a transaction was recorded. For example, if a merchant spent 10,000 lire to purchase a ship, the merchant's book of accounts would show a cash expenditure of 10,000 lire, but it would not show that a ship worth 10,000 lire was acquired in the transfer. Under Pacioli's system, both the expenditure and the acquisition of the ship were recorded. Double-entry bookkeeping provided a more scientific and mathematical basis for accounting that produced significantly better information.

The Industrial Revolution

The Industrial Revolution that centered in England during the eighteenth and nineteenth centuries changed the way products were manufactured, and new accounting techniques were required to accommodate the changes. Manufacturing of goods moved out of craftspersons' individual cottages and into factories. This shift from small, individual proprietorships to large manufacturing firms required accounting and reporting systems that provided managers with product and process cost data that had not been necessary when each craftsperson was his or her own manager. The needs of the factory led to the development of cost/managerial accounting systems that identify and report product costs to management.

Taxation and Public Investment

The importance of accounting and widespread interest in its practice were boosted significantly in the United States with the passage of the federal income tax in 1913 and the movement towards widespread public ownership of business entities during the past hundred years.

Federal Income Tax Influence. The federal income tax law required all businesses and individuals to maintain sufficient records to support the filing of tax returns. Further, successful implementation of a taxation system based on voluntary compliance with tax requirements meant that fair accounting rules and procedures were required.

The Securities Acts. During the late 1800s and early 1900s, expanding public ownership of business entities created a need for sharing financial information about businesses with the public at large. At first, rules and requirements for disclosure of financial information were established and policed by the stock exchanges that served as marketplaces for trading shares of ownership. However, rules established by each stock exchange often varied, and policing of the rules was difficult.

In the aftermath of the stock market collapse in 1929, investors demanded more uniform accounting and reporting standards for publicly held companies. In response to this demand, the Securities Act of 1933 and the Securities Exchange Act of 1934 were passed, creating the Securities and Exchange Commission (SEC). Under the Securities Acts, companies that want to offer investment opportunities to the general public are required to have their financial statements formally examined by independent accountants to verify their conformity with generally accepted accounting principles. Further, the SEC was given the authority to promulgate binding financial reporting requirements on a national scale. The continuing expansion of public investment has led to continuing refinements in accounting systems as publicly traded organizations have grown and diversified.

TYPES OF BUSINESS ORGANIZATIONS

As accounting grew from a single entry to a sophisticated system for providing information about and to organizations, the practice of accounting widened to include many kinds of entities. The primary focus of this text is on accounting for profit-oriented businesses. (Appendix G provides a framework for accounting in nonprofit organizations.) Three major types of business organizations exist in the United States—sole proprietorships, partnerships, and corporations, the characteristics of which are summarized in Exhibit 1.

CORPORATE FOCUS

Conceptually, the accounting principles and practices used in any profit-oriented business are similar. However, given the importance and economic prominence of the corporate form in the United States, this text focuses on corporate accounting. We use this perspective to enable us to describe the accounting process in the context of a pragmatic, realistic, and consistent framework. Because many sole proprietorships and partnerships do exist, we have included material specific to these organizations in Chapter 12.

ACCOUNTING TODAY AND ITS USERS

Users External to Organizations

External users of accounting include present and potential owners, the government, creditors, and financial analysts. These external users have become so important that one whole branch of accounting—financial accounting—has evolved to meet their information needs.

Users Internal to Organizations

The information needs of internal managers, although many times similar to those of people outside the organization, are often different. The needs of managers are

EXHIBIT 1

Characteristics of Sole Proprietorships, Partnerships, and Corporations

Characteristic	Sole Proprietorship	Partnership	Corporation
Method of creation	Created by an individual.	Created by agreement of the parties.	Charter issued by state—created by statutory authorization.
Legal position	Not a separate legal entity.	Not a separate legal entity in many states.	Always a legal entity separate and distinct from its owners—a legal entity for the purposes of owning property and being a party to litigation.
Liability of owners	Unlimited liability.	Unlimited liability (except for limited partners in a limited partnership).	Limited liability of shareholders—shareholders are not liable for the debts of the corporation.
Duration	Terminated at discretion, death, or retirement of the owner-manager.	Terminated by agreement of the partners, by the death of one or more of the partners, by withdrawal of a partner, or by bankruptcy.	Can have perpetual existence.
Transferability of ownership	Transferred at discretion of owner. (Transfer terminates old proprietorship and creates new one.)	Partnership interest can be transferred to someone else.	Ownership shares can be sold.
Management	Controlled and managed by owner.	Each general partner has a direct and equal voice in management unless expressly agreed otherwise in the partnership agreement. (Limited partners have no rights in management in a limited partnership.)	Owners elect directors who set policy and appoint key managers.
Taxation	Pays taxes as an individual.	Each partner pays his or her pro rata share of income taxes on net profits, whether or not distributed.	Double taxation—corporation pays income tax on net profits, and owners pay income tax on profits when distributed to them as dividends.
Organizational fees, annual license fees, and annual reports	None.	None.	All required.
Transactions of business in other states	No limitation.	Generally no limitation.	Normally must qualify to do business and obtain certificate of authority.
Accounting entity	Separate accounting entity.	Separate accounting entity.	Separate accounting entity.

covered by another branch of accounting—cost or management accounting. This book covers the underlying principles of both financial and managerial accounting.

THE PROFESSION OF ACCOUNTING

To meet the needs of different organizations, professional accountants usually work within one of four broad areas: public accounting, industrial accounting, government accounting, and accounting education.

Public Accounting

Perhaps the most widely publicized group of accountants is certified public accountants (CPAs), who offer professional services to clients on an independent fee basis much like lawyers and doctors. (CPAs provided the results service to the Los Angeles Olympics.) The license to practice as a CPA is granted by individual states after the candidate has obtained the required educational background, successfully completed a rigorous nationally uniform examination, and fulfilled certain experience requirements. CPAs practice in four broad areas: auditing, review and write-up, taxation, and management advisory services.

On-site with an industrial client. Gaining an understanding essential to the audit function.

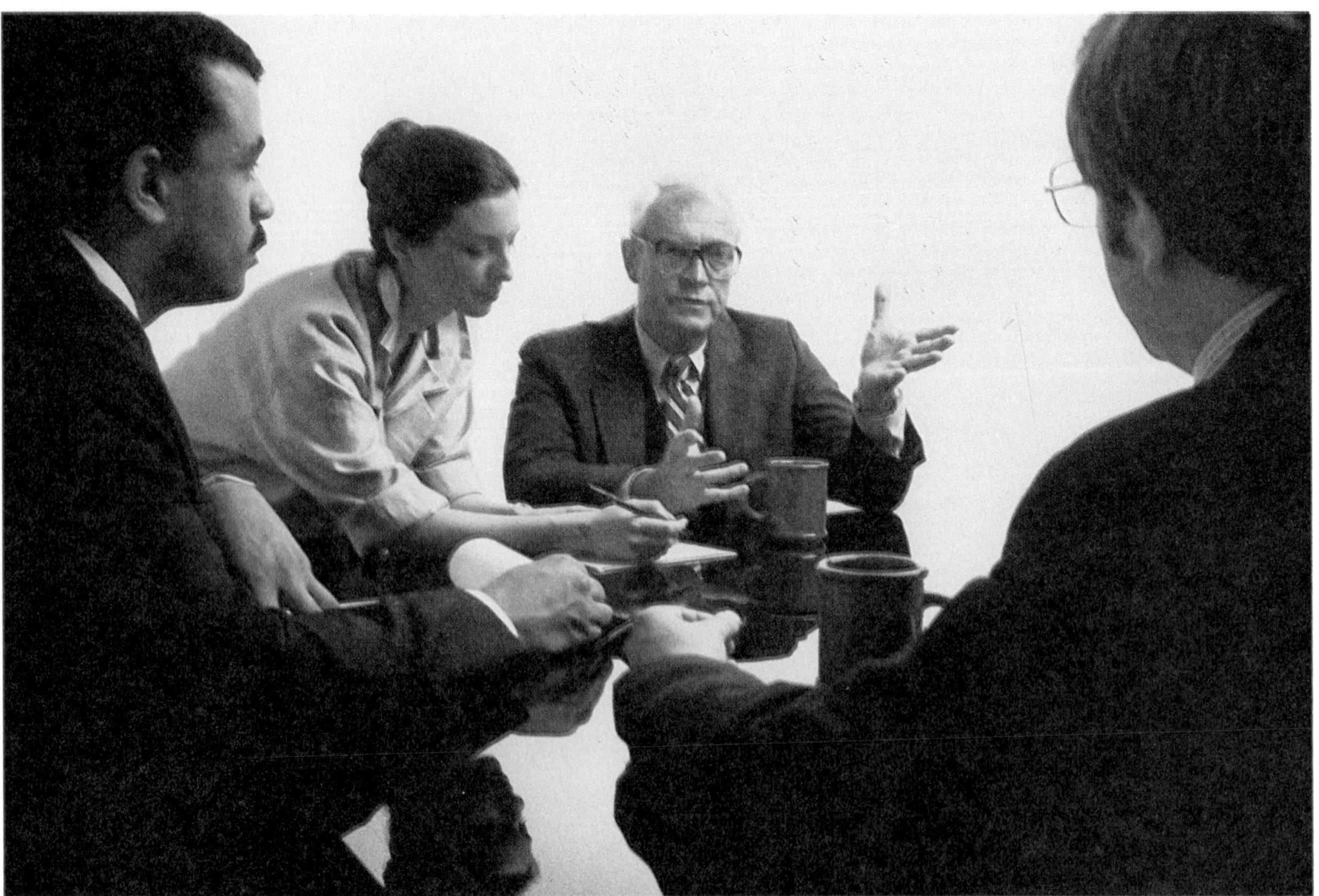

Auditing. During an audit a CPA examines the financial statements of an organization and gives an opinion as to whether the statements were prepared in accordance with generally accepted accounting principles (guidelines adopted by the accounting profession for preparation of financial statements). Outsiders to the organization, such as investors, employees, and creditors, are thus assured that the financial information that they use in making decisions concerning the organization is reliable.

Review and Write-up. Closely related to auditing is preparation of unaudited financial statements for clients (referred to as a review and write-up). Although the CPA needs to probe the client's records to a limited extent to assure that the statements prepared are reasonable given the client's bookkeeping system, no opinion as to compliance with any reporting standards is given. This review might be all that is required for corporations where the owners are known to one another, but it is generally inadequate for corporations with wide stock distribution and general public ownership.

Taxation. Some CPAs assist clients in preparing tax returns and in planning business transactions to minimize taxation in the future. As taxation becomes more complicated, tax practice grows in scope.

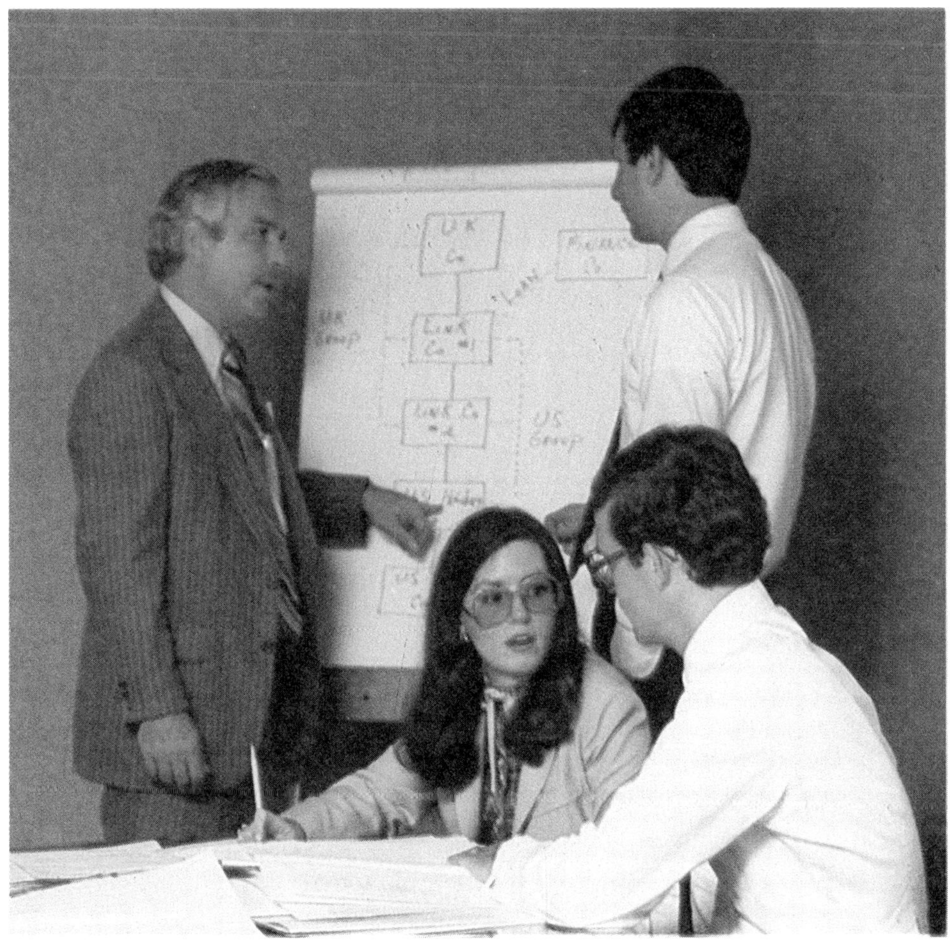

International tax specialists evaluate the tax implications of organizational alternatives for a British client's U.S. subsidiaries.

Management Advisory Services. The fourth area of practice for many CPAs is assisting clients with their management problems. CPAs are called on to give advice on a wide variety of problems, ranging from the design of accounting systems to marketing studies to executive searches. Because CPAs work with many different clients, they have a wide experience base to draw from for solutions.

Industrial Accounting

Unlike the CPA engaged in public practice for a number of different clients, the accountant performing services for an organization is an employee of the organization. No licensing or specific training requirements exist for private accounting practice, except in a voluntary fashion. Several organizations have developed professional certification programs for accountants in the industrial sector. Typical of such programs are the Certificate in Management Accounting (CMA) offered by the Institute for Management Accounting and the Certificate in Internal Auditing (CIA)

Today, the field of aerodynamics has transcended man's highest expectations. Over the years, Deloitte Haskins & Sells has provided numerous consulting services to Rockwell International, a major contributor to the U.S. space shuttle program.

offered by the Institute of Internal Auditors. The usual requirements for certification include an appropriate educational background, completion of a rigorous examination related to the certification area, and evidence of practical experience.

Professional opportunities in business and industry for accountants are generally found within one of the following areas:

- Cost/managerial accounting
- Systems design
- Financial accounting and analysis
- Internal auditing
- Corporate taxation

Cost Accounting. Information on product or service cost is vital to any organization for producing reliable external financial reports and for providing information for managerial decision making. Determination of reliable product and service costs for reporting and decision-making purposes is difficult and challenging in modern multinational, multiproduct organizations. Because of the difficulty involved, the cost accountant often plays a critical role in the decision process of and about an entity.

Systems Design. The accounting system must be properly designed if it is to record the data arising from an organization's operations and properly classify and summarize the data in a meaningful and useful manner. The design of the accounting system is the key to the results obtained. Specialists who work in systems design are often known as systems analysts.

Financial Accounting and Analysis. Development of overall financial reports for external users and the preparation of financial forecasts for management are necessary for business organizations. The incorporation of expectations (forecasts) into current plans provides benchmark data used both internally and externally in assessing performance. Accountants specializing in financial accounting and analysis work with management in preparing a firm's external reports and internal analyses.

Internal Auditing. The work of the internal audit staff is quite similar to certain reviews performed by the outside CPA in the auditing area discussed earlier, with two important distinctions:

1. The internal auditor is an employee of management and has no third-party liability to the general public.
2. The internal auditor usually goes far beyond the external auditor's review of financial statements for compliance with generally accepted accounting principles and is responsible for operational auditing to ensure that management policies are being followed throughout the entire organization.

In effect, the internal auditor is the eyes and ears of management, providing assurance that resources are accounted for and controlled appropriately and that operational policies are uniformly carried out throughout the organization. In many cases, the director of internal auditing reports directly to the board of directors or the audit committee of the corporation.

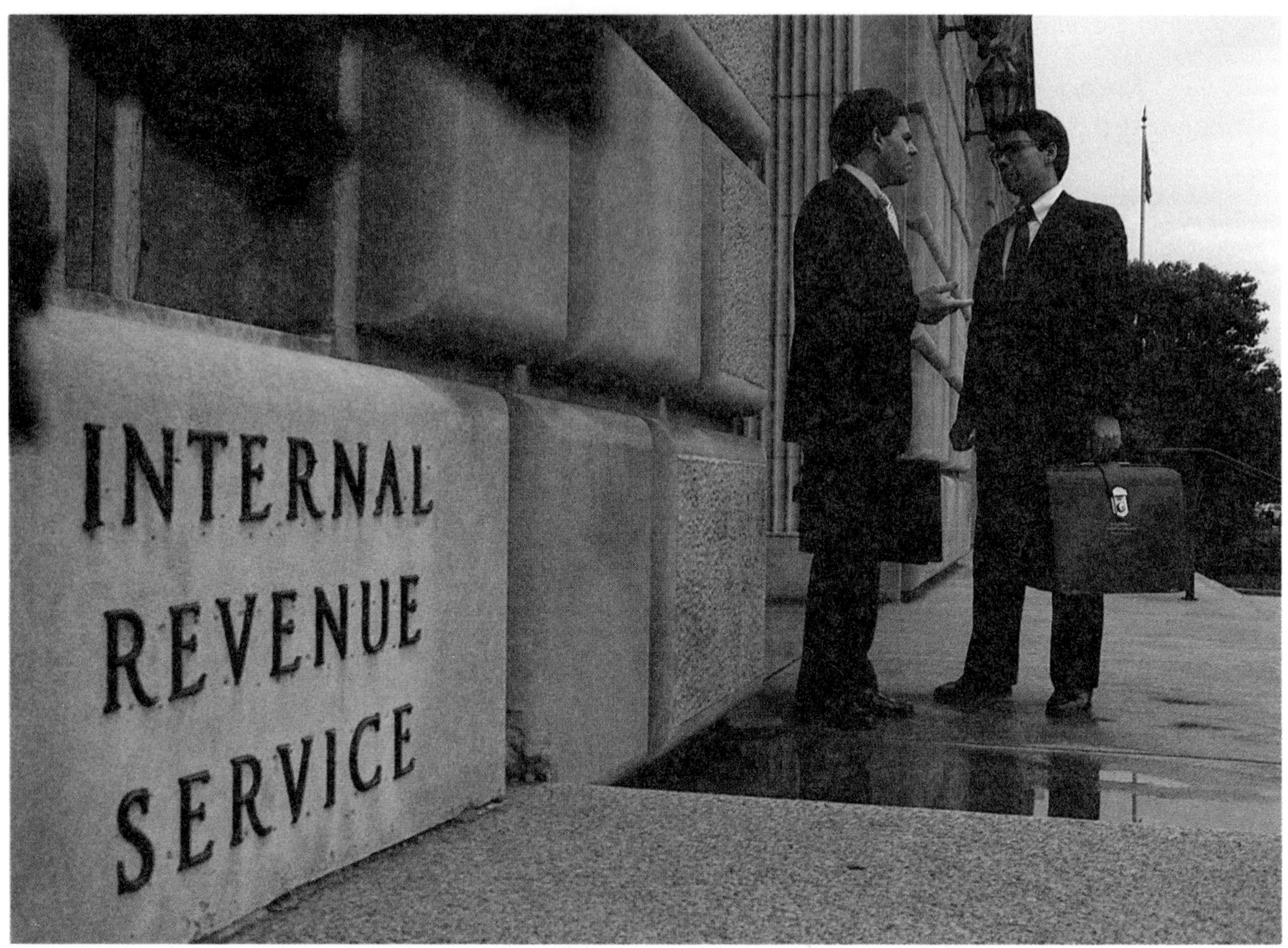

Corporate Taxation. Most businesses pay taxes on their income at the federal, state, and local levels. Often the tax consequences of a business transaction will vary depending upon the structure of the transaction. In addition, compliance with the various taxing authorities' reporting requirements has become exceedingly complex. For these reasons, business organizations are finding the need to establish a separate in-house tax staff not only for tax compliance purposes but also for formulating business strategies that minimize tax liability.

Government Accounting

Growth in government and in increasingly costly and complex government programs leads to large expenditures of public monies. Accountants serve not only to protect against misappropriation of funds but also to help government managers carry out their duties in a cost-effective fashion.

In addition to having traditional opportunities with the Internal Revenue Service or General Accounting Office, accountants today play a key role in a wide variety of governmental agencies, from white-collar-crime strike forces to welfare management to defense contracts.

Accounting Education

Over the years, tremendous change has occurred in the preparation of accountants for entry-level professional positions. Today, a formal four-year university education is generally accepted as the minimum accounting education required for entering the accounting profession. Accounting professors employed by the various colleges and universities are responsible for educating future practitioners of accounting.

The minimum preparation for an academic career is a masters degree, with a Ph.D. required in most major universities. Additionally, qualification as a practicing professional by obtaining the CPA or CMA certificate is desirable.

PROFESSIONAL RESPONSIBILITIES

The preceding sections clearly emphasized accounting as a profession in all areas of service (public, private, governmental, and educational). With the designation as a profession come certain obligations.

In the practice of public accounting, a distinct and well-established legal obligation exists to perform audit reviews thoroughly. Negligent work or fraudulent acts can be punished by the courts of law by suits brought by injured parties. However, the obligations of a professional go beyond courtroom liability. Professional accountants must follow the same codes of conduct whether they are engaged in public practice, private accounting, government work, or education.

Further, professional accountants are obligated to bring professional expertise to bear on societal issues and to provide needed services to all segments of society regardless of the ability of the recipient to pay. In recent years, such obligations have received increasing attention through professional organizations at the national, state, and local levels. Many accountants have become involved in direct assistance at a low or no-fee basis to minority businesses, charitable organizations, and government agencies such as boards of education.

Recently some accountants have become involved in public issue cases involving a wide variety of problems ranging from nuclear energy to health care delivery systems to land use questions. In public issue cases, the role of the accountant has been not to advocate a position but rather to report relevant financial information to all interested parties in an independent and unbiased fashion. In this new role, accountants are fulfilling their obligation by using their financial expertise to enable society to understand the complex financial overtones of important issues. By doing so, accountants today are enhancing society's efficiency in the allocation of scarce resources.

PART ONE 1
THE BASIC ACCOUNTING FRAMEWORK

1 BASIC ACCOUNTING PRINCIPLES AND THE STATEMENT OF FINANCIAL POSITION

CHAPTER OBJECTIVES
After studying Chapter 1, you should understand the following:

1. The assumptions and conventions of the accounting system.
2. The accounting equation and its importance.
3. The nature of assets, liabilities, and owners' equity.
4. The concept of a transaction and the transaction's impact on the accounting equation.
5. The contents and format of the statement of financial position.

Accounting is central to providing information about organizations to interested parties. This chapter explains the conceptual structure and underpinnings of the conventional accounting system, presents and explains the accounting equation that forms the framework for analyzing and recording economic events known as transactions, and describes the statement of financial position and the information contained therein.

REPORTING FINANCIAL INFORMATION

The purpose of an accounting system is to collect and organize economic data about an organization in a useful manner for decision making. Found in every type of institution, the accounting system aims to convert economic events into understandable information. Thus, accounting should provide a means of communicating financial information about an organization to interested parties. Before communication can occur, certain ground rules must be understood. Accounting reports are like game results: The scoring rules must be known if observers are to properly interpret player or team achievements.

Suppose you were told that The Grove Company had an income of 100. What would you know? You would *not* know the value of the 100, because the measuring unit was not given. You would *not* know the time span during which the income was earned, because this information was not provided. Interpretation of accounting reports is very difficult without a clear understanding of the assumptions underlying the preparation of such reports.

Because accounting serves a wide spectrum of users both inside and outside an organization, the variety of accounting reports is practically limitless. As discussed in the Invitation, management accounting focuses on the information needs of the internal managers of the entity while financial accounting focuses on the information needs of the users outside the organization, primarily investors (owners) and creditors (lenders).

Management can develop any set of rules for internal report preparation that appears useful for making decisions about the resources under its control. These rules are communicated throughout the organization so that all readers can understand the firm's internal accounting reports, which should be tailored to an organization's particular needs.

A vastly different problem exists in meeting the needs of external users of accounting information. Owners, creditors, government agencies, and labor groups are seldom part of the firm or organization that prepares accounting reports. If accounting data provided to outside parties are to be useful, both the preparer and the user must agree on the rules to be used in developing the reports.

In some societies, a government agency would establish the ground rules. In the United States, the Securities and Exchange Commission (SEC)[1] is the ultimate authority on accounting rules and public reporting requirements for corporations whose stock is publicly held. However, to a large extent, the SEC has allowed its rule-making authority to be exercised by the private sector through the Financial Accounting Standards Board (FASB).[2] The pronouncements of the FASB, sanctioned by

[1]The SEC is a federal agency charged with the oversight of the external accounting and reporting practices of corporations offering debt securities or stock to the general public. The SEC exercises its powers through five commissioners appointed by the President and confirmed by the Senate for terms of five years each.

[2]The FASB consists of seven full-time individuals representing public accounting, industry, and accounting education. The FASB conducts research on accounting problems and on basic theory. Additionally, the Board issues authoritative pronouncements that are mandatory rules for preparation of financial statements for external corporate reports. Although the FASB is a private entity, its actions are heavily monitored by the SEC and Congress.

the SEC, provide the basis for this text's exploration of accounting as a means of providing information to external users.

FUNDAMENTAL PRINCIPLES AND PRACTICES

Transactions

Accounting measures the financial results of operations by focusing on economic events known as transactions. A **transaction** is any identifiable economic event or activity that can be measured in money and recorded in the accounting system. Because of this focus, accounting is often said to be transaction-based. To understand accounting, the characteristics that define a transaction must first be identified.

TRANSACTION
An identifiable economic event or activity that can be measured in money and recorded in the accounting system.

Consider the following example. Jack invests $10,000 cash in machinery to produce clay pots, places another $10,000 cash in a bank account for business use, and produces and sells pots for ten years. At the end of ten years, Jack sells the equipment for $2,000 cash, pays the outstanding business bills, and finds that $100,000 remains in the bank. The $100,000 is the final result of everything that had affected Jack's business during the ten-year period. Because he started with $20,000 cash, Jack knows with certainty that the business earned $80,000. However, Jack does not know when the money was earned, because he measured his earnings only at the termination of his business. He had defined an economic event (or transaction) as occurring at only two points: when he invested his cash and when he terminated the business. To know specifically when the money was earned and to understand the ongoing operations of the business, Jack could have defined an economic event as some smaller, more frequently occurring event, such as the sale of one pot.

Basic Principles, Conventions, and Assumptions

Money Measurement. The transformation of economic events into useful information in dollar terms is known as **money measurement.** The use of dollars allows the uniform classification and summarization of diverse events.

MONEY MEASUREMENT
Transformation of economic events into useful information in dollar terms.

Stable Monetary Unit Assumption. The usefulness of money as a common denominator depends, in part, on the stability of the dollar as a measuring unit. The assumption that the economic value of the dollar does not change over time is called the **stable monetary unit assumption.**

STABLE MONETARY UNIT ASSUMPTION
The assumption that the economic value of the dollar does not change over time.

An analogy can be made to using the liter as a measurement of volume. If a liter does not measure the same volume from month to month or year to year, a liter of water collected in one year added to a liter of water collected in another year would not be equal to two liters of water collected at the same time. The constancy of the liter as a measuring unit is the trait that supports the liter's usefulness.

Exactly the same can be said of the dollar. The usefulness of accounting data expressed in dollars is dependent on the assumption that the dollar is a constant measuring unit. Although such an assumption is open to criticism, the conventional accounting model assumes dollar value constancy.

Historical Cost. Closely related to the assumption of dollar value constancy is the use of **historical cost,** which means that the purchase price in effect when an item is acquired is generally used as the value of that item in all future time periods within the accounting system.

HISTORICAL COST
The accounting convention that measures the value of an item within the accounting system by reference to its original purchase price.

Like the use of a constant dollar measure, criticism of the historical cost convention abounds. Suppose that many years ago the Holly Company purchased a tract of land for $15,000 on which to grow Christmas trees and that the land is now appraised at $100,000. Under the historical cost convention, the firm's accounting reports would still list the land as valued at $15,000. To alleviate such distortions, new systems are being designed and tested. Determination of fair market values is difficult and is not as objective as historical cost. Because of such difficulties, historical cost continues to form the basis for values used within the conventional accounting system.

Objectivity. To be most reliable, accounting data should be gathered on an objective basis. Two reasonable accountants reviewing the same transactions data should produce comparable financial reports. Basing accounting reports on historical cost information obtained from written documentation—invoices, order forms, time records, etc.—is known as the **objectivity principle** in accounting. Reliance on objective documentation for recording transactions assures users of accounting statements that the data contained therein are not simply figments of someone's imagination. This is not to imply that all accounting data are exact in nature. Although estimates must often be made, such estimates should be based on available documentation.

OBJECTIVITY PRINCIPLE
The accounting principle that requires basing accounting reports on historical cost information obtained from written documents.

The Accounting Entity Concept. The organization to be accounted for is known as an **accounting entity.** An accounting entity is defined by the interests and needs of a particular user group; ownership, legal, or physical considerations alone do not define an accounting entity. Although information sometimes can be sought on strictly legal bases, at other times information summaries are needed with a broader focus. For example, corporations can be combinations of several legally separate firms with common management teams and owner groups. In such cases, the combined resources and accounting activities of these legally separate organizations are reported as if the organizations were one organization which, in an economic sense, is true.

ACCOUNTING ENTITY
The organization that is being accounted for.

Information summaries with a narrower focus can also be useful. An individual plant, an operation within a plant, or even a particular work shift can be an entity for accounting purposes. Only a basis for linking the appropriate economic events to a particular entity is required.

Entity boundaries should be drawn with care. If the focus is on Tompkins and Company, for instance, Ms. Tompkins's personal financial affairs would not be included in the business records in any way.

Consistency. The underlying requirement that accounting systems be operated and accounting reports be prepared in a similar manner from year to year is known as the **consistency principle.** If a user of accounting data wishes to compare operations of one year with those of another for the same company, the reports of operating performance for each of the years should be consistently developed.

CONSISTENCY PRINCIPLE
The general requirement that accounting systems be operated and accounting reports be prepared in a similar manner from year to year.

Going Concern. Decisions are futuristic in nature. In accounting, the **going concern assumption** is that the accounting entity in question will continue to operate in the future. One of the reasons historical cost is used in accounting is that a firm planning on future operation must acquire many productive resources. Prospective investors might be more interested in the historical cost of such resources than in the market value. For example, the appropriate value of a building used to house an operating steel mill in Gary, Indiana, might be far different from the value of a closed mill in Youngstown, Ohio, being offered to the general public as real estate. Unless otherwise indicated, accounting reports are prepared on the assumption the entity will continue to operate in the future much as it has in the past.

GOING CONCERN ASSUMPTION
The assumption that the accounting entity will continue to operate in the future.

The preceding assumptions, coupled with widely accepted accounting practices and the pronouncements of bodies such as the FASB and SEC, form what is known as **generally accepted accounting principles** (GAAP). With an understanding of these principles, you can now begin to explore the accounting system in action.

GENERALLY ACCEPTED ACCOUNTING PRINCIPLES
The assumptions, conventions, practices, and authoritarian pronouncements that form the basis for accounting practices.

CONCEPT SUMMARY 1.1

Major Accounting Principles, Conventions, and Assumptions

ITEM	MEANING
Money measurement	The common denominator used for measuring and reporting accounting data is the dollar.
Stable monetary unit	The economic value of the dollar is assumed to be constant over time.
Historical cost	Transactions are recorded within the accounting system at amounts established at the time a particular transaction occurs. This historical value is used as the basis for subsequent accounting reports.
Objectivity	Transactions are recorded on the basis of objective, verifiable facts such as those contained in normal written business documents.
Accounting entity	The reporting unit is defined by the interests and needs of a particular user group, not by ownership or legal considerations alone.
Consistency	Accounting reports are prepared in a similar manner from year to year.
Going concern	An accounting entity will continue to exist as a viable operation in the future.

THE ACCOUNTING EQUATION

All the resources used by any business organization (referred to as assets) must be obtained from someone. An **asset** is a resource controlled solely by an organization that is expected to provide future economic benefits to the organization. Assets have two sources:

ASSET
A resource controlled solely by an organization that is expected to provide future economic benefits.

1. Assets can be loaned to the firm by third parties, known as creditors; the amount of such assets is represented by a firm's liabilities.
2. Assets can be provided by owners of the firm; the amount of such assets is represented by a firm's owners' equity.

Since the total assets held by a firm must have been provided by some combination of creditors and owners, the following relationship must always hold true:

Assets = Sources of Assets
or
Assets = Liabilities + Owners' Equity

The latter equation (frequently abbreviated as A = L + OE) is known as the **accounting equation.** Understanding the logic of the accounting equation is extremely important, because it forms the basis of the conventional accounting system.

ACCOUNTING EQUATION
Assets = Liabilities + Owners' Equity. This equation is the basis of conventional accounting.

When Does an Asset Cease To Exist?

In 1980, the federal government deregulated the nation's trucking industry. Until deregulation, each trucking company held exclusive rights to operate in certain territories. These rights, acquired by purchase in most cases, were reported on the books as assets. When deregulation allowed anyone to enter any territories, the rights ceased to have future economic benefit to their owners. As a result of this deregulation, one trucking company, Consolidated Freightways, reduced its assets and lowered its income by $32.1 million in 1980.

An asset ceases to exist for accounting purposes when control is lost or no future economic benefits are available. Although the normal reason for lack of future economic benefits is that the asset is used up in business operations, such is not always the case.

ASSETS, LIABILITIES, AND OWNERS' EQUITY

To fully understand the accounting equation, the terms *assets, liabilities,* and *owners' equity* need further consideration.

Assets

Not all things of value held by a business organization are included as assets within the accounting system. The skills of employees are of value to a business organization but would not be considered assets within the accounting system. These skills are not controlled solely by the business.

Whether or not a resource will yield future economic benefit to an organization must be determined from the surrounding facts and circumstances. If the resource can be used or sold in the foreseeable future, classification by the controlling firm as an asset is warranted. Consider the following:

> A utility company owns a nuclear power plant. An accident has damaged and contaminated the plant beyond any hope of salvage. In fact, the plant must now be removed from the property at great cost to the utility company. Clearly, the nuclear plant should not be classified as an asset.

Assets do not always possess physical characteristics such as those of machinery and buildings. Resources such as patents and copyrights that have future economic benefit can also be classified as assets, even though they lack physical attributes.

Sources of Assets—Liabilities and Owners' Equity

All the assets of an organization are provided by either owners or creditors. In exchange for asset investment, the provider receives a claim against the organization's resources and normally expects a fee for the use of the assets. Both owners and creditors expect to be compensated for providing assets to a business.

Nonowner Sources (Creditors). Business organizations often acquire assets by borrowing from outsiders. The lenders of assets to a business are known as **creditors** of the business. Creditors can provide assets to a business in any form, for example, cash, equipment, or office space. The original form of the assets acquired through borrowing is not important. All assets obtained from creditors are valued at their historical cost when they are received. **Liabilities** represent the dollar amount of assets provided by creditors and the claims of creditors against an entity's assets.

CREDITOR
Lender of assets to a business.

LIABILITIES
The dollar amount representation of assets provided by creditors and claims of the creditors against an entity's assets.

Owner Sources

Invested Assets. The amount of assets contributed (or invested) by owners in their business is part of owners' equity in the accounting equation. Most owner contributions are in the form of cash, which is then exchanged by the business for other assets. As with contributions from creditors, the form of contribution by owners is irrelevant.

Business Income. Companies are usually organized and operated to make a profit. If a company is successful, its earnings can flow into two channels. First, profits can be removed from the control of the business for the personal use of the owners. Second, the profits can remain in the business as additional assets. The assets earned by the company belong to the owners; if these assets are not distributed to the owners, the owners have made additional asset contributions (investments) to the business. Like assets invested directly into the business, assets earned by the business and not withdrawn by the owners are part of owners' equity in the accounting equation.

Thus, **owners' equity** represents the total amount of assets provided by owners either through investment from the owners' personal holdings or through undistributed earnings of the business and the claims of the owners against the assets of the entity.

OWNERS' EQUITY
Representation of the total amount of assets provided by owners to a corporation through either investment or undistributed earnings of the business and the claims of the owners against an entity's assets.

Comparison of Owners and Creditors. The following characteristics differentiate creditors from owners:

1. **Compensation for asset use.** Both creditors and owners expect to be compensated for the use of the assets they provide. This compensation can be thought of as fees for asset use. Fees for creditor-provided assets (interest) are usually payable at certain stated intervals, are a legal obligation of the company, and are fixed in amount. On the other hand, fees for owner-provided assets (dividends) are uncertain in amount and are not a legal obligation of the company unless a decision is made by the corporate board of directors to pay dividends.
2. **Return of assets to their owners.** Owner-provided assets are used by the business for the life of the organization. On the other hand, creditors expect to receive the cash equivalent of their asset contributions at a definite future time. The payment to creditors of amounts equivalent to the assets originally provided is known as repayment of debt or payment of a liability.

CONCEPT SUMMARY 1.2

Assets, Liabilities, and Owners' Equity

ITEM	DEFINITION
Assets	Resources expected to provide future economic benefits to an organization that are under the organization's sole control.
Liabilities	A representation of the total amount of assets provided by creditors and the claims of the creditors against an entity's assets.
Owners' equity	A representation of the total amount of assets provided by owners either through direct investment or through undistributed earnings of the business and the claims of the owners against an entity's assets.

CONCEPT SUMMARY 1.3

Comparison of Creditors and Owners

Source of Assets	Amount of Compensation	Timing of Compensation	Legal Status of Compensation	Return of Assets to Provider
Creditors	Fees for use (interest) are usually certain in amount.	Fees for use are payable at a definite stated time.	Fees for use are a legal obligation.	Repayment of assets is a legal obligation at a certain future point.
Owners	Fees for use (dividends) are uncertain in amount.	Fees for use are payable only at discretion of board of directors.	Fees for use are not a legal obligation.	Repayment of assets required only upon liquidation.

THE ACCOUNTING EQUATION AND TRANSACTION ANALYSIS

A transaction most often occurs because an organization undergoes a change in type or quantity of assets controlled. The following sections consider different types of transactions and analyze their impact on the accounting equation.

The fact that a transaction has occurred is usually evidenced by a source document, such as an invoice or a receipt (recall the objectivity principle). The source document triggers an accounting process that begins with the analysis of the transaction and the transaction's impact on the accounting equation. This impact is recorded within the accounting system as changes in two or more accounts.

ACCOUNT
A place to collect and record data arising from transactions.

An **account** is simply a place to collect and record data arising from transactions. Each account has a name—such as Cash or Accounts Payable—called the account title. The total set of accounts for any business can be compared to the set of mailboxes in an apartment building. Each box is identified by a name, and each is used to collect information for the person whose name appears thereon. Like the mail carrier delivering mail to the correct boxes, the accountant must assure that each transaction is recorded in the proper account.

Investment of Assets in the Business by Owners

Suppose that you and two friends have decided to begin a small corporation, the Star Corporation. On January 5, 1986, each of you invests $10,000 cash in Star, and in return, the three of you hold complete ownership.

What accounts are affected from the firm's viewpoint? One account, Cash (an asset), has increased $30,000. Since the company has gained an asset, we must also determine the source of the asset. Because the asset was contributed by the owners of Star, the second account that increases is Owners' Equity. All transactions produce changes in two or more accounts maintaining the balance of the accounting equation.

In what direction do the account balances change? Both Cash and Owners' Equity must be increased from zero (they did not exist before the corporation was formed) to $30,000. Star has more cash, and the owners have an additional claim against the corporation. The accounting equation is still in balance:

	Assets	=	**Liabilities**	+	**Owners' Equity**
	Cash	=			**Owners' Equity**
Old balance	$ 0	=	$ 0	+	$ 0
Transaction	+ 30,000	=			+ 30,000
New balance	$30,000	=	$ 0	+	$30,000

Obtaining Assets from Creditors

Suppose on January 10 that Star Corporation buys $7,000 of merchandise from the Supplier Corporation. The Supplier Corporation provides the goods to Star on credit and expects payment by January 25. The accounts to be changed to reflect this transaction are Merchandise (an asset), which should be increased from zero to $7,000, and Accounts Payable (a liability), which should also be increased from zero to $7,000. The effects of this transaction on the accounting equation are as follows:

	Assets			=	Liabilities	+	Owners' Equity
	Cash	+	Merchandise	=	Accounts Payable	+	Owners' Equity
Old balance	$30,000	+	$ 0	=	$ 0	+	$30,000
Transaction			+ 7,000	=	+ 7,000		
New balance	$30,000	+	$7,000	=	$7,000	+	$30,000

Exchange of One Asset for Another

On January 16, Star Corporation purchases a delivery truck for $10,000 cash. The two accounts affected by this transaction are Cash (an asset) and Delivery Truck (an asset). The Cash account is decreased by $10,000, and the Delivery Truck account is increased from zero to $10,000. The accounting equation is now:

	Assets					=	Liabilities	+	Owners' Equity
	Cash	+	Delivery Truck	+	Merchandise	=	Accounts Payable	+	Owners' Equity
Old balance	$30,000	+	$ 0	+	$7,000	=	$7,000	+	$30,000
Transaction	− 10,000		+ 10,000						
New balance	$20,000	+	$10,000	+	$7,000	=	$7,000	+	$30,000

Purchase of an Asset in Part for Cash and in Part on Credit

On January 18, Star Corporation purchases a building and equipment for a total of $20,000. The building is worth $15,000, and the equipment is worth $5,000. The seller agrees to take $9,000 in cash on the sale date with the remainder due on February 18. Four accounts are affected by this transaction. Cash (an asset) is decreased by $9,000, Building (an asset) is increased from zero to $15,000, Equipment (an asset) is increased from zero to $5,000, and Accounts Payable (a liability) is increased by $11,000. It is not unusual for one transaction to affect more than two accounts. You must analyze each transaction carefully. The accounting equation would remain in balance as follows:

	Assets									=	Liabilities	+	Owners' Equity
	Cash	+	Merchandise	+	Delivery Truck	+	Building	+	Equipment	=	Accounts Payable	+	Owners' Equity
Old balance	$20,000	+	$7,000	+	$10,000	+	$ 0	+	$ 0	=	$ 7,000	+	$30,000
Transaction	− 9,000						+15,000		+ 5,000	=	+ 11,000		
New balance	$11,000	+	$7,000	+	$10,000	+	$15,000	+	$5,000	=	$18,000	+	$30,000

Sale of an Asset

On January 23, Star sells merchandise for $4,000 cash. The merchandise originally cost Star $3,000. By selling assets (merchandise) for $4,000 that originally cost $3,000, Star has earned a $1,000 profit. Profits are part of owners' equity. Recall that the source of all assets must be either creditors or owners. Creditors did not provide any additional assets. Yet assets have increased by $1,000—the $4,000 cash received less the $3,000 of merchandise given up. This increase in assets must therefore be attributed to owners, and owners should have a claim against any profits made by the business they own. As a result of this transaction, Star's Cash (an asset) is increased by $4,000, Merchandise (an asset) is decreased by $3,000, and Owners' Equity is increased by $1,000. The accounting equation would now appear as follows:

	Assets					=	Liabilities	+	Owners' Equity
	Cash	+ Merchandise	+ Delivery Truck	+ Building	+ Equipment	=	Accounts Payable	+	Owners' Equity
Old balance	$11,000	+ $7,000	+ $10,000	+ $15,000	+ $5,000	=	$18,000	+	$30,000
Transaction	+ 4,000	− 3,000				=			+ 1,000
New balance	$15,000	+ $4,000	+ $10,000	+ $15,000	+ $5,000	=	$18,000	+	31,000

Repayment of a Liability

On January 25, Star pays the Supplier Corporation for the merchandise purchased on January 10. As a result of this transaction, Cash (an asset) is decreased by $7,000 and Accounts Payable (a liability) is decreased by $7,000. The accounting equation would now appear as follows:

	Assets					=	Liabilities	+	Owners' Equity
	Cash	+ Merchandise	+ Delivery Truck	+ Building	+ Equipment	=	Accounts Payable	+	Owners' Equity
Old balance	$15,000	+ $4,000	+ $10,000	+ $15,000	+ $5,000	=	$18,000	+	$31,000
Transaction	− 7,000					=	− 7,000		
New balance	$ 8,000	+ $4,000	+ $10,000	+ $15,000	+ $5,000	=	$11,000	+	$31,000

Distribution of Assets to Owners

DIVIDEND
Distribution of assets from a corporation's prior earnings to the owners.

On January 31, Star distributes $200 cash each to you and your two friends for personal use. The formal name for the distribution of assets from a corporation's prior earnings to the owners is **dividend.** The important thing to understand at this point is the impact on the accounting equation of this distribution of assets to owners. The asset Cash is reduced by $600. Because the $600 cash is a distribution of assets provided by owners (profits earned belong to the owners), logic dictates that you should reduce Owners' Equity by $600. The accounting equation remains in balance after the transaction as follows:

	Assets					=	Liabilities	+	Owners' Equity
	Cash	+ Merchandise	+ Delivery Truck	+ Building	+ Equipment	=	Accounts Payable	+	Owners' Equity
Old balance	$8,000	+ $4,000	+ $10,000	+ $15,000	+ $5,000	=	$11,000	+	$31,000
Transaction	− 600					=			− 600
New balance	$7,400	+ $4,000	+ $10,000	+ $15,000	+ $5,000	=	$11,000	+	$30,400

Transaction Summary

As the preceding examples show, the analysis of transactions and the effect on the accounting equation involves two steps:

1. Determine which accounts have been affected.
2. Determine the amount by which each account balance is to change to reflect the new data.

These tasks appear relatively straightforward at first. However, you can expect occasional difficulty as you confront the transactions that accountants must analyze. If you do not know what to call an account, use a descriptive name. As your study of accounting progresses, the more traditional names will become familiar to you.

Exhibit 1.1 summarizes the preceding transactions. Review it carefully to assure that you understand each transaction described and its impact on the accounting equation.

THE ACCOUNTING STATEMENTS

Overview

The purpose of accumulating accounting data is to produce reports for users. The accounting statement is the end product of the application of accounting principles and assumptions to transactions. Two primary accounting statements are the statement of financial position, often referred to as the balance sheet, and the income statement.

The **statement of financial position,** or **balance sheet,** is a listing of the Assets, Liabilities, and Owners' Equity accounts at some specified point in time. The statement of financial position tells interested parties what assets a corporation holds on that date and the sources of those assets. Throughout this text, the term *statement of financial position* will be used, representing a trend away from the term *balance sheet.* This choice emphasizes the material concerning the entity's financial condition. The fact that the assets = liabilities + owners' equity equation appears within the statement reflects mechanical accuracy in the bookkeeping system but does not provide assurance that the presentation conforms with generally accepted accounting principles.

STATEMENT OF FINANCIAL POSITION
A listing of the assets, liabilities, and owners' equity accounts at some specified point in time.

BALANCE SHEET
See Statement of Financial Position.

The income statement provides the user with information on the profits or losses for the organization over a period of time. Chapter 3 studies in detail the contents of the income statement. Corporations whose ownership is widespread and available for public investment must prepare and publish a statement of financial position and

EXHIBIT 1.1

Star Corporation
Transaction Analysis
For the Month of January 1986

	Assets					=	Sources of Assets: Liab. + Owners' Equity	
Trans. Date	**Cash**	**Merchandise**	**Del. Truck**	**Buildings**	**Equipment**		**Accounts Payable**	**Owners' Equity**
1/5	+$30,000							+$30,000
1/10		+$7,000					+$ 7,000	
1/16	− 10,000		+$10,000					
1/18	− 9,000			+$15,000	+$5,000		+ 11,000	
1/23	+ 4,000	− 3,000						+ 1,000
1/25	− 7,000						− 7,000	
1/31	− 600							− 600
1/31 Bal.	$ 7,400	$4,000	$10,000	$15,000	$5,000		$11,000	$30,400

an income statement along with certain other financial data and statements at least once each year.

An Extended Focus on the Statement of Financial Position

The statement of financial position is a detailed listing of the accounts represented by the accounting equation. Like the accounting equation, the statement of financial position has two major sections: assets and sources of assets. The sources of assets are broken down into the two major categories: liabilities and owners' equity.

If a statement of financial position were prepared immediately following the formation of the Star Corporation, it would appear as in Exhibit 1.2.

EXHIBIT 1.2

Star Corporation
Statement of Financial Position
January 5, 1986

Assets		Liabilities and Owners' Equity	
Cash	$30,000	Liabilities	$ 0
		Owners' equity	30,000
Total	$30,000	Total	$30,000

In addition to listing the assets, liabilities, and owners' equity, the statement of financial position presents three other important pieces of information: the name of the accounting entity, the report title, and the date. This information is generally found on all accounting reports and is essential for a proper interpretation of the contents of the report.

If Star Corporation were to prepare a statement of financial position at the end of January, the statement would reflect the net effect of the seven transactions recorded and would appear as in Exhibit 1.3.

EXHIBIT 1.3

Star Corporation
Statement of Financial Position
January 31, 1986

Assets		Liabilities and Owners' Equity	
Cash	$ 7,400	Liabilities	
Merchandise	4,000	Accounts payable	$11,000
Delivery truck	10,000	Owners' equity	30,400
Buildings	15,000		
Equipment	5,000		
Total	$41,400	Total	$41,400

From Exhibit 1.3, it is impossible to trace any specific asset to any specific source. After a business has been in operation for a while, specific assets cannot be traced to specific sources. The purpose of the Liabilities and Owners' Equity accounts is not to reflect specific asset contributions to the firm, but rather to show the portion of the total assets provided by owners and the portion provided by creditors.

Exhibit 1.4 highlights the assumptions of the accounting system discussed earlier with respect to the analysis of transactions for the Star Corporation and the statement of financial position previously presented.

A REPRESENTATIVE STATEMENT OF FINANCIAL POSITION

So that you can become more familiar with an actual statement of financial position, we have selected the Delta Airlines report for the fiscal year ending June 30, 1984, shown in simplified form in Exhibit 1.5.

The heading presents the name of the accounting entity (Delta Airlines), report title, and date. Assets are grouped by type, as are the sources of assets. Such grouping is common in statement presentation. The statement is known as a **classified statement of financial position** when assets and sources of assets are grouped by type for presentation. For Delta, the assets are grouped into three broad categories: current; operating property, plant, and equipment; and other. In general, **current assets** are those resources a business expects to consume or convert to cash within the upcoming year. Property, plant, and equipment and other assets will be useful for more than one year and are known as **long-term assets.**

Liabilities are divided into three groups: current liabilities, long-term debt, and other. **Current liabilities** generally are those obligations that must be repaid within the next year. **Long-term liabilities** might not require repayment for five, ten, twenty or more years.

Owners' equity in the Delta example represents asset financing provided by the owners and is divided into two parts: assets invested from the owners' personal

CLASSIFIED STATEMENT OF FINANCIAL POSITION
A statement of financial position that groups assets and sources of assets by type for presentation.

CURRENT ASSETS
Assets that an entity expects to use or convert to cash within one year.

LONG-TERM ASSETS
Assets that will be useful to an entity for more than one year.

CURRENT LIABILITIES
Obligations that must be repaid within one year.

LONG-TERM LIABILITIES
Liabilities that will not be repaid within the next year.

EXHIBIT 1.4

Assumption	Application to Star Corporation
Accounting entity	Neither the transaction analysis nor the statement of financial position for Star Corporation contains any information about the owners' personal financial affairs.
Going concern	It is assumed that the Star Corporation will continue to operate through 1986 and in future years.
Consistency	Although this business has just been formed, future statements of financial position would be prepared on the same basis as the one presented.
Money measurement	All transactions are measured in dollar terms.
Stable monetary unit	Inherent in the statement of financial position is the assumption that all dollars represent equal measures of value. If this were not true, the summation into totals would not make sense. (Recall the unequal liter example.)
Historical cost	All of the amounts recorded in the transaction analysis and presented in the statement of financial position were the amounts established when the transactions occurred.
Objectivity	The data used in preparing the reports were determined from the objective facts. Another accountant looking at the same facts would come to the same conclusions with respect to the transaction analysis and would prepare an identical statement of financial position.

EXHIBIT 1.5

Delta Airlines
Statement of Financial Position*
June 30, 1984
(in thousands)

Assets		**Liabilities and Shareholders' Equity**	
Current assets		Current liabilities	
Cash and short-term investments	$ 32,853	Loans payable to short-term creditors	$ 171,151
Accounts receivable	417,969	Accounts payable	615,419
Supplies	35,197	Liability for vacation pay	74,754
Other short-term assets	30,969		
Total current assets	$ 516,988	Total current liabilities	$ 861,324
		Long-term debt	672,737
Operating property, plant, and equipment	$2,695,690	Other liabilities	685,854
		Total liabilities	$2,219,915
Other assets	56,144	Owners' equity	
		Paid in for common stock	199,371
		Retained earnings	849,536
		Total shareholders' equity	$1,048,907
Total assets	$3,268,822	Total liabilities and shareholders' equity	$3,268,822

*Developed from the June 30, 1984, statement of financial position published by Delta Airlines.

holdings (paid in for common stock) and assets earned by the business that have not been paid out to the owners (retained earnings). Although some of the accounts in the Delta Airlines statement might be unfamiliar, each is explored in subsequent sections of the text. For now, simply focus on the general format of the statement and the broad asset, liability, and owners' equity groups previously defined.

FOR REVIEW

DEMONSTRATION PROBLEM

On January 1, 1986, Mary and Jo start a plumbing supply company, Flush, Incorporated. During January, the following events take place.

January 2 Mary invests $30,000 cash and Jo invests a building worth $30,000 in return for complete ownership of Flush.

January 6 Flush purchases a truck for $10,000. The seller agrees to accept $5,000 in cash, with the remaining $5,000 due on February 1.

January 10 Flush purchases $2,000 of merchandise. The supplier agrees to wait until January 17 for payment.

January 16 Flush finds that it does not need all of the space in the building for its business and sells a one-half interest in the building to another company for $15,000 cash.

January 17 Flush pays the supplier $2,000 that is owed for merchandise purchased on January 10.

January 19 Flush sells merchandise to a customer for $500 that had originally cost Flush $200. Flush thus makes a profit of $300 on the sale. The purchaser agrees to pay Flush by January 26.

January 26 Flush receives the $500 in payment for the merchandise sold.

Required

1. Analyze the preceding transactions and prepare a schedule similar to the one in Exhibit 1.1.

2. Prepare a statement of financial position for Flush as of January 31, 1986.

Demonstration Problem Solution

1.

Flush, Incorporated
Transaction Analysis
For the Month of January 1986

	Assets					=	Sources of Assets: Liabilities & Owners' Equity	
Trans. Date	**Cash**	**Accounts Receivable**	**Merchandise**	**Truck**	**Building**		**Accounts Payable**	**Owners' Equity**
1/2	+$30,000				+$30,000			+$60,000
1/6	− 5,000			+$10,000			+$5,000	
1/10			+$2,000				+ 2,000	
1/16	+ 15,000				− 15,000			
1/17	− 2,000						− 2,000	
1/19		+$500	− 200					+ 300
1/26	+ 500	− 500						
Bal 1/31	$38,500	$ 0	$1,800	$10,000	$15,000		$5,000	$60,300

2.

Flush, Incorporated
Statement of Financial Position
January 31, 1986

Assets		**Liabilities and Owners' Equity**	
Cash	$38,500	Liabilities	
Accounts receivable	0	Accounts payable	$ 5,000
Merchandise	1,800	Owners' equity	60,300
Truck	10,000		
Building	15,000		
Total	$65,300	Total	$65,300

SUMMARY

- Accounting focuses on economic events known as transactions.
- The statement of financial position shows the assets of an organization and the sources of those assets.
- The accounting equation, assets = liabilities + owners' equity, underlies the conventional accounting system and must always hold true.

- Nonowner sources of assets are known as creditors, and the amount of assets they provide a firm can be determined from the liabilities on the statement of financial position.
- Owners provide assets to an accounting entity either directly by investment from their personal assets or indirectly by not withdrawing assets earned by the business.
- Asset inflows, outflows, or exchanges form the basis for business transactions.
- Conventional accounting assumes the following:
  a. The dollar is a constant measuring unit of economic value over time.
  b. Transaction data are recorded at the historical amounts established at the time the transaction occurs. This means that an accounting entity's assets, liabilities, and owners' equity accounts are all valued at historical cost.
  c. Transactions are recorded on the basis of objective, verifiable facts such as those contained in normal business documents.
  d. Accounting focuses on an entity as an economic organization separate from its owners.
  e. Normally, accounting rules should be applied consistently over time to maximize the comparability of periodic reports.
  f. The accounting entity will continue to exist as a viable operation in the future (that is, it is a going concern).
- Current assets and current liabilities are those assets and liabilities that are expected to be used up or repaid within the next year, or operating cycle, of the business organization. Other assets and liabilities are known as long-term assets and long-term liabilities.

QUESTIONS

1-1. Define and comment on the significance of the following accounting system basics:

a. objectivity	**d.** historical cost
b. accounting entity	**e.** consistency principle
c. money measurement	**f.** going concern

1-2. A typical accounting system focuses on transactions. What is meant by this statement?

1-3. Give the accounting equation and comment on its significance.

1-4. What two characteristics must a resource held by a business organization possess to be classified as an asset?

1-5. What is the purpose of a statement of financial position?

1-6. Explain the two sources of assets.

1-7. What are the differences between liabilities and owners' equity?

1-8. Explain the role of the SEC and the FASB.

1-9. Why must assets always equal liabilities plus owners' equity?

1-10. Describe the two ways that owners provide assets to business organizations.

EXERCISES

1-E1. The following are several items that might appear in a firm's statement of financial position:

a. Merchandise inventory	**f.** Equipment
b. Cash	**g.** Office supplies
c. Accounts receivable	**h.** Bank note payable
d. Accounts payable	**i.** Property
e. Long-term debt payable	**j.** Furniture and fixtures

State the letter identifying in which of the following categories each item would appear on a statement of financial position.

A—Current assets
B—Other assets
C—Current liabilities
D—Other liabilities

1-E2. Given the following items and amounts taken from a company's statement of financial position, show that assets = liabilities + owners' equity:

a. Cash	$200,000
b. Owners' equity	$400,000
c. Accounts payable	$215,000
d. Accounts receivable	$40,000
e. Inventory	$25,000
f. Land	$600,000
g. Note payable to bank	$250,000

1-E3. Assuming that all accounts for a firm are as follows, compute owners' equity:

a. Long-Term Debt Payable	$200,000
b. Equipment	150,000
c. Property	400,000
d. Accounts Payable	75,000
e. Inventory	50,000
f. Bank Note Payable	25,000

1-E4. Prepare an analysis of the following facts on the accounts of ABC Corporation using the format in Exhibit 1.1:

a. ABC Corporation borrows $10,000 from National Bank on a 120-day note.
b. ABC Corporation collects $500 cash owed by customers from prior sales to them.
c. ABC Corporation purchases $20,000 of inventory with $10,000 cash and $10,000 on credit.
d. ABC Corporation pays a supplier $5,000 owed from prior purchases.
e. ABC Corporation sells equipment no longer needed for $6,000. The equipment was carried on ABC's books for $4,500.
f. ABC Corporation purchases $1,000 of supplies on credit.

1-E5. Indicate the effect of each of the following transactions on total assets by indicating (S) if total assets remain the same, (D) if total assets decrease, or (I) if total assets increase:

a. Owners invest cash in the business.
b. Equipment is purchased on credit.
c. A 90-day bank note is repaid.
d. Merchandise is sold to customers on credit. The sales price of the merchandise is more than the purchase cost to the seller.
e. Supplies are purchased with cash.

1-E6. For each of the following situations, describe a transaction that will cause the stated effects:

a. Increase assets, increase liabilities.
b. Increase one asset, decrease another asset.
c. Decrease assets, decrease liabilities.
d. Decrease assets, decrease owners' equity.
e. Increase assets, increase owners' equity.

1-E7. Indicate the impact of each of the following transactions on each element of the accounting equation. Indicate an increase with a "+", a decrease with a "−", and no change with a "0".

a. Owners invest cash in a corporation.
b. The corporation purchases merchandise for resale on credit.
c. The corporation purchases supplies for cash.
d. The corporation pays for the merchandise purchased in (b).
e. The corporation sells merchandise to customers on credit. The sales price is greater than the original purchase price to the corporation.
f. The corporation distributes some merchandise to the owners as a dividend.
g. The corporation borrows money from a bank.
h. The corporation collects cash from the customers for the merchandise sold in (e).

Transaction	Accounting Equation				
Letter	Assets	=	Liabilities	+	Owners' equity

PROBLEM SET A

1-A1. Basic Statement of Financial Position. The following items appear on the September 30, 1986, statement of financial position for Ace Corporation:

Long-term debt	$50,000
Inventory	80,000
Accounts receivable	30,000
Taxes payable	10,000
Cash	5,000
Accounts payable	15,000
Property	50,000
Owners' equity	?

Required

a. Compute the amount for Owners' Equity.
b. Prepare a statement of financial position in proper form as illustrated in Exhibit 1.3.

1-A2. Recognition of Transactions. Entertainment Enterprises, agent for several local musical groups, is owned by Barry Clayton. Clayton prepared the following statement of financial position as of March 31, 1986.

Entertainment Enterprises
Statement of Financial Position
March 31, 1986

Assets		Liabilities and Owners' Equity	
Cash	$ 500	Bank notes payable	$ 5,000
Accounts receivable	3,000	Accounts payable	9,000
Building	10,000	Taxes payable	4,000
Supplies	1,000	Total liabilities	$18,000
Furniture	2,000	Owners' equity	8,500
Other assets	10,000	Total liabilities and	
Total assets	$26,500	owners' equity	$26,500

After talking with Clayton and reviewing his accounting records, you discover the following facts:

1. Included in other assets is a lawsuit filed by Entertainment Enterprises for $5,000 against a client that Clayton is confident he will win.
2. Included in furniture is a $500 typewriter that Entertainment bought two years ago and that Clayton gave to his daughter last year to use in college.
3. Entertainment owes $1,000 in income taxes from previous years. Clayton did not include these taxes in the books because he is fighting the charge in tax court.
4. Included in accounts receivable is an IOU for $100 signed by an individual who died penniless five years ago.
5. Included in furniture is $100 for an antique telephone that Entertainment paid $50 for but put in the records at $100 because that is what Clayton really believed it was worth.

Required

a. For each of the facts, determine whether an adjustment in the company's accounts should be made. Give a reason for each change proposed.
b. Prepare a corrected statement of financial position as of March 31, 1986, for Entertainment Enterprises.

1-A3. Transaction Processing and the Statement of Financial Position. The following are the transactions for September 1986 for Xcell Corporation:

September 1 Owners invest $50,000 cash in Xcell.
September 5 Xcell purchases $15,000 of supplies with $1,000 cash and $14,000 on credit.
September 8 Xcell signs a 90-day bank note for a loan of $20,000.
September 15 Xcell pays $14,000 to suppliers for items purchased on September 5.
September 19 Xcell purchases $75,000 of merchandise inventory for $35,000 cash and $40,000 on credit.
September 23 Xcell sells merchandise to customers for $25,000. Of this amount, $10,000 is received in cash and customers promise to pay $15,000 later. The merchandise originally cost Xcell $12,000.
September 25 Xcell distributes $500 cash to the owners for their personal use.
September 30 Xcell collects $10,000 from customers in partial payment for goods sold on September 23.

Required

a. Using the format in Exhibit 1.1, analyze the September transactions of the Xcell Corporation.
b. Prepare a statement of financial position as of September 30 for Xcell.

1-A4. Recognition of Transaction Types. Mary Hunt and Tina Walker, owners of Decorators, Inc., have summarized the March transactions of Decorators, Inc., as follows:

						Sources of Assets		
	Assets				=	Liabilities + Owners' Equity		
Trans. Date	**Cash**	**Accounts Rec.**	**Inventory**	**Equipment**		**Accounts Payable**	**Bank Note Payable**	**Owners' Equity**
3/1 Bal.	$5,000	$600	$2,000	$20,000		$1,000	$15,000	$11,600
3/5	+ 100	− 100						
3/10				− 400				− 400
3/12	− 200		+ 300			+ 100		
3/13	+ 1,000						+ 1,000	
3/15	− 800							− 800
3/20	− 100					− 100		
3/25	+ 100	+ 400	− 200					+ 300
3/31 Bal.	$5,100	$900	$2,100	$19,600		$1,000	$16,000	$10,700

Required

Give a possible explanation for each of the transactions.

1-A5. Reconstruction of Transactions from Sequential Statements of Financial Position. Steve Adams formed Adams Apple Company on June 1, 1986, and prepared a statement of financial position after each of several days in June.

1.

Adams Apple Company
Statement of Financial Position
June 1, 1986

Assets		Liabilities and Owners' Equity	
Cash	$30,000	Owners' equity	$30,000

2.

Adams Apple Company
Statement of Financial Position
June 3, 1986

Assets		Liabilities and Owners' Equity	
Cash	$ 20,000	Long-term loan	$120,000
Building	100,000		
Equipment	30,000	Owners' equity	30,000
Total	$150,000	Total	$150,000

3.

Adams Apple Company
Statement of Financial Position
June 10, 1986

Assets		Liabilities and Owners' Equity	
Cash	$ 10,000	Accounts payable	$ 30,000
Inventory	40,000	Long-term loan	120,000
Building	100,000		
Equipment	30,000	Owners' equity	30,000
Total	$180,000	Total	$180,000

4.

Adams Apple Company
Statement of Financial Position
June 18, 1986

Assets		Liabilities and Owners' Equity	
Cash	$ 35,000	Accounts payable	$ 30,000
Accounts receivable	10,000	Long-term loan	120,000
Inventory	10,000		
Building	100,000		
Equipment	30,000	Owners' equity	35,000
Total	$185,000	Total	$185,000

5.

Adams Apple Company
Statement of Financial Position
June 28, 1986

Assets		Liabilities and Owners' Equity	
Cash	$ 20,000	Accounts payable	$ 15,000
Accounts receivable	10,000	Long-term loan	120,000
Inventory	10,000		
Building	100,000		
Equipment	30,000	Owners' equity	35,000
Total	$170,000	Total	$170,000

Required

Write a possible explanation for the transactions that resulted in each updated statement of financial position.

1-A6. Personal Versus Business Transactions. Pamela Jones is a penniless recent graduate with a degree in accounting. She has just won $200,000, after taxes, in a sweepstakes and decides to open up an accounting practice to service local small businesses. Jones has the following transactions during June 1986:

June 1 Deposits $100,000 in her personal checking account and $100,000 in a business checking account.
June 3 Purchases a small downtown office for $50,000, with $5,000 down and the rest mortgaged through First Federal Savings and Loan.
June 5 Purchases a condominium unit for $80,000, with $16,000 down and the rest mortgaged on a 20-year land contract with the seller.
June 8 Purchases furniture for $10,000. Half of the furniture is for her condominium unit and half is for her office. The $10,000 is due in 30 days.
June 10 Opens a charge account at Lord and Taylor and charges $2,000 for clothes.
June 12 Lends her brother $2,000 for his college expenses.
June 15 Hires a receptionist at $200 a week to start July 1.
June 18 Purchases $300 of office supplies and pays cash.
June 20 Invests $10,000 in various stocks as a personal investment.
June 25 Pays a decorator $1,000 to wallpaper and paint her condominium unit.
June 29 Pays $300 for a sign at the entrance to her office.

Required

Prepare two statements of financial position—one for Pamela Jones, Accountant, and one for Pamela Jones, Personal, as of June 30, 1986. (Hint: Prepare a transaction analysis for each of the accounting entities and summarize the information to prepare the required financial statements.)

1-A7. More Sophisticated Transaction Analysis Including Owner Contributions and Withdrawals. On August 1, Harvey Smith starts Smith Hardware and has the following transactions:

August 1 Harvey Smith, owner of Smith Hardware, invests $10,000 of his personal savings in the business.
August 4 Smith Hardware signs a six-month note payable for $30,000.
August 5 Smith Hardware purchases a used delivery truck for $8,000, with $2,000 cash down and $6,000 to be paid by August 9.
August 6 Smith Hardware purchases $6,000 of merchandise from a supplier; payment is due in ten days.
August 6 Smith Hardware sells merchandise to customers for $10,000. Of this amount, $2,000 is received in cash and customers promise to pay the remainder on or before September 6. The merchandise sold originally cost Smith $4,000.
August 9 Payment of $6,000 is made for the truck purchased on August 5.
August 10 A salesman leaves a $10,000 microcomputer for Smith Hardware to try out.
August 15 A dissatisfied customer who purchased a $10 item is refunded her money and allowed to keep the merchandise.
August 16 Checks totaling $1,500 arrive in the mail from customers in payment of prior sales.
August 16 Payment is made for merchandise purchased on August 6.
August 17 Smith provides a typewriter to the hardware company and takes home merchandise that originally cost Smith Hardware $500.
August 19 Smith Hardware decides to keep the microcomputer. Payment is to be made to the vendor by September 10.

August 20 Harvey Smith receives $1,000 cash as a dividend.
August 25 Smith Hardware purchases merchandise from suppliers for $500 cash.
August 26 Smith discovers that merchandise that had cost $100 was stolen during a burglary the night before.

Required

a. Prepare an analysis of the August transactions on the accounts of Smith Hardware using the format of Exhibit 1.1.
b. Prepare a statement of financial position for Smith Hardware as of August 31, 1986.

1-A8. Claims of Creditors and Owners. Just before the Buggy Whip Company goes out of business on September 30, its statement of financial position shows the following accounts and balances:

Cash	$ 75,000
Buggy whips	100,000
Accounts payable	125,000
Owners' equity	50,000

Required

For each of the following cases, show a new statement of financial position with account balances immediately after the sale of the buggy whips and tell how the available cash would be distributed between creditors and owners:

Case 1: The buggy whips are sold for $25,000 cash.
Case 2: The buggy whips are sold for $60,000 cash.
Case 3: The buggy whips are sold for $110,000 cash.

PROBLEM SET B

1-B1. Basic Statement of Financial Position. The following items were taken from the March 31, 1986, statement of financial position for Hart Automotive Supplies:

Merchandise inventory	$ 5,000
Accounts payable	12,000
Long-term note payable	50,000
Building	80,000
Equipment	10,000
Accounts receivable	?
Cash	1,000
Owners' equity	60,000

Required

a. Compute the amount for Accounts Receivable.
b. Prepare a statement of financial position in proper form as illustrated in Exhibit 1.3.

1-B2. Recognition of Transactions. Sally Taylor owns and operates Taylor Rental Agency. She prepared the following statement of financial position as of April 30, 1986:

Taylor Rental Agency
Statement of Financial Position
April 30, 1986

Assets		**Liabilities and Owners' Equity**	
Cash	$ 300	Accounts payable	$ 600
Accounts receivable	500	Bank note payable	1,000
Supplies	200	Total liabilities	$1,600
Furniture	1,000	Owners' equity	900
Other assets	500	Total liabilities and	
Total assets	$2,500	owners' equity	$2,500

After talking with Taylor and examining her records you discover the following facts:

1. A desk is included in furniture for $650. Taylor bought the desk on April 1 for $500, paying $50 cash down with the remainder due in June. Taylor believes the desk is worth $650 and has increased owners' equity to keep the books in balance.
2. Going through the accounts receivable, Taylor notes that one account of $50 is five years past due. The customer moved out of the country three years ago and has not been heard from since.
3. Taylor received notice in April for $500 due for late taxes. Sally is fighting the case in tax court and is confident she will win. The taxes were not included in the April 30 statement.
4. In April, Taylor gave her sister a calculator bought by the company in March for $20. The calculator was included in the Other Assets account.
5. Supplies on hand amount to $700 on April 30. Taylor did not include all the supplies in the April 30 statement because she had not yet put them out for general office use.

Required

a. For each of the foregoing facts, determine whether an adjustment in the accounts of Taylor Rental Agency should be made. Give a reason for each change proposed.
b. Prepare a corrected statement of financial position for Taylor Rental Agency as of April 30, 1986.

1-B3. Transaction Processing and the Statement of Financial Position. Bounty Bakery Company has the following transactions during April 1986:

April 2 The two owners of the company each invest $10,000 cash in the business.
April 5 Bounty purchases $3,000 of merchandise inventory on account.
April 10 Bounty purchases a $2,500 doughnut warmer, with $500 cash down and $2,000 due in ten days.
April 13 Bounty sells $5,000 of baked goods to customers for $4,000 cash and $1,000 to be received later. The baked goods originally cost Bounty $2,000.
April 17 Bounty pays $3,000 to suppliers for inventory purchased April 5.
April 18 Bounty collects $500 from customers from April 13 sale.
April 20 Bounty pays amount due on doughnut warmer purchased April 10.
April 27 Bounty distributes $1,000 cash to each owner as a dividend.

Required

a. Prepare an analysis of transactions for Bounty Bakery for the month of April in the format in Exhibit 1.1.
b. Prepare a statement of financial position for Bounty as of April 30, 1986.

1-B4. Recognition of Transaction Types. Steve Kent prepared the following analysis of October transactions for his business, Kent's Kitchen Kabinets, Incorporated:

	Assets				=	Sources of Assets: Liabilities + Owners' Equity		
Trans. Date	**Cash**	**Accounts Rec.**	**Inventory**	**Equipment**		**Accounts Payable**	**Notes Payable**	**Owners' Equity**
10/1 Bal.	$5,000	$1,100	$5,000	$10,000		$1,500	$ 8,000	$11,600
10/2	− 1,000		+ 5,000			+ 4,000		
10/5	+ 500	+ 300	− 300					+ 500
10/10	− 2,000							− 2,000
10/12	+ 400	− 400						
10/15				− 1,000				− 1,000
10/20				+ 3,000			+ 3,000	
10/26	+ 2,000	+ 1,300	− 1,000	− 500				+ 1,800
10/31 Bal.	$4,900	$2,300	$8,700	$11,500		$5,500	$11,000	$10,900

Required

Give a possible explanation for each of the October transactions of Kent's Kitchen Kabinets, Incorporated.

1-B5. Reconstruction of Transactions from Sequential Statements of Financial Position. Paula Vine, owner of The Print Shop, prepared a statement of financial position after each of several days in May 1986. The Print Shop was formed on May 1, 1986.

1.

The Print Shop
Statement of Financial Position
May 1, 1986

Assets		**Liabilities and Owners' Equity**	
Cash	$10,000	Bank note payable	$10,000
Equipment	20,000	Owners' equity	20,000
Total	$30,000	Total	$30,000

2.

The Print Shop
Statement of Financial Position
May 5, 1986

Assets		**Liabilities and Owners' Equity**	
Cash	$ 5,000	Accounts payable	$ 5,000
Inventory	10,000	Bank note payable	10,000
Equipment	20,000	Owners' equity	20,000
Total	$35,000	Total	$35,000

3.

The Print Shop
Statement of Financial Position
May 8, 1986

Assets		**Liabilities and Owners' Equity**	
Cash	$ 8,000	Accounts payable	$ 5,000
Accounts receivable	3,000	Bank note payable	10,000
Inventory	6,000		
Equipment	20,000	Owners' equity	22,000
Total	$37,000	Total	$37,000

4.

The Print Shop
Statement of Financial Position
May 15, 1986

Assets		Liabilities and Owners' Equity	
Cash	$ 3,000	Bank note payable	$10,000
Accounts receivable	3,000		
Inventory	6,000		
Equipment	20,000	Owners' equity	22,000
Total	$32,000	Total	$32,000

5.

The Print Shop
Statement of Financial Position
May 25, 1986

Assets		Liabilities and Owners' Equity	
Cash	$ 3,000	Accounts payable	$ 2,000
Accounts receivable	2,000	Bank note payable	12,000
Inventory	10,000		
Equipment	20,000	Owners' equity	21,000
Total	$35,000	Total	$35,000

Required

Write a possible explanation of the transactions that resulted in each updated statement of financial position.

1-B6. Personal Versus Business Transactions. Tim Adams has just been awarded $150,000 in a lawsuit and decides to establish Adams Automotive Supply. He has the following transactions during April 1986:

April 2 Deposits $50,000 in his personal checking account and $100,000 in his new business account.
April 4 Purchases a townhouse for $60,000, with $10,000 down and $50,000 on a 20-year mortgage.
April 8 Purchases a building for his business for $100,000, with $10,000 down and $90,000 financed through a ten-year land contract with the seller.
April 10 Purchases furniture for his home and his office for $4,000 to be paid in 15 days. The $4,000 of furniture is divided equally between his home and his office.
April 13 Purchases $15,000 of merchandise inventory, with payment due in ten days.
April 14 Hires a stock clerk to begin work May 1 for $200 a week.
April 15 Pays for the furniture purchased on April 10.
April 18 Purchases a delivery truck for $12,000, with $1,000 down and $11,000 to be paid over three years.
April 23 Pays for the inventory purchased on April 13.
April 29 Purchases fixtures for use in the business at an auction for $3,000. The fixtures are later appraised as worth $4,000.
April 30 Accepts $5,000 from his brother, who wishes to be a part owner of the business. The $5,000 is deposited in the business account.

Required

Prepare two statements of financial position as of April 30, 1986—one for Tim Adams, Personal, and one for Adams Automotive Supply.

1-B7. More Sophisticated Transaction Analysis Including Owner Contributions and Withdrawals. Jones contributes $10,000 cash, Adams contributes office supplies worth $3,000 and furniture and fixtures valued at $7,000, and Smith contributes a building worth $10,000, to form TDH Corporation on July 1, 1986. During the month of July, the following transactions take place:

July 2 TDH signs a three-month bank note payable for $25,000.
July 3 Merchandise inventory is purchased for $50,000, with $5,000 paid in cash and the rest obtained on credit.
July 3 TDH purchases a $700 typewriter at a 20% discount by paying cash.
July 5 A salesman from a copying company leaves a $1,000 office copier in the TDH office for a tryout.
July 6 TDH sells merchandise to Alpha Corporation for $25,000 on credit that originally cost $15,000.
July 9 TDH purchases a warehouse for $50,000 by paying $5,000 cash and financing the remainder through a mortgage held by First Federal Savings and Loan.
July 12 TDH finds that $1,000 of its merchandise inventory is damaged beyond salvage.
July 13 Alpha Corporation pays $25,000 in full settlement of its purchase of July 6.
July 14 TDH returns to the salesman the copier left on July 5.
July 15 TDH sells merchandise for $40,000 on credit that originally cost $25,000.
July 17 TDH pays $20,000 for the merchandise purchased on credit July 3.
July 19 TDH receives office supplies worth $1,000 from Adams and gives him furniture and fixtures worth the same amount.
July 24 TDH purchases merchandise inventory for $40,000 by paying $2,000 cash and obtaining the rest on credit.
July 25 TDH distributes $1,000 to each of the owners as a dividend.
July 27 TDH receives $30,000 cash from customers for sales made on July 15 and pays $30,00 to suppliers for inventory purchased on July 24.

Required

a. Prepare an analysis of the July transactions on the accounts of TDH Corporation using the format in Exhibit 1.1.
b. Prepare a statement of financial position for TDH as of July 31, 1986.

1-B8. Claims of Creditors and Owners. Just before The Lilac Shop goes out of business on June 30, 1986, its statement of financial position shows the following accounts and balances:

Cash	$ 50,000
Inventory	200,000
Accounts payable	100,000
Owners' equity	150,000

Required

For each of the following cases, show a new statement of financial position with account balances immediately after the sale of the inventory and tell how the available cash would be distributed between creditors and owners:

Case 1: The inventory is sold for $50,000 cash.
Case 2: The inventory is sold for $150,000 cash.
Case 3: The inventory is sold for $300,000 cash.

THE ACCOUNTING CYCLE: RECORDING TRANSACTIONS

2

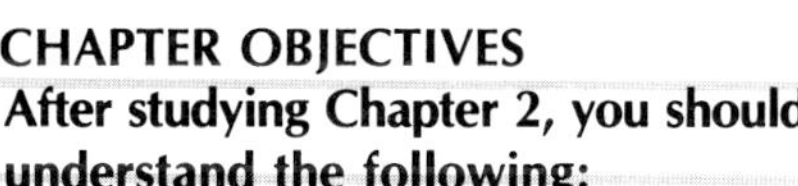

CHAPTER OBJECTIVES

After studying Chapter 2, you should understand the following:

1. The nature and purpose of a chart of accounts.
2. The debit/credit language of the double-entry accounting system.
3. The use of the general journal and general ledger.
4. The trial balance and its role in financial statement preparation.

Accounting is a cyclical process starting with transaction recognition and ending with the preparation of financial statements. Chapter 1 examined the concepts underlying the accounting system, the accounting equation, the nature of a transaction, and the statement of financial position. Chapter 2 focuses on the method of recording transactions and the method of summarizing data into a format useful for preparation of financial statements.

THE ACCOUNT

In Chapter 1, an account was compared to one mailbox in a set of mailboxes in an apartment building. Suppose the mail carrier delivering mail in the apartment building found a piece of mail addressed to someone without a separate mailbox. The mail carrier would not be able to deliver that particular piece of mail.

The Chart of Accounts

CHART OF ACCOUNTS
The total list of accounts of an organization.

Just as the mail carrier cannot deliver mail to an addressee without a mailbox, the accountant cannot record transaction data in an account that does not exist. The total list of accounts of an organization (the **chart of accounts**) provides the total range of recording possibilities for accounting data just as an apartment building's mailboxes provide the mail carrier with the total set of possible delivery points within the building.

Because organization and user needs differ, the type of data summarized varies among organizations. For example, both the management of a small shoe store and the management of a large manufacturing firm need to know the amount of money spent to pay employees. But the shoe store's management needs to know only the total spent for all employees in the store, whereas the manufacturer needs to know how much is spent for labor to produce each of its products. Although the manufacturer's set of accounts would include a separate labor cost account for each product, the shoe store would have only one account to collect all payments to employees.

The chart of accounts used by an organization must be responsive to user needs, yet not be so extensive as to require needless work that provides little, if any, useful information. A chart of accounts is not static, but evolves as the information needs of an organization change. One of the accountant's jobs is to design and maintain the necessary accounts and to recognize when the chart of accounts needs altering.

T-Accounts

In its simplest form, an account has three parts:

1. A title giving the account name.
2. A place to record increases.
3. A place to record decreases.

T-ACCOUNT
A simple form of an account shaped like a T.

A very simple account form (a **T-account**) is often used in classrooms and is used extensively in this text. The T-account designation is derived from its appearance, as illustrated for cash in the accompanying diagram.

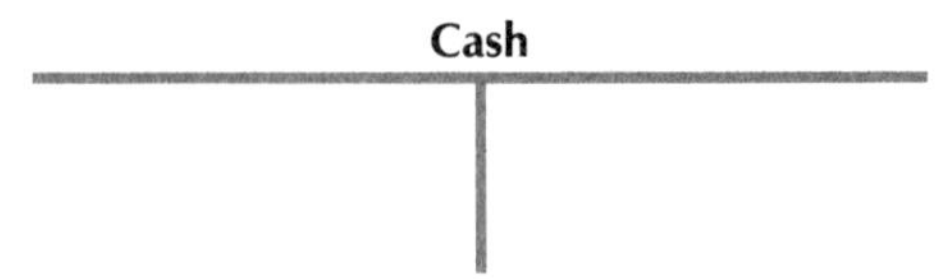

Although the position for the account title is self-evident, the locations to record increases and decreases in the account are not. Increases or decreases could be recorded on either side of the account as long as the sides are used consistently and the approach is understood by all. To simplify the process of recording transaction information within accounts and to communicate the results of business operations, accountants have developed a specialized language.

AN ACCOUNTING LANGUAGE: DEBIT AND CREDIT

The most important specialized words used by accountants are debit and credit, frequently abbreviated as "dr." and "cr." Debit and credit have meanings both in terms of position and as verbs when used in an accounting context: Any attempt to attach additional meanings to the two terms will cause confusion. **Debit** means left or increase in the left side of an account; **credit** means right or increase in the right side of an account. Exhibit 2.1 illustrates the use and meaning of the terms debit and credit.

DEBIT
An accounting term meaning left side or increase in the left side of an account.

CREDIT
An accounting term meaning right side or increase in the right side of an account.

Asset accounts must always equal their sources, as follows:

Total Assets		=	Total Liabilities		+	Owners' Equity	
+'s or debits				+'s or credits			+'s or credits

The total debits must always equal the total credits. Decreases in accounts can be analyzed in a similar fashion:

Total Assets		=	Total Liabilities		+	Owners' Equity	
	−'s or credits		−'s or debits			−'s or debits	

To debit an asset account means to increase the dollar amount of that asset; to credit an asset account means to decrease the dollar amount of that asset. Conversely, debiting a liability or owners' equity account decreases the balance in those accounts. Although the use of debits and credits to represent increases and decreases in accounts might seem confusing and unnecessary at first, such use helps to ensure that

EXHIBIT 2.1

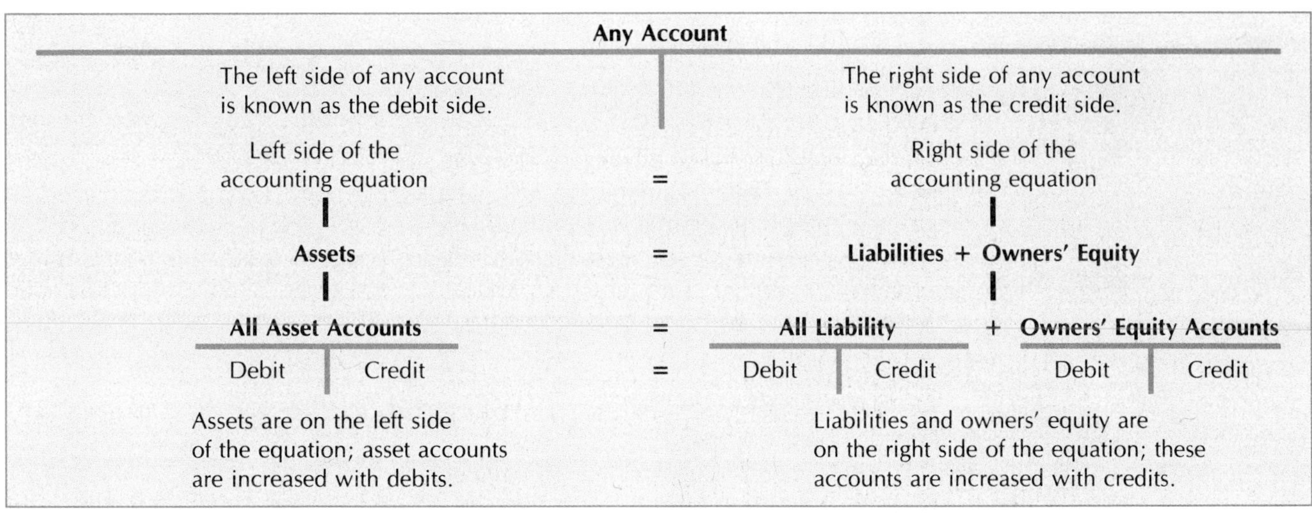

the accounting equation remains in balance after recording each transaction. The bookkeeping rule that the debits must equal the credits when recording any transaction is another way of stating that the accounting equation must always balance.

Suppose the Sarah Cookie Company borrows $1,000 cash from a bank. The company's asset account, Cash, would be debited (increased) by $1,000, and the liability account, Notes Payable to Banks, would be credited (increased) by $1,000. The debits of $1,000 equal the credits of $1,000, and the accounting equation would remain in balance. Conventional accounting is called a **double-entry system,** because each transaction is recorded twice—once on the debit side of one account and once on the credit side of a different account.

DOUBLE-ENTRY SYSTEM
A method of recording transactions whereby each transaction is recorded twice.

CONCEPT SUMMARY 2.1

EFFECTS OF DEBITS AND CREDITS ON ACCOUNTS

Accounts	Increased By	Decreased By
Assets	Debits	Credits
Liabilities	Credits	Debits
Owners' Equity	Credits	Debits

THE ACCOUNT BALANCE

ACCOUNT ENTRY
The recording of data in an account.

ACCOUNT BALANCE
The total amount in an account at a point in time.

The recorded data in an account are called **account entries.** By adding up all the debits and all the credits in a particular account and subtracting the smaller from the larger, we get the total amount in the account (the **account balance**). For example, suppose the Cash account has a beginning balance and entries as shown in Exhibit 2.2.

The total of the debits (left side) is $210,000. The total of the credits (right side) is $170,000. The account balance is $40,000, the number we would use for preparation of the statement of financial position. The account balance is really just a summary of the beginning balance plus all of the entries in the account.

Footing

FOOTING
The process of adding up a column of figures.

GENERAL LEDGER
A book containing the complete set of accounts for an entity.

Since the total of the debits in Exhibit 2.2 exceeds the total of the credits, the account has a debit balance. The process of adding up the debit columns and credit columns is known as **footing** the columns. Observe that the beginning account balance is added to the subsequent transactions when footing the account columns.

Normal Account Balances

We normally would expect cash to have a debit balance, since cash is an asset, and assets are increased by debits within the accounting system. The normal balance in any asset account is a debit balance, whereas the normal balance in any liability or owners' equity account is a credit balance. That is, the normal balance will be on the increase side of the account (debit side for assets or the credit side for liabilities and owners' equity). Throughout the text unless otherwise stated, when an account balance is given, think of the balance as normal in terms of debit or credit designation.

EXHIBIT 2.2

Cash		
Bal.	10,000	35,000
	100,000	70,000
	65,000	45,000
	35,000	20,000
	210,000	170,000
Bal.	40,000	

THE GENERAL LEDGER

The **general ledger** contains the complete set of accounts for a company. Each account is called a general ledger account. The simple T-account, although useful for classroom purposes and transaction analysis, is not feasible for recording all information a company might wish to retain concerning a particular transaction. In addition to including the account title, debit entries, and credit entries, the formal ledger account generally allows space to present three additional pieces of information:

1. The account number.
2. Cross-reference information to other accounting records.
3. Entry dates and descriptive information as required.

Although variations exist, the information in Exhibit 2.2 would appear in formal general ledger format as in Exhibit 2.3.

EXHIBIT 2.3

ACCOUNT Cash							**Account No. 101**
Date	**Explanation**	**Post Ref.**	**Debit**	**Date**	**Explanation**	**Post Ref.**	**Credit**
1986	Bal. 1/1		10,000	1/8		J1	35,000
1/3		J1	100,000	1/10		J1	70,000
1/15		J1	65,000	1/22		J2	45,000
1/25		J2	35,000	1/28		J2	20,000
	Total		210,000		Total		170,000
	Bal. 1/31		40,000				

Debits, Credits, and the General Ledger

The formal general ledger account retains the convention of entering debits on the left side and credits on the right. The formal account contains an account number (101 in our example), a beginning-of-the-period balance, subsequent transactions with cross-references (Post. Ref.) (discussed later in the chapter), and an end-of-period balance. (The entry dates are merely illustrative.)

Account Numbering

One other convention needs noting. Account numbers are generally assigned within the chart of accounts in accounting equation order. That is, lowest numbers are assigned to asset accounts, next lowest to liabilities, and the highest to owners' equity accounts. Exhibit 2.4 illustrates a simple chart of accounts and its relationship to the general ledger.

Debit and Credit Analysis

Analyzing transactions in Chapter 1 required two steps:

1. Determine which accounts were affected by the transaction.
2. Evaluate the amount and direction (+ or −) of the change.

To properly enter transactions in the general ledger, a third step is needed. You must decide whether to debit or credit the account on the basis of the direction of change and the account classification.

The most appropriate way to approach transaction analysis is to examine asset changes and the source of financing. Does the firm have more or less cash? Has the firm obtained a new building? Was the cash obtained from a bank loan, or did owners invest more money in the business? Once the asset and source of the asset

EXHIBIT 2.4

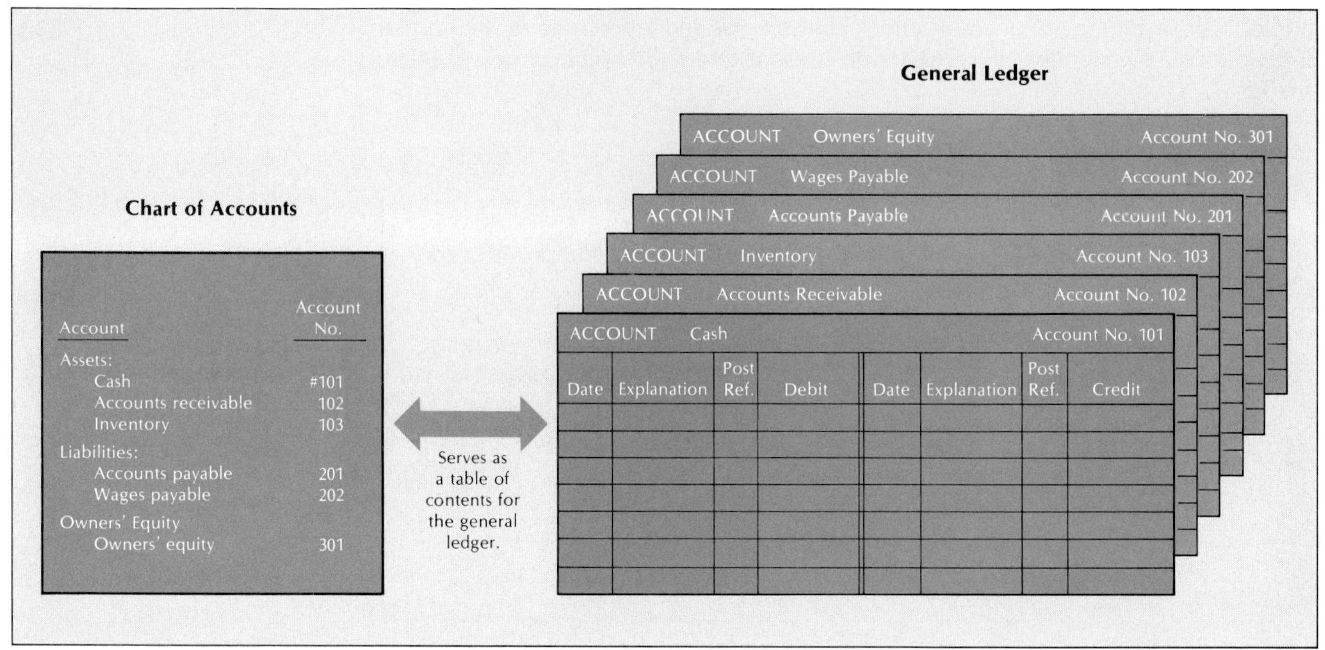

have been identified, you can determine whether to debit or credit the account by the rules presented earlier.

Exhibit 2.5 combines the transactions developed and analyzed for Exhibit 1.1 with the rules for debit and credit use.

The January 1986 transactions for Star Corporation would be entered in the general ledger as shown in the following T-accounts:

January 5—You and two friends invest $10,000 each in cash to start the Star Corporation.

Cash

Bal. 1/1	0		
1/5	30,000		

Owners' Equity

		0	Bal. 1/1
		30,000	1/5

January 10—Star Corporation purchases $7,000 of merchandise on credit.

Merchandise

Bal. 1/1	0		
1/10	7,000		

Accounts Payable

		0	Bal. 1/1
		7,000	1/10

January 16—Star Corporation purchases a delivery truck for $10,000 cash.

Cash

Bal. 1/1	0	10,000	1/16
1/5	30,000		

Delivery Truck

Bal. 1/1	0		
1/16	10,000		

The Running Balance Ledger Account

An alternative formal ledger account form (the **running balance ledger account**) is often found in practice. An example of this form of general ledger account is presented in the accompanying diagram using the entries from Exhibit 2.3. All the normal account elements are present, and the convention of putting debits on the left and credits on the right is observed within the form. The only difference is the addition of a column for the account balance. The balance in the account is determined after each entry. The term *running account* is derived from this practice. The running balance form of the ledger account is similar to your personal checkbook record.

ACCOUNT Cash					Account No. 101
Date	Explanation	Post Ref.	Debits	Credits	Balance
1986	Bal. 1/1				10,000
1/3		J1	100,000		110,000
1/8		J1		35,000	75,000
1/10		J1		70,000	5,000
1/15		J1	65,000		70,000
1/22		J2		45,000	25,000
1/25		J2	35,000		60,000
1/28				20,000	40,000

RUNNING BALANCE LEDGER ACCOUNT

A form of ledger account where the account balance is determined and shown following each entry made to the account.

January 18—Star Corporation purchases machinery for $5,000 and buildings for $15,000, with $9,000 paid in cash and the remainder due in February.

Cash

Bal. 1/1	0	10,000	1/16
1/5	30,000	9,000	1/18

Accounts Payable

		0	Bal. 1/1
		7,000	1/10
		11,000	1/18

Buildings

Bal. 1/1	0		
1/18	15,000		

Machinery

Bal. 1/1	0		
1/18	5,000		

EXHIBIT 2.5

Star Corporation
Transaction Analysis
For the Month of January 1986

	Assets					=	Sources of Assets	
Trans. Date	Cash	Merchandise	Delivery Truck	Buildings	Machinery		Accounts Payable	Owners' Equity
1/5	+$30,000 (Dr)							+$30,000 (Cr)
1/10		+$7,000 (Dr)					+$ 7,000 (Cr)	
1/16	− 10,000 (Cr)		+$10,000 (Dr)					
1/18	− 9,000 (Cr)			+$15,000 (Dr)	+$5,000 (Dr)		+ 11,000 (Cr)	
1/23	+ 4,000 (Dr)	− 3,000 (Cr)						+ 1,000 (Cr)
1/25	− 7,000 (Cr)						− 7,000 (Dr)	
1/31	− 600 (Cr)							600 (Dr)
1/31 Bal	$ 7,400 (Dr)	$4,000 (Dr)	$10,000 (Dr)	$15,000 (Dr)	$5,000 (Dr)		$11,000 (Cr)	$30,400 (Cr)

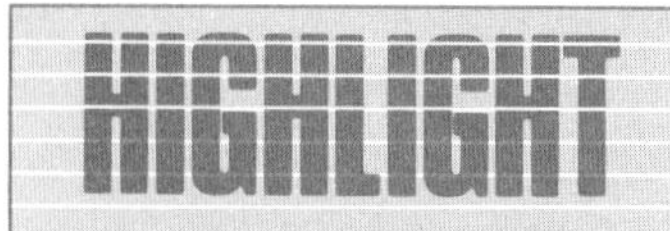

Computers and Bookkeeping Entries

You may have wondered if the bookkeeping procedures described in this chapter are really used in today's computerized world. The answer is emphatically yes! Although the general ledger and general journal along with all the entries may be nothing more than magnetized spots on a disk or tape, everything described in this chapter is still present. The overall control, logic, and efficiency of the double-entry system is simply implemented by computer systems. Using the computer to remove the drudgery of the required bookkeeping enables the accountant to spend more time analyzing the data and advising management on the data's proper interpretation.

January 23—Merchandise is sold for $4,000 cash; the original cost of the merchandise was $3,000.

Cash

Bal. 1/1	0	10,000	1/16
1/5	30,000	9,000	1/18
1/23	4,000		

Owners' Equity

		0	Bal. 1/1
		30,000	1/5
		1,000	1/23

Merchandise

Bal. 1/1	0	3,000	1/23
1/10	7,000		

January 25—Star pays suppliers for the merchandise purchased on January 10.

Cash

Bal. 1/1	0	10,000	1/16
1/5	30,000	9,000	1/18
1/23	4,000	7,000	1/25

Accounts Payable

1/25	7,000	0	Bal. 1/1
		7,000	1/10
		11,000	1/18

January 31—Star Corporation distributes $200 cash to you and each of your two friends as a dividend.

Cash

Bal. 1/1	0	10,000	1/16
1/5	30,000	9,000	1/18
1/23	4,000	7,000	1/25
		600	1/31

Owners' Equity

1/31	600	0	Bal. 1/1
		30,000	1/5
		1,000	1/23

Compare the preceding T-account entries to the debit and credit analysis presented in Exhibit 2.5. All of the entries follow the rules for debits and credits presented earlier. Note the usefulness of the account as a summarization device. All the transaction activity that affects a given account is collected in one place in the general ledger. Each account begins with an opening balance. Since Star Corporation did not exist before January 1986, all beginning balances are zero.

THE TRIAL BALANCE

TRIAL BALANCE
A listing of all of the accounts in the general ledger along with the balance in each.

A **trial balance** is a listing of all the accounts in the general ledger along with the balance in each account. The trial balance serves as a starting point for the preparation of financial statements. Exhibit 2.6 presents all the general ledger accounts for the Star Corporation with balances as of January 31, 1986.

Exhibit 2.7 presents a January 31, 1986, trial balance for the Star Corporation using the ledger account balances from Exhibit 2.6.

Several conventions should be observed in preparing a trial balance. Debit balances should be listed separately from and to the left of the credit balances. The accounts themselves should be listed in the order of the accounting equation, with assets first, liabilities second, and owners' equity last.

In addition to arranging the ledger accounts in an orderly fashion for use in preparing accounting statements, the trial balance helps to ensure accuracy within the bookkeeping system. If the total debits do not equal the total credits, a mechanical bookkeeping error probably exists in the general ledger. The simple fact that the

EXHIBIT 2.6

Cash

	Debit	Credit	
Bal. 1/1	0	10,000	1/16
1/5	30,000	9,000	1/18
1/23	4,000	7,000	1/25
		600	1/31
	34,000	26,600	
Bal. 1/31	7,400		

Merchandise

	Debit	Credit	
Bal. 1/1	0	3,000	1/23
1/10	7,000		
	7,000	3,000	
Bal. 1/31	4,000		

Delivery Truck

	Debit	Credit
Bal. 1/1	0	
1/16	10,000	
	10,000	0
Bal. 1/31	10,000	

Buildings

	Debit	Credit
Bal. 1/1	0	
1/18	15,000	
	15,000	0
Bal. 1/31	15,000	

Machinery

	Debit	Credit
Bal. 1/1	0	
1/18	5,000	
	5,000	
Bal. 1/31	5,000	

Accounts Payable

	Debit	Credit	
1/25	7,000	0	Bal. 1/1
		7,000	1/10
		11,000	1/18
	7,000	18,000	
		11,000	Bal. 1/31

Owners' Equity

	Debit	Credit	
1/30	600	0	Bal. 1/1
		30,000	1/5
		1,000	1/23
	600	31,000	
		30,400	Bal. 1/31

EXHIBIT 2.7

Star Corporation
Trial Balance
January 31, 1986

Account	Debit	Credit
Cash	$ 7,400	
Merchandise	4,000	
Delivery Truck	10,000	
Buildings	15,000	
Machinery	5,000	
Accounts Payable		$11,000
Owners' Equity		30,400
Totals	$41,400	$41,400

debits do equal the credits does not guarantee the absence of errors. For example, had Star Corporation entered the delivery truck it purchased in the Machinery account instead of the Delivery Truck account, the balance in both accounts would be incorrect. However, the debit column total in the trial balance would be the same, since both accounts represent assets, and the error in the Machinery account would exactly offset the error in the Delivery Truck account.

THE GENERAL JOURNAL

GENERAL JOURNAL
A book of record used to record transactions in chronological order.

Until this point, transaction data were entered directly into the accounts in the general ledger. Because the general ledger is organized by account, it is difficult to retrieve transaction data except by account. For example, retrieval of all transactions that occurred on a certain date would not be easy. Yet the natural flow of transactions is by date, since transactions occur chronologically.

Transactions thus are normally recorded as they occur in the **general journal** (a book used to record transactions in chronological order) before they are transferred into the general ledger. Because transactions are recorded first in the general journal, the general journal is known as the book of original entry. Recording transactions chronologically parallels the natural order of transaction occurrence, facilitates the bookkeeping process, and provides more flexibility to management for data retrieval.

Source Documents

SOURCE DOCUMENTS
Documents used to collect data about a transaction.

Soon after each transaction, details about it are relayed to accounting personnel by a **source document** (a document used to collect data about a transaction). Source documents include such items as bank notices, cash register tapes, invoices, and shipping documents. Information from the source document is first recorded in the general journal.

General Journal Entries

Each entry, in sequence by date, includes the accounts involved, amounts of the changes in the accounts, and the debit or credit for the type of change. Because the debit and credit information for the type of change to be made to an account is conveyed by the arrangement of the general journal entry, particular attention to format is essential. The standard format for a general journal entry is as follows:

Date	Title of account being debited	debit amount	
	Title of account being credited		credit amount
	(explanation or description of transaction)		

The indentation of the credit account title to the right of the debit account title is critical. Consistent with the conventions of the bookkeeping process, this indentation conveys the identification within the general journal entry of the type of change to be made to the account. The account titles to the left are to be debited, whereas those to the right are to be credited by the amounts shown in the journal entry.

Exhibit 2.8 presents the general journal entries for the transactions of the Star Corporation for January 1986.

EXHIBIT 2.8

Star Corporation
General Journal

Page 1

Date	Transaction	Post. Ref.	Debit	Credit
1986				
Jan. 5	Cash	101	30,000	
	Owners' equity	301		30,000
	(to record owners' investment)			
10	Merchandise	102	7,000	
	Accounts payable	201		7,000
	(to record purchase of			
	merchandise on account)			
16	Delivery truck	103	10,000	
	Cash	101		10,000
	(to record purchase of truck)			
18	Buildings	104	15,000	
	Machinery	105	5,000	
	Cash	101		9,000
	Accounts payable	201		11,000
	(to record purchase of			
	machinery and building)			
23	Cash	101	4,000	
	Merchandise	102		3,000
	Owners' equity	301		1,000
	(to record sale of			
	merchandise at a profit)			
25	Accounts payable	201	7,000	
	Cash	101		7,000
	(to record payment on account)			
31	Owners' equity	301	600	
	Cash	101		600
	(to record distribution of assets to			
	owners as a dividend)			

Posting

POSTING
The process of transferring data from the general journal to the general ledger.

Once transactions have been analyzed and recorded in the general journal, each part of the transaction must be entered in the appropriate account in the general ledger. The process of transferring data from the journal entry to the ledger account is known as **posting.**

For each line of the general journal entry posted to the appropriate account in the general ledger, four data items are transferred:

1. The transaction date is repeated in each ledger account affected.
2. The debit and credit amounts are entered in the respective debit and credit sides of the ledger accounts affected.
3. The general journal page containing the original entry is noted in the affected ledger accounts as a cross-reference.
4. The number of the ledger accounts affected is written in the general journal as a cross-reference.

These steps, usually followed in the order listed, are illustrated in Exhibit 2.9. Following a regular pattern helps to ensure that the bookkeeping process is accurately performed.

Exhibit 2.10 presents the formal general ledger records for the Star Corporation for January 1986. To understand the mechanics of posting, trace each part of every transaction from its general journal entry in Exhibit 2.8 to the formal general ledger account in Exhibit 2.10. (The only difference between the general ledger records in Exhibit 2.10 and those in Exhibit 2.6 is the addition of the account number and the cross-reference to the general journal entries presented in Exhibit 2.8.)

EXHIBIT 2.9

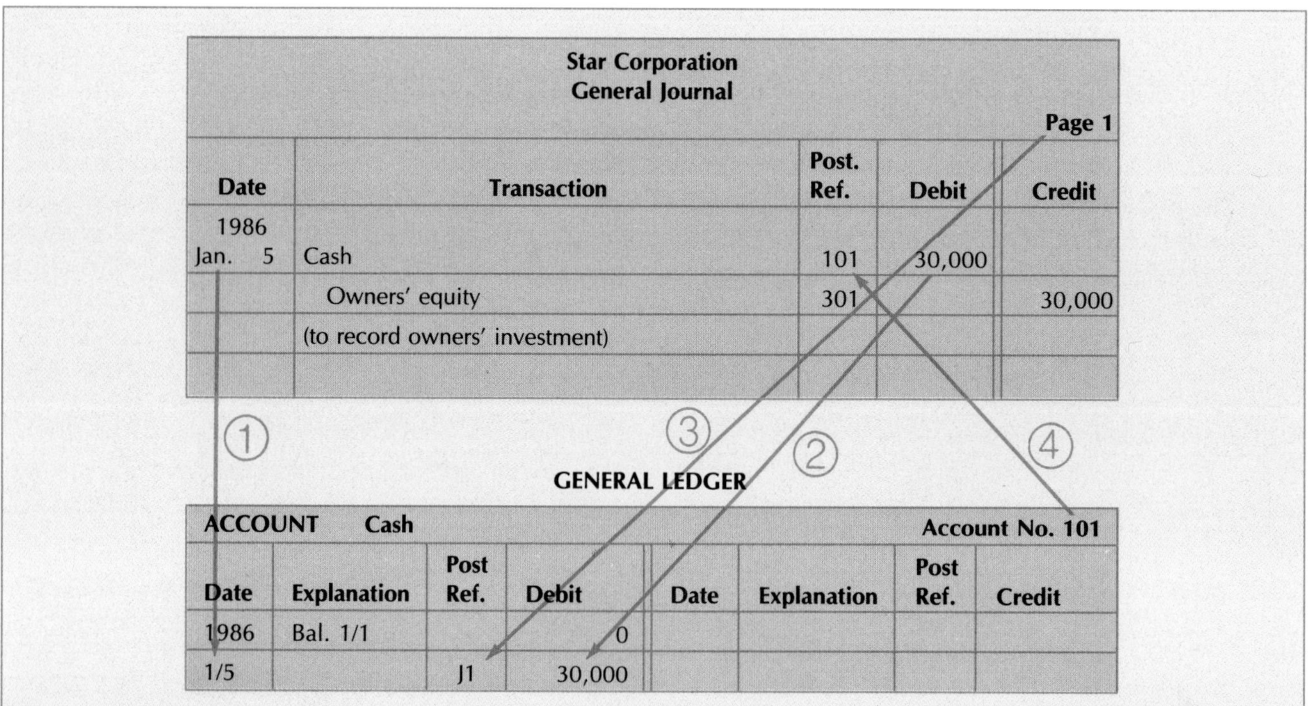

Star Corporation
General Journal

Page 1

Date	Transaction	Post. Ref.	Debit	Credit
1986				
Jan. 5	Cash	101	30,000	
	Owners' equity	301		30,000
	(to record owners' investment)			

GENERAL LEDGER

ACCOUNT Cash **Account No. 101**

Date	Explanation	Post Ref.	Debit	Date	Explanation	Post Ref.	Credit
1986	Bal. 1/1		0				
1/5		J1	30,000				

EXHIBIT 2.10

Star Corporation
GENERAL LEDGER

ACCOUNT	Cash					Account No. 101	
Date	Explanation	Post Ref.	Debit	Date	Explanation	Post Ref.	Credit
1986	Bal. 1/1		0	1/16		J1	10,000
1/5		J1	30,000	1/18		J1	9,000
1/23		J1	4,000	1/25		J1	7,000
				1/30		J1	600
	Total		34,000		Total		26,600
	Bal. 1/31		7,400				

ACCOUNT	Merchandise					Account No. 102	
Date	Explanation	Post Ref.	Debit	Date	Explanation	Post Ref.	Credit
1986	Bal. 1/1		0	1/23		J1	3,000
1/10		J1	7,000				
	Total		7,000		Total		3,000
	Bal. 1/31		4,000				

ACCOUNT	Delivery Truck					Account No. 103	
Date	Explanation	Post Ref.	Debit	Date	Explanation	Post Ref.	Credit
1986	Bal. 1/1		0				
1/16		J1	10,000				
	Total		10,000		Total		0
	Bal. 1/31		10,000				

ACCOUNT	Buildings					Account No. 104	
Date	Explanation	Post Ref.	Debit	Date	Explanation	Post Ref.	Credit
1986	Bal. 1/1		0				
1/18		J1	15,000				
	Total		15,000		Total		0
	Bal. 1/31		15,000				

(Continued on next page)

EXHIBIT 2.10 (Cont.)

ACCOUNT Machinery							Account No. 105
Date	Explanation	Post Ref.	Debit	Date	Explanation	Post Ref.	Credit
1986	Bal. 1/1		0				
1/18		J1	5,000				
	Total		5,000		Total		0
	Bal. 1/31		5,000				

ACCOUNT Accounts Payable							Account No. 201
Date	Explanation	Post Ref.	Debit	Date	Explanation	Post Ref.	Credit
1/25		J1	7,000	1986			0
				1/10		J1	7,000
				1/18		J1	11,000
	Total		7,000		Total		18,000
					Bal. 1/31		11,000

ACCOUNT Owners' Equity							Account No. 301
Date	Explanation	Post Ref.	Debit	Date	Explanation	Post Ref.	Credit
1/30		J1	600	1986			0
				1/5		J1	30,000
				1/23		J1	1,000
	Total		600		Total		31,000
					Bal. 1/31		30,400

■ CONCEPT SUMMARY 2.2 GENERAL JOURNAL VERSUS GENERAL LEDGER—A COMPARISON

General Journal	General Ledger
Transactions recorded by chronological sequence (from source documents).	Transactions recorded by account category (posted from the general journal).
Cross-referenced to general ledger by ledger account number.	Cross-referenced to general journal by journal page number.

AN OVERVIEW OF THE ACCOUNTING CYCLE

By now you should be recognizing the cyclical nature of the accounting process. An overview of this process is shown in Exhibit 2.11, which you should review carefully. This chapter covers steps 1, 2, and 3. Chapter 4 explores steps 4, 5, and 6.

EXHIBIT 2.11
The Accounting Cycle

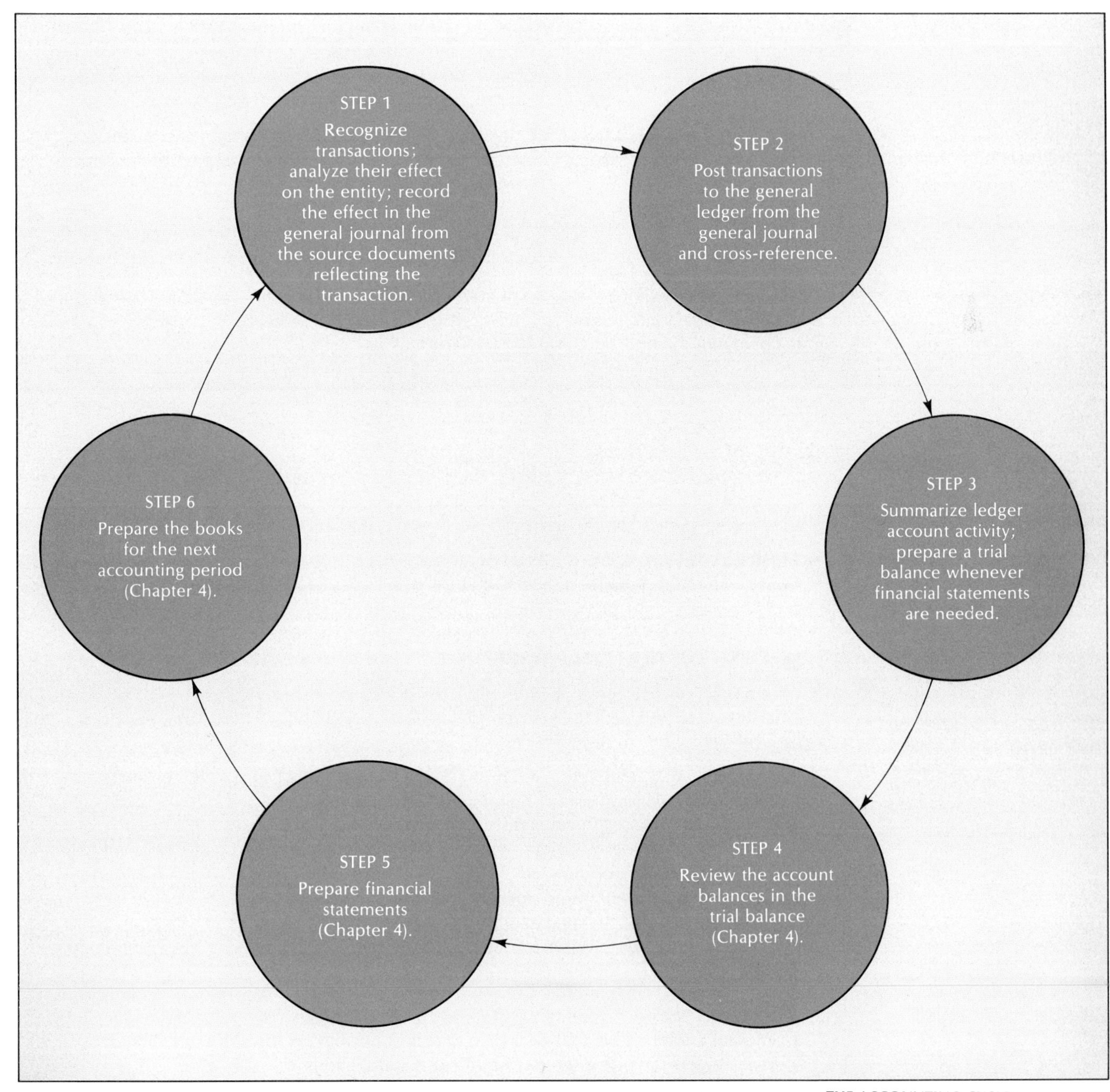

Error Checks

Many students make mechanical errors as they work their way through accounting assignments. If the debits do not equal the credits when you prepare a trial balance, the following suggestions can help you find your mechanical errors:

1. Check for accuracy the addition of the trial balance debit and credit columns.
2. If the trial balance debit column still does not equal the credit column, determine the difference between the two columns and do the following:

a. Look in the ledger to see if you omitted an account with this total from the trial balance and trace your ledger postings back to the general journal to see if you failed to post an entry in the amount of the difference.
b. Divide the difference by two. Look to see if you have placed this amount in the wrong column of the trial balance.
c. Divide the difference between the two columns by nine. If the difference is evenly divisible by nine, look for a transposition of digits in copying your ledger balances over to the trial balance. Perhaps you copied \$7,200 as \$2,700. Also check to make sure you placed the decimal point in the correct position in the trial balance. You may have written \$2,700 as \$27.00.

3. Recheck your trial balance with the general ledger account balances to make sure you copied each correctly.
4. Make sure each account balance in the general ledger was correctly determined.
5. Recheck the posting of each item in the general ledger from the general journal to see that it was made correctly.

Most errors can be found by following the preceding steps. In many instances, you will locate your error before you reach step three.

FOR REVIEW

DEMONSTRATON PROBLEM

Sid, Able, and Tom started the SAT Office Supply Corporation on June 1, 1986. During June, SAT has the following transactions:

June 1 Sid, Able, and Tom each invest \$15,000 cash in SAT to start the business.
June 4 SAT purchases a small building for \$30,000 cash.
June 5 SAT purchases merchandise from suppliers for \$3,000 cash.
June 11 SAT purchases \$4,000 of merchandise from suppliers on credit. Payment is due to the suppliers on June 30.
June 20 SAT purchases a used delivery truck for \$5,000 cash.
June 30 SAT pays for the merchandise purchased on June 11.
June 30 SAT borrows \$10,000 cash from a local bank, with payment due in six months.

Required

1. Prepare a transaction analysis in the format of Exhibit 2.5 for SAT's June transactions.
2. Prepare general journal entries for the June transactions.
3. Post the general journal entries to the general ledger.
4. Prepare a trial balance for SAT Office Supply Corporation as of June 30, 1986.
5. Prepare a statement of financial position for SAT as of June 30, 1986.

Demonstration Problem Solution

1.

SAT Office Supply Corporation
Transaction Analysis
For the Month of June 1986

	Assets				=	Sources of Assets: Liabilities		+ Owners' Equity
Trans. Date	**Cash**	**Merchandise**	**Delivery Truck**	**Buildings**		**Accounts Payable**	**Notes Payable to Banks**	**Owners' Equity**
6/1	+$45,000							+$45,000
6/4	− 30,000			+$30,000				
6/5	− 3,000	+$3,000						
6/11		+ 4,000				+$4,000		
6/20	− 5,000		+$5,000					
6/30	− 4,000					− 4,000		
6/30	+ 10,000						+$10,000	
Bal. 6/30	$13,000	$7,000	$5,000	$30,000		$ 0	$10,000	$45,000

2.

SAT Office Supply
General Journal

Page 1

Date	Transaction	Post. Ref.	Debit	Credit
1986				
June 1	Cash	101	45,000	
	Owners' equity	301		45,000
	(to record owners' investment)			
4	Building	117	30,000	
	Cash	101		30,000
	(to record purchase of building)			
5	Merchandise inventory	105	3,000	
	Cash	101		3,000
	(to record purchase of mdse.)			
11	Merchandise inventory	105	4,000	
	Accounts payable	201		4,000
	(to record purchase of mdse.)			
20	Delivery truck	115	5,000	
	Cash	101		5,000
	(to record purchase of truck)			
30	Accounts payable	201	4,000	
	Cash	101		4,000
	(to record payment on acct.)			
30	Cash	101	10,000	
	Notes payable to bank	205		10,000
	(to record borrowing from bank)			

3.

SAT Office Supply
GENERAL LEDGER

ACCOUNT Cash							Account No. 101
Date	Explanation	Post Ref.	Debit	Date	Explanation	Post Ref.	Credit
6/1		J1	45,000	6/4		J1	30,000
6/30		J1	10,000	6/5		J1	3,000
				6/20		J1	5,000
				6/30		J1	4,000
	Bal. 6/30		13,000				

ACCOUNT Merchandise Inventory							Account No. 105
Date	Explanation	Post Ref.	Debit	Date	Explanation	Post Ref.	Credit
6/5		J1	3,000				
6/11		J1	4,000				
	Bal. 6/30		7,000				

ACCOUNT Delivery Truck							Account No. 115
Date	Explanation	Post Ref.	Debit	Date	Explanation	Post Ref.	Credit
6/20		J1	5,000				
	Bal. 6/30		5,000				

ACCOUNT Buildings							Account No. 117
Date	Explanation	Post Ref.	Debit	Date	Explanation	Post Ref.	Credit
6/4		J1	30,000				
	Bal. 6/30		30,000				

ACCOUNT Accounts Payable							Account No. 201
Date	Explanation	Post Ref.	Debit	Date	Explanation	Post Ref.	Credit
6/30		J1	4,000	6/11		J1	4,000
					Bal. 6/30		0

ACCOUNT Notes Payable to Bank							Account No. 205
Date	Explanation	Post Ref.	Debit	Date	Explanation	Post Ref.	Credit
				6/30		J1	10,000
					Bal. 6/30		10,000

ACCOUNT Owners' Equity							Account No. 301
Date	Explanation	Post Ref.	Debit	Date	Explanation	Post Ref.	Credit
				6/1		J1	45,000
					Bal. 6/30		45,000

4.

SAT Office Supply Corporation
Trial Balance
June 30, 1986

Account	Debit	Credit
Cash	$13,000	
Merchandise	7,000	
Delivery Truck	5,000	
Buildings	30,000	
Accounts Payable		$ 0
Notes Payable to Bank		10,000
Owners' Equity		45,000
Totals	$55,000	$55,000

5.

SAT Office Supply Corporation
Statement of Financial Position
June 30, 1986

Assets		Liabilities and Owners' Equity	
Cash	$13,000	Liabilities	
Merchandise	7,000	Notes payable to bank	$10,000
Delivery truck	5,000	Owners' equity	45,000
Buildings	30,000		
Total	$55,000	Total	$55,000

SUMMARY

- Transactions are recorded in the accounting system as debits and credits.
- Debit denotes a left position and, as a verb, means to increase an asset account or to decrease a liability or owners' equity account.
- Credit denotes a right position and, as a verb, means to increase a liability or owners' equity account or to decrease an asset account.
- The account is the fundamental data collection point in an accounting system and summarizes transaction data.
- Transactions are recorded from source documents by time sequence in the general journal—the book of original entry.
- Transactions are recorded by account in the general ledger—the book of accounts.
- The chart of accounts lists all of the accounts for a firm and serves as a table of contents for the general ledger.
- The trial balance is a listing of all ledger account balances and provides a starting point for the preparation of financial statements.

QUESTIONS

2-1. Define the terms *debit* and *credit* as used in accounting.

2-2. What is a chart of accounts, and why is it significant?

2-3. What is a general journal, and what purpose does it serve?

2-4. List the steps necessary to properly analyze a transaction before it can be recorded in the general journal.

2-5. Explain the purpose of the general ledger and how it relates to the general journal.

2-6. Briefly outline the procedure for posting from the general journal to the general ledger.

2-7. Why must the debits always equal the credits when an accounting transaction is recorded?

2-8. Indicate the effects of debits and credits on assets, liabilities, and owners' equity.

2-9. Discuss the purpose and function of the trial balance.

2-10. Explain the difference between entries in an account and an account balance.

EXERCISES

2-E1. Classify each of the following accounts as either an asset account or a liability account. In addition, indicate the effect that debits and credits have on the account.

a. Cash
b. Accounts Payable
c. Accounts Receivable
d. Land
e. Notes Payable
f. Inventory

2-E2. Fill in the blanks in each of the following statements with the word *debit* or *credit:*

a. Cash is increased by a __________ and is decreased by a __________.
b. Accounts Receivable is increased by a __________ and decreased by a __________.
c. Accounts Payable is increased by a __________ and decreased by a __________.
d. Owners' Equity is increased by a __________ and decreased by a __________.
e. Taxes Payable is increased by a __________ and decreased by a __________.

2-E3. For each of the following independent errors, indicate (1) whether the trial balance will be out of balance because of the error and by how much and (2) whether the debit or credit side of the trial balance will have the larger total.

a. A debit of $125 was never posted to Accounts Receivable.
b. A credit of $54 to Accounts Payable was mistakenly posted as a credit of $45.
c. A debit of $250 to Accounts Receivable was mistakenly debited to cash.
d. A $100 credit to Accounts Receivable was posted as a $100 credit to Accounts Payable.
e. A credit of $500 to Owners' Equity was posted twice.

2-E4. The following account balances were taken from the general ledger of the Caustic Chemical Company:

Accounts Payable	$ 2,500
Cash	?
Accounts Receivable	4,000
Building	10,000
Notes Payable	3,000
Owners' Equity	19,500
Land	8,000

Determine the balance in the Cash account and prepare a trial balance for the Caustic Chemical Company as of December 31, 1986.

2-E5. Widget Retailers, a retailer of educational widgets used in college-level economics classes, opened its doors on June 1, 1986. The following transactions are for the company's first month of operations:

June 1 Wanda Widget, owner, invests $18,000 cash and office equipment worth $2,000 to form Widget.
June 12 Widget Retailers purchases a building for $25,000, giving $10,000 cash and a note payable of $15,000.
June 23 $3,000 of widgets are purchased on account.
June 30 $150 of supplies are purchased for cash.

Prepare the appropriate journal entry for each of the preceding transactions for Widget Retailers.

2-E6. Using the transactions from 2-E5, prepare ledger T-accounts to correspond to the accounts that would appear in Widget's general ledger. Post the transactions to the T-accounts and prepare a trial balance to assure that you have not made mechanical errors.

2-E7. For each of the following accounts, indicate whether the normal account balance is a debit or a credit:

a. Cash
b. Inventory
c. Accounts Payable
d. Notes Payable
e. Accounts Receivable
f. Equipment
g. Owners' Equity

PROBLEM SET A

2-A1. Transaction Analysis. The William Tell Telephone Company had the following transactions for February 1986:

	Assets				=	Liabilities		+	Owners' Equity
Trans. Date	Cash	Accounts Receivable	Buildings	Office Equipment		Accounts Payable	Notes Payable		Owners' Equity
2/1	+$ 5,000			+$4,000					+$9,000
2/7	− 5,000		+$22,000				+$17,000		
2/18	+ 2,000	+$3,000		− 5,000					
2/22				+ 1,500		+$ 1,500			
2/28	+$10,000					+$10,000			

Required

a. Prove that the accounting equation is correct in total for all February transactions.
b. Describe the nature of each of the five transactions that occurred during February.
c. Prepare the appropriate general journal entry for each of the February transactions.

2-A2. Journalizing Transactions. The S.A.C. Corporation is a manufacturer of paper and paper by-products. During the month of May, the corporation has the following transactions:

May 1 Owners invest $50,000 cash in the company.
May 10 S.A.C. purchases office supplies for $175 and a typewriter for $400 on account from Summit City Office Supply.

May 13 S.A.C. borrows $5,000 from the Mad Anthony Bank on a six-month note.
May 15 S.A.C. purchases $10,000 of timber for paper production on account.
May 20 S.A.C. issues check number 989 for $575 to pay for supplies and the typewriter purchased on May 10.
May 25 S.A.C. purchases a delivery truck from Don Hoage's Used Car and Truck Lot. The truck is purchased for a down payment of $15,000 and a note payable for the remaining $5,000 due in one year.
May 30 S.A.C. pays for the timber purchased on May 15.

Required

Prepare the proper general journal entry for each of the corporation's May transactions.

2-A3. General Ledger and Trial Balance. Using the information from 2-A2, and given that May was S.A.C.'s first month of operation, perform the following:

Required

a. Prepare a chart of accounts for S.A.C.
b. Post the general journal entries for the month of May to the general ledger.
c. Prepare a trial balance for S.A.C. as of May 31.

2-A4. Recognizing Impact of Journal Entries on Accounts. A review of the Crispy-Crunchy Potato Chip Company's general journal for the first ten days of August 1986 shows the following entries:

August	1	Inventory	$100,000	
		Accounts Payable		$100,000
	3	Cash	10,000	
		Accounts Receivable		10,000
	5	Machinery	30,000	
		Notes Payable		30,000
	6	Accounts Payable	60,000	
		Cash		60,000
	7	Cash	30,000	
		Notes Payable		30,000
	9	Accounts Receivable	30,000	
		Inventory		20,000
		Owners' Equity		10,000
	10	Owners' Equity	4,000	
		Cash		4,000

The bookkeeper has forgotten to give any explanations with the entries.

Required

a. For each part of each entry, indicate whether the account is being increased or decreased.
b. Provide a reasonable explanation for each transaction that results in each of the journal entries.

2-A5. Trial Balance. Clarence Gustava, Inc., owns a chain of German-American restaurants located in the Great Lakes region. The restaurants specialize in bratwurst, knockwurst, and knipplekaanocken. The following accounts were taken from the corporation's general ledger on January 1, the beginning of the corporation's fiscal year. All accounts had normal balances at that time.

Inventory	$ 3,000
Building	25,000
Accounts Payable	4,500
Accounts Receivable	?
Equipment	11,000
Owners' Equity	35,000
Cash	2,000
Notes Payable	4,300

Required

a. Determine the balance in accounts receivable.
b. Prepare a trial balance for Clarence Gustava, Inc., as of January 1, 1986.

2-A6. Correcting a Trial Balance. Malpractice, Inc., a highly reputable CBA (Certified Bumbling Accountant) firm, prepared the following trial balance for the Gullible Corporation. As can be seen, the trial balance does not balance.

The Gullible Corporation
Trial Balance
December 31, 1986

	Debit	Credit
Cash	$ 3,150	
Accounts Receivable		$ 5,400
Merchandise Inventory		6,600
Accounts Payable	2,300	
Notes Payable	4,300	
Wages Payable		12,000
Equipment	8,500	
Buildings	12,000	
Owners' Equity	16,500	
Totals	$46,750	$24,000

Upon examination of the general journal and general ledger, you find the following:

1. Each of the accounts really has its balance on the normal side of the account.
2. Total debits to Accounts Receivable equal $8,500 (including the beginning balance), and total credits equal $3,400.
3. A cash payment of $600 from a customer has been recorded as a debit to Accounts Receivable and a credit to Cash.
4. An $850 payment from a customer has been mistakenly posted to the Cash account twice.
5. Purchases of equipment on account totaling $1,500 have been entered in the general journal but have not been posted to the general ledger.
6. A $600 payment to a vendor for merchandise purchased on account has not been posted to the Accounts Payable account.

Required

Prepare a corrected trial balance.

2-A7. Journalizing, Posting, and Trial Balance. The Suave and Debonair Corporation sells distasteful clothing for the terminally unfashionable male. The trial balance of Suave and Debonair as of June 30, 1986, appears as follows:

The Suave and Debonair Corporation
Trial Balance
June 30, 1986

Account No.	Account Title	Debit	Credit
100	Cash	$ 3,500	
110	Accounts Receivable	5,000	
120	Merchandise Inventory	10,000	
130	Notes Receivable	4,000	
140	Office Equipment	6,000	
150	Trucks	10,000	
160	Buildings	20,000	
200	Accounts Payable		$ 4,000
210	Notes Payable		12,000
300	Owners' Equity		42,500
	Totals	$58,500	$58,500

Additional information:

July 1 To purchase a large quantity of purple 1970s' jackets, the corporation borrows $7,500 from the Decatur National Bank. The note is payable in two years.

July 5 S & D purchases $7,500 of 1970s' jackets on account from Behind-the-Times Wholesalers.

July 7 S & D purchases a delivery truck from Snakey Hedger's Used Trucks for $2,000 down and $4,000 on account.

July 11 S & D sells $1,500 of black sneakers on account to a punk basketball team from London, England. The sneakers cost S & D $750.

July 14 Feeling that a frog-shaped office building is neither suave nor debonair, Suave and Debonair decides to sell Kermit Towers. The building cost S & D $10,000 to build and is sold for $10,000, with the buyer, Piggy, Inc., paying $1,500 cash and the rest on a one-year note.

July 18 S & D issues a check for $7,500 to cover the 1970s' jackets purchased on July 5.

July 21 S & D receives $1,500 from the punk basketball team in payment of its account.

July 25 S & D pays $600 to the editor of *Gentlemen's Biannually* for future advertising space.

July 28 S & D purchases display racks for $1,800 cash.

July 30 Otis Guntley, part owner, invests an additional $8,000 cash and $2,000 worth of vinyl office furniture.

July 30 S & D purchases an assortment of 5-inch wide neckties and wide-lapel sport coats for $5,500.

Required

a. Prepare a general journal entry for each of the preceding transactions. You may need to prepare additional accounts to make some of your entries. Label and number these accounts reasonably.
b. Construct general ledger T-accounts using the June trial balance as a chart of accounts and enter the beginning balances in the appropriate accounts.
c. Post the journal entries from (a) to the ledger accounts.
d. Prepare a trial balance for Suave and Debonair as of July 31, 1986.

2-A8. Analysis of Ledger Accounts with Incomplete Information. The Walnut Creek Company has hired a new bookkeeper. In reviewing the work of the former bookkeeper, the new bookkeeper learns that certain information is missing. The new bookkeeper has reconstructed part of the ledger in T-account form as follows for the month of August:

Accounts Receivable

8/1 Bal.	40,000	?	Total Aug. cr.
Total Aug. dr.	80,000		
8/31 Bal.	?		

Accounts Payable

Total Aug. dr.	40,000	?	8/1 Bal.
		?	Total Aug. cr.
		60,000	8/31 Bal.

Cash

8/1 Bal.	100,000		
Total Aug. dr.	70,000	?	Total Aug. cr.
8/31 Bal.	?		

Inventory

8/1 Bal.	?	60,000	Total Aug. cr.
Total Aug. dr.	80,000		
8/31 Bal.	90,000		

The bookkeeper has also determined the following facts:

1. All increases in Cash during August are the result of customer payments on account.
2. All decreases in Cash during August are the result of payments made to suppliers on account.
3. All increases in Accounts Payable during August are the result of purchases of inventory on account, and all purchases of inventory are made on account.

Required

Determine the following amounts:

a. The total credits to Accounts Receivable during August.
b. The 8/31 balance in Accounts Receivable.
c. The total credits to Cash during August.
d. The 8/31 balance in Cash.
e. The 8/1 balance in Accounts Payable.
f. The total credits to Accounts Payable during August.
g. The 8/1 balance in inventory.

PROBLEM SET B

2-B1. Transaction Analysis. The Top Notch Office Supply Company enters into the following transactions during May 1986:

	Assets					= Liabilities		+ Owners' Equity
Trans. Date	Cash	Accounts Receivable	Merchandise Inventory	Office Equipment	Buildings	Accounts Payable	Notes Payable	Owners' Equity
5/1	+$ 5,000		+$5,000					+$10,000
5/4		+$1,500	− 750					+ 750
5/10	+ 10,000						+$10,000	
5/15	− 1,000		+ 4,000			+$3,000		
5/21	− 4,000				+$14,000		+ 10,000	
5/28				+$1,500		+ 1,500		

Required

a. Prove that the accounting equation is correct in total for the May transactions.
b. Describe a possible transaction that could have occurred for each of the May 1986 dates listed.
c. Prepare an appropriate general journal entry for each of the May transactions.

2-B2. Journalizing Transactions. Patricia Pastel and Louis Latex begin Perfect Finish Painting Supplies, Inc., on June 1, 1986. Perfect Finish's June transactions are as follows:

June 1	The owners each invest $6,000 of their personal funds to start the business.
June 2	Perfect Finish purchases a new truck for $7,500, with $2,500 paid in cash and the balance due in 90 days.
June 3	Perfect Finish purchases sprayers, scaffolding, and other equipment for use in the business for $1,100 cash.
June 6	Perfect Finish purchases supplies on account, $480.
June 8	Perfect Finish purchases paint, paint brushes, and scrapers for resale, $4,250 on account.
June 20	Perfect Finish hires two salespeople to begin work on July 1, each at a monthly salary of $1,200.
June 30	Perfect Finish issues a check for $2,000 in partial payment of merchandise purchased on June 8.

Required

Prepare general journal entries for each of the June transactions.

2-B3. General Ledger and Trial Balance Preparation. Using the information from 2-B2, and given that June 1986 was Perfect Finish's first month of operation, perform the following:

Required

a. Prepare a chart of accounts for Perfect Finish.
b. Post the general journal entries for the month of June to general ledger T-accounts.
c. Prepare a trial balance as of June 30, 1986.

2-B4. Recognizing Impact of Journal Entries on Accounts. A review of the Precision Flight Charter Company's general journal for the first ten days of June shows the following entries:

Date	Account	Debit	Credit
June 1	Cash	100,000	
	Owners' Equity		100,000
June 2	Inventory	60,000	
	Accounts Payable		60,000
June 4	Furniture	10,000	
	Notes Payable		10,000
June 5	Cash	40,000	
	Accounts Receivable		40,000
June 7	Accounts Payable	30,000	
	Cash		30,000
June 8	Accounts Receivable	20,000	
	Inventory		15,000
	Owners' Equity		5,000
June 10	Owners' Equity	1,000	
	Cash		1,000

The bookkeeper forgot to give any explanations with the entries.

Required

a. For each part of each entry, indicate whether the account is being increased or decreased.
b. Provide a reasonable explanation for each transaction that resulted in each of the journal entries.

2-B5. Trial Balance. The Two-for-One Book Company had the following account balances pulled from its general ledger on July 31, 1986. Assume that the fiscal year closes on July 31, 1986, and that all accounts have their normal balances.

Delivery Truck	$ 7,500
Merchandise Inventory	6,000
Cash	?
Accounts Payable	3,000
Accounts Receivable	2,500
Owners' Equity	30,000
Building	20,000
Note Payable	8,000

Required

a. Compute the appropriate account balance for Cash.
b. Prepare a trial balance for the Two-for-One Book Company as of July 31, 1986.

2-B6. Correcting a Trial Balance. Rinky Dink Accounting Services, a disreputable firm at best, prepared the following trial balance for the Naive Corporation. As can be seen, the trial balance does not balance.

Naive Corporation
Trial Balance
May 31, 1986

	Debit	Credit
Cash		$ 2,700
Accounts Receivable	$ 3,250	
Merchandise Inventory	4,000	
Supplies		800
Buildings	10,000	
Accounts Payable	2,700	
Notes Payable		5,000
Owners' Equity	14,250	
Totals	$34,200	$ 8,500

Upon examination of the general journal and general ledger, you find the following:

1. Each of the accounts really has its balance on the normal side of the account.
2. Total credits to the Accounts Payable account, including the beginning balance, amount to $4,700, and total debits equal $3,000.
3. A $200 payment to a vendor for merchandise purchased on account has not been posted to the Accounts Payable account.
4. Purchases of $1,000 of merchandise on credit have been entered in the general journal but not posted to the general ledger.
5. Purchases of supplies for $200 cash have been entered in the general journal but were never posted to the general ledger.

Required

Prepare a corrected trial balance.

2-B7. Journalizing, Posting, and Trial Balance. Plastic World, Incorporated, is a retailer of genuine imitation plastic products. The trial balance of the corporation as of January 31, 1986, is as follows:

Plastic World, Incorporated
Trial Balance
January 31, 1986

		Debit	Credit
100	Cash	$10,000	
110	Accounts Receivable	4,500	
120	Merchandise Inventory	6,750	
130	Office Supplies	1,500	
140	Furniture	3,250	
150	Trucks	10,500	
160	Buildings	20,000	
200	Accounts Payable		$ 3,500
210	Notes Payable		14,000
300	Owners' Equity		39,000
	Totals	$56,500	$56,500

The following transactions take place during February:

February 1 Plastic World purchases office supplies on account, $250.
February 5 The company sells a truck and office furniture recorded on the books at $5,000 and $3,000, respectively, for $2,000 cash each.
February 7 The company sells imitation plastic table tops to Mac's Fast Food Diner for $8,000 on account. The table tops originally cost Plastic World $3,000.
February 9 Plastic World purchases plastic novelty items from the Plasto Company for $3,000 on account.
February 14 The company issues a check to pay for office supplies purchased on February 1.
February 15 The company pays $550 for fire insurance for the next two years.
February 18 The owners invest an additional $10,000 cash into the corporation.
February 21 The company receives $5,000 from Mac's in partial payment for merchandise sold on February 7.
February 25 The company receives an order for $5,000 worth of plastic flowers from Ned's Mortuary to be delivered on March 16, 1986.
February 28 The company issues a check to pay for the plastic novelty items purchased on February 9.

Required

a. Construct general ledger T-accounts using the January 31 trial balance and enter the February 1 beginning balances in the accounts.
b. Prepare general journal entries for the February transactions. You might need to add accounts to complete your entries.
c. Post the journal entries from (b) to the appropriate T-accounts. You might need to add accounts to complete your entries.
d. Determine the balance in each account as of February 28 and prepare a trial balance for Plastic World, Incorporated, as of that date.

2-B8. Analysis of Ledger Accounts with Incomplete Information. Basic Sales Corporation has recently hired a new bookkeeper. In reviewing the ledger accounts for July, the bookkeeper learns that certain information is missing and reconstructs part of the ledger in T-account form as follows:

Accounts Receivable

7/1 Bal.	?	110,000	Total July cr.
Total July dr.	80,000		
7/31 Bal.	70,000		

Accounts Payable

Total July dr.	?	30,000	7/1 Bal.
		?	Total July cr.
		?	7/31 Bal.

Cash			
7/1 Bal.	70,000		
Total July dr.	?	?	Total July cr.
7/31 Bal.	100,000		

Inventory			
7/1 Bal.	60,000	80,000	Total July cr.
Total July dr.	70,000		
7/31 Bal.	?		

The bookkeeper also determines the following facts:

1. All increases in Cash during July are the result of customer payments on account.
2. All decreases in Cash in July are the result of payments made to suppliers on account.
3. All increases in Inventory during July are the result of purchases on account.

Required

Determine the following amounts:

a. The July 1 balance in Accounts Receivable.
b. The total debits to Cash during July.
c. The total credits to Cash during July.
d. The total debits to Accounts Payable during July.
e. The total credits to Accounts Payable during July.
f. The July 31 balance in Accounts Payable.
g. The July 31 balance in Inventory.

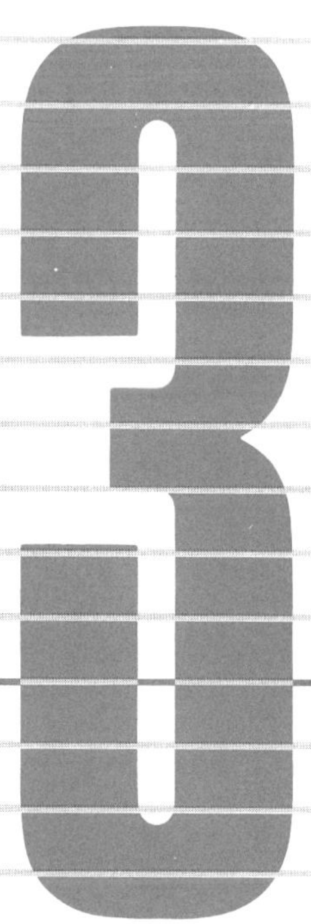

THE INCOME STATEMENT

3

CHAPTER OBJECTIVES
After studying of Chapter 3, you should understand the following:

1. The concept of business income and the accounting model.
2. The relationship between the statement of financial position and the income statement.
3. The framework for processing revenue and expense transactions within an accounting system.
4. The content of the income statement.

After examining transactions, the accounting equation, and the accounting language of debits and credits, we now take a closer look at the asset flows that occur when a business enters into transactions with customers to earn a profit.

INCOME BASICS

PROFIT
See Income.

INCOME
The excess of revenue and gains over expenses and losses for a given time period.

Most corporations are organized to make a profit for their owners. **Profit,** or **income,** is defined as the excess of revenue and gains over expenses and losses for a given time period. Chapter 1 explained transactions in terms of asset flows. When Star Corporation sold merchandise for $4,000 that had originally cost $3,000, we said the corporation made a profit on the sale: More assets were received ($4,000 in cash) than were used up ($3,000 in merchandise). The goal in a profit-oriented business is to enter into transactions with customers in which the business receives more assets from the customers than it uses up to support the transaction.

Revenue and Expense

REVENUES
Inflows of assets from customers in exchange for goods provided or services rendered.

EXPENSES
Assets consumed or traded to secure revenues.

Inflows of assets from customers in exchange for goods provided or services rendered are called **revenues.** In Star's case, the $4,000 revenue was received in the form of cash, but if the sale had been on account, Star would still have received $4,000 revenue in the form of accounts receivable. Assets consumed or traded to secure revenues are labeled **expenses.** In Star's case, the assets traded (consumed) were the $3,000 of merchandise used up. The difference between revenues (asset inflows from customers) and expenses (assets consumed to obtain the revenues) is Star's profit on the transaction.

The Income Statement

INCOME STATEMENT
A statement presenting an entity's revenue, expense, gain, and loss information for a given time period.

The **income statement** presents an entity's revenue and expense information (along with other gains and losses discussed later in the chapter) for a given time period. Assume that the foregoing sale was Star's only transaction involving revenue and/or expense during January 1986. Exhibit 3.1 presents Star's income statement for the month ending January 31, 1986.

COST OF GOODS SOLD
The amount paid to suppliers for merchandise sold to customers.

The income statement, like all accounting statements, bears a heading giving the entity's name, identification of the report, and the time period covered. By convention, revenues is the first category listed. Following are expenses listed by type. In Star's case, the only expense is **cost of goods sold,** which is the amount paid by the seller for merchandise sold. In general, the term *cost* denotes the amount paid by a company to acquire an asset or a service. The cost of an asset becomes an expense when the asset is used up in producing revenue.

EXHIBIT 3.1

Star Corporation
Income Statement
For the Month Ending January 31, 1986

Sales	$4,000
Less cost of goods sold	3,000
Net income	$1,000

The Importance of Income

For businesses today, income is the most widely accepted performance measurement and often is the basis for investor predictions of future economic outcomes. To understand accounting for income determination, one must first understand the framework in which accountants attempt to measure income.

THE INCOME FRAMEWORK

Cash Accounting Versus Accrual Accounting

Because income measurement is based on the recognition of revenues and expenses, the question of when revenue and expense transactions occur is central to income measurement. One of two basic approaches can be taken to determine the answer to this question.

1. Transaction recognition can be restricted to those occasions when cash is exchanged (known as the **cash basis**).
2. Transactions can be recognized whenever cash is exchanged *or* whenever the right to receive money or the obligation to pay money is established (known as the **accrual basis**).

CASH BASIS
The method of accounting where transaction recognition is restricted to those occasions when cash is exchanged.

ACCRUAL BASIS
The method of accounting where transactions are recognized whenever cash is exchanged or the right to receive money or the obligation to pay money is established.

Cash Basis of Accounting. Under the cash basis of accounting, transactions are recognized only when cash changes hands. Assume that you own a bookstore and that you sell five books on December 31 for $25 each. You agree to accept payment of $125 (5 × $25) in January.

Under the cash basis of accounting, you would not recognize any revenue until you received the cash; your records would thus show the following:

Revenue for December	$ 0
Revenue for January	125

Although seemingly unreasonable, you recognize zero revenue in December when you actually sold the books and you recognize $125 revenue in January when you did not sell any books.

Or consider the problem that you would face if you used the cash basis of accounting and purchased a used delivery truck on December 1 for $5,000 cash. Your records under the cash basis of accounting would record your expenses as follows:

Truck expense in December	$ 5,000
Truck expense in January	0

This makes even less sense. Clearly, the truck should be considered an expense as you wear it out making deliveries over time. You did not wear the truck out completely in December.

Accrual Accounting. In addition to recognizing transactions when cash is exchanged, accrual accounting recognizes a transaction when either the right to receive money or the obligation to pay money is established. Your work in December established your right to receive money.

Who Uses Cash Accounting?

Although the accrual method of accounting provides better financial information for decision making because it focuses on work efforts rather than cash flows, many small firms use the cash basis of accounting because it is simple.

The only book of record required under this system is a checkbook. The checkbook is a running total of cash receipts and disbursements. In addition to offering simplicity, the cash method fosters control of cash, one of the most important assets available to companies and individuals.

Many professionals, such as doctors, lawyers, and accountants, use the cash basis because it has certain advantages for tax purposes. For example, a medical doctor can defer billing of patients at the end of the year until the following year, thereby shifting income from one tax year to the next.

Under the accrual basis of accounting, you would recognize revenue as follows:

Revenue for December	$ 125
Revenue for January	0

Also, some allocation of the cost of the truck would be made to reflect the wear and tear of the vehicle from your use in December to deliver the books. For example, if you think the truck will last five years (60 months), you could divide the truck's cost by 60 ($5,000/60 = $83) and record $83 as the expense of using the truck each month. Under accrual accounting, you would recognize truck expense as follows:

Expense related to truck in December	$ 83
Expense related to truck in January	83

Accrual accounting links the revenue and expense you recognize and your work efforts much more closely than does cash accounting. Under the accrual basis of accounting, it makes no difference when you actually receive the cash from your customers or when you spend cash to acquire assets—what counts is the completion of the sale and the associated using up of assets.

Both the cash basis and the accrual basis of accounting would recognize the receiving and spending of the cash itself. The difference between the two methods lies in the timing of revenue and expense recognition.

In a simple business situation where economic events and cash exchanges are closely related in time, perhaps occurring simultaneously, the cash basis of accounting is an acceptable method. But for today's complex business world, the accrual basis of accounting generally provides a much better foundation for measuring the results of business operations, because it matches revenues and expenses with work efforts of a business. The text focuses on accrual accounting.

Revenue Recognition

REVENUE RECOGNITION
When revenues are recorded in the accounts. Generally, revenue recognition occurs in accrual accounting when services are rendered or when goods are delivered to customers.

Revenue recognition occurs when revenues are recorded in the accounts and generally occurs in an accrual accounting system when services are rendered or when goods are delivered to customers. However, three conditions must exist before revenue is recognized under conventional (accrual) accounting:

1. The earning process must be substantially complete. This point usually occurs when the goods have been delivered or the service has been provided to the customer.
2. The price of the goods or services (the amount of assets to be received from customers) must be known or be subject to reasonable estimation.
3. Collection of revenue (assets to be received from customers) is reasonably assured.

Normally, all three of the foregoing conditions are met at the point of sale. Whether the customer pays cash then or promises to pay at a later date has no bearing on when the revenue and expenses associated with the sale are recognized within the accounting system.

If the Computer Store sells goods for $30,000 on September 1 and the customers pay $10,000 in cash and promise to pay $20,000 by the end of the month, Computer would recognize revenue of $30,000 on September 1. When the customers pay the remaining $20,000 in cash on September 30, no further revenue is recognized. The Computer Store has simply collected $20,000 in cash in exchange for the noncash asset, accounts receivable (the customer's promise to pay).

Revenue Realization

Closely related to the concept of revenue recognition is the principle of **revenue realization,** which occurs when the business entity acquires the right to receive payment from its customers. In general, sellers acquire the right to receive payment from customers when ownership of goods passes to the customer or when services have been performed (for service organizations such as accounting firms).

REVENUE REALIZATION
The term applied to the point when the business entity acquires the right to receive payment from its customers.

Revenue is recognized whenever a revenue transaction is recorded in the accounting system. Businesses will sometimes record revenue before completion of the earnings process (before revenue is realized). For example, a construction firm building a nuclear power plant over a ten-year period might record and recognize revenue from the project throughout the construction period rather than wait ten years until the plant is finished to recognize its revenue.

For purposes of this text, we will ignore these timing differences and assume that when revenue is recognized and recorded it is completely realized (earned).

Recognition of Expenses

Once a revenue transaction has been recognized for accounting purposes, the assets used up to produce the revenue should be recorded as expenses. Expense recognition is therefore dependent on association of asset use with revenue. Associating expense recognition with revenue recognition is referred to as the matching principle and is essential to the accrual process of income determination.

The Matching Principle. The **matching principle** states that all expenses must be recorded in the same time period as their associated revenues are recognized. Timing of expense recognition is not dependent on the timing of payment to suppliers or simple use of assets in operations. Although an asset must be used up to create an expense, the consumption is not recorded as an expense until the revenue from a sale associated with that asset use is recognized.

MATCHING PRINCIPLE
The principle that requires all expenses to be recognized in the same time period as their associated revenues are recognized.

Some assets, such as office buildings and equipment, cannot be linked directly to products sold. Yet the use of such assets is required to operate the business and produce revenue. In such cases, the passing of time is often used as the basis for allocating asset cost to expense under the assumption that a portion of the asset wears out during each time period that the business operates. Subsequent chapters explore this concept more fully.

The Matching Principle Illustrated. The Brady Company uses two raw materials—molasses and seasoning—to produce syrup. No other asset expenditures are necessary. Producing a barrel of syrup requires one can of each raw material. A can of molasses costs $10, and each can of seasoning costs $20. The syrup sells for $100 per barrel. Brady purchases 100 cans of molasses and 100 cans of seasoning for cash and produces 100 barrels of syrup in January. The company sells 60 barrels of syrup in February.

Brady Company would not recognize any revenue or expense in January. All that has occurred is a change in asset types held by the firm. Cash in the amount of $3,000 was exchanged for $1,000 of molasses and $2,000 of seasoning. The molasses and seasoning were then transformed into $3,000 of syrup.

In February, 60 barrels of syrup are sold for $6,000 cash, and $6,000 of revenue is then recognized. To satisfy the matching principle, $1,800 of expense—the amount of assets used up—must also be recognized. This expense represents 60 barrels of syrup at a cost of $30 each. The syrup ceases to be an asset to Brady, because ownership has been transferred to customers, and the syrup will yield no additional economic benefits to the company. Exhibit 3.2 schematically presents the foregoing events.

EXHIBIT 3.2

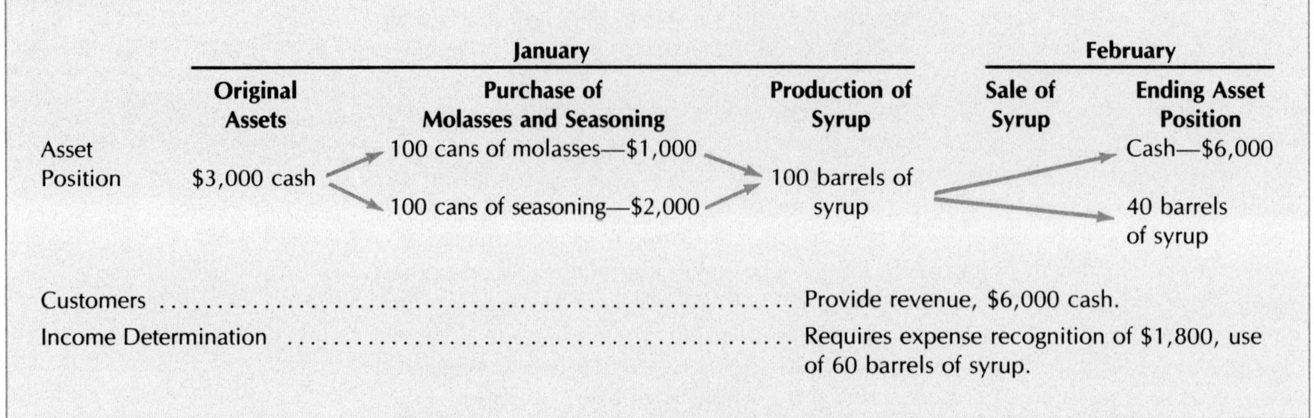

Customers .... Provide revenue, $6,000 cash.

Income Determination .... Requires expense recognition of $1,800, use of 60 barrels of syrup.

CONCEPT SUMMARY 3.1

THE RECOGNITION OF REVENUE AND EXPENSE

Account	Point of Recognition	Conditions
Revenue	When services are provided or goods are delivered to customers.	• The earning process must be substantially complete. • The price of the goods and services must be determinable. • Collection of revenue from customers must be reasonably assured.
Expense	In the same time period as their associated revenues are recognized (matching principle).	• Revenue must be recognized. (Some expenses are matched with revenue by time period.)

ACCOUNTING FOR REVENUE AND EXPENSE TRANSACTIONS

Revenue and Expense Transactions and the Accounting System

When recording revenue and expense transactions in the accounting language of debits and credits, the rules explained in Chapter 2 apply. Recall from Chapter 1 that profit belongs to the owners of a business. Therefore, revenue and expense accounts are subsets of owners' equity. Because revenues increase owners' equity, increases in revenue accounts must be recorded as credits. Because expenses decrease owners' equity, an increase in an expense account must be recorded as a debit. Exhibit 3.3 summarizes the debit and credit rules as they apply to revenue and expense accounts.

Revenue Accounts and Transactions

Both sides of the accounting equation are affected by revenue transactions. The increase in assets is added to the left side of the accounting equation and is reflected as an addition to owners' equity on the right side. The accounts used to record

EXHIBIT 3.3

Owners' Equity	
Decreased by debits	Increased by credits

Expenses	
Since expenses decrease owners' equity, expense accounts are increased with debits.	

Revenues	
	Since revenues increase owners' equity, revenue accounts are increased with credits.

revenue are most commonly labeled sales, fees earned, or revenue, depending on the source.

Consider the following transactions:

January 2 Marple Company sells merchandise for $30,000. The customers pay $10,000 cash and agree to pay the remaining $20,000 by January 31.

January 31 Marple subsequently receives $20,000 cash from customers.

Exhibit 3.4 shows the effects of these two transactions on the accounting equation.

EXHIBIT 3.4

Trans. Date	Assets		=	Liabilities	+	Owners' Equity
	Cash	Accounts Receivable				Sales
1/2	+$10,000	+$20,000	=	0		+$30,000
1/31	+ 20,000	− 20,000				

In general journal form, Marple would record the two transactions as follows:

Marple Company
General Journal

Page 1

Date	Transaction	Post Ref.	Debit	Credit
Jan. 2	Cash	110	10,000	
	Accounts receivable	120	20,000	
	Sales	410		30,000
	(to record sales to customers)			
31	Cash	110	20,000	
	Accounts receivable	120		20,000
	(to record customer payments on account)			

The revenue is completely recognized on the date of the sale, January 2. Assets (cash and accounts receivable) are increased by the revenue recognized, and owners' equity (sales) is likewise increased to reflect the owners' claims against these assets. On January 31, when the customers pay their bill of $20,000, the only change in the accounting equation is the exchange of one asset (accounts receivable) for another (cash). Remember, under accrual accounting, the timing of revenue recognition is not a function of when cash is received.

Expense Accounts and Transactions

Expenses arise from using assets in the production of revenues and include all asset consumptions necessary to attract and serve customers. Outflows of assets representing expenses are reflected on both sides of the accounting equation. On the left side of the accounting equation, assets are decreased to reflect the asset consumed, and on the right side of the equation, owners' equity must be decreased to reflect the reduction in the residual assets available to the owners. Many different account titles are used to record expenses; most include the term *expense,* such as Rent Expense and Salaries Expense. Because expenses are measured by the cost of assets consumed, some expense accounts are labeled with a cost title. For example, the cost of merchandise sold to customers (representing an expense always associated with a sale of merchandise) is referred to as Cost of Goods Sold. In general, the term **cost** is defined as the amount paid to acquire an asset or service.

COST
The amount paid to acquire an asset or service.

Consider the following January expenses for Marple Company:

1. The merchandise sold had originally been purchased by Marple for $20,000.
2. Marple's bookkeeper earns $500 for the first two weeks in January and is paid in cash on January 16.
3. By January 31, the bookkeeper has earned another $500, and this salary is to be paid on February 1.

Exhibit 3.5 presents the effect of these expenses on the accounting equation for Marple.

EXHIBIT 3.5

	Assets		=	**Liabilities**	+	**Owners' Equity**	
Trans. Date	**Cash**	**Merchandise**		**Salary Payable**		**Cost of Goods Sold**	**Salary Expense**
1/2		−$20,000	=			−$20,000	
1/16	−$500		=				−$500
1/31				+$500			− 500

In general journal form, Marple would record the expenses in Exhibit 3.5 as follows:

Marpple Company				
General Journal				
				Page 1
Date	**Transaction**	**Post Ref.**	**Debit**	**Credit**
Jan. 2	Cost of goods sold	510	20,000	
	Merchandise inventory	130		20,000
	(to record cost of goods sold			
	to customers as an expense)			
16	Salaries expense	530	500	
	Cash	110		500
	(to record salaries expense)			
31	Salaries expense	530	500	
	Salaries payable	210		500
	(to record salaries expense			
	and liability for payment)			

Although the revenues in Exhibit 3.4 are added to assets and owners' equity, the expenses are deducted from assets and owners' equity.

Note particularly the January 31 wages of $500. Since the bookkeeper worked in January, his labor was used up in the production of revenue. The amount of labor used is measured by the total cost of wages for the time worked. Common sense suggests that the cost of labor used in January should be recognized as an expense in January if all expenses are to be matched against their associated revenues. The January 31 changes in the accounting equation reflect both the liability to pay the bookkeeper (through an increase in the liability, salary payable) and the use of the bookkeeper's labor (through a decrease in owners' equity). Again note that the timing of cash payments does not govern recognition of events under accrual accounting concepts.

The transactions of Marple Company from Exhibits 3.4 and 3.5 are summarized with debit and credit indications in Exhibit 3.6. As you study Exhibit 3.6, keep in mind that increases in expense accounts are actually decreases in owners' equity (marked with an asterisk).

EFFECTS OF DEBITS AND CREDITS ON ACCOUNTS

CONCEPT SUMMARY 3.2

Accounts	Increased By	Decreased By
Revenue	Credits	Debits
Expense	Debits	Credits

EXHIBIT 3.6

Marple Company
Transaction Summary
January 1986

		Assets			= Liabilities +	Owners' Equity		
Transaction	**Trans. Date**	**Cash**	**Accounts Receivable**	**Merchandise**	**Salary Payable**	**Cost of Goods Sold**	**Salary Expense**	**Sales**
Record sale	1/2	+$10,000 Dr.	+$20,000 Dr.					+$30,000 Cr.
Record cost of goods sold	1/2			−$20,000 Cr.		−$20,000 Dr.*		
Record salary	1/16	− 500 Cr.					−$500 Dr.*	
Record cash collections	1/31	+ 20,000 Dr.	− 20,000 Cr.					
Record wages owed	1/31				+$500 Cr.		− 500 Dr.*	

*These decreases in owners' equity are recorded as increases in the expense accounts as indicated by the debit notation.

Journal and Ledger Entries for Revenues and Expenses

The Marple Company transactions described earlier and summarized in Exhibit 3.6 would have first been recorded chronologically in the general journal entries shown following Exhibits 3.4 and 3.5 and then posted to the general ledger as illustrated in Exhibit 3.7.

The process of posting from the journal entries to the general ledger accounts is exactly the same for revenue and expense transactions as that described in Chapter 2 for asset, liability, and owners' equity accounts. The general journal entries are tied to the ledger through posting references.

Exhibit 3.8 presents an income statement for the Marple Company based on the foregoing revenue and expense transactions.

GROSS MARGIN
See Gross Profit.

GROSS PROFIT
Sales revenue minus cost of goods sold. Also known as gross margin.

Exhibit 3.8 introduces a new element in the income statement—**gross profit** (also known as **gross margin**), defined as sales revenue less cost of goods sold. Gross profit is significant in that the difference between the amount paid by a company to its suppliers for merchandise and the amount it receives from customers for that same merchandise must be large enough to cover all other operating and selling expenses if the business is to earn a profit.

OPERATING INCOME AND NET INCOME

Thus far we have discussed income only in the context of regular recurring business operations. However, business organizations often engage in transactions that are not part of their regular operations. Generally accepted accounting principles require that income from regular operations (operating income) be shown separately from net income which includes both regular transactions and those not expected to occur regularly. In this way, income statement users can better analyze income from regular operations of the business.

Marple Company
GENERAL LEDGER

EXHIBIT 3.7

ACCOUNT Cash							Account No. 110
Date	Explanation	Post Ref.	Debit	Date	Explanation	Post Ref.	Credit
1/2		J1	10,000	1/16		J1	500
1/31		J1	20,000				

ACCOUNT Accounts Receivable							Account No. 120
Date	Explanation	Post Ref.	Debit	Date	Explanation	Post Ref.	Credit
1/2		J1	20,000	1/31		J1	20,000

ACCOUNT Merchandise Inventory							Account No. 130
Date	Explanation	Post Ref.	Debit	Date	Explanation	Post Ref.	Credit
				1/2		J1	20,000

ACCOUNT Salaries Payable							Account No. 210
Date	Explanation	Post Ref.	Debit	Date	Explanation	Post Ref.	Credit
				1/31		J1	500

ACCOUNT Sales							Account No. 410
Date	Explanation	Post Ref.	Debit	Date	Explanation	Post Ref.	Credit
				1/2		J1	30,000

ACCOUNT Cost of Goods Sold							Account No. 510
Date	Explanation	Post Ref.	Debit	Date	Explanation	Post Ref.	Credit
1/2		J1	20,000				

ACCOUNT Salaries Expense							Account No. 530
Date	Explanation	Post Ref.	Debit	Date	Explanation	Post Ref.	Credit
1/16		J1	500				
1/31		J1	500				

Operating Income

Operating income is defined as operating revenues less operating expenses. Think about the definitions of revenues and expenses. Implicit in the definition of revenues is an assumption that the revenue-producing exchange (normally called a sale) is

OPERATING INCOME
Operating revenues minus operating expenses.

EXHIBIT 3.8

Marple Company Income Statement For the Month Ending January 31, 1986	
Sales	$30,000
Less cost of goods sold	20,000
Gross profit	$10,000
Operating expenses	
Salary expense	1,000
Net income	9,000

part of the usual operation for a particular company. However, operating income might not include all transactions with customers.

For example, suppose the Marple Company owns three stores that are recorded on the books for $40,000 each and decides to sell one of the stores for $50,000 cash during January 1986. Marple does not sell stores as a regular part of its business, and the $50,000 received for the store would not be shown in the Sales account or included in operating income. Likewise, the $40,000 (cost of the store sold) would not be included in the Cost of Goods Sold account.

Rather, the $10,000 difference between the $50,000 cash received and the $40,000 store given up would be a gain and would appear as a separate item on the income statement after operating income. If the store were sold for $35,000, Marple would record a loss of $5,000. In general, **gains** and **losses** can be defined as the excess or deficiency of assets received over those given up in a transaction that is not a part of normal business operations. Owners' equity is increased by gains and decreased by losses.

GAIN
The excess of assets received over those given up in a transaction not part of normal business operations.

LOSS
The deficiency of assets received over those given up in a transaction not a part of normal business operations.

Net Income

The sale of merchandise (a usual and recurring item for Marple) is included in operating income, whereas the sale of the store (not a usual and recurring item for Marple) is excluded. Both the sale of merchandise and the sale of the store are included in net income. Net income, as generally used in accounting, is an all-inclusive concept reflecting all profit and loss items: **net income** = operating revenues − operating expenses + gains − losses. Exhibit 3.9 combines Exhibit 3.8 with Marple's sale of the store for $50,000 to illustrate this relationship.

NET INCOME
Operating revenue minus operating expenses plus gains minus losses.

INCOME, THE ACCOUNTING EQUATION, AND OWNERS' EQUITY

The income statement provides a report on asset flows that have occurred within a given time period as a result of transactions with customers. From your study of the accounting equation and statement of financial position, you know that asset exchanges are also reflected in these items. The income statement must mesh with the accounting equation and the statement of financial position.

Because income from a business belongs to the owners, it follows that all of the revenues, expenses, gains, and losses that make up the income statement must be placed in the owners' equity section on the statement of financial position. The relationship among the accounting equation, the statement of financial position, and the income statement is depicted in Exhibit 3.10.

EXHIBIT 3.9

Marple Company Income Statement For the Month Ending January 31, 1986	
Sales	$30,000
Less cost of goods sold	20,000
Gross profit	$10,000
Operating expenses	
Salary expense	1,000
Operating income	$ 9,000
Other income	
Gain from sale of store	10,000
Net income	$19,000

Income is depicted on both sides of the accounting equation—on the left side in assets and on the right side in owners' equity. Net income is equal to the net increase or decrease in assets as a result of all revenue, expense, gain, and loss transactions. The income statement is nothing more than the details of the changes in owners' equity corresponding to the changes in assets that occurred as a result of doing business with customers.

Revenues, Expenses, and Owners' Equity

Chapter 1 established that owners' equity represents assets provided to the business by owners from two sources:

1. Assets invested from the owners' personal store of assets.
2. Assets earned through operations but not distributed to the owners.

EXHIBIT 3.10

STATEMENT OF FINANCIAL POSITION

INCOME STATEMENT

Assets	=	Liabilities + Owners' Equity
Inflows of assets from customers in exchange for goods or services	=	Revenues—increase in owners' equity
Use of assets to produce revenues	=	Expenses—decrease in owners' equity
Net increase in assets from a transaction not typical of regular operations	=	Gains—increase in owners' equity
Net decrease in assets from a transaction not typical of regular operations	=	Losses—decrease in owners' equity
Net income (loss)—net asset change as a result of summarizing revenues, expenses, gains, losses	=	Net change in owners' equity

No distinction was made between these two owner sources either in the accounting equation or in the statement of financial position so that you could concentrate on understanding the accounting equation and transaction processing. However, the two sources do arise in different ways, and accountants do distinguish between them when recording transactional data in a formal system of accounts in a corporation.

PAID-IN CAPITAL
The term applied to the total amount of assets provided by owners in exchange for their original ownership interest in a corporation.

Paid-in Capital. Assets invested by owners from their personal store of assets can be thought of as assets paid in to the corporation. In general terms, the amount of owners' equity that corresponds to the assets invested by the owners from their personal holdings is labeled **paid-in capital,** representing the assets provided by owners in exchange for their original ownership interest in the corporation. Owners usually receive a document (a stock certificate) from the corporation as evidence of their ownership. Although many varieties exist, the most widespread is common stock. Chapters 13 and 14 examine paid-in capital more closely.

Retained Earnings. All revenue, expense, gain, and loss transactions could be entered directly into owners' equity. If a business had numerous transactions with customers (as most successful businesses do), not only would owners' equity be difficult to interpret, but also specific information on the nature and extent of the revenues, expenses, gains, and losses making up income would be lacking. Therefore, accounting systems provide separate revenue, expense, gain, and loss accounts for recording changes in owners' equity as transactions with customers occur.

RETAINED EARNINGS
The account that represents the portion of the total assets held by a corporation that came from profitable operations.

The link between the income statement accounts (revenues, expenses, gains, and losses) and owners' equity on the statement of financial position is found in a special owners' equity account—Retained Earnings. The income statement accounts are periodically summarized, and their total (net income for a particular time period) is added to **retained earnings,** which represents the portion of the total assets held by a corporation that comes from profitable operations.

When dividends are distributed to owners, the account of the asset distributed, usually cash, and the Retained Earnings account are each reduced by the amount of the dividend. However, it is important to understand that retained earnings is not cash itself or any other specific asset. Retained earnings simply represents owners' claims against assets accumulated through profitable operations, and assets distributed as dividends reduce those claims.

Suppose that Marple Company had been organized on January 1, 1986, and that the only two transactions other than those summarized in Exhibit 3.6 occur on January 1 and are as follows:

1. The owners invest $100,000 cash to start the business. This transaction would be recorded as follows:

Cash	100,000	
Common stock		100,000
(to record investment by owners)		

2. Marple purchases $40,000 of merchandise from suppliers, paying cash. This transaction would be recorded as follows:

Merchandise	40,000	
Cash		40,000
(to record purchase of merchandise for cash)		

Combining these two transactions with those summarized in Exhibit 3.6 results in Exhibit 3.11. Here again, note that the additions to expense accounts represent reductions in owners' equity (marked with an asterisk to help you analyze the exhibit).

EXHIBIT 3.11

Marple Company
Transaction Summary
January 1986

Transaction	Trans. Date	Cash	Accounts Receivable	Merchandise	Salary Payable	Common Stock	Cost of Goods Sold	Salary Expense	Sales
		Assets			= Liabilities +	Owners' Equity			
						Paid-in Capital	Retained Earnings		
Investment by owners	1/1	+$100,000				+$100,000			
Purchase merchandise	1/1	− 40,000		+$40,000					
Record sale	1/2	+ 10,000	+$20,000						+$30,000
Record cost of goods sold	1/2			− 20,000			−$20,000*		
Record salary	1/16	− 500						−$ 500*	
Record cash collections	1/31	+ 20,000	− 20,000						
Record wages owed	1/31				+$500			+ 500*	
Account Bal.	1/31	$ 89,500	$ 0	$20,000	$500	$100,000	$20,000	$1,000	$30,000

*These decreases in owners' equity are recorded as increases (debits) in the expense accounts.

Exhibit 3.12 presents a statement of financial position for Marple as of January 31. Note that the revenue and expense accounts contained in Exhibit 3.8 and displayed in Exhibit 3.11 have been summarized in retained earnings in Exhibit 3.12 ($30,000 − $20,000 − $1,000). Chapter 4 covers the bookkeeping mechanics of the process of summarizing revenue and expense accounts into retained earnings. For now, concentrate on grasping the relationship among revenues, expenses, and owners' equity (retained earnings).

EXHIBIT 3.12

Marple Company
Statement of Financial Position
January 31, 1986

Assets		Liabilities and Owners' Equity	
Cash	$ 89,500	Liabilities	
Accounts receivable	0	Salary payable	$ 500
Merchandise	20,000	Owners' equity	
		Common stock	100,000
		Retained earnings	9,000
Total	$109,500	Total	$109,500

CONCEPT SUMMARY 3.3

THE TWO PARTS OF OWNERS' EQUITY

Account	Represents
Common stock	Assets invested by owners from their personal holdings in exchange for ownership of the corporation.
Retained earnings	Assets earned by the business as a result of transactions with customers and not yet distributed to owners as dividends.

A REPRESENTATIVE INCOME STATEMENT

We have chosen Delta Airlines' income statement for the year ending June 30, 1984, as a representative example of an actual income statement (Exhibit 3.13). A distinction is made in Delta's case between income from operations and net income. Recall that operating income is the difference between operating revenues and expenses and net income is the result of combining income from operations with other expenses, gains, or losses. The other expenses, gains, and losses are shown separately from operating revenues and expenses so that the user can identify income from regular ongoing operations. Chapter 18 explores the analysis of the income statement and the statement of financial position.

CONSERVATISM AND MATERIALITY

Accounting reports are prepared in conformity with generally accepted accounting principles. However, in some cases, these principles are modified in actual practice. Two such modifications are based on the conventions of conservatism and materiality.

Conservatism Convention

CONSERVATISM CONVENTION
The convention that accountants are prudent or cautious in their approach to financial reporting. It means that in general, the accountant will select the alternative that has the least favorable impact on income.

The **conservatism convention** means that accountants are prudent or cautious in their approach to financial reporting. Not all accounting information is known with certainty. When faced with an uncertain situation, the response of the accountant is one of playing it safe. This means that given two alternatives, the accountant will select the one with the least favorable impact on income or assets. Most accountants believe that the potential danger of misinformation to the external user of financial statements is much less from understatement than from overstatement.

Materiality Convention

MATERIALITY CONVENTION
The convention that allows the accountant to overlook minor items not reported in conformity with generally accepted accounting principles.

The **materiality convention** allows the accountant to overlook minor items not reported in conformity with generally accepted accounting principles. If the dollar size of an item is small enough so that the accountant can be reasonably assured that it will not be significant to a decision maker, it may sometimes be reported in a way that is theoretically incorrect. The materiality convention allows for handling such small items in an expedient, cost-effective manner. For example, the cost of a pencil is generally considered an expense when purchased, although theoretically the cost should be considered as an expense only as the pencil is used up in the production of revenue.

EXHIBIT 3.13

Delta Airlines Income Statement* Twelve Months Ending June 30, 1984 (In Thousands)		
Operating revenues		
Passenger	$3,963,610	
Cargo	239,649	
Other	60,472	
Total operating revenues		$4,263,731
Operating expenses		
Salaries and related costs	$1,687,899	
Aircraft fuel	938,189	
Aircraft maintenance materials and repairs	66,397	
Rentals and landing fees	145,609	
Passenger service	151,317	
Agency commissions	303,362	
Other cash costs	413,086	
Depreciation and amortization	346,480	
Total operating expenses		$4,052,339
Operating income (loss)		$ 211,392
Other income		
Interest expense	$ (109,802)	
Gains on disposition of aircraft	129,511	
Realized and unrealized loss on foreign currency translation	60	
Miscellaneous income, net	9,054	
Total other income (expenses)		$ 28,823
Income before income taxes		240,215
Provision for income taxes		(64,611)
Net income		$ 175,604

*Developed from Delta Airlines annual report for 1984 (simplified for illustrative purposes).

INCOME MEASUREMENT AND WEALTH

Economists often define income as increases in wealth (increases in ability to purchase goods and services). Accountants define wealth in a much more restrictive fashion.

Because accounting is a transaction-based process, conventional accounting income measurement does not include all increases or decreases in wealth. For example, if the Lima Company holds $100,000 cash and the purchasing power of the dollar declines ten percent because of inflation, Lima is clearly less wealthy. Its $100,000 will not purchase as many goods and services as $100,000 would have purchased before inflation. Conversely, suppose Lima owns a building and the market value of the building has increased from $100,000 to $150,000 because of an expanding population base in the area. Lima Corporation has more wealth: The firm could sell or trade the building and obtain 50 percent more goods and services than before the population expansion (assuming no inflation). However, neither of the above wealth changes would be recognized by the conventional accounting income measurement process because a transaction has not occurred.

Additionally, conventional accounting principles include an objectivity requirement and, in most cases, the use of historical cost. The market value of the building is not the historical cost, and its estimation is less objective than the purchase price of the building.

INCOME MEASUREMENT AND TAXATION

Income as determined under generally accepted accounting principles is not the same as taxable income determined by applicable tax code, regulation, and court precedents. Most corporations maintain supplementary records that are used to convert accounting income to taxable income. This text is mainly concerned with accounting income.

You might ask why income developed under generally accepted accounting principles should vary from taxable income developed under applicable law, regulation, and court precedent. Accountants are concerned with an accurate portrayal of the results of economic events so that users of financial statements can make investment decisions. Taxing authorities, on the other hand, are concerned with matters of national economic policy, equitable distribution of the tax burden among taxpayers, wealth distributions in society, and other items that are a proper province of government. As the objectives of the accountant and governments differ, so too do the rules for determining income.

FOR REVIEW

DEMONSTRATION PROBLEM

The Little Giant Corporation, a wholesaler of canned and packaged goods, is organized on June 1, 1986. The corporation's chart of accounts follows:

110 Cash
120 Accounts Receivable
130 Merchandise Inventory
140 Office Furniture
150 Delivery Equipment
160 Computer
170 Warehouse
200 Accounts Payable
210 Notes Payable
300 Common Stock
310 Retained Earnings
400 Sales
500 Cost of Goods Sold
510 Wages Expense
520 Phone Expense
530 Utility Expense

During the corporation's first month of operation, the following transactions occur:

June 1 The owners invest $80,000 cash and delivery equipment worth $30,000 to start the business.

June 4 The company purchases a warehouse facility with a down payment of $20,000 cash and a note payable of $40,000.

June 5 While cleaning up the warehouse, the work crew discovers that the roof is in desperate need of repair. The company hires American Roofing to make repairs, after receiving an estimate of $1,500 for the work.

June 7 Little Giant purchases merchandise for $15,000, paying $5,000 in cash with the remainder due by June 30.

June 9 The firm purchases office furniture on account for $1,500.

June 11 The firm sells merchandise that had originally cost $3,000 to the Ranch Supermarket for $6,000. Ranch is given until June 18 to pay.

June 13 Merchandise that had been sold for $200 to Ranch Supermarket is returned.

June 15 Little Giant pays salaries for the first half of the month, $850.

June 16 A check from Ranch Supermarket is received for the remaining amount of the merchandise sold to it on June 11.

June 18 Little Giant pays for the office furniture purchased on June 9.

June 19 Merchandise that had originally cost $500 is sold to the Century Market for $1,500 cash.

June 21 Little Giant receives and pays phone bill, $550.

June 23 Repairs on the roof are completed, and American Roofing is paid the agreed-upon price.

June 25 Little Giant purchases a microcomputer from Computer Heaven for $5,500 on credit.

June 27 The utility bill for June of $800 is paid.

June 29 The firm pays the remaining balance owed for the merchandise purchased on June 7.

June 30 Salaries are paid for the second half of the month, $1,200.

Required

1. Prepare general journal entries for each of Little Giant's June transactions.
2. Post each general journal entry to the appropriate general ledger account.
3. Prepare a trial balance as of June 30.
4. Prepare an income statement for Little Giant Corporation for the month ending June 30, 1986.
5. Prepare a statement of financial position for Little Giant Corporation as of June 30, 1986.

Demonstration Problem Solution

1.

Little Giant Corporation
General Journal

Page 1

Date		Transaction	Post Ref.	Debit	Credit
1986					
June	1	Cash	110	80,000	
		Delivery equipment	150	30,000	
		Common stock	300		110,000
		(to record owners' investment)			
	4	Warehouse	170	60,000	
		Cash	110		20,000
		Notes payable	210		40,000
		(to record purchase of a warehouse)			
	5	No entry required. An agreement for future			
		services is not a transaction for accounting purposes.			
	7	Merchandise inventory	130	15,000	
		Cash	110		5,000
		Accounts payable	200		10,000
		(to record purchase of mdse.)			
	9	Office furniture	140	1,500	
		Accounts payable	200		1,500
		(to record purchase of office furniture)			
	11	Accounts receivable	120	6,000	
		Sales	400		6,000
		(to record sales on account)			
	11	Cost of goods sold	500	3,000	
		Merchandise inventory	130		3,000
		(to record cost of goods sold to customers)			
	13	Sales	400	200	
		Accounts receivable	120		200
		(to record sales reduction for goods returned)			
	13	Merchandise inventory	130	100	
		Cost of goods sold	500		100
		(to record goods returned by customers)			
	15	Wages expense	510	850	
		Cash	110		850
		(to record payment of wages)			
	16	Cash	110	5,800	
		Accounts receivable	120		5,800
		(to record collection of cash from customers)			

Little Giant Corporation
General Journal

Page 2

Date	Transaction	Post Ref.	Debit	Credit
1986				
June 18	Accounts payable	200	1,500	
	Cash	110		1,500
	(to record payment for office furniture)			
19	Cash	110	1,500	
	Sales	400		1,500
	(to record sales made to customers)			
19	Cost of goods sold	500	500	
	Merchandise inventory	130		500
	(to record cost of goods sold to customers)			
21	Phone expense	520	550	
	Cash	110		550
	(to record telephone expense)			
23	Warehouse	170	1,500	
	Cash	110		1,500
	(to record roof repairs as additional warehouse			
	cost)			
25	Computer	160	5,500	
	Accounts payable	200		5,500
	(to record purchase of computer)			
27	Utility expense	530	800	
	Cash	110		800
	(to record utility expense)			
29	Accounts payable	200	10,000	
	Cash	110		10,000
	(to record payment to suppliers)			
30	Wages expense	510	1,200	
	Cash	110		1,200
	(to record payment of wages)			

2.

GENERAL LEDGER

ACCOUNT Cash — Account No. 110

Date	Explanation	Post Ref.	Debit	Date	Explanation	Post Ref.	Credit
6/01		J1	80,000	6/04		J1	20,000
6/16		J1	5,800	6/07		J1	5,000
6/19		J2	1,500	6/15		J1	850
				6/18		J2	1,500
				6/21		J2	550
				6/23		J2	1,500
				6/29		J2	800
				6/29		J2	10,000
				6/30		J2	1,200
6/30	Balance		45,900				

ACCOUNT Accounts Receivable — Account No. 120

Date	Explanation	Post Ref.	Debit	Date	Explanation	Post Ref.	Credit
6/11		J1	6,000	6/13		J1	200
				6/16		J1	5,800
6/30	Balance		0				

ACCOUNT Merchandise Inventory — Account No. 130

Date	Explanation	Post Ref.	Debit	Date	Explanation	Post Ref.	Credit
6/07		J1	15,000	6/11		J1	3,000
6/13		J1	100	6/19		J2	500
6/30	Balance		11,600				

ACCOUNT Office Furniture — Account No. 140

Date	Explanation	Post Ref.	Debit	Date	Explanation	Post Ref.	Credit
6/09		J1	1,500				
6/30	Balance		1,500				

ACCOUNT Delivery Equipment — Account No. 150

Date	Explanation	Post Ref.	Debit	Date	Explanation	Post Ref.	Credit
6/01		J1	30,000				
6/30	Balance		30,000				

ACCOUNT Computer — Account No. 160

Date	Explanation	Post Ref.	Debit	Date	Explanation	Post Ref.	Credit
6/25		J2	5,500				
6/30	Balance		5,500				

ACCOUNT Warehouse — Account No. 170

Date	Explanation	Post Ref.	Debit	Date	Explanation	Post Ref.	Credit
6/04		J1	60,000				
6/23		J2	1,500				
6/30	Balance		61,500				

ACCOUNT	Accounts Payable						Account No. 200
Date	Explanation	Post Ref.	Debit	Date	Explanation	Post Ref.	Credit
6/18		J2	1,500	6/07		J1	10,000
6/29		J2	10,000	6/09		J1	1,500
				6/25		J2	5,500
				6/30	Balance		5,500

ACCOUNT	Notes Payable						Account No. 210
Date	Explanation	Post Ref.	Debit	Date	Explanation	Post Ref.	Credit
				6/04		J1	40,000
				6/30	Balance		40,000

ACCOUNT	Common Stock						Account No. 300
Date	Explanation	Post Ref.	Debit	Date	Explanation	Post Ref.	Credit
				6/01		J1	110,000
				6/30	Balance		110,000

ACCOUNT	Sales						Account No. 400
Date	Explanation	Post Ref.	Debit	Date	Explanation	Post Ref.	Credit
6/13		J1	200	6/11		J1	6,000
				6/19		J2	1,500
				6/30	Balance		7,300

ACCOUNT	Cost of Goods Sold						Account No. 500
Date	Explanation	Post Ref.	Debit	Date	Explanation	Post Ref.	Credit
6/11		J1	3,000	6/13		J1	100
6/19		J2	500				
6/30	Balance		3,400				

ACCOUNT	Wages Expense						Account No. 510
Date	Explanation	Post Ref.	Debit	Date	Explanation	Post Ref.	Credit
6/15		J1	850				
6/30		J2	1,200				
6/30	Balance		2,050				

ACCOUNT	Phone Expense						Account No. 520
Date	Explanation	Post Ref.	Debit	Date	Explanation	Post Ref.	Credit
6/21		J2	550				
6/30	Balance		550				

ACCOUNT	Utilities Expense						Account No. 530
Date	Explanation	Post Ref.	Debit	Date	Explanation	Post Ref.	Credit
6/27		J2	800				
6/30	Balance		800				

3.

Little Giant Corporation
Trial Balance
June 30, 1986

Account	Debit	Credit
Cash	$ 45,900	
Accounts Receivable	0	
Merchandise Inventory	11,600	
Office Furniture	1,500	
Delivery Equipment	30,000	
Computer	5,500	
Warehouse	61,500	
Accounts Payable		$ 5,500
Notes Payable		40,000
Common Stock		110,000
Sales		7,300
Cost of Goods Sold	3,400	
Wages Expense	2,050	
Phone Expense	550	
Utilities Expense	800	
Totals	$162,800	$162,800

4.

Little Giant Corporation
Income Statement
For the Month Ending June 30, 1986

Sales		$7,300
Less cost of goods sold		3,400
Gross margin		$3,900
Less operating expenses		
Wages expense	$2,050	
Phone expense	550	
Utilities expense	800	
Total operating expenses		3,400
Net income (loss)		$ 500

5.

Little Giant Corporation
Statement of Financial Position
June 30, 1986

Assets		Liabilities and Owners' Equity	
Cash	$ 45,900	Liabilities	
Accounts receivable	0	Accounts payable	$ 5,500
Merchandise inventory	11,600	Notes payable	40,000
Office furniture	1,500	Total liabilities	$ 45,500
Delivery equipment	30,000	Owners' equity	
Computer	5,500	Common stock	110,000
Warehouse	61,500	Retained earnings	500
		Total owners' equity	$110,500
Total assets	$156,000	Total liabilities and owners' equity	$156,000

SUMMARY

- Income is the most widely used measure of corporate financial performance and is measured by the increases in assets available to owners that have been provided through profitable operations.
- Revenues represent asset increases; expenses represent asset decreases.
- Increases in revenue accounts are recorded as credits; increases in expense accounts are recorded as debits.
- Income in every form is part of owners' equity; thus, revenues, expenses, gains, and losses are all part of owners' equity.
- Proper income determination requires that expenses be matched with the revenues they support.
- Proper presentation of income requires that the statement be headed with the entity name and the time period within which the income was earned.
- All cumulative increases or decreases in assets as a result of profitable or unprofitable operations that have not been distributed to the owners are represented on the statement of financial position by the owners' equity account, Retained Earnings.

QUESTIONS

3-1. Explain the two levels of performance in income determination.

3-2. When is revenue generally recognized (and recorded), and what three conditions must hold?

3-3. What is meant by the matching principle?

3-4. What is the difference between a statement of financial position and an income statement?

3-5. What is gross margin?

3-6. Explain why accounting income measurement does not include all increases or decreases in wealth.

3-7. Define expenses and revenue.

3-8. Is an increase in revenue shown as a debit or credit? Why?

3-9. Indicate the effects of debits and credits on revenue and expense accounts.

3-10. Why might income for financial reporting purposes differ from that for income tax purposes?

EXERCISES

3-E1. The Jones Company starts in business on June 1. The only record made of June's transactions is contained in the company's checkbook. For June, the checkbook shows the following transactions. Indicate for each transaction whether any revenue or expense would be recognized under accrual accounting concepts and, if so, how much.

June 1 Owners invest $50,000 in the business to get it started.
June 3 Jones buys $4,000 of merchandise from suppliers, paying cash.

June 5 Jones buys a delivery truck for $10,000 cash and expects to use the truck for five years.

June 10 Jones sells merchandise to customers for $3,000 cash. The merchandise sold originally cost Jones $1,800.

June 20 Jones pays salaries to its employees for the period June 1–15, $1,000 cash.

June 30 Jones pays June store rent of $500.

3-E2. The Doughnut Hole is a retail outlet for bakery products. Identify by answering "yes" or "no" which of the following items would be included in the calculation of operating income:

a. Salaries
b. Gain on sale of land
c. Interest expense
d. Sales
e. Income taxes
f. Cost of goods sold
g. Rental of building in which business is located
h. Selling expenses
i. Uninsured fire loss

3-E3. Given the following analysis of transactions for Better Books Company, prepare an income statement for January 1986 using the format in Exhibit 3.9.

	Assets			= Liabilities and Owners' Equity				
				Liabilities	Owners' Equity Revenue (Expenses)			
Trans. Date	**Cash**	**Accounts Receivable**	**Merchandise**	**Accounts Payable**	**Sales**	**Cost of Goods Sold**	**Salary Exp.**	**Comm. Exp.**
1/1 Bal.	$1,000	$500	$ 500	$2,000				
1/2	+ 500	− 500						
1/4	+ 500	+ 500	− 800		+ 1,000	(+ 800)		
1/10	− 700						(+ 700)	
1/14	− 200		+ 1,000	+ 800				
1/18	− 300							(+ 300)
1/20	+ 200	+ 300	− 300		+ 500	(+ 300)		
1/22	+ 500	− 500						
1/25	− 400							(+ 400)
1/27	− 300						(+ 300)	
1/30	− 400			− 400				

3-E4. From the following account balances of February 28, 1986, prepare an income statement for Allen Distributing using the format in Exhibit 3.9.

Common Stock	$30,000
Accounts Payable	2,000
Salaries Expense	2,000
Long-term Debt	10,000
Rent Expense	4,000
Sales Revenue	15,000
Cost of Goods Sold	7,000
Accounts Receivable	3,000
Commission Expense	1,000

3-E5. The following accounts and their balances appear on the February 28, 1986, trial balance of the Hoagette Scooter Company:

a. Salaries Expense	$ 5,000	**e.** Common Stock	15,000
b. Cost of Goods Sold	10,000	**f.** Sales	8,000
c. Accounts Receivable	5,000	**g.** Retained Earnings	20,000
d. Accounts Payable	2,500		

Indicate whether each of the accounts is an asset, liability, owners' equity, revenue, or expense account. In addition, determine whether a debit or credit increases the account balance.

3-E6. For each of the following account types, indicate the effects of a debit and a credit and state whether the account normally has a debit or a credit balance:

a. Assets
b. Liabilities
c. Owners' Equity
d. Revenues
e. Expenses

3-E7. Prepare the proper general journal entries for each of the following transactions:

a. Owners invest $20,000 in the corporation.
b. The corporation purchases a building for $10,000 cash and a note payable of $30,000.
c. The corporation purchases office equipment on account, $2,500.
d. The corporation purchases merchandise for resale on account, $5,000.
e. The corporation sells merchandise for $1,500 on account. The cost of the merchandise sold was $500.
f. The corporation pays employee salaries of $950.
g. The corporation collects $1,250 from customers on account.
h. The corporation pays $1,500 of the amount owed for the office equipment purchased in (c).

PROBLEM SET A

3-A1. **Income Statement Preparation.** Bigwheels Company, a manufacturer of skateboards, has the following expenses and revenues for November 1986:

Cost of skateboards sold	$20,000
Sales of skateboards	50,000
Salaries expense	8,000
Supplies expense	500
Administrative expense	5,000
Commission expense	2,000

Required

Prepare an income statement following the format in Exhibit 3.9.

3-A2. **Journalizing Transactions.** The Hoage Corporation enters into the following transactions during January:

January 2	Is organized under a corporate charter from the state and issues $100,000 of common stock for cash.
January 3	Purchases $5,000 of merchandise on account.
January 7	Purchases equipment from Widget Company for $20,000. Payment is made with a note payable.
January 10	Pays $800 rent for January.
January 12	Sells merchandise for $8,000 on account. The cost of the merchandise was $2,000.
January 14	Receives an order from a customer for merchandise that has a selling price of $10,000 and a cost of $5,000. The merchandise will be delivered at the end of February.

January 15	Pays $2,000 to employees for work performed during the first two weeks of January.
January 18	Pays $5,000 to suppliers for merchandise purchased on January 3.
January 21	Receives $8,000 from customers for merchandise sold on January 12.
January 26	Pays $1,200 utility bill.
January 31	Pays $2,000 to employees for work performed during the last two weeks of January.

Required

Prepare a general journal entry for each of the January transactions.

3-A3. Correcting Journal Entries. The Jewelry Box reports net income of $10,000 for December 1986. In reviewing the accounts, the following facts are noted:

1. Inventory sold for $8,000 cash has been recorded by debiting sales and crediting cash.
2. Salaries of $500 have been recorded by debiting salary expense and crediting accounts receivable.
3. The distribution of $800 cash to owners (dividends) has been recorded by debiting salary expense and crediting cash.
4. Interest expense of $100 has been recorded by debiting cash and crediting accounts receivable.
5. A cash refund of $200 for merchandise returned by a dissatisfied customer has been recorded by crediting sales and debiting miscellaneous expense. The merchandise returned originally cost The Jewelry Box $150 and is put back in the store's inventory.

Required

a. Prepare general journal entries that will correct each transaction improperly recorded.
b. Compute the correct net income for December 1986.

3-A4. Correcting Income Statement Errors. The following income statement was prepared for Consumer Rental Company and contains a number of errors:

Consumer Rental Company
Income Statement
Year Ending December 31, 1986

Revenues	
Security deposits received on apartments	$ 10,000
Bank loan	175,000
Rent revenue	180,000
Interest income	2,000
Gain from sale of apartment	40,000
Total revenue	$407,000
Expenses	
Return of security deposits	$ 8,000
Maintenance expense	20,000
Equipment rental expense	15,000
Administrative expense	25,000
Interest expense	1,000
Cleaning expense	5,000
Truck purchase	3,000
Purchase of apartment building	200,000
Total expenses	$277,000
Net income	$130,000

Required

Prepare a corrected income statement for the year ending December 31, 1986. Separate operating revenues and expenses from other income and expenses.

3-A5. Statement of Financial Position and Income Statement. Clay Construction Company prepared the following statement of financial position as of February 28, 1986.

Clay Construction Company
Statement of Financial Position
February 28, 1986

Assets		**Liabilities and Owners' Equity**	
Cash	$ 5,000	Accounts payable	$ 20,000
Accounts receivable	25,000	Long-term debt	30,000
Tools	15,000	Total liabilities	$ 50,000
Supplies	30,000	Common stock	50,000
Land	50,000	Retained earnings	25,000
Total	$125,000	Total	$125,000

Clay Construction Company has the following transactions during March:

1. Receives payment of $4,000 for a remodeling job completed in March. Costs are $1,500 for wages and $2,000 for supplies, all of which are used in March.
2. Sells a piece of land for $2,000 cash. The land was originally purchased for $8,000.
3. Signs a contract to build a house for $100,000, with construction to begin in April. Labor, materials, and supplies to build the house are estimated to be approximately $90,000.
4. Receives $5,000 payment for a construction job completed and billed in January.
5. Purchases $3,000 of tools for cash at an auction.
6. Purchases $10,000 of lumber on account for the house to be started in April.
7. Makes a payment of $2,500 on the long-term debt. $500 of the payment is for interest.

Required

a. Prepare an income statement for the month ending March 31, 1986.
b. Prepare a statement of financial position for Clay Construction as of March 31, 1986.

3-A6. Preparation of Financial Statements by Analysis of Accounts. Sunshine Toy Company has the following account balances for the dates given:

Cash, May 1	$20,000
Cash, May 31	30,000
Accounts Receivable, May 1	5,000
Accounts Receivable, May 31	7,000
Total Owners' Equity, May 1	?
Total Owners' Equity, May 31	?
Inventory, May 1	15,000
Inventory, May 31	12,000
Sales	50,000
Accounts Payable, May 1	3,000
Accounts Payable, May 31	?
Operating Expenses	14,000
Net Income	10,000
Cost of Goods Sold	?

Assume that the accounts represent all of the accounts of the Sunshine Toy Company.

Required

a. Prepare a statement of financial position as of May 1, 1986.
b. Prepare a statement of financial position as of May 31, 1986.
c. Prepare an income statement for the month ending May 31, 1986.

3-A7. Trial Balances and General Ledger. Clarence P. Arnold is the president and senior lawyer in a small legal services corporation, Arnold's While-U-Wait Legal Service. In an effort to cut costs, C. P. Arnold fires his accountant and prepares the trial balance for the month ending July 31, 1986, by himself. Mr. Arnold's incorrect trial balance is as follows:

Arnold's While-U-Wait Legal Service
Trial Balance
July 31, 1986

Account	Debits	Credits
Cash	$ 2,510	
Accounts Receivable		$ 2,500
Office Supplies	540	
Office Equipment		3,000
Accounts Payable		2,550
Notes Payable	2,000	
Common Stock	1,000	
Retained Earnings		500
Legal Service Revenue		5,500
Rent Expense	2,000	
Wages Expense		1,000
Utilities Expense	500	
Totals	$ 8,550	$15,050

After many hours of frustrating work, Mr. Arnold has asked you to review the July transactions and postings and prepare a corrected trial balance. Upon review, you find the following:

1. Total debits to accounts receivable in the general ledger, including the beginning balance in the account, are $7,000, and total credits to the account equal $5,000.
2. A $450 purchase of office supplies has been debited to office supplies and credited to cash for $540.
3. A $500 payment by a customer on his account has been posted as a debit to cash and a credit to accounts payable.
4. A $600 payment to one of the corporation's suppliers has been properly recorded in the general journal but never posted to the general ledger.

Required

Prepare a corrected trial balance.

3-A8. Journal Entries, General Ledger, Trial Balance, and Income Statement. Floods and Fires Furniture Company sells furniture and fixtures at discount prices. The company began operations on June 1, 1986. The company's chart of accounts is as follows:

100 Cash
110 Accounts Receivable
120 Inventory
130 Office Supplies
140 Office Furniture
150 Building
200 Accounts Payable
210 Notes Payable
300 Common Stock

310 Retained Earnings
400 Sales
500 Cost of Goods Sold
510 Wages Expense
520 Phone Expense
530 Utilities Expense

Floods and Fires has the following transactions during June:

June 1 Receives $40,000 cash and a building worth $30,000 from the owners as an investment to start the business.
June 2 Purchases merchandise on account, $50,000.
June 5 Receives a two-year $20,000 loan from First City Bank.
June 7 Sells merchandise for $6,000 on account. The merchandise cost Floods and Fires $3,000.
June 9 Purchases office furniture for $2,000 cash.
June 11 Returns merchandise purchased on June 2 to suppliers. The merchandise originally cost Floods and Fires $1,200, and the supplier gives Floods and Fires a full $1,200 reduction in what it owed for the returned goods.
June 15 Pays salaries for the first half of June, $1,200.
June 18 Sells merchandise for $9,000, with $5,000 received in cash and $4,000 on account. The merchandise originally cost Floods and Fires $5,000.
June 19 Issues a check for $48,800 to pay for the remainder of the merchandise purchased on June 2.
June 21 Purchases office supplies for $500 on account.
June 25 Receives a $6,000 check from a customer in payment for the merchandise purchased on June 7.
June 27 Receives and pays phone bill, $500.
June 29 Pays utility bill for June, $950.
June 30 Pays salaries for the second half of June, $1,100.

Required

a. Prepare a general journal entry for each of the June transactions.
b. Prepare general ledger T-accounts for Floods and Fires and post the journal entries from (a).
c. Determine the balance in the T-accounts and prepare a trial balance for Floods and Fires as of June 30.
d. Prepare an income statement for Floods and Fires for the month ending June 30.

PROBLEM SET B

3-B1. Simple Income Statement. The Stationer, Inc., a retailer of office supplies, has the following expenses and revenues for August 1986:

Salaries expense	$ 8,000
Sales	50,000
Cost of goods sold	?
Miscellaneous expense	5,000
Utilities expense	2,000

Required

If Stationer's net income for August 1986 is $5,000, prepare an income statement following the format in Exhibit 3.9.

3-B2. Journalizing Transactions. Sandy Lake Sport Shop carries a full line of sporting, camping, and recreational equipment. Transactions for September are as follows:

September 2	Sandy Lake purchases 80 football helmets on account from Midwest Supply Company for a total of $4,800.
September 4	Company sells three canoes on account to Lake-Front Rentals, Inc., for a total of $1,050. Sandy Lake's cost of the canoes was $855.
September 9	Company pays Score-More Sports Supplies for a shipment of footballs received in August, $630.
September 12	Company receives $500 payment on account from Lakeview schools for weight-training equipment purchased in August.
September 14	The owners invest an additional $2,000 cash in the corporation.
September 15	Company purchases a pickup truck for $6,700 to make deliveries of equipment to local schools. Sandy Lake makes a down payment of $1,700 and signs a note for the balance.
September 18	Company sells 40 of the helmets purchased from Midwest to Lake State University for $90 per helmet on account.
September 22	Company receives payment in full from Lake-Front Rentals for the canoes purchased on September 4.
September 24	Company purchases $4,300 of ski equipment on account from Haldeman's Sports Wholesalers.
September 29	Company pays Midwest for the helmets purchased on September 2.
September 30	Company pays rent for the month of September, $300.
September 30	Company pays a clerk/stockboy for September, $450.
September 30	Miscellaneous cash sales for the month total $9,750. The cost of the miscellaneous goods was $6,175.

Required

Prepare a general journal entry for each of the September transactions.

3-B3. Correcting Journal Entries. The Entertainment Company, a retail outlet for musical instruments, reported a net income of $4,000 for June 1986. The following facts concern the June transactions:

1. Inventory purchases for $3,000 cash were recorded by debiting cash and crediting sales.
2. Payment of $1,000 received from customers on account was recorded by debiting cash and crediting sales.
3. Salary expense of $2,000 was recorded by debiting inventory and crediting cash.
4. Merchandise originally sold on account for $150 was returned by a customer. The Entertainment Company debited inventory and credited cost of goods sold for $150. The merchandise returned had originally cost The Entertainment Company $75; since it was undamaged, the merchandise was returned to inventory.
5. The Entertainment Company distributed $1,000 cash to the owner as a dividend. This transaction was recorded as a debit to salary expense and a credit to cash.

Required

a. Prepare general journal entries that will correct each transaction improperly recorded.
b. Compute the correct income for the month ending June 30, 1986.

3-B4. Correcting Income Statement Errors. Business Accounting Service prepared the following income statement that contains several errors:

Business Accounting Service
Income Statement
Month Ending April 30, 1986

Revenues	
Bank loan	$ 15,000
Service revenue	125,000
Interest income	3,000
Total revenues	$143,000
Expenses	
Purchase of office building	$100,000
Accounts payable	20,000
Wages payable	5,000
Administrative expense	10,000
Return of customer overpayment (never billed)	2,000
Interest expense	2,000
Salaries expense	30,000
Total expenses	$169,000
Net income	($ 26,000)

Required

Prepare a corrected income statement for the month ending April 30, 1986. Separate operating revenues and expenses from other income and expenses.

3-B5. Statement of Financial Position and Income Statement. Fashion Flooring, Inc., has the following statement of financial position for September 30, 1986:

Fashion Flooring, Inc.
Statement of Financial Position
September 30, 1986

Assets		Liabilities and Owners' Equity	
Cash	$ 15,000	Accounts payable	$ 80,000
Accounts receivable	40,000	Bank loan	250,000
Inventory	100,000	Total liabilities	$330,000
Equipment	90,000	Common stock	70,000
Buildings	200,000	Retained earnings	45,000
Total assets	$445,000	Total liabilities and owners' equity	$445,000

The company has the following transactions during October:

1. Purchases $20,000 of carpeting on account.
2. Signs a contract for $7,000 to carpet a new home in November. Fashion estimates that its cost to complete this job will be $3,000 for the carpeting and $1,500 for labor.
3. Receives $1,200 for a flooring job. Fashion's cost for the job was $500 for materials and $200 for labor.
4. Sells a warehouse no longer being used for $100,000. The warehouse was being carried in the accounts for $60,000.
5. Pays $2,000 on a bank loan, $500 of which is for interest.
6. Receives $10,000 from customers on account.
7. Purchases fork lift for $5,000 cash at an auction.

Required

a. Prepare an income statement for October 1986.
b. Prepare a statement of financial position as of October 31, 1986.

3-B6. Preparation of Financial Statements by Analysis of Accounts. Stimson Training Center has the following account balances in December 1986:

Accounts Payable, December 1	$20,000
Accounts Payable, December 31	15,000
Common Stock, December 1	10,000
Common Stock, December 31	10,000
Retained Earnings, December 1	15,000
Retained Earnings, December 31	?
Cash, December 1	?
Cash, December 31	18,000
Accounts Receivable, December 1	10,000
Accounts Receivable, December 31	15,000
Inventory, December 1	30,000
Inventory, December 31	25,000
Cost of Goods Sold	20,000
Sales	?
Operating Expenses	10,000

Assume that the foregoing list constitutes all of the accounts of Stimson Training.

Required

a. Prepare a statement of financial position as of December 1, 1986.
b. Prepare a statement of financial position as of December 31, 1986.
c. Prepare an income statement for December 1986.

3-B7. Trial Balances and General Ledger. Eileen A. Hathaway is the president of and senior doctor in a medical services corporation, Hathaway's Feel Better Medical Services. In an effort to cut costs, E. A. Hathaway fires her accountant and prepares the trial balance for the month ending August 31, 1986, by herself. Dr. Hathaway's incorrect trial balance is as follows:

Feel Better Medical Services
Trial Balance
August 31, 1986

Account	Debit	Credit
Cash		$ 10,000
Accounts Receivable	$ 40,000	
Supplies	5,000	
Equipment		100,000
Accounts Payable	25,000	
Notes Payable	10,000	
Common Stock		50,000
Retained Earnings		39,000
Medical Fee Revenue	100,000	
Salary Expense		60,000
Rent Expense		10,000
Utilities Expense		3,000
Supplies Expense		1,000

After many hours of frustration, Dr. Hathaway has asked you to review August's transactions and postings and prepare a corrected trial balance. Upon review, you find the following:

1. Total credits to accounts payable in the general ledger, including the beginning balance in the account, are $70,000; total debits for August are $40,000.
2. Cash of $960 received from a customer on account has been entered in the proper accounts as $690.

3. A payment of $1,000 cash to suppliers on account has been posted as a debit to cash and a credit to accounts payable.
4. Utility expenses of $500 paid in cash have been properly recorded in the general journal but never posted to the general ledger.

Required

Assuming that all accounts have normal debit/credit balances, prepare a corrected trial balance as of August 31, 1986, for Feel Better Medical Services.

3-B8. Journal Entries, General Ledger, Trial Balance, and Income Statement. The Wilmington Company sells carriages, surreys, and other horse-drawn vehicles and has the following trial balance as of March 1, 1986.

The Wilmington Company
Trial Balance
March 1, 1986

Account	Debit	Credit
Cash	$ 1,200	
Accounts Receivable	2,900	
Inventory	4,300	
Furniture and Fixtures	1,850	
Delivery Equipment	2,400	
Accounts Payable		$ 2,200
Common Stock		4,200
Retained Earnings		4,700
Sales		5,800
Cost of Goods Sold	2,100	
Rent Expense	620	
Wages Expense	1,280	
Utilities Expense	250	
Totals	$16,900	$16,900

The company's chart of accounts is as follows:

100 Cash
110 Accounts Receivable
120 Inventory
130 Supplies
140 Furniture and Fixtures
150 Delivery Equipment
160 Machinery
200 Accounts Payable
300 Common Stock
310 Retained Earnings
400 Sales
500 Cost of Goods Sold
510 Rent Expense
520 Wages Expense
530 Utilties Expense

During the month of March, Wilmington Company has the following transactions:

March 1 Purchases a small carriage for $380 on account.
March 3 Sells a surrey for $360 cash. The surrey originally cost Wilmington $270.
March 5 Purchases a new drill press on account from The Manufacturing Company for $420.
March 7 Receives a $350 payment from Eli Byler on his account.
March 8 Purchases $200 of fixtures on account for the office.

March 12	Purchases nuts and bolts to use as repair parts for $75 cash.
March 15	Pays employee wages, $320.
March 17	Owners invest an additional $1,000 cash in the company.
March 18	Sells a special-order pony cart to Jim Callahan for $310 on account. The cart cost Wilmington $250.
March 18	Pays William's Wheel Company $360 owed on account.
March 20	Receives a $250 payment from Bob Timmerman on his account.
March 21	Pays March rent of $310.
March 22	Sells Mary Rickets a new lightweight racing sulky for $520 on account. The sulky cost Wilmington $370.
March 24	Pays for the small carriage purchased on March 1.
March 27	Pays for the drill press purchased on March 5.
March 28	Receives payment in full from Jim Callahan for his March 18 purchase.
March 29	Pays utilities bill of $110.
March 30	Pays employee wages, $320.

Required

a. Prepare a general journal entry for each of the March transactions.

b. Prepare general ledger T-accounts for Wilmington and post the general journal entries from (a). (Be sure to enter the beginning balances in your ledger.)

c. Determine the balances in the T-accounts and prepare a trial balance as of March 31, 1986.

d. Prepare an income statement for the Wilmington Company for the month ending March 31, 1986.

THE ACCOUNTING CYCLE CONCLUDED PREPARATION OF FINANCIAL STATEMENTS

4

CHAPTER OBJECTIVES

After studying Chapter 4, you should understand the following:

1. The nature of the accounting cycle.
2. The requirements for and nature of the adjustment process for financial statement preparation.
3. The makeup and use of the accounting worksheet.
4. The process of financial statement preparation.
5. The process of closing the books at the conclusion of the accounting cycle.

Previous chapters have examined the bookkeeping process of recording transactions and the content and form of the statement of financial position and income statement. We now turn our attention to the process of using the transaction data in the journals and ledgers to develop these two statements.

THE ACCOUNTING CYCLE

ACCOUNTING CYCLE
The sequence of events beginning with initial recognition of transactions and ending with financial statement preparation.

Although accounting is a continuous process due to the never-ending stream of transactions, it exists for the purpose of supporting the preparation of periodic financial statements. Corporate financial reports are usually produced annually but can be generated as often as needed. The **accounting cycle** is the sequence of events beginning with initial recognition of transaction data and ending with financial statement preparation. The following are the first steps in the process:

1. Recognizing and analyzing transactions.
2. Recording transactions in the general journal.
3. Posting transactions to the general ledger accounts.

These three steps are continuous in nature and occur concurrently with the flow of transactions themselves.

In contrast to these continuous steps, the other steps in the accounting cycle occur only at periodic intervals, either as a check on the mechanical accuracy of the bookkeeping process or as an aid for the preparation of financial statements. The periodic steps are as follows:

1. Taking a trial balance.
2. Reviewing the account balances in light of all available facts and, if an account balance is not appropriate, adjusting the balance to the appropriate amount.
3. Compiling the financial statements from the adjusted account balances obtained from step 2.
4. Closing the revenue and expense accounts to ready them for the next accounting cycle.
5. Taking a post-closing trial balance to assure that the system is ready to begin the next accounting cycle.

Taking a trial balance is often done by itself to ensure bookkeeping accuracy. Steps 2 and 3 are normally undertaken when financial statements are to be prepared; steps 4 and 5 are completed at the conclusion of each accounting cycle. Let us begin our journey through the completion of the accounting cycle by closely examining step 2, the potential need to adjust the accounts in support of financial statement preparation.

ADJUSTMENTS AND THE PERIODIC CONCEPT

If all transactions are started and completed within one income measurement period and if each transaction has been properly recognized and recorded, income determination becomes a relatively simple task. However, many revenue and expense transactions span more than one time period. When such transactions occur, the accountant is required to make estimates of the proper amount of revenue or expense to be recognized for each period.

Suppose a company borrows $100,000 from a bank on October 1, 1986, with an annual interest fee of 15 percent of the amount borrowed and with repayment of the loan and interest due on October 1, 1987. Although a portion of the interest fee becomes an expense every day, the recognition of the interest expense in the bookkeeping process would normally occur when repayment of the loan and interest is made on October 1, 1987. If the company waits to record the total interest expense until October 1, 1987, zero interest expense would be reported in 1986 and $15,000 ($100,000 × .15) would be reported in 1987. However, if the company prepares financial statements for the year ending December 31, 1986, interest expense appropriate to 1986 (3 months x $1,250 per month, or $3,750) would be included in the 1986 income statement, and a liability of $3,750 would be included in the statement of financial position.

Adjustments in General

Recall that accrual accounting is a process that attempts to match economic transactions with time periods independent of the exchange of cash. The periodic procedure by which accounting records are updated to reflect all transactions occurring up to a particular moment in time is known as **adjusting the accounts.** The accountant's aim is to develop a set of accounts that conforms to generally accepted accounting principles and reflects all transactions. Such accounts can then be used to prepare financial statements that fairly present the financial position and the results of operations for the business.

ADJUSTING THE ACCOUNTS
The periodic procedure by which accounting records are updated to reflect all transactions occurring up to a particular point in time.

The next section explores the more common types of adjustments found in the actual practice of accounting. The examples presented are only representative of a particular type of adjustment. In actual practice, many hundreds of different adjustments can exist within each type.

Types of Transactions Spanning Multiple Time Periods

Four types of transactions can have an impact on several time periods:

1. Assets can be acquired that will be useful over several time periods. The portion of the assets used each period to produce revenue must be recognized as an expense—an asset/expense adjustment.
2. An asset can be acquired and completely used up, with payment to the supplier not yet occurring. The asset use must be recognized as an expense and the appropriate liability established—a liability/expense adjustment.
3. Revenue can be earned but not yet recorded. The revenue must be recognized—an asset/revenue adjustment.
4. Revenue can be recognized but not yet earned. In this case, a liability exists to supply future services or merchandise. The records must reflect the liability, and revenue must be adjusted downward—a liability/revenue adjustment.

Asset/Expense Adjustments

Prepaid Current Items. Frequently, cash is paid for current assets before their actual acquisition or use. Prime examples are rent and insurance, which normally are prepaid for several periods at a time. The term **prepaid expense** is often used in reference to current assets that are paid for before their actual acquisition or use. At the end of an accounting period, an adjustment must be made to reclassify the portion of the assets consumed as an expense or to reclassify the portion of the expenditure not yet used as an asset. The exact nature of the adjustment required must be determined from the facts of each case, including the type of journal entry made when the asset was acquired.

PREPAID EXPENSE
Current assets that are paid for before their actual acquisition or use.

Suppose the High-Risk Company purchases a three-year insurance policy on July 1, 1986, for $12,000 cash. High-Risk makes the following general journal entry for the purchase:

July 1	Prepaid insurance	12,000	
	Cash		12,000
	(to record purchase of insurance policy)		

For financial statements being prepared on December 31, 1986, High-Risk needs to recognize that six months of the insurance coverage has been used and should be reclassified as an expense. The facts are that on December 31, 1986, High-Risk has prepaid insurance (an asset) of only $10,000 and insurance expense (a used-up asset) of $2,000 ($12,000 × 6/36). The accounts of High-Risk, however, contain the following amounts:

Prepaid Insurance

7/1	12,000		

Insurance Expense

1/1 Bal.	0		

To make the necessary adjustment, $2,000 must be subtracted from the Prepaid Insurance account and $2,000 added to the Insurance Expense account. In terms of debit and credit notation, the updating is achieved by the following adjusting entry:

Dec. 31	Insurance expense	2,000	
	Prepaid insurance		2,000
	(to record expired insurance as an expense)		

After posting this entry, the account balances reflect the facts and appear as follows:

Prepaid Insurance

7/1	12,000	12/31	2,000
12/31 Bal.	10,000		

Insurance Expense

1/1 Bal.	0		
12/31	2,000		
12/31 Bal.	2,000		

To review, the adjustment process is a three-step operation:

1. Determine the appropriate account balances from the surrounding facts.
2. Compute the relevant ledger account balances as currently recorded.
3. Prepare an adjusting entry that adds or subtracts amounts from the current account balances to produce the appropriate account balances.

Note that the adjusting entry does not determine the appropriate account balance. The facts in the company's situation determine this balance, and the adjusting entry simply changes the account to the balance indicated by the facts. Don't try to memorize adjusting entries, but rather concentrate on analyzing the facts surrounding each account to determine whether or not the account balance is appropriate. The variety of facts in actual practice is endless, as is the variety of adjustments required.

Suppose that High-Risk had made the following entry in the general journal on July 1 when it purchased the insurance policy:

July 1	Insurance expense	12,000	
	Cash		12,000
	(to record purchase of insurance policy)		

The accounts, before adjustment, would then have appeared as follows:

Prepaid Insurance

Debit		Credit	
1/1 Bal.	0		

Insurance Expense

Debit		Credit	
7/1	12,000		

The surrounding facts and the appropriate account balances on December 31, 1986, are the same: Unused insurance is $10,000 and insurance coverage of $2,000 has been used up. The required adjustment in journal entry form is as follows:

Dec. 31	Prepaid insurance	10,000	
	Insurance expense		10,000
	(to record unexpired insurance as an asset)		

The final account balances would be the same as before, as follows:

Prepaid Insurance

Debit		Credit	
1/1 Bal.	0		
12/31	10,000		
12/31 Bal.	10,000		

Insurance Expense

Debit		Credit	
7/1	12,000	12/31	10,000
12/31 Bal.	2,000		

Review these alternate methods of handling the accounting for the purchase of the insurance and the subsequent recognition of the amount of insurance consumed and remaining until you thoroughly understand the process.

Noncurrent Asset Adjustments. The service potential of noncurrent assets, such as property, plant, and equipment, is in the assets' capacity to support the production of revenue over a long time. Noncurrent assets used in producing revenue should have a portion of their cost charged to expense each accounting period over their useful lives. Because many of these assets are productive for five, ten, twenty, or more years, estimates are required as to the amount of the asset to appropriately charge as an expense in each time period.

The depreciation process. The accounting process by which the cost of long-term assets is allocated to expense over the asset's useful life is known as **depreciation.** The amount of an asset's cost to be charged against each reporting period is called depreciation expense.

DEPRECIATION
The accounting process by which the cost of a long-term asset is allocated to expense over the asset's useful life.

Suppose the High-Risk Company acquires a machine on January 1, 1986, for $100,000. The machine is expected to be useful for ten years and have no resale value at the end of its useful life. A common assumption is that the benefits of the

STRAIGHT-LINE DEPRECIATION
The depreciation method that allocates equal amounts of a long-term asset's cost to expense each period of the asset's useful life.

NET BOOK VALUE
See Book Value.

BOOK VALUE
The amount at which an item is carried in the accounting records and reported in accounting statements.

machine will be received evenly over the ten-year life. Thus, one-tenth, or $10,000, of the machine's cost should be recognized as expense each year for ten years. The depreciation method that allocates equal amounts of a long-term asset's cost to expense in each period of the asset's useful life is called **straight-line depreciation.** The remaining undepreciated cost of a fixed asset (i.e., original price less all depreciation to date) is known as the **net book value** of the asset. In general, the net book value, or **book value,** of an asset is the amount at which the asset is carried in the accounting records and reported in financial statements. The net book value of High-Risk's machine is $90,000 after one year and $80,000 after two years. The depreciation adjustment with respect to the machine could be made as follows:

Dec. 31	Depreciation expense	10,000	
	Machinery		10,000
	(to record a portion of machine cost as expense)		

The effects of this entry on the accounts would be as follows:

Depreciation Expense

1/1 Bal.	0		
12/31	10,000		
12/31 Bal.	10,000		

Machinery

1/1	100,000	12/31	10,000
12/31 Bal.	90,000		

However, note that no well-defined measurement of the actual amount of the machine's service potential used during 1986 exists. The $10,000 of depreciation recognized was a rough estimate based on the expected useful life of the machine.

CONTRA-ACCOUNT
An account whose balance is offset against another account—the primary account—to determine the primary account's net book value.

Contra-accounts. Because of this lack of precision, accountants generally do not directly reduce the original balance of the machine account as illustrated under the foregoing method. Rather, they use a **contra-account,** a separate account whose balance is offset against another account, the primary account, to obtain the primary account's net book value. Contra-accounts commonly appear in asset, liability, and owners' equity relationships. Exhibit 4.1 illustrates the nature of the bond between a primary asset account and a contra-account.

EXHIBIT 4.1

Primary Asset Account		Contra-Account			Primary Asset Account	
Normal balance (e.g. 20,000)			Reduction in primary account (e.g. 1,000)	**Equivalent to**	Normal balance (e.g. 20,000)	Reduction in balance (e.g. 1,000)

Primary asset account balance reduced indirectly by entry to contra-account (e.g., if we wished to reduce primary asset balance to 19,000)

When depreciating long-term assets, a contra-account (called **accumulated depreciation**) collects the reduction in the asset during each time period. Accumulated depreciation represents the sum of all prior periods' depreciation expense. Returning to our example, depreciation expense for the year 1986 would be recognized with this adjusting journal entry:

ACCUMULATED DEPRECIATION
The sum of all prior periods' depreciation expense.

Dec. 31	Depreciation expense	10,000	
	Accumulated depreciation—machinery		10,000
	(to record a portion of machine cost as expense)		

The ledger accounts would appear as follows after posting:

Machinery

1/1	100,000	
12/31 Bal.	100,000	

Accumulated Depreciation—Machinery

	1/1 Bal.	0
	12/31	10,000
	12/31 Bal.	10,000

1/1 Bal.	0	
12/31	10,000	
12/31 Bal.	10,000	

To determine the book value of the machine at any given time, the total of the accumulated depreciation account is subtracted from the machinery account. In our example, the book value of the machine on December 31, 1986, would be $100,000 w $10,000 z $90,000. The 1986 statement of financial position for the High-Risk Company would show the following information regarding the machine in the noncurrent assets section:

Machinery	$100,000
Less: Accumulated depreciation	10,000
Net book value	$90,000

Although you may find the use of contra-accounts to be a confusing way of handling a routine task, remember that the amount of property, plant, and equipment sacrificed to the production of revenue in any given time period is, at best, a rough estimate. The two-account method of valuation for depreciable long-term assets provides the user of financial statements with information on both the original cost of the asset *and* the total amount of the asset cost that has been matched against revenues of earlier periods. A more extensive discussion of depreciation is presented in Chapter 10.

Liability/Expense Adjustments

As of the financial statement date, services sometimes have been received and thus expenses have been incurred for which no asset use or liability has yet been recorded. An example would be wages earned by employees but not yet paid. The wages earned represent an expense, since labor has been both acquired (an asset acquisition) and used (an expense).

Suppose the High-Risk Company hires workers on August 1, 1986, and agrees to pay them collectively $10,000 per working day ($50,000 per week). Assume further that High-Risk agrees to pay the workers every two weeks for the period then ended. The first payday is set for August 8; this initial pay period includes only six working days. During August 1986, the following routine journal entries are made on August 8 and August 22 to record the payment of cash to the workers and to recognize wages expense:

Aug. 8	Wages expense	60,000	
	Cash		60,000
	(to record wages earned August 1–8)		
Aug. 22	Wages expense	100,000	
	Cash		100,000
	(to record wages earned August 11–22)		

On August 31, 1986, wages totaling $50,000 have been earned since the last pay date. Payment of these wages is scheduled for September 5. High-Risk wishes to prepare financial statements for the month ending August 31. The total wage expense for August is $210,000 (21 working days @ $10,000 per day), and the amount owed on August 31, is $50,000. Yet the current accounts on August 31 show the following figures:

Wages Expense

8/8	60,000	
8/22	100,000	
8/31 Bal.	160,000	

Wages Payable

	8/1 Bal.	0

The appropriate balances should be as follows:

Wages Expense

Debit	Credit
210,000	

Wages Payable

Debit	Credit
	50,000

Thus, the $50,000 of wages owed must be recorded. The adjusting journal entry is as follows:

Aug. 31	Wages expense	50,000	
	Wages payable		50,000
	(to record wages owed as of August 31)		

After adjustment, the accounts would be properly updated, as follows:

Wages Expense

8/8	60,000	
8/22	100,000	
8/31 Bal.	160,000	
8/31	50,000	
8/31 Bal.	210,000	

Wages Payable

	0	Bal. 8/1
	50,000	8/31
	50,000	Bal. 8/31

Note again that the purpose of the adjusting entry is to alter account balances so that the financial statements will reflect economic reality as of the statement date. If no financial statements were being prepared by High-Risk on August 31, the recording of the wages expense could be delayed until the payment date of September 5, at which time an entry identical to the August 22 entry would be made.

Since High-Risk did prepare financial statements on August 31, the September 5 payroll entry will need to reflect the August 31 adjustment. Thus, on September 5, the following entry will be recorded:

Sept. 5	Wages payable (from August)	50,000	
	Wages expense (for September)	50,000	
	Cash		100,000
	(to record payroll for August 25 to September 5)		

Note that before recognizing any September wages expense, the cash payment is offset against the amount in Wages Payable.

The relevant ledger accounts will now look like this:

Wages Expense

9/1 Bal.	0*	
9/5	50,000	

Wages Payable

9/5	50,000	50,000	Bal. 9/1

*All revenue and expense accounts are returned to zero at the end of each accounting period. This process is discussed later in the chapter.

Wages Expense shows five days of September payroll costs, and Wages Payable has been driven to zero. Both amounts are appropriate, since the workers have worked five days in September and no wages are owed as of September 5.

Asset/Revenue Adjustments

The inflow of assets representing revenue and the actual earning of revenue do not always coincide. An accounting entity may have to adjust its revenue accounts to reflect the actual amounts earned within any given time period. Frequently, revenue may have been earned but not yet received in cash or recorded.

In some situations, such as those dealing with rent or interest, revenue is earned continuously but recorded only at discrete intervals, normally when cash changes hands or billings occur. Unless, by coincidence, the recording of revenue is up-to-date at the end of a period, an adjustment is in order. Suppose the High-Risk Company made a one-year loan of $10,000 with 14 percent interest to another company on

October 1, 1986. Both the loan and the interest of 14 percent of the loan amount, or $1,400, will be due for repayment on October 1, 1987.

On December 31, 1986, High-Risk intends to prepare financial statements. During October, November, and December, High-Risk has been earning interest, but this has not yet been recorded. This unbilled and uncollected interest should be included in High-Risk's 1986 income, and the expected payments should be included as an asset on the statement of financial position. The relevant account balances before making December 31 adjustments would be as follows:

Interest Receivable

	Debit	Credit
Bal. 12/31	0	

Interest Revenue

Debit	Credit	
	0	Bal. 12/31

The facts indicate, however, that the actual balances on December 31 should be as follows:

Interest Receivable

Debit	Credit
350 (1/4 × $1,400)	

Interest Revenue

Debit	Credit
	350

Therefore, an adjusting journal entry adding the $350 to revenue and to assets is required. This entry would be as follows:

Dec. 31	Interest receivable	350	
	Interest revenue		350
	(to record unbilled interest revenue at Dec. 31)		

The accounts would then appear as follows:

Interest Receivable

	Debit	Credit
Bal. 12/31	0	
12/31	350	
Bal. 12/31	350	

Interest Revenue

Debit	Credit	
	0	Bal. 12/31
	350	12/31
	350	Bal. 12/31

Liability/Revenue Adjustments

In some industries, customers pay in advance for services or goods. Although cash may have been received, the company has not earned the revenue until the services have been performed or goods delivered. Because the customer has a claim on the firm, the liability must be presented in the financial reports.

Let us assume that the High-Risk Company publishes several magazines for which subscription payments are received two years in advance. On January 1, 1986, High-Risk receives $24,000 from subscribers for magazines to be delivered through December 31, 1987. High-Risk records the receipts of the money on January 1, 1986, as follows:

Jan. 1	Cash	24,000	
	Subscription revenue		24,000
	(to record subscription revenue received)		

High-Risk wishes to prepare financial statements for the six months ending June 30, 1986. Clearly, High-Risk has not earned the total revenue of $24,000 in the six months just ended. In fact, only one-fourth, or $6,000, has been earned, and High-Risk has an obligation to deliver magazines to subscribers for the next one and one-half years. This obligation can be valued at $18,000 and should be shown as a liability. The accounts require adjustment to reflect their proper balances on June 30 before preparing the financial statements. Based on this information, the accounts currently appear as follows:

Subscription Revenue			
		1/1	24,000

(liability) Subscription Revenue Received in Advance			
		0	Bal. 1/1

We know from the facts, however, that the June 30 account balances should be as follows:

Subscription Revenue	
	6,000

Subscription Revenue Received in Advance	
	18,000

Thus, $18,000 must be subtracted from the Subscription Revenue account and added to the liability account—Subscription Revenue Received in Advance. The adjusting entry to accomplish this would be as follows:

June 30	Subscription revenue	18,000	
	Subscription revenue received in advance		18,000
	(to record unearned revenue as a liability)		

After the adjustment, the accounts would look as follows:

Subscription Revenue			
6/30	18,000	24,000	1/1
		6,000	Bal. 6/30

Subscription Revenue Received in Advance			
		0	Bal. 1/1
		18,000	6/30
		18,000	Bal. 6/30

The subscription revenue received in advance is called **unearned** or **deferred revenue.** Unearned or deferred revenue is revenue received before completion of the earnings process and represents a liability. In this case, High-Risk has an obligation to deliver future publications to subscribers in return for the funds provided by the subscribers. In effect, the subscribers are creditors of the High-Risk Company. Again we emphasize that the appropriate account balances must determine the adjusting entry—the entry does not determine the appropriate account balances.

UNEARNED REVENUE
See Deferred Revenue.

DEFERRED REVENUE
Revenue received before completion of the earnings process.

Assume High-Risk had made the following entry on January 1 when the cash was originally received from subscribers:

Jan. 1	Cash	24,000	
	Subscription revenue received in advance		24,000
	(to record receipts of magazine subscriptions)		

The fact pattern would remain the same. The appropriate account balances at June 30 would still be as follows:

Subscription revenue: $6,000 credit balance

Subscription revenue received in advance: $18,000 credit balance

However, the actual account balances before adjustment would appear as follows:

Subscription Revenue			
		0	Bal. 6/30

Subscription Revenue Received in Advance			
		24,000	Bal. 6/30

The appropriate adjusting entry to change the accounts to their proper balances is as follows:

June 30	Subscription revenue received in advance	6,000	
	Subscription revenue		6,000
	(to recognize subscription revenue earned)		

After the adjustment, the accounts would appear as follows:

Subscription Revenue			
		0	Bal. 6/30
		6,000	6/30
		6,000	Bal. 6/30

Subscription Revenue Received in Advance			
		24,000	Bal. 6/30
6/30	6,000		
		18,000	Bal. 6/30

Note that the final account balances are exactly the same as with the prior adjustment.

Adjustments Summary

In summary, the adjustments that might be necessary before the preparation of financial statements are diverse. Each time financial statements are prepared, account balances and the facts involved must be reviewed. When the surrounding facts lead to the conclusion that an account balance is not appropriate, the proper balance should be determined and an adjusting journal entry prepared that will add or subtract the amount required. An adjustment will normally change an account balance both for income statement preparation (revenue or expense) and for statement of financial position preparation (asset or liability).

COMPLETION OF THE ACCOUNTING CYCLE

After completing the adjustment process, the accountant can prepare the financial statements. To facilitate financial statement preparation, the accountant often employs a tool known as the accounting worksheet.

ADJUSTMENT TYPES

■ **CONCEPT SUMMARY 4.1**

Type	Statement of Financial Position Purpose	Income Statement Purpose
Asset/Expense adjustment	To reduce an asset balance to its unused portion as of the statement date.	To recognize the portion of an asset used up during the current time period as an expense.
Liability/Expense adjustment	To recognize the liability for future payment for goods or services used up during the current period.	To recognize the cost of services or assets used up during the current time period as an expense.
Asset/Revenue adjustment	To record the asset received for goods or services provided during the current period.	To recognize the asset received and earned as revenue during the current time period.
Liability/Revenue adjustment	To recognize the liability for future delivery of goods or services.	To reduce recorded revenue by the amount not yet earned.

The Accounting Worksheet

ACCOUNTING WORKSHEET
An informal document used by accountants to organize their work.

The **accounting worksheet** is an informal document accountants use to organize their work. A worksheet is commonly used to organize the work that needs to be done at the conclusion of each cycle and is not a part of the financial statements supplied to interested parties. The normal process of recording business transactions in the journal and ledger can continue without interruption as the periodic reporting process goes forward. Perhaps the best way to demonstrate the interplay of the continuous process of transaction recording and the periodic preparation of financial statements (using a worksheet) is with a comprehensive example. This also gives you a chance to review the materials discussed in the preceding sections of the text.

The Downearth Company—A Comprehensive Example

The following transactions take place from January 1 through February 28, 1986. Downearth wishes to prepare an income statement for the two months ending February 28, 1986, and a statement of financial position as of February 28, 1986.

January 3 — Downearth is formed; the owners invest cash of $100,000 and receive common stock.

January 5 — Merchandise costing $40,000 is purchased, with payment due within 30 days.

January 6 — Downearth purchases and pays for equipment costing $20,000.

January 9 — A building is rented for $1,000 per month. Six months' rent ($6,000) is paid in advance.

January 10 — A one-year fire insurance policy is purchased for $3,000.

January 13 — Downearth opens for business and sells merchandise for $10,000 cash. The merchandise originally cost Downearth $5,000.

January 18 — Credit sales of merchandise total $20,000, with payment due from customers by February 18. This merchandise originally cost Downearth $10,000.

January 20 — An additional $20,000 of merchandise is purchased, with payment due suppliers by February 20.

January 20	Employees are paid $1,600 in wages for the work period ending January 13.
February 1	Downearth borrows $100,000 from a local bank at an annual interest rate of 15 percent. An expanded line of merchandise is purchased for $50,000 from suppliers. The other $50,000 is used to purchase delivery vehicles.
February 3	Wages of $2,000 are paid for the work period ending January 27.
February 4	Downearth pays for the goods purchased on January 5.
February 9	Merchandise is sold for $40,000 on credit, with payment from customers due by March 9. The merchandise originally cost Downearth $20,000.
February 17	Downearth pays $2,000 in wages for the work period ending February 10.
February 18	$20,000 is received from customers for goods sold on January 18.
February 20	Payment is made for the goods purchased by Downearth on January 20.

Using the chart of accounts for Downearth (Exhibit 4.2), the bookkeeper diligently records the transactions in the general journal and posts them to the general ledger as shown in Exhibit 4.3.

EXHIBIT 4.2

Chart of Accounts
The Downearth Company

Account Title	Number
Assets	
Cash	101
Accounts Receivable	102
Merchandise Inventory	103
Prepaid Rent	104
Prepaid Fire Insurance	105
Equipment	121
Accumulated Depreciation—Equipment	122
Delivery Vehicles	123
Accumulated Depreciation—Delivery Vehicles	124
Liabilities	
Accounts Payable	201
Notes Payable to Banks	202
Interest Payable	203
Wages Payable	204
Owners' Equity	
Common Stock	301
Retained Earnings	321
Revenues	
Sales	401
Expenses	
Cost of Goods Sold	501
Wages Expense	502
Rent Expense	503
Insurance Expense	504
Depreciation Expense	505
Interest Expense	506
Other	
Income Summary	901

EXHIBIT 4.3

Downearth Company
General Journal

Page 1

Date	Transaction	Post. Ref.	Debit	Credit
1986				
Jan. 1	Cash	101	100,000	
	Common stock	301		100,000
	(to record owners' investment)			
5	Merchandise inventory	103	40,000	
	Accounts payable	201		40,000
	(to record merchandise purchases)			
6	Equipment	121	20,000	
	Cash	101		20,000
	(to record purchase of equipment)			
9	Prepaid rent	104	6,000	
	Cash	101		6,000
	(to record prepayment of six months' rent)			
10	Prepaid fire insurance	105	3,000	
	Cash	101		3,000
	(to record purchase of fire insurance)			
13	Cash	101	10,000	
	Sales	401		10,000
	(to record sales to customers)			
13	Cost of goods sold	501	5,000	
	Merchandise inventory	103		5,000
	(to record cost of goods sold)			
18	Accounts receivable	102	20,000	
	Sales	401		20,000
	(to record sales on account)			
18	Cost of goods sold	501	10,000	
	Merchandise inventory	103		10,000
	(to record cost of goods sold)			
20	Merchandise inventory	103	20,000	
	Accounts payable	201		20,000
	(to record merchandise purchases)			
20	Wages expense	502	1,600	
	Cash	101		1,600
	(to record payroll for period ending Jan 13)			

EXHIBIT 4.3
Continued

Downearth Company
General Journal

Page 2

Date		Transaction	Post. Ref.	Debit	Credit
1986					
Feb.	1	Cash	101	100,000	
		Notes payable to banks	202		100,000
		(to record borrowing from bank)			
	1	Merchandise inventory	103	50,000	
		Cash	101		50,000
		(to record merchandise purchases)			
	1	Delivery vehicles	123	50,000	
		Cash	101		50,000
		(to record purchase of delivery vehicles)			
	3	Wages expense	502	2,000	
		Cash	101		2,000
		(to record payroll for			
		period ending Jan. 27)			
	4	Accounts payable	201	40,000	
		Cash	101		40,000
		(to record payment to suppliers)			
	9	Accounts receivable	102	40,000	
		Sales	401		40,000
		(to record sales on account)			
	9	Cost of goods sold	501	20,000	
		Merchandise inventory	103		20,000
		(to record cost of goods sold)			
	17	Wages expense	502	2,000	
		Cash	101		2,000
		(to record payroll for			
		period ending Feb. 10)			
	18	Cash	101	20,000	
		Accounts receivable	102		20,000
		(to record customers' payments)			
	20	Accounts payable	201	20,000	
		Cash	101		20,000
		(to record payment to suppliers)			

EXHIBIT 4.3

Continued

GENERAL LEDGER

ACCOUNT Cash — Account No. 101

Date	Explanation	Post Ref.	Debit	Date	Explanation	Post Ref.	Credit
1/01		J1	100,000	1/06		J1	20,000
1/13		J1	10,000	1/09		J1	6,000
2/01		J2	100,000	1/10		J1	3,000
2/18		J2	20,000	1/20		J1	1,600
				2/01		J2	50,000
				2/01		J2	50,000
				2/03		J2	2,000
				2/04		J2	40,000
				2/17		J2	2,000
				2/20		J2	20,000
2/28	Balance		35,400				

ACCOUNT Accounts Receivable — Account No. 102

Date	Explanation	Post Ref.	Debit	Date	Explanation	Post Ref.	Credit
1/18		J1	20,000	2/18		J2	20,000
2/09		J2	40,000				
2/28	Balance		40,000				

ACCOUNT Merchandise Inventory — Account No. 103

Date	Explanation	Post Ref.	Debit	Date	Explanation	Post Ref.	Credit
1/03		J1	40,000	1/13		J1	5,000
1/20		J1	20,000	1/18		J1	10,000
2/01		J2	50,000	2/09		J2	20,000
2/28	Balance		75,000				

ACCOUNT Prepaid Rent — Account No. 104

Date	Explanation	Post Ref.	Debit	Date	Explanation	Post Ref.	Credit
1/09		J1	6,000				
2/28	Balance		6,000				

ACCOUNT Prepaid Fire Insurance — Account No. 105

Date	Explanation	Post Ref.	Debit	Date	Explanation	Post Ref.	Credit
1/10		J1	3,000				
2/28	Balance		3,000				

ACCOUNT Equipment — Account No. 121

Date	Explanation	Post Ref.	Debit	Date	Explanation	Post Ref.	Credit
1/06		J1	20,000				
2/28	Balance		20,000				

EXHIBIT 4.3
Continued

GENERAL LEDGER

ACCOUNT	Delivery Vehicles						Account No. 123
Date	Explanation	Post Ref.	Debit	Date	Explanation	Post Ref.	Credit
2/01		J2	50,000				
2/28	Balance		50,000				

ACCOUNT	Accounts Payable						Account No. 201
Date	Explanation	Post Ref.	Debit	Date	Explanation	Post Ref.	Credit
2/04		J2	40,000	1/03		J1	40,000
2/20		J2	20,000	1/20		J1	20,000
				2/28	Balance		0

ACCOUNT	Notes Payable to Banks						Account No. 202
Date	Explanation	Post Ref.	Debit	Date	Explanation	Post Ref.	Credit
				2/01		J2	100,000
				2/28	Balance		100,000

ACCOUNT	Common Stock						Account No. 301
Date	Explanation	Post Ref.	Debit	Date	Explanation	Post Ref.	Credit
				1/02		J1	100,000
				2/28	Balance		100,000

ACCOUNT	Sales						Account No. 401
Date	Explanation	Post Ref.	Debit	Date	Explanation	Post Ref.	Credit
				1/13		J1	10,000
				1/18		J1	20,000
				2/09		J2	40,000
				2/28	Balance		70,000

ACCOUNT	Cost of Goods Sold						Account No. 501
Date	Explanation	Post Ref.	Debit	Date	Explanation	Post Ref.	Credit
1/13		J1	5,000				
1/18		J1	10,000				
2/09		J2	20,000				
2/28	Balance		35,000				

ACCOUNT	Wages Expense						Account No. 502
Date	Explanation	Post Ref.	Debit	Date	Explanation	Post Ref.	Credit
1/20		J2	1,600				
2/03		J2	2,000				
2/17		J2	2,000				
2/28	Balance		5,600				

Beginning the Accounting Worksheet. On February 28, 1986, the information recorded in the journal and ledger becomes the basis for financial statement preparation for the two-month period then ended. The accountant begins the task of financial statement preparation by copying the chart of accounts listing into the leftmost columns of the accounting worksheet.

Trial Balance. All of the account balances, determined from the general ledger, are listed on the worksheet as a trial balance. Entering the chart of accounts from Exhibit 4.2 along with the ledger account balances from Exhibit 4.3 provides the worksheet with the trial balance as in Exhibit 4.4. Of course, care must be taken to appropriately enter the account balances as debits or credits as indicated by the placement of each balance in the ledger. The trial balance serves to start the worksheet and to provide a check on the mechanical accuracy of the bookkeeping process. Keep in mind that the total debit balances should equal the total credit balances.

The Adjustment Process As discussed earlier, each account must be reviewed for potential adjustment. If the balance does not reflect all accounting events up to the statement date, the appropriate balance must be determined and an adjusting journal entry prepared. This adjustment process can involve the addition of new accounts to the worksheet.

A review of the accounts listed on the trial balance follows:

1. Cash—appropriate as shown on trial balance; no adjustment needed.
2. Accounts Receivable—appropriate as shown on trial balance; no adjustment needed.
3. Merchandise Inventory—appropriate as shown on trial balance; no adjustment needed.
4. Prepaid Rent—covers six months from January 1, 1986, through June 30, 1986. Two months' rent has been used up. The appropriate balance is therefore $4,000, representing the four months' rent not yet used. As with any asset consumed in the production of revenue, an expense equal to the rent used must be recognized. The following adjusting journal entry is required:

Feb. 28	Rent expense	2,000	
	Prepaid rent		2,000
	(to adjust prepaid rent and recognize rent expense—adjusting entry one)		

The adjusting journal entry is placed in the adjustments column on the worksheet, not in the general journal at this point. (Adjusting entries are entered into the books of record later in the statement preparation process.) Footnotes on the worksheet can be used to explain the adjustments. The ledger accounts will be affected as follows:

Prepaid Rent

Debit		Credit	
Bal. before adj.	6,000	Adj.	2,000
Bal. after adj.	4,000		

Rent Expense

Debit		Credit
Bal. before adj.	0	
Adj.	2,000	
Bal. after adj.	2,000	

EXHIBIT 4.4

Downearth Company
Financial Statement Worksheet
Two-Month Period Ending February 28, 1986

		1	2	3	4	5	6	7	8	9	10
Acct.		Trial Balance									
No.	Account Title	Dr.	Cr.								
101	Cash	35,400									
102	Accounts Receivable	40,000									
103	Merchandise Inventory	75,000									
104	Prepaid Rent	6,000									
105	Prepaid Fire Insurance	3,000									
121	Equipment	20,000									
122	Accum. Depreciation—Equip.		0								
123	Delivery Vehicles	50,000									
124	Accum. Depreciation—Del. Veh.		0								
201	Accounts Payable		0								
202	Notes Payable to Banks		100,000								
203	Interest Payable		0								
204	Wages Payable		0								
301	Common Stock		100,000								
321	Retained Earnings		0								
401	Sales		70,000								
501	Cost of Goods Sold	35,000									
502	Wages Expense	5,600									
503	Rent Expense	0									
504	Insurance Expense	0									
505	Depreciation Expense	0									
506	Interest Expense	0									
	Totals	270,000	270,000								

5. Fire Insurance—one-year policy, two months expired. Only ten months of future value remain. Consequently, the appropriate balance is $2,500 as of February 28, the other $500 having been used up. The $500 must be subtracted from the Prepaid Fire Insurance account and an equal expense of $500 recognized. The appropriate adjustments to be recorded on the worksheet and the effects of this entry are as follows:

Feb. 28	Insurance expense	500	
	Prepaid fire insurance		500
	(to reduce prepaid fire insurance and recognize insurance expense—adjusting entry two)		

Prepaid Fire Insurance

Bal. before adj.	3,000	Adj.	500
Bal after adj.	2,500		

Insurance Expense

Bal. before adj.	0	
Adj.	500	
Bal. after adj.	500	

6. Equipment—expected to last ten years, with no salvage value at the end of that time. Because it has been in use for two months, 2/120, or $333, of the cost has become an expense. Recall that long-lived assets such as equipment are adjusted for use (depreciated) by increasing the contra-account (Accumulated Depreciation). Therefore, the following adjusting entry is required to match part of the equipment cost to the revenue it helped to produce:

Feb. 28	Depreciation expense	333	
	Accumulated depreciation—equipment		333
	(to reduce equipment and recognize depreciation expense—adjusting entry three)		

The appropriate balances will be as follows:

Equipment

Bal. before adj.	20,000	
Bal. after adj.	20,000	

Accumulated Depreciation—Equipment

	Bal. before adj.	0
	Adj.	333
	Bal. after adj.	333

Depreciation Expense

Bal. before adj.	0	
Adj.	333	
Bal. after adj.	333	

(Note once again that the Equipment account itself is not affected directly by the adjustment for equipment use and that the contra-account, Accumulated Depreciation—Equipment, and the Equipment account taken together provide a net book value of $19,667 for the equipment.)

7. Delivery Vehicles—expected to be in use five years and then be worthless. Since 1/60 of their useful life has passed, $833 should be charged as expense. This account

is adjusted for use in the same way as is the Equipment account. The adjusting entry and ledger accounts would be as follows:

Feb. 28	Depreciation expense	833	
	Accumulated depreciation—delivery vehicles		833
	(to recognize delivery vehicle use expense—adjusting entry four)		

Delivery Vehicles

Debit		Credit	
Bal. before adj.	50,000		
Bal. after adj.	50,000		

Accumulated Depreciation—Delivery Vehicles

Debit		Credit	
		Bal. before adj.	0
		Adj.	833
		Bal. after adj.	833

Depreciation Expense

Debit		Credit	
Bal. before adj. (from equipment)	333		
Adj. (from del. veh.)	833		
Bal. after adj.	1,166		

The net book value of the delivery vehicles is $50,000 − $833, or $49,167, after this adjustment is made.

8. Accounts Payable—appropriate as shown on trial balance; no adjustment needed.
9. Notes Payable to Banks—appropriate as shown. However, interest has been accumulating for one month, and the obligation to pay the expense deriving from this "rental of money" (interest) must be recognized. The interest expense is calculated to be $1,250 [1/12 × (.15 × 100,000)]. The adjusting entry to recognize this increase in obligations and increase in expenses along with the ledger account effects are as follows:

Feb. 28	Interest expense	1,250	
	Interest payable		1,250
	(to recognize interest liability and expense—adjusting entry five)		

Interest Payable

Debit		Credit	
		Bal. before adj.	0
		Adj.	1,250
		Bal. after adj.	1,250

Interest Expense

Debit		Credit	
Bal. before adj.	0		
Adj.	1,250		
Bal. after adj.	1,250		

10. Common Stock—appropriate as shown on trial balance; no adjustment needed.
11. Sales—appropriate as shown on trial balance; no adjustment needed.
12. Wages Expense—last paid on February 17 for the two-week period ending February 10. Consequently, Downearth owes wages through February 28 of $2,800. Both the obligation to pay the wages and the additional amount of labor expense must be recognized to reflect the total labor used as of February 28. The adjusting entry recorded on the worksheet and posted ledger account effects are as follows:

Feb. 28	Wages expense	2,800	
	Wages payable		2,800
	(to recognize the obligation to pay wages and the labor used since the last payday —adjusting entry six)		

Wages Payable

Debit	Credit	
	Bal. before adj.	0
	Adj.	2,800
	Bal. after adj.	2,800

Wages Expense

Debit		Credit
Bal. before adj.	5,600	
Adj.	2,800	
Bal. after adj.	8,400	

Each adjustment has been placed on the worksheet as in Exhibit 4.5. Note how explanations are placed on the bottom of the worksheets as footnotes. The footnote numbers also tie together the associated debits and credits for easy reference.

After all entries are recorded, the adjustment columns are footed (totaled) to help detect mechanical errors before proceeding across the worksheet. The debit column, as usual, must equal the credit column.

The Adjusted Trial Balance. When the original account balances are combined with the end-of-period adjustments, the result is called an **adjusted trial balance.** The adjusted trial balance in columns 5 and 6 of the worksheet in Exhibit 4.6 was produced by combining the adjustments with the original account balances on a line-by-line basis. Keep in mind when totaling across that if both the initial balance of and the adjustment to an account are debits or credits, you should add. If one is a debit and the other a credit, subtracting is in order, with the new balance belonging to the larger side.

ADJUSTED TRIAL BALANCE
A trial balance that combines original account balances with end-of-period adjustments.

The adjusted trial balance columns should also be footed at this point. The worksheet is usually completed in pencil so that mistakes can be erased. (Journals and ledgers, on the other hand, are a part of a business's formal records and should be completed by permanent methods.)

EXHIBIT 4.5

Downearth Company
Financial Statement Worksheet
Two-Month Period Ending February 28, 1986

Acct. No.	Account Title	1 Trial Balance Dr.	2 Trial Balance Cr.	3 Adjustments Dr.	4 Adjustments Cr.	5	6	7	8	9	10
101	Cash	35,400									
102	Accounts Receivable	40,000									
103	Merchandise Inventory	75,000									
104	Prepaid Rent	6,000			2,000[1]						
105	Prepaid Fire Insurance	3,000			500[2]						
121	Equipment	20,000									
122	Accum. Depreciation—Equip.		0		333[3]						
123	Delivery Vehicles	50,000									
124	Accum. Depreciation—Del. Veh.		0		833[4]						
201	Accounts Payable		0								
202	Notes Payable to Banks		100,000								
203	Interest Payable		0		1,250[5]						
204	Wages Payable		0		2,800[6]						
301	Common Stock		100,000								
321	Retained Earnings		0								
401	Sales		70,000								
501	Cost of Goods Sold	35,000									
502	Wages Expense	5,600		2,800[6]							
503	Rent Expense	0		2,000[1]							
504	Insurance Expense	0		500[2]							
505	Depreciation Expense	0		333[3]							
				833[4]							
506	Interest Expense	0		1,250[5]							
	Totals	270,000	270,000	7,716	7,716						

1. To adjust prepaid rent and rent expense.
2. To adjust prepaid fire insurance and insurance expense.
3. To adjust equipment account for depreciation.
4. To adjust delivery vehicle account for depreciation.
5. To show interest expense and liability.
6. To show wages expense and liability as of Feb. 28.

EXHIBIT 4.6

Downearth Company
Financial Statement Worksheet
Two-Month Period Ending February 28, 1986

Acct. No.	Account Title	Trial Balance Dr. (1)	Trial Balance Cr. (2)	Adjustments Dr. (3)	Adjustments Cr. (4)	Adj. Trial Balance Dr. (5)	Adj. Trial Balance Cr. (6)	7	8	9	10
101	Cash	35,400				35,400					
102	Accounts Receivable	40,000				40,000					
103	Merchandise Inventory	75,000				75,000					
104	Prepaid Rent	6,000			2,000[1]	4,000					
105	Prepaid Fire Insurance	3,000			500[2]	2,500					
121	Equipment	20,000				20,000					
122	Accum. Depreciation—Equip.		0		333[3]		333				
123	Delivery Vehicles	50,000				50,000					
124	Accum. Depreciation—Del. Veh.		0		833[4]		833				
201	Accounts Payable		0				0				
202	Notes Payable to Banks		100,000				100,000				
203	Interest Payable		0		1,250[5]		1,250				
204	Wages Payable		0		2,800[6]		2,800				
301	Common Stock		100,000				100,000				
321	Retained Earnings		0				0				
401	Sales		70,000				70,000				
501	Cost of Goods Sold	35,000				35,000					
502	Wages Expense	5,600		2,800[6]		8,400					
503	Rent Expense	0		2,000[1]		2,000					
504	Insurance Expense	0		500[2]		500					
505	Depreciation Expense	0		333[3]		1,166					
				833[4]							
506	Interest Expense	0		1,250[5]		1,250					
	Totals	270,000	270,000	7,716	7,716	275,216	275,216				

1. To adjust prepaid rent and rent expense.
2. To adjust prepaid fire insurance and insurance expense.
3. To adjust equipment account for depreciation.
4. To adjust delivery vehicle account for depreciation.
5. To show interest expense and liability.
6. To show wages expense and liability as of Feb. 28.

The Income Statement and Statement of Financial Position

As Exhibit 4.7 shows, the adjusted balance in each of the revenue and expense accounts is repeated in the income statement columns (7 and 8 in our example), and all other balances are copied into the statement of financial position columns (9 and 10 in our example).

EXHIBIT 4.7

Downearth Company
Financial Statement Worksheet
Two-Month Period Ending February 28, 1986

		1	2	3	4	5	6	7	8	9	10
										Statement of	
Acct.		Trial Balance		Adjustments		Adj. Trial Balance		Income Statement		Financial Position	
No.	Account Title	Dr.	Cr.	Dr.	Cr.	Dr.	Cr.	Dr.	Cr.	Dr.	Cr.
101	Cash	35,400				35,400				35,400	
102	Accounts Receivable	40,000				40,000				40,000	
103	Merchandise Inventory	75,000				75,000				75,000	
104	Prepaid Rent	6,000			2,000[1]	4,000				4,000	
105	Prepaid Fire Insurance	3,000			500[2]	2,500				2,500	
121	Equipment	20,000				20,000				20,000	
122	Accum. Depreciation—Equip.		0		333[3]		333				333
123	Delivery Vehicles	50,000				50,000				50,000	
124	Accum. Depreciation—Del. Veh.		0		833[4]		833				833
201	Accounts Payable		0				0				0
202	Notes Payable to Banks		100,000				100,000				100,000
203	Interest Payable		0		1,250[5]		1,250				1,250
204	Wages Payable		0		2,800[6]		2,800				2,800
301	Common Stock		100,000				100,000				100,000
321	Retained Earnings		0				0				
401	Sales		70,000				70,000		70,000		
501	Cost of Goods Sold	35,000				35,000		35,000			
502	Wages Expense	5,600		2,800[6]		8,400		8,400			
503	Rent Expense	0		2,000[1]		2,000		2,000			
504	Insurance Expense	0		500[2]		500		500			
505	Depreciation Expense	0		333[3]		1,166		1,166			
				833[4]							
506	Interest Expense	0		1,250[5]		1,250		1,250			
	Totals	270,000	270,000	7,716	7,716	275,216	275,216				

1. To adjust prepaid rent and rent expense.
2. To adjust prepaid fire insurance and insurance expense.
3. To adjust equipment account for depreciation.
4. To adjust delivery vehicle account for depreciation.
5. To show interest expense and liability.
6. To show wages expense and liability as of Feb. 28.

Once again, the columns should be footed. However, this time the debits will probably not equal the credits for either set of columns. After totaling, the next step is to subtract expenses (column 7) from revenues (column 8) to determine net income. If the resulting figure is positive (a profit), it should be entered under the footing in columns 7 and 10, as in Exhibit 4.8. If the income figure was negative (a

EXHIBIT 4.8

Downearth Company
Financial Statement Worksheet
Two-Month Period Ending February 28, 1986

		1	2	3	4	5	6	7	8	9	10
Acct.		Trial Balance		Adjustments		Adj. Trial Balance		Income Statement		Statement of Financial Position	
No.	Account Title	Dr.	Cr.	Dr.	Cr.	Dr.	Cr.	Dr.	Cr.	Dr.	Cr.
101	Cash	35,400				35,400				35,400	
102	Accounts Receivable	40,000				40,000				40,000	
103	Merchandise Inventory	75,000				75,000				75,000	
104	Prepaid Rent	6,000			2,000[1]	4,000				4,000	
105	Prepaid Fire Insurance	3,000			500[2]	2,500				2,500	
121	Equipment	20,000				20,000				20,000	
122	Accum. Depreciation—Equip.		0		333[3]		333				333
123	Delivery Vehicles	50,000				50,000				50,000	
124	Accum. Depreciation—Del. Veh.		0		833[4]		833				833
201	Accounts Payable		0				0				0
202	Notes Payable to Banks		100,000				100,000				100,000
203	Interest Payable		0		1,250[5]		1,250				1,250
204	Wages Payable		0		2,800[6]		2,800				2,800
301	Common Stock		100,000				100,000				100,000
321	Retained Earnings		0				0				
401	Sales		70,000				70,000		70,000		
501	Cost of Goods Sold	35,000				35,000		35,000			
502	Wages Expense	5,600		2,800[6]		8,400		8,400			
503	Rent Expense	0		2,000[1]		2,000		2,000			
504	Insurance Expense	0		500[2]		500		500			
505	Depreciation Expense	0		333[3]		1,166		1,166			
				833[4]							
506	Interest Expense	0		1,250[5]		1,250		1,250			
								48,316	70,000	226,900	205,216
								A21,684			A21,684
	Totals	270,000	270,000	7,716	7,716	275,216	275,216	70,000	70,000	226,900	226,900

1. To adjust prepaid rent and rent expense.
2. To adjust prepaid fire insurance and insurance expense.
3. To adjust equipment account for depreciation.
4. To adjust delivery vehicle account for depreciation.
5. To show interest expense and liability.
6. To show wages expense and liability as of Feb. 28.

A. To show income summary and transfer income to statement of financial position.

loss), it would be entered in columns 8 and 9 below the previous footings. Entering the profit or loss figure in this way provides a check on mechanical accuracy. Finally, again compute column totals for these last four columns. The debits should now equal the credits for each pair of columns.

Recall from Chapter 3 that the income statement accounts are a part of owners' equity. Specifically, the revenue and expense accounts taken collectively represent an increase or decrease in retained earnings. Thus, the total of the revenue and expense accounts (income for the time period under review) must be added to the adjusted trial balance figure for retained earnings before the preparation of the statement of financial position. The fact that this income is not yet reflected in the Retained Earnings account is the reason we had to add net income to column 10 before the statement of financial position accounts would balance.

At this point, the formal income statement and statement of financial position can be prepared from the worksheet. These statements are presented in Exhibit 4.9 for the Downearth Company. Note that all account balances except retained earnings have been transferred exactly from the worksheet. Retained earnings on the new statement of financial position is increased by net income.

Following completion of the worksheet, the adjusting journal entries must be formally entered in the journal and posted to the ledger to bring the books of record up-to-date.

CLASSIFIED FINANCIAL STATEMENTS
Financial statements where accounts are grouped by category for presentation within the statements.

As with the Delta Airlines example in Chapters 2 and 3, accounts have been grouped by category in both the income statement and the statement of financial position for Downearth. When accounts are grouped by category (classified) for presentation, the financial statements are called **classified financial statements.**

Closing the Accounts

CLOSING THE ACCOUNTS
The process of summarizing revenue and expense account totals into retained earnings.

The process of summarizing revenue and expense account totals into retained earnings is known as **closing the accounts** and is performed on the income statement accounts at the end of each accounting period.

The Closing Process. Keep in mind that all asset inflows recognized as revenues have generated increases in asset accounts while all asset uses recognized as expenses have generated decreases in asset accounts. The summarization (closing) of the revenue and expense accounts into retained earnings simply changes retained earnings by an amount equal to the total of previously recognized asset increases and decreases on the statement of financial position. Thus, the integrity of the basic accounting equation—Assets = Liabilities + Owners' Equity—is preserved.

Because revenue and expense accounts are used to accumulate income transactions independently for the current time period, each revenue and expense account must start the period with a zero balance. The closing process is the mechanism used to achieve this zero starting point. The closing process is really quite simple. Each revenue and expense account, as listed on the worksheet in the income statement columns, is examined, and an appropriate debit or credit entry is made to each account so that the account ends up with a zero balance.

Although the second part of each closing entry could be entered directly into the Retained Earnings account, such multiple entries would make the Retained Earnings account difficult to interpret. For this reason, most accountants favor the creation and use of a special account—Income Summary—to serve as a collection point for all revenue and expense account balances. The final total in this Income Summary account then serves as a basis for one entry to the Retained Earnings account summarizing all of the revenue and expense accounts. The closing process using an Income Summary account has three steps:

EXHIBIT 4.9

Downearth Company
Income Statement
For the Two-month Period Ending February 28, 1986

Sales		$70,000
Less cost of goods sold		35,000
Gross margin		$35,000
General and administrative expenses		
Wages expense	$8,400	
Rent expense	2,000	
Insurance expense	500	
Depreciation expense	1,166	
Interest expense	1,250	
Total general and administrative expense		13,316
Net income		$21,684

Downearth Company
Statement of Financial Position
February 28, 1986

Assets			**Liabilities and Owners' Equity**	
Current assets			Current liabilities	
Cash		$ 35,400	Notes payable	$100,000
Accounts receivable		40,000	Interest payable	1,250
Merchandise inventory		75,000	Wages payable	2,800
Prepaid rent		4,000	Total current liabilities	$104,050
Prepaid fire insurance		2,500		
Total current assets		$156,900		
Property, plant, and equipment			Owners' equity	
Equipment	$20,000		Common stock	100,000
Less: Accum. depr.	333	19,667	Retained earnings	21,684
			Total owners' equity	$121,684
Delivery vehicles	$50,000			
Less: Accum. depr.	833	49,167		
Total property, plant, & equip.		$ 68,834		
Total assets		$225,734	Total liabilities and owners' equity	$225,734

1. Close all revenues by debiting the revenue accounts and crediting the Income Summary account.
2. Close all expenses by debiting the Income Summary account and crediting the expense accounts.
3. Close the Income Summary account by forcing it to zero with a debit or credit, as necessary, and assigning the other half of the entry to Retained Earnings.

HIGHLIGHT

Adjustment and Statement Preparation in Practice

Although the text material illustrates and discusses the adjustment and statement preparation process, it is difficult to convey the magnitude of the process as found in the large American multinational corporations. The adjustment process must be applied to hundreds, if not thousands, of operating units around the world, and all of these units must then be combined into one set of accounting reports representing the total of all of the separate operations. In recognition of the amount of work that must be done to complete the annual financial statement preparation and to allow time for an independent review of the statements by a CPA firm, the Securities and Exchange Commission allows corporations 90 days following the close of their fiscal year to complete the job. Even though a full independent review of quarterly financial reports is not required, corporations are nonetheless permitted 45 days following the close of their fiscal quarters to complete and file the appropriate financial statements with the Commission.

The flow of the closing process is as follows:

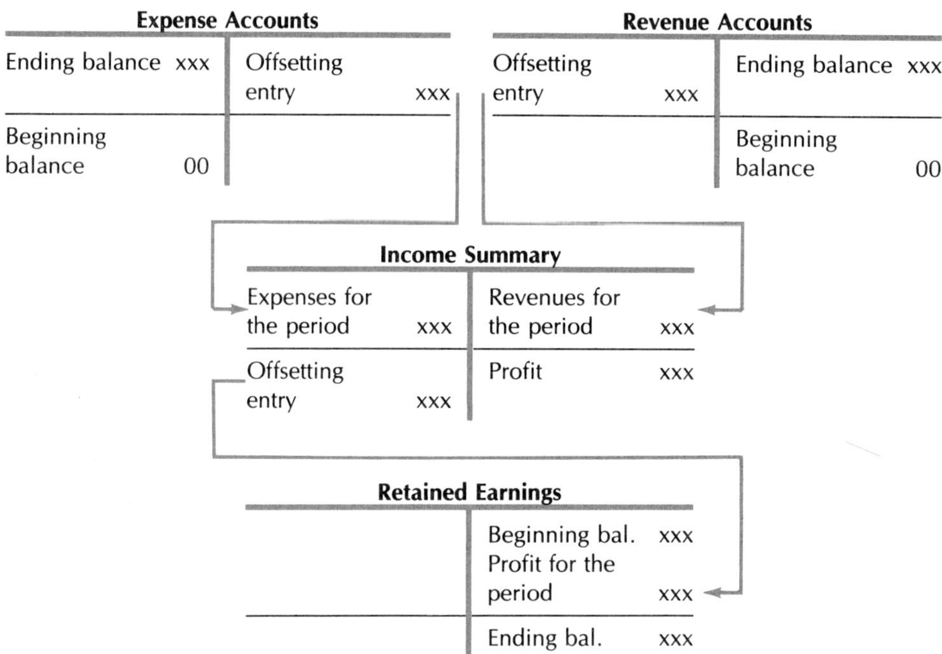

The Closing Process Illustrated. For Downearth, examination of the adjusted revenue and expense accounts shows the following balances before closing:

Sales		Cost of Goods Sold		Wages Expense		Rent Expense	
	70,000	35,000		8,400		2,000	

Insurance Expense		Depreciation Expense		Interest Expense	
500		1,166		1,250	

The first two required revenue and expense closing journal entries utilizing an Income Summary account are as follows:

Sales	70,000	
Income summary		70,000
(to close the revenue account)		
Income summary	48,316	
Cost of goods sold		35,000
Wages expense		8,400
Rent expense		2,000
Insurance expense		500
Depreciation expense		1,166
Interest expense		1,250
(to close the expense accounts)		

After posting the closing entries to the appropriate ledger accounts, the accounts would show the following results:

Sales

Closing entry	70,000	Bal. before closing	70,000
		Bal. after closing	0

Cost of Goods Sold

Bal. before closing	35,000	Closing entry	35,000
Bal. after closing	0		

Wages Expense

Bal. before closing	8,400	Closing entry	8,400
Bal. after closing	0		

Rent Expense

Bal. before closing	2,000	Closing entry	2,000
Bal. after closing	0		

Insurance Expense

Bal. before closing	500	Closing entry	500
Bal. after closing	0		

Depreciation Expense

Bal. before closing	1,166	Closing entry	1,166
Bal. after closing	0		

Interest Expense

Bal. before closing	1,250	Closing entry	1,250
Bal. after closing	0		

Income Summary

Closing entry	48,316	Bal. before closing	0
		Closing entry	70,000
		Bal. after closing revenue and expense	21,684

The last step in the closing process is the transfer of the balance of the Income Summary account to Retained Earnings. This balance should match the worksheet amount for net income. For Downearth, this entry is the following:

Income summary	21,684	
Retained earnings		21,684
(to close net income into retained earnings)		

The Income Summary and Retained Earnings accounts would appear as follows after the posting of this last entry:

Income Summary

Closing entry	21,684	Bal. after revenue and expense closing	21,684
		Bal. after final closing	0

Retained Earnings

		Bal. before closing	0
		Closing entry	21,684
		Bal. after closing	21,684

TEMPORARY ACCOUNTS
Accounts that are closed to zero at the end of each accounting period with their balances being transferred to retained earnings.

NOMINAL ACCOUNTS
See Temporary Accounts.

REAL ACCOUNTS
See Permanent Accounts.

PERMANENT ACCOUNTS
Accounts whose balances are not closed to retained earnings at the end of each accounting period.

POST-CLOSING TRIAL BALANCE
A listing of all account balances prepared following completion of the closing process.

Temporary and Permanent Accounts. **Temporary,** or **nominal, accounts** are accounts that are closed to zero at the end of each accounting period with their balances being transferred to Retained Earnings. All income statement accounts are temporary in nature. Accounts whose balances are not closed to Retained Earnings at the end of each accounting period are known as **real,** or **permanent, accounts.** All accounts found on the statement of financial position are permanent accounts. Although permanent accounts can have zero balances, they are not closed at the conclusion of an accounting cycle. Nominal accounts have temporary balances that are transferred to the real account—Retained Earnings—at the end of each time period through the closing process.

Post-Closing Trial Balance. A **post-closing trial balance** is a listing of all account balances prepared following completion of the closing process. The post-closing trial balance serves as a final check on mechanical accuracy of the closing process. If all adjusting and closing entries have been properly posted to the ledger as illustrated, the revenue and expense accounts (the nominal, or temporary, accounts) along with the special Income Summary account should have zero balances. The total debits should equal the total credits in all of the real, or statement of financial position, accounts. The post-closing trial balance for Downearth appears in Exhibit 4.10.

EXHIBIT 4.10

Downearth Company
Post-Closing Trial Balance
February 28, 1986

Account	Debit	Credit
Cash	$35,400	
Accounts Receivable	40,000	
Merchandise Inventory	75,000	
Prepaid Rent	4,000	
Prepaid Fire Insurance	2,500	
Equipment	20,000	
Accumulated Depreciation—Equipment		$ 333
Delivery Vehicles	50,000	
Accumulated Depreciation—Delivery Vehicle		833
Notes Payable to Banks		100,000
Interest Payable		1,250
Wages Payable		2,800
Common Stock		100,000
Retained Earnings		21,684
Totals	$226,900	$226,900

STEPS IN THE ACCOUNTING CYCLE

■ **CONCEPT SUMMARY 4.2**

Step	Action Taken
1. Journalize transactions	Prepare journal entries for each transaction.
2. Post transactions	Enter each part of the journal entry prepared in step 1 in the appropriate ledger account.
3. Prepare trial balance	List the title and balance of each ledger account on a worksheet. Foot debits and credits as a mechancial accuracy test.
4. Adjust the accounts	Review each account balance against generally accepted accounting principles. Change any balance not appropriate and prepare an adjusting journal entry on the worksheet to reflect the appropriate balance. Enter the adjusting entries in the general journal and general ledger.
5. Prepare financial statements	Using the appropriate account balances from step 4 (the adjusted trial balance), compile the income statement and statement of financial position.
6. Close the accounts	Reduce all revenue and expense accounts to zero by transferring all such account balances to Income Summary and Income Summary, in turn, to Retained Earnings.
7. Prepare post-closing trial balance	List the title and balance of each ledger account after the closing process has been completed. Foot debits and credits as a mechanical accuracy test.

FOR REVIEW

■ SUMMARY

■ The accounting cycle is the term applied to the accounting system's periodic summarization of transaction data into accounting reports. The accounting cycle begins with the recording of transaction data in the journal and ledger and ends with the preparation of the financial statements.

■ Proper income measurement usually requires adjusting the accounts so that all revenue and expenses are properly classified and recognized as determined from the facts surrounding the transaction data. Such adjustments also provide for proper measurement of assets and liabilities on the statement of financial position.

■ The accounting worksheet is a tool accountants use to facilitate financial statement preparation. It is not a formal part of the bookkeeping system.

■ In closing the books at the conclusion of an accounting cycle, all revenue and expense balances are transferred through Income Summary to Retained Earnings. The revenue and expense accounts (nominal accounts) are thus set equal to zero at the end of each accounting cycle, and the owners' equity is increased or decreased by an amount equal to the increase or decrease in assets represented by profit or loss. The increase or decrease in owners' equity is reflected in the Retained Earnings account.

QUESTIONS

4-1. What is the accounting cycle?

4-2. Define and explain the purpose of adjusting journal entries.

4-3. Give an example of and explain three types of transactions that might span several income reporting periods.

4-4. What is a contra-account, and why is it used?

4-5. Why must the revenue and expense accounts be closed after each income reporting period?

4-6. How do the income statement accounts and owners' equity on the statement of financial position relate to each other?

4-7. What is the function of the accounting worksheet, and how does the worksheet's status as a document compare to the income statement and statement of financial position?

4-8. List the steps in the closing process and state what is accomplished by the process itself.

4-9. Define each of the following:

- **a.** Trial balance.
- **b.** Adjusted trial balance.
- **c.** Post-closing trial balance.

4-10. Define each of the following:

- **a.** Depreciation.
- **b.** Straight-line depreciation method.
- **c.** Net book value.

EXERCISES

4-E1. Indicate which of the following accounts will be closed by an entry to the Income Summary account. If the account is closed to the Income Summary account, indicate whether the closing entry will be in the form of a debit or credit to the given account. Assume that all of the accounts have normal balances before closing.

- **a.** Cost of Goods Sold
- **b.** Retained Earnings
- **c.** Accounts Receivable
- **d.** Prepaid Rent
- **e.** Sales Revenue
- **f.** Depreciation Expense
- **g.** Notes Payable
- **h.** Accumulated Depreciation

4-E2. On June 30, 1986, O.V.S. Incorporated enters into a two-year janitorial service contract with Tidy-Rite Janitorial Service with a $10,000 cash payment. This transaction could be recorded in either of the following ways:

a. O.V.S. could debit prepaid janitorial expense and credit cash when the contract is purchased.
b. O.V.S. could debit janitorial expense and credit cash when the contract is purchased.

For both (a) and (b), give the originating journal entry at the payment date and the adjusting journal entry necessary at the close of O.V.S.'s fiscal year on December 31, 1986. Using T-accounts, show that the December 31 balance in all accounts related to the janitorial expense is the same under either method.

4-E3. Star Company purchases a machine for $120,000. The machine is expected to have a useful life of ten years with a salvage value of $10,000.

a. Using the straight-line method, compute the annual depreciation expense on the machine.
b. What would the net book value of the machine be at the end of four years?

4-E4. **1.** The premium on a three-year fire insurance policy purchased on September 30, 1986, is $9,000. Compute the amount of insurance expense that will be presented on the company's income statement for the year ending December 31, 1986.

2. A warehouse was originally purchased on January 1, 1979. The building is being depreciated on a straight-line basis at the rate of $15,000 per year. The net book value of the warehouse on January 1, 1986, is $45,000. In the following calculations, assume that the building will be worthless at the end of its estimated useful life.

a. Calculate the original purchase price of the warehouse.
b. Determine the amount of accumulated depreciation for the warehouse as of January 1, 1986.
c. What is the remaining useful life of the warehouse?

4-E5. The Hoosier Corporation is a sporting goods wholesaler specializing in quality basketball equipment. Which of the following accounts could appear on the post-closing trial balance with other than zero balances:

a. Accounts Receivable
b. Cost of Goods Sold
c. Depreciation Expense
d. Retained Earnings
e. Sales
f. Accumulated Depreciation
g. Prepaid Insurance
h. Deposits Received for Goods Not Yet Shipped

4-E6. For each of the following situations, indicate the effect that the error would have on reported earnings for the years 1986 and 1987:

a. Through an oversight, no adjusting entry was made for unpaid employee wages of $12,000 on December 31, 1986.
b. A three-year insurance policy was purchased on July 1, 1986, for $3,600. As is the custom of the company, this transaction was recorded as a debit to insurance expense and a credit to cash. No adjustment to the insurance expense account was made on December 31, 1986.
c. On December 31, 1986, the company received $3,000 for 1987 magazine subscriptions. The entire $3,000 was credited to a revenue account, and no adjustment was made for 1986 statement preparation.

4-E7. The Summit City Company's adjusted trial balance is as follows:

The Summit City Company
Adjusted Trial Balance
December 31, 1986

Account	Debit	Credit
Cash	$ 5,000	
Accounts Receivable	1,500	
Merchandise Inventory	3,000	
Equipment	6,000	
Accumulated Depreciation—Equipment		$ 2,000
Accounts Payable		600
Notes Payable		2,000
Common Stock		6,000
Retained Earnings		2,500
Sales		8,000
Cost of Goods Sold	2,500	
Rent Expense	800	
Wages Expense	1,000	
Advertising Expense	100	
Depreciation Expense	1,200	
Totals	$21,100	$21,100

Prepare the company's 1986 income statement; the closing entries for December 31, 1986; and the post-closing trial balance as it would appear on December 31, 1986.

PROBLEM SET A

4–A1. Analyzing Account Balances. The Fox Company has several insurance policies in force, with payments due at varying times. The following information relates to prepaid insurance and insurance expense at two successive financial statement dates:

	December 31, 1986	December 31, 1987
Prepaid insurance	$10,000	$ 8,500
Insurance expense	6,400	9,000

Required

Determine the amount of cash paid by Fox to insurance companies during 1987.

4-A2. Adjusting Entries. The account balances for the ABC Company as of July 31, 1986, are as follows:

Cash	$2,000
Prepaid Insurance	600
Wages Expense	800
Inventory	4,000
Equipment	6,000
Sales	5,000

1. Inventory on hand is $1,000; all other inventory has been sold to customers.
2. The insurance policy is a six-month policy covering the period July 1 through December 31, 1986.
3. ABC issued paychecks totaling $800 on July 20 for the two-week period ending July 15. The paychecks for $800 owed to employees for the two-week period ending July 31 will be issued August 5.

4. The equipment was purchased on July 1, 1986, and has an expected useful life of ten years with zero salvage value.

Required

Prepare any adjusting entries necessary to support preparation of the financial statements as of July 31, 1986.

4-A3. Financial Statement Preparation. National Services, Inc., prepared the following adjusted account balances for April 30, 1986:

Cash	$ 50,000
Accounts Receivable	40,000
Inventory	30,000
Prepaid Insurance	5,000
Building	80,000
Accumulated Depreciation—Building	20,000
Accounts Payable	10,000
Long-term Loan	25,000
Wages Payable	4,000
Common Stock	100,000
Retained Earnings	37,500
Sales	60,000
Cost of Goods Sold	35,000
Wages Expense	12,000
Rent Expense	?
Insurance Expense	1,000
Depreciation Expense	500

Required

a. Determine the balance in the rent expense account.
b. Prepare an income statement for the month ending April 30, 1986.
c. Prepare a statement of financial position as of April 30, 1986.
d. Prepare closing entries for April 30, 1986.

4-A4. Adjusting Journal Entries and Financial Statements.
The Indiana Horseshoe Company began business on June 1, 1986. The following is its trial balance:

The Indiana Horseshoe Company
Trial Balance
June 30, 1986

Account	Debit	Credit
Cash	$ 5,000	
Accounts Receivable	2,500	
Inventory	3,000	
Prepaid Rent	3,000	
Equipment	12,000	
Accumulated Depreciation—Equip.		$ 0
Accounts Payable		6,750
Notes Payable		2,000
Common Stock		13,000
Retained Earnings		0
Sales		18,000
Cost of Goods Sold	8,000	
Wages Expense	3,000	
Heating and Lighting Expense	2,000	
Administrative Expense	1,250	
Totals	$39,750	$39,750

Additional information:

1. The Indiana Horseshoe Company entered into a ten-year building lease on June 1, 1986. At that time, $3,000 was paid in advance to cover the rent for June through August, 1986.
2. Equipment purchased on May 31, 1986, for $12,000 has an estimated useful life of ten years and is not expected to have any salvage value. The company plans to use straight-line depreciation.
3. On June 1, 1986, the company borrowed $2,000 from the Hoagland City National Bank. The yearly interest on this note payable is 12% of the amount borrowed. The interest will be paid on June 1, 1987, when the note must also be repaid.
4. Due to an oversight, $500 of horseshoes sold and shipped to the International Horseshoe Pitchers Association on June 28, 1986, was not recorded in the accounting records. The company had purchased the horseshoes from a supplier for $300.
5. Salaries earned but not yet paid on June 30 amounted to $580.

Required

a. Prepare any adjusting journal entries you consider necessary in order to prepare financial statements for Indiana Horseshoe as of June 30, 1986.
b. Prepare an income statement for the month ending June 30, 1986.
c. Prepare a statement of financial position as of June 30, 1986.

4-A5. Correction of Errors in Financial Statements. Ace Hardware Company is good at selling hardware but not so good at preparing financial statements. Ace prepared the following income statement and statement of financial position as of December 31, 1986:

Ace Hardware Company
Income Statement
For the Year Ending December 31, 1986

Sales		$200,000
Less cost of goods sold		100,000
Gross margin		$100,000
Less selling and administrative expenses		
Wages expense	$40,000	
Rent expense	10,000	50,000
Net income		$ 50,000

Ace Hardware Company
Statement of Financial Position
December 31, 1986

Assets		**Liabilities and Owners' Equity**	
Cash	$ 70,000	Accounts payable	$ 62,000
Accounts receivable	90,000	Total liabilities	$ 62,000
Prepaid insurance	12,000	Common stock	100,000
Equipment	50,000	Retained earnings	50,000
Accum. deprec.—equipt.	(10,000)		
Total	$212,000	Total	$212,000

After reviewing Ace Hardware's statements and related facts, you have discovered the following:

1. The one and only insurance policy of Ace Hardware was purchased for $12,000 on July 1, 1986, and covers a three-year period.
2. The equipment was purchased on January 1, 1985, for $50,000 and was expected to last five years with zero salvage value.

3. Rent of $10,000 had been paid on October 1, 1986, covering the 12 months ending September 30, 1987.

4. Wages of $1,000 were owed on December 31, 1986. (The wages are not included in Accounts Payable.)

5. All of the sales of $200,000 were on credit. Of the $90,000 owed to Ace at the end of the year, $2,000 was not considered to be collectible due to the bankruptcy of one of Ace's customers. (This fact may give you trouble. Ask yourself if you have revenue if you do not expect to collect the cash owed. Refer to Chapter 3 for revenue recognition requirements.)

Required

a. Prepare any adjusting journal entries that are necessary to properly prepare an income statement and statement of financial position as of December 31, 1986.

b. Prepare a corrected income statement and statement of financial position for the Ace Hardware Company for the year ending December 31, 1986.

4-A6. The Accounting Cycle and Worksheet. Colonial Furniture has the following account balances on June 1, 1986:

Cash	$16,000
Accounts Receivable	2,000
Inventory	?
Prepaid Insurance	600
Equipment	15,000
Accumulated Depreciation—Equipment	3,000
Accounts Payable	6,000
Wages Payable	10,000
Bank Note Payable	8,000
Common Stock	5,000
Retained Earnings	13,600

Colonial Furniture has the following transactions during June:

June 3	Sells $6,000 of merchandise to customers for $5,000 cash and $1,000 on account. The merchandise originally cost Colonial $4,000.
June 5	Pays rent of $5,000 for June and July.
June 10	Issues paychecks for $10,000 for May.
June 15	Distributes $1,000 cash to the owners as a dividend.
June 20	Pays $1,000 on account to suppliers.
June 25	Purchases inventory for $15,000 on account.
June 29	Pays $100 interest on the bank note.

The following facts are in addition to the preceding transactions:

1. The equipment was purchased on June 1, 1985, and has an expected useful life of five years with zero salvage value.

2. The insurance was purchased in May for June and July.

3. Wages for June totaled $12,000 and will be paid July 10.

Required

a. Determine the June 1 balance in the Inventory account.

b. Enter the June 1, 1986, account balances in general ledger T-accounts.

c. Prepare general journal entries for the June transactions.

d. Post the journal entries in (c) to the ledger accounts. You may need to establish additional T-accounts to complete this step.

e. Prepare an accounting worksheet with columns for the trial balance, adjustments, adjusted trial balance, income statement, and statement of financial position and enter the ledger account balances into the trial balance columns.

f. Prepare any necessary adjusting entries in support of preparation of June 30 financial statements. Post them to the general ledger accounts and enter them on the worksheet.
g. Complete the remainder of the accounting worksheet.
h. Prepare closing entries for the month ending June 30, 1986, and post to the appropriate general ledger accounts.
i. Prepare an income statement and a statement of financial position for Colonial Furniture as of June 30, 1986.
j. Prepare a post-closing trial balance.

4-A7. Constructing Financial Statements from Partial Information. The Goodwin Company began operations several years ago and had an office fire on December 31, 1987. Goodwin was able to salvage only the following December 31, 1987, account balances. The account balances given are after all required adjustments have been made to complete the 1987 financial statements.

Cash	$ 10,000
Accounts Receivable	20,000
Accumulated Depreciation—Plant and Equipment	40,000
Accounts Payable	25,000
Common Stock	30,000
Cost of Goods Sold	120,000
Wages Expense	10,000
Retained Earnings 1/1/87	20,000

In addition to the above account balances, Goodwin has determined the following facts:

1. The only asset held by the company on December 31 other than cash, plant and equipment, and accounts receivable was inventory.
2. Plant and equipment was eight years old and had an estimated useful life of 20 years with no salvage value.
3. The Goodwin Company had borrowed $20,000 on January 1, 1987, at an annual interest rate of 16% of the amount borrowed and had not repaid either the loan or any interest as of December 31, 1987.
4. Gross margin was $70,000 for the year ending December 31, 1987.
5. Wages of $1,000 were owed on December 31, 1987.

Required

Given that no accounts exist other than those provided or suggested in the five facts, reconstruct the income statement and the statement of financial position for Goodwin for the year ending December 31, 1987. Keep in mind that all account balances given are after all necessary adjustments have been made for the year ending December 31, 1987.

4-A8. Interpreting the Worksheet and the Financial Statements. On December 31, 1986, The Maxout Company fired its chief computer programmer. In a final act of retribution, the programmer destroyed the computer files containing the adjusting journal entries that had just been completed. However, both the unadjusted and adjusted trial balances were recovered from backup files and are presented as follows:

Account	Unadjusted Trial Balance		Adjusted Trial Balance	
	Debit	Credit	Debit	Credit
Cash	$ 4,000		$ 4,000	
Accounts Receivable	12,000		12,000	
Office Supplies	1,000		1,200	
Merchandise Inventory	20,000		20,000	
Prepaid Insurance	2,000		3,000	
Building	80,000		80,000	
Accumulated Depreciation —Building		$ 4,000		$ 8,000
Office Equipment	6,000		6,000	
Accumulated Depreciation —Office Equipment		1,200		2,400
Accounts Payable		10,000		10,000
Notes Payable		30,000		30,000
Common Stock		40,000		40,000
Retained Earnings		36,600		36,600
Sales		15,000		15,000
Cost of Goods Sold	4,000		4,000	
Rent Expense	1,000		1,400	
Wages Expense	4,000		4,000	
Office Supplies Expense	800		600	
Insurance Expense	2,000		1,000	
Depreciation Expense			5,200	
Interest Expense			3,000	
Interest Payable				3,000
Rent Payable				400
Totals	$136,800	$136,800	$145,400	$145,400

Required

a. Analyze the trial balances and reconstruct the adjusting journal entries destroyed by the programmer.
b. Prepare the closing entries to be made on December 31, 1986.
c. Prepare an income statement and statement of financial position for the Maxout Company as of December 31, 1986.

PROBLEM SET B

4-B1. Analyzing Account Balances. Hermit Company owns several properties that it rents to numerous tenants. Some tenants pay rent in advance; others do not. The following information relates to rent receivable and unearned rent revenue at two successive statements of financial position dates:

	December 31, 1986	December 31, 1987
Rent receivable	$4,500	$3,800
Unearned rent revenue	1,700	2,300

Cash collections from tenants totaled $25,500 during 1987.

Required

Determine the rent revenue earned by Hermit Company for the year ending December 31, 1987.

4-B2. Adjusting Entries. The Wilkins Landscape Company has the following account balances as of September 30, 1986:

Cash	$ 2,000
Inventory	900
Prepaid Rent	800
Building	24,000
Sales	8,000
Cost of Goods Sold	2,600
Wages Expense	1,000

The following facts concern Wilkins Company as of September 30:

1. The prepaid rent is for a storage building. The $800 was paid on September 1 for the period September 1 through December 31.
2. The building was purchased on September 1 for $24,000 with an expected useful life of 20 years and zero salvage value.
3. Wages earned during the month of September but not yet paid totaled $950. The wages will be paid on October 5.

Required

Prepare the necessary adjusting entries for September 30, 1986, to support preparation of the company's financial statements.

4-B3. Financial Statement Preparation. A review of the Chemical Supply, Inc.'s, general ledger as of January 31, 1986, has provided the following list of accounts and their balances:

Cash	$ 15,000
Accounts Receivable	20,000
Inventory	25,000
Prepaid Insurance	3,000
Building	100,000
Accumulated Depreciation—Building	50,000
Accounts Payable	30,000
Wages Payable	2,000
Bank Loan Payable	20,000
Common Stock	5,000
Retained Earnings	24,300
Sales	90,000
Cost of Goods Sold	50,000
Wages Expense	5,000
Depreciation Expense	1,000
Interest Expense	800
Insurance Expense	?

Required

Assume that the above constitutes a complete list of accounts for Chemical Supply after all adjustments and that all accounts have normal balances as of January 31.
a. Compute the insurance expense for January.
b. Prepare an income statement for January 1986.
c. Prepare a statement of financial position as of January 31, 1986.
d. Prepare closing entries for the month ending January 31, 1986.

4-B4. Adjusting Journal Entries and Financial Statements. The November 30, 1986, trial balance taken from the general ledger for Bond Distributors is as follows:

Account	Debit	Credit
Cash	$ 40,000	
Accounts Receivable	90,000	
Inventory	100,000	
Prepaid Rent	20,000	
Equipment	120,000	
Accumulated Depreciation—Equipment		$ 2,000
Vehicles	30,000	
Accumulated Depreciation—Vehicles		2,000
Accounts Payable		50,000
Bank Note Payable		40,000
Long-term Loan		80,000
Common Stock		50,000
Retained Earnings		116,000
Sales		140,000
Cost of Goods Sold	80,000	
Totals	$480,000	$480,000

The following facts concern the accounts:

1. No adjustments have been made for the month ending November 30, 1986.
2. The rent payment of $20,000 made in November was for both November and December.
3. Wages totaling $20,000 are paid on the fifteenth of each month for all of the work performed during the preceding calendar month.
4. The equipment was purchased on September 1, 1986 with an expected useful life of ten years and zero salvage value.
5. An interest payment of $800 for November is due December 5.
6. The vehicles were purchased on July 1, 1986 with an expected useful life of five years and zero salvage value.

Required

a. Prepare any adjusting journal entries you consider necessary to prepare financial statements as of November 30, 1986.
b. Prepare an income statement for the month ending November 30, 1986.
c. Prepare a statement of financial position as of November 30, 1986.

4-B5. Correction of Errors in Financial Statements. The Cleaver Corporation is a knife wholesaler whose fiscal year ends on December 31, 1986. The company has prepared an income statement and a statement of financial position as of December 31, 1986, as follows:

The Cleaver Corporation
Income Statement
For the Year Ending December 31, 1986

Sales		$60,500
Less cost of goods sold		32,250
Gross margin		$28,250
Less operating expenses		
Wages expense	$10,500	
Depreciation expense	2,000	
Miscellaneous expense	5,500	18,000
Net income		$10,250

The Cleaver Corporation
Statement of Financial Position
December 31, 1986

Assets		Liabilities and Owners' Equity	
Cash	$ 25,000	Accounts payable	$ 28,250
Accounts receivable	30,000	Notes payable	25,500
Merchandise inventory	35,500	Total liabilities	$ 53,750
Prepaid rent	2,500	Common stock	50,000
Equipment	12,000	Retained earnings	19,250
Accumulated deprec.—equipment	(2,000)		
Building	24,000		
Accumulated deprec.—building	(4,000)		
Total assets	$123,000	Total liabilities & owners' equity	$123,000

On New Year's Day, the controller receives a frantic phone call from Cleaver, the president, informing him that the financial statements for 1986 appear to have omitted a number of year-end adjustments. Beaver, the controller, immediately calls you and describes the following facts that appear to support the need for adjustments:

1. Depreciation was recorded for the equipment only for the fiscal year 1986. The building was acquired on January 1, 1984, and is estimated to have a useful life of 12 years with a zero salvage value.
2. The Cleaver Corporation entered into a three-year equipment lease on November 30, 1986, at which time the corporation paid four months' rent, in advance, a total of $2,500.
3. Due to an oversight, a $4,000 cash sale on October 1, 1986, was recorded as a sale on account.
4. The Cleaver Corporation borrowed $25,500 on a note payable on April 1, 1986. Both the note and associated interest of 16% of the amount borrowed per year are due on April 1, 1987.
5. On December 31, 1986, the company received orders for knives totaling $2,500 with a full cash payment. Due to an order backlog, the knives will not be shipped until March 4, 1987. The bookkeeper deposited the cash and debited Cash for $2,500 and credited Sales for this same amount.

Required

a. Prepare any adjusting journal entries that are necessary to properly prepare an income statement and statement of financial position as of December 31, 1986.
b. Prepare a corrected income statement and statement of financial position for the year ending December 31, 1986.

4-B6. The Accounting Cycle and Worksheet. The following post-closing trial balance is for the Home Computer Services Corporation as of May 31, 1986:

Home Computer Services Corporation
Post-Closing Trial Balances
May 31, 1986

Account	Debit	Credit
Cash	$ 43,000	
Accounts Receivable	140,000	
Inventory	180,000	
Prepaid Rent	10,000	
Vehicles	18,000	
Accumulated Depreciation—Vehicles		$ 9,000
Accounts Payable		95,000
Bank Note Payable		30,000
Common Stock		130,000
Retained Earnings		?
Totals	$391,000	$?

The company has the following transactions during June:

June 5 Sells $120,000 of inventory on account. The inventory originally cost Home Computer $50,000.
June 12 Pays $1,000 for insurance for July through September, 1986.
June 14 Pays $6,000 as wages for the first half of June.
June 16 Receives payments of $50,000 on account.
June 21 Purchases $80,000 of inventory on account.
June 29 Pays interest for June of $450.
June 29 Pays suppliers $5,000 on account.

The following facts also concern the company for June:

1. Rent of $20,000 was paid in May for the months of May and June, 1986.
2. Wages for the second half of June total $6,000 and will be paid on July 2.
3. The vehicles were purchased on May 31, 1981 with an expected useful life of ten years and zero salvage value.

Required

a. Determine the balance of the Retained Earnings account as of May 31, 1986.
b. Post the May 31 account balances to general ledger T-accounts.
c. Prepare general journal entries for the June transactions and post them to the ledger T-accounts. (You may need to prepare additional ledger accounts to complete this step.)
d. Prepare an accounting worksheet for June 30, 1986, with columns for the trial balance, adjustments, adjusted trial balance, income statement, and statement of financial position.
e. Complete the accounting worksheet to prepare financial statements as of June 30. Prepare any adjustments necessary and post them to your ledger accounts in addition to placing them on the worksheet.
f. Prepare closing entries for the month ending June 30, 1986, and enter them into the accounts as appropriate.
g. Prepare an income statement and a statement of financial position for Home Computer Services Corporation as of June 30, 1986.
h. Prepare a post-closing trial balance.

4-B7. Constructing Financial Statements from Partial Information. The Cooke Company began operations some years ago and had an office fire on December 31, 1986. Cooke was able to salvage only the following December 31, 1986, account balances. (The account balances given are after all adjustments have been made to complete the 1986 financial statements.)

Cash	$ 20,000
Inventory	30,000
Accumulated Depreciation—Plant and Equipment	60,000
Accounts Payable	12,000
Retained Earnings, 1/1/86	40,000
Sales	120,000
Wages Expense	22,000

Cooke has also determined the following facts:

1. The only assets held by Cooke on December 31 other than cash, inventory, and plant and equipment were accounts receivable and prepaid insurance.
2. Cooke paid $12,000 for a three-year liability insurance policy on January 1, 1986. This was Cooke's only insurance.
3. Plant and equipment was three years old on December 31, 1986, and was being depreciated on a straight-line basis over its ten-year life with zero salvage value.
4. The company had borrowed $50,000 on July 1, 1986, at an annual interest rate of 12% and had not paid either the interest or the loan as of December 31, 1986.
5. Cooke owed wages of $2,000 on December 31.
6. Gross margin was $80,000 for the year ending December 31, 1986.

Required

Given that no accounts exist other than those provided or suggested in the six facts, reconstruct the income statement and the statement of financial position for Cooke for the year ending December 31, 1986. Keep in mind that all account balances given are after all necessary adjustments have been made for the year ending December 31, 1986.

4-B8. Interpreting the Worksheet and the Financial Statements. On December 31, 1986, Don Hoage, president of the Hoage Mobile Corporation, decided to lay off 25% of the company's white-collar employees. One of the employees affected by the layoff was the staff accountant, who had prepared the adjusting and closing entries for the year. In a final act of defiance, the staff accountant deliberately misplaced the adjusting journal entries that he had just finished. However, both the unadjusted and adjusted trial balances still exist and are as follows:

Account	Unadjusted Trial Balance		Adjusted Trial Balance	
	Debit	Credit	Debit	Credit
Cash	$ 5,000		$ 5,000	
Accounts Receivable	10,000		10,000	
Office Supplies	500		300	
Merchandise Inventory	15,000		15,000	
Prepaid Insurance	1,200		800	
Building	20,000		20,000	
Accumulated Depreciation—Building		$ 4,000		$ 8,000
Office Equipment	5,000		5,000	
Accumulated Depreciation—Office Equipment		1,000		2,000
Accounts Payable		11,200		11,200
Notes Payable		15,000		15,000
Common Stock		16,000		16,000
Retained Earnings		5,250		5,250
Sales		22,250		22,250
Cost of Goods Sold	6,500		6,500	
Rent Expense	3,750		3,750	
Wages Expense	4,000		4,750	
Advertising Expense	3,750		3,750	
Office Supplies Expense			200	
Insurance Expense			400	
Depreciation Expense			5,000	
Interest Expense			2,100	
Interest Payable				2,100
Wages Payable				750
Totals	$74,700	$74,700	$82,550	$82,550

Required

a. Analyze the company's trial balances and reconstruct the adjusting journal entries "lost" by the unhappy staff accountant.
b. Prepare the closing entries to be made on December 31, 1986.
c. Prepare an income statement and a statement of financial position for the Hoage Mobile Corporation as of December 31, 1986.

APPENDIX A
COMPUTERS AND ACCOUNTING

Today's business world has become extremely reliant on computers with their remarkable processing speeds and seemingly unlimited memories. Perhaps no area of business has been more affected than accounting, partly because accounting historically has been one of the first areas in nearly every company to become computerized. This appendix examines computers, explores the role computers have played in the field of accounting, and explains some of the implications of the new technology on accounting methods.

THE COMPUTER SYSTEM

A typical computer system has at least four hardware components: the computer itself, one or more devices for data input, one or more devices for data output, and some form of storage. Before the computer can accomplish any task, it must have instructions, referred to as software or programs. This section examines the usual hardware devices found in such a system. Software is discussed later.

The Central Processing Unit

CENTRAL PROCESSING UNIT
The heart of a computer consisting of an arithmetic-logic unit, a control unit, and primary memory.

PRIMARY MEMORY
The storage area contained inside the central processing unit of a computer.

KILOBYTE (K)
A common measure of computer memory consisting of approximately one thousand bytes or characters.

MEGABYTE (M)
A common measure of computer memory consisting of approximately one million bytes or characters.

READ-ONLY MEMORY
A memory area that can be read by a computer but the contents cannot be changed by the user's programs or data.

RANDOM ACCESS MEMORY
Computer storage area available to the user for instructions or data.

The heart of the system is the **central processing unit** (CPU). The CPU has three parts: an arithmetic-logic unit to do the mathematical and logical work; a memory, or storage, area to hold instructions and data; and a control unit to coordinate the activities of the computer. CPUs differ in power, with the more powerful computers having faster processing speeds and larger memories.

One of the more common characteristics of a computer is the size of the storage area contained inside the CPU (properly called **primary memory,** or main memory). Common memory sizes are 256K, where K stands for **kilobyte (K)** (which is approximately 1,000 bytes or characters), or 5M, where M represents a **megabyte (M)** (about one million bytes). The amount of memory contained in the CPU can be important because in general the more memory, the more sophisticated the tasks that the computer can perform.

Primary memory usually includes two different forms. The first is called **read-only memory (ROM),** a memory area that can be read by the computer but cannot be used to store your own data or instructions. ROM generally holds many of the programs the computer uses to manage its own operations. The second type of memory, **random-access memory (RAM),** is a storage area available to the user for instructions or data. In nearly all computers, RAM holds its contents only when the power is turned on. For most computer users, this necessitates supplementing primary memory resources with another type of memory—not contained in the CPU—for more permanent storage. We discuss this type of memory in a forthcoming section.

A CPU by itself is not very useful. The system needs some type of input device to get instructions and data into the computer for processing and an output device to find out the results of the processing.

Input Devices

TERMINAL
A common computer input device. Can be of many types but most often has a keyboard and a monitor.

A very common input device used with computers of all sizes is the terminal. Usually a **terminal** has a keyboard and a monitor. Most computer terminal keyboards closely resemble the standard electric typewriter. The keyboard acts as an input unit, allowing the computer user to communicate with the CPU. The messages sent to the computer are called **input.** Some keyboards have a number pad on the right side that allows the user to input numerical data in the same way one would with a 10-key adding machine. Many keyboards also have a few keys to perform special functions defined by the manufacturer or the user.

INPUT
Message sent to a computer.

Although the keyboard is the mainstay of business data entry, other methods are frequently found. Many retail operations collect data using terminals that look like cash registers or by using devices that can read sales tickets or universal product codes. Input is sometimes provided using optical character or magnetic ink character readers, punched cards, magnetic tape, magnetic disk, or voice recognition. However, the typical accountant deals with the computer on his or her keyboard.

Output Devices

When the CPU has a message for the user or is ready to report the information it was asked to produce (called **output**), it can do so by printing a document. This type of output is called **hard copy.** Two types of printers are common. **Dot-matrix printers** form each character as a pattern of dots and are relatively inexpensive. In an office where printed documents must look as though they were produced on a typewriter, **letter-quality printers** are used. They are capable of forming the entire character and are usually slower and more expensive than dot matrix printers.

When a printed document is not required, the computer can communicate by showing the output on a TV-like screen called a **monitor.** Sometimes the monitor is referred to as a CRT (cathode ray tube) or a VDT (video display terminal). Output displayed on the screen is called **soft copy.** The monitor also displays items being typed in on the system's keyboard. The typical screen size is 12 or 13 inches, and most business monitors can display 24 lines of 80 characters at one time. Monitors can have color capabilities, or they might display only two colors, usually green or orange characters on a black background. Other methods of output are sometimes used, including computer output microfilm, magnetic tape, magnetic disk, or voice response.

OUTPUT
Messages produced for users by a computer.

HARD COPY
Printed computer output.

DOT-MATRIX PRINTERS
Printers that form each character as a pattern of dots.

LETTER-QUALITY PRINTERS
Printers that produce documents that look as if they were produced on a typewriter.

MONITOR
A TV-like screen used to communicate computer output.

SOFT COPY
Computer output displayed on a computer's monitor.

Secondary Storage

A computer nearly always is supplemented with more memory than that contained in the CPU for two reasons. The first is that primary memory loses any data it contains when the power is shut off; the second reason is that primary memory is both limited and relatively costly. To store all the items needed for computer processing, **secondary storage**—a memory area not contained within the primary memory—is necessary. The most common forms of secondary storage used by firms today are magnetic tape and magnetic disk.

SECONDARY STORAGE
Additional memory that is not part of the CPU's primary memory.

Magnetic tape takes the form of a continuous plastic strip treated with an iron oxide coating. Typically the tape is one-half inch wide and is wound in lengths of from 400 to 3,200 feet. Data are stored on the tape by magnetizing small spots of the coating on the tape. Large volumes of information can be stored on a single tape; densities of 1,600 characters per inch are common. Because the tape is a continuous strip, records must be organized in some sequential manner on the tape before efficient processing can occur. In situations where just one or two items out

MAGNETIC TAPE
A continuous plastic strip treated with an iron oxide coating used as a form of secondary storage in a computer system.

MICROCOMPUTERS
Small computers.
MAGNETIC DISK
A plastic platter coated with ferric oxide used as a secondary storage device within a computer system.
DISK PACK
Several magnetic disks mounted together on a central shaft.
MAINFRAMES
Large computers.

of a large file normally are accessed at a time, tape is not a good storage medium because of its sequential nature.

Magnetic disk provides an efficient means of retrieving items in a more random manner. Small computers, or **microcomputers,** use a form of **magnetic disk** called a floppy disk, or diskette, which is a plastic platter coated with ferric oxide. The floppy disk comes in several sizes, with 5¼ inches being the most common. A conventional magnetic disk is a metal platter 14 inches in diameter, also coated on both sides with a magnetizable material. Several conventional disks are mounted together on a central shaft to form a **disk pack,** which is the most common form used with large business computers, called **mainframes.**

All of these secondary storage media must be used with a device upon which they can be mounted for reading from or writing to. Such a device is called a tape drive or disk drive. The drive itself must be linked to the CPU for communication to occur.

DEVELOPMENT OF THE COMPUTER-ACCOUNTING RELATIONSHIP

First Generation: 1951–1958

When computers first became commercially available, they were huge, generated lots of heat from the many vacuum tubes used for internal operations, and had little internal memory. Since computers were so new, programs had to be written for any job that was to be computerized, nearly always by people who were employed by the company using the computer. Because writing programs was laborious, the most common jobs to be programmed were those that were very repetitive and that followed strict procedures that could be well-defined. Thus, the first business jobs to be programmed were normally routine jobs like payroll processing and billing, since they could more easily be cost-justified.

BATCH PROCESSING
A method of processing data in which a large number of similar transactions are collected and then processed together.
PROGRAM
Instructions given to a computer to accomplish a given task.

Secondary storage as previously discussed did not yet exist. All input and output exchanges with the computer were made using punched cards. For any processing to be efficient, a method called **batch processing** was used. With batch processing, a fairly large number of similar transactions to be processed—credit payments and new charges, for example—would be collected and punched on cards. The instructions for the computer (called the **program**) would be punched onto cards and entered into the computer. Then the transaction file of punched cards would be sorted either in alphabetical or numerical order and entered along with a third set of cards that would contain the master file—the accounts receivable records for the customers, in this example. After processing, the computer would generate new punched cards containing output data—in our example, these cards would be a new master file of accounts receivable records.

Punched cards had a distinct advantage in being both human and machine readable, which provided a good audit trail of transaction processing. Other controls existed naturally in this environment as well. Access to the computer and to the punched card files was limited to authorized personnel, with all input, processing, and output activities confined to a separate, limited-access computer room. People with no access to the computer rarely had the knowledge necessary to carry out any fraudulent activities.

Second Generation: 1959–1964

In the late 1950s, tiny, solid-state transistors replaced vacuum tubes in computers. The elimination of vacuum tubes greatly reduced generated heat and made possible the development of computers significantly smaller and more reliable than those of the first generation. These new computers were faster, had increased storage capacity, and required less power to operate. In addition, secondary memory capabilities were increased some 50 times by the use of magnetic tape.

Programs were still being developed in-house, but business applications began to include the automation of the entire general ledger. In addition, some companies moved their budget-planning processes to the computer. Files started to be transferred from the bulky punched cards onto magnetic tape. Because by its very nature magnetic tape demanded sequential processing of records, batch processing was still used. Each application was separate—for example, accounts receivable would be processed separately from the inventory updating—as were master files.

Towards the end of this period, magnetic disk storage began to appear. Although it greatly enhanced processing methods, magnetic disk caused a major concern in the area of backup. When utilizing magnetic tape in a batch processing mode, a backup tape was created automatically. That is, updating a master file meant that a new tape was created with the new master records; the old master and the transaction file were not destroyed at all by this process and could be kept in case the new master was ruined and needed to be recreated. With disk storage, however, each new master record would be stored in exactly the same place as the old one was, a process that destroyed the old master record. Thus, with disk storage, a special effort had to be made to create extra copies of master files to use for backup purposes.

Third Generation: 1965–1970

As the years progressed, continual technological advances in electronics and solid-state physics brought further reductions in computer size, even greater reliability and speed, and lower hardware costs. The generation began as integrated circuits replaced the transistors of the previous generation's computers. Increasing numbers and types of businesses found that computers were both useful and affordable.

Computer power no longer was contained in just one room of the firm. Software to help run the computer had made **timesharing**—where several users could be connected to and use the same CPU resources—possible. Thus, terminals for input and output were placed throughout the firm. Although input was still usually processed in batch mode, output began to become available on an as-requested basis. Some integration of related master files began to occur; for example, accounts receivable and sales records might be kept in the same file and updated from the same program. Exception reports were produced and routed to the appropriate terminals to help control the firm's production processes. In addition, management realized that the computer could be programmed to run generalized simulation and modeling programs to help it plan for the firm's future needs and actions.

TIMESHARING
The term applied when several users are connected to and use the same central processing unit resources within a computer at the same time.

Control over computer records became an increasing concern. With distributed input/output terminals, control over access was not as limited as before. In addition, the general workforce was no longer so computer illiterate; combined with motivation, access and knowledge could be dangerous. Another control consideration was the audit trail. As input began to be entered nearer the transaction, some paper documents were no longer needed. Accountants in computerized firms started implementing special procedures necessary to that environment to protect the integrity of the data and the processing.

Fourth Generation: 1971–????

Although no radically different technology determined the start of a new generation, the computer industry had succeeded in packing even larger numbers of circuits on still smaller pieces of silicon. These chips offered significantly faster processing speeds and larger primary memories.

The larger memories allow more sophisticated software to be developed for controlling the computer's operations efficiently and making the interaction of human and computer easy enough to be referred to as user friendly. Files that before were kept separate can now be put on line to the computer and can be logically linked. This integration of files that have logical interrelationships is called a **data base.** Accountants soon realized that the general ledger itself is a database and started storing it as such. Manipulating such a wealth of information and keeping track of the relationships is made relatively simple by software called the data base management system. Thus, one general ledger entry can update related accounts in both the general ledger and any subsidiary ledger. Managers at all levels are finding that a better variety of information is easily available for strategic planning and have begun to use the computer for decision support. Reports that are not routine can be requested and, because of the data base links, timely processed and presented.

DATA BASE
An integrated set of files that have logical interrelationships.

Increased power of the computer means that input/output devices of all sorts can be scattered throughout the company, and all can be tied into the main computer. Order entry thus can occur from one or more of many remote locations. Some companies have even placed terminals in the offices of their customers so that orders placed by customers are entered directly into the seller's computer for processing. Not only are terminals being hooked to computers, but computer-to-computer hookups are not unusual. With such a computer-to-computer connection, some processing can occur at either location before the processed data are transmitted to the other computer for further manipulation and storage.

With such types of distributed environments allowing data to be entered into a computer for processing from literally hundreds of locations, control has become a primary concern. Access is essentially unlimited; records of assets are easily obtainable; links provided by the data base management system make alteration of related accounts possible; and the paper audit trail has virtually disappeared. Without proper attention to the control concerns, many systems became auditors' nightmares. After several disasters, the control issues inherent in computer use became more defined and procedures were instigated to deter further problems. (Refer to Chapter 7 regarding internal control.)

The fourth generation also brought the microcomputer revolution. Many of the desktop-size computers are as powerful as the large computers of the first and second generations, and they are so inexpensive that even small businesses can afford computer power. Distinct implications for gaining a competitive edge are evident from the commercial software available in the computer stores that have almost overnight appeared everywhere. Easy and complete budget planning and modeling are no longer the tools of only large corporate managers alone.

ACCOUNTING SOFTWARE

Since the early generations, when all programming was done in-house, to the current time, when many good software packages can be easily purchased, accounting tasks have been found to be efficiently handled by the computer. Thus, this section explores some of the more useful types of software being used by accountants. Keep in mind throughout this section that some accountants use large mainframe computers for such tasks and others use microcomputers. In general, the programs described operate the same way on any size computer. However, programs designed for mainframes will be faster and more sophisticated than their counterparts designed for use on microcomputers. This difference is natural due to the greater power of the mainframe.

Application Oriented

Most accounting software has been prepared in a modular fashion so that a firm can purchase just the programs it wants at its particular stage of growth and computer sophistication. Although various software developers combine the programs differently, usually the following modules are available: general ledger, order entry, inventory, accounts receivable, accounts payable, sales analysis, payroll, tax reporting, and job costing.

The General Ledger. The foundation of nearly any accounting system—whether it is manual or computer-based—is the general ledger. The general ledger is maintained in the memory of the computer in the form of a large data base. When a transaction is entered, all relevant accounts can be quickly updated.

Implementing such a system is rarely accomplished quickly, because planning is essential. To install a general ledger system, the accountant starts by designing a chart of accounts, with a numbering system that will be useful when requesting reports that refer to or summarize subgroups. Transaction types must be defined, data base space requirements estimated, and the report generation features of the program altered to suit the particular company. In addition, controls demand consideration. Passwords to enter the system are normal. A backup policy is essential, because with such systems the records are updated in place. This means that the previous record is destroyed and only one copy exists of the data base unless backups are made. Some general ledger packages provide a transaction logging feature that records transactions in a separate file, and records the transactions' effects in the general ledger data base. If something should occur that damages the data base, this computerized transaction log could be used to quickly update the most recent backup of the master data base to create a new one.

Other Modules. Modules other than the general ledger are also available that frequently interact with the data base maintained by the general ledger module. To give you an idea of what these accounting programs can do, Exhibit A-1 lists four typical modules and some of their characteristics. Keep in mind, however, that software from different companies will do different things in a variety of ways. For instance, sales reports can be generated by the order entry, the inventory, or the accounts receivable module, depending upon the system design.

Many software developers are now taking advantage of the microcomputer's increasing power and capacity and are marketing so-called integrated accounting packages that are simple to install and use. However, a truly integrated set of modules for the microcomputer—with data being easily shared among the modules and a

EXHIBIT A-1

Samples of Accounting Software

MODULE	OBJECTIVE	REPORTS PRODUCED
Accounts receivable	To show where funds will come from and when they will come.	Sales record Sales tax record Cash receipts journal Aged trial balances Customer statements Mailing labels
Accounts payable	To show where cash will be going and how much will be needed.	Purchase record Listing of unpaid invoices by vendor Checks Vouchers Payment schedule Expense account summary
Inventory	To track on a perpetual basis items in stock and how much they are worth (at cost or retail).	Shelf life activity Overstocked and understocked items Seasonal demand Future forecasts Audit trail listing
Payroll	To accurately pay employees and aid in acting as collection agent for various organizations (government, insurance companies, and others).	Payroll register Checks Tax liability statements W-2 forms Personnel data

common command set—that is quickly learned, installed, and used is still hard to find.

The Spreadsheet

SPREADSHEET
An electronic version of the accounting worksheet.

CELL
A spot at the intersection of a row and a column on a spreadsheet.

TEMPLATE
The form created with a spreadsheet that has a certain number of rows and columns with a specific amount of space allocated to each cell and names for the cells, rows, and columns.

One piece of software that is of primary importance to accountants is certainly the **spreadsheet software,** an electronic version of a tool that accountants have used for centuries—the accounting worksheet (see Exhibit A-2).

Formed like a matrix with its columns and rows, such a package allows the user to specify a label, a number, or a formula for each **cell** (a spot at the intersection of a row and a column). The formulas entered relate data in various cells, rows, and columns; and the software records the formulas. Whenever a change is entered by the user, other related figures are updated using the stored formulas. Thus, a spreadsheet package can quickly and easily give the accountant answers to key questions such as: How much cash will remain at the end of each month? and What is the effect on net income if the product's price is raised $10?

The accountant starts a spreadsheet by creating a **template,** a standard form that has a certain number of rows and columns with a specific amount of space allotted to each cell and, if desired, names for the cells, rows, and columns. With today's increased memory size and technological advances, some spreadsheet packages will

EXHIBIT A-2

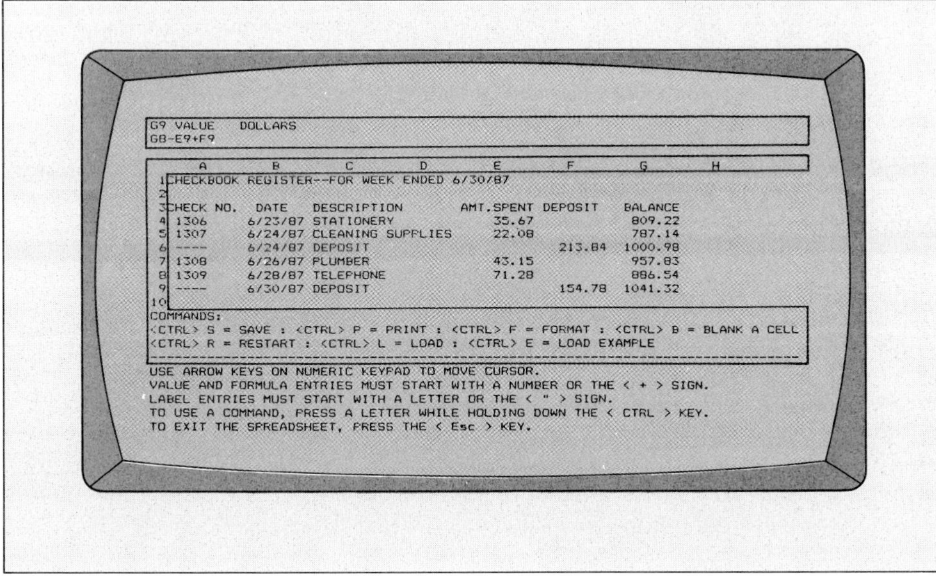
G9 VALUE DOLLARS
G8-E9+F9
A B C D E F G H
1 CHECKBOOK REGISTER--FOR WEEK ENDED 6/30/87
2
3 CHECK NO. DATE DESCRIPTION AMT.SPENT DEPOSIT BALANCE
4 1306 6/23/87 STATIONERY 35.67 809.22
5 1307 6/24/87 CLEANING SUPPLIES 22.08 787.14
6 ---- 6/24/87 DEPOSIT 213.84 1000.98
7 1308 6/26/87 PLUMBER 43.15 957.83
8 1309 6/28/87 TELEPHONE 71.28 886.54
9 ---- 6/30/87 DEPOSIT 154.78 1041.32
10
COMMANDS:
<CTRL> S = SAVE : <CTRL> P = PRINT : <CTRL> F = FORMAT : <CTRL> B = BLANK A CELL
<CTRL> R = RESTART : <CTRL> L = LOAD : <CTRL> E = LOAD EXAMPLE
USE ARROW KEYS ON NUMERIC KEYPAD TO MOVE CURSOR.
VALUE AND FORMULA ENTRIES MUST START WITH A NUMBER OR THE < + > SIGN.
LABEL ENTRIES MUST START WITH A LETTER OR THE < " > SIGN.
TO USE A COMMAND, PRESS A LETTER WHILE HOLDING DOWN THE < CTRL > KEY.
TO EXIT THE SPREADSHEET, PRESS THE < Esc > KEY.

allow as many as 256 columns and 2,048 rows—over half a million cells—even on a microcomputer. In some packages, certain cells can be protected from changes so that the spreadsheet user can enter data only where it is supposed to go.

Once the spreadsheet has been defined and data entered, the user can experiment with it by changing data or by moving around cells, rows, or columns. These experimental changes will not affect the original spreadsheet unless the user wants the change to become permanent and issues a special command. Portions of the spreadsheet can be saved separately or added to other spreadsheets (particularly useful in budgeting situations).

One of the major annoyances of using large spreadsheets has been the difficulty of viewing widely separated parts of the document. Unlike manual processing, where the accountant can spread papers across the desk, computer use allows the viewing of only one screenful—usually less than one page—at a time. Recent advances have addressed this problem by utilizing **windows,** which allow the viewing of parts of several items on the screen at one time. With windowing, the user can compare columns 2 through 4 with columns 222 through 225, for example.

WINDOW
A technique that allows a user to view parts of several items (e.g., pages of a large spreadsheet) on the monitor at the same time.

Many popular spreadsheet packages now offer special functions, such as automatic calculation of internal rates of return, future values and present values, standard deviations, and variances. Getting the computer to do certain user-defined functions might require the user to type a line of commands. With some packages, such a series of commands can be "taught" to the computer and then recalled with just two or three keystrokes. Also, since most packages today have many formatting options, the user can get printed reports with such niceties as up to 15 decimal places, dollars and cents, decimal alignment of columns, scientific notation, and negative numbers in parentheses.

Graphics

One of the newer developments in business software—particularly for micro-computers—is the graphics package. Although accountants frequently feel more comfortable with figures detailing the firm's financial status, they have found graphs very useful for spotting trends, comparing actual results to forecasts, highlighting exceptions, and communicating information to others.

The traditional charts have been of the line, bar, or pie type prepared manually. With computers, charts can be more exciting with, for example, three-dimensional bars or exploded pies; and the output options are numerous—paper, slides, transparencies, horizontal or vertical plots, oversized output, multiple charts per page, graphics combined with text, and dozens of colors.

Financial Planning

Because of their ready access to the current status of the business and their understanding of these figures, accountants are frequently involved with the task of planning for the firm's future. Computers are giving the word *forecasting* a new meaning; with the software currently available, predicting the firm's future performance under a great number of conditions is possible.

Software Aids. Programs are available to help the accountant in situations that call for sophisticated mathematical techniques. For example, an accountant might want to find out why sales are so much higher in one area than in another. The answer might be dependent upon many variables, such as the number of salespeople in the area, the advertising budget, and the population density of the locale. To analyze such a situation would involve multivariate regression—a technique that is much easier for a computer using a statistical package than for a human with a calculator. Two of the more popular statistical packages are SAS (Statistical Analysis System) and SPSS (Statistical Package for the Social Sciences).

Other software is designed to model the cash flow patterns of a firm. Although spreadsheet packages are frequently used for this purpose, packages such as IFPS (Interactive Financial Planning System) are more powerful and provide an English-like method of communicating the model to the computer. IFPS not only supports "what if . . ." types of inquiries, but can also perform goal seeking, where the user specifies the desired end result and the computer searches for the necessary action to achieve it.

Commercial Data Base Services. Sometimes the firm's internal data base is not able to supply enough information for future planning and the accountant might also need data about the world outside the firm. Several commercial computerized data bases exist. One of the most popular with business users is the Dow Jones News/Retrieval Service because of its 22 comprehensive business and financial data bases. This service carries excerpts from *The Wall Street Journal* (the night before the *WSJ* is circulated), *Barrons,* and the Dow Jones News Wire. Both current and historic stock quotations are available for most publicly traded firms, as well as ratio information (by firm or by industry), economic and earning forecasts, and SEC reports. Other data base network services that could be of help to accountants are the National Automated Accounting Research System (NAARS) and WESTLAW (for legal research information).

The cost to subscribe to an online data base service varies according to the service, the time of day, and how much and how well the service is utilized. For example,

Dow Jones has several subscriber plans. The standard plan has a password charge of $75 (one-time fee) and fees for use that are based on length of time in use, time of day, and the data base that is accessed. One minute of access to stock quotes during prime time currently costs $1.20. If access is during nonprime time, the cost drops to $.20. Cheaper rates are available by paying monthly or yearly subscription charges. In addition, if the firm is not located near a network service line (such as Tymnet or Net One), a long-distance phone charge accrues.

Online data bases might seem expensive after totaling the costs, particularly compared to library research. However, the service can be conveniently available at the accountant's desk 24 hours a day. If the financial data improve decision making, the money might be well spent.

COMPUTERS AND THE PROFESSIONAL ACCOUNTANT

This appendix has described the effect of the computer on the traditional accounting records of a firm. It has shown how the process of accounting for a firm's activities has become more and more efficient and how controls over the accounting process have been eroded by the use of computers. As you know, the task of reviewing the accounting records of a firm is called auditing, and you can see that this task can no longer be accomplished using the methods of the precomputer era. A 1984 Coopers and Lybrand survey tells a great deal about the impact of computers on auditing. Corporate auditors in 200 of the Fortune 500 reported that 25 percent of their work is currently being done by computer, compared to less than 10 percent five years ago. They predict that over half of all internal auditing will be computerized by 1990, and 90.5 percent consider computer education a necessity in college auditing programs.

Computers in general have freed the accountant from many of the tedious tasks associated with tracking a firm's financial progress. Microcomputers have gone one step further by giving the accountant a powerful, versatile personal tool to help in decision support. The accountant who is at ease with such a system has at his or her fingertips the historical data needed for exploring many future possibilities. By previewing the potential results of the firm's activities, the proper course of action to recommend can be made much clearer.

SUMMARY

- A computer system is composed of the central processing unit, at least one input device, at least one output device, and a secondary memory device.
- The central processing unit has three parts: the control unit, the arithmetic-logic unit, and primary memory.
- During the first generation of computer development, the primary processing method was batch processing, and a good audit trail was available.
- With the advent of the second generation of computers, magnetic disk storage devices were developed along with some on-line processing leading to loss of automatic backup records and the beginning of the disappearance of the audit trail.

- As the third generation of computers was developed, controls became a more widespread concern as more and more input-output devices were connected directly to the computer, providing more widespread access to systems and data therein. The audit trail continued to disappear with the replacement of paper inputs.
- The fourth generation of computers brought significant advances in user-friendly software, open access, and widespread microcomputer use. The audit trail continued to evaporate as paper was eliminated by terminal-to-computer and mainframe-to-mainframe connections.
- Accounting task-oriented software is usually modular, with the general ledger serving as the foundation of the system.
- A spreadsheet program is probably the handiest tool available to accountants. It resembles the accounting worksheet and can show the results of adjustments quickly and easily.
- Graphics packages are helpful for spotting trends and communicating information to others.
- Software aids for financial planning include statistical programs, financial planning languages, and commercial data base services.
- Auditors are learning to use the computer in audit tasks and to evaluate the results of a client's computer applications.

EXERCISES

A-E1. List the components and capabilities most likely to be found in a computer system in a business manager's office and in a retail sales office.

A-E2. For each of the following, state whether a batch or an on-line system is more appropriate:

a. Updating inventory records in a high-volume discount store.
b. Updating customer checking accounts at a bank.
c. Checking of license plates on a vehicle being investigated by the highway patrol.
d. Preparation of payroll for employees.
e. Recording stock exchange transactions.

A-E3. Design a spreadsheet template that could be used to record students' grades in one class for one term. Plan for 25 students; each student will be completing four quizzes, two projects, and three tests. Raw scores, not percents, are recorded. The final grade should be included; it is a weighted average based on the following formula:

$$\text{Final grade} = \left(\frac{\text{Total of 4 quiz scores}}{100}\right) 20 + \left(\frac{\text{Total of 2 project scores}}{50}\right) 20 + \left(\frac{\text{Total of 3 test scores}}{300}\right) 60$$

Enter these data for the first two students: Sue Black, quiz grades of 20, 22, 20, 25; project grades of 22 and 21; test grades of 89, 82, 91. Bob Smith, quiz grades of 16, 18, 23, 22; project grades of 20 and 24; test grades of 75, 87, 83.

A-E4. Refer to Exhibit A-2. For each column of data (excluding column titles), indicate whether the items entered would be considered labels, numbers, or formulas.

A-E5. The manager of the housewares division of a retail chain wants to compare her divisional sales to those of other divisions. Pertinent data for the previous quarter are as follows:

Total sales	$9,526,000
Divisional sales	
Apparel	$3,695,000
Hardware	657,000
Shoes	480,000
Housewares	1,803,000
Automotive	1,327,000
Health & beauty aids	1,564,000

Prepare a chart that highlights the divisional sales of the housewares manager. (How long did this take you? If a computer graphics package is available, try using it and compare times.)

APPLICATION

American Metal Treating Company

American Metal Treating Company (AMT), located in Cleveland, is not a corporate giant with hundreds of employees. In fact, in 1985, AMT had sales of a little over a million dollars and employed 26 office and plant workers. The company is in business to provide a service—heat treating metal parts, particularly gears, that go into making all kinds of machinery.

■ A Brief History

AMT began operations in 1932 as a sole proprietorship under the auspices of Jesse L. Teegarden, uncle of the present owner. At that time, the firm processed metal parts in furnaces. Herbert Summers, the present owner, joined the firm in 1937 as a furnace operator. Eight months later, he became the sales representative traveling throughout the Ohio area seeking new business.

By 1948, Summers was in charge of production, sales, and overall management. Teegarden was only marginally involved in operations, although he was still heavily involved in the decision-making process. Teegarden died in 1951, and the business was owned by his widow until 1958. When Mrs. Teegarden died, ownership passed to her estate. Summers and two partners bought the estate in 1960 for approximately $100,000.

Summers bought new equipment in 1961 and 1962 to replace the original equipment, and in 1964 the company added additional hardening processes to the business. In 1967, Summers bought out his partners and became the sole owner-manager of the company. The company was incorporated later that year, and corporate ownership was shared among Mr. Summers and his two key managers, Mr. Roenn and Mr. Davis. Mr. Summers retains majority ownership but eventually will have a minority share

because of a buyout agreement that allows Messrs. Roenn and Davis to purchase additional shares over a period of years. By the time Mr. Summers retires, Messrs. Davis and Roenn will have controlling interest.

It is Summers' view that what differentiates his company from many others is the personal service it renders. He points out that approximately 20 percent of AMT's current customers have been with the firm for 40 years, and he attributes this loyalty to his policy of providing advice, special services, and high-quality service. He also credits AMT's ability to provide a full range of heat treating, especially for parts that require more than one type of treatment. This saves customers the trouble and expense of transferring parts from company to company.

EXHIBIT 1

American Metal Treating Company
Statements of Financial Position
December 31

	1985		1984	
Assets				
Current Assets				
Cash		$158,867		$123,408
Accounts receivable		175,626		167,956
Shop supplies		7,790		1,002
Prepaid taxes		0		4,535
Other prepaid expenses		18,370		6,011
Total current assets		360,653		302,912
Property, Plant, and Equipment	$639,531		$577,820	
Less accumulated depreciation	243,017		209,176	
Total property, plant, and equipment		396,514		368,644
Other Assets		113,498		75,076
Total assets		$870,665		$746,632
Liabilities and Shareholders' Equity				
Current Liabilities				
Notes payable		44,742		47,806
Accounts payable		56,818		51,800
Taxes payable		24,967		3,649
Accrued expenses		60,211		66,711
Total current liabilities		186,738		169,966
Long-Term Debt		179,450		159,533
Shareholders' Equity				
Common stock	20,000		20,000	
Retained earnings	484,477		397,133	
Total shareholders' equity		504,477		417,133
Total liabilities and shareholders' equity		$870,665		$746,632

EXHIBIT 1
Continued

American Metal Treating Company Income Statement Year Ending December 31, 1985	
	1985
Sales	$1,201,342
Less cost of goods sold	897,024
Gross profit	304,318
Less operating expenses	
Selling	94,039
General and administrative	124,178
Total operating expenses	218,217
Income from operations	86,101
Other income	22,828
Less other expenses	21,765
Income before income taxes	87,164
Income taxes	23,369
Net income before sale of assets	63,795
Sale of assets—net of tax	24,349
Net income	$ 88,144

Overview of Financial Accounting System

Every month, AMT's accountant prepares an income statement and statement of financial position for the company. The income statement is prepared on a departmental basis as well as in total. Management uses these statements to determine how it is doing, to spot potential problem areas, and to plan for the future. These statements are management's financial report card. The financial statements are prepared using the principles and procedures described in Chapters 1–4. In particular, the accounting cycle described in Chapters 2 and 4 is followed. However, most of the bookkeeping work is done by computer rather than manually. The company uses the accrual basis of accounting.

AMT's fiscal year ends December 31, which is the slowest time of the year. This lull gives the accountant time to prepare year-end statements for the owners, management, and anyone else needing financial information (e.g., bankers, lawyers, pension fund managers).

Exhibit 1 shows the company's comparative statements of financial position for 1984 and 1985 and a statement of income for 1985. In addition, assume the following information for 1985:

1. AMT had no cash sales.
2. All operating expenses were paid on the fifteenth of the month following the month in which the expenses were incurred.
3. All other expenses were paid in 1985.

Exercises

1. Prepare a journal entry for each of the following transactions:

Sales revenue
Payment of operating expenses
Collections of accounts receivable
Recognition of other income
Payment of income tax
Payment of distribution of dividends
Payment of all other expenses

2. A comparison of the December 31, 1984, and December 31, 1985, statements of financial position indicates that cash increased by $35,459, yet retained earnings increased by $87,344. How can this happen?

PART TWO
TRANSACTION ANALYSIS AND FIXED ASSETS

2

THE SELLING CYCLE: PURCHASES AND SALES

CHAPTER OBJECTIVES

After studying Chapter 5, you should understand the following:

1. Purchase and sales transactions in a merchandising operation.
2. General purchase and sales terms and accounting procedures for each.
3. Revenue recognition associated with sales transactions.
4. The relationship between income and the purchasing/selling cycle.

This chapter contains a detailed discussion of the acquisition and sale of products in a merchandising business. It introduces purchase transactions and purchase contract conditions.

Sales transactions and revenue measurement arising therefrom are covered, with special emphasis on revenue recognition. The effects of both sales and purchases on income determination are explored.

SALES/INCOME AND THE GROSS PROFIT PERCENTAGE

As suggested in Chapter 3, income is the most often used measure of performance by external users of financial statements. Although the bottom line net income figure is the most often quoted item on the income statement, financial statement users often pay attention to the relationship between sales and cost of goods sold, since this relationship is paramount to profitability.

The markup of cost to selling price of goods sold must be sufficient to pay all administrative and selling expenses and provide a reasonable profit for the owners. The total markup from purchase cost of goods sold, expressed as a percentage of selling price, is generally referred to as the **gross profit** or **gross margin percentage.** For example, if the Nickel and Dime Toy Store were to purchase a puzzle for $1.00 and mark it up 60 cents to a selling price of $1.60, we would say the gross profit percentage equals $.60/$1.60 equals .375, or 37.5 percent of sales.

GROSS PROFIT PERCENTAGE
Total markup from purchase cost of goods sold expressed as a percentage of selling price (Sales Price – Purchase Cost)/Sales Price.

GROSS MARGIN PERCENTAGE
See Gross Profit Percentage.

The remainder of this chapter focuses on the measurement and recording of inventory acquisition costs (purchases) and sales revenue—the items that become the basis for gross profit measurement on the income statement.

INVENTORY AND COST OF GOODS SOLD

Before merchandise can be sold, it must be obtained from suppliers. The historical cost of merchandise forms the basis for the subsequent measurement of the Cost of Goods Sold account and the Inventory account.

Inventory

Inventory can be defined as assets held by a company either for resale or for use in production. For a merchandising firm, all goods purchased for resale in the normal course of business that are still on hand at a given point in time are classified as inventory. Exhibit 5.1 portrays the relationship between purchases, cost of goods sold, and inventory.

INVENTORY
Assets held by a company either for resale or for use in production.

At the end of an accounting period, the purchase costs of merchandise are classified in one of two ways: as inventory if the merchandise is still available for sale or as cost of goods sold if the merchandise was sold to customers. Inventory at the end of any time period consists of all goods available for sale at the beginning of the period (beginning inventory), plus all goods acquired from suppliers during the period **(purchases),** less any goods sold during the period (cost of goods sold). For example, if Acme Auto Parts had $170,000 of auto parts on January 1, purchased $300,000 of parts during the year, and sold $292,500 of parts during the year, we would expect ending inventory on December 31 to be $177,500 worth of parts. Exhibit 5.2 illustrates the computation of the ending inventory for Acme.

PURCHASES
All inventory items acquired from suppliers during a particular time period.

Note that the $292,500 figure is the *cost* of the inventory that was sold, not the *price* at which it was sold.

EXHIBIT 5.1

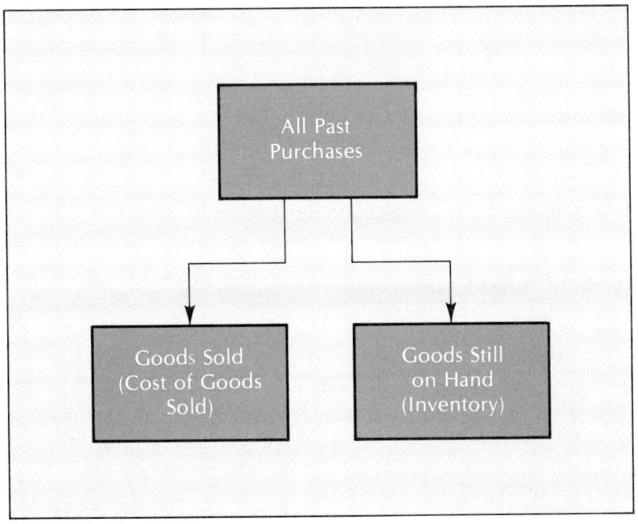

All Past Purchases → Goods Sold (Cost of Goods Sold) | Goods Still on Hand (Inventory)

Goods Available for Sale

The total value of **goods available for sale** for a period is the sum of beginning inventory and purchases. For Acme, goods available for sale totaled $470,000, as shown in Exhibit 5.2. Only two possibilities exist for Acme's goods available for sale: Either Acme has sold the parts or it still has them. Of course, the parts could have been stolen or destroyed, but we are ignoring this complication for now and assuming that the parts not on hand have been sold to customers. Thus, if Acme subtracts its year-end inventory from its goods available for sale, the difference must be equal to the cost of goods sold. Exhibit 5.3 illustrates this computation for Acme.

GOODS AVAILABLE FOR SALE
The sum of beginning inventory and purchases.

EXHIBIT 5.2

Beginning inventory, January 1	$170,000
Plus: Purchases during the year	300,000
Goods available for sale	$470,000
Less: Cost of goods sold	292,500
Ending inventory, December 31	$177,500

EXHIBIT 5.3

Inventory, January 1	$170,000
Plus: Purchases during the year	300,000
Goods available for sale	$470,000
Less: Inventory, December 31	177,500
Cost of goods sold	$292,500

PERIODIC AND PERPETUAL INVENTORY METHODS

Note that in Exhibit 5.3, it is not necessary to determine the original cost of each part sold by Acme to determine the total cost of goods sold. If Acme determines its inventory level at the beginning and end of the accounting period (January 1 and December 31 in Exhibit 5.3) and records its merchandise purchases, cost of goods sold can be determined by the preceding computation.

The Periodic Inventory Method

PERIODIC INVENTORY METHOD
The method of inventory record keeping where inventory levels are determined at the end of each accounting period, purchases are recorded as made in a separate purchases account, and cost of goods sold is determined by computation.

This method of inventory record keeping—where inventory levels are determined (usually by a physical count of items on hand) at the end of each accounting period, merchandise purchases are recorded as made in a separate Purchases account, and cost of goods sold is determined by computation—is known as the **periodic inventory method** and is widely used in merchandising firms.

Under periodic inventory, entries are made in the Inventory account only at the end of each accounting period to adjust the account to its appropriate end-of-period balance, which also serves as the beginning balance for the following period. Because all purchases are added together in the Purchases account, the cost of individual inventory items is not maintained within the accounting system and the cost of any particular item sold cannot be easily determined.

The Perpetual Inventory Method

PERPETUAL INVENTORY METHOD
The method of inventory record keeping where each purchase of inventory is separately recorded in the inventory account and the cost of each item sold is entered into the cost of goods sold account at the time of sale.

Rather than use the periodic inventory method, Acme could use the method used throughout Chapters 1 through 4—the **perpetual inventory method.** Under the perpetual inventory method, each item of inventory is separately recorded in the Inventory account at the time of purchase and the cost of each item sold is entered into a Cost of Goods Sold account at the time of sale. Since each item of inventory is separately tracked, the perpetual inventory method requires more complex record keeping and bookkeeping, although it provides more detailed and up-to-date information on the composition of a firm's inventory than does the periodic method. Of course, the accuracy of the firm's inventory records must be verified from time to time by a physical count of the inventory on hand. The perpetual inventory method is often used where each item of inventory is unique or has a high value, such as might be the case with a jewelry store.

Given its simplicity and focus on the totality of merchandise purchases, we will use the periodic method as a framework for our discussion in this chapter of accounting for purchases and sales. We will return to a more detailed discussion of perpetual and periodic inventory methods in Chapter 9.

MEASURING COST OF GOODS PURCHASED AND SOLD

NET PURCHASE COST
Gross price paid for merchandise plus any freight charges incurred less any price, quantity, or payment discounts granted and less any goods returned to the supplier.

Goods purchased are normally valued at their net acquisition price consistent with the historical cost convention and its reliance on transaction dollars. **Net purchase cost** is generally defined as gross price paid for merchandise, plus any freight charges incurred, less any price, quantity, or payment discounts granted and less any goods returned to the supplier.

Record Keeping for Purchases

The Purchases Account. Under the periodic inventory system, all goods purchased are recorded in a separate Purchases account. The Purchases account is functionally similar to the Income Summary account in that it is temporary in nature and serves only to collect data. The sole purpose of the Purchases account is to keep a record of goods acquired for resale purposes so that cost of goods sold can be determined at the end of each accounting period. At the end of the period, the Purchases account is closed to cost of goods sold. Under the periodic procedure, the balance in the Inventory account is neither increased for goods received nor decreased for sales made.

Purchases is not thought of as an asset account, although it does represent asset acquisitions and potential expense and is, therefore, increased by debits. For example, assume that the AC/DC Lighting Company purchases $10,000 of lamps on October 1 to be paid for at a future date. AC/DC would make the following entry:

Oct. 1	Purchases	10,000	
	Accounts payable		10,000
	(to record purchases of inventory on account)		

The Purchases account is used only for merchandise acquisitions under the periodic inventory method. Acquisitions of other assets not acquired for resale are not recorded as purchases. These other asset acquisitions are discussed in Chapters 10 and 11. The nature of accounts payable and the bookkeeping for such debts are covered in Chapter 6.

Inventory and Profit

Custom Car Products discovered that it was having serious financial problems in 1984 despite an apparently good gross profit percentage. Custom Car Products had started as a small business in 1975 making specialized plastic parts for restoration of high-performance cars of the 1960s. Outside specialists were called in who discovered that through carelessness, much inventory had been double counted on December 31, 1981, 1982, and 1983. As a result, computed cost of goods sold was much lower than actual cost of goods sold, and Custom Car Products had lowered its price each year based on the computed amount until it was actually selling at a loss.

Discounts on Purchases. Often a supplier will grant a discount from list price **(a purchase discount)** if a buyer will pay the bill promptly. Terms of the available discount are given in the purchase agreement and are usually written in shorthand notation, such as 3/10, n/30 (read three ten, net thirty). This shorthand means that if the buyer pays for the goods within 10 days from the invoice date, the supplier will allow a three percent purchase discount off the list price, but that in any event, the net amount (full amount without discount) is due within 30 days. Discounts such as this are extremely valuable and should normally be taken by making payment within the discount period.

PURCHASE DISCOUNT
A discount from list price granted for prompt payment.

Under terms of 3/10, n/30, the buyer must pay either within 10 days or within 30 days, depending upon whether or not the discount is taken. Stated another way, the buyer must pay three percent more in order to delay payment 20 days (30 − 10). The decision to delay payment from 10 days after date of purchase to 30 days after the date of purchase has a "cost" of three percent of the total purchase price. This decision, therefore, is exactly the same as borrowing enough money from a bank 10 days after the date of purchase to pay the supplier the net amount owed and then repaying the loan 20 days later with three percent interest added. If we had to pay three percent interest on borrowed money for every 20-day period in a year, we would be paying an effective annual rate of interest of 54 percent, since one year has eighteen 20-day periods. For example, assume that the AC/DC purchase of $10,000 of lamps on October 1 carries payment terms of 3/10, n/30. Exhibit 5.4 details the options for payment available to AC/DC.

EXHIBIT 5.4

Option 1: Pay on October 30	$10,000
Option 2: Pay on October 10 (purchase price less 3% discount)	9,700
Cost of waiting 20 days to pay	$ 300
Cost of waiting 20 extra days as a percentge of total purchase cost (300/10,000)	3%
Number of 20-day periods in one year (360/20)	18
Effective annual rate of interest for delayed payment	54%

The relationship between the purchase discounts permitted and the equivalent cost of borrowing funds should always be considered. The relationship between various purchase term discounts and simple interest is as follows:

Purchase Terms	Equivalent Simple Interest
1/10, n/30	18%
2/10, n/30	36%
1/15, n/30	24%
2/15, n/30	48%

Gross Method of Recording Purchases. Since discounts reduce the total purchase cost, a record must be kept of those discounts taken. Suppose AC/DC paid for the goods on October 9. AC/DC would record the disbursement of cash and the reduction of purchase cost represented by the discount as follows:

Oct. 9	Accounts payable	10,000	
	Cash		9,700
	Purchase discounts (.03 × 10,000)		300
	(to record payment to supplier with discount taken)		

The Purchase Discounts account is a contra-account to the Purchases account and, like the Purchases account, is a temporary account for use when later computing cost of goods sold.

GROSS METHOD OF RECORDING PURCHASES
The bookkeeping procedure where purchases are initially recorded at total purchase price and purchase discounts are recorded separately if payment is made within the discount period.

The bookkeeping procedure where purchases are initially recorded at total purchase price and purchase discounts are recorded separately if payment is made within the discount period is known as the **gross method of recording purchases.**

NET METHOD OF RECORDING PURCHASES
The bookkeeping procedure where purchases are initially recorded net of permitted discounts and only those discounts not taken are recorded in the accounts.

Net Method of Recording Purchases. An alternative bookkeeping method is available that more correctly records the amount of the purchaser's liability (accounts payable) and merchandise acquisition cost (purchases) under the assumption that the buyer will take advantage of the permitted discount. Under this bookkeeping procedure (the **net method of recording purchases**), purchases are initially recorded net of permitted discounts and only those discounts not taken are recorded in the accounts.

Under the net method, AC/DC would record its $10,000 purchase of lamps as follows if payment terms are 3/10, n/30:

Oct. 1	Purchases	9,700	
	Accounts payable		9,700
	(to record inventory purchases on account)		

When the account is paid on October 9, AC/DC would record the payment as follows:

Oct. 9	Accounts payable	9,700	
	Cash		9,700
	(to record payment on account)		

Suppose, however, that AC/DC did not make the required payment within ten days and therefore must pay an extra $300. The additional $300 now required in payment must be recorded as an added cost. If AC/DC delays payment until October 29, it would be required to pay out cash of $10,000, and the following journal entry would be required:

Oct. 29	Accounts payable	9,700	
	Purchase discounts lost	300	
	Cash		10,000
	(to record payment to supplier and forfeited discount)		

Besides recording the initial liability and purchase cost at the net amount owed at the date of purchase, the net method provides management with the total dollar cost of not paying within the discount period. Again, the cost of not taking allowed discounts can be quite high when compared with the cost of borrowing sufficient money to make payments. Since the total amount of discounts not taken is recorded under the net method of recording purchases, management is provided cost information that would otherwise be difficult to obtain.

Goods Returned to Suppliers. When merchandise for resale is received and inspected, some items might be defective or ultimately not needed. Unnecessary or defective merchandise often can be returned to the supplier with an allowance granted to the purchaser for all or most of the purchase price of the goods returned. Sometimes the supplier will grant an allowance from the original purchase price for defective goods as compensation to the purchaser for defects and allow the purchaser to retain the goods. Such returns and allowances reduce the total purchase cost of merchandise and ultimately reduce the cost of goods sold.

Rather than simply reduce the amount of purchases directly, most companies use a separate account to record the allowances received for returned or defective merchandise. In this way, management can readily obtain information on the amount of defective and returned goods and use this information for inventory management and supplier selection purposes. Order entry and merchandise handling processes are expensive, and returning excessive amounts of items purchased or replacing defective goods is costly. Of course, any allowances made by suppliers for defective or returned merchandise reduce the amount owed to suppliers and constitute a net reduction of the liability represented by accounts payable as well as a reduction in the cost of goods purchased.

PURCHASE RETURNS AND ALLOWANCES
The allowances granted by suppliers to purchasers for defective or returned goods.

The allowances granted to purchasers for defective or returned goods are usually recorded in a contra-account to Purchases entitled **Purchase Returns and Allowances.** Because the effect of the allowances is to reduce the cost of the goods purchased, the allowances are recorded as credits. Assume that AC/DC inspects its October 1 purchase of $10,000 of lamps on October 3 and discovers that $500 of the lamps are damaged. AC/DC notifies the supplier of the damaged lamps and receives an allowance of $500. If AC/DC records purchases at their gross purchase cost, the allowance would be recorded as follows:

Oct. 3	Accounts payable	500	
	Purchase returns and allowances		500
	(to record allowances for defective merchandise)		

remember →

If AC/DC had recorded the original purchase net of discount, the allowance entry would be the same, except the amount of the allowance would be entered net of discount at $485 (.97 × 500).

Freight Charges. If the purchasing company bears the freight charges for delivery of inventory items, the cost of the freight is added to the purchase cost and thus increases cost of goods. If the supplier bears the freight charges on goods sold, the price of the goods might be greater, but the purchaser does not need to perform any special bookkeeping. The purchase price will automatically include all freight charges.

F.O.B. SHIPPING POINT
A selling term that means ownership to goods changes from the seller to the purchaser when the goods are turned over to the shipping company.

F.O.B. DESTINATION
A selling term that means ownership to goods does not change from the seller to the purchaser until the goods are delivered by the shipping company to the purchaser's place of business.

Selling terms and freight charges. Standardized terms have been developed in purchase contracts that communicate the responsibility for freight charges to the purchaser and seller. A contract written with the pricing **f.o.b.** (free on board) **shipping point** means that ownership changes from the seller to the buyer when the goods are turned over to the shipping company and the buyer is responsible for all freight charges. **F.o.b. destination** means that ownership or title to the goods does not change from the seller to the purchaser until the goods are delivered by the shipping company to the purchaser. Therefore, the seller must bear the freight charges. Exhibit 5.5 summarizes standard contract terms in purchase agreements.

If the contract terms for AC/DC's purchase of $10,000 of lamps on October 1 were f.o.b. shipping point and the transportation charge was $400, AC/DC would be obligated to pay the $400 and would record the charge in a separate temporary account to keep track of what was paid or owed to transportation companies. If, on the other hand, the contract terms were f.o.b. destination, the supplier would have paid the $400 and AC/DC would not record any freight on the purchase.

EXHIBIT 5.5

Contract Language	Title Passes	Freight Is the Responsibility Of
f.o.b. shipping point	when seller places goods with carrier	buyer
f.o.b. destination	when buyer receives goods from carrier	seller

Bookkeeping for freight charges. Transportation charges paid by the purchaser are known as **freight-in** or **transportation-in,** and those paid by the seller are known as **freight-out** or **transportation-out.** Freight-in is an expense of the purchaser, while freight-out is an expense of the seller. Freight-in is normally added to the purchase cost at the end of an accounting period, whereas freight-out is normally carried as a separate expense of the seller. Assume that the selling terms for AC/DC's October 1 purchase were f.o.b. shipping point and that the freight charge was $400. AC/DC would record the purchase and freight charge (assuming gross purchase method used) as follows:

FREIGHT-IN
Transportation charges paid by the purchaser.

TRANSPORTATION-IN
See Freight-In.

FREIGHT-OUT
Transportation charges paid by the seller.

TRANSPORTATION-OUT
See Freight-Out.

Oct. 1	Purchases	10,000	
	Freight-in	400	
	Accounts payable		10,400
	(to record purchase of merchandise and freight charge)		

If the contract terms for the purchase also include a discount, say 3/10, n/30, the three percent discount would apply only to the $10,000 of lamps. AC/DC would have to pay the full freight charge of $400 regardless of payment date.

Cost of Goods Sold Summary

To see how all of the preceding fits together to produce cost of goods sold, assume the following data were obtained from the records of the AC/DC Company for October:

1.	Inventory taken on September 30	$200,000
2.	Purchases during October	500,000
3.	Freight-in on October purchases	1,000
4.	Purchase discounts taken on October purchases	10,000
5.	Purchase returns and allowances on October purchases	800
6.	Inventory taken on October 31	217,000

Exhibit 5.6 shows the computation of cost of goods sold for AC/DC for October.

EXHIBIT 5.6

AC/DC Lighting—Cost of Goods Sold
October

Beginning inventory, October 1		$200,000
Purchases		
Gross purchases	$500,000	
Plus: Freight-in	1,000	
	$501,000	
Less: Purchase discounts	10,000	
Purchase returns and allowances	800	
Net purchases		490,200
Goods available for sale		$690,200
Less: Ending inventory, October 31		217,000
Cost of goods sold, October		$473,200

Lost or Damaged Goods

In any business, inventory items can be damaged, lost, or stolen. The business can count only the goods on hand when taking inventory and would value damaged goods at less than original cost. Thus, the ending inventory is lowered to the extent that inventory items are missing or damaged. Since lowering ending inventory raises the cost of goods sold, the value of missing items and the reduced value of damaged items are automatically included as part of cost of goods sold for the time period under consideration when using the periodic inventory method. Under the materiality convention discussed in Chapter 1, lost or damaged inventory would be shown separately only if the losses or damages were large enough to affect decisions made by users of financial statements.

CONCEPT SUMMARY 5.1

PURCHASES SUMMARY—PERIODIC INVENTORY

Item	Recorded In	Effect on Total Purchases Amount
Goods purchased	Purchases account as a debit	Increase
Freight charges	Freight-in account as a debit	Increase
Purchase discounts allowed by seller	Purchase Discounts account as a credit	Decrease
Goods returned to supplier	Purchase Returns and Allowances account as a credit	Decrease

SALES OF MERCHANDISE

Once a firm has acquired merchandise, it can begin to earn revenue by selling items from inventory.

Gross Sales

GROSS SELLING PRICE
The initial price charged to customers for goods.

As Chapters 1 and 3 discuss, revenue represents an inflow of assets from the sale of goods or services. The initial price charged customers for goods is known as the **gross selling price** and serves as the beginning of the revenue measurement process. When a sale is made on credit, as most sales are, the seller records the revenue earned and adds the asset obtained to those already held. For example, if AC/DC sold lamps to customers for $3,000 on account on October 8, the gross sale would be recorded as follows:

Oct. 8	Accounts receivable	3,000	
	Sales		3,000
	(to record sales on account)		

Recall from the material in Chapter 3 that revenue recognition requires a good expectation of collection from customers of amounts owed. This chapter assumes that all amounts owed are collected. The next chapter presents material specific to the problem of uncollectible accounts.

Sales Discounts

Earlier we discussed purchase discounts for prompt payment. To the seller of merchandise, discounts from the sales price granted for prompt payment are called **sales discounts.** Such discounts constitute reductions in the amounts received from customers and therefore reductions in revenue from sales.

SALES DISCOUNTS
Discounts from sales price granted by sellers to buyers in return for prompt payment by the buyers.

Gross Method of Recording Sales. If, in the case of AC/DC, the selling terms had been 2/10, n/30, and the customer had paid on October 17, only $2,940 (.98 × 3,000) would be received and the $60 reduction in revenue would have to be recorded. Generally, a separate Sales Discounts account (a contra-account to sales) is used to record the reduction in revenue so that management can easily monitor its credit policies and their cost. Of course, since the customer has satisfied the $3,000 obligation by taking the discount and paying $2,940, AC/DC needs to reduce the amount owed by the customer by the full $3,000. The entry for the payment just described would be as follows:

Oct. 17	Cash	2,940	
	Sales discounts	60	
	Accounts receivable		3,000
	(to record payment from customers with discount taken)		

The bookkeeping procedure whereby sales are recorded at gross sales price and sales discounts are recorded when taken by customers is known as the **gross method of recording sales.**

GROSS METHOD OF RECORDING SALES
The bookkeeping procedure where sales are recorded at gross sales price and sales discounts are recorded only when taken by customers.

Net Method of Recording Sales. As with purchase discounts, an alternative bookkeeping procedure is available. Known as the **net method of recording sales,** it assumes that customers will pay within the discount period. Under this method, the sale is recorded net amount of permitted discounts and only those discounts not taken are recorded in the accounts. Recording sales at the net expected collection level is consistent with basic revenue recognition concepts discussed is Chapter 3, since the sale is recorded at an amount equal to the expected total future cash to be collected from the customer. The entry for the sale by AC/DC Lighting Company to customers of lamps for $3,000 with terms of 2/10, n/30, would be as follows:

NET METHOD OF RECORDING SALES
The bookkeeping procedure where sales are recorded net of permitted discounts and sales discounts not taken by customers are recorded separately.

Oct. 8	Accounts receivable	2,940	
	Sales		2,940
	(to record sales of goods to customers)		

As with purchase discounts, the actual payment on account will be one of two amounts, depending on whether or not payment is made within the discount period. If payment is made after the discount period, the additional cash received is recorded as "revenue from forfeited sales discounts."

For the preceding sale, either $2,940 or $3,000 will be received, depending on whether payment is made before or after October 18. Journal entries for the two possibilities are as follows:

(payment within 10 days)			
Oct. 17	Cash	2,940	
	Accounts receivable		2,940
	(to record payment from customer)		

(payment after 10 days)			
Sept. 5	Cash	3,000	
	Forfeited sales discounts		60
	Accounts receivable		2,940
	(to record payment from customer)		

In addition to being consistent with revenue recognition concepts, the net method of recording sales has the advantage of identifying customers who are forfeiting their discounts. Such forfeiture can indicate that a customer is facing financial difficulties and might become a greater credit risk. In spite of these advantages, the net method of recording sales is not widely used.

Sales Returns and Allowances

Just as purchase returns and allowances represent reductions in cost to buyers, allowances for goods returned by customers and allowances granted to customers for defective goods represent a reduction in revenue to sellers. Suppose AC/DC's customer returns some lamps on October 10 and AC/DC allows the customer $500 for the returned lamps. The allowance for goods returned might be for less than the original selling price, since the seller must perform extra bookkeeping and must employ a certain amount of labor for restocking the shelves, etc. Typically, however, the allowance granted will be equal to the original selling price of the goods to the customer.

SALES RETURNS AND ALLOWANCES
The allowances made by sellers for damaged or returned goods.

As with purchases, a separate contra-account to sales (**Sales Returns and Allowances**) is generally used to record allowances for damaged or returned goods so that management can more effectively monitor its selling operations. Excessive amounts of returned or damaged goods can indicate a problem in quality of merchandise, shipping practices, or some other aspect of order filling. Although a seller could issue a check to a customer for allowances for goods returned, the more common treatment is to reduce the amount that the customer owes by the amount of the allowance. AC/DC's entry for the $500 allowance granted October 10 is as follows:

Oct. 10	Sales returns and allowances	500	
	Accounts receivable		500
	(to record allowances for goods returned by customer)		

Had AC/DC been recording sales under the net method, the accounts would be the same, but the amount of the allowance permitted might have varied, depending upon whether the discount was granted as a percentage of net sales price (sales price minus allowed discount) or of gross sales price. The complexities involved in the problem of granting sales returns after the discount date when sales are recorded under the net method are best left to more advanced accounting courses.

Net Sales

NET SALES
Gross selling price for goods minus sales discounts minus sales returns and allowances.

Net sales equals the gross selling price of goods less sales discounts and less sales returns and allowances. To illustrate the computation of the net sales amount for a merchandising company, assume the records of the AC/DC Company indicate the following for October:

1. Gross sales revenue	$600,000
2. Sales discounts taken by customers on October sales	4,000
3. Sales returns and allowances from October sales	800

Exhibit 5.7 presents the computation of net sales and gross profit for AC/DC for October.

All other expenses are deducted from gross profit to arrive at net income. Exhibit 5.8 presents a complete income statement for AC/DC Company for October. The data for selling, administrative, and general expenses are assumed for illustrative purposes.

EXHIBIT 5.7

Sales		$600,000
Less: Sales discounts	$4,000	
Sales returns and allowances	800	4,800
Net sales		$595,200
Less: Cost of goods sold (from Exhibit 5.6)		473,200
Gross profit		$122,000

EXHIBIT 5.8

AC/DC Lighting
Income Statement
For the Month Ending October 31

Net sales		$595,200
Cost of goods sold		473,200
Gross profit		$122,000
Operating expenses		
Selling	$15,000	
Administrative	40,000	
General	30,000	85,000
Net income		$ 37,000

CONCEPT SUMMARY 5.2

SALES SUMMARY

Item	Recorded In	Effect on Revenue
Goods sold	Sales account as a credit	Increase
Discounts taken by customers	Sales Discounts account as a debit	Decrease
Goods returned by customers	Sales Returns and Allowances account as a debit	Decrease

Whether to show the details of the computation of cost of goods sold and net sales on the face of the income statement is optional under current accounting standards. In any event, all of the supporting accounts for cost of goods sold (Purchases, Purchase Returns and Allowances, etc.) and net sales (Gross Sales, Sales Returns and Allowances, etc.) are temporary accounts and are closed at the end of each accounting period.

FOR REVIEW

DEMONSTRATION PROBLEM

On July 3, the Kauber Lumber Company purchases $100,000 of lumber for resale from the Rain Forest Wholesale Company under terms of 2/10, n/30, f.o.b. shipping point. The freight charge on the lumber is $5,000. On July 5, Kauber discovers that $2,000 of the lumber is defective and returns the lumber to Rain Forest. Rain Forest grants a full allowance of $2,000 on the returned lumber. On July 12, Kauber pays for the goods, taking the allowed discount. Kauber also pays the freight charge at this time. Both Kauber and Rain Forest use the gross method of recording purchases and sales.

Required

1. Prepare journal entries for Kauber and for Rain Forest for the purchase/sale.
2. Prepare a schedule showing net purchase cost to Kauber and a schedule showing gross profit for Rain Forest on the purchase/sale.

Demonstration Problem Solution

1.

Kauber

July 3	Purchases	$100,000	
	Freight-in	5,000	
	Accounts payable		$105,000
	(to record purchase)		
July 5	Accounts payable	2,000	
	Purchase returns and allowances		2,000
	(to record return of defective merchandise)		
July 12	Accounts payable	98,000	
	Purchase discounts*		1,960
	Cash		96,040
	(to record payment for purchases)		
July 12	Accounts payable	5,000	
	Cash		5,000
	(to record payment for freight)		

Rain Forest

Accounts receivable	$100,000	
Sales		$100,000
(to record sale)		
Sales returns and allowances	2,000	
Accounts receivable		2,000
(to record return of defective merchandise)		
Cash	96,040	
Sales discounts	1,960	
Accounts receivable		98,000
(to record collection from sales)		

*Discount permitted on net amount owed Rain Forest: (.02 × $98,000 = $1,960)

2.

Kauber

Purchases	$100,000
Plus: Freight-in	5,000
	$105,000
Less: Purchase returns and allowances	2,000
Purchase discounts	1,960
Net purchases	$101,040

Rain Forest

Gross sales	$100,000
Less: Sales returns and allowances	2,000
Sales discounts	1,960
Net sales	$ 96,040

SUMMARY

- Gross profit is of prime importance to merchandising firms and is defined as net sales less cost of goods sold.
- Under the periodic inventory method, inventory values are obtained only at the beginning and end of each accounting period. Purchases are recorded as made in a separate Purchases account and cost of goods sold is computed as beginning inventory, plus net purchases, less ending inventory.
- Under the perpetual inventory method, inventory values can be obtained directly from the Inventory account at any time. Cost of goods sold is determined and recorded for each sale made, and the Inventory account is reduced by this cost. All inventory items purchased are entered directly into the Inventory account.
- Net purchase price of goods is equal to gross price paid or owed, plus any freight paid, less any discounts taken for prompt payment and/or allowances made for returned or defective merchandise.
- Net sales revenue in any time period is equal to gross selling price of merchandise, less any discounts granted to customers for early payment and/or allowances made to customers for returned or defective merchandise.
- F.o.b. destination means the seller pays the freight charges; f.o.b. shipping point means the buyer pays the freight charges.

QUESTIONS

5-1. Both sales and cost of goods sold reflect values for goods sold during the period. Explain.

5-2. How does a periodic inventory system differ from a perpetual inventory system?

5-3. What is a purchase discount, and why is it granted? What is the conceptual relationship of the discount to interest on borrowed money?

5-4. Indicate the major components of total purchase cost for inventory. State whether each increases or decreases the total purchase cost.

5-5. What is the gross profit percentage, and why is it important?

5-6. Both purchase returns and allowances and sales returns and allowances are recorded in separate accounts rather than just being offset against purchases and sales. What information is provided by the use of separate accounts, and how can it help management?

5-7. What is the difference between the selling terms *f.o.b. shipping point* and *f.o.b. destination?*

5-8. What is meant by purchase terms of 2/15, n/45? Why is it important to take all possible discounts?

5-9. What is the difference between gross sales and net sales?

5-10. Define goods available for sale.

EXERCISES

5-E1. During the current year, The Follet Corporation buys merchandise for $100,000. Follet uses the periodic inventory method. Determine the cost of goods sold for each of the following independent cases:

a. Beginning inventory $64,000; ending inventory 0.
b. Beginning inventory $49,000; ending inventory $16,000.
c. Beginning inventory $40,000; ending inventory $76,000.

5-E2. If the Herman Company has a gross profit margin of 40% and sales of $896,000, what is the cost of goods sold?

5-E3. The Zible Company purchases $7,500 of merchandise under terms of 3/10, n/30, on January 5. For each of the following payment dates, indicate the amount of the required payment:

a. January 12
b. January 30

Under the purchase terms, what is the latest date that Zible can delay payment to?

5-E4. The Wiley Company records indicate the following for June 1987:

Beginning inventory	$25,000
Purchases	50,000
Purchase discounts	1,000
Purchase returns and allowances	4,000
Freight-in	3,950

If ending inventory for June is 20% of the gross purchases, determine cost of goods sold for June.

5-E5. For each of the following purchase terms, determine the effective rate of interest if the purchase discount is not taken:

a. 2/10, n/30
b. 3/20, n/30
c. 2/15, n/45
d. 1/20, n/30

5-E6. The Moon Company records indicate the following for July 1986:

Sales	$100,000
Sales returns and allowances	1,000
Sales discounts	5,000
Freight-in	4,000
Purchase discounts	3,000
Purchase returns and allowances	2,000

Determine the net sales for Moon for July 1986.

5-E7. Quip Corporation's gross profit margin is 20%. The following information is available from Quip's records for August:

Purchase returns and allowances	$ 2,000
Purchase discounts	1,800
Beginning inventory	28,000
Ending inventory	19,000
Net sales	250,000

Determine Quip Corporation's gross purchases for August.

PROBLEM SET A

5-A1. Inventory and Net Income Percentage. Beegee Company has the following information for the year ending December 31, 1986:

Beginning inventory	$ 25,000
Ending inventory	27,000
Sales	110,000
Sales returns and allowances	6,000
Sales discounts	2,000
Purchases	64,000
Purchase discounts	3,000
Purchase returns and allowances	2,500
Freight-in	7,200
Selling and administrative expenses	16,500

Required

a. What is the gross profit percentage on net sales?
b. Prepare an income statement for Beegee for 1986.

5-A2. Inventory/Sales/Cost of Goods Sold Relationships. The following information has been taken from the records of Mercury Trading Company for the year ending December 31, 1986:

Beginning inventory	$ 32,000
Sales	400,000
Sales returns and allowances	4,000
Sales discounts	8,000
Net purchases	320,000
Gross profit percentage on net sales	20%

Required

Compute the cost of goods sold and the ending inventory for Mercury Trading for the year ending December 31, 1986.

5-A3. Recording Purchases and Sales. On June 18, 1986, the Olsen Company sells merchandise to the Crowe Company for $150,000, with terms of 2/10, n/60, f.o.b. shipping point. The freight charge is $2,500. On June 22, Crowe discovers that $2,500 of the merchandise is damaged and returns it to Olsen for a full allowance. On June 26, Crowe Company pays for the merchandise as well as the freight bill.

Required

Assume that Crowe takes all discounts to which it is entitled.

a. Prepare journal entries for both Olsen and Crowe for the preceding transactions, assuming both companies

(1) Use the gross method of recording purchases and sales.

(2) Use the net method of recording purchases and sales.

b. If Crowe delays payment until July 10, prepare the payment entry for both Olsen and Crowe, assuming both use the net method of recording purchases/sales.

5-A4. Analysis of Accounts to Determine Sales. The following information has been obtained from the accounting records of the Mangalore Company:

Accounts receivable balance, 12/31/85	$ 62,000
Accounts receivable balance, 12/31/86	56,000
Cash collections during 1986	926,000
Sales returns and allowances for 1986	9,000
Sales discounts for 1986	26,000

Required

If all sales during 1986 are credit sales and all sales are made on account, determine the gross and net sales figures for Mangalore for 1986.

SPREADSHEET PROBLEM

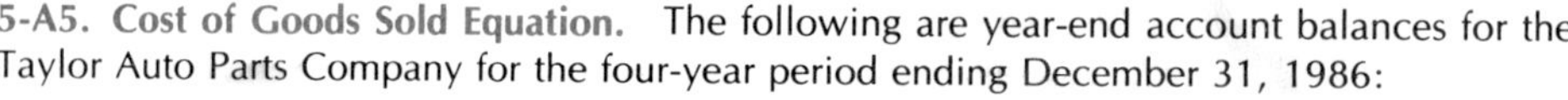

5-A5. Cost of Goods Sold Equation. The following are year-end account balances for the Taylor Auto Parts Company for the four-year period ending December 31, 1986:

	1983	1984	1985	1986
Sales	$250,000	$300,000	(h)	(m)
Less Cost of Goods Sold				
Beginning inventory	25,000	(d)	(i)	(n)
Purchases	275,000	(e)	$400,000	$450,000
Purchase returns and allowances	(a)	50,000	55,000	(o)
Ending inventory	(b)	(f)	(j)	(p)
Cost of Goods Sold	210,000	(g)	(k)	403,000
Gross profit	(c)	25,000	(l)	(q)

The following additional information is available:

1. Sales grow at the rate of 20% per year through 1986.
2. The ending inventory is always equal to 10% of the following year's sales. 1987 sales are expected to be $500,000.

Required

Fill in the unknowns in the above schedule.

5-A6. Discounts and Interest Rates. The Essex Supply Company has not been taking discounts on purchases. The company is considering borrowing the cash needed from a local bank to make payments within the discount period. Essex buys from a number of different vendors with different purchase terms as follows:

Vendor	Terms
A	3/10,n/30
B	2/20,n/30
C	1/10,n/60
D	3/15,n/40
E	3/20,n/60
F	1/10,n/40

Required

If Essex can borrow money from the local bank at an annual interest rate of 14%, determine for each vendor whether the money should be borrowed to make the payments within the discount period.

5-A7. Comprehensive Review. Consider each of the following independent cases:

	A	B	C
Assets, beginning of year	(a)	$100,000	(o)
Assets, end of year	$110,000	(h)	$150,000
Liabilities, beginning of year	40,000	60,000	20,000
Liabilities, end of year	50,000	70,000	(p)
Owners' equity, beginning of year	40,000	(i)	(q)
Owners' equity, end of year	(b)	(j)	70,000
Inventory, beginning of year	20,000	30,000	(r)
Inventory, end of year	(c)	(k)	60,000
Sales	(d)	70,000	60,000
Sales returns and allowances	2,000	0	(s)
Purchases	40,000	40,000	75,000
Purchase discounts	0	2,000	0
Freight-in	4,000	0	0
Cost of goods available for sale	(e)	(l)	95,000
Cost of goods sold	40,000	(m)	(t)
Gross profit	(f)	25,000	(u)
Selling and administrative expenses	7,000	(n)	5,000
Net income	10,000	20,000	20,000
Additional investment by owners	(g)	0	20,000
Dividends	0	0	10,000

Required

Fill in the unknowns in each of the preceding cases.

PROBLEM SET B

5-B1. Inventory and Net Income Percentage. B. G. Company learns that its store manager has been stealing inventory. On December 31, 1986, the company takes inventory and determines that $26,000 is on hand. Other account balances from the company's books on December 31 are as follows:

Inventory (January 1, 1986)	$ 28,000
Purchases	68,000
Purchase returns and allowances	2,000
Freight-in	4,000
Sales	101,000
Sales returns and allowances	1,000

Required

a. If the normal gross profit percentage on net sales is 35%, how much has the manager stolen?
b. If selling and administrative expenses are $14,500, prepare an income statement for the year ending December 31, 1986.

5-B2. Inventory/Sales/Cost of Goods Sold Relationships. The following information is from the books of Hightail Industries for the month of October:

Purchases	$140,000
Purchase discounts	10,000
Purchase returns and allowances	4,000
Freight-in	20,000
Sales returns and allowances	15,000
Sales discounts	6,000
Inventory, October 31	35,000
Cost of goods sold	150,000

Required

Compute the gross sales for October and October 1 inventory for Hightail Industries if the gross profit percentage is 25% of net sales.

5-B3. Recording Purchases and Sales. On June 26, 1986, Weilnau, Inc., purchases $120,000 of roofing materials from the Lyon Company. The terms of this sale are 3/15, n/30, f.o.b. destination. Lyon Company receives an invoice from Lar's Transportation for $1,000 on June 28, with terms of n/20. On June 29, Weilnau discovers that $4,000 of the goods are damaged. Lyon grants a full allowance for the damaged goods and lets Weilnau keep the goods. On July 7, Weilnau pays for the goods. Lyon pays the freight charge on July 7.

Required

Assume that Weilnau takes all discounts to which it is entitled.
a. Prepare journal entries for the preceding transactions for both Weilnau and Lyon, assuming that both companies
(1) Use the gross method of recording sales and purchases.
(2) Use the net method of recording sales and purchases.
b. If Weilnau delays payment until July 20, prepare the payment entry for both Weilnau and Lyon, assuming both use the net method of recording purchases and sales.

5-B4. Analysis of Accounts to Determine Sales. The following information is from the books of the DRT Corporation:

Accounts receivable, June 1	$45,000
Accounts receivable, June 30	70,000
Cash collections on account during June	50,000
Sales discounts during June	10,000
Sales returns during June	5,000

Required

If the only entries to accounts recéivable are related to sales, determine the gross and net sales dollars for June.

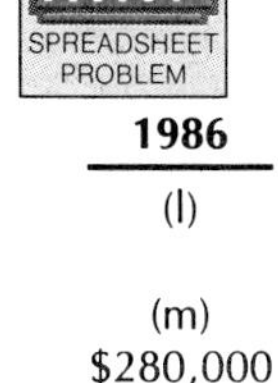

5-B5. Cost of Goods Sold Equation. The following are year-end account balances for the Hartley Baseball Supply Company for the four-year period ending December 31, 1986:

	1983	1984	1985	1986
Sales	(a)	$330,000	(h)	(l)
Less Cost of Goods Sold				
Beginning inventory	(b)	100,000	$120,000	(m)
Purchases	$190,000	(e)	(i)	$280,000
Purchase returns and allowances	5,000	7,000	10,000	(n)
Ending inventory	(c)	(f)	(j)	(o)
Cost of Goods Sold	(d)	220,000	(k)	249,300
Gross profit	70,000	(g)	120,000	(p)

The following additional information is available:

1. Sales grow at the rate of 10% per year through 1987.
2. The ending inventory in 1985 and 1986 is equal to one-third of 1986 and expected 1987 sales, respectively.

Required

Complete the unknowns in the above schedule.

5-B6. Discounts and Interest Rates. Sunny Landscape Supply has not been taking discounts on purchases. The company is considering borrowing the cash needed from a local bank to make the early payments. Several different suppliers give Sunny different purchase terms. The following purchase terms have been gathered from Sunny's records:

1. 2/10,n/30
2. 3/10,n/30
3. 3/15,n/40
4. 3/20,n/60
5. 3/10,n/60
6. 1/10,n/60

Required

If the company can borrow money from the local bank at an annual interest rate of 16%, determine for each case whether or not it should do so to make the payment within the discount period.

5-B7. Comprehensive Review. Consider each of the following independent cases:

	A	B	C
Assets, beginning of year	$ 75,000	$100,000	(o)
Assets, end of year	(a)	150,000	(p)
Liabilities, beginning of year	(b)	20,000	$ 75,000
Liabilities, end of year	50,000	(h)	100,000
Owners' equity, beginning of year	45,000	(i)	50,000
Owners' equity, end of year	(c)	85,000	(q)
Inventory, beginning of year	50,000	(j)	45,000
Inventory, end of year	45,000	35,000	(r)
Sales	100,000	165,000	(s)
Sales returns and allowances	0	15,000	25,000
Purchases	(d)	100,000	110,000
Purchase discounts	0	10,000	15,000
Freight-in	0	20,000	5,000
Cost of goods available for sale	(e)	(k)	(t)
Cost of goods sold	(f)	(l)	115,000
Gross profit	(g)	40,000	60,000
Selling and administrative expenses	10,000	(m)	25,000
Net income	20,000	12,000	(u)
Additional investment by owners	10,000	0	25,000
Dividends	0	(n)	18,000

Required

Fill in the unknowns.

THE SELLING CYCLE: RECEIVABLES AND PAYABLES

CHAPTER OBJECTIVES

After studying Chapter 6, you should understand the following:

1. The nature of accounts payable and accounts receivable.
2. The nature of notes payable and notes receivable.
3. Interest computations.
4. The nature of uncollectible accounts and their impact on income.
5. The major methods of determining the amounts of uncollectible accounts and the accounting associated with each.

Chapter 5 described purchases and sales of goods in a merchandising firm. Most purchases and sales are made on credit, giving rise to accounts payable and accounts receivable, respectively. This chapter continues the selling cycle by examining accounts payable and accounts receivable.

Accounts receivable and accounts payable are short-term or current assets and liabilities. Notes receivable and notes payable are more formal kinds of liabilities and assets and can be either short-term or long-term. The chapter examines these more formal kinds of assets and liabilities. Methods of computing interest, determining uncollectible accounts, and calculating discounted notes are presented along with the related effects on expense and revenue. The transactions are illustrated with T-accounts and journal entries.

ACCOUNTS PAYABLE

ACCOUNTS PAYABLE
Future obligations to remit cash to suppliers for previous purchases.

Accounts payable represent obligations to remit cash in the future to suppliers for prior purchases. Since the obligation to pay cash usually follows the purchase date rather closely, accounts payable are considered short-term obligations or current liabilities.

Accounts payable need to be recognized in the books as soon as ownership to the goods purchased passes from the seller to the buyer and the obligation to pay is created.

Valuation of Accounts Payable

Accounts payable are initially valued by reference to the price of goods purchased. For example, if the invoice amount (purchase price) for goods is $280, the account payable associated with this purchase is valued at $280. Until the purchaser remits cash to the seller for goods purchased, the seller is extending the assets as a form of loan to the purchaser.

Bookkeeping for Accounts Payable

If the Graybill Electronics Company purchases $1,000 of radios on open account, the purchase would be recorded in the accounting system as follows:

Purchases	1,000	
Accounts payable		1,000
(to record merchandise purchased on account)		

When Graybill remits cash to its supplier or, as is usually stated, when the account is paid, the liability is satisfied and is removed from the books as follows:

Accounts payable	1,000	
Cash		1,000
(to record payment on account)		

Note that payment represents the use of an asset (cash) to satisfy a liability. The payment to the seller is just like the repayment of a loan to a bank. Because neither revenue nor expense is affected, this payment of cash does not affect income.

Selling terms frequently include a provision requiring the purchaser to pay specific amounts of interest to the seller if payment is not made by the specified due date. **Interest** can be defined as a fee charged for the use of money for a period of time and is often stated as a percentage of the amount of money being used. A very common interest rate on unpaid accounts is 1.5 percent per month on the unpaid balance. This interest charge of 18 percent per year (1.5 percent × 12) begins to accumulate the first day after the agreed-upon accounts payable due date and continues until payment is finally made. This interest fee is recognized as a separate interest expense and is not considered to be part of the cost of goods purchased.

INTEREST
Fee charged for the use of money for a period of time.

Assume that the Graybill Company purchases $20,000 of wiring supplies with payment due 30 days after purchase with payment of interest at the rate of 1.5 percent per month due on any unpaid amounts after 30 days. Graybill is short on cash and does not pay the supplier until 60 days after making the purchase. At that time, Graybill would owe $20,000 plus interest for one month. The interest would be computed as follows (1.5 percent per month equals 18 percent per year):

$$\$20,000 \times .18 \times 1/12 = \$300$$

The payment would be recorded and interest expense recognized by Graybill as follows:

Accounts payable	20,000	
Interest expense	300	
Cash		20,300
(to record payment on account and interest)		

NOTES PAYABLE

A **note payable** is a liability represented by a written and signed promise to pay a stated amount of money at a stated time or upon demand, either with or without interest. Such a written promise is called a **promissory note** and can be short-term or long-term, depending upon its due date. More often than not, explicit payment of interest is required by a promissory note.

NOTE PAYABLE
A liability represented by a written and signed promise to pay a stated amount of money at a stated time or upon demand, either without interest or with a stated interest rate.

PROMISSORY NOTE
See Note Payable.

Notes payable can be created when a firm borrows short-term funds from a bank or negotiated as part of the original terms of sale, particularly if the buyer is making an unusually large purchase that might require a longer than normal payment period.

Sometimes when a purchaser cannot pay an account payable on the due date, the seller will insist on conversion of the account payable to a note payable. Such conversions provide a higher degree of legal protection for the seller. If Graybill were to convert its $20,000 account payable to a $20,000 note payable, the company would make the following entry to reflect the conversion:

Accounts payable	20,000	
Notes payable		20,000
(to record conversion of accounts payable to notes payable)		

BORROWER
One who borrows assets, usually cash.

MAKER OF A NOTE PAYABLE
A person who receives a loan of assets, usually cash, giving a promissory note in exchange.

PAYER
One who provides payment.

DUE DATE
The specified time when repayment on a note is due.

LENDER
One who lends resources, usually cash, to another.

CREDITOR
Lender of assets to a business.

PAYEE
One who receives payment.

TERM OF A NOTE
The period of time between the date on which borrowing occurs and the repayment date.

MATURITY VALUE
Total amount to be paid on a note. Includes both principal and interest.

Promissory Note Terminology

The firm or person making or signing a promissory note is known as the **borrower/maker/payer.** The borrower receives a loan of assets, usually cash, and promises to repay the loan to the other party at a specified future time (the **due date**).

The party providing the resources to the borrower in return for the borrower's promise to repay the same amount in the future, plus an additional interest fee for the use of the resources, is known as the **lender/creditor/payee.** The period of time between the date on which the borrowing occurs and the repayment date is known as the **term of a note.** The total amount paid (interest plus principal) is called the **maturity value** of the note.

Exhibit 6.1 is an example of a note payable made by Graybill, assuming that the company had borrowed $20,000 from the First National Bank of Example City on May 9, 1987.

Due Date

The due date of a promissory note must be precise. If the term of the note is expressed in months or years, the note is due on the same day as made in the appropriate month or year. Thus, a note made on November 23, 1986, and due in one year is due on November 23, 1987. If the term of the note is expressed in days, the days must be counted exactly. The day the note is made is excluded, but the due date is counted. Graybill's note made on May 9, 1987, to be repaid in 90 days is due on August 7, 1987, determined as follows:

Month	Number of Days
May (31 − 9)	22
June	30
July	31
August	7
Total	90

A Closer Look at Interest

To fully understand the accounting for borrowed funds, one must thoroughly understand interest and its computation. The dollar amount of interest is based on three things:

PRINCIPAL
The original amount of money borrowed or invested.

FACE VALUE
The amount of money stated on a debt or investment instrument as the total owed or invested.

1. The amount of money borrowed **(principal,** or **face value).**
2. The interest rate charged, expressed as an annual rate unless otherwise stated.
3. The time period of the loan.

The interest computation can be expressed as a formula:

$$\text{Interest} = \text{Principal} \times \text{Rate} \times \text{Time}$$

Interest Conventions. Consider the Graybill note for $20,000. Principal and interest at the rate of 12 percent are to be paid at the end of 90 days. The amount of interest payable at the end of the 90-day period is determined as follows:

$$\text{Interest} = \text{Principal} \times \text{Rate} \times \text{Time}$$

$$\text{Interest} = \$20{,}000 \times .12 \times 90/360 = \$600$$

EXHIBIT 6.1

Commercial Loan Note
Note Number 30010

First National Bank
Example City, California

lender/creditor/payee → FOR VALUE RECEIVED, the undersigned, jointly and severally if more than one, promise to pay to the order of FIRST NATIONAL BANK OF EXAMPLE CITY at its main office the sum of:

twenty thousand & 00/100----------------Dollars

(hereinafter called the "Principal Sum") together with interest as hereinafter provided. The undersigned promise to pay the Principal Sum and the interest thereon as hereinafter provided

term of the note → 90 days after May 9, 1987.

RATE OF INTEREST. Percentage Rate--Prior to maturity, the unpaid balance of the Principal Sum shall bear interest at the

interest rate → rate of twelve percent (12.00%) per annum. If the obligation evidenced by this note shall not be paid at maturity, whether maturity occurs by lapse of time or by acceleration, the unpaid portion of the Principal Sum and any unpaid interest shall, thereafter until paid, bear interest at the rate of twelve percent (12.00%) per annum.

borrower/maker/payer → The Graybill Company

by ____________________ May 9, 1987

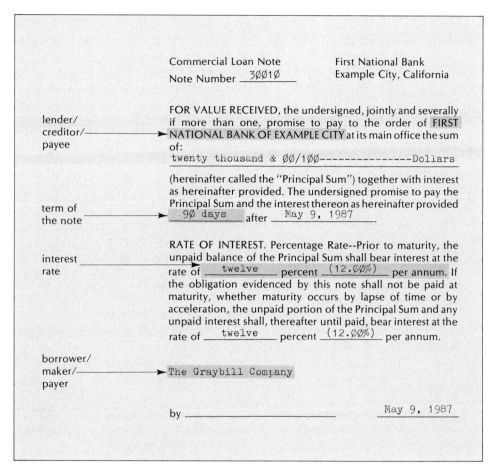

Note that a year was considered to consist of 360 days for interest computation purposes. Basing interest computations on a 360-day year (with 30-day months) is known as the ordinary method. Interest computations can also be based on a 365-day year (the exact method). Unless otherwise stated, all examples and problems in this chapter assume a 360-day year with respect to interest determination on notes payable.

Timing of Interest Recognition. Although interest expense accumulates continuously, journal entries to recognize the expense are made only at reasonable intervals: when the note payable is created, at the end of any accounting period when interest is accrued but remains unpaid, and when the note is paid.

when created
at end of acct. period
when paid

Assume that Graybill's fiscal year ends on June 30. Note that 52 days (22 + 30) will have elapsed by the end of the fiscal year. If payment is made on the due date, Graybill's bookkeeping system would trace the life cycle of the note as follows:

1. When Graybill borrows the money:

May 9	Cash	20,000	
	Notes payable		20,000
	(to record borrowing money by note)		

2. At the end of Graybill's fiscal year to state the Interest Expense and Interest Payable accounts at their appropriate year-end balances:

June 30	Interest expense	347	
	(20,000 × .12 × 52/360)		
	Interest payable		347
	(to record accrued interest—an adjusting entry)		

3. To record the repayment of the note, payment of the interest owed, and the interest expense since the last year-end date:

Aug. 7	Notes payable	20,000	
	Interest payable	347	
	Interest expense	253	
	(20,000 × .12 × 38/360)		
	Cash		20,600
	(to record repayment of note and interest)		

Defaulted Notes

DEFAULT
Term applied when repayment of a debt is not made on or before the due date.

If repayment is not made on or before the due date, the note is said to be in **default.** If an overdue note has not been paid by the end of the accounting year, the existence of notes in default should be disclosed in the financial statements.

Discounted Notes

ORDINARY NOTE
See Interest-Bearing Note.

INTEREST-BEARING NOTE
A note where interest is added to the face amount of the note to determine the total owed at the due date.

DISCOUNTED NOTE
See Noninterest-Bearing Note.

NONINTEREST-BEARING NOTE
Notes where the face value includes the interest and the maturity value of the note is equal to the face amount.

Thus far the discussion has been limited to straightforward notes payable. A note payable where the interest is added to the face amount of the note to determine the total owed at the due date is called an **ordinary,** or **interest-bearing, note.**

As an alternative, the interest can be deducted from the amount borrowed before the borrower receives the money. The borrower, in effect, pays the interest in advance. Although all notes bear interest, those where the principal or face value includes the interest and the maturity value is equal to the principal amount are known as **discounted,** or **noninterest-bearing, notes.**

Assume that Graybill borrows $20,000 but that the note is a discounted note with a maturity value of $20,000. Graybill would receive $19,400, computed as follows:

Face value of the note	$20,000
Less: Interest due at maturity (.12 × $20,000 × 90/360)	600
Amount received by borrower	$19,400

The amount to be repaid at maturity is $20,000. The interest deducted in advance is known as a discount on the note payable and is recorded separately. Over the life of the note, the discount will be recognized as interest as follows:

May 9	Cash	19,400	
	Discount on notes payable	600	
	Notes payable		20,000
	(to record borrowing money by note)		

June 30	Interest expense	347	
	(.12 × $20,000 × 52/360)		
	Discount on notes payable		347
	(to record accrued interest—a year-end adjusting entry)		

Aug. 8	Notes payable	20,000	
	Interest expense	253	
	(.12 × $20,000 × 38/360)		
	Discount on notes payable		253
	Cash		20,000
	(to record payment of note)		

The process of recognizing the discount as interest expense over the life of the note is known as amortization of the discount. Discounting of notes has the effect of increasing the real, or effective, rate of interest paid, since the borrower never has the use of the full principal amount of the loan. The effective, or real, rate of interest of the preceding discounted note is 12.36 percent as follows:

Interest rate paid for 90 days (600/19,400)	3.09%
Times number of 90-day periods in one year	4
Annual effective rate of interest	12.36%

The Discount on Notes Payable is a contra-account to the Notes Payable account. If financial statements were prepared on June 30, Graybill would show the remaining discount on notes payable ($600 − $347 = $253) as an offset to notes payable as follows:

Notes payable	$20,000
Less: Discount on notes payable	253
Net notes payable	$19,747

OTHER PAYABLES

Short-term liabilities are not limited to accounts payable or notes payable. Many other kinds of payables arise in conducting the day-to-day operations of a business. Such liabilities fall into two general categories: those that are definite in amount and those that can only be estimated.

CONCEPT SUMMARY 6.1 NOTES PAYABLE TERMINOLOGY

TERM	MEANING
Borrower/maker/payer	The individual or firm that borrows the money.
Lender/creditor/payee	The lender of the money.
Principal, or face value	The amount of money borrowed.
Term of a note	The length of time between borrowing and the required repayment of the money.
Due date, or maturity date	The date on which repayment is required.
Maturity value	The total amount, including interest, owed on the due date.
Defaulted note	A note not repaid when due.
Ordinary, or interest-bearing, note	Interest is added to the amount borrowed, and the total interest plus principal is repaid at the due date.
Discounted, or noninterest-bearing note	Interest is deducted from the principal amount borrowed, and the total principal repaid on the due date includes interest.

Payroll Liabilities

The payroll cycle gives rise to several of the first type of payables, including wages, withholding taxes, FICA taxes, and union dues. Chapter 8 discusses the payroll process and associated liabilities.

Estimated Liabilities

Estimated liabilities are recorded when a company knows that a future payment is required and has a reasonable basis for estimating the amount but does not know the exact amount. Examples of payables that can only be estimated include income taxes (where the exact payment cannot be determined until taxable income is known at year-end), property taxes (where the exact payment cannot be known until all property valuations and tax levies are known), and product warranty liability (where exact payments cannot be known until goods are sold to customers and product failures occur).

Proper matching of expense with revenue requires that such liabilities be currently estimated and recognized, because each liability represents an obligation arising from current revenue-producing operations. A company must use its historical experience and any other pertinent data to make its estimates of such liabilities. Methods vary, and detailed discussion of each is best left to more advanced study of accounting.

CONTINGENT LIABILITIES
Liabilities that arise from past activities where future outcomes and amounts owed are uncertain.

ACCOUNTS RECEIVABLE
Amounts owed to an entity by customers from past credit sales.

Contingent Liabilities

A class of potential liabilities exists called **contingent liabilities**—those that arise from past activities where future outcomes and amounts owed are uncertain. For example, a lawsuit might or might not result in a firm's having to pay damages to those bringing the suit. Such contingent liabilities are not formally entered into the accounting records unless two conditions are met:

1. Available information indicates a likelihood that either an asset has been impaired or a liability has been incurred.
2. The amount of the impairment or liability can be reasonably estimated.

If these conditions are met, the contingent liability must be formally recorded in the financial statements. In other cases, footnote disclosure of the potential liability is sufficient.

ACCOUNTS RECEIVABLE

Accounts receivable are amounts owed to the entity by customers from past credit sales. The receivables are short-term, since they will normally be converted to cash within one year or one accounting cycle.

Credit card sales might or might not create accounts receivable. In the case of bank credit cards, sales are almost equivalent to cash sales. The seller takes the credit card slips to the bank and receives an immediate addition to the business's bank account, less whatever fees are associated with the use of the credit card.

In the case of nonbank cards, such as American Express or Diner's Club, customer use of the cards results in a receivable until payment is received from the credit card firm. This receivable is normally carried in a separate account from other accounts receivable, perhaps titled Due from Credit Card Company, or something similar.

Health Hazards and Accounting Information

In the early 1980s, new information suggested a health hazard existed from exposure to asbestos dust. One outcome of these findings was the creation of large amounts of contingent liabilities for companies that had been suppliers of asbestos-inclusive products. As an example, Eagle-Pricher Industries supplied the following information to its 1984 annual report as part of a contingent liabilities footnote:

. . . Because of the uncertainties associated with this litigation a reasonable estimate of the Company's ultimate liability cannot be made at this time. Therefore, no such liability has been recorded in the financial statements. However, the Company's share of the current cost of this litigation . . . is expensed as incurred. While the impact of the litigation on earnings is significant, the Company does not feel that it will materially affect its financial stability.

Valuation of Accounts Receivable and Bad Debts

Accounts receivable are initially valued at an amount equal to the selling price of goods purchased by customers. However, it is difficult and costly to get 100 percent payment from all customers, and not all accounts receivable are collected. Sooner or later the uncollectible amounts, often called bad debts, must be determined, with appropriate adjustments made to both income and accounts receivable.

Timing of the Bad Debt Adjustment

Two approaches to accounting recognition of the amount of bad debts resulting from credit sales are the direct write-off method and the allowance method.

Direct Write-off Method. Under the **direct write-off method,** recognition of the amount of bad debts is delayed until evidence appears of noncollectibility of customer accounts. Because evidence showing that an account cannot be collected is usually discovered in an accounting period subsequent to the one in which the original credit sale was made, net income can be overstated in the period of the sale and understated in the period of discovery. In addition, the balance in the Accounts Receivable account on the statement of financial position at the end of the period in which the sale occurred will be higher than the amount that will be ultimately collected. As a result, the direct write-off method of accounting for bad debts is normally not allowed under generally accepted accounting principles.

DIRECT WRITE-OFF METHOD
A bookkeeping procedure where bad debt expense is not recognized until evidence of noncollectibility of customer accounts appears.

Allowance Method. The **allowance method** requires that an estimate of the bad debts be made in the same period in which credit sales giving rise to bad debts are made. In this way, both income and the amount of the accounts receivable to be collected (the net realizable value of the accounts receivable) will be more accurate both in the period of sale and in subsequent time periods. In general, the **net**

ALLOWANCE METHOD
A bookkeeping procedure where estimates of bad debts are made in the same period in which the credit sales giving rise to the bad debts are made.

NET REALIZABLE VALUE
The amount of future cash inflows that an asset is expected to generate.

realizable value of an asset is the amount of future cash inflows the asset is expected to produce.

Assume the following facts with respect to Hyperspace, Inc:

	1986	1987
Total credit sales made	$1,000,000	$2,000,000
Operating and selling expense other than bad debts	500,000	700,000
Year-end total accounts receivable balance	300,000	

During 1987, it becomes apparent that three percent of the 1986 credit sales ($30,000) will not be collected. This means that total revenue for 1986 is really only $970,000 rather than the $1,000,000 recorded as credit sales are made. Exhibit 6.2 compares the impact of the foregoing information on income and accounts receivable under the direct write-off and allowance methods of recognizing bad debts.

Although the total combined income for 1986 and 1987 is the same in either case ($1,770,000), the incomes considered for the two years taken individually more closely reflect the results of operations of those years under the allowance method. Further, as the exhibit shows, the use of the allowance method of estimating bad debts provides a year-end accounts receivable balance that more closely reflects future cash collection expectations.

The Concept of Bad Debts as an Expense

BAD DEBT EXPENSE
The estimated amount of uncollectible accounts for a given time period.

As Exhibit 6.2 shows, the estimated amount of uncollectible accounts is recorded and presented under an expense label such as **Bad Debt Expense.** Although this presentation is conventional, it is not conceptually correct. Recall from Chapter 5 that one condition required for revenue recognition is that collection of the sales price in cash must ultimately be expected. Because bad debts represents the amount of sales for which collection is not expected, the estimation and recognition of bad

EXHIBIT 6.2

	Direct Write-off 1986 Bad Debts Recognized in 1987		Allowance Method 1986 Bad Debts Recognized in 1986	
	1986	1987	1986	1987
Recorded sales	$1,000,000	$2,000,000	$1,000,000	$2,000,000
Less: Other exp.	500,000	700,000	500,000	700,000
Bad debt expense	—	30,000	30,000	—
Net income	$ 500,000	$1,270,000	$ 470,000	$1,300,000
Real net income—bad debts matched with sales that produced them	$ 470,000	$1,300,000	$ 470,000	$1,300,000
Income over/(under) stated	$ 30,000	$ (30,000)	$ 0	$ 0
Gross accounts rec. 12/31	$ 300,000		$ 300,000	
Less: Expected bad debts	0		30,000	
Net realizable value	$ 300,000		$ 270,000	
Amount actually collected	270,000		270,000	
Error in year-end balance	$ 30,000		$ 0	

debts are, conceptually, nothing more than an adjustment to obtain a more correct revenue figure for the income statement and to value accounts receivable at their net realizable amount. Conceptually, to get net sales, the amount of the bad debts estimated for each accounting period should be subtracted from gross sales (just like sales discounts and sales returns and allowances). In thinking about the following materials dealing with the specifics of bad debt "expense" recognition, it might be helpful to keep in mind the unique nature of the "expense."

Estimating Uncollectible Accounts

We cannot determine in advance which specific accounts will become uncollectible. If we knew which customers were not going to pay, we would not sell to them on credit. A general estimate of the dollar amount that will eventually be written off as uncollectible is therefore required.

Because the estimate of bad debts has implications for both the income statement and the statement of financial position, the adjustment required under the allowance method can be determined by analysis of either credit sales or accounts receivable. Basing the estimate of bad debt expense on past credit sales experience is known as the **percentage of sales method.** Basing the estimate on past collection experience for accounts receivable is known as the **aging of accounts receivable method.** The choice made between these two approaches to determining the appropriate adjustment for uncollectible credit sales can produce different adjustment amounts as explained in the following sections.

PERCENTAGE OF SALES METHOD
A method of estimating bad debt expense where the estimate is based on past credit sales experience.

AGING OF ACCOUNTS RECEIVABLE METHOD
A method of estimating bad debts expense where the estimate is based on past collection experience for accounts receivable.

Percentage of Sales Method. Under the percentage of sales method, a business firm would look to its own past experience in credit sales, experience figures for its industry, and future economic predictions to make an estimate of the percentage of current credit sales that will prove uncollectible. Using the percentage of credit sales figure thus developed, it becomes an easy matter to make an appropriate adjustment at the end of the accounting period to record an estimate of uncollectible amounts.

Assume that Hyperspace had credit sales during 1987 of $1,000,000. Hyperspace estimates that one percent of all credit sales will prove uncollectible. The appropriate adjustment for bad debt "expense" and reduction in gross accounts receivable is, therefore, $10,000 ($1,000,000 × .01). Under the allowance method of recording bad debt estimates, the appropriate bookkeeping entry would be as follows:

Bad debt expense	10,000	
Allowance for uncollectible accounts		10,000
(to record a bad debt estimate of 1% of credit sales)		

Like other expenses, bad debt expense becomes part of the 1987 income statement, and the allowance for uncollectible accounts is shown on the statement of financial position as a contra-account to Accounts Receivable. Netting the Allowance account against Accounts Receivable reduces Accounts Receivable to its net realizable value without affecting any specific customer accounts.

Suppose Hyperspace had the following relevant account balances before making any adjustments for estimated uncollectible accounts in 1987:

Accounts Receivable		Allowance for Uncollectible Accounts		Bad Debt Expense	
99,000			500	0	

The balances in the relevant accounts after making the adjustment for 1987 bad debts are as follows:

Accounts Receivable		Allowance for Uncollectible Accounts			Bad Debt Expense	
99,000			500	Bal. before adj.	0	
			10,000	Adj.	10,000	
			10,500	Bal. after adj.	10,000	

Under the percentage of sales method, the bad debt amount is determined solely by an analysis of credit sales on the income statement. With this income statement focus, the preadjustment balance in the allowance for uncollectible accounts is not considered in determining the amount of bad debts. The net realizable value of accounts receivable on the statement of financial position is simply a function of the bad debt expense determined by reference to credit sales. The balance in the allowance for uncollectible accounts is usually different in amount from bad debts expense on the income statement.

Aging of Accounts Receivable Method. Aging of accounts receivable is accomplished by examining the accounts receivable and listing each account according to how long it has been outstanding. Exhibit 6.3 is an example of such an aging schedule for Hyperspace's December 31, 1987, accounts receivable.

Based on past experience and future economic predictions, Hyperspace estimates the percentage of accounts receivable within each age category that it is not likely to collect. Applying the determined percentages to the total dollar amount of receivable found within each age category provides an estimate of the total dollar amount of the accounts receivable that will probably not be collected. Exhibit 6.4 demonstrates the development of the dollar estimate of accounts deemed uncollectible from the aging schedule presented in Exhibit 6.3. Percentages are assumed for illustrative purposes.

Again assume that the relevant account balances for Hyperspace before making any adjustments for bad debts in 1987 are as previously shown. Given that $8,800 of

EXHIBIT 6.3

Aging Schedule for Accounts Receivable

			Number of Days Past Due				
Customer	**Total**	**Not Yet Due**	**1–30**	**31–60**	**61–90**	**91–180**	**over 180**
Ace	$ 4,000					$4,000	
Drake	3,000						$3,000
Long	5,000				$5,000		
Tipton	15,000		$15,000				
Others	72,000	$25,000	20,000	$20,000	4,000	2,000	1,000
Totals	$99,000	$25,000	$35,000	$20,000	$9,000	$6,000	$4,000

EXHIBIT 6.4

Age of Accounts Days Past Due	Amount	% Estimated Uncollectible	Amount Estimated Uncollectible
Over 180 days	$ 4,000	75%	$3,000
91–180 days	6,000	35	2,100
61–90 days	9,000	15	1,350
31–60 days	20,000	10	2,000
1–30 days	35,000	1	350
not yet due	25,000	—	—
Totals	$99,000		$8,800

accounts receivable is estimated to be uncollectible, the appropriate adjustment for bad debts would be as follows:

	Debit	Credit
Bad debt expense	8,300	
Allowance for uncollectible accounts		8,300
(to record estimated bad debt amount)		

Relevant account balances after the adjustment is made are as follows:

Accounts Receivable		Allowance for Uncollectible Accounts			Bad Debt Expense	
99,000			500	Bal. before adjustment	0	
			8,300	Adj.	8,300	
			8,800	Bal. after adj.	8,300	

Under the aging of accounts receivable method, the bad debt amount is determined solely by analysis of accounts receivable. The final balance in the Allowance account must equal the estimated total of uncollectible accounts receivable. As previously shown, the amount of the adjustment is determined by subtracting the preadjustment balance in the allowance for uncollectible accounts from the total amount of accounts receivable projected as uncollectible. The aging of accounts receivable method focuses solely on the valuation of accounts receivable, making the bad debts expense shown on the income statement a function of the adjustment necessary to state accounts receivable at their net realizable value.

Writing Off an Uncollectible Account

The judgment that an individual account receivable is actually worthless is usually based on circumstantial evidence. How long the account has been outstanding, whether the customer is still a customer, and the general financial health of the customer are all factors to be considered. At any rate, at some point the judgment will be made that certain specific accounts are worthless and should be removed from the books.

Assume that the Hyperspace Company has the following balances in its accounts receivable and in its allowance for uncollectible accounts:

Accounts Receivable			Allowance for Uncollectible Accounts	
99,000				8,300

Further assume that John Black, one of Hyperspace's customers, declares bankruptcy and owes Hyperspace $1,000, and it appears that Hyperspace will not be able to collect any of Black's account. At this point, Black's account should be removed from the books. The entry that will remove John Black's $1,000 account from Hyperspace's books is as follows:

Allowance for uncollectible accounts	1,000	
Accounts receivable		1,000
(to write off John Black's worthless account)		

The ledger accounts after the write-off would appear as follows:

Accounts Receivable			Allowance for Uncollectible Accounts		
99,000				8,300	Balances before write-off
	1,000	Write-off	1,000		
98,000				7,300	Balances after write-off

Note that the net accounts receivable balance both before and after the write-off is $90,700. The write-off does not change either the net accounts receivable balance or the bad debt expense under the allowance method of estimating bad debts, because the earlier estimate for uncollectibles is deemed to have covered this specific write-off as well as all others.

Occasionally a customer pays an account already written off. Assume that John Black later pays $300 on his account. Hyperspace must restore John Black's account. The account can be restored for either the total amount originally owed or for just the amount of the payment if no further payments are expected. Assuming that the $300 payment is all that Hyperspace expects to ever receive from Black on his account, the restoration would be as follows:

Accounts receivable	300	
Allowance for uncollectible accounts		300
(to restore part of an account previously written off)		

The $300 payment can now be routinely recorded as follows:

Cash	300	
Accounts receivable		300
(to record collection on account)		

The preceding process of restoring an account previously written off when a payment is received and then recording the payment provides a complete record of all of the events surrounding Black's account.

Credit Considerations and Bad Debt Losses

The amount of credit sales that will prove uncollectible is a function of several things: the credit policies of the seller, the collection practices of the seller, and general economic conditions.

It is possible for a firm to have credit policies so restrictive that sales are unnecessarily limited and potential profits are lost. It is equally possible to have credit policies so loose that although very few sales are turned away, the loss on uncollectible accounts exceeds the profits gained through additional sales.

The longer an account is outstanding, the more difficult collection becomes. Collection procedures that recognize this fact and that consistently monitor accounts receivable so that appropriate action can be taken early will help prevent accounts from becoming uncollectible.

NOTES RECEIVABLE

Notes receivable represent formal loans to other entities and are the lender's side of notes payable. Notes receivable are assets. If the note is due to be paid within a year or within one operating cycle (whichever is longer), it is a current asset. Otherwise, it is a long-term asset.

NOTES RECEIVABLE
Represent formal loans to other entities.

Bookkeeping for Notes Receivable

When a promissory note is received, both the note and the assets given up in return must be recorded. Suppose that on November 1, the Patton Company loans $1,000 to the Post Company for 90 days, with an interest rate of 12 percent. Patton would record the note receivable as follows:

Nov. 1	Notes receivable	1,000	
	Cash		1,000
	(to record issuance of note receivable)		

As with notes payable, interest accumulates continuously on notes receivable but is recorded only at discrete intervals, usually when the note is repaid or financial statements are prepared. On December 31, Patton wishes to prepare financial statements. To correctly state revenue and asset values for the period then ending, interest revenue that has been earned must be recognized. The interest earned by Patton as of December 31 is $20 ($1,000 × .12 × 60/360) and is recognized as follows:

Dec. 31	Interest receivable	20	
	Interest revenue		20
	(to record interest revenue through December 31)		

When the note is paid on January 30, the due date, Patton records the receipt of the cash from the collection of the interest receivable established on December 31, the interest revenue earned during the month of January, and collection of the note itself.

Jan. 30	Cash	1,030	
	Interest receivable		20
	Interest revenue		10
	Notes receivable		1,000
	(to record collection of note and interest)		

Unless a company's primary business is the lending of money, interest revenue from notes receivable is generally considered incidental to operations and is classed as other revenue or nonoperating revenue on the income statement.

Dishonored Notes Receivable

DISHONORED NOTE
A note receivable that is not paid when due.

If a note is not paid when due, the note is in default and is called a **dishonored note** by the lender. The interest revenue has nevertheless been earned and is recognized in the accounts. The note and associated interest earned are usually reclassified as a current account receivable. Such reclassification recognizes the obligation of the maker of the note to repay currently and allows the Notes Receivable account in the general ledger to represent only those notes not yet due.

If the Post Company fails to repay the note to Patton on the due date, Patton makes the following entry:

Accounts receivable	1030	
Interest receivable		20
Interest revenue		10
Notes receivable		1000
(to reclassify note and interest in default as an account receivable)		

If dishonored notes are included within a firm's assets on the statement of financial position, their existence must be disclosed in a footnote to any published financial statements.

Discounted Notes Receivable

A firm holding notes receivable might find itself in need of cash before the note payments are due to be received. Rather than negotiate a loan itself, the firm can sell the notes (they are negotiable instruments) to a bank or finance company and receive cash. The substance of the sale of notes receivable is that the buyer (usually a bank) provides cash (a "loan") to the seller with repayment of the cash advanced plus interest expected on the due date of the note from the third party (the maker of the note).

The buyer of the note deducts the amount of interest expected on the cash advance from the total maturity value of the note. When the maker repays the note, the purchaser thus collects both the amount advanced (the "loan") and the interest fee expected.

Assume that after holding the thousand-dollar, 90-day, 12 percent note made by the Post Company for 15 days, the Patton Company discounts the note receivable at the First National Bank. First National wishes to earn 15 percent on its cash advance. Exhibit 6.5 presents a determination of the amount that the bank will pay Patton for the note.

EXHIBIT 6.5

Original value of the note receivable	
Face amount of the note	$1,000
Plus: Interest at 12% for 90 days (.12 × $1,000 × 90/360)	30
Maturity value of the note receivable	$1,030
Less: Bank's interest charge (.15 × $1,030 × 75/360)	32
Cash paid by First National to Patton	$ 998

Note that the interest amount charged by the bank is based on the number of days that the bank will hold the note before repayment by the maker (75 in this case). The $2.00 difference between principal amount of the note and the cash received is interest expense to Patton. Discounted notes can result in either interest revenue or interest expense to the seller, depending on the interest rate charged by the bank compared to the rate of interest on the note itself and the remaining term of the note at the time of discounting.

The seller remains secondarily responsible for the note's payment. That is, if the maker (Post) fails to pay the note when due, the lender (Patton) must pay the maturity value of the note to First National and try to collect from Post. Therefore, when the note is originally discounted and cash is received, the secondary liability is recognized in the bookkeeping process. Patton would make the following journal entry when it discounted Post's note:

Nov. 16	Cash	998	
	Interest expense	2	
	Discounted notes receivable		1,000
	(to record discounting of note receivable)		

The net balance of notes receivable is equal to the gross amount of notes receivable, less the discounted notes receivable, and is placed on the statement of financial position as an asset. However, the existence of discounted notes receivable must be made known to financial statement users through a footnote.

If the discounted note is paid to the bank by the maker (Post), the secondary liability ceases to exist, as does the note receivable itself. The bookkeeping to recognize this fact is as follows:

Jan. 30	Discounted notes receivable	1,000	
	Notes receivable		1,000
	(to remove paid discounted notes from the books)		

Should the discounted note be defaulted upon, Patton would be called upon to pay the total maturity value (principal plus interest) to the bank. The amount paid by Patton would be considered an account receivable due from Post, and both the note receivable and discounted note receivable would be removed from the books as follows:

Jan. 30	Accounts receivable	1,030	
	Cash		1,030
	(to record payment of dishonored discounted note)		
	Discounted notes receivable	1,000	
	Notes receivable		1,000
	(to remove discounted note and the original note itself from the books)		

PRESENTATION OF RECEIVABLES AND PAYABLES ON THE STATEMENT OF FINANCIAL POSITION

Exhibit 6.6 is a partial statement of financial position provided as an example of how a detailed presentation of accounts and notes receivable would appear.

EXHIBIT 6.6

The Example Company
Statement of Financial Position
December 31, 1987

Assets		
Current Assets		
Cash		$300,000
Accounts receivable	$100,000	
Less: Allowance for uncollectible accounts	10,000	90,000
Notes receivable	$20,000	
Less: Discounted notes receivable	15,000	5,000
Inventory		50,000
Other current assets		4,000
Total current assets		$449,000
Liabilities and Shareholders' Equity:		
Current Liabilities		
Accounts payable		$ 70,000
Notes payable		40,000
Interest payable		7,000
Total current liabilities		$117,000

More typical of an actual presentation is Exhibit 6.7 taken from the 1984 annual report of the U.S. Steel Corporation. Accounts receivable are shown at net realizable value, with the allowance for uncollectible accounts shown within the presentation

EXHIBIT 6.7

U.S. Steel Corporation
Consolidated Balance Sheet

(Dollars in millions) **December 31**	**1984**	**1983**
Assets		
Current assets:		
Cash and marketable securities *(Note 3, page 34)*	**$ 355**	$ 541
Receivables, less allowance for doubtful accounts of $39 and $53	**1,611**	1,612
Inventories *(Note 4, page 34)*	**2,164**	2,099
Other current assets	**59**	46
Total current assets	**4,189**	4,298
Liabilities and Stockholders' Equity		
Current liabilities:		
Notes payable *(Note 7, page 35)*	**$ 349**	$ 297
Accounts payable	**1,846**	1,684
Payroll and benefits payable	**440**	585
Accrued taxes *(Note 8, page 35)*	**493**	472
Accrued interest	**185**	195
Long-term debt due within one year *(Note 10, page 36)*	**220**	77
Current portion of provision for estimated costs attributable to shutdown of facilities *(Note 16, page 30)*	**115**	199
Total current liabilities	**3,648**	3,509

7. Notes Payable

(In millions) **December 31**	**1984**	**1983**	**1982**
Banks (principally demand basis)	**$349**	$ 297	$ 362
Average interest rate year-end	***7.4%***	*7.5%*	*9.0%*
Maximum aggregate amount at any month-end	**$596**	$ 508	$ 362
Weighted daily average:			
Borrowing	**$304**	$ 267	$ 229
Interest rate[(a)]	***7.4%***	*6.0%*	*10.0%*

[(a)] Computed by relating interest expense to average daily borrowing. The Corporation had available short-term credit agreements totaling $646 million at December 31, 1984. Two one-year agreements aggregating $400 million are with two Canadian banks, with interest based on their prime rate or London Interbank Offered Rate and carry a commitment fee of ⅛%. The remaining credit agreements, totaling $246 million, are with a number of banks and require maintenance of compensating balances of 3% on average. At December 31, 1984, a total of $160 million was outstanding under these agreements.

8. Accrued Taxes

(In millions) **December 31**	**1984**	**1983**
Income taxes—Current	**$ 298**	$ 242
—Deferred	**(91)**	(5)
Other taxes	**286**	235
Total	**$ 493**	$ 472

line. Other items are shown at net amounts, with details provided in appropriate footnotes. Footnotes 7 and 8 are included in Exhibit 6.7 as examples.

FOR REVIEW

DEMONSTRATION PROBLEM

During 1987, Yammy Company had credit sales of $3,000,000. Historically, 2% of all credit sales prove uncollectible. Yammy's fiscal year ends on December 31. On December 31, 1987, Yammy reviewed its accounts receivable and developed the following age distribution of the accounts:

Less than 31 days old	$400,000
Over 30 but less than 61 days old	300,000
Over 60 but less than 91 days old	100,000
Over 90 days old	60,000
Total accounts receivable	$860,000

Based on prior experience, Yammy expects that within each of the age groups the following percentage will prove uncollectible:

Less than 31 days old	2%
Over 30 but less than 61 days old	5%
Over 60 but less than 91 days old	20%
Over 90 days old	50%

Before any adjustments, the December 31, 1987, account balances relative to accounts receivable and bad debts are as follows:

Accounts Receivable		Allowance for Uncollectible Accounts		Bad Debt Expense	
860,000			5,000	0	

Required

1. If Yammy uses the allowance method of accounting for uncollectible accounts, make any necessary journal entries on December 31, 1987 if:

a. Yammy uses the percentage of sales method of estimating bad debts.

b. Yammy uses the aging of accounts receivable method of estimating bad debts.

2. Determine the balance of gross and net accounts receivable, allowance for uncollectible accounts, and bad debt expense that Yammy would have on December 31, 1987, after adjusting for estimated 1987 bad debts under each of the approaches in (1).

3. On January 1, 1988, a customer files for bankruptcy and Yammy writes off his account of $1,000. Present the journal entry for this write-off.

4. What would be the balance of gross and net accounts receivable, allowance for uncollectible accounts, and bad debt expense immediately after the write-off of the customer's account in (3) if Yammy uses the percentage of sales method to estimate uncollectible accounts?

Demonstration Problem Solution

1a. Percentage of Sales Method

Bad debt expense	60,000*	
Allowance for uncollectible accounts		60,000
(to adjust for estimated bad debts)		

*.02 × $3,000,000 = $60,000

1b. Aging of Accounts Receivable Method

Bad debt expense	68,000	
Allowance for uncollectible accounts**		68,000
(to adjust for estimated bad debts)		

**.02 × $400,000 =	$ 8,000
.05 × 300,000 =	15,000
.20 × 100,000 =	20,000
.50 × 60,000 =	30,000
Total estimated uncollectible accounts as of 12/31/87	$73,000
Less: 12/31/87 balance of allowance for uncollectible accounts	5,000
Adjustment required	$68,000

2a. Percentage of Sales Method

Accounts Receivable

Debit	Credit
Bal. 860,000	

Allowance for Uncollectible Accounts

Debit	Credit
	5,000
	60,000
	65,000

Bad Debt Expense

Debit	Credit
Bal. before adj. 0	
Adj. 60,000	
Bal. after adj. 60,000	

Net balance in Accounts Receivable = $860,000 − 65,000 = $795,000.

2b. Aging of Accounts Receivable Method

Accounts Receivable

Debit	Credit
Bal. 860,000	

Allowance for Uncollectible Accounts

Debit	Credit
	5,000
	68,000
	73,000

Bad Debt Expense

Debit	Credit
Bal. before adj. 0	
Adj. 68,000	
Bal. after adj. 68,000	

Net balance in Accounts Receivable = $860,000 − 73,000 = $787,000.

3.

Allowance for uncollectible accounts	1,000	
Accounts receivable		1,000
(to write off a bad debt)		

4.

Accounts Receivable		Allowance for Uncollectible Accounts		Bad Debt Expense*	
Bal. before adj. 860,000	1,000	Write-off 1,000	65,000	Bal. before adj. 0	
Bal. after adj. 859,000			64,000	Bal. after adj. 0	

*Zero balance, since bad debt expense is closed as of December 31, 1987. Net balance in Accounts Receivable = $859,000 − 64,000 = $795,000.

SUMMARY

- Short-term liabilities include both those whose amounts are known and those whose amounts can only be estimated and generally require repayment within one year.
- Accounts payable arise from previous purchases and are similar to short-term loans.
- Notes payable are formal, generally short-term, debt instruments and usually require specific interest payments.
- Interest is rental fee on money and is computed in conjunction with accounts and notes payable and receivable.
- The borrowing or lending of money at interest generates expense or revenue.
- Discounting a note has the effect of raising the note's true rate of interest.
- Contingent liabilities are those that can become liabilities, depending on future events.
- Accounts receivable are current assets arising from past sales.
- To properly value accounts receivable and revenue, one must estimate the amount of credit sales that will ultimately prove uncollectible.
- The allowance method of accounting for uncollectible accounts sets up a general allowance against which specific accounts are written off as they are determined to be uncollectible.
- The allowance for bad debts can be based on total credit sales or on the age of the accounts receivable.
- Notes receivable represent formal, generally short-term, loans and usually require specific interest payments by the borrower.
- Discounting notes receivable is a way to raise cash and results in contingent liabilities until the maker of the notes pays them off.

QUESTIONS

6-1. Why do accountants normally ignore interest fees when dealing with accounts receivable or accounts payable?

6-2. Explain the difference between the direct write-off and the allowance methods of handling bad debt expenses.

6-3. How do notes payable or receivable differ from accounts payable or receivable?

6-4. What are the three factors that determine the total amount of interest owed on a given debt instrument?

6-5. What is a discounted note?

6-6. What are contingent liabilities, and how are they recorded, if at all, on the financial statements?

6-7. Explain the two methods of estimating bad debts under the allowance method.

6-8. What is the difference between a discounted note receivable and a dishonored note receivable? How is each handled in the accounts?

6-9. Define the following terms with respect to notes:

a. maturity value
b. due date
c. maker
d. holder
e. principal amount

6-10. Briefly discuss the considerations in formulating a firm's credit policy for sales.

EXERCISES

6-E1. On December 12, 1986, Zee Company borrows $7,500 from the bank for 120 days at an interest rate of 14%, giving a noninterest-bearing note.

a. What is the maturity value of the note?
b. What is the maturity date of the note?
c. How much cash does Zee receive from the bank on December 12?

6-E2. Feld Transportation's allowance for uncollectible accounts had a credit balance of $450 on January 1, 1987. Other information taken from Feld's books is as follows:

Accounts receivable balance, December 31, 1987	$80,000
Estimate of uncollectible accounts based on the aging of the 12/31/87 accounts receivable	2,700

Given that no entries have been made to the allowance account during 1987, prepare the necessary adjusting entry(s) as of December 31. What is the December 31, 1987, balance in the allowance for uncollectibles following your adjustments?

6-E3. Jersey, Inc., accepts a 60-day, 12% note receivable of $6,000 in payment of an account receivable.

a. Prepare the general journal entry for the receipt of the note.
b. Twenty days later, Jersey discounts the note at its bank at an interest rate of 14%. Record the discounting transaction.
c. If the customer defaults on the note on the maturity date, what is Jersey's responsibility?

6-E4. The Tiger Company uses the allowance method of handling credit losses. The allowance for uncollectible accounts has a normal credit balance of $1,500 on January 1, 1986. During the first ten months of 1986, the company writes off $1,200 in bad accounts. In November, the company learns that another of its customers owing $550 has gone bankrupt.

a. Record the entry to write off the customer's account.
b. What is the new balance in the allowance account after the write-off?
c. How will this balance affect the 1986 bad debt expense for Tiger if the company uses the aging of accounts receivable as a basis for establishing the allowance for uncollectibles?

6-E5. Badger Company has the following balances in its end-of-year records:

Accounts receivable	$ 76,000
Allowance for uncollectible accounts	1,100 Cr.

Transactions during the year are:

Sales on account	216,000
Actual cash collected from customers on account	161,000
Sales discounts	17,000
Sales returns and allowances	2,400
Accounts written off as uncollectible	1,400

Total estimated uncollectibles at year-end using aging of accounts receivable method	3,900

a. What are Badger's net sales for the year?
b. What will be Badger's gross and net accounts receivable on the statement of financial position after all year-end adjustments?
c. What is Badger's bad debt expense for the year?

6-E6. If the Badger Company in 6-E5 were to use the direct write-off method of handling bad debts, what would Badger report as bad debt expense for the year-end? What would be the gross and net figures for accounts receivable on the statement of financial position? What would the income difference be between the user of the allowance method and the direct write-off method in Badger's income?

6-E7. The following data are from Apple Processor's accounts receivable as of December 31, 1986:

	Age of Accounts Receivable				
Customer	**Less than 30 days**	**30–60 days**	**61–90 days**	**91–180 days**	**More than 180 days**
TWP	$ 9,000	$7,000	$16,000	$6,000	$ 500
PDE	18,000	3,000	1,000	1,000	750
Others	21,000	—	—	2,500	3,500

Based on past experience, Apple uses the following percentages in estimating uncollectible accounts:

	Less than 30 days	**30–60 days**	**61–90 days**	**91–180 days**	**More than 180 days**
Percent uncollectible	1%	2.5%	3.75%	18%	62%

a. What estimate should Apple make for its uncollectible accounts for 1986 if its December 31, 1986, balance in the allowance account is $1,400 credit before adjustment?
b. If the company has a collection target of 95% of credit sales and the total credit sales for 1986 are $121,000, does it appear that the target will be met?

PROBLEM SET A

6-A1. Journalizing Transactions. Rush Company has the following transactions during 1986 and 1987:

October 1, 1986	Sells $10,000 of goods to Today's Products and accepts a 120-day, 16% note in payment.
October 10, 1986	Discounts the note at the First Bank at 14%.
February 1, 1987	Receives communication from First Bank that Today's Products note has been dishonored. Rush pays the bank.
February 15, 1987	Today's Products pays the maturity value of the note.
March 1, 1987	Rush gives a creditor a $15,000, 60-day, 12% note in payment of an account.
May 1, 1987	Rush pays off the note and interest given on March 1.
May 15, 1987	Rush receives an $8,000, 90-day, 14% note from Barometer Works in payment of its account.
August 15, 1987	Barometer repays the note and interest.

Required

Prepare general journal entries for Rush's transactions.

6-A2. Journalizing Transactions for Uncollectible Accounts. On January 1, 1986, Random, Inc., has the following balances on its books:

Accounts receivable	$80,000
Allowance for uncollectible accounts	1,600

During 1986, credit sales are $210,000 and collections on account are $201,000. Random, Inc., uses the allowance method for handling bad debts. The following additional transactions take place during 1986:

January 5	Bill Smith's account of $800 is written off.
February 7	Tom Jones's account of $1,253 is written off.
March 8	Tom Jones pays the $1,253 that has been written off.
November 15	Bill Smith pays $800 in full settlement.
December 31	Based on prior experience, Random estimates that 1% of credit sales would prove uncollectible.

Required

a. Prepare a general journal entry for each of the transactions.
b. Give the December 31, 1986, balances in accounts receivable and allowance for uncollectible accounts after all adjustments for 1986.

6-A3. Uncollectible Accounts and the Allowance Method. The July 31, 1986, balances in the accounts of Windows, Inc., include the following:

Accounts receivable	$285,000
Allowance for uncollectible accounts	1,650
Credit sales for the year ending July 31	825,000

Analysis of the accounts receivable provides the following data:

Percentage of Estimated Uncollectible	Age of Account	Amount
1.00%	Under 30 days	$142,500
1.75%	31–60 days	71,000
4.80%	61–90 days	67,000
16.00%	over 90 days	4,500

Based on past experience, the company has found that on the average, about 0.93% of all credit sales proves uncollectible.

Required

a. Determine the bad debt expense for the year ending July 31 if:

(1) Windows uses the percentage of sales method of estimating bad debts.

(2) Windows uses the aging of accounts receivable method of estimating bad debts.

b. Prepare adjusting journal entries for the estimates made in (a).

6-A4. Net Income, Statement of Financial Position, and Uncollectible Accounts. The Chef Company prepares an income statement for 1986 as follows:

Chef Company
Income Statement
Year Ending December 31, 1986

Sales	$630,000
Cost of goods sold	480,000
Gross margin	$150,000
Bad debt expense	5,000
Other general, selling, and admin. expenses	50,000
Net income	$ 95,000

The following information has been discovered through an examination of the records of Chef:

1. Dick Trent, whose account of $3,500 was written off as uncollectible during 1986, pays the full amount in December. No entry is made for Trent's payment.

2. The estimate of the allowance for uncollectibles should have been 1% of sales.

3. The accounts receivable balance as of December 31, 1986, is $32,000, and the allowance for uncollectibles balance as of that same date is $2,000 credit.

Required

a. Prepare a corrected income statement for Chef.

b. Prepare any journal entry(s) required to correct Chef's accounts.

c. Determine Chef's net balance in accounts receivable as of December 31.

6-A5. Discounted Notes and Interest Computations. Dynamics Inc. sells the Army a missile launcher for $15,000,000. The Army gives Dynamics a note due in one year with a maturity value of $16,200,000. Six months later, Dynamics discounts the note at a bank at 0.5% more than the implicit interest rate in the note. Dynamics takes the cash received from the discounting and purchases a short-term note receivable from a mutual savings company with an interest rate of 11.5% and a maturity date of six months hence.

Required

Determine the principal amount and maturity value of the note receivable that Dynamics has purchased from the mutual savings company.

6-A6. Analysis of Accounts Receivable for Cash Flows. Tamby Company estimates that it needs $100,000 cash on hand at the end of each month. The company normally expects to collect accounts receivable as follows:

Collected within the month of sale	50%
Collected within one month after the sale	20%
Collected within two months after the sale	15%
Collected within three months after the sale	14.85%
Estimated uncollectible amounts of credit sales	0.15%

Sales for the first six months of the year and estimates for the last six months are as follows:

	Jan.–June	July	August	Sept.	Oct.	Nov.	Dec.
Cash sales	$216,000	$33,000	$32,000	$32,000	$ 31,500	$33,000	$34,000
Credit sales	548,000	90,000	80,000	75,000	100,000	60,000	85,000

Of the $548,000 credit sales during the first six months, $210,000 has been collected, 50% of the balance will be collected in July, 40% of the balance in August, and the remainder of the collectible amount in September. Cash disbursements for various items average 90% of total sales in any given month.

Required

If the July 1 cash balance is $100,000, determine the amount of borrowing needed, if any, for the last six months of the year to meet the cash-on-hand target.

6-A7. Journalizing Transactions for Notes Payable and Receivable. The Holly Solly Company and one of its customers, Sneaky Pete, have the following transactions during 1986 and 1987:

July 1, 1986	Holly sells Sneaky Pete $5,000 merchandise on account.
July 31, 1986	Sneaky Pete offers a 60-day, 12% promissory note in payment of its July 1 purchase. Holly accepts the note.
Sept. 30, 1986	On the due date, Sneaky Pete cannot make payment.
Dec. 31, 1986	Since Holly has not been able to collect the note or interest due despite numerous attempts, both are written off as uncollectible.
Jan. 15, 1987	Sneaky Pete comes into some cash and pays half of the note and all of the original interest. Collection of the other half of the note is highly questionable.

Required

Prepare all required journal entries for the transactions on the books of Holly and Sneaky Pete, respectively. Assume that Holly follows the practice of reclassifying all amounts associated with defaulted notes as accounts receivable and is on the allowance method for bad debt recognition.

PROBLEM SET B

6-B1. Journalizing Transactions. London Fogs and Mists has the following transactions during 1986:

January 1 Borrows $200,000 from the bank on a six-month, 8% note, with interest to be paid at maturity.

January 7 Receives an $8,500, 90-day, 10% note from Dick Turpin in payment of his account.

January 8 Discounts Turpin's note at Bonclary's Bank at 9.5%.

March 7 Dick Turpin pays his note off at Bonclary's.

May 31 LF & M gives a creditor, Wimbledon Croquet Company, an $8,580, 180-day, 6% note in payment of an account.

July 1 Pays off the note given on January 1.

July 7 Receives an $8,000, 60-day, 5% note from Jim Thompson in payment of his account.

July 8 Discounts Thompson's note at Lloyds Bank at 5.5%.

October 7 Receives communication from Lloyds that Thompson's note had been dishonored.

Required

Prepare general journal entries for the transactions for London Fogs and Mists' books.

6-B2. Journalizing Transactions for Uncollectible Accounts. On January 1, 1986, Weeks Company has the following balances on its books:

Accounts receivable	$100,000
Allowance for uncollectible accounts	3,000

During 1986, credit sales are $210,000 and collections on account are $201,000. Random, Inc., uses the allowance method for handling bad debts. The following additional transactions take place during 1986:

January 5 Bill Smith's account of $800 is written off.

February 7 Tom Jones's account of $1,253 is written off.

March 8 Tom Jones pays the $1,253 that has been written off.

November 15 Bill Smith pays $800 in full settlement.

December 31 Based on prior experience, Random estimates that 1% of credit sales would prove uncollectible.

Required

a. Prepare a general journal entry for each of the transactions.
b. Give the December 31, 1986, balances in accounts receivable and allowance for uncollectible accounts after all adjustments for 1986.

6-B3. Uncollectible Accounts and the Allowance Method. Mini Cars has the following normal account balances (before any adjustment for 1986 bad debts) as of December 31, 1986:

Accounts receivable	$150,000
Credit sales	600,000
Allowance for uncollectible accounts	5,400

The company's accounting department has analyzed the accounts receivable and prepares the following aging schedule:

Percentage of Estimated Uncollectible	Age of Account	Amount
2.2%	1–30 days	$45,000
3.4%	31–60 days	60,000
7.2%	61–90 days	25,000
14.1%	Over 90 days	20,000

In the past, collectible accounts have totaled 99.21% of total sales.

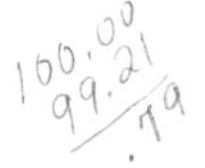

Required

a. Prepare an estimate for 1986 bad debt expense using:
  (1) The percentage of sales method.
  (2) The aging of accounts receivable method.
b. Prepare adjusting journal entries for the estimates made in (a).

6-B4. Net Income, Statement of Financial Position, and Uncollectible Accounts. Toupee Industry has a net income of $45,000 for the year ending December 31, 1987. This income includes a bad debt expense of $450. Selected account balances taken from Toupee's financial statements are as follows:

Accounts receivable	$38,000
Allowance for uncollectible accounts	300
Sales	70,000

In analyzing the books of Toupee, you discover the following information has not been taken into account in developing the 1987 financial statements:

1. An account of $210 written off during 1987 was fully collected in November. (No entry has been made for the collection.)
2. An account of $300 that should have been written off as uncollectible was converted by the bookkeeper to a note receivable.
3. The total amount of accounts receivable that should have been estimated as uncollectible as of December 31 is $350.

Required

a. Determine the correct net income for 1987.
b. Determine the correct net accounts receivable balance as of December 31.

6-B5. Notes Receivable and Interest Computations. Brigit Hillson Inc. accepts a note from a customer for $100,500, paying 10% interest due in 90 days. Hillson then discounts the note at the bank 9.5%. Three days later, the customer goes bankrupt, and only 50% of all of his liabilities are paid off. In the meantime, Hillson has invested the proceeds of the discounted note in a note receivable, paying 14% with a maturity date of one year hence. Since Hillson had guaranteed the discounted note, the company had to pay the bank the 50% not paid by the bankrupt customer. (This payment was made at the maturity date of the discounted note.) To make this payment, Hillson borrows the required amount from another bank at 16%. Hillson is able to pay back this 16% loan at the end of six months.

Required

Determine the amount of Hillson's net interest expense or revenue resulting from the foregoing transactions.

6-B6. Accounts Receivable and Cash Requirements. Watchword, Inc., is analyzing its cash needs for the next six months. The company believes it needs a minimum cash balance of $50,000 at the end of each of these months. Cash payments for all needs usually average 95% of total sales. The company's collection pattern for accounts receivable is as follows:

Collected in the month of sale	30%
Collected one month following sale	35%
Collected two months following sale	25%
Collected three months following sale	5%
Estimated to be uncollectible	5%

The December 31 balance in the cash account is $25,000; the balance in accounts receivable is $60,000. The company expects to collect 60% of the year-end receivables in January, 20%

in February, and 18% in March, with the remaining 2% expected to prove uncollectible. The following sales projections have been prepared:

	January	February	March	April	May	June
Cash sales	$30,000	$25,000	$20,000	$30,000	$30,000	$25,000
Credit sales	60,000	70,000	50,000	85,000	80,000	75,000

Required

Prepare a schedule showing the amount of borrowing needed, if any, at the end of each of the next six months.

6-B7. Journalizing Transactions for Notes Payable and Receivable. The Liberal Credit Hardware Company and one of its customers, Fly Be Gone, have the following transactions during 1986 and 1987:

June 1, 1986	Liberal sells Fly Be Gone $3,000 of hardware on account.
June 30, 1986	Fly Be Gone notifies Liberal that it lacks funds to pay its bill and offers a 90-day, 14% promissory note in payment. Liberal accepts the note.
Sept. 30, 1986	On the due date of the note, Fly Be Gone defaults on payment.
Dec. 31, 1986	After numerous attempts to collect the note, Liberal writes the note and associated interest off as uncollectible.
Feb. 15, 1987	Fly Be Gone comes into some cash and pays the note and interest owed as of the original due date.

Required

Prepare all required journal entries for the events on the books of Liberal Credit and Fly Be Gone, respectively. Assume that Liberal follows the practice of reclassifying all amounts associated with defaulted notes as accounts receivable and is on the allowance method for bad debt recognition.

7

CASH, SHORT-TERM INVESTMENTS, AND INTERNAL CONTROL

CHAPTER OBJECTIVES

After studying Chapter 7, you should understand the following:

1. The various types of forms pertinent to a firm's bank account.
2. How to construct a bank reconciliation and why one is necessary.
3. Why a firm would wish to invest temporarily idle cash and how to account for such investments.
4. What internal control is and why it is needed.
5. Several of the most valuable internal control guidelines.
6. How the computerized business environment has caused internal control changes.

In simpler times, the cash account represented the currency a firm used when doing business. Today, cash includes bank checks, bank deposits, money orders, and even credit cards. Cash is the most liquid of all assets. It is a medium of exchange readily transferred from person to person. Because cash can be easily misplaced or stolen, businesses adopt practices to maintain accounting records to prevent loss through theft or fraud. They also routinely invest cash not needed immediately so that interest or dividends can increase the amount of cash available. Since cash is not the only asset subject to misuse, internal control measures are necessary to safeguard all assets.

BANK TRANSACTIONS

Transaction-Oriented Documents

DRAWER
A person who fills out and signs a check.

DRAWEE
An entity—usually a bank—required to pay the amount of a check.

CHECK
A written command to a bank from its customer (depositor) to pay a certain sum of money to a person or organization.

DEPOSIT SLIP
A listing of cash and checks to be deposited in a bank used to deposit currency and checks received by a business from its customers.

DEBIT MEMORANDUM
A form issued to indicate a charge against a customer's account.

CREDIT MEMORANDUM
A form issued by a bank when it makes deposits directly to a customer's account from a third party.

Checks. Most firms handle as many cash transactions as possible through their checking accounts. Checks, like other bills of exchange, involve three parties in the payment process: the **drawer,** the person who fills out and signs the checks; the **drawee,** an entity required to transfer the amount, usually the bank; and the payee, the recipient of the transferred amount. A **check** is a written command to a bank by its customer (depositor) to pay a certain sum of money to a third person or organization.

Deposit Slip. A **deposit slip** lists currency or checks being deposited in the bank. A deposit slip usually is two-sided. One side is for summarizing the various items being deposited, and the reverse side is for listing additional checks.

Debit Memo. A **debit memorandum** is a form a bank issues to show a charge against the depositor's account for services rendered or to deduct amounts for payments made on the depositor's behalf, such as interest payments on a loan from the bank, rental for safe deposit boxes, or monthly mortgage payments. (Other businesses use debit memos for similar transactions.) A debit memo can also be used when a check that has been deposited to a company's account is returned uncollected, most commonly when the drawer has inadequate funds in his or her own bank account.

Exhibit 7.1 shows a debit memo. The top part is sent to the customer; the bottom section is the bank's source document.

Credit Memo. A **credit memorandum,** or credit advice, is a form issued by a bank when it makes deposits directly to a customer's checking account from a third party. For example, if a firm requests its bank to collect a note receivable on the firm's behalf, the bank most likely will deduct a service charge from the amount collected and will then deposit the balance of principal and interest to the firm's account. Exhibit 7.2 shows two copies of a credit memorandum; the top copy is sent to the checking account customer; the lower copy is the bank's copy.

BANK STATEMENT
A summarization of transactions in a bank account issued by a bank to its customer.

BANK RECONCILIATION
A report prepared to explain the differences between the balances in a firm's cash account and in the company's account as shown on the bank statement at a certain point in time.

Bank Statement

A **bank statement** is a summary of the transactions of a checking account customer issued by the bank to the customer. The account balance reflects the impact of checks, deposits, and debit and credit memos throughout the specified period.

The Bank Reconciliation

A **bank reconciliation** is a report that explains the differences between the balances on a certain day in the firm's Cash account and in the company's account as shown on the bank statement. These differences normally are caused by a time lag. The reconciliation process also helps locate potential errors in either the bank's records or the firm's books. For example, a company receives checks worth $10,000 from

EXHIBIT 7.1
Debit Memorandum

EAST LANSING STATE BANK
EAST LANSING, MICHIGAN

WE CHARGE YOUR ACCOUNT — DATE 11-25-86

DESCRIPTION	AMOUNT	
Check printing	25	80

ACCOUNT NUMBER 008697-262

MAIL TO →
G. Lucas Productions
16 West Lafayette
Detroit, Michigan 48613

North
DEPARTMENT OR BRANCH
S. Spielburger
MANAGER

EAST LANSING STATE BANK
EAST LANSING, MICHIGAN

WE CHARGE YOUR ACCOUNT — DATE 11-25-86

DESCRIPTION	AMOUNT	
Check printing	25	80

ACCOUNT NUMBER 008697-262

DEBIT →
G. Lucas--Royalty Account

North
DEPARTMENT OR BRANCH
S. Spielburger
MANAGER

customers on account on May 31, and the following entry is recorded in its cash receipts journal:

May 31	Cash	10,000	
	Accounts receivable—assorted		10,000
	(to record receipt of checks from credit customers)		

EXHIBIT 7.2
Credit Memorandum

EAST LANSING STATE BANK
EAST LANSING, MICHIGAN

DATE 11-16-86

Royalties--Check No.		1,000 00
63816, Star Studios		

WE CREDIT YOUR ACCOUNT SUBJECT TO TERMS AND CONDITIONS ON REVERSE SIDE OF STATEMENT OF ACCOUNT

CREDIT ADVICE - MAIL TO

G. Lucas Productions
16 West Lafayette
Detroit, Michigan 48613

APPROVED SS

008697-262 ACCOUNT NO.

EAST LANSING STATE BANK
EAST LANSING, MICHIGAN

DATE 11-16-86

Royalties--Check No.		1,000 00
63816, Star Studios		

WE CREDIT YOUR ACCOUNT SUBJECT TO TERMS AND CONDITIONS ON REVERSE SIDE OF STATEMENT OF ACCOUNT

CREDIT TO THE ACCOUNT OF

G. Lucas--Royalty Account

APPROVED SS

008697-262 ACCOUNT NO.

The company then deposits the checks in the bank late on the evening of May 31. The bank records the deposit of $10,000 in the customers' account on June 1. Thus, if the bank and company cash balances are compared as of May 31, the Cash account in the company's books will show a deposit of $10,000 that will not show on the May 31 bank statement. A deposit that a firm records in its Cash account but that has not yet been recorded by the firm's bank in the bank's accounting records is called a **deposit in transit.** Such a lag in recording is one reason the balances might differ and would appear on a bank reconciliation.

DEPOSIT IN TRANSIT
A deposit that a firm has recorded in its cash account but that the firm's bank has not yet recorded in its accounting records.

Other differences in the balances that might appear on a bank reconciliation are illustrated in the following example. The Cash account from the general ledger of Aaron Corporation, which reconciles its Cash account with the bank statement each month, follows:

Cash

June 1 balance	28,280	Payments during June	13,334
Receipts during June	19,365		
June 30 balance	34,311		

The cash receipts and cash payments records for June 1986 that provide the details regarding cash transactions are as follows:

Aaron Corporation
Cash Receipts for June 1986

Date	Particulars	Cash (Debit)	
June 1	Apple Company	$ 672	X
2	John Corporation	1,285	X
4	Haven & Sons	3,262	X
6	Jacobs, Inc.	929	X
9	O'Conner & Co.	2,110	X
10	Outslay, Inc.	655	X
12	Numberg & Sons	420	X
15	Bierman & Company	625	X
17	Janson Corporation	896	X
18	Anderson & Company	926	X
20	Wright & Son	1,627	X
22	McKenzie, Inc.	1,267	X
24	Wooten & Company	467	X
27	Snider Corporation	852	X
30	Steinbart, Inc.	1,679	(a)
30	Falk & Sons	582	(a)
30	Marshall & Company	1,111	(a)
	Total	$19,365	

Aaron Corporation
Cash Payments for June 1986

Check Number	Date	Particulars	Cash (Credit)	
856	June 1	Lester Corporation	$ 675	X
857	2	Connery Inc.	897	X
858	3	Hepburn & Company	1,286	X
859	4	Scarlett & Sons	982	(b)
860	6	Williamson Company	1,121	X
861	9	Void	—	X
862	10	Shaw, Inc.	900	X
863	11	Harris & Company	285	(d)
864	15	Huston Company	583	X
865	16	Giler & Sons	374	X
866	20	Spade, Inc.	755	X
867	23	Gutmen Corporation	1,344	X
868	25	Stander & Company	489	X
869	27	Patrick, Inc.	199	X
870	29	Cook & Sons	1,481	(b)
871	30	McGuire Corporation	681	(b)
872	30	Plummer, Inc.	1,282	(b)
		Total	$13,334	

The bank statement for Aaron Corporation for June 1986 shows the following details:

Aaron Corporation
Bank Statement
June 30, 1986

			Charges		Credits		Balance
June	1	Balance					28,280
	2	Deposit			672	√	28,952
	3	Deposit			1,285	√	30,237
	4	Check #856	675	√			29,562
	6	Deposit			3,262	√	32,824
		Check #858	1,286	√			31,538
	9	Deposit			929	√	32,467
		Check #857	897	√			31,570
	10	Deposit			2,110	√	33,680
		Check #860	1,121	√			32,559
	11	Deposit			655	√	33,214
	15	Deposit			420	√	33,634
	16	Deposit			625	√	34,259
		Check #863	258	(d)			34,001
		Check #862	900	√			33,101
	17	Check #864	583	√			32,518
	18	Deposit			896	√	33,414
		NSF Check	3,262	(e)			30,152
	20	Deposit			926	√	31,078
		Check #865	374	√			30,704
	22	Deposit			1,627	√	32,331
	23	Deposit			1,267	√	33,598
		Check #866	755	√			32,843
	25	Deposit			467	√	33,310
		Collections			855	(c)	34,165
	27	Check #867	1,344	√			32,821
	29	Deposit			852	√	33,673
		Check #869	199	√			33,474
	30	Check #868	489	√			32,985
		Service Charges—June	65	(f)			32,920

The charges noted on this statement represent amounts deducted from the account; credits represent increases to the account. Good internal control over cash requires that the bank reconciliation as of June 30, 1986, be prepared by someone who does not handle cash or record cash transactions.

The June 30 bank reconciliation for Aaron Corporation is as follows. (The lettered items are explained in detail in the following paragraphs.)

Aaron Corporation
Bank Reconciliation
June 30, 1986

Cash balance, June 30		$34,311	Bank balance, June 30	$32,920
Add: (c) Collection of note & interest receivable	$ 855		Add: (a) Deposits in transit	3,372
(d) Recording error	27	882	Less: (b) Outstanding checks	(4,426)
Less: (e) NSF check	$(3,262)			
(f) Service charges	(65)	(3,327)		
Adjusted cash balance, June 30		$31,866	Adjusted cash balance, June 30	$31,866

Note that the bank reconciliation has two parts. Each part leads to an adjusted cash figure that should match the firm's actual cash balance on the reconciliation date. The left part of the statement updates the Cash at Bank account on Aaron's books for June transactions. Any economic fact entered on this side must be recorded in Aaron's accounting records via a journal entry. The right side of the statement generally reflects differences that are only temporary in nature because of time lags in the cash flow process. Since the right side is the bank's viewpoint of the account, the firm does not journalize the entries affecting that side.

The reconciling entries are discovered by comparing the transactions in the cash receipts and payments journals with the bank statement. For example, check #856 for $675 issued to Lester Corporation was recorded in the cash payments journal on June 1; however, according to the bank statement, the check was not recorded until June 4. This time lag is common with checks. A check that has been written and issued by a firm but has not been paid by the bank is called an **outstanding check.** To identify any outstanding checks or deposits in transit, all transactions must be matched and cross-referenced. We have used a "√" on the bank statement and an "X" on the cash records in the example to indicate a transaction that shows up in both places. The items remaining unmarked after this process are those that cause the company and bank balances to differ and are the focus of the reconciliation process. Items not recorded by either the bank or the company in the example appear on Aaron's bank reconciliation as follows:

OUTSTANDING CHECK
A check that has been written and issued by a firm but has not been paid by the bank.

a. Deposits in transit, $3,372 ($1,679 + $582 + $1,111). This sum represents cash and checks received by the company from customers and other sources. However, since the money was deposited at night on June 30, the bank was unable to increase Aaron Corporation's account on June 30. Thus, the bank statement balance is understated compared with Aaron's balance. The $3,372 must be added to the bank statement balance to proceed to the correct cash total.

b. Outstanding checks, $4,426 ($982 + $1,481 + $681 + $1,282). These checks were issued in June, recorded as cash payments, and mailed to the payees. However, because some checks were not presented for payment by June 30, the bank has not yet charged Aaron Corporation's account. The bank statement balance is overstated, and we must subtract $4,426 from the bank's balance.

c. Collection of notes receivable, $855. A note receivable with a face value of $800 and accrued interest of $90 was collected by the bank on behalf of Aaron Corporation in June. The bank deducted a $35 service charge from the total proceeds of the note and sent the company credit memo #8293. Since the credit memo was received after June 30, the company did not record the collection as a cash receipt in June. However, since the cash actually was collected in June, the following general journal entry is in order:

June 30	Cash	855	
	Bank charges	35	
	Interest revenue		90
	Notes receivable		800
	(to record collection of note and interest by bank)		

d. Recording error, $27. Comparing the bank statement to the cash payments record shows that check #863 for $258 was incorrectly recorded as a payment of $285 by Aaron Corporation. The accounts affected therefore contain amounts as follows:

Cash				Accounts Payable—Harris & Co.			
		June 11	285	June 11	285		

Had the correct amount of $258 been recorded, the accounts would show the following amounts:

Cash				Accounts Payable—Harris & Co.			
		June 11	258	June 11	258		

Both Accounts Payable and Cash are reduced by $27 ($285 − $258). The error can be remedied by the following adjusting entry, which in effect returns $27 to the cash balance.

June 30	Cash	27	
	Accounts payable (Harris & Co.)		27
	(to correct error in recording payment on June 11)		

e. Nonsufficient funds (NSF) check, $3,262. The check received from Haven & Sons on June 4 was recorded as follows:

June 4	Cash	3,262	
	Accounts receivable (Haven & Sons)		3,262
	(to record receipt of check from customer)		

The check was deposited on June 5. Since Haven & Sons' own bank account did not have adequate funds to cover the check, the company's bank subtracted the $3,262 from Aaron's account when the check was returned by Haven & Sons' bank. A check returned because of inadequate funds is an NSF (nonsufficient funds) check. As far as Aaron Corporation is concerned, Haven & Sons has not paid its debt. A journal entry must be made to eliminate the payment recorded earlier. The updating entry would be as follows:

June 30	Accounts receivable (Haven & Sons)	3,262	
	Cash		3,262
	(to record receipt of NSF check from bank)		

f. Service charges, $65. Service charges of $65 accrued as an expense for June; the bank already has reduced Aaron's balance on the bank's books via debit memo #6285. To reflect the expense, Aaron Corporation must enter the following item:

June 30	Bank charges	65	
	Cash		65
	(to record bank fee expenditure)		

Accordingly, $65 is deducted from the cash balance of $34,311.

The June 30 adjusted cash balance of $31,866 at the bottom of the bank reconciliation is the cash balance for the June 30 statement of financial position. Since journal entries were made to record any items causing the account to differ from the adjusted, or true, cash figure, the Cash account is updated to this same figure as follows:

Cash

Balance, June 30	34,311	(e)	3,262
(c)	855	(f)	65
(d)	27		
Balance, June 30	31,866		

Although the adjustments to this account have been illustrated as four separate journal entries, many accountants prefer to do the updating in one combined entry. If this had been Aaron's method, the entry would have been as follows:

June 30	Bank charges	100	
	Accounts receivable (Haven & Sons)	3,262	
	Interest revenue		90
	Note receivable		800
	Accounts payable (Harris & Co.)		27
	Cash		2,445
	(to adjust account due to bank reconciliation)		

Note that the end results of either method yield identical account balances.

CASH MANAGEMENT CONCEPTS

For most people, cash has two functions: as a medium of exchange and as a store of value. A store of value means that people can hold their wealth in cash form—for example, in a bank or under a mattress—for later use. This is not very effective, however, for at least two reasons. First, if the cash is not used, invested, or loaned, the owner loses earnings potential. The second reason has roots in inflation: Holding cash results in a loss of purchasing power, or value. This purchasing power erosion is what prompts some individuals to invest spare cash in alternate stores of wealth, such as precious metals, paintings, and antiques, because the values of such items are normally not eroded by inflation.

A business can hardly expect to keep its wealth in oil paintings, since it needs liquidity in the form of assets easily exchanged for cash to run its day-to-day operations. To satisfy this need, a business must have an effective cash management system, allowing it to operate with the least possible actual cash. Efficient managers recognize that cash can earn interest if invested.

An effective cash management policy lets a business minimize the adverse impact of inflation. One procedure sometimes suggested is to collect all receivables as soon as possible and to delay payments as long as possible. This technique is based on the inflation-caused loss of purchasing power of money over a period of time. A manager is wise to collect all accounts and reinvest the funds to avoid a loss from holding cash. On the other hand, a business manager would prefer to postpone payments on account, since a later repayment can be made with dollars less costly in terms of purchasing power. Of course, payment should not be delayed beyond the date for taking available discounts.

Similarly, a business might find borrowing cash advantageous—even at high rates of interest—if inflation is expected to continue. For example, assume that on July 1, 1986, a company borrows $100,000 for one year at an interest rate of 18 percent and that inflation is expected to be 10 percent during the year. The company is obligated to pay back $118,000 ($100,000 principal + $18,000 interest) on July 1, 1987. Considering inflation, $118,000 in 1987 will be able to command the amount of goods or services that can be acquired with just $107,273 ($118,000/110%) in 1986. In terms of 1986 purchasing power, then, the company has paid interest of 7.27 percent ($7,273/$100,000), not 18 percent. If more than 7.27 percent in real terms can be earned on the loan, borrowing at 18 percent is a wise move.

SHORT-TERM INVESTMENTS

Cash managers normally invest a temporary excess of cash in short-term investments such as certificates of deposit, notes of other reputable companies, and stock. This type of investment earns revenue for the holder through interest or dividends, yet is in a form easily converted to cash.

The initial recording of such an investment is straightforward. For example, assume that a firm purchased short-term notes for $10,000 cash. The journal entry to recognize the investment is as follows:

Temporary investment in notes receivable	10,000	
Cash		10,000
(to record purchase of short-term notes)		

MARKETABLE DEBT SECURITIES Notes payable, certificates of deposit, or any other item that would eventually be repaid by a debtor.

Marketable debt securities include notes payable, certificates of deposit, or other items that are eventually repaid by the debtor. Such investments are carried at cost throughout the time held unless a permanent decline in their market value occurs. If for some reason the investment's market value drops below the investment's historical cost, the reduction in value is recorded only if the decline is considered permanent in nature and is material. If the value decline is expected to be offset shortly by a gain in value, no loss need be recognized. (Note: Although accounting treatment of investments described in this chapter is technically correct according to FASB Statement 12, current practice usually treats debt security investments in the same way as that described for equity security investments in the following section.)

MARKETABLE EQUITY SECURITIES Capital stock of an outside entity.

When an investment is made by purchasing stock of another company, the accounting treatment differs slightly. Investments in stock of another firm are frequently referred to as **marketable equity securities.** By including the word equity, a firm is saying that it has purchased an ownership interest in another company.

The initial recording of such a purchase is again at cost. Suppose that on July 10, Harris Company purchases 250 shares of stock in Xero Company for $5,000 cash as a temporary investment. The appropriate journal entry is as follows:

July 10	Temporary investment in equity securities	5,000	
	Cash		5,000
	(to record purchase of Xero Company stock)		

On financial statements, a company is required to value investments in equity securities at the lower of their original cost or their current market value. The lower of cost or market rule is to be applied to the total holdings (the portfolio) of short-term equity securities, not to the individual securities. The mechanism used to reduce the Investment account, which contains historic costs, to a lower current market value is an Allowance account similar to the one for expected bad debts.

To illustrate, assume that Harris holds the following marketable equity securities on a temporary basis:

Company	Number of Shares	Cost per Share	Total Cost
Ace Corporation	300	$10	$ 3,000
Lite Brothers	500	$25	$12,500
Xero Company	250	$20	$ 5,000

On July 31, Harris must list these investments on its statement of financial position. However, the market value of the stocks no longer equals the initial cost. The current market prices per share are as follows:

Ace Corporation	$11
Lite Brothers	$20
Xero Company	$22

Harris must compute the total market value of its stock portfolio and compare the resulting figure to the total cost of $20,500 ($5,000 + $3,000 + $12,500) to determine the proper carrying value of the Temporary Investment in Equity Securities account. In general, the **carrying value** is the amount at which an item is valued on an entity's books and reported on the financial statements. Since the market value totals $18,800 ($5,500 + $3,300 + $10,000), a loss of $1,700 has occurred. Exhibit 7.3 shows the loss computations.

CARRYING VALUE
The amount at which an item is valued on an entity's books and reported on the financial statements.

EXHIBIT 7.3

Marketable Equity Securities, July 31

	Company	Amount	Total
Cost			
	Ace Corporation	$ 3,000	
	Lite Brothers	12,500	
	Xero Company	5,000	$20,500
Market Value			
	Ace Corporation	$ 3,300	
	Lite Brothers	10,000	
	Xero Company	5,500	18,800
Allowance balance, ending			$ 1,700
Less: Allowance balance, beginning			0
Unrealized loss			$ 1,700

The Allowance account in this example is a contra-account to the Temporary Investment in Equity Securities account. It provides the necessary adjustment for presentation of temporary investments on the statement of financial position. Using a contra-account rather than a direct reduction of the Temporary Investments account itself provides an easy method of tracking changes in the market value of temporary investments.

The loss must be reflected by the accounting system with the following journal entry:

July 31	Unrealized loss on temporary equity investments	1,700	
	Allowance for decline in market value of temporary equity investments		1,700
	(to recognize loss on investment portfolio)		

UNREALIZED LOSS
The difference between the original amount paid and the current market value for unsold investments.

Note that we are recognizing an **unrealized loss,** which is the difference between the original amount paid and the current market value for unsold investments. The adjustment reflects the conservative approach that accountants feel is prudent. Since the investments are short-term and can be sold soon (thus realizing the lower value), the loss is placed on the income statement below operating income in the period in which it occurs, in this case the month ending July 31. Should the investments be held as long-term, different accounting treatment might be more appropriate for an unrealized change in market values. These long-term alternatives are covered in Chapters 15 and 16.

Sometimes after a marketable equity security portfolio is written down to reflect a value drop, the market prices go back up. If this occurs, the Temporary Investments account should be revalued. However, the lower of cost or market rule is still in effect, and the investments should never be listed at an amount higher than their historical cost.

For example, on August 31 Harris Company notes that the market prices (per share) of the three stocks it holds as short-term investments are now quoted as follows:

Ace Corporation	$11.50
Lite Brothers	$23.00
Xero Company	$21.00

Thus, the total value of Harris' holdings is $20,200 ($3,450 + $11,500 + $5,250) as shown in Exhibit 7.4.

Since Harris Company must record this change in the period the change arises, the following entry is in order:

August 31	Allowance for decline in market value of temporary equity investments	1,400	
	Recovery of unrealized loss on valuation of temporary equity investments		1,400
	(to recognize recovery on stock portfolio)		

EXHIBIT 7.4

Marketable Equity Securities, August 31

	Company	Amount	Total
Cost			
	Ace Corporation	$ 3,000	
	Lite Brothers	12,500	
	Xero Company	5,000	$ 20,500
Market Value			
	Ace Corporation	$ 3,450	
	Lite Brothers	11,500	
	Xero Company	5,250	20,200
Allowance balance, ending			$ 300
Less: Allowance balance, beginning			1,700
Recovery of unrealized loss			$ (1,400)

The recovery of unrealized loss is reported as a gain on the periodic income statement for the month ending August 31. Temporary equity investments are shown on the statement of financial position as of August 31 as follows:

Current assets	
Temporary equity investments, at cost	$20,500
Less: Allowance for decline in market value, as of August 31	300
Temporary equity investments, at market	$20,200

When a firm sells all or part of its temporary investments, any difference between the original cost and the sales price of the investment is considered to be a **realized gain or loss** and is recognized as such. For example, if Harris sold all 500 shares of Lite Brothers for $13,000 on September 15, it would recognize a gain of $500 as follows:

REALIZED GAIN/LOSS
The difference between the original cost and the sales price of an investment.

Price received on sale of Lite shares	$13,000
Original cost of Lite shares	12,500
Realized gain	$ 500

The journal entry to record the sale would be as follows:

Sept. 15	Cash	13,000	
	Temporary investment in equity securities		12,500
	Gain on sale of marketable securities		500
	(to record sale of temporary investments)		

No adjustment to the Allowance account is required at the sale date. The market valuation of the remaining temporary equity investments on the next financial statement date would determine any such adjustment.

CONCEPT SUMMARY 7.1

JOURNAL ENTRIES FOR HOLDING TEMPORARY INVESTMENTS PORTFOLIOS

Event	JOURNAL ENTRY		Amount
	For Debt Securities	For Equity Securities	
Initial purchase	Temporary investments Cash	Temporary investments Cash	Cost
Market value drops below cost (judged temporary)	None	Unrealized loss on temporary equity investments Allowance for decline in market value	Cost less market value less allowance balance
Market value drops below cost (judged permanent)	Unrealized loss on temporary debt investments Temporary investments	Unrealized loss on temporary equity investments Allowance for decline in market value	Cost less market value
Market value rises above cost—no amount in Allowance account	None	None	----
Market value rises above cost—Allowance account contains a previous balance	None	Allowance for decline in market value Recovery of unrealized loss on temporary investment	Allowance balance
Market value rises above carrying value of portfolio but below cost	None	Allowance for decline in market value Recovery of unrealized loss on temporary investment	Allowance balance less needed allowance

Note that for income tax purposes only realized gains or losses, such as the gain computed for the sale of the Lite shares, are recognized. Unrealized gains or losses are recognized for accounting statement purposes only.

INTERNAL CONTROL
The plan of organization and all of the coordinate methods and measures adopted within a business to safeguard its assets, check the accuracy and reliability of its accounting data, and promote operational efficiency and adherence to management's policies.

INTRODUCTION TO INTERNAL CONTROL

Objectives

Making wise use of cash and other assets is just one aspect of good management. Serious consideration must be given to **internal control,** which has been defined as follows:

> . . . the plan of organization and all of the coordinate methods and measures adopted within a business to safeguard its assets, check the accuracy and reliability of its accounting data, promote operational efficiency, and encourage adherence to prescribed managerial policies.[1]

In a broad sense, controls include accounting and administrative controls. **Accounting controls** are the methods and procedures an organization uses to safeguard assets and to ensure the accuracy and reliability of the financial records. These controls are specifically designed to reasonably assure the following:

ACCOUNTING CONTROLS
Methods and procedures an organization uses to safeguard assets and to ensure the accuracy and reliability of its financial records.

1. Transactions are executed as management has authorized.
2. Transactions are recorded as necessary to permit preparation of financial statements that conform to generally accepted accounting principles.
3. Access to assets is permitted only as management has authorized.
4. The recorded amounts for assets are periodically compared with the existing assets, and appropriate action is taken regarding any differences.[2]

Allowing access to cash to only those who do not reconcile the bank statement is an example of an accounting control.

Administrative controls are the methods and procedures designed to monitor the efficiency of management's authorization procedures and the adherence of workers to such authorizations. These controls are directly associated with the achievement of organizational objectives and are the starting point for establishing accounting control of transactions. Securing a supervisor's authorization before placing a purchase order is an example of an administrative control.

ADMINISTRATIVE CONTROLS
Methods and procedures designed to monitor the efficiency of management's authorization procedures and the adherence of workers to those authorizations.

Although the definition and objectives of internal control are equally applicable to manual or computerized systems, many special internal control considerations arise in the computerized environment. The remainder of the chapter focuses primarily on accounting controls: their importance, limitations, and features.

A Case in Point

Governments at all levels, as well as businesses, are learning that "an ounce of prevention is worth a pound of cure." Let's take Fairfax, Virginia, for example. This county seat of 22,000 held an election in November 1981 that turned into an upset for the position of treasurer. Wealthy and well-known Frances L. Cox had been city treasurer for twenty years and town clerk for nearly eight years before Fairfax became a city. Rumors told of lax administration in her office, and she lost by only 200 votes.

Ray M. Birch was elected, assuming the post on January 1, 1982. To everyone's surprise, however, he resigned just three weeks later, claiming that the treasurer's office was severely disordered. The city council then appointed John Coughlin, a local CPA, to the position until fall elections could be held. Coughlin was requested not only to fulfill the treasurer's responsibilities but also to examine current procedures and make recommendations. By May, Coughlin had uncovered another surprise for the city—money had been embezzled. The original treasurer had stolen at least $600,000 over a period of six years using a very unsophisticated scheme with several variations.

[1]AICPA. *Professional Standards,* Vol. I. Chicago, Ill.: Commerce Clearing House, Inc., July 1979, p. 243, A.V. Sec. 320.09.

[2]AICPA. *Professional Standards,* Vol. I. Chicago, Ill.: Commerce Clearing House, Inc., July 1979, p. 248, A.V. Sec. 320.28.

One variation involved taking currency that had been received in payment of real estate and property taxes. The cash was simply pocketed and never recorded. Payments meant that a computer card for that taxpayer would be moved from an "uncollected" drawer to the "collected" drawer. The control account for uncollected property taxes, kept in another office, never seemed to match the total of the cards in the uncollected drawer. That was easily remedied, however, with frequent and large write-downs of the control account to make the account match the cards. No one even seemed to wonder why such a write-down was necessary. And if anyone had, responsibilities were so unclearly delineated that no one could have immediately figured out the problem anyway.

Another variation of the scheme hinged on the nightly cash bank deposit that had been rung on the office cash register. On the deposit slip that the treasurer always handled, currency was correctly listed separately from checks. However, Coughlin noticed something unusual when comparing his deposit slips to those from a year ago. Although all the old deposit slips listed very small amounts of currency, such as 93 cents or 12 cents, currency amounts were now running from $400 to $1,000 daily. This was particularly odd, since nothing in the treasurer's office cost less than $5.

Upon closer examination, the deposits were found to total the amounts that had been rung on the cash register, but checks from other nonregistered sources had been substituted for nearly all of the daily currency receipts. The past treasurer had always opened the mail, and she had hoarded a supply of the checks received in the mail. At the end of each day, she simply assembled a combination of checks that nearly matched the daily cash and took the cash, substituting the checks.

To wrap up the Fairfax story, Frances Cox never admitted her guilt, but the evidence was overwhelming, including the obvious deposit of embezzled funds into her personal bank account. She was convicted and sentenced to ten years in prison. Several lawsuits are pending against her: Fairfax city is asking for $2.7 million, and a Fairfax citizen is suing for $1 million. And of course, the tax authorities are not missing their claim to unreported income.

Two lessons are particularly important in this tale. First, bear in mind that the Fairfax treasurer's office had been subjected to at least 14 routine audits by CPA firms and state authorities during the six years of known embezzling. Even though the amounts missing were very substantial, no audit uncovered the embezzlement. (Although audits are not designed primarily to detect fraud, most audit programs should be set up to detect material fraud.)

Second, if good internal control had been in place, the embezzlement probably could not have occurred. Certainly, good internal control calling for separation of duties and periodic reconciliation of subsidiary records with the control account would have detected such a simple embezzling scheme much earlier.

Essential Characteristics of Internal Accounting Control

The characteristics of internal accounting control are a sound accounting system, reliable personnel, sound personnel policies, and physical safeguards. These four items are essential for successfully accomplishing the objectives of internal accounting control.

Internal control is meant to detect errors, whether intentional or not. Since one person's work is automatically checked by another, most errors are found and corrected. However, no system can guarantee detection of fraud; controls can be circumvented by employees handling a particular transaction who cooperate in stealing from the company.

As you might suspect, the more sophisticated a system of internal control, the higher the cost to the company. In reality, a tradeoff must occur between the cost of internal control and the probable losses that would result from the absence of such a system.

Sound Accounting System. Effective internal control begins with a sound accounting system requiring several conditions. First, accounting procedures should be designed to ensure that transactions are properly executed and recorded. A procedures manual, which specifies the way documents should flow through the system, can facilitate this goal.

Second, the procedures manual should identify the means to ensure that the records are complete and accurate. For example, a periodic comparison could be made of recorded assets to the actual physical assets to verify that the recorded items exist. Other factors that aid efficient record keeping are adequate documentation and good equipment. All source documents should be serially numbered and accounted for periodically. Custom-designed documents and devices, such as cash registers and check protectors, can ease the recording process.

A third area requiring thoughtful planning is the proper authorization of transactions and a clear assignment of responsibility, neither of which should be shared. When one person is accountable for a function, praise or blame for results can be clearly assigned.

Finally, continuing review of the accounting system and procedures is important. Reviews should be conducted by both internal and external parties. The review of an organization's accounting system by independent external parties helps reduce theft and fraud.

Reliable Personnel. An effective system of internal control is not possible without reliable personnel. Employees should be carefully selected. Honest, competent workers are important to all phases of the accounting system, especially in the area of internal control. An otherwise strong system of internal control can be destroyed by dishonest or incompetent personnel.

Sound Personnel Policies. The most important personnel policy calls for the separation of duties into four parts. First, an employee who has custody of or access to an asset, particularly cash and inventories, should not maintain the accounting record of that asset. If one person has custody of assets and also maintains the accounting records, opportunity and incentive to falsify the records to conceal a shortage can be overwhelming. Second, responsibility for maintaining the accounting records should be separated from the responsibility for engaging in or initiating business transactions. By creating this independence, the accounting records serve as a check on business operations. Third, responsibility for related duties within the accounting function should be isolated, which will strengthen the internal checks and balances and reduce the risk of fraud. For example, the person who makes entries to accounts receivable for payments should not record customer sales. Finally, to the extent possible, persons who authorize transactions should not have control over the related asset. For instance, the person who signs checks (which implies having custody of cash in the checking account) should not authorize invoices for payment.

Other important personnel considerations include the bonding of employees, mandatory vacations, and a rotation of duties. Each of these policies reduces opportunity for fraud, since employees will be unable to cover up falsified records for long periods of time.

Physical Safeguards. A business needs to be insured adequately against losses from fire, theft, and other casualties. Cash on hand should be kept to a minimum and locked in a safe. Inventory should be in a secure location, and strict controls should be maintained over the issuance of stock. In some cases, security personnel must be hired to protect inventory and other company property.

Foreign Corrupt Practices Act

FOREIGN CORRUPT PRACTICES ACT
The 1977 law making internal accounting controls mandatory for many U.S. companies.

The **Foreign Corrupt Practices Act** of 1977 has made internal accounting control a matter of law for U.S. companies registered with the Securities and Exchange Commission. The act requires that management document its own evaluation of the firm's internal control practices. Since this law is concerned primarily with regulation of internal accounting controls, it specifies the objectives these controls should fulfill, which are essentially the same as those described earlier. Although the act makes little mention of administrative controls, management still must recognize the importance of both types of control to the overall system. With the increasing complexity of the internal control environment through the use of electronic data processing and databases, management will have a more difficult time complying with the requirements of the law.

Limitations

Virtually no system of internal control can be perfect. The right person or persons feasibly can circumvent the controls of any system, resulting in inaccurate records or outright embezzlement. An internal control system, therefore, is not expected to eliminate fraud but is aimed at reducing the temptation to commit fraud.

COLLUSION
When two or more employees of an organization conspire to circumvent the company's system of internal control.

The two major limitations to achieving a "perfect" system of internal control are collusion and cost. **Collusion** occurs when two or more employees conspire to circumvent the system of internal control. Suppose an accounts payable clerk prepares an invoice from a nonexistent supplier and submits it to the treasurer along with an unsigned check for approval. Normally, the treasurer would catch this "mistake," especially if it involves a large amount, and would not sign the check before investigating. But should these two employees plot together, the system of internal control could be ineffective in protecting the firm's assets.

Cost considerations are the biggest limitation to developing a perfect system of internal control. For example, if every sales receipt were re-added by a second person, fewer mistakes would go unnoticed. Doing so, however, would probably cost more than the benefit derived. A general rule provides that a specific control should not be implemented unless the benefit exceeds the cost.

GENERAL CONTROLS
In a data processing environment, the methods and procedures relating to the overall control of all data processing activities.

APPLICATION CONTROLS
In a data processing environment, the methods and procedures designed to control some particular accounting task.

AUDIT TRAIL
The forms and records that allow the accountant to trace an original transaction forward to a summarized total or to follow a summarized total back to the original transaction.

INTERNAL CONTROL: MANUAL VERSUS EDP VERSUS DATABASE

Although the introduction of computerized data processing affects the way operations are conducted, the essential aspects of business operations remain the same, as do the goals of internal control. Frequently, however, the methods for achieving internal control must be restructured to match the characteristics of a computer system. The subsequent changeover sometimes results in a series of "control gaps" causing new risks for organizations using computers.

Increase of Computerized Crime

Computer crime is much more of a problem than most people realize. Estimates of losses range from at least $2 billion to more than $40 billion a year. No one really knows how much is being stolen, but the total is growing. New problems appear as technology advances. The combination of home computers and electronic funds transfer systems (EFTS) threatens billions of dollars in banks accessible through telephone lines. Misguided people have already made illegal switches of money by phone, and more thefts are expected as transfer systems become increasingly common.

The Union Dime Savings Bank Case

A bank teller of the Union Dime Savings Bank embezzled approximately $1.5 million between 1970 and 1973. Michael Kessler was the bank's chief teller. When a customer made a deposit, Kessler pocketed the money. Then he used a computer terminal to update the customer's account by transferring money from one of many accounts that had been inactive for years. Kessler gambled away much of the embezzled cash and was caught when police raided his bookie's operation and found Kessler's name in the records. Kessler, whose annual salary was $11,000, was betting sums as high as $30,000 a day on horse races and basketball games. Kessler was charged with stealing, pleaded guilty, and was sentenced to only 20 months in jail. Fifteen months later, he was released.

Environmental Changes

The scope of internal control in computerized systems by necessity is more complex than in manual systems due to differing organizational and processing structures. The major difference in organizational structure is that in an electronic data processing (EDP) environment, many processing steps are concentrated within one department. Thus, the natural control made available by the separation of duties in the manual recording process is eliminated. Many well-documented cases of computer crime can be recounted. An illustration of such a weakness in internal control is the Union Dime Savings Bank case (see Highlight).

Electronic data processing (EDP) systems, as well as manual systems, use some accounting control procedures relating to all data processing activities **(general controls)** and some specifically keyed to particular accounting tasks **(application controls).**

General controls attempt to restructure the separation-of-duties concept weakened by the computer environment and include the following:

1. The plan for organizing and operating the EDP facility.
2. The procedures for documenting, reviewing, testing, and approving systems, programs, or changes thereto.
3. Controls built into the equipment by the manufacturer (hardware controls).
4. Control over access to equipment and data files.
5. Other data and procedural controls affecting overall EDP operations.[3]

With an EDP system, major differences are present in the processing of accounting transactions. The most notable variation is the change in the audit trail. In a manual system, the **audit trail** consists of the forms and records that allow the accountant to trace an original transaction forward to a summarized total or to follow a summarized total back to the original transaction. In a computerized system, this audit trail is no longer a natural by-product of the system and therefore must be well planned. Thus, application controls become essential. Application controls can be categorized as input, processing, and output controls. (See Concept Summary 7.2 for examples.)

Input controls are designed to provide reasonable certainty that data received for processing have been properly authorized, converted into machine-sensible form, and identified. Input controls assure that data (including data transmitted over communication lines) have not been lost, suppressed, added, duplicated, or otherwise improperly changed. Input controls also include procedures that relate to rejection, correction, and resubmission of data that were initially incorrect.

INPUT CONTROLS
Methods and procedures designed to provide reasonable certainty that data received for processing has been properly authorized, converted into machine-sensible form, and identified.

[3]AICPA. *Professional Standards*, Vol. I. Chicago, Ill.: Commerce Clearing House, Inc., July 1979, p. 308 A.V. Sec. 321.07.

PROCESSING CONTROLS
Methods and procedures designed to see that the processing has been performed as intended for the particular application.

OUTPUT CONTROLS
Methods and procedures designed to assure the accuracy and quality of data processing results and to guarantee that only authorized personnel receive the output.

Processing controls aim to see that the EDP has been performed as intended for the particular application. In other words, these controls ensure that all transactions are processed as authorized, that no authorized transactions are omitted, and that no unauthorized transactions are added.

Output controls are intended to assure that accuracy and quality of the processing results (such as account listings or displays, reports, magnetic files, invoices, and disbursement checks) and to guarantee that only authorized personnel receive the output.

CONCEPT SUMMARY 7.2

INTERNAL CONTROL TERMS

Term	Environment	Description	Examples
Accounting controls	Most types of organizations	Refer to safeguarding assets and reliability of financial records	• Separation of duties. • Limited access to cash and inventory. • Procedures manual. • Standard forms.
Administrative controls	Most types of organizations	Refer to the procedures and records leading to management authorization of transactions	• Manager's authorization needed before cashing large personal checks. • Managerial auditing of required procedures.
General controls	EDP	Relate to all EDP activities	• Librarian for programs and off-line storage devices. • Passwords to access computer system.
Application controls	EDP	Relate to specific EDP tasks	• (Input) Authorization for file updates. • (Processing) Control totals of figures. • (Output) Limited access to certain reports.

FOR REVIEW

SUMMARY

- In an accounting sense, cash is anything commonly acceptable as a medium of exchange. At one time, cash was considered an acceptable store of value; with inflation, this is not true.
- Banks keep records of the cash transactions of their checking account customers. Documentary support for the entries includes checks, deposit slips, and debit and credit memos. Transactions are reproduced on a bank statement, which is periodically sent to the customer.
- A bank reconciliation statement explains the differences between the balances on the bank statement and those in the cash account at a particular time.
- Good management of cash requires that temporarily idle cash be invested to yield a return.
- Temporary investments are recorded initially at cost. Investments in marketable equity securities must be shown at the lower of cost or market on the firm's balance sheet.
- Internal control is the firm's system for ensuring that assets are protected and transactions are recorded in accordance with management's authorization.
- Accounting controls are the methods and procedures an organization uses to safeguard its assets and to ensure the accuracy and reliability of the financial records.
- Administrative controls are primarily concerned with the efficiency of management's authorization of transactions procedures and the adherence to those guidelines in actual practice.
- The Foreign Corrupt Practices Act of 1977 has made internal accounting control a matter of law for all U.S. companies that are registered or file reports with the SEC.
- The two major limitations to achieving a perfect system of internal control are collusion and cost.
- Regardless of whether a processing environment is manual or computerized, all effective systems of internal control have several essential common characteristics: a sound accounting system, reliable personnel, sound personnel policies, and physical safeguards.
- Increase in computerized crime and environmental changes are characteristics of computer-based accounting systems. The environmental changes include new developments in organizational structure and in processing.
- In an EDP environment, many processing steps can be concentrated into one department, thus eliminating the spontaneous internal control made available by the separation of duties in the manual recording process. General controls attempt to restructure the separation-of-duties concept that was weakened by installation of the computerized environment.
- When switching to an EDP system, major changes occur in the processing of accounting transactions. The most significant change is to the audit trail. Application controls are essential and can be categorized as input, processing, and output controls.

QUESTIONS

7-1. Give three examples of situations where a bank would send a debit memo to its customers.

7-2. What is the main purpose of a bank reconciliation statement?

7-3. What is the significance of the book balance for cash on a bank reconciliation?

7-4. How does inflation affect business cash decisions?

7-5. What is the distinction between a marketable debt security and a marketable equity security?

7-6. For good internal control over cash, how should the duties and responsibilities be separated?

7-7. What impact does the Foreign Corrupt Practices Act have on accounting?

7-8. What is an audit trail?

7-9. What are the features of a strong system of internal control?

7-10. What are the major limitations to a perfect system of internal control? Why are they considered limitations?

EXERCISES

7-E1. The Daley Company ledger shows a cash balance of $10,200 on March 31. The bank's records state a balance of $12,600 on the same date. The reconciling items consist of an $800 deposit in transit, a bank service charge of $4, and 30 outstanding checks. What is the total of the outstanding checks?

7-E2. The following are several items that might appear in a firm's bank reconciliation:

1. Checks written that have not yet been presented by the payees for cashing.
2. Bank service charges.
3. Deposit in transit.
4. A cancelled check recorded on the books for less than the amount of the check.
5. A check deposited in the account but returned due to insufficient funds.
6. The collection by the bank of a note plus interest for the firm.
7. An error by the firm in recording a deposit of $1,523 as $1,503.

Identify by letter each item as it would appear on a bank reconciliation statement using the following:

A—add to the balance per books
B—deduct from the balance per books
C—add to the balance per bank
D—deduct from the balance per bank

7-E3. Pizza King Restaurants Incorporated has recently taken out a bank loan of $375,000. The interest payment for one year on the loan is $65,625. Annual inflation is forecasted at 8%. Ignoring income tax effects, what is the stated rate of interest on the loan and what will be the effective rate of interest on the loan for the next year, considering expected inflation?

7-E4. On July 1, Harrison Company holds the following temporary investments:

Holding	Cost	Current Market	Permanent?
Common stock of Future, Inc.	$ 6,000	$ 7,100	Yes
Common stock of Last Word Fashions	1,500	1,450	No
Preferred stock of Sapphire Mines	15,000	17,000	No
Bonds of Band Y Retailers	5,000	4,500	No

What amounts pertaining to these holdings should appear on the statement of financial position? The income statement? (No allowance account balance exists.)

7-E5. Identify an internal control procedure that would prevent the following situations in a company:

a. To cover his theft of cash receipts, the sales manager prepares fictitious sales returns vouchers that indicate the return of cash sales merchandise.
b. Checks mailed to the company in payment of accounts receivable are stolen by the cashier/bookkeeper, who then credits the proper accounts and creates false receivables to keep the records in balance.
c. The office manager issues checks to fictitious suppliers and deposits them in accounts under those names where he is listed as an authorized signer of checks. The books are kept in balance by charging the purchases to the Inventory account.

7-E6. Would the following items be general or application controls?

a. A computer control to see that no payroll check is issued for over $500.
b. Rules allowing only authorized personnel access to the computer.
c. A listing of exceptions produced after a particular program is run.
d. The restriction of computer programmers from routine computer operations.
e. The use of a librarian to check out and receive data files and programs.

7-E7. What four internal control rules were violated in the Fairfax situation described on pages 239–40? Even if controls had been in place, what limitation of internal control procedures might have allowed embezzlement anyway?

PROBLEM SET A

7-A1. Bank Reconciliation with Journal Entries. The ABC Company records show the following data for the month of May:

1.	Bank balance, May 31	$46,500
2.	Service charges for May	5
3.	NSF check returned with statement	60
4.	Note collected by the bank for ABC Company	7,000
5.	Debit memo for $389 that shows a correction for an error from previous month when the bank credited the ABC Company account for a check belonging to the BAC Corporation	389
6.	Interest received on the note collected in (4)	100
7.	Book balance, May 31	41,900
8.	Cash on hand	700
9.	Deposit unrecorded by bank	6,400
10.	Outstanding checks	4,665

Required

a. Prepare a bank reconciliation.
b. Give required journal entries for May 31.
c. Assuming that the foregoing information is all the cash-related data for the ABC Company, what cash figure should appear on the statement of financial position?

7-A2. Effective Interest Rates. Kite Loft Incorporated currently has a loan outstanding at the Eastern National Bank. Kite Loft makes semiannual payments for interest of $10,500. The stated rate of interest on the loan is 12%. Currently, inflation is at an annual rate of 10%.

Required

Ignoring income tax effects, compute the principal amount of the loan and the effective annual rate of interest, assuming the loan is repaid in one year and inflation occurs evenly throughout the year.

7-A3. Reporting on Temporary Equity Investments. O'Brien and Company holds only one type of stock as a temporary investment. O'Brien originally purchased 300 shares for $60 a share on January 15. One-third of this holding was sold on February 18 for $5,800. Fifty more shares were sold on March 26 for $3,100. The market price of the stock was $58 a share on January 21, $57 on February 28, and $61 on March 31.

Required

a. What information and amounts pertaining to this investment will be reported on the statement of financial position for each month?
b. What information and amounts will be reported on the income statement for each month?

7-A4. Journal Entries for Temporary Investments. Tracy Mills had the following transactions and information dealing with its short-term investments:

January 10	Purchased for $3,400 a note from Bonded Way.
February 16	Purchased $6,000 of Lotus Products common stock at $100 a share.
March 2	Sold 20 shares of the Lotus stock for $110 a share.
March 10	Purchased 100 shares of Iris Haven stock for $55 a share.
March 17	Sold 20 more shares of Lotus stock for $112 a share.

Market values for the investments on March 31 are as follows:

Bonded Way note, $3,300
Lotus Products stock, $112 a share
Iris Haven stock, $54 a share

Required

a. Prepare journal entries for the five transactions.
b. What items dealing with these holdings will appear on Tracy Mills' financial statements as of March 31?

7-A5. Bank Reconciliation Concepts. The following are the cash receipts and the cash payments for Mailer Corporation for the month of February:

Cash Receipts

Date	Particulars	Cost (Dr.)
Feb. 1	Anders Company	$ 285
2	J. T. Noonan & Company	1,976
4	McGill Brothers	258
8	Aramco	2,176
10	Konopka Mfg.	629
11	Conroy Limited	566
12	Hamstra & Sons	292
15	Temple University	2,110
18	Chaser Corporation	762
19	Hotel Plaza	1,420
21	Anders Company	467
27	Folk and Lewis	236
28	Mo Trio Motors	1,102
	Total	$12,279

Cash Payments

Check Number	Date	Particulars	Cash (Cr.)
2122	Feb. 2	Alsation Abbey	$ 300
2123	5	Herman Brothers	2,133
2124	8	Kaufman's	300
2125	9	Meadow Green	125
2126	11	Standforth Assn.	489
2127	13	Whiting Supply	285
2128	15	Arkie Corporation	1,186
2129	18	Helen's Travel Agency	2,235
2130	23	Lemmelin Ltd.	416
2131	25	Mish and Company	178
2132	25	Siragusa, Inc.	210
2133	26	Bestbyis Brokerage	1,500
2134	27	Municipal Utilities	142
		Total	$9,499

All cash receipts in February were deposited at the local bank at the end of the day they were received and were entered in the journal. On February 17, the bank returned Hamstra & Sons' check due to NSF. This amount is still uncollected, and the return of the check has not been recorded in the cash account. The beginning cash balance on February 1 was $43,121.

Promptly at the end of the month, the bank prepared and sent the following bank statement:

Mailer Corporation
Bank Statement
February 28, 1986

		Charges	Credits	
February 1	Balance			$48,965
	Deposit		6,115	55,080
2	Deposit		285	55,365
3	Deposit		1,976	57,341
5	Deposit		258	57,599
6	Check #2122	300		57,299
9	Deposit		2,176	59,475
10	Check #2110	6,959		52,516
	Check #2125	125		52,391
11	Deposit		629	53,020
	Check #2124	300		52,720
12	Deposit		566	53,286
13	Deposit		292	53,578
	Check #2108	5,000		48,578
16	Deposit		2,110	50,688
	Check #2127	285		50,403
17	Check #2126	489		49,914
	NSF Check	292		49,622
18	Check #2128	1,816		47,806
20	Check #2129	2,235		45,571
	Deposit		762	46,333
	Deposit		1,420	47,753
21	Deposit		467	48,220
22	Check #2123	2,133		46,087
26	Check #2131	178		45,909
	Check # 2132	210		45,699
28	Check #2134	142		45,557
	Deposit		236	45,793
	Service Charges	43		45,750

Required

a. What deposits were in transit on January 31? On February 28?
b. What checks were outstanding on January 31? On February 28? (Mailer uses checks in consecutive order; no pre-February checks continue to be outstanding at the end of February.)
c. What error in recording did Mailer's treasurer make? By how much?
d. Prepare a reconciliation dated February 28.
e. Prepare the necessary journal entry.

7-A6. Types of Internal Controls. Discuss the differences between control in a manual environment and control in an EDP environment. List five examples of general controls and five examples of application controls.

7-A7. Internal Control Concerns. Betty's Bakery, a small proprietorship, has been operating for ten years. For the past five years Betty's cousin Martha has handled all the cash activities of the store. Her responsibilities include counting and depositing cash receipts, handling accounts receivable and accounts payable, reconciling bank statements, doing payroll, and writing off bad debts.

Martha recently purchased a new Rolls Royce. Knowing that Martha is not wealthy and is not overpaid, Betty cannot help but wonder how Martha can afford the new car. She fears that some of the money has come from her bakery inappropriately.

Required

Upon reviewing the situation, determine how Betty might have left the firm vulnerable to illegal actions by Martha.

PROBLEM SET B

7-B1. Bank Reconciliation with Journal Entries. Hi-Point Productions deposits all cash in the First National Bank. The following activities are recorded on HPP's records in the month of January:

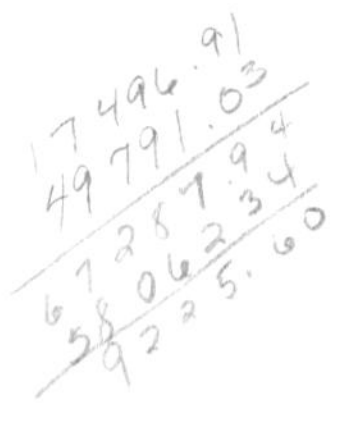

1. The ledger balance on January 1 is $17,496.91.
2. Cash receipts for the month total $49,791.03; checks written total $58,062.34.
3. The bank statement shows a January 31 balance of $6,637.02.
4. An NSF check on the account of Bob Hanna for $976.47 has been returned with the bank statement.
5. The following checks are outstanding as of January 31: #3142 for $40.30; #3347 for $110.58; #3581 for $127.20; #3969 for $69.12; #3970 for $6.82; #4001 for $39.30.
6. The bank has erroneously deducted a check of Petty Productions for $546.33 from the Hi-Point Productions account.
7. On January 31, a deposit of $2,349.30 is in transit.
8. The Hi-Point Productions accountant has made an error in recording a check received from Fox Industries. The check for $952.84, correctly handled by the bank, has been recorded as $52.84.
9. The January bank service charge is $9.80.

Required

a. Prepare a bank reconciliation as of January 31.
b. Prepare any required journal entries as of January 31.

7-B2. Effective Interest Rates. The Phyrst Company borrowed $250,000 from the State National Bank at a stated interest rate of 15% payable in one year. Currently, the annual inflation rate is 9%. (Ignore income tax effects.)

Required

a. What is the amount of interest Phyrst Company will have to pay for a year? For five months?
b. Considering inflation, find the amount of (current) money that is equivalent in purchasing power to the sum that will be repaid one year from now.
c. What is the effective interest rate in terms of current purchasing power?

7-B3. Reporting on Temporary Equity Investments. Benjamin's Outlet, Inc., carries three stocks in its temporary investment portfolio. Information relating to these stocks on the statement of financial position dates is as follows:

	Stocks		
	Azure Corp.	**Baleful Co.**	**Charisma, Inc.**
January 31			
Cost of shares held	$1,000	$19,000	$5,000
Current value	1,200	18,500	5,000
April 30			
Cost of shares held	1,000	12,000	5,000
Current value	1,050	11,500	5,000
July 31			
Cost of shares held	1,500	12,000	5,000
Current value	1,600	11,650	5,050
October 31			
Cost of shares held	1,500	6,000	5,000
Current value	1;600	5,900	5,100

Required

a. Show the portion of the statement of financial position pertaining to temporary investments on each of the preceding dates.
b. What amounts and descriptions would appear on the four income statements, excluding any gain or loss from the sale of holdings?

7-B4. Journal Entries for Temporary Investments. The Ludi-Starr Company has decided to regularly invest idle cash in stocks or bonds. It has made no previous temporary investments. During 1987, the following events take place:

January 16	Company purchases 50 shares of Northtown common stock for $30 a share.
March 12	Company purchases 50 additional shares of Northtown common stock for $32 a share.
June 22	Company purchases a $5,000 Feelie, Inc., note.
August 6	Company purchases 100 shares of Southside stock for a total price of $6,000.
October 15	Company sells 25 shares of Southside stock for $65 each.

Ludi-Starr prepares financial statements on a quarterly basis at the end of March, June, September, and December. At those times, the current market values of the investments are as follows:

	March 31	June 30	September 30	December 31
Northtown stock, per share	$35	$ 30	$ 30	$ 28
Feelie, Inc., note		5,025*	5,000	4,800*
Southside stock, per share			55	60

*Judged temporary in nature

Required

a. Prepare all necessary journal entries dealing with Ludi-Starr's temporary investments in 1987.
b. At what amounts should the temporary investments be listed on the quarterly statements of financial position?

7-B5. Bank Reconciliation Concepts. The Blazer Company has the following transactions during March:

March 1–30	Cash sales totaling $10,830 are deposited in the First Bank.
March 1–31	Checks #1832 through #1853 are written for a total amount of $7,308 in payment of operating expenses.
March 1–31	Cash received from customers on account in the amount of $3,695 is deposited.
March 5	A customer's check for $110 is returned from the bank marked NSF.
March 11	A computer is purchased for $10,000. A note is given as promise of payment.
March 31	Miscellaneous income of $350 is deposited.

Also during March, First Bank records the following transactions dealing with Blazer Company's account:

March 1–31	Deposits of $14,525 are credited.
March 1–31	Checks #1820 for $510 and #1832 through #1852 for $7,200 are presented and clear the account.
March 3	An NSF check for $110 is deducted from the account and returned to Blazer.
March 31	Service charges of $15 are deducted.

Additional data available shows the following:

March 1 balances	
Blazer's cash in bank account	$9,450
First Bank's balance for Blazer's account	9,960

Required

Determine the following amounts:

a. March 31 balance in Blazer's Cash in Bank account before reconciliation.
b. March 31 balance in First Bank's account for Blazer.
c. Deposits in transit, March 31.
d. Outstanding checks, March 31.
e. The actual March 31 amount of cash for Blazer.

7-B6. Types of Internal Controls. Define the following terms and give three examples of each

a. input control
b. processing control
c. output control

7-B7. Internal Control Concerns. The 4-R Corporation hired a certified public accountant to design a system of internal control especially suited to its operations. Assuming that the CPA has finished the work and the newly designed system of internal control is in use, will it be possible for any type of fraud to occur without immediate detection once the new system is in full operation? Describe two limitations inherent in any system of internal control that will prevent it from providing absolute assurance against inefficiency and fraud.

APPENDIX B
SPECIAL-PURPOSE ACCOUNTING RECORDS

Transactions involving sales, purchases, and cash usually occur with great frequency in business organizations. To record each transaction involving sales, purchases, or cash in the general journal and general ledger would be inefficient and would require continual use of the prime books of record. In addition, a very cluttered set of records would be difficult to use for data analysis in a decision context.

SPECIAL JOURNAL
A journal for keeping records of a specific type.

Most businesses, therefore, have adopted the practice of using a **special journal** that records the details of a particular type of transaction. Rather than post every transaction to the general ledger, businesses periodically enter transaction summaries in the general journal and general ledger. They use some special journals in conjunction with a special ledger showing more detail. This type of ledger is called a **subsidiary ledger,** and it contains the records of a set of accounts that, taken collectively, equal the balance in a general ledger account. Exhibit B.1 shows the relationship between the special-purpose sales journal and ledger and the general records of a business. Other special journals and ledgers are similarly related.

SUBSIDIARY LEDGER
A set of accounts that taken collectively equal an overall control account.

Using special journals and ledgers for recording frequently repeated transactions accomplishes the following:

1. Removes clutter from the general journal and general ledger.
2. Allows an efficient division of labor in the bookkeeping process.
3. Provides support for control purposes.
4. Supports efficiency in summarizing data for managerial analysis.

EXHIBIT B.1

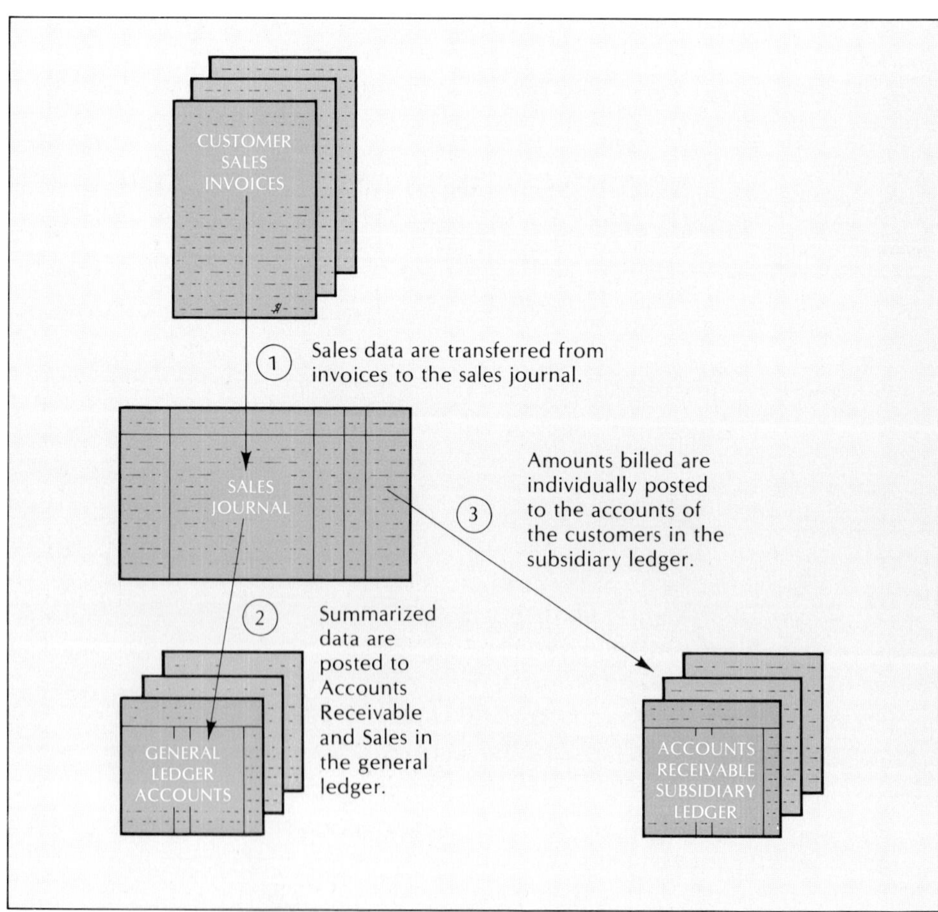
CUSTOMER
SALES
INVOICES
1
Sales data are transferred from invoices to the sales journal.
SALES
JOURNAL
3
Amounts billed are individually posted to the accounts of the customers in the subsidiary ledger.
2
Summarized data are posted to Accounts Receivable and Sales in the general ledger.
GENERAL
LEDGER
ACCOUNTS
ACCOUNTS
RECEIVABLE
SUBSIDIARY
LEDGER

Although specialized records can be adapted for any frequently repeated transaction, this appendix focuses on special journals for purchases, sales, and cash. It also describes the nature and use of a petty cash fund.

PURCHASES JOURNAL

The purchases journal is designed to record purchases efficiently. Although using the general journal would require at least three lines to record each purchase (a debit line, a credit line, and an explanation), a purchases journal allows each purchase to be recorded on a single line using multiple columns in place of separate lines. The columns used by specific firms can differ slightly to fit the firm's situation, but purchases journals always have columns for credits to accounts payable and debits to purchases (of inventory). The accounts payable and purchases columns can be combined if all transactions recorded in the journal are only for purchases of inventory. Exhibit B.2 shows an example of a purchases journal. This journal has columns to record the debit part of an entry for credit purchases of noninventory

EXHIBIT B.2

PURCHASES JOURNAL — **Page 15**

Date		Terms	Invoice Number	Creditor	Accounts Payable Cr. √	Accounts Payable Cr. Amount	Purchases Dr. Amount	Miscellaneous Accounts Dr. Account	P R	Amount
1987										
July	8	n/30	821	Matthew Corp.	24	3280 00	3280 00			
	10	2/10, n/30	16789	Uneeda Toy Co.	11	5610 00	5610 00			
	10	1/15, n/30	1402	Western Unlimited	27	235 00	235 00			
	11	n/15	61	Jason, Inc.	93	1200 00	1200 00			
	13	2/30, n/60	923	Seasons Greetings	72	2150 00	2150 00			
	14	3/10, n/45	7190L	Systems, Inc.	54	768 00	768 00			
	14	n/30	625	Smith and Co.	75	1115 00	1115 00			
	31	n/30	8001	Wales Corp.	86	495 00		Store supplies	123	495 00
	31			Totals		23682 00	23187 00			495 00
						(215)	(112)			(√)

items. The supplier is identified in the column labeled Creditor. Thus, any type of credit purchase could be recorded in this particular purchases journal.

When summaries from a specialized journal are entered in the general ledger, the total for any column with a specific account title is entered in the corresponding general ledger account. In Exhibit B.2, the totals of the columns for accounts payable ($23,682) and purchases ($23,187) are entered in the general ledger accounts for Accounts Payable and Purchases. The column total for accounts payable is entered as a credit to Accounts Payable; the column total for purchases is entered as a debit in the general ledger account, Purchases. When the special journal column total has been posted to the appropriate general ledger account, the general ledger account number is written under the column total to show that the posting has been completed.

Purchase transactions involving noninventory items require identification of the account to be debited and the amount of the purchase. Since the accounts are different in the miscellaneous columns, posting of a miscellaneous column total to the general ledger is not possible. Each account entered into the miscellaneous column must be individually posted to the appropriate general ledger account. In Exhibit B.2, store supplies provides an example of this procedure. The account number from the general ledger is entered in the posting reference column (123 in this case) to indicate that the posting of debits has been completed. The check mark under the total of Miscellaneous Accounts Dr. indicates that no column total should be posted.

Amounts owed to each supplier are also posted individually to each creditor's record in the accounts payable subsidiary ledger. This subsidiary record is vital. Determining whom the company owes and how much it owes to each creditor is practically impossible if all purchases and cash payments are recorded in one large payable account. Therefore, each individual vendor's account in the accounts payable subsidiary ledger is a record of the amount of charge purchases from and payments to that vendor. The amounts charged and paid to all vendors in total are recorded in the Accounts Payable control account in the general ledger. The sum of the balances of the individual vendor accounts should therefore always equal the balance in the general ledger account of Accounts Payable. We will demonstrate this detail-to-control-account relationship more fully when discussing the cash receipts journal.

SALES JOURNAL

The sales journal is similar to the purchases journal and is designed to record sales on account efficiently. Like credit purchases, sales on account all have the same repetitive general ledger effect (that is, a debit to Accounts Receivable and a credit to Sales for the amount of the transaction). Exhibit B.3 shows an example of a sales journal. Note that the only entry in this journal is for regular sales of merchandise on account to customers. Without a miscellaneous column, sales of items other than merchandise cannot be entered in this journal. In our example, the single column total is posted periodically to both the Accounts Receivable (Dr.) and the Sales accounts (Cr.) in the general ledger. Again, entry of the account numbers for Accounts Receivable and for Sales under the column total indicates that the posting has been completed for the column total. The amount each individual customer owes is posted to that particular customer's account in the accounts receivable subsidiary ledger. As with accounts payable, the total of the accounts receivable subsidiary ledger should always be equal to the total in the Accounts Receivable control account in the general ledger.

EXHIBIT B.3

SALES JOURNAL					Page 24
Date		Description	Invoice Number	P R	Accts. Rec. Dr. / Sales Cr.
1987					
Oct.	6	Larson Corp.	8123	626	7680 90
	6	Tiller Company	8124	678	2152 00
	6	Moon-Lion	8125	691	5690 45
	7	Frederick, Inc.	8126	685	4275 32
	7	Giant Productions	8127	656	8100 10
	8	April Showers, Ltd.	8128	617	1280 74
	31	Lastone Co.	8142	610	6123 00
	31	Totals	—		65827 00
					(162) (410)

■ CONCEPT SUMMARY B.1

JOURNALS AND LEDGERS

General journal	Receives entries when transactions do not fit a special journal. Requires more than one line per transaction. Each line posted to general ledger. Some lines also posted to subsidiary ledgers.
Special journal	Time-saving device adapted to firm's special needs. One line per transaction. Where feasible, totals posted to general ledger. Individual lines usually posted to subsidiary ledger.
General ledger	Contains data to support all balance sheet and income statement accounts. Total of debits always equals total of credits.
Subsidiary ledger	Provides detail for a particular account in the general ledger. Total of debits less total of credits (or vice versa) is always equal to the total recorded in the control account in the general ledger.

Cash Receipts Journal

Like other special journals, the cash receipts journal facilitates the accounting of similar economic events, in this case, transactions involving cash receipts. Instead of requiring the entry of a separate amount into the accounting system for each cash receipt, the specialized journal permits us to accumulate details and make a summary journal entry to the general journal at the end of a week or a month reflecting all the cash receipts of that period. Exhibit B.4 shows a page from a cash receipts journal for the week ending March 31.

The miscellaneous accounts credit column is used to record cash receipt events that are neither sales to nor collections from customers. In Exhibit B.4, the receipt of $3,000 for scrap sold to Kent Corporation is an example of such a miscellaneous entry.

The posting reference (PR) column provides space for the numbers assigned to the individual accounts that receive miscellaneous credits or to customer accounts maintained in an accounts receivable subsidiary ledger. (Again note that any line that is posted entirely by use of the column total, such as cash sales, has a check mark to indicate that no posting is necessary.) Cash receipts journal amounts are posted to the general ledger accounts, which then appear as in Exhibit B.5.

Payments from customers are posted individually to the proper accounts of the accounts receivable subsidiary ledger from the cash receipts journal. The subsidiary accounts are also shown in Exhibit B.5.

Note that the total of the five amounts posted to the right side of the subsidiary accounts equals $18,160, the same amount posted to the Accounts Receivable control account in the general ledger. A similar relationship exists between the posting of sales to the Sales account and to the customers' accounts from the sales

EXHIBIT B.4

Cash Receipts Journal **Page 9**

	Date	Account Credited	PR	Cash Dr.	Sales Discount Dr.	Accounts Receivable Cr.	Miscellaneous Accounts Cr.	Sales Cr.	
	1987								
1	Mar. 27	Cash sales	√	12650 00				12650 00	1
2	27	Larson Corp.	626	4280 00		4280 00			2
3	28	Cash sales	√	10620 00				10620 00	3
4	28	John Company	625	1280 00		1280 00			4
5	28	Frederick, Inc.	685	7625 00	175 00	7800 00			5
6	29	Cash sales	√	11826 00				11826 00	6
7	30	Cash sales	√	10680 00				10680 00	7
8	31	Cash sales	√	9400 00				9400 00	8
9	31	Johnson and Sons	630	3600 00		3600 00			9
10	31	Law and Co.	641	1200 00		1200 00			10
11	31	Misc. income (Kent Corp.)	525	3000 00			3000 00		11
12									12
13	31	Totals	√	76161 00	175 00	18160 00	3000 00	55176 00	13
14				(101)	(412)	(162)	(√)	(410)	14
15									15

EXHIBIT B.5

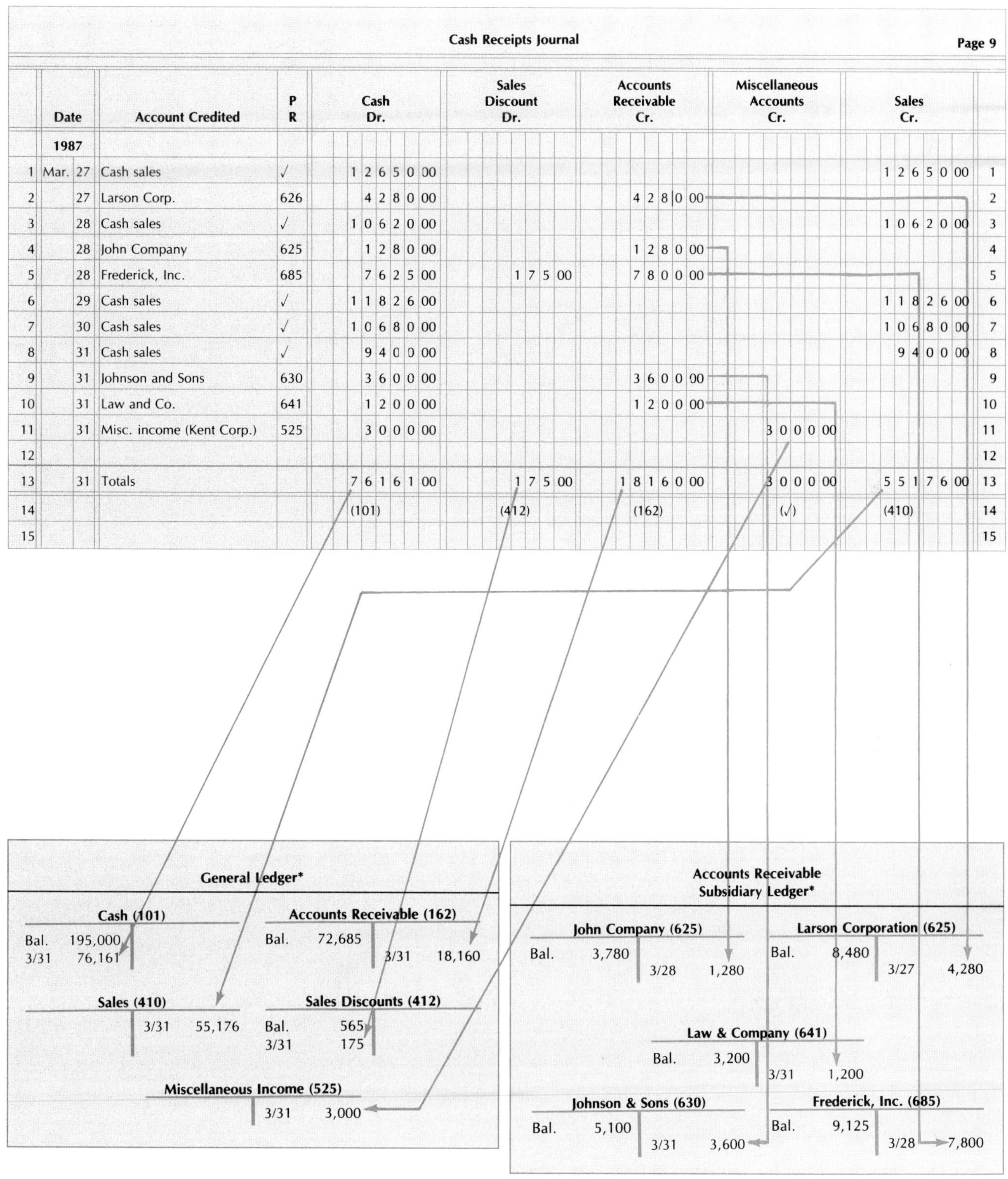

Cash Receipts Journal Page 9

	Date		Account Credited	P R	Cash Dr.	Sales Discount Dr.	Accounts Receivable Cr.	Miscellaneous Accounts Cr.	Sales Cr.	
	1987									
1	Mar.	27	Cash sales	√	12650 00				12650 00	1
2		27	Larson Corp.	626	4280 00		4280 00			2
3		28	Cash sales	√	10620 00				10620 00	3
4		28	John Company	625	1280 00		1280 00			4
5		28	Frederick, Inc.	685	7625 00	175 00	7800 00			5
6		29	Cash sales	√	11826 00				11826 00	6
7		30	Cash sales	√	10680 00				10680 00	7
8		31	Cash sales	√	9400 00				9400 00	8
9		31	Johnson and Sons	630	3600 00		3600 00			9
10		31	Law and Co.	641	1200 00		1200 00			10
11		31	Misc. income (Kent Corp.)	525	3000 00			3000 00		11
12										12
13		31	Totals		76161 00	175 00	18160 00	3000 00	55176 00	13
14					(101)	(412)	(162)	(√)	(410)	14
15										15

General Ledger*

Cash (101)

Debit		Credit	
Bal.	195,000		
3/31	76,161		

Accounts Receivable (162)

Debit		Credit	
Bal.	72,685	3/31	18,160

Sales (410)

Debit		Credit	
		3/31	55,176

Sales Discounts (412)

Debit		Credit	
Bal.	565		
3/31	175		

Miscellaneous Income (525)

Debit		Credit	
		3/31	3,000

Accounts Receivable Subsidiary Ledger*

John Company (625)

Debit		Credit	
Bal.	3,780	3/28	1,280

Larson Corporation (625)

Debit		Credit	
Bal.	8,480	3/27	4,280

Law & Company (641)

Debit		Credit	
Bal.	3,200	3/31	1,200

Johnson & Sons (630)

Debit		Credit	
Bal.	5,100	3/31	3,600

Frederick, Inc. (685)

Debit		Credit	
Bal.	9,125	3/28	7,800

*Only pertinent accounts are shown.

journal (described earlier). To ensure that this equality is maintained, the subsidiary ledger accounts are periodically reconciled to the general ledger control account (see Exhibit B.6).

EXHIBIT B.6

RECONCILIATION OF THE ACCOUNTS RECEIVABLE SUBSIDIARY LEDGER

Ceasar Corporation
Reconciliation of Accounts Receivable Ledger
March 31, 1987

Credit customers	
April Showers, Ltd.	$15,000
Frederick, Inc.	1,325
Giant Productions	9,500
John Company	2,500
Johnson & Sons	1,500
Kent Corporation	500
Law & Company	2,000
Larson Corporation	4,200
Lastone Company	8,500
Moon-Lion	7,000
Tiller Company	2,500
Total customers' balances	$54,525
Accounts receivable balance	$54,525

As you can see, a particular subsidiary ledger provides the detailed individual account data that have been summarized in a related control account from the general ledger.

Cash Payments Journal

A fourth specialized journal summarizes the cash payments over a certain period of time. Exhibit B.7 shows a typical cash payments journal. Most of the payments were made on accounts payable, but one miscellaneous payment was made on a long-term note. As with the posting process from the cash receipts journal, each supplier's account in the accounts payable subsidiary ledger is decreased by the total of the relevant individual payment, including any discount taken. The Accounts Payable control account in the general ledger will be decreased by $11,070. The other totals are posted to Note Payable, $1,000; Purchase Discounts, $170; and Cash, $11,900. The accounts payable subsidiary ledger also is reconciled periodically with its control account, Accounts Payable. The form of this reconciliation is the same as the format in Exhibit B.6 for accounts receivable.

CONCEPT SUMMARY B.2

COMMON USES OF SPECIAL JOURNALS

Transaction	Recorded In
Purchases on account	Purchases journal
Sales of merchandise on account	Sales journal
Receipt of cash from any source	Cash receipts journal
Payment of cash for any purpose	Cash payments journal

EXHIBIT B.7

	Cash Payment Journal							Page 12
	Date		Chk. No.	Account Debited	P R	Cash Cr.	Purchases Discounts Cr.	Accounts Payable Dr.	Miscellaneous Accounts Dr.
	1987								
1	Mar.	27	263	Joseph & Sons	810	2640 00		2640 00	
2		28	264	Matthew Corp.	824	1775 00	50 00	1825 00	
3		30	265	Hilary Company	863	4160 00	120 00	4280 00	
4		30	266	Jason, Inc.	893	2325 00		2325 00	
5		30	267	National Bank	285	1000 00			1000 00
6									
7		31		Totals		11900 00	170 00	11070 00	1000 00
8						(101)	(720)	(215)	(√)
9									
10									
11									

VOUCHER SYSTEMS

To increase control over expenditures, some companies, rather than keeping a purchases journal, utilize a system of preparing vouchers for each expected payment. A **voucher** is a special form that represents written authorization to pay cash. Voucher numbers are assigned in sequence to transactions of this type, and the voucher and the source document for future cash payment can then be conveniently filed according to the date due. The voucher register replaces the purchases journal, and the check register serves as a cash payments journal.

VOUCHER
A special form prepared to provide control over and authorization for expenditures.

The voucher system facilitates cash management. Bills are paid in time to take advantage of cash discounts, and the cash due to be disbursed on a given day is readily determinable. Voucher systems can also be adapted to cash receipts for similar reasons.

PETTY CASH RECORDS

Increasingly, our world is closer to being a cashless society; we can purchase almost anything with checks and credit cards. Running an active business, however, brings forth some situations for which cash is still appropriate, such as paying a cab fare or paying for a C.O.D. package. A company usually arranges to have a cash fund

PETTY CASH
A special cash fund for paying small expenditures where actual cash is required, such as cab fares and small C.O.D. packages.

IMPREST SYSTEM
A system that establishes an account or fund at a certain level and that requires periodic replenishment to that level.

close at hand to meet such expenses. This fund **(petty cash)** is a relatively small amount of cash kept by a business to meet certain incidental expenses.

Businesses frequently maintain petty cash under an imprest system. An **imprest system** requires that an account or fund, in this case Petty Cash, have a certain predetermined balance, with occasional replenishment occurring periodically or as needed. A reimbursement to the petty cash fund represents the actual amount of expenses incurred in the prior period and for which receipts should have been collected. This concept can be better explained with the help of the following example.

Ball Company has decided to keep a petty cash account under the imprest system. Experience has shown that incidental expenses have been less than $100 a week. To start the petty cash fund, the treasury department on May 11 draws a check for $100 on the Ball Company's checking account; the $100 in cash is withdrawn and entrusted to the petty cashier. The general journal entry would be as follows:

May 11	Petty cash	100	
	Cash at bank		100
	(to establish petty cash fund)		

As occasions to use cash from the fund arise, the cashier replaces the cash with a voucher. In this case, a voucher is simply an explanation of how the money has been spent. The total of the unreimbursed vouchers and cash in the fund should always total the authorized balance for control purposes, in our example $100. Assume that the expenses for the first week of operation of the petty cash account are logged routinely and appear in a format like that in Exhibit B.8.

Since the expenses paid out of petty cash total $85, the original $100 placed in the fund is nearly exhausted. To replenish the fund, a check is drawn for the amount of the expenditures, $85. The check is cashed, and the money is turned over to the custodian of the fund. The disbursement vouchers totaling the amount of the expenditure should be perforated to prevent their reuse. The journal entry to record the issuance of the check to replenish the fund (normally recorded in the cash payments journal) is as follows:

May 15	Supplies expense	8	
	Entertainment expense	44	
	Transportation expense	23	
	Cleaning expense	10	
	Cash at bank		85
	(to replenish weekly incidental expenses)		

The fact that normally an entry is made to the Petty Cash account only when the fund is first established should be emphasized. Each time the fund is replenished, the appropriate expense accounts are charged, and the Cash at Bank account (*not* Petty Cash account) is credited. Journal entries made to the Petty Cash account after the account is established would occur only if a decision is made to discontinue or to change the size of the fund.

EXHIBIT B.8

BALL COMPANY
Columnar Petty Cash Book

	Date		Particulars	Cash Cr. #101	Supplies Expense Dr. #521	Entertainment Expense Dr. #536	Transportation Expense Dr. #562	Miscellaneous Debits		
								Title	Acct. No.	Amount
	1987									
1	May	11	Mr. Themes	18 00			18 00			
2		11	Fox Stationery	8 00	8 00					
3		12	Ms. Lavell	5 00			5 00			
4		12	Ms. Sorenson	19 00		19 00				
5		13	Ms. Dunaway	25 00		25 00				
6		15	Bishop Laundry	10 00				Cleaning expense	552	10 00
7										
8			Totals	85 00	8 00	44 00	23 00			10 00
9										
10										
11										
12										
13										
14										

The petty cash fund is usually replenished at the end of an accounting period even if the fund is not running low. This allows the vouchers in the fund to be charged to the expense accounts before the accounts are closed and financial statements are prepared. If the total of cash and vouchers is not the required balance, the discrepancy should be recorded in an account called Cash Short and Over. The account is debited for shortages and credited for overages. A debit balance in the Cash Short and Over account is treated as an expense on the income statement. A credit balance, on the other hand, is considered to be additional revenue.

SUMMARY

- Special journals are used for efficient recording of frequently repeated transactions.
- Some special journals are used in conjunction with subsidiary ledgers that show details of a control account in the general ledger.
- Posting from special journals usually is done with summarized entries.
- A voucher system provides additional control over expenditures through the use of special forms that represent written authorization to pay cash.
- Petty cash is often handled under an imprest system.

EXERCISES

B-E1. The following journals are used by one firm. Identify the journal where each of the ten given transactions should be recorded:

a. General journal
b. Sales journal
c. Purchases journal
d. Cash receipts journal
e. Cash payments journal

1. Issued shares of the firm's stock in exchange for a building.
2. Sold goods for cash.
3. Bought merchandise on account.
4. Sold goods on account.
5. Sold for cash a display fixture no longer used by the firm.
6. Paid supplier for merchandise in (3).
7. Received payment from a customer for a previous purchase.
8. Purchased but did not pay for a new delivery truck.
9. Reimbursed petty cash for miscellaneous expenses.
10. Adjusted the insurance account for the expired amount.

B-E2. The Bolding Retail Company maintains a special journal for sales and one for cash receipts. (These journals follow the formats in the exhibits in this appendix.) Record the following transactions in the appropriate journal. If the transaction should be recorded in a journal other than the sales or cash receipts journals, indicate which one in lieu of making an entry.

August 1 Cash sales of merchandise, $8,350.
Credit sales of merchandise, $3,120, to the following:

Madison Co., Acct. #10	Inv. #7344	$1,210
Malloy, Inc., Acct. #20	Inv. #7345	$ 950
Tracy Fabrics, Acct. #30	Inv. #7346	$ 530
Wiggenthulers, Acct. #40	Inv. #7347	$ 430

August 2 Payment is received from Madison, $1,089, the full amount of the bill less a 10% discount.
August 4 Wiggenthulers paid in full, $430.
August 5 Goods that cost $800 are returned to the supplier, Handy Corp., for full credit.
August 8 Cash sales of merchandise, $10,200. Credit sales of $1,500, all to Madison Co., on Inv. #7348.
August 9 Malloy pays $300 on its account.
August 10 Jeffy Co. pays $5,900 for a piece of land Bolding no longer needs.
August 10 Tracy Fabrics settles its account in full, taking the allowed discount of 5%.

B-E3. The following is a cash payments journal:

Cash Payments Journal Page 35

	Date		Chk. No.	Account Debited	PR	Accounts Payable Dr.	Miscellaneous Accounts Dr.	Cash Cr.	Purchases Discounts Cr.	
	1988									
1	July	1	510	Wise Traffic		125 00		120 00	5 00	1
2		2	511	Kellicot		150 00		150 00		2
3		5	512	State Savings & Loan (Note)			400 00	400 00		3
4		5	513	Robeson and Sons		100 00		96 00	4 00	4
5		7	514	Kellicot		150 00		150 00		5
6										6
7		7	/	Totals	/	525 00	400 00	916 00	9 00	7
8										8
9										9

Accounts Payable balances at the start of the month are as follows:

Acct. #223 Robeson and Sons, $180
Acct. #215 Kellicot, $450
Acct. #241 Wise Traffic, $125

Post the balances and the entries to the general ledger and accounts payable subsidiary ledger. The State Savings and Loan account balance on July 1 is $1,200 (account #2311). Accounts Payable is #2001; Purchase Discounts is #2005. Cash on July 1 has a balance of $5,800 (account #1001).

B-E4. Superior Products maintains a petty cash record having the following columns:

Date
Received by
Cash credit
Supplies expense debit
Mailing expense debit
Delivery expense debit
Miscellaneous debits—title
Miscellaneous debits—acct. no.
Miscellaneous debits—amount

Enter the following petty cash transactions. Total and rule the page.

November 4	Postage stamps are purchased by F. Stevens for $21.75.
November 5	Gas and oil are put in the delivery van by S. Williams at a cost of $25.16.
November 8	New envelopes are delivered from Gray Print Shop. $20.00 is paid to the delivery person.
November 9	Several letters are sent by certified mail for $7.18. Fran Stevens handled the errand.
November 10	The parking lot is snowplowed by Stellar Lot Service for $35.00. Lot maintenance expense carries account #523.
November 11	Antifreeze for the delivery van is purchased by S. Williams for $6.58.

B-E5. How would accounting system procedures detect the following errors:

a. A purchase voucher is accurately entered in the petty cash book for $5.16, but cash is paid in the amount of $6.15.
b. An entry in the purchases journal is not posted to the subsidiary ledger for accounts payable.
c. A column total on the cash receipts journal is added incorrectly.
d. An entry in the sales journal is posted twice to the customer's account.

PAYROLL

CHAPTER OBJECTIVES

After studying Chapter 8, you should understand the following:

1. The internal control considerations of a payroll system.
2. Methods for computing gross earnings and the usual deductions necessary to complete a payroll register.
3. The accounting treatment for payroll items and related expenses.

Payroll is one of the largest single expenses of most businesses. This chapter discusses the components of a typical payroll and the accounting required and covers certain internal control aspects of a payroll system.

THE SIGNIFICANCE OF PAYROLL

The importance of payroll accounting to businesses is often underestimated. Payroll expense can consume a substantial portion of each sales dollar. Very few organizations have no payroll, and most realize that keeping good workers depends heavily on how pay for services is handled.

The purpose of payroll accounting is to keep adequate records regarding the firm's employees, such as the basis for computing pay, the salary or wages earned by each employee, and the deductions made on a worker's behalf. In addition, since federal, state, and city governments rely on an organization's payroll records to confirm tax collection, such data must be kept by a system in a readily retrievable form. As with all systems involving cash transactions, payroll procedures should be structured to minimize theft and fraud.

Internal Control for Payroll Transactions

A payroll system lacking adequate internal control is typified by a situation where one or two persons hire personnel, keep all employee records, compute the amounts to be paid, prepare and sign the checks, and distribute the payroll to the employees. Such a system can encourage such undesirable events as payments to fictitious employees and excessive payments to valid employees. To avoid such situations, a good internal control system divides the payroll process into the following separate functional areas.

Personnel Function. One of personnel's responsibilities involves the hiring and terminating of employees. Either action usually generates several documents, one of which either places employees on or removes them from the payroll. Every change in the terms of employment is first transmitted to someone in the personnel department who, in turn, informs the payroll department.

Timekeeping Function. Most workers are paid according to the number of hours worked. To aid accuracy, a manual or mechanical system of marking timecards is often located at the entrance of the workplace. Some companies station an employee at the entrance to prevent co-workers from checking in or out for absent friends.

The number of hours worked by each employee is totaled and entered on a timecard summary, which shows both regular and overtime hours. On the basis of such a summary, the payroll department is authorized to compute the period's gross earnings for each employee.

Payroll Function. Payroll functions are handled by departments that vary greatly in size. However, the payroll department's primary duty—maintaining the payroll register—must always be fulfilled. A **payroll register,** or payroll journal, is a listing of the gross earnings of each employee, the deductions and withholdings, and the net earnings payable. The necessary information for preparing the payroll register is retrieved from employee payroll record sheets that are kept up-to-date by personnel and timekeeping representatives.

PAYROLL REGISTER
A listing of the gross earnings, the deductions and withholdings, and the net earnings payable of each worker. Also known as a payroll journal.

Paychecks Around the World

Ever wonder how your paycheck would be affected if you lived in another country? A recent study shows that workers in the United States usually earn more than those doing the same type of work elsewhere. The study also reports that doctors and lawyers are usually the highest paid professions; teachers nearly always rank considerably lower.

Some exceptions are evident in the white-collar group. A receptionist in the United States earns an average of $10,900; in Switzerland a receptionist is paid $17,920. An army general in Great Britain receives $64,018; in Australia, $58,160; but in the United States, only $45,528.

In some of the jobs where the U.S. workers earn a lot more, workers in other countries are compensated with more than cash. For example, U.S. jet pilots earn from $80,000 to $160,000. Airline pilots in India receive only about $18,300, but they receive additional benefits, such as very nice away-from-home living accommodations. The occupation of pilot is thus considered the highest paid in India and carries considerable social prestige.

Another unexpected job that carries favorable social status is that of bus driver in the third-world nations. The reason is that in these mostly carless nations, the people depend on buses for transportation.

SOURCE: "Take-Home Pay," *Time*, June 28, 1982, p. 51, from *World Paychecks: Who Makes What, Where, and Why*, by David Harrop.

Treasury Function. After wage amounts have been determined by payroll personnel, checks can be prepared and sent to the treasurer's department for an authorized signature. The endorser is responsible for comparing the amounts payable on the payroll register with the amounts on the checks.

After the checks are signed, the workers receive them either through the mail, as direct deposits to their bank accounts, or in person. In the case of the latter, the paychecks are preferably distributed by a treasury department employee, with a supervisor present so that the workers can be identified as each receives his or her own paycheck.

THE PAYROLL REGISTER

The discussion of the payroll register is organized around three main parts: the determination of gross earnings, the computation of deductions from gross earnings, and the relevant accounting treatment of payroll transactions. Exhibit 8.1 at the end of the chapter shows a payroll register.

Determination of Gross Earnings

Salaries and Wages. Some employees, especially those not directly involved in production, are paid salaries, frequently determined on an annual basis. Employees directly connected with production are usually paid wages based on either the number of hours worked (a time rate) or on actual output (a piece rate). Determination of gross pay under either system requires the multiplication of the rate times the base of hours or pieces. Sometimes employees are paid under a system combining hourly pay with incentive piece rates.

EXHIBIT 8.1

Payroll Register

Page 1 of 1

Empl. No.	Employee	Hours: Reg.	Hours: Over-time	Hourly Pay Rate	Earnings: Regular	Earnings: Overtime		Earnings: Other*	Earnings: Total	T/S	DEDUCTIONS: FICA Tax	Federal Income Tax	State Income tax	Local Income Tax		Other*	Total	Net Pay
10	Lieberman, Kathy	48	—	N/A	695.00	—		—	695.00	M/3	49.00	112.00	13.90	6.95	P	25.00	206.85	488.15
14	Olson, David	48	—	N/A	610.00	—		—	610.00	M/5	43.01	80.00	12.20	6.10	P	25.00	166.31	443.69
22	Avery, Paul	44	—	N/A	535.00	—	C	100.00	635.00	S/0	44.77	141.00	12.70	6.35	P	17.50	222.32	412.68
24	Conners, Ray	44	—	N/A	500.00	—	C	120.00	620.00	M/0	43.71	109.00	12.40	6.20	U	5.00	176.31	443.69
27	Hinojosa, Marie	30	—	N/A	340.00	—	C	85.00	425.00	S/0	29.96	76.00	8.50	4.25		—	118.71	306.29
51	Taggart, James	40	10	8.00	320.00	120.00		—	440.00	M/1	31.02	59.00	8.80	4.40	P	25.00	128.22	311.78
52	Kellogg, Owen	40	9	7.00	280.00	94.50		—	374.50	S/1	26.40	58.00	7.49	3.75	U	5.00	100.64	273.86
55	Austin, John	40	3	8.10	324.00	36.45		—	360.45	M/2	25.41	39.00	7.21	3.60	P	25.00	100.22	260.23
58	Baker, Teresa	38	—	7.75	294.50	—		—	294.50	S/0	20.76	43.00	5.89	2.95		—	72.60	221.90
63	Zimmerman, Lori	36	—	5.50	198.00	—	B	10.00	208.00	S/0	14.66	26.00	4.16	2.08		—	46.90	161.10
	TOTALS	**408**	**22**		**4096.50**	**250.95**		**315.00**	**4662.45**		**328.70**	**743.00**	**93.25**	**46.63**		**127.50**	**1339.08**	**3323.37**
								***B: Bonus C: Commission**								***P: Pension U: United Way**		

Overtime Pay. In a business that is subject to cyclical labor needs, paying for overtime is one way of optimally utilizing the firm's personnel. Overtime occurs when an employee works longer than the company's regular work period. Organizations determine overtime hours in different ways, such as counting hours in excess of eight in a day or forty in a week or hours worked on a weekend or holiday.

Benefits and Perquisites. Very often a company compensates its employees by means other than salaries. The firm might offer bonuses or enter into profit sharing agreements to entice and retain top management personnel. One U.S. oil company, for example, recently paid its chairman and president a bonus of $825,000 in addition to his annual salary of $440,000. Some companies offer employees stock options that are convertible into cash. Providing medical and life insurance is commonly done. These noncash benefits (**perquisites** or "perks") are an important part of the total compensation agreement. Although such benefits do not constitute cash payments, employees frequently pay income tax on the cash value of some perquisites that are given in compensation for services rendered. The cost of the perquisite is included in the total salary expense of the firm.

PERQUISITES
Noncash benefits given to employees, for example, apartments, chauffeur-driven automobiles, and memberships in country clubs.

Gross Earnings. An employee's **gross earnings** generally equal the periodic regular pay plus any overtime pay. Holiday pay, bonuses, meal allowances, and other items can also be included. Payroll taxes, as discussed in the following section, are based on the employee's gross earnings.

GROSS EARNINGS
All that a worker earns in a given time period. Generally equal to regular pay plus overtime pay, if any, plus, if applicable, items such as holiday pay, bonuses, and meal allowances.

Deductions from Gross Earnings

Deductions from gross earnings stem from legal regulations binding the employer or from voluntary actions of the employee. An employee's **net earnings** equal gross earnings less all deductions. In all cases of deductions from gross pay, the employer is acting merely as an agent of the employee or the government when, instead of paying the employee the full amount of his or her gross earnings, the employer withholds certain amounts and remits only the balance to the worker.

NET EARNINGS
Gross pay less all deductions for a worker.

Federal Income Tax. A deduction from gross earnings to pay personal income taxes is required by the Internal Revenue Service (IRS). The deduction is scaled so as to accumulate the approximate amount of tax that the employee will owe on wages earned during the year. Thus, instead of the employee's paying the full tax bill on or before April 15 of the following year, a certain amount is deducted each period from the employee's pay. From the government's viewpoint, paying as you earn is beneficial for two reasons. First, the government's cash flow is enhanced by having employees' deductions forwarded periodically from the employer. Second, a person prone to evading taxes is hindered from doing so, since most of what eventually will be owed is withheld by the employer and transmitted directly to the government.

All new employees must complete the Employee's Withholding Allowance Certificate, commonly called a W-4. This form documents the employee's marital and exemption status. The payroll department must use the W-4 information to locate appropriate tax deductions found in charts such as those in Exhibits 8.2 and 8.3.

As the tax charts readily make apparent, an employee can reduce the amount of tax withheld by claiming additional exemptions. The company's responsibility rarely extends to challenging the truthfulness of a W-4 form; the tax status information is eventually verified by the IRS.

FEDERAL INSURANCE CONTRIBUTIONS ACT (FICA) The law regulating Social Security taxes and benefits.

FICA (Social Security) Tax. Social Security taxes and benefits are regulated by the **Federal Insurance Contributions Act (FICA).** The system originated to give the elderly a pension that could help support living costs during retirement or disability. Later, the act was revised to include health and education benefits. The Social Security system is funded in part by payments from the employee's salary up to a yearly maximum. The percentage paid and the maximum yearly tax are subject to legislative changes; in 1985, the FICA tax was 7.05 percent of gross earnings up to $39,600.

EXHIBIT 8.2

SINGLE Persons–**WEEKLY** Payroll Period

(For Wages Paid After December 1984)

And the wages are–		And the number of withholding allowances claimed is–										
At least	But less than	0	1	2	3	4	5	6	7	8	9	10
		The amount of income tax to be withheld shall be–										
140	145	16	13	10	7	4	2	0	0	0	0	0
145	150	16	13	10	8	5	2	0	0	0	0	0
150	160	18	14	11	9	6	3	1	0	0	0	0
160	170	19	16	13	10	7	4	2	0	0	0	0
170	180	21	18	14	11	9	6	3	1	0	0	0
180	190	22	19	16	13	10	7	4	2	0	0	0
190	200	24	21	18	14	11	9	6	3	1	0	0
200	210	26	22	19	16	13	10	7	4	2	0	0
210	220	27	24	21	18	14	11	9	6	3	1	0
220	230	29	26	22	19	16	13	10	7	4	2	0
230	240	31	27	24	21	18	14	11	9	6	3	1
240	250	33	29	26	22	19	16	13	10	7	4	2
250	260	35	31	27	24	21	18	14	11	9	6	3
260	270	37	33	29	26	22	19	16	13	10	7	4
270	280	39	35	31	27	24	21	18	14	11	9	6
280	290	41	37	33	29	26	22	19	16	13	10	7
290	300	43	39	35	31	27	24	21	18	14	11	9
300	310	46	41	37	33	29	26	22	19	16	13	10
310	320	48	43	39	35	31	27	24	21	18	14	11
320	330	50	46	41	37	33	29	26	22	19	16	13
330	340	53	48	43	39	35	31	27	24	21	18	14
340	350	55	50	46	41	37	33	29	26	22	19	16
350	360	58	53	48	43	39	35	31	27	24	21	18
360	370	60	55	50	46	41	37	33	29	26	22	19
370	380	63	58	53	48	43	39	35	31	27	24	21
$380	$390	$65	$60	$55	$50	$46	$41	$37	$33	$29	$26	$22
390	400	68	63	58	53	48	43	39	35	31	27	24
400	410	71	65	60	55	50	46	41	37	33	29	26
410	420	73	68	63	58	53	48	43	39	35	31	27
420	430	76	71	65	60	55	50	46	41	37	33	29
430	440	78	73	68	63	58	53	48	43	39	35	31
440	450	81	76	71	65	60	55	50	46	41	37	33
450	460	84	78	73	68	63	58	53	48	43	39	35
460	470	87	81	76	71	65	60	55	50	46	41	37
470	480	90	84	78	73	68	63	58	53	48	43	39
480	490	93	87	81	76	71	65	60	55	50	46	41
490	500	96	90	84	78	73	68	63	58	53	48	43
500	510	99	93	87	81	76	71	65	60	55	50	46
510	520	102	96	90	84	78	73	68	63	58	53	48
520	530	105	99	93	87	81	76	71	65	60	55	50
530	540	108	102	96	90	84	78	73	68	63	58	53
540	550	111	105	99	93	87	81	76	71	65	60	55
550	560	114	108	102	96	90	84	78	73	68	63	58
560	570	117	111	105	99	93	87	81	76	71	65	60
570	580	121	114	108	102	96	90	84	78	73	68	63
580	590	124	117	111	105	99	93	87	81	76	71	65
590	600	127	121	114	108	102	96	90	84	78	73	68
600	610	131	124	117	111	105	99	93	87	81	76	71
610	620	134	127	121	114	108	102	96	90	84	78	73
620	630	138	131	124	117	111	105	99	93	87	81	76
630	640	141	134	127	121	114	108	102	96	90	84	78
640	650	144	138	131	124	117	111	105	99	93	87	81
650	660	148	141	134	127	121	114	108	102	96	90	84
660	670	151	144	138	131	124	117	111	105	99	93	87
670	680	155	148	141	134	127	121	114	108	102	96	90

Thus, the highest FICA tax paid by any one worker in 1985 would have been $2791.80.

Social Security is a tax on both the employee and the employer; each party contributes an equal amount. The employer's FICA cost is discussed later in the chapter.

Other Deductions. An employee can instruct his or her employer to withhold a certain amount of pay and to forward the money to a specific organization or fund.

EXHIBIT 8.3

MARRIED Persons–**WEEKLY** Payroll Period

(For Wages Paid After December 1984)

And the wages are–		And the number of withholding allowances claimed is–										
At least	But less than	0	1	2	3	4	5	6	7	8	9	10
		The amount of income tax to be withheld shall be–										
300	310	36	32	29	26	23	20	17	14	11	9	6
310	320	38	34	31	28	24	21	18	16	13	10	8
320	330	39	36	32	29	26	23	20	17	14	11	9
330	340	41	38	34	31	28	24	21	18	16	13	10
340	350	43	39	36	32	29	26	23	20	17	14	11
350	360	45	41	38	34	31	28	24	21	18	16	13
360	370	47	43	39	36	32	29	26	23	20	17	14
370	380	48	45	41	38	34	31	28	24	21	18	16
380	390	50	47	43	39	36	32	29	26	23	20	17
390	400	52	48	45	41	38	34	31	28	24	21	18
400	410	55	50	47	43	39	36	32	29	26	23	20
410	420	57	52	48	45	41	38	34	31	28	24	21
420	430	59	55	50	47	43	39	36	32	29	26	23
430	440	61	57	52	48	45	41	38	34	31	28	24
440	450	63	59	55	50	47	43	39	36	32	29	26
450	460	66	61	57	52	48	45	41	38	34	31	28
460	470	68	63	59	55	50	47	43	39	36	32	29
470	480	70	66	61	57	52	48	45	41	38	34	31
480	490	73	68	63	59	55	50	47	43	39	36	32
$490	$500	$75	$70	$66	$61	$57	$52	$48	$45	$41	$38	$34
500	510	78	73	68	63	59	55	50	47	43	39	36
510	520	80	75	70	66	61	57	52	48	45	41	38
520	530	83	78	73	68	63	59	55	50	47	43	39
530	540	85	80	75	70	66	61	57	52	48	45	41
540	550	88	83	78	73	68	63	59	55	50	47	43
550	560	90	85	80	75	70	66	61	57	52	48	45
560	570	93	88	83	78	73	68	63	59	55	50	47
570	580	95	90	85	80	75	70	66	61	57	52	48
580	590	98	93	88	83	78	73	68	63	59	55	50
590	600	101	95	90	85	80	75	70	66	61	57	52
600	610	103	98	93	88	83	78	73	68	63	59	55
610	620	106	101	95	90	85	80	75	70	66	61	57
620	630	109	103	98	93	88	83	78	73	68	63	59
630	640	112	106	101	95	90	85	80	75	70	66	61
640	650	115	109	103	98	93	88	83	78	73	68	63
650	660	117	112	106	101	95	90	85	80	75	70	66
660	670	120	115	109	103	98	93	88	83	78	73	68
670	680	123	117	112	106	101	95	90	85	80	75	70
680	690	126	120	115	109	103	98	93	88	83	78	73
690	700	129	123	117	112	106	101	95	90	85	80	75
700	710	132	126	120	115	109	103	98	93	88	83	78
710	720	136	129	123	117	112	106	101	95	90	85	80
720	730	139	132	126	120	115	109	103	98	93	88	83
730	740	142	136	129	123	117	112	106	101	95	90	85
740	750	146	139	132	126	120	115	109	103	98	93	88
750	760	149	142	136	129	123	117	112	106	101	95	90
760	770	152	146	139	132	126	120	115	109	103	98	93
770	780	155	149	142	136	129	123	117	112	106	101	95
780	790	159	152	146	139	132	126	120	115	109	103	98
790	800	162	155	149	142	136	129	123	117	112	106	101
800	810	165	159	152	146	139	132	126	120	115	109	103
810	820	169	162	155	149	142	136	129	123	117	112	106
820	830	172	165	159	152	146	139	132	126	120	115	109
830	840	175	169	162	155	149	142	136	129	123	117	112

Such deductions often include contributions to pension plans and charitable organizations, union dues, health or life insurance premiums, and savings or loan payments to credit unions. The company, of course, must agree to help the workers in making such voluntary payments; the employee cannot specify payments to be remitted to organizations that have not made arrangements with the firm.

CONCEPT SUMMARY 8.1

DISPOSITION OF EMPLOYEE GROSS EARNINGS

ITEM	PAID TO
Federal income tax*	U.S. government—Internal Revenue Service
FICA tax*	U.S. government—Social Security Administration
State or local income tax	State or local government
Other authorized payments	Designated agency
Net pay	Employee

*Withheld federal income tax and FICA tax amounts are usually remitted together to a bank acting as a depository for the IRS, which serves as a collection agency for the FICA tax.

PAYROLL EXPENSES FOR THE EMPLOYER

Payroll expense of the firm includes, in addition to wages and salaries paid, amounts expended by the employer to various funds for the benefit of its workers. A business is required by law to match each employee's FICA tax deduction and to remit the combined amounts to the Social Security fund. Similarly, if the pension plan is funded by both parties, the employer would add its share to the amount withheld from the employee's gross earnings for the plan.

Certain payroll taxes must be paid by the employer for the benefit of the employee. Unemployment insurance is an example. Most states require companies to contribute to their state unemployment compensation funds an amount ranging from 2.7 percent to 8 percent of the first $7,000 paid to each employee. This money helps states to provide some level of compensation for jobless workers and to establish facilities that help the unemployed worker find suitable employment.

FEDERAL UNEMPLOYMENT TAX ACT (FUTA)
The federal law regulating unemployment taxation at the federal level.

The federal government also exacts such a tax based on the **Federal Unemployment Tax Act (FUTA).** This federal tax, which in 1985 was 6.2 percent on the first $7,000 paid to each employee annually, can be reduced by state unemployment compensation tax paid. In other words, a company in a state imposing a 4.2 percent tax for unemployment compensation would be required to remit only 2.0 percent to the national fund.

PAYROLL CHECKING ACCOUNT

A company often uses a special payroll bank account. A check is written against the firm's regular account for the amount of wages and salaries payable and is deposited in the payroll checking account. The firm then draws the payroll checks on that special account.

This procedure has several advantages. First, determining whose payroll check has not been cashed is possible. Since the exact total of the paychecks is transferred into the account and since most employees promptly cash their checks, any balance in the payroll checking account would be unusual, allowing for an early inquiry into any uncashed checks.

Increased convenience is another advantage. Payroll accounts are complemented by specially designed payroll checks containing space for the pertinent details of the transaction. These checks are usually easier for banks to identify and thus for employees to cash. Also, by diverting general cash into special payroll accounts, an organization can more easily split the job of reconciling the cash account with bank records.

AN EXTENDED PAYROLL EXAMPLE

Exhibit 8.1 shows a payroll register for a firm with ten employees, five of whom are salaried. The remaining workers earn their wages on an hourly basis. Overtime hours for nonsalaried employees are paid at one and one-half times the regular rate. The hours worked have been copied from a summary of time cards. Other earnings include commissions and bonuses.

The tax status column contains an entry for the employee's marital status (M or S for married or single) and the number of exemptions claimed. This information is required for determining (from Exhibits 8.2 and 8.3) the appropriate amount of federal (and frequently state) income tax to withhold. Amounts are also withheld from earnings on this payroll for Social Security tax (7.05 percent on all earnings; no one has yet accumulated earnings above $39,600), state income tax (2 percent), and local income tax (1 percent). Certain employees have authorized additional deductions for pension or charitable contributions. The net pay column indicates the amount that the employee will actually receive.

Once the payroll register is complete and cross-footed with totals, a journal entry is required. The entry that would be appropriate for the register in Exhibit 8.1 is as follows:

Jan. 14	Salaries and wages expense	4,662.45	
	FICA tax payable employee portion		328.70
	Employees' federal withholding payable		743.00
	Employees' state withholding payable		93.25
	Employees' local withholding payable		46.63
	Pension fund payable		117.50
	Donations payable—United Way		10.00
	Cash		3,323.37
	(to record weekly payroll)		

Note that the amounts withheld are entered as liabilities on the books of the company. As discussed earlier, a company merely acts as a collection agency in the withholding process. Once the funds are withheld from employee wages, the company is obligated to remit them to the appropriate agency.

Suppose that this firm is located in a state where the unemployment tax is 2.4 percent and the firm matches all pension contributions. The payroll register totals on January 14 would indicate that additional employer costs should be recorded as follows, assuming no employee has yet accumulated earnings over $7,000 this year:

Jan. 14	Payroll expense—taxes	617.77	
	Payroll expense—pension contributions	117.50	
	FICA tax payable employer portion		328.70
	Pension fund payable		117.50
	State unemployment tax payable		111.90
	Federal unemployment tax payable		177.17
	(to record liability for payroll expense)		

To complete the accounting for payroll, the employer must periodically transmit cash to settle the liabilities. Although having all these accounts settled at the same date and so soon is unlikely, should the above firm remit all amounts due on January 20, the entry required would be as follows:

Jan. 20	FICA payable	657.40	
	Pension fund payable	235.00	
	Employees' federal withholding payable	743.00	
	Employees' state withholding payable	93.25	
	Employees' local withholding payable	46.63	
	Donations payable—United Way	10.00	
	State unemployment tax payable	111.90	
	Federal unemployment tax payable	177.17	
	Cash		2,074.35
	(to settle payroll liabilities)		

These payments would conclude the payroll cycle for that period. Note that in practice most payments would be made separately. Also, FICA and federal income taxes withheld must be remitted periodically based on the amounts accumulated.

CONCEPT SUMMARY 8.2

FEDERAL TAXES RELATING TO PAYROLL

TAX	WHO PAYS
Federal income	Employee
FICA	Employee and employer
Unemployment	Employer

FOR REVIEW

SUMMARY

- Since payroll transactions involve cash, establishing a sound system of internal control is essential. Optimum assurance of minimized risk would require separating the payroll transaction into four functional areas: personnel, timekeeping, payroll, and treasury.

- The payroll register is the basic document for recording payroll transactions. First, gross earnings are computed, including salaries and wages, overtime pay, bonuses, and benefits. The various deductions from employee earnings, such as income taxes, FICA tax, and pension payments are determined. Finally, the net amount payable to the employee is calculated.
- The company incurs other costs, in addition to salaries and wages, relating to payroll, such as the employer's contributions to the Social Security fund, private pension plans, and unemployment compensation insurance. All such costs related to having employees are called payroll expenses.
- Most companies maintain a separate payroll checking account to help them keep track of uncanceled payroll checks and for convenience.

QUESTIONS

8-1. What information is found on a completed payroll register?

8-2. Why is a good system of internal control necessary for payroll transactions? How should the system operate?

8-3. What are the advantages of overtime from the point of view of the employer? Of the employee?

8-4. How do wages differ from salaries?

8-5. What tax payments must an employer handle on the employees' behalf? As a company expense?

8-6. What are some usual deductions from pay other than taxes?

8-7. List five common perquisites.

8-8. What is the purpose of a W-4 form?

8-9. Why is the pay-as-you-earn system of taxation good for the government?

8-10. What are the advantages of maintaining a separate payroll checking account?

EXERCISES

8-E1. Teeny Toys, Inc., has ten employees: a manager, two office clerks, one floor supervisor, and six production workers. A time clock is provided near the facility entrance, and payroll is remitted by check. How would you assign the four payroll functions for effective internal control?

8-E2. The firm of Curious and Sons pays an overtime rate of one and one-half times an employee's regular hourly rate for hours worked over eight in one day. Bea Curious's work record for the past week is as follows: Monday, 6 hours; Tuesday, 10 hours; Wednesday, 8 hours; Thursday, 4 hours; and Friday, 10 hours. If Bea's regular rate is $4.12, what is her gross pay that week?

8-E3. Refigure Bea's pay based on the hours listed in 8-E2, assuming that the company pays overtime rates only for hours over 40 in one week.

8-E4. Ralph Jackson's earnings to date total $39,482 for the year. His next gross salary payment will be $860. How much of this amount will be deducted for Social Security? (Assume 1985 FICA rates.)

8-E5. Earnings to date for the year for certain employees are as follows: Steve Brown, $20,000; Gayle Weinheimer, $18,500; Tom Maywhoor, $6,875; and Dawn Bergland, $4,880. This week's gross earnings for the four are $450, $620, $315, and $290, respectively. What journal entry will be appropriate to record the firm's unemployment insurance tax relating to the week's payroll? (Assume a state unemployment tax of 3.7% and a federal maximum rate of 6.2% on a base of $7,000.)

8-E6. Gwen West is employed as an office clerk for a local veterinarian, Hal Stone. Last week, Gwen noticed that her pay had been figured incorrectly. She had worked five hours of overtime for which she was not paid. Gwen's pay stub for that check showed gross earnings, $224.00; federal withholding, $29.00; FICA, $15.79; state withholding, $2.24; credit union, $10. Her additional pay amounts to $42; extra federal withholding is $3.15. FICA tax is 7.05%; state withholding is 1%. What correcting journal entries are required? Ignore federal and state unemployment taxes.

8-E7. Iris Maddock works for a tent-manufacturing firm. She is paid an hourly rate of $6 plus a piece rate that is keyed to the type of construction task being performed. Last week, Iris was assigned to window flap construction. For every completed flap, she is to be paid $.20. Iris has the following work record: Monday, 7½ hours, 24 pieces; Tuesday, 7¾ hours, 30 pieces; Wednesday, 7½ hours, 28 pieces; Thursday, 7 hours, 26 pieces; and Friday, 7¾ hours, 31 pieces. What is Iris's weekly gross pay?

PROBLEM SET A

8-A1. Payroll Register. The following is a payroll register dated January 7, 1985:

Payroll Register

Name	Withholding Allowances	Hourly Rate	Regular Hours	Overtime Hours	Insurance Premium
Sue Brady	S/1	$5.10	40	2	$10
Joseph Alian	S/1	6.05	39	0	15
Cynthia Jamison	M/4	7.75	40	0	15
Wanda Wooten	S/0	3.90	37½	0	—
Sifu Chang	M/3	7.95	40	2¼	15
Sarah Emcee	S/0	5.50	40	1	10

Required

Complete the payroll making columns for regular earnings, overtime earnings, gross earnings, federal withholding, FICA, state tax, local tax, other deductions, total deductions, and net pay using the given information. Use the federal tax charts in Exhibits 8.2 and 8.3; FICA is 7.05%. A state tax of 1% and a city tax of 2% must also be withheld. Overtime is paid at one and one-half times the regular rate. Insurance premiums are to be deducted at this time. Cross-balance the figures and write the corresponding journal entry.

8-A2. Employer Payroll Costs. The Windy City Cab Service is preparing the payroll expense section of next year's budget. Management has estimated the yearly gross payroll to be $225,000. Other costs that may accrue are as follows:

1. The employees' federal withholding will amount to 10% more than last year's total of $43,000.
2. FICA tax will rise from 7.05% to 7.15%.
3. State income tax will change from 1% to 1.25%.
4. Local tax remains at 2%.

5. The company's pension plan terms require the employees to pay 2% of their gross earnings; the firm matches that amount.
6. The company pays $30,000 annually for the employees' health insurance.
7. A state unemployment tax of 4.2% and the additional federal unemployment tax of 2.0% must be paid. Windy City Cab Service has 30 employees, each of whom will earn over $7,000 next year.

Required

Present in orderly form an estimate of the firm's coming year's payroll costs.

8-A3. Computing Gross Pay. The Formalwear Tailoring Shop (FTS) has six employees. The manager, Sam Dixon, earns a salary of $25,000 annually. The three sales and fitting clerks are paid hourly; Lisa Lemmon and Jay Trumbull earn $4 an hour; Pat Riley receives $5 an hour. The other two employees, Sally Baker and Mamie Bidlack, are paid a piece rate for each garment finished. FTS pays employees every other week.

For the period ending May 27, Lisa worked 75 hours; Jay, 80 hours; Pat, 78 hours; Sally, 50 hours; Mamie, 60 hours; and Sam, 90 hours. Sally completed seven prom dresses at a piece rate of $30, and Mamie tailored six suits that carry a piece rate of $50.

Required

a. What is the periodic gross pay for each employee? What is the total payroll for the period?
b. How much did Sally earn per hour this period? Mamie?
c. If FTS is located in your college town, what would be the payroll costs from this period?

8-A4. Planning for Payroll Costs. Homestead Industries has a seasonal demand for many of its products. Over the company's ten-year existence, it has met increased labor needs by having regular employees work overtime. As Homestead's work force has been very stable, the average worker now earns $9.15 an hour; overtime pay, obviously, at one and one-half times this rate is even more costly. Management is considering the alternative plan of hiring additional help. The following options are available:

Overtime Plan: Use of an expected 40 regular hours per week per employee; 10 employees year around; average hourly rate, $9.15; yearly seasonal need of 500 overtime hours (50 hours a week during the 10-week peak season).

Hiring Plan: Use of 40 regular hours per week per employee; 11 employees; average hourly rate per employee, $8.65; yearly seasonal need of 100 overtime hours.

The following additional data may bear on the decision:

1. All employees work the full year and receive a two-week paid vacation.
2. Payroll taxes include FICA, 7.05%; state withholding, 3%; local withholding 1.5%; state unemployment, 4%; additional federal unemployment, 2.2%. (Federal and state unemployment taxes have a $7,000 base.)
3. Nontaxable employee benefits, excluding vacations, paid by the firm cost $1,500 per employee per year.

Required

Which plan would you recommend for Homestead? Present your cost data for both options in orderly form.

8-A5. Payroll Journal Entries. Gregg Industries has the following payroll transactions during August:

Aug. 6 Payroll figures for the two-week pay period ending August 4 are gross pay, $6,283; federal withholding, $1,230; FICA, $443; state income tax, $628; bond deductions, $180; medical insurance deductions, $560.

Aug. 10 Payroll checks are distributed.

Aug. 10 Payroll expenses are computed and entered: unemployment insurance, exempting $5,200 of the payroll (rates are 3.8% to the state and, an additional 2.4% to the federal government); life insurance provided to eligible employees ($80 premium total for all eligible employees); and FICA.

Aug. 14 A new employee is hired at $400 a week and will start on the 15th.

Aug. 20 Payroll figures for the period ending August 18 are gross pay, $6,157; federal withholding, $1,195; FICA, $434; state income tax, $616; bond deductions, $180.

Aug. 24 Payroll expenses: unemployment insurance on $1,563 and FICA.

Aug. 24 Payroll checks are distributed.

Required

Prepare journal entries as necessary for the above transactions.

8-A6. Internal Control Over Payroll. The following flowchart depicts a typical manual system of figuring payroll:

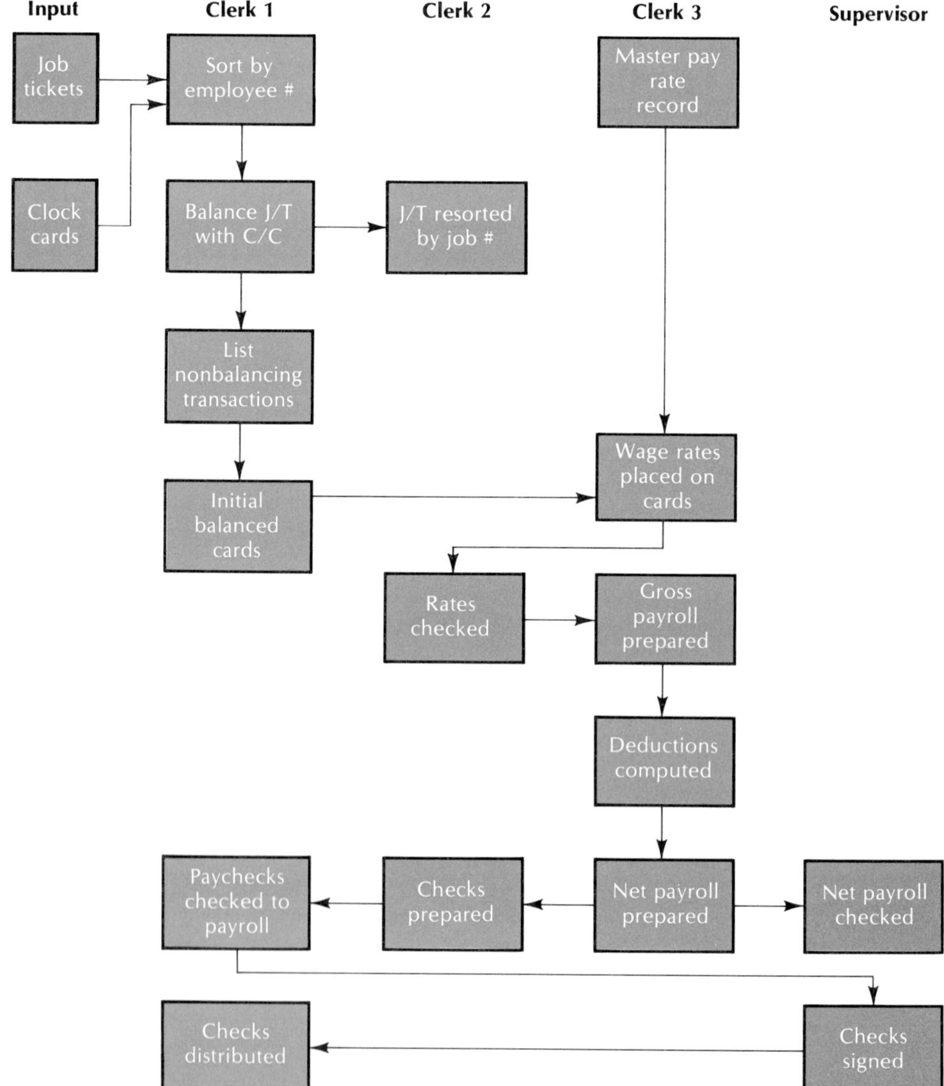

Required

List the controls that appear to be operating.

8-A7. Planning for Payroll Cash Flows. Lester Manley has just purchased a new car with monthly payments of $220. Lester, who is single, still lives with his parents, and his budget contains expenditures of $300 a month in addition to the car payment. He also wishes to save at least $100 each month.

Lester works 40 hours a week in a factory that pays him an hourly wage of $3.50. He also receives a piece rate of $.15 for each unit he finishes. Lester claims no exemptions. The FICA rate is 7.05%, state tax is 2%, and local tax is 1%.

Required

Approximately how many units must Lester finish each week to take home enough cash to cover his budget? (Assume that each month is equal to four weeks.)

PROBLEM SET B

8-B1. Payroll Register. Employer pays an overtime rate of one and one-half times the regular rate for hours in excess of 40. The following information is pertinent for the week ending December 7:

Empl. No.	Name	Tax Status	Hourly Rate	Hours Worked	Year-to-Date Gross Pay	Additional Deductions
12	Alan Essex	M/2	$15.50	48	$40,100	$20 credit union
16	Val Peters	S/0	6.75	44	14,180	$10 pension contribution
17	Jamie Fisher	M/1	15.00	46	39,450	—
21	Amy Cooke	S/1	13.10	40	25,190	—
23	Jeff Reiter	S/0	4.75	40	3,750	$30 credit union
30	Jan Hollister	S/3	4.00	37	5,925	—
45	Brian Irwin	S/0	8.00	41	15,375	$18 pension contribution

Note that the year-to-date gross pay does *not* include the amounts on the December 7 payroll.

Required

Complete the above payroll dated December 7 using the payroll register format and tax charts presented in the chapter. Assume a FICA rate of 7.05% on earnings up to $39,600, state tax of 2%, and local tax of 1%.

8-B2. Employer Payroll Costs. Refer to 8-B1. Assume also that the federal unemployment tax is 6.2% and the state unemployment tax is 4.4% on a base of $7,000. The employer incurs a weekly health insurance premium cost of $10 each for single workers and $15.50 each for married workers. Alan Essex and Jamie Fisher have life insurance coverage paid by the employer at an annual cost of $200 each. All employee pension contributions are equally matched by the employer.

Required

What journal entry is appropriate to record all of the employer's payroll expenses for the week of December 7?

8-B3. Computing Gross Pay. Jim, Rick, and Luke sell major appliances in a department store. Each receives a base hourly rate plus a scaled sales commission. The commission is based on the amount of the sale before tax, as follows:

Category	Sales Value	Commission Rate
A	$100–$199	0.5%
B	$200–$299	1%
C	$300–$399	2%
D	$400–$499	2.5%
E	$500 and over	3%

Last week's payroll register and sales log yield the following condensed information:

1. Jim Laststand: hourly rate, $4.25; worked 40 regular hours; sales—Category C, $942; Category D, $1,280; Category E, $1,816.
2. Richard Robnolte: hourly rate, $4.30; worked 35 regular hours; sales—Category B, $803; Category D, $2,305; Category E, $1,610.
3. Luke Heath: hourly rate, $5.10; worked 40 regular hours; sales—Category B, $1,160; Category C, $1,974; Category D, $2,114; Category E, $4,080.

Required

Calculate the gross pay of each salesperson for last week.

8-B4. Planning for Payroll Costs. Samson Caterers has recently revamped its entire operation, making the forecasting of payroll costs more complicated. The following factors seem significant:

1. New equipment will require employee training time of four hours per person for ten employees.
2. The average pay rate will change because of new workers and pay raises for continuing personnel to $5.40 an hour from $5.15.
3. One supervisor, whose annual salary is $15,000, has retired effective December 31 and is not being replaced.
4. Using the old arrangement, Samson has been able to cater 150 social gatherings a year at an average work load of 20 employee hours per engagement. The new equipment and organization will permit the firm to handle an expected 175 functions annually while reducing average employee hours needed to 18 per job.
5. The proportion of payroll costs to gross pay is expected to remain stable. Last year's figures were total gross pay to hourly employees, $15,450; total hourly payroll expenses, $2,850.
6. Supervisors' salaries are not figured into the average hourly rate nor are supervisors' hours included in (4). Last year, supervisors earned $36,000, and payroll costs were proportionate to those of hourly workers.

Required

What are the total payroll and payroll costs that can be expected during the coming year?

8-B5. Payroll Journal Entries. The following are the transactions of Adelaide, Inc., for January:

Jan. 9 Payroll figures for the week ending January 7 are gross pay, $3,984; federal withholding, $570.12; FICA, $281; state tax, $398.40; Blue Cross premium, $425; United Way contributions, $284.
Jan. 9 FICA and unemployment insurance taxes are entered: 4.6% to the state and an additional 1.6% to the federal government.
Jan. 10 Paychecks are distributed.

Jan. 11 Dee Leffler reports an error on her paycheck. After refiguring, her gross pay is increased by $30; federal withholding, up $4.10; FICA, $2.11; state tax, $3. A new check is issued for the increase. Payroll tax expense is not adjusted until January 23.

Jan. 23 Payroll figures amount to: gross pay, $4,444; federal withholding, $616.10; FICA, $313.30; state tax, $444.40; pension fund contributions, $220.

Jan. 23 Related taxes are accrued, including those due to Dee Leffler's additional pay.

Jan. 24 Paychecks are distributed.

Jan. 31 All withholdings and accrued payroll taxes are forwarded to the appropriate agents, except for the pension contributions.

Required

Prepare the general journal entries for the payroll transactions of Adelaide, Inc., during the month.

8-B6. Internal Control Over Payroll. Bespectacled, Inc., a new bookstore, has a manager, two office clerks, six sales clerks, and two stock clerks. Employees record their hours worked on a clipboard under the sales counter. The shop is very informal, and if someone forgets to write "in" or "out," an office clerk fills in the missing information from the schedule unless she knows that the person was not actually present.

The store is open every day except Sunday. On Monday mornings, the office clerk in charge of payroll (the pay clerk) collects last week's work record from the clipboard and totals the number of hours each employee worked. The pay clerk then completes the payroll register, figuring each paycheck completely, footing and balancing the computations, and transferring the amounts to the general journal. The pay clerk then prepares the checks and places them on the manager's desk for signing.

The manager will have the checks signed by noon on Tuesday. At that time, the checks are placed under the cash register drawer until their respective owners come in and pick them up.

Required

Identify possible internal control weaknesses in the above scenario. How would you improve the system?

8-B7. Planning for Payroll Cash Flows. Mr. Wiggons, a local manager, is faced with a directive from his regional supervisor to cut his total payroll cost by 10%. His branch office currently employs two supervisors who each earn $15,000 annually, ten full-time staff members who each average $10,000 in annual wages, and four part-time workers who have average yearly wages of $4,000 each.

Additional payroll costs include taxes (7.05% for FICA and 6.2% on the first $7,000 of each employee's wages for unemployment) and benefits (about $1,000 yearly for each supervisor, $800 yearly for each full-time staff member, and $250 each for part-time help).

Required

a. What is the dollar amount by which Mr. Wiggons must reduce his payroll costs?
b. Can he manage the reduction by laying off only one full-time worker or supervisor?

INVENTORIES

CHAPTER OBJECTIVES
After studying Chapter 9, you should understand the following:

1. The nature of inventory and the alternative valuations possible.
2. The relationship between inventory valuation and income determination.
3. The fact that physical inventory movements are not the focus of accounting for inventory costs.
4. The periodic and perpetual methods of maintaining inventory records.
5. The presentation of inventories on the statement of financial position.

This chapter explores inventory valuation and its importance in income determination and presents alternative assumptions about inventory cost flows. It discusses alternative methods of inventory record keeping and actual determination of quantities on hand and describes financial statement presentations of inventory and related bookkeeping requirements.

THE NATURE AND SIGNIFICANCE OF INVENTORY

Chapter 5 defined inventory as an asset held for resale or use in manufacturing goods in a business. In general, inventory falls into one of four categories: merchandise, raw materials, work-in-process, and finished goods. Exhibit 9.1 describes these categories.

EXHIBIT 9.1

Inventory Category	Description
Merchandise	Held for resale in the normal course of business.
Raw materials	Held for use in the production process of a manufacturing firm.
Work in process	Held as partially finished goods still in the process of being manufactured.
Finished goods	Held as finished goods that have been completely manufactured and are awaiting sale.

This chapter focuses on merchandise inventories normally associated with wholesale and retail operations and is not concerned with raw materials, work-in-process, or finished goods inventories found in a manufacturing operation. Although much of the material in the chapter can be applied to manufacturing inventories, detailed discussion of such inventories is deferred until Chapter 20 dealing with manufacturing cost systems.

The goods held for resale within either a wholesale or a retail operation are significant to wholesale and retail firms for two reasons. First, as discussed earlier, inventory items that have been sold to customers become expenses (cost of goods sold) and are generally the largest single expense on the income statement. Second, the dollar value of the asset, inventory, is often one of the largest asset amounts on the statement of financial position.

UNDERLYING INVENTORY THEORY

Since inventory is an asset, each item it contains must meet two critical tests to be considered part of the firm's inventory for accounting purposes. First, the item must be owned by the firm. Second, the goods must be of future economic benefit to the organization. That is, in general, each merchandise inventory item must be saleable to be considered part of a firm's inventory for accounting purposes. People often believe that if an item physically exists and is owned by a firm, it is included as inventory on the firm's statement of financial position. That is not the case. Items that cannot be sold or otherwise used in the future are not included in inventory.

Normally, inventory items are valued by reference to their original acquisition cost, or purchase price. However, if the expected selling price of an inventory item suddenly falls below the original cost, the inventory value on the statement of financial position must reflect this fact to fulfill the basic requirement that an asset not be valued at more than its future economic benefit.

We will return to the problem of fluctuations in purchase cost and market value later in the chapter. For now we will assume that appropriate inventory valuations can be based on purchase prices.

INVENTORY VALUES AND THE INCOME DETERMINATION PROCESS UNDER THE PERIODIC INVENTORY SYSTEM

You may recall from Chapter 5 that under the periodic method of inventory accounting, inventory quantities on hand, the value of these quantities, and the cost of goods sold are determined at the end of each accounting period. The cost of goods sold is computed as beginning inventory, plus purchases, less ending inventory.

As Chapter 5 explained, the periodic method of inventory determination makes record keeping for inventory and cost of goods sold quite simple. For any business with a large volume of sales involving many units of a homogeneous product, such as gasoline, the periodic method of valuing inventory and determining cost of goods sold is the only practical system.

Inventory Errors and Income

Because the periodic method of inventory accounting and the cost of goods sold computation depend on the values placed on the inventory at the beginning and end of the accounting period, errors in the values will produce errors in the cost of goods sold computation and in the income reported on the income statement. Errors in either counting or valuing the merchandise on hand would result in incorrect inventory balances being used in these computations.

Consider the three condensed income statements in Exhibit 9.2. In each case, the beginning inventory on January 1, 1986, the merchandise purchased during 1986 and 1987, and the ending inventory on December 31, 1987, are assumed to be correct as stated. Net sales and expenses are also assumed to be correct.

The three cases are identical, except that in Case 2, ending inventory on December 31, 1986, is understated by $25,000 while in Case 3, ending inventory on December 31, 1986, is overstated by $25,000. Exhibit 9.2 gives the income determination for each case.

Note that in each case, total income for the two years combined is the same—$275,000. Errors in determining inventory amounts affect the income recognized in each of two time periods—the period in which the error is made and the following period. However, the errors are equal and offsetting when the two time periods are considered together.

On the statement of financial position, the inventory errors would have the effect of either overstating or understating total assets and therefore of overstating or understating total owners' equity. For example, the understatement error in Case 2 would result in the understatement of both assets and owners' equity on December 31, 1986, by $25,000. However, both assets and owners' equity would be correct on December 31, 1987, because the two years' errors are equal and offsetting.

Water Tec Incorporated

In the early 1980s, Water Tec Incorporated, a regional manufacturer of water softeners and related water treatment equipment, became convinced that industrial scale water reclamation units for use in automatic car washes would be highly profitable. The company began the manufacture and sale of such units. However, it was soon learned that the operating costs of the units exceeded the savings generated by reuse of the water. The per unit manufacturing cost was $100,000, and by 1984, Water Tec had reclamation units in its inventory valued at $1.2 million. Total inventory was only $2 million at the time. Review of pertinent facts indicated that no units had been sold during 1983 or 1984, and prospects for future sales were nonexistent. Disassembly for parts was not considered worthwhile because of high labor costs involved. From an accounting point of view, the units were no longer inventory, because they could not be sold and therefore had no future economic value.

EXHIBIT 9.2

	Case 1 Inventory Correctly Stated on 12/31/86 as $125,000		Case 2 Inventory Understated on 12/31/86 by $25,000		Case 3 Inventory Overstated on 12/31/86 by $25,000	
	1986	1987	1986	1987	1986	1987
Inv. Jan. 1	$100,000	$125,000	$100,000	$100,000	$100,000	$150,000
Plus: Goods purchased	500,000	600,000	500,000	600,000	500,000	600,000
Total goods avail. for sale	$600,000	$725,000	$600,000	$700,000	$600,000	$750,000
Less: Inv. Dec. 31	125,000	75,000	100,000	75,000	150,000	75,000
COGS*	$475,000	$650,000	$500,000	$625,000	$450,000	$675,000
	Income Statement for the Year Ending		Income Statement for the Year Ending		Income Statement for the Year Ending	
	12/31/86	12/31/87	12/31/86	12/31/87	12/31/86	12/31/87
Net sales	$650,000	$950,000	$650,000	$950,000	$650,000	$950,000
COGS*	475,000	650,000	500,000	625,000	450,000	675,000
Gross profit	$175,000	$300,000	$150,000	$325,000	$200,000	$275,000
Expenses	100,000	100,000	100,000	100,000	100,000	100,000
Net profit	$ 75,000	$200,000	$ 50,000	$225,000	$100,000	$175,000

*Cost of goods sold

Determination of Physical Inventory Amounts

In attempting to determine correct inventory balances, the accountant is faced with two problems:

1. How many inventory items are owned by the business?
2. What dollar value should be assigned to each item owned?

TAKING THE INVENTORY
The process by which inventory items are counted, weighed, or otherwise physically examined.

Taking the Inventory. Under the periodic inventory system, all inventory items owned by an organization are counted, weighed, or otherwise physically examined as of the end of each accounting period—a process often referred to as **taking the inventory.** Since sales and purchase transactions continuously alter inventory levels, inventory taking is often performed during nonworking hours. At times, operations are suspended while the inventory is examined.

Inventory observation teams often include two or more persons so that one person can verify the work of another. Frequently, prenumbered tags with written descriptions and amounts are attached to each inventory item or to a group of similar items to make collection of inventory information easier and help ensure completeness. The individuals examining the inventory must be alert for unsaleable or unuseable items. Such items should not be included in the inventory amounts, as they offer no future economic benefit.

Goods in Transit. Since one of the requirements for including an item in inventory is that the business have legal title to it, a review of ownership must be part of the inventory-taking process. Recall from Chapter 5 that the timing of the passage of title to goods depends on the selling terms. Thus, although all goods purchased under terms of f.o.b. destination are excluded from the purchaser's inventory until received, goods purchased under terms of f.o.b. shipping point should be included in the purchaser's inventory even if they are in transit and have not yet arrived as of the end of an accounting period.

Consigned Goods. A further inventory problem is presented by goods held on consignment. **Consigned goods** are goods shipped from a supplier (the consignor) to a seller (the consignee) that remain the legal property of the supplier until sold. Therefore, consigned goods held by a merchandising firm consignee should not be included in the consignee's inventory at the end of an accounting period. The goods are included in the inventory of the consignor at the end of the accounting period.

CONSIGNED GOODS
Goods shipped from a supplier to a seller that remain the property of the supplier until sold.

Simple physical possession of goods does not always imply ownership, nor should it be assumed that taking the physical inventory will identify all inventory items owned by a company. The firm must examine purchase and sales agreements, shipping and receiving reports, invoices, and any other available inventory-related documentation relevant to the period shortly before and after the end of an accounting period to complete the physical inventory.

Determination of Inventory Values

The Role of Historical Cost. Following the process of taking the inventory, some value must be assigned to each inventory item. As discussed in Chapter 5, historical cost, or purchase price, adjusted by freight charges and purchase discounts and allowances, serves as the basis for assigning dollar values to inventory quantities. We will assume that the purchase prices used in the remainder of this chapter are net purchase prices so that no further adjustments for freight charges or purchase discounts are necessary.

A review of purchase documents, invoices, and other related materials provides the accountant with purchase cost data. However, some assumption must be made about which purchase costs are associated with items sold during the prior accounting period and which are associated with items still on hand. This assumption is generally based on one of four costing methods:

1. Specific identification.
2. Weighted average.
3. First-in, first-out (FIFO).
4. Last-in, first-out (LIFO).

These methods do not necessarily reflect the actual physical flow of goods through a firm. For accounting purposes, it is often irrelevant which specific items are actually sold and which remain in inventory at the end of an accounting period.

For example, assume that a grocery store always places the oldest cans of pears at the front of the shelf when restocking merchandise. The oldest pears are the items sold and the newest pears remain in inventory on the shelf. However, the ending inventory value can be determined from the purchase cost of the specific cans on the shelf, the oldest purchase costs on record, the most recent purchase costs incurred, or some average of the oldest and most recent costs.

SPECIFIC IDENTIFICATION METHOD
An inventory costing method by which the cost of goods sold and ending inventory amounts are determined by tracing the purchase cost of each inventory item as it moves through the business.

Specific Identification Method. Under the **specific identification method,** the cost of goods sold and ending inventory amounts are determined by tracing the purchase cost of each inventory item as it moves through the business. Consider the case of High Tech Corporation, which sells small radios and has inventory data for January as shown in Exhibit 9.3.

EXHIBIT 9.3

Beginning inventory 1/1	600 units @ $10		$ 6,000
Purchases			
1/4	300 units @ $12	$ 3,600	
1/10	200 units @ 13	2,600	
1/16	400 units @ 11	4,400	
1/30	100 units @ 14	1,400	
Total purchases	1,000 units	$12,000	12,000
Total goods available for sale 1,600 units			$18,000
Average unit price			$ 11.25

700 radios were listed on the physical inventory on January 31.

Further investigation indicates that 700 radios in ending inventory and 900 radios sold came from the following purchases:

	Units Sold	Units on Hand
From beginning inventory	500	100
From 1/4 purchase	250	50
From 1/10 purchase	100	100
From 1/16 purchase	50	350
From 1/30 purchase	0	100
Totals	900	700

The cost of goods sold and ending inventory values under specific identification are as follows:

	Cost of Goods Sold	1/31/Inventory
From beginning inventory	500 @ $10 = $5,000	100 @ $10 = $1,000
From 1/4 purchase	250 @ 12 = 3,000	50 @ 12 = 600
From 1/10 purchase	100 @ 13 = 1,300	100 @ 13 = 1,300
From 1/16 purchase	50 @ 11 = 550	350 @ 11 = 3,850
From 1/30 purchase	0	100 @ 14 = 1,400
Totals	$9,850	$8,150

WEIGHTED AVERAGE COSTING METHOD
An inventory costing method by which all units sold during a period and all units remaining in physical inventory at the end of the period are assumed to have the same average cost per unit.

Weighted Average Method. Under the **weighted average costing method,** all units sold during a period and all units remaining in physical inventory at the end of that period are assumed to have the same average cost per unit. This cost is determined by first adding together the costs of beginning inventory and purchases for the period and then dividing the sum by the total number of units available for sale (beginning inventory plus purchases) for the period.

Applying the weighted average costing method to High Tech yields a unit price of $11.25 for each radio, as follows:

$$\frac{\text{Cost of beginning inventory plus purchases}}{\text{Total number of radios available for sale}} = \frac{\$18{,}000}{1{,}600} = \$11.25$$

The January 31 inventory would be valued at $7,875 (700 units × $11.25 per unit). The cost of goods sold for the month ending January 31 would be $10,125 ($6,000 beginning inventory + $12,000 purchases − $7,875 ending inventory).

Note that it was not necessary to determine the specific source of the 700 units in ending inventory. The value of the ending inventory would be the same no matter which specific radios High Tech sold during January.

FIFO Method. Under the **first-in, first-out (FIFO) costing method,** the value of the ending inventory is determined from the most recent purchase costs and the cost of goods sold is determined from the oldest purchase costs in the goods available for sale. For inventory valuation purposes, the FIFO cost flow assumption can be thought of as "last-in, still-here."

FIRST-IN, FIRST-OUT (FIFO)
An inventory cost flow assumption by which the value of ending inventory is determined from the most recent purchase costs and the cost of goods sold is determined from the oldest purchase costs in goods available for sale.

For High Tech, the ending physical inventory of 700 radios on January 31 would be valued under FIFO as follows:

Radios Assumed To Be in Inventory on 1/31		Cost Assigned	
1/30 purchase	100 units @ $14	$1,400	Most recent purchase
1/16 purchase	400 units @ $11	4,400	Next most recent purchase
1/10 purchase	200 units @ $13	2,600	Third most recent purchase
Totals	700 units	$8,400	

The cost of goods sold for January would be computed as $9,600 ($6,000 beginning inventory + $12,000 purchases − $8,400 ending inventory). Again note that High Tech did not specifically consider which radios were sold during January in determining either the cost of goods sold or ending inventory.

LIFO Method. Under the **last-in, first-out (LIFO) costing method,** the value of the ending inventory is determined from the oldest purchase costs and the cost of goods sold is determined from the most recent purchase costs in the goods available for sale. For inventory valuation purposes, the LIFO cost flow assumption can be thought of as "first-in, still-here."

LAST-IN, FIRST-OUT (LIFO)
An inventory cost flow assumption by which the value of ending inventory is determined from the oldest purchase costs and cost of goods sold is determined from the most recent purchase costs in the goods available for sale.

High Tech's ending inventory of 700 units at January 31 would be valued under LIFO as follows:

Units Assumed To Be in Inventory on 1/31		Cost Assigned	
Beg. inv. 1/1	600 units @ $10	$6,000	Oldest purchase
Purchase 1/4	100 units @ $12	1,200	Next oldest purchase
Totals	700 units	$7,200	

The cost of goods sold for January would be $10,800 ($6,000 beginning inventory + $12,000 purchases − $7,200 ending inventory). Again, note that the specific radios sold were irrelevant to the computations.

Comparison of Inventory Cost Flow Assumptions

As you have just seen, the values assigned to ending inventory and cost of goods sold for a time period are different under each cost flow assumption, even though the physical movement of goods is the same in each case. Assuming total sales of $30,000 and other expenses of $2,000, the income statement in Exhibit 9.4 uses the High Tech data to compare the four inventory costing methods in relation to net income and ending inventory values.

EXHIBIT 9.4

	Specific Identification	Weighted Average	FIFO	LIFO
Net sales	$30,000	$30,000	$30,000	$30,000
Cost of goods sold—per above	9,850	10,125	9,600	10,800
Gross margin	$20,150	$19,875	$20,400	$19,200
Other expenses	2,000	2,000	2,000	2,000
Net income for January	$18,150	$17,875	$18,400	$17,200
Inventory, January 31	$ 8,150	$ 7,875	$ 8,400	$ 7,200

Price Trends and Inventory Costing Methods. Note in Exhibit 9.3 that the general price trend was upward. Except for the purchase of January 16, each purchase was higher priced than the one before. Exhibit 9.4 shows that the LIFO costing method produced the lowest net income, while the FIFO costing method produced the highest. In a period of rising inventory prices, using LIFO will always result in a lower income than using FIFO, since LIFO determines the cost of goods sold by the more recent higher prices.

Since sales prices of goods tend to rise as purchase costs of goods rise, some LIFO proponents argue that LIFO is the best cost flow assumption to use during inflationary periods, since it associates current cost dollars with current revenue dollars. However, LIFO does not completely match equivalent dollars of revenue and expense. Some time lag still exists between the time goods are purchased and the time they are sold. This argument also ignores the value of inventory on the statement of financial position.

Examining the inventory balances in Exhibit 9.4 shows that in periods of generally rising prices, LIFO places the lowest dollar amounts on the statement of financial position while FIFO places the highest dollar amounts on the statement. FIFO proponents argue that the inventory value on the statement of financial position under FIFO is closest to current value, since it is based on the most recent purchase prices and is therefore more useful to users of financial statements than are LIFO values.

Inventory Costing and Income Taxation. Which costing method assumption to use is a free choice of management, with one exception. Although the rules for tax accounting and financial reporting are generally separate and distinct, companies that choose LIFO for income tax purposes are legally required to use LIFO for general financial reporting purposes as well. Tax considerations can thus influence management's choice in the selection of an inventory valuation and related cost of goods sold methodology.

Inflation and Inventory Profits

Some accountants and analysts argue that using FIFO or weighted average cost during inflationary periods produces "inventory profits" that are not true profits in an economic sense. The argument advanced is that FIFO or weighted average cost of goods sold computations are based on "old" costs that are much lower than the current market value of the goods sold.

To illustrate, assume that High Tech uses FIFO and that its only assets immediately before January 31 are its radio inventory. Therefore, at the close of business on January 30, High Tech had total assets of 1,600 radios valued at $18,000 (goods available for sale per Exhibit 9.3). If High Tech sells 900 radios on January 31 for $30,000 cash, its assets at the close of business on January 31 would be as follows:

Cash	$30,000
Inventory (700 radios)	8,400
Total	$38,400

As illustrated in Exhibit 9.4, gross profit earned on January 31 appears to be $30,000 − $9,600, or $20,400. But if High Tech buys 900 radios (to replace those sold) for $14 each, its assets will be as follows:

Cash	$17,400	[$30,000 − (900 × $14)]
Inventory (1,600 radios)	21,000	[$8,400 + (900 × $14)]
Total	$38,400	

In real terms, High Tech now has the same number of radios that it had before the January 31 sales (1,600), but it has $17,400 more cash than before as follows:

	Number Owned Immediately Before January 31 Sale	Number Owned After January 31 Sale and Repurchase of Inventory
Radios	1,600	1,600
Cash	$0	$17,400

The "real" gross profit must be only $17,400. The $3,000 difference between the FIFO gross profit of $20,400 and the gross profit computed after looking at replacement cost of the inventory sacrificed is often called an inventory profit. Adding to the foregoing problem is the fact that High Tech would be required to pay tax on its reported profits, not on its real profits.

FASB 33 and 82—Inflation Disclosure

The Financial Accounting Standards Board (FASB) passed Statement No. 33[1] in 1979 in response to criticism of historical cost accounting procedures in inflationary periods. Statement 33 was modified in 1984 by FASB Statement No. 82[2] and requires that large corporations disclose both the current replacement cost of inventories on their statement of financial position and their cost of goods sold determined by

[1]FASB "Financial Reporting and Changing Prices," Statement of Financial Accounting Standards No. 33 (Stamford, Conn., 1979).

[2]FASB "Financial Reporting and Changing Prices: Elimination of Certain Disclosures," Statement of Financial Accounting Standards No. 82 (Stamford, Conn., 1984).

looking at the current value of the items sold at the date of sale. In addition to requiring these inventory disclosures, Statement 33 as amended, requires current value disclosures with respect to plant assets. Although Statement 33 applies only to large corporations, smaller companies are urged to disclose similar information.

CONCEPT SUMMARY 9.1

COMPARISON OF INVENTORY VALUATION METHODS

	Specific Identification	Weighted Average	FIFO	LIFO
Cost of goods sold	Specifically identified costs assigned	Weighted average costs assigned	Costs associated with oldest purchase dates assigned	Costs associated with most recent purchase dates assigned
Inventory valuations	Specifically identified costs assigned	Weighted average costs assigned	Costs associated with most recent purchase dates assigned	Costs associated with oldest purchase dates assigned

Consistency of Inventory Value Determination

A further requirement for inventory accounting under generally accepted accounting principles is consistency of application. Since changes in the use of inventory cost flow methods can cause differences in inventory valuations, in cost of goods sold computations, and in overall profit levels of a business, the inventory valuation method chosen should be applied consistently over time. Changing from one inventory method to another would cause wide fluctuations in reported income and would make income statements difficult to analyze from year to year. Therefore, if a change is made in the cost flow method used, the dollar effect of the change in inventory values and income levels should be presented to the users of the financial statements so that they can accurately compare the results of several years' operations.

Lower of Cost or Market Rule

Inventory is an asset. As with any asset, its value should not exceed its future economic benefit. If the end-of-period replacement (purchase) cost of an inventory item were less than the value on a firm's books, the recorded value of the item would exceed the future economic benefit. For example, if High Tech had recorded $8,400 as its January 31 inventory value and could replace all 700 radios for $7,000 on January 31, then surely the radios have a real value of only $10 each.

It is not unusual for market prices of merchandise inventory items to decline because of such things as shifts in consumer preferences and normal obsolescence. In such circumstances, many firms adopt the lower of cost or market rule. The **lower of cost or market (LCM) rule** assigns the lower of the historical purchase cost or current replacement value to an item for financial statement purposes. For inventory, this rule requires that the value of the inventory be the lower of the historical purchase cost assigned under the firm's cost flow method or the current market value. The current market value refers to replacement purchase cost and not to sales price to

LOWER OF COST OR MARKET (LCM) RULE
A rule that assigns the lower of the historical purchase cost or current replacement value to an item for financial statement purposes.

customers. LCM can be applied to each inventory item individually, to collections of similar inventory items on a group basis, or to total inventory. Regardless of the application, the methodology is the same.

First, ending inventory values are determined based on historical purchase cost. Then, market price is compared with the historical cost. The lower of these values is selected as the basis for inventory valuation and related cost of goods sold determination. Usually, LCM is applied on an item-by-item basis, since this is the only method acceptable for federal income tax purposes, and most companies do not wish to do the work required by the LCM method more than once. Exhibit 9.5 is an example of item-by-item computations of LCM values for High Tech.

EXHIBIT 9.5

Inventory Item	Quantity in Physical Inv.	Historical Cost/Unit	Current Market Purchase Cost/Unit	Total Historical Cost	Total Market Price	Lower of Cost or Market
Tubes	100	$ 2.00	$ 3.00	$ 200	$ 300	$ 200
Transistors	300	8.00	7.00	2,400	2,100	2,100
Connectors	200	4.00	3.50	800	700	700
Radios	700	12.00	13.00	8,400	9,100	8,400
		Total costs and market prices		$11,800	$12,200	$11,400

Although High Tech determined purchase cost by the FIFO method in Exhibit 9.5, the company could have used LCM regardless of the cost method used. If High Tech had applied LCM on a total inventory basis, it would have valued its inventory at $11,800, since total historical cost ($11,800) is less than total market price ($12,200).

Under LCM, the accountant departs from historical cost when market prices decline below purchase cost but not when market prices rise above purchase cost. This inconsistency is an application of the principle of conservatism.

INVENTORY ESTIMATION METHODS

Gross Profit Method

The **gross profit method** is a way to estimate the value of ending inventory using the relationship among sales dollars, cost of goods sold, and gross profit rather than physically counting and valuing the inventory items. For example, if an inventory were destroyed by fire, counting would not be possible. Yet management would need to establish a value for the loss. In other cases, management might wish to estimate inventory and cost of goods sold to develop financial statements at times other than year-end. Even though some accuracy is sacrificed in estimation, the cost of interim statements would be prohibitive if actual inventory levels had to be taken each time such statements were prepared.

GROSS PROFIT METHOD
A method of estimating ending inventory value by using the relationship among sales dollars, cost of goods sold, and gross profit.

If the relationship among sales dollars, cost of goods sold, and gross profit is known and is consistent over time, it can be used in estimating the value of inventory. Let's say that an examination of the historical relationship among sales, cost of goods sold, and gross profit for Rigid Company, which sells sterling silver salad forks, provides the data in Exhibit 9.6.

EXHIBIT 9.6

	Total Dollar Amounts	Percentage of Sales Dollars
Average sales in preceding time periods	$225,000	100%
Average cost of goods sold in preceding time periods	135,000	60%
Average gross profit in preceding time periods	$ 90,000	40%

Cost of goods sold = 60 percent of sales dollars
Gross profit = 40 percent of sales dollars

Suppose a fire at Rigid Company destroyed the company's inventory of forks, but management had the following data:

Merchandise inventory, March 1	$ 75,000
Purchases during March	90,000
Goods available for sale during March	$165,000
Sales during March	$200,000

Inventory on March 31 could then be estimated as follows:

Goods available for sale during March		$165,000
Less: Estimated cost of goods sold for March		
Sales during March	$200,000	
Cost of goods sold percentage of total sales dollars	.60	
		120,000
Estimated ending inventory, March 31		$ 45,000

Retail Inventory Method

Retail businesses often have many different items in inventory (consider a grocery store) and a corresponding high volume of purchase transactions. Tracing inventory on hand to specific purchase cost records can be very difficult in such an environment. However, retail price information is usually readily available because items are displayed for sale with retail prices attached. Under the **retail inventory method,** ending physical inventory is maintained at the more easily determined selling (or retail) price and is reduced to historical cost by using the ratio of purchase cost to selling price of goods available for sale.

RETAIL INVENTORY METHOD
A method of valuing inventory by which inventory records are maintained at selling prices and are reduced to historical cost by using the ratio of purchase cost to selling price of goods available for sale.

Assume that the Little Giant Department Store takes inventory on July 31 and determines that the retail value of its inventory is $1.25 million. Historical records of Little Giant provide the following information:

	At Retail Selling Prices	At Historical Purchase Cost
Beginning inventory, July 1	$1,000,000	$ 700,000
Merchandise purchases during July	4,000,000	2,900,000
Goods available for sale during July	$5,000,000	$3,600,000
Ending inventory, July 31	$1,250,000	

From these records, Little Giant determines that the ratio of purchase costs to selling prices of the goods available for sale during July is $\frac{\$3,600,000}{\$5,000,000}$, or 72 percent. Little Giant then estimates the historical purchase cost of its July 31 inventory as $1,250,000 × .72 = $900,000.

Like the gross profit method, the retail inventory method can be used to estimate the dollar level of inventory on hand at any time without physically taking inventory. If Little Giant knows that total retail value of the goods available for sale for the month ending October 31 is $5 million and net sales for October are $3.5 million, Little Giant can estimate inventory value on October 31 as follows:

Goods available for sale at retail	$5,000,000
Less: Net sales	3,500,000
Inventory, October 31 at retail	1,500,000
Ratio of purchase cost to selling price	.72
Estimated October 31 inventory, at cost	$1,080,000

Of course, a periodic physical inventory still must be taken at year-end to verify the computations and provide information as to inventory losses. However, the retail inventory method does provide an economical way of determining the historical cost of inventory where large numbers of small items make review of purchase documents infeasible.

Comparison of the Gross Profit and Retail Inventory Methods

Although both the retail inventory method and the gross profit method rely on ratios of cost to selling price to determine inventory values, the data used in the retail method tend to be more recent. Exhibit 9.7 contrasts the data used in the retail and gross profit methods of inventory determination.

Although both methods share the weakness that they use past data to estimate current cost, the problem is more severe with the gross profit method, which relies on older data. Problems in application of either the retail or gross profit methods of inventory estimation occur when changes in sales mix, inventory mix, or selling prices take place. Adjustments can be made for these problems, but the details of these adjustments are best left to those who take more advanced accounting courses.

JOURNAL ENTRIES REQUIRED UNDER THE PERIODIC INVENTORY SYSTEM

Under the periodic inventory method, no journal entries are made in the Inventory or Cost of Goods Sold accounts at the time of sale. As discussed in Chapter 5, the

EXHIBIT 9.7

Retail Method	Gross Profit Method
Inventory cost as a percentage of selling price determined by beginning of *current* period inventory and *current* purchase cost/selling price ratios.	Inventory cost as a percentage of selling price determined by *historical* (prior period) cost/selling price ratios.

only account used with respect to merchandise inventories during day-to-day operations of the business is the Purchases account. All purchases of goods for resale made during a particular period are recorded in this account. The Inventory account is merely updated at the end of each accounting period to record the dollar value change in inventory that has occurred since the end of the preceding period. Under the periodic inventory method, changes in the Inventory account are made through adjusting entries in conjunction with financial statement preparation.

Earlier in the chapter, High Tech Corporation was shown to have FIFO inventory balances as follows:

Inventory balance, January 1	$ 6,000
Purchases during January	12,000
Inventory balance, January 31	8,400

A worksheet for High Tech is presented in Exhibit 9.8. All figures except those for inventory-related accounts simply represent assumptions for purposes of completeness. Note that the amount entered in the trial balance for inventory is as of January 1. To complete the worksheet, we need to adjust the inventory balance to its January 31 level of $8,400 as follows and in the first adjusting entry on the worksheet:

Inventory	2,400	
Cost of goods sold		2,400
(to adjust ending inventory to actual balance)		

We also need to close the Purchases account; this task is accomplished by the following entry labeled as adjusting entry 2 on the worksheet:

Cost of goods sold	12,000	
Purchases		12,000
(to close the purchases account)		

After these adjustments have been posted to the general ledger, the Inventory, Purchases, and Cost of Goods Sold accounts appear as follows:

Inventory

	Debit	Credit	
Bal. before adj.	6,000		
Adj. 1	2,400		
Bal. after adj.	8,400		

Purchases

	Debit	Credit	
Bal. before adj.	12,000		
		12,000	Adj. 2
Bal. after adj.	0		

Cost of Goods Sold

	Debit	Credit	
Bal. before adj.	0		
		2,400	Adj. 1
Adj. 2	12,000		
Bal. after adj.	9,600		

EXHIBIT 9.8

The High-Tech Company
Financial Statement Worksheet—Periodic Inventory
For the Month Ending January 31

		1	2	3	4	5	6	7	8	9	10
Acct.		Trial Balance		Adjustments		Adj. Trial Balance		Income Statement		Statement of Financial Position	
No.	Account Title	Dr.	Cr.	Dr.	Cr.	Dr.	Cr.	Dr.	Cr.	Dr.	Cr.
101	Cash	20,000				20,000				20,000	
102	Accounts Receivable	600				600				600	
103	Merchandise Inventory	6,000		2,400[1]		8,400				8,400	
201	Accounts Payable		1,400				1,400				1,400
202	Notes Payable		1,000				1,000				1,000
301	Common Stock		5,000				5,000				5,000
401	Retained Earnings		3,200				3,200				3,200
501	Sales		30,000				30,000		30,000		
601	Purchases	12,000			12,000[2]						
602	Cost of Goods Sold			12,000[2]	2,400[1]	9,600		9,600			
503	Salary Expense	1,500				1,500		1,500			
504	Utilities Expense	500				500		500			
								11,600	30,000	29,000	10,600
								18,400[3]			18,400[3]
	Totals	40,600	40,600	14,400	14,400	40,600	40,600	30,000	30,000	29,000	29,000

[1]To adjust inventory to ending balance

[2]To close purchases account

[3]To show income summary and transfer income to the statement of financial position

Note that the balance in the Cost of Goods Sold account before the Revenue and Expense accounts are closed is equal to the amount obtained in Exhibit 9.4. The effect of the adjusting entries in Exhibit 9.8 is to add the change in inventory amount and the purchases to the Cost of Goods Sold account. This is consistent with the formula for cost of goods sold since, if

Cost of goods sold = Beginning inventory + Purchases − Ending Inventory

then

Cost of goods sold = (Beginning inventory − Ending inventory) + Purchases

or

Cost of goods sold = Change in inventory + Purchases

PERPETUAL INVENTORY SYSTEM

Firms that need day-to-day information about inventory and cost of goods sold use the perpetual inventory system. Under this system, all inventory items are immediately recorded in the Inventory account when purchased and, when sold, are immediately removed from the Inventory account and added to Cost of Goods Sold. Any of the cost flow methods—LIFO, FIFO, weighted average, or specific identification—can be used with the perpetual inventory system. A simple examination of the perpetual inventory records and the Cost of Goods Sold account provides data on the current historical cost of inventory on hand and the amount of the cost of goods sold up to that moment. Of course, the firm must periodically verify these records by taking a physical inventory. Discrepancies between the physical inventory and the perpetual records indicate the need for follow-up internal control reviews.

A Perpetual Inventory Example

Although simple memoranda records of inventory quantities can be used, records more commonly include quantity and dollar value information for each inventory item. An example of an inventory card that could be used under the perpetual inventory system is shown in Exhibit 9.9. Note that entries are made on this card

EXHIBIT 9.9

Inventory Number 13ZQ: Digital watch—Perpetual inventory record

	Purchases			Sales				
		Cost			Cost		Balance on Hand	
Date	Quantity	Unit	Total	Quantity	Unit	Total	Quantity	Total Cost
3/1							200	$2,000
3/5	100	$11	$1,100				300	3,100
3/10				100	$11	$1,100	200	2,000
3/10				100	10	1,000	100	1,000
3/15	300	12	3,600				400	4,600
3/20	200	13	2,600				600	7,200
3/22				200	13	2,600	400	4,600
3/25				100	12	1,200	300	3,400
3/28	100	14	1,400				400	4,800
3/31							400	$4,800

for each purchase or sale of a watch. Note also that the LIFO cost flow assumption was used to determine the cost of the watches sold.

You can see by now that perpetual inventory systems require more detailed record keeping than do periodic systems. Each individual inventory addition or deletion must be recorded as it occurs, whereas the only bookkeeping required under the periodic system consists of purchase costs and year-end inventory adjustments. Perpetual inventory systems are therefore more expensive to operate and must be justified on a cost/benefit basis. Does the benefit derived from the system justify the operational costs? With the advent of small computer-based systems, costs of operating perpetual systems have fallen, and many more companies are implementing such systems to gain the day-to-day inventory control benefits they provide.

Journal Entries Under the Perpetual Inventory System

The journal entries required to capture transactions under the perpetual inventory system are as follows for the March 5 and March 10 purchases and sales of the 13ZQ watches from Exhibit 9.9, assuming a selling price of $30 per unit:

March 5	Merchandise inventory	1,100	
	Cash or accounts payable		1,100
	(to record the purchase of inventory)		
March 10	Cash or accounts receivable	6,000	
	Sales		6,000
	(to record the sales transaction)		
March 10	Cost of goods sold	2,100	
	Merchandise inventory		2,100
	(to reclassify the inventory used as an expense)		

As shown, the perpetual inventory system requires entries for each item sold not only to record the sales amount but also to reduce the Merchandise Inventory account and increase the Cost of Goods Sold account.

INVENTORIES ON THE STATEMENT OF FINANCIAL POSITION

Merchandise inventory is a current asset, since the goods are normally turned over (sold) and replaced several times during one operating cycle of the business. Presentation normally follows Cash and Accounts Receivable on the statement of financial position and generally includes a footnote describing the cost flow assumption used. Exhibit 9.10 shows the partial statement of financial position taken from the 1984 annual report of R. J. Reynolds Industries. Details concerning the inventory amount shown on the face of the statement are provided in a footnote. Note that R. J. Reynolds uses both LIFO and FIFO cost flow assumptions for portions of its inventory.

EXHIBIT 9.10

R. J. Reynolds Industries, Inc.
CONSOLIDATED BALANCE SHEETS
December 31

(Dollars in Millions)	**1984**	1983
ASSETS		
Current assets:		
Cash and short-term investments (Note 4)	**$1,323**	$ 363
Accounts and notes receivable (less allowances of $46 and $42, respectively)	**1,226**	1,344
Inventories (Note 5)	**2,493**	2,690
Prepaid expenses	**72**	64
Total current assets	**5,114**	4,461

Note 5
Inventories

The major classes of inventory and the amount of each at December 31 were:

	1984	1983
Leaf tobacco	$1,174	$1,418
Manufactured products	659	637
Bulk whiskey and wine	125	124
Excise tax on manufactured products	97	131
Raw materials	256	247
Other	182	133
	$2,493	$2,690

At December 31, 1984 and 1983, $1,657 million and $1,827 million, respectively, of the inventory was valued by the LIFO method. The balance of the inventory was valued by various other methods, principally FIFO.

The current cost of inventories at December 31, 1984 and 1983 was greater than the amounts at which these inventories were carried on the balance sheets by $1,727 million and $1,675 million, respectively.

FOR REVIEW

DEMONSTRATION PROBLEM

Magrom Company makes the following purchases of X-glow during June 1986:

Date	Units Purchased	Unit Price	Total Cost
6/1	10,000	$3.00	$ 30,000
6/10	15,000	4.00	60,000
6/15	14,000	4.10	57,400
6/20	11,000	4.05	44,550
6/30	7,000	4.20	29,400
Totals	57,000 units		$221,350

On June 1, Magrom has 5,000 units of X-glow in inventory at a cost of $2.75 per unit, or $13,750 total. Sales of X-glow total 52,000 units during June at $10 each.

On June 30, 1986, Magrom counts its inventory and finds that it has 10,000 units of X-glow on hand.

Required

1. If Magrom uses a periodic inventory system, determine cost of goods sold and ending inventory values for June under each of the following cost flow methods:

a. weighted average
b. FIFO
c. LIFO

2. Under requirement 1, which cost flow assumption will minimize income reported for June on sale of X-glow? All expenses other than cost of goods sold total $50,000 during June.

Demonstration Problem Solution

1. a. Weighted Average (WA)
Total X-glow available for sale

Transaction Date	Units	Cost
Beginning inventory	5,000	$ 13,750
6/1 purchase	10,000	30,000
6/10 purchase	15,000	60,000
6/15 purchase	14,000	57,400
6/20 purchase	11,000	44,550
6/30 purchase	7,000	29,400
Totals	62,000 units	$235,100

$$\text{WA cost/unit} = \frac{\$235{,}100}{62{,}000} = \$3.79/\text{unit}$$

Ending inventory = 10,000 × $3.79 = $37,900

Cost of goods sold computations

Beginning inventory	$ 13,750
Plus: Purchases	221,350
Less: Ending inventory	(37,900)
WA cost of goods sold	$197,200

b. FIFO
Ending inventory

7,000 @ $4.20 =	$29,400
3,000 @ $4.05 =	12,150
Total	$41,550

Cost of goods sold

Beginning inventory	$ 13,750
Plus: Purchases	221,350
Less: Ending inventory	(41,550)
FIFO cost of goods sold	$193,550

c. LIFO

Ending inventory

5,000 @ $2.75 =	$13,750
5,000 @ $3.00 =	15,000
Total	$28,750

Cost of goods sold

Beginning inventory	$ 13,750
Plus: Purchases	221,350
Less: Ending inventory	(28,750)
LIFO cost of goods sold	$206,350

2. Income is lowest if LIFO is assumed, since this method yields the highest cost of goods sold.

	WA	FIFO	LIFO
Sales 52,000 @ $10	$520,000	$520,000	$520,000
Cost of goods sold	197,200	193,550	206,350
Gross margin	$322,800	$326,450	$313,650
Other expenses	50,000	50,000	50,000
Net income	$272,800	$276,450	$263,650

SUMMARY

- Inventory items are assets that must be owned and offer future economic benefit to an organization to be included in the Inventory account.
- Inventory costing and the related cost of goods sold measurement can be accomplished under a variety of methods. The primary concern is how useful the resulting economic data will be to users of financial statements and not how well the method matches the physical movement of items through a firm.
- Inventory value and cost of goods sold computations are normally based on historical costing procedures.
- With the periodic method of inventory accounting, identification of items owned at the beginning and end of the accounting period and purchases made during the period form the basis for determining the Inventory balance on the statement of financial position and Cost of Goods Sold on the income statement.
- With the perpetual method of inventory accounting, identification of the cost of each item sold at the time of sale forms the basis for determining Cost of Goods Sold and the Inventory account balances.
- Weighted average costing assumes that the cost of each item sold during a period and of each item on hand at the end of that period is the same.
- First-in, first-out (FIFO) costing assumes that the dollars associated with the oldest inventory items purchased are to be assigned to cost of goods sold first.
- Last-in, first-out (LIFO) costing assumes that the dollars associated with the most recently purchased inventory items are to be assigned to cost of goods sold first.

- LIFO costing procedures produce lower reported incomes in periods of rising prices than do FIFO costing procedures.
- FIFO costing procedures produce more current values for inventory on the statement of financial position than do LIFO or weighted average costing procedures.
- Inventory valuation procedures should be applied consistently over time to avoid misleading users of financial statements when they make period-to-period comparisons.
- Inventory is a current asset and generally follows Cash and Accounts Receivable on the statement of financial position.

QUESTIONS

9-1. misstatement of inventory results in an error in net earnings one year and in an opposite, equal, and compensating error in the following year. That being true, why is so much emphasis placed on the correct determination of ending inventory?

9-2. On which financial statement do the following appear?

a. Ending inventory.

b. Cost of goods sold.

How are the two related under the periodic inventory method?

9-3. What are weaknesses of the retail inventory and gross profit methods of determining inventory values?

9-4. FIFO, LIFO, and weighted average all deal with historical costs. How does lower of cost or market differ from historical cost?

9-5. Which "market" is meant in the expression "lower of cost or market"?

9-6. If Jobs Company buys Wheels, Inc., and finds six wheels used for covered wagons, how would the wagon wheels inventory be valued?

9-7. When is it acceptable to use an indirect estimation of inventory? What are two acceptable methods for indirectly estimating inventory?

9-8. If purchase prices for inventory do not change for an entire year, and if beginning inventory unit costs are the same as the purchase prices for the year, would net income vary depending on whether FIFO, LIFO, or weighted average is assumed?

9-9. What are the advantages and disadvantages of using a perpetual inventory system? A periodic inventory system?

9-10. Would having a computer available for inventory record keeping affect the decision on whether to use a periodic or perpetual system? If so, how?

EXERCISES

9-E1. A firm manufacturing washroom soap dispensers is forced to modify one model when it can no longer obtain its usual internal valve assembly. Costs are similar for both models, and the modified model is indistinguishable from the original model by sight. Inventory records are as follows:

1/1	Inventory on hand, 100 units (original) @ $5.05/unit
3/31	Manufacture and placement in merchandise inventory of 45 units (original) @ $5.10/unit
6/30	Manufacture and placement in inventory of 50 units (modified) @ $5.10/unit
10/10	Manufacture and placement in inventory of 30 units (modified) @ $5.15/unit

The firm uses periodic inventory and the LIFO flow assumption. It wishes to sell all original model units before selling any modified units. Is it possible to do so and continue to use LIFO?

9-E2. The Zilch Company, which follows a periodic inventory system, purchased inventory item 217XJZ during the past year as follows:

February 1	$11.00 per unit
June 15	11.20 per unit
December 20	11.60 per unit

a. Given the preceding cost pattern, which of the three inventory flow assumptions will result in the highest net earnings if sales prices remain constant?
b. Suppose that the price trend had been opposite that given (February 1 purchase was at $11.60 with June 15 at $11.20 and December 20 at $11.00). Now which cost flow assumption will likely result in the highest net earnings if sales prices remain constant?

9-E3. Sauterly Corporation, which uses the periodic inventory system, is finishing its inventory calculations for the year ending December 31, 1986. The physical inventory shows 62,000 units of Item K on hand. The following additional information has been obtained from shipping and receiving reports, purchase orders, invoices, and other records:

1. Sauterly held 1,000 units of Item K on consignment from Prix Company.
2. Sauterly purchased 5,000 units of Item K from Bixby Manufacturing, Nashville, Tennessee. Terms were f.o.b. Nashville, and the goods were shipped on December 30, 1986, and received on January 7, 1987.
3. Sauterly sold 2,000 units of K to Amber Tool Company in Minneapolis, f.o.b. Minneapolis. Amber received the goods on January 3, 1987. The goods were shipped on December 28, 1986.
4. Sauterly sent 5,000 units of K to Blackbury Machine Company on December 29, 1986. Blackbury is taking the goods on consignment.

Calculate the number of units of Item K that should be included in Sauterly's December 31, 1986, inventory.

9-E4. The following information is from the records of the Tri-D Corporation, which uses periodic inventory:

12/31/86	Inventory on hand, 100 units @ $6.00/unit
2/10/87	Purchase of 100 units @ $5.75/unit
5/5/87	Purchase of 200 units @ $5.50/unit
10/11/87	Purchase of 100 units @ $5.25/unit

It is determined that there are 150 units in 12/31/87 inventory. Calculate the dollar amount of ending inventory and derive the cost of goods sold for 1987 using the following flow assumptions:

a. Weighted average.
b. FIFO.
c. LIFO.

9-E5. Wilson Company calculates its year-end inventory at cost using the FIFO assumption as follows:

Item	Cost
151-B	$ 1,210
152-B	6,200
154-B	8,900
158-B	16,600
Total	$32,910

The cost of replacing all items on hand with the same new items would be as follows:

Item 151-B	$ 1,200
Item 152-B	6,500
Item 154-B	8,690
Item 158-B	16,600

At what amount will Wilson's ending inventory be valued using lower of cost or market applied on an item-by-item basis?

9-E6. The accounts of Wilson Company (refer to 9-E5) show this additional information:

Beginning inventory	$25,000
Purchases	52,910
Sales	90,000
Operating expenses	30,000

Calculate gross profit and net earnings for Wilson if ending inventory is valued at the following:

a. Cost.
b. Lower of cost or market.

9-E7. Anderson Company has the following transactions in its inventory accounts during March 1986:

March 3	Purchases $10,000 of goods on account.
March 10	Sells $4,000 of inventory for cash; inventory originally cost $3,000.
March 15	Purchases $12,000 of goods for cash.
March 25	Sells $8,000 of inventory that originally cost $5,000. Half the sales are on account and half are cash.

Prepare journal entries required for the following:

a. A perpetual inventory system.
b. A periodic inventory system.

PROBLEM SET A

9-A1. **Inventory Methods and Journal Entries.** The following transactions and data relate to the Tate Corporation for the month of October. Tate uses LIFO inventory procedures.

October 1	Inventory on hand, 100 units	$100,000
October 5	Purchase of 600 units on account	660,000
October 8	Sale of 600 units on account	750,000
October 10	Sale of 20 units on account	30,000
October 15	Purchase of 400 units on account	450,000
October 20	Purchase of 200 units on account	222,000
October 25	Sale of 300 units on account	450,000

Required

Present general journal entries for each transaction and any adjusting entries necessary to prepare financial statements for the month ending October 31 if:

a. Tate uses periodic inventory methods.
b. Tate uses perpetual inventory methods.

9-A2. Effect of Inventory Errors. Donleavy, Donleavy, and Shearson, CPAs, have discovered the following inventory errors in the process of auditing the accounts of the Buckminster Company:

Inventory Date	Originally Stated As	Correct Amount
12/31/84	$60,000	$64,000
12/31/85	80,000	78,000
12/31/86	75,000	75,000

Required

At the end of each of the years 1984, 1985, and 1986, what are the errors, if any, in the originally calculated:

a. Net earnings for the year.
b. Owners' equity section of the statement of financial position.
c. Assets section of the statement of financial position.

9-A3. Fire Loss and Gross Profit. Beltrak Corporation has a normal gross profit of 45%. On the night of October 5, 1986, welders remodeling a section of the warehouse neglected to turn off all of their equipment, and the warehouse and most of the inventory burned.

Required

To make an insurance claim, estimate the inventory on hand before the fire using the following information:

Inventory on January 1, 1986	$150,000
Purchases, 1/1/86 through 10/5/86	200,000
Sales, 1/1/86 through 10/5/86	295,000

9-A4. Fire Loss and Retail Method. Kelly-Smithson Company suffers an inventory fire loss on November 1, 1986. However, since it usually employs the retail method of estimating inventory for quarterly financial statements, if has the following information available:

	At Retail Selling Prices	At Historical Purchase Cost
Inventory 1/1/86	$1,000,000	$ 700,000
Purchases, 1/1/86 through 11/1/86	3,000,000	2,100,000
Sales, 1/1/86 through 11/1/86	2,000,000	

Required

Estimate the cost of the inventory destroyed by fire.

9-A5. LIFO, FIFO, Perpetual, and Periodic Inventory. Alex-Lid, Incorporated's, records show the following information:

1/1/86	Inventory on hand, 1,000 units @ $100.00/unit
3/31/86	Sale of 800 units
5/15/86	Purchase of 1,200 units @ $102.50/unit
6/30/86	Sale of 500 units
9/29/86	Sale of 800 units
11/12/86	Purchase of 1,500 units @ $105.00/unit

Required

a. If Alex-Lid uses the perpetual inventory system, calculate the December 31, 1986, inventory and cost of goods sold for the year under FIFO and LIFO.
b. What will be the ending inventory as of December 31, 1986, and the cost of goods sold for the year if a periodic inventory system is used assuming FIFO and LIFO.

9-A6. Periodic Inventory, LIFO, FIFO, and Weighted Average. The Bill Bailey Corporation accounts show the following for the year ending December 31, 1986:

Sales	$1,000,000
Beginning inventory	200,000 (20,000 units @ $10/unit)
Purchases: 2/10	138,375 (13,500 units @ $10.25/unit)
8/20	157,500 (15,000 units @ $10.50/unit)
12/1	199,950 (18,600 units @ $10.75/unit)
Ending inventory	15,000 units
Operating expenses	400,000

Required

a. Prepare comparative earnings statements for the year ending December 31, 1986, under a periodic inventory system and assuming weighted average, FIFO, and LIFO.
b. What amount of merchandise inventory will appear on the December 31, 1986, statement of financial position in the cases in (a)?

9-A7. Lower of Cost or Market. Dempsey Corporation's 12/31/86 inventory is as follows:

Item	Number of Units	Historical Purchase Cost	Current Market Value
N23	200	$ 1.00	$1.10
M15	300	2.00	2.60
Q60	100	10.00	9.00
A12	50	6.00	4.00
C89	150	8.00	9.00

Required

a. Compute ending inventory under the lower of cost or market rule applied on an item-by-item basis.
b. Compute ending inventory under the lower of cost or market rule applied on a total inventory basis.
c. What is the impact of the lower of cost or market rule on reported profits of Dempsey in (a) over what profit would have been if inventory values had been based only on purchase cost if Dempsey uses the periodic method of inventory?

PROBLEM SET B

9-B1. Inventory Methods and Journal Entries. The Kit Kat Corporation has the following transactions during June. Kit Kat uses LIFO inventory costing procedures.

June 1	Inventory on hand, 300 units	$30,000
June 6	Purchases 200 units on account	22,000
June 9	Sells 400 units on account	60,000
June 15	Purchases 500 units on account	52,500
June 20	Sells 100 units on account	15,000
June 25	Purchases 50 units on account	5,750
June 30	Sells 60 units on account	9,000

Required

Present general journal entries for each transaction and any adjusting entries necessary to prepare financial statements for the month ending June 30 if:

a. Kit Kat uses periodic inventory methods.
b. Kit Kat uses perpetual inventory methods.

9-B2. Effect of Inventory Errors. The following inventory errors have been noted in the accounts of Lake Company:

Inventory Date	Originally Stated As	Correct Amount
12/31/84	$100,000	$ 90,000
12/31/85	80,000	85,000
12/31/86	110,000	110,000

Required

For each of the three years, calculate the errors, if any, contained in the original:

a. Net earnings for the year.
b. Owners' equity section of the statement of financial position.
c. Assets section of the statement of financial position.

9-B3. Inventory Theft and Gross Profit. The Ross Company was burglarized on June 20. In addition to stealing all of the company's inventory, the thieves destroyed most of the company's accounting records. However, Ross was able to put together the following information:

Inventory, January 1, 1986	$ 300,000
Purchases 1/1/86 through 6/20/86	700,000
Sales 1/1/86 through 6/20/86	1,500,000

Required

If Ross has a normal gross profit of 60%, estimate the inventory on hand before the theft.

9-B4. Inventory Theft and Retail Method. Kelly Auto Parts was burglarized on November 12, 1986, by thieves who stole the entire inventory. The company uses the retail method of estimating inventory and has the following information:

	At Retail Selling Prices	At Historical Purchase Cost
Inventory, 1/1/86	$ 85,000	$ 68,000
Purchases, 1/1/86 through 11/12/86	150,000	120,000
Sales, 1/1/86 through 11/12/86	100,000	

Required

Estimate the amount of inventory stolen from Kelly Auto Parts.

9-B5. LIFO, FIFO, Perpetual, and Periodic Inventory. Blair Distributors has the following transactions in its inventory accounts:

January 1, 1986	Inventory on hand, 2,000 units at $80/unit
March 1, 1986	Sale of 500 units
April 1, 1986	Sale of 800 units
June 1, 1986	Purchase of 1,000 units at $85/unit
August 1, 1986	Sale of 700 units
November 1, 1986	Purchase of 600 units at $75/unit

Required

a. Assuming a perpetual inventory system, calculate the December 31, 1986, inventory and cost of goods sold using FIFO and LIFO.
b. If Blair Distributors uses a periodic inventory system, calculate the December 31, 1986, inventory and cost of goods sold using FIFO and LIFO.

9-B6. Periodic Inventory, LIFO, FIFO, and Weighted Average. Following are accounts relating to the periodic inventory system for Gray Company for 1986:

Sales	$1,100,000
Beginning inventory	100,000 (5,000 units at $20/unit)
Purchases: 3/1	200,000 (8,000 units at $25/unit)
6/15	400,000 (16,000 units at $25/unit)
10/31	300,000 (10,000 units at $30/unit)
Operating expenses	250,000
Ending inventory	12,000 units

Required

a. Prepare comparative earnings statements for 1986 using weighted average, FIFO, and LIFO.
b. Calculate the amount of inventory that will appear on the statement of financial position for December 31, 1986, in (a).

9-B7. Lower of Cost or Market. Sanders Corporation's ending inventory is as follows for the year ending December 31, 1986:

Item	Number of Units	Historical Purchase Cost	Current Market Value
KLM	100	$ 9.00	$11.00
MJQ	300	8.00	7.00
NOP	200	20.00	24.00
CAL	500	30.00	29.00
NPW	50	4.00	7.00

Required

a. Compute ending inventory under the lower of cost or market rule applied on an item-by-item basis.
b. Compute ending inventory under the lower of cost or market rule applied on a total inventory basis.
c. What is the impact of the lower of cost or market rule on reported profits of Sanders in (a) over what the profit would have been if inventory values had been based only on purchase cost if Sanders uses the periodic method of inventory.

PROPERTY, PLANT, AND EQUIPMENT

CHAPTER OBJECTIVES

After studying Chapter 10, you should understand the following:

1. The nature of tangible long-lived assets.
2. Depreciation accounting and its relationship to income determination.
3. Repair and maintenance versus asset improvement expenditures.
4. Disposition of long-lived assets, including sale and exchange transactions.

Property, plant, and equipment involves large outlays and has a long useful life. This chapter explores accounting for the acquisition, use, and disposition of property, plant, and equipment; discusses the difference between capitalizing and expensing asset expenditures; and explains how to calculate gain or loss on disposition of assets.

CATEGORIES OF FIXED ASSETS

LONG-LIVED ASSETS
Assets expected to yield economic benefits to an organization for longer than one year or one operating cycle.

FIXED ASSETS
See Long-Lived Assets.

TANGIBLE ASSETS
Assets that have physical characteristics that can be seen or touched.

INTANGIBLE ASSETS
Assets that do not possess physical characteristics.

Long-lived assets, often called **fixed assets,** are expected to yield economic benefits to an organization for longer than one year or one operating cycle. Long-lived assets are subdivided into tangible and intangible assets. **Tangible assets** have physical characteristics that you can see or touch. Buildings, land, equipment, and natural resources such as timber, iron ore, or oil are examples of tangible assets. **Intangible assets** are those that do not possess physical characteristics. Rather, they confer certain rights upon the owner. Patents, copyrights, trademarks, franchises, organization costs, leaseholds, and goodwill are examples of intangible assets.

Tangible assets can be subdivided into categories of manufactured or naturally occurring assets. Manufactured assets include buildings, equipment, and vehicles. Naturally occurring assets include land and natural resources.

Manufactured assets wear out or become obsolete in the course of use and time. Most naturally occurring assets do not wear out but are used up or depleted. Land usually is neither used up nor worn out.

This chapter discusses land (property) and manufactured assets (plant and equipment). Natural resources and intangible assets are considered in Chapter 11.

TANGIBLE LONG-LIVED ASSETS

PROPERTY, PLANT, AND EQUIPMENT
Long-lived tangible assets used in the operation of a business that are not intended primarily for resale.

Property, plant, and equipment assets are tangible long-lived assets used in the operation of a business that are not intended primarily for resale. Buildings, production equipment, office equipment, tools, vehicles, land, and land improvements are all examples of property, plant, and equipment.

A purchase of property, plant, and equipment represents the acquisition of a package of future services. The purchase of a building with a useful life of 40 years is the equivalent of the purchase of shelter for 40 years. Purchase of an automobile with an estimated life of 100,000 miles is the equivalent of the purchase of 100,000 miles of transportation. Property, plant, and equipment assets are very similar to current assets, such as prepaid insurance, prepaid rent, prepaid interest, or supplies. The main difference is that the future benefits of property, plant, and equipment are used up over several future time periods, whereas current assets are generally used up within the period of acquisition.

DEPRECIATION ACCOUNTING

As you may recall, depreciation is the term applied to the accounting measurement of the extent of wearing out of manufactured assets in a given period. Depreciation is simply the recognition that by the end of any accounting period, some of the future benefits of plant and equipment have been used up to support the production of revenue during the period.

The cost of using fixed assets must be matched with the revenues that the assets helped to produce, accomplished either by recognizing depreciation as an expense of the periods during which the assets were used or by including depreciation as part of the cost of products produced by the assets. Depreciation as a part of product costing is covered in Parts V and VI of the text. In this chapter, depreciation is treated as an expense of the current period.

DETERMINING AND RECORDING ACQUISITION COST

Purchased Assets

Acquisition cost includes all reasonable and necessary costs to acquire an asset and put it into place and condition for use. Typically, such costs include the purchase price, transportation, insurance while in transit, installation costs, testing costs, and repair or parts costs if reconditioning is required. In accounting terms, all expenditures included in the acquisition costs are said to be **capitalized expenditures;** that is, they are added to an asset account rather than to an expense account.

CAPITALIZED EXPENDITURES
All expenditures that are added to an asset account rather than to an expense account.

For example, Crafty Printing purchases a new printing press for $110,000. Transportation charges are $2,000, insurance during transit is $800, a new concrete pad is poured to accommodate the press at a cost of $3,000, and Crafty pays its own employees $4,200 to install and test the press. During testing one of Crafty's employees drops a washer into the press causing $5,000 damages. Crafty's acquisition, or capitalized, cost for this press is as follows:

Purchase price	$110,000
Transportation	2,000
Insurance	800
Concrete pad	3,000
Installation and testing	4,200
Total acquisition cost	$120,000

Since the $5,000 for damage repair was the result of carelessness and not a necessary cost, it is classified as a repair expense rather than as part of the cost of the press.

Interest Costs. In general, acquisition cost does not include interest incurred to finance the asset. However, under certain conditions specified in Financial Accounting Standards Board Statement No. 34[1], interest costs can be considered part of the acquisition cost. This is called capitalizing interests costs and is best left to more advanced accounting courses.

Basket Acquisitions. In cases where assets of different character are purchased as a package, acquisition cost must be allocated among the different assets, using some rational basis such as relative market or tax assessment value.

Assume that Crafty Printing Company purchases a building on an acre of land for $560,000 and that half of the land is used as a parking lot. The building is appraised

[1] FASB "Accounting for Interest Costs," Statement of Financial Accounting Standards No. 34 (Stamford, Conn., 1981).

at $280,000, the land at $200,000, and the paving and lighting in the parking lot at $60,000. The acquisition cost is allocated to each asset as follows:

Building	$\frac{\$280,000}{\$540,000} \times \$560,000 = \$290,370$
Land	$\frac{\$200,000}{\$540,000} \times \$560,000 = \$207,407$
Parking lot improvements	$\frac{\$\ 60,000}{\$540,000} \times \$560,000 = \$\ 62,222$

Self-Constructed Assets

Assets can be constructed by the user. In such cases, only the reasonable and necessary costs of construction are included in the acquisition cost. Costs considered reasonable and necessary are determined the same way as those discussed earlier for Crafty's purchase of the printing press.

Suppose Crafty needs a new building and decides to use its own employees to construct the building. Since the employees are not experienced at plant construction, the building costs 20 percent more than an outside contractor would have charged. The 20 percent differential is not reasonable and necessary and should not be considered part of the acquisition cost of the building. The extra 20 percent should be charged off as a loss on Crafty's income statement during the construction period.

Asset Acquisitions for Other Than Cash

The cost of a fixed asset acquired for other than cash is considered equal to the value of the assets given up in exchange or to the value of the asset received, whichever is more clearly determinable.

Accounting for Asset Acquisitions

Ledger Accounts Used. For recording purposes, assets are grouped into like categories in ledger accounts. Production equipment would be accounted for in one ledger account, office equipment in another, and buildings in still another. The individual pieces of equipment or buildings are listed in subsidiary records in the same way that individual records are kept for each separate account receivable.

Land, which is not depreciable, must be carried in an account separate from buildings, which are depreciable. Separate accounts are required even if land and buildings are purchased as a package and physically located together. Land improvements, if they have a limited life, must be carried in an account separate from land. For instance, the paving in a parking lot has a limited life and is depreciable even though the land it sits upon has an unlimited life and is not depreciable.

Journal Entries Required. The journal entries for fixed asset acquisitions are relatively straightforward. The appropriate asset account is increased, and some other asset is decreased or a liability increased. If Crafty acquires the new printing press for $60,000 cash and $60,000 in notes payable, the required journal entry would be as follows:

Printing press	120,000	
Cash		60,000
Notes payable		60,000
(to record acquisition of printing press)		

RESIDUAL VALUE AND USEFUL LIFE

Residual value, sometimes called **salvage value,** is the value remaining when a fixed asset's useful life to an enterprise is at an end. When no longer useful, equipment can be sold as reconditionable equipment, for parts, or for the scrap value of the contained materials.

RESIDUAL VALUE
See Salvage Value.

SALVAGE VALUE
The value remaining when a fixed asset's useful life to an enterprise is at an end.

The useful life of the asset can be a function of time, units of use, or units of output. Estimates of residual value and useful life are based on one or more of the following sources of information:

1. The firm's own experience with similar assets.
2. The manufacturer's estimates.
3. Industry or trade average figures, usually available from trade publications.
4. Consultation with other firms with similar equipment.
5. Analysis of the probable factors and time frame of deterioration in asset usefulness.

The factors that cause asset deterioration can be physical or functional. Physical deterioration factors include normal wear and tear or damages from climate or the elements. Functional deterioration occurs when the asset no longer provides economical service. Computers are a good example of assets that frequently become obsolete long before they physically wear out.

ALLOCATION OF LONG-LIVED ASSET COSTS TO EXPENSE

How do accountants allocate a fixed asset's cost to expense? How can the rate of decline in future usefulness of assets be determined? How long will an asset last? What is the true residual value of an asset at the end of its useful life?

Obviously, answers to these questions cannot be known with certainty until an asset is discarded. Estimates must therefore be made of useful life, residual value, and rate of decline in future utility. The estimates required in the depreciation process mean that the expense computed in any one time period is not a precise measure of asset use during that period.

estimates
of useful life
residual value
rate of decline

Accountants have evolved several systematic methods for determining depreciation for fixed assets. The four most common depreciation methods are the straight-line, units-of-production, declining-balance, and sum-of-the-years' digits methods.

Crafty's new printing press acquired for $120,000 will be used to illustrate the different methods of determining depreciation. Assume that the press's estimated useful life is five years or 30,000 hours of use and that the press can be sold for $15,000 (residual value) at the end of five years.

Straight-Line Depreciation

The straight-line method yields equal amounts of depreciation expense in each year of the asset's life. If the depreciation expense is plotted over time, the graph is a straight line as shown in Exhibit 10.7, hence the name, straight-line method.

The formula for determining depreciation under the straight-line method is as follows:

$$\frac{\text{Acquisition cost} - \text{Residual value}}{\text{Life (in time units)}} = \text{Depreciation per time unit}$$

DEPRECIABLE COST
Acquisition cost of an asset less the asset's residual value.

Acquisition cost less residual value is called **depreciable cost.** Since residual value will presumably be recovered when disposing of assets, it is excluded from the depreciable cost.

Straight-line depreciation on Crafty's printing press would be as follows:

$$\frac{\$120{,}000 - \$15{,}000}{5 \text{ years}} = \frac{\$105{,}000}{5} = \$21{,}000 \text{ depreciation per year, or } \$1{,}750 \text{ per month}$$

Exhibit 10.1 gives the complete straight-line depreciation schedule for the five-year life of the press.

EXHIBIT 10.1

Year		Depreciation Expense This Year	Accumulated Depreciation At Year-End	Book Value Beginning Of Year	Book Value End Of Year
1		$21,000	$ 21,000	$120,000	$99,000
2		21,000	42,000	99,000	78,000
3	$\frac{\$105{,}000}{5}$ =	21,000	63,000	78,000	57,000
4		21,000	84,000	57,000	36,000
5		21,000	105,000	36,000	15,000
Total deprec.		$105,000			

Accumulated depreciation is the total of all depreciation charged against the asset in the past. Book value is acquisition cost less accumulated depreciation. The adjusting entry for depreciation in Exhibit 10.1 for each year would be as follows:

Depreciation expense	21,000	
Accumulated depreciation—equipment		21,000
(to record depreciation expense)		

This adjusting entry is the same, except for the dollar amounts, for each depreciation method and is not repeated within the following discussion.

Units-of-Production Depreciation

UNITS-OF-PRODUCTION METHOD
A depreciation method that assigns equal amounts of depreciation expense to each unit of an asset's input or output.

The **units-of-production method** assigns equal amounts of depreciation expense to each unit of an asset's input or output. Units of output refers to items produced by the asset. Units of input refers to the number of hours or days the asset is used. The units-of-production method is particularly applicable to production-related assets.

Under the units-of-production method, depreciation expense for a period is determined as follows:

$$\frac{\text{Acquisition cost} - \text{Residual value}}{\text{Estimated life (in units of input or output)}} = \text{Depreciation per unit of input or output} \times \text{Units for this time period} = \text{Depreciation for the period}$$

Suppose that Crafty's printing press is used 5,800 hours in the first year and 6,300 hours, 6,200 hours, 6,000 hours, and 5,700 hours, respectively, in the four following years. Depreciation expense for the first year would be as follows:

$$\frac{\$120{,}000 - \$15{,}000}{30{,}000 \text{ hours}} = \$3.50 \text{ per hour} \times 5{,}800 \text{ hours} = \$20{,}300$$

Exhibit 10.2 illustrates depreciation over the life of the press under units-of-production.

EXHIBIT 10.2

Year		Hours of Use	Depreciation Expense This Year	Accumulated Depreciation At Year-End	Book Value Beginning Of Year	Book Value End of Year
1	3.50 ×	5,800 =	$ 20,300	$ 20,300	$120,000	$99,700
2	3.50 ×	6,300 =	22,050	42,350	99,700	77,650
3	3.50 ×	6,200 =	21,700	64,050	77,650	55,950
4	3.50 ×	6,000 =	21,000	85,050	55,950	34,950
5	3.50 ×	5,700 =	19,950	105,000	34,950	15,000
Total deprec.			$105,000			

Declining-Balance Depreciation

Depreciation expense under the **declining-balance method** is determined by multiplying a constant percentage times an asset's book value at the beginning of each period. Since the book value is computed by subtracting accumulated depreciation from acquisition cost, book value must decline each year as accumulated depreciation increases, hence the name, declining-balance method.

DECLINING-BALANCE METHOD
A depreciation method that determines depreciation expense by multiplying a percentage (usually 150 or 200 percent of the straight-line rate) times an asset's book value at the beginning of each period.

Depreciation under the declining-balance method is determined as follows:

$$\text{Rate} \times \text{Book value at beginning of period} = \text{Depreciation for the period}$$

where rate is some multiple of straight-line percentage, usually 150 percent or 200 percent. To obtain the declining-balance rate, first determine the straight-line percentage:

$$\frac{100\%}{\text{Useful life in years}} = \text{Yearly straight-line percentage}$$

Next, multiply the straight-line rate by 1.5 or 2.0, depending on whether the 150 percent or 200 percent multiple of straight-line is being used. When the 200 percent rate is used, the depreciation method is called the **double-declining balance method.**

DOUBLE-DECLINING BALANCE METHOD
A depreciation method that determines depreciation expense by multiplying 200 percent of the straight-line rate times an asset's book value at the beginning of the period.

Combining the preceding formulas, we get the following:

$$\frac{100\%}{\text{Useful life}} \times \begin{matrix}2\\ \text{or}\\ 1.5\end{matrix} \times \begin{matrix}\text{Book value at}\\ \text{beginning of}\\ \text{period}\end{matrix} = \begin{matrix}\text{Depreciation}\\ \text{for}\\ \text{the period}\end{matrix}$$

Double-declining balance depreciation for Crafty's press for Years 1 and 2 is as follows:

Year 1 $\frac{100\%}{5} \times 2 \times \$120{,}000 = \$48{,}000$

Year 2 $\frac{100\%}{5} \times 2 \times (\$120{,}000 - \$48{,}000) = \$28{,}800$

Residual value is ignored in declining-balance depreciation computations for most years. However, an asset should not be depreciated below its residual value regardless of the method used. Therefore, depreciation expense must be limited if normal computations would reduce year-end book value below residual value. Year 5 of the double-declining balance depreciation schedule in Exhibit 10.3 illustrates the effect of the $15,000 residual value in the case of Crafty's press.

EXHIBIT 10.3

Year		Book Value Beg. of Yr.		Deprec. Expense This Year	Accumulated Depreciation At Year-End	Book Value Beginning Of Year	Book Value End of Year
1	40% ×	$120,000	=	$ 48,000	$ 48,000	$120,000	$72,000
2		72,000	=	28,800	76,800	72,000	43,200
3		43,200	=	17,280	94,080	43,200	25,920
4		25,920	=	10,368	104,448	25,920	15,552
5		15,552		552	105,000	15,552	15,000
Total deprec.				$105,000			

As you can see, depreciation expense is limited to $552 in Year 5, even though 40 percent of the beginning-of-the-year book value ($15,552 × 0.4) is $6,221.

Comparing Exhibit 10.3 with Exhibit 10.1, note that depreciation expense is greater in the early years of the press's life under declining-balance than under straight-line and is less in later years. A depreciation method that yields a greater expense in the early years of an asset's useful life than in the later years is referred to as an **accelerated depreciation method.**

ACCELERATED DEPRECIATION METHOD
A depreciation method that yields a greater expense in the early years of an asset's useful life than in the later years.

Sum-of-the-Years' Digits Depreciation

The **sum-of-the-years' digits (SYD) method** is an accelerated depreciation method where depreciation expense is determined by multiplying an asset's depreciable cost by a fraction, with the numerator equal to the remaining years of asset useful life at the beginning of each year and the denominator equal to the sum-of-the-years' digits.

SUM-OF-THE-YEARS' DIGITS METHOD
A depreciation method that determines depreciation expense by multiplying an asset's depreciable cost by the remaining years of the asset's useful life at the beginning of the year divided by the sum-of-the-years' digits in the useful life.

$$\frac{\text{Remaining years of life at beginning of the year}}{\text{Sum-of-the-years' digits}} \times \begin{matrix}\text{Acquisition cost}\\ -\ \text{Residual value}\end{matrix} = \begin{matrix}\text{Depreciation expense}\\ \text{for the year}\end{matrix}$$

The sum-of-the-years' digits can be obtained in two ways: sum the digits in the asset's useful life, i.e., 10 + 9 + 8 + 7 + 6 + 5 + 4 + 3 + 2 + 1 = 55, in the case of a ten-year life, or use the following formula:

$$\frac{n(n+1)}{2}, \text{ where } n = \text{asset life}$$

Crafty's $120,000 printing press has a five-year life. The SYD denominator is [5(5 + 1)]/2 = 15. Depreciation allocations are as follows and as in Exhibit 10.4.

Year 1: 5/15 × ($120,000 − $15,000) = $35,000
Year 2: 4/15 × ($120,000 − $15,000) = $28,000

EXHIBIT 10.4
Sum-of-the-Years' Digits Depreciation Schedule

Year			Depreciation Expense This Year	Accumulated Depreciation At Year-End	Book Value Beginning Of Year	Book Value End of Year
1	5/15	× $105,000 =	$ 35,000	$ 35,000	$120,000	$85,000
2	4/15	× $105,000 =	28,000	63,000	85,000	57,000
3	3/15	× $105,000 =	21,000	84,000	57,000	36,000
4	2/15	× $105,000 =	14,000	98,000	36,000	22,000
5	1/15	× $105,000 =	7,000	105,000	22,000	15,000
Total deprec.			$105,000			

Partial Years' Depreciation

The preceding illustrations assume that the press is in service for a full year in the year of acquisition. In reality, this seldom happens. Assets are normally acquired throughout the year. Whenever an asset is acquired at a time other than the beginning of the year, the first and last years' depreciation expense is based on partial years.

Assume that Crafty acquires the press on October 1 and ends its fiscal year on December 31. Straight-line depreciation over the press's life would be as shown in Exhibit 10.5.

EXHIBIT 10.5

	Computation		Amount	Period
Year 1:	$\frac{\$120,000 - \$15,000}{5}$	× 3/12 =	$ 5,250	(1/4 year)
Year 2:	$\frac{\$120,000 - \$15,000}{5}$	=	21,000	(4 years)
Year 3:		=	21,000	
Year 4:		=	21,000	
Year 5:		=	21,000	
Year 6:	$\frac{\$120,000 - \$15,000}{5}$	× 9/12 =	15,750	(3/4 year)
Total depreciation and years			$105,000	5 years

Similar prorating of the first and last years' depreciation expense would hold for the declining-balance method for fixed assets acquired at other than the beginning of a firm's fiscal year. Of course, depreciation expense in the last year would still be limited by residual value. Since the units-of-production method is not time dependent, no special computations are needed to accommodate partial years.

Because the sum-of-the-years' digits depreciation method requires different fractions for each year of an asset's life, partial years' depreciation expense computations are more complex. Exhibit 10.6 presents the depreciation expense for Years 1, 2, and 6 if Crafty purchases the press on October 1.

EXHIBIT 10.6

Depreciable amount = \$120,000 − \$15,000 = \$105,000

				Depreciation Expense
Year 1	5/15 × \$105,000 × 3/12	=		\$ 8,750
Year 2	5/15 × \$105,000 × 9/12	=	\$26,250	
	+			
	4/15 × \$105,000 × 3/12	=	7,000	33,250
Year 6	1/15 × \$105,000 × 9/12	=		5,250

Depreciation expense for whole Years 3, 4, and 5 would be determined like Year 2 in Exhibit 10.6.

Comparison of Methods

Regardless of the depreciation method used, the goal is to match the cost of using the asset with the time periods that benefit from the asset's use. Comparing the preceding depreciation schedules, note that different methods result in very different amounts of depreciation expense per time period. Thus, the act of selecting one depreciation method over another will have a direct effect on a firm's earnings.

The line graph in Exhibit 10.7 illustrates the differences in annual depreciation expense for Crafty under the different depreciation methods.

If Crafty has earnings of \$50,000 each year before depreciation expense is deducted and all other factors remain unchanged, net earnings before taxes would be as shown in Exhibit 10.8 under the different depreciation methods.

Criteria for Selection of a Depreciation Method

It would seem reasonable to select the method that most closely mirrors the decline in the asset's future utility as the asset is used. For example, an automobile might lose future usefulness at an even pace, assuming that mileage each period is fairly equal. In such a case, straight-line would appear to be an appropriate method. However, because a computer tends to lose future usefulness through obsolescence rapidly in the early part of its life, an accelerated method of depreciation would appear reasonable. Professional accounting standards say only that any method used must be rational and systematic and, once selected, must be used consistently for

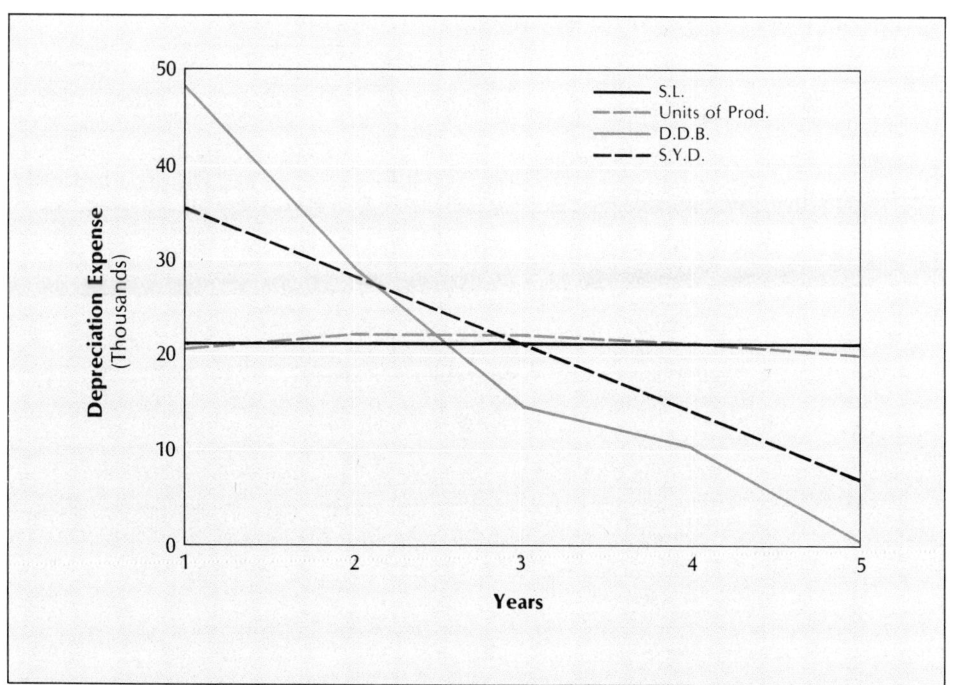

EXHIBIT 10.7

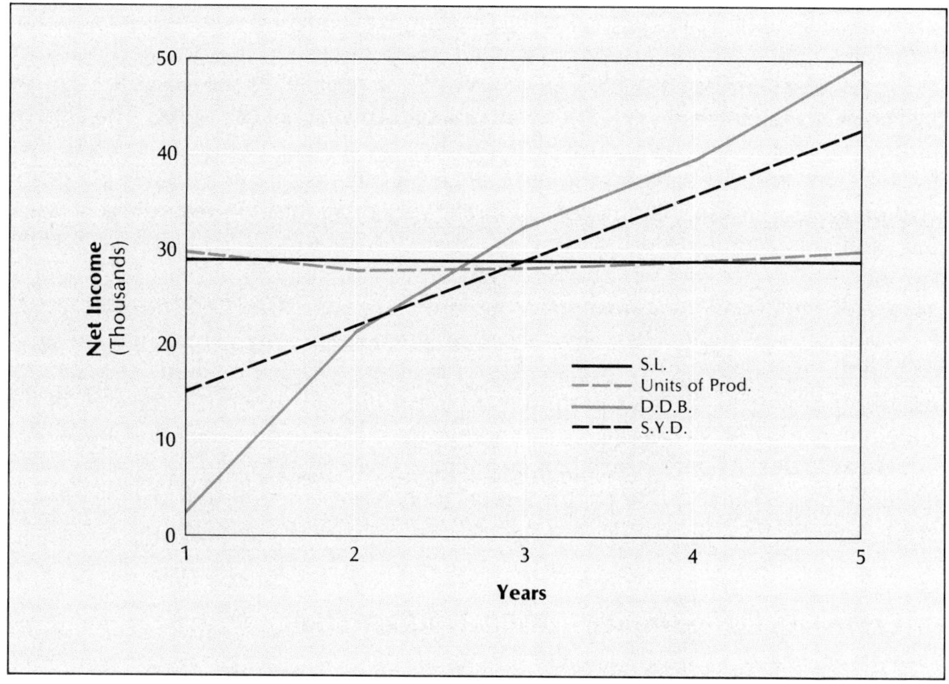

EXHIBIT 10.8

that asset. Nearly three-fourths of 777 large firms surveyed for 1983 used straight-line depreciation.[2]

[2] *1984 Accounting Trends and Techniques*, American Institute of Certified Public Accountants (New York, 1984), p. 277.

CONCEPT SUMMARY 10.1 DEPRECIATION METHODS SUMMARIZED

Method	Basic Computation	Income Effect
Straight-line	$\frac{\text{Acquisition cost} - \text{Residual value}}{\text{Useful life}}$	Expense is even over asset life, affects income by the same amount each year.
Units-of-Production	$\frac{\text{Acquisition cost} - \text{Residual value}}{\text{Total productive units expected}}$ × Number of units used in each time period	Expense is related to use. The larger the use in a time period, the larger the expense, thus lowering income.
Declining-Balance	Beginning-of-period book value times a multiple (usually 1.5 or 2) of the straight-line percentage	Expense drops each year of asset life. Thus, income will be greater as asset ages.
Sum-of-the-Years' Digits	Acquisition cost − Residual value $\times \frac{\text{Inverse order year of life}}{\text{Sum-of-the-years' digits}}$	Expense drops each year of asset life. Thus, income will be greater as asset ages.

DEPRECIATION AND FEDERAL INCOME TAXES

The depreciation rules used to determine taxable income are different from those used by accountants to determine income under generally accepted accounting principles. The method currently employed was established in 1981 and is known as the Accelerated Cost Recovery System (ACRS). Under ACRS, all assets are defined by law as having three, five, ten, fifteen, or eighteen years of useful life. The amount of original cost to be charged off as depreciation expense each year is determined by the Code and depends on the life category of the assets. Fifteen percent of the cost of a five-year asset is charged off in the year of acquisition regardless of when the asset was acquired during the year. Twenty-two percent is charged off in the second year of the asset's life, and 21 percent is charged off in Years 3, 4, and 5. Most machinery and equipment used by businesses are considered five-year assets.

As you can see, the ACRS system is not designed in any way to match the revenue earned through asset use with the cost of the asset. Allowed methods of asset cost recovery for federal taxation purposes are the result of a desire on the part of the government to either encourage or discourage fixed asset acquisitions and are altered from time to time as government policy changes. We will return to some accounting problems caused by the difference between accountants' income and taxable income in Chapter 14.

CHANGES OF ESTIMATES DURING ASSET LIFE

Estimates as to asset life and residual value are based on the best information available at a given time. As can happen with any estimate, subsequent events can require changes. New depreciation calculations are based on the remaining book value and asset life at the time new estimates are necessary and apply from the change point forward.

Assume that Crafty purchases a used press for $80,000 on July 1, 1980, estimates its useful life as ten years with zero residual value, and uses straight-line depreciation.

In 1986 it becomes apparent that the machine will last only until mid-1988—a total of only eight years—and it will be worthless at that time. The remaining book value must be considered an expense over the remainder of the asset's life—two and one-half years. At the end of 1985, the relevant ledger accounts appear as follows:

Machinery			Accumulated Depreciation—Machinery	
80,000			4,000	(1980)
			8,000	(1981)
			8,000	(1982)
			8,000	(1983)
			8,000	(1984)
			8,000	(1985)
			44,000	Balance

Depreciation charges between December 31, 1985, and mid-1988 would be based on the remaining depreciable amount of $80,000 − $44,000 = $36,000. Therefore, depreciation for 1986 and beyond would equal $36,000 ÷ 2.5 yrs, or $14,400 per year.

On the other hand, suppose that the market for used presses has grown, and by the end of 1985, Crafty estimates that its press will have a value of $9,000 at the end of its original estimated life in 1990. The remaining four and one-half years of depreciation expenses would be based on a depreciable amount of $80,000 − $44,000 − $9,000, or $27,000. Depreciation expense over the press's remaining life would equal $27,000 ÷ 4.5 yrs, or $6,000 per year.

Depreciation and Income Relationships

Estimating fixed asset life and residual value accurately is a difficult task that can influence a firm's financial picture. In a footnote to its 1984 financial statements, Trans World Airlines reported that its estimate of resale values of all B747-100 aircraft was being extended an average of four and one-half years effective January 1, 1985. TWA estimated that this change would increase 1985 pretax income approximately $16.6 million over what would have been earned without this change. In a 1983 change, TWA had increased the estimated residual value of all of its widebodied aircraft by 5–10 percent. The 1983 change increased 1983 pretax income by $11 million.

ADDITIONAL EXPENDITURES DURING ASSET LIFE

Additional expenditures made for an asset during its useful life are of two types. One is routine maintenance—an automobile must have periodic oil changes and tuneups. An expenditure for routine maintenance is classified as a **repair expense** of the period in which it occurs.

REPAIR EXPENSE
An expenditure for routine maintenance on a long-lived asset.

A second type is an expenditure to improve an asset by increasing its capacity or efficiency or extending its life. Remodeling a building to accommodate more machinery in the same space (increased capacity) and putting a new roof on a building (extended life) are examples. Since these expenditures add to the future usefulness of the asset, they should be charged to expense over future periods through depreciation and not charged to expense in the period in which they are made.

Suppose Crafty has a building that cost $100,000 with an estimated useful life of 50 years and zero salvage value, and Crafty uses straight-line depreciation. The building needs a new roof costing $5,000. Without the new roof, the building would become unuseable before the end of its remaining 45 years of life.

Technically speaking, if the building is improved in nature or capacity, the expenditure should be added to the asset account. If the expenditure only extends the life of the building or can be characterized as extraordinary repairs, it should be deducted from the Accumulated Depreciation account, since the basic nature of the asset itself is unchanged and therefore the Asset account itself should remain unchanged.

The net effect of either bookkeeping method is the same: The book value of the building is increased and, therefore, subsequent depreciation is increased.

The equality of the alternative bookkeeping procedures is illustrated in the following examples.

If the $5,000 is added to the building account:

Buildings	5,000	
Cash		5,000
(to record addition of new roof)		

Buildings

	Debit	Credit
	100,000	
	5,000	
Bal.	105,000	

Accumulated Depreciation—Buildings

Debit	Credit	
	2,000	
	2,000	
	2,000	
	2,000	
	2,000	
	10,000	Bal.

Book value: $105,000 − $10,000 = $95,000

If the $5,000 expenditure is deducted from accumulated depreciation:

Accumulated depreciation—buildings	5,000	
Cash		5,000
(to record addition of new roof)		

Buildings

	Debit	Credit
	100,000	
Bal.	100,000	

Accumulated Depreciation—Buildings

Debit	Credit	
	2,000	
	2,000	
	2,000	
	2,000	
5,000	2,000	
	5,000	Bal.

Book value: $100,000 − $5,000 = $95,000.

In either case, straight-line depreciation for each remaining year would equal $95,000/45 = $2,111 per year.

ASSET DISPOSITION

When a property, plant, and equipment item is no longer useful, it is usually sold or discarded as junk. If sold, the purchaser exchanges some assets (usually cash) that might differ in amount from the book value of the equipment or property sold. In such cases, the difference between the book value of the assets disposed of and the amount of assets received is known as a gain or loss on disposition of fixed assets. Assets received from customers in exchange for normal goods and services are known as revenue; assets received from sales of property, plant, and equipment in excess of the book value of the property, plant, and equipment are considered to be supplemental gains. Review Chapter 3 if this distinction is unclear.

Assume that Crafty purchased a delivery truck for $8,000 three years ago and has depreciated it at the rate of $2,500 per year. The truck is now sold for $300. The loss is as follows:

Original cost	$8,000
Less: Accumulated depreciation	7,500
Book value	$ 500
Cash received	300
Loss on disposition	$ 200

The bookkeeping required in this case would reflect the facts given. Before disposition of the truck, the relevant ledger account balances would be as follows:

Truck		Accumulated Depreciation—Truck	
8,000			7,500

The truck is removed from the books, the cash received is added, and the loss is recorded. Note that the removal of the book value of the truck requires entries to both the Truck account itself and to the contra-account, Accumulated Depreciation—Truck. The appropriate journal entry is as follows:

Cash	300	
Accumulated depreciation—truck	7,500	
Loss on disposition of truck	200	
Truck		8,000
(to record disposition of truck at a loss)		

If assets received exceed the book value of the disposed item, a gain is recognized. If the truck had been sold for an $800 note receivable, the gain on disposition would be as follows:

Original cost	$8,000
Less: Accumulated depreciation	7,500
Book value	$ 500
Note receivable	800
Gain on disposition of truck	$ 300

In bookkeeping terms, this transaction would be recorded as follows:

Notes receivable	800	
Accumulated depreciation—truck	7,500	
Truck		8,000
Gain on disposition of truck		300
(to record sale of truck at a gain)		

If an asset is discarded as junk rather than sold, no new assets are received in exchange and the entire book value is considered to be a loss. If Crafty simply discards the worn out truck, it would make the following entry:

Accumulated depreciation—truck	7,500	
Loss on disposition of truck	500	
Truck		8,000
(to record disposition of truck)		

The preceding examples assume that Crafty has recorded all depreciation on the old truck up to the date of disposition. If this were not the case, Crafty would need to compute and record depreciation up to the date of disposition before making the disposition entry itself.

ASSET EXCHANGES

Not uncommonly, businesses dispose of used assets by trading the assets for similar new ones. "Similar" in this case means that the new assets acquired are of the same general nature or render the same general service as do the old assets. In such cases, it may be difficult, if not impossible, to determine the real purchase cost of the new asset. Without a firm purchase cost, computation of gains or losses on the disposition of the old asset is difficult, since the trade-in value of the old asset may or may not reflect the asset's market value.

To achieve a consistent basis of handling trades of similar assets, the Accounting Principles Board ruled in Opinion No. 29[3] that when trade-in value is less than book value of the old asset, a loss should be recognized at the time of the trade, but when the trade-in value is greater than book value, the apparent gain should be subtracted from the cost of the new asset.

Loss Recognition Illustrated

Assume that three years after purchase, Crafty trades its old truck for a new truck with a list price of $10,000 and pays cash of $9,700 plus the old truck. Since the trade-in allowance was only $300 ($10,000 − $9,700) and the book value was $500, a loss of $200 must be recognized at the time of the trade. The acquisition entry would be as follows:

New truck	10,000	
Accumulated depreciation—truck	7,500	
Loss on trade-in of truck	200	
Old truck		8,000
Cash		9,700
(to record exchange of an asset at a loss)		

[3] "Accounting for Nonmonetary Transaction, Accounting Principles Board, Opinion No. 29" (New York: American Institute of Certified Public Accountants, 1973), paragraph 22.

Gain Deferral

If the trade requires only a cash payment of $9,000, the trade-in allowance is $1,000 ($10,000 − $9,000) and a gain of $500 ($1,000 − $500) appears to exist. APB No. 29 disallows recognition of this apparent gain and requires that the cash paid be added to the book value of the old asset to determine the cost of the new asset. The entry for the trade with the apparent gain would be as follows:

New truck	9,500	
Accumulated depreciation—truck	7,500	
Old truck		8,000
Cash		9,000
(to record trade of old truck for new truck)		

The effect of this requirement is to treat the gain as a reduction of the cost of the new asset. This reduction in cost means that Crafty will have less depreciation expense in the future or will have a higher gain if it sells the new asset for more than book value. The net effect of this nongain recognition on trades is to increase future income by the amount of the current gain, as illustrated in Exhibit 10.9. Support for this position is found in the often artificial nature of list prices that could lead to recognition of gains that have no basis in economic reality. For illustrative purposes, we have assumed that Crafty will depreciate the new truck over five years with no salvage value and will earn $100,000 exclusive of truck depreciation over this period.

EXHIBIT 10.9

	Nongain Treatment As Required By APB 29	$500 Gain Recognized At Point of Trade-in
Income exclusive of truck depreciation	$100,000	$100,000
Depreciation expense over life of truck (equals recorded cost of truck)	9,500	10,000
Net income after depreciation of truck	$ 90,500	$ 90,000
Gain recognized at point of trade-in	0	500
Total income recognized	$ 90,500	$ 90,500

Note that neither gain nor loss on trade-ins is recognized for federal income tax purposes.

DEMONSTRATION PROBLEM

On July 1, 1985, the Tulip Ditching Corporation purchases a new digging machine for $175,000. Transportation costs total $25,000. The estimated useful life of the machine is ten years, and the estimated salvage value is $10,000.

Required

1. Present the general journal entry to record the purchase of the machine.
2. Present the depreciation expense to be charged for the years ending December 31, 1985, and December 31, 1986, with respect to the digging machine if Tulip uses the following:

a. Straight-line depreciation.
b. Sum-of-the-years' digits depreciation.
c. Double-declining balance depreciation.

3. Present the general journal entry to record straight-line depreciation for the year ending December 31, 1985.
4. What balance would Tulip have with respect to the digging machine in each of the following accounts after all adjustments have been made but before closing the accounts for the year ending December 31, 1986, if Tulip uses straight-line depreciation?

a. Digging Machine
b. Accumulated Depreciation—Digging Machine
c. Depreciation Expense

5. If Tulip uses straight-line depreciation and sells the digging machine on June 30, 1991, for $50,000, present the general journal entry(s) to record the sale. No depreciation has been recorded on the machine since December 31, 1990.

Demonstration Problem Solution

1.

Digging machine	200,000	
Cash		200,000
(to record acquisition of machine)		

2a. Straight-line depreciation:

$$1985 \quad \frac{\$200,000 - \$10,000}{10} \times 1/2 = \$\ 9,500$$

$$1986 \quad \frac{\$200,000 - \$10,000}{10} = \$19,000$$

2b. Sum-of-the years' digits depreciation:

$$1985 \quad (\$200,000 - \$10,000) \times \frac{10}{55} \times 1/2 = \$17,273$$

1986	$(\$200{,}000 - \$10{,}000) \times \frac{10}{55} \times 1/2 =$	$17,273
	$(\$200{,}000 - \$10{,}000) \times \frac{9}{55} \times 1/2 =$	15,545
		$32,818

2c. Double-declining balance depreciation:

1985	$\$200{,}000 \times .20 \times 1/2$	= $20,000
1986	$(\$200{,}000 - \$20{,}000) \times .2$	= $36,000

3.

Depreciation expense	9,500	
Accumulated depreciation—digging machine		9,500
(to record depreciation expense)		

4a. Digging machine	$200,000
4b. Accumulated depreciation—digging machine	28,500
4c. Depreciation expense	19,000

5.

Depreciation expense	9,500	
Accumulated depreciation—digging machine		9,500
(to record 6 months depreciation)		
Cash	50,000	
Accumulated depreciation—digging machine	114,000	
Loss on sale of digging machine	36,000*	
Digging machine		200,000
(to record sale of digging machine)		

*Computed as:

Digging machine	$200,000
Less: Accumulated depreciation	114,000
Net book value	$ 86,000
Less: Sales amount	50,000
Loss on sale	$ 36,000

SUMMARY

- Property, plant, and equipment consists of long-lived assets expected to yield economic benefits for periods longer than one year or one operating cycle and not intended primarily for resale.
- Long-lived assets can be tangible (have physical characteristics) or intangible (not have physical characteristics).

- Depreciation is the process by which accountants measure the recognition of declines in future usefulness of manufactured assets.
- The normal cost of an item of property, plant, and equipment includes historical purchase price plus all other expenditures necessary to make the item ready for use.
- To compute depreciation, estimates of useful life, residual value, and rate in decline of future utility must be made.
- Depreciation can be accounted for in any systematic, consistent, rational manner, but the four most common methods are straight-line, units-of-production, declining-balance, and sum-of-the-years' digits.
- Straight-line depreciation yields equal expense each year over the useful life of the asset; declining-balance and sum-of-the-years' digits yield decreasing expense over the useful life of the asset. Units-of-production allows depreciation to vary with actual asset use.
- Repairs that do not improve an asset or extend the asset's useful life are charged to expense when incurred. Alterations that improve an asset or extend the asset's useful life are capitalized and increase future depreciation charges.
- When property, plant, and equipment assets are sold, a gain or loss is recognized if the sales price is greater or less than the book value of the assets, respectively.
- If property, plant, and equipment assets are traded in for similar assets, losses on such trades are recognized at the time of the trade, whereas gains are treated as a reduction in the cost of the new asset.

QUESTIONS

10-1. What is the major difference between long-lived assets and other assets in terms of economic benefits provided? What accounting process does this difference require for long-lived assets?

10-2. What is the process of depreciation designed to do in accounting?

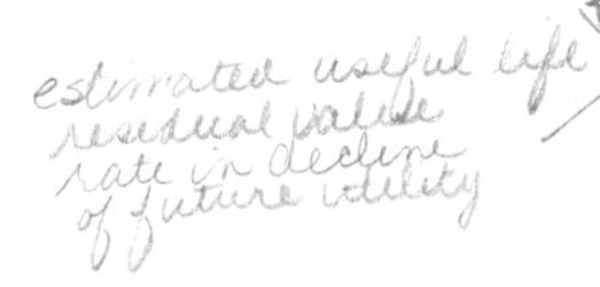

10-3. What three things must be known about an asset before depreciation can be determined?

10-4. What is generally included in the acquisition cost of a long-lived asset?

10-5. Are interest costs paid on loans taken out to acquire long-lived assets usually included in the acquisition cost?

10-6. If an asset is acquired in a noncash exchange, how is the cost of the asset determined?

10-7. Describe the differences in timing of depreciation deductions between straight-line and either sum-of-the years' digits or double-declining balance methods.

10-8. When can an expenditure be considered an asset improvement expenditure?

10-9. What criteria should be used in selecting a particular depreciation method?

10-10. Distinguish between functional deterioration and physical deterioration of long-lived assets.

EXERCISES

10-E1. Jenkins Manufacturing purchases land, buildings, and equipment for $4 million. Independent appraisals are made of each item, with land being appraised at $900,000, the buildings at $3,150,000, and the equipment at $450,000. What cost should Jenkins assign to each of the assets acquired?

10-E2. Harvey Company purchases land and a vacant building for $3 million. The building is demolished at a cost of $1 million, and a new building is constructed at a cost of $10 million. How much total cost should be assigned to the new building? The land? Why?

10-E3. Ronald Cookie Company purchases a new cookie press for $400,000. In the process of installation, a part breaks that costs $600 to repair. How much cost should Ronald assign to the cookie press? Why?

10-E4. The Wegman Company acquires a new truck on January 1, 1986, for $50,000. The estimated useful life of the truck is five years, and the estimated salvage value is $5,000. Wegman expects to drive the truck 200,000 miles over its five-year life. During 1987, Wegman actually drives the truck 50,000 miles. Determine the depreciation expense with respect to this truck for the year ending December 31, 1987, under each of the following depreciation methods:

a. Straight-line.
b. Sum-of-the-years' digits.
c. Double-declining-balance.
d. Units-of-production.

Which method will produce the highest income for Wegman if all other factors remain the same?

10-E5. The Hubbard Cupboard Company purchases a piece of equipment for $100,000 on January 1, 1986. The estimated salvage value is $10,000 at the end of the equipment's ten-year useful life, and Hubbard uses straight-line depreciation. Determine the gain or loss under each of the following assumptions and provide appropriate general journal entries to record the transaction in each case. Each transaction is independent and occurs on January 1, 1990.

a. The equipment is sold for $60,000.
b. The equipment is traded in on similar new equipment with a list price of $140,000. Hubbard receives a trade-in allowance of $80,000.
c. The equipment is found to be worthless, hauled to the dump, and discarded.

10-E6. The Chase Furniture Company purchases a shaping machine for $500,000 on January 1, 1986, at which time the machine's estimated useful life is five years and its estimated salvage value is $100,000. Chase uses straight-line depreciation. After two years, during 1988, Chase reevaluates the machine and makes changes in the original estimates. The machine is now expected to be useful for another five years beyond January 1, 1988, and its salvage value is estimated to be $50,000.

a. Determine the 1988 depreciation expense for the machine.
b. What effect do these revisions have on reported 1988 income for Chase compared to what would have been reported without the changes?

10-E7. On December 31, 1986, after all adjustments have been made, the accounts of the Smith Corporation with respect to the company's one delivery truck that was originally purchased on January 1, 1985, appear as follows:

Delivery Truck		Accumulated Depreciation—Delivery Truck	
40,000			25,600

a. If the truck is driven 10,000 miles in 1985 and 10,000 miles in 1986, and was originally expected to be useful for 100,000 miles, and if no changes have been made in the estimated life of five years, cost structure, or estimated salvage value of $4,000 since the truck was purchased, what depreciation method might Smith be using to account for the use of the truck?
b. What would be the expected depreciation in 1986?

PROBLEM SET A

10-A1. Comparison of Four Depreciation Methods. The Blasiman Company purchases a new truck on January 1, 1986, for $75,000. The estimated salvage value is $10,000, and estimated useful life is five years. Blasiman expects to drive the truck 250,000 miles over the truck's five-year life. The truck is driven 60,000, 50,000, 40,000, 70,000, and 30,000 miles in Years 1 through 5, respectively.

Required

a. Prepare a comparative schedule of depreciation expense computations and truck carrying values under each of the following depreciation methods:

1. Straight-line.
2. Sum-of-the-years' digits.
3. Double-declining balance.
4. Units-of-production.

b. If income each year before deducting truck depreciation charges is $50,000, prepare a schedule showing the income that Blasiman Company would have after deducting depreciation for each of the methods in (a).

10-A2. Cost Allocation to Assets or Expense. The Tom and Jerry Company purchases a vacant piece of land, builds a plant, and installs production machinery. In doing so, Tom and Jerry incur the following costs:

Land purchase cost	$ 142,000
Parking lot lights	10,000
Legal fees in connection with land purchase	10,000
Land grading to promote drainage	9,000
Contract cost of building (payment made by paying $100,000 cash and borrowing $900,000 at 16% interest)	1,000,000
Replacement of shrubs stolen from grounds before plant is put into operation	1,000
Parking lot grading and paving	100,000
Machinery purchase cost (payment made by borrowing $4,000,000 at 16% interest)	4,000,000
Delivery charges on machinery	40,000
Installation costs on machinery	5,000
Replacement of parking lot lights shot out by vandals before plant is put into operation	500
Architect fees for building plans	200,000

Required

a. Compute what Tom and Jerry should show on their books as the cost of land, buildings, and equipment.

b. Provide the name and amount of any other categories of costs capitalized.

10-A3. Depreciation and Asset Disposition. On July 1, 1986, the Sycamore Company decides to retire one of its machines. The machine originally cost $200,000 on January 1, 1983, at which time Sycamore estimated the useful life of the machine at four years and the salvage value at $20,000. Straight-line depreciation has been used. Sycamore is considering two alternatives as follows:

Plan 1—Sell the machine for $10,000 cash and shop for a new machine, which Sycamore thinks would cost $240,000 cash.

Plan 2—Trade the old machine for a new one. Sycamore has found a machine manufacturer willing to accept the old machine in trade. The manufacturer has priced its new machine at $260,000 and is willing to grant a trade-in allowance of $30,000.

Required

a. Present the journal entry(s) required assuming that Sycamore follows Plan 1.
b. Present the journal entry(s) required assuming that Sycamore follows Plan 2.
c. If the new machine has a four-year useful life and is being depreciated on a straight-line basis with zero salvage value, what will the annual depreciation charges be under Plan 1? Under Plan 2?
d. Compare the gain or loss on sale of the machine under Plan 1 with the total difference in depreciation charges over the life of the new machine between Plan 1 and Plan 2, and the gain or loss on disposition under Plan 2.

10-A4. Basket Purchase. On June 1, 1986, the Gibson Company purchases a plant complete with machinery for use in producing auto parts. The total purchase cost is $4 million. Independent appraisals of the land, buildings, and equipment provide the following valuations:

Land	$1,050,000
Buildings	1,680,000
Equipment	1,470,000
	4,200,000

Required

a. How should Gibson allocate the $4 million purchase price to the land, buildings, and equipment?
b. If Gibson could choose any purchase price allocation it wished without regard to the relative appraisal values, what would it most likely choose? (Ignore any income tax considerations.) Why?

10-A5. Acquisition Price in Noncash Exchange. Mitchell and Co., CPAs, acquire a computer in exchange for 600 hours of professional service. The list price of the computer is $35,000, and Mitchell's professional service billing rate averages $50 per hour. Mitchell has computed the average cost of providing an hour of professional service at $40.

Required

Compute the cost that Mitchell and Co. should record for the acquisition of the computer. Explain your answer.

10-A6. Depreciation and Improvements. The following transactions all pertain to the acquisition, use, and disposition of an accounting machine of the Kean Auto Parts Company. Kean uses straight-line depreciation and closes its books and prepares financial statements annually on December 31.

7/1/83	Machine purchased (estimated life eight years, zero salvage value)	$100,000
12/31/83	Main drive motor replaced	4,000
1/1/84	Machine modified and improved to newer model (estimated life extended for ten years until 12/31/93; no change in salvage value)	30,000
7/1/85	Routine two-year preventive maintenance	5,000
10/1/86	Machine sold for cash	50,000

Required

Present all journal entries required with respect to this machine from July 1, 1983, to October 1, 1986. Round all entries to the nearest dollar.

10-A7. Amounts for Asset Acquisition, Depreciation, and Disposition. On January 1, 1980, Harold Dracula, a distant relative of Count Dracula, organized the Transylvania Company. The sole purpose of the company was to develop a process by which blood could be obtained from turnips. After seven years of operations, Harold concluded that it was impossible to get blood from a turnip and thereby terminated operation of the Transylvania Company on December 1, 1986.

The following data are on four of the machines used by the Transylvania Company from 1980 to 1986:

Type of Machine	Acquisition Date	Cost	Est. Salvage Value	Est. Useful Life	Depreciation Method	Disposition Information
Grinder	1/3/80	$15,000	$4,000	10	Double-declining balance	Sold on 3/1/86 for $3,500 cash.
Juicer	1/1/81	24,000	1,500	8	Sum-of-the-years' digits	Exchanged on 9/1/84 for a new model with a list price of $26,000. Gave old machine and $16,208 cash for new model.
Smasher	9/2/83	25,500	2,500	30,000	Units-of-production	Exchanged on 6/1/85 for a new model with a list price of $30,000. Gave old machine and $21,833 cash for new model.
Separator	11/3/82	39,250	4,250	7	Straight-line	Sold for $19,500 cash on 12/1/86.

The company operates on a fiscal year that ends on December 31. The Smasher smashed 2,000 units in 1983, 12,000 units in 1984, and 6,000 units in 1985.

Required

Prepare a schedule for each machine showing the acquisition cost, the annual depreciation expense, and the gain or loss, if any, on disposition.

PROBLEM SET B

10-B1. Comparison of Four Depreciation Methods. The Mercer Corporation acquires a new stamping machine for $500,000 on January 1, 1986. The machine is expected to last five years, produce 7.75 million parts, and have a salvage value of $35,000 at the end of its useful life. Over the five-year life, 2 million, 2.5 million, 1.5 million, 750,000, and 1 million parts are produced in Years 1 through 5, respectively.

Required

a. Prepare a comparative schedule of depreciation expense and book value for each year over the life of the machine under each of the following depreciation methods:

1. Straight-line.
2. Sum-of-the-years' digits.
3. Double-declining balance.
4. Units-of-production.

b. Given that all factors other than depreciation are the same regardless of the depreciation method chosen and that net income each year before deducting depreciation expense is $1,000,000, $1,100,000, $900,000, $500,000, and $800,000 for Years 1 through 5, respectively, prepare a schedule showing each year's income after depreciation deductions that would be obtained under each of the depreciation methods in (a).

10-B2. Cost Allocation to Assets or Expense. During 1986, Crocke-Crocke Company builds a new bottle-blowing plant. The total costs incurred on this plant are as follows:

Purchase price of plant site	$ 175,000
Building materials (includes $10,000 of materials wasted due to worker inexperience)	700,000
Machinery installation charges	40,000
Grading and draining plant site	20,000
Labor costs of construction (Crocke-Crocke used its own workers to build the plant rather than lay them off since business is slack. However, the labor to build the plant is $40,000 higher than outside contractors would have charged due to worker inexperience and inefficiency.)	500,000
Machinery purchase cost	1,000,000
Machinery delivery charges	10,000
Parking lot grading and paving	60,000
Replacement of building windows shot out by vandals before production start-up	7,000
Architect's fees	40,000

Required

Compute the total cost that Crocke-Crocke should capitalize as land, as building, and as equipment or other category. Provide the name and amount of any other category of costs that should be capitalized.

10-B3. Depreciation and Asset Disposition. On July 1, 1983, the Stedd Company purchased a truck for $40,000. Stedd estimated salvage value after four years would be zero. Stedd uses straight-line depreciation.

Required

a. For each of the following independent situations, present the journal entry(s) to reflect the facts as given:

1. On July 1, 1986, Stedd sells the truck for $30,000 cash.
2. On July 1, 1986, Stedd trades the truck for a new one. The list price of the new truck is $60,000, and Stedd receives a trade-in allowance of $30,000 for the old truck.
3. On July 1, 1986, Stedd wrecks the truck and has no insurance. The vehicle is hauled to the junkyard, and Stedd receives $100 for its remains.

b. Suppose that Stedd sells the old truck for $25,000 cash and purchases the new truck outright for $55,000 cash instead of making the trade described in (a2). What journal entry(s) would Stedd make to reflect these two transactions?
c. From a cash flow point of view, is Stedd better off, worse off, or indifferent between (a2) and the sale and purchase described in (b). (Ignore any income tax considerations.)
d. From a profit point of view, is Stedd's case in (a2) better, worse, or the same as would result from the facts as described in (b)?

10-B4. Basket Purchase. On September 1, 1986, the Popular Brush Company purchases a warehouse complete with equipment for use in distributing its brushes. The total purchase cost is $2 million. An examination of property tax records indicates the following tax bases for the land, building, and equipment:

Land	$280,000
Building	980,000
Equipment	140,000

Required

a. How should Popular Brush allocate the $2 million purchase price to the land, buildings, and equipment?
b. If Popular Brush could choose any purchase price allocation it wished without regard to the relative appraisal values, what would it most likely choose? (Ignore any income tax considerations.) Why?

10-B5. Acquisition Price in Noncash Exchange. The Johnson Company acquires an earth-moving scraper in exchange for 10,000 tons of stone from its quarry. The list price of the earthmover is $120,000, and the normal selling price of the stone is $10 per ton. The cost of the stone to Johnson was computed at $7 per ton.

Required

Compute the cost that Johnson should record for the acquisition of the earthmover. Explain your answer.

10-B6. Depreciation and Improvements. On March 1, 1986, Leonnard Company purchases a building for one million dollars. The estimated life of the building is 25 years, and the estimated salvage value is zero. Leonnard uses double-declining balance depreciation and prepares annual financial statements on December 31. After the acquisition of the building, the following events occur:

8/1/86	Building painted.	$ 40,000
11/1/86	Roof blown away by the wind. $100,000 collected from the insurance company. New roof installed.	125,000
7/1/87	Building sold.	1,100,000

Required

Present all journal entries required with respect to the building from March 1, 1986, to July 1, 1987. Round answers to the nearest dollar.

10-B7. Journal Entries for Asset Acquisition, Depreciation, and Disposition. After issuing its 1986 financial statements, the Summit City Manufacturing Company decides that it is no longer satisfied with the services provided by its current auditor. As a result, the board of directors votes to have Straight & Arrow, CPAs, as the company's new auditor. Straight & Arrow, as part of its initial engagement, performs a comprehensive review of Summit City's 1983–1986 financial statements. This review reveals that a number of purchases and sales of long-term assets have gone unrecorded. The following describes each of the assets whose purchase and sale went unrecorded:

Type of Machine	Acquisition Date	Cost	Est. Salvage Value	Est. Useful Life	Depreciation Method	Disposition Information
Stamping press	7/1/83	$79,000	$ 5,000	10 yrs.	Units-of-production	Exchanged on 12/31/86 for a new model with a list price of $85,000. Old machine and $45,000 cash given for the new model.
Stacking machine	1/1/82	$45,000	$12,000	8 yrs.	Double-declining balance	Sold for $13,000 cash on 12/31/86.
Press brake	1/1/83	$55,000	$10,000	5 yrs.	Sum-of-the-years' digits	Exchanged for new press brake with a list price of $60,000 on 10/1/86. Old brake and $40,000 cash given for new brake.
Truck	3/2/83	$18,500	$ 1,000	10 yrs.	Straight-line	Sold for $2,000 cash on 7/1/86.

Summit is on a fiscal year ending December 31. The stamping press is expected to last for one million cycles. Cycles completed during 1983, 1984, 1985, and 1986 totaled 25,000, 100,000, 125,000, and 75,000, respectively.

Required

For each of the four assets, prepare a schedule showing the acquisition cost, the annual depreciation expense, and the gain or loss, if any, on disposition.

11 NATURAL RESOURCES AND INTANGIBLES

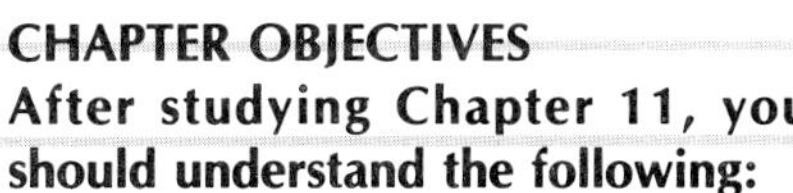

CHAPTER OBJECTIVES

After studying Chapter 11, you should understand the following:

1. The nature of natural resources and intangible assets.
2. The allocation of natural resource cost to operations through depletion charges.
3. The cost of intangible assets and allocation of their cost to operations through amortization charges.
4. Presentation of long-lived assets on the statement of financial position.

NATURAL RESOURCES

Chapter 11 takes a closer look at accounting for natural resources and intangible assets. It discusses changes in the character of natural resources when severed from the land, explains methods of allocating natural resource cost to depletion, presents intangible asset existence criteria, explains and illustrates amortization of intangible assets, and shows statements of financial position presentation of long-term assets.

Natural resources are assets that are long-lived, tangible, and naturally occurring. Some common examples of natural resources are oil, gas, standing timber, all types of minerals, clays, and gravel. A natural resource that is still attached to the land (whether on the land or in it) is not in a useful condition. Until a natural resource is removed from the land, it must be considered a long-lived asset.

THE CONCEPT OF DEPLETION

After natural resources have been severed from the land, they can be processed further, combined with other resources to manufacture products, or sold as raw materials to another entity. In every case, when the resources are severed from the land, they are transformed from a long-lived asset into inventory.

When natural resources are severed from the land, their removal lessens the future utility of the remaining property. An oil well has less remaining oil after each barrel is pumped; a timber stand has fewer remaining trees after each tree is cut. In other words, the natural resource is being depleted.

DEPLETION
The recognition that a naturally occurring asset has been reduced and some of the asset is now inventory.

Depletion is the recognition that a naturally occurring asset has been reduced and some of the asset is now inventory. The inventory is a current asset until it is sold; its cost then is subtracted from the revenue generated by its sale as cost of goods sold.

THE COST OF NATURAL RESOURCES

The cost of a natural resource inventory includes the cost of obtaining the land containing the resource and the costs of severing the natural resource from the land. Severance costs include the cost of labor, machinery, and other directly related items. Exhibit 11.1 shows the cost flow for a typical natural resource—coal.

As Exhibit 11.1 shows, all natural resource (depletion) cost is attached to a product (becomes inventory) and then becomes an expense (cost of goods sold) when that product is sold. Depletion cost thus stands in contrast to depreciation, which can be either a product or a period cost, depending on how the assets are used. The time period when the natural resources are severed from the land is not relevant to determining when depletion cost becomes an expense.

COMPUTATIONS FOR DEPLETION

Depletion computations are similar to those for the units-of-production depreciation method. To calculate depletion, the following information must be known:

1. Acquisition and development cost of the natural resource.
2. Total estimated output available from the resource.
3. Amount of the resource actually severed during the period.
4. The residual value of the property, if any.

EXHIBIT 11.1

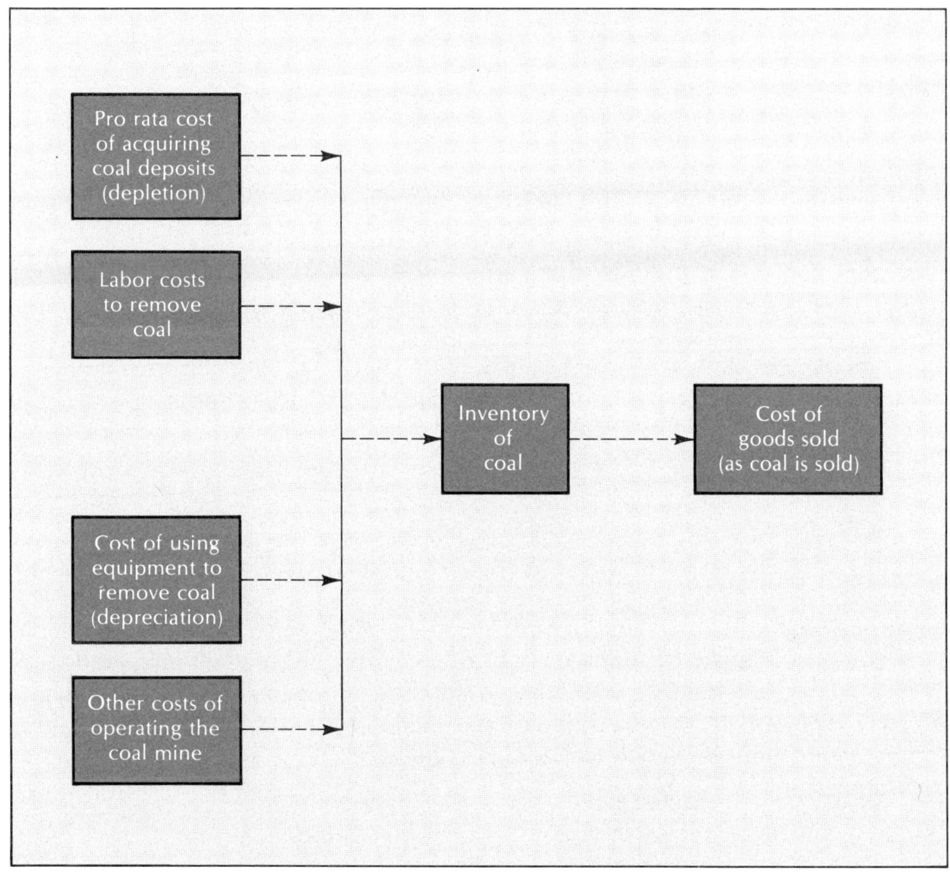

The formula for determining depletion in a period is as follows:

$$\frac{\text{Acquisition and development cost} - \text{residual value}}{\text{Total units of asset available}} \times \begin{array}{c}\text{Units}\\\text{severed}\\\text{in this}\\\text{period}\end{array} = \begin{array}{c}\text{Depletion}\\\text{in this}\\\text{period}\end{array}$$

Acquisition and Development Costs

Acquisition costs include purchase price, attorney's fees, document filing fees, and any other costs incurred in buying the asset. Development costs include all expen-

CONCEPT SUMMARY 11.1

DEPLETION AND DEPRECIATION COMPARED

Depreciation	Depletion
Amount is based on cost and useful life.	Amount is based on cost and amount of material removed.
Depreciation might or might not be attached to a product.	Depletion is *always* attached to a product.
Depreciation can occur even if asset is not used.	Depletion can occur only if resource is physically severed from the land.

ditures required to remove the resource from the land. For instance, for a timber stand in a remote area, it might be necessary to build roads before any timber can be removed.

Unit Estimation and Residual Value

Frequently, the amount of the natural resource available might not be known with precision, particularly if the resource comes from beneath the ground. Businesses must rely on geologists, mining engineers, or other experts to estimate the number of resource units available.

A natural resource can have residual value that must be subtracted from the acquisition and development cost to determine depletion. For instance, after coal or oil has been removed from the land, the surface can be reclaimed for agricultural uses or home sites.

Depletion Example

Suppose that the Great Plains Mining Company purchases a lignite coal deposit containing an estimated 100 million tons of coal. The cost of acquiring the deposit is $95 million, and development costs of stripping off the topsoil and stockpiling it for later replacement total $5 million. Ten million tons of coal are mined during 1986. Great Plains' depletion for 1986 is as follows:

$$\frac{\$95{,}000{,}000 + \$5{,}000{,}000}{100{,}000{,}000 \text{ tons}} = \$1 \text{ per ton} \times 10{,}000{,}000 \text{ tons} = \$10{,}000{,}000$$

The Bookkeeping Mechanics

Initial Recording of Depletion. Depletion costs are usually added to a Depletion Expense account, because a very large percentage of the natural resource severed is sold within the period of severance. However, as previously explained, natural resource costs become inventory before expense. Bypassing the Inventory account with depletion is justified on the basis of bookkeeping ease. If a company adds all depletion charges to a Depletion Expense account and any of the removed resource remains unsold at the end of an accounting period, an adjusting entry to record some of the depletion costs as inventory is required.

The initial journal entry to record depletion is similar to a depreciation entry. Typically, a contra-account—Accumulated Depletion—is used to record depletion. The initial journal entry to record Great Plains' 1986 depletion is as follows:

Depletion expense	10,000,000	
Accumulated depletion—coal mine		10,000,000
(to record depletion on coal mine)		

Relevant ledger accounts will then appear as follows:

Coal Mine	
100,000,000	

Accumulated Depletion—Coal Mine	
	10,000,000

Depletion Expense	
10,000,000	

The book value of the coal mine at the end of 1986 is $90 million.

Although use of an Accumulated Depletion account is widespread, some firms reduce natural asset accounts directly for depletion. The support for the direct reduction method is that unlike property, plant, and equipment, natural assets cease to exist once used up, and a direct reduction in original investment is therefore considered appropriate. If Great Plains used the direct write-off method, 1986 depletion would initially be recorded as follows:

Depletion expense	10,000,000	
Coal mine		10,000,000
(to record 1986 depletion)		

Adjusting for Unsold Resources. If all of the coal mined during the year is sold before the end of the year, all the depletion expense becomes part of cost of goods sold. But if some of the coal mined in 1986 is still on hand on December 31, the depletion costs associated with the unsold portion must be recorded as inventory. This is accomplished through an adjusting entry.

For example, suppose Great Plains has one million tons of coal on hand on December 31, 1986. Depletion associated with the one million tons or one million dollars (1,000,000 tons × $1) must be recorded as inventory.

Coal inventory	1,000,000	
Depletion expense		1,000,000
(to transfer depletion costs to inventory)		

Relevant ledger accounts now appear as follows:

Coal Mine	
100,000,000	

Accumulated Depletion—Coal Mine	
	10,000,000

Depletion Expense	
10,000,000	
	1,000,000

Coal Inventory	
1,000,000	

Cost of goods sold for 1986 now includes only $9 million of depletion expense. The other one million dollars becomes expense in a later year as the additional one million tons of coal are sold.

Related Buildings and Equipment

Some depreciable assets are so closely related to extraction of natural resources that they are useful only as long as the natural resources are being worked. Without the underlying resource, the buildings and equipment used to sever that resource lose all their future utility unless they can be moved to another site and used in that place. In such cases, depreciation of the related assets is tied to the depletion of the natural resource.

Assume that the Great Plains Mining Company constructs a building and acquires several large pieces of machinery to mine the coal. The building cost $100,000 and has a 30-year life. It would not be feasible to move it. The machinery cost $500,000. Its life is estimated as 12 years or 20,000 hours, and its residual value is estimated as $50,000. The machinery could be moved to other sites. All of the assets are put into service on January 1, 1986. Depreciation on the building for 1986 is determined as follows:

Cost	$100,000
Applicable life	100,000,000 tons of coal
Residual value	none

Depreciation for 1986:

$$\frac{10{,}000{,}000 \text{ tons}}{100{,}000{,}000 \text{ tons}} \times \$100{,}000 = \$10{,}000$$

Depreciation on the equipment for 1986 is determined as follows:

Cost	$500,000
Applicable life	12 years
Residual value	$50,000

Depreciation for 1986:

$$\frac{\$450{,}000}{12} = \$37{,}500$$

Note that the 1986 depreciation on the building is tied to the depletion rate of the coal mine while the depreciation for the machinery is based on the expected useful life of the equipment. The different methods arise because the building is tied directly to the coal mine. When the coal is gone, the building is worthless, but the equpiment can be moved and used at another location.

INTANGIBLE ASSETS

Intangible assets were defined in Chapter 10 as long-lived assets without physical characteristics. They confer a right on their owner—the right to use certain property or the right to sell specified products in a specified area. The right is frequently evidenced by a contract or other legal document, but the right itself is not something you can see or touch. Common examples of intangible assets are patents, copyrights, franchises, leaseholds, leasehold improvements, goodwill, and trademarks.

The measurement of an intangible's future utility and the decline in that future utility are fraught with uncertainties. For instance, an intangible asset can be something as definite and measurable as the right to use a piece of property—a lease—but it can also be something as indefinite as the right to control the manufacture and sale of a product represented by a patent. Until the patent has been challenged and upheld in court, no one can know for sure whether it has any value, much less how to estimate the useful life of that value.

A trademark is another common and nebulous intangible asset. Unless the trademark has some value in increasing sales revenue, it has no utility, future or otherwise. How does a firm associate the amount of its sales revenue with use of the trademark? Obviously, the Coca-Cola trademark is valuable. However, the existence of value in the trademark of other colas is very difficult to assess.

Acquisition Costs and Value for Intangibles

Like tangible assets, intangible assets are valued for accounting purposes at historical cost. The original valuation or exchange price of an intangible asset is presumed to represent the market's assessment of its future usefulness at the time of acquisition. However, many intangible assets are created—not purchased. In such cases, the historical cost can have little or no relationship to the asset's future usefulness.

Owner-created artistic or literary works that result in a copyright are a good example. An author might work for two years to produce a novel that subsequently sells hundreds of thousands of copies. The value of the copyright is the cost of obtaining and defending it—a very small amount compared with the revenue that the copyright will ultimately generate. If the original cost of an intangible asset is so insignificant in relationship to a firm's total revenues and expense as to be immaterial, the total cost should be considered expense when incurred.

The following questions must be answered to account for intangible assets:

1. Does the intangible asset have any value? If it has no future usefulness, it is not an asset, regardless of the cost to produce or acquire it.
2. What is the cost of producing or acquiring the intangible asset? Some special rules apply here that are discussed later.
3. Is the cost material? If not, it should be treated as an operational expense rather than an asset.
4. What is the asset's useful life?
5. How should the decline in the intangible asset's future utility be measured?

Exhibit 11.2 illustrates the decision structure used to distinguish between capitalization and expense treatment for outlays made to acquire intangible assets.

Determining Whether an Intangible Asset Has Value

Determining the existence of future usefulness of an intangible asset necessarily involves subjective judgments. Each case should be judged on its own circumstances. Some bases for making such judgments might include the entity's experience with similar items; the experience of other firms in the same trade; and estimates of marketing, advertising, legal, and real estate experts and others as to an intangible item's future utility.

Determining the Cost of Intangible Assets

If an intangible is purchased, the accounting is similar to that for a tangible asset and includes the purchase cost and all legal or filing fees. However, if the intangible is developed internally, the only expenditures included in the cost of the asset are legal and filing fees required to secure and defend the intangible. All research and development expenditures are considered expenses of the time period in which they are incurred.

EXHIBIT 11.2

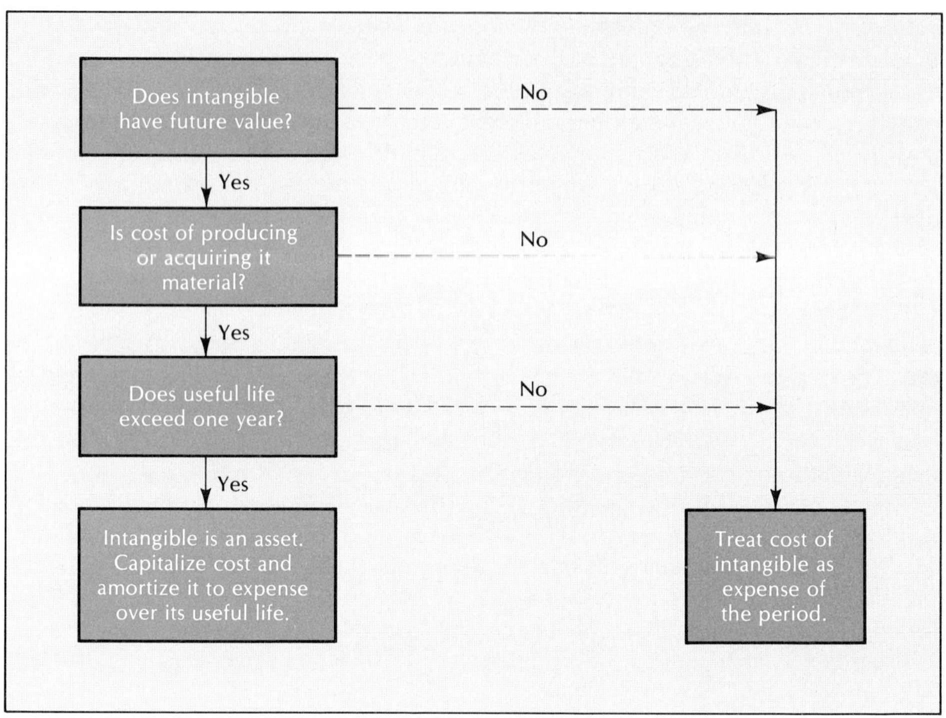

Although capitalizing research and development cost would be consistent with good accounting theory, other considerations win out over the purely theoretical ones. Financial Accounting Standards Board (FASB) Statement No. 2 requires that research and development costs be considered expense in the period incurred.[1]

The following are some of the reasons for requiring the expensing of research and development costs:

1. Difficulty of apportioning research and development costs to specific products in an environment where many products are being worked on simultaneously.
2. Uncertainty of the future utility of the costs—not all research efforts result in development of new products, and not all new products developed are ultimately successful.
3. Abuses of the option to expense or capitalize research and development costs. Because financial statements are extremely influential in the judgments that investors and creditors make about an entity, some managements might not pass up the opportunity to try to treat accounting decisions as merely tactical decisions. When that happens, management can choose between expensing or capitalizing research and development costs based not on what is fair but rather on what makes the company look the best. The major objective of financial accounting is to produce financial reports that give a fair and objective picture of the economic happenings of any given entity. It is believed in general that financial statements will be more objective and less misleading if no option exists and expensing of research and development cost is required.

[1]FASB, "Accounting for Research and Development Costs, Statement of Financial Accounting Standards No. 2," Financial Accounting Standards Board (Stamford, Conn.: 1974).

Estimating Useful Life

Estimating the expected useful life of an intangible asset can be considerably more difficult than estimating the useful life of a tangible asset. Most intangibles have a legal life determined by government regulation (patents, copyrights, and trademarks), by terms of a contract (franchises, leaseholds, leasehold improvements), or by the accounting profession (goodwill). The useful life may or may not be the same as the legal life. Certainly the useful life cannot exceed the legal life, but it can be a good deal shorter. For instance, the legal life of a copyright is the life of the author plus 50 years. The useful life is the number of years over which the author expects to sell copies of the copyrighted material.

The Amortization Process

The process of recognizing and measuring the periodic decline in future usefulness of intangible assets is called **amortization.** The options that exist in selecting a method for depreciable assets do not exist for intangible assets. Straight-line amortization must be used unless it can be demonstrated that another method is superior in a given case. Furthermore, an intangible does not have residual or scrap value. When its useful life has expired, there is no secondary purpose that it can fulfill, and thus zero value remains.

AMORTIZATION
The process of recognizing and measuring the periodic decline in future usefulness of intangible assets.

The formula for amortization is the same as for straight-line depreciation:

$$\frac{\text{Acquisition cost}}{\text{Life in time periods}} = \text{Amortization per time period}$$

Suppose that High, a pharmaceutical firm, purchases a drug patent on January 1, 1986, for $10 million. The legal life of the patent is seventeen years, but seven years have already passed. It is expected that demand for the drug will continue indefinitely. High reports on a calendar year. Amortization for 1986 equals $10,000,000 ÷ 10 years = $1,000,000 per year, and the following journal entry to recognize 1986 amortization is required:

Amortization expense	1,000,000	
Patent		1,000,000
(to record amortization on patent)		

Note that the intangible asset account is decreased directly rather than through a contra-account. After the preceding adjustment, High's relevant ledger accounts would appear as follows:

Patent		Amortization Expense	
10,000,000		1,000,000	
	1,000,000		

Intangible assets should be periodically reviewed to determine if they still retain value. If subsequent events prove that future value does not exist or has been lost, the remaining book value should be written off as expense immediately.

CONCEPT SUMMARY 11.2 AMORTIZATION OF INTANGIBLES AND DEPRECIATION COMPARED

Depreciation	Amortization
Amount is based on cost and useful life.	Amount is based on cost and useful or legal life, whichever is shorter.
Cost can include both purchase cost and internal expenditures for self-constructed assets.	Cost includes purchase costs but excludes internal expenditures for self-developed intangibles, except for legal and filing fees.
Depreciation methods vary depending on nature and use of asset.	Amortization is always straight-line, unless another method can be shown to be superior.
Salvage value can exist.	No salvage value ever exists.

Common Types of Intangible Assets

PATENT
The right granted by the federal government to an inventor to control a design or invention.

Patents. A **patent** is a right granted by the federal government to an inventor to control a design or invention and thus profit from the idea. The inventor can profit by manufacturing the product and selling it, selling the rights to someone else, or licensing others to manufacture the product. Again, the legal life of a patent is 17 years.

The cost of an internally developed patent includes all of the legal costs incurred to complete the paperwork necessary to obtain and, if required, to defend the patent but includes none of the cost of developing the patentable product. Purchased patents are valued at their purchase price plus any expenditures necessary to defend the patent against infringement.

TRADEMARK
A word, term, symbol, name, or design to identify a product or service.

Trademarks. A **trademark** is a word, term, symbol, name, or design to identify a product or service. A trademark can be registered with the government for a small fee and, when registered, gives the owner the exclusive right to its use. As with a patent, a large difference can exist in carrying value between an internally developed trademark and a purchased trademark. Trademarks must be amortized over their useful life, not to exceed 40 years.

COPYRIGHT
The right granted by the federal government to a writer or artist to control the use of his or her work.

Coyprights. A **copyright** is the right granted by the federal government to a writer or an artist to control the use of his or her work and the benefits deriving therefrom. The legal life is the life of the author plus 50 years. Frequently, a copyright is expected to have a useful life shorter than its legal life. For accounting purposes, the life of a copyright is the shorter of its useful life or 40 years. Like patents, copyright costs of internally developed works are limited to the legal costs incurred in connection with securing and defending the copyright. Development costs, such as writers' salaries, are charged to expense when incurred. Also, like purchased patents, purchased copyrights are valued at their purchase price plus legal costs, if any, necessary to defend the copyright against infringement.

FRANCHISE
The right granted to sell specified products under a specified name in specified geographic area.

Franchises. A **franchise** grants the holder the right to sell specified products under a specified name in a specified geographic area. Franchises have become widespread in the past 25 years, and some are extremely valuable. Fast-food franchises are perhaps the most visible, but many other types exist.

Franchises are acquired by purchase, since no need exists to franchise oneself. Their cost is usually significant. As with other intangible assets, determining whether franchises possess real value is difficult. At least two national fried chicken chains were launched that later became defunct. Presumably, purchasers of those franchises found they had an intangible on the books that was not an asset.

Franchise agreements are a matter of contract between the seller (franchiser) and buyer (franchisee). They vary widely as to length of life and other terms and must be amortized over their useful life, not to exceed 40 years.

Franchising and McDonald's

According to a 1984 article in *Forbes* magazine, franchising is still growing as a way of doing business in the United States, and the cost of acquiring a franchise is rising. *Forbes* reported that the cost of a McDonald's franchise was around $10,000 in the late 1950s. The 1984 cost ranges from $225,000 to $400,000, depending on location. On the other hand, the McDonald's franchise is certainly one of value, since the average revenue for a McDonald's was over one million dollars in 1984, with some operators taking home a net profit of over $100,000.

Leaseholds. A **lease** is a transfer of the right to use certain tangible property for a specified time. It is a contract between the property owner (lessor) and the party leasing the property (lessee) and can embody any terms acceptable to the two parties.

The two major types of leases are operating leases and capital leases. **Operating leases** transfer the right to use property, not the ownership of the property. In accounting for an operating lease, lease payments are changed to expense on the income statement. **Capital leases** are, in substance, sales of property from the lessor to the lessee. Capital leases result in an increase in tangible assets and liabilities on the statement of financial position. Neither type of lease is considered an intangible asset, but if operating leases are long-term and some type of advance payment has been made, the advance payment is recorded as an intangible asset. The advance payment is amortized to expense over the life of the lease.

Leasehold Improvements. An improvement made by the lessee that becomes a permanent part of leased property is known as a **leasehold improvement.** Examples are shelving attached to the walls, painting and decorating, carpeting attached to the floor, partitions added, and an attached garage added to a house. Such improvements become part of the property and, when the lease expires, become the property of the lessor. Their useful life to the lessee can be no more than the term of the lease, and they must be amortized accordingly.

Goodwill. **Goodwill** is a catchall term that includes any factor that allows a firm to earn more than a normal return on assets for the type of business in which it is engaged. Such factors can include superior products, service, distribution systems, management, location, or a monopolistic or semimonopolistic position within an industry. Even goodwill has a limited life, and it must be amortized over the period of its expected useful life, not to exceed 40 years.

Although goodwill can exist in any business, it can be entered into the accounts as an intangible asset only if it is acquired through purchase of another company. Determining goodwill is discussed further in Chapter 16.

LEASE
A transfer of the right to use certain property for a specified time.

OPERATING LEASE
A lease that transfers the right to use property but not the ownership of the property.

CAPITAL LEASE
A lease that is, in substance, a sale of property from the lessor to the lessee.

LEASEHOLD IMPROVEMENT
An improvement made by a lessee that becomes a permanent part of leased property.

GOODWILL
Any factor that allows a firm to earn more than a normal return on assets for the type of business in which it is engaged.

LONG-LIVED ASSETS ON THE STATEMENT OF FINANCIAL POSITION

Generally, long-lived assets are presented in a separate section of the statement of financial position following current assets under a general property, plant, and equipment caption. Intangibles can be shown separately in another asset section or included within property, plant, and equipment. The gross acquisition cost along with the accumulated depreciation, depletion, and amortization amounts are generally provided on the face of the statement, with additional details relative to the property placed in a footnote to the financial statements. The example in Exhibit 11.3, taken from the December 31, 1984, annual report of Revlon, Incorporated, is typical.

EXHIBIT 11.3

Consolidated Balance Sheets
REVLON, INC. AND SUBSIDIARIES
December 31, 1984 and 1983
(thousands of dollars)

	1984	1983
ASSETS		
Current assets		
Cash and time deposits	**$ 304,585**	$ 254,150
Short-term investments at cost, plus accrued interest, which approximates market	**114,451**	62,238
Accounts receivable—trade, less allowances of $17,645 and $20,391	**463,784**	429,979
Inventories	**420,386**	446,635
Prepayments	**98,111**	78,445
Other	**23,312**	21,272
Total current assets	**1,424,629**	1,292,719
Property, plant and equipment, at cost:		
Land and land improvements	**44,325**	46,554
Buildings and leasehold improvements	**392,892**	387,092
Machinery and equipment	**396,231**	384,419
Construction in progress	**24,554**	18,348
	858,002	836,413
Less accumulated depreciation and amortization	**267,402**	226,125
Total property, plant and equipment	**590,600**	610,288
Other assets:		
Excess of cost over net assets acquired, less accumulated amortization of $44,316 and $39,041	**181,717**	192,421
Patents, less amortization	**8,350**	10,241
Other	**106,069**	109,661
Total assets	**$2,311,365**	$2,215,330

Depreciation and Amortization—Property, Plant and Equipment:

Depreciation and amortization expense is computed on all classes of assets based on their estimated useful lives, as indicated below, using principally the straight-line method.

	Years
Land improvements	5 to 40
Buildings and building improvements	5 to 50
Machinery and equipment	3 to 15
Office furniture and equipment	5 to 15
Leasehold improvements	Life of lease or estimated life of improvements, whichever is shorter

Excess of Cost Over Net Assets Acquired: This represents trade names, trademarks, formulas and goodwill acquired in purchase transactions. Such intangibles are generally being amortized on a straight-line basis over appropriate periods not exceeding forty years.

Patents: The costs of patents are amortized from the date marketing of the related product commences over the estimated useful life of the product.

FOR REVIEW

SUMMARY

- Natural resources are tangible, naturally occurring resources that are considered long-lived until they are severed from the land.
- As natural resources are severed from the land, they are transformed into inventory, a current asset.
- Depletion is calculated on a units-of-production basis, assigned to a product, and passed on to cost of goods sold when the product is sold.
- The depreciation of buildings and equipment used in conjunction with natural resources severance should be linked to the depletion of the natural resources.
- Before it can be established that an intangible item is an asset, it must be determined that the item has future value, that its cost is material, and that it has a useful life exceeding one year.
- Intangible assets are typically amortized on a straight-line basis.
- Research and development costs must be treated as expense when incurred rather than as intangible assets.
- If an intangible asset proves to have no value, any remaining book value should be written off as an expense.

REVIEW QUESTIONS

11-1. How does a naturally occurring asset, such as a coal mine, differ from a manufactured asset, such as a building, in terms of accounting for its use in the production of revenue?

11-2. Give four examples of intangible assets and characterize the nature and life of each one.

11-3. In general, how is the useful life of an intangible asset determined?

11-4. How do companies account for research and development expenditures? Does this accounting methodology represent a good application of the matching principle?

11-5. What costs are included in the depletion base for naturally occurring assets?

11-6. What is a franchise? In general terms, how do companies account for the cost of a franchise?

11-7. What is goodwill? How is it handled in the accounting system?

11-8. Sometimes buildings and equipment are attached to naturally occurring assets in order to extract the underlying resource. If the useful life of the buildings and equipment differs from that of the naturally occurring asset to which they are attached, what is the basis for determining the useful life of the buildings and equipment for depreciation purposes?

11-9. Distinguish between an operating lease and a capital lease. What is the major difference in accounting for these two types of leases?

11-10. If one million tons of coal are mined at a cost of $2 million, including depletion of one million dollars in a given year, and 800,000 of those tons are sold to customers, how should the $2 million of costs be handled in the accounts?

EXERCISES

11-E1. Tiber Company purchases a timber stand containing an estimated 500,000 board feet of lumber for $200,000. The purchase does not include the land on which the timber stands. If Tiber harvests 300,000 board feet in the year of purchase, how much depletion expense should be recognized that year if all the timber is sold?

11-E2. Prepare general journal entries for 11-E1 for the following:

a. The acquisition of the timber stand.
b. The depletion, assuming all the timber harvested is sold.
c. The depletion, assuming only three-fourths of the timber harvested is sold by year-end.

11-E3. Ernest Nielsen, owner of Nielsen's Paint Store, leases a building for the store. The lease runs until December 31, 1991 and will not be renewed. Nielsen decides that a new display window and interior remodeling would increase his business and spends $5,000 making the investments, finishing the job on July 1, 1986. He estimates the store will not need remodeling for another ten years. Make the journal entries, recording the expenditure of the $5,000 and amortization for 1986 and 1987. Round to the nearest dollar.

11-E4. Krazy Kola is a well-known soft drink in its five-state market region. The owner sells the Krazy Kola name and trademark to Six Pac Soft Drink Company for one million dollars. Six Pac estimates that it will sell $500,000 of Krazy Kola each year after purchasing the trademark if it also spends $50,000 per year on advertising.

a. At what dollar figure should the trademark be carried on Six Pac's books?
b. Over how many years should the trademark be amortized?

11-E5. Refer to the data in 11-E4. If the trademark is acquired on August 1, 1986, and has an unlimited life remaining, how much amortization should be recognized in 1986?

11-E6. Current Publishing Company publishes books and sometimes buys manuscripts outright from authors for a fixed dollar amount. It currently owns copyrights for the following books:

Number of Copyrights	Type of Book	Date of Copyright(s)	Total Purchase Price
2	Mystery/detective	1/1/79	$10,000
1	Historical novel	1/1/80	2,000
15	Gothic romances	1/1/84	30,000
1	Contemporary novel	1/1/85	8,000

How much amortization of copyrights should Current record at the end of 1986, assuming that all of the books are selling well and appear to have virtually unlimited future sales potential?

11-E7. Refer to the data in 11-E6. In 1986, the vice president of Current determines that the detective stories and the historical novel will sell for ten more years, the contemporary novel will have a market for only five more years, and the Gothic romances for three more years. How much amortization should be recorded at the end of 1986? At the end of 1990?

PROBLEM SET A

11-A1. Depletion, Depreciation, and Natural Assets. A gold mine is purchased for $20 million. It is estimated to contain 100,000 ounces of gold, and it is expected that the mine will be in production for 25 years. In the first year after purchase, 5,000 ounces of gold are mined. In the second and third years, 15,000 and 25,000 ounces, respectively, are mined.

A system of water flues and sluices was constructed to be able to mine the gold. The system cost $300,000 to build and has an estimated life of ten years. Since the cost of removing the flues and sluices from the mountainside would exceed their value at any time after installation, no salvage value exists. The company uses straight-line depreciation.

Required

a. How much depletion expense should be recognized in Years 1, 2, and 3?
b. What is the carrying value of the gold mine at the end of Year 3?
c. How much depreciation expense on the flues and sluices should be recognized in Years 1, 2, and 3?

11-A2. Leases. George Williams leases space in a shopping mall for his retail clothing store. He signs a five-year lease effective January 1, 1986, paying $25,000. In addition, he agrees to pay 5% of the year's sales at the end of each year. Sales in 1986 and 1987 are $1 million and $1.2 million, respectively.

Required

a. Present the general journal entry showing how the original $25,000 payment should be recorded.
b. Present the general journal entries necessary at the end of 1986 and 1987.

11-A3. Research, Development, and Patents. The Sheerluck Company acquires a patent from Donovan Corporation on March 31, 1986. The patent has a remaining life of 17 years. Sheerluck wants it badly and agrees to pay $150,000 cash plus $50,000 per year for five years. It also incurs $10,000 for legal and accounting fees related to the negotiations and transfer of patent ownership. Sheerluck estimates that ownership of the patent will mean additional sales of $300,000 per year in selling the patented item.

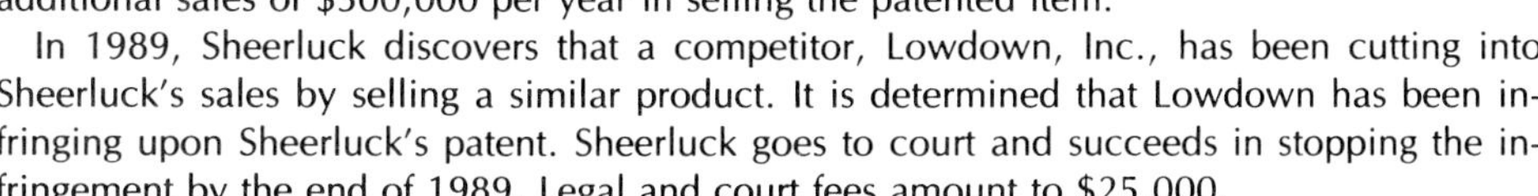

In 1989, Sheerluck discovers that a competitor, Lowdown, Inc., has been cutting into Sheerluck's sales by selling a similar product. It is determined that Lowdown has been infringing upon Sheerluck's patent. Sheerluck goes to court and succeeds in stopping the infringement by the end of 1989. Legal and court fees amount to $25,000.

Required

a. At what value should the patent be entered on Sheerluck's books on March 31, 1986?
b. How much amortization should be recognized in 1986? In 1987? In 1989?
c. Assume Sheerluck does not go to court and allows the infringement to proceed. How much expense should be recognized in 1989 in connection with the patent?
d. Present general journal entries for the patent acquisition on March 1, 1986, the amortization in 1987, and the loss in 1989 if Sheerluck does not go to court.

11-A4. Sale of a Patent. Refer to 11-A3. Assume Sheerluck goes to court, wins its case, and amortizes the proper amount of patent expense in 1989. On January 2, 1990, Sheerluck sells the patent for $300,000 cash.

Required

a. Using a T-account, enter the events in the life of the patent through 1990.
b. How much profit or loss is realized on the sale of the patent?
c. Present the general journal entry to record the sale of the patent.

11-A5. Financial Statements and Long-Term Assets. Carp Industries is the world's largest supplier of carp and carp-related by-products. During 1986, the firm had a number of transactions involving intangible assets.

Required

As a result of your extensive experience in this area, you have been asked by the controller to determine the 1986 amortization expense and the value to be placed on the company's statement of financial position for each of the following assets:

a. A four-year-old patent for the Carp-O-Matic was purchased for $600,000 on February 1, 1986. At the time of its initial development, the patent was expected to have an economic useful life of nine years. This estimate remained unchanged at the time of Carp Industries' acquisition.

b. On April 3, 1986, a patent was acquired for a process that deodorized carp scales. The process had been developed by Carp Industries chief researcher and had cost the company $75,000 in research and development funds. The process was a quantum leap forward and as a result was estimated to be commercially worth $150,000. The patent had an economic useful life of 15 years and associated legal fees of $12,000.

c. On November 1, 1986, a series of room partitions costing $50,000 were purchased and permanently installed in offices leased by Carp Industries from another firm. The partitions had a physical life of 20 years. At the time of the partitions' installation, the building's lease had eight more years to run and its renewal is doubtful.

d. Goodwill of $55,000 was acquired from the purchase of a business on January 1, 1986. Carp Industries wishes to amortize the goodwill over the maximum period of time allowed under generally accepted accounting principles.

e. Land was acquired on July 1, 1986, for a new warehouse at a cost of $200,000.

f. Equipment was acquired for use in distributing the Carp products on September 1, 1986, at a cost of $100,000. The equipment was expected to last ten years and have a salvage value of $10,000. Carp uses double-declining balance depreciation on equipment.

11-A6. Intangible Asset Acquisition and Amortization. On January 1, 1982, the Alfonz Scarpette Spaghetti Company established an American subsidiary in Fort Wayne, Indiana. A lack of familiarity with generally accepted accounting principles resulted in a number of problems for the company in recording various transactions involving certain assets. The following transactions were found by the auditor to be in error:

1. Alfonz Scarpette developed a process for producing a new type of spaghetti at a cost of $200,000. The company also incurred legal costs of $50,000 in the process of applying for a patent. On January 1, 1986, Alfonz Scarpette capitalized $250,000 as the cost of the patent and decided that this cost should be amortized over an economic useful life of 20 years.

2. On January 1, 1986, Alfonz Scarpette paid $22,000 of legal costs to defend a copyright from infringement by a competitor. The copyright had originally been purchased on January 1, 1983, at a cost of $150,000. The copyright was being amortized over a 20-year period, with the current year's amortization expense recorded as $7,500.

3. On July 1, 1986, the company acquired goodwill amounting to $50,000 from the purchase of a small pasta company. The goodwill was expected to have an indeterminable life and, as a result, was being amortized over a 50-year period.

4. On October 1, 1986, Alfonz Scarpette permanently installed a number of service counters and partitions costing $10,000 in a store leased from another firm. The lease did not state that Alfonz would be able to recover the fixtures installed. Alfonz amortized the counters and partitions over their expected 20-year physical life. However, at the time of installation, only ten years remained on the lease and its renewal was doubtful.

Required

Present any journal entries you consider necessary to correct any errors made during 1986. Identify each entry with the described situation by number.

11-A7. Natural Resources Cost Flows. On Janaury 1, 1986, the King Cole Coal Company bought land with mineral rights to coal reserves estimated at 4 million tons for $1.5 million. Before starting operations, King Cole made the following expenditures:

Geological survey fees	$100,000
Legal fees	10,000
Construction of access roads	250,000
Surface grading and leveling	140,000

The land, upon extraction of all the coal reserves, is expected to have an estimated resale value of $100,000. The machinery necessary to extract the coal was purchased on January 3, 1986, for one million dollars in cash. This equipment is expected to have a physical life of 15 years. However, the equipment will have no further value to King Cole when the coal reserves are exhausted in eight to ten years.

During 1986, 800,000 tons of coal were extracted from the mine. As of December 31, 1986 (the end of King Cole's fiscal year), only 600,000 of the 800,000 tons of coal had been sold. The remaining 200,000 tons of coal were sold in 1987.

Required

a. Determine the total "cost" to be allocated to the 800,000 tons of coal mined during 1986.
b. Will all of the cost allocated in (a) be an expense in 1986? If not, how will the nonexpense portion be treated in the 1986 financial statements of King Cole, and when will this portion become an expense, if ever?

PROBLEM SET B

11-B1. Depletion, Depreciation, and Natural Resources. Trinidad Nickel Company buys mineral rights to nickel reserves estimated at five million tons, paying $50 million. To reach the mining site, which is in a remote area, it is necessary to build a road at a cost of $5 million. The cost of opening the mine and putting a mine shaft down totals $2 million. The mining equipment is new when it is brought to this mine. It has an estimated life of ten years, cost $103,000, and will have a salvage value of $3,000 at any time after installation. Five hundred thousand tons of nickel are removed in the first year after the mine is opened, and one million tons are removed in the second year. Trinidad expects to exhaust all of the nickel from the mine in five years.

Required

a. At what value should the mine be carried on the books of Trinidad Nickel Company?
b. How much depletion should be recognized in the first year? In the second?
c. How much depreciation on the equipment should be recognized in the first year? In the second? (Trinidad uses straight-line depreciation.)
d. If Trinidad sold 800,000 tons of nickel from the mine in the second year, how should the depletion be accounted for in the company's financial statements?

11-B2. Leases. Julian Lopez leases space in a shopping mall for his sporting goods store. He signs a five-year lease effective January 1, 1986, paying $10,000 at that time. In addition, he agrees to pay 5% of sales at the end of each year. Sales in 1986, 1987, and 1988 are $100,000, $110,000, and $115,000, respectively.

Required

a. Present the general journal entry showing how the original $10,000 payment should be handled.
b. What is the lease (or rent) expense for 1986 and 1987.
c. Lopez occupies the store through 1988, at which time he decides to move to a better location. According to the existing lease, he must forfeit any remaining part of the original payment plus pay $1,000. Present the general journal entry to record these events.

11-B3. Research, Development, and Patents. Tryhard, Inc., has a small but brilliant research staff. Over the course of two years, it develops an exciting new product. Research costs traceable to this project are as follows:

Salaries	$250,000
Depreciation of equipment	45,000
Depreciation on building	20,000
Research reference materials	2,000
Research materials	48,000
Testing costs	35,000
Total	$400,000

Since the company estimates the product would generate $300,000 of sales per year, it decides to obtain a patent. Legal fees and other costs of obtaining the patent amount to $10,000.

Required

a. At what value should the patent be carried on Tryhard's books?
b. If the patent becomes effective on March 31, 1986, what amount of patent amortization should be recognized in 1986?
c. In 1987, Tryhard is forced to go to court to stop another manufacturer from making Tryhard's patented product without permission. Tryhard wins the case, incurring $25,000 of legal fees in the process. What amount of amortization should Tryhard recognize in 1987?
d. Assume Tryhard loses the 1987 case. What amount of patent amortization expense should it record in 1987?
e. Present general journal entries to record the events in (a) through (d).

11-B4. Sale of a Patent. Refer to the data in 11-B3. Assume that Tryhard goes to court, wins its case, and amortizes the proper amount of patent expense in 1987. On January 2, 1988, it sells the patent for $300,000 cash.

Required

a. Using a T-account, enter the events in the life of the patent through 1988.
b. How much gain or loss is realized on the sale of the patent.
c. Present the general journal entry to record the sale of the patent.

11-B5. Financial Statements and Long-Term Assets. Dog-Metics, Inc., is the world's only manufacturer of cosmetics for dogs. The company aims its product at those dogs who have everything except looks. During your first week of employment at the firm, the controller asks you to prepare the long-term asset portion of the 1986 statement of financial position. The controller gives you the following information on the accounts:

Account	Description
Patents	*Patent A.* The Doggie Lipstick patent was acquired on January 1, 1980, for $25,000. Its estimated economic life at that time was 20 years. *Patent B.* The Doggie Nose Dewetter patent was acquired on April 3, 1984, for $45,000. When purchased, the patent had been used for eight years and was expected to have an economic useful life of eleven years for Dog-Metics.
Copyright	The copyright to *Tips on the Perfect Doggie Facial* was acquired on July 2, 1981, for $60,000. The copyright was expected to have an economic useful life of 15 years.
Equipment	Packaging machine was purchased on January 3, 1982, for $32,000. The machine was expected to have a ten-year useful life with a salvage value of $2,000. Dog-Metics uses sum-of-the-years' digits method for depreciation of all machinery.
Mineral Mine	Mineral mine was acquired on October 1, 1986, the output of which will be used in the production of various doggie cosmetics. The mine cost $1.5 million and was estimated to have mineral reserves of one million tons. During the period 10/1/86 through 12/31/86, 20,000 tons of minerals were removed from the mine.
Land	Land was purchased on January 3, 1979, for $200,000.
Building	On July 1, 1978, Dog-Metics purchased a manufacturing facility for $250,000. The facility had an estimated economic useful life of 20 years with zero salvage value. Dog-Metics uses the straight-line depreciation method for all buildings.

Required

Prepare the long-term asset portion of the December 31, 1986, statement of financial position for Dog-Metics, Inc.

11-B6. Intangible Asset Acquisition and Amortization. Widget World, Inc., was organized on January 1, 1986. Widget World manufactures a wide assortment of educational widgets designed specifically for use in the teaching of college level economics and production courses. Wanda Widget, the company's accountant, is not sure about the appropriate journal entries to record those transactions involving the firm's intangible assets. As a result, Wanda has come to you for help in determining the correct journal entries for the following transactions:

January 3—Widget World, Inc., pays $1.5 million for the patent for a widget that could be used in the instruction of Ph.D. seminars. Because of the dynamic nature of the widget industry, the patent is expected to have an economic useful life of only eight years. On July 1, the company successfully prosecutes an infringement of its patent by Wankel Widget. The cost of the litigation amounts to $8,000.

April 2—Winslow Widget, president of Widget World, notices a marked increase in the demand for European widgets used in international business classes. As a result, Widget World acquires a franchise that entitles it to be the sole distributor of Euro-Widget in the United States. The franchise costs $85,000. Widget World pays cash of $35,000 and signs a 10% note payable for the remaining balance. The initial principal payment, due on December 31, amounts to $15,000.

November 1—Widget World, Inc., is granted the patent rights for the Adjusto-Widget by the U.S. federal government. The patent is the result of a ten-month research and development effort by the chief chemist, Woodrow Widget. The project cost $75,000. The legal fees and paperwork needed to obtain the patent total $3,500. On December 31, the company pays $25,000 to obtain patents that could make Adjusto-Widget useless if used by its competitors. The patents obtained will not be used and were obtained for the protection of its earlier patent.

Required

a. For each of the preceding transactions, prepare the general journal entries necessary to properly record the acquisition of the intangible asset.
b. Prepare the general journal entry to record the amortization of the intangible assets at the end of the year.

11-B7. Natural Resources Cost Flows. On July 10, 1986, the Gypsum Mining Company purchases the mineral rights only (not the land) to dolomite reserves estimated at ten million processed tons for $200,000. Before starting operations, Gypsum makes the following expenditures:

Legal fees	$ 20,000
Mine shaft and tunnel construction	10,000,000
Access road construction	100,000
Mining machinery (nonremovable)	1,000,000

During 1986, one million tons of rock are removed from the mine yielding 100,000 tons of processed dolomite. The market for dolomite is severely depressed in 1986, and Gypsum cannot sell any of its production. During 1987, the company does not mine any more rock but manages to sell 90,000 tons of processed dolomite.

Required

a. Determine the total "cost" to be allocated to the dolomite mined during 1986.
b. Will all of the cost allocated in (a) be an expense in 1986? If not, how will the nonexpense portion be treated in the 1986 financial statements of Gypsum Mining, and when will this portion become an expense, if ever?

APPLICATION

Owens-Illinois

Owens-Illinois, Inc., traces its corporate ancestral tree to a glass plant founded in 1779 by the seven Stanper brothers of Glassboro, New Jersey. In 1918, the small glass plant became part of the Owens Bottle Company, which had been formed shortly after 1900 following Michael J. Owens' invention of the automatic bottle-making machine, the most significant development in glassmaking since the invention of the blowpipe two thousand years earlier. The Owens Bottle Company and the Illinois Glass Company were merged to form Owens-Illinois Glass Company in 1929, and in 1935 Owens-Illinois Glass Company acquired the Libbey Glass Company. The corporate name was shortened in 1965 to Owens-Illinois, Inc., to reflect the ever-broadening scope of company operations.

Today Owens-Illinois (O-I) ranks among the largest American corporations, with 45,000 employees located in 110 domestic and foreign facilities. Headquartered in Toledo, Ohio, Owens-Illinois had sales in 1984 of $3.5 billion, with net profits of $135.8 million.

Exhibit 1 shows Owens-Illinois' consolidated statement of financial position. As of December 31, 1984, the company had total assets of approximately $3.2 billion, consisting of current assets; investments; and property, plant, and equipment.

Current Assets

Current assets of Owens-Illinois are $1.04 billion, or 32.6 percent of total assets. Cash and short-term investments have decreased by more than 13 percent from their 1983 level to $189.1 million. However, a look at the composition of this figure (see Exhibit 2[a]) reveals that O-I has very wisely placed the majority of this money in short-term investments, where it earns interest income.

Another major component of O-I's current assets is accounts receivable. As noted in Chapter 6, an account receivable has its origins in a credit sale. Like all companies extending credit, Owens-Illinois occasionally has customers who are unable to pay their bills. In such cases, O-I credit managers will make several attempts to collect payment. If these attempts are unsuccessful, the bad debt must be accounted for. O-I uses the allowance method to estimate bad debts. The balance of the Allowance for Loss account is determined by examining credit sales and using the aging of accounts receivable method. Each month, the Allowance for Loss account is credited with a percentage of the month's credit sales expected to prove uncollectible. The balance within the

EXHIBIT 1

Owens-Illinois, Inc. Consolidated Statement of Financial Position Millions of dollars December 31	1984	1983
Assets		
Current assets:		
Cash (including time deposits of $54.2 in 1984 and $34.3 in 1983)	**$ 94.4**	$ 65.7
Short-term investments (at cost, which approximates market)	**94.7**	152.6
Receivables, less allowances of $18.0 ($16.0 in 1983) for losses and discounts	**414.5**	491.1
Inventories	**393.3**	353.6
Prepaid expenses	**41.7**	8.4
Total current assets	**1,038.6**	1,071.4
Investments and other assets:		
Foreign investments and advances	**155.9**	156.7
Domestic investments	**52.5**	27.8
Repair parts inventories	**104.1**	103.5
Deferred charges	**77.7**	24.4
Deposits, receivables and other assets	**109.3**	68.6
Total investments and other assets	**499.5**	381.0
Property, plant and equipment:		
Land and timberlands, at cost less depletion	**95.9**	95.4
Buildings and equipment, at cost:		
Buildings and building equipment	**621.2**	556.7
Factory machinery and equipment	**2,006.9**	1,898.3
Transportation, office and miscellaneous equipment	**111.4**	109.4
Construction in progress	**86.5**	52.7
	2,826.0	2,617.1
	2,921.9	2,712.5
Less accumulated depreciation and amortization	**1,276.9**	1,229.0
Total property, plant and equipment	**1,645.0**	1,483.5
Total assets	**$3,183.1**	$2,935.9

EXHIBIT 1

Continued

Owens-Illinois, Inc. **Consolidated Statement of Financial Position** Millions of dollars except share amounts December 31	**1984**	1983
Liabilities and Shareholders' Equity		
Current liabilities:		
Short-term loans and notes payable	**$ 101.9**	$ 22.1
Accounts payable	**231.8**	217.7
Salaries and wages	**92.1**	87.3
U.S. and foreign income taxes	**24.0**	12.6
Other accrued liabilities	**194.9**	207.1
Long-term debt due within one year	**28.2**	28.7
Total current liabilities	**672.9**	575.5
Long-term debt	**571.8**	544.8
Deferred taxes and other credits:		
Deferred taxes	**289.1**	260.1
Obligations under foreign pension plans	**67.4**	72.8
Other liabilities and reserves	**106.8**	103.3
Total deferred taxes and other credits	**463.3**	436.2
Minority shareholders' interests	**48.3**	52.9
Redeemable preferred shares	**4.4**	4.8
Shareholders' equity (excluding redeemable preferred shares):		
Preference shares (liquidation preference, $12.8 in 1984 and $18.7 in 1983)	**2.6**	3.7
Common shares (outstanding, 29,573,776 in 1984 and 27,747,312 in 1983)	**92.4**	86.7
Capital in excess of stated value	**203.3**	154.7
Retained earnings	**1,265.0**	1,178.3
Cumulative foreign currency translation adjustment	**(140.9)**	(101.7)
Total shareholders' equity (excluding redeemable preferred shares)	**1,422.4**	1,321.7
Total liabilities and shareholders' equity	**$3,183.1**	$2,935.9

EXHIBIT 2

Owens-Illinois (Tabular Data in Millions of Dollars)

2(a)

Cash and short-term investments at December 31, 1984 and 1983, were as follows:

	1984	**1983**
Cash	$ 40.2	$ 31.4
Time deposits	54.2	34.3
Short-term investments, at cost, which approximate market	94.7	152.6
	$ 189.1	$ 218.3

2(b)

Major classes of inventory at December 31, 1984 and 1983, were as follows:

	1984	1983
Finished goods	$ 227.1	$ 219.1
Work in process	21.6	22.4
Construction inventory in process	18.6	——
Raw materials	90.6	77.6
Operating supplies	35.4	34.5
	$ 393.3	$ 353.6

2(c)

The major classes of property, plant, and equipment at December 31, 1984 and 1983, were as follows:

	1984	1983
Land and timberlands, at cost less depletion	$ 95.9	$ 95.4
Buildings and equipment, at cost		
Buildings and building equipment	621.2	556.7
Factory machinery and equipment	2,006.9	1,898.3
Transportation, office, and miscellaneous equipment	111.4	109.4
Construction in progress	86.5	52.7
	2,826.0	2,617.1
	2,921.9	2,712.5
Less accumulated depreciation and amortization	1,276.9	1,229.0
Total property, plant, and equipment	$1,645.0	$1,483.5

account is reviewed quarterly and annually against all potential bad debts identified by the aging, and any needed adjustment to the total of the monthly bad debt accruals is made. Using this method, O-I has set the balance of its Allowance for Loss account at $18 million, which represents 4.2 percent of total accounts receivable.

The last major component of O-I's current assets is inventory. As of December 31, 1984, O-I had $393.3 million of inventory. Because Owens-Illinois is a manufacturing organization, this amount is divided among finished goods, work in process, raw materials, and operating supplies (see Exhibit 2 [b]). O-I values inventories on the LIFO cost basis. Because costs were lower when these inventory units were produced (due to inflation), the balance of the Inventory account is less than it would have been had FIFO or weighted average costing been used.

Investments and Other Assets

Investments and other assets represents 15.7 percent of total assets. The investments represent O-I's ownership interests in domestic and foreign corporations.

Property, Plant, and Equipment

The final group of Owens-Illinois' assets is property, plant, and equipment, which represents 51.7 percent of total assets. The majority of property, plant, and equipment is depreciable. As we saw in Chapter 10, there are several methods for accounting for depreciation. O-I has elected to use straight-line depreciation. O-I deducts the amount of annual depletion directly from the Land and Timberlands asset account. Thus, there is no separate listing on the statement of financial position of the land's original cost and the amount of accumulated depletion (see Exhibit 2 [c]).

Exercises

1. Why would Owens-Illinois, Inc., prefer to value its inventories under the LIFO method when the FIFO method would have resulted in a higher value for inventories and higher reported earnings?

2. If Owens-Illinois had used double-declining balance depreciation for its buildings and equipment, would the net value of fixed assets be higher or lower than it is now? Why would any company prefer to use a depreciation method that results in lower net fixed asset values?

3. Using the information given in Owens-Illinois' statement of financial position, what portion of the building and equipment's estimated useful life has already expired (on the average)?

PART THREE
SOURCES AND USES OF INVESTED CAPITAL

PARTNERSHIPS

CHAPTER OBJECTIVES
After studying Chapter 12, you should understand the following:

1. The features of a partnership, including advantages and disadvantages of the partnership form of organization.
2. How to account for partners' investments in and withdrawals from the firm.
3. The government's approach toward taxation of partnership earnings.
4. Specialized situations that can arise when a person joins or leaves a partnership.

Organizing a business as a partnership lends a particular framework to sharing the ownership of a business, dividing the profits and losses, and allowing for new members or eventual dissolution of the partnership. This chapter discusses the advantages and disadvantages of a partnership as well as accounting procedures developed to record partnership transactions.

WHAT IS A PARTNERSHIP?

PARTNERSHIP
An association of two or more persons to carry on as co-owners of a business for profit.

The Uniform Partnership Act (UPA) defines a **partnership** as an association of two or more persons to carry on as co-owners of a business for profit. When the finances needed to run a business exceed what one owner can contribute, that owner looks for alternative forms of organization. A partnership offers a new source of capital without requiring numerous shareholders with a subsequent loss of control over the business.

Most partnerships are created by written contract. To govern those for which no written agreement exists, almost 90 percent of the states have adopted the UPA. Partnerships in the other ten percent of the states are governed by common law.

FEATURES OF A PARTNERSHIP

A partnership is a voluntary association in which each member has the right to act on behalf of the entire firm and new partners must be approved by all existing partners.

Unlike corporations, partnerships have a limited life and are dissolved with the withdrawal or death of a partner. Although the old partnership is ended, the business can continue with existing or new partners.

MUTUAL AGENCY
The characteristic of a partnership that each partner has the power to represent the firm.

A partnership requires absolute trust among the partners, since each partner has the power to represent the firm. This characteristic is called **mutual agency.** To afford some protection, the partners can agree among themselves that a particular partner should not have the authority to represent the firm. In such a case, the business world must be notified that the specific partner has no authority to act on behalf of the partnership.

Unlimited liability is probably the most noteworthy feature of the partnership form of organization. Each partner is responsible for a share of the debts and losses of the firm. A partner whose capital investment is inadequate must use his or her personal property to satisfy the debt or loss. If a partner is bankrupt and cannot cover his or her share of the partnership debts, the remaining owners are liable just as if the debt were their own.

Some limitations to a partner's liability exist. For example, new partners are responsible only for losses that occur after their admission. Similarly, a partner's liability ceases at the date of his or her retirement or death.

Partnerships are easy to form and operate. A partnership can be formed when the partners create an agreement specifying such details as owning and running the business and sharing profits. Government permission is not required, nor is the completion of any preliminary forms. A partnership is not required to submit operational reports to governmental agencies such as the Securities and Exchange Commission (SEC). This important advantage can help the firm maintain the confidentiality of its affairs.

The Big Eight

Partnerships can be *big*. The following eight American-based accounting firms—each organized as a partnership—are so large that they are frequently referred to as the Big Eight:

— Arthur Andersen
— Coopers and Lybrand
— Deloitte, Haskins, and Sells
— Ernst and Whinney
— Peat Marwick Mitchell
— Price Waterhouse
— Touche Ross
— Arthur Young and Company

Approximately 150,000 people work for Big Eight firms in 2,500 offices in over 100 nations. These firms annually interview some 160,000 U.S. college students and hire close to 10,000 graduates.

Combined revenues of the eight firms approach $5 billion per year. Although some partners earn nearly one million dollars annually, most earn around $130,000, which might seem like a comfortable figure. However, since the firms are partnerships, the owners must invest capital in the business. Thus, the amount a partner might "take home" is frequently much less than his or her share of the partnership earnings.

All partnership property is owned jointly by the partners. Although the property may have been contributed by an individual partner, the partnership is deemed to have purchased the assets from the owner at fair market value and will increase the donating owner's capital account for that amount.

A partner has an ownership right in the partnership profits; however, simply sharing the profits does not make someone a partner. For example, a senior employee of the partnership might get a bonus based on profits but have no other partnership rights or obligations.

ADVANTAGES AND DISADVANTAGES OF A PARTNERSHIP

Organizing a business as a partnership is attractive because a partnership offers flexibility, ease in formation, possible tax benefits, and employee inducements. A partnership is flexible because it can raise more capital or acquire additional talent by admitting an acceptable partner. Formation is easy because paperwork is simple and government requirements are minimal. Since a partnership is not considered a separate entity for tax purposes, it has tax benefits. Partnership profits are taxed only once; a specified portion must be reported on the personal tax return of each partner. (In contrast, as explained in Chapter 13, corporate profits are taxed twice, once as corporate income and again as dividend income to the owner/shareholders.) A partnership can induce valuable employees to continue their association with the business by offering full, limited, or potential partnerships as rewards for their contributions to the business.

The disadvantages of partnerships originate in the principles of mutual agency and unlimited liability. As discussed earlier, the risk of mutual agency can be reduced. Total elimination of the risk is impossible, however; a partner might become financially overwhelmed, particularly if the partnership sustains heavy losses.

THE PARTNERSHIP AGREEMENT

PARTNERSHIP AGREEMENT
A contract between the partners specifying how the business is to be run.

A **partnership agreement** is a contract between the partners specifying how the business is to be run. The contract preferably will be written, although an oral or implied agreement is still enforceable. The normal contents of the agreement include the following:

1. The name and location of the partnership business.
2. The names of the partners and the duties that each partner has accepted in the day-to-day operation of the business.
3. The individual investment obligations and drawing rights of each partner. Like any other business, a partnership obtains its assets from its creditors and owners. Hence, the agreement must specify how much each partner is expected to contribute. Since partners need money for personal living expenses, they normally can make withdrawals at specified times from the business **(drawings)** up to certain ceilings. The rights to drawings are outlined in the agreement.

DRAWINGS
Amounts partners withdraw from a partnership for their personal use.

4. The method of sharing profits or losses, interest on partners' loans, and related details. The UPA or common law applies when no agreement exists for distribution of profits or losses. The UPA provides for equal sharing of profit or loss. However, the partners can specify how profits and losses are to be distributed. Such specifications can include salaries payable to partners or interest payable on the partners' capital and loan balances.
5. Relevant details about insurance on the lives of the partners. When a partnership is dissolved due to the death of a partner, the remaining owners must supply a payment equal to the value of the deceased partner's share of the firm to the executors of the estate. To ensure sufficient cash to forward to a deceased partner's estate, the partnership might carry insurance policies on the life of each partner, with the partnership named as beneficiary.
6. The planned accounting period and provisions for audit. The agreement should specify the accounting period over which profit will be computed. Although not required, owners of large partnerships need assurance that the organization is being managed in their best interests. Thus, some partnership agreements call for audits and specify the auditor to be used.
7. The procedure for arbitration of disputes. If a conflict should arise, an arbiter named in the agreement and acceptable to all partners will resolve the dispute.

Although the law does not recognize a partnership as distinct from the partners, accounting does. All journal entries that we discuss are from the point of view of the partnership and not of individual partners.

CAPITAL FORMATION OF A PARTNERSHIP

Any business needs investment from its owners. In the case of a partnership, each partner must contribute assets to the business in accordance with the partnership agreement. If Ash, Black, and Cole contribute $100,000, $130,000, and $180,000, respectively, on June 1, the partnership would record the investment as follows:

June 1	Cash	410,000	
	Ash, capital		100,000
	Black, capital		130,000
	Cole, capital		180,000
	(to record initial cash contributions from owners)		

Unlike corporate owners' equity, where the investments of all owners are merged into one account, the amount of each partner's contribution must be identified separately. Each partner's **capital account** shows the accumulated personal investment of the partner.

CAPITAL ACCOUNT
An account that shows each partner's accumulated personal investment.

Generally, partners can withdraw cash during the year for their personal use. If Ash withdraws $1,000 on August 2, the withdrawal would be recorded as follows:

Aug. 2	Ash, drawing	1,000	
	Cash		1,000
	(to record the withdrawal of funds by Ash)		

A partner's **drawing account** is used to record all withdrawals by the partner and is a contra-account to his or her capital account. At the end of each period, the debit balance in a partner's drawing account is closed against the credit balance in his or her capital account. The net amount remaining in the capital account represents the partner's current investment in the business.

DRAWING ACCOUNT
An account used to record a partner's drawings; a contra-account to the partner's capital account.

Although partners normally supply cash as their contribution to the firm's capital, they sometimes furnish other assets. In such cases, the fair market value of their assets forms the basis for recording the partner's capital contribution. If Cole contributed a building valued at $130,000 to the partnership on September 10, the partnership would record Cole's contribution as follows:

Sept. 10	Buildings	130,000	
	Cole, capital		130,000
	(to record contribution of building by Cole)		

Sometimes two persons already operating businesses independently combine to form a partnership. Then the capital accounts for each partner should reflect the fair market value of the net assets contributed by each. Suppose Apple and Berry wish to form a partnership. On November 1, 1987, their assets and liabilities have the following fair market values:

	Apple	Berry
Assets	$200,000	$150,000
Liabilities	60,00	100,000

The journal entries to record the Apple-Berry partnership formation are as follows:

Nov. 1	Miscellaneous assets	200,000	
	Miscellaneous liabilities		60,000
	Apple, capital		140,000
	(to record investment)		
Nov. 1	Miscellaneous assets	150,000	
	Miscellaneous liabilities		100,000
	Berry, capital		50,000
	(to record investment)		

The statement of financial position for the Apple-Berry partnership as of the formation date is as follows:

Apple-Berry Partnership
Statement of Financial Position
November 1, 1987

Miscellaneous assets ($200,000 + $150,000)	$350,000	Miscellaneous liabilities ($60,000 + $100,000)		$160,000
		Partners' capital accounts		
		Apple	$140,000	
		Berry	50,000	190,000
Total assets	$350,000	Total equities		$350,000

PARTNERSHIP PROFITS AND TAXES

PROFIT-SHARING RATIO The ratio that determines how profits and losses in a partnership are shared among the partners.

The profits and losses of a partnership can be shared in any manner agreeable to all. The most common method of allocation is to split the profits and losses by a predetermined **profit-sharing ratio** showing the relative proportion of the profits and losses for each partner. The ratio, perhaps 50:50 or 2:2:6, normally is based on the contribution of funds, time, and expertise each partner is expected to make to the earning capacity of the firm. In many cases, partners do not devote equal time or expertise to the business nor do they invest equal amounts of assets. To reflect such differences, the profit-sharing agreement can be adjusted. Some of the more common adjustments take the form of salary payments or interest payments on contributed capital. These adjustments become unavoidable commitments of the partnership. Partners who contribute funds or take an active role in the business have given up the opportunity for earnings by investing their time or money elsewhere, and they should be compensated for their sacrifice.

ACTIVE PARTNERS Those partners actively involved in the day-to-day operations of a partnership.

SILENT PARTNERS Those partners who, although they can participate in certain policy-making decisions, do not work actively in the business.

Salary Allowance Paid to a Partner

Although all partners can participate in the day-to-day operation of the business, sometimes a few partners, called **active partners,** manage the firm's operation. The others, called **silent partners,** can participate in certain policy-making decisions but do not work actively in the business.

Since active partners are willing to devote time and energy to operating the business, fairness demands that the partnership reward them with salary allowances in addition to their normal share of the profits. Since a partner legally cannot be distinguished from the partnership, a partner's salary allowance is not treated as salary expense on the income statement but as a distribution of earnings to an owner. As an example, assume Ash, Black, and Cole share profits and losses in the ratio of 30:40:30. Black runs the business on a day-to-day basis and is allotted a "salary" of $30,000 per year. The partnership profit before paying Black was $50,000. The partnership earnings would be allocated to the partners as in Exhibit 12.1

EXHIBIT 12.1

Profit before Black's salary allowance	$50,000
Less: Black's salary allowance	30,000
Remaining profit to be divided in ratio of 30:40:30	$20,000

Partnership earnings allocation:

	Earnings Allocated As Salary	Earnings Allocated After Deduction Of Salary	Total Allocation To Partners
Ash (30%)	0	$ 6,000	$ 6,000
Black (40%)	$30,000	8,000	38,000
Cole (30%)	0	6,000	6,000
Total allocation	$30,000	$20,000	$50,000

The following journal entry would close the income summary account and recognize the earnings allocation:

Dec. 31	Income summary	50,000	
	Ash, capital		6,000
	Black, capital		38,000
	Cole, capital		6,000
	(to close profit to capital accounts)		

The closing entries for a partnership are similar to the closing entries for any business organization: All revenue and expense accounts are closed into the Income Summary account. As previously stated, amounts paid or payable to a partner cannot be considered an expense and are excluded from the Income Summary account. The income summary discloses the profit or loss of the partnership exclusive of all distributions made to the owners. The summary account along with the drawing accounts are closed to partners' capital accounts.

Interest on Partners' Capital

Partnership agreements often provide for interest payments on partner capital to differentiate between partners who invest varying amounts of cash or other assets.

The rate of interest need not be the market rate, but it should be high enough to recognize the partner's contribution. As with partners' salaries, interest is deducted from overall partnership earnings to determine residual profit available for distribution under the profit-sharing ratio.

For example, assume Apple and Berry share profits and losses in the ratio of 70:30 and their capital account balances at the beginning of the year are $150,000 and $200,000, respectively. The partnership agreement requires payment of interest on capital at 15 percent, and the profit before any allocations is $100,000. The partnership profits would be distributed as in Exhibit 12.2.

EXHIBIT 12.2

Profit before allocations		$100,000
Less interest on capital balances:		
Apple (15% on $150,000)	$22,500	
Berry (15% on $200,000)	30,000	52,500
Balance of profits to be shared in ratio of 70:30		$ 47,500
Apple (70% × $47,500)		$ 33,250
Berry (30% × $47,500)		14,250
		$ 47,500

The total allocation to Apple and Berry is as follows:

	Earnings Allocated As Interest on Partner Capital	Earnings Allocated After Deduction For Interest on Partner Capital	Total Allocation To Partner
Apple	$22,500	$33,250	$ 55,750
Berry	30,000	14,250	44,250
Total	$52,500	$47,500	$100,000

The following journal entry would recognize the distribution of partnership profits for the year:

Dec. 31	Income summary	100,000	
	Apple, capital		55,750
	Berry, capital		44,250
	(to allocate yearly earnings to owners)		

Interest on a Partner's Loan

When the partnership needs additional funds, it can approach a bank or other financial agency, or the firm can ask one or more of the partners to lend it the money for a short period of time. Normally, the partnership agreement provides the rate of interest to be paid on loans from partners.

Assume that Ash, Black, and Cole are partners sharing profits and losses in the ratio of 50:20:30. Cole lends the business $120,000 on January 1. The rate of interest on a partner's loan is set at 12 percent. The journal entry recognizing the receipt of $120,000 from Cole on January 1 is as follows:

Jan. 1	Cash	120,000	
	Note payable—Cole		120,000
	(to record receipt of funds borrowed from Cole)		

Assume that the profit before any allocation to the partners is $50,000. The interest on Cole's loan has priority over other distributions of earnings to the partners. As with partner salaries and interest on invested capital, any interest paid on loans from a partner is considered a distribution of partnership earnings to that partner. Thus, Cole's share of the partnership's earnings is the interest on his loan plus his 30 percent share of remaining earnings. Allocations are as follows:

Profit before allocation to partners	$50,000
Less: Interest on Cole's loan at 12% (12% × 120,000)	14,400
Balance of profits to be shared in the ratio 50:20:30	$35,600
Ash (50%)	$17,800
Black (20%)	7,120
Cole (30%)	10,680
	$35,600

The journal entry to recognize the allocation of earnings in this case would be as follows:

Dec. 31	Income summary	50,000	
	Ash, capital		17,800
	Black, capital		7,120
	Cole, capital ($14,400 interest + $10,680)		25,080
	(to allocate earnings to partners)		

Usually several of these profit allocation adjustments exist simultaneously. Consider the following problem as a more typical case. Amber, Brown, and Clay share profits and losses equally. Interest on the partners' capital balances (at the beginning of the year) and partners' loan balances is payable at 12 percent. Brown is allowed a salary of $50,000 per year. Clay lends the partnership $60,000 on July 1, 1986. The partners' capital balances on January 1, 1986, are $130,000, $85,000, and $185,000, respectively. Balances on December 31, 1986, in the drawing accounts for Amber, Brown, and Clay are $12,000, $25,000, and $23,000, respectively. The partnership earnings before any allocations for 1986 are $98,000. The allocation of earnings to each partner would be determined as follows:

Earnings before any allocation		$98,000
Less: Salary allowance for Brown	$50,000	
Interest on Clay's loan: 12% on $60,000 for 6 months	3,600	53,600
Available for interest on capital		$44,400

The total amount owed for interest on capital is as follows:

Amber	(.12) × ($130,000)	$15,600
Brown	(.12) × ($ 85,000)	10,200
Clay	(.12) × ($185,000)	22,200
		$48,000

The partnership profits are, therefore, short $3,600 ($48,000 − $44,400) of the amount needed for interest. This shortage constitutes a decrease in capital to the partners. Since the partners share residual profits equally, they must also share decreases equally unless their agreement specifies otherwise. In this case, each partner will bear $1,200 ($3,600/3) of the loss. The total allocation to each partner is shown in Exhibit 12.3.

EXHIBIT 12.3

Earnings Allocation to Each Partner

Partner	Partner Salary	Interest On Loans	Interest On Capital	Residual Profit (Loss)	Total Allocations To Partner
Amber	$ 0	$ 0	$15,600	$(1,200)	$14,400
Brown	50,000	0	10,200	(1,200)	59,000
Clay	0	3,600	22,200	(1,200)	24,600
Totals	$50,000	$3,600	$48,000	$(3,600)	$98,000

The following journal entry to close the Income Summary account and recognize the earnings distribution would be required:

Dec. 31	Income summary	98,000	
	Amber, capital		14,400
	Brown, capital		59,000
	Clay, capital		24,600
	(to allocate profits to owners)		

Finally, the following entry should be made to close the drawing accounts to their respective capital accounts:

Dec. 31	Amber, capital	12,000	
	Brown, capital	25,000	
	Clay, capital	23,000	
	Amber, drawing		12,000
	Brown, drawing		25,000
	Clay, drawing		23,000
	(to close drawing accounts to capital accounts)		

The capital accounts in the ledger would appear as shown after closing. Drawing accounts have been reduced to zero.

Amber, Capital

		1/1/86	130,000
Drawing	12,000	Allocation	14,400
		12/31/86	132,400

Brown, Capital

		1/1/86	85,000
Drawing	25,000	Allocation	59,000
		12/31/86	119,000

Clay, Capital

		1/1/86	185,000
Drawing	23,000	Allocation	24,600
		12/31/86	186,600

CONCEPT SUMMARY 12.1

DIFFERENCES IN ACCOUNTING FOR OWNERS' EQUITY

Transaction Type	Partnership Account	Corporation Account
Asset contributions.	Partners' capital.	Common stock (or other paid-in capital).
Asset distributions.	Partners' drawing.	Dividends declared or retained earnings.
Past earnings of firm.	Partners' capital.	Retained earnings.
Closing of Income Summary account.	Partners' capital.	Retained earnings.
Owner disposition of interest in the business.	Partners' capital.	None. The transaction does not involve the corporation directly.

TAXATION OF PARTNERSHIP INCOME

As stated earlier, the income from a partnership is not taxed in the name of the firm, since a partnership is not recognized as a legal entity for tax purposes. However, a partnership files an information tax return for IRS purposes. Partnership income is taxed when allocated to the partners as personal income whether the partners withdraw it or not. The tax authorities do not differentiate a partner's profits from such transactions as salary allowances and interest on capital. All allocations to a partner add to the partner's personal income. In the previous example, partners Amber, Brown, and Clay would be required to include $14,400, $59,000, and $24,600, respectively, on their personal tax returns.

ADMISSION OF A NEW PARTNER

When a new partner is admitted to the firm, a new partnership is formed. Several different procedures facilitate partnership admission.

Purchase of Retiring Partner's Interest

Sometimes a new partner is admitted by purchase of an existing partner's interest in the firm. A purchase agreement is made between the new partner and the old partner, not with the firm itself, although the old partners usually must give their consent. Upon payment to the existing partner, the new member assumes the rights and obligations of that share of the firm.

The only entry that the partnership must make is to close the old capital account and open a new capital account with the same balance. For example, Able sells his partnership interest to Baker on March 2 for $120,000. Able's capital account balance on the date of the purchase is $110,000. The journal entry to record this transaction is as follows:

Mar. 2	Able, capital	110,000	
	Baker, capital		110,000
	(to record transfer of ownership)		

Exactly the same entry would have been made whether Able had sold his interest to Baker for $120 or for $1,200,000.

Investment into Partnership

Situations often arise when a new partner is admitted to a firm but no existing partner retires. In such a case, the original partners would decide among themselves the duties and responsibilities of the new partner, the capital to be contributed, and the new partner's share of future profits. Since the existing owners are selling an interest in the partnership to the new partner, they must reduce their own investments or increase the total owners' equity.

Assume Xavier joins an existing partnership on April 1 by contributing $80,000 for a ten percent share of the profits. The journal entry to record the receipt of Xavier's investment would be the following:

Apr. 1	Cash	80,000	
	Xavier, capital		80,000
	(to record initial investment of new partner)		

This entry would increase the total owners' equity available for the firm's use.

Bonus Paid to Existing Partners

A person might want to be admitted to a very profitable partnership. The existing owners might believe that the new partner is going to benefit from the extra earning capacity of the firm and that they should be rewarded for having built up the business. In such a case, the new partner would be asked to invest a fair amount for capital and some additional amount as a bonus to the existing partners. The bonus portion would be divided by the existing partners in their former profit-sharing ratio.

Assume Arrow, Batt, and Cane, sharing profits in the ratio of 3:2:1, respectively, admit Davit into the partnership on June 1. Davit is required to invest $100,000 as a share of the firm's capital and $60,000 as a bonus to the old partners. Davit will then receive ten percent of the profits, with the remainder being shared by Arrow, Batt, and Cane in their previous profit-sharing ratio. The bonus is shared by the old partners in their old profit ratio of 3:2:1. After Davit's admission, the new profit-sharing ratio is 9:6:3:2 for Arrow, Batt, Cane, and Davit, respectively. The following journal entry is required to record the capital contribution and admission of Davit:

June 1	Cash	160,000	
	Davit, capital (initial investment)		100,000
	Arrow, capital (share of bonus)		30,000
	Batt, capital (share of bonus)		20,000
	Cane, capital (share of bonus)		10,000
	(to record initial investment of capital and bonus paid to existing partners)		

Bonus Paid to New Partner

If the new partner commands a unique talent needed by the firm, his or her admission can be crucial to the continued profitability or even the very survival of a partnership. The prospective new partner would then have a strong bargaining position. In addition to relinquishing a sizable share of future profits, the existing partners might be compelled to provide a bonus, reducing the amount of cash that the new partner must invest in the business to obtain an ownership share.

For example, Xero and Young are partners sharing profits and losses in the ratio of 60:40. Zurgen is admitted to the partnership on May 2, and the partners agree that the new profit-sharing ratio will be 48:32:20. Although the investment required for Zurgen's 20 percent interest in the partnership is $100,000, the existing partners are willing to provide $60,000 of the $100,000 as a bonus to entice Zurgen to join the firm. Therefore, Zurgen is required to invest only $40,000 in cash to become a 20 percent partner. The following journal entries regarding the admission of Zurgen to the partnership would reflect the arrangement:

May 2	Cash	40,000	
	Zurgen, capital		40,000
	(to record initial investment by new partner)		
May 2	Xero, capital	36,000	
	Young, capital	24,000	
	Zurgen, capital		60,000
	(to record bonus provided by existing partners)		

RETIREMENT OF A PARTNER

When a partner retires or resigns, the existing partnership essentially is dissolved. To continue the firm's business, the remaining members can form a new partnership among themselves or can admit new partners. In any case, the retiring owner must be paid his or her proportionate share of the partnership's assets.

As you know, the real value of a firm's net assets is usually not the same as the book value of the net assets. Recall that the book value of net assets equals owners' equity. Since a retiring partner has a claim on the real value of his or her share of the firm's net assets, the retiring partner usually receives a cash payment different from his or her capital balance.

Since the retirement of a partner terminates the old partnership and requires the formation of a new one if the business is to continue, revaluation of the assets and liabilities of the firm to reflect its fair market value as of the date of formation of the new firm is appropriate. Further, revaluation is required to maintain the integrity of the relationship between net assets and owners' equity before and after payment to the retiring partner. The current market value of the net assets may or may not be formally recognized in the accounts. Both variations are discussed in the following paragraphs.

Assets Adjusted to Market Values

If the net assets are adjusted to current values, the partners share the gain or loss from revaluation according to their profit-sharing ratio. Once this revision is made, the retiring partner is given assets equal to the amount of his or her capital account balance. In this way, the retiree receives a due share of any change in the value of assets over time.

For example, Prinz, Queen, and Riegal share profits and losses in the ratio of 50:30:20 and have capital account balances on December 31, 1988, of $80,000, $120,000, and $140,000, respectively. Riegal retires on December 31, 1988, and the assets recorded on the books at $500,000 are adjusted upward to $550,000 to reflect their current market values. The liabilities of $160,000 are expected to be paid in full and need not be adjusted; therefore, the total gain in net assets is $50,000. The following journal entries (summaries) on the partnership books relate to the retirement of Riegal:

Dec. 31	Miscellaneous assets (new value)	550,000	
	Miscellaneous assets (old value)		500,000
	Gain on revaluation of assets		50,000
	(to revalue assets at current market)		
Dec. 31	Gain on revaluation of assets	50,000	
	Prinz, capital		25,000
	Queen, capital		15,000
	Riegal, capital		10,000
	(to record allocation of revaluation gain to owners)		
Dec. 31	Riegal, capital ($140,000 + $10,000)	150,000	
	Cash		150,000
	(to record retirement withdrawal of Riegal)		

Note that Riegal's capital is increased by his share of the revaluation gain before the computation and payment of his capital interest for retirement. After the distribution on December 31, the statement of financial position would appear as follows:

Prinz-Queen
Statement of Financial Position
December 31, 1988

Miscellaneous assets ($550,000 − $150,000)	$400,000	Miscellaneous liabilities	$160,000
		Capital accounts	
		Prinz ($80,000 + $25,000)	105,000
		Queen ($120,000 + $15,000)	135,000
Total assets	$400,000	Total liabilities and capital	$400,000

Assets Not Adjusted to Market Value

Although practitioners generally agree that partnership assets should be revalued before computing the amount a retiring partner can withdraw, accounting practice usually dictates the use of original historical cost valuations for the remaining firm. The revaluation of assets necessary to give the retiree fair treatment is not formally recorded, and the book value of the firm's net assets is not altered. The purpose of the asset revaluation is to compute, not record, each partner's share of any profit or loss due to changing values. The retiring partner's capital is adjusted by a transfer from nonretiring partners' capital accounts.

Let's return to the preceding example and assume that Prinz and Queen expect to share profits and losses equally following Riegal's retirement. If historical book value of net assets is to be maintained, capital would be transferred equally from Prinz and Queen to Riegal in order to equate Riegal's capital balance with the real value of his proportionate share of the net assets, $150,000.

Because Riegal's share of the gain on revaluation was $10,000 in the previous case, his capital account should be increased by $10,000. Since only Prinz and Queen will now share the benefit of the increase in asset values, they are essentially buying Riegal's right to a share in the increased asset values. After the $10,000 increase, Riegal's capital account stands at $150,000—the same as in the previous case—and this is the amount Riegal will withdraw. The capital transfer and subsequent distribution of assets to Riegal would be recorded by the following entries:

Dec. 31	Prinz, capital	5,000	
	Queen, capital	5,000	
	Riegal, capital		10,000
	(to record provision for revaluation gain belonging to Riegal)		
Dec. 31	Riegal, capital ($140,000 + $10,000)	150,000	
	Cash		150,000
	(to record withdrawal due to Riegal's retirement)		

Observe that the only difference between the two procedures is that the first method revalues the assets and records them at their new values while the second method revalues the assets but continues to carry them at the old value, or cost.

A partnership is automatically dissolved upon the death of a partner, and the heirs of the deceased partner's estate are reimbursed in the same way as a retiring partner. The journal entries to record a partnership dissolution due to death of a partner are the same as those for retirement.

LIQUIDATION OF THE PARTNERSHIP BUSINESS

Even though a partnership is dissolved when a partner dies or retires, the partnership business usually continues with the remaining or new partners. The assets and liabilities, though they can be revalued, are not sold.

Sometimes the partnership comes to an end either because the business for which it was formed is over or the remaining partners no longer wish to operate the business. In such cases, the partnership business could be sold in its entirety to any interested buyer or its assets and liabilities could be disposed of piecemeal. In either instance, all of the assets are converted into cash, the liabilities are satisfied, and the remaining cash (if any) is distributed to the owners, a process called **liquidation.** Any gain or loss on sale of assets is divided among the partners in their profit-sharing ratio before each partner is paid his or her share of the remaining partnership assets.

LIQUIDATION
A process whereby all assets are converted into cash, liabilities are satisfied, and remaining cash is distributed to the owners.

Assume that the partnership of Angle, Bent, and Cuela has the following statement of financial position on December 31, 1986, just before liquidation, and that Angle, Bent, and Cuela share profits and losses in the ratio of 40:20:40.

Angle, Bent, Cuela
Statement of Financial Position
December 31, 1986

Assets			**Liabilities and Owners' Equity**		
Cash		$ 30,000	Accounts payable		$ 50,000
Accounts receivable		140,000	Wages payable, etc.		5,000
Equipment	$70,000		Capital		
Less: Accumulated			Angle	95,000	
depreciation	35,000	35,000	Bent	45,000	
			Cuela	10,000	150,000
Total assets		$205,000	Total liabilities and owners' equity		$205,000

The business is liquidated on December 31, 1986. The accounts receivable and equipment are sold for $115,000 and $10,000 in cash, respectively; and the liabilities are paid in full. The firm also learns that Cuela had filed for bankruptcy a few days earlier. The journal entries to record the sale of the assets and payment of the liabilities are as follows:

Dec. 31	Cash ($115,000 + $10,000)	125,000	
	Accumulated depreciation	35,000	
	Loss on sale of assets	50,000	
	Accounts receivable		140,000
	Equipment		70,000
	(to record sale of assets)		
Dec. 31	Accounts payable	50,000	
	Wages payable	5,000	
	Cash		55,000
	(to record settlement of liabilities)		

After sale of assets and payment of liabilities, the loss on sale of assets must be allocated to the partners according to their profit-sharing ratio. This allocation would be recorded as follows:

Dec. 31	Angle, capital (40%)	20,000	
	Bent, capital (20%)	10,000	
	Cuela, capital (40%)	20,000	
	Loss on sale of assets		50,000
	(to allocate liquidation loss of owners)		

After the losses are recorded in each partner's capital account, the account balances are as follows:

Angle, Capital

Loss	20,000	Beg. bal.	95,000
		End. bal.	75,000

Bent, Capital

Loss	10,000	Beg. bal.	45,000
		End. bal.	35,000

Cuela, Capital

Loss	20,000	Beg. bal.	10,000
End. bal.	10,000		

The statement of financial position following sale of the assets, payment of the liabilities, and allocation of the loss is as follows:

Angle, Bent, Cuela
Statement of Financial Position
December 31, 1986

Assets		**Liabilities and Owners' Equity**		
Cash	$100,000	Capital		
		Angle	75,000	
		Bent	35,000	
		Cuela	(10,000)	100,000
Total assets	$100,000	Total liabilities and owners' equity		$100,000

If all the partners' capital accounts are positive, the firm could be dissolved by distribution of cash to the partners equal to their account balances. Since Cuela's capital account has a debit (negative) balance of $10,000, Cuela owes the partnership $10,000. However, since she is bankrupt, Cuela is unable to pay anything. In this case, the other partners must bear the loss of $10,000 in line with their 40:20 profit-sharing ratio. The journal entry to recognize the loss generated by Cuela's inability to make the required payment is as follows:

Dec. 31	Angle, capital	6,667	
	Bent, capital	3,333	
	Cuela, capital		10,000
	(to record transfer of loss to solvent partners)		

After this journal entry, Angle's capital account equals $68,333 and Bent's equals $31,667. The cash is distributed to Angle and Bent, and a final journal entry is made to complete the liquidation process:

Dec. 31	Angle, capital	68,333	
	Bent, capital	31,667	
	Cash		100,000
	(to liquidate partnership business)		

This chapter's preoccupation with owners' equity accounts for a partnership demonstrates the primary difference between accounting for a partnership and other forms of business organization. Most other transactions are recorded the same as those of a corporation or a proprietorship.

FOR REVIEW

DEMONSTRATION PROBLEM

Janning and Deen decide to form a partnership that will operate a food concession at the World's Fair. The partnership is formed on January 1, 1986, when Janning contributes $5,000 cash and equipment worth $7,000 and Deen turns over $20,000 cash to the firm. The partners agree to share profits and losses in a 1:2 ratio for Janning and Deen, respectively.

Interest of 10% is paid on partner loans, but no interest is paid on capital. Both partners are to be active in daily operations, and each agrees to a salary of $12,000, payable in monthly allotments of $2,000 from April through September.

Before the fair opens in April, the partners have the following transactions:

January 15	Purchase a van for $7,500 cash.
February 18	Lease fair space for six months. A security deposit of $300 is made, to be returned in October. The rental payments are $400 a month payable on the 5th.
February 28	Pay workers who installed equipment, $750, charged to "Assorted Expenses."
March 1	Janning's sister, Berry, is admitted to the partnership. Janning and Deen agree to give her a 20% interest in capital and profits in return for her secret recipe for sugared pretzels. Berry will receive no salary. The new profit and loss ratio is 4:8:3.
March 30	Deen lends the firm $5,000 on a note.
April 1– September 30	The fair is open. The partnership accumulates sales revenue of $113,500 and miscellaneous expenses (excluding those before April) of $43,000. All cash has passed hands. The only noncash expense is depreciation totaling $3,500. Withdrawals by Janning total $13,000; by Deen, $12,000; and by Berry, $1,500.
September 30	The $300 deposit on fair space is returned, and Deen's loan is repaid. (The interest expense is included in the $43,000 of expenses entered above.)
October 1	All equipment is removed and sold. Net proceeds total $4,200. The van is sold for $6,800.
October 4	The partnership dissolves. All profits are distributed. Before closing, the drawing accounts have the following balances: Janning, $13,000 Deen, $12,000 Berry, $1,500

How will the partnership record the preceding events? (Ignore tax considerations.) How much cash will each receive on October 4 at dissolution?

Demonstration Problem Solution

The transactions will be recorded in the journal as follows:

1986			
Jan. 1	Cash	25,000	
	Equipment	7,000	
	Janning, capital		12,000
	Deen, capital		20,000
	(to show initial investments)		
Jan. 15	Van	7,500	
	Cash		7,500
	(to record purchase of van)		
Feb. 18	Deposits	300	
	Cash		300
	(to record deposit made on fair space leased)		
Feb. 28	Assorted expenses	750	
	Cash		750
	(to record payment for installation of equipment)		
Mar. 1	Janning, capital	2,133	
	Deen, capital	4,267	
	Berry, capital ($32,000 × .20)		6,400
	(to record entrance of new partner)		
Mar. 30	Cash	5,000	
	Note payable		5,000
	(to record loan from Deen)		
Apr. 1–Sept. 30	Assorted expenses	43,000	
	Cash	74,000	
	Accumulated depreciation		3,500
	Sales		113,500
	(to record sales/expenses during fair)		
Apr. 1–Sept. 30	Janning, drawing	13,000	
	Deen, drawing	12,000	
	Berry, drawing	1,500	
	Cash		26,500
	(to record distribution to partners)		
Sept. 30	Cash	300	
	Deposit		300
	(to record receipt of security deposit repayment)		
Sept. 30	Note payable	5,000	
	Cash		5,000
	(to record repayment of loan from Deen)		
Oct. 1	Cash ($4,200 + $6,800)	11,000	
	Accumulated depreciation	3,500	
	Equipment		7,000
	Van		7,500
	(to record proceeds from sale of assets)		
Oct. 4	Sales	113,500	
	Expenses		43,750
	Income summary		69,750
	(to close revenue and expense accounts)		

Date	Account	Debit	Credit
Oct. 4	Income summary	69,750	
	Janning, capital		24,133
	Deen, capital		36,517
	Berry, capital		9,100
	(to allocate profits to owners (see earnings allocation table))		
Oct. 4	Janning, capital	13,000	
	Deen, capital	12,000	
	Berry, capital	1,500	
	Janning, drawing		13,000
	Deen, drawing		12,000
	Berry, drawing		1,500
	(to close drawing accounts)		
Oct. 4	Janning, capital	21,000	
	Deen, capital	40,250	
	Berry, capital	14,000	
	Cash		75,250
	(to dissolve the firm by distributing cash to partners (see T-accounts))		

Earnings Allocation

Partner	Partner Salary	Interest On Loan	Allocation of Remaining Earnings[b]	Total Allocations
Janning	$12,000	0	$12,133	$24,133
Deen	12,000	$250[a]	24,267	36,517
Berry	0	0	9,100	9,100
Totals	$24,000	$250	$45,500	$69,750

[a] $5,000 × 10% × ½ year

[b] Available earnings = $69,750 − ($24,000 + $250) = $45,500; split 4:8:3 to Janning, Deen, and Berry.

Cash

Date	Debit	Date	Credit
1/1	25,000	1/15	7,500
3/30	5,000	2/18	300
4/1–9/30	74,000	2/28	750
9/30	300	4/1–9/30	26,500
10/1	11,000	9/30	5,000
10/4	75,250		
		10/4	75,250

Janning, Capital

Date	Debit	Date	Credit
3/1	2,133	1/1	12,000
10/4	13,000	10/4	24,133
		10/4	21,000
10/4	21,000		

Deen, Capital

Date	Debit	Date	Credit
3/1	4,267	1/1	20,000
10/4	12,000	10/4	36,517
		10/4	40,250
10/4	40,250		

Berry, Capital

Date	Debit	Date	Credit
10/4	1,500	3/1	6,400
		10/4	9,100
		10/4	14,000
10/4	14,000		

SUMMARY

- A partnership's unique features include voluntary association, limited life, mutual agency, unlimited liability, ease of formation and operation, and ownership of property and profits.
- A partnership contract defines the duties and responsibilities of each partner, the method of sharing profits and losses, investment in the firm, drawing rights, insurance on the lives of the partners, the accounting year, and provisions for audit and arbitration of disputes.
- A partnership is formed by partners investing cash or other assets in the partnership business. If a noncash asset is brought into the business, the partner is credited with its fair market value.
- Profits and losses of a partnership can be shared in many ways—as salary to a partner, interest on partners' capital accounts, interest on a partner's loan, or simply in a predetermined profit-sharing ratio.
- A partner can purchase an old partner's interest, or equity, for admittance into the partnership. Often a new partner will get (or give) a bonus depending on his or her value to the partnership.
- A partnership can be dissolved on the death or retirement of a partner. In such a case, the partnership assets would have to be revalued at fair market values, and the retiring or deceased partner's share would be computed on the basis of the revalued assets.
- A partnership business can be liquidated, in which case the assets and liabilities would be converted into cash and shared according to the provisions of the partnership agreement.

QUESTIONS

12-1. What are the main features of a partnership?

12-2. Why is a partnership agreement important? What kind of information is normally contained in such an agreement?

12-3. What are some ways in which partners can share the profits and losses?

12-4. Why would a partnership be willing to pay an incoming partner a bonus to join?

12-5. Why are insurance policies taken out by the partnership on the lives of the partners? Who normally is named the beneficiary of such a policy? How would the proceeds from the policy be used?

12-6. What is the principal area of difference in accounting for a partnership versus accounting for a corporation?

12-7. Describe the process of taxing partnership profits.

12-8. What are some considerations when deciding how to account for revaluation profit or loss?

12-9. What are the disadvantages of belonging to a partnership?

12-10. Contrast the roles of an active partner and a silent partner.

EXERCISES

12-E1. Brummel and Beatty, who have both previously been in business, decide to form a partnership on November 4. Brummel contributes $5,000 cash and a delivery van with a book value of $1,500 and a fair market value of $1,800, accounts receivable worth $250, and a note payable of $1,000. Beatty's additions to the partnership are $10,000 in cash, $5,000 of equipment, and $500 of accounts payable. What journal entry is necessary on the partnership books?

12-E2. Green, Kelley, and Jade own a partnership that had net earnings of $118,000 this year. Their profit-sharing ratio is 40:30:30, respectively. Prepare journal entries necessary to close the revenue and expense summary on December 31, the end of their fiscal year.

12-E3. Assume from 12-E2 that Jade actively manages the firm, for which the partnership agrees to pay him a $20,000 annual salary. What would be the allocation of profit?

12-E4. Samuels decides to retire on May 1. Blessing, his son-in-law, has secured approval from the remaining partners to buy Samuels' share for $90,000. On the retirement date, Samuels' capital account balance is $150,000. What is the appropriate journal entry?

12-E5. Estrada and Lerma feel that their partnership would be much more profitable with the addition of McHale as a partner. Currently, profits are split 50:50. McHale agrees to join when offered a bonus of $20,000 plus a share of the profits; he will have an investment of $50,000. The present capital account balances are Estrada, $75,000, and Lerma, $85,000. What is the journal entry to add McHale on July 24?

12-E6. If assets recorded on the books at $10,000 have a market value of $12,500 and liabilities recorded at $5,000 will be paid in full, what is the revaluation profit or loss?

12-E7. A partnership, Jack and Jake's Place, sustains a loss in 1986 of $8,200. Jack and Jake share profits and losses 70:30. How will the loss be allocated if capital earns 7% interest and the appropriate balances are $10,000 and $4,000 for Jack and Jake? What would be the consequences for Jack if Jake is bankrupt at this time?

PROBLEM SET A

12-A1. Partnership Formation. Waters and Meadows form a partnership on January 1, 1986, and agree to share profits and losses 60:40. Interest is to be paid on capital amounts as of January 1 at 11% annually. Capital contributions on January 1 consist of the following:

Waters		Meadows	
Cash	$10,000	Cash	$45,000
Inventory	5,000	Accounts receivable	200
Accounts receivable	1,000	Equipment	30,000
Building	80,000	Accounts payable	750
Note payable	1,500		

Required

a. Prepare the journal entry on January 1, 1986, to form the firm.
b. Prepare a classified statement of financial position as of January 1, 1986, for Waters-Meadows Company.

12-A2. Allocation of Net Earnings. The partners of Luminous Illustrators—Ray, Bright, and Drew—share earnings in the ratio of 25:35:40, respectively. Bright and Drew earn salaries of $25,000 each year; interest is paid on beginning capital at 7%. Capital account balances on January 1, 1986, were Ray, $150,000; Bright, $90,000; and Drew, $100,000. During the year of 1986, no new capital investment was made. On December 31, the total year's revenues totaled $340,000; expenses summed to $220,000. Drawing accounts had balances of Ray, $20,000; Bright, $22,500; and Drew, $23,100.

Required

a. Prepare a schedule allocating net earnings to the partners.
b. Journalize the allotments; make necessary closing entries. (Expenses and revenues have already been closed to the summary account.)
c. What is the balance of each capital account as of December 31, 1986?

12-A3. Bonus to New Partner. The partnership of Allen and Joseph is very interested in having Thomas join it. Both partners feel that Thomas has accounting skills previously lacking in their operation. Thomas is being wooed by several companies. Allen and Joseph thus agree to pay Thomas a bonus of $75,000 to join. Thomas will add to her investment in the firm an additional $75,000 ($35,000 cash and $40,000 of securities). Allen and Joseph have had an earnings ratio of 55:45; the new ratio will give Allen 40%, Joseph 30%, and Thomas 30%.

Required

a. Prepare the journal entries for May 1 when Thomas joins the company.
b. If allocable net earnings are $90,000 for the fiscal year, of which 60% was earned after May 1, how much would each partner receive?

12-A4. Termination of a Partnership Interest. Woo, Kim, and Rashti have been partners of Oriental Imports sharing earnings in the ratio of 35:30:35. Kim has decided to retire from the business at the close of the 1987 fiscal year. On that date, November 30, the books reveal the following balances: Cash, $205,000; Inventory, $100,000; Furniture and Fixtures, $10,000; Showroom, $90,000; Accounts Payable, $15,000; Note Payable, $208,000; Woo, capital, $57,000; Kim, capital, $75,000; and Rashti, capital, $50,000. Appraisals show that the current value of inventory is $125,000; of the furniture and fixtures, $12,000; and of the showroom, $175,000. Woo and Rashti plan to continue the business and will share profits and losses 50:50. The assets are to be maintained at book value.

Required

a. Compute the profit or loss from revaluation.
b. Prepare the journal entries necessary to retire Kim.
c. Prepare a statement of financial position as of December 1.

12-A5. Owners' Equity Relationships. Selected accounts for the partnership firm of McAllister and Petersen are as follows:

McAllister, Capital

		Jan. 1	Bal. 30,000
Dec. 31	7,000		D
		Dec. 31	Bal. I

Petersen, Capital

		Jan. 1	Bal. 50,000
Dec. 31	20,000		E
			J

McAllister, Drawing

XXXXXX	
XXXXXX	
F	G

Petersen, Drawing

XXXXXX	
XXXXXX	
20,000	H

Income Summary

B	A
	C

Revenues				Expenses		
		XXXXXX			XXXXXX	
		XXXXXX			XXXXXX	
		XXXXXX			XXXXXX	
Z	Dec. 31 Bal.	240,000		Dec. 31 Bal.	95,000	XXXXXX

The partners share profits and losses 50:50. Petersen receives an annual salary allowance of $20,000; McAllister withdraws at will with Petersen's consent. Interest is allowed on capital at the start of the year at the rate of 10%. No other payments are authorized in the partnership agreement.

Required

Indicate the missing amounts and a probable reason for each entry. (Note: X's represent amounts not pertinent to your computations.) Example: Z = $240,000—entry to close revenues at end of year.

12-A6. Allocating Earnings with Complications. The Market partnership has four partners, Evans, Pigge, McFee, and Brune, who share profits and losses equally. Partners receive 8% interest on capital and 10% interest on loans. Interest is computed and credited on January 1 and July 1 each year, and the computation is based on beginning balances for that six-month period. Earnings, except for the interest amounts, and withdrawals are not entered in the capital accounts until December 31 each year.

A new partner, Phillips, joins the firm on July 1. He receives a 20% interest in capital and profits in return for a building valued at $80,000.

Partnership earnings for the year total $300,000 before allocating any interest or profits. ($120,000 had been earned before July 1.) Capital balances on January 1 and drawing balances on December 31 are as follows:

	Capital, January 1	Drawing, December 31
Evans	$ 60,000	$11,000
Pigge	115,000	22,000
McFee	85,000	18,000
Brune	140,000	29,500
Phillips	0	10,000

The firm owes Evans $100,000. The debt has been outstanding all year. No new assets have been invested by any partners except Phillips.

Required

a. How should earnings be allocated?
b. Show T-accounts for capital for this year as they would appear after closing drawing accounts and allocating earnings.

12-A7. Alternative Allocation Plans. Valerie Gross and Susan Hale have decided to form a partnership. By agreement, Gross will invest $30,000 and Hale, $45,000. Gross will devote full time to the business, and Hale will devote half time. The partners are considering several plans of allocation:

1. Equal division.
2. In the ratio of the initial investment.
3. In the ratio of time devoted to the business.
4. Salaries of $20,000 to Gross, $10,000 to Hale, and the remainder divided equally.

Required

Determine the allocation of net income under each alternative plan if net income is:
a. $45,000
b. $33,000

12-A8. Entering Partner. Jensen and Hanks are in a partnership and share profit or loss in a 6:4 ratio. They are considering admitting Dale as a new partner. The following is a listing of the partnership account balances before such admission:

Cash	$ 50,000
Other assets	120,000
Liabilities	50,000
Jensen, capital	80,000
Hanks, capital	40,000

Required

a. Determine the amount that Dale should contribute to acquire a one-fifth interest.
b. If, by agreement, Dale contributes $20,000 for that one-fifth interest, determine the capital account balances after Dale's admission.

PROBLEM SET B

12-B1. Partnership Formation. Rebecca Ryatt has run her sole proprietorship, Crystal Cranny, for many years. Her twins, Rachel and Rya, have just finished college, and the three of them have exciting plans for Crystal Cranny. The first step is to re-form the business as a partnership. Rebecca plans to maintain half interest, with the twins sharing the other half equally. Each twin will invest $10,000, which is available in a trust fund. Rebecca will furnish the remaining amount of the twins' interest, a total of $30,000, from her own account as a graduation gift. The business is worth $80,000 on the date of forming the partnership, July 1.

Required

Prepare journal entries to form the partnership.

12-B2. Allocation of New Earnings. Cain, Baker, and Coe form a partnership on January 1. They initially invest $100,000, $220,000, and $250,000, respectively. By agreement, Cain will receive an annual salary of $40,000. Baker and Coe will receive $20,000 each. Additionally, the partners are to receive 10% interest on their respective capital balances at the start of the year. Any income remaining after payment of salaries and interest will be divided equally.

The partnership net income for the year is $170,000. On June 1, Cain invests an additional $30,000 in the partnership. Coe withdraws $50,000 from the partnership on October 1.

Required

a. Determine how the net income will be allocated among the three partners.
b. Determine each partner's capital balance at year-end.

12-B3. Bonus to New Partner. The partnership of Bennett and Brennan wants to lure Johnson, a successful salesman, away from a competing firm. It has submitted an offer to Johnson whereby Johnson can buy a 20% interest in the partnership and receive a $20,000 bonus for entering. Bennett and Brennan's capital balances before Johnson's admission are $100,000 and $140,000, respectively. Bennett and Brennan share profits equally and will continue to do so *after* Johnson has paid his 20%.

Required

a. Prepare the necessary journal entries to admit Johnson.
b. Determine how a net income of $120,000 will be allocated.

12-B4. Termination of a Partnership Interest. Seraphic Sessions suffered an unfortunate loss when one of its active partners, Art Camlan, died unexpectedly on March 10. The owners had prepared for such an event by insuring each partner's life for $150,000. This fund is to be used to pay the Camlan estate administrators. On March 10, the firm's accounts showed assets totaling $300,000; liabilities amounting to $120,000; and owners' equity for Art Camlan, $60,000, Gwen Morgan, $80,000, and Merle Mila, $40,000. The partners had shared profits and losses in the ratio of 30:40:30, respectively. Assets are currently on the books at an amount $20,000 lower than actual value. Earnings of the firm net to $192,000 as of March 10.

Required

a. What journal entries are necessary on March 10?
b. How much money is due to be paid to the Camlan estate?
c. Is the firm carrying an adequate amount of life insurance?

12-B5. Owners' Equity Relationships. Following are T-accounts showing paid-in capital for Covenant and Company:

Lilly, Capital

Debit	Credit
	Jan. 1 Bal 40,000
D	E
	F

Lucky, Capital

Debit	Credit
	Jan. 1 Bal. 60,000
H	G
	Dec. 31 Bal. 65,000

Lilly, Drawing

Debit	Credit
Jan. 1 3,500	
Mar. 1 Z	
Sept. 1 5,000	
Dec. 31 Bal. 15,500	Dec. 31 XXXXX

Lucky, Drawing

Debit	Credit
Jan. 30 I	
May 1 12,000	
Sept. 1 7,000	
XXXXX	J

Revenues

Debit	Credit
	XXXXXX
	XXXXXX
	XXXXXX
XXXXXX	Dec. 31 Bal. 170,000

Expenses

Debit	Credit
XXXXXX	
XXXXXX	
XXXXXX	
Dec. 31 Bal. 105,000	XXXXXX

Income Summary

Debit	Credit
A	B
XXXXXX	C

Profits and losses of the firm are shared 40:60 by Lilly and Lucky. No other payments are authorized in the partners' agreement; withdrawals are made at will with mutual consent.

Required

Indicate the missing amounts and a probable reason for each entry. (Note: X's represent amounts not pertinent to your computations or that can be implied from other problem facts.) Example: Z = $7,000—Lilly withdrew assets from the firm.

12-B6. Allocating Earnings with Complications. The owners of Calaway Caterers—Matee, Kirk, and Taiya—have the following items listed in their partnership agreement:

1. Taiya will receive a $30,000 salary yearly.
2. Interest is paid on partners' loans at 10%.
3. Interest is paid on capital (beginning-of-the-year balances) at 7.5%.
4. Remaining profits and losses will be split 30:30:40 among Matee, Kirk, and Taiya, respectively.

The 1986 partnership earnings netted $325,000 before any payment to the partners. Selected account balances on December 31 are Cash, $20,000; Inventory, $35,800; Note Payable to Matee, $10,000, dated January 1, 1975; Note Payable to Kirk, $5,000, dated July 1, 1986; Capital: Matee, $60,000, Kirk, $65,000, and Taiya, $50,000; Drawing: Matee, $32,000, Kirk, $27,000, and Taiya, $28,000. The capital accounts have had no transactions throughout 1986.

Required

a. Prepare a schedule showing the allocation of Calaway Caterers' 1986 net earnings.
b. Journalize the necessary year-end entries.
c. What are the new capital account balances?

12-B7. Alternative Allocation Plans. Carol Tapp and Paul Cole agree to form a partnership. By agreement, Tapp will invest $80,000 and will devote full time to the business. Cole will invest $120,000 and will devote only one-fourth the time. Tapp and Cole are considering several plans for the allocation of income:

1. Equal division.
2. In the ratio of original investment.
3. In the ratio of time devoted to the business.
4. Interest of 10% on original investment and the remainder based on time devoted to the business.
5. Interest of 12% on original investment, salaries of $45,000 to Tapp and $20,000 to Cole, and the remainder divided equally.

Required

Determine the allocation of net income under each alternative plan if net income is:
a. $90,000
b. $200,000

12-B8. Entering Partner. The firm of Leto and Silvers has decided to admit Pohl into the partnership. Pohl is required to pay the partners a bonus of $25,500 for a 30% interest. Leto and Silvers, up to Pohl's arrival on September 1, shared profits and losses equally; this respective ratio will not change. Pohl, of course, must pay for his interest in the firm in addition to the bonus. Total capital will be $300,000 after Pohl contributes his $120,000 investment.

Required

a. Prepare the entries to admit Pohl.
b. If net yearly earnings are $96,000, how much will each partner receive?

CORPORATIONS 13

CHAPTER OBJECTIVES
After studying Chapter 13, you should understand the following:

1. The unique features of the corporate form of business.
2. The roles of the shareholders, the board of directors, and management in the corporation's affairs.
3. The characteristics of common and preferred stocks.
4. The terminology frequently used in reference to stock.
5. The meaning of treasury stock and how to account for it.

A corporation is a business association that is legally separate from its owners. This chapter presents the advantages and disadvantages of organizing a business in the corporate form and the alternative ways that a corporation can raise funds from its owners. It also presents the accounting treatment for the sale or exchange of capital stock in a corporation.

WHAT IS A CORPORATION?

CORPORATION
An artificial legal entity distinct from its owners and representatives.

A **corporation** is an artificial legal entity distinct from its owners and representatives. It can carry out, through its management, all of the same acts that a sole proprietor or a partner in a partnership can. Since a corporation is lifeless, it cannot be indicted for criminal activities as can partners or sole proprietors. Laws, such as the Foreign Corrupt Practices Act, prescribe fines and prison terms for a corporation's management personnel if certain unlawful practices are discovered.

CHARACTERISTICS OF A CORPORATION

Separate Legal Entity

Since a corporation is a separate legal entity, the corporation's authorized representatives, whether majority shareholders or professional managers, can conduct the company's business without fear of personal liability for noncriminal acts on behalf of the firm. If a corporation goes bankrupt, the owners are not in jeopardy of losing personal belongings—other than their investments in the firm—to pay the corporation's debts. This feature makes part ownership of a corporation very attractive to many persons looking for an investment who are unwilling to risk their personal assets.

SHAREHOLDER
Part owner or investor in a corporation.

A corporation is structured so that an unlimited number of contributors, called **shareholders,** can invest in the business as part owners. For example, Ford Motor Company has about 300,000 shareholders.

BOARD OF DIRECTORS
A body elected by the shareholders to strategically manage the company on their behalf.

Having the owners actively running the business becomes impractical when many part owners are involved. Thus, the shareholders elect a board of directors, who in turn employ professional managers to run the company. The **board of directors** is a body elected by the shareholders to strategically manage the company on their behalf.

Separation of Organization from Ownership

STOCK EXCHANGE
An organization where stocks are bought and sold.

Unlike a partnership, the ownership shares in many corporations are easily transferred from one owner to another. A shareholder who needs funds can sell his or her stock, often through a **stock exchange,** an organization that acts as a marketplace for many stocks. The selling shareholders do not need permission of the other owners to transfer their holdings, or shares, in the corporation to another.

Since a corporation is separate from its owners, the corporation has a potentially unlimited life. The death of a shareholder has no legal impact upon the corporation. This assurance of continuity allows a corporation to attract large amounts of capital.

Corporate Taxation

Under U.S. law, a corporation must pay income tax on its earnings as a separate entity. The tax is based on a progressive scale, which for 1985 is as follows:

Taxable Income	Rate
$25,000 and under	15%
over $25,000 but not over $50,000	18%
over $50,000 but not over $75,000	30%
over $75,000 but not over $100,000	40%
Over $100,000	46%

In addition to this corporate income tax, the individual shareholder must pay income taxes on the dividends received from the corporation. In effect, shareholders pay tax twice on the distributed earnings of the corporation, once collectively in the name of the corporation and again individually on the personal returns of the shareholders.

To relieve this double tax burden for the owners of very small corporations, a special tax treatment can be elected by some corporations under the S corporation regulations in the tax code. This tax election allows the firm to maintain the legal characteristics of a corporation, such as limited liability for the owners, but to be taxed like a partnership. That is, all corporate income is assigned to the owners for taxation; generally the S corporation does not pay any tax on its own behalf.

FORMATION OF A CORPORATION

When one or more persons of legal age decide to form a corporation to conduct business, they are required to declare their intention to the appropriate state government. The founders, or incorporators, must fulfill the state corporation law requirements. The incorporators then apply for a **corporate charter,** a document that serves to create the corporation and grants it the right to do business. Before a charter is issued, the incorporators must prepare articles of incorporation.

CORPORATE CHARTER
The document that serves to create the corporation and grants it the right to do business.

Articles of incorporation provide the legal framework for the operation of the corporation and usually include the following provisions:

ARTICLES OF INCORPORATION
The document that provides the legal framework for the operation of a corporation.

1. The name of the corporation and the location of its principal office.
2. The type of business and where branches, if any, are to be located.
3. The types of capital stock to be issued, the number of shares authorized to be issued, and the rights attendant to each class of capital stock.
4. Any limitations on the authority of the board of directors or the managers of the corporation.

MANAGEMENT OF A CORPORATION

Though the shareholders do not usually participate in the day-to-day management of the business, they are vitally concerned that the business is run in a professional manner. Therefore, the shareholders authorize their immediate spokespersons, the board of directors, to establish certain rules, referred to as **bylaws,** for the corporation.

BYLAWS
Rules established by the board of directors for operation of a corporation.

The overall managing of a corporation is typically carried out by the board of directors and the officers. Members of the board of directors are initially selected at a meeting called by the incorporators after the charter has been secured. In later years, the directors are elected at shareholders' meetings, called at least once a year to discuss and vote on matters of general interest.

Traditionally, a board of directors supplies part-time management to the corporation and protects the interests of the shareholders. The board of directors is responsible for making strategic policy decisions, authorizing dividend payments, appointing auditors, and completing important contractual agreements with third parties.

The board members are empowered to seek qualified persons to handle policy implementation and the day-to-day running of the business. Thus, the board generally appoints a president to head the corporation and gives him or her the power to hire assistants. The president and the vice presidents run the corporation and report to the board of directors.

SOURCES OF CORPORATE CAPITAL

A corporation can obtain funds for its operations either from shareholders or creditors. If the corporation seeks financing from the shareholders, it can obtain funds either directly through the issuance of stock or indirectly by retaining part of its past earnings. This chapter discusses transactions involving funds from the issuance of stock. Chapter 14 covers transactions dealing with retained earnings.

A corporation obtains financing directly from its owners by issuing shares of stock in exchange for cash. A share certificate is given to each investor to reflect the owner's interest in the corporation and to assign the rights accorded to holders of that particular type of stock.

Key Terms and Concepts

The following paragraphs will help you to become familiar with some key terms and concepts necessary to understand a discussion of various stock characteristics.

AUTHORIZED SHARES
The number of shares of each category of stock that a corporation can issue.

Authorized Shares. **Authorized shares** represent the number of shares of each category of stock that the corporation can issue. This number is found in the articles of incorporation filed with the state. Since quite a few formalities, including shareholders' approval, must precede an articles of incorporation amendment to increase the authorized capital, most corporations deliberately overestimate their initial capital needs.

ISSUED SHARES
Shares that have been issued at some time to the investing public.

Issued Shares. **Issued shares** are those that have been issued at some time to the investing public. They include shares traded for cash or in exchange for other assets or services received.

OUTSTANDING SHARES
The amount of stock that actually is in the hands of investors at a particular moment and on which a dividend could be paid.

Outstanding Shares. **Outstanding shares** indicate the amount of stock that actually is in the hands of investors at a particular moment and on which a dividend could be paid. Outstanding shares can be different from issued shares, since stock that was once issued might no longer be outstanding. Sometimes a company will repurchase and hold its own stock (called treasury stock). Such holdings are discussed more fully later in the chapter.

Book Value. The book value of a corporation is equal to the corporation's net assets (total assets minus total liabilities). The book value per share of a firm having only one class of stock can be easily computed by dividing the number of shares of stock outstanding into the net assets.

Market Value. The **market value per share** of stock is the price at which the sale of such shares is occurring at the stock exchange. Prospective purchasers can have different perceptions regarding the value of a share. Information such as the annual dividend per share, the value of assets at both book and market, the type of management, and future earnings potential usually is included in the shares' evaluations and is reflected in the price paid.

MARKET VALUE PER SHARE
The price at which the sale of a share of stock is occurring at the stock exchange.

Par Value. **Par value per share** represents an artificial amount often required by the laws of the state of incorporation. Note that par value is not the same as book value or market value. For example, the annual report of Kellogg Company for the year ending December 31, 1984, shows the par value of common stock at $.50, the book value at $7.91, and the market value fluctuating between $34.75 and $42.75 during the last quarter.

PAR VALUE PER SHARE
An artificial amount per share required by the laws of the state of incorporation.

Requiring a par value for stock arises from the belief that shareholders should contribute some minimal amount to protect the interests of the creditors. Most states therefore prohibit a corporation from issuing its stock for less than par value. Most corporations are able to issue stock at a price higher than the par value, which indicates that investors believe the company's past prosperity will continue. For instance, IBM Corporation's common stock has a par value of $1.25 per share, but the market value is usually above $100 per share. If IBM wishes to issue more shares of common stock, its management would be foolish not to ask for more than par value. Thus, par value is an artificial and arbitrary figure, selected by the issuing corporation to comply with state law, and is rarely pertinent to purchasers of stock.

No Par Stock. Stock issued without an assigned par value is known as **no par stock.** No par stock originated when the concept of par value created more problems than it solved. Few readers of financial statements understood the meaning of par value and were confused as to its significance relative to market and book values.

NO PAR STOCK
Stock issued without an assigned par value.

When stock does not have a par value, the board of directors usually assigns a stated value to the stock. The **stated value** is an arbitrary assignment of value that has no significance in terms of shareholder liability and should not be considered equivalent to par value in that regard. Stated value does serve to limit the amount that can be distributed as dividends.

STATED VALUE
An arbitrary assignment of value that has no significance in terms of shareholder liability and serves only to limit the amount that can be distributed as dividends.

Issuance of Capital Stock

Issuance for Cash. Stock can be issued either for cash, for other assets, or on a subscription basis. When stock is issued for cash, both the cash and stock accounts are increased. For example, assume that Jensen Corporation issues 1,000 shares of $100 par value common stock for $100 per share. The journal entry to record this is as follows:

Cash	100,000	
Common stock		100,000
(to record issue of common stock at par)		

Stock issued for an amount equal to its par value is said to sell at par. However, a corporation often finds that because of its overall profitability and financial strength investors value its common stock at a price above par value. The corporation, of course, will issue the stock at the highest price the market will bear. If Jensen Corporation issues the same 1,000 shares of common stock at $175 each, the corporation would make the following entry:

Cash	175,000	
Common stock		100,000
Paid-in capital in excess of par, common stock		75,000
(to record issue of common stock at $175 per share)		

The account—Paid-in Capital in Excess of Par—is a part of shareholders' equity. Recall that paid-in capital is a classification that includes all assets received by the firm in exchange for stock. Paid-in Capital in Excess of Par, however, is an account that shows the amount by which assets received from investors have exceeded the par value of the stock issued.

If the Jensen Corporation's common stock has neither a par value nor a stated value, no paid-in capital in excess of par would be recorded. The journal entry to record the issue of the stock in this case is the following:

Cash	175,000	
Common stock, no par value		175,000
(to record sale of no par stock for $175 per share)		

If, on the other hand, the Jensen Corporation's common no par stock has a stated value of $65 per share and the 1,000 shares are issued for $175 per share, the appropriate journal entry would be as follows:

Cash	175,000	
Paid-in capital in excess of stated value, common stock		110,000
Common stock		65,000
(to record issuance of $65 stated value stock for $175 per share)		

Note that stated value is treated exactly like par value in the accounting process.

Issued on a Subscription Basis. Sometimes stock is issued on a subscription basis, particularly when it is offered to employees through an employee stock participation plan or when small, closely-held corporations publicly offer stock. Under the subscription method of stock issuance, full cash price is received through installment payments.

To illustrate, suppose that Andrews Corporation offers 1,000 shares of $100 par value common stock to selected employees for $135 each. The employees who accept the offer are expected to pay $60 on February 1 and the balance by September 30. When Andrews receives the subscriptions and partial payments on February 1, it makes the following entries:

Feb. 1	Subscriptions receivable	135,000	
	Common stock subscribed		100,000
	Paid-in capital in excess of par, common stock		35,000
	(to record common stock subscriptions at $135 per share)		
Feb. 1	Cash	60,000	
	Subscriptions receivable		60,000
	(to record initial payment on subscribed stock)		

If a statement of financial position is prepared on February 2, the paid-in capital section of shareholders' equity would show Common Stock Subscribed—$100,000 and Paid-in Capital in Excess of Par, Common Stock—$35,000 below the caption for any fully issued and outstanding stock. The Subscriptions Receivable account balance of $75,000 ($135,000 − $60,000) is a current asset. Most states give the holders of capital stock subscriptions the same rights that accrue to holders of fully paid shares of the same class of stock.

On September 30, Andrews Corporation receives the $75,000 due from the employees and issues the stock certificates. The following journal entries are required on September 30 to record the collection of cash and issuance of stocks:

Sept. 30	Cash	75,000	
	Subscriptions receivable		75,000
	(to record receipt of cash from stock subscriptions)		
Sept. 30	Common stock subscribed	100,000	
	Common stock		100,000
	(to record issuance of stock certificates)		

The final position of Andrews Corporation after the cash collection on September 30 is the same as if the corporation had issued the stock for $135,000 cash on February 1.

Sometimes, after making the initial payment, a prospective shareholder is unable to pay the balance. In such a case, the corporation can either issue the number of shares represented by the original cash payment or return the initial payment, less a fee for incidental expenses, to the investor. The choice is usually determined by the laws of the state in which the corporation is organized. Occasionally the subscriber is forced to forfeit the down payment. Such forfeitures would be recorded as an addition to paid-in capital from subscription forfeiture.

Exchange of Capital Stock for Assets or Services Rendered. Usually the incorporators incur organizational costs in setting up the corporation and are often reimbursed for their expenses with stock rather than cash. Sometimes a corporation will purchase expensive machinery and arrange to pay the seller with common stock rather than cash. In these and similar cases, the transaction should be valued at the fair market value of either the asset acquired or the stock issued, whichever is more clearly determinable.

Suppose that Burns Corporation wants to acquire a machine with a list price of $145,000 and the seller agrees to accept 1,000 shares of Burns' $100 par value common stock in exchange for the machine. If no readily available market price for the stock exists, the machine's list price would serve as the basis for recording the transaction. The seller must believe that the 1,000 shares of common stock are worth at least $145,000, because he or she would not give up a machine valued at $145,000 for common stock worth less. Burns would therefore record the issuance of the stock in exchange for the machine as follows:

Machinery	145,000	
Common stock		100,000
Paid-in capital in excess of par, common stock		45,000
(to record acquisition of machine for stock)		

Alternatively, if Burns Corporation stock was regularly traded and had an established market price of $140 per share when the machine was acquired, the real value of the equipment must be $140,000, since the seller is willing to accept stock with this total market value in payment. The difference between the list price of $145,000 and the stock market value of $140,000 simply reflects the often artificial nature of list prices. The general journal entry for the acquisition of the machine in this case is as follows:

Machinery	140,000	
Common stock		100,000
Paid-in capital in excess of par, common stock		40,000
(to record acquisition of machine for stock)		

OWNER-TO-OWNER TRANSACTIONS

Understand that exchanges between individual shareholders have no impact on the corporation. The majority of stocks bought and sold on the nation's stock exchanges represent transactions between two individuals, with one person selling all or part of his or her ownership interest in a corporation to another. The only transactions of this nature that a corporation records are those where it either issues shares of its own stock, as previously shown, or repurchases those shares directly from investors, which is demonstrated at the end of the chapter.

STOCK CHARACTERISTICS

CAPITAL STOCK
All of the firm's stock taken collectively.

COMMON STOCK
Stock that usually gives its holders voting rights and represents the residual owners' equity in the corporation.

PREFERRED STOCK
Stock that generally confers some preferential rights to its holders over those of common shareholders but that generally lacks voting privileges.

Our discussion of the accounting methods for stock up to this point is applicable to any type of stock. In most firms, only two major types of stock exist—common stock and preferred stock. All of a firm's stock is considered **capital stock;** if only one class of capital stock exists, it will be common. **Common stock** usually gives its holder voting rights (discussed below) and represents the residual owners' equity in the corporation.

Preferred stock generally confers some rights that are preferential over the rights of common shareholders. The typical rights of common shareholders and the types of preferences frequently assigned to preferred stock issues are discussed in the following sections.

Rights of the Shareholders

Voting Rights. Common shareholders can vote for directors and thus have a voice in the management policies of the firm. Preferred shareholders usually lack voting rights. Since the common shareholders carry greater risk in relation to their investment and expected dividends, they are compensated with the power to vote on the important decisions of the company.

Preemptive Right. Generally, shareholders hold the right to purchase more stock from any new issue of their class of stock in order to keep the same percentage of ownership as was held before the new issue. This right of existing shareholders to maintain a certain proportionate share of ownership by purchasing shares from a new stock issue is called the **preemptive right.**

PREEMPTIVE RIGHT
The right of existing shareholders to maintain a proportionate share of ownership by purchasing shares of stock from any new stock issue before the stock is offered to others.

Dividends. Recall from Chapter 1 that a distribution of earned assets to owners is called a dividend. Such a distribution must be made on a pro rata basis to all shareholders of a given class of stock.

In cases where both preferred and common shareholders exist, the preferred shareholders have a right to receive dividends before the common shareholders do. Preferred stock usually specifies a rate for annual dividend payment (although no dividend will be paid until declared by the board of directors). The amount of dividends paid on common stock is never specified until declared. A common shareholder cannot receive any dividends if profits are low but can receive dividends in excess of those paid to preferred shareholders if profits are high and the board of directors is willing to distribute the funds. Preferred stocks are favored by investors who want a steady stream of yearly dividends and are willing to forgo the potentially greater dividend potential of common stock.

Since the board of directors is not obligated to declare dividends, including the preferred dividend, some years might pass with no dividend being paid. Holders of preferred stock might have the right to receive unpaid dividends from prior years before any payments are made to common shareholders. This right of the preferred shareholders depends on whether the stock is cumulative or noncumulative.

If the stock is **cumulative preferred stock,** all dividends not paid in prior years must be paid along with the current year's dividend before the common shareholders can receive any dividends. Preferred dividends on cumulative stock not paid out in prior years are known as **dividends in arrears.** For example, assume that Jaras Corporation's net earnings were $100,000 for the year ending December 31, 1987, and this amount was declared to be paid as dividends to shareholders. Dividends of $2 each on 5,000 shares of cumulative preferred stock have not been paid since 1982. Exhibit 13.1 presents the net earnings available for dividends to the common shareholders.

CUMULATIVE PREFERRED STOCK
A preferred stock issue where all dividends not paid in prior years must be paid along with the current year's dividends before the common shareholders can receive any dividends.

DIVIDENDS IN ARREARS
Dividends on cumulative preferred stock not paid out in prior years.

EXHIBIT 13.1

Net earnings for 1987		$100,000
Less: Preferred dividends in arrears		
(5,000 shares × $2 × 4 yrs)	$40,000	
Preferred dividends for 1987	10,000	(50,000)
Net earnings available for dividends on common stock		$ 50,000

EXHIBIT 13.2

> Cash dividends at the rate of $.6875 per quarter were paid on the $2.75 Cumulative Preferred Stock each quarter from the date such stock was issued on June 20, 1978, through the third quarter of 1979. As of December 31, 1982, dividend payments had been omitted for 13 consecutive quarters and the dividend arrearage on the $2.75 Cumulative Preferred Stock was $89.4 million.

Preferred dividends in arrears are not recorded in the accounts as liabilities until the board of directors declares the dividend payment. (Chapter 14 contains a detailed discussion of accounting for dividend distributions. Here we are concerned only with the division of available dividends between common and preferred shareholders.) Any unpaid preferred dividends are shown in a footnote to the financial statements as illustrated in Exhibit 13.2 for the 1982 financial statements of the Chrysler Corporation.

A **noncumulative preferred stock** does not guarantee the priority of preferred dividends in arrears. If preferred dividends are not declared, the dividends lapse. If the preferred stock of the Jaras Corporation in Exhibit 13.1 is noncumulative, earnings available to the common shareholders are as follows:

Net earnings for 1987	$100,000
Less: Preferred dividends for 1987	(10,000)
Net earnings available for common dividends	$ 90,000

Because very few investors are willing to purchase noncumulative preferred stock, very few corporations offer such issues.

NONCUMULATIVE PREFERRED STOCK
A preferred stock that does not guarantee that its holders receive dividends in arrears before the common shareholders receive any dividends.

PARTICIPATING PREFERRED STOCK
A stock that offers its holders the right to receive additional dividends when the total dividends declared exceed the normal preferred amount.

Sometimes a preferred stock, known as **participating preferred stock,** offers its holders the right to receive additional dividends when the total dividends declared exceed the normal preferred amount. A preferred issue that specifies a dividend equal to the greater of the preferred guarantee or the rate to the common shareholder is called fully participating.

Assume that Olsen Corporation has issued 10,000 shares of eight percent, $100 par value, participating preferred stock and 20,000 shares of $10 par value common stock. The preferred contract specifies that once the common shareholders are paid $5 per share, the remaining dividends are to be divided between preferred and common shareholders in the ratio of their total par values. Exhibit 13.3 shows the relative distribution if dividends for the year total $300,000.

Asset Claims. Preferred shareholders are entitled to receive assets before any distribution to the common shareholders in the event of a corporation's liquidation if

EXHIBIT 13.3

	Total	Preferred	Common
Amount available	$300,000		
Less: Basic dividends	(180,000)		
Preferred (10,000 sh. × .08 × $100 par value)		$ 80,000	
Common (20,000 sh. × $5)			$100,000
Amount remaining	$120,000		
Additional dividend			
Preferred ($120,000 × $1,000,000 / $1,200,000)		100,000	
Common ($120,000 × $200,000 / $1,200,000)			20,000
Total dividend payable		$180,000	$120,000
Dividend per share		$18	$6

assets remain after satisfying creditor claims. Preferred shareholders' claims include the par or stated value of the shares or an expressly provided liquidation value plus any dividends in arrears if their stock is cumulative.

Assume Boyer Corporation has 5,000 shares of nine percent, $100 par value, cumulative preferred stock with a liquidation value of $105 and 10,000 shares of $100 par value common stock outstanding. The corporation is liquidated on December 31, 1986, and after converting the assets into cash and paying the liabilities, one million dollars remains. The preferred stock is preferred as to assets, and the last preferred dividend was paid in (and for) 1983. Exhibit 13.4 shows the amount available for distribution to common shareholders.

EXHIBIT 13.4

Cash available on liquidation		$1,000,000
Less: Preferred stock at liquidation value		
(5,000 × $105)	$525,000	
Preferred dividends in arrears		
(5,000 × $100 × .09 × 3 yrs)	135,000	(660,000)
Available for common shareholders		$ 340,000

If the preferred stock did not have an asset preference in liquidation, the one million dollars would be divided proportionately between the preferred shareholders' claim of $660,000 (as computed in Exhibit 13.4) and the common shareholders' claim of one million dollars (10,000 shares × $100 par value). In this case, Boyer's preferred shareholders would receive $397,590 ($660,000/$1,660,000 × $1,000,000), and the common shareholders would receive the remaining $602,410.

Other Types of Preferred Stock

Callable Preferred Stock. When the issuing corporation can repurchase its outstanding preferred stock at its option, the stock is known as **callable preferred stock.** Practically all preferred stock carries this call option. The option is retained by the corporation in the event that repurchasing the stock makes financial sense. Redemption can arise if the corporation no longer wishes to pay the required preferred dividends or if a corporation finds that money can be obtained more cheaply from some other source.

CALLABLE PREFERRED STOCK
Preferred stock that can be repurchased by the issuing corporation at its option.

Normally the preferred stock agreement calls for redemption at a certain price. Any difference between the price paid and the amounts recorded in the preferred stock accounts should be added to or subtracted from other additional paid-in capital accounts. Exhibit 13.5 displays an extract of the shareholders' equity section of DuPont Company's 1984 annual report showing an example of callable preferred stock.

In this case, DuPont must pay $272.1 million to its preferred shareholders to reacquire the stock. However, once conditions are met and DuPont calls the stock, each shareholder must surrender his or her shares for the redemption price.

The redemption price is generally set at par value plus some additional amount, known as a **call premium on the stock.** If the redemption price is above the original

CALL PREMIUM ON STOCK
The difference between the par value of callable preferred stock and the amount that must be paid to the shareholders if a company decides to repurchase its callable preferred stock.

EXHIBIT 13.5

Consolidated Statement of Stockholders' Equity
(Dollars in millions, except per share)

See Note	1984	1983	1982
Preferred Stock, without par value—cumulative			
23,000,000 shares authorized; issued at Dec. 31:			
$4.50 Series—1,672,594 shares (callable at $120)	**$167**	$167	$167
$3.50 Series—700,000 shares (callable at $102)	**70**	70	70
	237	237	237

issue price of the stock, the extra amount paid is a distribution of assets to owners and is reflected by a reduction in retained earnings. For example, if the Beckwith Company had originally issued for $105 each 1,000 shares of $100 par preferred stock with a call premium of $15 per share, its paid-in capital accounts would include the following:

Preferred stock	100,000
Paid-in capital in excess of par	5,000

If Beckwith exercises its call option and redeems all of the stock, it would make the following entry:

Preferred stock	100,000	
Paid-in capital in excess of par	5,000	
Retained earnings	10,000	
Cash		115,000
(to record redemption of stock)		

If the call premium of the Beckwith stock was only $3 per share, the shareholders would receive less in redemption than the amount originally provided the corporation when they purchased the shares. In such a case, redemption would create a new class of paid-in capital—redemption premium on preferred stock. The following entry would record the redemption of all of the preferred stock in this case:

Preferred stock	100,000	
Paid-in capital in excess of par	5,000	
Redemption premium on preferred stock		2,000
Cash		103,000
(to record redemption of stock)		

The redemption premium on preferred stock represents the portion of the original preferred shareholders' contributions that becomes a new class of capital for the life of the firm.

Convertible Preferred Stock. A **convertible preferred stock** is a stock that can be exchanged for common stock or cash at the option of the holder, usually within a specified period of time. Convertible preferred stock issues are not generally welcomed by the common shareholders, since after conversion, more common stock would be outstanding, thus diluting both control and earnings per share.

CONVERTIBLE PREFERRED STOCK
Stock that can be exchanged for common stock or cash at the option of the holder, generally within a specified period of time.

To illustrate, assume that Johnson Corporation issues 10,000 shares of seven percent, $100 par value, cumulative preferred stock for $100 a share. Each preferred share is convertible into three shares of no par common stock at the option of the holder. The preferred shareholders can retain the preferred stock as long as desired (unless the corporation redeems the issue). But if the common stock is selling at a price greater than one-third (in this case) of the preferred stock price, investors could convert their holdings into common stock and make a profit.

Conversion of this stock into common shares would not affect total owners' equity in the Johnson Corporation. If all preferred shareholders elect to convert, Johnson would simply reclassify the one million dollars (10,000 × $100) of preferred stock into common stock. The journal entry to effect such a reclassification would be as follows:

Preferred stock	1,000,000	
Common stock		1,000,000
(conversion of 10,000 preferred shares for 30,000 common shares with no par value)		

note

CONCEPT SUMMARY 13.1

PREFERRED STOCK CHARACTERISTICS

Term	Implication
Asset preference	In case of corporate liquidation, preferred holders will receive a set amount, if assets are available, before common shareholders receive anything.
Callable	The stock can be repurchased at the firm's option for a set price.
Convertible	The stock can be traded for another type of security issued by the firm at the holders' options.
Cumulative	Dividends not paid in past and current years must be paid before common shareholders receive any dividends.
Noncumulative	When a dividend is not declared in a particular year, it is permanently forfeited.
Participating	The preferred shareholder will share in additional dividends once the common shareholder has received some basic amount.

if stock goes up - call it back in & buy it

can convert preferred to common

OTHER SOURCES OF PAID-IN CAPITAL

Treasury Stock

TREASURY STOCK
Shares reacquired by the corporation that originally issued them for purposes other than share retirement.

When a corporation reacquires shares of its own outstanding stock for purposes other than share retirement, the reacquired shares are called **treasury stock.** Treasury

Rise of the Dow Jones

When most people talk about the stock market, they refer to its activity by noting the rise or fall of the Dow Jones industrial average. Charles Henry Dow developed the formula for the average in 1884 while he was a financial reporter in New York City. Dow wanted to track the stock market's changes and felt that an average of the 12 stocks he chose to watch would indicate the general flavor of trading. Dow added up the 12 stock prices and divided the total by 12. This average was printed in a two-page bulletin and hand delivered throughout Wall Street.

Since then, the company that Dow formed with Edward Davis Jones to collect and distribute business information has grown considerably. That two-page "Customer's Afternoon Letter" is now the *Wall Street Journal*. (The first *WSJ* sold for two cents.)

The Dow Jones industrial average is still reported, although it has undergone some changes. Now, 30 stocks are included in the average, as follows:

Allied Corp.
Aluminum Co. of America
American Brands
American Can
American Express
A T & T
Bethlehem Steel
DuPont
Eastman Kodak
Exxon
General Electric
General Foods
General Motors
Goodyear
Inco
IBM
International Harvester
International Paper
Merck
Minnesota Mining & Mfg.
Owens-Illinois
Procter & Gamble
Sears, Roebuck
Standard Oil of Calif.
Texaco
Union Carbide
United Technologies
U.S. Steel
Westinghouse Electric
F.W. Woolworth

The average computation has been changed to maintain comparability over time. At first the average was simple—add the 30 prices and divide by 30—but stock splits and stock dividends occurring after the formation of the list have required adjustments to the divisor. For example, suppose that on one day IBM stock sells for $70 per share. If IBM splits its stock two for one, the price per share should drop to around $35 and twice as many shares would be outstanding. If the new price for one share is used and no adjustment is made, the Dow Jones average would drop without cause from the buyers in the market. So when the $35 price goes into the sum of prices for the dividend, the divisor must be adjusted accordingly from, say, 30 to 29.5. This procedure has had to be applied so many times since the 1920s that the current divisor is only 1.359. This is why the Dow Jones average can be well over 1000 and still represent an "average" of stock prices currently selling for less than $100 each.

stock is held for a variety of reasons: to have stock available for employee stock purchase plans and employee bonuses, to support the market price of the company's stock, or to have stock reserved for the acquisition of other companies. Since a corporation cannot own itself, treasury stock does not have voting rights and cannot receive dividends.

When a corporation acquires its own stock, it reduces its outstanding shareholders' equity. When treasury shares are reissued, shareholders' equity and assets are increased by the amount contributed by the new owners. Revenue is not involved, because a company cannot earn profits or suffer losses by engaging in the sale of its own stock. Thus, the sale of treasury stock affects only the statement of financial position.

The most common procedure for recording the purchase of treasury stock is the cost method. Under the **cost method of accounting for treasury stock,** the Treasury Stock account is increased by the cost of the shares, regardless of their par values. Suppose Holland Corporation purchases 1,000 shares of its $25 par value common stock on the open market for $100 per share. Holland would make the following general journal entry:

COST METHOD OF ACCOUNTING FOR TREASURY STOCK
A bookkeeping method where the total cost of purchasing treasury stock is charged to the treasury stock account.

Treasury stock	100,000	
Cash		100,000
(to record purchase of treasury stock at cost)		

Note that the $25 par value has been ignored in the preceding entry.

If Holland Corporation later sells some of the treasury shares, the Treasury Stock account is reduced in proportion to the shares sold, and any difference between cost and selling price is generally credited to Paid-in Capital from Sale of Treasury Stock. For example, if Holland sells 100 shares at a price of $125 each, the transaction would be recorded as follows:

Cash	12,500	
Treasury stock		10,000
Paid-in capital from sale of treasury stock		2,500
(to record sale of treasury shares)		

A special problem arises if the selling price of the treasury shares is less than the cost and paid-in capital from sale of treasury stock is insufficient to absorb the deficit. For example, suppose the total balance in Holland's Paid-in Capital from Sale of Treasury Stock account is the $2,500 previously shown and Holland sells 400 additional shares for $75 each. The amount received—$30,000—is less than Holland's cost, and the difference—$7,500— would be charged against any paid-in capital in excess of par on the books. If that is exhausted, the remaining deficit would be charged against Retained Earnings. If Holland has a $3,000 balance in Paid-in Capital in Excess of Par, the following entry would be made to record the sale of the treasury shares:

Cash	30,000	
Paid-in capital from sale of treasury stock	2,500	
Paid-in capital in excess of par	3,000	
Retained earnings	4,500	
Treasury stock		40,000
(to record sale of treasury stock)		

Since treasury stock is a reduction of outstanding shareholders' equity but not of the number of shares issued, the total cost of any treasury stock held is shown as a reduction from total owners' equity on the statement of financial position. Any paid-in capital from the sale would be treated the same as other paid-in capital accounts. Exhibit 13.6 shows an example of treasury stock presentation in an excerpt from the Sherwin-Williams Company annual report.

EXHIBIT 13.6

Consolidated Balance Sheets
The Sherwin-Williams Company and Subsidiaries
(Thousands of dollars)

December 31	1984	1983	1982
Shareholders' equity			
Capital stock:			
Serial preferred	—	386	5,521
Common	**25,852**	158,364	73,552
Other capital	**145,402**	6,220	12,728
Retained earnings	**305,175**	257,527	279,103
Cumulative foreign currency translation adjustment	**(12,530)**	(11,741)	(9,987)
	463,899	410,756	360,917
Treasury stock, at cost	**(59,759)**	(39,786)	(12,085)
Total shareholders' equity	**404,140**	370,970	348,832

Donated Capital

Occasionally a shareholder will donate his or her shares to the issuing corporation. Because stock held by the issuing corporation is not an asset, the donation is reflected on the books only by way of a memorandum entry. The donation decreases the number of shareholders but not the amount of owner-contributed assets (capital) of the firm. If the donated treasury shares are sold, the value of the assets received is considered donated capital and recorded as follows:

Cash	10,000	
Donated capital		10,000
(to record sale of 200 donated treasury shares)		

Donated capital could also arise from the donation of tangible property to a company, such as a building site provided by a city as an inducement for plant location. In such instances, the donated capital would be recognized immediately upon receipt. Note that fair market or appraisal value, not cost, is used for valuation of donated property.

For example, Bailey and Company receives land appraised at $100,000 as a donation from the estate of the founder, who recently died. The entry for this event is as follows:

Land	100,000	
Donated capital		100,000
(to record receipt of donated land)		

FOR REVIEW

DEMONSTRATION PROBLEM

The Fast Track, a new organization providing athletic facilities to clients, has decided to incorporate. The firm has been authorized to issue 15,000 shares of common stock, $10 par, and 3,000 shares of nine percent cumulative preferred stock, $20 par. The preferred stock is callable at $30 a share and is nonparticipating.

During the month of January, The Fast Track has the following transactions:

January 5	5,000 shares of common stock are sold by subscription for $40 a share. Half the money is collected; the remainder is due by the end of January, at which time the shares will be issued.
January 7	1,000 shares of common stock are sold outright for $35 a share.
January 8	1,500 shares of preferred stock are sold for $55 a share.
January 15	500 shares of common stock are issued in exchange for a building with a fair market value of $22,500.
January 20	100 shares of common stock are reacquired for a total of $3,300.
January 25	The remainder of the cash due on the 5,000 subscribed shares is received. The new shares are issued.

Required

1. Using journal entries, record the effects of these transactions on the firm's accounts.
2. How will the paid-in capital section of The Fast Track's statement of financial position appear on January 31?

Demonstration Problem Solution

1. Journal entries for the January transactions would be as follows:

January 5	Cash	100,000	
	Subscriptions receivable	100,000	
	Common stock subscribed		50,000
	Paid-in capital over par, common		150,000
	(to enter subscriptions for 5,000 shares at $40 each)		
January 7	Cash	35,000	
	Common stock		10,000
	Paid-in capital over par, common		25,000
	(to record sale of 1,000 shares at $35 each)		
January 8	Cash	82,500	
	Preferred stock		30,000
	Paid-in capital over par, preferred		52,500
	(to enter sale of 1,500 shares at $55 each)		

January 15	Building	22,500	
	Common stock		5,000
	Paid-in capital over par, common		17,500
	(to enter exchange of stock for building)		
January 20	Treasury stock	3,300	
	Cash		3,300
	(to record purchase of treasury stock, at cost)		
January 25	Cash	100,000	
	Common stock subscribed	50,000	
	Subscriptions receivable		100,000
	Common stock		50,000
	(to record receipt of cash due and issuance of stock)		

2. The Fast Track will have the following section on the January 31 statement of financial position:

Paid-in capital:

Preferred stock, $20 par, 3,000 shares authorized, 1,500 shares issued and outstanding	$ 30,000
Paid-in capital over par on preferred	52,500
Common stock, $10 par, 15,000 shares authorized, 6,500 shares issued, 6,400 shares outstanding	65,000
Paid-in capital over par on common	192,500
Less: Treasury stock, at cost (100 shares)	(3,300)
Total paid-in capital	$336,700

SUMMARY

- A corporation is formed by filing articles of incorporation with state authorities, receiving a corporate charter, selecting a board of directors, and determining the bylaws under which the corporation will be operated.
- A corporation is an artificial but legal entity created under state law. It has all the rights and responsibilities of a business organization, but owners escape personal liability for criminal acts of the firm.
- Corporate features include legal separation of owners from the organization, professional management, limited liability, no mutual agency, ease of transfer of shares, ease of raising capital, and continuity of life.
- A corporation can issue either preferred or common stock. A preferred stock can be preferred as to dividends, preferred as to assets, callable, convertible, or any combination of the foregoing.
- Common stock carries voting privileges and residual ownership.
- Capital stock can be issued either for cash or on a subscription basis. Sometimes stock is exchanged for assets other than cash.
- Treasury stock—a firm's own repurchased shares—is a reduction of shareholders' equity. Treasury stock can be reissued.
- Paid-in capital includes any donated capital. Donations are valued at fair market prices rather than at historical cost.

QUESTIONS

13-1. Briefly explain the major advantages and problems of a corporation.

13-2. What purpose do the articles of incorporation and the bylaws fulfill?

13-3. Briefly explain the possible advantages a common shareholder could hope to achieve if the corporation issues nonvoting preferred stock.

13-4. Briefly describe the process of incorporation and the line of authority for a corporation.

13-5. In what ways can stock be preferred? What do you feel would be the most favorable combination of features for the investor?

13-6. Distinguish between capital stock, common stock, and preferred stock.

13-7. What is a stock subscription?

13-8. Why should shareholders protest double taxation of income?

13-9. What corporate characteristics are unavailable to a partnership?

13-10. What is treasury stock? Is treasury stock considered to be outstanding?

EXERCISES

13-E1. A corporation's charter says that the corporation can sell up to 100,000 shares of common stock. As of June 30, 75,000 shares had been purchased by investors, but 3,000 of those shares have since been reacquired by the firm. What number of shares are issued? Outstanding? Authorized?

13-E2. A firm sells 5,000 shares of common stock, par value $125, for $675,000 on October 17. What journal entry must be made? At what price did a share sell? Why is this different from the par value?

13-E3. The board of directors authorized payment of a $50,000 dividend on a date when 8,000 shares of $10 par common stock and 6,000 shares of 6% preferred stock, with a par value of $20, were issued and outstanding.

a. If the preferred stock is participating on the basis of par value per share, how much will the holder of one share of preferred earn? Common?
b. What would be the dividend per share to each class of stock if the preferred is nonparticipating?

13-E4. Harry Vale owns 100 shares of Centuri Corporation's cumulative preferred stock. The yearly share dividend of $8 has not been paid for 1983 or 1984. Centuri has 10,000 shares of preferred issued and outstanding and 20,000 shares of common stock outstanding; 22,500 shares of common stock have been issued. If, for 1985, the board authorizes the full preferred dividend amount and a $5 common dividend per share, how much is the total authorization? How much will Vale receive?

13-E5. A corporation is forced out of business and sells its assets with a book value of $150,000 for $95,000. The firm has no other cash but does have debts to creditors amounting to $65,000. Shareholders' equity consists of 200 shares of preferred stock, $100 par, with a liquidation value of $110 per share, and 5,000 shares of $8 par common stock. How will the firm's cash be divided?

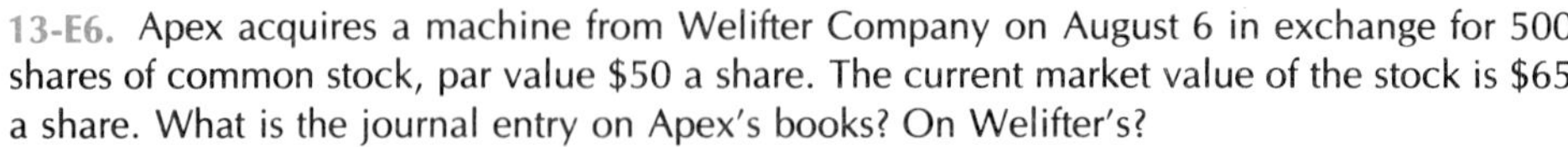
13-E6. Apex acquires a machine from Welifter Company on August 6 in exchange for 500 shares of common stock, par value $50 a share. The current market value of the stock is $65 a share. What is the journal entry on Apex's books? On Welifter's?

13-E7. Maura Chin, Inc., receives subscriptions for 10,000 shares of common stock, par value $40 a share, along with the required down payments of $20 each share on June 1. Subscribers must remit the balance of the sales price, $30 per share, in two equal monthly payments. What entries are necessary on Maura Chin's journals for June 1, July 1, and August 1?

PROBLEM SET A

SPREADSHEET PROBLEM

13-A1. Preferred Stock Effect on Dividend. Frames and Finishes, Inc., has shareholders' equity of common stock, $30 par, 10,000 shares issued and outstanding; additional paid-in capital, common, $15,000; preferred stock, $100 par, 7%, 3,000 shares outstanding; and retained earnings, $80,000. On November 30, the board of directors declares a total dividend of $60,000 to be paid on December 15.

Required

Considering each of the following items separately, prepare a short schedule showing allocation of the dividend between stock classes if the preferred stock is:

a. Cumulative and no dividend was paid last year.
b. Noncumulative and no dividend was paid last year.
c. Fully participating on the basis of the number of shares after common shareholders receive a 7% dividend.

13-A2. Allocating Cash at Liquidation. Golden East is closing its business entirely. It currently has outstanding 60,000 shares of common stock that sold for $20 a share and has a par value of $12 a share. Also outstanding are 800 shares of a preferred stock that carries a liquidation value of $10 a share. Each preferred share has an $8 par value and was sold for $15 each. Golden East has auctioned all assets and is left with $75,000 cash and $50,000 of liabilities yet to be paid.

Required

a. How will the cash be allocated?
b. If the cash proceeds from selling assets had been $53,000, how would that amount have been distributed?

13-A3. Convertible Preferred Stock. On September 1, Noah's Ark, Inc., issues 7,000 shares of 8% convertible preferred stock, $80 par, at 1.09 (109% of par). The stock can be converted to common at the holder's option in the ratio of one preferred share for two common shares, par value $40 each. On December 1, 3,000 shares of preferred stock are converted.

Required

a. What amount is received for the preferred issue?
b. What amount of preferred paid-in capital will be transferred to common paid-in capital on December 1?
c. How much will the *total* preferred dividend be on September 1 one year after issue? Per share?

13-A4. Subscription of Stock. Creativity Corner recently offered common stock for sale by subscription. As of May 15, Creativity Corner had received subscriptions for 35,000 shares at a share price of $60. The stock carries a par value of $35. Terms of the offer required a down payment of $35 per share with the subscription. The balance was due in 30 days. On May 25, one subscriber cancelled his order for 300 shares; his down payment was refunded in accordance with company policy. All other payments were received, and the certificates were issued.

Required

a. Journalize all entries dealing with this stock.
b. Where would the accounts dealing with the stock subscription appear on the statement of financial position of May 31? June 30?

13-A5. Callable Preferred Stock. On March 2, Scott Friedman purchases 500 shares of Lanan's Turn, Inc., 10.5% preferred stock, par value $25 a share. The stock's market price is $40 a share, and the issue is callable at $48 a share. On May 1, the stock is called by the firm and Friedman relinquishes his shares.

Required

a. Journalize entries for March 2 and May 1 on the books of both Friedman and Lanan's Turn, Inc.
b. What is Friedman's return on his investment in dollars? In percent?
c. Why would Lanan's Turn, Inc. call the stock?

13-A6. Paid-in Capital Relationships. The following is Unity Corporation's schedule for paid-in capital and details:

TUTORIAL PROBLEM

Paid-in capital:	
10% preferred stock, $2 par; 100,000 shares authorized; 80,000 shares issued and outstanding	$ A
Paid-in capital over par, preferred	240,000
Common stock, $1 par; 500,000 shares authorized; _B_ shares issued, and 380,000 shares outstanding	400,000
Paid-in capital over par, common	320,000
Less: Treasury stock, _G_ shares, at cost	(30,000)
Total paid-in capital	$ C
Price at which average preferred share sold	D
Price at which average common share sold	E
Amount of yearly preferred dividend to be paid	F

Required

Compute the missing amounts for Unity Corporation's schedule of paid-in capital and details.

13-A7. Journal Entries for Stock Transactions. The Monroe Company, an organization that provides data processing services to health care facilities, decides to incorporate. In January 1988, Monroe is issued a charter that authorizes 50,000 shares of common stock. During 1988, the following transactions occur:

February 2 Monroe sells 10,000 shares for a total of $20,000. The stock is issued immediately.
March 1 Monroe sells an additional 5,000 shares of common stock for $15,000. The stock is issued immediately.
March 27 Monroe exchanges 3,000 shares for a truck valued at $7,500.

Required

Give the entries for the preceding transactions under each of the following three assumptions:

a. The par value is $2 per share.
b. The stock has no par value.
c. The no par stock has a stated value of $1.50 per share.

PROBLEM SET B

13-B1. Preferred Stock Effect on Dividend. On January 1, Lucky Walla, Inc., has capital stock consisting of 9% cumulative, nonvoting preferred stock, par value $20 a share, 30,000 shares authorized, 25,000 shares issued at an average of $43 a share, all 25,000 shares outstanding; and common stock, par value $15 a share, 50,000 shares authorized, 35,000 shares issued and outstanding. The common stock is sold at an average $27 a share. Retained earnings amount to $250,000.

Required

a. Prepare the portion of the Lucky Walla statement of financial position on January 1 that shows the owners' equity interest.
b. (Consider each portion independently.) If the board of directors authorizes a dividend payment of $125,000, how much would the holder of one common share earn if:
  1. The preferred dividend is in arrears for one year previously.
  2. The preferred dividend is in arrears for two years previously.

13-B2. Allocating Cash at Liquidation. To finance a new operation, Tourist Trappings, Inc., had some years ago issued 10,000 shares of 5% preferred stock, par value $100 per share, for $120 a share. The stock is preferred as to assets and carries a liquidation value of $145 a share. Tourist Trappings is forced out of business and shuts down on March 12. On this date, assets with a book value of $2,915,000 are sold, realizing a total of $1,870,000 cash. Liabilities totaling $35,000 remain to be paid. Common stock outstanding consists of 30,000 shares, carrying no par value, that sold for an average of $56 per share. The current year's dividend has already been paid, and no retained earnings remain.

Required

a. How will the company's cash be allocated?
b. Prepare journal entries to record the final transactions.
c. If the assets had been sold for only one million dollars, how would the cash have been allocated?

13-B3. Convertible Preferred Stock. Rosa L'Amaine owns 1,000 shares of Twilight Entertainment, Inc., 12% preferred stock, $60 par, for which she paid $75,000. This issue is convertible by trading two shares of preferred for three shares of common stock, $40 par. L'Amaine must decide whether to hold her investment or exchange it on the next conversion date, May 1. After that date, the conversion feature expires.

Required

Discuss the implications to L'Amaine of the following situations:

a. During the most recent months, a share of the common stock has been selling at a steady average of $65, and the preferred has been selling for $70. The common dividend last year totaled $3.15 per share.

b. The common stock's average market price has climbed recently from $50 per share to $90 due to public speculation about a new satellite facility being acquired. The last quarterly common dividend was $2 per share. Preferred stock currently sells at an average of $100 per share and is nonparticipating.

13-B4. Subscription of Stock. The Optic Lens, Inc., offers for sale 25,000 shares of 8% cumulative preferred stock with a par value of $125 per share at a subscription price of $180. Half of the payment must be made with the subscription. Of the balance, half is due in 30 days and the remainder in 60 days. By September 15, Optic Lens receives subscriptions for 22,000 shares. On October 10, a subscriber cancels his order for 1,200 shares, and his down payment is refunded. The remaining orders are paid in full.

Required

Journalize all necessary entries pertaining to the subscribed stock.

13-B5. Callable Preferred Stock. Incidental Items, Inc., has the following section included on its statement of financial position dated December 31:

Preferred stock, 6%, $50 par value, callable at $60 per share, 1,000 shares issued and outstanding	$ 50,000
Additional paid-in capital—preferred	4,000
Common stock, $30 par value, 3,000 shares issued and outstanding	90,000
Additional paid-in capital—common	120,000
Retained earnings	200,000
Total shareholders' equity	$464,000

On January 1, Incidental Items calls in all of the preferred stock. (No dividends are payable.) The stock had originally sold for $54 a share.

Required

What accounts will change and by how much?

13-B6. Paid-in Capital Relationships. The following are some account balances and additional facts for a firm:

Account balances:	12/31/87	12/31/88
Total assets	$ C	$340,000
Total liabilities	85,000	110,000
Retained income	100,000	H
Common stock	A	F
Paid-in capital over par, common stock	10,000	10,000
*Preferred stock, 9%	24,000	G
Paid-in capital over par, preferred stock	15,000	32,000
Treasury stock, at cost	-0-	5,000

Additional facts:

Dividends declared on 12/30	$ 15,000	$ I
Common shares issued	20,000	20,000
Common shares outstanding	20,000	16,000
Preferred shares issued and outstanding	12,000	14,000
Net income, year ending 12/31	30,000	60,000
Dividends to preferred class	D	J
Dividends to common class	E	K
Par value, common	$1	
Par value, preferred	B	
Treasury shares purchased during year		L

*Nonparticipating, cumulative; no dividends in arrears.

Required

Compute the missing amounts for the firm.

13-B7. Journal Entries for Stock Transactions. The Rudy Corporation is granted a charter that authorizes the following capital stock:

Common stock, no par, 100,000 shares
Preferred stock, 5%, $10 par, 40,000 shares

During the year, the following transactions occur:

January 12	Sells 15,000 shares of common stock for cash at $2 per share.
February 17	Sells 10,000 shares of preferred stock for cash at $10.50 per share.
March 21	Sells 10,000 shares of preferred stock for cash at $10 per share.
April 15	Exchanges 10,000 shares of common stock for equipment valued at $22,000.
May 12	Reacquires 1,000 shares of common to hold as treasury stock at a cost of $1 per share.
August 24	Exchanges 3,000 shares of preferred stock for land valued at $15,000 and equipment valued at $25,000.
September 15	Sells 500 of the treasury stock shares for $1.75 each.
October 17	Sells 6,000 shares of common stock for cash at $1 per share.

Required

Prepare journal entries for the preceding transactions.

CORPORATE SHAREHOLDERS' EQUITY: RETAINED EARNINGS AND OTHER RELATED TOPICS

14

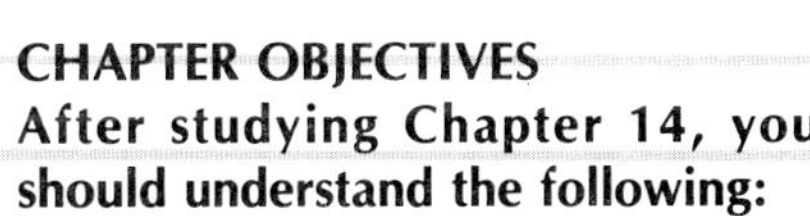

CHAPTER OBJECTIVES

After studying Chapter 14, you should understand the following:

1. The second source of shareholders' equity—retained earnings.
2. The impact of net income, prior-period adjustments, dividends, and appropriations on retained earnings.
3. Unusual items (discontinued operations, extraordinary items, and changes in accounting principles) and how they are summarized on the income statement under the all-inclusive concept of net income.
4. The accounting treatment of cash and stock dividends.
5. The preparation of a retained earnings statement and of the shareholders' equity section of the statement of financial position.

Chapter 13 examined shareholders' equity arising from contributed capital. This chapter discusses the other primary component of shareholders' equity—retained earnings. Recall from Chapter 3 that retained earnings represents the accumulation of net income reinvested in a company rather than paid out in dividends. This chapter will therefore include net income and the unusual items affecting retained earnings. The chapter also examines accounting procedures for retained earnings, dividends, and corporate income taxes. So that you can complete your understanding of retained earnings, you will be asked to prepare a retained earnings statement and the equity section of a corporate statement of financial position.

RETAINED EARNINGS

Chapter 13 discussed the sources of paid-in capital that are components of shareholders' equity. The other major component of shareholders' equity is retained earnings. To understand the nature of retained earnings, one must first understand each of the factors that influence it. In addition to some infrequent transactions, such as the redemption of preferred stock at a price exceeding original issuance price, retained earnings is affected by four primary factors: net income, dividends, prior-period adjustments, and appropriations.

Net Income

Most corporations are in business to earn a profit. Operating income is determined by subtracting expenses from revenues, while net income may include other nonoperating items. Though little controversy exists over the operating income concept, some differences do exist over how to handle unusual items sometimes found within the "other income and expense" category.

Concepts of Income

ALL-INCLUSIVE CONCEPT OF NET INCOME
A method of determining net income where all unusual and nonrecurring items are included in the calculation of net income.

CURRENT OPERATING METHOD OF NET INCOME
A method of determining net income where only items arising from normal operations are included in the calculation of net income. All unusual and nonrecurring events are reported directly in retained earnings.

Under the **all-inclusive concept of net income,** all unusual and nonrecurring items are included in the calculation of net income. The rationale behind this concept is that it permits financial statement users to understand all items that affect net income while still differentiating between items generated from normal operations and those created from unusual or nonrecurring events.

Some accountants advocate the **current operating method** of reporting net income rather than the all-inclusive approach. Under this method, the only items reported on the income statement are those arising from normal operations. All unusual or nonrecurring events are recorded directly in retained earnings. Because users of income statements prepared under the current operating method might not be fully cognizant of all occurrences that affect either the short-run or long-run profitability of the company, the accounting profession has endorsed the all-inclusive concept as the only acceptable method for income statement presentation. However, even under the all-inclusive concept, controversy exists as to the exact placement of certain items on the income statement. The following sections discuss issues that have been specifically addressed by the accounting profession in an attempt to achieve consistency of income presentation among companies.

Discontinued Operations. When a company sells or otherwise disposes of a segment of its business, any gain or loss should be reported in the income statement after presentation of income from continuing operations but before any extraordinary items. Disclosure should include information on any predisposal profits or losses from operation of the discontinued segment, information concerning the level of assets of the segment, and information on any gains or losses arising from the final disposal. Exhibit 14.1 illustrates these required disclosures.

EXHIBIT 14.1

Eaton Corporation Discontinued Operations Presentation

Statement of Consolidated Operations
Eaton Corporation and Subsidiaries

Year Ended December 31	1984	1983	1982
(Millions of Dollars)			
Income (Loss) From Continuing Operations Before Income Taxes	411.1	116.2	(123.1)
Income taxes (credits)	156.7	22.9	(52.1)
Income (Loss) From Continuing Operations	254.4	93.3	(71.0)
Loss from discontinued operations	-0-	-0-	(118.6)
Net Income (Loss)	$254.4	$ 93.3	$(189.6)

Discontinued Materials Handling Vehicles Operations

On January 26, 1983, the Company's Board of Directors approved the discontinuance of its Materials Handling Vehicles business segment. Accordingly, in 1982 the Company provided $143.0 million, less income tax credits of $50.2 million, for the estimated loss on disposal of these operations, including $35.0 million for operating losses to estimated dates of disposal.

On December 31, 1983, the Company transferred its industrial truck operations in the United States and the United Kingdom to Yale Materials Handling Corporation (Yale), a newly established subsidiary. Simultaneously with this transaction, the Company sold common stock of Yale totaling 41% to outside investors for $7.8 million. In September 1984, the Company reached an agreement in principle for the sale in early 1985 of an additional 54.5% of Yale's common stock. Accordingly, the investment being sold has been classified in other current assets at December 31, 1984.

In July 1984, the Company sold its woodland vehicles business for $27.5 million. During 1983, the Company sold certain portions of its industrial truck operations in West Germany.

The consolidated financial statements and related notes of the Company have been classified to report separately the operating results and net assets of discontinued operations. Net sales and operating results are summarized below:

Results of Discontinued Operations

Year Ended December 31	1984	1983	1982
(Millions of Dollars)			
Net sales	$249.4	$244.0	$241.6
Operating income (loss) before income taxes (credits)	$ 13.6	$ (16.9)	$ (36.9)
Income taxes (credits)	2.4	(6.5)	(11.1)
Operating income (loss) before accrued loss on disposal	11.2	(10.4)	(25.8)
Minority interest in income of Yale	(4.4)	-0-	-0-
Accrued estimated loss on disposal and subsequent operating results	(6.8)	10.4	(92.8)
Loss from discontinued operations	$ -0-	$ -0-	$(118.6)

EXTRAORDINARY ITEMS
Items that are both unusual in nature and infrequent in occurrence for a particular company.

Extraordinary Items. **Extraordinary items** are items *both* unusual in nature *and* infrequent in occurrence for a particular business entity. What is extraordinary for one company may be normal for another. Consider, for example, a gain or loss on the sale of an investment in stocks and bonds. Sale of stock is part of normal operations for a stock brokerage company; and for a company that has several investments in securities, the sale of stock might be unusual but certainly likely to happen again. In neither case would the sale of stock be an extraordinary item. However, if a company owning only one large block of stock sold the stock and never expected to buy any other stock, the gain or loss on the sale could be considered an extraordinary item.

Other types of extraordinary items include casualty losses from catastrophies such as floods and earthquakes. (Note, however, that if a business is located in a flood plain and is subject to periodic flooding, losses from floods would be recurring and, therefore, not extraordinary.) Although a gain or loss from early repayment of long-term debt is always considered unusual or nonrecurring, any item from normal operations, such as a large bad debt write-off or the sale of plant assets, would not be treated as an extraordinary item no matter how large the dollar amount involved.

Extraordinary items are shown on the income statement following discontinued segment disclosures, if any, but before information on the impact of changes in accounting principles (discussed below). Exhibit 14.2 illustrates a disclosure of extraordinary items.

EXHIBIT 14.2
Extraordinary Item Presentation Pacificorp

Year Ended December 31 (Thousands of Dollars)	**1982**	**1983**	**1984**
Income Before Income Taxes, Extraordinary Items and Cumulative Effect of Unbilled Revenue Accrual	294,916	408,725	389,196
Income Taxes	96,759	131,592	144,571
Income Before Extraordinary Items and Cumulative Effect of Unbilled Revenue Accrual	198,157	277,133	244,625
Extraordinary Items:			
Gain from debt extinguishment	55,153	—	—
Provision for nuclear projects unrecoverability, net of income tax benefits: 1982—$28,901 and 1983—$121,236	(55,996)	(228,282)	—
Total	(843)	(228,282)	—
Cumulative Effect to January 1, 1983 of Unbilled Revenue Accrual, Net of Deferred Taxes of $20,556 (Note 1)	—	22,069	—
Net Income	197,314	70,920	244,625

Changes in Accounting Principles. A change in accounting principle is a change from one generally accepted accounting principle to another. Since a company must normally apply the same accounting principles from one period to another to be consistent, it should make changes only if the new principle is preferable. If a change is made, full disclosure of the change (including the reason for it and the dollar impact on the company) should be included in the financial statements. The income statement of the period of change must disclose the cumulative effect of the change on net income of prior periods as well as the effect of the change on the income of the current period.

The cumulative effect of the change is equal to the total difference between all prior-period incomes and the incomes that would have existed had the new accounting principle been in use. The cumulative effect should be shown in the income statement after net income from continuing operations and immediately following any extraordinary items. When financial statements of prior periods are presented along with the current financial statements for comparative purposes, a change in accounting principle should be applied retroactively to all statements presented and the result should be disclosed either in the body of the statement itself or in the footnotes to the financial statements. Exhibit 14.3 illustrates the disclosure for a change in accounting principles.

EXHIBIT 14.3
Change in Accounting Principle
Uniroyal

In thousands, except per share amounts	1984	1983	1982
Sales	$2,121,688	1,935,578	1,836,001
Costs and Expenses			
Cost of goods sold	1,700,359	1,553,397	1,502,361
Selling and administrative	271,444	260,059	267,325
Interest expense	38,543	39,373	52,971
Other income, net	(34,559)	(15,628)	(40,274)
Provision for income taxes	45,736	27,187	21,823
	2,021,523	1,864,388	1,804,206
Income from Continuing Operations	100,165	71,190	31,795
Unusual Items			
Loss from discontinued operations (1984 includes $29,734 loss on disposal)	(45,549)	(18,907)	(6,197)
Extraordinary credits	79,240	14,715	—
Cumulative effect of accounting change	(56,710)	—	—
	(23,019)	(4,192)	(6,197)
Net Income	$ 77,146	66,998	25,598

In 1984 the company changed to a preferable method of accounting for pension costs for vested active employees impacted by plant closings. Under this method, the unfunded liability for such employees is expensed at the time of a plant closing. Prior to this change, only actuarial gains or losses resulting from the closings were expensed. The cumulative effect of this accounting change, which amounted to $56,710,000, after recognizing income tax benefits of $5,063,000, has been recorded as of January 1, 1984. The impact of the change on net income for prior years presented was not material; accordingly, pro forma data has been omitted.

Income Taxes—Intraperiod and Interperiod Tax Allocation

INTRAPERIOD TAX ALLOCATION
The distribution of the current year's tax expense among the components of net income responsible for the tax.

Intraperiod Tax Allocation. Up to this point, the focus has been on pretax accounting income. However, a major determinant of earnings that may be retained from profitable operations is income taxes levied by governments on the profitable operations of a corporation. Discontinued operations, extraordinary items, and the cumulative effects of changes in accounting principles should be shown separately in the income statement net of their related tax effects. This distribution of the current year's tax expense among the components of income responsible for the tax is known as **intraperiod tax allocation.** However, income determined for taxation purposes may be different from income determined for accounting purposes. The income tax expense shown on published financial statements is based on accounting income, while the amount actually paid in any one period may be different from the amount shown as an expense. This difference gives rise to the interperiod tax allocation.

Interperiod Tax Allocation.

Permanent Differences. Some of the differences between taxable income and accounting income arise because certain revenue or expense items included in the calculation of accounting income can be legally and permanently excluded from taxable income. Such differences are called permanent differences. As an example, interest revenue on municipal bonds is included in accounting income but excluded from taxable income. Likewise, goodwill must be amortized as an expense for financial accounting purposes, although it is never deductible as an expense for tax purposes. If only permanent differences exist, the tax expense reported on the income statement will be the same as the tax computed and paid per the federal income tax return.

Timing Differences. Sometimes an item may be included in one period for accounting income determination but in a different period for determination of taxable income. Unlike the permanent differences discussed above, however, all such items must ultimately be included in both accounting and taxable incomes. Any differences between taxable and accounting incomes in one period are therefore offset by equal and opposite differences between the two incomes in some future period. Since the total amounts of accounting and taxable incomes will be the same in the long run, the income taxes paid over time must be the same on both taxable and accounting incomes.

The income tax expense reported on the accounting income statement should relate to pretax accounting income and not to taxable income or actual tax paid. If a company's taxable income is less than the accounting income in 1985, the amount of taxes the company would actually pay in 1985 would be less than the amount of income tax expense it reports on its accounting income in 1985. If the company's 1986 taxable income is greater than its 1986 accounting income, the reverse would be true: The amount of taxes the company would actually pay in 1986 would be greater than the amount of income tax expense it reports on its 1986 accounting income. For example, assume that pretax incomes for accounting and taxable income are as follows:

	Pretax Accounting Income	Pretax Taxable Income
1985	$125,000	$100,000
1986	50,000	75,000

If income tax expense was 40 percent of pretax income, accounting income tax expense and income tax actually paid would be as follows:

	1985		1986	
	Accounting Income	**Taxable Income**	**Accounting Income**	**Taxable Income**
Pretax income	$125,000	$100,000	$50,000	$75,000
Accounting income tax expense (40%)	50,000		20,000	
Taxes actually paid (40%)		40,000		30,000
Net income after taxes	$ 75,000	$ 60,000	$30,000	$45,000

Note that total income tax expense computed and reported on accounting income for 1985 and 1986 combined is equal to total income taxes actually paid on taxable income ($70,000). Likewise, net income after taxes reported under both accounting and taxable incomes for the combined years are equal ($105,000).

Allowing for the temporary differences between income tax expense shown on accounting income statements and income taxes actually paid is known as **interperiod tax allocation.** The difference between income taxes actually paid in a period and tax expense computed on the basis of accounting income is recorded in an account called **deferred income taxes.** To illustrate interperiod tax allocation, consider the example of the Andrews Corporation.

INTERPERIOD TAX ALLOCATION
The term applied to accounting for the temporary differences between income tax expense shown on accounting income statements and income taxes actually paid.

DEFERRED INCOME TAXES
The difference between income taxes actually paid in a period and tax expense computed on the basis of accounting income reported in that same period.

Andrews had accounting and taxable income before depreciation and taxes of $50,000 for each of five years. At the beginning of year one, Andrews paid $60,000 for a machine with an expected useful life of five years and no salvage value. The company decided to depreciate the machine on a straight-line basis for accounting purposes. Tax depreciation is prescribed by law under a system known as Accelerated Cost Recovery System (ACRS) and is a fixed percentage of the asset's cost as follows:

Year 1	15%
Year 2	22%
Year 3	21%
Year 4	21%
Year 5	21%

Using the above data, the actual tax owed can be calculated as follows:

	Year 1	**Year 2**	**Year 3**	**Year 4**	**Year 5**
Earnings before depreciation and taxes	$50,000	$50,000	$50,000	$50,000	$50,000
Depreciation (ACRS)	9,000	13,200	12,600	12,600	12,600
Taxable income	$41,000	$36,800	$37,400	$37,400	$37,400
Income tax liability (35%)	14,350	12,880	13,090	13,090	13,090

Based on accounting income, tax expense would be:

	Year 1	**Year 2**	**Year 3**	**Year 4**	**Year 5**
Earnings before depreciation and taxes	$50,000	$50,000	$50,000	$50,000	$50,000
Depreciation (S-L)	12,000	12,000	12,000	12,000	12,000
Accounting income	$38,000	$38,000	$38,000	$38,000	$38,000
Income tax expense (35%)	13,300	13,300	13,300	13,300	13,300

For year 1, income taxes owed (based on taxable income) are $14,350, but income tax expense based on accounting income is $13,300. The bookkeeping to reflect this difference is shown in the following journal entry:

Income tax expense	13,300	
Deferred income taxes	1,050	
Income taxes payable		14,350
(to record year-1 tax liability and expense)		

The deferred taxes at the end of year one are considered an asset, since future taxes paid will be less than future computed tax expenses. If, after considering all timing differences, Andrews actually owed less taxes than shown as accounting income tax expense, the deferred taxes account would be a liability. The journal entries for years two and three would be as follows:

Year 2	Income tax expense	13,300	
	Deferred income taxes		420
	Income taxes payable		12,880
	(to record year-2 tax liability and expense)		

Year 3	Income tax expense	13,300	
	Deferred income taxes		210
	Income taxes payable		13,090
	(to record year-3 tax liability and expense)		

After five years, the balance in the deferred taxes account would be zero, since the total tax over the five years is the same ($66,500) whether computed on the basis of accounting income or taxable income.

If the accounting income statement reported the actual taxes paid rather than an expense computation based on accounting income rules, Andrews would show varying amounts of net income as follows:

	Year 1	**Year 2**	**Year 3**	**Year 4**	**Year 5**
Accounting income	$38,000	$38,000	$38,000	$38,000	$38,000
Actual income taxes	14,350	12,880	13,090	13,090	13,090
Net income	$23,650	$25,120	$24,910	$24,910	$24,910

The result is that years with identical operations have different net incomes. Interperiod tax allocations solve this problem by relating income tax expense to the income that gave rise to the tax. Thus, years with identical operating results have identical net incomes.

Prior-Period Adjustments

Even under the all-inclusive concept of net income, certain rare items, known as **prior-period adjustments,** are excluded from the income statement. These rare prior-period adjustments are entered directly into retained earnings. One such item would be an error made in determining income in a prior accounting period discovered and corrected in the current period.

PRIOR-PERIOD ADJUSTMENT
A rare item that is entered directly into retained earnings even under the all-inclusive concept of net income.

The definition of an error requiring prior-period adjustment is very limited. For example, an incorrect estimate made in a prior period does not give rise to a prior-period adjustment. However, correction of an error in a mathematical calculation would be a prior-period adjustment. For example, if bad debts were estimated as two percent of credit sales during the previous year and experience during the current year shows the allowance should have been five percent, bad debt expense of the current period is simply increased for the additional amount. Two percent was the best estimate possible based upon the information available at the time, and no error exists. However, if last year's depreciation expense was accidentally recorded at one-half the correct amount, the error,if material in amount, would be corrected by adjusting the beginning balance in retained earnings for the current year, and a prior-period adjustment exists.

A change from an unacceptable accounting principle to a generally accepted accounting principle always qualifies as a prior-period adjustment. For example, it is unacceptable for a company to write off its buildings entirely as an expense in the year of acquisition, because generally accepted accounting principles state that buildings must be established as assets and depreciated over several years. Thus, a company that had always expensed its buildings upon acquisition would record a prior-period adjustment when it switched to the accepted practice of capitalizing and depreciating its buildings. Although other prior-period adjustments are possible, the criteria for qualifying any one item as this type of adjustment are quite rigid, and prior-period adjustments are rarely found in practice.

Dividends

Liquidating Dividends. Since dividends normally represent the distribution of past earnings to owners, retained earnings is reduced by the amount of the dividend. Sometimes, when a firm is permanently reducing its operations or going out of business, paid-in capital is reduced by the amount of the dividend. In such unusual cases, the distribution is termed a **liquidating dividend.** For purposes of this discussion, let us assume the more usual case: The distribution is recognized within owners' equity by a reduction in retained earnings. Although dividends can be paid in cash, in stock of the distributing corporation, or in other property, the most common dividends are **cash dividends** and **stock dividends.**

LIQUIDATING DIVIDEND
The term applied to a dividend distribution that reduces paid-in capital such as when the firm is permanently reducing its operations or going out of business.

CASH DIVIDEND
Dividends that are paid in cash.

STOCK DIVIDEND
A dividend that is paid in stock of the distributing corporation.

Cash Dividends. Paying cash dividends has three prerequisites: sufficient unappropriated retained earnings, sufficient cash, and formal declaration of a dividend by the board of directors.

Recall that retained earnings represent owner sources or claims to the assets, not the assets themselves. The presence of a substantial amount of retained earnings does not necessarily mean that the corporation is able to pay cash dividends. Before distributing a cash dividend, the board of directors assesses the corporation's current cash position.

If current cash resources are adequate and future needs seem assured, the board may decide to pay some cash to owners as dividends on their investments. Although corporations are not required to distribute dividends to their owners, once the board of directors formally declares a dividend, the dividend becomes a legal obligation of the corporation.

Three dates are of interest with regard to dividends: (1) the date of declaration, (2) the date of record, and (3) the date of payment. The date of declaration is the date the board of directors takes formal action in declaring the dividend, at which time the corporation must record its liability to pay the dividend. The date of record is the date on which the shareholders entitled to receive the dividend are identified. No entry is made on the date of record. Finally, the date of payment is the date on which the corporation must discharge its liability and send dividend checks to the appropriate shareholders.

To illustrate, assume that on August 20 the board of directors of Gold Corporation declared a $1.00 per share dividend on its 25,000 outstanding shares of common stock payable on October 1 to shareholders of record as of September 2. The journal entries to record this dividend would appear as follows:

Aug. 20	Dividends	25,000	
	Cash dividends payable		25,000
	(to record declaration of dividends)		
Sept. 2	No entry—shareholders to receive dividend are identified		
Oct. 1	Cash dividends payable	25,000	
	Cash		25,000
	(to record payment of dividends)		

As part of the closing process, the balance in the dividends account would be closed to retained earnings. If financial statements were prepared between the date of declaration and the date of payment, dividends payable would be shown as a current liability.

Stock Dividends. In some cases, a company might want to declare a dividend but might not have the cash available to pay the dividend because of a cash shortage or a desire to use the cash for some other reason. In such a situation, the company could issue a stock dividend, which represents a pro rata distribution of shares of new stock to existing shareholders, accompanied by a reclassification of part of retained earnings to paid-in capital. Stock dividends are generally paid on common stock and are stated as a percentage of par value, such as "a 10 percent stock dividend."

Stock dividends are different from cash dividends in that the shareholders do not receive any corporate assets when a stock dividend is distributed. As an example, assume the Higlo Corporation has only one asset—cash—and its statement of financial position as of June 30, 1986, is as follows:

The Higlo Corporation
Statement of Financial Position
June 30, 1986

Assets		**Liabilities and Owners' Equity**	
Cash	$2,610,000	Total liabilities	$1,000,000
		Owners' Equity:	
		Common stock, $1 par, 150,000 shares authorized, 100,000 shares issued and outstanding	100,000
		Paid-in capital in excess of par	10,000
		Retained earnings	1,500,000
		Total owners' equity	$1,610,000
Total assets	$2,610,000	Total liabilities and owners' equity	$2,610,000

If Higlo distributes a cash dividend of $1.25 per share, both cash and retained earnings will be reduced by $125,000. The corporation will have less cash after the distribution ($2,610,000 − $125,000 = $2,485,000) than it had before the distribution ($2,610,000). However, if Higlo declares and distributes a 10 percent common stock dividend, assets before the distribution would be the same as assets after the distribution. The corporation would simply send 10,000 shares (10 percent of 100,000 shares outstanding) to its existing common shareholders. These 10,000 shares are available because 150,000 shares are authorized and, prior to the stock dividend, only 100,000 shares had been issued.

Not only have the shareholders not received any assets from Higlo, but each individual shareholder has the same proportionate ownership interest in the corporation after the stock dividend as he or she had before the dividend. Before the dividend, total shareholders' equity was $1,610,000. Since 100,000 shares were outstanding, each share represented $16.10 ($1,610,000/100,000) of ownership equity. After the stock dividend, 110,000 shares of stock are outstanding, and each share represents $14.64 ($1,610,000/110,000) of ownership equity. A person holding one share before the stock dividend (representing an equity interest of $16.10) would hold one and one-tenth shares after the stock dividend, representing an equity interest of 1.1 × $14.64, or $16.10. Although the ownership equity per share has been reduced, the ownership equity per shareholder is the same, since all shareholders have 10 percent more shares.

If, in reality, nothing of substance has occurred, how should a stock divdend be recorded? The accounting for stock dividends is related to the stock market's reaction to the dividend. If the stock dividend is small (defined by generally accepted accounting principles as less than a 20 percent dividend), the increase in the number of shares is not considered great enough to cause a reduction in the market price of the stock. The stock received by the shareholders will therefore have a market value per share approximately the same as the original stock. When a large stock dividend is distributed (i.e., the total number of shares outstanding increases by 20 percent or more), the market price of each share of stock is assumed to decrease somewhat, though not below par value.

Given these valuations of the dividend shares, the stock dividend is treated as if the company had distributed a cash dividend (in an amount equal to the value of the dividend shares) and the receiving shareholders had instantly reinvested the cash. Thus, the accounting treatment provides that retained earnings are decreased by the amount of the assumed cash dividend and that paid-in capital is increased by the amount of the assumed reinvestment. The resulting transfer of retained earnings to paid-in capital is termed a "capitalization" of retained earnings. Since small stock dividends do not decrease the market value of the firm's stock, when the dividends are distributed, retained earnings are capitalized in an amount equal to the full market value of the dividend shares. Since large stock dividends do reduce the market value of the firm's stock, when the dividends are distributed, retained earnings are capitalized only in an amount equal to the par value of the dividend shares.

To illustrate, suppose that Higlo Corporation distributes a 10 percent stock dividend to its shareholders. If the current market price of the stock is $15 per share, Higlo makes the following entries:

Declaration date	Stock dividends	150,000	
	Stock dividends distributable		10,000
	Paid in capital in excess of par, common		140,000
	(to record declaration of stock dividend)		

Payment date	Stock dividends distributable	10,000	
	Common stock		10,000
	(to record distribution of stock dividend)		

If, instead, Higlo declared a 25 percent stock dividend, the dividends would be recorded as follows:

Declaration date	Stock dividends	25,000	
	Stock dividends distributable		25,000
	(to record declaration of stock dividend)		

Payment date	Stock dividends distributable	25,000	
	Common stock		25,000
	(to record distribution of stock dividend)		

As with the cash dividends account, the stock dividends account would be closed as a reduction in retained earnings at the end of the period. Unlike cash dividends payable, stock dividends distributable are not a liability. Cash dividends payable are a current liability, because they represent a contractual obligation to distribute a certain sum of cash (an asset) to shareholders at a specified future time. Stock

The Dividend Habit

Shareholders without a doubt enjoy receiving dividends. Potential investors who feel that receiving dividends is important will carefully analyze the dividend record of a company before investing. Likewise, corporations that pay dividends take great pride in establishing a consistent record of ever-increasing dividend payments, since such a record is a sign of financial strength.

How far would a company go to maintain its dividend record, especially when faced with declining earnings and inadequate cash to make the payment? A recent article in *Forbes* ("High Risk Dividends," June 18, 1984, p. 194) indicates that many companies in such a situation would do anything to preserve the payment record—even if it meant borrowing money.

Why would a company go to such extremes? There seem to be at least two reasons. First, a company would be embarrassed to admit that it did not have the cash available. Shareholders might see this as a sign of weakness, and the image of the company could be tarnished. Second, corporate managers often believe that a reduction in dividends adversely affects the market value of the stock. They are probably correct, at least in the short run. Investors are likely to evaluate a dividend payment reduction as a sign of financial troubles; as a result, demand for the stock decreases. Yet in the long run, this dividend action may not have any adverse impact on market price, especially if the cash savings were used for a good purpose.

dividends distributable do not represent a contractual obligation to distribute any assets to anyone and are therefore considered part of owners' equity.

Because stock dividends do not provide shareholders with additional assets, one might wonder whether they have any real value to their owners. Theoretically, the per share market price of the stock should fall in direct proportion to the increase in the number of shares represented by a stock dividend. In the long run, this does not usually happen. In fact, in the long run, a change in the stock price is usually not affected by the dividend. Therefore, shareholders generally receive an increase in the market value of their investment because they own more shares than they did before the stock dividend.

Stock Splits. **Stock splits** are similar to large stock dividends, because they divide the corporation's equity into smaller shares. However, they involve the issuance of a relatively large number of shares which is expected to reduce the market price of the stock. Even though a stock dividend can increase outstanding stock by the same number of shares as a stock split, the market price of a company's stock generally will fall more in the case of a stock split.

STOCK SPLIT
The division of a company's stock into smaller shares while reducing the par or stated value per share proportionately.

The purpose of a stock split is different from that of a stock dividend. Corporations might split their stock to lower the price and induce new owners to invest in the corporation. A lower market share price might encourage more individuals to invest in the stock because the stock is more affordable. Stock dividends are declared to provide a return to the shareholders for their current investment. Because of this difference in purpose, stock splits are recorded differently from stock dividends.

To maintain legal capital both before and after a stock split (by law the minimum paid-in capital must equal the total par value of stock issued), the par value of the splitting stock must be reduced proportionately. For example, if Higlo were to split its 150,000 shares of $1.00 par value common stock two for one, each of the 300,000 shares of common stock that existed after the split would have a par value of $.50.

Since nothing of substance had occurred, the stock splits would not require formal journal entries. Higlo would merely make a memorandum entry to reflect the reduction in par value of the stock.

Appropriations of Retained Earnings

APPROPRIATION OF RETAINED EARNINGS
A restriction on the amount of assets represented by retained earnings that are available for dividends.

Occasionally the board of directors might wish to indicate to the company's shareholders that not all assets represented by retained earnings are available for dividends. The restriction is indicated on the company's financial statements by an **appropriation of retained earnings.** Because the amount of assets distributed as dividends is normally limited to unrestricted retained earnings, appropriations of retained earnings highlight for shareholders that some assets are not available for distribution. The appropriation is made by the board of directors and can be a voluntary restriction, a contractual requirement, or a legal requirement. Some states require a corporation to appropriate retained earnings equal to the purchase price of any treasury stock. A contractual requirement might occur if a bank extending a loan requires the company to restrict dividends. A voluntary restriction is usually made for some specific purpose, such as a million-dollar plant expansion. For this example, the following entry would be made:

Retained earnings	1,000,000	
Appropriation for plant expansion		1,000,000
(to record appropriation of retained earnings)		

At the end of the year, the retained earnings section of the statement of financial position would show the appropriation as follows:

Retained earnings	
Appropriated for plant expansion	$ 1,000,000
Unappropriated	12,500,000
Total retained earnings	$13,500,000

When the restriction is no longer needed, the appropriation is eliminated. For example, when the plant expansion was completed, the appropriation of retained earnings would be eliminated as follows:

Appropriation for plant expansion	1,000,000	
Retained earnings		1,000,000
(to reverse appropriation of retained earnings)		

Note that no cash or other assets are actually set aside when an appropriation is established. All the appropriation does is indicate to financial statement users that a certain amount of assets will not be used to pay dividends. Today, companies generally disclose restrictions of retained earnings in the footnotes to the financial statements, and formal appropriations of retained earnings are relatively rare.

SELECTED ITEMS AND THEIR INFLUENCE ON RETAINED EARNINGS

CONCEPT SUMMARY 14.1

Item	Effect on Retained Earnings
Net income (loss)	Increase (decrease) by total amount.
Cash dividend	Decrease by total amount.
Stock dividend	Decrease by market value of stock issued if stock dividend less than 20 percent; decrease by par value of stock issued if stock dividend equal to or greater than 20 percent.
Stock split	No change.
Prior-period adjustment	Change by the amount of the adjustment; will be an increase or decrease depending on the nature of the adjustment.
Appropriation	Divide retained earnings into appropriated and unappropriated portions—no change in total.

RETAINED EARNINGS STATEMENT

The preceding sections analyzed each of the major factors influencing the balance of retained earnings: net income, income taxes, prior-period adjustments, dividends, and appropriations of retained earnings. We are now ready to prepare the statement of retained earnings, using the following steps:

1. State the amount of unappropriated retained earnings at the beginning of the period.
2. Adjust this balance (i.e., increase or decrease) by the amount of any prior-period adjustments.
3. Combine these figures (i.e., add them or net them) to arrive at "Beginning balance of retained earnings—as adjusted."
4. Add (deduct) the period's net income (loss).
5. Adjust for any current appropriations of retained earnings to arrive at "Retained earnings available for dividends."
6. Deduct any current dividends to arrive at the amount of unappropriated retained earnings at the end of the period.
7. List the balance of appropriated retained earnings at the beginning of the period.
8. Adjust for changes in appropriations of retained earnings during the period.
9. Add the ending balances of unappropriated retained earnings and appropriated retained earnings to arrive at "Total retained earnings—end of period."

An example of a separate retained earnings statement compiled by following these steps is shown in Exhibit 14.4. All items shown have been assumed for illustrative purposes.

As an alternative to the separate statement shown in Exhibit 14.4, some firms combine retained earnings presentation with other components of owners' equity and prepare a "Statement of Shareholders' Equity." Such statements include changes in paid-in capital accounts in addition to retained earnings. More commonly, however, firms will append the retained earnings statement to the income statement in a "Combined Statement of Income and Retained Earnings," thereby combining retained earnings with its source.

EXHIBIT 14.4

Delta Corporation
Statement of Retained Earnings
For the Year Ending December 31, 1986

Balance—unappropriated 1/1/86		$ 90,000
Prior-period adjustment (correction of inventory error)		10,000
Beginning balance of retained earnings—as adjusted		$100,000
Net income for 1986		30,000
Total		$130,000
Less appropriation made during 1986		5,000
Retained earnings available for dividends		$125,000
Less dividends to common shareholders		25,000
Balance—unappropriated 12/31/86		$100,000
Appropriated balance 1/1/86	$20,000	
Plus 1986 appropriation	5,000	
Balance—appropriated 12/31/86		25,000
Total retained earnings 12/31/86		$125,000

SHAREHOLDERS' EQUITY SECTION OF STATEMENT OF FINANCIAL POSITION

After completing the retained earnings statement, we have all of the information necessary to prepare the shareholders' equity section of the statement of financial position. The shareholders' equity section has three distinct parts: paid-in capital, retained earnings, and treasury stock. The following general rules guide the preparation of this section:

1. Within the paid-in capital presentation, capital stock and other paid-in capital account balances must be listed. The description of capital stock accounts should include the name of the class of stock; the stock's par value; and the number of shares authorized, issued, and outstanding. For preferred stock, the liquidation preference amount should also be included.
2. Presentation of retained earnings should follow paid-in capital. The balances of appropriated and unappropriated retained earnings accounts should be listed separately.
3. Treasury stock, if any, should be deducted from the total of paid-in capital and retained earnings as the last line item before "Total shareholders' equity."

Exhibit 14.5 shows the full shareholders' equity section of the B. F. Goodrich Corporation statement of financial position. From this it is clear that Goodrich has very carefully followed the above rules.

EXHIBIT 14.5

The BFGoodrich Company and Subsidiaries
Consolidated Statement of Shareholders' Equity
(Dollars in millions, except per share amounts)

Year ended December 31,	1984	1983	1982
$3.125 Cumulative Convertible Preferred Stock—Series C			
Stated at involuntary liquidation value of $25 per share; shares issued and outstanding at December 31: none in 1984 and 1983 and 2,568,291 in 1982	**$ —**	$ —	$ 64.2
Common Stock—$5 Par Value			
Authorized 50,000,000 shares; issued at December 31: 23,718,948 in 1984; 23,696,136 in 1983 and 17,751,579 in 1982	**118.6**	118.5	88.8
Additional Capital			
Balance at beginning of year	**296.7**	139.7	136.7
Changes resulting from:			
Conversion or redemption of Series C Preferred Stock—net	**—**	52.5	—
Exercise of warrants to purchase Common Stock	**—**	36.6	—
Issuance of new Common Stock—net	**.5**	67.0	2.0
Reissuance of treasury shares	**—**	.7	.4
Difference between redemption price and purchase price of Series A and B Preferred Stock	**—**	.2	.6
Tax benefit applicable to stock option shares	**.3**	—	—
Balance at end of year	**297.5**	296.7	139.7
Cumulative Unrealized Translation Adjustments			
Balance at beginning of year	**(23.3)**	(17.1)	(7.4)
Aggregate adjustments for the year	**(9.7)**	(6.5)	(9.7)
Net amount realized from sale of investments in foreign subsidiaries	**—**	.3	—
Balance at end of year	**(33.0)**	(23.3)	(17.1)
Income Retained in the Business			
Balance at beginning of year	**720.4**	739.5	809.8
Net income (loss)	**60.6**	18.4	(32.8)
Dividends:			
Preferred Stock:			
Series A, $7.85 a share	**(1.3)**	(1.3)	(1.5)
Series B, $.975 a share	**(.3)**	(.4)	(.4)
Series C, $3.125 a share annually	**—**	(2.0)	(8.0)
Common Stock—$1.56 a share	**(36.3)**	(33.8)	(27.6)
Total dividends	**(37.9)**	(37.5)	(37.5)
Balance at end of year	**743.1**	720.4	739.5
Treasury Stock			
Shares of Common Stock held in treasury at December 31: 1,313,900 in 1984; 140,381 in 1983 and 99,171 in 1982	**(45.1)**	(4.0)	(1.9)
Total Shareholders' Equity	**$1,081.1**	**$1,108.3**	**$1,013.2**

FOR REVIEW

DEMONSTRATION PROBLEM

Part A. On January 1, 1986, Jonesfield Quarry, Inc., purchased a granite cutting saw for $100,000. The saw had a useful life of five years with no salvage value. Jonesfield uses straight-line depreciation for financial statement purposes and ACRS depreciation for tax purposes. Because of this, accounting income before taxes and taxable income are different, even though income before depreciation and taxes is the same for both income computations, as follows:

	Year 1	Year 2	Year 3	Year 4	Year 5
Income before depreciation and taxes	$100,000	$100,000	$100,000	$100,000	$100,000
Straight-line depreciation	20,000	20,000	20,000	20,000	20,000
ACRS depreciation	15,000	22,000	21,000	21,000	21,000

Part B. The shareholders' equity of Jonesfield Quarry, Inc., as of January 1, 1986, is as follows:

6% preferred stock, $30 par value, 20,000 shares authorized, 15,000 shares issued and outstanding	$ 450,000
Common stock, $10 par value, 60,000 shares authorized, 20,000 shares issued and outstanding	200,000
Paid-in capital in excess of par-common stock	100,000
Retained earnings appropriated for plant expansion	50,000
Unappropriated retained earnings	420,000
Total shareholders' equity	$1,220,000

The following transactions took place during the year:

1. On February 20, it was discovered that the 1985 year-end inventory had been undercounted by $6,000.
2. On May 19, a 5% stock dividend was declared on all shares of common stock issued and outstanding. The market price of the stock was $20 per share.
3. On August 14, the stock dividend was issued.
4. On October 14, the board of directors appropriated $10,000 of retained earnings for equipment purchases.
5. On December 10, the annual cash dividend on the preferred stock and a cash dividend of 50 cents per share on the common stock were declared, payable on January 10 to shareholders of record on December 25.

Required

a. Present the journal entries required in each of the five years for the proper allocation and elimination of deferred taxes. Assume a tax rate of 40%.
b. Prepare a retained earnings statement for the year ending December 31, 1986, and the shareholders' equity section of the statement of financial position as of December 31, 1986.

Demonstration Problem Solution

a. The accounting tax expense and income tax liability in each of the five years may be computed as follows:

	Year 1		Year 2		Year 3		Year 4		Year 5	
	Acctg	Taxes	Acctg	Taxes	Acctg	Taxes	Acctg	Taxes	Acctg	Taxes
Income before depreciation and taxes	100,000	100,000	100,000	100,000	100,000	100,000	100,000	100,000	100,000	100,000
Straight-line depreciation	20,000		20,000		20,000		20,000		20,000	
ACRS depreciation		15,000		22,000		21,000		21,000		21,000
Pretax accounting income	80,000		80,000		80,000		80,000		80,000	
Taxable income		85,000		78,000		79,000		79,000		79,000
Tax rate	40%	40%	40%	40%	40%	40%	40%	40%	40%	40%
Accounting tax expense	32,000		32,000		32,000		32,000		32,000	
Income tax liability		34,000		31,200		31,600		31,600		31,600

The necessary journal entries to record these accounting tax expenses and income tax liabilities would appear as follows:

Year 1	Income tax expense	32,000	
	Deferred income taxes	2,000	
	Income taxes payable		34,000
	(to record year-1 income tax expense and liability)		

Year 2	Income tax expense	32,000	
	Deferred income taxes		800
	Income taxes payable		31,200
	(to record year-2 income tax expense and liability)		

Year 3	Income tax expense	32,000	
	Deferred income taxes		400
	Income taxes payable		31,600
	(to record year-3 income tax expense and liability)		

Year 4	Income tax expense	32,000	
	Deferred income taxes		400
	Income taxes payable		31,600
	(to record year-4 income tax expense and liability)		

Year 5	Income tax expense	32,000	
	Deferred income taxes		400
	Income taxes payable		31,600
	(to record year-5 income tax expense and liability)		

b. The calculations to determine the impact of the above transactions and the journal entries necessary to record them are as follows:

1. If we assume that the understatement of inventory is material, the following entry is necessary:

Inventory	6,000	
Retained earnings		6,000
(to correct inventory error of prior period)		

2. Because 20,000 shares of common stock are outstanding, the declaration of a 5% stock dividend requires that another 1,000 shares be issued (.05 × 20,000). Since the market price per share was $20, the amount to be transferred from retained earnings is $20,000 (1,000 × $20). Part of this is credited to the account stock dividend to be issued, in the amount of $10,000 (1,000 × $10 par value). The remainder is credited to the account paid-in capital in excess of par value.

Retained earnings	20,000	
Stock dividend distributable		10,000
Paid-in capital in excess of par value		10,000
(to record declaration of 5% stock dividend on common shares.)		

3. At the time the shares are issued, the entry would be:

Stock dividend distributable	10,000	
Common stock		10,000
(to record issuance of stock dividend on common shares.)		

4. The following entry would be made to indicate that the board of directors wishes to restrict dividends in order to use the funds for a specific purpose:

Retained earnings	10,000	
Retained earnings appropriated for equipment purchases		10,000
(to record appropriation of retained earnings)		

5. Dividends to be paid on the preferred and common shares are computed as follows:

Preferred: 6% × $450,000 (par value) = $27,000
Common: $0.50/share × 21,000 shares = $10,500

The following entry would be made on the declaration date:

Retained earnings	37,500	
Dividends payable—preferred stock		27,000
Dividends payable—common stock		10,500
(to record declaration of 6% dividend on preferred stock and $0.50 dividend on common stock)		

The retained earnings statement of Jonesfield Quarry, Inc., for 1986 would appear as follows:

Jonesfield Quarry, Inc.
Retained Earnings Statement
For the Year Ending December 31, 1986

Balance—unappropriated 1/1/86		$420,000
Prior-period adjustment (correction of inventory error)		6,000
Beginning balance of retained earnings—as adjusted		$426,000
Net income for 1986		48,000
Total		$474,000
Less appropriation for equipment purchases		10,000
Retained earnings available for dividends		$464,000
Less stock dividend issued		20,000
		$444,000
Less cash dividends declared		
Preferred	$27,000	
Common	10,500	
		37,500
Balance—unappropriated 12/31/86		$406,500
Appropriated balance 1/1/86	50,000	
Plus 1986 appropriation	10,000	
Balance appropriated 12/31/86		60,000
Total retained earnings 12/31/86		$466,500

The shareholders' equity section of the statement of financial position for Jonesfield Quarry, Inc., would appear as follows:

Jonesfield Quarry, Inc.
Statement of Shareholders' Equity
As of December 31, 1986

6% preferred stock, $30 par value, 20,000 shares authorized, 15,000 shares issued and outstanding	$ 450,000
Common stock, $10 par value, 60,000 shares authorized, 21,000 shares issued and outstanding	210,000
Paid-in capital in excess of par—common stock	110,000
Retained earnings appropriated for plant expansion	50,000
Retained earnings appropriated for equipment purchases	10,000
Unappropriated retained earnings	406,500
Total shareholders' equity	$1,236,500

SUMMARY

- Retained earnings, typically the largest item of shareholders' equity, is affected by four major factors: net income, dividends, prior-period adjustments, and appropriations.
- Taxable income is often different from accounting income. Some of the differences are permanent differences, such as amortization of goodwill, while others are timing differences that result in an interperiod tax allocation.
- Under the all-inclusive concept of income, events that are unusual or nonrecurring in nature (discontinued operations, extraordinary items, and changes in accounting principles) are included in the income statement.
- Dividends are a distribution of income to corporate owners. The most common dividend payments are either cash or stock.

- An appropriation of retained earnings is used to communicate to owners that some assets are not available for payment of dividends.
- The shareholders' equity section of the statement of financial position is made up of three distinct portions: paid-in capital, retained earnings, and treasury stock.

QUESTIONS

14-1. Discuss the four major factors that affect retained earnings.

14-2. What is meant by a change in accounting principles, and how should it appear in the financial statements?

14-3. Distinguish between permanent differences and timing differences with regard to tax rules and regulations.

14-4. What is meant by the all-inclusive concept of net income?

14-5. On March 15, 1986, J Company sold a segment of its business for an after-tax gain of $100,000. That particular segment of the business had incurred a $40,000 loss in 1986. How should this transaction be reported on the income statement of J Company?

14-6. Give three examples of extraordinary items and explain why they are listed separately on the income statement.

14-7. What is a prior-period adjustment? How are prior-period adjustments reported on the financial statements?

14-8. On March 15, the board of directors of Alan Corporation declared a $100,000 cash dividend to shareholders on record as of April 1 that will be paid on April 15. Record the journal entries needed on March 15, April 1, and April 15.

14-9. How would a corporation show declared but unpaid cash dividends on interim financial statements? How would the corporation show declared but unissued stock dividends?

14-10. What does an appropriation of retained earnings indicate to users of financial statements?

EXERCISES

14-E1. The Medium Corporation has 5,000 shares of common stock outstanding (par value $10) and a balance in retained earnings of $75,000. On April 30, the board of directors declares a 10% stock dividend and a cash dividend of $1.00 per share. At the declaration date, the market price of the stock is $30 per share. Record the journal entries required for the preceding transactions.

14-E2. The Big Byte Company has decided to purchase a new computer system in 1989. In both 1987 and 1988, the company appropriates $45,000 of retained earnings for the future acquisition. In 1989, Big Byte acquires the new system for $74,000. Prepare the journal entries to record the appropriations of retained earnings in 1987 and 1988 and the disposition of the amount remaining after the acquisition.

14-E3. The accounting income and taxable income for Karen Company for the past three years are as follows:

	Accounting Income	Taxable Income
1982	$110,000	$ 80,000
1983	$110,000	$120,000
1984	$110,000	$130,000

Differences in accounting and taxable income were attributable to depreciation schedules. The current tax rate is 30%. Prepare the journal entries for each year to allocate income tax expense and the income tax liability.

14-E4. Cardiac Company had revenues for 1986 of $3 million. Expenses, excluding taxes for the same year were $2,600,000. Cardiac also had a $125,000 gain from the early extinguishment of a long-term bond. In addition, the company changed from the straight-line depreciation to the accelerated depreciation method. The cumulative effect, before taxes, of this change in accounting principle was to decrease retained earnings by $125,000. The current tax rate for Cardiac is 40%. Prepare an income statement for Cardiac Company for 1986.

14-E5. Shown below is the shareholders' equity section of the statement of financial position for Wadsworth Company. On September 22, 1986, the board of directors declared a 5% stock dividend. The market price of Wadsworth Company stock on September 22 is $35 per share.

a. Prepare the journal entries necessary for the declaration of the dividend and the issuance of the stock.
b. Determine the equity per share before and after the stock dividend.
c. Determine the equity before and after the dividend for an individual owning 150 shares of Wadsworth Company before the dividend was declared.

Wadsworth Company
Shareholders' Equity

Common stock, $10 par	$300,000
Paid-in capital in excess of par	200,000
Retained earnings	250,000
	$750,000

14-E6. Pierre Company has 25,000 shares of its $10 par stock outstanding. On July 1, when the stock was selling for $12 a share, the company announced a two-for-one stock split and reduced the par value to $5.

a. Prepare the journal entry required for the stock split.
b. Assume instead that Pierre Company issued a 15% stock dividend. Prepare the appropriate journal entry for the declaration and issuance of the stock.

14-E7. The following information applies to De Fleur Oil Company for 1986:

a. Net income before taxes was $115,000.
b. In 1985, an undercalculation of $50,000 (net of the tax effect) was made for depreciation.
c. Current dividends are $60,000.
d. On 12/31/86, retained earnings were appropriated for the amount of $50,000. This was the only appropriation.
e. Balance of the retained earnings account for 1985 was $850,000.

The current tax rate is 30%. From this information, prepare a statement of retained earnings for De Fleur Oil Company.

PROBLEM SET A

14-A1. Intraperiod Tax Allocation. Geworhte Iron Works, Inc., has the following income statement items affecting its federal income taxes for the year:

Income from continuing operations, before income taxes	$253,795
Extraordinary loss on early extinguishment of debt, before income taxes	95,650
Gain from operation of discontinued segment, before income taxes	43,875
Loss from disposal of discontinued segment, before income taxes	143,250

Geworhte has a tax rate of 46% for the year.

Required

For proper intraperiod tax allocation purposes, determine the tax effect of each of the preceding items and the net (i.e., after-tax) amounts of each.

14-A2. Interperiod Tax Allocation. Differences in the accounting methods used in the determination of accounting income and taxable income have yielded the following amounts during the first five years of a corporation's operations:

	Year 1	Year 2	Year 3	Year 4	Year 5
Pretax income	$210,000	$260,000	$250,000	$270,000	$230,000
Taxable income	$150,000	$175,000	$270,000	$300,000	$325,000

The income tax rate for each of the years was 45% of taxable income, and each year's taxes were promptly paid.

Required

a. Determine for each year the amounts described in the following columnar titles, presenting the information in the form indicated:

			Deferred Income Taxes Payable	
Year	Income Tax Deducted on Income Statement	Income Tax Payments for the Year	Current Addition (Deduction)	Year-end Balance

b. Total the first three amount columns.

14-A3. Shareholders' Equity Journal Entries. The shareholders' equity of the Opus Corporation as of January 1, 1986, is as follows:

Common stock, $10 par value, 50,000 shares authorized, 25,000 shares issued and outstanding	$250,000
Paid-in capital in excess of par value—common stock	125,000
Unappropriated retained earnings	200,000

The following transactions take place during the year:

June 6	The board of directors authorizes an appropriation of retained earnings of $50,000 for future purchases of plant and equipment.
December 17	The board of directors declares a stock dividend of 6% and a cash dividend of $1.00 per share. (At the time, the market value of the stock is $25 per share.)
December 31	The Income Summary account, with earnings of $100,000, is closed to retained earnings.
December 31	The Dividends account is closed to retained earnings.

Required

a. Prepare general journal entries to record the preceding transactions.
b. Prepare a statement of retained earnings for the year ending December 31, 1986.

14-A4. Shareholders' Equity Section of The Statement of Financial Position. The following data are from the trial balance of the Nash Corporation as of December 31, 1986:

Unappropriated retained earnings	$200,000
Common stock, $30 par value, 20,000 shares issued	600,000
Preferred stock, $40 par value, 9%, 5,000 shares issued and outstanding	200,000
Paid-in capital in excess of par value—common	100,000
Paid-in capital in excess of par value—preferred	25,000
Treasury stock, at cost (common), 1,000 shares	25,000
Appropriated retained earnings (equipment)	150,000

Required

Present the shareholders' equity section of the statement of financial position.

14-A5. Statement of Retained Earnings. The following information relates to the F.C.P.A. Corporation for the year 1986:

Net earnings for the year	$515,000
Dividends declared on common stock	79,000
Dividends paid on common stock	150,000
Dividends declared on preferred stock	25,000
Dividends received on investments	15,500
Retained earnings, January 1, unappropriated	275,635
Appropriation for retirement of debt	250,000
Paid-in capital in excess of par from common stock issued during the year	15,000
Balance in "Appropriation for possible loss of lawsuit" no longer needed due to favorable court decision; returned to unappropriated status	100,000

Required

Prepare a statement of retained earnings for the year ending December 31, 1986.

14-A6. Multistep Income Statement. The following data were selected from the books of Pristine Enterprises for the current fiscal year ending October 31:

Merchandise inventory (November 1)	$ 77,500
Merchandise inventory (October 31)	62,900
Depreciation expense—store equipment	5,000
Sales	810,150
Office salaries	26,000
Sales commissions	83,900
Advertising expense	10,250
Rent expense	25,000
Purchases	469,000
Delivery expense	4,500
Store supplies expense	1,030
Office supplies expense	860
Insurance expense	3,500
Depreciation expense—office equipment	1,750
Miscellaneous selling expense	3,035
Miscellaneous general expense	2,169
Interest expense	1,300
Loss from operation of disposed segment	10,500
Loss from disposal of a segment of the business	15,750
Gain on early retirement of debt	25,000
Income tax	
Applicable to continuing operations	63,300
Applicable to early retirement of debt	6,250
Reduction due to loss from operation of discontinued segment	2,630
Reduction due to loss on disposal of discontinued segment	3,938

Required

Prepare a multistep income statement summarizing the preceding data for Pristine Enterprises for the year ending October 31.

14-A7. Shareholders' Equity Section of the Statement of Financial Position. The trial balance of Marina Corporation as of December 31, 1986, contains the following account balances:

Bonds payable, 12%, due May 1, 1995	$1,000,000
Allowance for doubtful accounts	19,000
Common stock, $10 par, 200,000 shares authorized, 150,000 shares issued, 140,000 shares outstanding	1,500,000
Retained earnings, unappropriated	197,000
Dividends payable in cash	5,000
Stock dividends distributable	100,000
Appropriation for pending litigation	250,000
Preferred stock, 8%, par value $50, 10,000 shares authorized, issued, and outstanding (liquidation preference of $60/share)	500,000
Paid-in capital from donation of stock	100,000
Paid-in capital in excess of par—common	3,000
Treasury stock, at cost	150,000

Required

Present the shareholders' equity section of the statement of financial position.

PROBLEM SET B

14-B1. Intraperiod Tax Allocation. The following data were selected from the financial statements of various corporations:

Item	Amount Before Tax	Tax Rate	Tax Effect	Amount After Tax
Continuing operations	$ 150,000	30%	$______	$______
Extraordinary items	(53,450)	______	(25,656)	______
Discontinued operations	89,625	______	______	53,775
Cumulative effect of change in accounting principle	______	46%	60,057.60	______
Prior-period adjustment	______	50%	______	(12,565)
Continuing operations	______	______	(43,987.50)	(131,962.50)

Required

Make the computations necessary and fill in the missing numbers in the above table.

14-B2. Interperiod Tax Allocation. Differences in the accounting methods used in the determination of accounting income and taxable income have yielded the following amounts during the first five years of a corporation's operations:

	Year 1	Year 2	Year 3	Year 4	Year 5
Pretax income	$175,000	$225,000	$200,000	$250,000	$225,000
Year-end balance of deferred taxes payable	10,000	30,000	10,000	10,000	16,000

The income tax rate for each of the years was 40% of taxable income, and each year's taxes were promptly paid.

Required

Calculate the amount of taxable income for each of the first five years. The following format may be useful:

	Deferred Taxes Payable				
(1)	(2)	(3)	(4)	(5)	(6)
Year	Beginning Balance	Addition During Year	Income Differential [(3) ÷ t]	Accounting Income	Taxable Income [(5) − (4)]

14-B3. Shareholders' Equity Journal Entries. The shareholders' equity of the Mars Corporation as of January 1, 1986 is given below.

Common stock, $10 par value, 150,000 shares authorized, 90,000 shares issued and outstanding	$900,000
Preferred stock, $20 par value, 8%, 10,000 shares authorized, issued, and outstanding	200,000
Paid-in capital in excess of par value—common	100,000
Appropriated retained earnings—plant expansion	110,000
Unappropriated retained earnings	295,000

During the year, the following transactions took place:

January 22	Mars Corporation discovered that some of the inventory had been double-counted during the previous year's physical inventory. Thus, the beginning inventory was overstated by $66,000.
July 16	The board of directors authorized a 5% stock dividend on the common stock. At the time, the market price per share was $20.
August 25	The board of directors authorized another $40,000 of retained earnings to be appropriated for plant expansion.
October 19	The stock dividend declared on July 16 was issued.
December 14	The annual cash dividend on the preferred stock was declared, payable on January 22, 1987, to shareholders on record as of December 28, 1986.
December 31	The Income Summary account, with net earnings of $225,000, was closed to retained earnings.
December 31	The Dividends account was closed to retained earnings.

Required

a. Prepare journal entries to record the preceding transactions.
b. Prepare a statement of retained earnings for the period ending December 31, 1986.

14-B4. Shareholders' Equity Section of the Statement of Financial Position. The shareholders' equity accounts of the World Corporation as of January 1, 1988, are as follows:

Common stock, $20 par value, 50,000 shares authorized, 40,000 shares issued and outstanding	$800,000
Paid-in capital in excess of par value	200,000
Appropriated retained earnings (litigation)	100,000
Unappropriated retained earnings	234,000

During the year, the following transactions also took place:

Feb. 1	World paid cash dividends of $0.34 per share, declared on December 29, 1987.
May 9	World declared a 7% stock dividend. The current market price of the stock was $29.
Aug. 18	World issued the stock dividend declared on May 9.
Nov. 16	The board authorized an additional $50,000 of retained earnings to be appropriated for future litigation.
Dec. 31	World closed the Income Summary account, with a credit balance of $346,000, to retained earnings.

Required

Prepare the shareholders' equity section of the statement of financial position for the year ending December 31, 1988.

14-B5. Statement of Retained Earnings. The following data have been collected regarding Shaky Company for the year 1986:

1. A computational error was made last year resulting in depreciation expense being $50,000 less than it should have been.
2. An appropriation of $100,000 from retained earnings was made for modernization.
3. The applicable tax rate for the past five years was 40%.
4. Net earnings for 1986 are $275,000.
5. Dividends for 1986 amounted to $110,000.

6. An error was made last year in recording interest income for bond investments. The amount recorded was $1,000. The correct amount is $10,000.
7. The balance in the unappropriated retained earnings account on 12/31/85 was $420,000.

Required

Prepare a statement of retained earnings for the year 1986 for Shaky Company.

14-B6. Financial Statement Presentation of Unusual Items. The following data were selected from the books of Ritchard Corporation for the current fiscal year ending May 31, 1986:

Net income from continuing operations	$130,092
Loss from operation of discontinued segment	15,900
Loss from disposal of a segment of the business	25,980
Loss on destruction of plant by earthquake	150,000
Loss on write-off of accounts receivable from a major customer	30,000
Income taxes	
Applicable to continuing operations	86,728
Reduction due to earthquake loss	60,000
Reduction due to write-off of receivables	12,000
Reduction due to loss from operation of discontinued segment	6,360
Reduction due to loss on disposal of discontinued segment	10,392
Paid on $150,000 reported taxable income for 1985	49,750
Applicable to $200,000 corrected taxable income for 1985	72,750
Retained earnings balance, June 1, 1985	136,790

Required:

Prepare the financial statements necessary to report the preceding unusual items.

14-B7. Shareholders' Equity Section of the Statement of Financial Position. The following data have been collected for Rinakor Corporation as of December 31, 1989:

1. Bonds payable, 18%, due June 30, 2010, were issued at a market rate of 17%. The current book value of the bonds is $2,500,000.
2. Accumulated depreciation on the buildings amounts to $950,000.
3. The balance of unappropriated retained earnings on December 31 is $565,000.
4. On June 30, 1989, the city donated to Rinakor a tract of land to be used as a plant site. The market value of the land at the date of donation is $250,000.
5. On December 15, 1989, Rinakor declared a $75,000 stock dividend on common stock outstanding. The dividend shares are to be distributed on January 31, 1990.
6. On December 15, 1989, Rinakor also declared a $90,000 cash dividend on preferred stock outstanding. The dividend is to be paid on January 31, 1990.
7. On June 1, 1989, the corporation purchased 10,000 shares of its own common stock at a total cost of $150,000.
8. The following is known about Rinakor Corporation capital stock:

		Number of Shares			
Stock Class	Par Value	Authorized	Issued	Outstanding	Issue Price
10%, preferred	$45	20,000	20,000	20,000	$50
Common	20	500,000	450,000	440,000	20

Corporate records indicate that the preferred stock has a liquidation preference of $60 per share.

9. On December 31, 1989, Rinakor board of directors authorized a $150,000 appropriation of retained earnings for the retirement of debt.

Required

Prepare the shareholders' equity section of the statement of financial position for financial statements for the year ending December 31, 1989.

LONG-TERM DEBT AND INVESTMENT IN BONDS

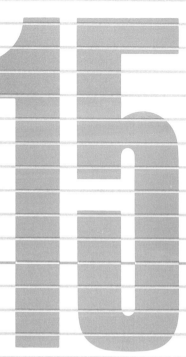

CHAPTER OBJECTIVES
After studying Chapter 15, you should understand the following:

1. The nature of long-term debt.
2. The basic concepts of present value computations and their application to long-term debt.
3. Accounting for long-term debt from the point of view of both the borrower and lender.
4. Presentation of long-term debt on the statement of financial position.

This chapter explains long-term debt as a source of assets. Bonds are presented as a source of financing and as marketable securities. Accounting for bonds from both a debtor and creditor point of view are covered, with emphasis on the debtor. Present value concepts are introduced as a natural part of valuing bonds, with an appendix to the chapter (Appendix C) providing detailed support material.

BONDS—A DEBT INSTRUMENT

A **bond** is nothing more than a promise to pay a given sum of money at some future point and to pay periodic interest amounts for the use of the funds until loan repayment. The creditor who lends money by purchasing bonds is known as a **bondholder.** The corporation borrowing the money is known as an **issuer of bonds,** and the act of borrowing through bonds is commonly referred to as selling bonds. You should immediately recognize that "selling bonds" is not a sale and does not generate revenue. To avoid confusion, we will use the term **issuance of bonds** rather than sale of bonds to denote the act of borrowing money through long-term debt. Likewise, we will use the term **investment in bonds** rather than purchase of bonds to denote the act of lending money through bond acquisitions.

The total amount borrowed through one group of bonds is known as the **bond issue.** Typically, a bond issue is made up of a group of $1,000 denomination bonds totaling some larger amount. For example, a $10 million bond issue would typically contain 10,000 bonds for $1,000 each. This allows many different investors to participate in the process. Each investor in a bond would receive a **bond certificate** as evidence of the issuer's debt to the investor. The total amount specified in the bond issue ($10 million in this case) is known as the **face amount of the bond issue.**

BOND
A promise to pay a given sum of money at some future point and to pay periodic interest amounts for the use of the funds until loan repayment.

BONDHOLDER
A creditor who lends money by purchasing bonds.

ISSUER OF BONDS
The corporation borrowing money through the issuance of bonds.

ISSUANCE OF BONDS
The act of borrowing money through long-term debt.

INVESTMENT IN BONDS
The lending of money through bond acquisitions.

BOND ISSUE
The total amount borrowed through one group of bonds.

BOND CERTIFICATE
A document providing evidence of the issuer's debt to the investor.

FACE AMOUNT OF THE BOND ISSUE
The total amount specified in the bond issue.

The only difference between short-term borrowing and long-term borrowing represented by bonds lies in the nature of the promise to repay and the relationship between the debtor and creditor. For short-term borrowing of relatively small amounts of money, a business typically deals directly with the lender, and repayment is promised at some near future date, usually less than one year away. This direct contact between lenders and borrowers does not exist when borrowing through bonds, and repayment may not be required for ten, twenty, or thirty or more years in the future. The debt represented by bonds on the books of the borrower is somewhat like stock in that one lender might transfer the debt to another lender (sell the bond) in a regulated organized market (the money market) at will, usually without the borrower's consent or even immediate knowledge. However, in no way does the bondholder (creditor) become an owner of the corporation.

Since one bond issue can involve thousands of individual investors, the issuing (borrowing) corporation signs a master agreement known as a **bond indenture** with a **trustee** (usually a bank) who represents the bondholders. The bond indenture sets forth all of the details of the debt agreement, such as repayment date (also known as the maturity date), interest rates and interest payment requirements, and any other provisions such as call features, convertible features, or other restrictions and privileges of either the issuer or the investor. The trustee stands independent of the issuer and administers the bond agreement on behalf of the many bondholders.

BOND INDENTURE
The master agreement between the bond issuer and the bondholder.

TRUSTEE
A person or organization that represents the interests of third parties.

Coverage of all of the possible provisions contained within bond indenture agreements is nearly impossible and is well beyond the scope of this text. The following sections, however, describe some of the more common alternatives found in bond indenture agreements.

BOND INDENTURE ALTERNATIVES

Security Behind the Bond

Bonds can be secured with specific assets of the issuing corporation or can rest solely on the general value of the corporation's total assets and reputation. If the bond indenture agreement pledges specific assets to the creditors (bondholders) in the event the bonds are not repaid when due, the bonds are referred to as **secured bonds** (also known as **mortgage bonds**). If, on the other hand, the bond indenture is not secured by the pledge of certain assets, the bonds are referred to as **unsecured bonds** (also known as **debenture bonds**).

SECURED BOND
A bond that pledges specific assets to the creditors in the event the bond is not repaid when due.

MORTGAGE BOND
See Secured Bond.

UNSECURED BOND
A bond that is not secured by the pledge of certain assets to the bondholders in the event of nonpayment by the bond issuer.

DEBENTURE BOND
See Unsecured Bond.

Time of Repayment

Serial Bonds. Some bond issues are repaid in stages. For example, a corporation might issue one million dollars of bonds (borrow one million dollars) and repay $200,000 at the end of Years 2, 4, 6, 8, and 10 from the date of issue. Such bonds are known as **serial bonds,** since repayment occurs over a series of dates.

SERIAL BOND
A bond issue where repayment occurs over a series of dates.

Term Bonds. A corporation might borrow one million dollars by issuing bonds and pledge repayment only at one specific future date for the total amount borrowed, say ten years after the date of issue. Bonds where repayment is made at only one specified future date for the total amount borrowed are known as **term bonds.** Note that we are discussing only bond repayment dates, not interest payment requirements.

TERM BOND
A bond where repayment is made only at one specified future date for the total amount borrowed.

Interest Payment Arrangements

Coupon Bonds. Interest is usually paid to creditors (bondholders) either once or twice a year. To facilitate interest payments, some bonds have a series of attached future-dated checks known as **coupons.** Each coupon is payable to the bondholder on the date specified for the interest due on that date. To collect the interest, the bondholder detaches each check from the bond and presents it to any bank for payment on the appropriate date. Such bonds are known as **coupon bonds** or **bearer bonds.** The issuer does not need to know the identity of the individual bondholder.

COUPONS
Future-dated checks attached to a bond and payable on the date specified for the interest due on that date.

COUPON BOND
A bond that is issued with coupons attached covering interest payments over the life of the bond.

BEARER BOND
See Coupon Bond.

Registered Bonds. Most bonds issued today are known as **registered bonds.** With registered bonds, the bond issuer keeps a record of the name and address of each of the bondholders and sends each one an interest check on each interest payment date.

REGISTERED BOND
A bond where the issuer keeps a record of the name and address of each bondholder and sends each one an interest check on each interest payment date.

Bond Call and Conversion Privileges

Convertible Bonds. Sometimes bonds (called **convertible bonds**) can be traded for stock at the option of the creditor (bondholder). If the bondholders convert all of the bonds to stock, repayment of the debt is no longer required, since the bondholder ceases to be a creditor and becomes an owner of the bond-issuing corporation.

CONVERTIBLE BOND
A bond that can be traded for stock at the option of the bondholder.

Callable Bonds. Very often a corporation might wish the option of paying off (retiring) the bonds before the normal repayment date. Bonds allowing early repayment at the option of the issuer are termed **callable bonds.** Such early repayment might be inconvenient for the bondholder, who must now find a new place in which to invest the returned money. Most bond agreements, therefore, require that the issuing corporation pay a penalty (known as a **call premium on bonds**) to the bondholder for the privilege of early repayment.

CALLABLE BOND
A bond that provides for early repayment at the option of the issuer.

CALL PREMIUM ON BONDS
The penalty payment required for the privilege of early repayment of callable bonds.

ISSUANCE OF BONDS

Bond issuance is typically a long process. The issuing company must take such steps as preparing certain financial and operating information for the prospective investor, selecting a trustee, and drawing up an indenture agreement. The bond's interest rate and maturity dates must be selected well ahead of the actual issue date.

The Problem of Interest Rates

Nominal and Effective Interest Rates. Because of the lead time required and because bond agreements, once written, cannot be altered easily, the interest rate agreed to in the bond indenture might not be the same as the rate of interest that investors will demand when the bonds are actually issued. For example, the Teak Company might agree to pay 14 percent in the indenture agreement, but by the time the bonds are issued, investors might demand 16 percent or perhaps only 12 percent on their money, depending on prevailing general interest rates. The actual interest rate paid on a bond is known as the **effective rate, real rate,** or **market rate of interest** and takes into account the relative financial market conditions and the risk involved in the loan. The rate of interest agreed to in the indenture is known as the **face rate (nominal rate) of interest.**

EFFECTIVE RATE OF INTEREST
The actual rate of interest paid on debt.

REAL RATE OF INTEREST
See Effective Rate of Interest.

MARKET RATE OF INTEREST
See Effective Rate of Interest.

FACE RATE OF INTEREST
The rate of interest agreed to in a debt instrument.

NOMINAL RATE OF INTEREST
See Face Rate of Interest.

Interest Rates and Bond Market Values. Because the bond agreement cannot be changed, reconciliation of the face rate to the market rate of interest takes place through adjustment of the market value of the bonds. For example, assume Teak Company offers one million dollars of ten-year maturity bonds on January 1, 1985, bearing interest at 14 percent, payable each January 1 (starting on January 1, 1986). Investors are unwilling, however, to lend money to Teak for ten years for anything less than 16 percent annual interest.

Consider the two promises made by Teak in issuing the bonds:

1. Teak has promised to pay 14 percent of one million dollars ($140,000) as interest at the end of each year for ten years.
2. Teak has promised to pay the face amount (one million dollars) to the lender at the end of the tenth year.

These two promises cannot be easily altered, since both are specified in writing in the bond agreement. However, if lenders provide Teak with less than one million dollars when the bonds are issued, the effective rate of interest must be greater than 14 percent, as illustrated in Exhibit 15.1.

Since all payments received by the lender above the amount originally provided to the borrower are really interest payments regardless of how paid, the effective rate of interest actually paid by Teak in Case 2 must be greater than 14 percent. To understand the exact determination of the effective interest rate on bonds issued for

EXHIBIT 15.1

	Case 1 Bonds Issued For $1,000,000	Case 2 Bonds Issued For $900,000
Interest payments (10 × $140,000)	$1,400,000	$1,400,000
Face amount paid	1,000,000	1,000,000
Total paid	$2,400,000	$2,400,000
Less total amount originally provided by lenders	($1,000,000)	($ 900,000)
Total interest paid by borrower over life of bond	$1,400,000	$1,500,000
Effective rate of interest	14%	Greater than 14%

amounts other than the face rate, you need to understand that all money to be received in the future has a lower present value. If you are unfamiliar with present value concepts, thoroughly study Appendix C before reading further.

CONCEPT SUMMARY 15.1
BOND TERMINOLOGY

TERM	MEANING
Bond indenture	Agreement between borrower (bond issuer) and lender (bondholder).
Callable bonds	Bonds that can be repaid early at the borrower's option; usually requires payment of a penalty, known as a call premium.
Convertible bonds	Bonds that can be converted to stock at the bondholder's option.
Face rate and face amount	The rate of interest specified on the bond indenture and the total amount to be repaid.
Effective rate, or market rate	The actual rate of interest on the bonds—determined by the market.
Maturity date	When the debt must be repaid.

Present Value and Bond Interest

A present value amount can be computed for any future stream of payments, for any interest rate, for any time period. As Exhibit 15.1 shows, if investors wish to earn 16 percent rather than 14 percent on the loan to Teak, all they need to do is lend Teak some amount less than one million dollars. The amount lent must be

Bond Sweeteners and Interest Rates

In addition to accepting prevailing market conditions and assessing the risk of investing, investors might be willing to accept a lower rate of interest if a bond agreement provides the investor with certain options, known as sweeteners. The right to convert bonds to stock discussed earlier is an example of such a provision.

In October 1984, Chrysler Financial Corporation issued $200 million of 15-year bonds, giving investors the option of returning the bonds to Chrysler and receiving face value for them in 1989 regardless of prevailing interest rates. The bonds were issued with an interest rate of 13.25 percent while comparable Chrysler bonds without this right would have cost Chrysler 13.95 percent. Investors were willing to accept $35 less per $1,000 bond in interest between 1984 and 1989 for this right, or sweetener. If interest rates are above 13.25 percent in 1989, investors will exercise their right and reinvest their money at the then higher interest rates. Without this right (or put option, as it is known), the investors would not be able to take advantage of the higher interest rates. Of course, if the interest rates go down, the option is worthless.

equal to the present value, at 16 percent, of the total amount to be received in the future from Teak. We have computed this amount to be $903,335 as follows:

Present value of repayment	$1,000,000 × .2266836 =	$226,684
Present value of interest payments	140,000 × 4.8332275 =	676,651
Total amount received as a loan		$903,335

For further information on how we computed this amount, study Appendix C.

Thus, if the investors provide $903,335 for the one million dollars of bonds issued by Teak, the actual interest earned over the ten-year period would be $1,496,665 ($2,400,000 − $903,335), and this amount of interest would be sufficient for the investors to earn 16 percent on the amount lent, as illustrated in Exhibit 15.2.

EXHIBIT 15.2

Comparison of Market and Face Rate on Bonds Issued at a Discount

Year	Loan at Beginning Of Year		Effective Interest Rate		Yearly Interest Expense	Cash Paid January 1	Portion of Discount Added To Loan Amount
1	903,335	×	.16	=	144,534	140,000	4,534
2	907,869	×	.16	=	145,259	140,000	5,259
3	913,128	×	.16	=	146,101	140,000	6,101
4	919,229	×	.16	=	147,077	140,000	7,077
5	926,306	×	.16	=	148,209	140,000	8,209
6	934,515	×	.16	=	149,522	140,000	9,522
7	944,037	×	.16	=	151,046	140,000	11,046
8	955,083	×	.16	=	152,813	140,000	12,813
9	967,896	×	.16	=	154,863	140,000	14,863
10	982,759	×	.16	=	157,241	140,000	17,241
11	1,000,000						
Total interest payments						$1,400,000	$96,665
Total interest expense					$1,496,665		

DISCOUNT ON BONDS
The excess of the face amount of a bond over the actual cash provided by creditors when the bond is issued.

PREMIUM ON BONDS
The excess of cash received from investors over the face amount of a bond issue.

The difference between the face amount of the bond and the actual cash provided by creditors is called a **discount on bonds** when the cash received is less than the face amount and a **premium on bonds** when the cash received is greater than the face amount. In the case of Teak, the discount is $96,665 ($1,000,000 − $903,335).

As Exhibit 15.2 shows, the interest paid annually in cash is determined by the face rate given on bonds, but the interest expense is determined by multiplying the loan balance at the beginning of the year by the effective interest rate. The interest expense in excess of amount paid each year is added to the total debt. The unpaid interest over the life of the bonds equals the difference between the amount of cash received and the face value of the bonds at issue date. All of this unpaid interest will be paid at the maturity date of the bond. Thus, present value computations can always be used to adjust the cash received for a bond issue to accommodate the difference between the face rate and market rate of interest.

The market value (price) of bonds is generally quoted as a percentage of face value. A bond valued at its face amount in the marketplace is said to be **issued at**

par. A bond issued for less than par is said to be **issued at a discount,** while one valued at greater than par is said to be **issued at a premium.** The bonds for the Teak Company would have a market value quoted as 90.3335 ($903,335/ $1,000,000 × 100).

The process of increasing the debt for the unpaid interest as demonstrated in Exhibit 15.2 is known as amortization of the discount. If the bonds are issued at a premium because the market rate of interest is less than the face rate, the opposite of Exhibit 15.2 would occur. The loan value would initially be greater than the face amount, each interest payment would be greater than the interest expense based on the market rate, and the extra amount paid would be a reduction of the loan amount over the life of issue. The face amount and loan amount would be the same at the maturity date. The premium would thus be amortized over the life of the bond issue.

ISSUED AT PAR
The term applied when a bond is valued at its face amount when it is issued.

ISSUED AT A DISCOUNT
The term applied when a bond is issued for less than its face amount.

ISSUED AT A PREMIUM
The term applied when a bond is issued for more than its face amount.

CONCEPT SUMMARY 15.2

BOND ISSUE AMOUNTS, INTEREST RATES, AND CASH RECEIVED

WHAT	WHEN	EXPLANATION/TREATMENT
Discount	Market rate of interest is above face rate of the bond.	A discount. The discount is amortized over the life of the bond as an addition to interest expense. Discount amount amortized equals interest *computed* at market rate minus interest *paid* at face rate.
Premium	Market rate of interest is below face rate of the bond.	A premium. The premium is amortized over the life of the bond as a reduction of interest expense. Premium amount amortized equals interest *paid* at face rate minus interest *computed* at market rate.
Bond issue amount	Determined when bond is issued.	Sum of the present value of the future amounts of actual interest payments promised *and* the future repayment of the bond itself.
Cash received	Determined when bond is issued.	The bond issue amount plus interest owed, if any, since the last interest payment date.

ACCOUNTING FOR BOND ISSUANCE

To translate all of the preceding issuance problems into accounting language, we must make entries that correspond to the facts in each case.

Bonds Issued at Par

If the Teak Company issues the one million dollars of 14 percent, ten-year bonds on January 1, 1985, at 100 with interest payable annually on January 1, it would make the following entries for the period January 1, 1985, to January 1, 1986, assuming a fiscal year ending December 31:

Jan. 1, 1985	Cash	1,000,000	
	Bonds payable		1,000,000
	(to record issuance of $1,000,000 bonds at par)		
Dec. 31, 1985	Interest expense	140,000	
	Interest payable		140,000
	(to record interest expense adjustment for financial statement purposes—an adjusting entry)		
Jan. 1, 1986	Interest payable	140,000	
	Cash		140,000
	(to record payment of 1985 interest)		

The December 31 adjustment for interest is necessary to have a correct account balance in interest expense and interest payable at December 31, 1985. This sequence of entries would continue each year until the maturity date of January 1, 1995, when Teak would make the last interest payment and repay the loan. The final entry would be as follows:

Jan. 1, 1995	Bonds payable	1,000,000	
	Interest payable	140,000	
	Cash		1,140,000
	(to record interest payment and bond repayment)		

Bonds Issued at a Discount

For this example, let's assume that the Teak Company issues its one million dollars of bonds on January 1, 1985, for $903,335. The entries would follow the facts presented earlier and for the period ending January 1, 1986, would be as follows:

Jan. 1, 1985	Cash	903,335	
	Discount on bonds	96,665	
	Bonds payable		1,000,000
	(to record bonds issued at a discount)		
Dec. 31, 1985	Interest expense	144,534	
	Discount on bonds		4,534
	Interest payable		140,000
	(to record interest on bonds as of Dec. 31—an adjusted entry)[1]		
Jan. 1, 1986	Interest payable	140,000	
	Cash		140,000
	(to record distribution of cash on Jan. 1)		

(Note that the entries correspond exactly to Exhibit 15.2.)

[1]See note on p. 459

Bonds Issued Between Interest Payment Dates

One other issuance problem can exist with bonds. Interest is normally paid either annually or, more commonly, semiannually. The dates of payment are fixed in the bond indenture agreement and cannot be changed. If the bonds of Teak are dated January 1, 1985, pay interest each year starting on January 1, 1986, and are actually issued on January 1, 1985, at par, all of the $140,000 first-year interest is earned by the bondholders as of January 1, 1986. But suppose that delays occur and the bonds are not actually issued until April 1, 1985. Since the bondholders have lent money to Teak for only three-fourths of a year by January 1, 1986, they are only entitled to $105,000 (3/4 × $140,000) interest. Nevertheless, on January 1, 1986, Teak Company must pay $140,000 under the bond indenture agreement.

To adjust for this problem, the investor (lender) must advance money to the bond issuer (borrower) equal to the accrued interest from the last interest payment date to the date of issue. In our example, the investors in the Teak Company bonds would advance Teak an additional $35,000 over the issue amount.

The additional $35,000 would not affect the price quotation or the face amount of the bond. The bond in this case would be quoted at 100 plus accrued interest. The entry for the bond issued on April 1 is as follows:

Apr. 1, 1985	Cash	1,035,000	
	Bonds payable		1,000,000
	Interest payable		35,000
	(to record issuance of bonds, receipt of cash, and liability for interest)		

As previously shown, Teak's 1985 interest expense is $105,000, recorded as follows:

Dec. 31, 1985	Interest expense	105,000	
	Interest payable		105,000
	(to record interest on bonds as of Dec. 31—an adjusting entry)		

[1]Some texts apply straight-line amortization to bond discounts and premiums when presenting the bookkeeping entries for bonds issued at prices other than par. Under the straight-line approach, the total discount or premium is divided by the number of payment periods and the resulting equal amount of discount or premium is amortized at each interest payment date. Under this method, interest expense for each period is determined by adding the amount of discount amortized to (or subtracting the amount of premium amortized from) the cash paid each period. If straight-line amortization were used, this entry would be as follows:

Dec. 31,1985	Interest expense	149,666.50	
	Discount on bonds		9,666.50
	Interest payable		140,000.00
	(to record interest on bonds as of Dec. 31)		

The straight-line method is not permitted in actual practice, since the interest computation is not correct. We believe that regular interest computations are easier for students to follow and support a far greater understanding of bond premiums and discounts. For these reasons, we have chosen to use regular interest computations throughout the text.

Teak would make the following entry on January 1, 1986, when the actual cash payment required by the bond agreement occurs:

Jan. 1, 1986	Interest payable	140,000	
	Cash		140,000
	(to record cash disbursement)		

After this payment, the investors' net cash inflow is $105,000 and Teak's net cash outflow is $105,000 ($140,000 − $35,000), which corresponds to the correct interest expense on the bonds from the date of issue to the end of the year. Note again that the entries follow the facts and the interest payable balance as of January 1, 1986, is now zero, as it should be.

Bonds Issued at a Discount Between Interest Payment Dates

Although the entries appear complicated, this case is simply a combination of the two preceding cases. Assume that Teak issues the bonds on April 1, 1985, to yield an effective rate of 16 percent. The present value amount received would not be $903,335, since only 9¾ rather than 10 years remain until maturity. The present value of the bonds as of April 1 at an effective rate of 16 percent would be $904,348. The entries with key computations would be as follows:

Apr. 1, 1985	Cash ($904,348 + $35,000)	939,348	
	Discount on bonds ($1,000,000 − $904,348)	95,652	
	Bonds payable		1,000,000
	Interest payable		35,000
	(to record bonds sold at a discount between interest dates)		
Dec. 31, 1985	Interest expense (.16 × 904,348 × 3/4)	108,521	
	Discount on bonds		3,521
	Interest payable		105,000
	(to record interest expense, amortize the discount, and record liability as of December 31—an adjusting entry)		
Jan. 1, 1986	Interest payable	140,000	
	Cash		140,000
	(to record cash disbursement)		

Note the similarity between these entries and the preceding set of entries. The only change is in the present value of the bonds and the resultant interest expense and discount amortization. All other facts and, thus, other parts of the entries are the same.

Bonds Issued at a Premium

Suppose that the Teak Company issues the one million dollars of 14 percent, ten-year bonds on January 1, 1985, at an effective rate of interest of 12 percent with annual interest payments due on January 1. The bonds would then have an issue value of 111.3005. If the lender provided $1,113,005, Teak would pay total interest over the life of the bonds of $1,286,995 rather than $1.4 million as in Exhibit 15.3.

EXHIBIT 15.3

Total amount paid by Teak over the life of the bonds	
Interest payments 10 × $140,000	$1,400,000
Face amount paid	1,000,000
Total paid	$2,400,000
Less: Amount originally provided by lender	$1,113,005
Total interest	$1,286,995

This case is, of course, opposite that for discounts presented earlier. Exhibit 15.4 presents a schedule of expense and interest payments for this type of bonds similar to the discount in Exhibit 15.2.

EXHIBIT 15.4

Comparison of Market and Face Rate on Bonds Issued at a Premium

Year	Loan Beginning Of Year	Effective Interest Rate	Yearly Interest Expense	Cash Paid January 1	Portion of Premium Deducted From Loan Amount
1	$1,113,005 ×	.12	= $ 133,561	$ 140,000	$ 6,439
2	1,106,566 ×	.12	= 132,788	140,000	7,212
3	1,099,354 ×	.12	= 131,922	140,000	8,078
4	1,091,276 ×	.12	= 130,953	140,000	9,047
5	1,082,229 ×	.12	= 129,867	140,000	10,133
6	1,072,096 ×	.12	= 128,651	140,000	11,349
7	1,060,747 ×	.12	= 127,290	140,000	12,710
8	1,048,037 ×	.12	= 125,764	140,000	14,236
9	1,033,801 ×	.12	= 124,056	140,000	15,944
10	1,017,857 ×	.12	= 122,143	140,000	17,857
11	1,000,000				
Total interest payments				$1,400,000	$(113,005)
Total interest expense			$1,286,995		

Note that since Teak pays more cash each year under the bond agreement than the actual interest expense, the excess reduces the loan amount. At maturity, the loan amount will be one million dollars and repayment will be the same as that for bonds sold at par.

The entries for Teak for the period January 1, 1985, through January 1, 1986, are as follows:

Date	Account	Debit	Credit
Jan. 1, 1985	Cash	1,113,005	
	Premium on bonds payable		113,005
	Bonds payable		1,000,000
	(to record bond issued at a premium)		
Dec. 31, 1985	Interest expense		
	(.12 × 1,113,005)	133,561	
	Premium on bonds payable	6,439	
	Interest payable		140,000
	(to record interest expense)		
Jan. 1, 1986	Interest payable	140,000	
	Cash		140,000
	(to record cash paid out on January 1)		

General Approach to Journal Entries

The types of bond entries are endless, and many students have great difficulty making the entries properly. The entries are not difficult, however, if you analyze each one carefully and remember the following conventions:

1. Bonds payable are always recorded at face amounts. Adjustments for discounts or premiums, if any, are handled through separate premium and discount accounts.
2. Interest is always computed at the market rate for the period of time covered within a particular interest payment period. The loan amount for any time period is always equal to the face amount minus any unamortized discount or plus any unamortized premium.
3. Premium or discount amortization amounts are always equal to the difference between the interest earned as computed in (2) and the amount paid. In cases where bonds are issued between interest payment dates, the amount paid in the first period must be adjusted for the investor's (lender's) initial payment to the issuer to determine proper premium or discount amortization.

Bond Issue Costs

Corporations incur legal, accounting, and investment banking fees when they decide to borrow money by issuing bonds. These expenditures relate to the entire life of the loan and are charged to expense over the life of the bond issue. Such bond issue costs decrease the amount received from the bond issue and are considered to be adjustments to the premium or discount on the bonds. None of our examples included these costs, and we will continue to assume that all bond prices are given after deducting issue costs.

EARLY REPAYMENT OF BONDS

The loans represented by bonds are normally repaid to the investor when the bonds mature. An example of an entry to record such repayment was presented on page 458.

As discussed earlier, many bond indenture agreements contain a provision allowing for repayment of the bonds before their maturity date if a call premium is paid to the bondholders. Suppose that Teak has the right to repay the one million dollars of bonds issued at par on January 1, 1985, before maturity for 105 and it exercises this right on January 1, 1989. This means that Teak must pay 105 percent of face, or $1,050,000, to the bondholders on January 1, 1989. The difference between the bond carrying value and the price paid would be considered an extraordinary loss for income determination purposes in 1989. The **carrying value of bonds** is equal to the face amount less any unamortized discount or plus any unamortized premium. In this case, since no discount or premium exists, the carrying value is equal to the face value. The loss would be $50,000, and the early retirement would be recorded as follows:

CARRYING VALUE OF BONDS
Face amount of the bonds less any unamortized discount or plus any unamortized premium.

Jan. 1, 1989	Bonds payable	1,000,000	
	Loss on early retirement of bonds payable	50,000	
	Cash		1,050,000
	(to record early retirement of bonds)		

If a premium or discount had existed, any unamortized amounts would also be completely removed from the books of record.

CONVERSION OF BONDS TO STOCK

As introduced earlier in the chapter, some indenture agreements allow the bondholder the option of converting the bonds into stock of the issuing corporation. When and if a bondholder elects to convert his or her loan into ownership, the bonds are exchanged for stock, and the debt must be reclassified as stock on the corporation's books. For example, assume that Teak Corporation has convertible bonds outstanding that allow the bondholders to exchange each $1,000 bond for ten shares of Teak $10 par value common stock. Further assume that carrying value of the bonds is $950,000 on January 1, 1988, and one-half of all bondholders elect to convert their bonds into stock at that date. Four hundred seventy-five thousand dollars would be removed from the debt classification and placed in the ownership class as follows:

Jan. 1, 1988	Bonds payable	500,000	
	Discount on bonds payable		25,000
	Common stock		50,000
	Paid-in capital in excess of par		425,000
	(to reclassify debt as owners' equity)		

Note that the additional common stock is put on the books at par value, with the remainder added to paid-in capital in excess of par consistent with the presentations in Chapter 13.

SINKING FUNDS

SINKING FUND
Funds set aside each year for repaying a loan at maturity.

Sometimes when companies borrow money through issuance of bonds, they agree to set aside funds each year for repaying the loan at maturity. This money is called a **sinking fund** and is owned by the company issuing the bonds but is under the control of the bond trustee as protection for the investors. Sinking funds may not be used for any purpose except bond repayment and are invested by the trustee until the repayment date. The bond issuer need not put aside the full amount necessary for repayment, since the trustee will invest the funds, and the earnings from this investment will provide additional money for repayment. The exact amount of money put under the control of the bond trustee is determined by the amount of expected investment earnings.

Since the funds really belong to the bond issuer, all earnings on the funds are reported as income of the bond issuer. Likewise, any gains or losses that occur as investment decisions are made are also reported as part of the bond issuer's income.

At maturity, the trustee will sell all of the sinking fund investments and pay out the cash to the bond investors in repayment of their loans to the bond-issuing company. If insufficient funds are available for repayment, the bond issuer must make up the difference. If more funds are available than are needed, the extra amount is made available for any purpose the issuer wishes.

The assets in the sinking fund are reported as one total on the bond issuer's statement of financial position as a long-term investment, since such funds are not useable by the reporting company for current operating purposes.

BONDS ON THE STATEMENT OF FINANCIAL POSITION

Bonds are shown after current liabilities and before owners' equity on the statement of financial position unless they are due to mature in less than one year. Those bonds maturing within the next year are shown as current liabilities. The bond indebtedness is generally shown as one figure net of all discounts or premiums. Details concerning the various parts of the net carrying value are usually disclosed in a footnote to the financial statements. Exhibit 15.5 presents a typical example taken from the 1984 annual report of the Corning Glass Works of New York.

THE INVESTOR IN BONDS

From the investor's point of view, a long-term loan has been made when bonds are acquired and the loan is treated as an investment. Although most bonds are acquired by individual investors, one corporation might lend idle funds to another through bond acquisitions. Whether the investment is long-term or short-term depends upon the intention of the investor. Chapter 7 details the distinctions between long-term and short-term investments.

The investor is a mirror image of the bond issuer. All of the details concerning issue amounts and conditions, real and nominal interest rates, and interest payment

EXHIBIT 15.5

Consolidated Balance Sheets
Corning Glass Works of New York

Liabilities and Stockholders' Equity	**December 30, 1984**	**January 1, 1984**
Current Liabilities		
Loans payable	**$ 31.7**	$ 29.4
Accounts payable	**98.6**	82.8
Taxes on income payable	**56.5**	61.3
Wages and employee benefits accrued	**101.8**	68.6
Accrued costs of business restructuring	**17.0**	28.4
Other accrued liabilities	**71.5**	73.9
Total current liabilities	**377.1**	344.4
Accrued Furnace Repairs	**22.7**	21.3
Other Liabilities and Deferred Credits	**38.5**	29.5
Loans Payable Beyond One Year[9]	**309.1**	315.3
Deferred Investment Credits and Deferred Taxes on Income	**42.3**	29.9
Minority Interest in Subsidiary Companies		1.5
Common Stockholders' Equity		
Common stock, including excess over par value in 1983—Par value $5 per share; authorized—60,000,000 shares (net of cost of 1,554,678 and 1,572,826 shares of common stock in treasury)	**167.5**	122.1
Retained earnings	**969.7**	959.9
Translation adjustments	**(70.1)**	(49.3)
Total common stockholders' equity	**1,067.1**	1,032.7
Total Liabilities and Stockholders' Equity	**$1,856.8**	$1,774.6

[9]Loans Payable Beyond One Year

	December 30, 1984	January 1, 1984
Sinking fund debentures, 7¾%, due November 15, 1998	**$ 25.0**	$ 25.0
Income debentures, 3¾%, due March 1, 2002	**8.1**	8.1
Debentures, 7%, due March 15, 2007	**48.7**	48.5
Industrial revenue bonds, average rate 7.8%, due through 2014	**55.8**	47.9
Subordinated exchangeable debentures, 8¼%, due December 1, 2007	**100.0**	100.0
MetPath subordinated debentures, 13¼%, due August 1, 2000	**27.5**	27.4
MetPath mortgage payable, 9¼%, due through February, 2011	**7.6**	7.7
Other notes payable, average rate 12.1%, due through 2011	**36.4**	50.7
	$ 309.1	$ 315.3

The 7% Debentures, due March 15, 2007, at December 30, 1984, are net of unamortized discount of $51.3 million.

The 8¼% Subordinated Exchangeable Debentures due December 1, 2007, are exchangeable beginning in 1983 into Owens-Corning Fiberglas (OCF) Corporation common stock held in escrow for Corning at an exchange rate of 26.2295 shares per $1,000 principal amount of debentures.

Bank revolving credit agreements in effect at December 30, 1984, provided for Corning Glass Works to borrow up to $265 million and certain subsidiaries to borrow up to $108.6 million. At the end of 1984, $31.9 million of borrowings were outstanding under these agreements. The revolving credit agreements provide for borrowings of U.S. dollar and Eurocurrency at various rates—equal to or above prime, London interbank offered rate, or bank certificate of deposit rate, during the revolving period. U.S. dollar borrowings are convertible in 1987–1990 to term notes repayable through September, 1994. Eurocurrency borrowing agreements terminate in 1988–1990.

Loans payable in 1985 are presented as current liabilities in the consolidated balance sheet. The company may, at its option, accelerate retirements of portions of this debt.

At December 30, 1984, loans payable beyond one year become payable:

1986	1987	1988	1989	1990	1991–2014
$6.4	$3.4	$5.7	$4.0	$4.6	$285.0

During 1983, Corning's Mexican subsidiaries entered into an exchange risk protection program known as FICORCA. Participation in this program resulted in borrowing and, in turn, depositing with FICORCA the peso equivalent of $23.7 million of which $13.7 million remained in the program as of December 30, 1984. Under terms of the program, the deposit with FICORCA can be used to fully offset the related Peso debt (principal and accrued interest) at anytime during the life of the program. Therefore, the FICORCA deposit and Peso debt have been offset against one another and are not included in the Consolidated Balance Sheets of Corning as of December 30, 1984.

dates are the same for the investor as for the issuer. The only difference is that investors do not use separate premium or discount accounts. Amortization of the premium or discount amounts are reflected directly in the investment in bonds account, and thus the investment in bonds account is always shown at net carrying value. Of course, bond interest expense to the issuer is interest revenue to the investor.

Accounting for Bond Investment

To illustrate the accounting process, assume that Investor Corporation acquires all of the bonds of the Teak Company as a long-term investment. Further assume that the acquisition takes place on April 1, 1985, at a value of 90.4348 paralleling the issuance described on page 460. In nonaccounting terms, Investor Corporation lends Teak $904,348 on April 1, 1985, for 9¾ years at 16 percent effective annual interest (face rate of 14%). Repayment is due January 1, 1995.

Since the acquisition date is between interest payment dates, Investor must give Teak an extra $35,000 at the investment date. Thus, Investor gives $939,348 cash to Teak representing an investment (loan) of $904,348 and returnable cash of $35,000. The entry would be as follows:

Apr. 1, 1985	Investment in bonds	904,348	
	Interest receivable	35,000	
	Cash		939,348
	(to record the investment in bonds of Teak)		

Note that the discount was not recorded separately as it was on the books of Teak on page 460.

Accounting for Interest Revenue

Assume that Investor is on a calendar year basis for financial reporting purposes. Since no entries have been made for the interest earned, an adjusting entry would be required on December 31, 1985, to have a correct interest revenue figure on the books for 1985. This entry is as follows:

Dec. 31, 1985	Interest receivable	105,000	
	Investment in bonds	3,521	
	Interest revenue		
	(.16 × $904,348 × 3/4)		108,521
	(to record interest revenue and adjust the balances in the receivable and investment accounts)		

Note that the interest revenue corresponds to the interest expense on the part of Teak. Note further that the interest earned but not expected to be currently received is an increase in the loan corresponding to the increase in debt explained earlier. The only accounting difference lies in the fact that the additional loan amount is added directly to the investment account balance, whereas a separate discount account was decreased on the debtor's (Teak) books. On January 1, 1986, Investor would receive $140,000 cash from Teak and would record the receipt as follows:

Jan. 1, 1986	Cash	140,000	
	Interest receivable		140,000
	(to record receipt of cash from bond investment)		

The balance in the Interest Receivable account would now be zero.

In 1985 and beyond until maturity, the only accounting required is to record interest revenue on December 31 as 16 percent of the January 1 investment carrying value, to record the amortization of discount, and to record the interest receivable. On January 1 of each year, the cash received would be recorded. Entries for December 31, 1986, and January 1, 1987, are as follows:

Dec. 31, 1986	Interest receivable	140,000	
	Investment in bonds	5,259	
	Interest revenue		
	(.16 × 907,869)		145,259
	(to record 1986 interest revenue on bonds)		
Jan. 1, 1987	Cash	140,000	
	Interest receivable		140,000
	(to record receipt of cash from bond investment)		

At the maturity date, January 1, 1995, the loan would be repaid by Teak to Investor. By this date, the discount would be fully amortized and the Investment in Bonds account would have a balance of one million dollars. The receipt of cash in repayment of the loan would be recorded by reducing the Investment in Bonds account to zero and adding one million dollars to cash.

Jan. 1, 1995	Cash	1,000,000	
	Investment in bonds		1,000,000
	(to record repayment of loans made to Teak)		

Sale of Bonds Before Maturity

Since investment in bonds is an asset, one investor can choose to sell the investment in bonds to another investor at will. Such a sale does not constitute repayment of the loan and has no effect on the bond issuer. The issuer simply owes the money to a new creditor.

An investor selling an investment in bonds treats the sale like any other sale of an asset. The carrying value of the asset is subtracted from the proceeds of the sale, and any difference is treated as a gain or loss. The assets received in the sale, usually cash, are recorded. The carrying value of the asset given up is removed from the books, and gain or loss is recorded and reported as part of income for the period in which the sale took place.

As an example, suppose that Investor Corporation sells its investment in bonds to the Zee Company on January 1, 1987, for $925,000. The gain would be computed as follows:

Proceeds of the sale		$925,000
Carrying value of the investment		
Original investment	$904,348	
Plus: Discount amortization for 1985 and 1986	8,780	913,128
Gain on sale		$ 11,872

The reason Zee Company is willing to pay more for the bonds is that Zee is willing to accept an effective interest rate lower than 16 percent. From the point of view of Teak (the issuer), the effective interest rate is still 16 percent. How can the issuer have an effective rate of 16 percent when the new creditor Zee Company has an effective rate of less than 16 percent? Because the present value of the difference between Zee Company's earnings and Teak's expense is the gain recorded by Investor on the sale, it all evens out.

Investor would record the sale of the bonds in the books as follows:

Jan. 1	Cash	925,000	
	Investment in bonds		913,128
	Gain on sale of bonds		11,872
	(to record the sale of bonds at a gain)		

Of course, had the sale of the bond not been on an interest payment date, Investor would have recognized and recorded the interest earned up to the date of sale and amortized the appropriate amount of discount, and Zee Company would have given Investor extra cash, since the cash payment Zee Company will receive on January 1, 1988, will be for all of 1987.

OTHER LONG-TERM DEBT

Mortgages

MORTGAGE
A borrower's pledge of title to property made as security for a loan.

Purchases of real estate and some types of equipment are often financed through mortgages. When title to the property is pledged by the borrower as security for the loan, the pledge is known as a **mortgage.** In the event of nonpayment, the lender forces sale of the pledged property and recovers the amount lent from the sale proceeds.

Mortgages are typically repaid on a fixed monthly installment basis, with each payment representing interest owed for the period plus some loan balance reduction. As the outstanding loan is reduced, the portion of the payment representing interest expense declines and the portion representing loan repayment increases. Exhibit 15.6 shows the interest and loan repayments for the first five months of a $200,000 real estate mortgage loan bearing annual interest of 15 percent and with monthly payments of $2,528.89.

EXHIBIT 15.6

End of Month	Monthly Payment	Interest Amount	Loan Repayment	Unpaid Loan Balance End of Month
1	$2,528.89	$2,500.00	$28.89	$199,971.11
2	2,528.89	2,499.64	29.25	199,941.86
3	2,528.89	2,499.27	29.62	199,912.24
4	2,528.89	2,498.90	29.99	199,882.25
5	2,528.89	2,498.53	30.36	199,851.89

Each payment would be recorded as interest expense and loan reduction per the schedule in Exhibit 15.6. The portion of the mortgage due in the following year would be classified as short-term debt, with the remainder being added in with other long-term debt on the borrower's statement of financial position.

Pensions

A corporation's obligation to pay pensions to workers as they retire can be quite large. The disclosure of long-term future pension obligation in a corporation's annual financial statement is highly controversial as to computation of amount and manner of presentation. Certain requirements for reporting pension obligations to the federal government were imposed by the Employee Retirement Income Security Act of 1974 (ERISA) and are currently being studied by the FASB. Coverage in detail is a topic that must be reserved to advanced accounting courses. Be aware, however, that the obligations can be quite large and might not show up directly in the main body of a corporation's annual financial statements.

Leases

Operating and capital leases were defined in Chapter 11. From the point of view of the lessee, either operating or capital leases can constitute future long-term liabilities if the lease period extends beyond one year. Obligations under operating leases are not shown on the main body of the statement of financial position but are disclosed in the footnotes to the statement.

On the other hand, the present value of future lease obligations is recorded as a liability when a corporation enters into a capital lease. Each lease payment is divided into an interest amount and a repayment of the amount of the loan represented by the lease. The accounting methodology is very similar to that for mortgages. Detailed coverage of the subtleties in determining the present value of the future lease obligation and the considerations involved in properly classifying a lease as either operating or capital are well beyond the scope of this text.

FOR REVIEW

DEMONSTRATION PROBLEM

On January 1, 1985, the Suflo Corporation issues $20 million of 15-year, 14 percent bonds dated January 1, 1985, for $17,769,400. Interest is payable annually on January 1. One-half of the bonds are acquired by the Ragus Corporation on the issue date. Both Suflo and Ragus end their fiscal year and prepare financial statements on December 31.

Required

1. What is the effective rate of interest on the bonds?
2. Determine the amount of interest expense and interest revenue incurred and earned by Suflo and Ragus, respectively, for 1985 and 1986.
3. Present general journal entries for Suflo and Ragus for:

- **a.** The issuance and acquisition of the bonds.
- **b.** Any adjustments required at December 31, 1985, for preparation of financial statements.
- **c.** Payment and receipt of interest on January 1, 1986.

4. Suppose the bonds had been issued at the same price on April 1, 1985, instead of January 1. Present the journal entries required for both Suflo and Ragus. Is the effective rate of interest on the bonds the same as, less than, or more than that incurred when the bonds were issued on January 1? Why?

Demonstration Problem Solution

1. To find the effective rate of interest on the bonds, we must find an interest rate with present value factors such that the sum of the present value of the future interest payments ($2.8 million per year) plus the present value of the future bond repayment itself ($20 million to be received in 15 years) is equal to the issue price ($17,769,400).

Let x = PVIF of $1.00 received at the end of 15 years (Table 2, Appendix C)
Let y = PVIF of $1.00 received at the end of each year for 15 years (Table 4, Appendix C)
Then $20,000,000 times x plus $2,800,000 times y = $17,769,400

We examine Tables 2 and 4 in the 15-year row and try the present value factors corresponding to various rates of interest in the preceding formula. By trial and error we eventually try the present value factors that correspond to 16 percent interest. These factors are as follows:

for x—.1079 (Table 2, 15-year row, 16% column)
for y—5.5755 (Table 4, 15-year row, 16% column)

Using these present value factors wer find the following:

$20,000,000 (.1079) + $2,800,000 (5.5755) = $17,769,400

Thus, the effective rate of interest on the bond equals 16 percent.

2. The interest expense or revenue for any time period on the bonds must be equal to the effective rate of interest times the carrying value of the bonds at the beginning of the time period. The carrying value of the bonds is, of course, equal to the face amount of the bonds less any unamortized discount.

	For the Year Ending 12/31/85	For the Year Ending 12/31/86
Face amount of the bonds	$20,000,000	$20,000,000
Unamortized discount on bonds 1/1/85	2,230,600	2,187,496*
Net carrying value	$17,769,400	$17,812,504
Effective rate of interest	.16	.16
Interest expense	$ 2,843,104	$ 2,850,001

*The unamortized discount is determined as follows:

Discount 1/1/85	$ 2,230,600
Amortization for 1985 (effective interest less face interest)	43,104
	$ 2,187,496

Since Ragus acquired only one-half of the bonds, its interest revenue for the years ending 12/31/85 and 12/31/86 would be one-half of the interest expense amounts previously computed.

For 1985:	$1,421,552
For 1986:	$1,425,001

3.

Entries for Suflo

Jan. 1, 1985	Cash	17,769,400	
	Discount on bonds	2,230,600	
	Bonds payable		20,000,000
	(to record bond issue)		
Dec. 31, 1985	Interest expense	2,843,104	
	Interest payable		2,800,000
	Discount on bonds		43,104
	(to record 1985 interest expense)		
Jan. 1, 1986	Interest payable	2,800,000	
	Cash		2,800,000
	(to record payment of interest)		

Entries for Ragus

Jan. 1, 1985	Investment in bonds	8,884,700	
	Cash		8,884,700
	(to record bond investment)		
Dec. 31, 1985	Investment in bonds	21,552	
	Interest receivable	1,400,000	
	Interest revenue		1,421,552
	(to record 1985 interest revenue)		
Jan. 1, 1986	Cash	1,400,000	
	Interest receivable		1,400,000
	(to record receipt of interest)		

4. If the bonds had been issued on April 1, three months' interest at the face rate would have been accumulated. Cash equal to the accrued interest would have been given by the investors

to the issuer of the bonds (Suflo). This cash would have been given back to the investors by Suflo when the first annual interest payment was made on January 1, 1986, for the full year 1985. The following journal entries would have been made:

Suflo

Apr. 1, 1985	Cash	18,469,400	
	Discount on bonds	2,230,600	
	Bonds payable		20,000,000
	Interest payable		700,000
	(to record issue of bonds and accrued interest)		

Ragus

Apr. 1, 1985	Investment in bonds	8,884,700	
	Interest receivable	350,000	
	Cash		9,234,700
	(to record investment in bonds and accrued interest)		

The effective rate of interest on the bonds if the issue date is April 1 and the issue prices are the same ($17,769,400) would be higher, since the time to maturity is smaller. A smaller time to maturity would yield a higher issue price if the effective rate of interest is the same. The present value of any future sum becomes greater as you move towards the date of receipt, as long as the interest rate is constant.

SUMMARY

- When bonds are issued by a corporation, the corporation is borrowing money from investors who acquire those bonds. Bonds, therefore, represent a liability from the point of view of the issuer and an asset from the point of view of the investor.
- The agreement between the bond issuer (debtor) and the bond investor (creditor) is contained in the bond indenture agreement, and a trustee is generally appointed to ensure compliance with the agreement.
- Bonds can be secured (mortgage bonds) or unsecured (debenture bonds), serial (repayment in installments) or term (one repayment at maturity), convertible (changeable into stock), or callable (early repayment permitted). They can have any of a host of other special features as defined by the bond indenture agreement.
- Interest rates and dates of payment are fixed by the bond indenture agreement, but this fixed rate (the face or nominal rate) can be altered by market value subtractions (discounts) or additions (premiums) to the amount borrowed so that the real or effective interest rate is determined when the bonds are issued.
- The market value of a bond issue is the present value at the effective rate of interest of the sum of the future interest payments and the ultimate loan repayment amounts.
- Discounts on bonds have the effect of raising the real rate of interest above the face rate; premiums on bonds have the effect of lowering the real rate of interest below the face rate.
- Long-term debt other than bonds can exist in the form of mortgages, pensions, and leases.
- The long-term debt disclosed on a corporation's statement of financial position is combined and shown at net carrying value with details provided in the footnotes to the statement.

QUESTIONS

15-1. Define the following terms:

a. bondholder
b. issuer of bonds
c. bond certificate
d. bond indenture
e. mortgage bonds
f. debenture bonds
g. serial bonds
h. term bonds

15-2. Explain the fact that real and nominal rates of interest can be different on a particular bond issue.

15-3. Explain why it can be said that all money to be received in the future has a lower present value today.

15-4. What happens to the amount of money received for a bond issue compared to the face value of the bond when the bond is issued at par? At a discount? At a premium?

15-5. Is the real rate of interest on a bond higher or lower than the face rate when the bond is issued at a discount? At a premium?

15-6. Suppose that the bond issued by the Holly Cookie Company calls for interest payments of 12% payable on July 1 and January 1. If a $1,000 bond dated on January 1 is issued at par on April 1, how much money will Holly Cookie pay the bondholder on July 1? How much interest will have been earned by the bondholder on that date?

15-7. What is a call provision in a bond agreement? Why is a premium generally attached to the call privilege?

15-8. What is the purpose of a provision in a bond agreement allowing the bondholder to convert his or her bonds into common stock? What effect does the conversion of bonds to stock have on the statement of financial position?

15-9. What is a sinking fund?

15-10. How is a conventional home mortgage different from a bond? How is it the same?

EXERCISES

15-E1. If Ada Company issues $400,000 of 10% bonds on January 1 and the bonds are dated January 1, what are the proceeds to Ada if the bonds are issued at 100? At 90? At 104?

15-E2. On March 1, the Quest Company issues $500,000 of 10-year, 10% bonds dated March 1, with an annual interest payment date of March 1. Prepare the March 1 journal entry for the Quest Company assuming the bonds are issued at par. Prepare the March 1 journal entry for the issue of bonds if the issue price is 110.

15-E3. On June 1, the Big D Company is authorized to issue $100,000 of 15% bonds, with semiannual interest payment dates of December 1 and June 1. The bonds are issued on September 1, or three months after authorization. Prepare journal entry(s) to record the issue of the bonds if:

a. The bonds are issued at par.
b. The bonds are issued at 90.

15-E4. On July 1, Cooper Chemical Company is authorized to issue $300,000 of 10% bonds, with an interest payment date of July 1. The bonds are issued six months later on January 1.

The Sure Thing Company invests in $10,000 of these bonds. Prepare journal entries for Sure Thing if the acquisition is made:

a. At par on January 1.
b. At a price of 97 on January 1.

15-E5. Assume that on January 1, 1986, Electronics Corporation issues $600,000 of 10-year, 12% bonds dated January 1, with an annual interest payment date of January 1 to yield an effective interest rate of 14%. Determine the cash proceeds from the bond issue. Determine the price of the bonds. How much interest expense would Electronics recognize during 1986? 1987? Over the life of the bonds?

15-E6. Suppose the bonds in 15-E5 are issued on July 1, 1986, for $539,489 plus accrued interest, representing an effective interest rate of 14% on the bonds. How much interest expense would Electronics Corporation recognize during 1986 in this case? What journal entry(s) would Electronics make:

a. For the issue of the bonds on July 1.
b. On December 31, 1986, if financial statements were to be prepared as of that date.

15-E7. On January 1, 1986, Smith Enterprises invests $8,994 for a $10,000, 5-year, 12% bond dated January 1, 1986, to earn an effective rate of interest of 15%. Interest is paid annually on January 1. Prepare an amortization schedule following the format of Exhibit 15.2. What will Smith earn in interest over the life of the bond? Can you equate this with the cash that Smith receives as interest payments?

PROBLEM SET A

15-A1. Bonds Issued at Par. Abacus Computing Company issues $10 million of 10-year, 16% bonds at par on January 1, 1985. The bonds are dated January 1, 1985, and interest is paid annually on January 1. Abacus closes its books and prepares financial statements on December 31 each year.

Required

a. Prepare journal entries to record the following:

1. The issuance of the bonds on January 1, 1985.
2. Any adjustments necessary on December 31, 1985.
3. The payment of interest on January 1, 1986.
4. The repayment of the bonds on January 1, 1995.

b. What is Abacus's bond interest expense for 1985? For the entire life of the bond issue?

15-A2. Bonds Issued at a Discount. On July 1, 1985, Barley Company issues $500,000 of 5-year, 15% bonds at a price of 90.3736 for an effective yield of 18%. Interest is payable semiannually on July 1 and January 1, and Barley closes its books and prepares financial statements annually on December 31.

Required

a. Prepare an amortization schedule following the format of Exhibit 15.2.
b. Prepare journal entries to record the following:

1. The issuance of the bonds on July 1, 1985.
2. Any adjusting entry(s) for preparation of the financial statements on December 31, 1985, and interest payment on January 1, 1986. Discounts are amortized at each interest payment date and for financial statement preparation.
3. The payment of interest on July 1, 1986.
4. The repayment of the bonds on July 1, 1990.

c. What is Barley's bond interest expense for 1985? For 1986? Over the entire life of the bonds?

15-A3. Bonds Issued at a Discount—Investors' Books. Glenn Insurance Company invests in $10,000 of the bonds issued by Barley in 15-A2 on July 1, 1985. Glenn closes its books and issues financial statements annually on December 31.

Required

a. Prepare journal entries for Glenn to record the following:

1. The investment in the bonds on July 1, 1985.
2. Any adjusting entry(s) for preparation of the financial statements on December 31, 1985, and interest payment received on January 1, 1986. Discounts are amortized at each interest payment date and for financial statement preparation.
3. The receipt of interest on July 1, 1986.
4. The repayment of the bond on July 1, 1990.

b. What is Glenn's interest revenue for 1985? For 1986? Over the entire life of the bond issue?

15-A4. Bonds Issued Between Interest Payment Dates. On March 1, 1985, News Corporation issues one million dollars of 10-year, 15% bonds dated January 1, 1985, at a price of 100 plus accrued interest. Interest is payable annually on January 1. All of the bonds are acquired by the Investor Corporation. Both companies close their books and publish financial statements on December 31.

Required

Prepare general journal entries for both News and Investor for the following:
a. The issuance of the bonds on March 1.
b. Any adjustments required for preparation of financial statements on December 31, 1985, and December 31, 1986.
c. The payment of interest on January 1, 1986, and January 1, 1987.

15-A5. Mortgages. The Stanford Company is financing the purchase of a warehouse through a $100,000, 30-year, 16% mortgage with monthly payments of $1,344.76. The company obtains the mortgage on March 15, with the first payment due on April 15.

Required

Prepare general journal entries to record the following:
a. The acquisition of the warehouse on March 15.
b. Any adjusting journal entries needed to support preparation of financial statements on March 31.
c. The payments made on the mortgage on April 15 and May 15.

15-A6. Bonds Issued Between Interest Payment Dates at a Premium. On January 1, 1985, the Value Furniture Company is authorized to issue $300,000 of 5-year, 12% bonds with an annual interest payment date of January 1. The bonds are issued on April 1, 1985, at a price of 103.559 plus accrued interest to yield an effective annual rate of interest of 11%. The Value Furniture Company closes its books and prepares financial statements annually on December 31.

Required

a. Prepare an amortization schedule for bond interest payments similar to Exhibit 15.4.
b. Prepare all necessary journal entries with respect to the bonds for Value for the years ending December 31, 1985, and December 31, 1986.

15-A7. Bonds Issued at a Premium—Investors' Books. On January 1, 1985, Blizzard Air Conditioning Company issues $500,000 of 5-year, 10% bonds. The bonds are priced to yield 8%. Interest is payable semiannually on June 30 and December 31. Dan Dover buys $200,000 (40%) of Blizzard's bonds on January 1.

Required

a. Determine the price at which the bonds are issued.
b. Prepare journal entries for Blizzard and Dover on January 1, 1985.
c. Prepare journal entries for Blizzard and Dover on June 30, 1985, and December 31, 1985.
d. Assume Dover sells his bonds for $214,343 on January 1, 1986. Prepare a journal entry for Dover's sale.

15-A8. Determination of Issue Price. On July 1, 1986, Calhoun Company issues $400,000 of 4-year, 11% bonds at a price to yield an effective interest rate of 14%. The bonds are dated July 1, 1986, and require semiannual interest payments on January 1 and July 1. Calhoun closes its books and prepares financial statements on December 31.

Required

a. Determine the issue price of the bonds.
b. Prepare all necessary journal entries with respect to the bonds for the years ending December 31, 1986, and December 31, 1987.
c. What carrying value would the bonds have at the close of fiscal 1986 and fiscal 1987? How would these values be shown in Calhoun's statement of financial position?
d. Determine the total interest expense of Calhoun over the life of the bonds.
e. Why is the issue price different from the face amount of the bonds?

PROBLEM SET B

15-B1. Bonds Issued at Par. Charlie's Door Company issues $15 million of 20-year, 14% bonds at par on January 1, 1986. The bonds are dated January 1, 1986, and pay interest annually on January 1. Charlie's Door Company closes its books and prepares financial statements as of December 31 each year.

Required

a. Prepare journal entries to record the following:

1. The issuance of the bonds on January 1, 1986.
2. Any adjustments necessary on December 31, 1986.
3. The payment of interest on January 1, 1987.
4. The repayment of the bonds on January 1, 2006.

b. What is Charlie's bond interest expense for 1986? For the entire life of the bond issue?

15-B2. Bonds Issued at a Discount. On January 1, 1986, Browning Corporation issues $800,000 of 5-year, 16% bonds at a price of $701,654 to yield an effective rate of 20%. The bonds are dated January 1, 1986, and pay interest semiannually on January 1 and July 1.

Required

a. Prepare an amortization schedule of bond interest expense similar to Exhibit 15.2.
b. Prepare general journal entries to record the following:

1. The issuance of the bonds on January 1, 1986.
2. The payment of interest and amortization of discount on July 1, 1986, and any adjustments required on December 31, 1986, with respect to the bonds.
3. The repayment of the bonds on January 1, 1991.

c. How much interest expense does Browning incur in 1986? In 1987? Over the life of the bonds?

15-B3. Bonds Issued at a Discount—Investors' Books. Thomas Investors invests in $20,000 of the bonds issued by Browning in 15-B2.

Required

a. Determine the purchase price of the bonds.
b. Prepare general journal entries for Thomas Investors for the following:

1. The acquisition of the bonds on January 1, 1986.
2. The receipt of interest and amortization of discount on July 1, 1986, and December 31, 1986.
3. The repayment of the bonds on January 1, 1991.

c. Compare the amount of interest income recorded by Thomas over the life of the bonds before repayment with the amount of cash received in interest payments. Explain how the two amounts differ.

15-B4. Bonds Issued Between Interest Payment Dates. On April 1, 1986, Xray Corporation issues $4 million of 15-year, 16% bonds dated January 1, 1986, at a price of 100 plus accrued interest. Interest is payable annually on January 1. All of the bonds are acquired by the Ace Insurance Company. Both companies close their books on December 31.

Required

Prepare general journal entries for both Xray and Ace for the following:
a. The issuance of the bonds on April 1.
b. Any adjustments required for preparation of financial statements on December 31, 1986, and December 31, 1987.
c. The payment of interest on January 1, 1987, and January 1, 1988.

15-B5. Mortgages. Lucas Brothers Incorporated purchases an office building for $400,000 and pays $100,000 down in cash, with the remainder financed through a 20-year, $300,000 mortgage with monthly payments carrying an annual interest rate of 18%. The company purchases the building on May 15, with the first payment of $4,630 due on June 15.

Required

Prepare general journal entries for the following:
a. The acquisition of the building on May 15.
b. Any adjusting journal entries required if Lucas wishes to prepare financial statements on May 31.
c. The first two mortgage payments due on June 15 and July 15.

15-B6. Bonds Issued Between Interest Dates at a Premium. E. F. Mutton Corporation, a sheep ranch in Idaho, authorizes one million dollars of 5-year, 12% bonds on January 1, 1986. Interest is paid annually on December 31. The bonds are issued on April 1, 1986, at a price of 107.2927 for an effective yield of 10%.

Required

a. Determine the issue price and premium on the bonds and prepare the journal entry for E. F. Mutton on April 1, 1986.
b. Prepare an amortization schedule following the format of Exhibit 15.4.
c. Prepare general journal entries for the payment of interest on December 31, 1986, and December 31, 1987 (assume fiscal year ends December 31).

15-B7. Bonds Issued at a Premium—Investors' Books. Steven Shepard purchases $100,000 of the bonds issued by E. F. Mutton in 15-B6 on April 1.

Required

a. Prepare general journal entries for Steven Shepard to record the following:

1. The purchase of the bonds on April 1.
2. Receipt of interest on December 31, 1986, and December 31, 1987.

b. Steven Shepard sells his bonds on June 30, 1988, for $111,000 plus accrued interest. Prepare all general journal entries necessary to close out the bonds on Shepard's books.

15-B8. Determination of Effective Rate. On January 1, 1985, Light Company issues one million dollars of ten-year, 14% bonds for $903,348. The bonds are dated January 1, 1985, and interest payments are to be made annually on that date.

Required

a. Determine the effective rate of interest on the bonds.
b. Prove your answer in (a) by preparing an amortization schedule similar to the one in Exhibit 15.2.
c. Determine the total interest expense of Light over the life of the bonds.
d. Why might the effective rate of interest on these bonds be different from the face rate?

APPENDIX C
PRESENT VALUE CONCEPTS

THE LOGIC BEHIND TIME-VALUED ADJUSTMENTS

When you deposit money into your savings account, you expect to reclaim your investment at a later date and to be paid for the use of your money. If you make no withdrawals, when the fund is reclaimed, it will be larger because of the interest that has accumulated. In today's world, we naturally expect that the value at a later date of a wise investment will exceed the investment's value today. The value of a current investment at a future point in time is called **future value.**

FUTURE VALUE
The value of an investment at a point in time subsequent to the date at which the investment is made.

SIMPLE INTEREST
Interest where the principal amount used in the computation is the original investment at the beginning of the time period.

Payments made by a borrower for the use of money can be figured by the simple interest method or the compound interest method. **Simple interest** is calculated using the familiar formula: Interest = Principal × Rate × Time, where the principal is the original investment at the beginning of the time period. The rate is quoted on an annual basis unless noted otherwise, and the time period measurement is also based on one year. For example, if $125 is deposited in an account paying eight percent simple interest, the account would produce $30 in interest ($125 × 8% × 3 years) at the end of three years. Note that although the invested amount had grown to $135 at the end of the first year, the interest calculations for succeeding years are based on the original principal of $125.

COMPOUND INTEREST
Interest calculations where the principal amount includes accumulated interest that has not been withdrawn or paid to the investor.

Investors usually prefer compound interest to be paid. **Compound interest** calculations are based on the currently invested amount as opposed to the original investment. This current principal includes accumulated interest that has not been withdrawn or paid to the investor. In theory, interest is earned every fraction of every second that the debt exists. In actual practice, interest is not compounded quite so frequently.

Exhibit C.1 examines the previous example assuming the eight percent interest to be compounded annually.

EXHIBIT C.1

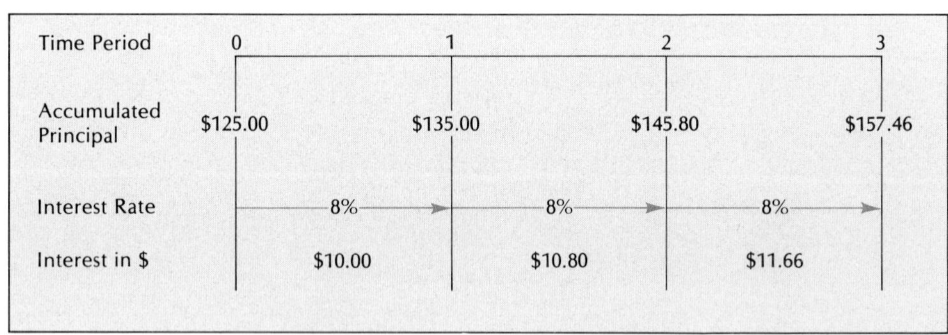

As the chart in Exhibit C.1 shows, interest at the end of each year is a function of the beginning-of-the-period principal. If interest is not remitted to the investor, the unpaid amount adds to the capital invested and produces additional interest in succeeding periods. The principal amount from Year 2 of $10.80 includes $10.00 earned on the original amount plus $.80 earned on the Year 1 interest of $10.00.

PRESENT VALUE
The current value of amounts to be received or paid in the future discounted at some interest rate; the amount that must be invested today at some interest rate to accumulate to some specified future value.

Time graphs, such as the one in Exhibit C.1, can be helpful when visualizing present and future value concepts. **Present value** is the name given to the current value of amounts to be received or paid in the future that have been discounted at some interest rate. The term also applies to an amount invested currently at some interest rate to accumulate to a specified future value. In the example in Exhibit C.1,

Year 0 represents the present time, and the present value of the investment is \$125. Several future, or compound, values are depicted; the investment's future value at the end of Year 3 is \$157.46. (Note that when using simple interest, the future accumulation totals only \$155—\$125 principal plus \$30 interest.)

Interest can be compounded more frequently than once a year and is sometimes compounded as often as once a day. Let's turn again to the \$125 deposit; this time the funds are placed into an account that carries interest at eight percent compounded semiannually. In other words, four percent times the beginning-of-the-period investment is earned at the end of each six-month period. The sequence can be shown as in Exhibit C.2:

EXHIBIT C.2

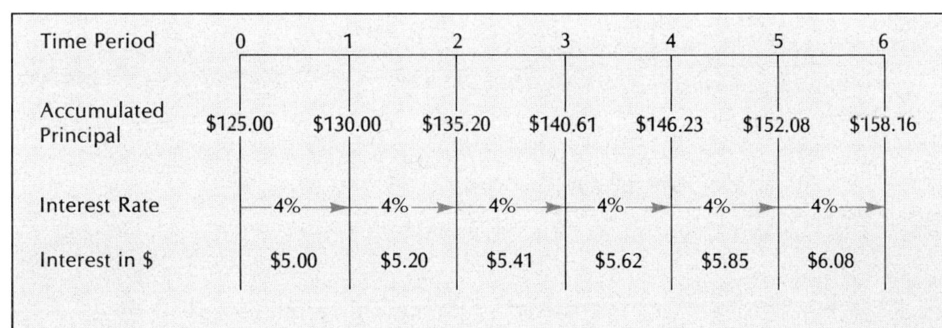

Time Period	0		1		2		3		4		5		6
Accumulated Principal	\$125.00		\$130.00		\$135.20		\$140.61		\$146.23		\$152.08		\$158.16
Interest Rate		4%		4%		4%		4%		4%		4%	
Interest in \$		\$5.00		\$5.20		\$5.41		\$5.62		\$5.85		\$6.08	

The interest now totals \$33.16, exceeding the interest in the first two examples. The more frequently interest is compounded, the greater the interest that will accrue, assuming the same annual rate and no withdrawals.

Calculations for compound interest are represented by the following formula:

$FV = PV\,(1 + i)^t$ where FV = future value of the investment
PV = original investment (present value)
i = interest rate for the period
t = number of time periods

The total of \$158.16 reached in Exhibit C.2 can also be found by formula: $\$125\,(1 + .04)^6 = \$158.16$.

Sometimes future, or compound, values are known for a particular situation, and the present value can be found from that information. As you can see by formula, if $FV = PV\,(1 + i)^t$, it follows that $PV = FV \div (1 + i)^t$, or, written another way, $PV = FV\,[1 \div (1 + i)^t]$. Given these two formulas, we can determine the present value or future value of any sum of money, given the applicable interest rates and time periods.

Suppose, for example, we want to determine the following:

1. The future value of \$125 invested at six percent for four years.
2. The present value of \$125 to be received after four years given a six percent interest rate.

The solution is as follows:

1. The future value of any amount can be determined as $FV = PV(1 + i)^t$. In this case, $FV = \$125(1 + i)^t$. $(1 + i)^t$ is called the future value interest factor (FVIF). There-

fore, FVIF = $(1.06)^4$ = 1.2625, and the future value of $125 at six percent for four years = $125 × 1.2625 = $157.81.

2. The present value of any amount can be determined as PV = FV $[1 \div (1+i)^t]$. In this case, PV = 125 $[1 \div (1+i)^t]$. $[1 \div (1 + i)^t]$ which is called the present value interest factor (PVIF). Therefore, the PVIF = 1 ÷ $(1.06)^4$ = .792, and the present value of $125 received after four years at a rate of interest of six percent is ($125)(.792) = $99.00.

Rather than actually calculate interest factors, you can use precalculated tables that list values for various time periods at assorted rates. Thus, if we wish to calculate the present value of $125 at six percent for four years, we would look up the PVIF in Table 2 (at the end of the appendix) where the 6% column and Year 4 row intersect. This PVIF is .792. Therefore, our answer is the same, i.e., ($125)(.792) = $99.00. (See also Table 1 at the end of the appendix for future values.)

The relationship between the two interest factors and future and present value is as follows:

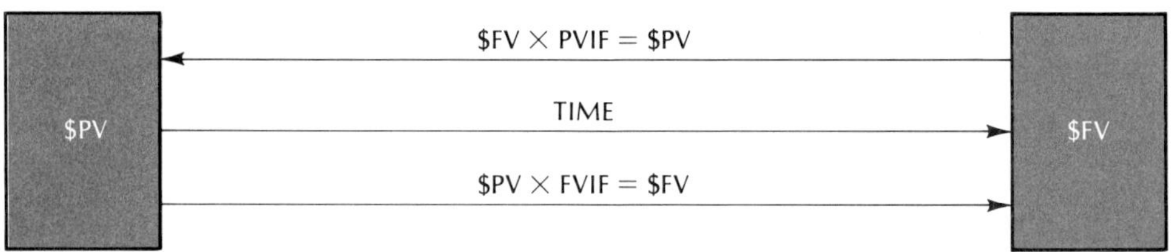

To find an unknown present amount, the future amount must be multiplied by the present value interest factor for the appropriate rate and number of time periods. Similarly, finding an unknown future value requires multiplying the present value of the investment times the appropriate future value interest factor.

PV-FV APPLICATIONS

The following examples and their solutions will help you reinforce your understanding of present value and future value concepts and give you practice using the tables:

1. You have determined that based on your budget you can add $1,000 to your savings this month. If the bank will pay you interest of 12%, assuming no withdrawals, how much interest will your money earn in nine months using the following:
   a. Simple interest.
   b. Compound interest, paid quarterly.

2. If you invest $2500 at the rate of 8%, compounded semiannually, how much will your investment be worth in five years?

3. Sam Smith is willing to sell Jim Johns a machine for $100 down and $500 due in one year. What must be the current value of the machine, assuming a desired rate of return of 10%?

Solution 1: (a) $P \times R \times T = \$1{,}000 \times .12 \times 9/12 = \$90$

(b) PV= $1,000 —— × FVIF (3 periods) ——→ FV= $??

$\$1000 \times \text{FVIF}_{3\%,\ 3\ \text{periods}} = \text{FV}$

(Remember to adjust interest quoted on an annual basis to fit the compounding time period.)

$\$1{,}000 \times 1.0927 = \$1{,}092.70$
$\$1{,}092.70 - \$1{,}000 = \$92.70$ interest

Solution 2: $\$2{,}500 \times \text{FVIF}_{4\%,\ 10\ \text{periods}} = \text{FV}$
$\$2{,}500 \times 1.4802 = \$3{,}700.50$

Solution 3:

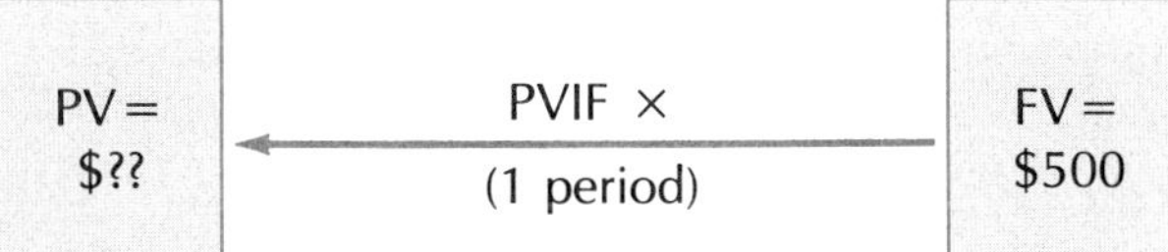

$\$500 \times \text{PFIV}_{10\%,\ 1\ \text{period}} = \text{PV}$
$\$500 \times .9091 = \$454.55$
Value of the machine $= \$454.55 + \$100 = \$554.55$

NATURE OF ANNUITIES

Business transactions frequently involve more than just one payment. A periodic series of equal payments, called rents, is an **annuity.** Usually the interest is compounded once each period. Although the procedure and reasoning for time valuation of annuity payments are quite similar to the examples just explored, annuity calculations involve multiple time periods.

ANNUITY
A periodic series of equal payments.

For example, suppose that a company, the lessee, leases an automobile for five years for $2,000 annually. The payments are made at the end of each year, and the lessor wishes to earn 12 percent on its invested capital. As Exhibit C.3 shows, each rental payment can be reduced to its present value using Table 2. By summing the present values for the payments, we can arrive at the total present value of the series of payments as shown in Exhibit C.3. In our example, although the lease payments will total $10,000, their value at the current time is considerably less because of the interest that is inherent in the transaction.

Since businesses frequently need to know the present value of annuity payments, tables are available that supply future and present value interest factors for annuities of $1 (see Tables 3 and 4 at the end of the appendix). The annuity of $1 tables are prepared based on ordinary annuity payments paid at the end of each period.

EXHIBIT C.3

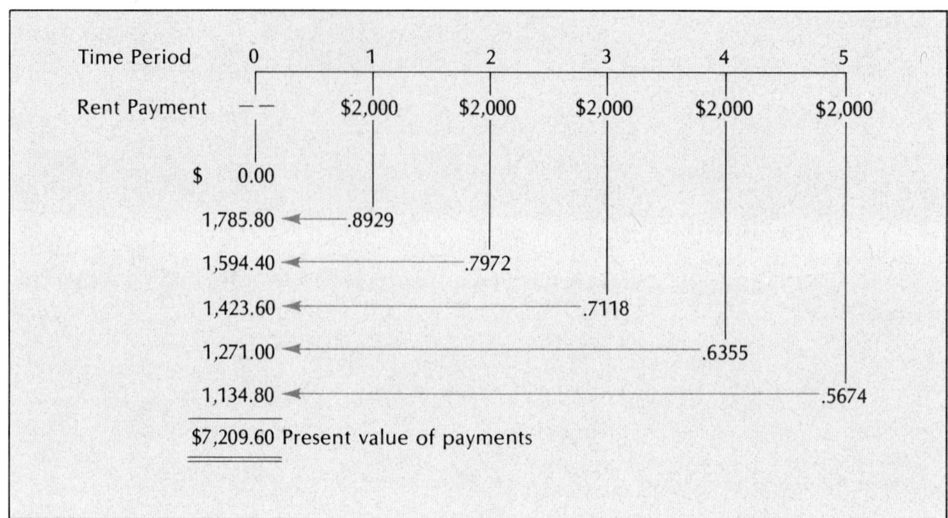

Determining the present value of an annuity of $2,000 from Table 3 is easier than using the preceding computations:

$2,000 × PVIF for an annuity at 12%, 5 periods = $2,000 × 3.6048 = $7,209.60

If the transaction involves both a payment immediately and a series of equal payments, additional computation will be necessary.

PV-FV OF ANNUITY APPLICATIONS

The following examples and their solutions will help you understand the calculation of annuities. (As we explore several examples, we will utilize the value of an annuity of $1 tables, but note that the problems can also be solved using only the value of $1 tables.)

1. Your parents want to take a vacation in two years. They think that they can put $3,000 in their savings account every three months from now until then. How much will the account hold after two years at an annual interest rate of 8%?

2. You recently participated on a televised game show and won the grand prize. You can take this prize in one of four forms of payment:
   - **a.** A camping trailer package worth $25,000 to be delivered in six months.
   - **b.** $22,500 cash payable immediately.
   - **c.** $10,000 cash now and $3,500 each year for five years.
   - **d.** No cash now and $6,000 each year for five years.

   Your family could use the camping gear, but you want to pick the choice with the highest present value. If the appropriate interest rate is 16%, which is the best choice?

Solution 1: Future value of an annuity of $3,000 for 8 periods at 2% each period = $3,000 × FVIFA at 2%, 8 periods = $3,000 × 8.583 = $25,749. (Note: FVIFA is an abbreviation for future value interest factor of an annuity. PVIFA represents the present value interest factor of an annuity.)

Solution 2: Reduce each choice to its present value, a process sometimes called discounting. Calculations are as follows:

(a) Find the PV of $25,000 in 6 months at 16% annually:

PV = $??	← PVIF (1 period)	FV = $25,000

PV = $25,000 × $PVIF_{8\%,\ 1\ period}$ = $25,000 × .9259 = $23,147.50

(b) $22,500 is the present value.

(c)

Time Period	0	1	2	3	4	5
Payment	$10,000	$3,500	$3,500	$3,500	$3,500	$3,500

Present value of $10,000 at Time 0 = $10,000
Present value of annuity of $3,500 at 16%, 5 years = $3,500 × 3.2743 = $11,460.05.

PV of this alternative = $10,000 + $11,460.05 = $21,460.05.

(d)

Time Period	0	1	2	3	4	5
Payment	—	$6,000	$6,000	$6,000	$6,000	$6,000

Present value of annuity of $6,000 at 16%, 5 years = $6,000 × 3.2743 = $19,645.80.

Alternative (a) is the best choice in terms of present value.

PRESENT VALUE BUSINESS APPLICATION—BONDS

To apply present value concepts to the issuance of bonds, assume the following facts: A company issues for cash $100,000 of five-year bonds at eight percent, with interest payable semiannually. The bondholder receives the following:

1. Ten payments of $4,000 ($100,000 × 8% × ½) each over five years (semiannual payments).
2. $100,000 at the end of five years.

The present value of these payments is computed as follows:

Item	Amount	PV Factor	Present Value
Principal	$100,000	.6756	$ 67,560*
Interest	$ 4,000	8.1109	32,440**
			$100,000

* $100,000 at 8% compounded semiannually = $67,560
**$4,000 *annuity* at 8% compounded semiannually = $32,440 rounded

In this example, present values have been calculated at four percent, since the eight percent interest is payable semiannually. The $67,560 represents an amount that, if invested at eight percent compounded semiannually, will have a future value of $100,000 in five years. The $32,440 is the present value of $4,000 received semiannually over the next five years. Viewed another way, a current deposit of $32,440 at eight percent would yield ten semiannual withdrawals of $4,000 each, as follows:

	Beginning Balance	Interest Multiplier	Total Amount with Interest	Withdrawal	Amount Carried Forward
1st 6-month period	$32,440.00	1.04	$33,737.60	$4,000.00	$29,737.60
2nd 6-month period	$29,737.60	1.04	$30,927.10	$4,000.00	$26,927.10
.	.	.	.	.	.
.	.	.	.	.	.
.	.	.	.	.	.
9th 6-month period	$ 7,539.47	1.04	$ 7,841.05	$4,000.00	$ 3,841.05
10th 6-month period	$ 3,841.05	1.04	$ 3,994.69	$3,994.69*	–0–

*$5.31 difference due to rounding

Present value concepts are utilized in many accounting areas other than bonds. Lease agreements, pension plans, sinking funds, and capital budgeting decisions also involve finding present values of future cash flows.

OTHER CONSIDERATIONS

During your study of this topic and the PV tables, you should become aware of several important details. First, a lower interest, or discount, rate will yield a higher present value. (Test this for yourself: $1,000 to be paid in ten years is of what value now if the interest rate is 15% compounded annually? 10%? 5%?) The reverse is, of course, also true.

Second, in some situations, the amount to be received in the future is much less significant than the time period or the interest rate to be used when determining the present value. For instance, compare the present values of $10,000 and $20,000 to be paid in 15 years when the rate is 18%. How much of the payment is the return of the original investment (the present value), and how much represents interest? To see the effects of time periods, figure the present value of $10,000 and $20,000 to be paid after 30 years. Now how much represents the original investment and how much interest?

Finally, note that we have not discussed inflation for any of these examples. Present value concepts operate independent of inflation. Inflation adjustments can be necessary in computations that determine the value of cash flows over time. We will not deal with such adjustments here.

TABLE 1

Future Value of $1

FVIF = $(1 + i)^n$

Period	1%	2%	3%	4%	5%	6%	7%	8%	9%	10%	12%	14%	15%	16%	18%	20%	24%	28%	32%	36%
1	1.0100	1.0200	1.0300	1.0400	1.0500	1.0600	1.0700	1.0800	1.0900	1.1000	1.1200	1.1400	1.1500	1.1600	1.1800	1.2000	1.2400	1.2800	1.3200	1.3600
2	1.0201	1.0404	1.0609	1.0816	1.1025	1.1236	1.1449	1.1664	1.1881	1.2100	1.2544	1.2996	1.3225	1.3456	1.3924	1.4400	1.5376	1.6384	1.7424	1.8496
3	1.0303	1.0612	1.0927	1.1249	1.1576	1.1910	1.2250	1.2597	1.2950	1.3310	1.4049	1.4815	1.5209	1.5609	1.6430	1.7280	1.9066	2.0972	2.3000	2.5155
4	1.0406	1.0824	1.1255	1.1699	1.2155	1.2625	1.3108	1.3605	1.4116	1.4641	1.5735	1.6890	1.7490	1.8106	1.9388	2.0736	2.3642	2.6844	3.0360	3.4210
5	1.0510	1.1041	1.1593	1.2167	1.2763	1.3382	1.4026	1.4693	1.5386	1.6105	1.7623	1.9254	2.0114	2.1003	2.2878	2.4883	2.9316	3.4360	4.0075	4.6526
6	1.0615	1.1262	1.1941	1.2653	1.3401	1.4185	1.5007	1.5869	1.6771	1.7716	1.9738	2.1950	2.3131	2.4364	2.6996	2,9860	3.6352	4.3980	5.2899	6.3275
7	1.0721	1.1487	1.2299	1.3159	1.4071	1.5036	1.6058	1.7138	1.8280	1.9487	2.2107	2.5023	2.6600	2.8262	3.1855	3.5832	4.5077	5.6295	6.9826	8.6054
8	1.0829	1.1717	1.2668	1.3686	1.4775	1.5938	1.7182	1.8509	1.9926	2.1436	2.4760	2.8526	3.0590	3.2784	3.7589	4.2998	5.5895	7.2058	9.2170	11.703
9	1.0937	1.1951	1.3048	1.4233	1.5513	1.6895	1.8385	1.9990	2.1719	2.3579	2.7731	3.2519	3.5179	3.8030	4.4355	5.1598	6.9310	9.2234	12.166	15.916
10	1.1046	1.2190	1.3439	1.4802	1.6289	1.7908	1.9672	2.1589	2.3674	2.5937	3.1058	3.7072	4.0456	4.4114	5.2338	6.1917	8.5944	11.805	16.059	21.646
11	1.1157	1.2434	1.3842	1.5395	1.7103	1.8983	2.1049	2.3316	2.5804	2.8531	3.4785	4.2262	4.6524	5.1173	6.1759	7.4301	10.657	15.111	21.198	29.439
12	1.1268	1.2682	1.4258	1.6010	1.7959	2.0122	2.2522	2.5182	2.8127	3.1384	3.8960	4.8179	5.3502	5.9360	7.2876	8.91961	13.214	19.342	27.982	40.037
13	1.1381	1.2936	1.4685	1.6651	1.8856	2.1329	2.4098	2.7196	3.0658	3.4523	4.3635	5.4924	6.1528	6.8858	8.5994	10.699	16.386	24.758	36.937	54.451
14	1.1495	1.3195	1.5126	1.7317	1.9799	2.2609	2.5785	2.9372	3.3417	3.7975	4.8871	6.2613	7.0757	7.9875	10.147	12.839	20.319	31.691	48.756	74.053
15	1.1610	1.3459	1.5580	1.8009	2.0789	2.3966	2.7590	3.1722	3.6425	4.1772	5.4736	7.1379	8.1371	9.2655	11.973	15.407	25.195	40.564	64.358	100.71
16	1.1726	1.3728	1.6047	1.8730	2.1829	2.5404	2.9522	3.4259	3.9703	4.5950	6.1304	8.1372	9.3576	10.748	14.129	18.488	31.242	51.923	84.953	136.96
17	1.1843	1.4002	1.6528	1.9479	2.2920	2.6928	3.1588	3.7000	4.3276	5.0545	6.8660	9.2765	10.761	12.467	16.672	22.186	38.740	66.461	112.13	186.27
18	1.1961	1.4282	1.7024	2.0258	2.4066	2.8543	3.3799	3.9960	4.7171	5.5599	7.6900	10.575	12.375	14.462	19.673	26.623	48.038	85.070	148.02	253.33
19	1.2081	1.4568	1.7535	2.1068	2.5270	3.0256	3.6165	4.3157	5.1417	6.1159	8.6128	12.055	14.231	16.776	23.214	31.948	59.567	108.89	195.39	344.53
20	1.2202	1.4859	1.8061	2.1911	2.6533	3.2071	3.8697	4.6610	5.6044	6.7275	9.6463	13.743	16.366	19.460	27.393	38.337	73.864	139.37	257.91	468.57
21	1.2324	1.5157	1.8603	2.2788	2.7860	3.3996	4.1406	5.0338	6.1088	7.4002	10.803	15.667	18.821	22.574	32.323	46.005	91.591	178.40	340.44	637.26
22	1.2447	1.5460	1.9161	2.3699	2.9253	3.6035	4.4304	5.4365	6.6586	8.1403	12.100	17.861	21.644	26.186	38.142	55.206	113.57	228.35	449.39	866.67
23	1.2572	1.5769	1.9736	2.4647	3.0715	3.8197	4.7405	5.8715	7.2579	8.9543	13.552	20.361	24.891	30.376	45.007	66.247	140.83	292.30	593.19	1178.6
24	1.2697	1.6084	2.0328	2.5633	3.2251	4.0489	5.0724	6.3412	7.9111	9.8497	15.178	23.212	28.625	35.236	53.108	79.496	174.63	374.14	783.02	1602.9
25	1.2824	1.6406	2.0938	2.6658	3.3864	4.2919	5.4274	6.8485	8.6231	10.834	17.000	26.461	32.918	40.874	62.668	95.396	216.54	478.90	1033.5	2180.0
26	1.2953	1.6734	2.1566	2.7725	3.5557	4.5494	5.8074	7.3964	9.3992	11.918	19.040	30.166	37.856	47.414	73.948	114.47	268.51	612.99	1364.3	2964.9
27	1.3082	1.7069	2.2213	2.8834	3.7335	4.8223	6.2139	7.9881	10.245	13.110	21.324	34.389	43.535	55.000	87.259	137.37	332.95	784.63	1800.9	4032.2
28	1.3213	1.7410	2.2879	2.9987	3.9201	5.1117	6.6488	8.6271	11.167	14.421	23.883	39.204	50.065	63.800	102.96	164.84	412.86	1004.3	2377.2	5483.8
29	1.3345	1.7758	2.3566	3.1187	4.1161	5.4184	7.1143	9.3173	12.172	15.863	26.749	44.693	57.575	74.008	121.50	197.81	511.95	1285.5	3137.9	7458.0
30	1.3478	1.8114	2.4273	3.2434	4.3219	5.7435	7.6123	10.061	13.267	17.449	29.959	50.950	66.211	85.849	143.37	237.37	634.81	1645.5	4142.0	10143.

TABLE 2

Present Value of $1

$$PVIF = \frac{1}{(1 + i)^n}$$

Period	1%	2%	3%	4%	5%	6%	7%	8%	9%	10%	12%	14%	15%	16%	18%	20%	24%	28%	32%	36%
1	.9901	.9804	.9709	.9615	.9524	.9434	.9346	.9259	.9174	.9091	.8929	.8772	.8696	.8621	.8475	.8333	.8065	.7813	.7576	.7353
2	.9803	.9612	.9426	.9246	.9070	.8900	.8734	.8573	.8417	.8264	.7972	.7695	.7561	.7432	.7182	.6944	.6504	.6104	.5739	.5407
3	.9706	.9423	.9151	.8890	.8638	.8396	.8163	.7938	.7722	.7513	.7118	.6750	.6575	.6407	.6086	.5787	.5245	.4768	.4348	.3975
4	.9610	.9238	.8885	.8548	.8227	.7921	.7629	.7350	.7084	.6830	.6355	.5921	.5718	.5523	.5158	.4823	.4230	.3725	.3294	.2923
5	.9515	.9057	.8626	.8219	.7835	.7473	.7130	.6806	.6499	.6209	.5674	.5194	.4972	.4761	.4371	.4019	.3411	.2910	.2495	.2149
6	.9420	.8880	.8375	.7903	.7462	.7050	.6663	.6302	.5963	.5645	.5066	.4556	.4323	.4104	.3704	.3349	.2751	.2274	.1890	.1580
7	.9327	.8706	.8131	.7599	.7107	.6651	.6227	.5835	.5470	.5132	.4523	.3996	.3759	.3538	.3139	.2791	.2218	.1776	.1432	.1162
8	.9235	.8535	.7894	.7307	.6768	.6274	.5820	.5403	.5019	.4665	.4039	.3506	.3269	.3050	.2660	.2326	.1789	.1388	.1085	.0854
9	.9143	.8368	.7664	.7026	.6446	.5919	.5439	.5002	.4604	.4241	.3606	.3075	.2843	.2630	.2255	.1938	.1443	.1084	.0822	.0628
10	.9053	.8203	.7441	.6756	.6139	.5584	.5083	.4632	.4224	.3855	.3220	.2697	.2472	.2267	.1911	.1615	.1164	.0847	.0623	.0462
11	.8963	.8043	.7224	.6496	.5847	.5268	.4751	.4289	.3875	.3505	.2875	.2366	.2149	.1954	.1619	.1346	.0938	.0662	.0472	.0340
12	.8874	.7885	.7014	.6246	.5568	.4970	.4440	.3971	.3555	.3186	.2567	.2076	.1869	.1685	.1372	.1122	.0757	.0517	.0357	.0250
13	.8787	.7730	.6810	.6006	.5303	.4688	.4150	.3677	.3262	.2897	.2292	.1821	.1625	.1452	.1163	.0935	.0610	.0404	.0271	.0184
14	.8700	.7579	.6611	.5775	.5051	.4423	.3878	.3405	.2992	.2633	.2046	.1597	.1413	.1252	.0985	.0779	.0492	.0316	.0205	.0135
15	.8613	.7430	.6419	.5553	.4810	.4173	.3624	.3152	.2745	.2394	.1827	.1401	.1229	.1079	.0835	.0649	.0397	.0247	.0155	.0099
16	.8528	.7284	.6232	.5339	.4581	.3936	.3387	.2919	.2519	.2176	.1631	.1229	.1069	.0930	.0708	.0541	.0320	.0193	.0118	.0073
17	.8444	.7142	.6050	.5134	.4363	.3714	.3166	.2703	.2311	.1978	.1456	.1078	.0929	.0802	.0600	.0451	.0258	.0150	.0089	.0054
18	.8360	.7002	.5874	.4936	.4155	.3503	.2959	.2502	.2120	.1799	.1300	.0946	.0808	.0691	.0508	.0376	.0208	.0118	.0068	.0039
19	.8277	.6864	.5703	.4746	.3957	.3305	.2765	.2317	.1945	.1635	.1161	.0829	.0703	.0596	.0431	.0313	.0168	.0092	.0051	.0029
20	.8195	.6730	.5537	.4564	.3769	.3118	.2584	.2145	.1784	.1486	.1037	.0728	.0611	.0514	.0365	.0261	.0135	.0072	.0039	.0021
25	.7798	.6095	.4776	.3751	.2953	.2330	.1842	.1460	.1160	.0923	.0588	.0378	.0304	.0245	.0160	.0105	.0046	.0021	.0010	.0005
30	.7419	.5521	.4120	.3083	.2314	.1741	.1314	.0994	.0754	.0573	.0334	.0196	.0151	.0116	.0070	.0042	.0016	.0006	.0002	.0001

TABLE 3

Future Value of an Annuity of $1

$$FVIFA = \frac{(1 + i)^n - 1}{i}$$

Number of Periods	1%	2%	3%	4%	5%	6%	7%	8%	9%	10%	12%	14%	15%	16%	18%	20%	24%	28%	32%	36%
1	1.0000	1.0000	1.0000	1.0000	1.0000	1.0000	1.0000	1.0000	1.0000	1.0000	1.0000	1.0000	1.0000	1.0000	1.0000	1.0000	1.0000	1.0000	1.0000	1.0000
2	2.0100	2.0200	2.0300	2.0400	2.0500	2.0600	2.0700	2.0800	2.0900	2.1000	2.1200	2.1400	2.1500	2.1600	2.1800	2.2000	2.2400	2.2800	2.3200	2.3600
3	3.0301	3.0604	3.0909	3.1216	3.1525	3.1836	3.2149	3.2464	3.2781	3.3100	3.3744	3.4396	3.4725	3.5056	3.5724	3.6400	3.7776	3.9184	4.0624	4.2096
4	4.0604	4.1216	4.1836	4.2465	4.3101	4.3746	4.4399	4.5061	4.5731	4.6410	4.7793	4.9211	4.9934	5.0665	5.2154	5.3680	5.6842	6.0156	6.3624	6.7251
5	5.1010	5.2040	5.3091	5.4163	5.5256	5.6371	5.7507	5.8666	5.9847	6.1051	6.3528	6.6101	6.7424	6.8771	7.1542	7.4416	8.0484	8.6999	9.3983	10.146
6	6.1520	6.3081	6.4684	6.6330	6.8019	6.9753	7.1533	7.3359	7.5233	7.7156	8.1152	8.5355	8.7537	8.9775	9.4420	9.9299	10.980	12.135	13.405	14.798
7	7.2135	7.4343	7.6625	7.8983	8.1420	8.3938	8.6540	8.9228	9.2004	9.4872	10.089	10.730	11.066	11.413	12.141	12.915	14.615	16.533	18.695	21.126
8	8.2857	8.5830	8.8923	9.2142	9.5491	9.8975	10.259	10.636	11.028	11.435	12.299	13.232	13.726	14.240	15.327	16.499	19.122	22.163	25.678	29.731
9	9.3685	9.7546	10.159	10.582	11.026	11.491	11.978	12.487	13.021	13.579	14.775	16.085	16.785	17.518	19.085	20.798	24.712	29.369	34.895	41.435
10	10.462	10.949	11.463	12.006	12.577	13.180	13.816	14.486	15.192	15.937	17.548	19.337	20.303	21.321	23.521	25.958	31.643	38.592	47.061	57.351
11	11.566	12.168	12.807	13.486	14.206	14.971	15.783	16.645	17.560	18.531	20.654	23.044	24.349	25.732	28.755	32.150	40.237	50.398	63.121	78.998
12	12.682	13.412	14.192	15.025	15.917	16.869	17.888	18.977	20.140	21.384	24.133	27.270	29.001	30.850	34.931	39.580	50.894	65.510	84.320	108.43
13	13.809	14.680	15.617	16.626	17.713	18.882	20.140	21.495	22.953	24.522	28.029	32.088	34.351	36.786	42.218	48.496	64.109	84.852	112.30	148.47
14	14.947	15.973	17.086	18.291	19.598	21.015	22.550	24.214	26.019	27.975	32.392	37.581	40.504	43.672	50.818	59.195	80.496	109.61	149.23	202.92
15	16.096	17.293	18.598	20.023	21.578	23.276	25.129	27.152	29.360	31.772	37.279	43.842	47.580	51.659	60.965	72.035	100.81	141.30	197.99	276.97
16	17.257	18.639	20.156	21.824	23.657	25.672	27.888	30.324	33.003	35.949	42.753	50.980	55.717	60.925	72.939	87.442	126.01	181.86	262.35	377.69
17	18.430	20.012	21.761	23.697	25.840	28.212	30.840	33.750	36.973	40.544	48.883	59.117	65.075	71.673	87.068	105.93	157.25	233.79	347.30	514.66
18	19.614	21.412	23.414	25.645	28.132	30.905	33.999	37.450	41.301	45.599	55.479	68.394	75.836	84.140	103.74	128.11	195.99	300.25	459.44	700.93
19	20.810	22.840	25.116	27.671	30.539	33.760	37.379	41.446	46.018	51.159	63.439	78.969	88.211	98.603	123.41	154.74	244.03	385.32	607.47	954.27
20	22.019	24.297	26.870	29.778	33.066	36.785	40.995	45.762	51.160	57.275	75.052	91.024	102.44	115.37	146.62	186.68	303.60	494.21	802.86	1298.8
21	23.239	25.783	28.676	31.969	35.719	39.992	44.865	50.422	56.764	64.002	81.698	104.76	118.81	134.84	174.02	225.02	377.46	633.59	1060.7	1767.3
22	24.471	27.299	30.536	34.248	38.505	43.392	49.005	55.456	62.873	71.402	92.502	120.43	137.63	157.41	206.34	271.03	469.05	811.99	1401.2	2404.6
23	25.716	28.845	32.452	36.617	41.430	46.995	53.436	60.893	69.531	79.543	104.60	138.29	159.27	183.60	244.48	326.23	582.62	1040.3	1850.6	3271.3
24	26.973	30.421	34.426	39.082	44.502	50.815	58.176	66.764	76.789	88.497	118.15	158.65	184.16	213.97	289.49	392.48	723.46	1332.6	2443.8	4449.9
25	28.243	32.030	36.459	41.645	47.727	54.864	53.249	73.105	84.700	98.347	133.33	181.87	212.79	249.21	342.60	471.98	898.09	1706.8	3226.8	6052.9
26	29.525	33.670	38.553	44.311	51.113	59.156	68.676	79.954	93.323	109.18	150.33	208.33	245.71	290.08	405.27	567.37	1114.6	2185.7	4260.4	8233.0
27	30.820	35.344	40.709	47.084	54.669	63.705	74.483	87.350	102.72	121.09	169.37	238.49	283.56	337.50	479.22	681.85	1383.1	2798.7	5624.7	11197.9
28	32.129	37.051	42.930	49.967	58.402	68.528	80.697	95.338	112.96	134.20	190.69	272.88	327.10	392.50	566.48	819.22	1716.0	3583.3	7425.6	15230.2
29	33.450	38.792	45.218	52.966	62.322	73.639	87.346	103.96	124.13	148.63	214.58	312.09	377.16	456.30	669.44	984.06	2128.9	4587.6	9802.9	20714.1
30	34.784	40.568	47.575	56.084	66.438	79.058	94.460	113.28	136.30	164.49	241.33	356.78	434.74	530.31	790.94	1181.8	2640.9	5873.2	12940.	28172.2

Interest

TABLE 4

Present Value of an Annuity of $1

$$PVIFA = \frac{1 - \frac{1}{(1 + i)^n}}{i}$$

Number of Periods	1%	2%	3%	4%	5%	6%	7%	8%	9%	10%	12%	14%	15%	16%	18%	20%	24%	28%	32%
1	0.9901	0.9804	0.9709	0.9615	0.9524	0.9434	0.9346	0.9259	0.9174	0.9091	0.8929	0.8772	0.8696	0.8621	0.8475	0.8333	0.8065	0.7813	0.7576
2	1.9704	1.9416	1.9135	1.8861	1.8594	1.8334	1.8080	1.7833	1.7591	1.7355	1.6901	1.6467	1.6257	1.6052	1.5656	1.5278	1.4568	1.3916	1.3315
3	2.9410	2.8839	2.8286	2.7751	2.7232	2.6730	2.6243	2.5771	2.5313	2.4869	2.4018	2.3216	2.2832	2.2459	2.1743	2.1065	1.9813	1.8684	1.7663
4	3.9020	3.8077	3.7171	3.6299	3.5460	3.4651	3.3872	3.3121	3.2397	3.1699	3.0373	2.9137	2.8550	2.7982	2.6901	2.5887	2.4043	2.2410	2.0957
5	4.8534	4.7135	4.5797	4.4518	4.3295	4.2124	4.1002	3.9927	3.8897	3.7908	3.6048	3.4331	3.3522	3.2743	3.1272	2.9906	2.7454	2.5320	2.3452
6	5.7955	5.6014	5.4172	5.2421	5.0757	4.9173	4.7665	4.6229	4.4859	4.3553	4.1114	3.8887	3.7845	3.6847	3.4976	3.3255	3.0205	2.7594	2.5342
7	6.7282	6.4720	6.2303	6.0021	5.7864	5.5824	5.3893	5.2064	5.0330	4.8684	4.5638	4.2883	4.1604	4.0386	3.8115	3.6046	3.2423	2.9370	2.6775
8	7.6517	7.3255	7.0197	6.7327	6.4632	6.2098	5.9713	5.7466	5.5348	5.3349	4.9676	4.6389	4.4873	4.3436	4.0776	3.8372	3.4212	3.0758	2.7860
9	8.5660	8.1622	7.7861	7.4353	7.1078	6.8017	6.5152	6.2469	5.9952	5.7590	5.3282	4.9464	4.7716	4.6065	4.3030	4.0310	3.5655	3.1842	2.8681
10	9.4713	8.9826	8.5302	8.1109	7.7217	7.3601	7.0236	6.7101	6.4177	6.1446	5.6502	5.2161	5.0188	4.8332	4.4941	4.1925	3.6819	3.2689	2.9304
11	10.3676	9.7868	9.2526	8.7605	8.3064	7.8869	7.4987	7.1390	6.8052	6.4951	5.9377	5.4527	5.2337	5.0286	4.6560	4.3271	3.7757	3.3351	2.9776
12	11.2551	10.5753	9.9540	9.3851	8.8633	8.3838	7.9427	7.5361	7.1607	6.8137	6.1944	5.6603	5.4206	5.1971	4.7932	4.4392	3.8514	3.3868	3.0133
13	12.1337	11.3484	10.6350	9.9856	9.3936	8.8527	8.3577	7.9038	7.4869	7.1034	6.4235	5.8424	5.5831	5.3423	4.9095	4.5327	3.9124	3.4272	3.0404
14	13.0037	12.1062	11.2961	10.5631	9.8986	9.2950	8.7455	8.2442	7.7862	7.3667	6.6282	6.0021	5.7245	5.4675	5.0081	4.6106	3.9616	3.4587	3.0609
15	13.8651	12.8493	11.9379	11.1184	10.3797	9.7122	9.1079	8.5595	8.0607	7.6061	6.8109	6.1422	5.8474	5.5755	5.0916	4.6755	4.0013	3.4834	3.0764
16	14.7179	13.5777	12.5611	11.6523	10.8378	10.1059	9.4466	8.8514	8.3126	7.8237	6.9740	6.2651	5.9542	5.6685	5.1624	4.7296	4.0333	3.5026	3.0882
17	15.5623	14.2919	13.1661	12.1657	11.2741	10.4773	9.7632	9.1216	8.5436	8.0216	7.1196	6.3729	6.0472	5.7487	5.2223	4.7746	4.0591	3.5177	3.0971
18	16.3983	14.9920	13.7535	12.6593	11.6896	10.8276	10.0591	9.3719	8.7556	8.2014	7.2497	6.4674	6.1280	5.8178	5.2732	4.8122	4.0799	3.5294	3.1039
19	17.2260	15.6785	14.3238	13.1339	12.0853	11.1581	10.3356	9.6036	8.9501	8.3649	7.3658	6.5504	6.1982	5.8775	5.3162	4.8435	4.0967	3.5386	3.1090
20	18.0456	16.3514	14.8775	13.5903	12.4622	11.4699	10.5940	9.8181	9.1285	8.5136	7.4694	6.6231	6.2593	5.9288	5.3527	4.8696	4.1103	3.5458	3.1129
25	22.0232	19.5235	17.4131	15.6221	14.0939	12.7834	11.6536	10.6748	9.8226	9.0770	7.8431	6.8729	6.4641	6.0971	5.4669	4.9476	4.1474	3.5640	3.1220
30	25.8077	22.3965	19.6004	17.2920	15.3725	13.7648	12.4090	11.2578	10.2737	9.4269	8.0552	7.0027	6.5660	6.1772	5.5168	4.9789	4.1601	3.5693	3.1242

EXERCISES

C-E1. Sam Jackson would like to purchase a new car in three years upon his graduation. He thinks $10,000 will be enough, and he plans to make equal savings deposits every three months until then. If his account pays 8% interest on a quarterly basis, how much must he deposit every three months to reach his goal?

C-E2. Seneca Tool and Die Company recently purchased a new machine that is expected to generate cash savings of $6,500 every year for 15 years. Assuming that the purchase price is equal to the present value of the savings, what was the purchase price if the appropriate rate is 18%?

C-E3. Sue and Don Hanna would like to purchase a home. Their banker has offered to lend them $50,000 at 15% interest. They can choose to repay the loan in annual installments over 20 or 30 years. Assuming no other costs of financing, how much will the yearly payments be and how much will be repaid over a 20-year period? Over a 30-year period? (Note the implications of your answers. Do you think taking the extra ten years for repayment is financially wise?)

C-E4. Sally Darling, who recently turned eight years old, has just inherited $300,000. Sally's parents have decided to place the money into an investment account that bears an average return of 12%. Sally will then get the inherited money (and accumulated earnings) on turning 21. How much should be available?

C-E5. Jason and Holly Hammer want to be able to take an extended cruise in ten years after their children are grown. Jason thinks that they can lay aside $1,200 every six months for that purpose. How much will they have for their anticipated vacation if the savings can earn 14%?

C-E6. Bob Hoffman's daughter has just started college and plans to become an accountant. Bob has high hopes for her future and wants to be able to help her start her own business as a CPA. He thinks she will be ready to do so in six years. Bob has $10,000 available now and can set aside an additional $3,000 every year until then. How much will this fund yield in six years if it grows at a 10% rate?

C-E7. Pat Harkness has $25,000 in a savings account that pays 12% semiannually. How much can Pat withdraw each period so that the withdrawals continue for ten years before the fund is used up?

C-E8. The Davis Company is issuing 15-year bonds that have a face value of $400,000 and that pay 10% interest semiannually. What is the present value of the principal, and what is the present value of the interest payments using a 10% rate?

16 LONG-TERM STOCK INVESTMENTS AND CONSOLIDATED STATEMENTS

CHAPTER OBJECTIVES
After studying Chapter 16, you should understand the following:

1. The basic concepts underlying consolidated financial reports of corporations.
2. The nature of long-term investments by one corporation in the stock of another.
3. The basic alternative accounting methods permitted with respect to acquisition of one corporation by another.
4. Concepts of economic control versus legal control of business entities.

This chapter introduces the unique accounting requirements and practices involved in the preparation of a set of consolidated financial statements. Complete coverage of the complexities of the consolidation process are well beyond the scope of this text. The material herein is designed to cover the basics and to provide a general framework for understanding and interpreting a set of consolidated financial statements.

Control of one corporation by another through stock purchase is one of the most popular business expansion methods in the United States today and often involves large amounts of money and hard-fought acquisition battles. Both the acquiring and the acquired corporation remain separate legal entities and conduct business independently. Accounting focuses on economic entities and is not bounded by legal parameters. Because one group of owners is in economic control of both companies, the financial reports of the legally separate companies must be combined into one consolidated set of financial statements to provide complete information to the owners.

LONG-TERM STOCK INVESTMENTS

Chapter 7 covered the investment by one corporation in the stock of another for the purpose of generating a cash return on nonessential funds. These investments in marketable securities were expected to be sold in the near future. This chapter is concerned with the investment by one corporation in the voting stock of another for the purpose of gaining influence or control. Such investments are long-term and are without any expectation of resale in the short-term.

Purchase and Pooling of Interests

POOLING OF INTERESTS
A business combination in which the shareholders of the acquired corporation exchange their voting stock for that of the acquiring corporation and little or no cash is exchanged.

The acquisition of the voting stock of one corporation by another is usually accomplished through a cash purchase of the stock from existing shareholders. In some cases, shareholders of the acquired corporation exchange their voting stock for that of the acquiring corporation, and little or no cash is exchanged. These stock-for-stock acquisitions are not considered true purchases but rather a **pooling of interests.** The ensuing discussion assumes a purchase for cash has occurred when one corporation acquires another. The post-acquisition principles of consolidation remain essentially the same for both pooling and purchase acquisitions, but pooling of interests mandates different valuations with respect to the assets and earnings of the acquired corporation prior to and at the point of merger. These differences are covered in a separate section of this chapter.

Levels of Control

COST METHOD
An accounting method for long-term investments in which the only income recognized by the investor is dividends and the long-term investment account is valued on the basis of the lower of cost or market rule.

Initially the investment of one corporation in the stock of another is recorded at purchase price. However, unlike most corporate assets where the future economic benefits represented by the assets are realized through use, long-term investments in stock can be held indefinitely, and the benefits of ownership revolve around the exercise of influence or control of the investor corporation over the investee. The Accounting Principles Board in Opinion No. 18 distinguishes three different methods of accounting for long-term investments in the stock of one corporation by another subsequent to the original purchase transaction.[1] The three methods are known as the cost method, the equity method, and full consolidation.

The choice of method is determined by the amount of investment by one corporation in the voting stock of another. Each method is different in the way that the long-term investment account is valued and in the amount and timing of investment income recognition. The differences among the methods arise because different amounts of ownership of one firm by another give rise to potential differences in the amount of future economic benefits expected from the investment.

Long-Term Investments Without Significant Influence. In general, when one corporation owns less than 20 percent of the voting stock of another, the investor corporation has little real influence or control over the actions of the investee. For such long-term investments, the cost method of accounting for the investment is normally employed.

The Cost Method. Under the **cost method,** the only income recognized by the investor is actual dividend payments received from the investee, and the value of the long-term investment account is based on a lower of cost or market rule. That is, if less than 20 percent ownership exists and the total market value of the stock held as a long-term investment is less than the total original cost of the stock, valuation on the statement of financial position is at market value. However, if the total market value of the portfolio is above the total cost, valuation for financial statement purposes is at cost. The source of the decline in value when market is below cost is owners' equity, and the adjustment thus does not affect income. If, in a subsequent time period, the market value of the stock previously written down increases, investment in long-term assets would be increased upward to the new market value with a maximum permissible account value of original cost.

Illustration of the Cost Method. Assume the following transactions occur in 1986 and 1987:

6/1/86 Demee purchases 100,000 shares of Filo common stock at a price of $23 per share. Those shares represent 15 percent of the voting stock of Filo.
9/1/86 Filo declares and pays a cash dividend of $.50 per share.
12/31/86 Filo common has a market price of $20 per share.
9/1/87 Filo declares and pays a dividend of $.50 per share.
12/31/87 Filo common has a market price of $26 per share.

Exhibit 16.1 gives the market and cost values for the Filo stock.

EXHIBIT 16.1

Investment	Number of Shares	Market Value 12/31/86 Per Share	Market Value 12/31/86 Total	Market Value 12/31/87 Per Share	Market Value 12/31/87 Total	Original Cost
Filo	100,000	$20	$2,000,000	$26	$2,600,000	$2,300,000

Of Corporate Raiders, Sharks, and White Knights

Not all acquisitions of one corporation by another are friendly. Managers of one corporation who attempt to gain control over another corporation that does not wish to be acquired are often called corporate raiders or sharks. The defense set up by the target corporation is sometimes called a shark repellant or poison pill, and if those defenses fail, the target might ask a third corporation (known as a white knight) to beat the shark by gaining control of the target. For example, in 1984, Mesa Petroleum Company, led by Chairman T. Boone Pickens (the raider), attempted to gain control of Gulf Oil. Mesa put together a $1.7 billion war chest to gain a controlling interest in Gulf's stock. Gulf's management did not want the company to be acquired by Mesa but lacked an effective shark repellant. So Gulf asked Standard Oil of California (the white knight) to acquire control. Standard Oil of California did so, beating out Mesa (the shark) for control. Standard Oil of California changed its name to Chevron Corporation following its acquisition of Gulf.

[1] "The Equity Method of Accounting for Investments in Common Stock," *Opinions of the Accounting Principles Board No. 18*, American Institute of Certified Public Accountants (New York: 1971).

Exhibit 16.2 shows the 1986 and 1987 income and year-end investment values for Demee's investment in Filo under the cost method of accounting for long-term investments.

EXHIBIT 16.2

	Income Recognized	Value of Long-Term Investment Account at 12/31
1986	$50,000—dividend of 9/1/86	$2,000,000
1987	$50,000—dividend of 9/1/87	$2,300,000

Accounting Under the Cost Method. The following bookkeeping entries that Demee would have in 1986 and 1987 reflect the example transaction and market value adjustments:

Date	Account	Debit	Credit
1986			
6/1	Long-term investment in common stock	2,300,000	
	Cash		2,300,000
	(to record purchase of Filo stock)		
9/1	Cash	50,000	
	Dividend income		50,000
	(to record dividends received)		
12/31	Unrealized loss on long-term investment	300,000	
	Allowance to reduce long-term investments to market		300,000
	(to adjust long-term investment in Filo to market value)		
1987			
9/1	Cash	50,000	
	Dividend income		50,000
	(to record dividends received)		
12/31	Allowance to reduce long-term investments to market	300,000	
	Unrealized loss on long-term investments		300,000
	(to adjust long-term investment in Filo up to original cost)		

Note that the adjustment to the asset Long-Term Investment in Common Stock and the corresponding adjustment to owners' equity are mechanically accomplished through the contra-asset (Allowance to Reduce Long-Term Investments to Market) and contra-owners' equity (Unrealized Loss on Long-Term Investments) accounts.

These contra-asset and contra-owners' equity accounts are used in conjunction with the investment account itself and with overall owners' equity in the same manner as accumulated depreciation was used to value long-term assets in Chapters 4 and 10.

Long-Term Investments With Some Influence But Without Control. In some cases, an investor acquires over 20 percent but less than 50 percent of the voting stock of another company. In such cases, absolute control of the investee by the investor does not exist, although significant influence does. The investor company is required in such cases to use the equity method of accounting for its long-term investment as a reflection of its influence.

The Equity Method. Under the **equity method,** the investor company includes its proportionate share of the income of the investee for its period of ownership in its income whether or not any dividend payments are actually made by the investee. Valuation of the Long-term Investment in Common Stock account is not based on either cost or market value under the equity method. Rather, the investment account value is original purchase price plus all proportionate income recognized by the investor less any dividends paid by the investee to the investor.

EQUITY METHOD
An accounting method for long-term investments where the investor includes its proportionate share of the income of the investee in its income whether or not any dividends are actually received.

The value of the long-term investment account under the equity method more closely approximates the underlying economic realities of the investment and reflects the amount of the investee's assets over which the investor can exert some influence. Dividend payments by the investee to the investor can be thought of as an exchange of asset types. Cash is received, and the investment account (another asset) is exchanged for this receipt.

Illustration of the Equity Method. Assume in the Demee Company example that the original purchase of 100,000 common shares of Filo represents 30 percent of the total voting stock of Filo, the net income of Filo is $450,000 in 1986 and $500,000 in 1987, and dividends of $50,000 are received from Filo each year. Exhibit 16.3 shows the income Demee would report in 1986 and 1987 from its investment in Filo and the value of Demee's investment account at the end of each year.

EXHIBIT 16.3

	Year Ending 12/31/86	Year Ending 12/31/87
Income from Investment		
(.3 × $450,000 × 7/12)	$ 78,750	
(.3 × $500,000)		$ 150,000
Value of Investment Account		
($2,300,000 + 78,750 − 50,000)	2,328,750	
($2,328,750 + 150,000 − 50,000)		2,428,750

Accounting Under the Equity Method. Bookkeeping entries for Demee under the equity method of accounting for long-term investments are as follows:

1986			
6/1	Long-term investment in common stock	2,300,000	
	Cash		2,300,000
	(to record purchase of Filo stock)		
9/1	Cash	50,000	
	Long-term investment in common stock		50,000
	(to record dividend received)		
12/31	Long-term investment in common stock	78,750	
	Income from long-term investment in common stock		78,750
	(to record proportionate share of Filo income for 1986)		
1987			
7/1	Cash	50,000	
	Long-term investment in common stock		50,000
	(to record dividends received)		
12/31	Long-term investment in common stock	150,000	
	Income from long-term investment in common stock		150,000
	(to record proportionate share of Filo income for 1987)		

Comparison of the Cost and Equity Methods. The equity method of accounting requires the investor to recognize more income each year on the investment than does the cost method under normal profit-making conditions. However, if stock held as a long-term investment is sold, the investor recognizes a greater gain under the cost method than under the equity method, since the basis for the investment account is not affected by earnings of the investee during the holding period.

The difference between the cost and equity methods considering the totality of a purchase, holding period, and sale of stock is zero in terms of total income. For example, assume that Demee has a change in strategic plans and decides to sell all of its Filo stock for $2.7 million on December 31, 1987. Exhibit 16.4 presents the 1986 and 1987 income from investment in Filo under the cost and equity methods.

EXHIBIT 16.4

	Cost Method	Equity Method
1986 per above	$ 50,000	$ 78,750
1987 per above	50,000	150,000
Gain on sale of stock	400,000	271,250
Total income for the two years	$500,000	$500,000

The only real difference between the cost and equity methods of accounting for long-term investments in common stock may be the timing of income recognition.

Long-Term Investments with Absolute Control. When one corporation acquires over 50 percent of the voting stock of another, absolute control over the acquisition is assured. The acquiring corporation becomes known as the **parent company,** and the acquired corporation is referred to as a **subsidiary company.**

PARENT COMPANY
A corporation that acquires over 50 percent of the voting stock of another corporation.

SUBSIDIARY COMPANY
A corporation where over 50 percent of the voting stock is owned by another corporation.

CONSOLIDATED FINANCIAL STATEMENTS

The users of a parent's financial statements need an integrated set of financial statements that includes information on all of the entities within the economic sphere of the parent's control. Such integrated statements are known as **consolidated financial statements** and are the result of adding together the parent's and subsidiary's separate statements. Thus, for example, consolidated cash is the sum of all of the cash held by all of the combined companies, and other accounts are likewise summed. As a part of the consolidation process, certain eliminations must be made. For example, you cannot owe money to yourself or sell something to yourself. Nor can a corporation. Therefore, sales and debt relationships between parent and subsidiary companies must be eliminated from the consolidated financial statements. Many other kinds of intercompany transactions must likewise be eliminated to prepare a set of consolidated financial statements and to report fairly the results of operations between the consolidated group and other nonaffiliated companies.

CONSOLIDATED FINANCIAL STATEMENTS
Integrated financial statements that are the result of adding together the parent's and the subsidiary's separate statements.

Just as with many other accounting rules, the use of the consolidated format or the equity or cost method of accounting for long-term investments does not rest solely on percentage ownership. If, in the professional judgment of management and its accountants, control is lacking or businesses are so dissimilar that consolidation makes no sense, financial statements should not be consolidated even if over 50 percent of the voting stock of one corporation is owned by another. For example, foreign law might prevent control over subsidiaries located in other nations, or a bank might own a retail store. In the first case, control is lacking, and in the second, the businesses are completely different; in neither case would you consolidate the financial statements.

The same reasoning can apply to carrying investments on the cost or equity basis. If an investor cannot achieve any influence in spite of valid attempts to do so, it may well be that the cost method of accounting is preferable to the equity method, even if the ownership level of the investor is over 20 percent.

CONCEPT SUMMARY 16.1 CONTROL AND ACCOUNTING

Degree of Ownership Control	Method of Accounting
Less than 20 percent.	Cost—only income from investment is dividend income.
Equal to or over 20 percent but less than 50 percent plus one share.	Equity—income from investment includes investor share of investee income whether paid as dividends or not.
Over 50 percent.	Consolidate financial statements into one economic report, and/or equity income from investment includes investor share of investee income whether paid as dividends or not.

THE CONSOLIDATION PROCESS

Let's approach the process of consolidation of financial statements with examples. *Because a consolidated company does not exist from an operational point of view, consolidated journals, ledgers, and other such books of record do not exist.* Preparation of consolidated financial statements is a two-phase process. Phase one consists of an independent review of the accounts of each of the companies to be consolidated and adjustment of the independent trial balances to appropriate numbers as discussed throughout the text. Phase two, which is the focus of this section of this chapter, consists of preparation of a consolidated trial balance adjusted specifically for consolidation purposes, using the adjusted trial balances from each of the independent companies. In general, accountants use the worksheet as a tool to facilitate the task, and the most important question they ask about each consolidated account is whether or not the balance represents only those transactions between outside entities and the consolidated group taken as a whole. Since no consolidated books of record exist, adjusting entries are worksheet items only.

Consolidated Statements of Financial Position

Assume that two independent corporations, Parent and Subsidiary, have statements of financial position on January 1, 1986, as in Exhibit 16.5.

The following additional facts are relevant:

1. Parent Company owes Subsidiary Company $50,000 on open account. This amount is included in Accounts Receivable of Subsidiary and Accounts Payable of Parent.
2. The other assets of Parent Company consist of an investment in bonds of Subsidiary Company. Subsidiary has properly shown this amount as a long-term debt.

Purchase at Book Value of 100 Percent of the Voting Stock. Assume that on January 1, 1986, Parent purchases all of Subsidiary's voting stock for $625,000, the net book

EXHIBIT 16.5

Assets	Parent Company	Subsidiary Company
Cash	$ 900,000	$100,000
Accounts receivable	600,000	200,000
Inventory	400,000	100,000
Property, plant, and equipment	1,000,000	500,000
Other assets	100,000	25,000
Total	$3,000,000	$925,000
Liabilities and Owners' Equity		
Accounts payable	$ 500,000	$200,000
Long-term debt	500,000	100,000
Common stock	600,000	500,000
Retained earnings	1,400,000	125,000
Total	$3,000,000	$925,000

value of Subsidiary Company's assets. This payment does not go to Subsidiary Company but to the owners of Subsidiary. In combining the two companies' statements of financial position, the following adjustments are needed:

1. Since Parent now owns all of Subsidiary and cannot owe money to itself, the Parent debt of $50,000 to Subsidiary and the Subsidiary debt of $100,000 to Parent must be eliminated to avoid double counting.
2. The $625,000 investment that Parent has made is represented by the assets on Subsidiary's books. To place both the investment and the assets in the consolidated statements would be double counting. Thus, we eliminate Parent's investment in Subsidiary account and the owners' equity of Subsidiary. Remember that Subsidiary no longer has any owners other than Parent and the owners of the consolidated entity are Parent's shareholders.

Exhibit 16.6 shows the consolidation worksheet used to prepare consolidated financial statements for Parent and Subsidiary based on the preceding facts.

Now review the consolidated statement of financial position. Cash is what the two companies together have in the bank. Accounts receivable in total is what the combined companies are owned by outsiders. Inventory and property, plant, and equipment represent the combined holdings of the two companies. Obviously, you cannot invest in yourself, and the investment account is therefore zero when the two companies are considered as one. Other assets are the combined amounts after subtracting out the long-term loans made within the combined companies. Accounts payable and long-term debt are net to the consolidation as a whole, and the common stock and retained earnings represent Parent only. Remember that because Subsidiary is totally owned by Parent, Parent's owners are also the sole owners of the consolidated entity. Thus, intuitively, the consolidation makes sense.

Purchase of Less Than 100 Percent of the Voting Stock at Book Value. Suppose that Parent were to purchase 80 percent of the voting stock of Subsidiary on January

EXHIBIT 16.6

Parent Company and Consolidated Subsidiary
Worksheet for Consolidated Statement of Financial Position
As of January 1, 1986 (at purchase date)
100% Ownership

	1	2	3	4	5
					Consolidated
			Intercompany		Statement
	Parent	Subsidiary	Eliminations		of Financial
Account Title	Company	Company	Dr.	Cr.	Position
Cash	$ 275,000	$100,000			$ 375,000
Accounts receivable	600,000	200,000		$ 50,000[1]	750,000
Inventory	400,000	100,000			500,000
Property, plant, and equipment	1,000,000	500,000			1,500,000
Investment in Sub. Company	625,000			625,000[3]	
Other assets	100,000	25,000		100,000[2]	25,000
Totals	$3,000,000	$925,000			$3,150,000
Accounts payable	$ 500,000	$200,000	$ 50,000[1]		$ 650,000
Long-term debt	500,000	100,000	100,000[2]		500,000
Common stock	600,000	500,000	500,000[3]		600,000
Retained earnings	1,400,000	125,000	125,000[3]		1,400,000
Totals	$3,000,000	$925,000	$775,000	$775,000	$3,150,000

[1]To subtract $50,000 from accounts payable and accounts receivable, representing internal debt only.
[2]To subtract $100,000 from other assets and long-term debt, representing internal debt only.
[3]To eliminate the investment account and corresponding owners' equity, as these items do not exist for the consolidated entity.

1, 1986, for $500,000 (0.8 × $625,000). Now we have a slightly different consolidation in that two owner classes exist. Parent's owners are still in control of all of the actions and assets of Subsidiary by virtue of possession of over one-half of the voting stock, but some of the assets of Subsidiary—and therefore of the consolidated group—can be thought of as being provided by the independent owners not affiliated with Parent. These independent owners are called a minority interest for consolidation purposes.

MINORITY INTEREST
A separate class of owners on consolidated statements of financial position that have no rights with respect to the primary company around which the consolidation is built.

Minority Interest. The **minority interest** represents a separate class of owner on a consolidated statement of financial position. Although they have provided assets to one of the subsidiaries included in the consolidation, the minority interest owners are not in control in any way, nor do they have any rights with respect to the primary company around which the consolidation is built. It is important to understand that minority interest never exists outside a set of consolidated financial statements, since the minority interest represents regular owners within the separate companies outside the consolidation.

Consolidated Working Papers. Consolidated working papers for the 80 percent purchase are shown in Exhibit 16.7.

As with adjustments discussed here and in earlier chapters, new accounts might be needed that are not found on any of the included company's books as with minority interest. The formal consolidated statement of financial position for Parent

EXHIBIT 16.7

Parent Company and Consolidated Subsidiary
Worksheet for Consolidated Statement of Financial Position
As of January 1, 1986 (at purchase date)
80% Ownership

	1	2	3	4	5
			Intercompany Eliminations		Consolidated Statement of Financial Position
Account Title	Parent Company	Subsidiary Company	Dr.	Cr.	
Cash	$ 400,000	$100,000			$ 500,000
Accounts receivable	600,000	200,000		$ 50,000[1]	750,000
Inventory	400,000	100,000			500,000
Property, plant, and equipment	1,000,000	500,000			1,500,000
Investment in Sub. Company	500,000			500,000[3]	
Other assets	100,000	25,000		100,000[2]	25,000
Totals	$3,000,000	$925,000			$3,275,000
Accounts payable	$ 500,000	$200,000	$ 50,000[1]		$ 650,000
Long-term debt	500,000	100,000	100,000[2]		500,000
Common stock	600,000	500,000	500,000[3]		600,000
Retained earnings	1,400,000	125,000	125,000[3]		1,400,000
Minority interest				125,000[3]	125,000
Totals	$3,000,000	$925,000	$775,000	$775,000	$3,275,000

[1]To subtract $50,000 from accounts payable and accounts receivable, representing internal debt only.

[2]To subtract $100,000 from other assets and long-term debt, representing internal debt only.

[3]To eliminate the investment account and corresponding owners' equity and reclassify minority owners in Subsidiary as minority interests outside the consolidated parent company.

is presented in Exhibit 16.8. Note the classification of minority interest as a separate kind of owners' equity. All other accounts except cash are the same as discussed following the first consolidation for 100 percent ownership. Cash is $125,000 higher because Parent paid out less to Subsidiary's shareholders in purchasing 80 percent rather than 100 percent of the voting stock of Subsidiary.

EXHIBIT 16.8

Parent Company and Consolidated Subsidiary
Statement of Financial Position
January 1, 1986

Assets		**Liabilities and Owners' Equity**	
Cash	$ 500,000	Liabilities	
Accounts receivable	750,000	Accounts payable	$ 650,000
Inventory	500,000	Long-term debt	500,000
Property, plant, and equipment	1,500,000	Total liabilities	$1,150,000
Other assets	25,000	Owners' equity	
		Minority interest	125,000
		Common stock	600,000
		Retained earnings	1,400,000
Total assets	$3,275,000	**Total liabilities and owners' equity**	$3,275,000

Purchase of a Controlling Interest at Other Than Book Value. You'll recall that book value of ownership units often has no relationship to current market value. By purchasing the voting stock of a subsidiary corporation, the new parent is, in effect, purchasing the assets of the new subsidiary by achieving control over the destiny of the subsidiary and thus the subsidiary's assets. For this reason, more often than not, the price paid by one company to the shareholders of another in exchange for some or all of their stock does not coincide with book value. Since the usual case is one in which the price paid is greater than the book value, we will confine our discussion to such a case. Purchases of stock at less than the stock's underlying book value, although similar, can lead to complex questions in accounting theory well beyond the scope of this text.

No problem exists stemming from purchases of stock by a company at prices greater than the underlying book value of the stock as long as consolidated statements are not prepared. The purchaser simply records the investment at its cost. However, when consolidated financial statements are prepared, a simple elimination of the investment account and the appropriate owners' equity of the subsidiary will not be possible. When the price paid is greater than the book value, it is also greater than the appropriate proportion of owners' equity of the subsidiary, since owners' equity is equal to net book value. Some reclassification of the excess paid is needed.

Asset Revaluation and Goodwill. Theoretically, when an investor company pays more than book value for all of an investee's stock, the extra amount paid should simply be added to the appropriate assets when the consolidation is performed so that the statement of financial position reflects the new market value of the assets of the investee company. In fact, this is precisely what is required under APB Opinion No. 16.[2] But if management and the accountants of the purchasing company cannot determine which, if any, of the acquired company's assets should be revalued upwards for consolidation purposes, the extra amount paid is assigned to a new asset account called Goodwill.

We cannot stress too strongly that this possible departure from historical cost (possible write-up of assets) and the possible establishment of the asset goodwill are consolidation items only. The write-ups and establishment of goodwill never appear on any company's books but arise only when consolidated financial statements are prepared and these items do not go beyond the statements and the supporting worksheet.

Consolidated Working Papers. Going back to the data in Exhibit 16.5, assume now that Parent purchases 100 percent of Subsidiary's voting stock for $800,000. Further assume that Parent is willing to pay more for Subsidiary than the underlying book value ($625,000) of its assets because of the following:

1. Property, plant, and equipment of Subsidiary has a market value of $600,000 instead of the $500,000 book value.
2. Subsidiary enjoys a reputation for possessing an excellent customer base for expansion of Parent's business.

For consolidation purposes only, the combined property, plant, and equipment value wili be increased by $100,000 and the remainder of the excess paid over book value, or $75,000 ($800,000 − $100,000 − $625,000), will be shown on the consolidated statement of financial position as the asset goodwill. It might occur to you that the asset goodwill is unique in that it is a derived intangible whose future economic benefit (the test for any asset) might be questionable. Accountants have long argued concerning the nature of goodwill, with volumes written on the topic. Suffice it to say that the concept of goodwill is highly controversial, but under current accounting practice, it arises as previously discussed and is mechanically handled as shown in the consolidation worksheet in Exhibit 16.9.

Note carefully in the worksheet in Exhibit 16.9 that the only difference between this case and that in Exhibit 16.7 is found in the cash and investment account of Parent and in the consolidated statement accounts. Goodwill and the increase in the value of property, plant, and equipment do not appear on the books of either Parent or Subsidiary as presented in the second and third columns of the worksheet.

Consolidated Income Statements

Conceptually, the preparation of consolidated income statements is the same as preparation of consolidated statements of financial position. Just as a consolidated entity cannot owe money to itself, neither can it make a profit by selling to itself or

[2] "Business Combinations," *Accounting Principles Board Opinion No. 16,* The American Institute of Certified Public Accountants (New York: 1970).

EXHIBIT 16.9

Parent Company and Consolidated Subsidiary
Worksheet for Consolidated Statement of Financial Position
As of January 1, 1986 (at purchase date)
100% Ownership

	1	2	3	4	5
			Intercompany Eliminations		Consolidated Statement of Financial Position
Account Title	Parent Company	Subsidiary Company	Dr.	Cr.	
Cash	$ 100,000	$100,000			$ 200,000
Accounts receivable	600,000	200,000		$ 50,000[1]	750,000
Inventory	400,000	100,000			500,000
Property, plant, and equipment	1,000,000	500,000	$100,000[3]		1,600,000
Investment in Sub. Company	800,000			800,000[3]	
Other assets	100,000	25,000		100,000[2]	25,000
Goodwill			75,000[3]		75,000
Totals	$3,000,000	$925,000			$3,150,000
Accounts payable	$ 500,000	$200,000	$ 50,000[1]		$ 650,000
Long-term debt	500,000	100,000	100,000[2]		500,000
Common stock	600,000	500,000	500,000[3]		600,000
Retained earnings	1,400,000	125,000	125,000[3]		1,400,000
Totals	$3,000,000	$925,000	$950,000	$950,000	$3,150,000

[1]To subtract $50,000 from accounts payable and accounts receivable, representing internal debt only.
[2]To subtract $100,000 from other assets and long-term debt, representing internal debt only.
[3]To remove investment in Subsidiary, eliminate Subsidiary's owners' equity, write up property, plant, and equipment to its market value in consolidation, and establish goodwill arising from the consolidation process.

performing services for itself. All intercompany revenue, expense, gain, or loss transactions must be eliminated in the process of consolidating multiple company income statements into one overall presentation. The goal of proper presentation of a consolidated income statement is to present only those items of revenue, expense, gain, or loss that represent transactions between those companies within the consolidated group and entities completely outside the consolidated group.

Intercompany Transactions. Assume the original purchase of 100 percent of the stock of Subsidiary by Parent at book value is as presented following Exhibit 16.5.

Now suppose that during 1986 Parent sells goods to Subsidiary for $300,000 that originally cost Parent $250,000. In turn, Subsidiary sells all of the goods to outside customers for $330,000. Subsidiary also pays Parent $14,000 interest on the long-term debt held by Parent.

Taken independently, the two companies would report the following in their respective 1986 income statements with regard to the two items:

1. Parent would report sales revenue of $300,000 and cost of goods sold of $250,000, for a gross profit on the sale of $50,000 and interest income of $14,000 from the long-term loan held under other assets.
2. Subsidiary would report sales revenue of $330,000 and cost of goods sold of $300,000, for a gross profit on the sale of $30,000 and interest expense of $14,000 on its long-term debt.

Taken as a whole, the consolidated entity has sold goods to outsiders for $330,000 with an original cost of $250,000 and therefore made a gross profit on the sale of $80,000. No interest revenue or expense has been earned or paid on Subsidiary's long-term debt when the two companies are considered as a whole. Looking at the arithmetic sum of the original independent income statements, we would find that revenues total $630,000 ($300,000 from Parent and $330,000 from Subsidiary) and cost of goods sold total $550,000 ($250,000 from Parent and $300,000 from Subsidiary), for a total gross profit of $80,000 from the original sale of goods. Further, Subsidiary would report interest expense of $14,000, and Parent would report $14,000 interest income. Therefore, to consolidate the two income statements, we would need to reduce sales to $330,000 (a reduction of $300,000), cost of goods sold to $250,000 (a reduction of $300,000), interest expense by $14,000, and interest income by $14,000. Note that gross profit is correct at $80,000. Once goods are sold outside the consolidated group, all of the profit has been earned and will be correct. It makes no difference which company within the consolidation "earned" which part of the profit. The individual parts must add to the correct total.

Income Statement Worksheet. Exhibit 16.10 presents a worksheet for preparation of a consolidated income statement for Parent and Subsidiary for 1986. We have assumed that all revenue and expense transactions recorded by either company in the worksheet, other than the two preceding transactions, are with outside entities. Exhibit 16.10 concludes our discussion of the consolidated income presentation. To be sure, more complex problems exist, but such discussions are well beyond the scope of this text.

POOLING OF INTERESTS

Sometimes one company will acquire another by exchanging its voting stock for all or substantially all of the voting stock held by the owners of the acquired company. This is known as a pooling of interests. Suppose, in our example based on Exhibit 16.5, Parent Company issues 12,500 shares of its no par, no stated value common stock held in its treasury to the shareholders of Subsidiary Company in return for 100 percent of Subsidiary's voting stock. At the time, Parent's stock has a market value of $64 per share. It can be argued that Parent, in this case, has not purchased

EXHIBIT 16.10

Parent Company and Consolidated Subsidiary
Worksheet for Consolidated Income Statement
For the Year Ending December 31, 1986
100% Ownership

	1	2	3	4	5
			Intercompany		Consolidated
	Parent*	Subsidiary	Eliminations		Income
Account Title	Company	Company	Dr.	Cr.	Statement
Sales	$1,000,000	$500,000	$300,000[1]		$1,200,000
Interest revenue	14,000	—	14,000[2]		—
Total revenue	$1,014,000	$500,000			$1,200,000
Cost of goods sold	700,000	400,000		$300,000[1]	800,000
Selling, general, and adm. expense	100,000	20,000			120,000
Interest expense	70,000	14,000		14,000[2]	70,000
Total expenses	$ 870,000	$434,000			$ 990,000
Net income	$ 144,000	$ 66,000	$314,000	$314,000	$ 210,000

[1]To reduce sales and cost of goods sold by intercompany amount.
[2]To reduce interest revenue and interest expense by intercompany amounts.
*Technically, Parent's accounts would include Income from Subsidiary Company of $66,000, with a corresponding increase in the account Investment in Subsidiary Company. In consolidating, the Income from Subsidiary Company would be eliminated against the Investment in Subsidiary Company account. This elimination is purely mechanical, and the essence of income consolidation is as portrayed in the foregoing text.

Subsidiary. In fact, Subsidiary's owners have now joined up with the original shareholders of Parent to own and control the combined companies. In the earlier case of cash purchases by Parent of Subsidiary's stock, the original owners of Parent became the only owners of the combined companies. Now, in the stock-for-stock exchange, Subsidiary's former owners are pooled with Parent's former owners to form the new ownership group, thus the name, pooling of interests.

Valuation of Pooling Acquisitions

Since no cash changes hands, some question arises as to the proper dollar value to assign to the acquisition. If the market price of the stock were used as a basis for valuing the transaction, we would conclude that Parent "paid" $800,000 ($64 × 12,500) for all of Subsidiary and the case would be similar to that presented in Exhibit 16.9. However, since the transaction is not considered a purchase by Parent from Subsidiary's owners but rather a combining (pooling) of two independent owner groups into a new common owner group (pool), market value of the stock paid out is ignored, and the new stock issued is considered to be equal to the book value of the assets acquired.

Retained Earnings, Income, and Pooling of Interests

Retained Earnings. Two other major differences between pooling-of-interests accounting and purchase accounting are worth noting. Under purchase accounting, the assets provided by owners through prior earnings of the consolidated companies are considered to be equal to the sum of the retained earnings of the parent plus any new income earned by either the parent or its subsidiaries after acquisition. Under pooling-of-interests accounting, the assets provided by owners through prior earnings of the consolidated entity are considered equal to the sum of the retained earnings of both companies at the point of acquisition plus all new income earned by either company.

Income. Similar to the retained earnings difference, under purchase accounting, the earnings of the consolidated group are equal to the earnings of the parent company plus all of the earnings of both companies after the date of acquisition. Under pooling of interests, the earnings of the consolidated group are considered equal to the sum of the earnings of both companies for the entire reporting period regardless of the point of acquisition. If Parent Company pools with Subsidiary Company on December 31, 1986, Parent would include all of its earnings plus all of Subsidiary's earnings for 1986 when reporting consolidated income for 1986. Under purchase accounting, the consolidated income statement for Parent would include only Parent's earnings, since Subsidiary was not acquired until December 31.

CONCEPT SUMMARY 16.2

PURCHASE VERSUS POOLING OF INTERESTS

Item	Purchase	Pooling of Interests
Resource used to acquire.	Can be cash or stock.	Must be an exchange of voting stock.
Valuation of acquisition.	At amount paid, cash plus fair market value of stock.	At book value of assets acquired.
Acquired company's income.	Consolidated income includes only that amount earned after date of acquisition.	Consolidated income includes total amount regardless of date of acquisition.
Acquired company's retained earnings.	Consolidated retained earnings includes only amount accumulated after date of acquisition.	Consolidated retained earnings includes total amount regardless of date of acquisition.

Worksheet for Pooling of Interests

Pooling-of-interests accounting has been heavily criticized, and its use has been severely limited by Accounting Principles Board Opinion No. 16.[3] Further discussion is well beyond the scope of this text, and we will conclude by presenting a worksheet for a consolidated statement of financial position for Parent Company and Subsidiary Company on January 1, 1986, assuming that Parent acquires 100 percent of the voting stock of Subsidiary in exchange for 12,500 shares of its own stock as described earlier. Of particular interest, compare the results obtained in Exhibit 16.11 with those in Exhibits 16.6 and 16.9.

[3]Accounting Principles Board Opinion No. 16, *op cit.*

EXHIBIT 16.11

Parent Company and Consolidated Subsidiary
Worksheet for Consolidated Statement of Financial Position
As of January 1, 1986 (at pooling date)
100% Ownership

	1	2	3	4	5
			Intercompany Eliminations		Consolidated Statement of Financial Position
Account Title	Parent Company	Subsidiary Company	Dr.	Cr.	
Cash	$ 900,000	$100,000			$1,000,000
Accounts receivable	600,000	200,000		$ 50,000[1]	750,000
Inventory	400,000	100,000			500,000
Property, plant, and equipment	1,000,000	500,000			1,500,000
Investment in Sub. Company	625,000			625,000[3]	
Other assets	100,000	25,000		100,000[2]	25,000
Totals	$3,625,000	$925,000			$3,775,000
Accounts payable	$ 500,000	$200,000	$ 50,000[1]		$ 650,000
Long-term debt	500,000	100,000	100,000[2]		500,000
Common stock	1,100,000	500,000	500,000[3]		1,100,000
Retained earnings	1,525,000	125,000	125,000[3]		1,525,000
Totals	$3,625,000	$925,000	$775,000	$775,000	$3,775,000

[1]To subtract $50,000 from accounts payable and accounts receivable, representing internal debt only.
[2]To subtract $100,000 from other assets and long-term debt, representing internal debt only.
[3]To eliminate the investment account and equity of Subsidiary for consolidation purposes.

FOR REVIEW

SUMMARY

- When one company holds a long-term investment of less than an influential owner position in another (generally less than 20 percent ownership), the investment is carried at cost and only dividends received are considered income.
- When one company holds a long-term investment of an influential but noncontrolling position in another (generally over 20 percent but less than 50 percent ownership), the investment is accounted for by the equity method, and the investor records income equal to its share of the investee's income whether or not any dividends are paid by the investee to the investor.
- When one company owns over 50 percent of another as a long-term investment, consolidated financial statements are prepared unless it can be shown that control does not exist or consolidation would not make economic sense.
- Purchase accounting and pooling-of-interests accounting are two methods of accounting for acquisition of one company by another.
- When one company purchases the stock of another for more than book value, write-ups in asset values can occur and goodwill can be created in the process of consolidation of the financial statements.
- When consolidated financial statements are prepared, all intercompany debts, investments, revenues, expenses, gains, or losses must be eliminated from the consolidated account balances.
- Minority interest refers to owners of a subsidiary company not directly having ownership interests in the parent company and thus not being in any position to control the consolidated entity.
- No separate books of account exist for consolidated entities, since financial statement consolidation is solely an economic report prepared from separate company data via a worksheet.

QUESTIONS

16-1. Explain the difference between short-term and long-term investment in the stock of another company.

16-2. What is meant by pooling of interests?

16-3. Explain the two major differences between pooling-of-interests accounting and purchase accounting with respect to retained earnings and income.

16-4. How is acquisition cost determined under pooling of interests?

16-5. Describe the two methods of accounting for long-term investments in the stock of one corporation by another.

16-6. Explain when each of the methods defined in 16-5 would be appropriate.

16-7. What are consolidated financial statements?

16-8. Under what circumstances would financial reports of legally separate companies but with one group of owners not be combined into one consolidated set of financial statements?

16-9. Define minority interest and explain its placement in the consolidated financial statements.

16-10. If a company pays more than book value for all of another company's stock, where is the extra amount paid recorded on the financial statements?

EXERCISES

16-E1. Elmtree Company purchases 10,000 shares, or 10%, of Maple Company's common stock for $50 a share on January 1 as a long-term investment. On December 1, Maple pays a cash dividend of $1 per share. On December 31, the market value of Maple's stock is $40 per share. Prepare journal entries to record the foregoing information on Elmtree's books.

16-E2. Assume that the 10,000 shares of Elmtree purchased in 16-E1 constitute 40% of Maple's common stock. Further assume that both Elmtree and Maple are domestic corporations in similar businesses. Maple's net income for the year ending December 31 is $160,000. Prepare journal entries to record the foregoing information on Elmtree's books.

16-E3. Ace Corporation purchases 100% of Bay Company's common stock for $300,000 on December 31. Bay Company's statement of financial position at that time includes $200,000 of common stock and $50,000 of retained earnings. The book value of all of Bay's assets are equal to the assets' fair market value on December 31. Prepare the eliminating worksheet entry for the consolidation of the statements of financial position as of the date of acquisition, December 31.

16-E4. Suppose that Ace Corporation in 16-E3 purchases 70% of Bay Company's common stock, or 70,000 shares, for $3 per share on December 31. Prepare the eliminating entry (including minority interest) necessary to consolidate the statements of financial position at the date of acquisition.

16-E5. On January 1, May Company purchases 100% of Nale Company's common stock for $850,000. The book value of the stock is $750,000. May Company believes that Nale Company's fixed assets have a market value of $400,000 rather than the $310,000 book value. Compute the amount of goodwill that will be shown in the consolidated statement of financial position and explain your answer.

16-E6. Accounts from the statements of financial position for Taylor Company and its wholly owned subsidiary, Samson Company, are as follows:

	Taylor	Samson
Accounts receivable	$ 500,000	$ 300,000
Investment in Samson Company	1,000,000	
Rent receivable from Samson	50,000	
Interest receivable from Samson	20,000	
Notes receivable from Samson	200,000	
Property, plant, and equipment (net)	930,000	1,220,000
Accounts payable	300,000	250,000
Interest payable to Taylor		20,000
Rent payable to Taylor		50,000
Notes payable to Taylor		200,000
Common stock	2,000,000	800,000
Retained earnings	400,000	200,000

Included in Samson's accounts receivable is $100,000 that Taylor owes Samson. For each account, determine the amount that would appear on the consolidated statement of financial position.

16-E7. The Dandy Company exchanges 20,000 shares of its no par value common stock for all of Poorboy's no par common stock. The shareholders' equity sections for the two companies immediately after the acquisition are as follows:

	Dandy	Poorboy
Common stock	$1,000,000	$500,000
Retained earnings	500,000	200,000
Total shareholders' equity	$1,500,000	$700,000

Using the pooling-of-interests accounting method, what would be the amounts for the two accounts on the consolidated statement of financial position? Explain your answer.

PROBLEM SET A

16-A1. Investment Purchase of Less Than 20% of Voting Stock. Investment Corporation has the following transactions in 1986 regarding its long-term investment in Beta common stock:

January 1	Purchases 10,000 shares (10%) of Beta Company common stock at $50 per share.
March 1	Receives cash dividend of $1 per share from Beta Company.
September 1	Receives cash dividend of $2 per share from Beta Company.
December 31	Market value per share of the Beta stock is $48.

Required

a. Prepare journal entries to record Investment's transactions.
b. What is the net carrying value of Investment's long-term investment in Beta common stock account on December 31, 1986?

16-A2. Investment Purchase of Between 20% and 50% of Voting Stock. Given the same transactions as in 16-A1, assume that the stock purchased by Investment Corporation represents 25% of Beta Company. The net income of Beta Company for 1986 is $160,000.

Required

a. Prepare all necessary journal entries for Investment Corporation for 1986 with respect to the company's investment in Beta Company common stock.
b. What is the net carrying value of the long-term investment in Beta common stock account as of December 31, 1986?

16-A3. Investment in Varying Percentages of Voting Stock. Security Investments Company has the following 1986 long-term investment transactions. All stocks are purchased with cash.

January 1	Purchases 40% of Ace Company's voting stock (10,000 shares) for $40 per share.
January 2	Purchases 10% of Bay Company's voting stock (20,000 shares) for $10 per share.

March 1	Receives cash dividends of $.50 per share from Ace Company.
May 1	Receives cash dividends of $.10 per share from Bay Company.
December 31	Market values per share for stocks are Ace Company, $38; Bay Company, $12.
December 31	Net incomes for 1986 for the companies are Ace Company, $200,000; Bay Company, $50,000.

Required

a. Prepare journal entries to record the preceding transactions using the cost method or equity method, whichever is appropriate.
b. What is the net carrying value of the long-term investment in common stock account for each of the stocks, Ace and Bay?

16-A4. Preparation of Consolidated Worksheet—100% Purchase. The following statements of financial position are for Parent Company and Subsidiary Company as of December 1, 1986:

	Parent Company	Subsidiary Company
Assets		
Cash	$200,000	$ 50,000
Accounts receivable	50,000	30,000
Inventory	80,000	40,000
Fixed assets (net)	150,000	50,000
Other assets	50,000	10,000
Total assets	$530,000	$180,000
Liabilities and Owners' Equity		
Accounts payable	$100,000	$ 20,000
Long-term debt	50,000	15,000
Common stock	200,000	100,000
Retained earnings	180,000	45,000
Total liabilities and owners' equity	$530,000	$180,000

On December 1, 1986, Parent Company purchases all of Subsidiary Company's voting stock for $165,000 to become more vertically integrated. Parent Company believes that Subsidiary Company's fixed assets have a true market value of $70,000.

Required

Prepare a consolidated worksheet for preparation of a consolidated statement of financial position for Parent and Subsidiary for December 1, 1986.

16-A5. Preparation of Consolidated Worksheet—80% Purchase. The following statements of financial position are for Parent Company and Subsidiary Company as of June 15, 1986:

	Parent Company	Subsidiary Company
Assets		
Cash	$200,000	$ 80,000
Accounts receivable	150,000	50,000
Inventory	250,000	100,000
Fixed assets (net)	300,000	90,000
Other assets	50,000	5,000
Total assets	$950,000	$325,000
Liabilities and Owners' Equity		
Accounts payable	$100,000	$ 75,000
Long-term debt	125,000	50,000
Common stock	500,000	100,000
Retained earnings	225,000	100,000
Total liabilities and owners' equity	$950,000	$325,000

The following facts are relevant:

1. Subsidiary Company owes Parent Company $50,000 on account.
2. Part of Parent Company's long-term debt is held by Subsidiary Company in the form of a $5,000 bond.
3. On June 15, 1986, Parent purchased 80% of Subsidiary's voting stock for $160,000.

Required

Prepare a consolidated worksheet for preparation of a consolidated statement of financial position for June 15, 1986, with a minority interest class of owners.

16-A6. Preparation of Consolidated Income Statement—100% Purchase. The following income statements are for Gaylord Company and Harris Company for 1986:

	Gaylord Co.	Harris Co.
Sales	$400,000	$50,000
Rent revenue	20,000	10,000
Interest revenue	10,000	5,000
Total revenue	$430,000	$65,000
Cost of goods sold	200,000	20,000
Selling, general, and adm. exp.	120,000	10,000
Rent expense	20,000	5,000
Interest expense	15,000	10,000
Total expenses	$355,000	$45,000
Net income	75,000	20,000

The following 1986 facts are relevant:

1. Harris Company paid $5,000 rent to Gaylord Company.
2. Harris Company received $5,000 interest from Gaylord Company for long-term bonds.
3. Harris Company sold $30,000 of goods to Gaylord Company that originally cost $15,000. Gaylord Company sold the goods to other customers for $40,000.
4. Harris Company paid $5,000 interest to Gaylord Company.
5. Gaylord Company paid $10,000 rent to Harris Company.

6. Gaylord Company sold $10,000 of goods to Harris Company that originally cost $8,000. Harris Company sold the goods for $12,000 to outside customers.
7. Gaylord Company purchased 100% of Harris Company's voting stock for $300,000 on January 1, 1986.

Required

Prepare a consolidated worksheet for the preparation of a consolidated income statement for 1986.

16-A7. Consolidated Worksheets: Purchase and Pooling Methods. The statements of financial position as of December 31, 1986 for Jones Company and Katz Company are as follows:

Assets	Katz	Jones
Cash	$ 300,000	$ 80,000
Accounts receivable	120,000	40,000
Fixed assets (net)	1,080,000	250,000
Total assets	$1,500,000	$370,000
Liabilities and Owners' Equity		
Accounts payable	$ 100,000	$ 20,000
Common stock	800,000	200,000
Retained earnings	600,000	150,000
Total liabilities and owners' equity	$1,500,000	$370,000

On December 31, 1986, Katz issues 10,000 shares of its no par value common stock for all the no par common shares of Jones. The market value of Katz stock is $40 per share, and all of Jones's assets have a fair market value equal to the assets' book value on December 31. Net income for the year ending December 31, 1986, is $40,000 for Jones and $250,000 for Katz.

Required

a. Prepare a consolidated worksheet for a consolidated statement of financial position for Katz and Jones as of December 31, 1986 using:
  1. the pooling-of-interests method of accounting
  2. the purchase method of accounting.
b. What would be the consolidated net income for Katz and Jones for the year ending December 31, 1986 using:
  1. the pooling-of-interests method of accounting
  2. the purchase method of accounting?

PROBLEM SET B

16-B1. Purchase of Less Than 20% of Voting Stock. Money Makers, Inc., has the following transactions relating to long-term investment in Alpha Company during 1986:

January 1	Purchases 5,000 shares (15%) of Alpha Company for $20 per share.
March 1	Receives cash dividend of $.40 per share from Alpha Company.
July 1	Receives cash dividend of $.40 per share from Alpha Company.
December 31	Market value of Alpha stock on December 31, 1986, is $15 per share.

Required

a. Prepare journal entries to record the preceding transactions.
b. What is the net carrying value of Money Makers' long-term investment in Alpha common stock account on December 31, 1986?

16-B2. Investment Purchase of Between 20% and 50% of Voting Stock. Given the same transactions as in 16-B1, assume that the stock purchase made by Money Makers, Inc., represents 30% of Alpha Company. The net income of Alpha Company for 1986 is $70,000.

Required

a. Prepare all necessary journal entries for Money Makers, Inc., for 1986, given the transactions and net income.
b. What is the balance in the long-term investment in Alpha common stock account at December 31, 1986?

16-B3. Investment in Varying Percentages of Voting Stock. Financial Experts Corporation has the following 1986 long-term investment transactions. All stocks are purchased with cash.

January 1	Purchases 30% of Lane Company's voting stock (15,000 shares) for $20 per share.
January 1	Purchases 5% of Mead Company's voting stock (1,000 shares) for $10 per share.
April 1	Receives cash dividend of $.25 per share from Mead Company.
May 1	Receives cash dividend of $.10 per share from Lane Company.
December 31	Market values per share of stocks are Lane Company, $18; Mead Company, $15.
December 31	Net incomes for 1986 for the companies are Lane Company, $50,000; Mead Company, $25,000.

Required

a. Prepare journal entries to record the preceding transactions using the cost method or equity method, whichever is appropriate.
b. What is the balance in the long-term investment in common stock account for each of the stocks, Lane and Mead?

16-B4. Preparation of Consolidated Worksheet—100% Purchase. The following are the statements of financial position for Echo Company and Foxtrot Company as of October 31, 1986:

Assets	**Echo**	**Foxtrot**
Cash	$ 300,000	$ 5,000
Accounts receivable	200,000	30,000
Inventory	500,000	40,000
Fixed assets (net)	800,000	25,000
Other assets	10,000	15,000
Total assets	$1,810,000	$115,000
Liabilities and Owners' Equity		
Accounts payable	$ 250,000	$ 35,000
Long-term debt	600,000	15,000
Common stock	700,000	50,000
Retained earnings	260,000	15,000
Total liabilities and owners' equity	$1,810,000	$115,000

On October 31, 1986, Echo purchases 100% of Foxtrot's voting stock for $80,000 to foster horizontal integration. Echo believes that Foxtrot's fixed assets have a fair market value of $30,000 on the acquisition date.

Required

Prepare a consolidated worksheet for preparation of a consolidated statement of financial position as of October 31, 1986.

16-B5. Preparation of a Consolidated Worksheet—60% Purchase. The Gaaf Company and the Hoot Company have the following statements of financial position as of August 1, 1986:

Assets	Hoot	Gaff
Cash	$ 500,000	$ 100,000
Accounts receivable	900,000	200,000
Inventory	700,000	400,000
Fixed assets (net)	950,000	400,000
Other assets	150,000	50,000
Total assets	$3,200,000	$1,150,000
Liabilities and Owners' Equity		
Accounts payable	$ 700,000	$ 200,000
Long-term debt	500,000	250,000
Common stock	900,000	400,000
Retained earnings	1,100,000	300,000
Total liabilities and owners' equity	$3,200,000	$1,150,000

The following facts are relevant:

1. Hoot owes Gaaf $100,000 on account.
2. Part of Gaaf's long-term debt is held by Hoot in the form of a $50,000 bond.
3. On August 1, 1986, Hoot purchased 60% of Gaaf's voting stock for $420,000.

Required

Prepare a consolidated worksheet for preparation of a consolidated statement of financial position for August 1, 1986, with a minority class of owners.

16-B6. Preparation of a Consolidated Income Statement—100% Purchase. The following income statements are for Macy Company and Salter Company for the year ending December 31, 1986:

	Salter Company	Macy Company
Sales	$800,000	$120,000
Rent revenue	30,000	20,000
Interest revenue	40,000	5,000
Total revenue	$870,000	$145,000
Cost of goods sold	$500,000	$ 70,000
Selling, general, and adm. exp.	200,000	20,000
Rent expense	50,000	10,000
Interest expense	30,000	5,000
Total expense	$780,000	$105,000
Net income	$ 90,000	$ 40,000

The following facts are relevant:

1. Macy Company paid $10,000 rent to Salter Company during 1986.
2. Salter Company paid $5,000 interest to Macy Company during 1986.
3. During 1986, Salter Company sold Macy Company $30,000 of goods that originally cost $20,000. Macy Company sold these goods for $50,000 to outside customers.
4. Macy Company received $15,000 rent from Salter Company during 1986.
5. During 1986, Salter Company purchased $10,000 of goods from Macy Company that originally cost $7,000. Salter Company sold these goods for $15,000 to outside customers.
6. Salter Company received $3,000 interest from Macy Company during 1986.
7. Salter Company purchased 100% of Macy Company's voting stock for $500,000 on January 1, 1986.

Required

Prepare a consolidated worksheet for the preparation of a consolidated income statement for the year ending December 31, 1986.

16-B7. Consolidated Worksheets: Purchase and Pooling Methods. The statements of financial position as of June 30, 1986, for the Ackers Company and the Bait Company are as follows:

Assets	Ackers	Bait
Cash	$130,000	$ 20,000
Accounts receivable	125,000	100,000
Fixed assets (net)	495,000	180,000
Total assets	$750,000	$300,000
Liabilities and Owners' Equity		
Accounts payable	$150,000	$ 75,000
Common stock	400,000	100,000
Retained earnings	200,000	125,000
Total liabilities and owners' equity	$750,000	$300,000

On June 30, 1986, Ackers issues 5,000 shares of its no par value common stock for 100% of the no par common stock of Bait. The market value of Ackers stock is $50 per share, and the fair market value of all of Bait's assets is equal to the assets' book value on June 30, 1986. Net income for the year ending June 30, 1986, is $120,000 for Ackers and $35,000 for Bait.

Required

a. Prepare a consolidated worksheet for preparation of a consolidated statement of financial position for Ackers and Bait as of June 30, 1986 using:
   1. the pooling-of-interests method of accounting
   2. the purchase method of accounting.

b. What would be the consolidated net income for Ackers and Bait for the year ending June 30, 1986 using:
   1. the pooling-of-interests method of accounting
   2. the purchase accounting method?

APPLICATION

Levi Strauss & Company

The Story of Levi Strauss

Behind the development of the denim jeans we often take for granted lies a history that reads like a classic American rags-to-riches tale. The story centers around two men, both immigrants in the mid-1800s: Levi Strauss and Jacob W. Davis.

Strauss came to New York from Bavaria knowing no English and having no trade. Six years later at the age of 24 he had progressed to San Francisco where he opened a small store to sell goods, some of which were shipped to him by his brothers in New York.

In those days, merchandise had to travel between coasts by the Cape Horn route, making retail business quite different from today's practice. Even in this environment, Levi Strauss & Co. thrived. The merchandising company prospered continuously, particularly after the transcontinental railroad made transporting merchandise less difficult.

The second figure in this tale is Jacob Davis, who also arrived in New York and promptly headed west. At the age of 39, he found himself in Reno with few dreams remaining and barely making ends meet with his sewing, fashioning not well-tailored suits but horse blankets, wagon covers, and tents. He constructed these items from duck cloth that had come from Levi Strauss & Co. in San Francisco.

The Company, 100 Years Later

Through assorted events, such as the 1906 San Francisco earthquake and occasional merchandising blunders, Levi Strauss has emerged in the 1980s as an international enterprise with sales of $2.5 billion. Levi Strauss and Company's financial position is indicated by the company's 1984 income statement and statement of financial position (reproduced in Exhibit A).

The changes in shareholders' equity accounts were summarized in the annual report in a statement of shareholders' equity (see Exhibit B). This statement indicates that no new shares of common stock have been issued in the three years presented. A change in paid-in capital occurred when shares were issued to employees. A decrease in paid-in capital resulted because treasury stock, accounted for at Levi Strauss' acquisition cost, was issued to employees at a price below the acquisition cost. For example, the treasury stock account for the first year presented would appear as follows:

Treasury Stock

11-29-81	69,280,000		
		Issued to Employees	6,477,000
11-28-82	62,803,000		

EXHIBIT A

Consolidated Statements of Income
Levi Strauss & Co.
and Subsidiaries

	Year (52 Weeks) Ending		
	November 25, 1984	**November 27, 1983**	**November 28, 1982**
	(Dollars in Thousands Except Per Share Amounts)		
Net sales	$ 2,513,536	$ 2,731,273	$ 2,572,172
Cost of goods sold	1,652,476	1,648,502	1,635,539
Gross profit	861,060	1,082,771	936,633
Marketing, general and administrative expenses	674,322	710,442	665,660
Operating income	186,738	372,329	270,973
Interest expense	28,763	39,793	42,766
Other (income) expense, net	46,612	(44,287)	(21,624)
Income before taxes	111,363	376,823	249,831
Provision for taxes on income	69,976	182,300	123,256
Net income	$ 41,387	$ 194,523	$ 126,575
Net income per share	$ 1.07	$ 4.61	$ 3.05
Average common and common equivalent shares outstanding	38,517,526	42,206,980	41,553,553

The accompanying notes to consolidated financial statements are an integral part of these financial statements.

EXHIBIT A

Continued

Consolidated Statements of Financial Position
Levi Strauss & Co. and Subsidiaries

	November 25, 1984	November 27, 1983
	(Dollars in Thousands)	
Assets		
Current Assets:		
Cash	$ 37,452	$ 16,967
Temporary investments of cash	225,937	449,351
Trade receivables (less allowance for doubtful accounts: 1984—$8,676; 1983—$9,682)	339,798	425,464
Inventories		
Raw materials and work-in-process	170,510	183,739
Finished goods	217,150	280,927
Other current assets	51,732	70,995
Total current assets	1,042,579	1,427,443
Property, Plant and Equipment (less accumulated depreciation: 1984—$208,217; 1983—$182,573)	330,455	347,150
Other Assets	48,068	57,282
	$1,421,102	$1,831,875
Liabilities and Shareholders' Equity		
Current Liabilities:		
Current maturities of long-term debt	$ 9,359	$ 32,440
Short-term borrowings	21,077	58,429
Accounts payable	83,361	128,658
Accrued liabilities	123,023	96,496
Compensation and payroll taxes	72,923	74,508
Pension and profit sharing	4,257	26,397
Taxes based on income	40,235	72,724
Dividends payable	17,070	19,375
Total current liabilities	371,305	509,027
Long-Term Debt—Less current maturities	199,017	225,045
Deferred Taxes and Other Items	43,339	44,094
Shareholders' Equity:		
Common stock—$1.00 par value: authorized 100,000,000 shares; issued 43,998,808 shares	43,999	43,999
Additional paid-in capital	63,266	63,063
Retained earnings	1,066,068	1,093,417
Translation adjustment	(81,051)	(56,993)
Employee Stock Ownership Plan shares purchased with debt	(38,638)	(36,499)
Treasury stock, at cost: 1984—7,091,288 shares; 1983—2,108,120 shares	(246,203)	(53,278)
Total shareholders' equity	807,441	1,053,709
	$1,421,102	$1,831,875

The accompanying notes to consolidated financial statements are an integral part of these financial statements.

EXHIBIT B

Consolidated Statements of Shareholders' Equity Levi Strauss & Co. and Subsidiaries (In Thousands Except Per Share Amounts)

	Common Stock	Additional Paid-In Capital	Retained Earnings	Translation Adjustment	Employee Stock Ownership Plan	Treasury Stock
Balance November 29, 1981	$43,999	$60,614	$ 913,722			$ (69,280)
Net income			126,575			
Shares issued to employees		(410)				6,477
Cash dividends declared ($1.65 per share)			(68,292)			
Translation adjustment:						
Cumulative adjustment at the beginning of the year				$ (3,154)		
Adjustment for the year (less income tax benefit of $5,907)				(40,259)		
Balance November 28, 1982	43,999	60,204	972,005	(43,413)		(62,803)
Net income			194,523			
Shares issued to employees		2,859				9,525
Cash dividends declared ($1.75 per share)			(73,111)			
Translation adjustment (less income tax benefit of $839)				(13,580)		
Purchase of shares by ESOP with company guaranteed debt					$(46,918)	
Payment by ESOP of company guaranteed debt					10,419	
Balance November 27, 1983	43,999	63,063	1,093,417	(56,993)	(36,499)	(53,278)
Net income			41,387			
Purchases of treasury stock						(199,692)
Shares issued to employees		203				6,767
Cash dividends declared ($1.85 per share)			(68,736)			
Translation adjustment				(24,058)		
Purchase of shares by ESOP with Company guaranteed debt					(2,139)	
Balance November 25, 1984	$43,999	$63,266	$1,066,068	$(81,051)	$(38,638)	$(246,203)

The following journal entry would summarize the employees' stock receipt:

Cash (or employee benefit costs)	6,067,000	
Additional paid-in capital	410,000	
Treasury stock		6,477,000

The cash debit would equal the money received from employees for the stock at the offered price; a debit to employee benefit costs would be the amount that the company paid out of its own earnings.

The fourth account included in shareholders' equity—retained earnings—has risen substantially over the period. We can see that the shareholders are enjoying the benefits of this wealth through increased yearly dividends. The fifth account included in shareholders' equity—employee stock ownership plan—represents company stock purchased by a trust established to oversee an employee pension plan. In recent years, liberal tax incentives provided by Congress have encouraged many companies to set up such a plan.

EXERCISES

1. How is the statement of shareholders' equity related to the statement of financial position?
2. In 1984, the company paid approximately $69 million in cash dividends, yet at the end of the year it had a cash balance of only approximately $37 million. How can this be? Prepare a journal entry to record the declaration and subsequent payment of the cash dividend.
3. Our discussion demonstrated the journal entry for the employees' stock receipt for the year ending November 28, 1982. What entries would have been made for the years ending November 27, 1983, and November 25, 1984?
4. On November 25, 1984, the company had approximately $43 million in deferred taxes and other items. Explain the origins of this amount.
5. Analyze the change in the company's current liabilities and long-term debt from the beginning of the year to the end of the year and provide an explanation for these changes.

PART FOUR
TRANSITION TOPICS

STATEMENT OF CHANGES IN FINANCIAL POSITION

17

CHAPTER OBJECTIVES

After studying Chapter 17, you should understand the following:

1. The third major financial statement—the statement of changes in financial position—and its purpose and uses.
2. The meaning of the fund for which the statement summarizes sources and applications.
3. The two major approaches to the preparation of the statement—working capital and cash.
4. The all financial resources concept that must be employed in preparing the statement no matter which approach is used.

The first 16 chapters of the text have focused on issues and procedures associated with the preparation of a company's statement of financial position and income statement. These two statements are generally accepted as being of most interest to both internal and external users. However, they do not provide a comprehensive picture of a company's financial situation. Even though the income statement is a link between successive statements of financial position, it does not provide complete information about how a company's financial position changes during a given period.

Neither the income statement nor the statement of financial position provides answers to such questions as, How did the firm finance its recent capital assets acquisition program? What are the company's primary sources and uses of funds? Why is a highly profitable company sometimes unable—or unwilling—to pay dividends? To answer such questions, a different analysis is needed. Answers can be obtained by combining a careful analysis of changes in account balances on successive statements of financial position with information from the income statement.

To meet the needs of financial statement users, companies are required to undertake the analysis and publish the results in a financial statement commonly called the statement of changes in financial position. This chapter discusses this statement's objectives, format, content, and preparation.

STATEMENT OF FINANCIAL POSITION AND THE CONCEPT OF FUNDS

STATEMENT OF CHANGES IN FINANCIAL POSITION
A statement presenting a summary of all significant changes in a company's financial position occurring during a specified time period.

The **statement of changes in financial position** presents a summary of all significant changes in a company's financial position occurring during a specified period of time and discloses information about important aspects of the company's financing and investing activities. Typically, a statement is made up of two sections: One presents the company's sources of funds during the accounting period, and the other indicates the way in which the enterprise uses the funds.

The Concept of Funds

Central to the preparation of a statement of financial position is the concept of funds. Although the term *funds* can be defined in several different ways, most companies define it as either working capital (current assets − current liabilities) or cash.

If funds are defined as working capital, changes in financial position are measured in terms of changes in the firm's current assets and current liabilities. On the other hand, if funds are defined as cash, changes in financial position are measured in terms of changes in the cash account. Although most companies define funds as working capital, the trend seems to be towards more companies reporting on changes in cash basis. The 1984 edition of *Accounting Trends and Techniques* reported that 227 of 600 companies surveyed defined funds as cash, while the 1982 edition reported that only 134 of 600 were using the cash flow approach.

The All Financial Resources Concept

ALL FINANCIAL RESOURCES CONCEPT
The preparation concept for the statement of changes in financial position where all significant changes are included whether or not cash or working capital is affected.

Regardless of the funds concept employed, all significant changes in financial resources occurring during the reporting period must be included in the statement whether or not working capital or cash is affected. The inclusion of all significant changes in the statement without regard to the definition of funds is known as the **all financial resources concept.**

WORKING CAPITAL APPROACH TO THE STATEMENT

Working Capital Defined

Working capital is defined as the difference between current assets and current liabilities. Consider the Upjack Company in Exhibit 17.1.

WORKING CAPITAL
The difference between current assets and current liabilities.

Upjack had working capital of $31,000 at the end of 1985 and $93,000 at the end of 1986. The third column of Exhibit 17.1 identifies how each individual component of working capital changed during 1986. Because the changes given are net changes in the accounts (i.e., simply calculated on the basis of changes in the year-end account balances), no information is provided as to the specific events and transactions that caused the changes. For example, we do not know if the increase in cash came from selling off some of the firm's fixed assets, from the issuance of long-term bonds, or from some other source. To fully understand why and how working capital changed during the period, it is necessary to identify the events and transactions causing the changes. It is these events and transactions, along with other significant nonworking capital changes in financial resources, that are reported in the statement of changes in financial position.

Transactions and Events That Change Working Capital

Exhibit 17.2 presents examples of common transactions that affect working capital. The effects of transactions on working capital and their relationship to the statement of changes in financial position are presented in Exhibit 17.3.

EXHIBIT 17.1

Upjack Company
Working Capital Analysis
As of December 31

	1985	**1986**	**Increase (Decrease)**
Current Assets			
Cash	$ 10,000	$ 22,000	$ 12,000
Short-term investments	177,000	227,000	50,000
Accounts receivable	32,000	50,000	18,000
Inventories	25,000	18,000	(7,000)
Prepaid expenses	5,000	6,000	1,000
Totals	$249,000	$323,000	$ 74,000
Current Liabilities			
Accounts payable	$ 89,000	$101,000	$ 12,000
Notes payable	75,000	89,000	14,000
Taxes payable	54,000	40,000	(14,000)
Totals	$218,000	$230,000	$ 12,000
Working capital	**$ 31,000**	**$ 93,000**	**$ 62,000**

EXHIBIT 17.2

	Transaction	Example
Sources of working capital	Decrease in noncurrent assets	Sale of a machine
	Increase in noncurrent liabilities	Issuance of bonds
	Increase in shareholders' equity	Issuance of stock
Applications of working capital	Increase in noncurrent assets	Purchase of land
	Decrease in noncurrent liabilities	Repayment of long-term loan
	Decrease in shareholders' equity	Payment of dividends

Changes in Noncurrent Assets. As Exhibit 17.3 shows, whenever a noncurrent asset such as machinery is decreased, working capital is increased. However, the amount of funds generated might not be the same as the reduction in the noncurrent account. For example, if a machine with a book value of $50,000 is sold for $150,000, funds will increase by $150,000 (the cash received), but the machine account will go down by only $50,000 (the book value given up).

Likewise, whenever current assets are used to purchase noncurrent assets, working capital is reduced. However, not all increases in noncurrent asset accounts reduce working capital. For example, if a machine with a fair market value of $10,000 is donated to a company, noncurrent assets increase, but working capital is not affected.

Changes in Noncurrent Liabilities. Increases in noncurrent liabilities generally increase working capital. For example, the issuance of long-term bonds provides an increase in cash, a working capital item. Since current liabilities are unchanged by the long-term bond issuance, working capital is increased.

The reduction in any noncurrent liability ordinarily uses up working capital. When a company repays a $100,000 long-term loan, cash (a working capital item) is used

EXHIBIT 17.3

Transactions	Statement Presentation
Transactions affecting only current asset or current liability accounts.	Will not change amount of working capital. Will not appear in statement of changes in financial position.
Transactions affecting a current asset or current liability and a noncurrent account.	Will change amount of working capital. Will appear in statement of changes in financial position.
Transactions affecting only noncurrent accounts (exchange transactions).	Will not change amounts of working capital but will appear in statement of changes in financial position.

up without a corresponding reduction in current liabilities. Working capital must therefore decrease.

Changes in Shareholders' Equity. Profitable operations are normally accompanied by increases in working capital. Recall that revenues represent an inflow of current assets (generally accounts receivable or cash), and expenses represent, for the most part, consumption of current assets (inventories). If revenues are greater than expenses, it follows that current asset inflows will exceed current asset consumption and working capital will increase.

The amount that working capital increases as a result of profitable operations is not necessarily equal to the amount of net income earned by a company. Some expenses, such as depreciation and amortization, represent the use of noncurrent assets and therefore do not affect working capital. Reported net income must be adjusted for such nonfund-consuming expenses to determine the amount of working capital provided by profitable operations.

Although profitable operations normally generate an inflow of working capital to a firm, realized losses normally represent a use of working capital. However, net losses, like net profits, must be adjusted for nonfund-consuming expenses to determine the total working capital change from operations.

Working capital normally increases when stock is issued, since cash is generally received for the stock, while payment of cash dividends reduces working capital. Stock dividends do not affect working capital and are not reported on the statement of changes in financial position.

Other Changes in Financial Position. Under the all financial resources concept, nonworking capital transactions that have a significant financing or investing impact on a company are included on the statement of changes in financial position. Examples of such transactions are issuance of long-term debt to purchase noncurrent assets, conversion of long-term debt or preferred stock to common stock, and repayment of long-term debt with long-term sinking funds. Although each of these transactions represents a significant financing or investing activity, none affects working capital.

The significant nonworking capital transactions are included on the statement of changes in financial position as both a source and a use of funds. For example, when long-term debt is issued to acquire a building, the issuance of the debt is shown as a source of funds and the acquisition of the building is shown as a use of funds.

Preparing the Statement of Changes in Financial Position

Most of the information needed for preparation of the statement of changes in financial position (hereafter called the statement of changes) is contained in comparative statements of financial position, the income statement, the statement of retained earnings, and the general ledger accounts for noncurrent assets, noncurrent liabilities, and shareholders' equity. Using information from these sources, we will illustrate the preparation of the statement of changes through a series of increasingly complex examples.

Case #1—Net Income as the Only Source of Working Capital

Exhibit 17.1 illustrates working capital components and changes for the Upjack Company. Assume the following additional financial data for Upjack:

Upjack Company
Statement of Financial Position
December 31

	1985	1986
Current assets	$249,000	$323,000
Current liabilities	$218,000	$230,000
Long-term liabilities	10,000	10,000
Shareholders' equity	21,000	83,000
Totals	$249,000	$323,000

If Upjack did not issue any stock or pay any dividends during 1986, the change in shareholders' equity must equal the income for 1986—$62,000. If we assume that all revenue and expense items represent changes in current assets and current liabilities, the 1986 income of $62,000 is a source of working capital to Upjack. For profitable firms, net income is often the largest single source of working capital. Combining the information in Exhibit 17.1 with the foregoing information about Upjack provides Upjack's statement of changes as presented in Exhibit 17.4.

As Exhibit 17.4 shows, a statement of changes has two sections: The first shows the sources and applications of funds for the year, and the second shows the changes in the individual fund components for the year.

Case #2—Net Income with Other Sources and Uses of Working Capital

Exhibit 17.5 shows the most recent comparative statements of financial position for Upjack for 1985 and 1986. Assume the company paid no cash dividends and net income is $75,000 for 1986. Working capital still increased by $62,000 during the year, as reflected in the difference between the increase in current assets ($74,000)

EXHIBIT 17.4

Statement of Changes in Financial Position
For the Year Ending December 31, 1986

Sources of working capital			
Net income			$62,000
Application of working capital			
Increase in working capital			$62,000
Changes in components of working capital			
Increase (decrease) in current assets			
Cash	$12,000		
Short-term investments	50,000		
Receivables	18,000		
Inventories	(7,000)		
Prepaid expenses	1,000		
		$74,000	
Increase (decrease) in current liabilities			
Accounts payable	$12,000		
Notes payable	14,000		
Taxes payable	(14,000)		
		$12,000	
Increase in working capital			$62,000

EXHIBIT 17.5

Upjack Company
Comparative Statement of Financial Position
As of December 31, 1986, and December 31, 1985

	1985	1986	Difference Dr.	Difference Cr.
Assets				
Current assets	$249,000	$323,000	74,000	
Land, plant, property				
Land	50,000	50,000		
Plant	100,000	130,000	30,000	
Accum. depr.—plant	(30,000)	(35,000)		5,000
Property	60,000	75,000	15,000	
Accum. depr.—property	(10,000)	(15,000)		5,000
Long-term investments	10,000	20,000	10,000	
Total assets	$429,000	$548,000		
Liabilities and Equity				
Current liabilities	218,000	230,000		12,000
Long-term liabilities	126,000	158,000		32,000
Shareholders' equity	85,000	160,000		75,000*
Total liabilities and equity	$429,000	$548,000	$129,000	$129,000

*Assuming no payment of dividends and no changes in paid-in capital, this entire amount represents net income for the year.

and the increase in current liabilities ($12,000). However, unlike Case #1, where all of the working capital change is explained by net profits, several other factors impacted the working capital change in Case #2.

Upjack's 1986 profits in this case are $75,000. However, the increases in accumulated depreciation for plant and property of $5,000 each indicate that depreciation expense for 1986 was $10,000. As previously explained, depreciation expense does not use up any funds, and net income must therefore be adjusted upward to reflect this fact when determining the amount of working capital generated from operations. The From Operations section of Exhibit 17.6 shows this adjustment. A further analysis of the changes presented in Exhibit 17.5 indicates that additional funds were acquired by the company through issuance of additional long-term liabilities. This $32,000 increase is a source of working capital as shown in Exhibit 17.6. The total sources of working capital for 1986 are $117,000, as shown.

Exhibit 17.5 shows that funds were used in three ways during 1986. An additional $30,000 of plant assets were acquired, property was purchased for $15,000, and long-term investments were increased by $10,000. When these three uses of working capital are subtracted from the total sources ($117,000 − $30,000 − $15,000 − $10,000 = $62,000), we see that the net change in funds—$62,000—equals the change in working capital arrived at by analysis of current asset and current liability changes. This equality must always hold.

Case #1 and Case #2 show the basic approach used to prepare a statement of changes in financial position. In actual practice, the process is more complex, because each noncurrent asset and noncurrent liability account must be analyzed

EXHIBIT 17.6

Upjack Company Statement of Changes in Financial Position For the Year Ending December 31, 1986			
Sources of working capital			
From operations			
Net income	$75,000		
Add: Depreciation	10,000	$85,000	
Additional long-term indebtedness		32,000	
Total sources			$117,000
Applications of working capital			
Plant and property additions		$45,000	
Additional investments in long-term securities		10,000	
Total applications			55,000
Increase in working capital			$ 62,000
Changes in components of working capital			
Increase (decrease) in current assets			
Cash	$12,000		
Short-term investments	50,000		
Receivables	18,000		
Inventories	(7,000)		
Prepaid expenses	1,000	$74,000	
Increase (decrease) in current liabilities			
Accounts payable	$12,000		
Notes payable	14,000		
Taxes payable	(14,000)	12,000	
Increase in working capital			$ 62,000

in detail to determine the effect of any change on working capital. During a period of time, dozens of transactions are reflected in a particular ledger account, and each one can affect working capital. A simple examination of the net change in the account balance during a time period might not provide sufficient information for statement of changes preparation. Case #3 is a comprehensive example indicating the subtleties involved in preparation of a statement of changes in a more complex situation.

The general approach followed in Case #3 is the same as that for the first two cases:

1. Determine the net change in working capital from the current asset and current liability changes during the period.
2. Analyze all of the transactions affecting noncurrent assets, noncurrent liabilities, and shareholders' equity to pinpoint the sources and uses of working capital.
3. Consider all significant changes in the company's financing and investment activities that bypass current accounts and are not otherwise reflected in working capital.

Case #3—A Comprehensive Example

Exhibit 17.7 shows comparative statements of financial position for 1985 and 1986 for the Felco Company; the company's general ledger accounts for 1986 are shown

EXHIBIT 17.7

Felco Company
Comparative Statements of Financial Position
For the Years Ending 1985 and 1986

	as of 12/31/85	as of 12/31/86
Assets		
Current assets		
Cash	$ 24,000	$ 41,800
Accounts receivable (net)	38,600	47,000
Inventories	123,500	112,500
Prepaid expenses	2,670	3,600
Total current assets	$188,770	$204,900
Long-term investments	$ 15,000	—
Plant and equipment		
Equipment	187,750	$222,500
Less accumulated depreciation	(37,750)	(46,000)
	$150,000	$176,500
Plant	120,500	215,500
Less accumulated depreciation	(11,300)	(15,600)
	$109,200	$199,900
Land	25,000	25,000
Total plant and equipment	$284,200	$401,400
Total assets	$487,970	$606,300
Liabilities and Shareholders' Equity		
Current liabilities		
Accounts payable	$ 45,000	$ 18,700
Income tax payable	7,800	7,700
Total current liabilities	$ 52,800	$ 26,400
Long-term liabilities		
Bonds payable	—	$100,000
Less discount	—	4,750
Total long-term liabilities	-0-	$ 95,250
Total liabilities	$ 52,800	$121,650
Shareholders' equity		
Common stock, $25 par value	$300,000	$310,000
Paid-in capital in excess of par	22,500	26,500
Retained earnings	112,670	148,150
Total shareholders' equity	$435,170	$484,650
Total liabilities and shareholders' equity	$487,970	$606,300

in Exhibit 17.8. A systematic analysis of these statements and accounts will provide the data necessary to prepare the company's statement of changes in financial position. Before we begin this analysis, let's first calculate the net change in working capital for 1986. The statements of financial position in Exhibit 17.7 indicate that

EXHIBIT 17.8

Felco Company
General Ledger Accounts for 1986

Investments

Debit		Credit	
Balance 1/1	15,000	10/17 Sold investments (received $20,000 cash)	15,000
Balance 12/31	0		

Equipment

Debit		Credit	
Balance 1/1	187,750	2/10 Discarded equipment with no salvage value	13,000
8/17 Purchased equipment for cash	47,750		
Balance 12/31	222,500		

Accumulated Depreciation—Equipment

Debit		Credit	
2/10 Equipment discarded	13,000	Balance 1/1	37,750
		12/31 Depreciation for year	21,250
		Balance 12/31	46,000

Plant

Debit		Credit	
Balance 1/1	120,500		
8/10 Acquired with bonds	95,000		
Balance 12/31	215,500		

Accumulated Depreciation—Plant

Debit		Credit	
		Balance 1/1	11,300
		12/31 Depreciation for year	4,300
		Balance 12/31	15,600

Long-Term Bonds

Debit		Credit	
		Balance 1/1	0
		9/1 Issued 10-year bonds	100,000
		Balance 12/31	100,000

Discount on Bonds Payable

Debit		Credit	
Balance 1/1	0	12/31 Amortization of discount	250
9/1 Issued 10-year bonds	5,000		
Balance 12/31	4,750		

Land

Debit		Credit	
Balance 1/1	25,000		
Balance 12/31	25,000		

Common Stock, $25 Par

Debit		Credit	
		Balance 1/1	300,000
		12/20 Stock dividend	10,000
		Balance 12/31	310,000

Paid-in Capital in Excess of Par

Debit		Credit	
		Balance 1/1	22,500
		12/20 Stock dividend	4,000
		Balance 12/31	26,500

Retained Earnings

Debit		Credit	
12/20 Stock dividend	14,000	Balance 1/1	112,670
12/31 Cash dividend	11,000	12/31 Net income for year	60,480
		Balance 12/31	148,150

current assets increased by $16,130 between 1985 and 1986 and current liabilities decreased by $26,400, with a net increase in working capital of $42,530. Now we must identify the transactions that led to this increase.

To aid in the preparation of the statement of changes, we introduce the hypothetical account, Working Capital, to which debits are sources and credits are uses. As we go through each of the noncurrent balance sheet accounts, we will see what journal entries need to be made, and we will post them to our hypothetical Working Capital account. After analyzing the noncurrent accounts and posting all items that must appear in the statement to the Working Capital account, the balance of the Working Capital account will be the net increase/decrease in working capital for the period.

Working Capital

Sources	Uses
Bal. net increase	Bal. net decrease

Investments. The comparative statements of financial position indicate a decrease in the company's long-term investment of $15,000 during the year. The general ledger (refer to Exhibit 17.8) shows that investments with a book value of $15,000 were sold for $20,000 cash on October 17, 1986. The sale created a source of working capital equal to $20,000. However, in reporting this amount on the statement of changes, caution must be exercised. The $20,000 comprises two parts: (1) a recovery of the $15,000 book value of the investment and (2) a gain of $5,000, which has already been included in net income. To ensure proper reporting, the $20,000 should be shown on the statement of changes as a source of working capital (proceeds of a sale of investment), and the $5,000 gain should be deducted out of the net income figure. Thus, the entry for the sale (using our hypothetical account) would be as follows:

Working capital	20,000	
Investments		15,000
Gain on sale of investments		5,000
(to record sale of investment)		

Equipment and Accumulated Depreciation. Felco's statements of financial position indicate that equipment increased by $34,750 during the year. The Equipment account shows that two factors caused the change. First, on February 10 the company disposed of an asset that was fully depreciated and had zero salvage value. This transaction reduced the Equipment balance but had no impact on Working Capital, because the equipment was simply discarded. Therefore, this particular transaction would not be reflected in the statement of changes, and no entry to the Working Capital account would be made.

The second factor affecting the account balance was the purchase for cash of a piece of machinery worth $47,750. This equipment purchase resulted in an appli-

When Depreciation Is a Genuine Source of Funds

On the statement of changes in financial position, depreciation expense is added back to net income as an expense not requiring the outlay of funds rather than listed as a separate source of funds. Depreciation reduces income tax expense, an expense that does require the outlay of funds. Thus, depreciation creates funds in the amount of the income tax reduction.

To illustrate, assume Company X and Company Y have the same level of income before depreciation and income taxes and that both have the same tax rate. Company Y has depreciation expense this year; Company X does not. The amount of funds provided by operations for the two firms would be as follows:

	Company X	Company Y
Income before depreciation and taxes	$100,000	$100,000
Depreciation expense	-0-	10,000
Income before taxes	$100,000	$ 90,000
Funds outlay for tax expense (@40%)	(40,000)	(36,000)
Net income	$ 60,000	$ 54,000
Add: Expenses not requiring the outlay of funds—depreciation expense	-0-	10,000
Funds provided by operations	$ 60,000	$ 64,000

Note that funds provided by Y exceed those provided by X. This is due to depreciation, which has been a source of $4,000 of funds.

cation of working capital and would be reflected as such on the statement of changes. Thus, the entry to show the impact on Working Capital would be as follows:

Equipment	47,750	
Working capital		47,750
(to record purchase of equipment)		

Finally, we should note that the Accumulated Depreciation account shows that the depreciation expense for the year on the company's equipment was $21,250. This expense was accounted for on the income statement as a deduction from revenue. As previously discussed, this nonfund-consuming expense does not represent a use of working capital, and this fact must be reflected in funds from operations (to be discussed shortly).

Plant and Accumulated Depreciation, Bonds Payable, and Discount on Bonds Payable. In 1986, Felco had a significant increase in plant capacity. The balance sheet indicates a $95,000 increase in Plant. This increase in a noncurrent asset represents an application of funds. A review of the plant general ledger account indicates that the expansion was financed with the issuance of ten-year bonds. This observation is supported through an analysis of the bond account, which shows an increase of $100,000. This issuance of bonds thus created a source of working capital that was subsequently used to finance the plant purchase. Both transactions would appear on the statement of changes—one as a source, the other as an application. The issuance of bonds would appear as a source for $95,000 (not $100,000), because the bonds were issued at a discount. The entries would be as follows:

Working capital	95,000	
Discount on bonds payable	5,000	
Bonds payable		100,000
(to record issuance of bonds)		

Plant	95,000	
Working capital		95,000
(to show purchase of plant)		

Because the interest expense represented by amortization of bond discount is a nonfund-consuming expense, the amount of discount amortized in any year has to be reflected in the funds provided by operations.

Finally, changes in the Accumulated Depreciation—Plant account total $4,300, indicating that plant depreciation expense for 1986 was $4,300. As with depreciation on equipment and amortization of bond discount, this expense does not require funds and thus needs only to be reflected in the funds provided by operations.

Land. Both the statements of financial position and the land general ledger account indicate no changes in this noncurrent asset during the year; thus, no reference is made to this account on the statement of changes, and no entry is made to Working Capital.

Common Stock and Paid-In Excess. The comparative statements of financial position indicate that common stock at par and paid-in capital in excess of par increased during the year by $10,000 and $4,000, respectively. However, an inspection of the appropriate general ledger accounts shows that the increases were the result of a $14,000 stock dividend. In the case of stock dividends, the Common Stock and Paid-in Capital in Excess of Par accounts are proportionately increased by the amount of the dividend, with a corresponding reduction in Retained Earnings. Thus, this stock dividend does not represent either a source or a use of working capital. Consequently, it is not reflected in the statement, and no entry to Working Capital is made.

Retained Earnings. The statement of financial position in Exhibit 17.6 shows a $35,480 increase in Retained Earnings in 1986. Basically, three transactions affected this account. First, there was the declaration of the previously discussed stock dividend, which reduced the Retained Earnings balance but had no impact on the sources or uses of funds.

Second, the company paid a cash dividend of $11,000 on December 31. This transaction resulted in a use of working capital—in this case cash—and would be reflected as such in the statement of changes with the following entry:

Cash dividends	11,000	
Working capital		11,000
(to show impact of dividends paid)		

Finally, the company earned $60,480 for the year. Although this profit figure represents a source of working capital, it must be adjusted for items having an impact on the profit calculation but having no impact on working capital. The $60,480 really understates the amount of working capital provided through operations, because it includes such nonworking capital items as depreciation and amortization of bond discount discussed earlier. An analysis of the plant and equipment accumulated depreciation accounts indicates a total depreciation expense of $25,550 for the year. Likewise, the bond discount account indicates a nonfund amortization expense of $250. Also, remember that the net income figure included a gain from the sale of long-term investments of $5,000, which is not a component of income from normal operations. Thus, this amount should be deducted from net income in arriving at working capital provided by normal operations. The entry to Working Capital would be as follows:

Working capital	81,280	
Gain on sale of investment	5,000	
Net income		60,480
Depreciation expense (plant & equip.)		25,550
Discount on bonds payable		250
(to show impact of funds provided by operations)		

Based on the preceding information, it is possible to calculate the working capital provided by operations during the year as follows:

Net income		$60,480
Add: Expenses not requiring use of working capital		
Depreciation expense	25,550	
Amortization of bond discount	250	25,800
Deduct: Gain not due to normal operation		
Gain on sale of long-term investment		(5,000)
Working capital provided by operations		$81,280

The Statement

Provided below is the completed account, Working Capital. Note that it records everything needed for the final statement of changes in financial position (other than the changes in components of working capital) and that all of the sources are separated from all of the uses. Exhibit 17.9 contains the final draft of the statement of changes in financial position for Felco Company. It is divided into two parts. The first part summarizes the sources and uses of funds; the second part shows the changes in components of working capital. The net increase (or decrease) shown in part 1 must equal the final amount in part 2.

EXHIBIT 17.9

Felco Company
Statement of Changes in Financial Position
For Year Ending December 31, 1986

Sources of working capital				
Operations during the year				
Net income		$60,480		
Add expenses not requiring use of working capital				
Depreciation expense	$25,550			
Amortization of bond discount	250	25,800		
Deduct gain not due to normal operations				
Gain on sale of long-term investment		(5,000)	$ 81,280	
Proceeds from sale of investment			20,000	
Issuance of long-term bonds for plant, net of discount of $5,000			95,000	$196,280
Applications of working capital				
Purchase of equipment			$ 47,750	
Acquisition of plant by issuance of bonds			95,000	
Payment of cash dividends			11,000	153,750
Increase in working capital				$ 42,530
Changes in components of working capital				
Increase (decrease) in current assets				
Cash			$ 17,800	
Accounts receivable (net)			8,400	
Inventories			(11,000)	
Prepaid expenses			930	$16,130
Increase (decrease) in current liabilities				
Accounts payable			$(26,300)	
Income tax payable			(100)	(26,400)
Increase in working capital				$ 42,530

Working Capital

From sale of investments	20,000	Purchase of equipment	47,750
From bonds issued in exchange for plant	95,000	Purchase of plant with bonds payable	95,000
From operations	81,280	Cash dividends	11,000
Total sources	196,280	Total uses	153,750
Net increase	42,530		

DIVERSITY OF PRACTICE

Many approaches can be used in preparing a statement of changes. Our previous example used the working capital approach using a format where the net change in working capital was isolated. Exhibit 17.10 shows an example of a statement using this approach for Apple Computers, Inc. Let's now turn our attention to illustrating how such a statement can be prepared using a cash approach.

Focus on Changes in Cash

In recent years, corporate managers, financial analysts, and investors have become more and more interested in a company's cash position as well as its profit picture. Why this interest? Because, in reality, a firm's ultimate success depends on how much cash is generated and how this cash is used. Profits are not cash. It is quite conceivable to find a company with profits that lacks cash. Of course, even the opposite situation is possible. There are instances of companies that have losses but have been able to continue operating because they had sufficient cash to pay their bills and stay solvent.

The term *cash flow* refers to the amount of cash coming into and going out of a company. The net effect of cash flow is reflected at any moment in time in a

EXHIBIT 17.10

Apple Computers, Inc.
Consolidated Statements of Changes in Financial Position

Three years ended September 28, 1984 (In thousands)	**1984**	**1983**	**1982**
Working capital was provided by			
Operations			
Net income	$ 64,055	$ 76,714	$ 61,306
Charges to operations not affecting working capital:			
Depreciation and amortization	37,963	22,440	16,556
Deferred income taxes (non-current)	20,453	35,697	7,625
Total working capital provided by operations	122,471	134,851	85,487
Increases in common stock and related tax benefits, net of changes in notes receivable from shareholders	23,242	44,095	18,399
Increases in non-current obligations under capital leases	—	—	1,172
Total working capital provided	145,713	178,946	105,058
Working capital was applied to:			
Purchase of property, plant, and equipment, net of retirements	39,614	52,666	26,470
Other	13,939	11,531	4,421
Total working capital applied	53,553	64,197	30,891
Increase in working capital	$ 92,160	$114,749	$ 74,167
Increase (decrease) in working capital by components:			
Cash and temporary cash investments	$ (28,396)	$ (9,772)	$ 80,222
Accounts receivable	121,818	64,942	29,148
Inventories	122,162	67,089	(22,972)
Prepaid income taxes	(1,198)	25,860	2,089
Other current assets	4,172	9,660	1,156
Accounts payable	(56,337)	(27,576)	1,488
Accrued compensation and employee benefits	(4,686)	(3,996)	(4,015)
Income taxes payable	(11,268)	15,307	(6,686)
Accrued marketing and distribution and other current liabilities	(54,107)	(26,765)	(6,263)
Increase in working capital	**$ 92,160**	**$114,749**	**$ 74,167**

COMPONENTS OF THE STATEMENT OF CHANGES IN FINANCIAL POSITION UNDER THE ALL FINANCIAL RESOURCES APPROACH—WORKING CAPITAL DEFINITION OF FUNDS

CONCEPT SUMMARY 17.1

I. SOURCES OF WORKING CAPITAL	
Item	**Examples**
Working capital provided by operations	
Net income	Net income
Add expenses not requiring use of working capital	Depreciation, amortization
Add other sources of working capital	Sale of equipment, issuance of bonds, sale of stock
Add significant investing activities	Issuance of bonds to purchase plant facilities
II. APPLICATIONS OF WORKING CAPITAL	
Item	**Examples**
General applications of working capital	Purchase of equipment, retirement of long-term bonds, declaration of dividends
Add significant investing activities	Purchase of plant facilities through issuance of bonds
III. CHANGES IN COMPONENTS OF WORKING CAPITAL	
Item	**Examples**
Increase (decrease) in current assets	Cash, accounts receivable, inventory
Less increase (decrease) in current liabilities	Accounts payable, notes payable, dividends payable

Note: The statement of changes in financial position following a cash definition of funds will differ from the foregoing primarily in the Funds Provided from Operations section. See Exhibit 17.12 for these differences.

company's cash balance. Many companies spend a great deal of time and effort managing this asset. A firm's main source of cash is its cash receipts from customers in payment of accounts receivable. Similarly, a firm's main use of cash is its cash payments to suppliers in payment of its accounts payable. Let's see how we can determine cash flow from the accounting records.

Cash Inflow from Accounts Receivable. When a firm makes a sale to a customer, the customer generally charges the purchase to his or her account with the firm. Later the firm bills the customer for the amount of the purchase, and the customer pays off the balance of the account. The accounting records recognize revenue when the sale is made; however, the firm does not receive any cash until the customer makes a payment on the account. For this reason, sales revenue and cash inflow are not the same. Nevertheless, the two are related, for the current sales trigger the future cash inflow. The relationship can be thought of as someone filling a leaky bucket.

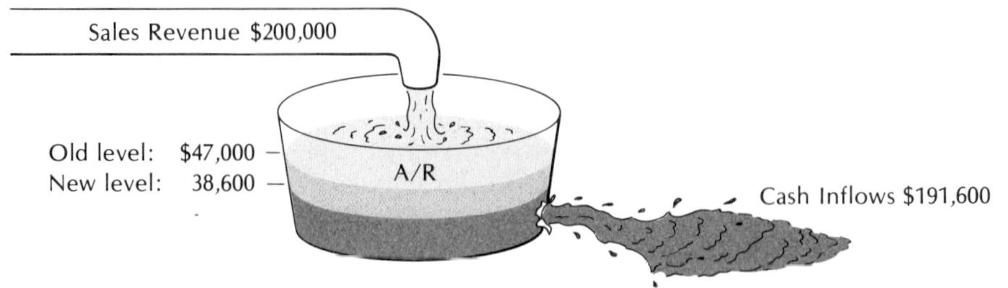

The bucket represents the firm's accounts receivable. Sales revenue constantly pours from customers into accounts receivable. Eventually, customers pay off their accounts: The firm receives cash, and the level of accounts receivable drops.

At any moment in time, the difference between the sales revenue flow and the cash flow is reflected in the balance of the firm's accounts receivable. With this relationship in mind, one can easily determine the firm's cash inflow from accounts receivable. When sales revenue pours into accounts receivable, it can do only one of two things: It can flow out of accounts receivable as cash, or it can increase the balance of accounts receivable. In other words, the amount of sales must equal the amount of cash inflow plus the increase in the balance of accounts receivable. This means that the amount of cash inflow must equal the amount of sales minus the increase (or plus the decrease) in accounts receivable. Therefore, to derive the firm's cash inflow from accounts receivable, one must take the firm's sales and subtract the change in accounts receivable. For example, if Felco Company had $200,000 of sales revenue in 1986, its cash inflow from accounts receivable would be $191,600, because accounts receivable increased by $8,400.

Cash Outflow to Accounts Payable. When a firm makes a purchase from a supplier, it generally charges the purchase to its account with the supplier. Later the supplier bills the firm, and the firm pays off the balance of its account. Although the accounting records recognize the purchase when the purchase is made, the firm does not use any cash until it pays the supplier's bill. For this reason, purchases and cash outflow are not the same. As with sales and cash inflow, purchases and cash outflow are related, and this relationship can be thought of in terms of the leaky bucket analogy.

This time, the bucket represents the firm's accounts payable. Purchases constantly pour into accounts payable. When the firm pays its suppliers' bills, it uses cash, and the level of accounts payable drops.

At any moment in time, the difference between the purchases expense flow and the cash flow is reflected in the balance of the firm's accounts payable. As with accounts receivable, it is easy to determine the firm's cash outflow to accounts payable, given this relationship. When purchases expense pours into accounts payable, it can do only one of two things: It can flow out of accounts payable as cash, or it can increase the balance of accounts payable. In other words, the amount of purchases must equal the amount of cash outflow plus the increase in the balance of accounts payable. This means that the amount of cash outflow must equal the amount of purchases minus the increase (or plus the decrease) in accounts payable. To derive the firm's cash outflow to accounts payable one must therefore take the firm's purchases and subtract the change in accounts payable. For example if Felco Company had $100,000 of purchases expense in 1986, its cash outflow to accounts payable would be $126,300, because accounts payable had decreased by $26,300.

Cash Basis Statement of Changes in Financial Position

It would be very tedious to identify all of the firm's cash flow by analyzing the company's accounts in the above fashion. Therefore, to ensure the availability of such cash flow information, some people strongly advocate that the statement of changes in financial position be prepared using a cash approach. Such an analysis is typically done internally to assist financial managers in financial analysis and in effectively planning and controlling for utilization of corporate cash, and the accounting profession is now encouraging companies to use the cash approach for external reporting.

To illustrate, we have included in Exhibit 17.11 another statement for the Felco

EXHIBIT 17.11

Felco Company
Statement of Changes in Financial Position
For Year Ending December 31, 1986

Sources of cash				
Operations during the year				
Net income		$60,480		
Add deductions not decreasing cash during the year:				
Depreciation	$25,550			
Amortization of discount on bonds payable	250			
Decrease in inventories	11,000	36,800		
		$97,280		
Deduct additions not increasing cash during the year:				
Increase in account receivables (net)	8,400			
Increase in prepaid expenses	930			
Decrease in accounts payable	26,300			
Decrease in income taxes payable	100	(35,730)		
Deduct gain not due to ordinary operations				
Gain on sale of long-term investment		(5,000)	$56,550	
Proceeds from sale of long-term investment			20,000	
Issuance of long-term bonds for plant			95,000	$171,550
Applications of cash				
Purchase of equipment			47,750	
Acquisition of plant by issuance of bonds			95,000	
Payment of cash dividends			11,000	153,750
Increase in cash				**$ 17,800**
Change in cash balance				
Cash balance, December 31, 1986				$ 41,800
Cash balance, December 31, 1985				24,000
Increase in cash				**$ 17,800**

Company using a cash approach. Let's examine for a moment the differences between this statement and the one in Exhibit 17.9.

The first item to note in the statement of changes is the isolation of changes in cash rather than in working capital. This change in focus impacts on the form and content of the entire statement. For example, in the Sources of Cash section, the increase in accounts receivable is included as a reduction of cash because such accounts represent sales for which cash has not yet been received. Similarly, the decrease in accounts payable is included as a reduction of cash because cash was expended in making payment on the account.

A simple principle will help explain the presence of this additional data in the cash basis statement of changes: Changes in noncash accounts frequently cause changes in the cash account. Keep in mind that working capital, which is defined as net current assets minus current liabilities, is affected by almost any change in the noncurrent accounts, and this requires analysis of all of the noncurrent accounts. It is thus analogous that the statement of changes on a cash basis requires analysis of all noncash accounts. When preparing the statement of changes on a cash basis, the noncurrent accounts must still be analyzed, and their analysis will proceed the same as before. For this reason, the changes in noncurrent accounts listed on the cash basis statement of changes are identical to those changes listed on the working capital statement.

The only additional work needed is the analysis of the noncash current asset and liability accounts. The analysis is very similar to that previously shown for accounts receivable and accounts payable, except that only the net changes in the account balances need review (since the amounts of sales, purchases, etc., are already included in net income). As in preparing the working capital basis T-account, when nonfund (i.e., noncash) accounts are credited, the fund (i.e., cash) is increased with a debit.

The main difference between the working capital basis statement of changes and the cash basis statement of changes lies in the section of the statement titled Funds Provided by Operations. To obtain working capital provided by operations, we are required to make certain adjustments to net income. To obtain cash provided by operations, we must make these same adjustments and others to net income. These adjustments (from Exhibit 17.11) are summarized in Exhibit 17.12.

The sources of data and general approach for the preparation of the statement of changes based on cash flow are similar to those for the statement of changes based on working capital. Comparative statements of financial position and general ledger accounts must be analyzed to identify the specific transactions occurring that have

EXHIBIT 17.12
Cash Provided by Operations

Item	Example
Net income	Net income
Add expenses not reducing cash	Depreciation
Add net credit changes in current accounts	
Decreases in current assets	Inventories
Increases in current liabilities	Accounts payable
Deduct net debit changes in current accounts	
Increases in current assets	Accounts receivable
Decreases in current liabilities	Income taxes payable
Cash provided by operations	Increase in cash

affected cash. Also, as was the case when following the working capital approach, there are variations in the preparation of the statement under the cash concept. Exhibit 17.13 contains IBM's statement for 1984 using a cash approach.

EXHIBIT 17.13

International Business Machines Corporation
and Subsidiary Companies
Consolidated Statement of Funds Flow
for the year ended December 31
(Dollars in millions)

	1984†		1983‡		1982‡	
Funds (Cash and Marketable Securities) at January 1		**$5,536**		$3,300		$2,029
Provided from (used for) Operations:						
Sources:						
Net earnings	**$ 6,582**		$ 5,485		$4,409	
Items not requiring the current use of funds:						
Depreciation charged to costs and expenses	**2,987**		3,362		3,143	
Net book value of rental machines and other property retired or sold	**1,483**		2,108		1,642	
Amortization of program products	**486**		311		249	
Other (principally deferred income taxes)	**1,004**		749		84	
	12,542		12,015		9,527	
Depreciation of manufacturing facilities capitalized	**228**		265		419	
	12,770		12,280		9,946	
Uses:						
Investment in rental machines	**858**		1,412		3,293	
Investment in plant and other property	**4,615**		3,518		3,392	
	5,473		4,930		6,685	
Investment in program products	**803**		588		468	
Increase (decrease) in investments and other assets	**1,764**		1,887		(320)	
Net change in working capital (excluding cash, marketable securities and loans payable)	**4,043**		855		370	
	12,083		8,260		7,203	
Translation effects	**(324)**		(147)		30	
Net provided from operations		**363**		3,873		2,773
Provided from External Financing:						
Net change in long-term debt	**595**		(177)		182	
Net change in loans payable	**302**		3		(244)	
Net provided from external financing		**897**		(174)		(62)
Provided from Employee and Stockholder Plans		**73**		788		613
		6,869		7,787		5,353
Less: Cash Dividends Paid		**2,507**		2,251		2,053
Funds (Cash and Marketable Securities) at December 31		**$4,362**		$5,536		$3,300

†1984 includes, on the appropriate lines, the amounts expended for the acquisition of the net assets of ROLM Corporation.

Net change in long-term debt for 1984 includes $1,285 million face value of 7⅞% convertible subordinated debentures issued in connection with the acquisition of ROLM Corporation.

‡Amounts have been reclassified, where applicable, to conform with 1984 presentation.

DEMONSTRATION PROBLEM

Following is a comparative schedule of working capital for Wessex Corporation for the year ending April 30, 1985:

	April 30	
	1985	**1984**
Cash	$ 15,000	$ 19,560
Marketable securities	25,750	18,250
Accounts receivable	79,600	85,400
Inventory	125,000	150,750
Prepaid expenses	10,500	11,250
	$255,850	$285,210
Accounts payable	18,500	17,400
Wages payable	25,500	20,200
Taxes payable	5,000	8,500
	$ 49,000	$ 46,100
	$206,850	$239,110

Additional information:

a. Net income amounts to $75,000 for the year.
b. Net income includes a deduction of $15,000 for depreciation expenses.

Required

Calculate the amount of cash provided by operations.

Demonstration Problem Solution

Cash provided by operations			
Net income		$75,000	
Add (deduct) items not affecting cash			
Noncash expenses			
Depreciation expense	$15,000		
Decrease in current assets or increase in current liabilities			
Accounts receivable	5,800		
Inventory	25,750		
Prepaid expenses	750		
Accounts payable	1,100		
Wages payable	5,300		
Increase in current assets or decrease in current liabilities			
Marketable securities	(7,500)		
Taxes payable	(3,500)	42,700	
Total cash provided by operations			$117,700

SUMMARY

- The statement of changes in financial position summarizes significant changes in a company's financial position during a specified period of time.
- The working capital approach to the statement of changes in financial position measures fund changes in terms of current assets and current liabilities. The cash approach to the statement of changes in financial position measures fund changes in terms of changes in cash.
- Companies are required under APB 19 to include all significant financing or investing activities of the firm in the statement of changes in financial position.
- Increases in working capital generally occur if noncurrent assets are decreased, noncurrent liabilities are increased, or a company makes a profit.
- Decreases in working capital generally occur if noncurrent assets are increased, noncurrent liabilities are decreased, or a company suffers a loss.
- Working capital provided by operations equals income adjusted upward or downward for nonfund-consuming expense items, such as depreciation.
- Information for preparing the statement of changes in financial position is obtained from comparative statements of financial position, the income statement for the period, the statement of retained earnings for the period, and the general ledger.

QUESTIONS

17-1. What is meant by the term *funds* when referring to the statement of changes in financial position?

17-2. What does the all financial resources concept mean to a business when it is preparing its financial statements?

17-3. Where would an accountant find the necessary information to prepare a statement of changes in financial position?

17-4. What are the major sources and uses of working capital for a business?

17-5. What does the term *cash flow* mean? How is this concept used by companies?

17-6. How might a company have an increase in cash and show an operating loss for a period?

17-7. Which of the following items is included in the statement of changes in financial position because of the all financial resources concept.

- **a.** Depreciation
- **b.** Issuance of capital stock
- **c.** Purchase of treasury stock
- **d.** Retirement of long-term debt by issuance of preferred stock

17-8. A company reports net income of $26,000, which includes $4,500 of depreciation expense and $2,500 amortization of goodwill. By what amount would working capital be increased or decreased?

17-9. Ranger Manufacturing declares a 10% stock dividend. What effect does this dividend have on working capital?

17-10. Skyco Company reports a net loss from operations of $15,000. Depreciation expense for the period is $7,200. How will the loss from operations appear in the statement of changes in financial position?

EXERCISES

17-E1. The following information is from Sunshine Company's records.

Proceeds from 90-day note	$ 320,000
Proceeds from long-term bonds	4,000,000
Purchase of capital equipment	840,000
Purchase of inventory	200,000
Proceeds from sale of common stock	1,000,000

What is the effect on working capital as a result of these transactions?

17-E2. Net income for Ellis Corporation for 1986 is $3 million, with the following additional information.

Capital expenditures	$1,250,000
Depreciation on fixed assets	180,000
Dividends paid on common stock	800,000
Amortization of goodwill	98,000

What is Ellis Corporation's working capital provided from operations for 1986?

17-E3. Working capital provided from operations in Goliath Company's statement of changes in financial position for 1986 is $4 million. For 1986, depreciation on fixed assets is $1.9 million, amortization of goodwill is $50,000, and dividends on common stock are $1 million. What is Goliath's net income for 1986?

17-E4. Cavalier Company sold a piece of equipment that originally cost $20,000 for $12,000. Book value of the equipment was $8,000. The gain on this sale was included as part of net income. What informtion should Cavalier Company show in its statement of changes in financial position regarding this sale?

17-E5. The following information is from the books of Miller Company.

	12/31/85	12/31/86
Accounts payable (for merchandise purchases)	15,000	21,000

Additional information shows purchases of $135,000. Calculate the amount of cost paid to vendors during 1986.

17-E6. Dividends payable for Yale Corporation went from $24,000 to $30,000. Dividends of $120,000 were declared. Determine the amount that should be shown in the statement of changes in financial position for dividends. Also determine what should be shown in the cash flow statement.

17-E7. Examine the following shareholders' equity accounts of Edwards Corporation and determine sources and uses of working capital and the amounts:

Common Stock, $50 Par					
				Balance	
Date	Item	Dr	Cr	Dr	Cr
1986					
Jan. 1	Balance, 50,000 shares				2,500,000
June 1	3,000 shares issued for cash		150,000		
Oct. 1	2,000 shares stock dividend		100,000		2,750,000

Paid-in Capital in Excess of Par on Common Stock					
				Balance	
Date	Item	Dr	Cr	Dr	Cr
1986					
Jan. 1	Balance				500,000
June 1	3,000 shares issued for cash		60,000		
Oct. 1	Stock dividend		20,000		580,000

Retained Earnings					
				Balance	
Date	Item	Dr	Cr	Dr	Cr
1986					
Jan. 1	Balance				750,000
Oct. 1	Stock dividend	120,000			
Dec. 31	Net income		950,000		
Dec. 31	Cash dividends	500,000			1,080,000

PROBLEM SET A

17-A1. Working Capital Adjustments. Indicate whether the following items are sources of working capital, are applications of working capital, or do not affect working capital and enter in the appropriate column the amount of working capital provided or applied (or 0 if not affected).

	Working Capital Provided	Working Capital Applied	Working Capital Not Affected
a. Net income for the year is $41,000.			
b. Issue of 8% bonds due in 1987 retired by payment of $80,000 to bondholders.			
c. Furniture and fixtures for the offices purchased on account for $6,150.			
d. Dividend declared of $9,000.			
e. Machinery sold for $15,000 cash; book value is $10,000 at the date of sale, and the company realizes a gain of $5,000 on the sale.			
f. 1,000 shares of stock issued, par $100, at $120 per share for cash.			
g. Land purchased for $300,000; no down payment; 10-year mortgage given for full purchase price.			
h. New 9% bonds issued having face value of $200,000 for $195,000 cash.			
i. Bondholders exchange their convertible bonds for common stock, paying $75,000 in addition to turning in bonds shown at $150,000 in the accounts.			

17-A2. Working Capital Provided by Operations. The following information is from the books of Cannon Company.

Accounts payable, January 1	$10,000
Accounts payable, December 31	8,750
Accounts receivable, January 1	18,750
Accounts receivable, December 31	10,000
Cash purchases of merchandise	40,000
Credit purchases of merchandise	25,000
Depreciation expense	3,000
General, administrative, and selling expense (excluding depreciation)	2,000
Inventory, January 1	2,750
Inventory, December 31	30,000
Prepaid expenses, January 1	1,000
Prepaid expenses, December 31	1,500
Sales of merchandise	62,500

Required

Determine the working capital provided by operations.

17-A3. Working Capital Provided by Operations. The following information is from the records of S.N.U. Corporation.

Notes receivable, January 1	$ 75,000
Notes receivable, December 31	63,950
Cash purchases of merchandise	85,000
Depreciation expense	22,750
Wages payable, January 1	6,550
Wages payable, December 31	9,380
Credit purchases of merchandise	150,000
General, administrative, and selling expense	15,550
Amortization of goodwill	2,500
Sales of merchandise	275,000
Working capital provided by operations	65,560
Inventory, January 1	?
Inventory, December 31	?

Required

Determine the corporation's cost of goods sold for the year.

17A-4. Working Capital Basis of Statement of Changes in Financial Position. Following are comparative statements of financial position and statement of retained earnings for Chapman Corporation for the fiscal year ending June 30, 1986.

Chapman Corporation
Statements of Financial Position
As of June 30

	1986	1985
Assets		
Cash	$ 28,000	$ 22,400
Marketable securities	8,000	9,600
Accounts receivable	46,400	57,600
Inventories	56,000	40,000
Investment in subsidiary	36,000	32,000
Land	24,000	20,000
Building and equipment	180,000	152,000
Patents	5,600	6,400
	$384,000	$340,000
Liabilities and Shareholders' Equity		
Accounts payable	$ 36,000	$ 25,600
Taxes payable	6,400	4,800
Accumulated depreciation	32,000	24,000
Bonds payable	80,000	80,000
Common stock, $40 par	160,000	160,000
Retained earnings	69,600	45,600
	$384,000	$340,000

Chapman Corporation
Statement of Retained Earnings
Year Ending December 31, 1986

Balance, June 30, 1985	$45,600
Net income	40,000
	85,600
Dividends declared	16,000
Balance, June 30, 1986	$69,600

Additional information:

1. A piece of land was purchased for plant expansion.
2. Depreciation of $12,800 and amortization of a patent of $800 were charged to expense.
3. New equipment was purchased for $32,800. Fully depreciated equipment, which cost $4,800, was discarded.
4. Additional shares of stock of the subsidiary company were acquired for cash.

Required

Prepare a comparative schedule of working capital and a statement of changes in financial position.

17-A5. Cash Basis of Statement of Changes in Financial Position. Using the information from 17-A4, prepare a statement of changes in financial position for Chapman Corporation using the cash concept of funds.

17-A6. Working Capital and Cash Bases of Statement of Changes in Financial Position. The following statements of financial position and income statement provide financial information for London Company.

London Company
Statements of Financial Position
As of December 31

Assets	1986	1985
Cash	$ 145,500	$ 90,750
Marketable securities	121,875	—
Accounts receivable	150,750	178,750
Inventories	425,000	364,500
Prepaid expenses	6,625	5,250
Investments	—	227,500
Equipment	731,250	650,000
Accumulated depreciation—equipment	(275,750)	(203,500)
Buildings	775,000	475,000
Accumulated depreciation—buildings	(155,250)	(140,000)
Land	175,000	125,000
	$2,100,000	$1,773,250

Liabilities and Shareholders' Equity	1986	1985
Accounts payable	$ 112,250	$ 121,500
Income tax payable	35,000	20,000
Dividends payable	22,500	15,000
Mortgage note payable	225,000	—
Bonds payable	375,000	525,000
Common stock, $25 par	675,000	625,000
Premium on common stock	125,000	100,000
Retained earnings	530,250	366,750
	$2,100,000	$1,773,250

London Company
Income Statement
For Year Ending December 31, 1986

Sales		$2,875,000
Cost of goods sold		1,935,250
Gross profit on sales		$ 939,750
Operating expenses (including depreciation of $87,500)		520,000
Income from operations		$ 419,750
Other income		
Gain on sale of land	$37,500	
Gain on sale of investments	25,000	
Interest income	1,500	64,000
		$ 483,750
Interest expense		15,250
Income before income tax		$ 468,500
Income tax		217,500
Net income		$ 251,000

Additional information:

1. Equipment was purchased for $81,250.
2. Long-term investments were sold for $252,500.
3. Marketable securities were purchased for $121,875.
4. Land, which was carried on the books at $50,000, was sold for $87,500.
5. Building valued at $300,000 and land valued at $100,000 were purchased, using $175,000 in cash and a five-year mortgage for the balance.
6. Bonds payable of $150,000 were retired by payment of their face amount.
7. Cash dividends of $87,500 were declared.
8. 2,000 shares of common stock were issued for cash at 37½.

Required

a. Prepare a statement of changes in financial position using the working capital concept. Include a section for changes in components of working capital.
b. Prepare a statement of changes in financial position using the cash concept. Include a summary of the change in cash balance.

17-A7. Working Capital and Cash Flow. The following statements of financial position and income statement show the working capital, cash flow, and earnings information for Carder Company.

Carder Company
Statements of Financial Position
As of April 30

Assets	**1986**	**1985**
Current assets		
Cash	$ 61,000	$ 61,000
Marketable securities	12,000	20,000
Accounts receivable, net	98,000	60,000
Inventories	250,000	100,000
Prepaid expenses	10,000	15,000
Total current assets	$431,000	$256,000
Land	60,000	65,000
Buildings and equipment	330,000	250,000
Allowance for depreciation	(80,000)	(65,000)
Total assets	$741,000	$506,000

Liabilities and Shareholders' Equity		
Current liabilities		
Accounts payable	$100,000	$ 60,000
Bank loans	60,000	—
Accrued expenses payable	32,000	15,000
Federal income tax payable	70,000	75,000
Total current liabilities	262,000	150,000
Bonds payable (5%)	200,000	200,000
Premium on bonds payable	1,800	2,000
Capital stock—common $100 par	200,000	140,000
Capital in excess of par	10,000	—
Retained earnings	67,200	14,000
Total liabilities and shareholders' equity	$741,000	$506,000

Carder Company
Income Statement
For Year Ending April 30, 1986

Net sales		$800,000
Less: Cost of goods sold	$500,000	
Selling and administrative expenses	148,000	648,000
Net earnings from operations		152,000
Gain on sale of land		8,000
		$160,000
Loss on sale of marketable securities	1,000	
Interest expense	10,800	
Loss on sale of equipment	4,200	16,000
Net earnings before income taxes		$144,000
Federal income taxes		70,000
Net income		$ 74,000

Additional information:

1. Dividends of $20,800 were declared during the year.
2. Equipment sold during the year had an original cost of $20,000, and depreciation of $12,000 had been recorded to time of sale.
3. The capital stock was issued for a building valued at $70,000 erected on company property.
4. Premium on bonds payable of $200 was amortized during the year.

Required

a. Compute the change in working capital.
b. Prepare a statement of changes in financial position (emphasizing working capital).
c. Using the foregoing data and the following information, prepare a cash flow statement:

—Depreciation of $27,000 is included in selling and administrative expenses.
—Accounts payable arose solely from the purchase of merchandise.
—Prepaid expenses consist of prepaid store rent.
—All of the accrued expenses payable relate to selling and administrative expenses, except that the balance on April 30, 1986, includes $1,000 of accrued interest payable on bank loan.

PROBLEM SET B

17-B1. Working Capital Adjustments. Following is a description of transactions for Mayfair Manufacturing Company.

1. 4,000 shares of common stock issued at $30 a share.
2. $2,500 collected on account from a current customer.
3. A 20-year, $2 million bond issued.
4. $25,000 borrowed from the bank to be repaid in 60 days.
5. Cash dividends declared totaling $3 million.
6. $940 of uncollectible accounts written off against the allowance for doubtful accounts.
7. Net income reported of $42,000, including $2,300 of depreciation.
8. A $3 million building acquired through a donation.
9. $900,000 stock dividend issued.

Required

For each transaction, indicate the effect on working capital, using the appropriate code, and the amount.

NC = No change in working capital.
I = Increase in working capital from regular operations.
D = Decrease in working capital from regular operations.
SS = Separate source of working capital.
SU = Separate use of working capital.

17-B2. Working Capital Provided by Operations. The following information is from the books of James Company.

Accounts payable, January 1	$ 20,000
Accounts payable, December 31	17,500
Accounts receivable, January 1	37,500
Accounts receivable, December 31	20,000
Cash purchases of merchandise	80,000
Credit purchases of merchandise	50,000
Depreciation expense	6,000
General, administrative, and selling expenses (excluding depreciation)	4,000
Inventory, January 1	5,500
Inventory, December 31	60,000
Prepaid expenses, January 1	2,000
Prepaid expenses, December 31	3,000
Sales of merchandise	125,000

Required

Determine the working capital provided by operations.

17-B3. Working Capital Applied to Operations. Selected data from the records of Cation Chemicals, Incorporated, are as follows:

Inventory, January 1	$ 75,450
Inventory, December 31	25,000
Wages payable, January 1	18,750
Wages payable, December 31	9,490
Notes receivable, January 1	16,500
Notes receivable, December 31	19,750
Amortization of copyright costs	2,600
Sales of merchandise	175,000
General, administrative, and selling expenses	5,250
Working capital applied to operations	15,750

Required

Calculate Cation's merchandise purchases for the year.

17-B4. Working Capital Basis of Statement of Changes in Financial Position. Comparative statements of financial position for Craig Corporation are as follows.

Craig Corporation
Statements of Financial Position
As of December 31

	1986	1985
Cash	$152,000	$ 75,000
Accounts receivable	138,000	102,000
Inventories	186,000	112,000
Investments	—	120,000
Equipment	420,000	234,000
Accumulated depreciation	(116,000)	(80,000)
Land	110,000	64,000
	$890,000	$627,000
Accounts payable	$124,000	$110,000
Dividends payable	24,000	13,000
Common stock, $50 par	400,000	300,000
Premium on common stock	30,000	—
Retained earnings	312,000	204,000
	$890,000	$627,000

Additional information:

1. Equipment and land were purchased for cash.
2. Investments were sold for $158,000.
3. There were no dispositions of equipment during 1986.
4. Common stock was issued for cash.
5. Net income was $148,000.
6. Cash dividend of $5 per share was declared.

Required

Prepare a statement of changes in financial position using the working capital concept.

17-B5. Cash Basis of Statement of Changes in Financial Position. Using the information in 17-B4, prepare a statement of changes in financial position for Craig Corporation using the cash concept of funds.

17-B6. Working Capital and Cash Bases of Statement of Changes in Financial Position. Comparative statements of financial position for Richardson Corporation for 1985 and 1986 and selected general ledger accounts are as follows.

Richardson Corporation
Statement of Financial Position
As of December 31

Assets	1986	1985
Cash	$ 242,250	$ 268,200
Accounts receivable	283,200	234,600
Inventories	886,800	748,050
Prepaid expenses	18,360	18,720
Investments	—	150,000
Equipment	1,375,500	1,261,500
Accumulated depreciation—equipment	(273,000)	(234,000)
Buildings	1,173,000	573,000
Accumulated depreciation—buildings	(154,260)	(130,800)
Land	120,000	120,000
	$3,671,850	$3,009,270

Liabilities and Shareholders' Equity

	1986	1985
Accounts payable	$ 69,330	$ 247,890
Income tax payable	53,400	43,500
Notes payable	630,000	—
Discount on long-term notes payable	(27,750)	—
Common stock, $75 par	2,340,000	2,250,000
Premium on common stock	240,000	180,000
Appropriation for contingencies	120,000	60,000
Retained earnings	246,870	227,880
	$3,671,850	$3,009,270

Investments

Date	Item	Dr	Cr	Balance Dr	Balance Cr
1986					
Jan. 1	Balance			150,000	
Dec. 17	$150,000 cash realized from sale		150,000		

Equipment

Date	Item	Dr	Cr	Balance Dr	Balance Cr
1986					
Jan. 1	Balance			1,261,500	
Apr. 19	Discarded, no salvage		90,000		
June 7	Purchased for cash	120,000			
Sep. 22	Purchased for cash	84,000		1,375,500	

Accumulated Depreciation—Equipment

Date	Item	Dr	Cr	Balance Dr	Balance Cr
1986					
Jan. 1	Balance				234,000
Jan. 24	Equipment discarded	90,000			
Dec. 31	Depreciation for year		129,000		273,000

Buildings					
Date	Item	Dr	Cr	Balance Dr	Balance Cr
1986					
Jan. 1	Balance			573,000	
Sep. 1	Purchase for long-term note payable	600,000		1,173,000	

Accumulated Depreciation—Buildings					
Date	Item	Dr	Cr	Balance Dr	Balance Cr
1986					
Jan. 1	Balance				130,800
Dec. 31	Depreciation for year		23,460		154,260

Land					
Date	Item	Dr	Cr	Balance Dr	Balance Cr
1986					
Jan. 1	Balance			120,000	

Long-Term Notes Payable					
Date	Item	Dr	Cr	Balance Dr	Balance Cr
1986					
Sep. 1	5-year notes issued		630,000		630,000

Discount on Long-Term Notes Payable					
Date	Item	Dr	Cr	Balance Dr	Balance Cr
1986					
Sep. 1	Notes issued	30,000		30,000	
Dec. 31	Amortization		2,250	27,750	

Common Stock, $25 Par					
				Balance	
Date	Item	Dr	Cr	Dr	Cr
1986					
Jan. 1	Balance				2,250,000
Dec. 10	Stock dividend		90,000		2,340,000

Paid-in Capital in Excess of Par on Common Stock					
				Balance	
Date	Item	Dr	Cr	Dr	Cr
1986					
Jan. 1	Balance				180,000
Dec. 10	Stock dividend		60,000		240,000

Appropriation for Contingencies					
				Balance	
Date	Item	Dr	Cr	Dr	Cr
1986					
Jan. 1	Balance				60,000
Dec. 31	Appropriation		60,000		120,000

Retained Earnings					
				Balance	
Date	Item	Dr	Cr	Dr	Cr
1986					
Jan. 1	Balance				227,880
Dec. 10	Stock dividend	150,000			
31	Net income		408,990		
31	Cash dividends	180,000			
31	Appropriation	60,000			246,870

Required

a. Prepare a statement of changes in financial position using the working capital concept. Include a section for changes in components of working capital.
b. Prepare a statement of changes in financial position using the cash concept. Include a summary of the change in cash balance.

17-B7. Working Capital and Cash Flow. The following are the comparative statements of financial position for Healy Company.

Healy Company
Statement of Financial Position
As of December 31

Assets	**1986**	**1985**
Cash	$ 51,000	$ 50,000
Receivables	60,000	68,000
Inventory	110,000	112,000
Prepaid expenses	9,000	8,000
Plant assets	312,000	217,000
Accumulated depreciation	(86,000)	(63,000)
Patents	35,000	41,000
	$494,000	$433,000

Liabilities and Shareholders' Equity		
Accounts payable	$ 75,000	$ 83,000
Taxes payable	70,000	65,000
Mortgage payable	—	100,000
Preferred stock	150,000	—
Additional paid-in capital—preferred	4,000	—
Common stock	150,000	150,000
Retained earnings	45,000	35,000
	$494,000	$433,000

Additional information:

1. The only entries in the Retained Earnings account are for dividends paid in the amount of $18,000 and for the net income for the year.
2. The income statement for 1986 is as follows.

Sales	$130,000
Cost of sales	94,000
Gross profit	36,000
Operating expenses	8,000
	$28,000

3. The only entry in the Accumulated Depreciation account is the depreciation expense for the period.

Required

a. Prepare a statement of changes in financial position using the working capital approach.
b. Prepare a statement of changes in financial position using the cash approach.

ANALYSIS AND INTERPRETATION OF FINANCIAL STATEMENTS

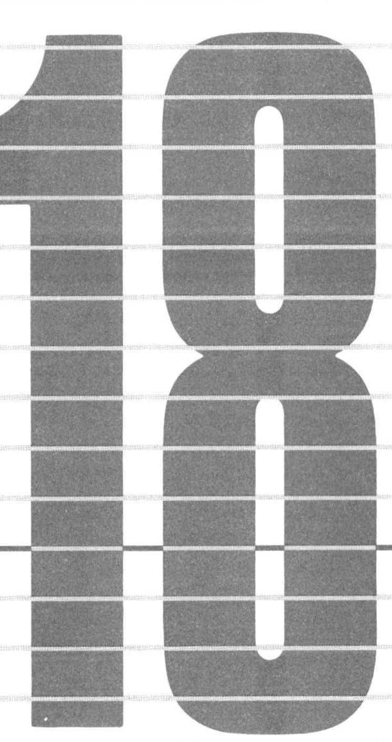

CHAPTER OBJECTIVES
After studying Chapter 18, you should understand the following:

1. The concepts and tools of financial statement analysis that are used to support the financial decision-making process.
2. Comparative statement analysis, including dollar and percentage changes, trend percentages, and common-size statements.
3. Ratio analysis, including the calculation and interpretation of liquidity, activity, leverage, profitability, and market ratios.
4. The limitations of financial analysis.
5. How to organize and conduct a financial analysis and properly interpret the results.

To this point, we have described in much detail the concepts and practices underlying financial accounting and the preparation of financial statements. Although to many people financial statements appear to be dry collections of numbers, they really are quite revealing. The challenge is knowing how to evaluate them. With that in mind, we attempt in this chapter to describe various approaches to analyzing and interpreting financial statements.

ANALYTICAL FRAMEWORK

INTRACOMPANY ANALYSIS
Evaluation of a company's financial performance against its own past performance or stated objectives.

INTERCOMPANY ANALYSIS
Comparison of a company's performance against similar companies or industry averages.

There are many different ways to organize a financial analysis. This chapter demonstrates specific techniques in the context of either an intracompany analysis or intercompany analysis. An **intracompany analysis** involves evaluating a company's financial performance against its own past performance or its own stated objectives. An **intercompany analysis** involves comparing a company's performance against similar companies or industry averages. The differences between these two approaches can be illustrated through a simple example.

Assume you invested in a company in 1982 with a growth rate in earnings as shown in Row A of the following table:

Percentage Increase in Net Income Over Prior Years

	1982	1983	1984	1985	1986
A. Your company	6	6	7	10	12
B. Competitor	15	15	9	9	8

The company's stated objective was to achieve a 15 percent increase per year. In contrast, this company's chief competitor has an earnings growth rate as shown in Row B. What can you conclude from this information? First of all, if you were doing an intracompany analysis, you would ignore the competitor's information and focus on how your company was doing. From the information provided, you would observe that the earnings growth pattern has consistently improved but remains below the company's stated objective. You would then try to find out why this is occurring and examine the company's future prospects. If you decided to conduct an intercompany analysis, the competitor's data would become important. Even though your competitor has a higher five-year average growth trend in earnings, its performance has deteriorated in the past four years, while your situation has improved. Assuming the trends continue with both companies, it appears your company's performance is superior.

In reality, most financial analysts use both approaches to study a company's financial performance, because each approach provides valuable insights into how a company is progressing and how it stacks up against its competitors. Of course, each approach has pros and cons, and one approach might be more appropriate than the other in certain circumstances. For example, for intercompany analysis to be effective, a company must be compared with some other similar company or companies. To the extent that the other companies are not similar, the comparisons might not be valid. Thus, intercompany analysis must be done cautiously to ensure that apples are not being compared with oranges. In some situations, even an intracompany analysis using historical information can be inappropriate. This is particularly true if there have been significant changes in the company's products, structure, or management, or in external factors affecting the operations of the company, such as price and wage controls, significant increases in inflation, or shortages of raw materials. We will present problems associated with these analyses later in the chapter when we discuss their limitations. For now, let's turn to the specific techniques of financial analysis.

COMPARATIVE FINANCIAL STATEMENTS

Comparative financial statements present a company's statements for two or more accounting periods so that dollar and percentage changes can be analyzed. We determine the percentage change for each number by dividing the dollar increase or decrease by the earlier year's data. To illustrate, assume a company had $100,000 invested in inventory in 1985 and $110,000 in 1986. The comparative statement of financial position would indicate that inventory increased $10,000 between 1985 and 1986, representing a 10 percent ($10,000/$100,000) increase.

COMPARATIVE FINANCIAL STATEMENTS
A company's statements presented for two or more accounting periods so that dollar and percentage changes can be analyzed.

Comparative financial statements can be analyzed in several ways, including analyses of dollar and percentage changes, trend percentages, and common-size statements. Each method is described in the following sections in conjunction with the IBM financial statements in Exhibits 18.1 and 18.2

Dollar and Percentage Changes

The two middle columns of Exhibits 18.1 and 18.2 contain the dollar and percentage changes in statement items between 1983 and 1984. An analyst first looks at the percentage changes in aggregate statement numbers, such as total assets, current assets, fixed assets, current liabilities, total revenue, and net earnings. In addition, particular attention is focused on the larger percentage changes, with an effort made to determine why they occurred, and the internal consistency of certain changes. Note, for example, that IBM's total assets increased by approximately $5.3 billion, or 14.3 percent, in 1984. Most of the expansion occurred in inventories ($2.2 billion, or 50.6 percent).

The analyst might also check to see what impact the increase in assets had on revenue, because the firm's assets are used to produce products that generate revenue. In IBM's case, total revenue increased in 1984 by approximately $5.8 billion, or 14.3 percent, which equaled the increase in assets. This indicates that the company's assets were utilized very productively; the company is realizing the benefits of its expanded assets base. Another interesting comparison on the statement of financial position involves the difference between current assets and current liabilities. Normally, we might expect these two items to be fairly consistent, as current assets are the sources used to liquidate current liabilities. In IBM's situation, the increase in current assets ($3,045 million, or 17.6 percent) exceeded the increase in current liabilities ($478 million, or 5.2 percent).

In IBM's statement of earnings, we see that net earnings increased by $1,097 million (20.0 percent). The dollar and percentage increase in the company's revenues ($5.8 billion, or 14.3 percent) was greater than increases in operating expenses, leading to an overall increase in operating income of $1,624 million, or 17.7 percent. Sometimes, a penalty for increased earnings is increased income taxes. However,

EXHIBIT 18.1

International Business Machines Corporation
Comparative Statement of Financial Position
(millions of dollars)

	1984	1983	Increase or (Decrease) 1984 Over 1983 Dollars	Percentage	Percentage of Total Assets 1984	1983
Assets						
Current assets						
Cash	$ 600	$ 616	(16)	−2.6%	1.4%	1.6%
Marketable securities, at cost	3,762	4,920	(1,158)	−23.5%	8.8%	13.1%
Notes and accounts receivable—trade	7,393	5,577	1,816	32.6%	17.3%	14.9%
Other accounts receivable	718	645	73	11.3%	1.7%	1.7%
Inventories	6,598	4,381	2,217	50.6%	15.4%	11.7%
Prepaid expenses	1,304	1,191	113	9.5%	3.0%	3.2%
Total current assets	20,375	17,330	3,045	17.6%	47.6%	46.3%
Plant, rental machines, and other property	29,423	29,187	236	0.8%	68.7%	77.9%
Less: Accumulated depreciation	13,060	13,045	15	0.1%	30.5%	34.8%
Total fixed assets	16,363	16,142	221	1.4%	38.2%	43.1%
Investments and other assets	6,070	3,989	2,081	52.2%	14.2%	10.6%
Total assets	$42,808	$37,461	5,347	14.3%	100.0%	100.0%
Liabilities and Shareholders' Equity						
Current liabilities						
Taxes	2,668	3,220	(552)	−17.1%	6.2%	8.6%
Loans payable	834	532	302	56.8%	1.9%	1.4%
Accounts payable	1,618	1,253	365	29.1%	3.8%	3.3%
Compensation and benefits	2,223	2,105	118	5.6%	5.2%	5.6%
Deferred income	340	382	(42)	−11.0%	0.8%	1.0%
Other accrued expenses and liabilities	1,957	1,670	287	17.2%	4.6%	4.5%
Total current liabilities	9,640	9,162	478	5.2%	22.5%	24.5%
Long-term debt	3,269	2,674	595	22.3%	7.6%	7.1%
Other liabilities	1,353	1,475	(122)	−8.3%	3.2%	3.9%
Deferred income taxes	2,057	931	1,126	120.9%	4.8%	2.5%
Shareholders' equity						
Capital stock, par value $1.25	5,998	5,800	198	3.4%	14.0%	15.5%
Retained earnings	23,486	19,489	3,997	20.5%	54.9%	52.0%
Translation adjustments	(2,948)	(2,070)	(878)	42.4%	−6.9%	−5.5%
Less: Treasury stock, at cost	47	0	47		0.1%	0.0%
Total shareholders' equity	26,489	23,219	3,270	14.1%	61.9%	62.0%
Total liabilities and shareholders' equity	$42,808	$37,461	5,347	14.3%	100.0%	100.0%

EXHIBIT 18.2

International Business Machines Corporation
Comparative Statement of Earnings
(millions of dollars, except per share figures)

	Year Ending December 31		Increase or (Decrease) 1984 over 1983		Percentage of Total Revenue	
	1984	**1983**	**Dollars**	**Percentage**	**1984**	**1983**
Sales	$29,753	$23,274	6,479	27.8%	64.8%	57.9%
Rentals	9,605	7,676	1,929	25.1%	20.9%	19.1%
Services	6,579	9,230	(2,651)	−28.7%	14.3%	23.0%
Total revenue	45,937	40,180	5,757	14.3%	100.0%	100.0%
Cost of sales	12,374	9,748	2,626	26.9%	26.9%	24.3%
Cost of rentals	4,347	3,506	841	24.0%	9.5%	8.7%
Cost of services	2,198	3,141	(943)	−30.0%	4.8%	7.8%
Selling, general, and administrative expense	11,587	10,614	973	9.2%	25.2%	26.4%
Research, development, and engineering expense	4,200	3,582	618	17.3%	9.1%	8.9%
Interest expense	408	390	18	4.6%	0.9%	1.0%
Total operating expenses	35,114	30,981	4,133	13.3%	76.4%	77.1%
Total operating income	10,823	9,199	1,624	17.7%	23.6%	22.9%
Other income	800	741	59	8.0%	1.7%	1.8%
Earnings before income taxes	11,623	9,940	1,683	16.9%	25.3%	24.7%
Provision for income taxes	5,041	4,455	586	13.2%	11.0%	11.1%
Net earnings	$ 6,582	$ 5,485	1,097	20.0%	14.3%	13.7%
Earnings per share	$ 10.77	$ 9.04				
Dividends per share	$ 4.10	$ 3.71				
Average no. of shares outstanding	611,426,324	606,769,848				

IBM's increase in net earnings (20.0 percent) was larger than the increase in operating income (17.7 percent) because of an increase in other income (8.0 percent). The increase in the cost of sales accounted for the largest percentage increase in operating expenses (26.9 percent), as well as the largest dollar change ($2.6 billion). From this limited intracompany analysis of dollar and percentage changes between years, an analyst might conclude that the company's financial position improved significantly between 1983 and 1984.

Trend Percentage Analysis

The next logical refinement of our analysis is to explore some of the changes in these numbers over a longer time period than two years. This type of analysis, referred to as trend percentage analysis, provides additional insights into the significance of dollar and percentage changes.

TREND PERCENTAGES
Dollar figures stated as a percentage of some base-year figure.

Trend percentages are useful in analyzing the changes in financial statement figures over a number of years. For most companies, multiyear data to use in such an analysis are readily available in the annual report. **Trend percentages** are simply dollar figures stated as a percentage of some base-year figure. In essence, these percentages are a form of indexing (that is, of expressing numbers as a percentage of a base-year number), as the federal government does when it calculates inflation indicators such as the Consumer Price Index (CPI) and Gross National Product deflator.

Exhibit 18.3 demonstrates the process of how trend percentages are calculated for IBM. The first line of Part I of the exhibit presents four years of dollar sales figures. The next line shows the numbers converted into trend percentages, with 1981 used as the base year. The base-year percentage is 100 percent; any subsequent year's sales trend percentage is determined by dividing that year's dollar sales figure by the base-year figure. Thus, for 1982, the trend percentage is calculated as follows:

$$\frac{\text{1982 sales of \$34.4 billion}}{\text{1981 sales of \$29.1 billion}} = 118\%$$

This percentage indicates that sales in 1982 were 18 percent higher than in 1981; 138 percent for 1983 indicates that sales that year were 38 percent higher than in 1981. Finally, sales over the four-year period increased by an average of 14.5 percent per year (58 percent/4 years = 14.5 percent per year).

Part II of Exhibit 18.3 shows the trend percentages for all income statement items and a few selected figures from the statement of financial position. An analysis of these data shows some interesting aspects of IBM's past financial performance. During the years 1981 to 1984, sales increased at an average annual rate of 14.5 percent, while net earnings grew at a rate of 20.5 percent (82 percent/4 years = 20.5 percent per year). Thus, sales growth exceeded the increase in operating expenses, net investment in fixed assets, and long-term debt and resulted in earnings growing more rapidly than sales. This indicates that the company was able to effectively control operating expenses during the period.

As might be expected, the growth rate in earnings per share (e.p.s.) paralleled the growth in net earnings; however, it is interesting to note that dividends per share did not grow as much. Firms often keep their dividends constant to maintain investors' confidence in the stability of the company.

Finally, note that there has actually been a slight decline in IBM's net investment (original cost less accumulated depreciation) in plant, rental machines, and other property. At the same time, working capital (current assets less current liabilities) has shown a very dramatic increase. There has also been a substantial increase in shareholders' equity during this period, which reflects the excellent earnings record of the company as well as the changes in the asset accounts on the statement of financial position.

Trend percentages, as well as dollar and percentage changes between years, must be interpreted with caution. They are helpful in identifying significant changes and their direction, but it is important to remember that they are founded on some base-year figure. Therefore, the magnitude of the percentages can be misleading unless the nature of the item and the amount of the dollar change are also considered. For example, assume a company with assets of $5 million has $100 invested in marketable securities. The next year, the company has $120 invested, representing a 20 percent increase. An analyst seeing only the 20 percent increase might be misled unless he or she also noted that this increase amounted to only $20—hardly sig-

EXHIBIT 18.3
Selected Trend Percentages for IBM Corporation

Part I	**1984**	**1983**	**1982**	**1981**
Total revenues (in billions of $)	45.9	40.2	34.4	29.1
Total revenues trend percentage (1981 revenues = 100%)	158	138	118	100
Part II				
A. Statement of earnings trends				
Gross income from				
Sales	231	180	130	100
Rentals	61	85	103	100
Service	180	144	121	100
Cost of sales	240	189	129	100
Cost of rentals	54	78	98	100
Cost of service	172	138	120	100
Selling, general, and administrative	138	127	111	100
Research, development, and engineering	171	146	124	100
Interest expense	100	96	112	100
Other income	217	201	89	100
Earnings before taxes	180	154	127	100
Income taxes	177	156	134	100
Net earnings	182	152	122	100
Earnings per share	175	147	120	100
Dividends per share	119	108	100	100
B. Statement of financial position trends				
Net investment in plant, rental machines, and other property	97	96	105	100
Long-term debt	122	100	107	100
Working capital	336	256	159	100
Total assets	147	129	112	100
Shareholders' equity	150	131	113	100

nificant in light of the company's $5 million investment in assets. To minimize the problems associated with interpreting trend percentages and other financial statement percentages, analysts often supplement these percentages with common-size statements.

Common-Size Statements

In **common-size statements,** each item is expressed as a percentage of some aggregate number in the statement. For example, in constructing a common-size statement of financial position, the firm expresses every item on the statement—cash, inventory, long-term debt, and so on—as a percentage of total assets. Thus, if a company has $5 million invested in inventory and its total assets are $100 million, inventory represents five percent of total assets and is expressed as five percent on the statement. Similarly, income statement items are typically stated as a percentage of total revenue.

COMMON-SIZE STATEMENTS
Statements in which each item is expressed as a percentage of some aggregate number in the statement.

The last two columns of Exhibits 18.1 and 18.2 are, in essence, common-size statements for IBM Corporation for 1983 and 1984. In the common-size statements of financial position in Exhibit 18.1, we see that IBM's current assets represented 47.6 percent of its total assets in 1984, an increase over the 46.3 percent in 1983. This percentage increase in current assets was offset by a reduced investment in fixed assets. In 1984, IBM's fixed assets accounted for 38.2 percent of its total assets, compared with 43.1 percent in 1983. On the liability and equity side, we note an increase in long-term debt as a percentage of total assets (7.6 percent in 1984 compared with 7.1 percent the year before) and a decrease in shareholders' equity (from 62.0 percent of total assets in 1983 to 61.9 percent in 1984). With this strong equity position, the majority of the firm's assets can be financed with owners' equity.

A common-size income statement is equally helpful. For example, in Exhibit 18.2, it is interesting to note that IBM's sales mix (equipment sales versus rental and service sales) changed from 1983 to 1984, with equipment sales gaining in importance and service sales declining significantly. However, operating expenses as a percentage of total revenue decreased from 77.1 percent in 1983 to 76.4 percent in 1984. The majority of this decrease involved cost of services, which reflects the decline in service sales previously pointed out. It is also interesting that even though interest expense increased by 4.6 percent in 1984, this expense as a percentage of total revenue was relatively small (0.9 percent in 1984 and 1.0 percent in 1983) and did not have a significant impact on earnings before income taxes. Finally, as expected, net earnings as a percentage of total revenue increased from 13.7 percent in 1983 to 14.3 percent in 1984. An analysis of the common-size income statement helps identify the items that contributed to this increase.

RATIO ANALYSIS

RATIO ANALYSIS
An approach to financial statement analysis that examines key relationships by means of ratio comparisons.

In the comparative financial statement analysis previously described, the feature of greatest value to the analyst is the identification and discussion of logical relationships between certain items in the statement, for example, the previously cited relationship between changes in assets and changes in revenue. **Ratio analysis** is another approach used by analysts to examine such relationships. There are a number of ways to organize a ratio analysis study; most analysts, however, classify ratios into five interrelated categories: liquidity ratios, turnover, or activity, ratios (sometimes referred to as efficiency ratios), leverage ratios, profitability ratios, and market ratios.

Liquidity Ratios

LIQUIDITY RATIOS
Ratios that provide insight into a firm's short-run solvency.

LIQUIDITY
A term that refers to how readily convertible a company's assets are to cash—the more convertible the assets, the more liquid they are.

Liquidity ratios provide insight into a firm's short-run solvency. **Liquidity** refers to how readily convertible a company's assets are to cash—the more convertible the assets, the more liquid they are. In essence, liquidity ratios measure the company's ability to meet its current liabilities. Short-term creditors—bankers, vendors, employees—are particularly interested in a company's short-term solvency, because they expect to receive payment from the conversion of current assets into cash.

The ratios most commonly used to measure liquidity are the current ratio and the acid-test (or quick) ratio. The current ratio is computed as follows:

CURRENT RATIO
Current assets divided by current liabilities.

$$\textbf{Current ratio} = \frac{\text{Current assets}}{\text{Current liabilities}}$$

$$\text{IBM's 1984 current ratio} = \frac{\$20{,}375}{\$9{,}640} = 2.11$$

The ratio is usually stated in dollars and indicates how many dollars of current assets the company has for each dollar of current liabilities. For example, as previously shown, IBM had a current ratio of 2.11 to 1 in 1984. That means it had $2.11 invested in current assets for every dollar in current liabilities. (Instead of saying the ratio is 2.11 to 1, we can simply say it is 2.11.)

In essence, the current ratio is another way to evaluate the company's working capital management. Working capital is determined by subtracting current liabilities from current assets. A positive difference indicates that the company has more current assets than current liabilities; it does not, however, indicate the relative margin of difference. The current ratio corrects this deficiency by providing the margin of safety on a relative basis (that is, a percentage basis) rather than on a dollar basis.

The closer a company's current ratio is to 1, the more likely the company will have difficulty in meeting its short-term obligations. In general, a current ratio of at least 2 to 1 is considered desirable. However, the acceptability of a particular current ratio depends on the trend in the ratio over time and how it compares with those of similar companies. It is also important to note that too high a current ratio can be undesirable; it can indicate that the company has too much money invested in current assets, which are normally nonincome-producing, rather than in fixed assets, which do produce income.

As you know from previous chapters, current assets normally consist of cash, receivables, marketable securities, inventory, and prepaid expenses. Of these five items, inventory and prepayments are considered least liquid. Given this fact, analysts often calculate an additional liquidity ratio (the acid-test ratio) to refine the current ratio by leaving out these less liquid items. This ratio is calculated as follows:

$$\textbf{Acid-test ratio} = \frac{\text{Cash + Receivables + Marketable securities}}{\text{Current liabilities}}$$

$$\text{IBM's 1984 acid-test ratio} = \frac{\$600 + 8{,}111 + 3{,}762}{\$9{,}640} = 1.29$$

ACID-TEST RATIO
(Cash plus receivables plus marketable securities) divided by current liabilities.

From a creditor's perspective, the acid-test ratio provides a more meaningful evaluation of the company's liquidity and ability to meet payments when due. IBM's 1984 acid-test ratio of 1.29 would normally be considered excellent, because it exceeds 1 and indicates that the company had more than enough cash and cash equivalents to meet its short-term obligations.

Turnover, or Activity, Ratios

Turnover or activity ratios indicate how efficiently management utilizes its assets. The acquisition and use of assets are costly. Unless the assets generate sufficient sales, overall profitability will suffer. Four commonly used activity ratios are total asset turnover, fixed asset turnover, accounts receivable turnover, and inventory turnover.

TURNOVER RATIOS
Ratios that indicate how efficiently management utilizes its assets.

ACTIVITY RATIOS
See Turnover Ratios.

The total asset turnover ratio is obtained as follows:

$$\textbf{Total asset turnover}\text{ (TAT)} = \frac{\text{Total sales}}{\text{Average total assets}}$$

$$\text{IBM's 1984 total asset turnover} = \frac{\$45{,}937}{\$40{,}134} = 1.145$$

TOTAL ASSET TURNOVER
Total sales divided by average total assets.

This ratio measures the amount of sales dollars earned for each dollar invested in assets. Ideally, a 12-month average of assets should be used, but in reality the average is typically calculated by summing the beginning-of-year and end-of-year balances

HIGHLIGHT

Ratios as Predictive Indicators

Many people believe that the primary use of financial ratio analysis is for dissecting a company's financial performance after the fact. Although this is basically correct, it is also quite possible to use the findings of such an analysis to predict future performance.

In recent years, a number of accounting studies have examined the potential uses of ratios. Most of them have focused on historical ratios' predictive value. In particular, researchers have examined the usefulness of ratios in predicting such things as bankruptcy, the likelihood that a loan applicant will receive a loan, the likelihood that a loan recipient will successfully liquidate his or her debt, bond ratings, future financial performance, and stock prices.

The bankruptcy of the W. T. Grant Company is certainly a case in point. Until formal bankruptcy proceedings began in October 1975, W. T. Grant was the nation's largest retailer, its stock selling for nearly 20 times earnings. The stock market was obviously shocked by the bankruptcy, but the firm's demise should not have come as a surprise to anyone who had carefully analyzed the firm's financial performance. A look at the downturn in W. T. Grant's liquidity, activity, leverage, and profitability ratios could have signaled the firm's problems as early as 1970, and a look at the firm's net cash flows *used* in operations could have foretold of impending doom as early as 1966.

Clearly for W. T. Grant Company, the ratios had predictive value. As a result of this and other such cases, ratio analysis has become an analytical tool widely applied by both internal and external users of financial statements.

and dividing by 2. Unless otherwise specified, all average figures subsequently used in this chapter will have been calculated this way.

IBM realized $1.14 of sales for every dollar invested in assets in 1984. Obviously, a company would like to have this number as high as possible, because that would indicate high asset productivity. Of course, too high a number could indicate that the company is merely milking old assets that will need to be replaced in the short term. Some analysts modify the total asset turnover calculation by including only operating assets (that is, assets really in use) in the denominator of the ratio. That way they get a truer picture of the productivity of the assets in use. As we will see later, a very important relationship exists between a firm's total asset turnover and its profitability as measured by a company's return on investment (ROI).

Once the total asset turnover ratio has been calculated, the analyst commonly calculates the turnover for the major components of total assets, that is, fixed assets, accounts receivable, and inventory. Because fixed assets are considered a company's most significant income-producing assets, the fixed asset turnover ratio is particularly important.

FIXED ASSET TURNOVER
Total sales divided by average fixed assets.

$$\textbf{Fixed asset turnover} \text{ (FAT)} = \frac{\text{Total sales}}{\text{Average fixed assets}}$$

$$\text{IBM's 1984 fixed asset turnover} = \frac{\$45{,}937}{\$16{,}252} = 2.83$$

A relatively low ratio would likely indicate that the company's largest asset group (in terms of dollars invested) was inefficiently used.

In calculating IBM's fixed asset turnover we used the book value of the assets in the denominator. All other things being equal, when book value is used, the fixed asset turnover ratio will improve each year simply because the book value of the assets will decline as a result of depreciation writeoffs. In contrast, if the gross value of these assets is used, the ratio decline will not occur. This problem is discussed in more detail in Chapter 22.

Accounts receivable turnover indicates how many times a year a company collects its receivables.

$$\textbf{Accounts receivable turnover} = \frac{\text{Credit sales}}{\text{Average net accounts receivable}}$$

$$\text{IBM's 1984 accounts receivable turnover} = \frac{\$45{,}937}{\$7{,}166} = 6.41$$

ACCOUNTS RECEIVABLE TURNOVER
Credit sales divided by average net accounts receivable.

Typically, no information on credit sales is available in a company's financial statements, in which case, total sales are used instead. This modification will not cause any real problem as long as the proportion of cash sales to total sales is relatively small.

Once calculated, the accounts receivable turnover ratio can be used to determine the average number of days required to collect a receivable, commonly referred to as the collection period.

$$\textbf{Collection period} = \frac{365}{\text{Accounts receivable turnover}}$$

$$\text{IBM's 1984 collection period} = \frac{365}{6.41} = 57 \text{ days}$$

COLLECTION PERIOD
365 divided by accounts receivable turnover.

At IBM, an account receivable remained outstanding for an average of 57 days in 1984. The acceptability of this number depends on the company's policy. If IBM's stated policy was n/30, the 1984 situation would not look favorable. If, however, the policy allowed 120 days, the 1984 figure would be most acceptable.

The final activity ratio of interest to an analyst is inventory turnover—the number of times a year a company sells its inventory.

$$\textbf{Inventory turnover} = \frac{\text{Cost of goods sold}}{\text{Average inventory}}$$

$$\text{IBM's 1984 inventory turnover} = \frac{\$12{,}374 + 4{,}347 + 2{,}198}{\$5{,}490} = 3.45$$

INVENTORY TURNOVER
Cost of goods sold divided by average inventory.

IBM turned over its inventory approximately 3.45 times a year, or every 106 days (365/3.45) in 1984. Obviously, a firm could maximize its inventory turnover and minimize inventory costs by keeping inventory amounts small. However, this policy could lead to lost sales and a decline in customer goodwill. As a result, management attempts to maximize inventory turnover while ensuring that enough is available to meet customer needs.

Inventory turnover is another ratio that must be calculated and interpreted with caution. How the inventory is valued (FIFO, LIFO) and what specific items inventory comprises (raw materials, work in process, finished goods) can distort the ratio and result in misleading conclusions.

Leverage Ratios

LEVERAGE
A term that refers to the amount of debt a company uses in its capital structure.

Leverage refers to the amount of debt a company uses in its capital structure. The more the debt, the more highly leveraged the company. The use of leverage has advantages and disadvantages. Its chief advantage is that by using someone else's

■ CONCEPT SUMMARY 18.1 LIQUIDITY AND TURNOVER RATIOS

RATIO	INTERPRETATION	FORMULA
Liquidity Ratios	Provide insight into a firm's short-run solvency.	
Current	Evaluates working capital management. Measures relative margin of safety of the excess of current assets over current liabilities.	$\frac{\text{Current assets}}{\text{Current liabilities}}$
Acid-test	Evaluates ability to meet payments when due. Measures the margin of safety of liquid assets (cash and cash equivalents) over current liabilities.	$\frac{\text{Cash + Receivables + Marketable securities}}{\text{Current liabilities}}$
Turnover Ratios	Indicate how effectively management utilizes the resources at its disposal.	
Total asset turnover	Indicates asset productivity. Measures the amount of sales dollars earned for each dollar invested in assets.	$\frac{\text{Total sales}}{\text{Average total assets}}$
Fixed asset turnover	Indicates efficiency of use of the largest, most significant income-producing group of assets.	$\frac{\text{Total sales}}{\text{Average fixed assets}}$
Accounts receivable turnover	Indicates how many times a year the company collects its receivables.	$\frac{\text{Credit sales}}{\text{Average net accounts receivable}}$
Collection period	Measures the average number of days required to collect a receivable.	$\frac{365}{\text{Accounts receivable turnover}}$
Inventory turnover	Measures the number of times a year a company sells its inventory.	$\frac{\text{Cost of goods sold}}{\text{Average inventory}}$

money, owners can maximize their returns. This phenomenon, commonly referred to as trading on the equity, and its impact on owner return are illustrated later. The primary disadvantage of leverage is that it increases the riskiness of a firm. Increased leverage brings with it increased interest payments (a fixed expense) and the possibility that the company will not have the cash available to meet either this expense or future principal payments. As long as a company earns more on its investments than it has to pay in interest, no problems occur. If this is not the case, however, the company can find itself defaulting on its debts and going into bankruptcy.

LEVERAGE RATIOS
Ratios that measure the extent to which a company uses debt and the impact of leverage on the company's ability to meet its interest payments.

Leverage ratios measure the extent to which a company uses debt and the impact of leverage on the company's ability to meet its interest payments. The most basic measure of leverage is the debt ratio.

$$\textbf{Debt ratio} = \frac{\text{Total debt}}{\text{Total assets}}$$

DEBT RATIO
Total debt divided by total assets.

$$\text{IBM's 1984 debt ratio} = \frac{\$16,319}{\$42,808} = 38.1\%$$

$$\text{IBM's 1983 debt ratio} = \frac{\$14,242}{\$37,461} = 38.0\%$$

The resulting number represents the percentage of assets financed by debt. In 1984, IBM financed 38.1 percent of its total assets with debt and the rest—61.9 percent—with equity. This 61.9 percent represents the company's equity ratio. The **equity ratio** is equal to 1.00 minus the debt ratio, or total equity divided by total assets. IBM's 1983 debt ratio is included to show that the company's position did not change in 1984. As pointed out earlier, that is because the company's retained earnings expanded substantially in 1984, with a resulting increase in its equity position, even though long-term debt also increased.

A commonly used modification of the debt ratio includes only interest-bearing debt in the numerator. Because other debt (usually in the form of accounts payable) does not increase the company's interest expenses, its existence does not adversely affect risk. In practice, a creditor evaluating the financial solvency of a potential loan applicant would be interested in both debt ratios. One without the other could be misleading.

Another leverage ratio commonly used with the debt ratio is the times interest earned ratio. Creditors often want to know how secure their interest payments are. One way of measuring this is to determine how much earnings before interest and taxes exceed interest payments. This figure shows how much earnings could decline before the payment of interest was jeopardized.

$$\textbf{Times interest earned} = \frac{\text{Earnings before interest and taxes}}{\text{Interest payments}}$$

TIMES INTEREST EARNED
Earnings before interest and taxes divided by interest payments.

$$\text{IBM's 1984 times interest earned} = \frac{\$11,623 + \$408}{\$408} = 29.5$$

$$\text{IBM's 1983 times interest earned} = \frac{\$9,940 + 390}{\$390} = 26.5$$

IBM's earnings available to meet interest payments in 1984 were 29.5 times the amount of these payments—an excellent margin of safety. The ratio has increased since 1983, even though IBM's leverage position has slightly increased. Nonetheless, IBM's leverage may, as we will see later, have been to the advantage of the common shareholders.

Before leaving the times interest earned ratio we should note that this ratio, appropriately modified, can be used to determine the margin of safety of payments to any investor group. For example, if preferred shareholders were concerned about the margin of safety surrounding their dividend payments, they could calculate a times preferred dividend payment ratio. This ratio would use earnings after taxes in the numerator and dividend payments in the denominator.

Profitability Ratios

PROFITABILITY RATIOS
Ratios that measure the overall effectiveness of management in operating the business.

Profitability ratios measure the overall effectiveness of management in operating the business and are therefore probably the most important to financial statement users. Several of the profitability ratios described in the following paragraphs serve as aggregate measures of performance; that is, they represent the firm's bottom line.

The bottom line normally refers to a company's net earnings. However, this measure is often misleading in performance evaluation because it is an absolute number when, in fact, profits should be evaluated in the context of the company's size and competitive position. As a result, analysts typically construct profitability ratios to compare some measure of earnings with either total assets, sales, or shareholders' equity. The most commonly used ratios are return on sales, gross profit margin, return on investment, and return on shareholders' equity.

The return on sales (also known as the **profit margin**) measures how much the company earns on every dollar of sales.

RETURN ON SALES
Net earnings divided by total revenue (also known as profit margin).

$$\textbf{Return on sales} = \frac{\text{Net earnings}}{\text{Total revenue}}$$

$$\text{IBM's 1984 return on sales} = \frac{\$6{,}582}{\$45{,}937} = 14.33\%$$

$$\text{IBM's 1983 return on sales} = \frac{\$5{,}485}{\$40{,}180} = 13.65\%$$

In 1983, IBM earned approximately $0.137 on every dollar of sales, while in 1984 the amount increased to $0.143. As we will see shortly, a company's profit margin is an important variable in analyzing ROI and is closely related to total asset turnover. For example, most retailers, such as grocery store and department store owners, have very small profit margins; their turnover of products, however, is high. Without this turnover, profits would be low. In contrast, manufacturers of heavy-duty equipment, such as tractors and computers, have low asset turnover but high profit margins. Thus, each sale generates a significant profit for the company.

Another variation of the profit margin, used in particular by retailers, is the gross profit margin.

GROSS PROFIT MARGIN
(Sales minus cost of goods sold) divided by sales.

$$\textbf{Gross profit margin} = \frac{\text{Sales} - \text{Cost of goods sold}}{\text{Sales}}$$

$$\text{IBM's 1984 gross profit margin} = \frac{\$45{,}937 - 18{,}919}{\$45{,}937} = 58.82\%$$

$$\text{IBM's 1983 gross profit margin} = \frac{\$40{,}180 - 16{,}395}{\$40{,}180} = 59.20\%$$

You could also calculate separate gross margin ratios for equipment sales, rentals, and services for IBM from the data for each major sales category provided in Exhibit 18.2.

The ratios show a slight decrease in the total gross profit margin from 1983 to 1984. The 1984 figure of 58.82 percent indicates that the company earned $0.59 in gross profit for each dollar generated in sales and that the other $0.41 was used to cover manufacturing costs. Normally, the higher the gross profit margin, the better off the company, because the gross profit margin shows how much is available to cover nonmanufacturing expenses and provide net earnings. The only way management can increase the gross profit margin is to raise prices or to reduce manufacturing costs. Thus, these figures are helpful in evaluating potential price increases and assessing plans to reduce manufacturing costs.

The profitability ratio most important to management is return on investment (ROI), because it measures how well the company is doing given its investment in assets. For example, two companies had net earnings of $10,000 in 1985: however, Company A had total assets of $100,000; Company B, $80,000. What can we conclude from these data? All other things equal, Company B earned a greater return on its investment than did Company A. A had a return on investment of 10 percent ($10,000/$100,000), while B realized a return of 12.5 percent ($10,000/$80,000). Without relating net earnings to some measure of investment—in this case, total assets—a misleading picture of performance could result.

There are many ways to define ROI. For our purposes, it is calculated as follows:

$$\textbf{ROI} = \frac{\text{Net earnings}}{\text{Average total assets}}$$

$$\text{IBM's 1984 ROI} = \frac{\$6{,}582}{\$40{,}134} = 16.40\%$$

RETURN ON INVESTMENT (ROI) Net earnings divided by average total assets.

In place of net earnings, a company might use operating income or earnings before taxes, while operating assets, fixed assets, or some other variant could be used in place of total assets. IBM's ROI of 16.4 percent indicates that after taxes, the company earned $0.164 on every dollar invested in assets.

As previously mentioned, ROI is a function of profit margin and total asset turnover. In fact, the multiplication of the profit margin ratio by the total asset turnover ratio equals ROI.

$$\text{ROI} = \text{Profit margin} \times \text{Total asset turnover}$$

$$\frac{\text{Net earnings}}{\text{Average total assets}} = \frac{\text{Net earnings}}{\text{Sales}} \times \frac{\text{Sales}}{\text{Average total assets}}$$

IBM's 1984 figures:

ROI	=	Profit margin	×	Total asset turnover
16.40%		14.33%		1.145

This relationship has some significant implications for managing a business. If, as for the makers of tractors or computers mentioned earlier, turnover is expected to be low, management can significantly affect ROI only by increasing profit margins. Conversely, companies with relatively low margins (such as grocery or department stores) will generate profits only by increasing asset turnover. Thus, the ROI model implies a strategy of how profits might be achieved in different types of businesses.

DuPont Corporation, the first company to popularize the ROI framework, envisioned it in the form of an "ROI tree," as depicted in Exhibit 18.4. The base of the tree represents the company's ROI; the branches leading from it depict the factors affecting ROI. The ROI framework depicted in the exhibit is often used by management for planning and control as well as for diagnostic purposes. In planning, management often sets targets for return on investment and its components, then compares performance with plans. In this situation, management is also using the ROI model as a diagnostic tool to identify and better understand the factors affecting corporate financial performance.

Despite the usefulness of ROI, shareholders are often more interested in determining the return of their own investment than in the return to creditors and shareholders as measured by ROI. From the shareholders' vantage point, a company's return on equity (ROE) is of particular importance.

$$\textbf{ROE} = \frac{\text{Net earnings available to common shareholders}}{\text{Average common shareholders' equity}}$$

$$\text{IBM's 1984 ROE} = \frac{\$6{,}582}{\$24{,}854} = 26.48\%$$

RETURN ON EQUITY (ROE) Net earnings available to common shareholders divided by average common shareholders' equity.

EXHIBIT 18.4
Dupont ROI Tree

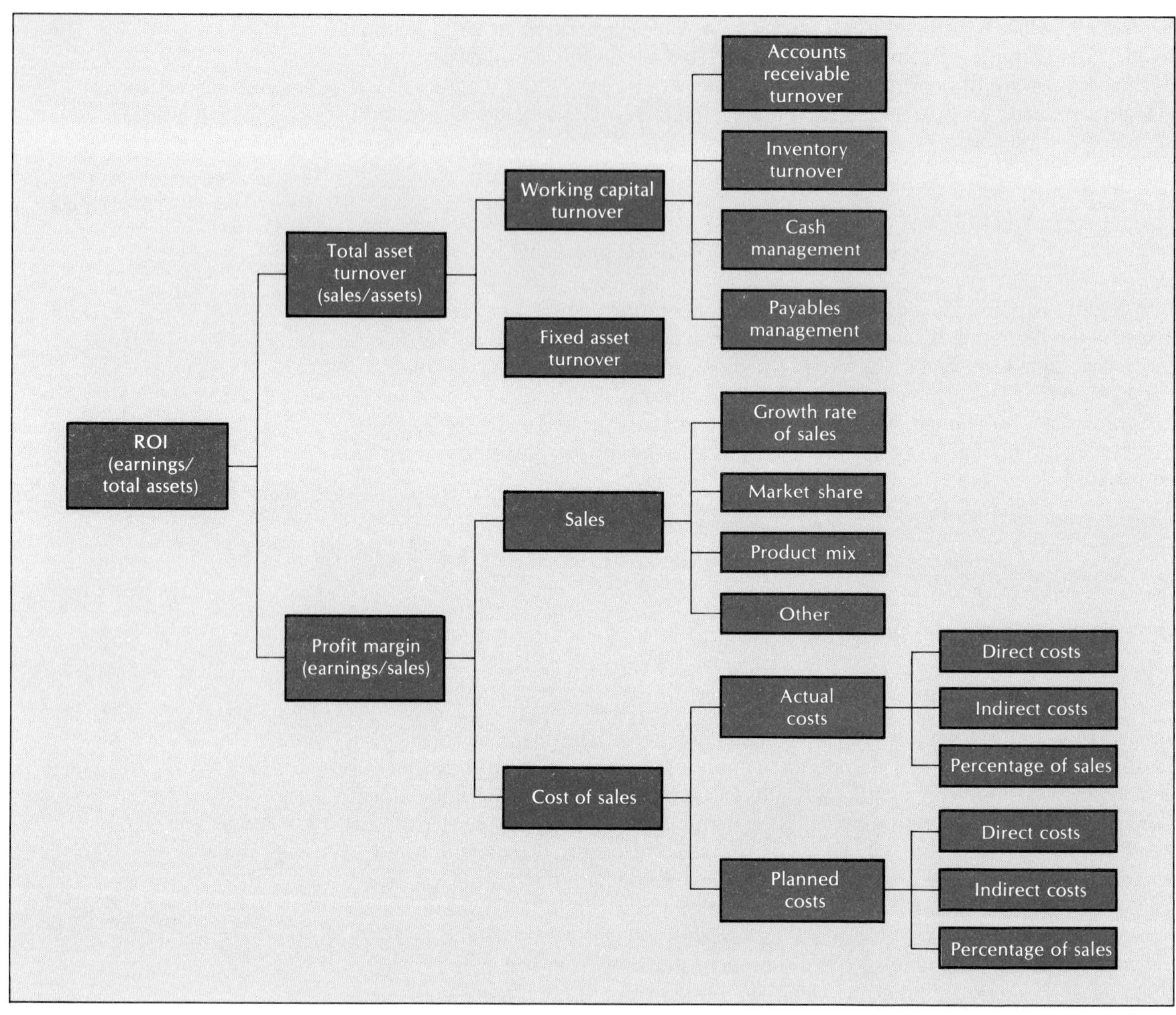

It is interesting to note that although IBM's 1984 ROI was 16.4 percent, its ROE was 26.5 percent. Why is this true?

Let's assume a company has no debt. In such a case, its total assets would equal its total equity, and ROI would equal ROE. Now, to the extent that a firm uses debt, ROE will be different from ROI. For example, if a company realizes a return on borrowed capital greater than the amount of interest paid, ROE will be higher than ROI, because any excess returns accrue to the shareholders without their having to increase their investment.

In reality, ROE is a function of ROI and leverage. In a firm with a relatively simple capital structure (that is, one with only common stock) ROE is equal to ROI divided by the equity ratio.

$$\text{ROE} = \frac{\text{ROI}}{\text{Equity ratio}}$$

$$\text{IBM's 1984 ROE} = \frac{16.40\%}{62\%} = 26.45\%^*$$

*difference from 26.48% due only to rounding.

This relationship indicates that ROE can be increased by increasing leverage or ROI. Of course, there is a delicate balance between ROI and a firm's leverage position,

■ **CONCEPT SUMMARY 18.2**

LEVERAGE AND PROFITABILITY RATIOS

RATIO	INTERPRETATION	FORMULA
Leverage Ratios	Measure the extent to which a company uses debt and the impact of leverage on the company's ability to meet its interest payments.	
Debt	Represents the percentage of total assets financed by debt.	$\frac{\text{Total debt}}{\text{Total assets}}$
Interest-bearing debt	Represents the percentage of total assets financed by interest-bearing debt.	$\frac{\text{Total interest-bearing debt}}{\text{Total assets}}$
Equity	Represents the percentage of total assets financed by shareholders' equity.	$\frac{\text{Total equity}}{\text{Total assets}}$
Times interest earned	Approximates creditors' margin of safety by indicating how much earnings could decline before the payment of interest would be jeopardized.	$\frac{\text{Earnings before interest and taxes}}{\text{Interest payments}}$
Profitability Ratios	Measure the overall effectiveness of management in operating the firm.	
Return on sales	Measures how much earnings the company makes on every dollar of sales.	$\frac{\text{Net earnings}}{\text{Total revenue}}$
Gross profit margin	Measures how much gross profit the company makes on every dollar of sales.	$\frac{\text{Sales} - \text{Cost of goods sold}}{\text{Sales}}$
Return on investment	Measures how well the company is doing given its investment in assets.	$\frac{\text{Net earnings}}{\text{Average total assets}}$
Return on equity	Measures how well the company is doing given the investment by shareholders.	$\frac{\text{Net earnings}}{\text{Average equity}}$

and a change in one will probably affect the other. However, under most circumstances, increased leverage will positively affect ROE.

Market Ratios

MARKET RATIOS
Ratios that provide information on the attractiveness of a stock investment.

Although current and potential shareholders are interested in the ratios we have described, investors are probably most concerned with the amount of dividends paid by the company and the potential for capital appreciation on their stock investment. In determining the attractiveness of a stock investment, individuals look at a number of **market ratios.** The most commonly used include the earnings/price ratio and its reciprocal, the price/earnings (P/E) ratio, book value per share, and dividend yield and dividend payout.

MARKET VALUE PER SHARE
Current selling price of a stock in the open market.

One of the first things an investor might look at to determine if a stock is undervalued or overvalued is the relationship between market value per share and book value per share. As discussed in Chapter 13, the market value per share equals the current selling price in the open market. It is the price the investor would have to pay to acquire the stock. In contrast, the book value per share is determined as follows:

BOOK VALUE PER SHARE
Common shareholders' equity divided by number of shares outstanding.

$$\textbf{Book value per share} = \frac{\text{Common shareholders' equity}}{\text{Number of shares outstanding}}$$

$$\text{IBM's 1984 book value per share} = \frac{\$26{,}489{,}000{,}000}{611{,}426{,}324} = \$43.32$$

$$\text{IBM's market value per share at December 31, 1984} = \$123.13$$

Book value per share is an approximation of the liquidation value per share, that is, the amount per share that would be realized by the common shareholders if a company sold all its assets, once all the debts to creditors had been liquidated. In IBM's case, market value exceeds book value, which indicates that the value investors place on the firm is higher than that indicated by the accounting numbers. It is not uncommon to see companies whose stock sells for less than book value. These companies are often prime candidates for takeover, because a buyer could sell the company for more than he or she paid for it. Book value figures must be interpreted cautiously, as they are based on the book values of assets, which are determined by cost. As you will see in Appendix D, during periods of inflation, historical cost can be a poor indicator of true value. Nevertheless, book value per share can provide some insight into how the market views a company.

Shareholders are also interested in knowing a stock's earnings and dividend yields.

EARNINGS YIELD
Earnings per share available to common shareholders divided by market value per share.

$$\textbf{Earnings yield} = \frac{\text{Earnings per share available to common shareholders}}{\text{Market value per share}}$$

$$\text{IBM's 1984 earnings yield} = \frac{\$10.77}{\$123.13} = 8.75\%$$

$$\text{IBM's 1984 price/earnings ratio} = \frac{\$123.13}{\$10.77} = 11.43$$

The earnings yield is a rough approximation of the percentage return shareholders earn on their investment, especially if a company pays out all its earnings in dividends.. The reciprocal of this ratio (the **price/earnings ratio**) is probably of more interest to investors, because it measures investors' perspectives on the quality of the company and its stock. The higher this P/E multiple, the more investors are willing to pay for the company's earnings stream. By analyzing the trend in a company's P/E ratio and by comparing it with those of other companies, an investor can get a feel for whether a stock is overvalued or undervalued and how attractive it is to other investors. In the late 1960s, during the age of "go-go" stocks and funds, it was not unusual to see stocks selling at ridiculously high P/E ratios. For example, stock of the Levitz Furniture Company once sold for more that *200 times earnings*. Investors had so much faith in the market and the potential of companies such as Levitz that they were willing to pay outlandish prices for shares of these companies. As it turned out in most cases, these prices were out of proportion to the real economic value of the company, and the potential returns envisioned simply did not occur.

PRICE EARNINGS RATIO
Market value per share divided by earnings per share available to common shareholders.

Many investors purchase stocks expecting to receive dividends in addition to realizing some capital appreciation on their investment. Dividends, much like interest payments on borrowed money, offer shareholders a fixed dollar return on their investment. However, unlike interest, dividends need not be paid; the decision to pay a dividend and the amount to be paid are strictly at the discretion of management. Once a company begins these payments, however, it usually makes every effort to continue and to increase them. To do otherwise might seem to indicate a weakness in the company's financial position, resulting in an adverse effect on share prices.

In evaluating a company's dividend policy, investors usually are interested in the stock's dividend yield and the company's dividend payout.

$$\textbf{Dividend yield} = \frac{\text{Dividend per share}}{\text{Market value per share}}$$

$$\text{IBM's 1984 dividend yield} = \frac{\$4.10}{\$123.13} = 3.33\%$$

DIVIDEND YIELD
Dividend per share divided by market value per share.

The resulting percentage, analogous to an interest rate, is the current yield a shareholder is earning on his or her investment. The total amount of dividends a company pays is a function of the company's dividend payout policy, which in turn is a function of the company's growth potential, cash position, and investment opportunities. Dividend payout is determined as follows:

$$\textbf{Dividend payout} = \frac{\text{Dividends}}{\text{Net earnings}}$$

$$\text{IBM's 1984 dividend payout} = \frac{\$2{,}507}{\$6{,}582} = 38.1\%$$

DIVIDEND PAYOUT
Dividends divided by net earnings.

Normally, high-growth companies have relatively low payout percentages, because they find it more advantageous to reinvest their earnings in the business. In contrast, companies with slower growth patterns or in no-growth positions distribute a larger percentage of earnings to shareholders under the assumption that the investor can earn a higher return on this distributed capital than if the earnings were reinvested by the company. Thus, the level of a company's dividend payout and dividend yield provides insight into the company's investment policy and growth potential.

■ CONCEPT SUMMARY 18.3 MARKET RATIOS

RATIO	INTERPRETATION	FORMULA
Market Ratios	Indicate the attractiveness of investment in a company's stock.	
Market value per share	Measures the price investors must pay to acquire the stock.	Current selling price in the open market
Book value per share	Approximates the amount that would be realized by common shareholders if the company sold all its assets, paid all its debt, and distributed the rest.	$\frac{\text{Common shareholders' equity}}{\text{Number of shares outstanding}}$
Earnings yield	Measures the amount of earnings due the shareholder per dollar of investment in stock.	$\frac{\text{EPS to common shareholders}}{\text{Market value per share}}$
Price/earnings	Measures the price an investor must pay to obtain one dollar of corporate earnings.	$\frac{\text{Market value per share}}{\text{EPS to common shareholders}}$
Dividend yield	Measures the return on investment the shareholder receives from dividend payments.	$\frac{\text{Dividend per share}}{\text{Market value per share}}$
Dividend payout	Measures the percentage of total earnings paid out in the form of dividends.	$\frac{\text{Dividends}}{\text{Net earnings}}$

A Comparative Ratio Analysis

Exhibit 18.5 summarizes IBM's ratios for 1983 and 1984. On the basis of an intracompany analysis, it appears that the company's financial performance improved in 1984. All the key ratios indicate an upward trend. Without any other measurement standards, though, it is difficult to put IBM's financial performance in perspective. To get a clearer and more complete picture of how efficiently and effectively the company performed in recent years, we should compare IBM's performance against that of similar companies. The comparative data in Exhibit 18.6 will help us do that.

These data from Standard & Poor's (S&P) Industry Surveys[1] include several of IBM's key ratios[2] along with those of similar companies. Examining five years of data tells us a number of interesting things not clearly indicated by the two-year intracompany analysis. First, although IBM's record of financial performance was outstanding during the five years, profitability increased only slightly from 1979 to 1983. Second,

[1]Other sources of comparative data are available from Moody's, Dunn & Bradstreet, Robert Morris Associates, and various U.S. government agencies such as the IRS, Federal Trade Commission, and U.S. Department of Commerce.

[2]Several of the S&P ratios for IBM might not be equal to those presented in this chapter because of differences in the method of calculation. However, the data do permit a comparative analysis, because they show the relative performances of the firms.

Summary of IBM's Key Ratios

	1984	1983
Liquidity		
Current	2.11	1.89
Quick	1.29	1.28
Activity Turnover		
TAT	1.14	1.15
Fixed asset turnover (gross)	2.83	2.38
A/R turnover	6.41	6.89
Number of days	57	53
Inventory turnover	3.45	4.16
Leverage Ratios		
Debt (all)	38.12	38.02
Debt (long-term)	7.64	7.14
Equity	61.88	61.98
Times interest earned	29.49	26.49
Profitability Ratios		
ROI	16.40	15.67
Return on sales	14.33	13.65
ROE	26.48	25.41
Gross margin		
Sales	58.41	58.12
Services	54.74	54.33
Rentals	66.59	65.97
Market Ratios		
Book value/share	$43.32	$38.27
Market value/share (at 12/31)	$123.13	$122.00
Dividend yield (average price)	3.33%	3.04%
Dividend payout	38.09%	41.04%
P/E ratio	11.43	13.50

compared with its competitors, IBM has had a more consistent and favorable record of financial performance. In fact, the company's performance in 1981—a down year—still exceeded that of most of its competitors. IBM was one of the leaders in its field while maintaining a relatively conservative capital structure, that is, one with a small proportion of long-term debt. Interestingly, despite the company's increase in debt since 1979, IBM is still not as highly leveraged as its competitors.

In summary, IBM appears to be a well-managed, profitable company with an impressive history of outstanding financial performance. Although the slight decline in 1981, viewed in the context of other similar firms, does not appear to be too serious, it still is something worth watching in the future.

REFINING THE ANALYSIS

Most financial analysts believe that the results of a ratio analysis can be misleading unless consideration is given to the impact of inflation and differing accounting

EXHIBIT 18.6

Comparative Ratio Data

Operating Income (as a % of revenues)

Company	1979	1980	1981	1982	1983
Computer Manufacturers					
Amdahl Corp.	18.9	17.4	14.4	8.2	17.1
Burroughs Corp.	27.4	14.6	18.6	13.1	17.0
Computer Automation	NM	12.4	6.1	6.6	2.5
Computervision Corp.	21.7	21.6	25.1	19.5	19.8
Control Data	13.3	14.7	15.0	19.7	17.9
Cray Research	50.3	45.3	45.3	38.0	37.0
Data General	21.0	20.3	15.4	9.7	11.1
Datapoint Corp.	26.8	27.1	25.3	12.1	13.1
Digital Equipment	18.9	19.1	20.0	19.0	13.3
Electronic Associates	10.4	9.0	5.2	8.0	NM
Floating Point Systems	15.6	22.0	20.2	22.2	24.2
Hewlett-Packard	19.9	19.9	19.6	19.6	19.5
Honeywell, Inc.	15.2	13.8	13.3	11.6	11.5
Int'l. Bus. Machines	31.6	30.9	30.7	32.6	33.0
Modular Comp. Systems	18.0	9.9	4.3	6.8	NM
NCR Corp.	20.8	20.6	17.1	18.0	19.4
Prime Computer	22.1	22.1	19.8	20.5	15.4
Sperry Corp.	16.3	16.4	14.4	11.1	13.0
Tandem Computers	19.8	20.1	21.4	16.3	16.3
Wang Laboratories	22.5	22.8	20.4	19.4	21.0

Net Income (as a % of revenues)

Company	1979	1980	1981	1982	1983
Computer Manufacturers					
Amdahl Corp.	5.7	3.9	6.0	1.1	5.6
Burroughs Corp.	11.0	2.9	4.5	2.2	4.5
Computer Automation	def.	5.7	2.2	2.5	NM
Computervision Corp.	9.9	10.4	13.2	10.0	8.8
Control Data	5.3	5.3	5.5	3.6	3.5
Cray Research	18.3	17.9	17.9	13.5	15.4
Data General	9.8	8.4	5.5	2.5	2.6
Datapoint Corp.	10.9	10.5	12.3	0.5	1.5
Digital Equipment	9.9	10.6	10.7	10.7	6.6
Electronic Associates	5.7	4.0	2.1	4.1	NM
Floating Point Systems	6.8	10.0	11.0	13.3	13.0
Hewlett-Packard	8.6	8.7	8.7	9.0	9.2
Honeywell Inc.	5.7	5.7	4.8	4.9	4.7
Int'l. Bus. Machines	13.2	13.6	11.4	12.8	13.7
Modular Comp. Systems	6.5	4.7	1.3	1.9	NM
NCR Corp.	7.8	7.7	6.1	6.6	7.7
Prime Computer	11.1	11.7	10.3	10.3	6.3
Sperry Corp.	5.8	5.8	4.0	2.3	4.1
Tandem Computers	8.8	9.8	12.7	9.6	7.4
Wang Laboratories	8.9	9.6	9.1	9.2	9.9

Return on Assets (%)

Company	1979	1980	1981	1982	1983
Computer Manufacturers					
Amdahl Corp.	5.4	3.8	6.2	0.9	6.4
Burroughs Corp.	9.7	2.3	3.6	2.1	4.8
Computer Automation	NM	6.7	3.3	3.8	NM
Computervision Corp.	15.9	17.7	17.8	12.8	11.2
Control Data	5.6	5.9	6.3	3.2	2.0
Cray Research	20.9	14.0	15.0	10.3	10.4
Data General	12.0	9.7	5.9	2.6	2.8
Datapoint Corp.	16.8	16.8	13.1	0.4	1.4
Digital Equipment	10.6	10.5	10.3	11.1	6.6
Electronic Associates	9.0	7.5	3.7	7.4	NM
Floating Point Systems	7.5	12.3	10.2	12.7	11.5
Hewlett-Packard	12.0	12.6	12.1	12.2	11.2
Honeywell Inc.	7.7	7.7	6.2	6.2	5.0
Int'l. Bus. Machines	13.3	13.9	11.7	14.1	15.6
Modular Comp. Systems	7.0	3.6	1.4	2.0	NM
NCR Corp.	8.5	8.0	6.2	6.9	8.3
Prime Computer	15.0	15.9	13.8	12.8	7.9
Sperry Corp.	6.5	6.5	4.1	2.1	3.4
Tandem Computers	13.9	14.2	14.3	9.9	8.0
Wang Laboratories	12.0	11.6	9.9	10.3	10.2

Return on Equity (%)

Company	1979	1980	1981	1982	1983
Computer Manufacturers					
Amdahl Corp.	11.0	6.8	10.5	1.8	12.9
Burroughs Corp.	15.1	3.8	6.9	4.3	8.9
Computer Automation	NM	19.2	5.9	5.7	NM
Computervision Corp.	38.2	30.4	28.0	19.9	17.4
Control Data	10.7	10.8	11.3	9.4	9.0
Cray Research	31.7	20.3	21.2	15.5	16.4
Data General	22.2	19.0	11.5	4.8	5.1
Datapoint Corp.	21.9	22.2	19.0	0.7	2.5
Digital Equipment	17.5	17.2	14.8	14.2	8.4
Electronic Associates	16.5	12.0	5.7	11.0	NM
Floating Point Systems	12.1	21.0	16.0	18.9	16.7
Hewlett-Packard	18.0	19.2	17.9	17.8	16.4
Honeywell Inc.	15.6	15.7	12.7	12.9	10.2
Int'l. Bus. Machines	21.2	22.7	19.0	22.9	25.2
Modular Comp. Systems	14.3	5.4	1.8	2.6	NM
NCR Corp.	16.9	15.9	11.7	12.3	14.5
Prime Computer	48.3	42.0	31.1	23.7	13.0
Sperry Corp.	14.3	14.1	9.2	4.8	7.1
Tandem Computers	20.0	19.8	18.3	12.9	10.7
Wang Laboratories	29.6	33.0	22.6	20.5	19.3

Debt/Capital Ratio (%)

Company	1979	1980	1981	1982	1983
Computer Manufacturers					
Amdahl Corp.	25.8	9.0	8.6	19.3	11.0
Burroughs Corp.	7.9	14.4	26.1	27.8	19.8
Computer Automation	9.3	5.5	21.7	7.1	6.7
Computervision Corp.	28.2	15.2	16.9	14.6	12.7
Control Data	21.1	17.6	18.7	65.8	71.5
Cray Research	8.2	8.9	10.7	17.1	16.3
Data General	19.9	29.7	25.8	23.3	21.8
Datapoint Corp.	1.9	2.3	24.3	28.8	26.8
Digital Equipment	23.1	22.4	3.1	2.8	2.5
Electronic Associates	16.1	8.5	3.3	2.4	4.3
Floating Point Systems	19.8	14.1	5.6	6.2	3.2
Hewlett-Packard	1.2	1.8	1.3	1.5	2.2
Honeywell Inc.	19.5	16.2	20.2	21.9	21.6
Int'l. Bus. Machines	9.5	11.2	12.7	12.3	10.1
Modular Comp. Systems	16.7	1.6	4.1	8.6	9.3
NCR Corp.	18.4	15.4	13.5	14.6	13.3
Prime Computer	45.2	33.3	24.3	5.7	4.7
Sperry Corp.	14.4	20.8	19.2	22.2	18.0
Tandem Computers	3.4	2.2	1.0	7.3	6.7
Wang Laboratories	47.4	53.4	33.5	34.8	26.5

LTD as % of Net Working Capital

Company	1979	1980	1981	1982	1983
Computer Manufacturers					
Amdahl Corp.	55.6	17.2	17.7	43.9	26.4
Burroughs Corp.	24.1	48.5	84.6	66.4	48.9
Computer Automation	11.8	8.7	26.5	8.8	8.6
Computervision Corp.	56.8	27.1	36.8	32.7	39.7
Control Data	84.1	65.4	69.2	NA	NA
Cray Research	21.8	14.7	20.0	33.1	29.1
Data General	28.1	40.1	34.7	31.5	32.9
Datapoint Corp.	3.8	4.1	35.3	72.5	56.9
Digital Equipment	31.7	29.5	4.3	4.2	3.9
Electronic Associates	21.0	11.1	4.3	3.1	2.3
Floating Point Systems	36.3	25.4	9.6	10.8	4.9
Hewlett-Packard	2.2	3.6	2.6	2.9	4.1
Honeywell Inc.	54.2	48.1	61.7	59.0	59.6
Int'l. Bus. Machines	36.1	61.7	89.5	59.3	34.4
Modular Comp. Systems	20.4	1.9	5.4	11.4	13.2
NCR Corp.	35.1	31.1	28.0	29.8	26.4
Prime Computer	67.0	51.4	39.8	10.4	8.0
Sperry Corp.	42.5	62.4	60.2	101.9	65.6
Tandem Computers	4.2	2.7	1.1	10.8	9.4
Wang Laboratories	80.9	85.8	56.4	82.3	58.6

policies. Appendix D deals with accounting for inflation and the requirements of FASB 33. As you will see, inflation-adjusted accounting numbers can have a significant impact on reported earnings and particular asset values. When these adjusted numbers are used in a ratio analysis, the result can be a different evaluation of a company's financial performance.

A second type of refinement, especially useful in intercompany analysis, involves adjusting for differing accounting policies. For example, a firm's turnover ratios depend on how the company values inventory, depreciates assets, and accounts for leases. An analyst must be aware of the impact of different accounting policies on these ratios and adjust them accordingly. If no adjustment is made, the comparative analysis will not be accurate.

LIMITATIONS OF FINANCIAL ANALYSIS

We could not conclude this chapter without briefly mentioning some of the limitations of ratio analysis. Many of them have been touched on already, but we repeat them for emphasis.

1. There are problems inherent in using financial statement data. As already pointed out, financial statements are based on the historical cost model and a certain set of accounting policies. To the extent that these policies change and the accounting numbers are affected by inflation, the results of a financial analysis can be misleading.
2. External factors affect company performance. It is difficult to determine how much a company's performance is affected by factors outside its control, such as economic problems and raw material shortages. Since information about these factors might not be readily available, an analyst must be sensitive to and knowledgeable about how general business and economic conditions affect the company under study.
3. An interindustry analysis requires the use of comparative data. An analyst must exercise caution in determining where to get this information and how to use it. The biggest problems in using comparative data are ensuring that ratios have been calculated similarly, that the companies or industry averages used are appropriate benchmarks for comparison, and that no unusual events occurred to distort the data during the time period under study.

Remember that financial analysis is much more than a mechanical process. Informed judgments can be made only when the results of such an analysis are coupled with other, nonfinancial information and good sense.

FOR REVIEW

SUMMARY

- Management and owners use financial information for planning and control; creditors, shareholders, and other external users are interested in the financial solvency and cash flow position of a company.

- An intracompany analysis compares a company's current performance with the company's own past performance; an intercompany analysis compares a company's performance with that of similar companies.
- Dollar and percentage changes, trend percentages, and common-size statements are three tools of financial analysis. Each has limitations, and analysts must choose carefully among the tools for meaningful analyses.
- Ratio analysis examines logical relationships between particular items in the financial statements. The five categories of ratios are liquidity, turnover or activity, leverage, profitability, and market.
- Liquidity measures the ability of a company to convert its assets to cash. The current ratio and the acid-test ratio are used to assess liquidity.
- Turnover, or activity, ratios measure how productively a company uses its assets. Key turnover ratios include total asset turnover, fixed asset turnover, accounts receivable turnover, and inventory turnover.
- Leverage refers to the amount of debt a company has in its capital structure. The debt ratio and times interest earned ratio help analysts determine optimal leverage positions.
- Profitability ratios measure the overall effectiveness of management in operating a business. Key profitability ratios include gross profit margin, return on investment, and return on equity.
- Market ratios are used by investors to determine where to invest their money. Commonly used market ratios are market value per share, book value per share, earnings yield, price/earnings ratio, dividend yield, and dividend payout.
- Analysts must consider items such as the impact of inflation, differing accounting policies, consistency of accounting policies, and other external factors when evaluating the financial health of a company.

QUESTIONS

18-1. What is the difference between an intercompany analysis and an intracompany analysis?

18-2. What is a trend percentage analysis, and how is it used? How are the percentages determined?

18-3. With the following figures, determine trend percentages for each year, using 1982 as the base year. Why is the figure for 1985 particularly interesting?

	1986	**1985**	**1984**	**1983**	**1982**
Total sales (in thousands)	\$91.0	\$72.4	\$88.9	\$62.3	\$45.4
	200	159	196	137	100

18-4. What are common-size statements, and why are they useful to persons reading financial information?

18-5. Why would short-term creditors be particularly interested in a firm's liquidity, and what measures would a creditor use to determine liquidity?

18-6. Total sales for Ynot Company are \$180,000. Assets at January 1, 1986, were \$92,000 and at December 31, 1986, were \$98,000. What is the company's total asset turnover? What does this figure represent?

18-7. Qbee Company has an accounts receivable turnover for the year of 4. The credit terms it extends to customers is n/35. Given this information, what would you suggest to the credit manager?

18-8. Rogers Corporation has a debt ratio of 42%. What does this figure tell us about the debt and equity level of the company?

18-9. Why are profitability ratios so important? Indicate how each of the following profitability measures would be calculated.

a. Gross profit margin
b. Return on sales
c. Return on investment
d. Return on equity

18-10. List some of the limitations of ratio analysis.

EXERCISES

18-E1. Following is selected information from R & J Sales Corporation statement of financial position for 1986.

Cash and marketable securities	$275,000	Accounts payable	$300,000
Accounts receivable	140,000	Long-term debt	325,000
Inventory	400,000	Shareholders' equity	210,000
Prepaid expenses	20,000		

How would you analyze R & J's liquidity position? What is working capital? Current ratio? Acid-test ratio?

18-E2. Selected information for Mountain View Ski Corporation is as follows.

	1986	1985
Net sales on account	$180,000	$135,000
Average account receivables	15,000	16,875

Mountain View has a credit policy of 1/10, N30. Determine the accounts receivable turnover and average collection period. What is your evaluation of Mountain View's credit department?

18-E3. Delicious Cheese Company sells a brand of cheese with a shelf life of 45 days. Financial information for 1986 for Delicious is as follows.

Purchases	$7,400
Beginning inventory	1,000
Ending inventory	1,160

Calculate the inventory turnover and evaluate Delicious Cheese Company inventory performance.

18-E4. Total assets for Image Manufacturers are $720,000. Short-term and long-term debt amount to $360,000. Earnings before taxes for 1986 were $62,000. Interest charges for the year amounted to $3,800. Determine the debt ratio and times interest earned and compare them to an industry average of 22.

18-E5. Joyson Company has a gross profit of $156,000. Total sales for 1986 were $390,000. Assuming a tax rate of 30%, what is Joyson's profit margin after taxes?

18-E6. Total assets for Joyson Company (18-E5) at December 31, 1985, were $256,000. At the end of 1986, total assets were $394,000. What was the ROI for Joyson at the end of 1986?

18-E7. Financial information for Leadway Distribution Company is as follows. Leadway stock is currently selling for $42 per share. Determine Leadway's price/earnings ratio.

Sales	$300,000
Inventory, Jan. 1, 1986	50,000
Inventory, Dec. 31, 1986	60,000
Purchases	190,000
Operating expenses	78,000
Income tax rate	20%
Number of shares outstanding	10,000

PROBLEM SET A

18-A1. Working Capital and Current Ratio. S & J Manufacturing Company has a current ratio of 2:1. Indicate the effect on working capital and on the current ratio for each of the following transactions. (Consider each transaction independently.)

	Working Capital	Current Ratio
a. Collected account receivable.		
b. Paid cash for piece of machinery.		
c. Obtained a 3-month loan from the bank.		
d. Sold a piece of capital equipment for cash.		
e. Sold merchandise with terms of n/25.		
f. Wrote off an overdue account receivable as uncollectible.		
g. Paid a cash dividend to preferred shareholders. (Dividend had been previously declared.)		
h. Exchanged a piece of wornout equipment for new equipment.		
i. Issued stock dividend to common shareholders.		
j. Purchased merchandise inventory for cash.		

18-A2. Quick Ratio, Long-Term Debt Ratio, and Equity Ratio. Stone Works Manufacturing, Inc., currently has a quick ratio of 3:1, a long-term debt ratio of 30%, and an equity ratio of 60%. Indicate the effect on each of these ratios for each of the following transactions. (Consider each transaction independently.)

	Quick Ratio	LT Debt Ratio	Equity Ratio
a. Purchased merchandise inventory for cash.			
b. Issued a short-term note payable for cash.			
c. Sold marketable securities at their book value.			
d. Paid off mortgage note (before maturity) with cash.			
e. Purchased new equipment by issuing a 5-year mortgage note payable.			
f. Purchased treasury stock with cash.			

	Quick Ratio	LT Debt Ratio	Equity Ratio
g. Sold merchandise on account.			
h. Sold merchandise in exchange for installment note receivable.			
i. Sold marketable securities at book value for installment note receivable.			
j. Converted bonds payable outstanding into common stock.			

18-A3. Common-Size Statement of Financial Position. The following is the consolidated statement of financial position at November 30, 1984, of Avery International Corporation as it appeared in the company's 1984 annual report.

November 30, 1984 **Assets**	
Current assets	
Cash and cash equivalents	$ 3,189,000
Trade accounts receivable, less allowance for doubtful accounts of $4,449,000	128,679,000
Other receivables	7,541,000
Inventories	126,056,000
Prepaid expenses	6,403,000
Deferred taxes on income	2,744,000
Total current assets	274,612,000
Property, plant, and equipment, at cost	
Land	11,785,000
Buildings	100,044,000
Machinery and equipment	218,460,000
Construction in progress	29,728,000
	360,017,000
Accumulated depreciation	134,503,000
	225,514,000
Other assets and deferred charges	30,723,000
	$530,849,000
Liabilities and Shareholders' Equity	
Current liabilities	
Short-term and current portion of long-term debt	13,422,000
Accounts payable	73,949,000
Accrued payroll and employee benefits	30,285,000
Other accrued liabilities	33,696,000
Dividends payable	2,963,000
Taxes on income	1,778,000
Total current liabilities	156,093,000
Long-term debt	75,365,000
Deferred taxes on income	28,866,000
Shareholders' equity	
Common stock, $1 par value	19,749,000
Capital in excess of par value	62,300,000
Retained earnings	220,888,000
Cumulative foreign currency translation adjustments	(32,412,000)
Total shareholders' equity	270,525,000
	$530,849,000

Required

Convert the statement into a common-size statement of financial position.

18-A4. Comparative Common-Size Financial Statements. The following are statement of financial position figures and selected revenue and expense accounts for Kenco Company for December 31, 1985, and December 31, 1986.

Kenco Company
(thousands of dollars)

	1986	1985
Assets		
Cash	$ 11,000	$ 8,400
Marketable securities	3,000	4,800
Accounts receivable	123,200	104,000
Inventory	152,000	126,000
Prepaid expenses	1,800	1,200
Property, plant, and equipment	90,000	80,000
Investments	3,600	3,200
Liabilities & Shareholders' Equity		
Notes payable	$ 11,400	$ 6,000
Accounts payable	44,000	48,200
Accrued liabilities	60,000	54,600
12% bonds payable	50,000	40,000
10% preferred stock	16,000	16,000
Common stock, $5 par	40,000	28,000
Paid-in capital	15,000	11,000
Retained earnings	148,200	123,800

Kenco Company
(thousands of dollars)

Sales	$830,000	$640,000
Cost of goods sold	580,000	460,000
Selling expenses	79,000	54,600
Administrative expenses	100,880	66,200
Interest expense	4,400	3,800
Income taxes	28,200	24,600

Required

a. Prepare a comparative statement of financial position showing the percentage change in each account and each item as a percent of total assets.
b. Prepare a comparative income statement showing the percentage change for each item and each account as a percent of total revenue.
c. Comment on the findings from your analysis.

18-A5. Ratio Analysis. The statement of financial position for Champion Company at the end of 1986 indicates the following:

Total current liabilities (noninterest-bearing)	$ 900,000
Bonds payable, 12% (due in 1995)	1,500,000
Preferred 9% stock, $100 par	600,000
Common stock, $10 par	1,500,000
Paid-in capital	225,000
Retained earnings	1,275,000

Income for 1986 was $652,500, and taxes totaled $316,500. Cash dividends on common stock totaled $225,000. Common stock of Champion Company was selling for $20 per share.

Required

Determine each of the following for Champion Company:

a. Rate earned on total assets.
b. Return on equity.
c. Number of times preferred dividends were earned.
d. Number of times bond interest was earned.
e. Earnings per share on common stock.
f. Dividend yield.
g. Price/earnings ratio.
h. Return on investment.

18-A6. Ratio Analysis. Selected data from the statement of financial position of Proportio, Inc., show the following.

TUTORIAL PROBLEM

	12/31/86	12/31/85
Cash	$150,000	$125,000
Marketable securities	25,000	5,000
Accounts receivable	53,650	75,900
Inventory	35,850	43,900
Current liabilities	75,000	68,000

The income statement provided information including the following.

Sales	$750,000
Cost of goods sold	500,000
Earnings per common share	$5.00

Additionally, it is reported that the average market value of Proportio's common stock is $75 per share and that Proportio has paid $2.15 per share in dividends.

Required

Compute the following ratios for Proportio, Inc.

a. Current ratio as of 12/31/86
b. Quick ratio as of 12/31/86
c. Accounts receivable turnover
d. Number of days sales in 12/31/86 accounts receivable
e. Inventory turnover
f. Dividend yield
g. Dividend payout
h. Price/earnings ratio

18-A7. Ratio Analysis. Following are the statement of financial position and income statement of Difficult, Inc., for 1986 with all dollar amounts missing.

Difficult, Inc.
Statement of Financial Position
December 31, 1986

Assets		Equities	
Cash	$?	Accounts payable	$?
Accounts receivable (net)	?	Bonds payable (16%)	?
Inventory	?	Common stock	?
Equipment	?	Retained earnings	?
Total assets	$?	Total equities	$?

Difficult, Inc.
Income Statement
For Year Ending December 31, 1986

Net sales	$?
Cost of goods sold	?
Gross profit	$?
Operating expenses	?
Net operating income	$?
Interest expense	?
Income before income taxes	$?
Income tax expense (40%)	?
Net income	$?

Additional information:

1. The quick ratio is 1.6:1.
2. The inventory turnover (with beginning inventory of $170,000) is two times.
3. The return on sales is 6%.
4. The average collection period for accounts receivable is 25.55 days. The balance of the allowance for doubtful accounts is $5,000.
5. The gross profit margin is 30%.
6. The return on assets (with total assets at 1/1/86 of $350,000) is 14%.
7. The equity ratio is 70%.
8. All interest expense relates to bonds payable, which were issued on September 1, 1986.
9. In the market, the 100,000 shares of common stock outstanding (all of which had been issued at par value of $2 per share) enjoyed a market price of $9 per share and a price/earnings ratio of 30.
10. Book value (equity) per share of common stock outstanding is $3.15.

Required

Complete the missing amounts in Difficult, Inc.'s, financial statements. (Hint: Complete the shareholders' equity section of the statement of financial position before proceeding to the income statement.)

18-A8. Computation and Evaluation of Ratios. The following data were taken from the financial statements of Lennon Drug Company, wholesaler of drugs, drug properties, and sundries, for calendar year 1986. Assume all sales are credit sales.

Lennon Drug Company
Statement of Financial Position
December 31, 1986
(thousands of dollars)

Assets		**Liabilities**	
Cash	$ 200	Accounts payable	$ 300
Receivables	800	Notes payable (at 10%)	200
Inventory	600	Other current liabilities	300
Total current assets	$1,600	Total current liabilities	$ 800
Net fixed assets	600	Long-term debt (at 10%)	600
Total assets	$2,200	Net equity	800
		Total liabilities	$2,200

Lennon Drug Company
Income Statement
For Year Ending December 31, 1986
(thousands of dollars)

Sales	$4,000	
Cost of goods sold	3,400	
Gross profit		$600
Selling expenses	$ 250	
Administrative expenses	200	450
Net operating income		$150
Interest expense		80
Income before taxes		$ 70
Federal income taxes		15
Net income		$ 55

Required

a. Fill in name and type of ratios and compute firm's ratios on the accompanying analysis sheet.
b. Indicate by comparison with the industry norms (industry averages for wholesale drugs, drug properties, and sundries) the possible weaknesses in management policies reflected in Lennon's financial statements.

	Name and Type of Ratio	Ratio	Firm's Ratio	Industry Norm
1.	______ ______	$\frac{\text{Current assets}}{\text{Current liabilities}}$	______	1.97 times
2.	______ ______	$\frac{\text{Debt}}{\text{Total assets}}$	______	60%
3.	______ ______	$\frac{\text{Earnings before interest and taxes}}{\text{Interest payments}}$	______	3.79 times
4.	______ ______	$\frac{\text{Cost of goods sold}}{\text{Inventory}}$	______	6.7 times
5.	______ ______	$\frac{365}{\text{Accounts receivable turnover}}$	______	36 days

Name and Type of Ratio	Ratio	Firm's Ratio	Industry Norm
6. ______ ______	Sales / Total assets	______	2.94 times
7. ______ ______	Net income / Sales	______	1.14%
8. ______ ______	Net income / Total assets	______	3.35%
9. ______ ______	Net income / Net equity	______	8.29%

PROBLEM SET B

18-B1. Working Capital and Current Ratio. Lincoln Incorporated has a current ratio of 1.5:1. Indicate the effect on working capital and on the current ratio for each of the following transactions. (Consider each transaction independently.)

	Working Capital	Current Ratio
a. Purchased equipment for cash.		
b. Invested cash in marketable securities.		
c. Issued 5-year bonds for cash.		
d. Wrote off a long overdue account receivable as uncollectible.		
e. Declared a stock dividend on common stock.		
f. Purchased merchandise inventory on account.		
g. Sold capital equipment for cash.		
h. Accepted a 3-month note from a customer in settlement of customer's account receivable.		
i. Paid a cash dividend that had been declared 45 days earlier.		
j. Wrote off goodwill to retained earnings.		

18-B2. Quick Ratio, Long-Term Debt Ratio, and Equity Ratio. Class Glass Crystal Manufacturing Company currently has a quick ratio of 0.5:1, a long-term debt ratio of 40%, and an equity ratio of 50%. Indicate the effect on each of these ratios for each of the following transactions. (Consider each transaction independently.)

	Quick Ratio	LT Debt Ratio	Equity Ratio
a. Issued bonds payable to creditor in settlement of account payable.			
b. Issued common stock for cash.			
c. Paid account payable with cash.			

d. Purchased merchandise on account from creditor.
e. Obtained short-term cash loan from bank.
f. Mortgage note issued five years ago now has less than one year until maturity.
g. Received memorandum from bank stating that account had been charged its monthly service charge.
h. Received memorandum from bank stating that interest coupons from bonds receivable had just been redeemed.
i. Accrued current income taxes payable.
j. Accrued deferred income taxes payable.

18-B3. Common-Size Income Statement. In the 1984 annual report of Avery International Corporation, the income statement for the year ending November 30, 1984, is as follows.

Net sales	$913,021,000
Cost of goods sold	608,641,000
Marketing, general, and administrative expense	214,708,000
Interest expense	10,753,000
Tax expense	31,358,000
Net income	$47,561,000

Required

Convert Avery International's income statement to a common-size income statement.

18-B4. Comparative Common-Size Income Statement. The following is the revenue and expense information for Widmark Die Casting Company along with information for the die casting industry in general.

	Widmark Company	Die Casting Industry Average
Sales	1,518,000	101.0%
Sales returns and allowances	18,000	1.0%
Cost of merchandise sold	1,005,000	66.5%
Selling expenses	135,000	7.2%
General expenses	99,000	5.8%
Other income	9,000	0.1%
Other expenses	24,000	1.4%
Income tax	94,500	6.1%

Required

Prepare a common-size income statement comparing Widmark Company's performance to that of the industry.

18-B5. Ratio Analysis. Selected statement of financial position items for Brown Corporation are as follows for the year ending 1986.

Current liabilities	$100,000
Mortgage note payable, 8% (due 1997)	175,000
Preferred 8% stock, $100 par	50,000
Common stock, $10 par	300,000
Retained earnings	200,000

After-tax income for 1986 was $53,070. Taxes totaled $40,000. Dividends of $1 per share were paid to common shareholders. Common stock for Brown Corporation was selling for $4.50.

Required

Determine each of the following for Brown Corporation.

a. Debt ratio.
b. Times interest earned.
c. Return on investment.
d. Number of times preferred dividends were earned.
e. Price/earnings ratio.
f. Dividend yield.
g. Number of times bond interest earned.
h. Return on equity.

18-B6. Ratio Analysis. The income statement of Avery International Corporation for the year ending November 30, 1984, showed the following:

Net sales	$913,021,000
Cost of goods sold	608,641,000
Marketing, general, and administrative expense	214,708,000
Interest expense	10,753,000
Tax expense	31,358,000
Net income	$ 47,561,000

Required

Calculate the following ratios for Avery International (referring also to information from 18-A3).

a. Gross margin
b. Net profit margin
c. Return on total assets
d. Long-term liabilities to capital (i.e., long-term liabilities and shareholders' equity) ratio
e. Earnings per share
f. Number of times interest earned
g. Return on shareholders' equity

18-B7. Ratio Analysis. Following are the statement of financial position and income statement of Simple, Inc., for 1986 with almost all dollar amounts missing.

Simple, Inc.
Statement of Financial Position
December 31, 1986

Assets		**Equities**	
Cash	$?	Accounts payable	$?
Accounts receivable (net)	?	Bonds payable (12%)	?
Inventory	?	Common stock	?
Equipment (net)	?	Retained earnings	116,000
Total assets	$360,000	Total equities	$360,000

Simple, Inc.
Income Statement
For Year Ending December 31, 1986

Net sales	$?
Cost of goods sold	?
Gross profit	$?
Operating expenses	?
Net operating income	$?
Interest expense	?
Income before income taxes	$?
Income tax expense (40%)	?
Net income	$54,000

Additional information:

1. The quick ratio is 1.5:1.
2. The inventory turnover (with beginning inventory of $122,000) is six times.
3. The return on sales is 5%.
4. The average collection period for accounts receivable is 27.375 days. The balance of the allowance for doubtful accounts is $1,000.
5. The gross profit margin is 30%.
6. The return on assets (with total assets at 1/1/1986 of $280,000) is 30%.
7. The equity ratio is 60%.
8. All interest expense relates to bonds payable, which were outstanding all year.

Required

Fill in the missing amounts in Simple, Inc.'s, financial statements. (Hint: Complete the income statement first.)

18-B8. Ratio Analysis. The Planting Company is listed on the Akron Stock Exchange. The market value of its common stock is quoted at $10 per share at December 31, 1986, and December 31, 1985. Planting's statement of financial position at December 31, 1986, and December 31, 1985, and statement of income and retained earnings for the years then ended are as follows:

Planting Company
Statement of Financial Position

	December 31	
	1986	**1985**
Assets		
Current assets		
Cash	$ 3,500,000	$ 3,600,000
Marketable securities, at cost which approximates market	13,000,000	11,000,000
Accounts receivable, net of allowance for doubtful accounts	105,000,000	95,000,000
Inventories, lower of cost or market	126,000,000	154,000,000
Prepaid expenses	2,500,000	2,400,000
Total current assets	250,000,000	266,000,000
Property, plant, and equipment, net of accumulated depreciation	311,000,000	308,000,000
Investments, at equity	2,000,000	3,000,000
Long-term receivables	14,000,000	16,000,000
Goodwill and patents, net of accumulated amortization	6,000,000	6,500,000
Other assets	7,000,000	8,500,000
Total assets	$590,000,000	$608,000,000

Liabilities and Shareholders' Equity		
Current liabilities		
Notes payable	$ 5,000,000	$ 15,000,000
Accounts payable	38,000,000	48,000,000
Accrued expenses	24,500,000	27,000,000
Income taxes payable	1,000,000	1,000,000
Payments due within one year on long-term debt	6,500,000	7,000,000
Total current liabilities	75,000,000	98,000,000
Long-term debt	169,000,000	180,000,000
Deferred income taxes	74,000,000	67,000,000
Other liabilities	9,000,000	8,000,000
Shareholders' equity		
Common stock, par value $1.00 per share; authorized 20,000,000 shares; issued and outstanding 10,000,000 shares	10,000,000	10,000,000
5% cumulative preferred stock, par value $100 per share; $100 liquidating value; authorized 50,000 shares; issued and outstanding 40,000 shares	4,000,000	4,000,000
Additional paid-in capital	107,000,000	107,000,000
Retained earnings	142,000,000	134,000,000
Total shareholders' equity	263,000,000	255,000,000
Total liabilities and shareholders' equity	$590,000,000	$608,000,000

Planting Company
Statement of Income and Retained Earnings

	Year Ending December 31,	
	1986	1985
Net sales	$600,000,000	$500,000,000
Costs and expenses		
Cost of goods sold	490,000,000	400,000,000
Selling, general and administrative expenses	66,000,000	60,000,000
Other, net	7,000,000	6,000,000
Total costs and expenses	563,000,000	466,000,000
Income before income taxes	37,000,000	34,000,000
Income taxes	16,800,000	15,800,000
Net income	20,200,000	18,200,000
Retained earnings at beginning of period	134,000,000	126,000,000
Dividends on common stock	12,000,000	10,000,000
Dividends on preferred stock	200,000	200,000
Retained earnings at end of period	$142,000,000	$134,000,000

Required

Compute (for the year 1986 only) the following, showing supporting computations:

a. Current (working capital) ratio.
b. Quick (acid-test) ratio.
c. Number of days' sales in average receivables, assuming a business year consisting of 300 days and all sales on account.
d. Inventory turnover.
e. Book value per share of common stock.
f. Earnings per share on common stock.
g. Price/earnings ratio on common stock.
h. Dividend payout ratio on common stock.

APPENDIX D
INFLATION ACCOUNTING

In recent years, a number of changes have been made in the content of annual reports. One of the most significant of these changes has been the inclusion of price-level adjusted information as a supplement to the financial statements. You might ask, Why should a corporation discuss the effects of inflation with its shareholders?

"REAL" RESULTS VERSUS "NOMINAL" RESULTS

NOMINAL MEASURES
Measures that use dollar valuations without concern for the possible inequalities of purchasing power.

REAL MEASURES
Measures using dollar valuations adjusted to create equality of purchasing power.

During periods of inflation, published historical cost data and economic reality can be significantly different. To understand this, we need to understand the difference between nominal and real. **Nominal measures** are those using dollar valuations without concern for the possible inequalities of purchasing power. The units used are equivalent in name only, hence the term *nominal*. **Real measures** are those using dollar valuations adjusted to create equality of purchasing power. Such units are equivalent in reality, hence the term *real*. (Under conditions of no inflation, nominal and real measures will, of course, be equal.)

Because investors, management, and others are concerned with the reality of their situations, accounting information properly adjusted to reflect real results is helpful in decision making. The use of nominal results can be misleading.

Corporate management is no less affected by distortions due to inflation than are outside investors. As discussed in Chapter 18, a figure commonly used by corporate management to measure performance is the rate of return on investment (ROI), defined as the ratio of operating income to average total assets. Because the measurements of both operating income and total assets are dependent upon historical cost data, this key ratio is also subject to the limitations of the historical cost method. The distortions that can result from ratios calculated on the basis of historical cost data were illustrated in Chapter 18.

NECESSITY OF AN INFLATION MODEL

Does this mean that the historical cost model must be adjusted or abandoned altogether? After all, shouldn't the prudent investor be aware of the effects of inflation and be able to adjust published financial data himself or herself? The answer to the latter question is no. Although an investor should be aware of inflation, it is impossible to properly adjust financial data himself or herself, for every corporation is affected differently by inflation. This is illustrated in Exhibit D.1. Note how the change in income from continuing operations (IFCO) due to restatement is different for each industry shown. It is because of this discriminatory nature of inflation that financial data must be adjusted separately by each corporation.

GENERAL PRICE-LEVEL ACCOUNTING
An approach to accounting where adjustments are made to historical costs to account for the general effects of inflation.

CONSTANT-DOLLAR ACCOUNTING
See General Price-Level Accounting.

APPROACHES TO INFLATION

Now that we have seen that the financial statements must be supplemented with information on the effects of inflation, what type of data should be presented? Two approaches are used. Under one approach, known as **general price-level (or constant-dollar) accounting,** adjustments are made to the historical costs to account for the general effects of inflation.

EXHIBIT D.1

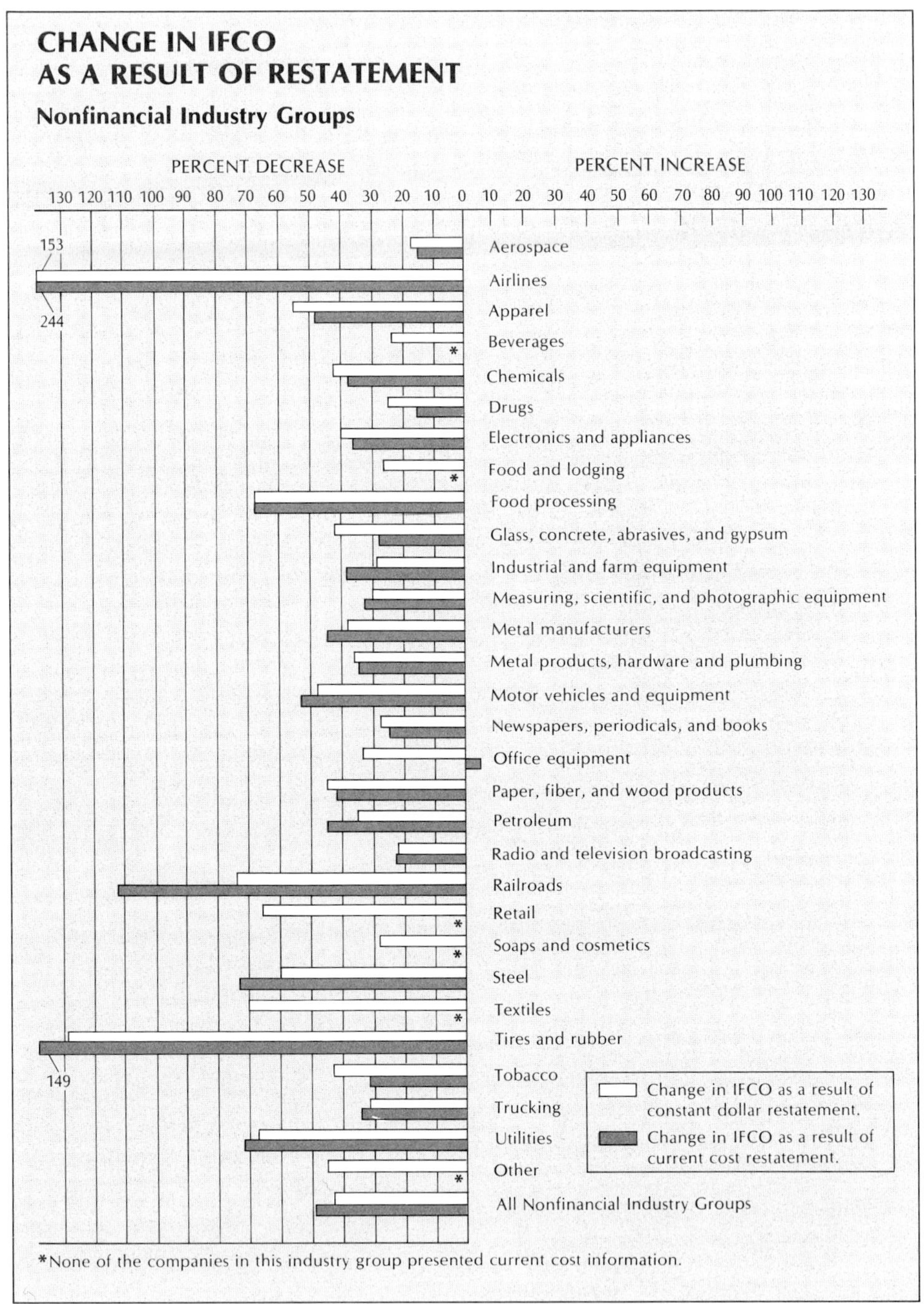

Under the second approach, known as **current-cost (or current value) accounting,** historical costs are ignored and accounts are restated in terms of their current market values. The current value approach thus includes the effects of market supply and demand on each account in measuring the impact of inflation on accounting data. The current value method goes beyond simply measuring inflationary impacts (to be discussed shortly).

CURRENT-COST ACCOUNTING
An approach to accounting that ignores historical costs and restates accounts in terms of their current market values.

CURRENT-VALUE ACCOUNTING
See Current-Cost Accounting.

General Price-Level (Constant-Dollar) Accounting

In 1969, the Accounting Principles Board offered the first authoritative pronouncement aimed toward dealing with inflation. In its Statement No. 3, "Financial Statements Restated for General Price-Level Changes," the APB recommended that corporations follow the general price-level approach to reflect the effects of changing prices in the overall economy. This reflection of general inflation through the periodic adjustment of historical cost records is the objective of price-level accounting.

Monetary Versus Nonmonetary Items. In discussing price-level accounting, a distinction must be made between two types of accounts found on the statement of financial position. The nominal market values of certain accounts, such as cash, accounts receivable, investments in bonds to be held to maturity, and most liabilities, are unaffected by inflation, because they represent the right to receive or the obligation to pay a fixed number of dollars. Such accounts are called **monetary items.** All other asset, liability, or owners' equity accounts represent **nonmonetary items,** because their nominal market values are impacted by inflation. For example, as prices rise, an average package of groceries that could once be purchased for $10 will now cost $20, whereas a cash balance of $10 will remain exactly $10. Exhibit D.2 lists some of the more commonly encountered monetary and nonmonetary items.

MONETARY ITEMS
Accounts that represent the right to receive or the obligation to pay a fixed number of dollars.

NONMONETARY ITEMS
Accounts whose nominal market values are impacted by inflation.

General Price-Level Gains and Losses. As a result of holding monetary items, changes in the general price level give rise to real gains and losses known as **general**

EXHIBIT D.2
Monetary and Nonmonetary Items

	Monetary	Nonmonetary
Assets	Cash Accounts receivable Allowance for doubtful accounts Notes receivable Long-term investment in bonds	Marketable securities Inventories Furniture and fixtures Property, plant, and equipment Accumulated depreciation on all fixed assets
Liabilities	Accounts payable Notes payable Wages payable Taxes payable Bonds payable Premium on bonds payable Discount on bonds payable	Accrued warranty obligation Contingent liabilities
Shareholders' Equity		Common stock Preferred stock Paid-in capital in excess of par Retained earnings

price-level (or purchasing power) gains and losses. The ownership of assets that are monetary items (monetary assets) results in a loss of purchasing power when the general price-level index is rising. On the other hand, the presence of liabilities that are monetary items (monetary liabilities) results in a gain, because fixed-dollar liabilities can be paid with cheaper dollars. For example, if CAM Corporation held $30,000 of accounts receivable at a time that the consumer price index rose from 100 to 120, it would suffer a $6,000 purchasing power loss, because its customers would be able to pay their accounts with dollars worth only five-sixths as much as when they made their purchases. However, if CAM held $30,000 worth of inventory (a nonmonetary item), it would have no loss, because the inventory's value would rise with inflation to the amount of $36,000. Such gains and losses might cancel each other out, but the gains will exceed the losses if the corporation is in a net monetary liability position (monetary liabilities exceed monetary assets), and the losses will exceed the gains if the corporation is in a net monetary asset position (monetary assets exceed monetary liabilities). In exploiting this fact, most nonfinancial corporations are in net monetary liability positions.

GENERAL PRICE-LEVEL GAINS AND LOSSES
Gains and losses that arise from holding monetary items during periods when price levels change.

PURCHASING POWER GAINS AND LOSSES
See General Price-Level Gains and Losses.

Current-Cost Accounting

In 1976, the Securities and Exchange Commission announced its preference for a second viewpoint, believed to be an accurate approach to inflation—current-cost accounting. In its Accounting Series Release No. 190, the SEC required corporations to disclose in their annual report to the SEC certain replacement cost information to reflect the effect of changing prices on its specific industry. This attempt at an accounting basis that would automatically reflect specific inflation is the objective of current-cost accounting.

Specific Indexes Versus General Index. As we saw earlier, different industries appear to be affected differently by inflation. This discriminatory nature also extends to individual assets: Different assets appear to be affected differently by inflation.

This is demonstrated when, during periods of rising prices, an asset's nominal value changes relative to the nominal values of other assets. Thus, adjustment for general inflation (rise in the general price-level index) does not seem to be sufficient to reflect economic reality. However, the economic reality of a rise in the price of a specific asset is due to two distinct causes: The price can rise because of general inflation or because of changes in the market supply and demand for the asset.

Although general price-level accounting measures only the price rise due to general inflation, current-cost accounting includes in its measurement the price rise due to changes in supply and demand. (It is this inclusion of the effects of supply and demand that prevents current-cost accounting from being a technique of measuring true inflation.) By combining general inflation with the action of supply and demand, current-cost accounting develops specific indexes, which measure the rise in prices of a specific asset or class of assets. The specific indexes can then be used to determine the current costs to be disclosed in the financial statements.

REPLACEMENT COST
The cost that an organization would incur to replace its existing assets.

Replacement Costs. The use of replacement costs is an alternative way for companies to determine the current cost of their assets. **Replacement cost** is the cost a corporation would incur to replace its existing assets. Corporations can obtain replacement cost information by asking vendors for the price of identical assets with equal productive capacity. Alternatively, corporations can derive the replacement cost of an asset by adding up the replacement cost of all of the asset's component parts.

If identical assets do not exist because they have been replaced by technologically superior assets, a company can use functional pricing to estimate the replacement costs of its existing assets. Under **functional pricing,** the replacement cost of existing assets is determined as a percentage of the cost of the newer, technologically superior asset. For example, if an old asset can produce only one-half as much as a new, technologically superior asset, the replacement cost of the old asset is considered to be one-half the cost of the new asset.

FUNCTIONAL PRICING
A method of estimating replacement cost where the replacement cost is determined as a percentage of the cost of a newer, technologically superior asset.

By using these more direct techniques, the corporation does not have to find asset-specific indexes to determine current costs. However, we use specific indexes in the illustrations in this appendix to facilitate the computations and maintain consistency between current-cost restatement and general price-level restatement.

Holding Gains and Losses

As a result of holding nonmonetary items, changes in specific indexes give rise to cost savings and dissavings known as **holding gains and losses.** (Compare this to purchasing power gains and losses that result from holding monetary items.) For example, if Alpha Corporation purchased 1,000 units of inventory for $10 each, and later (before the inventory was sold) the corporation's purchase price of the units increased 50 percent to $15 each, Alpha would experience a $5,000 cost savings, because it paid only $10,000 for inventory that otherwise would have cost $15,000. This would be a $5,000 holding gain. If, however, the purchase price of the inventory had *decreased* 50 percent to $5 each, Alpha would have experienced a $5,000 cost dissavings, because it paid $10,000 for inventory that otherwise would have cost only $5,000. This would be a $5,000 holding loss. Thus, as you can see, when the specific indexes decrease, the corporation will have holding losses. Such gains and losses might cancel each other out, or one might outweigh the other. However, because each asset might have a different index, it is impossible to make generalizations about the nature of the overall holding gain or loss.

HOLDING GAINS AND LOSSES
Cost savings and dissavings that occur as a result of holding nonmonetary items.

CURRENT PRACTICE

In 1979, the Financial Accounting Standards Board issued FASB Statement No. 33, prescribing generally accepted practice. Thus, Accounting Principles Board Statement No. 3 has been superseded, and the SEC Accounting Series Release No. 190 has been withdrawn. More recently, the disclosure requirements under FASB 33 have been amended with the release of FASBs 70 and 82. In its original FASB 33 statement, the FASB expressed a need for further experimentation: Preparers and users of financial reports had not yet reached a consensus on the practicality of price-level data or current-cost data. To provide for the additional experience needed by users to enable them to reach a consensus, FASB Statement No. 33 originally required supplemental disclosure of both price-level data and current-cost data. The issuance of FASB 82—"Financial Reporting and Changing Prices: Elimination of

Certain Disclosures"—in November 1984 deleted the requirement for supplementary disclosure of historical cost/constant-dollar information. Companies are required only to disclose information on current-cost/constant purchasing power.

The supplemental disclosure on the effects of inflation has two major parts: information concerning the current year and a summary of selected information from the five most recent years.

ILLUSTRATION OF INFLATION DISCLOSURE

The General Electric Company has been an outspoken proponent of inflation accounting in recent years, because the company believes that the historical cost model does not adequately reflect the impact of inflation on business operation and performance. The company's 1984 annual report contains an extended discussion of inflation and its impact on General Electric. Exhibit D.3 contains excerpts from this report (containing both historical and current-cost information) that vividly illustrate how the company's financial results are affected by inflation. As a result, General Electric's management is actively seeking new operating strategies to counter this inflationary effect. Recent investments in service and manufacturing companies are seen as ways the company can combat the financial impact of inflation.

EVALUATION OF INFLATION ACCOUNTING

Despite the issuance of FASBs 33 and 82, the desirability of publishing inflation-adjusted financial reports remains controversial. Opponents of inflation accounting generally believe that attempts to adjust for inflation are so complex that the resulting numbers are subjective, misleading, and difficult to interpret. They feel that the existence of current-cost and constant-dollar figures serves only to confuse users of financial statements rather than to assist them in decision making.

Supporters of inflation accounting base their position on the principle of economic reality. The existence of inflation in recent years is real and demonstrates the instability of the dollar. To facilitate an efficient allocation of capital in the market, supporters of inflation accounting feel that the historical cost model must be modified to reflect the impact on earnings, productivity, and capital investment of inflation. Without this adjustment, it is difficult, if not impossible, to evaluate the "real" economic performance of companies and their managements. Supporters also believe that corporate managers are more likely to make inappropriate decisions based on historical numbers rather than on the inflation-adjusted ones.

No doubt this controversy will continue in the future as long as inflation is an economic reality. However, there has been evidence in recent years that corporations are becoming believers of inflation accounting. Until three or four years ago, practically all of the attention focused on inflation accounting had concentrated on external financial reporting. However, companies are now examining the usefulness of inflation-adjusted information for internal purposes.

EXHIBIT D.3

Effect of changing prices
For the year ending December 31, 1984

(In millions)	As reported	Adjusted for current costs[A]
Sales of products and services to customers	$27,947	$27,947
Cost of goods sold	19,460	19,560
Selling, general and administrative expense	4,542	4,542
Depreciation, depletion and amortization	1,100	1,386
Operating costs	25,102	25,488
Operating margin	2,845	2,459
Other income	989	989
Interest and other financial charges	(333)	(333)
Earnings before unusual items	3,501	3,115
Unusual items	(145)	(762)
Earnings before income taxes	3,356	2,353
Provision for income taxes	(1,065)	(1,065)
Minority interest	(11)	(9)
Net earnings	$ 2,280	$ 1,279
Earnings per share (in dollars)	$ 5.03	$ 2.82
Share owners' equity at December 31	$12,573	$15,774

[A]In dollars of average 1984 purchasing power.

Selected financial data adjusted for the effect of changing prices in dollars of average 1984 purchasing power

(Dollar amounts in millions; per-share amounts in dollars)	1984	1983	1982	1981	1980
Sales	$27,947	$27,949	$28,524	$31,110	$31,469
Current cost information					
Net earnings before unusual items[a]	1,896	1,609	1,269	1,330	1,262
Net earnings per share before unusual items[a]	4.18	3.54	2.80	2.92	2.77
Share owners' equity at December 31	15,774	16,043	16,025	16,090	16,281
Excess of increase in general price level over increases in specific GE price levels[b]	547	592	584	803	246
Other					
Purchasing power loss on net monetary items	112	84	52	96	249
Dividends per share	2.05	1.96	1.80	1.79	1.87
Market price per share at December 31	56	60	51	31	38
Average Consumer Price Index (CPI-U; 1967 = 100)	311.1	298.4	289.1	272.4	246.8

[a]Unusual items affected current cost earnings in 1984 only. Net earnings and net earnings per share including unusual items in 1984 were $1,279 million and $2.82, respectively

[b]At December 31, 1984, in end-of-year dollars, the current cost of inventory was $5,704 million and of property, plant and equipment was $9,095 million. In dollars of average 1984 purchasing power, the increase that might have been expected from general inflation was more than the increase in specific GE current costs by the amount shown. A similar pattern is shown in the other years.

SUMMARY

- During inflationary periods, historical cost accounting might not adequately serve the needs of users of accounting statements.
- General price-level adjustments can be used to restate historical cost accounting statements into dollars of constant value.
- Current-cost accounting ignores historical purchase prices and is used to restate assets, liabilities, and equities at current replacement value.
- Monetary accounts represent either the right to receive or the obligation to pay a fixed-dollar amount. Nonmonetary accounts represent items whose dollar value changes with inflation.
- Replacement cost represents the sacrifice that would be required to replace the assets used up during a particular time period.
- Holding nonmonetary items during inflationary periods can give rise to either cost savings or dissavings.
- Generally accepted accounting standards require that certain companies provide supplementary data showing the impact of inflation on their financial statements within their annual reports to shareholders.

EXERCISES

D-E1. Distinguish between nominal measures and real measures.

D-E2. Classify the following accounts as monetary or nonmonetary items:

a. Inventory
b. Accounts Receivable
c. Prepaid Expenses
d. Machinery and Equipment
e. Long-Term Debt
f. Common Stock
g. Notes Payable
h. Retained Earnings
i. Cash
j. Buildings

D-E3. Distinguish between a net monetary liability position and a net monetary asset position. Which position would most corporations choose to be in today and why?

D-E4. How are replacement costs determined?

D-E5. Distinguish between the price-level adjustments made for constant-dollar accounting and for current-cost accounting.

APPLICATION

Avon Products, Inc.

When was the last time you answered your door and heard "Avon calling"? Chances are it hasn't been long. Since Avon's founding in 1886, the firm has been selling its products to Avon representatives who sell to customers in their own homes and, frequently nowadays, at work. Being a representative has appealed traditionally to women who wish to earn money but who want to have flexible hours and work close to home. The success of this marketing mode is shown by Avon Products' steadily rising sales, which were more than $3.1 billion in 1984.

The Avon Sales representative is not a company employee; she is an independent contractor who purchases from Avon the merchandise she sells to her customers. Each sales campaign lasts two weeks in the United States. At the end of each campaign, the representative forwards her order to an assigned distribution center. Avon assembles the merchandise and delivers it to the representative, who then takes the ordered goods to the customer, collects payment, and forwards the money in fulfillment of her account when she places an order at the end of the next sales campaign.

The prosperity of both the company and the representatives is enhanced by the efforts of district sales managers. These district managers are Avon employees who receive a salary as well as a commission based upon sales of the representatives in their charge. Thus, it is to everyone's advantage that the district manager actively recruits, trains, and rewards sales representatives.

Avon is committed to helping those representatives improve their earnings which are linked to sales revenues. The representatives can earn from 35 percent to 50 percent of their customer sales, depending on the size of their orders for each sales campaign. They can also earn a five percent bonus on the net sales of each new representative they introduce to Avon. Finally, representatives are encouraged to improve their earnings by taking responsibility for sales in larger areas, selling to 200 or more homes.

In view of current social and consumer trends in the United States, Avon must do more than employ strategies to increase revenues. With more women entering the labor force, it has become more difficult to sell to them at home, as well as to recruit them as representatives. This has led the management of Avon to develop new business

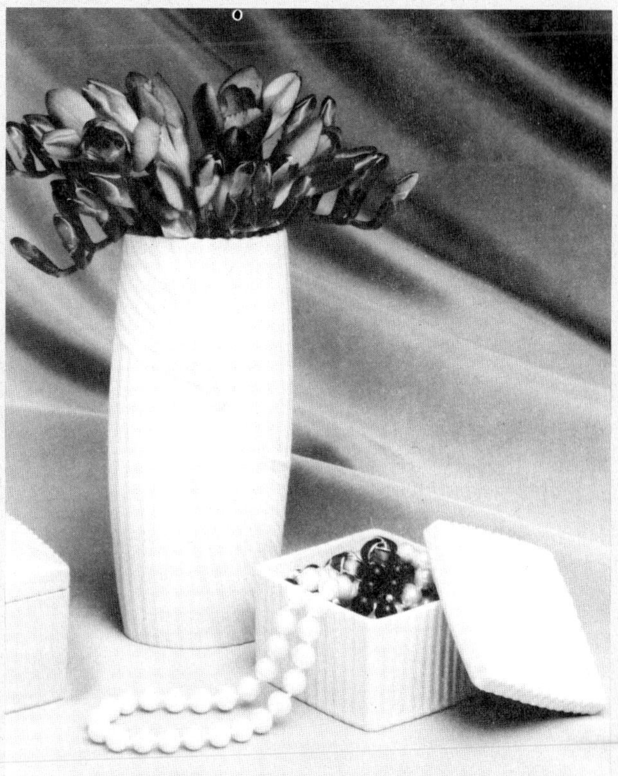

EXHIBIT 1

PART A

The consolidated summary of earnings adjusted for changing prices for the year ending December 31, 1984, follows (in millions):

	As shown in the financial statements (historical cost)	Adjusted for changes in specific prices (current cost)
Net sales	$3,141.3	$3,141.3
Cost of goods sold	1,330.4	1,372.0
Marketing, distribution and administrative expenses	1,435.0	1,458.0
Interest income	35.3	35.3
Interest expense	(54.6)	(54.6)
Other income (deductions)—net	(20.4)	(20.4)
Taxes on earnings	154.5	154.5
Net earnings	$ 181.7	$ 117.1
Income tax rate	46.0%	56.9%
Depreciation included in:		
Cost of goods sold	$ 39.2	$ 60.4
Marketing, distribution and administrative expenses	33.3	56.3
	$ 72.5	$ 116.7
Purchasing power gain on net monetary items		$ 22.0
Increase in current cost of inventory and property held during the year		$ 135.3
Effect of increase in the general price level		72.2
Increase in current cost over rate of increase in the general price level		$ 63.1
Adjustment—foreign currency translation		$ (54.5)
At December 31, 1984:		
Inventories		$ 510.9
Property—net of accumulated depreciation		$1,416.4

PART B

Selected financial data adjusted for changing prices in average 1984 dollars (in millions, except per share amounts):

	Year ended December 31				
	1984	1983	1982	1981	1980
Net sales	$3,141.3	$3,261.1	$3,376.2	$3,112.2	$3,239.1
Net earnings	117.1	144.8	158.5	239.0	265.2
Earnings per share	1.40	1.73	2.07	3.78	4.41
Purchasing power gain on net monetary items	22.0	19.1	9.9	8.3	3.7
Increase in current cost over (under) increase in the general price level	63.1	232.3	130.0	(.1)	(29.8)
Adjustment—foreign currency translation	(54.5)	(53.5)	(171.4)	(75.1)	(2.4)
Net assets, December 31	1,789.2	2,065.8	1,871.8	1,460.3	1,595.8
Dividends per share	2.00	2.09	2.69	3.42	3.72
Market price, December 31	21.57	25.76	28.53	33.16	41.08
Average consumer price index (1967 = 100)	311.1	298.4	289.1	272.4	246.8

EXHIBIT 2

Consolidated Statement of Financial Position
Avon Products, Inc. and Subsidiaries
(in millions of dollars)

	December 31 1984	December 31 1983
Assets		
Current assets		
Cash	$ 25.0	$ 29.3
Short-term investments	99.5	170.5
Accounts receivable (less allowance for doubtful accounts of $29.7 and $20.6)	299.9	309.7
Inventories		
Finished goods	276.6	259.5
Raw material	189.8	188.6
	466.4	448.1
Prepaid expenses	154.1	126.6
Total current assets	1,044.9	1,084.2
Property		
Land	41.7	44.9
Building and improvements	549.2	529.8
Equipment	485.2	413.0
Construction in progress	57.6	70.9
	1,133.7	1,058.6
Less accumulated depreciation	326.0	281.0
	807.7	777.6
Excess of cost over net assets acquired	446.8	413.4
Deferred charges	138.3	109.2
	$2,437.7	$2,384.4
Liabilities and Shareholders' Equity		
Current liabilities		
Notes payable	$ 96.4	$ 71.2
Accounts payable	171.7	203.3
Accrued expenses	143.9	114.6
Accrued compensation	40.4	40.7
Retail sales and other taxes	67.2	74.9
Taxes on earnings	123.9	104.1
Total current liabilities	643.5	608.8
Long-term debt	440.5	331.3
Foreign employees benefit plans	38.9	40.8
Other liabilities	15.6	11.2
Deferred income taxes	142.1	119.2
Shareholders' equity		
Common stock, par value $.50		
Authorized 200,000,000 shares		
Issued 85,421,032 and 84,897,354 shares	42.7	42.4
Additional paid-in capital	466.5	461.1
Adjustement—foreign currency translation	(153.6)	(132.0)
Retained earnings	925.5	901.6
Treasury stock, at cost—5,457,332 shares	(124.0)	
Total shareholders' equity	1,157.1	1,273.1
	$2,437.7	$2,384.4

EXHIBIT 2

Continued

Consolidated Statement of Earnings and Retained Earnings

Avon Products, Inc. and Subsidiaries
(in millions, except per share amounts)

	Year Ended December 31		
	1984	**1983**	**1982**
Net sales:			
United States	$2,075.9	$2,106.4	$1,976.3
International	1,065.4	1,020.3	1,160.4
	3,141.3	3,126.7	3,136.7
Cost of goods sold	1,330.4	1,363.2	1,375.7
Gross profit	1,810.9	1,763.5	1,761.0
Marketing, distribution and administrative expenses	1,435.0	1,409.3	1,342.1
Operating profit	375.9	354.2	418.9
Interest income	35.3	40.1	41.4
Interest expense	(54.6)	(46.8)	(39.8)
Other income (deductions)—net	(20.4)	(27.3)	(38.5)
Earnings before taxes	336.2	320.2	382.0
Taxes on earnings	154.5	147.3	195.4
Net earnings	181.7	172.9	186.6
Cash dividends	157.8	149.7	174.5
Addition to retained earnings	23.9	23.2	12.1
Retained earnings, January 1	901.6	878.4	859.9
Businesses acquired			6.4
As restated, January 1			866.3
Retained earnings, December 31	$ 925.5	$ 901.6	$ 878.4
Per share of capital stock:			
Net earnings	$ 2.16	$ 2.06	$ 2.43
Cash dividends	2.00	2.00	2.50
Average shares outstanding	83.84	83.58	76.75

strategies, such as selling more effectively to working women and using other distribution channels besides direct selling.

World-wide inflation has also had an impact on Avon's revenues and earnings. Exhibit 1 (taken from Avon's 1984 annual report) summarizes the effects of inflation on Avon Products, Inc. Part A shows two single-step versions of Avon's statement of earnings, prepared following historical cost and current-cost assumptions, respectively. Here only cost of goods sold and depreciation expense have been restated to current-cost bases. In accordance with FASB No. 33, all items are assumed to accrue evenly throughout the year. All other items have been left unchanged.

It is important to note that cost of goods sold and depreciation expense increase for the restatement to current cost. This means that specific prices are increasing—the company is facing a period of inflation. As a result of this inflation, the company's real earnings are less than the nominal (historical cost) earnings. This is shown in the restatement of net earnings: The restated net earnings figure is less than historical cost net earnings.

Part B of Exhibit 1 shows a five-year summary of selected financial data adjusted for changing specific prices. Here we can assess any trends in the company's *real* results. As shown by the growth in the consumer price index, Avon has had to cope not only with inflation (rise in the consumer price index) but also with an increasing rate of inflation (speed of rise in the consumer price index).

Avon Products, Inc., obviously believes such inflation-adjusted information is valuable to its shareholders, since it places the data within the financial review section of its annual report *preceding* the traditional historical-cost financial statements. (Ordinarily a corporation places the FASB No. 33 disclosure in the footnote section of the annual report following the financial statements.) Following this financial review section are the consolidated financial statements of Avon Products, Inc. (reproduced in Exhibit 2).

Looking at Avon's consolidated statement of financial position at December 31, 1984, we see a significant amount of liabilities (debt ratio = 52.53 percent). Corporations frequently use such debt to increase the return earned on shareholders' equity. All that is necessary to accomplish this is that the borrowed resources be invested to earn profits in excess of the interest expense due on the loan. The excess profits then become additional earnings to the shareholders which in turn increase the rate earned on shareholders' equity. In this case, most debt is current (long-term debt is only 34.39 percent of all liabilities), and interest payments are lower than they would be if the debt were primarily long-term (since many current liabilities, such as accounts payable, are interest-free). As a result, assets are earning in excess of interest costs, and return on shareholders' equity (ROE = 14.95 percent) exceeds return on investment (ROI = 7.54 percent) by a wide margin.

To handle all of the currently maturing debt, Avon carries a high level of current assets (42.86 percent of all assets are current assets), of which cash and short-term investments represent a significant portion (11.92 percent). Undoubtedly these short-term investments are responsible for the $35.3 million of interest income Avon realized in 1984.

This high level of current assets also enables Avon to pay out high cash dividends to its shareholders. In 1984, the company distributed $157.8 million in dividends, representing a payout ratio of 86.85 percent. Thus, Avon shareholders enjoy not only a high return on their equity, but also a high level of cash flows from their investment. This is an indication of good management: The company must be managing its resources well to be able to provide both of these benefits. Therefore, with the company managing its resources this well and the shareholders continually receiving high dividends, Avon shareholders should be pleased with their investments for many years to come.

Exercises

1. In Exhibit 1, Part A, Avon's effective income tax rate is shown to increase upon restatement to current-cost basis. Why is this so?

2. Avon Products, Inc., has maintained a high level of dividend payouts. Is such a high dividend payout ratio in the shareholders' best interests?

3. The price/earnings (P/E) ratio has become a very popular analysis tool in recent years. How might one go about calculating a *real* P/E ratio. (that is, one adjusted for the effects of general inflation)? What would Avon's real P/E ratio be for 1983 and 1984?

4. Calculate the current and quick ratios for Avon Products, Inc., at December 31, 1984. Are they within tolerable limits? What does this say about Avon's short-term liquidity in light of the company's high current liability burden?

PART FIVE
COST SYSTEMS

5

INTRODUCTION TO MANAGEMENT ACCOUNTING

CHAPTER OBJECTIVES
After studying Chapter 19, you should understand the following:

1. The difference between financial accounting and management accounting.
2. The concepts of planning and control.
3. The components of product cost for a manufacturing firm.
4. The difference between product cost and period cost.
5. The types of accounts used in keeping the books for a manufacturing company.
6. The kinds of financial statements prepared by a manufacturing company.
7. The variety of cost classification systems and how they are used for decision making.

Until now, we have focused on accounting for wholesalers and retailers. Additionally, we have described financial statements that provide information to external and internal users—the statement of financial position, the income statement, and the statement of changes in financial position. We now shift our discussion of accounting in two important ways. First, we will discuss accounting in manufacturing firms. Unlike wholesalers and retailers, manufacturers both produce and sell products. Consequently, the accounting requirements of a manufacturing company are quite different from those of a retailer. Second, we will focus more on the managerial use of accounting information.

FINANCIAL VERSUS MANAGEMENT ACCOUNTING

MANAGEMENT ACCOUNTING
Accounting directed at individuals internal to an organization.

Accounting can be broadly divided into two areas: financial accounting and management accounting. The primary difference between these areas lies in the different user groups to which each is directed. Financial accounting focuses on the needs of individuals external to the firm, such as shareholders, creditors, and the government. **Management accounting** is directed at individuals internal to the firm, that is, management. The information contained in reports for external users—the financial statements—might not provide all of the information required by a firm's management. Management accounting serves to bridge the gap between the needs of internal management and the information provided by a firm's financial accounting system. This is not meant to imply that financial and management accounting are unrelated. In practice, changes in one often have an effect on the other. Management accounting should be thought of as an extension of financial accounting, but it differs from financial accounting in some significant ways, as summarized in Exhibit 19.1.

As Exhibit 19.1 illustrates, the key point to note about management accounting is its flexibility. Because management accounting is not bound by law or generally accepted accounting principles, information can be prepared and presented in any way useful to managers in planning, controlling, and decision making.

NATURE OF PLANNING AND CONTROLLING

PLANNING
The process of setting goals and developing strategies to accomplish those goals.

GOAL
Something you would like to accomplish within a particular time period.

PLAN
A course of action developed by a manager.

Planning is the process of setting goals and developing strategies, or approaches, for attaining those goals. A **goal** is something you would like to accomplish within a particular time period. In other words, it is a target—something to strive for. Besides setting goals in the planning process, managers decide how they will go about accomplishing their goals. The course of action developed by the manager is called a **plan.**

Planning is vital for the success of a company. Consider two manufacturers of toy airplanes, Big Wing Company and Hifly Company. In 1985, each produced and sold 100,000 airplanes. An increase in demand caused sales to rise to 150,000 airplanes in 1986. It costs each firm $20 in materials and $10 in labor (2 hours @ $5) to produce one airplane, which sells for $50. Big Wing Company makes no plans for 1986 and assumes it will sell 100,000 airplanes. Much to the surprise of Big Wing managers, sales volume is up. To satisfy the extra demand, management has 100 employees work overtime (at $7.50 per overtime hour). Hifly Company, on the other hand, has planned for the extra demand and has hired 50 new employees at the base rate of $5 per hour. None of Hifly's employees are required to work overtime. At the end of 1986, Big Wing and Hifly summarize their performances as follows:

	Big Wing Company	Hifly Company
Sales (150,000 airplanes @ $50)	$ 7,500,000	$ 7,500,000
Material costs (150,000 @ $20)	(3,000,000)	(3,000,000)
Labor costs		
Base rate (@ $5)	(1,000,000)	(1,500,000)
Overtime (@ $7.50)	(750,000)	–0–
Profit	$ 2,750,000	$ 3,000,000

It is obvious from this example that the lack of planning has caused Big Wing Company to lose $250,000 of profit it might otherwise have earned. Had there been other consequences of the lack of planning (such as greater material waste during the overtime hours), Big Wing might have realized an even smaller profit than planned.

CONTROLLING Assuring that plans are completed and goals are achieved.

Controlling is assuring that plans are completed and goals are achieved; plans alone do not assure that work will get done. Control is implemented by comparing actual results to planned results and correcting any significant differences. For example, assume Hifly had predicted its performance to be as follows:

	Planned	Actual	Difference
Sales	$8,000,000	$7,500,000	$ (500,000)
Material costs	(3,000,000)	(3,000,000)	–0–
Labor costs	(2,500,000)	(1,500,000)	1,000,000
Profit	$2,500,000	$3,000,000	$ 500,000

EXHIBIT 19.1
Differences Between Financial Accounting and Management Accounting

Aspect	Financial Accounting	Management Accounting
Users	Groups external to firm	Internal management
Purpose	To provide useful financial information to external statement users	To provide management with information for use in planning, controlling, and decision making
Data	Historically oriented	Future oriented
Approach to information gathering	Primarily by analysis of corporate financial records	Interdisciplinary—using techniques of accounting, operations research, economics, finance, and behavioral sciences
Guiding principles	Generally accepted accounting principles	No binding set of principles
Necessity of activity	Required by law, e.g. SEC, IRS	Required to ensure success and profitability
End product	Historically oriented financial statements	Produces data useful for management; no definitive product
Cost basis used	Resources given up in return for goods and services acquired	Resources sacrificed to attain a particular objective

Keeping the Score

Until the 1970s, most controllers were considered "bean counters" or "scorekeepers." Their primary function was to keep track of how the organization was doing financially and provide financial information to other managers to assist them in decision making. Controllers were not part of the top management team, nor was their function considered to be particularly challenging or critical to organizational success.

However, the increased inflation rate during the 1970s and early 1980s, coupled with high interest rates throughout the latter half of the 1970s, has made controllers more visible. Managing companies in times of high cost capital and high inflation requires a keen understanding of a firm's financial structure and a creative approach to the management of financial resources. Controllers are particularly equipped to be of assistance. Although they are still responsible for "keeping score," controllers are now more involved in decision making. In fact, most of the people being promoted to the presidency or chairmanship of large companies in the 1980s have a background in accounting, and many of them are former controllers.

In fact, the company earned $500,000 more profit than anticipated. To understand how and why this favorable event occurred, management would analyze the differences between actual and planned sales and costs. The results of this analysis will help with future planning.

Managers can control their organizations by continually monitoring the use and performance of resources—especially people and money—and providing feedback to all concerned if the plan is not fulfilled. Control systems are not intended to be punitive; that is, such systems are not designed to catch people doing a bad job and punish them. Rather, managers want to provide employees with timely information about their performance to assist their self-development and to ensure that the organization keeps moving forward.

The following are characteristics of an effective control system:

- Differences between planned and actual results are reported as promptly as possible.
- The system is as objective as possible so that feedback is not biased and reflects reality.
- Feedback indicates what actions should be taken to correct any unfavorable deviations from goals or plans.

The management accounting process can assist managers in planning and control in many ways. In fact, each of the remaining chapters of the text describes in detail the various applications of management accounting concepts and techniques in decision making.

■ PRODUCT COSTING

One of the most fundamental uses of accounting information is product costing. The determination of product cost is an important issue to both financial accountants and management accountants. Financial accountants use product cost information to determine inventory values and profits for external reporting purposes, and management accountants and other managers use product cost information in pricing and in determining product profitability.

The accurate determination of product costs is of great importance, and errors can have far-reaching effects. Consider the following example. Alpha Corporation, which makes tiny toy space ships, has determined it costs $50 to produce and sell one unit of its product, Starship X. Consequently, a sales price of $55 per unit is established. At the end of the year, after Alpha has sold 100,000 units of Starship X, it learns that the true cost of production is $75 per unit. Thus, by incorrectly setting the sales price, Alpha has incurred a loss of $2 million.

Up to now we have touched only lightly on product costing, and this discussion has been in the context of either a retail business or service company. Even though many of the accounting concepts and techniques previously described for retail and service companies are equally appropriate for a manufacturing company, accounting for manufacturing operations is more complex. The increased complexity results from the nature of the production process in a manufacturing company and the impact this process has on how a manufacturing company accounts for inventory and cost of goods sold.

PRODUCTS AND PROCESSES

Products can be tangible or intangible. A tangible product, such as a car or an appliance, has form and substance. In contrast, an intangible product or service cannot be held or felt. For example, lawyers provide an intangible product in the form of legal services. Although services do not have a physical form, they involve the conversion of scarce resources (the time expended by the legal staff) into a finished product (the settlement of a suit or the resolution of some legal matter).

Because products can possess many characteristics, the processes used to create them vary. In addition, the input required to produce a product or service is diverse. Despite such diversity, any tangible product can be produced from four basic input items: labor, material, manufacturing overhead, and administrative overhead.

The nature of the production process and the relative amount of each input item used depends on the business. There are basically three types of businesses—sales, service, and manufacturing. Exhibit 19.2 outlines the production process and the relative use of items of input for each type of business.

COMPONENTS OF PRODUCT COST

Product costs are all the costs necessary to complete a product. These costs are also considered to be inventory costs. Until a product is sold, the costs incurred to purchase or manufacture it are accumulated in inventory. Inventory is an asset and, as such, is reflected in a company's statement of financial position. Once the product is sold, the costs in inventory are transferred to the income statement as part of cost of goods sold—an expense account. This flow of costs through inventory and the statement of financial position to cost of goods sold and the income statement is referred to as the cost flow concept.

A retailer or wholesaler purchases goods, such as packaged foods, jewelry, or showroom cars, from a manufacturer or supplier for resale without changing the goods' form. Unsold goods are held in merchandise inventory, and the cost of goods sold is charged off to the income statement as an expense. Any noninventory costs

EXHIBIT 19.2

Types of Business and the Production Process

Type of Business	Specific Example	Major Input Items Used in Production	Nature of Conversion Process	End Product
Service	Auto repair shop	• Labor • Materials	Skilled labor used to repair car is largest cost. Customer also pays for material.	Repaired car
Manufacturing	Cola	• Materials • Labor • Manufacturing overhead	Raw materials converted into a finished product (cola) through the use of mechanized production process.	A six-pack of cola
Sales/Wholesaler	Fruit and vegetable dealer	• Materials • Labor	Dealer purchases produce from the farmers and, in turn, sells it to the large grocery stores. Labor plays a significant role in process, but overhead normally is low.	Fresh vegetables and fruits for grocery stores
Sales/Retailer	Department store	• Materials • Labor • Administrative overhead	Store purchases finished goods from manufacturer or wholesaler and subsequently sells the goods to customers at a higher price. Salespeople are required in the process, as well as store space and administrative help.	Various goods for consumers

incurred to sell the product are classified as operating expenses and deducted from gross profit to arrive at operating income before interest and taxes.

In a service business, all expenses incurred to provide the service are treated as operating expenses and are deducted from sales to arrive at operating income before taxes and interest. No product inventory accounts are maintained.

Unlike a sales or service organization, a manufacturing firm obtains saleable products by producing them in a factory. To do this, the manufacturer must buy raw materials, hire workers to convert the raw materials into finished goods, and provide a factory with the necessary equipment to house the production process. In a retail or wholesale firm, the cost of goods sold is determined by the amounts paid to suppliers or manufacturers. In a manufacturing process, the cost of goods sold is the sum of the costs of the raw materials used, the labor hired, and the factory and its equipment used to produce the products. Exhibit 19.3 contrasts the product cost flows of a manufacturing and a retail merchandising firm. Understanding the nature of direct materials, direct labor, and manufacturing overhead is the key to understanding and using manufacturing cost data, and each is explored in this chapter.

A second difference between sales and manufacturing firms is shown in Exhibit 19.3 in the inventory accounts. Manufacturing firms have three types of inventory: unprocessed raw materials, unfinished work in process, and finished goods.

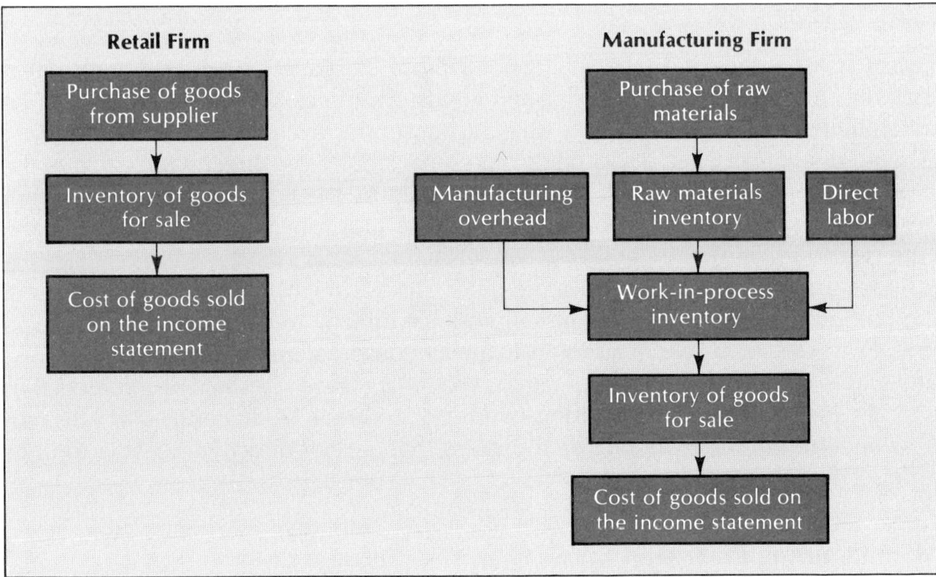

EXHIBIT 19.3

The first two—raw materials and work in process—are not found in retail or wholesale firms, since such firms obtain all their products in finished form.

PRODUCT COSTS IN A MANUFACTURING ENVIRONMENT

In a manufacturing process, the total cost of goods produced is equal to the cost of raw materials, direct labor costs, and factory overhead incurred in the production cycle. These three costs are collectively referred to as factory costs, manufacturing costs, or product costs.

Raw Materials

Direct materials (also known as **raw materials**) comprise all of the important raw materials that can be traced directly to the manufacture of a product. Examples include iron ore in steelmaking, steel sheets in automobile manufacturing, and integrated circuits in computer manufacturing.

DIRECT MATERIALS
All of the important raw materials that can be traced directly to the manufacture of a product.

RAW MATERIALS
See Direct Materials.

The cost of the materials consumed is measured in the same way a retail or wholesale firm measures its cost of goods purchased for resale, that is, the sum of the purchase price, plus transportation, and applicable discounts. Any of the inventory methods discussed in Chapter 9—LIFO, FIFO, weighted average, or specific identification—can be used to value the raw materials consumed in the production process.

In addition to the major raw materials traceable to a product, other materials might be required that cannot be easily traced to a specific product or batch of products. Examples are miscellaneous supplies, such as glue or nails in a furniture plant. Such materials are known as indirect materials and are accounted for as part of manufacturing overhead. **Indirect materials** are defined as all those materials costs incurred in a manufacturing process that are not traced directly to production of given units or batches of products.

INDIRECT MATERIALS
Those material costs incurred in a manufacturing process that are not traced directly to production of given units or batches of products.

Direct Labor

DIRECT LABOR
Total labor charges for those employees who work with direct materials to convert them into finished goods.

Direct labor is the total labor charges for those employees who work with direct materials to convert them into finished goods. Examples include assemblers in an automobile factory, welders in a shipyard, and bricklayers in a construction firm. As with direct materials, direct labor represents labor costs directly traceable to the products produced. Generally, workers are paid by the hour, and the direct labor cost includes the base pay for the hours worked plus fringe benefits such as health care, vacation time, and pension payments.

Like costs of direct materials, some labor charges might be incurred that benefit the production process but are difficult to trace directly to production of any given unit. Examples are wages of handlers in a warehouse, salaries of factory supervisors, and wages of janitorial personnel. Such labor charges are classified as indirect labor and are included in manufacturing overhead. **Indirect labor** consists of all labor costs incurred in the manufacturing process that are not directly traceable to units produced.

INDIRECT LABOR
All labor costs incurred in the manufacturing process that are not directly traceable to units produced.

Manufacturing Overhead

MANUFACTURING OVERHEAD
All manufacturing costs other than direct materials and direct labor.

Manufacturing overhead consists of all manufacturing costs other than costs of direct materials and direct labor and includes all costs that cannot be traced directly to specific units or batches of products. Manufacturing overhead (sometimes called factory overhead or factory burden) can include costs that, although theoretically direct in nature, are not worth the effort to trace to specific products because of the amounts involved. Exhibit 19.4 shows examples of manufacturing overhead costs.

Note in Exhibit 19.4 that overtime premiums are normally included in manufacturing overhead. Including such premiums in overhead rather than direct labor costs is common. The usual reason for overtime is a general backlog of work to be done. The fact that a particular product or batch of products is produced during the overtime hours does not mean that a higher cost should apply only to those products. The fact that the factory is working overtime should be reflected in a slightly higher average cost for all units produced, not just those that are produced during the overtime hours. For cost accounting to make sense, careful decisions are required when costs are classified as either direct or indirect to a cost objective. Such decisions are commonly required when production costs are accounted for.

Prime Costs and Conversion Costs

PRIME COSTS
Direct materials plus direct labor costs.

CONVERSION COSTS
Direct labor plus factory overhead costs.

Manufacturing costs can be divided into two categories: prime and conversion. **Prime costs** include direct materials and direct labor costs, and **conversion costs**

EXHIBIT 19.4

- Repairs and maintenance on factory buildings
- Taxes and insurance on factory buildings
- Depreciation on factory buildings and equipment
- Indirect materials (cleaners, lubricants, glue, nails)
- Indirect labor (supervisors' salaries, timekeepers, stockroom personnel, janitors, cost accountants)
- Overtime premiums
- Utilities
- Disposal of waste materials

include direct labor and factory overhead costs. Prime costs are considered those costs directly traceable to production. Conversion costs are considered those costs required to turn raw materials into finished products.

PRODUCT VERSUS PERIOD COSTS

Costs are often classified as either product or period costs.

Product Costs

Product costs are those costs associated with the production of inventory and usually include direct materials, direct labor, and manufacturing overhead. Such costs are similar to the purchase cost of inventory in a retail firm. The costs become expenses only when the products are sold. Until then, they are classified as inventory on the statement of financial position.

PRODUCT COSTS
Those costs associated with the production of inventory, usually inclusive of direct materials, direct labor, and manufacturing overhead.

Period Costs

Period costs (sometimes referred to as nonmanufacturing expenses) are those costs that are considered an expense of the period in which they are incurred. Most selling and administrative costs are considered period costs. **Administrative costs** are those expenditures incurred for general administration of the company. Examples are central office salaries, legal and accounting fees, and depreciation on the general office facilities. All firms have some administrative costs. **Selling costs** (sometimes referred to as selling expenses) are those expenditures required to obtain and fill customer orders for finished goods. Examples are sales staff salaries, delivery and storage costs, depreciation on sales staff automobiles, and advertising costs. Often a fine line exists between selling and administrative and production costs. For example, storage of finished products is often included in selling costs, since the production cycle has ended when the goods are placed in the warehouse. On the other hand, raw materials storage is often classified as a production cost.

PERIOD COSTS
Those costs considered an expense of the period in which they are incurred.

ADMINISTRATIVE COSTS
Those expenditures incurred for general administration of the company.

SELLING COSTS
Those expenditures required to obtain and fill customer orders for finished goods.

The actual timing of sales does not affect the time at which period costs become an expense as it does with product costs. It can be argued that treatment of all selling and administrative expenses as period costs is improper in terms of matching expense with revenue. For example, it is difficult to argue that advertising expenditures benefit only the time period in which the expenditure is made. Clearly, future time periods are also benefited in most cases. However, linking advertising benefits to future time periods is very difficult, and the principle of conservatism dictates that the expenditure be treated as an expense of the time period in which it is incurred.

Exhibit 19.5 presents a diagram of product and period costs and their relationship to the income statement and statement of financial position in a manufacturing firm.

MANUFACTURING ACCOUNTS

Inventory Accounts

A manufacturer can use any of the inventory accounting methods discussed in Chapter 9 for recording inventories of raw materials, work in process, and finished goods. Further, these accounts can be maintained on either a periodic or perpetual basis. For illustrative purposes, we will use the first-in, first-out inventory costing method with periodic inventory procedures.

EXHIBIT 19.5

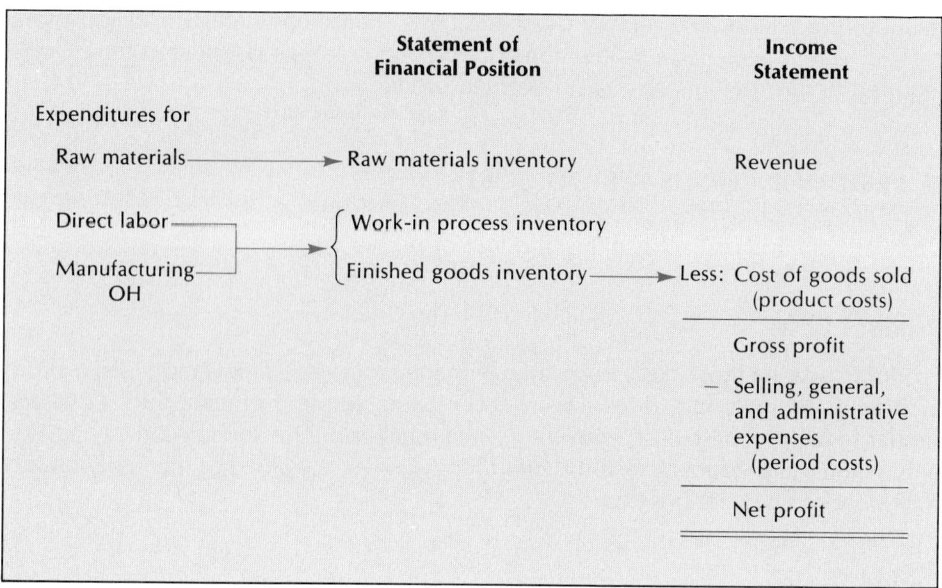

Raw Materials Inventory

RAW MATERIALS INVENTORY
Materials purchased for use in the production process.

Raw materials inventory is the term applied to materials purchased for use in the production process. Accounting for raw materials is very similar to accounting for inventories in the case of retail firms. Purchases of raw materials, transportation charges, purchase discounts, and purchase returns and allowances are all charged to representative accounts just as they are in retail firms. All of these accounts are charged to cost of production at year-end. Raw materials consumed during the year must be equal to the beginning balance of raw materials plus net purchases of material less the ending balance in raw materials. (Recall that cost of goods sold in a retail firm is equal to beginning inventory plus purchases less ending inventory under periodic procedures.)

The worksheet in Exhibit 19.6 illustrates the bookkeeping required for the Barron Manufacturing Company, manufacturers of Crazy Quilt dolls, for the year ending December 31, 1985. In addition to using the balances in the trial balance columns of Exhibit 19.6, assume that the 12/31/85 raw material inventory of Barron was $65,000.

The 1/1 raw materials inventory is added and the 12/31 raw materials inventory is subtracted within the cost of goods manufactured columns on the worksheet. These figures are labeled 1 and 2 on the worksheet. The raw materials purchase costs are carried to the cost of goods manufactured columns as item 3.

Work-in-Process Inventory

WORK IN PROCESS
The inventory of products started but not yet finished at a given point in time.

Work in process represents the inventory of products started but not yet finished. For Barron, work in process represents the amount of unfinished Crazy Quilt dolls on hand. To determine raw materials inventory, all that Barron needed to do was to physically count the quantities of material on hand and value the inventory by reference to purchase documents. Work in process differs from raw materials in two important aspects. First, no purchase documents exist. Second, since work in process represents only partially completed products, some estimate of the degree

EXHIBIT 19.6

BARRON MANUFACTURING COMPANY
Worksheet for the Year Ending December 31, 1985

Account Titles	Trial Balance		Adjustments		Cost of Goods Manufactured		Income Statement		Statement of Financial Position	
	Debit	Credit	Debit	Credit	Debit	Credit	Debit	Credit	Debit	Credit
Cash	47,000								47,000	
Accounts receivable	102,000								102,000	
Allow. for uncoll. accts.		1,000		1,040[e]						2,040
Prepaid rent	24,000			12,000[f]					12,000	
Inventories										
Raw materials	50,000				50,000[1]	65,000[2]			65,000	
Work in process	75,000				75,000[4]	99,200[5]			99,200	
Finished goods	80,000						80,000[6]	53,000[7]	53,000	
Factory building	500,000								500,000	
Accum. deprec.—fac. bldg.		250,000		10,000[a]						260,000
Factory equipment	300,000								300,000	
Accum. depre.—fac. equip.		100,000		20,000[b]						120,000
Office building	25,000								25,000	
Accum. deprec.—office bldg.		15,000		1,000[c]						16,000
Land	100,000								100,000	
Accounts payable		45,000								45,000
Long-term loan (12%)		200,000								200,000
Common stock		300,000								300,000
Retained earnings 1/1		276,000								276,000
Sales		575,000						575,000		
Raw materials purchases	100,000				100,000[3]					
Transportation in	5,000				5,000[3]					
Purchase discounts		4,000				4,000[3]				
Direct labor	120,000		10,000[g]		130,000					
Indirect labor	10,000				10,000					
Factory super. salaries	30,000				30,000					
Repairs	10,000				10,000					
Utilities	48,000				36,000		12,000			
Advertising	25,000						25,000			
Sales staff salaries	40,000						40,000			
Administrative salaries	50,000						50,000			
Income tax expense	25,000						25,000			
	1,766,000	1,766,000								
Depreciation expense										
Factory building			10,000[a]		10,000					
Factory equipment			20,000[b]		20,000					
Office building			1,000[c]				1,000			
Bad debt expense			1,040[e]				1,040			
Interest expense			24,000[d]				24,000			
Interest payable				24,000[d]						24,000
Rent expense			12,000[f]				12,000			
Wages payable				10,000[g]						10,000
			78,040	78,040	476,000	168,200				
Cost of goods manufactured						307,800	307,800			
					476,000	476,000	577,840	628,000		
Net income							50,160			50,160
							628,000	628,000	1,303,200	1,303,200

[1]To add 1/1 raw materials inventory to cost of goods manufactured
[2]To subtract 12/31 raw materials inventory from cost of goods manufactured
[3]To add raw materials purchased to cost of goods manufactured
[4]To add 1/1 work in process to cost of goods manufactured
[5]To subtract 12/31 work in process from cost of goods manufactured
[6]To add 1/1 finished goods inventory to cost of goods sold
[7]To subtract 12/31 finished goods inventory from cost of goods sold

[a]To recognize depreciation on factory building
[b]To recognize depreciation on factory equipment
[c]To recognize depreciation on office bulding
[d]To recognize interest expense and interest payable
[e]To increase allowance for uncollectibles to estimate
[f]To recognize rent expense
[g]To recognize wages owed at year-end and expense

of completion is required to assign a value to the inventory. Barron must estimate the amount of direct materials cost, direct labor, and factory overhead contained within each partially completed doll.

Direct Materials Cost. Direct materials cost can be determined by reference to a listing of materials required for each doll and when that material is introduced into the production process. To illustrate, let's assume that Barron places all direct materials into the dolls when each doll is started through the production process. At December 31, 1985, Barron has 4,000 incomplete dolls in production. Each doll requires $5 of raw materials. Therefore, the direct materials component of work in process is $20,000.

Direct Labor Cost. The amount of labor required to produce a product is normally given as an hourly amount. Multiplying the hourly amount by the wage rate per hour provides a direct labor cost per finished unit. In Barron's case, 1.5 hours of direct labor at a cost of $12 per hour are required to complete each doll. To determine the direct labor cost of the work in process, an estimate of the average percentage of completion of the unfinished production is required. Barron estimates that on average, the 4,000 unfinished dolls are 60 percent complete. With this estimate, Barron determines its 12/31/85 direct labor component of work in process as $43,200 (1.5 hrs. × $12/hr. × 4000 dolls × 60% completion level).

Manufacturing Overhead Cost. Unlike direct materials and direct labor, manufacturing overhead is not traced directly to any specific units produced. Rather, the total is accumulated and is then allocated to production at some predetermined rate. Selection of an overhead allocation rate that accurately reflects overhead consumption is not always easy and is covered in detail in future chapters. A common base for allocation of overhead is direct labor hours. Since Barron consumes direct labor at a steady rate throughout the production cycle for Crazy Quilt dolls, manufacturing overhead allocation is based on direct labor hour consumption. Barron estimates that it spends $10 on manufacturing overhead for each hour of direct labor consumed. Barron can then allocate $36,000 of manufacturing overhead to work in process at 12/31/85 ($10/DLH × 1.5 hrs./doll × 4,000 dolls × 60%).

Total December 31, 1985, work in process for Barron is the sum of direct materials, direct labor, and allocated manufacturing overhead as follows:

Work-in-process inventory 12/31/85	
Direct materials	$20,000
Direct labor	43,200
Manufacturing overhead	36,000
Total	$99,200

As with the cost of raw materials, the current cost of production must be increased by the beginning balance in the work-in-process account and decreased by the ending balance. This is shown as items 4 and 5 on Barron's worksheet in Exhibit 19.6.

Finished Goods Inventory

FINISHED GOODS INVENTORY **Inventory of completely finished but unsold units.**

Finished goods inventory represents completely finished but unsold units. The account is handled in the same way that inventory is handled in a retail firm. The beginning inventory is added to cost of goods sold along with the cost of goods manufactured during the current period. The ending finished goods inventory is then subtracted to determine cost of goods sold. The only difference is that instead of looking to purchase documents to determine the value of the ending inventory, the manufacturing firm must look to its own manufacturing cost records. Barron has determined its ending finished goods inventory as $53,000. Item 6 on the worksheet adds beginning finished goods inventory to expense on the income statement, and item 7 subtracts ending finished goods inventory from expense. Keep in mind that we are assuming periodic FIFO inventory procedures.

Completion of the Manufacturing Worksheet

As you have no doubt noticed, the only difference between the worksheet in Exhibit 19.6 and those in earlier chapters is the addition of cost of goods manufactured columns. From this point forward, the worksheet is completed in the same way as described earlier in the text. Care must be taken, however, to separate product costs from period costs. All product costs must be carried to the cost of goods manufactured columns, and period costs are carried directly to the income statement as expenses. For example, an analysis of Barron's accounts shows that all repairs during 1985 were for the factory, while one-fourth of the utility expenditures made during the year were for the office building. Thus, all the repairs—a product cost—would be added to the cost of goods manufactured, while one-fourth of the utilities—an administrative expense—would be shown on the income statement. The remainder of the utilities is considered to be a product cost. Likewise, depreciation on the factory and its equipment is a product cost, and depreciation on the office is a period cost. Rent expense is considered a selling expense in Barron's case, because it is payment for warehouse space for finished dolls, not for space to produce dolls.

The following facts will allow us to complete the worksheet in Exhibit 19.6:

1. The factory building is being depreciated over 50 years on a straight-line basis, with zero salvage value.
2. The factory equipment is being depreciated over 15 years on a straight-line basis, with zero salvage value.
3. The office building is being depreciated over 25 years on a straight-line basis, with zero salvage value.
4. The long-term loan has been outstanding all year, and no interest has been recorded.
5. Bad debts are estimated at two percent of year-end receivables.
6. Prepaid rent represents rents on warehouse facilities that were paid on January 1, 1985, covering the next 24 months.
7. Factory wages for direct labor of $10,000 were owed on December 31. All other wages and salaries are paid up for the year.

The following entries are required to reflect the preceding facts. Each entry is cross-referenced to its posting to the worksheet in Exhibit 19.6 by entry letter.

a. Depreciation expense	10,000	
Accum. deprec.—factory building		10,000
(to record depreciation on factory building)		
b. Depreciation expense	20,000	
Accum. deprec.—factory equipment		20,000
(to record depreciation on factory equipment)		
c. Depreciation expense	1,000	
Accum. deprec.—office building		1,000
(to record depreciation on office building)		

		Debit	Credit
d.	Interest expense	24,000	
	Interest payable		24,000
	(to record interest expense on long-term loan)		
e.	Bad debt expense	1,040	
	Allowance for uncollectible accounts		1,040
	(to recognize estimate of uncollectible accounts)		
f.	Rent expense	12,000	
	Prepaid rent		12,000
	(to recognize expiration of prepaid rent)		
g.	Direct labor	10,000	
	Wages payable		10,000
	(to recognize wages owed at year-end)		

CLOSING THE ACCOUNTS

Closing the accounts of a manufacturing company at the end of an accounting period differs slightly from the process used to close the accounts of a retail firm. First, all of the product cost accounts used to develop the statement of the cost of goods manufactured are closed to the Manufacturing Summary account. This account in total will then equal the cost of goods manufactured, and it, in turn, is closed to the Income Summary account (where it becomes part of cost of goods sold). The process is illustrated in the following closing entries for Barron Manufacturing Company:

Date	Account	Debit	Credit
Dec. 31	Manufacturing summary	476,000	
	Raw materials 1/1		50,000
	Work in process 1/1		75,000
	Raw materials purchases		100,000
	Transportation in		5,000
	Direct labor		130,000
	Indirect labor		10,000
	Factory supervisors' salaries		30,000
	Repairs		10,000
	Utilities		36,000
	Depreciation expense		30,000
	(to close all of the debit column accounts to manufacturing summary)		
Dec. 31	Raw materials 12/31	65,000	
	Work in process 12/31	99,200	
	Purchase discounts	4,000	
	Manufacturing summary		168,200
	(to close all of the credit column accounts in manufacturing cost worksheet)		
Dec. 31	Income summary	577,840	
	Finished goods 1/1		80,000
	Utilities		12,000
	Advertising		25,000
	Sales staff salaries		40,000
	Administrative salaries		50,000
	Income tax expense		25,000
	Depreciation expense		1,000
	Interest expense		24,000
	Rent expense		12,000
	Bad debt expense		1,040
	Manufacturing summary		307,800
	(to close all of the debit column accounts in income statement worksheet)		

Dec. 31	Finished goods 12/31	53,000	
	Sales	575,000	
	Income summary		628,000
	(to close all of the credit column accounts in income statement worksheet)		
Dec. 31	Income summary	50,160	
	Retained earnings		50,160
	(to close income summary to retained earnings)		

At this point, all of the manufacturing cost, revenue, and expense accounts would have a zero balance, and the bookkeeping system would be ready for use in reporting the next period's operations.

FINANCIAL REPORTING FOR MANUFACTURING COMPANIES

Following completion of the worksheet, Barron can prepare financial statements. A new financial statement—statement of cost of goods manufactured—is needed for manufacturing firms.

Statement of Cost of Goods Manufactured

The **statement of cost of goods manufactured** is an accounting statement that sets forth the details of the cost of goods produced in a given period. Exhibit 19.7 presents the cost of goods manufactured statement for Barron Manufacturing.

STATEMENT OF COST OF GOODS MANUFACTURED
An accounting statement that sets forth the details of the cost of goods produced in a given period.

The statement of cost of goods manufactured presents the details of direct materials, direct labor, and manufacturing overhead that have been combined to produce

EXHIBIT 19.7

Barron Manufacturing Company
Statement of Cost of Goods Manufactured
For the Year Ending December 31, 1985

Work in process, 1/1		$ 75,000
Direct materials		
Raw materials inventory 1/1	$ 50,000	
Raw materials purchases	100,000	
Transportation in	5,000	
Purchase discounts	(4,000)	
Raw materials available for use	$151,000	
Less: Raw materials inventory 12/31	65,000	
Direct materials cost		$86,000
Direct labor		130,000
Manufacturing overhead		
Indirect labor	$ 10,000	
Factory supervisors' salaries	30,000	
Repairs	10,000	
Utilities	36,000	
Depreciation expense	30,000	
Total manufacturing overhead		$116,000
Total manufacturing cost		$407,000
Less: Work in process, 12/31		99,200
Total cost of goods manufactured		$307,800

goods in a given period. Note the third from the last line in Exhibit 19.7 titled Total Manufacturing Cost. Total manufacturing cost must not be confused with total cost of goods manufactured. Total manufacturing cost includes all costs entered into production during the current period, including beginning work in process. Total cost of goods manufactured is the total cost of goods completed during the current period. Ending work in process is not included in total cost of goods manufactured, since it represents unfinished production.

Review carefully the Manufacturing Overhead section of the cost of goods manufactured statement. Note that factory and equipment depreciation is included in manufacturing overhead as a product cost along with indirect labor, factory supervisors' salaries, and three-fourths of the utilities. A cost need not be paid in cash during the current period to be a product cost. All that is required is that the cost represent a resource consumed in the production of goods.

The Income Statement

The income statement of a manufacturer is similar to that of a retail firm. Even though the manufacturing process is complex, the details of the process are not included in the income statement. Rather, the details are shown in the cost of goods manufactured statement, and only the total from this statement is used to prepare the income statement. The total cost of goods manufactured is similar to the net purchase account for a retail firm and is combined with beginning and ending inventories of finished goods to determine cost of goods sold as shown in Exhibit 19.8 for the Barron Manufacturing Company.

EXHIBIT 19.8

Barron Manufacturing Company
Income Statement
For the Year Ending December 31, 1985

Sales		$575,000
Cost of goods sold		
Finished goods inventory 1/1	$ 80,000	
Plus: Cost of goods manufactured	307,800	
Cost of goods available for sale	$387,800	
Less: Finished goods inventory 12/31	53,000	
Total cost of goods sold		334,800
Gross profit		$240,200
Selling and administrative expenses		
Advertising	$ 25,000	
Sales staff salaries	40,000	
Rent expense	12,000	
Utilities	12,000	
Administrative salaries	50,000	
Depreciation on office	1,000	
Interest expense	24,000	
Bad debt expense	1,040	
Total selling and administrative expenses		$165,040
Income before income taxes		$ 75,160
Income tax expense		25,000
Net income		$ 50,160

The Statement of Financial Position

The statement of financial position for a manufacturing company differs from that of a retail company only in inventory presentation. A manufacturing company shows raw materials, work-in-process, and finished goods inventories, while a retail company has only one inventory account. To illustrate, the statement of financial position for Barron Manufacturing is presented in Exhibit 19.9.

EXHIBIT 19.9

Barron Manufacturing Company
Statement of Financial Position
As of December 31, 1985

Assets		
Current assets		
Cash		$ 47,000
Accounts receivable	$102,000	
Less: Allowance for uncollectibles	2,040	
		99,960
Prepaid rent		12,000
Inventories		
Raw materials	$65,000	
Work in process	99,200	
Finished goods	53,000	217,200
Total current assets		$376,160
Property, plant, and equipment		
Factory building	$500,000	
Less: Accumulated depreciation	260,000	240,000
Factory equipment	$300,000	
Less: Accumulated depreciation	120,000	180,000
Office building	$ 25,000	
Less: Accumulated depreciation	16,000	9,000
Land		100,000
Total property, plant, and equipment		$529,000
Total assets		$905,160
Liabilities and Owners' Equity		
Current liabilities		
Accounts payable		$ 45,000
Interest payable		24,000
Wages payable		10,000
Total current liabilities		$ 79,000
Long-term loan payable		200,000
Total liabilities		$279,000
Owners' equity		
Common stock		300,000
Retained earnings		326,160
Total owners' equity		$626,160
Total liabilities and owners' equity		$905,160

■ **CONCEPT SUMMARY 19.1** MANUFACTURING INVENTORY ACCOUNTS

Account	Used for Recording	Normally Found on Statement Of		
		Cost of Goods Manufactured	Income	Financial Position
Raw materials	Cost of raw materials on hand	Yes	No	Yes
Work in process	Sum of raw materials, direct labor, and factory overhead for partially completed products	Yes	No	Yes
Finished goods	Sum of raw materials, direct labor, and factory overhead for unsold completed units	No	Yes	Yes

■ MANUFACTURING ACCOUNTING AND DECISION MAKING

Although the bookkeeping framework previously presented is adequate for external reporting purposes, it does not provide managers with information on the costs of manufacturing products as the process occurs. The periodic inventory system summarizes manufacturing cost information at the end of a reporting period. For this reason, most manufacturing companies use a perpetual inventory system. Direct materials, direct labor, and manufacturing overhead are entered directly into work in process as these costs occur. When goods are finished, entries are made to remove the cost of the finished goods from work in process. In this way, cost flows are traced from their source through the production process. A review of the work-in-process account entries at any point provides managers with cost information paralleling the production process that can be used for day-to-day operational control. (Manufacturing cost systems based on perpetual inventories are the topic of Chapter 20.)

■ OTHER COST CONCEPTS AND DECISION MAKING

An understanding of manufacturing costs is necessary to prepare financial statements and to assist management in decision making. However, for decision-making purposes, it must be remembered that the term *cost* has no single meaning in accounting—it has meaning only in the context in which it is used. To complicate matters even further, there are many different ways to classify cost information. Once again, the particular classification scheme used depends on how the cost information is used. Some simple examples illustrate what we mean.

Concepts Relevant to Decision Making

SUNK COSTS
Costs that have already been incurred and will not change regardless of the decision made.

Assume for a minute that you want to buy a car and you have to choose between two cars. You have all kinds of financial information at your disposal and are now in a position to analyze the information. What is the first thing you should do? Most decision makers believe that you should separate the relevant from the irrelevant information. Irrelevant costs, or **sunk costs,** are those that have already been incurred and will not change regardless of the decision made. If each car costs $6,000, the information regarding cost is irrelevant to the decision, because there is no difference between the cost of the two cars. **Differential costs** refer to those costs that are different between the alternatives and are relevant to the decision.

DIFFERENTIAL COSTS
Those costs that are different between the alternatives and are relevant to a decision.

Another distinction you might make in this decision-making situation is to identify the opportunity costs and the out-of-pocket costs. **Out-of-pocket costs** refer to those costs that require the use of cash. For example, a $100 dealer preparation charge would involve an out-of-pocket cost, because you must use cash to pay this expense. In contrast, an **opportunity cost** is the benefit forgone by using resources in one way as opposed to another. If you were to pay cash for your car by taking money out of your savings account, there is an opportunity cost associated with this decision. In this case, the opportunity cost is equal to the interest income you would earn if you left your money in the bank.

OUT-OF-POCKET COSTS
Costs that require the use of cash.

OPPORTUNITY COST
The benefit forgone by using resources in one way as opposed to another.

Cost Behavior Patterns

Many times in decision-making situations, business people analyze costs by how the costs change with changes in output. They classify costs as fixed, variable, or mixed. A **fixed cost** is one that remains constant over a particular range of output, often referred to as the **relevant range.** Graphically, a fixed cost appears as in Exhibit 19.10(a). Some practical examples of fixed costs are rent, depreciation, and supervisors' salaries. Because fixed costs are normally expected to remain constant over the relevant range, increasing output from one point to another does not affect them.

FIXED COST
A cost that remains constant over a particular range of output.

RELEVANT RANGE
The range of output for which fixed costs do not change.

Variable costs are those that change in proportion to changes in output. Normally, variable costs are fixed on a unit basis but increase in total as more units are produced and sold. Factory labor, materials, and sales commissions are examples of variable costs. As Exhibit 19.10(b) shows, if no units are produced, variable costs are zero. For each additional unit produced, variable costs increase by a given amount. In management accounting, we usually assume that variable costs remain constant on a unit basis regardless of how many units are produced. In contrast, economists believe that these unit variable costs change based on the level of production.

VARIABLE COSTS
Costs that change in proportion to changes in output.

Some costs by their very nature are neither exclusively fixed nor exclusively variable. Such costs are referred to as **mixed costs.** An example of such a cost is a company's utility bill. The amount of utility charges might be based on a combination of usage and a fixed amount for the service availability. Such a cost pattern might look like the one in Exhibit 19.10(c). In this case, the company pays $1000 per

MIXED COSTS
Costs that are neither exclusively fixed nor exclusively variable.

EXHIBIT 19.10

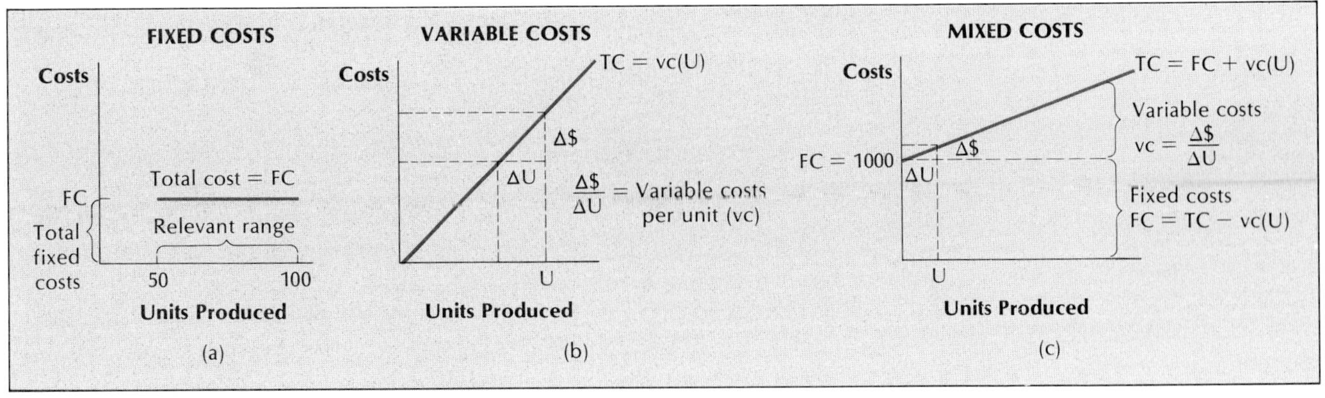

month for telephone service regardless of the number of calls made. In addition to paying the fixed charge, it pays a fee for each call it makes. In reality, most costs are mixed in nature, and the challenge to the accountant is to identify such costs and be able to determine whether mixed cost will change over a particular output range.

The subject of mixed, fixed, and variable costs is explored in more detail in Chapter 24—Cost-Volume-Profit Analysis. However, it is important to understand that the ability of an analyst to properly classify costs based on behavior patterns is often essential for effective decision making.

Traceability of Costs to Cost Objectives

DIRECT COSTS Those costs that can be physically traced to a cost objective.

COST OBJECTIVE The item or object for which a cost measurement is being made.

A question frequently raised in business is, What will happen to profits if we delete this product line or eliminate this department? To answer this question, management must be able to identify direct costs and indirect costs. **Direct costs** refer to those costs that can be physically traced to a cost objective. If the cost objective is eliminated, the costs would also be eliminated. The term **cost objective** refers to the item or object for which we are making a cost measurement. A cost objective could be a product, person, department, piece of machinery, or company. Assume for a minute that the cost objective is a product. Direct costs related to that product might include the labor and material required to make the product, as well as the rent the company pays on the building that houses the product. Clearly, if the product were eliminated, the company would not have to incur these labor, material, and rental costs.

INDIRECT COSTS Those costs that cannot be physically traced to a cost objective but nonetheless are allocated to cost objectives on some basis.

Indirect costs are those that cannot be physically traced to a cost objective but nonetheless are allocated to cost objectives on some basis. For example, assume that within a particular plant hundreds of different products are made. It costs the company one million dollars per year to lease the building. To determine the full cost of each product, management would probably attempt to distribute the lease cost to each product on the basis of square footage occupied. Normally, the elimination or reduction of a cost objective does not reduce the indirect costs. The subject of indirect costs and such costs' allocation to cost objectives is covered in Chapter 22.

Other Classification Schemes

The preceding discussion illustrates three methods of classifying costs. In reality, there are many other methods. One important point of the discussion is to understand that the way in which you classify costs is dictated by the type of decision you are making. There is no single best method of cost classification—the "best" method depends on the decision to be made. Another point is that the classification systems are not mutually exclusive; that is, in a particular decision setting, you might classify costs in a number of ways. For example, if you were making a decision whether to drop a product line, you would have to analyze product costs from several perspectives. You would certainly want to know the indirect and direct costs associated with the product. Within each category it would also be useful to determine the fixed and variable expenses. This information would provide insight on what impact dropping the product line would have on the overall profitability of the company.

COST CONCEPTS

■ CONCEPT SUMMARY 19.2

Aspect	Cost Categories	Example
Relevance to decisions	• *Sunk costs* cannot be changed regardless of the decision and are therefore irrelevant.	The original purchase price of old equipment.
	• *Differential costs* are different among alternatives.	The price of new equipment to be purchased.
	• *Out-of-pocket costs* are explicit costs that require the outlay of resources.	The price paid to acquire supplies.
	• *Opportunity costs* are benefits forgone by using resources in one way as opposed to another.	Future savings account interest on a cash withdrawal.
Behavior with respect to changes in activity	• *Fixed costs* remain constant over the relevant range of output.	Rent.
	• *Variable costs* change in proportion to changes in output.	Factory labor.
	• *Marginal costs* are the increase in total costs due to producing one more unit.	Materials used in last unit of output.
	• *Mixed costs* are partially fixed and partially variable.	Utility expense.
Traceability to cost objectives	• *Direct costs* can be physically traced to a cost objective.	Product materials.
	• *Indirect costs* cannot be physically traced but are allocated to cost objectives on some basis.	Lease expense of a multiproduct production plant.
Relevance to inventory	• *Product costs* are all costs necessary to complete a product.	Direct materials, direct labor, overhead.
	• *Period costs* are nonproduct costs charged directly to the income of the period.	Interest expense.

FOR REVIEW

■ SUMMARY

■ Management accounting is directed at individuals internal to the firm, whereas financial accounting is directed at individuals external to the firm.

■ Management accounting serves to bridge the gap between the needs of internal management and the information provided by a firm's accounting system.

■ Planning is the process of setting goals and developing strategies to obtain those goals.

■ Controlling is assuring that plans are completed and goals achieved and is accomplished by comparing actual results to planned results and correcting for material differences.

■ Unlike a retail firm that purchases the goods it sells in finished form from suppliers, a manufacturer obtains saleable products by producing them in a factory.

■ To produce saleable goods, a manufacturer must buy and use raw materials (direct materials), hire workers to convert the raw materials into finished goods (direct labor), and provide a factory with necessary equipment to house the production process (manufacturing overhead).

■ Direct materials and direct labor include all materials and labor charges that can be traced directly to specific units or batches of products. All other manufacturing costs are classified as part of manufacturing overhead.

■ Selling and administrative costs are charged to expense in the period in which they are incurred in manufacturing environments just as they are in retail businesses.

■ Raw material inventory consists of goods waiting to be put into production. Work-in-process inventory consists of products started but not yet finished.

■ The statement of cost of goods manufactured presents details of direct materials, direct labor, and manufacturing overhead that were used to produce goods in a given period.

■ Many different cost classification methods exist, and the choice of method depends on how the cost information is used.

QUESTIONS

19-1. What is management accounting?

19-2. What is the main difference between financial accounting and management accounting?

19-3. What is planning? What is meant by the term *controlling?*

19-4. Name the three types of businesses and describe their basic items of input and resulting output.

19-5. Identify and discuss the components of product cost for a manufacturing organization.

19-6. What is the difference between product costs and period costs?

19-7. What is the difference between the cost of goods sold calculation for a retail company and that for a manufacturing company?

19-8. How is the statement of financial position reporting of inventory different for retail firms from that of manufacturing firms?

19-9. In terms of decision-making purposes, what is the difference between sunk costs and differential costs? Opportunity costs and out-of-pocket costs?

19-10. In terms of traceability, what is the difference between direct and indirect costs?

EXERCISES

19-E1. Following are certain costs incurred for a bicycle manufacturer. Classify each cost as direct materials, direct labor, or manufacturing overhead.

a. Salary of the assembly-line inspector.

b. Cost of tires used on the bicycles.

c. Salary of the cost accountant.
d. Cost of assembly-line workers' services.
e. Payroll taxes based on factory employees' wages.
f. Supplies used in the cost accountant's office.
g. Machinery repair parts used in scheduled maintenance.
h. Cost of industry journals supplied to the senior design engineer.
i. Cost of factory employees' overtime premium.

19-E2. Review the costs in 19-E1 and indicate which are likely to vary directly with the level of bicycle output and which are likely to remain fixed.

19-E3. Tynof Clock Company had a merchandise inventory on January 1, 1986, of $5,000 and on December 31, 1986, of $7,500. The cost of purchases for the year was $12,000. What was Tynof's cost of goods sold for the year?

19-E4. What would the cost of goods sold in 19-E3 be if Tynof were a manufacturer (rather than a merchandiser) with finished goods inventories of $5,000 (beginning) and $7,500 (ending) and total cost of goods manufactured of $12,000.

19-E5. Printwright Typewriters, Inc., recorded the following costs for the year 1986. Calculate the cost of goods manufactured.

Raw materials used	$25,675
Direct labor used	53,980
Manufacturing overhead incurred	10,125
Work-in-process inventory, 1/1/86	89,163
Work-in-process inventory, 12/31/86	74,899

19-E6. Ic Gewite, accountant for Commuter Train Manufacturers, Inc., is preparing an income statement for the company's manufacturing operations. Following are data collected for the costs of goods sold calculation. Determine the amount that Ic Gewite will derive from its calculation.

Raw materials used	$153,756
Direct labor used	275,950
Manufacturing overhead incurred	598,875
Work in process, 1/1/86	423,450
Work in process, 12/31/86	516,795
Finished goods, 1/1/86	43,850
Finished goods, 12/31/86	94,713

19-E7. Following are data from Aleph Company's cost records. Determine the beginning work-in-process inventory.

Raw materials used	$ 45,000
Direct labor used	95,500
Manufacturing overhead incurred	63,450
Work in process, 12/31/89	50,190
Finished goods, 1/1/89	10,175
Finished goods, 12/31/89	5,615
Cost of goods sold during 1989	201,915

PROBLEM SET A

19-A1. Distinguishing Manufacturing, Sales, and Service Organizations. John Smith has been analyzing three corporations and is considering purchasing stock in one of them. One of the corporations is Johnson Electronics, Inc., manufacturer of computerized integrated circuits. Another is the Computer Store, Inc., an organization that purchases personal computers for resale to the general public. The third is The Fixit Factory, Incorporated, which services nonworking computer components.

Although Smith had carefully labeled the statements of financial position he had analyzed, he failed to do so for the income statements. Subsequently, his stack of work papers became disorganized, and he could not remember which income statement went with which corporation. The condensed income statements he had prepared are as follows.

(a)

Sales	$1,000
Cost of goods sold	
Beginning inventory	150
Purchases	350
Ending inventory	(175)
	$ 325
Gross profit	$ 675
Operating expenses	250
Income before taxes	425
Income taxes	170
Net income	255
Earnings per share	$ 5.10

(b)

Sales	$2,000
Cost of goods sold	
Beginning inventory	400
Cost of goods manufactured	1,100
Ending inventory	(200)
	1,300
Gross profit	700
Operating expenses	325
Net income before income taxes	375
Income taxes	113
Net income	$ 262
Earnings per share	$ 5.24

(c)

Fees		$1,500
Operating expense		
Labor	$750	
Other	200	950
Net income before income taxes		550
Income taxes		253
Net income		297
Earnings per share		$ 4.95

Required

Determine which income statement belongs to which corporation. Be sure to support your conclusions with specific information.

19-A2. Classification of Costs. The following are various costs incurred by an automobile manufacturer:

1. Cost of tires for the new cars.
2. Cost of overtime premium for the assembly-line workers.
3. Cost of the president's salary.
4. Cost of the assembly-line workers' basic wages.
5. Cost of storing the new F-cars in the warehouse currently occupied by several product lines.
6. Cost of lease payments on factories no longer used but held under a 30-year lease.
7. Cost of utilities used in the corporate headquarters.
8. Cost of glass windshields for the cars.
9. Cost of the die workers' salaries.
10. Cost of taxes on the corporation's income.

Required

Classify each of the preceding costs in each of the following three ways:

a. As a direct materials, direct labor, factory overhead, or other cost.
b. As a direct cost or an indirect cost.
c. As a product cost or a period cost.

19-A3. Cost of Goods Manufactured Statement. During the year ending October 31, 1987, C.G.M. Company purchased raw materials and paid for direct labor. It incurred the following additional overhead costs.

Indirect labor	$10,500
Indirect supplies	20% of indirect labor
Utilities	?

Trial balances as of October 31, 1986, and October 31, 1987, show the following inventory amounts.

	10-31-87	10-31-86
Raw materials inventory	$10,000	$ 9,750
Work-in-process inventory	25,000	27,850
Finished goods inventory	50,100	42,350

Additional information:

1. C.G.M. ordinarily maintains raw materials inventory equal to 13% of annual purchases. Though inventory was slightly higher on October 31, 1987, this observation was true on October 31, 1986.
2. C.G.M.'s direct labor costs for the year were twice raw material purchase costs.
3. Total factory overhead costs equal 9.4% of direct labor costs.

Required

a. Prepare a cost of goods manufactured statement.
b. Compute the amount of cost of goods sold that C.G.M. Company should report on its income statement for the year ending October 31, 1987.

19-A4. Statement of Cost of Goods Manufactured and Income Statement. The Carter Corporation has the following accounts (in millions).

Selling and administrative expenses	$100
Work in process, December 31, 1986	10
Factory supplies used	10
Direct materials, December 31, 1987	20
Factory utilities	30
Finished goods, December 31, 1987	55
Indirect labor	60
Work in process, December 31, 1987	5
Purchases of direct materials	125
Direct labor	200
Depreciation—factory building and equipment	80
Factory supervisory salaries	5
Miscellaneous factory overhead	35
Sales	700
Finished goods, December 31, 1986	70
Direct materials, December 31, 1986	15

Required

a. Prepare a schedule of cost of goods manufactured.
b. Prepare an income statement.

19-A5. Statements from Incomplete Data. Sally Hardluck, chief accountant of Johnson Enterprises, accidentally tossed the company's cost records into a wastebasket. Realizing her error, she raced to the incinerator but was successful in retrieving only a few scraps from the roaring blaze. From these scraps she has determined the following facts about the current year, 1986.

1. Sales totaled $100,000 during 1986.
2. The beginning inventories for the year were as follows:

Work in process	$12,000
Finished goods	6,000

3. Direct labor is equal to 25% of the manufacturing overhead combined with direct labor.
4. The work-in-process inventory decreased by $2,000 during 1986.
5. Gross profit during 1986 was equal to 55% of sales.
6. Manufacturing overhead totaled $24,000 for 1986.
7. Direct labor is equal to 40% of direct materials combined with direct labor.
8. Administrative expenses for 1986 were twice as great as net income but only 25% of selling expenses.

Required

Prepare a cost of goods manufactured and income statement for Sally Hardluck.

PROBLEM SET B

19-B1. Distinguishing Manufacturing, Sales, and Service Organizations. Robert Jones owns stock in three different corporations: Ore Metals Company, which manufactures various metal products from raw ore; Durable Hardware Company, which purchases finished hardware items and retails them to the public; and Quickserve Appliance Repair, Inc., which repairs customers' appliances.

Jones recently received annual statements of financial position from each of the companies, but the statements had been damaged in a recent home fire. The remaining portions of the statements of financial position are as follows:

(1)

Cash	$25,000
Marketable securities	1,000
Accounts receivable	15,000
Supplies inventory	2,000
Total assets	$43,000
Accounts payable	$ 2,000
Wages payable	17,500
Total liabilities	$19,500
Common stock	$15,000
Retained earnings	8,500
Total shareholders' equity	$23,500
Total liability and shareholders' equity	$43,000

(2)
November 30, 1985

Cash	$ 15,000
Accounts receivable	12,000
Raw materials inventory	4,000
Work-in-process inventory	15,000
Finished goods inventory	3,500
Total current assets	$ 49,500
Machinery and equipment (net)	$ 10,500
Buildings (net)	50,975
Total fixed assets	$ 61,475
Total assets	$110,975
Accounts payable	14,950

(3)
Balance Sheet
December 31, 1986

Cash	$ 11,000
Accounts receivable	2,500
Merchandise inventory	89,250
Total current assets	$ 97,750
Buildings	150,000
Accumulated depreciation	75,000
Total fixed assets	225,0
Total assets	

Required

Although the remnants have little value, Robert Jones would still like to identify which statement of financial position belongs to which firm (since the firms' names had been burned off the pages). You, acting as Jones's accountant, must match the corporations with their proper statements of financial position. Support your conclusions with specific information.

19-B2. Classification of Costs. Following are various costs incurred by a retailer:

1. Cost of an employee's current wages.
2. Interest income that could be earned if profits are placed in a bank account rather than reinvested in the business.
3. Cost for which the store is purchased.
4. The warehouse leasing cost when deciding which warehouse to lease.
5. The salary of a new employee when deciding between two applicants with different levels of experience and education.
6. The capital gain that could have been realized at sale if the profits from two years ago had been invested in appreciating real estate rather than in depreciating machinery.

Required

Classify each of the preceding costs in each of the following three ways.
a. As fixed cost or variable cost.
b. As sunk or differential cost.
c. As opportunity or out-of-pocket cost.

19-B3. Cost of Goods Manufactured and Sold Statement. During the month ending February 28, 1986, Cosco, Inc., purchases raw materials and pays $15,000 for labor costs (10% of which was for indirect labor). Cosco incurs the following additional overhead costs.

Indirect materials	$1,100
Rent	2,500
Small tools	400
Heat, power, and light	1,600

Trial balances as of February 28, 1986, and January 31, 1986, show the following inventory figures.

	2-28-86	1-31-86
Raw materials inventory	$ 1,000	$?
Work-in-process inventory	18,400	17,250
Finished goods inventory	4,300	5,900

One other piece of information is available: Cosco tries to maintain raw materials inventory equal to 20% of monthly purchases. Although Cosco was successful in this regard as of February 28, 1986, inventory had fallen to 19% on January 31, 1986.

Required

a. Prepare a statement of cost of goods manufactured.
b. Determine Cosco's cost of goods sold for the month.

19-B4. Schedule of Cost of Goods Manufactured and Income Statements. Following are various sales and cost data for White Enterprises for 1986.

Direct labor	$ 18,000
Indirect labor	5,500
Work in process, beginning	14,000
Work in process, ending	13,500
Sales	100,000
Selling expenses	10,000
Finished goods, beginning	10,000
Finished goods, ending	9,000
Depreciation, factory	27,000
Administrative expenses	8,000
Utilities, factory	2,000
Direct materials	13,000
Maintenance, factory	2,000
Indirect materials	4,000
Insurance, factory	1,000

Required

a. Prepare a schedule of cost of goods manufactured for 1986.
b. Prepare an income statement for 1986.

19-B5. Missing Production and Sales Data. JOX, Incorporated, has five operating divisions. The controller needs complete production and sales data from each division to prepare the annual reports. You have the following information.

Division	Sox	Sneak	Liniment	Shoelace	Sweat Suit
Sales	$12,500	$18,000	$20,000	$10,000	$15,000
Opening finished goods	3,000	?	6,000	2,000	4,000
Cost of goods manufactured	11,000	?	11,000	8,000	?
Ending finished goods	?	4,000	7,000	?	3,000
Cost of goods sold	10,000	13,000	?	7,000	?
Gross profit	?	5,000	?	3,000	5,000
Operating expenses	1,500	2,000	5,000	1,000	1,500
Net income	1,000	3,000	5,000	2,000	3,500
Direct materials	3,000	2,000	5,000	3,000	4,000
Direct labor	4,000	4,000	3,000	?	2,000
Manufacturing overhead	?	3,000	5,000	4,000	2,000
Total manufacturing costs	?	?	?	9,000	?
Beginning work in process	2,500	5,000	?	2,000	?
Ending work in process	2,500	2,000	4,000	?	4,000
Cost of goods manufactured	11,000	?	?	8,000	9,000

Required

Supply the missing data. Each division is independent of the others.

MANUFACTURING COST SYSTEMS

CHAPTER OBJECTIVES

After studying Chapter 20, you should understand the following:

1. The two cost accumulation systems of job-order costing and process costing, how each system is applied, and where each is likely to be used.
2. The three basic types of costs collected by product costing systems: actual costs, normal costs, and standard costs.
3. The formulation of predetermined overhead rates and their usage by management.
4. How process costing is used to provide management with comparative cost data, transfer costs from one process to the next, and provide a basis for inventory valuation.
5. The method for computing equivalent units of production and calculating unit costs under a process costing system.
6. The difference between single-stage and multi-stage process costing and when they are used.

How does IBM determine the cost of a computer or Exxon the cost of a gallon of gas? Do product costing procedures differ among firms? If so, what accounts for such differences? This chapter provides some answers to these questions by focusing on the topic of product costing. It describes ways that companies accumulate product costs, the kinds of costs accumulated, and opposing viewpoints on methods of defining product cost.

PRODUCT COST SYSTEMS

In designing any product cost system, one must answer two basic questions: How will costs be traced to the product? What kinds of cost information must be collected? Each of these questions must be answered in the context of a specific company, because product cost systems must be tailor-made.

Cost Accumulation Systems

JOB-ORDER COSTING
A method of cost accounting where direct labor, direct material costs, and factory overhead are physically traced to individual jobs or products.

Two contrasting methods exist for tracking costs to products: job-order costing and process costing. The principle difference between these methods is the cost objective. In **job-order costing,** direct labor, direct materials costs, and factory overhead are physically traced to individual jobs or products. This cost accumulation approach is typically found in the construction, printing, and computer industries, where each unit or batch of units tends to be unique and easily identifiable. In this environment, products are often custom-made, and it is economically feasible to trace costs to products.

In contrast, process costing is typically found in companies that mass produce similar products. In industries such as chemical, cement, flour, steel, and petroleum, output consists of like units, with each unit processed in the same manner. It is therefore assumed that the same amounts of materials, labor, and overhead costs are chargeable to each unit produced. The cost of a unit at the end of any manufacturing process can be determined if costs are accumulated on a departmental (process) basis and a record of units produced is available.

PROCESS COSTING
A method of cost accounting where material, labor, and overhead costs are accumulated for all units worked on in a department for a given period of time and all units produced are assigned the same average cost for that period.

Unlike job-order costing, where costs are recorded separately for each job or order going through the plant, **process costing** emphasizes the accumulation of costs for all units worked on in a department during a given period of time. The units processed in a department are homogeneous, and the average unit cost is computed before transferring costs from one department to another.

Types of Costs Collected

A dimension of any product cost system is the decision as to the type of costs to be collected. Basically, three types of systems can be followed: actual, normal, and standard costing.

ACTUAL COST SYSTEM
A cost system where only actual product cost data for labor, materials, and overhead are accumulated.

In an **actual cost system,** management accumulates only actual product cost data for labor, materials, and overhead. Overhead is distributed to products on the basis of the actual overhead expenses incurred. This method of allocating overhead expenses is difficult to accomplish promptly and accurately, because often a time lag exists between the manufacture of products and the recognition of overhead expenses. For example, 100 units of a product might be manufactured and sold in January, yet the actual overhead expenses incurred to produce these units might not be entered into the accounts until February or March. It is therefore difficult to determine the full cost of these units in January.

Another problem associated with an actual cost system is the difficulty in tracing actual overhead to specific products. By definition, overhead costs are not physically traceable to specific products and must therefore be distributed equitably to products on some predetermined basis. In an actual cost system, this allocation is typically not done, and it is difficult to ever determine the full manufacturing cost of a particular product.

As a result of the foregoing potential problems, many companies use a normal cost system. A normal cost system differs from an actual cost system in only one respect. In a **normal cost system,** overhead is allocated to products on a predetermined basis rather than on an actual basis. Actual overhead data are still accumulated in a normal cost system, but overhead is estimated and allocated to products as the products are manufactured rather than when actual overhead costs are collected. A lengthy discussion of overhead allocation is deferred for the moment, but the following example illustrates how the process might work.

NORMAL COST SYSTEM
A cost system where overhead is allocated to products on a predetermined basis rather than on an actual basis.

Assume that the Helio Company makes two products, Zippo and Beta. The manufacturing process for these two products is highly labor intensive. The company uses a normal cost system, tracking actual direct labor and direct materials to its two products as they are manufactured. Overhead, however, is allocated to the products on a predetermined basis. The company has estimated that manufacturing overhead will be $100,000 in the next year. Helio has also estimated that overhead should be allocated to products on the basis of the direct labor hours spent on each product. Management has forecast that 100,000 hours of direct labor will be used in 1986. Therefore, one dollar of overhead is allocated to a product for each direct labor hour spent on the product. If it takes five direct labor hours to manufacture a unit of Beta, $5 of overhead will be charged to that unit. This dollar rate is commonly referred to as the burden or **predetermined overhead rate.** This is the rate at which overhead costs are allocated to units of product. As the discussion of overhead allocation will illustrate, periodic comparisons are made between the amount of overhead allocated to products and the actual amount incurred. Any differences are handled through an adjustment to net income.

PREDETERMINED OVERHEAD RATE
A predetermined amount of overhead charged to each unit produced regardless of actual overhead costs.

The primary benefit of a normal cost system is that it allows management to determine product costs more accurately and more promptly. This assists in product pricing, job estimating, and cost control.

The most sophisticated approach to product costing is standard costing. In a **standard cost system,** management collects and reports both actual and predetermined labor, materials, and overhead costs. This method differs from a normal cost system, because it establishes a predetermined cost for materials and labor as well as for overhead. By predetermining all components, management can calculate a standard cost per unit and an actual cost per unit. The standard cost information is beneficial to management in planning and control in general and in product costing and pricing in particular. As a matter of fact, a standard cost system has so many uses and benefits, it is the subject of Chapter 21.

STANDARD COST SYSTEM
A cost system where management collects and reports both actual and predetermined labor, materials, and overhead costs.

JOB-ORDER COSTING

As previously mentioned, job-order costing is normally used in companies with distinguishable products and services. Such products are often custom-made and unique in their physical characteristics, making it possible and cost-effective to trace materials, labor, and overhead costs to them. In a job-order system, the cost objective is a job. It must be remembered, however, that a job can be the production of a single tangible product (or multiple units of the same product) or the providing of an intangible service such as consulting, auditing, or hospital services. Regardless of the tangibility of the product, a job-order system can be used if it is possible to trace costs to individual jobs. Let's see how this is accomplished.

An overview of the job-order cost process is reflected in Exhibit 20.1 (a). Job costs are accumulated on a job-order cost sheet much like the one in Exhibit 20.1 (b). The **job-order cost sheet** physically moves with the product as it is being produced and functions as a subsidiary ledger account for inventory. At any point in time, the total costs shown on the job-order cost sheets for jobs still in process are equal to the total work-in-process inventory, and the total of all job-order cost sheets for jobs completed but not yet sold equals the total finished goods inventory. Additionally, the total of all job-order cost sheets for jobs completed and sold equals the total cost of goods sold for the period.

CONCEPT SUMMARY 20.1

PRODUCT COSTING SYSTEMS

Cost Dimension	Technique	Issues
Cost accumulation systems	**Job-order costing.** Direct materials, direct labor, and factory overhead are physically traced to individual jobs or products.	Requires distinguishable products or services to trace costs to specific jobs.
	Process costing. Direct materials, direct labor, and factory overhead are physically traced to individual process departments during a given period of time.	Used where homogeneous products are mass-produced. Requires assumption that the same amount of materials, labor, and overhead are chargeable to each unit processed.
Type of costs collected	**Actual costing.** Only actual material, labor, and overhead cost data are collected.	Overhead cost data are not available on a timely basis. Actual overhead is difficult to physically trace to cost objectives. Creates difficulty in estimating and controlling product costs and setting realistic prices. Suitable only when prime costs are the major elements of total product cost.
	Normal costing. Actual material, labor, and overhead costs are collected, but estimated (predetermined) overhead is allocated to products.	Estimates of overhead are available on a timely basis. Predetermined overhead rates must be computed. Under-applied overhead is deducted from income of the period. Over-applied overhead is added to income of the period.
	Standard costing. Actual and predetermined material, labor, and overhead costs are collected.	Useful in planning and controlling, especially in product costing and pricing. Facilitates evaluation of manufacturing efficiency.

EXHIBIT 20.1

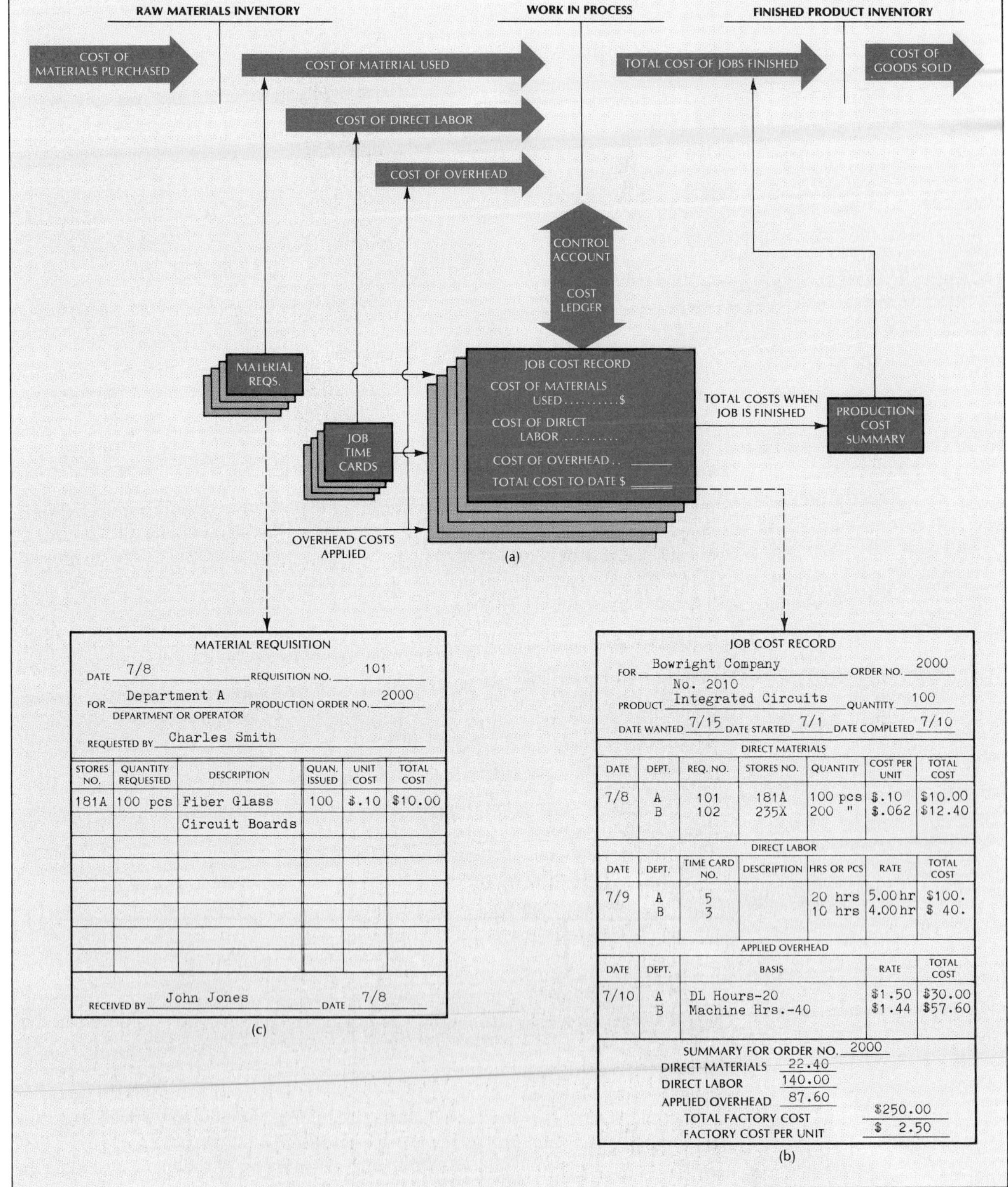

MATERIAL REQUISITION

DATE 7/8 REQUISITION NO. 101

FOR Department A PRODUCTION ORDER NO. 2000

DEPARTMENT OR OPERATOR

REQUESTED BY Charles Smith

STORES NO.	QUANTITY REQUESTED	DESCRIPTION	QUAN. ISSUED	UNIT COST	TOTAL COST
181A	100 pcs	Fiber Glass Circuit Boards	100	$.10	$10.00

RECEIVED BY John Jones DATE 7/8

(c)

JOB COST RECORD

FOR Bowright Company ORDER NO. 2000

PRODUCT No. 2010 Integrated Circuits QUANTITY 100

DATE WANTED 7/15 DATE STARTED 7/1 DATE COMPLETED 7/10

DIRECT MATERIALS

DATE	DEPT.	REQ. NO.	STORES NO.	QUANTITY	COST PER UNIT	TOTAL COST
7/8	A	101	181A	100 pcs	$.10	$10.00
	B	102	235X	200 "	$.062	$12.40

DIRECT LABOR

DATE	DEPT.	TIME CARD NO.	DESCRIPTION	HRS OR PCS	RATE	TOTAL COST
7/9	A	5		20 hrs	5.00hr	$100.
	B	3		10 hrs	4.00hr	$ 40.

APPLIED OVERHEAD

DATE	DEPT.	BASIS	RATE	TOTAL COST
7/10	A	DL Hours-20	$1.50	$30.00
	B	Machine Hrs.-40	$1.44	$57.60

SUMMARY FOR ORDER NO. 2000

DIRECT MATERIALS	22.40	
DIRECT LABOR	140.00	
APPLIED OVERHEAD	87.60	
TOTAL FACTORY COST		$250.00
FACTORY COST PER UNIT		$ 2.50

(b)

Job-Order Costing in a Public Accounting Firm

Job-order systems are commonly used in service companies as well as in manufacturing. Let's take the example of a CPA firm.

A CPA company normally provides three types of services for clients: auditing, taxation, and consulting. These services are tailored to the needs of each client, and even though the nature of the services is similar for each customer, the services might be performed differently. Because clients are distinguishable from one another, it is possible and economically feasible to physically trace costs to each job.

In public accounting, the largest cost incurred to provide a service is labor. As a result, professional accountants in CPA firms are often required to account for their time in 15-minute intervals, making sure to either charge time to a specific client or account for the time as indirect labor.

Hours charged to clients are billed out at rates in excess of the actual cost per hour. This is because the rate includes an amount of overhead and profit. Materials costs are considered part of overhead and thus are not traced to jobs. Therefore, a job-order system is particularly appropriate in this type of business.

Tracking Direct Materials Costs

Direct materials costs are assigned to jobs on the basis of materials requisition slips (Exhibit 20.1 (c)). Whenever materials are needed for a particular job, they are requisitioned by a department from inventory and charged directly to the job as used (Exhibit 20.1 (b), part (1)). The following accounting entry would reflect this cost assignment:

Work in process (Dept. A)	10.00	
Work in process (Dept. B)	12.40	
Inventory		22.40
(to transfer raw materials to work in process)		

This entry can be viewed as a transfer between the raw materials inventory and the work-in-process inventory.

Inventory (Raw Materials) Depts. A and B		Work in Process Depts. A and B	
Raw materials purchases	22.40 →	Job 2000: 22.40	

Unused excess materials are returned to inventory, and the job is relieved of the cost.

On the surface, it would appear that the accounting for direct materials cost is straightforward. However, many problems can arise in accumulating materials costs. For example, a distinction must be made between direct and indirect materials costs. For example, miscellaneous supplies such as glue and nails are not charged directly to a job but are charged to factory overhead. Since the cost of such items is relatively immaterial in proportion to the total job cost, it is not worth management's time and effort to trace the use of such supplies to particular jobs. In practice, such distinctions are not easy to make, and often subjective evaluations are required. Additionally, accounting and costing procedures are required for the handling of materials waste and spoilage. These issues, among others, are treated in greater detail in more advanced management accounting courses, and their resolution poses a challenge to cost accountants.

Tracking Direct Labor Costs

The tracking of direct labor costs to jobs parallels the procedures followed for tracking direct materials costs. As employees in a department work on a job, their hours are charged directly to the job and are posted to the job's job-order cost sheet. Subsequently, labor hours are converted to labor dollars by multiplying the hours charged to each job by the employees' appropriate hourly wage rates. This procedure is illustrated in section (2) of Exhibit 20.1 (b). The following accounting entry in Department A is needed to reflect this transaction:

Work in process (Dept. A)	100.00	
Work in process (Dept. B)	40.00	
Wages payable		140.00
(to transfer wages to work in process)		

This entry can be viewed as the recognition of a liability to increase an asset (i.e., work in process).

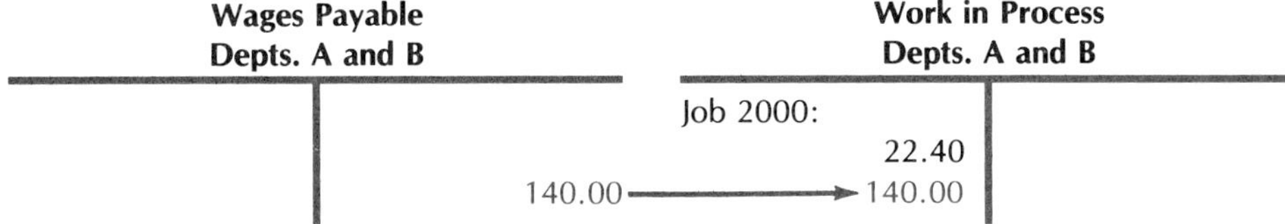

Indirect labor, such as janitorial expenses and supervisors' salaries, are not charged directly to jobs but are classified as part of manufacturing overhead.

As with materials costs, practical problems arise in accounting for labor costs. Management must determine whether certain labor costs should be considered direct or indirect. For example, how should overtime premiums, shift differentials, and rework time be handled? It obviously makes a difference to product cost, with a possible further impact on product pricing and profitability. In addition, management must decide how to calculate the hourly wage rate. Should, for example, this rate include fringe benefits such as health insurance and workers' compensation, or should such costs be charged to overhead? In the past, most companies have charged such costs to overhead. In more recent years, however, as fringe benefit costs have significantly increased, they are being incorporated into the direct hourly wage rate.

Accounting for Overhead

As with all cost systems, manufacturing overhead poses the greatest difficulties in accounting control. Management needs to know the amount of manufacturing overhead by type of cost for each department in total and the way it is distributed, or applied, to jobs. Accounting for overhead can pose problems even for small single-product companies. Seasonal or cyclical variations in production require careful handling of overhead costs. Overhead accounting is even more complex in multiple-product companies, because overhead costs must be distributed equitably over several products. In those single-product industries where there is little variation in the production flow, all manufacturing overhead is charged directly to the product. However, if multiple products are produced, an appropriate distribution of overhead must be made to each job.

In many job-order cost companies, a predetermined overhead rate is used to apply manufacturing overhead to jobs. This method is particularly useful where production fluctuates during the year without a complete shutdown, as in many seasonal industries. Thus, overhead can be distributed to jobs on the basis of actual or predetermined overhead rates. Using predetermined rates has the effect of averaging overhead costs over all jobs.

Predetermined rates for manufacturing overhead are used in most multiproduct plants. To apportion actual costs would give widely fluctuating unit costs that would not have much meaning to management. Another good reason for using a predetermined rate is to provide management with an index of efficiency by comparing actual manufacturing overhead with overhead assigned to jobs on a predetermined rate. This is particularly the case where the rate is based on standard costs. Finally, unit costs for each job can be computed at any time—daily, weekly, or monthly. Materials and labor costs are frequently available or easily accessible, and using predetermined overhead rate provides management with total unit costs to manufacture. Being able to determine unit costs helps management in formulating pricing policies and in preparing bids by the sales department.

The formulation of predetermined overhead rates is accomplished in three steps:

OVERHEAD ALLOCATION BASE
A base for assignment of overhead costs to production.

1. Classification and accumulation of overhead items on an estimated basis for each department in the manufacturing process.
2. Selection of a suitable **overhead allocation base,** the one most directly associated with incurrence of overhead costs. Overhead for labor-intensive products is generally allocated based on direct labor hours, whereas for machine-intensive products (such as those produced by automated equipment), allocation is generally based on machine hours.
3. Determination of the overhead application rate to be applied to production, found by dividing the departmental overhead cost totals by the estimated level of the allocation base.

Let's illustrate this process through a simple example. Assume the Hyppo Publishing Company has two manufacturing departments. Each department incurred overhead costs as in Exhibit 20.2. In forecasting departmental overhead for the upcoming year, each departmental manager has assumed an increase in overhead of 20 percent. In the past, overhead has been allocated to jobs in Department A on the basis of direct labor hours, and allocation in Department B has been based on machine hours. The allocation bases were selected because they were directly associated with the incurrence of overhead costs. For example, in Department A (an assembly operation), overhead costs varied with the number of direct labor hours used. Management thus believed that the most equitable distribution of overhead to jobs should be based on the number of direct labor hours incurred on each job.

A predetermined overhead rate for each department would be calculated by dividing the annual estimated departmental overhead costs by the allocation base. This procedure is illustrated in Exhibit 20.2, where Department A has a burden rate of $1.50 per direct labor hour and Department B has a rate of $1.44 per machine

	Dept. A	Dept. B
Manufacturing overhead incurred, 1985	$20,000	$30,000
Direct labor hours	15,000	
Machine hours		20,000
Estimated manufacturing overhead, 1986	$24,000	$36,000
Estimated direct labor hours	16,000	
Estimated machine hours		25,000

Departmental overhead rate: $\frac{\$24,000}{16,000} = \$1.50$ per DLH

$\frac{\$36,000}{25,000} = \$1.44$ per machine hour

EXHIBIT 20.2
Hyppo Publishing Company

hour. Assume Job 2000 was worked on in Departments A and B. In Department A, 20 direct labor hours were charged to the job, and in Department B, 40 machine hours were used. In this situation, the job would be charged with $87.60 of applied overhead as follows:

Dept. A: 20 hours @ $1.50 per hour =	$30.00
Dept. B: 40 hours @ $1.44 per hour =	57.60
Total overhead charged to Job 2000	$87.60

The following journal entry would be needed to reflect this transaction:

Work in process (Dept. A)	30.00	
Work in process (Dept. B)	57.60	
Manufacturing overhead applied		87.60
(to apply overhead to work in process)		

In T-account format, this application of overhead would be as follows:

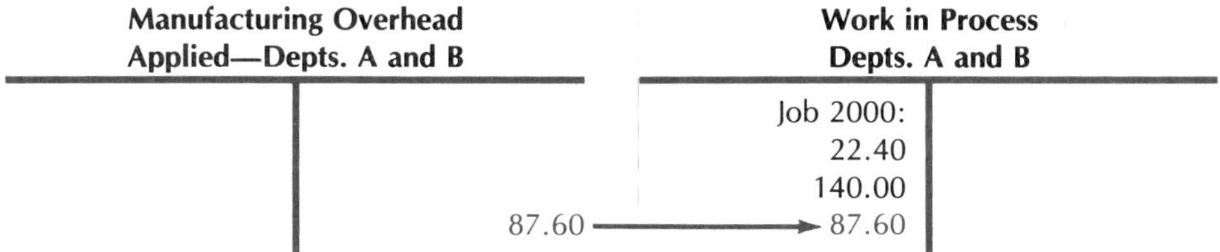

Note that an account entitled Manufacturing Overhead Applied was credited in the preceding entry. This is because actual and applied overhead costs are accumulated separately in the accounts. The incurrence of actual overhead would be recorded in a different account. For example, if Hyppo had incurred $93.00 of actual overhead during the production of Job 2000, its entry would be as follows:

Manufacturing overhead	93.00	
Accounts payable		93.00
(to record incurrence of actual overhead)		

This incurrence of overhead can be viewed as the purchase of various items from suppliers.

Accounts Payable		Manufacturing Overhead	
	93.00	93.00	

Periodically, comparisons will be made between the balances of Manufacturing Overhead and Manufacturing Overhead Applied by simply netting the two accounts together. If the debit balance of Manufacturing Overhead exceeds the credit balance of Manufacturing Overhead Applied, a net debit will exist, signifying under-applied overhead that will reduce net income of the period. Likewise, if the credit balance of Manufacturing Overhead Applied exceeds the debit balance of Manufacturing Overhead, a net credit will exist, signifying over-applied overhead that will increase net income of the period. Whenever there is a balance in the Manufacturing Overhead account, either it can be allocated to Work in Process, Finished Goods, and Cost of Goods Sold (in proportion to the amount remaining in each of these accounts), or it can be closed to Cost of Goods Sold. Most firms choose the latter method because it is a simpler procedure.

The total cost of a job is determined by adding the direct labor, direct materials, and manufacturing overhead applied costs accumulated for a job, as shown on the job's cost sheet. As shown in Exhibit 20.1 (b), the total cost of Job 2000 is $250. The unit product cost for the job would be calculated by dividing the job cost, $250, by the number of units in the job, in this case, 100. This results in a unit cost of $2.50. Once completed, this job would be transferred to finished goods by the following journal entry:

Finished goods (Job 2000)	250.00	
Work in process (Job 2000)		250.00
(to record completion of Job 2000 and its transfer to finished goods)		

This entry is viewed as a transfer between work-in-process inventory and finished goods inventory.

Work in Process Depts. A and B		Finished Goods	
Job 2000:	Job 2000:	Job 2000:	
22.40	250.00 →	250.00	
140.00			
87.60			
250.00			

PROCESS COSTING

The emphasis in process costing is on the accumulation of costs for all units worked on in a department during a given period of time. The units processed in a department typically are similar, and average costs are computed to determine the basis for transferring costs from one department to the next. The typical procedure used to calculate product cost under process costing consists of five steps:

1. Identify the physical flow of production through the various process centers.
2. Accumulate materials, labor, and manufacturing overhead costs by process for a given period of time.
3. Determine each process center's output for the same period of time.
4. Compute an average cost per unit produced in each process by dividing each department's accumulated costs for the period by its output for the same time period.
5. Add the average unit costs of various process centers to obtain the unit cost of individual products.

Keeping Track of Production

In a process cost system, management accumulates and records materials, labor, and overhead costs by processes or departments. Furthermore, costs are recorded on a time basis and are periodically summarized (normally monthly) on a cost of production report, which includes the cost of materials, labor, and manufacturing overhead for a definite time period for a specific department. In addition, each department will usually prepare a monthly production report including a summary of the units accounted for in that department during the month, a schedule of production, and a schedule of work in process.

Records of production quantities are intended to measure the flow of products through the plant from the time of the receipt of raw materials to the time of shipment of the finished product. Daily production reports are compiled. These reports keep management informed of actual achievements with respect to scheduled production quotas and furnish one of the necessary elements in cost computations by the cost department.

Production figures can often be obtained from meters attached to machines, with readings being taken at the beginning and end of each day or run. In some plants, finished units are counted by timekeepers or inspectors by either physical count or automatic scales. Daily reports of production for each process are summarized to constitute a monthly end-of-the-period production report.

Tracking Material Costs. Accounting for materials under process costing is similar to accounting for materials under other cost systems. Where the number of raw material items is large, ledger cards are usually maintained for each type of item of material, with a materials control account in the general or factory ledger.

Raw materials are requisitioned in the usual manner by formal materials requisitions. The requisitions must indicate the department in which the materials are used and the product for which they are requisitioned.

Tracking Labor Costs. In a process cost system, the following information relating to the use of labor must be determined and reported for each process center:

1. The amount of labor time used during the time period.
2. The cost of the labor used to include wages, fringes, and any other wage-related expenditures.

This information must be accumulated by worker and properly identified with the departments benefiting from the labor usage.

An analysis of labor costs by process is another essential requirement of product costing. This involves classification and analysis of labor in all process departments in addition to listing the indirect labor of service departments. Instead of job time tickets used in job-order cost accounting, a daily time ticket for each employee furnishes an analysis by process or service department and gives the breakdown by direct and indirect labor.

The distinction in process cost accounting between direct and indirect labor is usually unnecessary, because both can be charged to the same process account or department. Although no distinction is needed in determining the cost of a process, it should be pointed out that combining direct and indirect labor costs makes the control of each more difficult. This is particularly the case where labor standards are used.

Accounting for Overhead. The accounting for manufacturing overhead in a process cost environment is essentially the same as in a job costing company. However, overhead is charged to and accumulated by process or department rather than by job.

Inventory Valuation and Unit Cost Determination. The distinguishing characteristic of process costing is the requirement to compute unit costs to give essential comparative cost data to management, provide a basis for transferring costs from one process to the next, and provide a basis for inventory valuation.

Unit costs are easily determinable in a production environment where only one product is manufactured in a single step and where there is no unfinished product. In this simplified situation, the following formula would be used to determine the average cost per unit:

$$\text{Unit cost} = \frac{\text{Cost of material} + \text{Labor} + \text{Overhead charged to department}}{\text{Quantity produced by department}}$$

Quantity produced can be expressed in units, weights, or similar measures of production.

Equivalent Units of Production. It is somewhat more complicated to determine unit costs when there are unfinished units on hand at the beginning or end of an accounting period and when there is more than one process step in producing the product. In this case, it is necessary to spread the total costs over all work done in a department—including both completed and unfinished units—to obtain correct unit costs. To accomplish this, the work output of a department must be expressed in terms of a common denominator that represents the total work of a department or process in terms of fully completed units. This common denominator has a number of different names: equivalent units, effective production, equivalent production, or effective efforts. **Equivalent units** represent the number of complete units that would have been produced if all work had been directed toward producing *completed* units, as if there had been no beginning or ending inventories of partially completed units worked on during the period. The number of complete units represented by the equivalent production is divided into the total costs accumulated in the process center during a particular time period to obtain the cost per equivalent unit produced. This calculation rests on the assumption that the work done in producing 100 units of a half-completed product is equivalent to the work done in fully completing 50 units.

EQUIVALENT UNITS
The number of complete units that would have been produced if all work had been directed toward producing completed units, as if there had been no beginning or ending inventories of partially completed units worked on during the period.

Stage of Completion. To obtain a figure for equivalent units of production, management must have complete information as to the stage of completion of both opening and closing inventories. In many cases, the stage-of-completion figures must be given separately for materials, labor, and overhead. For example, if materials are issued at the beginning of a process, the stage of completion of materials in that process will be 100 percent, and the full materials cost must be charged to work-in-process inventory. As for labor and overhead, the work-in-process inventory might be only partially completed, and only partial labor and overhead costs can be charged to the work-in-process inventory. Frequently, however, labor and overhead are at the same stage of completion.

As you will recall from our earlier discussion of predetermined overhead rates, overhead is commonly applied to production based on the amount of direct labor hours or direct labor cost charged to production. This means that in such cases where direct labor is the overhead allocation base, overhead and direct labor are at the same stage of completion. Thus, one calculation is sufficient to obtain the equivalent units for both labor and overhead.

If materials, labor, and overhead are all consumed uniformly throughout the process, only a single computation of effective production is needed. Therefore, the general formula to calculate equivalent units equals physical units times the percentage of completion. Equivalent units must be calculated for labor, materials, and overhead.

Methods of Computing Equivalent Units of Production

The two methods for computing equivalent units of production are the weighted-average method and the first-in, first-out (FIFO) method. The former method treats units from the beginning inventory as though they were both started and completed in the current period, whereas the latter method considers only those units actually completed in the current period (i.e., work completed in the prior period is deducted in computing equivalent units). Here we will use the FIFO method (illustrated in Exhibit 20.3).

In this example, IC Processors has two T-accounts for work in process: one for tracking physical units and one for tracking equivalent units. In tracking physical units, we see that IC Processors began the period with 12,000 units in process. During the period, 100,000 units were added to the process; thus, IC worked on a total of 112,000 units during the period. Since only 8,000 units remained in process at the end of the period, IC must have completed 104,000 units. With this information, we can now determine IC Processors' equivalent units of production. IC began the period with 4,000 equivalent units in process (i.e., 12,000 units, one-third complete). By the end of the period, IC had completed and transferred out 104,000 equivalent units (the same as the number of physical units completed). This left IC with 2,000 equivalent units (i.e., 8,000 units, one-fourth complete) in process at the end of the period. Since IC began with 4,000 equivalent units and ended up with a total of 106,000 equivalent units (104,000 complete + 2,000 still in process), production must have added 102,000 equivalent units during the period.

Calculating Per Unit Costs. IC Processors' costs for the current month were $10,000 for materials, $51,000 for labor, and $25,500 for overhead; its beginning work-in-process inventory was $4,200. IC Processors adds all materials at the beginning of processing. With this information, IC Processors can calculate its costs per equivalent unit as shown in Exhibit 20.3 (b) by merely dividing total costs by equivalent units.

SINGLE-STAGE PROCESS COSTING
A process cost system applied when only one product is manufactured and this product requires only one step in the manufacturing process.

Single-Stage Process Costing. In **single-stage process costing,** only one product is manufactured, and this product requires only one step in the manufacturing process. Information regarding the physical flow of units and the unit costs is required to

EXHIBIT 20.3

Equivalent Units Calculation (a) and Costs Per Equivalent Unit (b)

A

Work in Process (Units)

BI	12,000	COMP	104,000
ADDED	100,000		
EI	8,000		

BI + ADDED − EI = COMP

12,000 + 100,000 − 8,000 = 104,000

Work in Process (Equivalent Units)

BI 12,000 @ 1/3 =	4,000	COMP	104,000
Production	102,000		
EI 8,000 @ 1/4 =	2,000		

Production = COMP + EI (SOC_{EI}) − BI(SOC_{BI})

Production = 104,000 + 8,000(1/4) − 12,000(1/3)

102,000 = 104,000 + 2,000 − 4,000

B

	Materials	Labor	Overhead	Total
(a) Costs of current month	$ 10,000	$ 51,000	$ 25,500	$86,500
(b) Equivalent units				
Materials—same as ADDED, since added at beginning of process	100,000			
Labor—see Production above		102,000		
Overhead—same as Labor, since overhead is applied based on labor			102,000	
(c) Cost per equivalent unit c = a ÷ b	$ 0.10	$ 0.50	$ 0.25	$ 0.85

Work in Process ($)

BI: (12,000 @ .10) + (4,000 @ .75)	$ 4,200	COMP: 104,000 @ .85 = 88,400
ADDED: 102,000 @ .85 =	86,500	
EI: 8,000 @ .1 = 800		
2,000 @ .75 = 1500		
	2,300	

Key: BI = Beginning inventory
EI = Ending inventory
COMP = Units completed
SOC = Stage of completion

determine the ending inventory and the value of product transferred to finished goods or cost of goods sold.

The physical flow of units is summarized in a production report, which accounts for all units placed in production. The production report for IC Processors can be easily prepared from the data in the work in process (units) T-account in Exhibit 20.3 (a). In proper form, the report would appear as follows:

IC Processors
Production Report

	Units
Beginning inventory	12,000
Units put into production	100,000
Units to account for	112,000
Units completed and transferred out	104,000
Ending inventory	8,000
Units accounted for	112,000

The cost figures are frequently summarized in a cost of production report, which normally includes the following information:

1. Costs incurred for the current month, including materials, labor, and manufacturing overhead.
2. Costs of items completed and on hand at the beginning and end of the accounting period.
3. Costs of work in process at the beginning and end of the accounting period.
4. Costs of items transferred to finished goods.

As discussed earlier, the form of this report will vary. One format for this statement is shown in Exhibit 20.4 for IC Processors. As you can see, this report can be easily prepared from the data in the work in process ($) T-account in Exhibit 20.3 (b).

EXHIBIT 20.4

IC Processors
Cost of Production Report

Costs to be accounted for	
Costs for current month	
Materials (from total of materials requisitions—100,000 units @ $.10)	$10,000
Labor (from total of time tickets—102,000 units @ $.50)	51,000
Manufacturing overhead (from balance of account—102,000 units @ $.25)	25,500
Total costs for the current month	$86,500
Completed and on hand at beginning of month (from inventory balance)	0,000
Work in process at beginning of month (from inventory balance)	4,200
Total costs to be accounted for	**$90,700**
Costs accounted for as follows	
Transferred to finished goods (104,000 units @ $.85)	$88,400
Completed and on hand at end of month (units completed × unit cost)	0,000
Work in process at end of month (8,000 units material @ $.10 + 2,000 units conversion @ $.75)	2,300
Total costs accounted for	**$90,700**

MULTI-STAGE PROCESS COSTING A process cost system used when a product must pass through several process steps before it is completed.

Multi-Stage Process Costing. In **multi-stage process costing,** the product must pass through several process steps before it is completed. Thus, when one process department has completed its work on a batch of output, the units are transferred to another department for further processing rather than transferred directly to finished goods. As with single-stage processing, information regarding the physical flow of units and the unit costs is required to determine the transferring department's ending inventory and the value of the products transferred to other process departments.

Multi-stage processing complicates the product costing by introducing a fourth type of cost: costs transferred in to later process departments from earlier process departments. In the multi-stage processing environment, when a department finishes processing a product, it transfers the costs to another processing department rather than to finished goods. The transferring department treats the costs as if they were being transferred to finished goods, and the receiving department treats the costs as if they represented raw materials from inventory. These costs are merely called by a different name—**transferred-in costs**—and can require a separate equivalent unit calculation.

TRANSFERRED-IN COSTS Costs transferred in from earlier process departments to later ones.

EXHIBIT 20.5

Multi-Stage Processing

	Dept. A	Dept. B
A. Total Costs Incurred		
Material X	$ 100,000	
Material Y		$ 127,500
Labor	770,000	673,750
Manufacturing overhead	440,000	385,000
Total costs incurred	$1,310,000	$1,186,250
B. Production Report		
Beginning inventory	0,000	0,000
Units put into production	100,000	85,000
Units to account for	100,000	85,000
Units completed and transferred out	85,000	75,000
Ending inventory (one-fifth complete in each dept.)	15,000	10,000
Units accounted for	100,000	85,000

C. Equivalent Unit Calculation

	Dept. A			Dept. B			
	Matl. X	Labor	OH	Matl. Y	Trans. in	Labor	OH
To complete beginning inventory (no inventory)	0,000	0,000	0,000	0,000	0,000	0,000	0,000
For units started and finished during the month							
(100,000 − 15,000)	85,000	85,000	85,000				
(85,000 − 10,000)				75,000	75,000	75,000	75,000
To start ending inventory							
(15,000 @ one-fifth complete)	15,000	3,000	3,000				
(10,000 @ one-fifth complete)				10,000	10,000	2,000	2,000
Equivalent units of production	100,000	88,000	88,000	85,000	85,000	77,000	77,000

For our purposes, we will illustrate the multi-stage situation involving ending inventory but no beginning inventory. Assume product Z goes through two process departments during production. Materials are added at the beginning of each process, and labor and overhead costs are incurred evenly throughout each process. Costs and production data, along with all reports, for each department for the current month are shown in Exhibit 20.5.

As the exhibit shows, Department A starts with no inventory, adds 100,000 units to process, completes 85,000 units and transfers them to Department B, and ends the month with 15,000 units (one-fifth complete) still in process. Department B starts with no inventory, receives 85,000 units from Department A, completes 75,000 of these units, and ends the month with 10,000 units (one-fifth complete) still in process.

The equivalent units calculation proceeds as before. Since no beginning inventories exist, no equivalent units of production are expended in completing them. Units started and finished during the month (85,000 units for Department A and 75,000 units for Department B) represent completed units and thus receive one full equivalent unit of production each for materials, transferred-in, labor, and overhead costs.

EXHIBIT 20.5
(Continued)

D. Cost Per Equivalent Unit Calculation

	Dept. A				Dept. B		
	Matl. X	Labor	OH		Matl. Y	Labor	OH
Costs	$100,000	$770,000	$440,000		$127,500	$673,750	$385,000
Equivalent units	100,000	88,000	88,000		85,000	77,000	77,000
Cost per equivalent unit	$ 1.00	$ 8.75	$ 5.00		$ 1.50	$ 8.75	$ 5.00
Conversion cost per unit		$13.75					$13.75
Dept. cost per unit		$14.75				$15.25	
Total completion cost per unit				$30.00			

E. Cost of Production Report

	Dept. A	Dept. B
Costs to be accounted for		
Current month		
Materials	$ 100,000	$ 127,500
Transferred in	—	1,253,750
Labor	770,000	673,750
Manufacturing overhead	440,000	385,000
Total costs to be accounted for	$1,310,000	$2,440,000
Costs accounted for		
Completed and transferred out		
(85,000 units @ $14.75)	$1,253,750	
(75,000 units @ $30.00)		$2,250,000
Ending work in process		
(15,000 material @ $1.00 + 3,000 conversion @ $13.75)	56,250	
(10,000 material @ $1.50 + 10,000 trans. in @ $14.75 + 2,000 conversion @ $13.75)		190,000
Total costs accounted for	$1,310,000	$2,440,000

Transferred-in costs in Department B are treated *exactly* as if they were raw materials requisitioned from inventory: They merely have come from a different department. At the end of the month, the two departments each have an inventory of incomplete units for which some equivalent units have been used. Since all materials are added at the beginning of processing, each incomplete unit receives one full equivalent unit of materials cost. Because transferred-in costs *always* enter at the beginning of processing, each incomplete unit receives one full equivalent unit of transferred-in costs. Labor and overhead costs, however, enter production evenly throughout the process. Since the ending inventories are only one-fifth complete, each incomplete unit receives only one-fifth of one equivalent unit of labor and overhead costs.

Once these equivalent units have been computed, the unit costs can be determined. This calculation also follows the pattern set for single-stage processing. Each of the materials, labor, and overhead cost totals for the departments is divided by its respective numbers of equivalent units to determine the unit costs of each product cost component. These individual product cost components can then be aggregated. By adding a department's unit labor cost and unit overhead cost, one can compute the department's unit conversion cost (the cost to convert one unit of raw materials into one unit of department output). By adding a department's unit material cost and unit conversion cost, one can compute the department's total unit cost (the total cost of producing one unit of department output). Note that the cost per equivalent unit calculation did not include a separate column for Department B's transferred-in costs. Since these transferred-in costs represent nothing more than the total materials, labor, and overhead costs of Department A's output, the transferred-in cost per unit is simply equal to Department A's total unit cost—$14.75. Finally, by adding the total unit costs of both departments, one can compute the firm's total unit cost ($30)—the total cost of producing one unit of *finished* product.

These calculations would have been much more complex if beginning inventories were present. Although such complexity is beyond the scope of this text and thus is not presented here, you will be introduced to it in more advanced accounting courses. In practice, process costing is a simpler and easier cost accumulation system to implement than is job-order costing, because it is easier and less time-consuming to track costs to a process than to specific jobs.

Bookkeeping for Product Costs

In addition to preparing all of the preceding unit cost computations and production reports, management must maintain the normal bookkeeping records. Journal entries must be prepared every time materials are requisitioned, labor is used, overhead is applied, or products are completed and transferred to the finished goods inventory or other process departments. Exhibit 20.6 illustrates the journal entries typically made in a product costing system.

EXHIBIT 20.6

Representative Product Costing Journal Entries

Transaction	Entry (Job-Order Costing)	Amount

Purchase of raw materials	Raw materials inventory
	  Accounts payable
		Total purchase cost
		  Total purchase cost

Requisition of direct materials	Work-in-process inventory (Job X)
	  Inventory
		Units @ unit purchase cost
		  Units @ unit purchase cost

Use of indirect materials	Manufacturing overhead
	  Inventory
		Units @ unit purchase cost
		  Units @ unit purchase cost

Use of direct labor	Work-in-process inventory (Job X)
	  Wages payable
		DLHs @ wage rate
		  DLHs @ wage rate

Use of indirect labor	Manufacturing overhead
	  Wages payable
		ILHs @ wage rate
		  ILHs @ wage rate

Incurrence of other overhead items	Manufacturing overhead
	  Accounts payable
		Total cost
		  Total cost

Application of overhead to job	Work-in-process inventory (Job X)
	  Manufacturing overhead applied
		Base units @ predetermined rate
		  Base units @ predetermined rate

Completion of job	Finished goods inventory (Job X)
	  Work-in-process inventory (Job X)
		Total on job-order cost sheet
		  Total on job-order cost sheet

Sale of job	Cost of goods sold
	  Finished goods inventory (Job X)
		Total on job-order cost sheet
		  Total on job-order cost sheet

Closing of overhead accounts and disposition of under-applied overhead	Manufacturing overhead applied
	Cost of goods sold
	  Manufacturing overhead
		Balance of applied overhead
		Net amount under-applied
		  Balance of incurred overhead

Closing of overhead accounts and disposition of over-applied overhead	Manufacturing overhead applied
	  Cost of goods sold
	  Manufacturing overhead
		Balance of applied overhead
		  Net amount over-applied
		  Balance of incurred overhead

Note: Process costing entries are identical to the job-order costing entries illustrated here, except that departments (rather than jobs) represent subsidiary accounts and inventory transfers require equivalent unit computations.

FOR REVIEW

DEMONSTRATION PROBLEM

Duplex Products, Inc., uses a process cost system to account for the costs incurred during production of its single product, Z89Y. Z89Y requires a single process in which two materials are used: Z8 is added (one unit per unit finished product) at the beginning of production, and 9Y is added (one unit per unit of finished product) at the 60% completion stage. Labor and overhead costs are incurred evenly throughout production.

Cost data for April 1988 are as follows.

April 1, Work-in-process inventory	
Units	10,000
Stage of completion	50%
Units started in process	20,000
Units completed and transferred out	25,000
April 30, Work-in-process inventory	
Units	5,000
Stage of completion	75%
Costs incurred	
Material Z8	$100,000.00
Material 9Y	270,000.00
Labor	106,875.00
Overhead	48,093.75

Required

In schedular format, prepare the equivalent unit calculation, the units of production report, and the cost of production report. (You can assume that unit costs of production are the same as those for the previous month.) Use the FIFO method to compute the equivalent units of production.

Demonstration Problem Solution

Duplex Products, Inc.
Equivalent Unit Calculation
For April 1988

	Matl. Z8	Matl. 9Y	Labor	Overhead
To complete beginning inventory 10,000 units, 50% complete	–0–	10,000	5,000	5,000
Units started and finished during month 20,000 started, 5,000 left in WIP	15,000	15,000	15,000	15,000
To start the ending inventory 5,000 units, 75% complete	5,000	5,000	3,750	3,750
Total equivalent units of production	20,000	30,000	23,750	23,750

Duplex Products, Inc.
Units of Production Report
For April 1988

	Units
Beginning inventory	10,000
Units put into production	20,000
Units to account for	30,000
Units completed and transferred out	25,000
Ending inventory	5,000
Units accounted for	30,000

Using the equivalent units of production data, the costs per equivalent unit can be calculated as follows.

	Matl. Z8	Matl. 9Y	Labor	Overhead
Total costs for April	$100,000.00	$270,000.00	$106,875.00	$48,093.75
Equivalent units	20,000	30,000	23,750	23,750
Cost per equivalent unit	$ 5.00	$ 9.00	$ 4.50	$ 2.025

These data can now be used to calculate total inventory values.

	Beginning Work in Process	Completed & Transferred	Ending Work in Process
Material Z8			
10,000 units	$50,000		
25,000 units		$125,000	
5,000 units			$25,000
Material 9Y			
0 units	–0–		
25,000 units		225,000	
5,000 units			45,000
Labor and overhead			
5,000 units	32,625		
25,000 units		163,125	
3,750 units			24,468.75
Total costs	$82,625	$513,125	$94,468.75

Using these inventory values, the cost of production report would appear as follows.

Duplex Products, Inc.
Cost of Production Report
For April 1988

Costs to be accounted for	
Costs for the current month	
Material Z8	$100,000.00
Material 9Y	270,000.00
Labor	106,875.00
Overhead	48,093.75
Total costs for the month	$524,968.75
Completed and on hand at beginning of month	000.00
Work in process at beginning of month	82,625.00
Total costs to be accounted for	$607,593.75
Accounted for as follows	
Transferred to finished goods	$513,125.00
Completed and on hand at end of month	000.00
Work in process at end of month	94,468.75
Total costs accounted for	$607,593.75

SUMMARY

- Product cost systems must be designed to fit individual company needs, and the method of tracking costs and the types of information needed must be considered in their design.
- Under job-order costing, direct labor, direct materials, and factory overhead are physically tracked to a product or a group of products.
- Under process costing, unit costs are determined by finding the total costs of materials, labor, and overhead and dividing the amounts by the quantities of products produced.
- Under an actual cost system, actual amounts of materials, labor, and overhead incurred are recorded and assigned to products as cost.
- Under a normal cost system, materials and labor are accumulated on an actual basis but overhead is allocated to production using a predetermined rate.
- When a standard costing system is in use, actual and predetermined costs for materials, labor, and overhead are accumulated and reported.
- Overhead is the most difficult of all product costs to identify with specific products or groups of products and is therefore usually allocated to production at a predetermined rate.
- Equivalent units represent the number of complete units that would have been produced during a period if all units had been started and finished during that period.
- In a multi-stage manufacturing process using process cost accounting, transferred-in costs are treated by the receiving department just like any other raw materials introduced at the beginning of the process.

QUESTIONS

20-1. What two dimensions can be used to characterize any product cost system?

20-2. List and briefly describe the two cost accumulation systems. What nature of product is produced under each system?

20-3. Identify and discuss the components of product cost.

20-4. List and briefly describe the three types of costs that can be collected by a product costing system.

20-5. Describe the function of the job-order cost sheet.

20-6. What is a predetermined overhead rate? How is one calculated?

20-7. What steps must be followed to calculate product costs in a process costing environment?

20-8. What is the distinguishing characteristic of process costing?

20-9. What are equivalent units of production?

20-10. What items should the cost of production report contain?

EXERCISES

20-E1. Following are various costs incurred by Jackson Corporation, manufacturers of bicycles for a large sporting goods retailer. Classify these costs as either product or period costs, and if they are product costs, further classify them as either direct labor, direct materials, or manufacturing overhead.

a. Payroll taxes for assembly line.
b. Cost of labor of workers who put fenders on the bicycles.
c. Office supplies for officers, e.g., stationery and envelopes.
d. Salary of in-house accountant.
e. Supplies used by in-house accountant.
f. Costs incurred by salespeople for overnight stay in hotel.
g. Repair costs for assembly-line machine.
h. Cost of tires for bicycles.

20-E2. Job No. 532 had accumulated total costs of $8,350 by the end of last week. During this week, $1,500 of direct materials were used on the job, 100 hours of direct labor were charged to the job at a cost of $25 per hour, and manufacturing overhead was applied at a rate of $3.50 per direct labor hour. Job No. 532 was completed this week. Compute its total cost and present the journal entry to record its completion.

20-E3. Hamilton, Inc., applies manufacturing overhead based on a predetermined rate of 120% of direct labor cost. Job No. 157 has a total of $7,500 of applied overhead. Determine the direct labor cost charged to Job. No. 157.

20-E4. Compute the equivalent production in each of the following cases.

Case	Units in Process At Beginning	Units Started	Units Completed And Transferred	Units in Process At End
1	125, 40% complete		2,750	250, 20% complete
2	230, 10% complete	3,100		200, 25% complete
3	150, 1/6 complete	2,500	2,250	? , 50% complete
4	? , 25% complete	4,000	4,200	100, 15% complete

20-E5. Assume the data for Case 3 in 20-E4 relate to labor product for the current month in Department A. If total labor cost for the department was $20,248.75, compute the following.

a. The labor cost per equivalent unit of production for the month.
b. The labor cost component of the ending inventory of the department.

20-E6. The Crew Company uses a job-order cost system with normal costing. In manufacturing an order of 1,000 units for one of its customers, Crew uses $2,500 of direct materials and 200 direct labor hours, which cost $8.50 per hour. The annual budget estimates that total labor for the year will be $1.25 million, while total overhead will be $5 million. If the predetermined overhead rate is expressed as a percentage of direct labor cost, what is the total cost and unit cost of the customer's order?

20-E7. The following data pertain to H.S.P. Corporation for the year 1986.

Sales (10,000 units)	$250,000
Raw materials used (15,000 units @$4)	60,000
Direct labor cost incurred	15,000
Manufacturing overhead incurred	
Variable	15,000
Fixed	30,000
Selling and administrative expenses	75,000

Assume that one unit of raw materials enters each finished unit, that there is an ending inventory of finished goods of 5,000 units, and that there are no other beginning or ending inventories. If H.S.P. uses a process costing system with actual costs, what costs must it attach to its total ending finished goods inventory and its total cost of goods sold for the year?

PROBLEM SET A

20-A1. Journal Entries for Job-Order Costing. The following activities relate to Hallace, Inc.'s, job-order cost system for May 1986.

May 1 Purchased 1,000 units of raw materials for cash at a price of $10 per unit.
5 Requisitioned 100 units of raw materials for manufacture of Job No. 125.
10 Recorded wages due employees for work on Job No. 125—100 hours at $8.50 per hour.
10 Applied overhead to Job No. 125 based on the predetermined rate of $2.50 per direct labor hour.
24 Recorded wages due employees for work on Job No. 125—50 hours at $8.50 per hour.
24 Applied overhead to Job No. 125 based on the predetermined rate of $2.50 per direct labor hour.
24 Recorded completion of Job No. 125, since all costs had been applied.
25 Recorded sale of Job No. 125 to customer on account for $50 per unit. Hallace uses a perpetual inventory system.

Job No. 125 required one unit of raw materials for each unit of finished product.

Required

Prepare the general journal entries to be used by Hallace, Inc., to record the information relevant to Job No. 125.

20-A2. Inventory Valuation Under Job-Order Costing. The Fabtell Company began business on October 1, 1986, and incurred the following manufacturing costs in the month of October.

Raw materials purchased	$25,000
Factory payroll costs (@$10 per hour)	20,000
Manufacturing overhead costs	8,500

The following costs were charged to the three jobs worked on during the month.

	Job 1	Job 2	Job 3
Direct materials	$10,000	$ 5,000	$ 4,500
Direct labor	?	?	?
Overhead applied at $4.25 per direct labor hour	4,335	2,890	1,275

Job No. 1 was completed and sold for $30,000; Job No. 2 was completed but not sold; and Job No. 3 is incomplete.

Required

Compute the balances of the three inventory accounts and of Cost of Goods Sold as of October 31, 1986.

20-A3. Analysis of Cost Flows. Selected ledger accounts of the King Corporation are as follows for 1986.

Raw Materials Inventory

Jan. 1 bal.	$15,000	1986 credits	$?
1986 debits	50,000		
Dec. 31 bal.	12,000		

Manufacturing Overhead

1986 debits	$74,000	1986 credits	$?

Work in Process

Jan. 1 bal.	$35,000	1986 credits	$188,000
Direct materials	48,000		
Direct labor	60,000		
Overhead	75,000		
Dec. 31 bal.	?		

Factory Wages Payable

1986 debits	$67,000	Jan. 1 bal.	$ 4,000
		1986 credits	66,000
		Dec. 31 bal.	?

Finished Goods

Jan. 1 bal.	$60,000	1986 credits	$?
1986 debits	?		
Dec. 31 bal.	48,000		

Cost of Goods Sold

1986 debits	$?		

Required

a. What was the actual manufacturing overhead cost incurred during 1986?
b. How much of the actual manufacturing overhead in (a) consisted of indirect materials?
c. How much of the actual manufacturing overhead in (a) consisted of indirect labor?
d. What was the cost of goods manufactured for 1986?
e. What was the cost of goods sold for 1986?
f. If overhead is applied to production on a basis of direct costs, what rate was in effect for 1986?
g. Was manufacturing overhead over-applied or under-applied for 1986? By how much?

20-A4. Manufacturing Overhead Under Job-Order Costing. Manusys, Incorporated, uses a job-order cost system, applying overhead based on a predetermined rate. Manusys has two departments, A and B. Machine hours is used as the overhead allocation base in Department A, and direct labor hours is used as the base in Department B. Budget estimates for the next month are as follows.

	Dept. A	Dept. B
Direct labor cost	$6,000	$6,500
Manufacturing overhead	7,200	9,600
Direct labor hours	1,500	1,600
Machine hours	3,000	800

Cost records show the following for Job No. 1503.

	Dept. A	Dept. B
Materials used	$4,500	$5,500
Direct labor cost	6,250	7,000
Direct labor hours	1,570	1,700
Machine hours	3,000	750

Required

a. Compute the predetermined overhead rates for the next month for Departments A and B.
b. Compute the amount of overhead that would be applied to Job No. 1503, which was started and finished during the next month.
c. Compute the total cost of Job No. 1503.

20-A5. Inventory Valuation Under Process Costing. Following are cost and production information for Littlan Corporation's Department B, in which all raw materials are added at the beginning of the process (one unit of raw material per unit of finished product).

Raw materials placed in production in April, 2,000 units	$8,000
Direct labor, 600 hours @$5	3,000
Overhead applied, 150% of direct labor cost	4,500
Work-in-process inventory, April 30, 200 units, 50% complete as to labor and overhead	?

Required

Calculate the following:

a. The number of units completed and transferred out of Department B.
b. The cost per equivalent unit of materials, labor, and manufacturing overhead for Department B for April.
c. The cost of the units transferred out.
d. The cost of the ending work in process of Department B for the month of April.

20-A6. Multi-Stage Equivalent Units of Production. Sceytco, Incorporated, manufactures a product that requires a three-step production process. Each step is performed by a separate process departmment. Inventory data for the three departments are as follows.

	Dept. A		Dept. B		Dept. C	
	Units	**% Completion**	**Units**	**% Completion**	**Units**	**% Completion**
Inventory, May 1	1000	30	300	50	400	80
Raw materials added to process (one unit per unit output)	5000		–0–		–0–	
Inventory, May 31	500	45	250	10	1100	20

Required

Compute the number of equivalent units of production for each of the three departments for May. (Hint: Compute the number of units completed and transferred to the next department as part of your calculations.)

20-A7. Cost of Production Report. Strake Company uses a process cost system to account for the costs incurred in making its single product, Beta. Beta requires one process in which materials are added entirely at the beginning of processing. Cost data for May 1986 are as follows.

Units started in process	300,000
Units completed and transferred out	250,000
Stage of completion on May 31	
Materials	100%
Labor	50%
Overhead	50%
Direct materials cost	$200,000
Direct labor costs	150,000
Overhead costs	300,000

There were no May 1 inventories.

Required

Prepare a cost of production report for May.

PROBLEM SET B

20-B1. Journal Entries for Process Costing. The following activities relate to Malrose Company's process cost system for August 1986.

August	1	Purchased raw materials for processing: 1,500 units of A at $15 per unit and 10,000 units of B at $1.50 per unit.
	2	Process Department A requisitioned 750 units of material A to be entered at the beginning of processing.
	15	Recorded wages due Department A employees—100 hours at $12.75 per hour.
	15	Applied Department A overhead to process based on the predetermined rate of 200% of direct labor cost.
	15	Recorded completion of 500 units of product and their transfer from Department A to Department B. 250 units remained in Department A work in process, 50% completed.
	16	Process Department B requisitioned 5,000 units of material B to be entered at the beginning of processing.
	31	Recorded wages due Department B employees—500 hours at $15.50 per hour.
	31	Applied Department B overhead to process based on the predetermined rate of 80% of direct labor cost.
	31	Recorded completion of 400 units of product and their transfer to finished goods. 100 units remained in Department B work in process, 75% completed.

Each unit of finished product required one unit of raw material A and ten units of raw material B.

Required

Prepare the general journal entries to be used by Malrose Company to record the preceding information relevant to the process cost system.

20-B2. Inventory Valuation Under Job-Order Costing. Dragic, Inc., uses a job-order cost system for its two-process manufacturing activities. It incurred the following costs during April 1986.

Raw materials purchased	
For Department A	$57,000
For Department B	40,000
Factory payroll costs	
For Department A (@ $10 per hour)	?
For Department B (@ $20 per hour)	45,000
Manufacturing overhead costs	?

The following costs were charged to four jobs worked on during the month.

	Job 1	Job 2	Job 3	Job 4
Department A costs				
Direct materials	$5,000	$15,000	$ 2,000	$30,000
Direct labor	?	?	?	?
Overhead applied at $5 per direct labor hour	5,000	7,500	15,000	2,500
Department B costs				
Direct materials	–0–	2,000	20,000	7,000
Direct labor	–0–	10,000	5,000	30,000
Overhead applied at 150% of direct labor cost	?	?	?	?

Job No. 4 was completed and sold for $150,000, Job No. 3 was completed but not yet sold, Job No. 2 has not yet been finished in process Department B, and Job No. 1 has not yet been finished in process Department A.

Required

Compute the balances of the three inventory accounts and of Cost of Goods Sold as of April 30, 1986.

20-B3. Incomplete Data for Analysis of Cost Flow. A fire at CoCo Company partially destroyed the company's records. The fragments left readable are as follows.

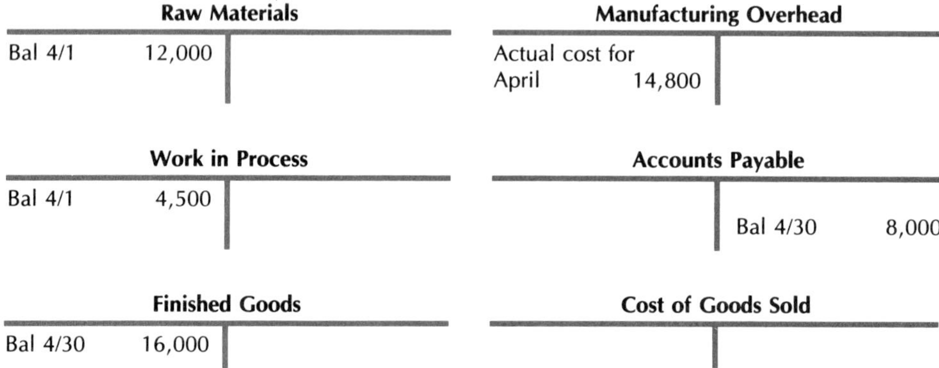

Raw Materials	
Bal 4/1 12,000	

Manufacturing Overhead	
Actual cost for April 14,800	

Work in Process	
Bal 4/1 4,500	

Accounts Payable	
	Bal 4/30 8,000

Finished Goods	
Bal 4/30 16,000	

Cost of Goods Sold	

Sifting through the ashes and talking to selected employees have turned up the following information:

1. The controller remembers clearly that the predetermined overhead was based on an estimated 60,000 direct labor hours to be worked over the year and an estimated $180,000 in manufacturing overhead costs.

2. The production superintendent's cost sheets showed only one job in process on April 30. Materials of $2,600 had been added to the job and 300 direct labor hours expended at $6 an hour.

3. The accounts payable are for raw materials only, according to the accounts payable clerk, who remembers that the balance in the account was $6,000 on April 1. An analysis of cancelled checks unaffected by the fire shows payments of $40,000 made to suppliers during the month.

4. A charred piece of payroll ledger shows that 5,200 direct labor hours were recorded during the month. The personnel department has verified that there were no variations in pay rates among employees.

5. Records in the finished goods warehouse indicate that finished goods inventory was $11,000 on April 1.

6. Another charred piece in the vault revealed the cost of goods manufactured for April was $89,000.

Required

Determine the following amounts:

a. Work-in-process inventory, April 30.

b. Raw materials purchased during April.

c. Overhead applied to work in process.

d. Cost of goods sold for April.

e. Over-applied or under-applied overhead for April.

f. Raw material usage for April.

g. Raw material inventory, April 30.

20-B4. Manufacturing Overhead Under Process Costing. Prosic Company uses a process cost system with direct costing, applying variable overhead based on a predetermined rate. At the end of the period, actual overhead is calculated and compared to applied overhead. If actual overhead is greater than that applied (under-applied), the difference is deducted from income for the period; conversely, if actual overhead is less than that applied (over-applied), the difference is added to income.

Prosic has one process department in which direct labor hours are used as the overhead allocation base. Budget estimates for the current month had shown the following to be relevant to this.

Direct labor cost	$12,000
Direct labor hours	3,000
Variable overhead	$15,000
Fixed overhead	$10,000

Cost records show the following for the current month.

Beginning work-in-process inventory	$ –0–
Materials entered at beginning of processing, 10,000 units	5,000
Labor cost incurred, 3,500 hours	14,000
Actual overhead	
Variable	16,000
Fixed	10,000
Ending work-in-process inventory, 3,000 units, 1/3 complete	?

Each unit of finished output required one unit of raw material.

Required

a. Compute the predetermined overhead rate that would have been used in the current month.
b. Compute the cost of the ending work-in-process inventory and of the goods completed and transferred out.

20-B5. Inventory Valuation Under Process Costing. Flour-works, Incorporated, began business on January 1, 1986. On January 31, the following information was taken from the corporation's process cost records.

Work in process balance Jan. 1	$ –0–
Materials requisitioned for process, 10,000 units	15,000
Factory labor costs incurred	37,500
Manufacturing overhead costs at actual amounts	
Variable	22,500
Fixed	10,000
Work in process balance Jan. 31, consisting of 5,000 units, 50% complete	?

Raw materials enter the process at the beginning, one unit per unit of finished output. The corporation uses a direct costing system.

Required

Compute the balances of Work in Process and Finished Goods (assuming none of the completed units have been sold) as of January 31, 1986.

20-B6. Multi-Stage Equivalent Units of Production. Fischer Industries, Inc., uses process costing for its manufacturing activities, which involve three related processing departments. Raw materials enter Department A; goods completed by Department A are transferred to Department B; goods completed by Department B are transferred to Department C; and goods completed by Department C are transferred to finished goods inventory.

Inventory and production data relevant to the three departments for the current month are as follows.

	Dept. A		Dept. B		Dept. C	
	Units	% Completion	Units	% Completion	Units	% Completion
April 1 inventory	150	30	200	?	?	60
Raw materials entering process (2 units per unit output)	1400		–0–		–0–	
Equivalent production for the month	1250		1364		1378	
April 30 inventory	300	?	100	50	180	20

Required

Calculate the missing amounts from the table. (Hint: You must determine the number of goods completed and transferred by one department to find the amount of goods entering the next department.)

20-B7. Cost of Production Report. Laster Corporation uses a process cost system to account for the costs incurred in the production of its single product, Digamma. Digamma requires three processes for its production, one each for the production of its two major subassemblies and one to join the subassemblies into the finished product. Raw materials are added at the beginning of each process. Cost data for process Department C, the final process, for July 1989 are as follows.

Units started in process	150,000
Units completed and transferred out	100,000
Stages of completion on July 31	
Subassembly A transferred in	100%
Subassembly B transferred in	100%
Material C	100%
Labor	50%
Overhead	50%
Subassembly A costs	$450,000
Subassembly B costs	900,000
Direct materials costs	75,000
Direct labor costs	125,000
Overhead costs	250,000

There were no July 1 inventories.

Required

Prepare a cost of production report for the month ending July 31, 1989, for process Department C.

STANDARD COSTS

CHAPTER OBJECTIVES
After studying Chapter 21, you should understand the following:

1. The nature and purpose and advantages and disadvantages of standard costs.
2. How product cost standards are developed and used for purposes of planning and control.
3. The way in which standard costs flow through the ledger accounts.
4. How to compute and interpret the different variances from standard costs.
5. The manner in which variances are isolated in accounting systems and disposed of at the end of the period.
6. The income statement presentation of product cost standards and variances from these standards.

Chapter 20 described how direct materials, direct labor, and predetermined overhead costs are applied to products under a normal cost system. This chapter expands the discussion of product costing by considering standard costing. This chapter also discusses how such systems can enhance management planning and control.

NATURE AND PURPOSE OF STANDARD COSTS

STANDARD COSTS
Predetermined estimates of the amounts and costs of raw materials, direct labor, and factory overhead.

Standard costs are predetermined estimates of the amounts and costs of raw materials, direct labor, and factory overhead required to produce finished goods in a manufacturing operation. These estimates provide management with an expectation of what the product *should* cost, assuming the manufacturing process operates smoothly and standards are reasonable and accurate.

Standard costs facilitate management planning and control. For planning purposes, standard costs provide management with information on the total expected cost for producing a given amount of output. Such information is useful for pricing decisions, financial planning, and overall decisions about whether to produce at all. For control purposes, standard costs provide benchmarks against which actual results can be compared. Management can then focus its efforts on those areas where results do not coincide with plans. This method of focusing the managerial process on areas that show deviations from standards is known as **management by exception.**

MANAGEMENT BY EXCEPTION
The focusing of management's attention on areas that show deviations from standards.

Standard Costs and Predetermined Overhead Rates

Standard costs are not quite the same as predetermined overhead rates discussed in Chapter 20. Although predetermined overhead rates apply to only one area of cost accumulation (i.e., factory overhead), a standard cost system includes direct materials and direct labor as well as factory overhead. Additionally, standard costs are likely to be more rigorously determined than simple predetermined overhead rates. The primary function of a predetermined overhead rate is to facilitate product costing. Standard cost systems, on the other hand, provide a tool for management in planning and control. To be useful for planning and control, a standard cost, whether for materials, labor, or overhead, must be carefully determined under existing manufacturing conditions.

Advantages and Disadvantages of Standard Costs

Advantages. As just stated, standard costs serve management in planning and control. Projections of total production costs allow management to determine future cash requirements more accurately. This, in turn, enables management to work with banks to obtain financing on favorable terms. (We will return to these financing aspects of the planning cycle in Chapter 23 when we cover the budgeting process.)

Projections of total costs also assist management in pricing decisions. By adding desired profits to total projected costs and dividing by the number of units to be produced and sold, management can determine selling prices. Obviously, the computed price can be adjusted for competitive considerations, economic conditions, and other variables, but at least it gives management a starting point. If it appears that actual cost will be greater than the standard costs, management can begin to work on cost reductions or product redesigns. The use of standard costs lets management make decisions about a product in advance of its actual production. These decisions would not be possible without such projections.

Standard Costing in Las Vegas Casinos

In the casinos, few efforts have been made to develop budgeting standards. For exmple, how many rooms should a maid be able to service in one day? How many tables should a waitress be able to serve in a given time period? For an estimated drop, how many blackjack tables must be used, and how many dealers are needed per shift to staff these tables? These areas are virtually unplowed ground for casino labor, although engineered work standards based on time and motion studies or methods-time-measurement have been adopted in the hotel-restaurant area.

As an example of how standards could be applied, one casino company calculates potential costs for its beverage sales. The actual costs are then compared with potential costs to determine if the actual costs are within acceptable limits. The potential cost is based on the beverage sales potential. The following is a simplified example of the calculation:

Size of drink	1.5 oz.
Size of bottle	32 oz.
Price of drink	$2
Drinks per bottle	(32 oz./1.5 oz.) = 21.3 drinks
Potential sales per bottle	(21.3 × $2) = $42.60
Cost of bottle	$6
Potential cost in relation to potential sales	($6/$42.60) = 14.1%

A wide disparity between historical costs and potential costs for a given beverage outlet is a signal for management to review the operation.

SOURCE: Hames H. Bullock and Virginia H. Bakay, "How Las Vegas Casinos Budget," *Management Accountant*, July 1980, p. 37.

Once final plans are made and production begins, use of standard costs lets management control operations on a more timely basis. Actual results with respect to materials, labor, and overhead used in the production process can be compared to the expected costs of each, and problems can be pinpointed for corrective action. Such comparisons can be made as often as management wishes, even on a daily or hourly basis. Of course, the more frequent the comparisons, the more costly the system is to operate. Just as with any accounting system, the costs of operating the system must be measured against the benefits it produces.

Standard costs also facilitate the bookkeeping process. In a standard cost system, raw materials, work-in-process, and finished goods inventory accounts are kept in terms of standard costs. Thus, bookkeepers need to trace only records of *quantities* through the system. All additions to or subtractions from the accounts are made at the standard cost. Bookkeeping then becomes a simple process of tabulating production in quantities and making standardized entries for the production amounts obtained. Of course, actual costs must also be accumulated for control purposes, but at any point in time, data are immediately available on the standard amounts of materials, labor, and factory overhead consumed and the amount of inventory on hand.

Disadvantages. Perhaps the greatest problem of a standard cost system is the difficulty in establishing and maintaining meaningful standards for each of the three components of product cost. Standards must be continuously examined and modified as conditions change so that they are always reasonable and reliable for planning and control. It is important that standards be set at reasonably attainable levels if they are to be useful to management. Loosely established standards do not provide much motivation for employees, because employees can easily beat them. Likewise, unobtainable standards based on perfect operating conditions will not be very useful, because employees will rarely be able to meet them. As a result, morale and attitude problems can arise.

Standards are usually established on the basis of historical performance or engineering studies. Standards based on prior years' performance might not reflect what will or should happen in the future. Consequently, standards are most effectively established on the results of engineering studies that determine how much labor and materials should go into making a specific product. This approach to standard setting is further discussed in a subsequent section.

The initial investment required to establish a standard cost system is both time-consuming and expensive. Not only must management undertake expensive studies to determine initial standards, but personnel within the business—from top management to production workers—must be educated in the purpose, usage, and limitations of the system. Without such education, not even the best standards in the best system can provide benefits to the organization.

For a standard cost system to be successful, top management must support the project, both financially and organizationally. Finally, as stated earlier, a standard cost system must meet a cost-benefit test just as any other potential investment. Simply put, the expected benefits of the system must be greater than the expected costs of installing and operating the system.

DIRECT MATERIALS STANDARDS

Development of Direct Materials Standards

Standards for direct materials focus on the amounts and costs of direct materials used in the production of one unit of output. The amount of direct materials expected to be consumed is known as the **direct materials usage standard,** while the expected cost per unit of direct materials used is known as the **direct materials price standard.**

DIRECT MATERIALS USAGE STANDARD
The amount of direct materials expected to be used to produce one unit of output.

DIRECT MATERIALS PRICE STANDARD
The expected cost per unit of direct materials.

For example, to produce one wood coffee table, the Fine Furniture Company expects that ten board feet of oak will be needed at a cost of $2.10 per board foot (see Exhibit 21.1). The materials usage standard is ten board feet per table, while the materials price standard is $2.10 per board foot. Taken together, the standard direct materials cost of one coffee table is $21.

The materials usage standard can be developed from historical experience or industrial engineering studies or can simply be management's best expectation of what should occur. The standard can be influenced by such factors as the age of the production machinery, the experience of the work force, output quality tolerances, product designs, and the quality of the materials available. Usually a reasonable standard includes an allowance for normal materials spoilage and waste in the production process.

Materials price standards can be developed from supplier price quotations or historical data for similar materials used in other products. The price standards can vary if projected production quantities are altered, since quantity discounts might be available on the materials purchases.

Direct Materials Standards in the Planning Cycle

For planning purposes, direct materials standards provide a basis for estimating purchasing requirements, determining inventory levels, and determining materials handling requirements. Combining the direct materials usage projections with the direct materials price standard, management can project the total estimated dollar commitment required to support the direct materials acquisition. This then becomes part of the cash flow budgeting process (to be explored more fully in Chapter 23). It should be apparent that projections of direct materials costs or any other costs to be incurred in production are exceedingly important. If a business does not have sufficient resources, production becomes impossible.

Direct Materials Standards in the Control Cycle

For control purposes, the direct materials price and usage standards provide a basis for establishing responsibility and identifying potential problems. Deviations of actual results from standard are known as **variances.** Such variances provide the basis for identifying and resolving problems.

VARIANCES
Deviations of actual results from standard expectations.

Suppose the Fine Furniture Company purchases 2,000 board feet of oak for $4,400 and uses 1,600 board feet to produce 150 coffee tables (as listed in Exhibit 21.1). Without a standard cost system, Fine Furniture would attach a direct materials cost of $3,520 (4,400/2,000 × 1,600) to the tables. However, the standard direct materials cost of 150 tables is only $3,150 (150 tables × 10 ft. × $2.10). Such variances in which actual costs are greater than standard costs are called unfavorable. In those cases where actual costs are less than standard, the variance is termed favorable.

Two different reasons exist for direct materials cost variances. First, the *price* paid for the materials might have been more or less than the standard price. Second, the *quantity* of materials used might have been more or less than the standard quantity. Differences in the materials price from standard are called **direct materials price variances,** while differences in the amount of direct materials used from standard are called **direct materials usage variances.**

DIRECT MATERIALS PRICE VARIANCE
The difference between actual material price and standard materials price.

DIRECT MATERIALS USAGE VARIANCE
The difference between the amount of direct materials used and the standard expectation.

Direct Materials Price Variances. The purchasing department is normally responsible for obtaining direct materials at standard costs. Therefore, responsibility for product cost variances traceable to materials acquisition is charged to purchasing. The direct materials price variance is computed as the difference between the actual and the standard cost per unit multiplied by the total number of units of direct materials purchased. Differences between actual and standard prices paid can be

EXHIBIT 21.1
Fine Furniture Company

Cost Component	Standard	Actual Experience
Direct materials		
Price	$2.10 per bd. ft.	$4400 for 2000 bd. ft.
Usage	10 bd. ft. per table	1600 bd. ft. for 150 tables
Direct labor		
Rate	$14.00 per hour	$23,625 for 1575 hours
Usage	10 hours per table	1575 hours for 150 tables
Variable overhead		
Spending	$0.24 per hour	$400 for 1575 hours
Efficiency	10 hours per table	1575 hours for 150 tables
Fixed overhead		
Budget	$320 per month	$350 for one month
Volume	2000 DLH	1500 DLH

caused by a number of factors. For example, the purchasing department might not have predicted the standard price accurately, might have ordered in uneconomic lot sizes, or might not have received anticipated purchase discounts. The purchasing department would try to isolate direct materials price variances as quickly as possible and correct any problems that caused significant variances. In the case of the Fine Furniture Company, the direct materials price variance is equal to the following:

Materials price variance	
Actual price	$2.20 per ft.
Standard price	2.10 per ft.
Variance—unfavorable	$0.10 per ft. × actual qty. purchased, 2000 = $200 unfavorable

The direct materials price variance is based on the total amount purchased, not just the materials used in production. In practice, the direct materials price variance can be calculated at the point of either purchase or usage. However, for control purposes, it is best calculated at the time of purchase. Earlier we indicated that inventory records under a standard cost system are maintained at standard costs rather than at actual costs. This use of standard cost means that the inventory valuation process does not require the use of FIFO, LIFO, or any other inventory cost-flow assumption until the firm prepares financial statements at year-end under generally accepted accounting principles.

Materials price variances are normally determined at the point of purchase and are excluded from the amounts entered as direct materials inventory. Further, the purchase creates the variances, and for control purposes, the amount of the variance, if any, needs identifying at this time for early attention by management. The journal entry for the materials acquisition by Fine Furniture Company would thus be as follows:

Materials price variance (2000 @ $.10)	200	
Direct materials inventory (2000 @ $2.10)	4,200	
Accounts payable		4,400
(to record materials acquisition)		

Direct Materials Usage Variances. Normally, the production department is responsible for the amount of direct materials used to produce a given amount of acceptable output. Therefore, responsibility for such variances would be assigned to production personnel.

In its simplest form, the direct materials usage variance is the difference between the amount of materials actually used to produce a given amount of acceptable output and the standard usage expected for that output. For Fine Furniture, the direct materials usage variance would be 100 board feet unfavorable (1600 bd. ft. actually used − 1500 bd. ft. projected use). Information on materials usage variances is probably best expressed in quantities only for feedback to production personnel. However, because accounting records are maintained in dollar terms, the variances must be translated into dollars for entry into the accounting system. Because price differences from standard for direct materials purchases are the responsibility of purchasing, materials usage variances are translated into dollars at the standard cost per unit. In the case of Fine Furniture, the direct materials usage variance would be as follows:

Materials usage variance	
Actual usage	1600 bd. ft.
Standard usage	1500 bd. ft.
Variance—unfavorable	100 bd. ft. × std. price/unit, $2.10 = $210

As with price variances, materials usage variances are removed from the cost of the finished product by charging finished goods only with the standard cost of the direct materials required for the number of acceptable units of output produced. For Fine Furniture, the journal entry to charge work in process with the standard quantity of materials would be as follows:

Work in process (1500 @ $2.10)	3,150	
Direct materials inventory		3,150
(to charge work in process with materials)		

Later, when additional materials are required to complete the work (due to materials spoilage or defective units), the usage variance would be recorded for Fine Furniture as follows:

Materials usage variance (100 @ $2.10)	210	
Direct materials inventory		210
(to recognize requisition of additional materials)		

Of course, if production uses less than the standard quantity of materials to complete the work, the remaining materials would be returned to inventory and the favorable usage variance would be recorded. For example, if Fine Furniture had used only 1400 board feet of the wood previously requisitioned, it would return 100 board feet to inventory as follows:

Direct materials inventory	210	
Materials usage variance		210
(to record return of unused materials)		

Management Analysis of Direct Materials Variances. It is tempting to consider all favorable variances as beneficial and rewardable and all unfavorable variances as bad and as a sign of inadequate performance. However, such analysis is too simplistic and can lead to improper action on the part of managers. For instance, it might be that the production manager used more than the standard amount of materials in the Fine Furniture Company example because the purchasing manager obtained lower quality wood. Or perhaps the sales manager is accepting rush orders that disrupt or overload the normal production schedule. Perhaps the personnel manager has not been able to obtain workers with the skills expected when the materials usage standard was developed.

Variances should be treated as flags signaling the need for management investigation, not as conclusive evidence of good or bad performance on the part of some individual. On the other hand, care must be exercised to avoid a situation where each manager attempts to shift blame to another and responsibility is never established. Finally, all variances—not just unfavorable ones—are signals for management attention. Most managers can take action to obtain favorable variances, but that action might not be desirable when viewed on an overall basis.

DIRECT LABOR STANDARDS

Development of Direct Labor Standards

Just as with direct materials, past experience can be used as the starting point to predict the future amounts of direct labor needed for production. If prior records are not available or substantial changes have been made in the production process, time and motion studies might be needed to determine appropriate direct labor usage standards. These studies can be employed when new standards must be developed for labor usage. A detailed discussion of time and motion studies is beyond the scope of this text, but it should be noted that great care must be exercised in doing these studies. When workers are observed, their behavior patterns can change. As a result, the standards developed might not be applicable to the regular production process.

Simulation of full-scale production in an experimental setting can also be used to develop direct labor usage standards. One advantage of this approach is that the process allows the production procedures to be modified before actual operation. Thus, the most efficient production arrangement can be determined at the same time as the labor standard.

DIRECT LABOR USAGE (EFFICIENCY) STANDARD
The expected amount of direct labor hours required to produce one unit of output.

The **direct labor usage** (or **efficiency**) **standard** is usually expressed in terms of direct labor hours required to produce one unit of output. For example, the direct labor usage standard for the Fine Furniture Company could be expressed as ten labor hours for each coffee table produced. Just as materials standards must allow for normal waste, reasonable labor efficiency standards must allow for normal amounts of unproductive time, such as coffee breaks, startup, and cleanup.

DIRECT LABOR RATE STANDARD
The normal pay rate per hour of labor.

The **direct labor rate standard** (the normal pay rate per hour of labor) is usually determined by reference to union contracts or established rates of pay. Although the determination of direct labor rate standards appears simple, managers must be careful to ensure that the most recent pay schedules are employed and that the correct pay rates are applied to each direct labor hour used in production if more than one type of worker is needed.

Direct Labor Standards in the Planning Cycle

For planning purposes, direct labor usage standards provide information to the personnel department on the amount and type of labor (skill) required to produce the level of planned production. Combining the amount of labor with the cost of that labor (estimated by the direct labor rate standard), management can determine the organization's future cash needs to meet payroll costs. Like expected direct materials cost, expected direct labor cost becomes an important part of the cash budgeting process.

Direct Labor Standards in the Control Cycle

Like direct materials costs, direct labor costs can vary from expectations for two reasons. First, more or less labor than standard can be used to produce a given amount of output—a **direct labor usage** (or **efficiency**) **variance.** Second, the actual direct labor used can cost more or less than standard—a **direct labor rate variance.**

DIRECT LABOR USAGE (EFFICIENCY) VARIANCE The difference between the standard amount of labor required to produce a given amount of output and the actual amount of labor used.

DIRECT LABOR RATE VARIANCE The difference between actual direct labor cost per hour and the standard labor rate.

Direct Labor Rate Variances. Suppose the standard direct labor cost for the Fine Furniture Company is $14 per direct labor hour. Assume further that the Fine Furniture Company pays $23,625 for the 1575 direct labor hours ($15 per direct labor hour) used in the production of 150 tables. Because the standard cost expected for 1575 labor hours is $14 × 1575,or $22,050, Fine Furniture has an unfavorable direct labor rate variance as follows:

Labor rate variance	
Actual rate	$15 per hour
Standard rate	14 per hour
Variance—unfavorable	$ 1 per hour × actual hours, 1575 = $1575

Note we did not consider the level of production in determining the direct labor rate variance for Fine Furniture Company. The direct labor rate variance is the difference between the amount actually paid ($23,625) and the standard for the total amount of labor used ($22,050). Responsibility for rates of pay is usually assigned to the personnel department.

Standard cost bookkeeping systems recognize that direct labor rate variances should not be included in production cost by charging work in process only with the standard costs of the labor used. Variances from standard rates are maintained in separate accounts for management review.

Direct Labor Usage (Efficiency) Variances. The direct labor usage variance is similar to the direct materials usage variance. It is the difference between the actual amount of direct labor used to produce a given amount of output and the standard direct labor usage expected for that same output. Given our earlier assumptions (refer to Exhibit 21.1) concerning coffee table production by the Fine Furniture Company, we would expect that 150 coffee tables would have required 1,500 direct labor hours. Because Fine Furniture actually used 1,575 direct labor hours to produce the 150 tables, there is an unfavorable direct labor usage variance of 75 hours.

Like direct materials usage variances, the most useful information to provide production supervisors is the labor usage variance in hours. Translation of direct labor usage variances into dollars for entry into the bookkeeping system is done by multiplying the hour variance by the standard direct labor rate per hour. For example, in dollar terms, the direct labor usage variance is equal to $1,050:

Labor usage variance	
Actual usage	1575 hours
Standard usage	1500 hours
Variance—unfavorable	75 hours × std. rate/hour, $14 = $1,050

The direct labor rate and usage variances are recognized within the bookkeeping system as goods are completed, just before the transfer of the work in process to finished goods. Prior recognition is not possible, because variances cannot be determined until the number of units produced is known. For the Fine Furniture Company, the journal entry to record direct labor costs is as follows:

Work in process (150 × 10 hrs @ $14)	21,000	
Direct labor usage variance	1,050	
Direct labor rate variance	1,575	
Wages payable		23,625
(to record direct labor applied to work in process)		

Management Analysis of Direct Labor Variances. Direct labor rate and usage variances are signals for management attention and not conclusions. Although primary responsibility for controlling labor rates rests with personnel and primary responsibility for labor usage rests with production, variances can occur that are beyond the control of these persons. For instance, if sufficiently skilled labor is unavailable, it is unreasonable to expect production supervisors to meet standards for labor usage. By the same token, perhaps the personnel department should not be rewarded because obtaining such underskilled workers costs less than standard. Or labor rates might be determined by a labor contract negotiated by top management and so might not be completely controllable by the personnel department. Clearly, although computation of direct labor variances is reasonably easy, interpretation of the variances requires judgment, experience, and skill.

FACTORY OVERHEAD STANDARDS

Development of Factory Overhead Standards

Recall from Chapter 20 that factory overhead has two components: a variable portion consisting of indirect labor, supplies, etc., that varies with production levels and a fixed portion whose total tends to remain relatively constant for a relevant range of production. Because the behavior of these two components of factory overhead is different with respect to variations in the level of production, separate standards and analyses of variations from standards are needed. Standards for factory overhead, whether fixed or variable, are usually established on the basis of historical experience. As discussed earlier, standards for factory overhead are similar to predetermined overhead rates. The major difference lies in the precision of the standard as a basis for predicting future costs.

To describe and illustrate the calculation of overhead variances, we will use the data in Exhibit 21.2 for the Fine Furniture Company. In this example, overhead is allocated to products on the basis of direct labor hours. In the current year, management estimates the firm's *normal capacity* at 2000 direct labor hours. This is the production volume needed to satisfy the firm's average consumer demand. Based on this figure, budgeted overhead is $800, consisting of $480 of variable costs and $320 of fixed costs. Therefore, overhead would be $.40 per direct labor hour, with

EXHIBIT 21.2

Overhead Data Fine Furniture Company	
Total budgeted overhead	$800
Variable	$480
Fixed	320
Normal capacity	2000 DLH
Overhead per direct labor hour	
Variable ($480/2000 DLH)	$ .24
Fixed ($320/2000 DLH)	$ .16
Total	$ .40
Actual overhead incurred	$750
Actual direct labor hours used	1575

$.24 representing the variable portion and $.16 representing the fixed portion. This $.40 figure is referred to as the **standard overhead rate.** This rate is set before the start of the fiscal year, during the annual budget process. Often during this process, managers use a **flexible overhead budget** to determine overhead rates. A flexible overhead budget shows the budgeted amount of overhead at different levels of activity. An illustration of a simple flexible budget is shown in Exhibit 21.3.

STANDARD OVERHEAD RATE
The expected overhead rate per unit of allocation base.

FLEXIBLE OVERHEAD BUDGET
An overhead budget that shows the budgeted amount of overhead at different levels of activity.

For product costing purposes, managers must choose one level of activity. Overhead rates are then established on that basis. In our example, Fine Furniture chose 2000 direct labor hours as the appropriate level. The selected activity level is commonly referred to as the **standard volume of output.** In practice, this level can be expressed in any unit of measure, such as direct labor hours, machine hours, or units of production. It is on the basis of the standard volume of output that managers calculate the standard overhead rate.

STANDARD VOLUME OF OUTPUT
Selected activity level chosen by managers for product costing purposes.

Factory Overhead Standards in the Planning Cycle

For planning purposes, variable overhead efficiency standards provide management with information on the amounts and types of overhead items (e.g., varnish, nails,

EXHIBIT 21.3

Flexible Budget: Fine Furniture Company

Direct labor hours	1800	2000	2200
Percent of normal capacity	90%	100%	110%
Total variable overhead	$ 432	$ 480	$ 528
Total fixed overhead	320	320	320
Total overhead	$ 752	$ 800	$ 848

lighting) required to produce the level of planned output. Similarly, fixed overhead volume standards give management estimates of the capacity needed for production. When these usage standards are combined with their related price standards (i.e., variable overhead spending standards and fixed overhead budget standards), managers can determine the firm's future cash needs to meet overhead costs. As with direct materials and direct labor, such estimates of overhead costs are vital to the budgeting process.

Factory Overhead Standards in the Control Cycle

The example for the Fine Furniture Company indicated the company had used 1575 direct labor hours and incurred actual overhead of $750 during the period. However, the standard for the actual production of 150 coffee tables was 1500 direct labor hours. This represents the number of hours that *should* have been used to make the actual number of tables produced. Under a "pure" standard cost system, overhead is applied to products on the basis of standard rather than actual hours. In this example, $600 (1500 DLH × $.40) of overhead would have been applied to products. As a result, there would be a $150 ($750 − $600) total unfavorable overhead variance at the end of the period. This $150 unfavorable variance can be further analyzed by segmenting it into fixed and variable portions and then further subdividing these portions into what is commonly referred to as a **four-way analysis of overhead variances.**

FOUR-WAY ANALYSIS OF OVERHEAD VARIANCES
A method of analyzing factory overhead that divides overhead into fixed and variable portions and further divides each portion into spending and usage variances.

ALLOCATION BASE
The activity measurement used to allocate variable overhead costs to production.

Variable Factory Overhead Standards. Variable overhead costs are generally assigned to production on the basis of some activity measurement, commonly referred to as an **allocation base,** rather than directly traced to production as are direct materials and direct labor. The standard for variable factory overhead is thus expressed as a function of standard units of activity such as direct labor hours or machine hours. For example, the Fine Furniture Company expects that variable factory overhead will amount to $.24 per direct labor hour. We would expect then that Fine Furniture would incur a cost of $2.40 in variable factory overhead for each coffee table produced, because it takes ten direct labor hours to make one unit.

Just as with direct materials and direct labor, two deviations from standard occur that explain the variable overhead variance. Fine Furniture could use more overhead items, such as supplies and varnish, than standard and create a **variable overhead efficiency variance,** or the variable overhead items could collectively cost more or less than normal and produce a **variable overhead spending variance.**

VARIABLE OVERHEAD EFFICIENCY VARIANCE
The difference between the actual amounts of variable overhead items used and the standard usage expected for a given level of output.

VARIABLE OVERHEAD SPENDING VARIANCE
The difference between the actual amounts spent on the variable overhead items used and the standard costs for the collective total.

Variable Overhead Spending Variances. Variable overhead spending variances result when the individual overhead items, such as supplies and varnish, cost more or less than the standard amounts. The amount of this variance is measured by the difference between the actual variable overhead rate and the standard variable overhead application rate, multiplied by the actual usage of the overhead allocation base (direct labor hours). For the Fine Furniture Company, this would be as follows:

Variable overhead spending variance	
Actual rate ($400/$1575)	$.254 per DLH
Standard rate	.240 per DLH
Variance—unfavorable	$.014 per DLH × actual use, 1575 = $22

Note that the spending variance is determined by the difference between the *total* actual variable overhead application rate and the *total* standard variable overhead application rate, not by variations in any one item included in overhead. Thus, some individual variable overhead items might cost more than expected while others might cost less. Control is typically exercised in the aggregate.

Variable Overhead Efficiency Variances. Use of variable factory overhead is dependent on use of the activity base that associates variable factory overhead with production. The variable factory overhead efficiency variance is the difference between the total variable factory overhead applied to production and that which should have been used to produce a given amount of output. For the Fine Furniture Company, the variable overhead efficiency variance is equal to the following:

Variable overhead efficiency variance	
Actual usage	1575 DLH
Standard usage	1500 DLH
Variance—unfavorable	75 DLH × variable overhead std. rate, \$.24 = \$18

Bookkeeping for Variable Factory Overhead. A variety of bookkeeping techniques can be used to record the actual and standard costs for variable overhead. One method is to debit an account entitled Variable Factory Overhead Control for the actual cost of the variable overhead incurred and credit the appropriate liability or asset account. As units are produced, variable overhead would be applied to production by debiting work-in-process inventory for the standard variable overhead cost and crediting the variable factory overhead control account. These journal entries would appear as follows:

Variable factory overhead control	400	
Accounts payable		400
(to record purchase of variable overhead items)		
Work in process (1500 @ \$.24)	360	
Variable factory overhead control		360
(to apply factory overhead to production)		

Once these entries are made, the balance in the variable factory overhead control account will equal the total variable overhead variance.

Bookkeeping recognition of variable factory overhead variances takes place when goods are in process. As with other costs, only standard amounts are charged to work-in-process and finished goods inventories. The following additional journal entry is required for Fine Furniture to recognize the variable overhead spending and efficiency variances:

Variable factory overhead spending variance	22	
Variable factory overhead efficiency variance	18	
Variable factory overhead control		40
(to close overhead account and record variances)		

Management Analysis of Variable Factory Overhead Variances. Unlike with direct materials and direct labor, it is difficult to separate the cost of variable overhead items from their usage because individual items included in variable factory overhead tend to be small. Further, the "usage" of variable overhead tends to be closely tied to usage of the activity base. In the Fine Furniture Company, for example, the more direct labor hours used, the more variable factory overhead costs incurred. In terms of management control, then, more emphasis is placed on the spending variance than on the usage variance in analyzing variable factory overhead.

Responsibility for control of variable factory overhead spending can be difficult to identify. Because many small items are included from several different sources within the company, responsibility for cost control can be divided. Further, the costs of identifying precise responsibilities can exceed the benefits of the additional accuracy. Nevertheless, like other variances, unusual variable factory overhead variances signal the need for management attention.

Responsibility for variable factory overhead efficiency parallels that for control of the activity base. Because Fine Furniture's activity base is direct labor hours, primary responsibility lies with production managers. However, the same careful use of judgment is required for intelligent follow-up on variable factory overhead efficiency variances as is required in interpreting direct labor efficiency variances.

Fixed Factory Overhead Standards. Fixed factory overhead represents the basic cost of productive capacity. Within a reasonable range of activity, the cost of this capacity is constant and known from prior experience. Thus, the only real variations that exist within the overhead are in the prices paid for the elements of fixed cost (**fixed overhead budget variances**).

FIXED OVERHEAD BUDGET VARIANCE
The difference between the amounts paid for items included in fixed overhead and the standard cost of the items.

However, given a fixed capacity cost, failure to use capacity at a reasonable level results in higher unit costs. That is, if the capacity used is only 60 percent of standard, the result will be a higher unit cost for items produced, because the total amount of fixed factory overhead does not change. Standard cost systems recognize the importance of capacity utilization and thus include analyses of over-utilization or under-utilization of capacity, the dollar measurement of which is known as the **fixed overhead volume variance.**

FIXED OVERHEAD VOLUME VARIANCE
The dollar measurement of over- or under-utilization of plant capacity.

Fixed Overhead Budget Variances. The fixed overhead budget variance is the counterpart of the price variances in direct materials, direct labor, and variable factory overhead. If, in the case of the Fine Furniture Company, budgeted fixed costs are $320 per month and actual fixed costs are $350, the fixed overhead budget variance is $30 unfavorable, as follows:

Fixed overhead budget variance	
Actual cost	$350 total
Standard cost	320 total
Variance—unfavorable	$ 30

The fixed overhead budget variance equals the difference between budgeted and actual fixed overhead.

Fixed Overhead Volume Variances. The volume variance is the counterpart of the usage variances in direct materials, direct labor, and variable factory overhead. It can be measured by the difference between the actual volume of activity and the standard volume, multiplied by the standard fixed overhead application rate. For example, if the budgeted fixed factory overhead for the Fine Furniture Company is $.16 per direct labor hour and the expected volume of activity is 2000 direct labor hours, the fixed overhead volume variance would be computed as follows:

Fixed overhead volume variance	
Actual volume	1500 std DLH
Standard volume	2000 std DLH
Variance—unfavorable	500 std DLH × std. rate, $.16 = $80

The variance is unfavorable, because Fine Furniture did not fully utilize its capacity during the period.

Note that we applied fixed factory overhead on the basis of standard direct labor hours worked, not on the basis of actual direct labor hours worked. If the application of fixed factory overhead had been dependent on actual direct labor hours worked, any differences in labor usage from standard would have influenced the amount of fixed factory overhead applied to production. This would have, in turn, changed the computation of the fixed overhead volume variance. If fixed overhead represents a capacity cost, the important consideration is not how efficiently labor was used but how many units were produced with the capacity within a given period of time.

Bookkeeping for Fixed Factory Overhead. If fixed factory overhead is entered into the accounting system based on the number of units completed, the bookkeeping is relatively easy. Since the total costs involved will vary little, no great loss of control occurs if fixed factory overhead is not entered into work in process until the units are ready for transfer to finished goods inventory.

The journal entries for the Fine Furniture Company for fixed factory overhead would be as follows:

Fixed factory overhead control	350	
Miscellaneous credits		350
(to record actual fixed factory overhead)		
Work in process (1500 @ $.16)	240	
Fixed factory overhead control		240
(to record overhead applied to production)		
Fixed factory overhead volume variance	80	
Fixed factory overhead budget variance	30	
Fixed factory overhead control		110
(to record fixed overhead variances)		

Management Analysis of Fixed Factory Overhead Variances. Responsibility for both the fixed factory overhead budget variance and volume variance is generally shared by a number of different management levels and areas. Top management planning of capacity and utilization of that capacity are starting points in the analysis. Budget variances suggest either that the fixed cost standard is unrealistic or that elements of fixed cost incurrences need to be reviewed.

Fixed overhead volume variances suggest that either planning, execution of plans, or actual production levels are not consistent with the planned capacity. Responsibility for volume variances can lie with any number of different areas, starting with top management capacity decisions, sales force execution of plans, or production control. It is very difficult to interpret fixed overhead volume variances properly. However, even if responsibility for the volume variance is difficult to identify, its computation provides managers with valuable information on the costs of capacity over-utilization and under-utilization.

TRANSFER OF GOODS TO COST OF GOODS SOLD AND DISPOSITION OF VARIANCES

When goods are completed, they are transferred from work in process to finished goods at standard cost. In the Fine Furniture Company example, the following journal entry is required to make this transfer:

Finished goods	24,750	
Work in process		24,750
(to transfer completed products to finished goods)		

The explanation for this amount can be found in the T-account analysis in Exhibit 21.4. Entries to the accounts are based on the preceding journal entries. After the last entry is made, there is a zero balance in the Work in Process account, indicating that there is no inventory left in process. Units sold during the period would also be transferred to cost of goods sold from finished goods at standard. Assuming all 150 tables were sold during the current period, the entry to reflect the transfer would be as follows:

Cost of goods sold	24,750	
Finished goods		24,750
(to reflect sale and transfer of inventory)		

Product cost variances are generally considered to be nonstandard costs incurred during a particular time period. Therefore, the normal practice is to treat all variances as costs of the time period in which they occur and charge them to cost of goods sold.

Some would argue that not all variances are associated with the goods sold during a particular period and that the practice of charging variances to cost of goods sold distorts income. For example, direct materials price variances could well be associated with direct materials not yet placed into production. Or work remaining in process might represent part of the labor usage, materials usage, or overhead usage variances. Although these arguments have merit, the difference in income that would occur if variances were allocated between inventories and cost of goods sold would be immaterial in most cases. Therefore, the practice of charging all variances off as period expenses would not, in most cases, cause any serious distortions of income.

EXHIBIT 21.4

Summary of Product Cost Flows in a Standard Costing System

Accounts Payable

		4,400	(a)
		400	(e)

Direct Materials Inventory

(a)	4,200	3,150	(b)
		210	(c)

Variable Factory Overhead Control

(e)	400	360	(f)
		40	(g)

Wages Payable

		23,625	(d)

Work-in-Process Inventory

(b)	3,150	24,750	(k)
(d)	21,000		
(f)	360		
(i)	240		

Finished Goods Inventory

(k)	24,750	24,750	(l)

Cost of Goods Sold

(l)	24,750		
(m)	3,185		

Miscellaneous Credits

		350	(h)

Fixed Factory Overhead Control

(h)	350	240	(i)
		110	(j)

Direct Materials Price Variance

(a)	200	200	(m)

Direct Labor Rate Variance

(d)	1,575	1,575	(m)

Variable Factory Overhead Spending Variance

(g)	22	22	(m)

Fixed Factory Overhead Budget Variance

(j)	30	30	(m)

Direct Materials Usage Variance

(c)	210	210	(m)

Direct Labor Usage Variance

(d)	1,050	1,050	(m)

Variable Factory Overhead Efficiency Variance

(g)	18	18	(m)

Fixed Factory Overhead Volume Variance

(j)	80	80	(m)

(a) Purchase of direct materials; recognition of price variances.
(b) Requisition of standard quantity of direct materials.
(c) Requisition of additional materials beyond standard.
(d) Recording of direct labor costs; recognition of direct labor variances.
(e) Purchase of variable overhead items.
(f) Application of variable overhead to process.
(g) Recognitiion of variable overhead variances.
(h) Procurement of fixed overhead items.
(i) Application of fixed overhead to process.
(j) Recognition of fixed overhead variances.
(k) Transfer to finished goods.
(l) Transfer to cost of goods sold.
(m) Disposition of product cost variances.

Further, the increase or decrease in inventory values as a result of the variance allocation could in itself represent a distortion of inventory valuations. Since the variances are not expected to recur, they take the nature of overhead expenses, representing inefficiencies or overachievements of a particular time period—not permanent asset values. Clearly, the value of materials or work-in-process inventories should not be dependent upon operational efficiencies or managerial performances that vary from period to period.

For the Fine Furniture Company example, then, the journal entry to charge the variances to cost of goods sold is as follows:

Cost of goods sold	3,185	
Direct materials price variance		200
Direct materials usage variance		210
Direct labor rate variance		1,575
Direct labor usage variance		1,050
Variable factory overhead spending variance		22
Variable factory overhead efficiency variance		18
Fixed factory overhead budget variance		30
Fixed factory overhead volume variance		80
(to write off all variances to cost of goods sold)		

Once again Exhibit 21.4 provides a summary of all of these cost flows in the standard costing system using data from the Fine Furniture Company example. Transfers between T-accounts parallel the journal entries presented in the chapter.

EXHIBIT 21.5

(a)
Fine Furniture Company
Partial Internal Management Income Statement

Sales	$45,000
Cost of goods sold (at standard)	24,750
Gross profit (at standard)	$20,250
Variances	
Direct materials price variance	(200)
Direct materials usage variance	(210)
Direct labor rate variance	(1,575)
Direct labor usage variance	(1,050)
Variable factory overhead spending variance	(22)
Variable factory overhead efficiency variance	(18)
Fixed factory overhead budget variance	(30)
Fixed factory overhead volume variance	(80)
Adjusted gross profit (at actual)	$17,065

(b)
Fine Furniture Company
Partial External Reporting Income Statement

Sales	$45,000
Cost of goods sold	27,935
Gross profit	$17,065

INCOME STATEMENT PRESENTATION

Before the disposition of the variances, management will often prepare an income statement for internal use that delineates the standard costs of production from the actual costs. An example of such an internal income statement for the Fine Furniture Company is shown in Exhibit 21.5 (a). We have assumed sales were $45,000 for the period. Following the disposition of variances, an income statement for external reporting purposes can be prepared. Such an income statement would appear as shown in Exhibit 21.5 (b) for the Fine Furniture Company.

CONCEPT SUMMARY 21.1

SUMMARY OF DIRECT MATERIALS AND DIRECT LABOR STANDARDS

			Control Considerations		
Standard	**Development**	**Planning Considerations**	**Variance**	**Formula***	**Responsibility**
Standards in general	Determined on item-by-item basis	Provide estimates of total expected costs for a given level of output	Provide benchmarks against which actual results can be compared		
Direct materials usage standard	Developed from historical experience or industrial engineering studies	Determines purchasing requirements, inventory storage capacity needs, materials handling requirements	Direct materials usage variance	(AQ − SQ) × SP	Production department
Direct materials price standard	Developed from supplier price quotations or historical experience	Determines projected cost of direct materials acquisition for cash budgeting	Direct materials price variance	(AP − SP) × AQ	Purchasing department
Direct labor usage standard	Developed from time and motion studies or from production simulations	Determines the size and skill of work force needed to be hired by the personnel department	Direct labor usage variance	(AQ − SQ) × SP	Production department
Direct labor rate standard	Developed from contracts with labor unions or historical experience	Determines projected cost of labor force, cash needs to meet payroll costs	Direct labor rate variance	(AP − SP) × AQ	Personnel department

***Key**

AQ = Actual quantity of materials units, direct labor hours, or overhead allocation base units.
SQ = Standard quantity of materials units, direct labor hours, or overhead allocation base units.
AP = Actual price of materials units, actual direct labor rate, or actual level of overhead costs per unit.
SP = Standard price of materials units, standard direct labor rate, or standard level of overhead costs per unit.

■ CONCEPT SUMMARY 21.2
SUMMARY OF FACTORY OVERHEAD STANDARDS

Standard	Development	Planning Considerations	Control Considerations		
			Variance	Formula*	Responsibility
Variable overhead spending standard (predetermined variable overhead rate)	Developed by dividing total projected variable overhead costs by the projected total of the allocation base	Determines the projected cost of variable overhead for cash budgeting	Variable overhead spending variance	(AP − SP) × AQ −or− AC − (AQ × SP)	Can be divided among several departments
Variable overhead efficiency standard	Identical to the standard for the allocation base (i.e., direct labor usage standard)	Determines the total amount of variable overhead items needed to be acquired	Variable overhead efficiency variance	(AQ − SQ) × SP	Same as the responsibility for allocation base
Fixed overhead budget standard (predetermined fixed overhead rate)	Set by the flexible budget at the standard volume of output	Determines the projected cost of providing productive capacity for cash budgeting	Fixed overhead budget variance	AC − SC	Inaccuracies in the budget: components or prices of fixed overhead are not as expected
Fixed overhead volume standard	Set at the standard volume of output on the flexible budget	Determines the expected volume of production, the quantity of productive facilities needed	Fixed overhead volume variance	(SV − AV) × SP −or− SC − (AV × SP)	Planning or execution of plans was insufficient to allow actual production to meet planned capacity

***Key**
AQ = Actual quantity of materials units, direct labor hours, or overhead allocation base units.
SQ = Standard quantity of materials units, direct labor hours, or overhead allocation base units.
AP = Actual price of materials units, actual direct labor rate, or actual level of overhead costs per unit.
SP = Standard price of materials units, standard direct labor rate, or standard level of overhead costs per unit.
AC = Actual total cost of overhead.
SC = Standard total cost of overhead.
AV = Actual volume of productive direct labor hours.
SV = Standard volume of productive labor hours, i.e., the standard volume of output.

FOR REVIEW

DEMONSTRATON PROBLEM

Prepared December 15, 1985, the budgeted income statement for January 1986 of CFL Corporation is as follows:

CFL Corporation
Budgeted Income Statement
For the Month Ending January 31, 1986

Sales (25,000 units @ $4)			$100,000
Less cost of goods sold			
Beginning inventory (15,000 units)		$ 45,000	
Cost of goods manufactured			
Raw materials used	$ 15,000		
Direct labor	25,000		
Variable factory overhead	20,000		
Fixed factory overhead	5,000		
		65,000	
Goods available for sale		$110,000	
Ending inventory (10,000 units)		30,000	
Cost of goods sold			80,000
Gross profit			$ 20,000
Less operating expenses			
Variable selling and administrative expense		$ 10,000	
Fixed selling and administrative expense		2,500	
			12,500
Net income			$ 7,500

On February 15, 1986, CFL Corporation management received the following statement from the accounting department:

CFL Corporation
Income Statement
For the Month Ending January 31, 1986

Sales (20,000 units @ $4)			$ 80,000
Less cost of goods sold			
Beginning inventory (15,000 units)		$ 45,000	
Cost of goods manufactured			
Raw materials used	$ 21,200		
Direct labor	34,320		
Variable factory overhead	32,890		
Fixed factory overhead	4,750		
		93,160	
Goods available for sale		$138,160	
Ending inventory (20,000 units)		60,000	
Cost of goods sold			78,160
Gross profit			$ 1,840
Less operating expenses			
Variable selling and administrative expense		$ 10,000	
Fixed selling and administrative expense		2,500	
			12,500
Net income			$ (10,660)

Additional information:

a. On January 1, 30,000 units of raw materials were purchased for a total cost of $24,000. They enter production one unit for each unit of output.
b. On January 2, a new agreement was made with the labor union that provided for a temporary pay cut from $5.00 per hour to $4.80 per hour.
c. Variable factory overhead is applied to production as a cost per direct labor hour.
d. There were no work-in-process inventories on January 1, 1986, or on January 31, 1986, and none were expected.

Required

1. Based on the master budget and the additional information provided, determine the standards (i.e., standard cost per unit input and standard number of units input per unit output) employed by CFL Corporation.
2. Compute the direct materials, direct labor, and factory overhead (four-way) variances.

Demonstration Problem Solution

1. Standards employed

a. The standard volume of production is 20,000 units. This is found by comparing the projected change in inventory level with the projected level of sales.

Projected sales		25,000 units
Ending inventory	10,000 units	
Beginning inventory	15,000 units	(5,000) units
Projected production		20,000 units

b. Direct materials standards
Usage standard: Given—one unit per unit output.
Price standard: $15,000 projected cost ÷ 20,000 projected units = $.75 per unit

c. Direct labor standards
Rate standard: Given—$5.00 per hour.
Efficiency standard: $25,000 projected cost ÷ 20,000 projected units = $1.25/unit

$1.25 projected cost per unit ÷ $5.00 per hour = 0.25 DLH/unit

d. Variable factory overhead standards
Efficiency standard: Since overhead is applied based on rate per direct labor hour, the efficiency standard is the same as that for labor—0.25 hour/unit.
Spending standard: $20,000 projected cost ÷ (20,000 projected units × 0.25 hour/unit) = $4.00 per hour

e. Fixed factory overhead standards
Volume standard: The standard volume of production—20,000 units.
Budget standard: The budgeted cost of fixed factory overhead—$5,000 total, or $0.25 per standard unit.

These standards can be summarized as follows:

	Rate Standard	Usage Standard
Direct materials	$ .75/unit	1 unit/unit output
Direct labor	5.00/hour	0.25 DLH/unit output
Variable overhead	4.00/hour	0.25 hour/unit output
Fixed overhead	$5,000 total or $0.25/unit output	20,000 units output per month

2. Variances from standards

a. Actual costs and usage can be determined from the actual income statement in the same manner as standard costs and usage were determined from the master budget. This yields the following:

	Actual Rate	Actual Usage	
		Total	Per Unit Output
Direct materials	$ .80/unit	26,500 units	1.06 units
Direct labor	4.80/DLH	7,150 DLH	0.286 DLH
Variable overhead	4.60/hour	7,150 hours	0.286 hour
Fixed overhead	$4,750 total	25,000 units output	—

b. Direct materials variances

Price variance: DMPV = ($.75 std. − $.80 act.) × 30,000 units purchased = $1,500 unfavorable

Usage variance: DMUV = (25,000 units std. − 26,500 units act.) × $0.75 std. = $1,125 unfavorable

c. Direct labor variances

Rate variance: DLRV = ($5.00 std. − $4.80 act.) × 7,150 DLH actual = $1,430 favorable

Efficiency variance: DLEV = (6,250 DLH std. − 7,150 DLH act.) × $5.00 std. = $4,500 unfavorable

d. Variable factory overhead variances

Spending variance: VOSV = ($4.00 std. − $4.60 act.) × 7,150 hours actual = $4,290 unfavorable

Efficiency variance: VOEV = (6,250 hours std. − 7,150 hours act.) × $4.00 std = $3,600 unfavorable

e. Fixed factory overhead variances

Budget variance: FOBV = $5,000 std. − $4,750 act. = $250 favorable

Volume variance: FOVV = (25,000 units act. − 20,000 units std.) × $.25 std. = $1,250 favorable

These variances can be summarized as follows:

	Rate Variance	Usage Variance
Direct materials	$1,500 U	$1,125 U
Direct labor	1,430 F	4,500 U
Variable overhead	4,290 U	3,600 U
Fixed overhead	250 F	1,250 F

SUMMARY

- Standard costs are predetermined estimates of the amounts and costs of raw materials, direct labor, and factory overhead required to produce finished products.
- Standard costs provide planning information to management for use in estimating total expected costs for producing a given level of output.
- Standard costs provide control information to management by providing benchmarks against which actual results can be compared.

- Each component of product cost has two standards: usage (efficiency) establishing the amount of input needed to produce one unit of output and price (rate) establishing the cost per input unit.
- Because variable factory overhead varies with production levels and fixed factory overhead does not, separate standards are needed for each.
- Standard overhead rates are often determined through the use of a flexible overhead budget and are applied to production on the basis of some activity measurement known as the allocation base.
- Direct materials standards provide a foundation for estimating materials purchase, storage, and handling requirements, while direct labor standards serve to identify both the amount and type of labor (skill) required.
- Deviations of actual results from standard expectations are known as variances and provide the basis for problem identification and resolution.
- Incurrence of variable overhead depends on use of the activity base that associates the overhead with production.
- Incurrence of fixed overhead does not depend on activity. The dollar measurement of over-utilization or under-utilization of capacity is known as the fixed overhead volume variance and suggests that actual production levels are not consistent with planned levels.
- All variances should be treated as flags signaling the need for management investigation, not as conclusive evidence of good or bad performance.
- Only standard costs (i.e., standard prices for standard usage) are charged to work in process, finished goods, and cost of goods sold under a standard cost system.
- Variances from standard are generally charged off as an adjustment to cost of goods sold in the time period in which they are identified.

QUESTIONS

21-1. How do standard costs facilitate management planning? How do standard costs facilitate control?

21-2. What is the major disadvantage of standard costing?

21-3. What is meant by management by exception?

21-4. Should standards be based on ideal, expected normal, or lax activity?

21-5. What are variances? Describe the two major types of variances.

21-6. Who is normally charged with the responsibility for each of the variances?

21-7. Compute the materials price and usage variances from the following data:

Standard—2,000 units at $15 per unit
Purchased—3,000 units at $16 per unit
Used—1,750 units

21-8. What would be a reasonable explanation for a company having a large *favorable* materials price variance and a large *unfavorable* materials usage variance?

21-9. Identify the type of variance in each of the following situations and indicate whether it is favorable or unfavorable:

a. A sawmill obtained 300 board feet of lumber from three logs, each 25 feet long and one foot in diameter. Normally, four logs are required to obtain 300 board feet of lumber.

b. Feower Construction Company considers metal rivets to be variable overhead items. 1,000 pounds of rivets were purchased at $50 per hundred pounds. The rivets are normally purchased for $65 per hundred pounds.
c. Seawell Optical Company operates its own lens-grinding lab. The owner's son had been working the lens-grinding machine for $15 per hour. The owner later hired someone else for $10 per hour.

21-10. How should the *existence* of variances be interpreted?

EXERCISES

21-E1. During the month of July, Department A manufactured 1000 units. The standard materials cost per unit is 20 square feet at a cost of 25¢ per square foot. The actual materials used consisted of 19,600 square feet at a cost of $5880. Compute the materials price and usage variances, and explain why the variances exist.

21-E2. Given the following data, calculate the labor rate and efficiency variances:

Units produced	1000
Actual direct labor hours	3000
Standard labor allowed per acceptable unit	2½ hours
Standard wage rate per hour	$5
Total payroll costs for the month	$18,000

21-E3. In December, the Aaron Company budgeted total overhead costs of $14,000, $8000 of which was variable and the remainder fixed. Actual overhead during the month was $15,000, $7500 of which was fixed and the remainder variable. Normal production for the month is 14,000 units; actual production was 12,000 units. Assuming that overhead is allocated on the basis of units produced, calculate the following variances:

Variable overhead spending
Variable overhead efficiency
Fixed overhead volume
Fixed overhead budget

Present the necessary journal entries to account for the variances.

21-E4. In 21-E3, if overhead is allocated on the basis of direct labor hours, recalculate the overhead variances assuming that the standard labor per unit is 2 hours and the actual labor per unit was 2¼ hours.

21-E5. Prepare an income statement for management using the following data:

Cost of goods sold (at standard)	$15,000	
Direct labor rate variance	$ 200	U
Direct labor efficiency variance	$ 450	F
Materials price variance	$ 125	F
Materials quantity variance	$ 65	F
Variable overhead spending variance	$ 50	U
Variable overhead efficiency variance	$ 100	F
Fixed overhead budget variance	$ 25	U
Fixed overhead volume variance	$ 40	U
Revenue	$25,000	

21-E6. Using the data in 21-E5, establish T-accounts for the variances, enter the balances in these accounts, and prepare journal entries to record the closing of these variance accounts.

21-E7. Following are the standard costs for one unit of the company's product:

Materials (3 lbs., $1 per lb.)
Direct labor (½ hour, $7 per hour)
Factory overhead (allocated on the basis of direct labor hours @ $1.50 per hour)

a. What is the standard cost per unit produced?
b. Assuming the following actual cost data, calculate the variance per unit and explain what portion of it is due to materials, labor, or overhead:

Actual materials (2 lbs., $.75 per lb.)
Direct labor (1 hour, $5 per hour)
Factory overhead ($1.75 per hour)

PROBLEM SET A

21-A1. Material Price and Usage Variances. During the month, a production department completed 10,000 units of a product that had a standard materials cost of 5,000 square feet at $0.50 per square foot. The actual amount of materials used was 5,950 square feet, for a total actual cost of $3,272.50. The actual purchase of the materials was for 10,000 square feet at a total cost of $5,500.

Required

Prepare the journal entries to record the purchase of materials, the materials' entry into process, and the transfer to finished goods of the units completed.

21-A2. Labor Rate and Efficiency Variances. The assembly department of Passal, Inc., completed 150,000 units of output during the month of March. Labor standards for this product are as follows:

Standard DLH per unit output	0.20
Standard DL rate per hour	$10.50

During March, 35,000 hours of direct labor were used at a total cost of $376,250.

Required

Prepare the journal entries necessary to apply labor costs to work in process and to transfer completed work to finished goods.

21-A3. Standards and Variances from Incomplete Data. Tates, Inc., produces a single product line. The following data are available for the corporation:

	Direct Materials	Direct Labor
Standard quantity per unit	3 feet	? hours
Standard price or rate	$5 per foot	? per hour
Standard cost per unit	$15	?

During the most recent period, the company paid $55,650 for direct materials, all of which were used in the production of 3,200 units of the product, and worked 4,900 direct labor hours at a cost of $36,750. The following variance data are available:

Materials quantity variance	$ 4,500 U
Total labor variance	1,600 F
Labor efficiency variance	800 U

Required

a. Compute the actual cost paid per foot for direct materials.
b. Compute the materials price variance.
c. Compute the standard direct labor rate per direct labor hour.
d. Compute the standard hours allowed for the production of the period and per unit.

21-A4. Four-Way Analysis of Overhead. During a standard month of production at Somserve Company, 15,000 direct labor hours are employed and overhead costs of $1,500 variable and $600 fixed are incurred. During the current month, the following actual data were recorded:

Total standard DLH of output	16,000
Total DLH of output	20,000
Total variable overhead costs	$ 1,900
Total fixed overhead costs	700

Required

Compute the variances associated with a four-way analysis of factory overhead variance.

21-A5. Material Price and Usage Standards. On June 10, 1986, the cost accountant of Nickle Cage Products, Inc., prepared a schedule comparing budgeted and actual variable cost of goods sold of the company's line of steel bird cages for May 1986. This schedule, with several amounts missing, is as follows:

Nickle Cage Products, Inc.
Comparative Schedule of Budgeted vs. Actual Variable Cost of Goods Sold
For the Month Ending May 31, 1986

	Budgeted	Actual	Variance
Variable cost of goods sold			
Beginning inventory (5000 units)	$4,500.00	$4,500.00	
Cost of goods manufactured			
Raw materials used	$?*	$ 4,762.00**	Price:
Direct labor	2,305.00	2,305.00	$793.75 U
Variable factory overhead	1,000.00	1,000.00	Usage:
Cost of goods manufactured	$?	$ 8,067.50	$531.25 U
Goods available for sale	$?	$12,567.50	
Ending inventory (4000 units)	3,600.00	3,600.00	
Cost of goods sold	$?	$ 8,967.50	

*Based on the standard materials costs per unit output
Steel wire

Usage	? feet
Price	? per foot
Standard cost	?

**Based on the actual materials costs per unit output
Steel wire

Usage	63.5 feet
Price	$.015 per foot
Actual cost	$.9525

Required

Given that 6000 bird cages were sold in May (as expected), complete the missing amounts.

21-A6. Flow of Standard Costs. Chair and Chair Alike, Inc., uses a standard costing system with a four-way analysis of overhead to control its chair production process. The standard cost of each chair is as follows:

Direct materials	
10 board feet of wood @ $0.50 per foot	$ 5.00
Direct labor (2 hours @ $15.00)	30.00
Overhead	
Variable	15.00
Fixed (based on 20,000 DLH per month output)	7.50
	$57.50

During June, the following data were accumulated:

Wood purchased and requisitioned for process	175,000	bd. ft.
Direct labor used	33,000	hours
Variable overhead costs incurred	$250,000	
Fixed overhead costs incurred	$ 50,000	
Units started and completed during month	15,000	
Units left in work in process	–0–	
Units sold during month	10,000	

Required

Compute the following:

a. The standard costs for materials, labor, and overhead put into production in June.
b. The standard cost of goods completed and transferred.
c. The standard cost of goods sold.

21-A7. Materials, Labor, and Overhead Variances. During June, Chair and Chair Alike, Inc., found that its actual cost of materials was $0.60 per board foot and its actual cost of labor was $14.75 per hour.

Required

Using the above information and the data from 21-A6, calculate the eight variances discussed in the chapter.

21-A8. Standard Costing Financial Statements. The bookshelf production process of Shelfworks Company is controlled through the use of a standard costing system. The standard costs for production of one good bookshelf are as follows:

Direct materials	
20 board feet of walnut @ $2.30 per board feet	$ 46.00
Direct labor (3.5 hours @ $16.80)	58.80
Overhead	
Variable (based on $4.90 per DLH)	17.15
Fixed (based on 35,000 DLH per year output)	3.50
Total standard cost	$125.45

During 1986, Shelfworks collected the following information:

Actual price paid for 250,000 board feet of walnut	$600,000
Total walnut requisitioned for process	234,000 bd. ft.
Total labor cost for 36,000 hours used	$603,000
Variable overhead costs incurred	$178,200
Fixed overhead costs incurred	$ 33,000
Units completed during year	12,000
Units left in work in process	–0–
Units sold during year (@ $175.00)	11,500
Selling expenses	125,000
Administrative expenses	175,000
Effective income tax rate	40%

As of December 31, 1985, Shelfworks' statement of financial position appeared as follows:

Shelfworks Company
Statement of Financial Position
December 31, 1985

Assets			
Cash		$ 10,000	
Accounts receivable		15,000	
Inventories*			
Raw materials	$ 2,000		
Finished goods	5,000	7,000	
Machinery and equipment, net		10,000	
Building, net		150,000	
Total assets			$192,000
Liabilities			
Accounts payable	$ 12,000		
Wages payable	5,000		
Taxes payable	5,000		
Long-term debt	55,000		
Total liabilities		$ 77,000	
Shareholders' Equity			
Common stock, $1 par	$100,000		
Retained earnings	15,000		
Total shareholders' equity		115,000	
Total liabilities and shareholders' equity			$192,000

*As of 12/31/85, there were no work-in-process inventories.

Required

Prepare the financial statements (income statement and statement of financial position) for Shelfworks Company for the year ending December 31, 1986. Where necessary, use the following assumptions:

a. All inventories are carried on the LIFO basis; that is, cost of goods sold is based on units produced during the current year, and raw materials expenses are based on materials purchased during the current year.

b. All sales are made on account uniformly throughout the year. Payments on account are received in the month following the sale.

c. All purchases are made on account uniformly throughout the year. Payments on account are made in the month following the purchases.
d. Labor is used uniformly throughout the year. Wages are paid in the month following use of the labor.
e. Fixed overhead results entirely from depreciation of the building, which reached its salvage value during the year.
f. Income tax expense is incurred uniformly throughout the year and is paid in the month following its incurrence.
g. Selling and administrative expenses are entirely paid during 1986.

PROBLEM SET B

21-B1. Material Price and Usage Variances. During November 1986, Jefferson Electronics, Inc., engaged in the following activities:

Nov. 1	Purchased 10,000 circuit boards for a total cost of $15,650.
Nov. 2	Requisitioned 5,000 circuit boards for production for the month.
Nov. 30	Completed 2,410 units of output and transferred them to finished goods. There were no beginning or ending work-in-process inventories.
Nov. 30	Disposed of the accumulated materials variances.

Jefferson Electronics had determined the standard materials costs to be as follows:

Raw materials	
2 circuit boards @ $1.50	$3.00
Standard materials cost per unit	$3.00

Required

Prepare the general journal entries to be used by Jefferson Electronics, Inc., to record the activities of November.

21-B2. Labor Rate and Efficiency Variances. The finishing department of Lacquer Wood Products Company completed 17,500 units of output during the month of June. The following labor standards were employed for this product:

Standard DLH per unit output	1.35
Standard DL rate per hour	$20.75

During June, 23,030 hours of direct labor were used for a total cost of 472,115.

Required

Prepare the journal entries to be used by Lacquer Wood Products Company to record the use of direct labor by the finishing department and to transfer completed units to finished goods.

21-B3. Standards and Variances from Incomplete Data. The following information is available on the single product produced by Quality Plastic Products, Inc., for the month of June:

	Materials Used	Direct Labor	Variable Overhead
Total standard costs*	$260	$1,900	$950
Actual costs incurred	276	?	985
Materials price variance	?		
Materials quantity variance	0		
Labor rate variance		?	
Labor efficiency variance		?	
Overhead spending variance			?
Overhead efficiency variance			?

*For one month's production.

Additional information:

Number of units produced	100
Actual direct labor hours	410
Standard overhead rate per hour	$2.50
Standard price of one pound of materials	$0.40
Overhead based on	direct labor hours
Difference between standard and actual cost per unit during June	$1.19 U

Required

a. What is the standard cost of a single unit of product?
b. What was the actual cost of a unit of product produced during June?
c. How many pounds of materials are required at standard-per-unit of product?
d. What was the materials price variance for June?
e. What was the labor rate variance? The labor efficiency rate?
f. What was the overhead spending variance? The overhead efficiency variance?

21-B4. Four-Way Analysis of Overhead. During May, Univest Company faced the following overhead cost data:

Total DLH of output	30,000
Total standard DLH of output	25,000
Total variable overhead costs	$22,500
Total fixed overhead costs	$10,300

Overhead cost standards are based on a flexible budget that shows $22,000 total overhead (variable and fixed) at a level of 20,000 DLH and $25,000 total overhead (variable and fixed) at a level of 25,000 DLH. Management expected that the activity during May would be 25,000 standard DLH.

Required

Calculate the variances associated with a four-way analysis of overhead for May for Univest Company.

21-B5. Labor Rate and Efficiency Standards. During January, Tungol Exploratory Equipment Corporation paid its production factory employees $2 million for the 80,000 actual direct labor hours they produced. This resulted in an unfavorable labor rate variance of $20,000, a favorable labor efficiency variance of $495,000, and production of 20,000 units of finished goods.

Required

Calculate the labor rate and efficiency standards employed by Tungol.

21-B6. Flow of Standard Costs and Variances. Feohtende Fixtures Company controls its plumbing fixtures production process with a standard costing system (including a four-way analysis of overhead). For product LY79, the standard costs per unit are as follows:

Direct materials	
2 pounds of iron for casting @ $0.30 per pound	$0.60
0.25 pound of chromium for plating @ $2.00 per pound	0.50
Direct labor (0.100 hour @ $20.00)	2.00
Overhead	
Variable (based on $7.50 per DLH)	0.75
Fixed (based on 10,000 DLH per month output)	0.50
	$4.35

During April, the following data were accumulated:

Actual price paid for 250,000 lbs. of iron	$ 0.33/lb.
Actual price paid for 50,000 lbs. of chromium	$ 1.95/lb.
Total iron requisitioned for process	205,000 lbs.
Total chromium requisitioned for process	20,000 lbs.
Actual labor rate paid	$ 25.00/hr.
Direct labor used	9,300 hrs.
Variable overhead costs incurred	$70,000
Fixed overhead costs incurred	$50,000
Units started and completed during month	95,000
Units left in work in process	–0–
Units sold during month	90,000

Required

Prepare T-accounts for the ledger accounts to be used by Feohtende for standard costing purposes and post to those accounts the journal entries necessary to record the above data (including variances). (Note: Only one Direct Materials Inventory account is needed, but there will be separate entries for the two varieties of direct materials. Also, remember to dispose of the variances at the end of the month.)

21-B7. Materials, Labor, and Overhead Variances. Based on a standard volume of output of 160,000 units per month, the standard cost of the product manufactured by Medico, Incorporated, is as follows:

Direct materials (0.50 ounce)	$5.00
Direct labor (0.125 hour)	2.00
Variable overhead	1.75
Fixed overhead	.75

During the month of October, 164,000 units were produced and the following costs incurred:

Direct materials (5,250 pounds @ $200)	$1,050,000
Direct labor (21,000 hours @ $20)	420,000
Variable overhead	300,000
Fixed overhead	125,000

Required

Compute the materials, labor, and overhead (four-way) variances for Medico for October.

21-B8. Standard Costing Income Statement. Mirror Image, Inc., uses a standard costing system to control manufacture of its single product, plate glass mirrors. The standard costs per mirror are as follows:

Direct materials	
2′ × 3′ glass plate @ $10 per 4′ × 6′ sheet	$2.50
0.01 ounce of silver @ $11 per ounce	.11
Direct labor	
2 minutes glass cutting @ $22.50 per hour	.75
1 minute silvering @ $15 per hour	.25
Overhead	
Variable	
Glass cutting dept. (based on $78 per DLH)	2.60
Silvering dept. (based on $120 per DLH)	2.00
Fixed	
Glass cutting dept. (based on 10,000 DLH per yr. output)	.15
Silvering dept. (based on 5,000 DLH per yr. output)	.25
Total standard cost per mirror	$8.61

During 1985, the following data were accumulated:

Actual price paid for 80,000 4/pr × 6′ sheets of glass		$920,000
Actual price paid for 200 pounds of silver		$ 34,400
Total glass requisitioned for process	74,000 4′ × 6′ sheets	
Total silver requisitioned for process	175 pounds	
Actual glass cutters' wage rate	$23.60 per hour	
Actual silvering workers' wage rate	$13.00 per hour	
Actual glass cutters' labor used	9,800 hours	
Actual silvering workers' labor used	4,950 hours	
Variable overhead costs incurred		
Glass cutting dept.	$775,000	
Silvering dept.	550,000	
Fixed overhead costs incurred		
Glass cutting dept.	50,000	
Silvering dept.	67,500	
Units started and completed during year	295,000 mirrors	
Units left in work in process	–0–	
Units sold during year (@ $35)	275,000 mirrors	
Selling expenses	$ 50,000	
Administrative expenses	75,000	

Required

Prepare an income statement for Mirror Image, Inc., for the year ending December 31, 1986. Be sure to adjust gross profit (at standard) for any variances in the company's costing data.

APPLICATION

The Weatherchem Corporation

■ Background

What do Morton Salt, Carnation, Procter and Gamble, General Foods, Kraft, DuPont, and R. J. Reynolds have in common? They are all customers of the Weatherchem Corporation, a $5 million company located in Twinsburg, a rural community in Ohio. Weatherchem is an excellent example of how a small company can develop a product concept, transform this concept into reality, and build a growing, profitable, and exciting organization.

Weatherchem was formed 12 years ago when A. J. Weatherhead, III, purchased the assets of the Ankey Company, whose main business was to build molds for injection molding equipment.[1] Shortly before Ankey was sold to Weatherhead, it had begun to switch from a builder of molds for injection molding equipment to a manufacturer of injection molded parts. Prominent customers for this new product line were the R. J. Reynolds Tobacco Company and the Clevepak Corporation, a large corporation that produced composite, or metal tubelike, containers. By the time Weatherhead purchased Ankey, plastic molding had totally replaced mold building as the company's main business.

■ Company Products

The products manufactured and sold to the two early, primary customers differed considerably in function but were produced by the same injection molding process. For R. J. Reynolds, the company made the small, plastic filter for Doral cigarettes. The Clevepak job called for a two-piece, round dispensing closure for its composite cans. This closure was later patented with the trademark Dispenz-R-Top and made in different sizes to fit different cans. An example of this product can be found today on the Morton's picnic size salt and pepper containers.

Up to this point, the traditional closures for composite cans were made of metal. Plastics were new to packaging and were touted as less expensive, attractive, and clean

1. Injection molding is a process where plastic resin pellets are melted and then injected under heat and pressure into a mold of a particular shape. The resins are then cooled in the mold and take the shape of the inside mold cavity. The product produced is determined by the type of plastic resin, the shape of the mold cavity, and the heat and pressure settings used in molding the part. The key capital equipment needed for this process is the press (machine that holds the mold) and the mold (tool that shapes the resins).

alternatives to metal. The newness of plastics in this market allowed for corporate growth with no entrenched competition within the plastic molding industry.

In the early years of Weatherchem's existence, the product line was virtually unchanged. Weatherhead established sales growth as the company's primary goal, with the composite can industry as the focus of the selling effort. Direct salespeople and manufacturers' representatives sold the product to firms in that industry. End users used composite can companies' containers and Weatherchem's closures for a wide variety of products, including specialty foods and spices, salt, and household and garden chemicals. This orientation is explicitly stated in Weatherchem's first promotional brochure, published in 1973: "Weatherchem aims toward becoming the container industry's prime supplier of dispenser-closures—and to this end applies technical skills, facilities and quality second to none."

During the next four years, additions were made to the product line. The basic closure was modified to allow a "friction" fit of the top to the can, which replaced the sometimes messy gluing operation. This proved to be a successful innovation. Other innovations were less successful. For example, a plastic spice can was developed but was never profitable. From each failure, however, the company learned and the number of subsequent product failures significantly decreased.

Over the years, the manufacturing system continued to be clean and well-run. Innovations such as a method of distributing resins in bulk were introduced (i.e., resins were distributed to presses in pipes, therefore eliminating manual handling). Engineering and mold-building support activities allowed the firm to maintain its molds inexpensively and promptly, thereby assuring quality while avoiding molding inefficiencies caused by poor mold maintenance. Such support activities were also key advantages in dealing with some customers who were unfamiliar with injection molding operation and who welcomed the advice Weatherchem could offer.

The first seven years of the company witnessed growth of sales along the traditional product line (with some modifications) and to a growing customer base, though still concentrated in the composite can industry. Assets and equity showed consistent growth, though net income and returns were more volatile, due in part to costs of increasing the sales force and developing new products. In addition, the company was still in the process of developing a standard cost system and was having difficulty in determining product costs.

■ Product Costing

Weatherchem has a job order, full-absorption, standard cost system. The company continually makes bids on potential jobs with existing and potential customers. For example, a customer wanting a closure for a new product would provide the company with detailed specifications of the end package and ask the company to quote a price to design and build the needed closure.

Three cost components are built into each cost estimate: materials, labor, and overhead (which includes the costs of machinery, tooling, and indirect labor). Assume the Hidro Company asked Weatherchem to determine a cost estimate for a closure for a package the company was developing. Weatherchem would go through the four steps to determine the cost estimate:

1. Materials cost. Amount of materials required × price per pound, e.g., 50 lbs (resin) × \$3.00/lb. = \$150.00.
2. Direct labor cost. Amount of direct labor hours required to manufacture product × wage rate per hour, e.g., 50 hours × \$7.50/hr = \$375.00.
3. Overhead cost. Number of machine hours required to make part × cost per hour for manufacturing overhead, e.g., 30 hours × \$15.00/hr = \$450.00.
4. Final price. Total cost to produce × (1 + profit markup), e.g., (150.00 + 375.00 + 450.00) (1.10) = (975.00)1.10 = \$1,072.50.

If the customer feels the final price is too high, Weatherchem can reduce its estimate by finding a less expensive way to produce the part or by accepting a lower profit markup.

Exercises

1. Does Weatherchem have an appropriate cost system, given the nature of the company?
2. Discuss how the company determines the following:

—overhead rate
—number of labor and machine hours required to produce the part
—direct labor wage rate
—amount and types of materials used in production.

3. How can the company use the cost estimate to help it in planning and controlling operations?

PART SIX

PLANNING, CONTROL, AND DECISION MAKING

RESPONSIBILITY ACCOUNTING

CHAPTER OBJECTIVES

After studying Chapter 22, you should understand the following:

1. The concept of responsibility accounting and how it is used by companies as a method of internal control.
2. The four types of responsibility centers typically found in organizations.
3. The method and importance of establishing a responsive reporting structure.
4. The concept of transfer pricing.
5. Commonly used procedures for evaluating responsibility center performance.

The initial chapters of the management accounting section have focused on specific issues related to product costing. This and the remaining chapters take a different perspective of management accounting by discussing how organizations should structure themselves internally to facilitate planning and control and describe what role accounting plays in a planning and control system.

One of the backbones of an effective planning and control system is a responsibility center structure. A **responsibility center** is a separate, identifiable segment of an organization managed by an individual who is responsible for the performance of his or her center and for many of the planning and control dimensions of the unit. To facilitate planning and control in these centers, many companies have adopted what we call a responsibility accounting system. That is, management accountants not only do the accounting for the company in the aggregate, but also establish a reporting system that allows accounting for the individual entities, or segments, within the organization. This subunit accounting is known as **responsibility accounting** and is the focus of this chapter.

RESPONSIBILITY CENTER
A separate, identifiable segment of an organization that is managed by an individual.

RESPONSIBILITY ACCOUNTING
Accounting for responsibility centers.

RESPONSIBILITY ACCOUNTING SYSTEMS AND MANAGEMENT STRUCTURES

Responsibility Accounting Systems

Responsibility accounting involves providing accounting information to subunits within the organization. Although we all realize that it is necessary to provide accounting information for an organization in its entirety, it is less obvious that this information is needed for individual subunits.

Each subunit in an organization is responsible for performance. To facilitate performance and to increase the effectiveness of planning and control, subunit managers need accounting information. This information should provide valuable feedback to let managers know whether or not they are on course and, if not, to pinpoint problem areas. Managers also need information to assist in planning for the future. Therefore, one of the important roles of the management accountant is to design responsibility accounting systems.

Probably one of the more interesting questions regarding responsibility accounting concerns how we go about implementing such a system. Basically, there are three steps: 1) establishing the proper responsibility structure, 2) developing a reporting system consistent with this structure, and 3) instituting a performance evaluation system that allows top management to evaluate the effectiveness and efficiency of subunits.

Responsibility Structure

The first step in implementing a responsibility accounting system is organizing the company properly. To accomplish this, top management segments the company into responsibility centers where each center is responsible for its own performance. Normally, there are four types of responsibility centers: cost centers, revenue centers, profit centers, and investment centers.

COST CENTER
A subunit in an organization that has primary responsibility for the incurrence of cost.

Cost Centers. A **cost center** is a subunit that has primary responsibility for the incurrence of cost for a given level of service. In the planning process, the department manager is responsible for determining the center's future costs and for controlling actual performance, in terms of cost incurrence, as measured against planned results. Cost centers have no responsibility to generate revenue. This is not meant to imply that they do not provide a service. However, many times this service is intangible and cannot easily be dollar quantified. For this reason, the output produced in cost centers is usually measured in a unit other than dollars, and control of these centers is focused on how much money is spent or what inputs are used to produce a certain level of output.

In some organizations, a distinction is made between discretionary and engineered cost centers. An **engineered cost center** is one where there is a direct and observable relationship between the costs incurred in that unit and the output provided, such as in a manufacturing department. This relationship is direct enough that many of the standard costing techniques studied in Chapter 21 can be applied in controlling the costs generated by the unit. In contrast, **discretionary cost centers** (such as the personnel department) do not exhibit a direct relationship between input and output. Because the direct relation does not exist, standard costing techniques are not appropriate in a discretionary cost center. Thus, other mechanisms must be developed to help in planning, controlling, and evaluating performance in these units.

ENGINEERED COST CENTER
A cost center where there is a direct and observable relationship between the costs incurred in that unit and the output provided.

DISCRETIONARY COST CENTER
A cost center that does not exhibit a direct relationship between input and output.

Revenue Centers. In contrast to a cost center, a **revenue center** is a subunit responsible for the generation of revenue. An excellent example of a revenue center is a sales department that sells products provided by a production department. The primary measure of performance in a sales department is the quantity and dollar amount of revenue generated. This is not meant to imply that a sales department is not responsible for controlling costs. Even in a revenue center, costs will be incurred and the subunit will be held accountable for these costs. In measuring the performance of the unit, however, emphasis is put on planning and controlling output such as the volume of sales and the product mix rather than the cost input.

REVENUE CENTER
A subunit of an organization responsible for the generation of revenue.

Profit Centers. Decentralized companies often create subunits known as profit centers. A **profit center** is a subunit where the manager is responsible for both the generation of revenue and the incurrence of costs. In other words, the managers have profit responsibility because they have control over the components that make up profit and loss. An excellent example of an organization that uses the profit center concept is the highly decentralized General Motors. We are all familiar with GM's individual divisions, such as the Chevy Division, the Buick Division, and the Cadillac Division. Each of these divisions is run as a profit center, with divisional managers held responsible for the profit of the division. Companies frequently decentralize in this fashion, as such a system allows them to institute proper control methods.

PROFIT CENTER
A subunit in an organization where the manager is responsible for both the generation of revenues and the incurrence of costs.

Since managers are held responsible for their subunits' profit or loss, it is important in a profit center for the manager of the unit to have independence and autonomy. If this were not the case, it would be unreasonable to hold managers responsible for the profits they could not actually control. In such situations, they would justly complain that any profit variances were not their fault. As a general rule, then, managers of responsibility centers should not be held responsible for actions beyond their influence.

INVESTMENT CENTER
A subunit in an organization where the manager is responsible for profits and the level of investment (asset base) of the subunit.

Investment Centers. In many decentralized companies, divisions are known as investment centers rather than profit centers. An **investment center** is a subunit where the manager is responsible for profits *and* the level of investment (the asset base) of the subunit. The primary difference between a profit center and an investment center lies in whether or not the manager is responsible for assets. For example, in service organizations, which are not capital intensive and have a low level of assets (typically controlled by top management), it would be most appropriate to organize the divisions as profit centers. However, in decentralized manufacturing companies, such as General Electric, each of the various divisions has assets at its disposal. Thus, the divisions are more appropriately treated as investment centers and are held accountable for profits in comparison to investment bases.

RESPONSIBILITY REPORTING SYSTEMS

Once a company has been organized properly, the next step is to establish a reporting system consistent with the differing needs of each level within the organization.

Illustration of Responsibility Reporting Systems

An illustration of an effective responsibility reporting system can be seen in the context of the organizational chart in Exhibit 22.1. The organization has three layers of management. The president is the top manager, with two product divisions (profit centers) under him or her. Reporting to the divisional managers are department managers responsible for sales (a revenue center), manufacturing (a cost center), and administrative services (a cost center).

As shown in Exhibit 22.2, reports at the departmental level are fairly detailed, focusing on the areas of responsibility of each department. For example, in the sales department, the key reporting items are the amount of sales generated in each of the geographical territories where the company operates. Control of these individual responsibility centers is maintained through a comparison of actual versus budgeted results. For example, in the sales department, the actual revenue generated for the last period was greater than originally budgeted. This difference (known as a variance in accounting) would provide feedback to the departmental manager and his or her superiors in evaluating the performance of the department.

At the division managers' level, the reporting system is modified from what it was at the departmental level. The division managers do not need to see the details for

EXHIBIT 22.1

Organization Chart Depicting Management Responsibility

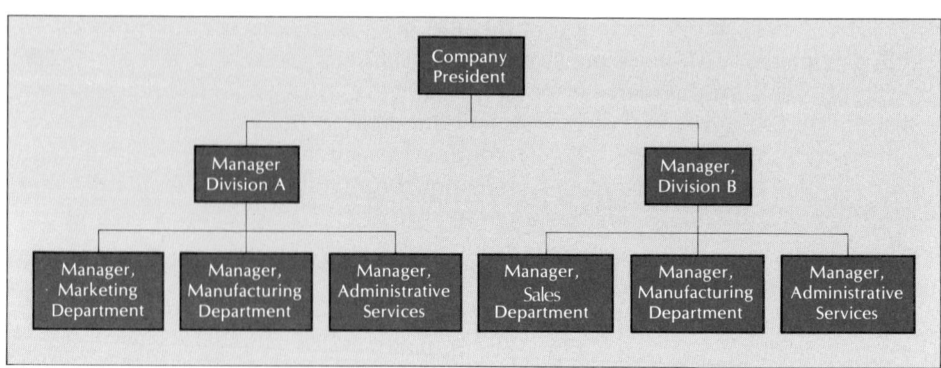

■ CONCEPT SUMMARY 22.1

RESPONSIBILITY ACCOUNTING: SUBUNITS WITHIN AN ORGANIZATION

Subunit	Responsibility	Evaluation
Cost Center 1. Engineered cost center—a direct, observable relationship exists between costs incurred and output provided. 2. Discretionary cost center—no direct, observable relationship exists between input and output.	Responsible for the incurrence (i.e., planning and controlling) of costs. Not responsible for revenue.	Based on the amount of costs incurred (i.e., money spent) to produce a certain level of output (physical units). 1. Budgeted versus actual costs. 2. Controllable versus uncontrollable variances.
Revenue center	Responsible for the generation of revenue. Not responsible for all costs.	Based on the dollar volume of revenue, number of physical units sold, product mix. 1. Budgeted versus actual revenues. 2. Controllable versus uncontrollable variances.
Profit center	Responsible for the generation of profits. Responsible both for the generation of revenue and for the incurrence of costs.	Based on the level of profits (before-tax profits, after-tax profits, segment contribution margin, or segment margin) generated. 1. Targeted versus actual profits. 2. Controllable versus uncontrollable variances.
Investment center	Responsible for the generation of profits and for the level of investment (asset base).	Based on the profit (return) generated from the employment of assets. 1. Targeted versus actual ROI. 2. ROI tree performance: targeted versus actual asset turnover, profit margins, etc. 3. Residual income—covering of opportunity costs.

EXHIBIT 22.2

Responsibility Reporting

XYZ Company
Budget Performance Report
For the Month Ending October 31, 1986

Item	Budget	Actual	Over	Under
Division A, profit	$ 17,200	$ 45,200	$ 28,000	
Division B, profit	20,000	16,000		$ 4,000
	$ 37,200	$ 61,200	$ 28,000	$ 4,000

Division A
Budget Performance Report
For the Month Ending October 31, 1986

Item	Budget	Actual	Over	Under
Sales dept., revenue	$230,000	$311,000	$ 81,000	
Direct costs				
Manufacturing dept.	150,000	204,000	(54,000)	
Administrative services	32,800	31,800		$ (1,000)
Indirect costs	30,000	30,000		
	$ 17,200	$ 45,200	$ 27,000	$ (1,000)

Division A, Sales Dept.
Budget Performance Report
For the Month Ending October 31, 1986

Item	Budget	Actual	Over	Under
Northeast sales	$100,000	$110,000	$ 10,000	
Southeast sales	50,000	54,000	4,000	
Northwest sales	65,000	72,000	7,000	
Southwest sales	10,000	50,000	40,000	
Export sales	5,000	25,000	20,000	
	$230,000	$311,000	$ 81,000	$ –0–

each individual department. Instead, they need to have aggregate information showing how each department did overall, as well as information about important deviations from budgeted items. In this way, divisional managers do not waste time analyzing reports of departments performing effectively. Note that the information required by the president is even more streamlined and summarized than the data provided to divisional managers. The president is basically concerned with whether the overall objectives of the company have been achieved. If the objectives have not been met, the president must determine why the company fell short and what can be done to rectify the situation.

Principles of Reporting

Establishing an effective responsibility reporting system has two guiding principles. The first is that the level of reporting becomes more specific the lower the level of

EXHIBIT 22.2 (Continued)

Division A, Manufacturing Dept.
Budget Performance Report
For the Month Ending October 31, 1986

Item	Budget	Actual	Over	Under
Direct costs				
Materials				
Material A	$ 50,000	$ 70,000	$ 20,000	
Material B	60,000	90,000	30,000	
Labor				
Labor class A	2,000	2,500	500	
Labor class B	3,000	3,000		
Labor class C	5,000	5,500	500	
Overhead				
Materials	11,000	15,000	4,000	
Labor	2,000	2,000		
Power	2,000	2,000		
Depreciation	5,000	5,000		
Indirect costs	10,000	9,000		$ 1,000
	$150,000	$204,000	$ 55,000	$ 1,000

Division A, Administrative Dept.
Budget Performance Report
For the Month Ending October 31, 1986

Item	Budget	Actual	Over	Under
Salaries expense	$ 30,000	$ 31,000	$ 1,000	
Bonuses expense	2,000	–0–		$ 2,000
Depreciation expense	500	500		
Utilities expense	200	200		
Supplies expense	100	100		
	$ 32,800	$ 31,800	$ 1,000	$ 2,000

management. This specificity is necessary to guide managers in effective and efficient operation of their units. The second important principle is that in reporting to higher levels of management, the reporting by exception principle is followed. That is, only upward information significantly different than planned is reported so that management focuses on significant items. An effective system should ensure that top management is not overwhelmed with unnecessary details.

In designing an effective reporting system, certain key issues must be resolved. The first issue is to determine the format of reports at each reporting level. These formats should be tailor-made to meet the needs of management and ensure that corporate management has the information necessary to prepare consolidated financial statements. For example, in some companies, control is maintained by comparing budgeted versus actual items, and an effective reporting system must provide budgeted versus actual performance data.

A second important issue is to determine the direct and indirect costs associated with responsibility centers. The purpose of establishing a responsibility center structure is to hold managers accountable for their performances. A manager will be able to influence only certain items. Therefore, we need to identify direct (i.e., controllable) and indirect (i.e., uncontrollable) costs by responsibility center.

A third issue involves the procedures to evaluate responsibility center performance. One approach is to compare actual versus budget; another is to compare actual this year versus actual in a prior time period. In addition to these methods of measuring managerial performance, we can discuss aggregate performance measures, such as return on investment and residual income.

The fourth issue in establishing an effective responsibility reporting system is to identify the interdependencies among the various departments and the impact these interdependencies have on financial performance. If, for example, the sales department in Division A buys its products from the manufacturing department, one would wonder at what prices these goods are transferred between the departments. Such prices charged for goods moving from one part of an organization to another are called **transfer prices.** Transfer pricing is critical because the way in which prices are set can impact the managerial performance of the units providing and acquiring goods.

TRANSFER PRICE
The internal price paid by one division of a company to obtain goods from another.

Indirect Versus Direct Costs

Chapter 19 discussed the concept of direct and indirect costs. Recall that direct costs are physically traceable to a cost objective, such as a department or product. In contrast, indirect costs cannot be physically traced to a cost objective but are allocated to a cost objective on some predetermined basis.

Indirect costs are allocated to cost objectives for many reasons, one of which is to determine a full-absorption cost of products to assist management in setting realistic product prices and thereby generating desired profit levels. Indirect costs can also be allocated to cost objectives to produce some desired motivation. For example, computer service costs are sometimes allocated to departments. Since departments must pay for the services, managers are motivated to use them efficiently. A third reason cost allocations are made is to get a better idea of the income and asset valuations associated with units in the organization. This is especially true in decentralized firms, which try to create a small company atmosphere in their divisions. If these divisions operated as independent companies, they would bear the cost of the indirect charges. Therefore, most large decentralized companies believe such costs should be allocated to divisions.

Exhibit 22.3 provides an overview of the cost allocation system typically used in an organization. All costs, both manufacturing and nonmanufacturing, including the president's salary, are allocated through the various layers of management until they are reflected in product cost. As the exhibit shows, the allocation of costs from one level of the organization to another can involve many different allocation bases. The key issue involves the identification of an appropriate allocation base. In essence, we are looking for the base most closely associated with overhead costs.

Let us examine, for example, the allocation of the personnel department's cost to the manufacturing units. The most rational allocation base in this situation would be number of people, because the personnel department exists to provide services to employees. Exhibit 22.4 shows how the personnel department's costs might be allocated to the two manufacturing departments based on the number of people in each department relative to the total employees in both manufacturing departments. We ignored the people working in the personnel department as well as in some of the other service departments. This method of allocating service department costs is known as **direct cost method.** Costs are directly allocated from the service de-

DIRECT COST METHOD
A method of allocating costs from service departments to manufacturing departments.

EXHIBIT 22.3

Overview of Cost Allocation

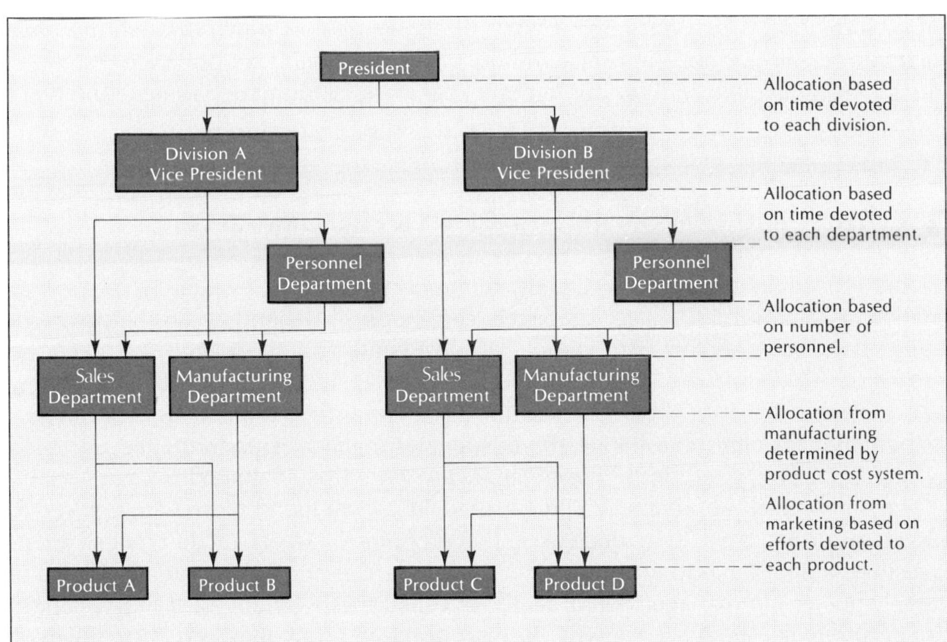

partments to the manufacturing departments, ignoring any interrelationships among service departments.

Such cause and effect relationships are much more difficult to determine at higher levels in an organization, and thus such high-level allocations tend to be arbitrary. For this reason, companies should design reporting systems that use the principles of direct costing (a more extensive discussion of which is included in Chapter 24). In this way, by reflecting the differences between the costs directly related to a unit and those that are allocated, the income statement accomplishes several objectives. The segment margin or direct costs associated with a unit could be used as a measure

EXHIBIT 22.4

Direct Method for Allocation of Service Department Costs

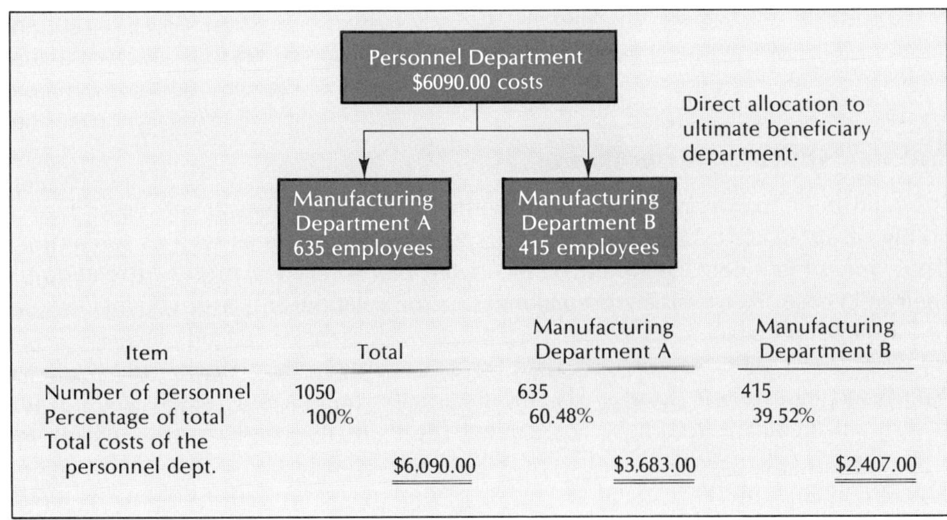

Item	Total	Manufacturing Department A	Manufacturing Department B
Number of personnel	1050	635	415
Percentage of total	100%	60.48%	39.52%
Total costs of the personnel dept.	$6.090.00	$3.683.00	$2.407.00

of performance. Top management goals of allocating cost down through the organization can also be accomplished without distorting subunit performance. Examples are shown in Exhibit 22.5 for our hypothetical manufacturing department and product division.

EVALUATING RESPONSIBILITY CENTER PERFORMANCE

As the preceding discussion indicates, different methods for evaluating the performance of responsibility center managers can be used, depending on the nature of the responsibility center. For example, in cost centers, performance will likely be measured by comparing actual and budgeted costs and analyzing the variances. Whether or not the manager can control these variances can then be determined. If the variances are controllable, the cost center manager's performance, in terms of his or her ability to control these variances, would be evaluated.

The same basic approach would be used in a revenue center. Actual revenue targets are compared to budgeted or predetermined targets. If differences exist, questions are raised as to the reasons for the differences and a determination is made as to whether the manager could have controlled these variances. If the variances are controllable, we must ask why they occurred and how they can be rectified.

The procedures used in evaluating the performance of a profit center and an investment center differ to a degree, even though the principles are quite the same as they were for revenue and cost centers.

Profit Center Performance

The overall performance of a profit center is evaluated in terms of the manager's ability to meet predetermined profit targets. If a division exceeds its profit target, its performance would be considered favorable, and top management would then probably examine how the surplus was achieved and whether it was large enough, given the changes in assumptions and operating conditions of the unit. In contrast, if the unit fails to meet its target, questions would be raised as to why and whether the factors that led to the below-target performance were controllable by the manager. If they were, what could the manager have done to correct the situation? Even though it is probably too late for the manager to do anything to correct the situation, by asking such questions, managers receive feedback that can be used in subsequent years.

Investment Center Performance

It would be inappropriate to evaluate performance in an investment center based solely on profit, since the manager is responsible for assets as well as for profits. Thus, investment centers should be evaluated based on their profits *in relation* to their asset base. Two tools are used to measure this relationship: return on investment and residual income.

Return on Investment (ROI). The most common measure of performance in an investment center is return on investment (ROI). In its simplest form, return on investment is calculated by dividing profits (pretax in the case of a division) by assets. The ROI figure is predetermined for each division, and performance is then measured on the basis of how well each unit attained its target. The ROI method of measuring

EXHIBIT 22.5(a)
Direct Cost Reporting for Departments

Division A, Manufacturing Department
Statement of Departmental Expenses
For The Month Ending October 31, 1986

Direct departmental expenses			
Materials		$160,000	
Labor		11,000	
Overhead			
Materials	$ 15,000		
Labor	2,000		
Power	2,000		
Depreciation	5,000	24,000	
Total direct costs			$195,000
Indirect departmental expenses			
Officers' salaries expense		$ 4,000	
Office staff salaries expense		2,000	
Rent expense		1,500	
Heating and lighting expense		500	
Advertising expense		475	
Miscellaneous expense		525	
Total indirect costs			9,000
Total departmental costs			$204,000

EXHIBIT 22.5(b)
Direct Cost Reporting for Divisions

Division B
Direct Costing Income Statement
For The Month Ending June 30, 1986

Net sales		$614,700
Variable manufacturing expenses		323,350
Contribution margin from manufacturing		$291,350
Direct divisional expenses		
Sales salaries expense	$30,900	
Advertising expense	9,100	
Property tax expense	3,740	
Uncollectible accounts expense	1,380	
Depreciation expense	1,760	
Insurance expense	2,145	
Total direct divisional expenses		49,025
Contribution margin (net)		$242,325
Indirect expenses allocated to division		
Officers' salaries expense	$26,000	
Office staff salaries expense	8,600	
Rent expense	9,400	
Heating and lighting expense	2,500	
Advertising expense	2,700	
Miscellaneous expense	4,500	
Total indirect expenses		53,700
Segment margin		$188,625

divisional performance is very popular and is used by the majority of decentralized companies in the United States having investment centers.

ROI is used in a decentralized company in two ways: as a static measure and as a diagnostic tool. Some companies simply set ROI targets for the various divisions and analyze, after the fact, whether these targets have been met. If the target has been exceeded, performance is deemed good. If the target has not been met, performance is considered poor. Little or no attention is devoted to analyzing how the ROI, whether good or bad, was achieved; rather, attention is focused on whether or not the target was met.

The preferable way to use ROI is as a diagnostic tool. Recall from Chapter 18 that the ROI calculation was originally formulated and used by the DuPont Corporation. Management at DuPont used the ROI framework as a way of evaluating the overall performance of a division. In doing this, it developed the ROI tree that was presented in Exhibit 18.5, repeated here in Exhibit 22.6.

EXHIBIT 22.6

DuPont ROI Tree

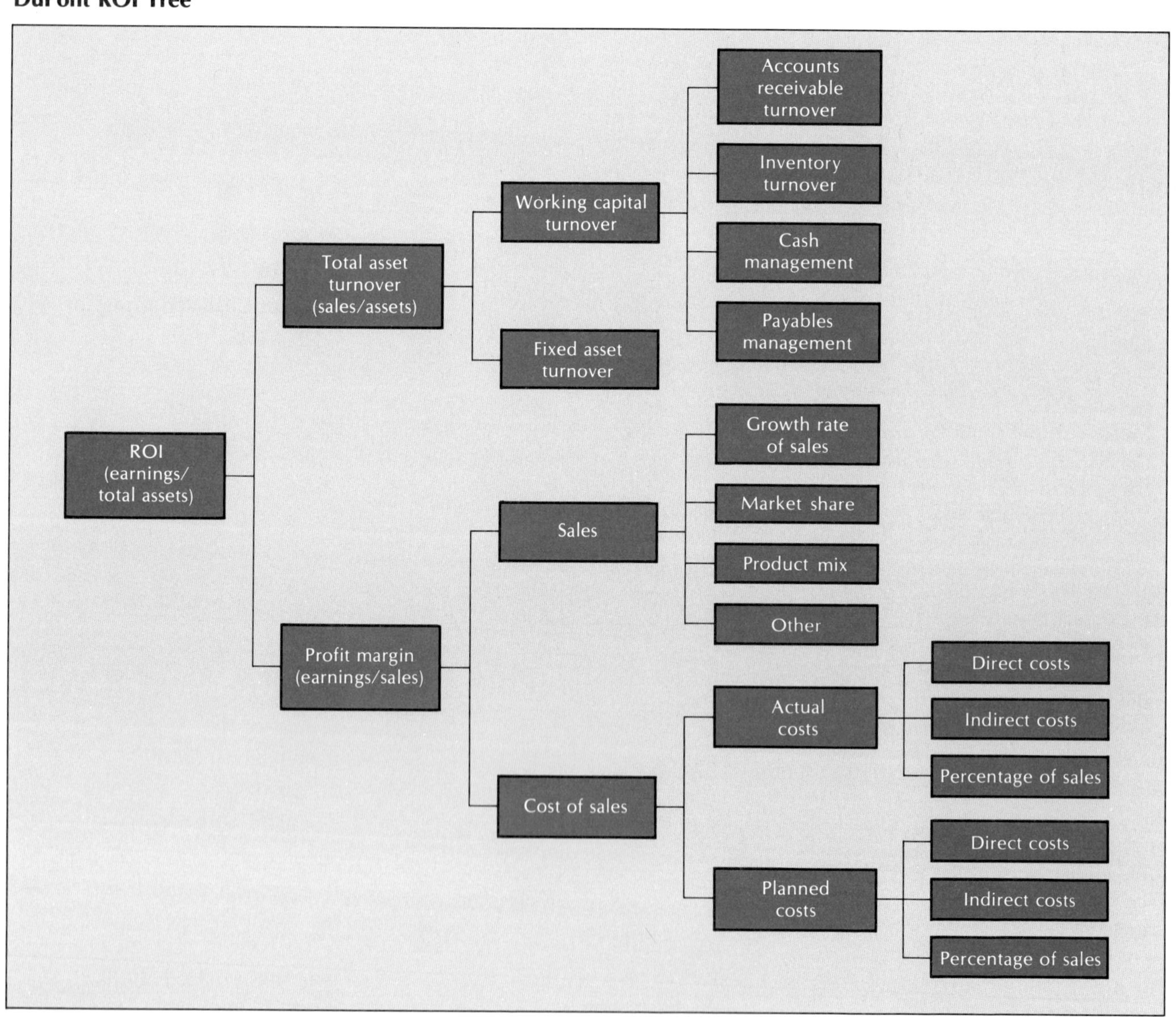

As indicated in Chapter 18, ROI is a function of two factors: total asset turnover and profit margin. Total asset turnover is defined as sales divided by assets—the higher the turnover, the higher the ROI. In analyzing total asset turnover, however, we can see it is a function of working capital turnover and fixed asset turnover and that ratios can be specified to identify effective utilization of each of these resources. Profit margin is defined as earnings divided by sales. In analyzing this profit margin, we can see it is a function of both sales and the ability to control costs and that measures can be specified for these variables as well. In this way, by branching the ROI from the aggregate measure to its smaller components, we have a more dynamic way to analyze the organization: We can systematically analyze how the ROI was achieved. It is in this context that DuPont uses the ROI method.

DuPont and other companies using ROI set targets each year for this figure at corporate and divisional levels. In addition to setting targets, management sets standards for the factors that impact ROI, such as total asset turnover, accounts receivable turnover, inventory turnover, and sales growth. Therefore, a manager is responsible for achieving an ROI target in a certain way.

If actual ROI exceeds planned, it might not indicate a favorable condition, since the superior performance might have been accomplished at the expense of something else. For example, a manager might have achieved a higher total asset turnover by refusing or ignoring to replace assets. In the short run, this would make ROI look very good, but the long-term impact of such a decision could be disastrous. When the ROI method is used as a diagnostic tool, however, management can identify and correct the causes of such seemingly superior ROI performances.

Residual Income. In recent years, another popular method has arisen to evaluate investment center performance. This other approach is known as the residual income method. This method, illustrated in Exhibit 22.7, holds divisions accountable for achieving a certain residual income target. In this context, **residual income** is defined as the difference between divisional profits and the divisional cost of capital. The cost of capital for a division is calculated by taking the assets of the division and multiplying them by an appropriate opportunity cost percentage, which represents the opportunity cost of using the assets. For example, assume a division has one million dollars in assets and the company has decided that there is a 10 percent opportunity cost of using this money; that is, the money could be invested elsewhere to earn 10 percent. Therefore, the division would have a cost of capital of $100,000.

RESIDUAL INCOME
The difference between divisional profits and the divisional cost of capital.

In many ways, the residual income method is similar to the ROI method. However, performance targets are based on absolute dollars of residual income rather than on ROI percentages. The residual income method is conceptually superior to the ROI method, because if a company is to maximize shareholder wealth, it must generate profits in excess of its cost of capital. By doing this, the company is creating wealth for shareholders. In practice, the use of residual income has resulted in response to the criticism that ROI causes managers of very profitable divisions to reject projects that should be accepted from the corporate viewpoint. For example, if ROI company-wide is 16 percent, a manager of a division that normally earns 20 percent might reject an investment earning 17 percent. This decision will ultimately hurt corporate profits.

The residual income method motivates managers to accept projects or make decisions yielding a profit greater than the opportunity cost. Despite the theoretical advantages of the residual income method, it is rarely used in practice, and ROI tends to be the primary measure of investment center performance.

EXHIBIT 22.7

Residual Income Reporting

Division B
Statement of Residual Income
For The Month Ending July 31, 1986

Net sales			$262,900
Cost of merchandise sold			125,000
Gross profit			137,900
Operating expenses			
Selling expenses			
Sales salaries expense	$ 24,600		
Advertising expense	4,300		
Miscellaneous expense	1,210		
Total selling expenses		$ 30,110	
General expenses			
Officers' salaries expense	$ 19,800		
Office staff salaries expense	7,140		
Rent expense	5,320		
Property tax expense	2,160		
Heating and lighting expense	1,815		
Uncollectible accounts expense	1,450		
Insurance expense	1,895		
Miscellaneous expense	1,302		
Total general expenses		40,882	
Total operating expenses			70,992
Income from operations			$ 66,908
Other expenses			
Interest expense			2,500
Income before income taxes			$ 64,408
Division cost of capital (@10%)			50,000
Residual income			$ 14,408

Transfer Pricing

Another primary issue involved in measuring investment center performance is the pricing of goods transferred internally. This is typically a problem in decentralized companies where one unit of the organization makes products that it sells internally. In this situation, prices (known as transfer prices) must be set for these products. How they are set is important for the following reasons:

1. Transfer prices can affect how divisional performance is measured. From the perspective of the selling division, the price received for the transferred goods becomes part of the division's revenue; in the buying division, the price paid becomes part of the cost of goods sold. Thus, the transfer price affects the income of both the buying and selling divisions.
2. Another important reason transfer pricing is critical is that depending on how these prices are established, they can impact managerial behavior. In the absence of any rules, buying managers will want to pay as little as possible for goods while selling units are probably trying to get the highest price possible. The transfer price set should lead to a transaction maximizing overall corporate profits.

3. The third objective of a good transfer pricing system is that it assures an efficient allocation of resources among and within subunits. Accurate and reasonable transfer prices will not distort divisional profit measurement, consequently resulting in an efficient allocation of resources.

Transfer Pricing Systems

Basically, two broad-based approaches are used in establishing transfer prices: Market-based prices and cost-based prices.

Market-Based Systems. A market-based transfer pricing system normally is the preferred method for measuring the profitability of intercompany transfers, because if a ready external market exists for the product, the price outsiders are willing to pay for it would be an objective and verifiable measure of the product's value. Such use of prevailing market prices encourages managers to be more concerned with cost control, because cost allocations are based on realistic rather than artificial prices.

If a ready outside market does not exist for the transferred product but similar products are available, the transfer price could be based on the price of similar products. However, such prices must be properly adjusted for any differences in product quality, technical specifications, and so on.

Cost-Based Systems. Transfer prices based on product cost should be used if market prices are unavailable or unsuitable. Cost-based prices can be determined using several concepts of costs. Each method has obvious advantages and disadvantages. For example, although transfer prices based on actual costs have the advantages of simplicity and understandability, this method might not encourage selling divisions to be efficient, because they are able to pass all of their costs on to the buying division. The use of standard costs can overcome this problem, assuming standards are reasonable and equitable. Even when standard costs are used, a markup should be added to product cost to arrive at a transfer price. This cost-plus approach allows the selling division to earn a profit on the transaction. Without this profit margin, there is no incentive for the division to make an internal sale, because it will not favorably impact its profits.

In certain circumstances (e.g., when excess capacity exists), transfer prices based on incremental, marginal, or variable costing methods might be more appropriate. Under incremental and marginal costing, transfer prices are equal to the increase in direct production costs incurred by the transferor (division or affiliated company). Under variable costing procedures, the transfer price includes direct labor, direct materials, and variable overhead costs. For example, if an affiliated company incurred \$5 in direct materials costs, \$5 in direct labor, and \$2 in variable overhead to produce product A, the transfer price under variable costing would be \$12. Under incremental or marginal costing, the transfer price would be only \$10 if the transferor was operating under conditions of excess capacity.

Transfer Pricing To Minimize Income Taxes

Although the primary purpose of transfer pricing systems is to maximize achievement of management objectives (such as provision of a measure with which to evaluate responsibility center performance), companies with operations in foreign countries can also use their systems to minimize their federal income taxes. Three methods are available for accomplishing this:

1. Utilize low ordinary tax rates. If a country imposes a high rate of income taxes, a corporation in that country might transfer goods or provide services at unusually low prices to an affiliate operating in a low-tax-rate country. This would effectively shift most or all of the corporation's overall profit to the affiliated company in the "tax haven" country.

2. Utilize low special tax rates. Regular U.S. domestic corporations can transfer goods at low prices to specially taxed corporations (such as corporations set up in U.S. possessions). The profits of the special corporation arising from the transfers would be taxed at preferential (i.e., lower) rates.

3. Utilize foreign tax credits. U.S. corporations receive tax credits for income taxes paid to foreign countries. If a company had unused credits, it could benefit by transferring goods at low prices to foreign affiliates that would resell at higher prices. Foreign taxes on the resulting profits would be offset by the tax credits, which might otherwise have gone unused.

These techniques provide management with a useful tool for reducing federal income taxes. Caution must be exercised in their application, however, for the Internal Revenue Service has the authority to disallow any transfer pricing system it believes to be tax-evasion motivated.

FOR REVIEW

SUMMARY

- A responsibility accounting system provides information to managers on subunit performance. Responsibility accounting system success depends on the establishment of the proper responsibility structure, design of a responsibility accounting system that fits the structure, and establishment of an effective subunit evalution system.
- The four types of responsibility centers are cost centers, revenue centers, profit centers, and investment centers.
- Cost centers are responsible for level of cost incurred; the primary focus is on input.
- Revenue centers are responsible for level of revenue generated; the primary focus is on output.
- Profit centers are responsible for both cost and revenue and thus focus on both input and output.
- Investment centers are similar to profit centers but bear additional responsibility for the level of assets employed by the subunit.
- In an effective responsibility reporting system, information presented in accounting reports is increasingly summarized as the reporting level in the organization moves up.
- Effective responsibility reporting systems require that (1) the format of the reports be appropriate for each reporting level, (2) direct and indirect costs be carefully established for

each responsibility center, (3) procedures for evaluating responsibility centers be established, and (4) structural interdependencies among various subunits be thoroughly understood.

■ Cost and revenue centers are usually evaluated by comparing actual and budgeted figures. Profit centers are usually evaluated by comparing actual results to target income levels. Investment centers are usually evaluated by return on investment or residual income computations.

■ Transfer pricing refers to the price at which goods are transferred internally from one department to another. Transfer prices are usually based on either market prices for similar goods or cost of production of the goods.

QUESTIONS

22-1. What is a responsibility center, and how is the concept of the responsibility center used as a method of planning and control within an organization?

22-2. What are the four types of responsibility centers typically found in organizations? What factors influence the type of responsibility center established?

22-3. Distinguish between a discretionary cost center and an engineered cost center.

22-4. How does a revenue center differ from a profit center?

22-5. Explain the principle of upward information flow in implementing a responsibility accounting system.

22-6. What is a transfer price, and why is the determination of a transfer price important?

22-7. Discuss some reasons why it is often necessary to allocate indirect costs to a cost objective.

22-8. What is the most likely way to evaluate cost center performance?

22-9. What are the two main components for determining ROI, and how is ROI calculated?

22-10. Identify the two approaches used to establish transfer prices and explain how these approaches are used.

EXERCISES

22-E1. Following are operating data for two divisions of the Soco Company for 1986:

	Computer Division	Components Division
Sales	$100,000	$250,000
Average operating assets	50,000	125,000
Divisional contribution margin	20,000	50,000
Identifiable assets	75,000	140,000

Required

a. Compute the return on investment for each division using the ROI formula.
b. Calculate for each division the total asset turnover and profit margin and explain the differences between how each division achieves its ROI figure.

22-E2. Using the data from 22-E1, assume that the computer division has been charged with a cost of capital of 10% and the components division has been charged with a capital charge of 15%. Calculate the residual income for each division using this information. What are the differences between the residual income method and the ROI method, and under what circumstances might they lead to different numbers and therefore to different evaluations by management?

22-E3. The seals division of the PH Company produces seals that it sells for $175 per thousand. The seals division's cost per 100,000 seals is as follows:

Variable costs are $50, and fixed overhead is $50, based on production of one million seals.

Total cost per 1,000 seals is $100.

The seals division has recently been asked to provide the data division of the same company with 200,000 seals. It has quoted a price of $175 per thousand, which is the customary charge to outside customers. However, the data division feels that it should be charged a lower price than what the seals division would charge an outside firm. Therefore, it has offered to pay $100 per thousand plus a small return.

Required

a. If each division is treated as an independent investment center, what transfer price would you recommend for the seals? Fully justify your answer.
b. What factors influence whether the transfer price should be based on market prices or cost?

22-E4. Provide the missing data in the following tabulation:

	Division		
	X	Y	Z
Sales	$200,000	?	?
Segment income	10,000	?	$ 20,000
Average operating assets	?	$500,000	
Profit margin	?	5%	6%
Total asset turnover	?	4	
Return on investment	15%		18%
Residual income	?	50,000	3,333
Cost of capital charge	10%	?	

22-E5. Alpha Company has assets of $2 million and a long-term 10% debt of $500,000. Beta Company has assets of $2 million and no long-term debt. The operating income of each company before interest is $150,000. Compute the return on investment on assets available and shareholders' equity. Why are there significant differences in the two rate-of-return computations for Alpha and Beta companies, and what are the implications for the management of the companies?

22-E6. The Amanda Division of the Super Toy Company produces dolls that it sells to its company's distributors. Following are cost-of-production data for the most recent years:

Dolls produced	100,000
Direct materials	$200,000
Direct labor	200,000
Manufacturing overhead (50% are variable expenses)	150,000
Administrative overhead	100,000

What is the transfer price per unit for the dolls using absorption costing, variable costing plus a 50% markup, a desired divisional income of 10% on sales, and variable manufacturing cost plus 50%?

22-E7. The Tommy Corporation has three product plants: L, K and M. The plants are treated as investment centers. The following data summarize the results for 1986:

	Revenue	Expenses	Investment Base (gross assets)
Plant L	$ 100,000	$ 50,000	$ 1,000,000
Plant K	200,000	80,000	4,000,000
Plant M	5,000,000	3,000,000	10,000,000

Required

a. If the plants are treated as investment centers, which plant manager appears to have done the best job?
b. If the plants are treated as profit centers, which plant manager has done the best job?
c. What criteria would you use to decide whether these plants should be treated as investment centers or profit centers? Do the results of your profit center and investment center analyses give different findings? If so, why, and how would this affect whether you made the plants investment or profit centers?

PROBLEM SET A

22-A1. Profit Centers Versus Investment Centers. Ledman Enterprises operates three manufacturing plants (A, B, and C) as responsibility centers. The following data summarize the results for 1986:

Plant	Revenue	Expenses	Investment Base
A	$2,500,000	$1,250,000	$ 4,375,000
B	5,000,000	1,600,000	7,895,000
C	7,500,000	3,550,000	19,500,000

Required

a. If the manufacturing plants are considered to be profit centers, which plant manager has done the best job?
b. If the manufacturing plants are considered to be investment centers, which plant manager has done the best job?
c. Do the results of the investment center analysis (b) differ from the results of the profit center analysis (a)? If so, why?

22-A2. Budget Performance Reports. Following is information relevant to Johnson Industries for the year ending December 31, 1985:

Controllable Expenses	Shop A Supervisor		Manufacturing Plant Manager		Vice President of Manufacturing	
	Budget	Actual	Budget	Actual	Budget	Actual
Office expense	$5,000	$2,500	$10,000	$12,500	$25,000	$22,500
Supervision	6,000	8,000				
Supplies	4,000	5,000				
Tools	7,500	9,000				
Shop B			27,000	30,000		
Shop C			33,000	36,000		
Purchasing					28,000	34,000
Receiving					30,000	30,000
Inspection					32,000	16,000

Required

Prepare the responsibility accounting reports for the three levels of management—supervisor, plant manager, and vice president of manufacturing.

22-A3. Segmental Direct Costing Income Statement. Willwood, Inc., operates two segments (A and B) and a home office. All home office expenses are allocated to the profit center segments. Following are the home office expense accounts and data upon which allocations are made, along with other segmental data:

Home Office Account	Amount	Basis of Allocation
Home office salaries	$25,000	Net sales
Purchase order expense	7,000	Net purchases
Bad debts	2,300	Net sales
Depreciation on home office equipment	2,500	Net sales
Indirect advertising expense	10,000	Segment direct advertising
Insurance expense	3,000	Equipment plus average inventory

Item	Segment A	Segment B	Total
Purchases (net)	$130,000	$270,000	$400,000
Sales (net)	350,000	550,000	900,000
Equipment (cost)	75,000	160,000	235,000
Direct advertising	3,000	4,500	7,500
Average inventory	16,750	25,900	42,650
Other direct expenses			
Cost of goods sold	150,000	230,000	380,000
Selling expenses	45,000	25,000	70,000
Depreciation expense	5,000	7,500	12,500
Insurance expense	8,000	5,000	13,000
Interest expense	2,000	1,500	3,500

Required

a. Prepare a schedule showing the allocation of the home office expense accounts to Segments A and B.
b. Based on the indirect expenses allocated in (a) and the direct expense data provided, prepare a segmental direct costing income statement for Willwood, Inc., for the year ending December 31, 1986. Your statement should include columns for Segment A, Segment B, and Total.

22-A4. Margin, Turnover, and Return on Investment. The manager of the northwest division of National Wholesaling, Inc., found the following data for 1986:

Contribution margin (net)	$ 1,000,000
Assets directly used by and identified with the segment	12,500,000
Sales	20,000,000

Required

a. Determine the margin, turnover, and return on investment for the division in 1986.
b. Determine the effect on margin, turnover, and return on investment of the division in 1987 if each of the following independent changes were to occur. Assume that any item not specifically mentioned remained the same as in 1986.

—A cost reduction plan decreased direct expenses by $200,000.
—New advertising resulted in increasing sales by $4 million, cost of goods sold by $3 million, and advertising expense by $300,000.
—Higher selling prices increased sales revenue by $2 million.
—Old, nonproductive assets were sold. As a result, direct assets decreased by $1 million and expenses decreased by $100,000.
—New assets were purchased. As a result, direct assets increased by $1 million, cost of goods sold decreased by $500,000, and other expenses increased by $50,000.

22-A5. Return on Investment and Residual Earnings. American Printers, Inc., operates three segments, A, B, and C. The segment managers are Mr. Arnold, Miss Bobbing, and Mrs. Charleson, respectively. Under American Printers' responsibility reporting system, data are collected for segments and segmental managers separately, as follows:

	Segment A	Segment B	Segment C
Contribution margin of the segment	$ 180,000	$ 150,000	$ 60,000
Earnings controllable by the manager	250,000	225,000	96,000
Assets directly used by the segment	1,000,000	1,200,000	300,000
Assets controllable by the manager	880,000	900,000	270,000

Required

a. Calculate the rate of return on investment for each segment and each segment manager. Rank the three segments from highest to lowest for both segment ROI and manager ROI.
b. Assume the minimum desired rate of return for a segment is 12% and for a segment manager is 20%. Calculate the residual earnings for each segment and manager, and rank them from highest to lowest.
c. Repeat (b), assuming the minimum ROI for a segment is 18% and for a manager is 26%. Again rank the residual earnings from highest to lowest.
d. Comment on the rankings achieved by the segments and managers.

22-A6. Transfer Pricing. Division X produces a product that can be sold either to Division Z or to outside customers. During 1986, the following activity occurred in Division X:

Units produced	500
Units sold to Division Z	100
Units sold to outside customers	400
Unit selling price	$10
Unit production cost	$ 6

The units purchased by Division Z were processed further at a cost of $4 per unit and sold to outside customers for $15. All transfers between divisions are made at market price.

Required

a. Prepare income statements for 1986 for Division X, Division Z, and the company as a whole.
b. Assume that Division X's manufacturing capacity is 500 units. In 1987, Division Z wants to purchase 200 units from X rather than only 100 units as in 1986. Should Division X sell the extra units to Division Z or continue selling the units to outside customers? Explain.

PROBLEM SET B

22-B1. Cost, Revenue, Profit, and Investment Centers. S.N. Corporation has two major divisions: South and North. Each division has a vice-presidential manager responsible for the level of investment of the division. Beneath the vice president are divisional managers responsible for the profits of the subdivisions. Beneath these managers are two departmental managers: The manufacturing department manager is responsible for the cost of production, and the marketing department manager is responsible for the revenue from sales. This is depicted in the following organizational chart:

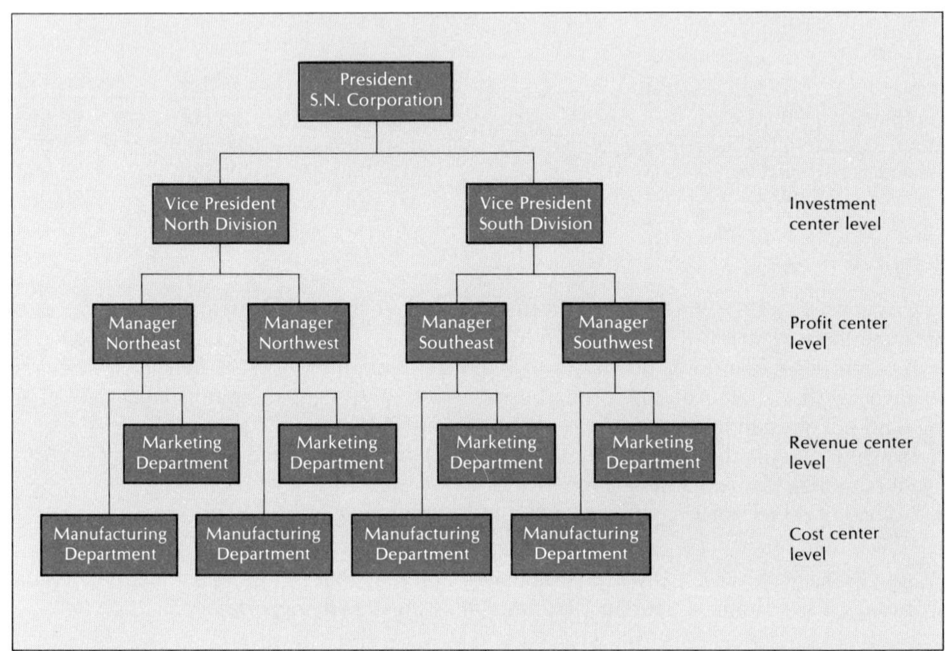

Financial data for the year ending December 31, 1986, are as follows.

	North Division		South Division	
	Northeast	**Northwest**	**Southeast**	**Southwest**
Manufacturing dept. costs	$ 600,000	$ 700,000	$ 900,000	$ 500,000
Marketing dept. revenues	1,000,000	1,500,000	1,100,000	450,000
Total assets	$5,000,000		$1,000,000	

Required

a. Which manufacturing department (cost center) manager appears to have done the best job?

b. Which marketing department (revenue center) manager appears to have done the best job?

c. Determine the net profit of each subdivision. Which subdivision (profit center) manager appears to have done the best job?

d. Calculate the net profit and return on investment for each of the major divisions. Which vice president appears to have managed his or her investment center better?

e. Should the president suggest a reallocation of resources between the divisions? Why or why not?

22-B2. Budget Performance Reports. S.N. Corporation subdivisions had the following budgeted amounts for the year ending December 31, 1986, as follows:

SPREADSHEET PROBLEM

	North Division		South Division	
	Northeast	Northwest	Southeast	Southwest
Manufacturing dept. costs	$ 575,000	$ 695,000	$1,000,000	$ 550,000
Marketing dept. revenues	900,000	1,300,000	1,000,000	400,000

Required

a. Using the actual data from 22-B1, prepare the budget performance reports for the vice presidents and for the president.
b. Based on the budget performance, which vice president appears to have done the better job?
c. What does this suggest about the viability of South Division?

22-B3. Direct Costing Income Statement. Willows Corporation prepared the following conventional income statement for Division B:

Division B
Income Statement
For the Year Ending May 31, 1986

Net sales			$500,000
Cost of merchandise sold			300,000
Gross profit			$200,000
Operating expenses			
Selling expenses			
Sales staff salaries expense	$25,000		
Advertising expense	11,000		
Miscellaneous expense	2,000		
Total selling expenses		$38,000	
General expenses			
Officers' salaries expense	$24,000		
Office staff salaries expense	7,500		
Rent expense	6,500		
Property tax expense	5,000		
Heating and lighting expense	2,100		
Insurance expense	2,000		
Miscellaneous expense	1,500		
Total general expenses		48,600	
Total operating expenses			86,600
Income from operations			$113,400
Other expenses			
Interest expense			10,000
Income before income taxes			$103,400

Additional information:

1. Of the advertising expense, $9,000 is applicable to Division B's needs. The remaining $2,000 was the division's allocation of general corporate advertising.
2. Heating and lighting expense is paid by general corporate management and allocated to divisions based on relative floor space. Division B's direct allocation for the year is $2,100.
3. Insurance is taken out by general corporate management and allocated to divisions based on relative cost of equipment and inventory, with $2,000 directly allocable to Division B for the year.
4. The interest expense is from a loan taken out by the supervisor in charge of Division B.

5. Miscellaneous selling expense is incurred by Division B salespeople. Miscellaneous general expense has been allocated from corporate headquarters.
6. Like insurance expense, property taxes are paid by general corporate management and then directly allocated to divisions based on relative property values.
7. Of the rent expense, $6,000 is incurred to pay for Division B's rent. The remaining $500 is an allocation of the rent due for general corporate headquarters.

Required

Convert the conventional income statement of Division B to a direct costing format. Note that segment income before income taxes should remain the same.

22-B4. Margin, Turnover, and Return on Investment. Selected financial data of Woodings Corporation for 1989 are as follows:

	Segment A	Segment B
Turnover of current assets	2.500	1.950
Turnover of fixed assets	0.625	0.750
Total current assets	$200,000	$250,000
Total fixed assets	800,000	650,000
Cost of merchandise sold	250,000	190,000
Operating expenses	100,000	60,000

Required

a. Calculate the total operating income of Woodings Corporation.
b. Determine the margin, turnover of total assets, and return on total investment for each segment of Woodings Corporation.
c. Determine for each segment the margin, turnover, and return on investment, as well as the total operating income of Woodings Corporation under each of the following independent situations:
—Woodings' president takes $100,000 of Segment A's assets and transfers it to Segment B, with the result that Segment A's ROI increases by 5% and Segment B's ROI decreases by 5%. Assume that the segments' profit margins remain constant.
—Woodings' president takes $100,000 of Segment B's assets and transfers it to Segment A, with the result that Segment B's ROI increases by 5% and Segment A's ROI decreases by 5%. Assume that the segments' profit margins remain constant.
d. Which situation in (c) resulted in higher total income for Woodings Corporation? What does this suggest about how the ROI method can be used to maximize total profit?

22-B5. Return on Investment and Residual Earnings. The trial balance of the central division of E. C. W., Incorporated, showed the following amounts for the year ending November 30, 1986:

Sales	$315,000
Merchandise inventory, 12/1/85	50,000
Merchandise inventory, 11/30/86	35,300
Purchases	120,000
Sales staff salaries expense	24,100
Officers' salaries expense	18,500
Office staff salaries expense	5,500
Advertising expense	3,100
Rent expense	2,500
Property tax expense	1,750
Miscellaneous general expense	500
Miscellaneous selling expense	650

E. C. W. management has calculated the central division's cost of capital to be 15% on the $500,000 of assets employed.

Required

a. Prepare a statement of residual income for the central division of E. C. W., Incorporated, for the year ending November 30, 1986.
b. Determine the central division's return on investment for the year ending November 30, 1986.
c. Which do you think gives a better measure of the central division's performance for the year ending November 30, 1986? Why?

22-B6. Transfer Pricing. Martin Manufacturing Company has two divisions. Division A produces machine fittings that it can sell to retail outlets for $15 or it can sell to Division B. The cost of each machine fitting is as follows:

Variable costs	
Direct materials	$6/unit
Direct labor	2/unit
Variable overhead	1/unit
Total variable costs	$9/unit
Total fixed overhead	$1,600,000

Capacity of Division A is one million machine fittings a year. Division B uses machine fittings in a coupler it makes. Each coupler requires one machine fitting. The couplers are sold to industry for $25. Division B requires 200,000 machine fittings a year and incurs costs of $8 for transforming a machine fitting into a coupler. These costs can be considered totally direct. Machine fittings can be purchased from many manufacturers for $13. Management will set transfer prices to maximize company profits.

Required

a. Assuming demand for machine fittings is 700,000 a year:
—What transfer price would you recommend and why?
—What are the effects on company profitability?
—Without doing any computations, would ROI for Division A increase, decrease, or remain the same? What would be the effect on ROI for Division B?
b. Assuming demand for machine fittings rises to 900,000 units a year:
—How many units should Division A sell to Division B to maximize profitability for the company as a whole?
—What transfer price would you recommend?

BUDGETING

CHAPTER OBJECTIVES
After studying Chapter 23, you should understand the following:

1. What a budget is and how it is used.
2. How budgets aid planning and control.
3. Why the key or limiting factor must be identified.
4. How to compile a master budget.

WHAT IS BUDGETING?

BUDGETING
A continuous process by which an organization attempts to anticipate the future and to see if the future, when it comes around, is as planned.

CONTROL
Monitoring actual events to see if they turned out as planned.

Budgeting is a continuous process by which an organization attempts to anticipate the future and to see if the future, when it comes around, is as planned. Recall that the process of predicting the future is called planning. Monitoring actual events to see if they turned out as planned is called **control.** Planning gives a corporation time to act before the event; control comes during and after it. Control involves a constant comparison of the present results with those previously predicted for the current period. If substantial divergences, or variances, exist, they must be analyzed. Thus, budgeting involves both planning and control. This chapter deals essentially with planning.

TYPES OF BUDGETS

OPERATING BUDGET
A plan that describes the desired future operations in terms of expected revenues and costs.

CAPITAL EXPENDITURES BUDGET
A plan that evaluates the desirability of incurring expenditures on plant, equipment, buildings, and so on, over a long time period.

Budgets can be either operating budgets or capital expenditures budgets. An **operating budget** is a plan that describes the desired future operations in terms of expected revenues and costs. These budgets normally cover a yearly time span, although operating budgets for shorter time periods are often found. On the other hand, a **capital expenditures budget** evaluates the desirability of incurring such expenditures as plant, equipment, and buildings over a longer time period, say five to ten years. This chapter deals with operating budgets; capital expenditures budgets are covered in Chapter 26.

ADVANTAGES OF BUDGETING

The budgeting process has several benefits that lead most successful corporations to utilize budgets to help achieve corporate goals. The four general advantages are outlined as follows:

1. **Focus on the future.** The budgeting process by its very nature focuses on the future. Every corporation wishes to anticipate the future so as to be better able to face it. Budgeting thus allows a corporation time to set up its goals and gives it advance information about impending problems. For example, a corporation that depends heavily on gas for its power might want to plan to change its system from gas to some less expensive power source. For such a move to be successful, the corporation must predict the price and availability of gas as well as the price and availability of substitutes.

2. **Coordination and communication.** Budgeting allows management to set corporate goals towards which all the company's segments should direct their energies. These segments are then encouraged to develop individual goals leading to the achievement of the corporate goals. Such communication negates situations where different company segments tend to act at cross-purposes, hurting overall profitability.

3. **Motivation.** When the different units are allowed to set their own objectives in line with the corporation's overall goals, a certain pride can be instilled within them. Incentives can be based on a performance that surpasses the budget goals, and the employees thus have an opportunity to improve their situations through hard work.

Boston Symphony Orchestra

When Major Henry Lee Higginson founded the Boston Symphony Orchestra (BSO) in 1881, he anticipated annual expenses of about $115,000. Since annual income to the BSO was only about $65,000, Major Higginson paid the 43 percent deficit each year out of his own pocket.

Today the orchestra's annual budget is over $10 million, its earned income is only about $7 million, and no founding father pays the deficit. The BSO thus follows the policy of museums and other similar nonprofit organizations—making up the balance from contributions, governmental grants, and endowment income. In inflationary times, such a task is not easy.

Walter Hill was hired by the BSO in 1977 to be its Director of Business Affairs. When he joined the BSO organization, Hill found that it waited until the end of each year to balance the books and determine the year's losses. By then, it was too late to take corrective action. So much for timely accounting.

Some attempt was made at planning. Unfortunately, the BSO was so far behind on its books that no previous year's statistics were available for reference.

Mr. Hill set out to develop a formal system of planning, budgeting, and control for the BSO. A minicomputer was purchased, and the programs modified suitably. Budgets were time-phased by month, since the orchestra's income fluctuates throughout the year. Monthly budgets are now planned for the current and following years, and annual forecasts are made for two more years. The computer produces regular reports that show comparisons to budgets for the current month and the year-to-date and any unpaid purchase commitments. All significant variances must be explained and dealt with. Year-to-date comparisons are also made to the previous year, showing the percentage of change.

Shrewd planning, careful budgeting, and conscientious control such as this helps keep such organizations as the Boston Symphony Orchestra afloat.

An example of such an incentive would be product sales quotas accompanied by incentive pay schemes for salespeople who exceed their goals.

4. Evaluation of performance. Control can be facilitated when the company segments themselves have had a say in setting their budget goals. If substantial variances do appear under such conditions, management naturally expects the segment to be able to explain them. This placement of responsibility is the basic element of control and is not meant to constitute placing blame. Rather, the aim of performance evaluation is to inquire of the persons who are most familiar with a system the reason that the system did not operate as planned. (This aspect of standard costs was discussed in Chapter 21.)

■ THE KEY OR LIMITING FACTOR IN BUDGETING

Every budget needs a starting point to serve as the basis for the budgeting process. In most cases, the starting point, also called the **key** or **limiting factor,** is sales revenue, since sales usually are not under the complete control of the corporation. However, situations do arise where other elements could become key factors. One example would be limited productive capacity—witness IBM's inability to meet the

KEY FACTOR
See Limiting Factor.

LIMITING FACTOR
In budgeting, the starting point for the budget process.

demand for its new PC-AT computers in 1984. In a period of fund scarcity and high interest rates, another example could be funds for working capital and capital expenditures.

Assuming that sales are indeed the limiting factor, quite a few important items must be considered before the future period's sales revenue can be predicted. Normally the first stage in such an effort is to examine the previous year's sales in terms of quantities of units sold and the prices per unit. The manager must then explore how the following factors could affect a repeat of the previous year's sales performance:

- economic conditions
- market research
- competition
- educational level of target customer group
- governmental action
- pricing policies

After assessing those factors that have an impact on the sales forecast, expected future sales revenue can be determined. Once this key figure is set, management can proceed to outline the budget. A detailed example of this planning process is the master budget.

THE MASTER BUDGET

MASTER BUDGET
A comprehensive picture of the results expected from a firm's future operations.

A **master budget** is a comprehensive picture of the results expected from the firm's future operations. Its preparation normally begins with selection of the key factor and ends with the preparation of a budgeted income statement and statement of financial position.

During this process, the firm will plan not only sales, production, and purchases but also its cash flow so that no important resource will be lacking during the coming period. Although the accrual basis of accounting is useful for taxation and external reporting purposes, it does not indicate the liquidity of the firm vis-a-vis available cash reserves. The cash flow can be ascertained only through the cash budget. As an example, the income statement can show high profits resulting from a spurt in sales at the same time that the cash budget shows a deficit. This is because credit sales with lagging cash inflow have been allowed. Depreciation is another example. Although the income statement treats depreciation as a deductible expense, the cash budget does not, since depreciation (or amortization) is a noncash charge.

The stages of preparing a master budget are outlined as follows:

1. Determine the key or limiting factor, assuming that the limiting factor for most manufacturing corporations is sales.

2. Once the expected sales revenue is forecast, determine the cost of producing and selling the expected number of units. This procedure involves, among other factors, predicting the direct costs of materials and labor, indirect manufacturing costs, and selling and administrative expenses.

3. Calculate expected cash collections and payments on the basis of the preceding transactions. This step helps the corporation with plans to either raise cash when necessary or invest cash when an excess is available.

4. Prepare projections of future income and ending financial position based on the information contained in the anticipated transactions stemming from the preceding actions. Such projections are called the **budgeted income statement** and the **budgeted statement of financial position.**

BUDGETED INCOME STATEMENT
A projected income statement covering anticipated future transactions.

BUDGETED STATEMENT OF FINANCIAL POSITION
A projected statement of financial position for anticipated future transactions.

All of the preceding steps produce figures contained in the master budget. This all-inclusive budget contains several subcategories:

1. Sales budget
2. Production budget and, based on it, the following:
   a. raw materials purchases budget
   b. direct labor budget
   c. manufacturing overhead budget
3. Selling and administrative budget
4. Cash budget and its parts:
   a. expected collection budget
   b. expected payment budget
5. Budgeted income statement
6. Budgeted statement of financial position

Let us consider the compilation of a one-month master budget for a manufacturing company. The budgeting process normally is pursued at least six months to a year in advance of operations. All the information presented must therefore be based on price predictions.

ILLUSTRATION OF MASTER BUDGET PREPARATION

The following information relates to the expected operations of Jones Corporation in the manufacturing of clay jars. Management is preparing a master budget for February 1987.

1. **Sales.** Sales for the months of January and February, 1987, are expected to be 80,000 and 90,000 jars, respectively. The planned selling price of each jar is $10. Thirty percent of each month's sales probably will be sold for cash, with the balance sold on credit.

2. **Production.** Production is to be scheduled so that at the end of each month the corporation will have in its inventory finished products that represent 25 percent of the next month's expected sales. Sales for March and April are expected to be 100,000 and 105,000 units, respectively. The probable inventory of finished goods on January 1 is 20,000 jars.

3. **Raw materials.** Each unit of finished product should consume two pounds of clay with an expected cost of $2 per pound. The company wishes to schedule its purchases of clay so that the ending inventory is 50 percent of the next month's production needs. The inventory of clay on January 1 is forecast to be 82,500 pounds.

4. **Direct labor.** A finished product usually takes one-half hour of direct labor; the expected rate per hour is $4.

5. Manufacturing overhead. Variable manufacturing overhead costs accrue at the rate of $1.50 per direct labor hour. Fixed manufacturing overhead costs are $23,000 per month, including depreciation on factory buildings, plant, machinery, and so on, of $10,000 per month. Fixed overhead is applied at $.50 per direct labor hour for product costing purposes.

6. Selling and administrative expenses. Variable selling expenses total $1 per unit sold. Fixed selling and administrative expenses, including depreciation on office equipment of $6,000, are expected to be $95,000 per month.

7. Expected collection budget. Predictions place 60 percent of the credit sales as collectible in the month of sale; thus, 40 percent of the credit sales will be collected in the month following sale.

8. Expected payment budget. These expenses are projected based on the following fact pattern:

a. Raw materials. 40 percent of the cost of materials purchased is remitted in the month of purchase; the remaining 60 percent is paid in the following month.
b. Direct labor. 75 percent of the direct labor cost is paid in the current month; 25 percent is paid in the following month.
c. Manufacturing overhead and selling and administrative expenses are paid in the month following the month of incurrence.
d. Other payments, including dividends of $50,000 and an advance payment of $380,000 towards the purchase of equipment are made in February.

9. Cash budget. The corporation believes that its cash balance at the end of each month should be at least $100,000. It has arranged with its bank to borrow any amount—in multiples of $10,000—needed to bring the balance over $100,000. This short-term financing would be received at the beginning of the appropriate month and carries interest at 15 percent, payable when the principal loan amount is repaid.

The following is the previously budgeted statement of financial position predicted for January 31, 1987, for Jones Corporation. (Note that this date is the beginning of the period currently being planned.)

Jones Corporation
Budgeted Statement of Financial Position
January 31, 1987

Assets			**Liabilities and Owners' Equity**		
Current assets			Current liabilities		
Cash		$ 150,000	Accounts payable		
Accounts receivable		224,000	Materials	$210,000	
Inventories			Overhead	74,875	
Materials	$ 185,000		Selling and administration	169,000	$ 453,875
Finished goods	157,500	342,500	Wages payable		41,250
Total current assets		$ 716,500	Total current liabilities		$ 495,125
Property, plant, and equipment			Owners' equity		
Land		$1,000,000	Capital stock		$1,200,000
Equipment	$1,006,700		Retained earnings		301,675
Less: Allowance for depreciation	726,400	280,300	Total owners' equity		$1,501,675
Total property, plant, and equipment		1,280,300			
Total assets		$1,996,800	Total liabilities and owners' equity		$1,996,800

Statement A—sales budget for January, February and March

	January	February	March
Expected sales at $10 per unit	$800,000	$900,000	$1,000,000
Cash sales (30%)	240,000	270,000	300,000
Credit sales (70%)	560,000	630,000	700,000

The sales budget is the starting point of this master budget, because sales are considered the key factor. As you can see, total sales have been split into cash and credit sales based on the mix observed in the past. The amount of cash sales will be transferred to the cash budget (statement I); the credit sales will be analyzed in the expected collections budget (statement G), which is a part of the cash budget. In addition, the total expected sales for February will be transferred to the budgeted income statement (statement J).

Statement B—production budget for January, February, and March

	January	February	March	April
Expected sales (units)	80,000	90,000	100,000	105,000
Add: Desired ending inventory at 25% of next month's sales	22,500	25,000	26,250	
Total units needed	102,500	115,000	126,250	
Less: Desired opening inventory	(20,000)	(22,500)	(25,000)	
Budgeted production (units)	82,500	92,500	101,250	

Since the production budget is dependent on the expected unit sales, we started this process with the expected sales in units. Although the Jones Corporation expects to sell 90,000 jars in February, it should not automatically plan to produce 90,000 jars. As statement B shows, the company plans to have 25 percent of the following month's sales in its ending inventory. Since most production processes take more than a day, the company must have some inventory on hand to satisfy its customers while the next batch of saleable goods is being produced.

Planning for inventory can avoid stockouts and the subsequent loss of customers. Holding inventory, however, can be costly in terms of both storage costs and the interest cost on capital committed to in inventory. The company must therefore weigh the obvious advantages and disadvantages to arrive at an optimum level of inventory. In this illustration, the corporation decided to maintain enough inventory to meet 25 percent of the following month's sales forecast. The ending inventory for February should thus be 25 percent of March sales of 100,000, or 25,000 jars.

The total of expected sales and desired ending inventory represents the amount of goods that should be available during the month. However, we already have 22,500 jars available on February 1—the ending inventory for January, which was computed at 25 percent of February's expected sales. Therefore, the production in February must be planned at 92,500 units. The information for January and March is displayed because it will be useful in later computations.

Statement C—raw materials purchases budget for January and February

	January	February	March
Expected production in units (statement B)	82,500	92,500	101,250
Clay—needed for one finished unit	2 lbs.	2 lbs.	2 lbs.
Clay—needed for production (in lbs.)	165,000	185,000	202,500
Add: Desired ending inventory at 50% of next month's production needs (in lbs.)	92,500	101,250	
Less: Desired opening inventory	(82,500)	(92,500)	
Clay—to be purchased (in lbs.)	175,000	193,750	
Expected purchase cost at $2 a lb.	$350,000	$387,500	

Once the expected production level is computed, the quantity of ingredients needed to produce goods at that level must be determined. Generally, three kinds of production costs are incurred: direct materials, direct labor, and manufacturing overhead. Statement C analyzes the direct materials needed; direct labor and manufacturing overhead are considered in statements D and E.

When planning for raw materials, we have to consider everything in pounds: 185,000 pounds of clay are expected to be consumed in February's production. The corporation wishes to have on hand an inventory of clay that could meet 50 percent of next month's expected production needs. The suppliers of clay have a production process that takes, say, a week; another week might be necessary to ship the raw materials. Rather than have production shut down for want of raw materials, the corporation prefers to keep a safety stock readily available.

After adding the materials needed for production to the desired ending inventory, we get 286,250 pounds of clay that should be available during February. However, since the Jones Corporation already should have on hand 92,500 pounds—the ending inventory for January—it needs to purchase only 193,750 pounds at $2 per pound during February. The predicted purchase cost of raw materials for January and February will be transferred to the expected payments budget (statement H).

Statement D—direct labor budget for January and February

	January	February
Expected production in units (statement B)	82,500	92,500
Direct labor hours needed per unit of finished product	0.5	0.5
Total number of direct labor hours needed	41,250	46,250
Expected cost per direct labor hour	$4	$4
Total direct labor cost	$165,000	$185,000

Since the cost of direct labor is dependent on the quantity of goods produced, we start with the expected production figures computed in statement B. Since one-half hour normally must be sacrificed to make one unit of finished product and Jones Corporation expects to pay $4 per hour, direct labor costs of $165,000 and $185,000 for January and February, respectively, will likely be incurred. These amounts will be transferred to the expected payments budget (statement H).

Statement E—manufacturing overhead budget for January and February

	January	February
Total direct labor hours needed (statement D)	41,250	46,250
Variable overhead rate per direct labor hour	$ 1.50	$ 1.50
	$61,875	$69,375
Fixed overhead costs	23,000	23,000
Total manufacturing overhead	$84,875	$92,375
Less: Depreciation	(10,000)	(10,000)
Total cash-related manufacturing overhead	$74,875	$82,375

Since we have already studied how the variable overhead rate of $1.50 per hour is computed and why direct labor often is selected as an activity base, we shall not repeat the discussion here. This budget obviously depends on the direct labor budget (statement D) and is computed in a like manner. Depreciation, being a noncash charge, is deducted from the total overhead; and the cash-related balances of $74,875 and $82,375 for January and February are transferred to the expected payments budget (statement H).

Statement F—selling and administrative expenses budget for January and February

	January	February
Expected sales (units)	80,000	90,000
Variable selling expense	$1	$1
	$ 80,000	$ 90,000
Fixed selling expense	95,000	95,000
Total selling and administrative expenses	$175,000	$185,000
Less: Depreciation	(6,000)	(6,000)
Cash-related selling and administrative expense	$169,000	$179,000

Note that expected production was not used as a starting point in this budget. The reason, as discussed in earlier chapters, is that the administrative and selling functions do not vary with production but can vary with sales.

Again, the expected depreciation charge is deducted from the total, since depreciation does not consume cash, and the balance to be disbursed in cash each month will be transferred to the expected payments budget (statement H).

Statement G—expected collections budget for February

	January	February
Expected credit sales (statement A)	$560,000	$630,000
February collections		
January credit sales—40% collected		224,000
February credit sales—60% collected		378,000
Total expected collections		$602,000

The expected collections budget is based on the forecasted credit sales computed in statement A and shows an estimate of the cash receipts expected to be received in February. Collections in February depend on the projected credit sales in January and February. In fact, Jones Corporation expects to collect 40 percent of January's credit sales and 60 percent of February's credit sales in February. These figures do not imply that each customer will pay 60 percent of his or her debt in the month of sale and 40 percent in the following month. Rather, sales are assumed to be made evenly during the month; and based on past experience, receivables representing about 60 percent of the sales are collected in the current month. The remaining 40 percent will be received in the following month. The amount of $602,000 represents the expected collections in February from credit sales and will be transferred to the cash budget (statement I).

Statement H—expected payments budget for February

Raw materials	60% of January purchases of $350,000 (statement C)	$210,000	
	40% of February purchases of $387,500 (statement C)	155,000	$ 365,000
Direct labor	25% of January labor cost of $165,000 (statement D)	41,250	
	75% of February labor cost of $185,000 (statement D)	138,750	180,000
Manufacturing overhead	100% of January cash cost of $74,875 (statement E)		74,875
Selling and administrative expense	100% of January cash cost of $169,000 (statement F)		169,000
Dividends payable in February			50,000
Advance payment for purchase of equipment			380,000
Total payments to be made in February			$1,218,875

The expected payments budget is similar to the expected collections budget (statement G), except that it estimates cash flows of the opposite direction. Since the budgeted items are quite similar, we shall discuss only one of them, the purchase of raw materials. Because materials suppliers are reimbursed over a period of two months—the month of sale and the month after—January and February purchases must be considered when computing February payments for raw materials. February's expected cash outlay for such materials is computed by adding 60 percent of January's purchase cost and 40 percent of February's purchase cost. As with collections of accounts receivable, these percentages are formed from the firm's past experience with creditors' payment terms. The total of $1,218,875, representing expected payments in February, will be transferred to the cash budget (statement I).

Statement I—cash budget for February

Projected cash balance on February 1		$ 150,000
Add: Expected collections		
February cash sales (statement A)	$270,000	
Sales on account (statement G)	602,000	872,000
Expected total cash available		$1,022,000
Less: Expected payments (statement H)		(1,218,875)
Cash balance before financing		$ (196,875)
Add: Financing from bank (in multiples of $10,000)		300,000
Expected cash balance, February 28		$ 103,125

As just demonstrated, a cash budget is composed of three elements: collections, payments, and financing. For all practical purposes, it is a projected cash account, with collections increasing the balance and payments decreasing it. Since we have already discussed the expected collections and payments, we confine our discussion here to the financing aspect.

Corporations can profit from budgeting because budgeting warns them of an impending dangerous cash shortage or informs them of an anticipated cash surplus. A corporation that knows its expected cash position can arrange to borrow or invest funds at more favorable rates than it would be forced to accept on short notice.

In this illustration, the corporation expects a cash deficit of $196,875. Since the corporation must have at least $100,000 in cash at the end of each month, it would inform its bank about the expected shortage and arrange to get a short-term loan for $300,000. Although it is unlikely that $300,000 will be exactly adequate, the balance at the end of February should be close to $100,000 after receiving the loan if the budgeting process has been reasonably accurate.

Alternatively, if the cash balance before financing was, say, $400,000 and the corporation had borrowed $200,000 six months ago (when the prevailing rate of interest was 14 percent, the corporation might wish to repay the loan and the interest.

Cash balance before financing	$400,000
Principal repayment	(200,000)
Interest payment (14 × $200,000 × ½ year)	(14,000)
Cash balance carried forward	$186,000

Note that the interest payment would be routinely deducted from operating income as an expense under the accrual system whether or not paid at that time.

Statement J—budgeted income statement for February

Sales (statement A)			$900,000
Cost of sales			
Direct materials cost per unit, 2 lbs. at $2/lb.	$4		
Direct labor cost per unit, ½ hr. at $4/hr.	2		
Overhead cost per unit, ½ hr. at $2/hr. ($1.50 variable; $.50 fixed)	1		
Total projected cost per unit	$7		
Budgeted cost of goods sold		$(630,000)	
Fixed overhead over-applied*		125	
Expected cost of sales		$(629,875)	
Gross margin			$270,125
Selling and administrative expenses (statement F)			(185,000)
Operating income			85,125
Interest expense ($300,000 × 15% × 1/12)			(3,750)
Net income before taxes			$ 81,375

*This amount is due to production's 92,500 units being assigned fixed overhead of $.25 per unit when actual fixed overhead totals only $23,000.

Although most of the preceding information was derived from budgets already prepared, the information on cost of sales per unit comes from the fact pattern assumed. The interest expense represents one month's interest at 15 percent on the short-term loan of $300,000 (statement I) accrued as of the beginning of February. Since the interest accrues but will not be paid in February (being payable along with the principal amount), the amount of $3,750 was not shown in the cash budget (statement I) for February.

Statement K—budgeted statement of financial position as of February 28

Jones Corporation
Budgeted Statement of Financial Position
February 28, 1987

Assets			**Liabilities and Owners' Equity**		
Current assets			Current liabilities		
Cash (statement I)		$ 103,125	Accounts payable		
Accounts receivable (note A)		252,000	Materials (note E)	$ 232,500	
Inventories			Overhead (note F)	82,375	
Materials (note B)	$202,500		Selling and adm. (note G)	179,000	$ 493,875
Finished goods			Wages payable (note H)		46,250
(note C)	175,000	377,500	Interest payable (statement J)		3,750
			Loan from bank (statement I)		300,000
Total current assets		$ 732,625	Total current liabilities		$ 843,875
Property, plant, and equipment			Owners' equity		
Land		$1,000,000	Capital stock	$1,200,000	
Equipment	$1,006,700		Retained earnings (note I)	333,050	1,533,050
Less: Allowance for					
depreciation (note D)	742,400	264,300			
Advance payment (statement H)		380,000			
Total assets		$2,376,925	Total liabilities and owners' equity		$2,376,925

The budgeted statement of financial position is the last part of the master budget, since it depends on everything that has been done earlier. To explain how these figures have been calculated, the following self-explanatory T-accounts show the results of February's transactions.

Note A

Accounts Receivable

Feb. 1 bal.	224,000	Collections (statement G)	602,000
Sales (statement A)	630,000		
Feb. 28 bal.	252,000		

Note B

Inventory—Materials

Feb. 1 bal.	185,000	Transferred to production ($92,500 \times 2 \times 2$) (statement C)	370,000
Purchases (statement C)	387,500		
Feb. 28 bal.	202,500		

Note C

Inventory—Finished Goods

Debit		Credit	
Feb. 1 bal.	157,500	Cost of sales (90,000 × 7) (statement A)	630,000
Production (92,500 × 7) (statement B)	647,500		
Feb. 28 bal.	175,000		

Note D

Allowance for Depreciation

Debit		Credit	
		Feb. 1 bal.	726,400
		Depreciation (statement E)	10,000
		(statement F)	6,000
		Feb. 28 bal.	742,400

Note E

Accounts Payable—Materials

Debit		Credit	
Payments (statement H)	365,000	Feb. 1 bal.	210,000
		Purchases (statement C)	387,500
		Feb. 28 bal.	232,500

Note F

Accounts Payable—Overhead

Debit		Credit	
Payments (statement H)	74,875	Feb. 1 bal.	74,875
		Expenditures (statement E)	82,375
		Feb. 28 bal.	82,375

Note G

Accounts Payable—Selling and Administrative

Debit		Credit	
Payments (statement H)	169,000	Feb. 1 bal.	169,000
		Expenditures (statement F)	179,000
		Feb. 28 bal.	179,000

Note H

Wages Payable

Debit		Credit	
Payments (statement H)	180,000	Feb. 1 bal.	41,250
		Labor cost (statement D)	185,000
		Feb. 28 bal.	46,250

Note I

Retained Earnings

Debit		Credit	
Dividends (statement H)	50,000	Feb. 1 bal.	301,675
		Net income (before taxes) (statement J)	81,375
		Feb. 28 bal.	333,050

STATIC VERSUS FLEXIBLE BUDGETS

STATIC BUDGET
A budget process that focuses on one level of corporate activity.

FLEXIBLE BUDGET
A budget that provides guidelines for different levels of activity.

The budgetary process just presented examines one level of corporate activity, that is, a particular sales forecast and a master budget based on that forecast. Such a plan is considered a **static budget.** To provide better incentive and more accurate evaluation, many firms prepare **flexible budgets,** which provide guidelines for different levels of activity.

The first step in flexible budgeting is to determine the nature of the costs involved. As you have previously studied, some costs vary with sales or production though not always in a strict one-to-one ratio (variable costs). Other costs remain at a certain level for a range of production or sales volume (fixed costs). Once the costs are identified and classified, budgets can be prepared for selected volumes of activity. An example of a flexible selling and administrative budget for one month is shown in statement L.

Statement L—selling and administrative budget for February

Sales volume in units	80,000	90,000	100,000
Variable costs			
Payroll	$ 80,000	$ 90,000	$100,000
Supplies	12,000	13,500	15,000
Utilities	24,000	27,000	30,000
Travel	28,000	31,500	35,000
Total variable costs	$144,000	$162,000	$180,000
Fixed costs			
Managers' salaries	$ 4,000	$ 4,000	$ 4,000
Rent	2,000	2,000	2,000
Depreciation	6,000	6,000	6,000
Total fixed costs	$ 12,000	$ 12,000	$ 12,000
Total selling and administrative costs	$156,000	$174,000	$192,000

As the period progresses, managers using flexible budgets should thus be able to predict and control costs even when the activity level is above or below the one originally expected. When the next period arrives and with it the time for evaluation of the prior period, the evaluation process can be more accurate and informative.

STATIC AND FLEXIBLE BUDGETS

■ CONCEPT SUMMARY 23.1

Type of Budget	Static	Flexible
Activity level	Budget is based on one projected level of future activity.	Budget covers a range of possible future activity levels.
Cost classification	Costs are broadly classified by function, such as production, administrative.	Costs are broadly classified by behavior (fixed or variable).
Interpretation and control usefulness	Difficult to interpret and use when actual activity varies from planned activity level.	Facilitates management interpretation and use over a wide range of activity levels.

■ ZERO-BASED BUDGETING—AN ALTERNATIVE APPROACH

The zero-based budgeting (ZBB) technique recently was popular with budget makers, especially in the government, because the method attempts to remedy the faults of traditional practices. Traditional budgeting takes the figures of the previous year and raises them a step higher, assuming implicitly that what happened in the previous year is an acceptable base. For example, if last year's salary expense totaled $100,000 and the employees are expected to get increases of five percent, salary expense of the coming period will be estimated at $105,000. This incremental approach contains a serious flaw—displayed very clearly by governmental departments in a frenzy at a fiscal year-end trying to spend their allocated funds. With probable cause, administrators fear that if they save any money they will get less in the coming years. Hence, wasteful expenditures result.

Alternatively, the concept of **zero-based budgeting** accepts no expenditure as reasonable unless the initiating department can substantiate the need for that recurring expenditure. Each department has to start fresh each period and rank all its projected expenditures according to priority. Thus, to focus on a single expense, last period's salary cost would be irrelevant. The department would review all positions and salaries and put them in order of preference. The authorities would then allot a set amount—say $110,000—and the department could fund those positions with higher priorities. In this way, money can be spent on only the most worthwhile projects. This technique also prevents spending money on projects that were relevant some years before but no longer need support. Under a more traditional budgeting system, such projects might continue getting funds. Thus, with ZBB, unnecessary and wasteful expenditures can be avoided or minimized.

ZERO-BASED BUDGETING
A method of budgeting that accepts no expenditure as reasonable unless the initiating department can substantiate the need for that recurring expenditure.

Zero-based budgeting became particularly prominent when then-Governor Carter had applied it in Georgia and attempted unsuccessfully to introduce it to Washington. The principal drawback of ZBB is that it is time-consuming, and when huge expenditures are involved, evaluating each expenditure every year—or even every five years—can be quite impractical. However, ZBB's applicability in industry is greater and ZBB is sometimes used, although not always in pure form.

FOR REVIEW

SUMMARY

- Budgeting involves planning and control. Planning means looking ahead to predict the actions that should be taken and the likely results of those actions. Control involves monitoring what happened and comparing the actual results with the plan.
- Budgets can be operational or capital. Operational budgets are involved with the short run and predict resources and expenses. Capital budgets evaluate the desirability of investing in capital goods, such as equipment or buildings, involving a longer time period.
- A budgeting process needs a starting point, called a key, or limiting, factor. This element is normally not under the complete control of management. Although most often sales is the limiting factor, the key element could be the productive capacity, an essential raw material, or a scarcity of funds for investment.
- Once a key factor is selected, the master budgeting process can be set into motion, and a bevy of budgets—ending with the budgeted income statement and the budgeted balance sheet—can be produced.
- Flexible budgets can be designed to predict and control costs at varying levels of activity. Doing so helps management evaluate performance and provide incentive when the activity level does not meet prior expectations.
- The traditional budgeting process sometimes causes inefficiency and waste. As an alternative, the zero-based budgeting concept has been applied with mixed success.

QUESTIONS

23-1. Briefly explain the two essential elements of budgeting.

23-2. What usefulness do budgets possess? Is it reasonable to believe that budgeting would help a business to be better run and more profitable? Why?

23-3. What are the factors to be considered before a sales forecast can be made?

23-4. What is the concept of zero-based budgeting? Why is it not more widely used?

23-5. What would be some common key or limiting factors upon which budgets can be built?

23-6. What are probable causes for variances between the budgets and the actual events?

23-7. How do budgets help aid communication about corporate goals?

23-8. What is the purpose of preparing flexible budgets?

23-9. On what does management base its predictions of cash collections and payments?

23-10. What is the treatment of depreciation when budgeting cash needs? Why?

EXERCISES

23-E1. What is a likely key or limiting factor to consider when constructing budgets for the following entities:

a. The operation of the local high school.
b. The toy department of a downtown department store.
c. The production of handmade quilts by a nonprofit group.
d. The publishing of a new novel.
e. A unique manufacturing process that utilizes a petroleum derivative.
f. The operation of an air traffic control tower.

23-E2. Carpentry Services Inc. expects to realize service fees during its third quarter on the following schedule: July, $400,000; August, $500,000; and September, $500,000. Normally, 50% of CSI's sales are for cash. Credit sales are billed in the month of the service; terms are 2/10, net/45. Seventy percent of the credit customers pay in the month after the service; the remaining pay in the following month. Prepare expected collections budgets for August and September.

23-E3. Factoria X, Inc., produces an improved widget. The company's sales are projected at $150,000 in November; $187,500 in December; $172,500 in January; and $150,000 in February. Each widget sells for $.75. At the end of each month, inventory should hold enough widgets to meet 15% of the following month's sales. Factoria X projects the ending inventory on October 31 to be 25,500 widgets. Prepare a production budget for November through January.

23-E4. An average of 3½ cups of unbleached flour is used in each loaf of Aunt Kerrie's muffin bread. The Aunt Kerrie Company buys this flour in 100-pound bags for $25 each; each bag contains an average of 500 cups. Aunt Kerrie expects the flour to increase in price in April and wants to buy a supply to last through June. Budgeted production is 120,000 loaves from April 1 to June 30, spread evenly. Current inventory holds 40 bags; the June 30 inventory is anticipated to be the same. How much flour should be purchased to supply Aunt Kerrie's Company during the April–June period?

23-E5. Recently the workers' union negotiated for and received a new contract with the Auto Care Products Company, calling for across-the-board pay raises of 3% on each of the following dates: April 1, July 1, and October 1. The average base pay per hour on January 1 is $4.15, with a direct labor need of one hour for every four units. Forecasted production has been set for the first quarter at 95,000 units; second, 110,000 units; third, 115,000 units; and fourth, 125,000 units. Prepare the next year's direct labor budget by quarters; the firm operates on a calendar year basis. If necessary, round average pay rates to the nearest cent.

23-E6. Food for Flocks, Inc., applies overhead at the rate of $.15 for each direct labor hour used in its annual production of two million pounds of birdseed. Direct labor needs will be 80,000 hours in January and 87,000 hours in February; depreciation of $2,000 per month will be taken. Prepare a manufacturing overhead budget for January and February.

23-E7. Inflatables, Inc., has a policy of maintaining a $75,000 cash balance and expects that balance to be on hand on December 1. Cash sales for December should be 60% of the projected total sales of $90,000. Payments from credit customers received in December will be about $30,000. Expected payments will go out to suppliers in the amount of $50,000; to shareholders, $25,000; and to redemption of matured company bonds, $25,000. Prepare a cash budget for December. If financing is required, the firm can borrow up to $100,000 from the bank in $1,000 increments at 16% on a short-term basis.

PROBLEM SET A

23-A1. Sales and Production Budget. Meadowview Dairy's records show that in 1988, it had cottage cheese sales as follows:

1st quarter —60,000 quarts
2nd quarter—65,000 quarts
3rd quarter—70,000 quarts
4th quarter —66,000 quarts

Ending inventory of cottage cheese on December 31, 1988, is 5,000 quarts. Sales in 1989 are expected to be 5% higher than those of 1988.

Production cost per quart was $.55 in 1988. The rising cost of milk and labor will result in the production cost increasing to about $.68 in 1989. Accordingly, Meadowview will raise the selling price per quart from $.90 to $1.25 on January 1.

Management would like an opening inventory each quarter of one-twelfth (one week's worth) the projected sales of that quarter. The inventory on December 31, 1989, should be 6,000 units.

Required

a. Calculate quarterly sales figures for 1989.
b. Prepare a quarterly production budget for 1989.

23-A2. Production and Materials Purchases Budget. The Trendy Tablecloth Company has forecast 1986 unit sales—at an average of $10 each—for the first four months to be January, $200,000; February, $217,000; March, $218,000; and April, $225,000. TTC has a policy of maintaining the period's finished goods ending inventory at one-third the following month's sales. In April, production will be stepped up to 40,000 units because of the addition of a new line.

Each tablecloth consumes 1.25 yards of material, costing an average of $3.25 per yard. Raw materials in inventory should equal one-half the following month's production needs; each finished product requires half an hour of direct labor. The average hourly rate paid to direct laborers is $4.75.

Required

a. Prepare for TTC the first-quarter production budget.
b. Prepare the first-quarter materials purchases budget.

23-A3. Cash Budget. Nirvana Greenhouses, Inc., has assembled the following estimates for 1986:

	Quarter			
	1	2	3	4
Sales	$627,300	$650,700	$648,100	$645,900
Purchases	544,610	563,980	557,100	553,550
Cash payments for other expenses	67,360	72,970	85,130	78,620

Actual results of the last quarter 1985 are sales, $590,100; purchases, $478,300; and cash payments for expenses, $74,330. The balance of cash on hand is $31,500 on January 1, 1986. In each quarter, Nirvana receives cash equal to 65% of the current quarter's sales plus 35% of the sales for the preceding quarter. Also, each quarter, Nirvana pays cash for half of the current quarter's purchases and half of the preceding quarter's purchases. Payments for other cash expenses are made in the current quarter. Nirvana will pay its shareholders a $60,000 dividend on January 10.

Required:

Prepare the quarterly cash budget for 1986.

23-A4. Budgeted Income Statement. Management at LaPasta, Inc., has determined the following projected figures and facts:

- Total net sales for 1987 will be $1,325,000.
- The cost of producing the goods sold is 60% of the net sales.
- Fixed expenses for 1987 will total:

Depreciation—selling	$ 4,500
Depreciation—administrative	$ 3,750
Operating expenses	$36,000

- Variable cash expenses for 1987 are estimated as a percentage of net sales. Operating expenses are a total of 2% of net sales. Selling expenses are 9.8%, and administrative expenses are 8.6%.
- Income taxes are 45% of estimated net income.
- Sales for the first quarter of 1988 are projected to be 8% higher than the 1987 average.
- 1988 fixed expenses will remain at 1987's cost level through the first quarter.
- All selling, administrative, and operating expenses are incurred evenly throughout the year.

Required

Prepare a budgeted income statement for the year ending December 31, 1987. Also, prepare a selling and administrative budget for cash expenditures for the first quarter of 1988, based upon projected sales.

23-A5. Budgeted Statement of Financial Position. The statement of financial position for Hillyvale, Inc., for last year is as follows:

Hillyvale, Inc.
Statement of Financial Position
December 31, 1985

Assets		**Liabilities and Shareholders' Equity**	
Current assets		Current liabilities	
Cash	$ 21,000	Accounts payable	$ 11,900
Accounts receivable	100,000	Note payable	5,000
Raw materials	4,900	Total liabilities	$ 16,900
Finished goods	23,000		
Total current assets	$148,900		
Plant and equipment		Shareholders' equity	
Land	$ 80,000	Common stock, no par	$200,000
Buildings and equipment	100,000	Retained earnings	88,000
Accumulated depreciation	(24,000)	Total shareholders' equity	$288,000
Plant and equipment, net	$156,000	Total liabilities and shareholders' equity	
Total assets	$304,900		$304,900

Additional information:

1. Raw materials purchases will amount to 3,690 pounds at $5 per pound.
2. 3,640 pounds of raw materials will enter production.
3. Two pounds of raw materials are used in each finished product.
4. No work in process will remain on January 31.
5. Each finished product requires five hours of labor at an average cost of $10 per hour.
6. Overhead is applied at the rate of $4.40 per labor hour. $4,000 of the total overhead is for depreciation.
7. Sales of 1,800 units at $200 each were all on account.
8. Accounts receivable collections will total $298,000.
9. Accounts payable is all for raw materials purchases. Half of the month's purchases are paid for in the month of purchase and the remainder in the next month.
10. Selling and administrative cash expenses will be $16,000.

Required

a. For each numbered item, state the budget(s), if any, where it will initially be entered.
b. Prepare a budgeted statement of financial position for Hillyvale as of January 31, 1986.

23-A6. Flexible Budgeting. Reception Unlimited, Inc., needs a budget for March but cannot accurately estimate sales. Sales of new client contracts may be as low as 2,000 or as high as 7,500. Variable costs for each new contract total $25. In addition, operating profits are expected from the 10,000 continuing contracts. Variable costs of handling these continuing commitments are $15 for each contract. Expenses that are fixed within the relevant range are depreciation, $9,200; salaries, $40,000; lease payments, $122,000; and miscellaneous, $15,000. Contract sales revenue is $40 per month per contract.

Required

Prepare a flexible budgeted income statement for March utilizing new contract levels of 2,000, 5,000, and 7,500.

23-A7. Production and Materials Budget. American Chair Corporation is setting up its production and materials budget for the last quarter of 1986. Expected unit sales are as follows:

September (actual)	1,100	October	2,000	November	3,000
December	5,000	January	1,000	February	2,000

The inventory of chairs as of September 30, 1986, was 800 units. It takes 30 board feet of lumber and one pound of nails to make one chair. On September 30, 1986, inventory records showed 10,000 board feet of lumber and 600 pounds of nails. Management wants the following inventory levels:

Finished chairs: 20% of next month's sales
Lumber: 30% of next month's production needs
Nails: 50% of next month's production needs

Required

a. Prepare a production budget for the fourth quarter of 1986.
b. Prepare a raw materials budget for the fourth quarter of 1986 (in units).

23-A8. Cash Budget. Downunder Oil Inc. is preparing its cash budget for the second half of the year. Sales estimates are as follows:

April	$150,000 (actual)	September	$250,000
May	210,000 (actual)	October	300,000
June	190,000	November	325,000
July	190,000	December	275,000
August	200,000		

The sales collection pattern is 50% cash collected in the month of sale, 40% on account collected the month after the sale, and 10% collected two months after the sale. Purchases average 70% of sales; 40% of purchases are paid for in the month incurred, with the remaining 60% being paid the following month. The cash balance is to be maintained at $10,000. Bank borrowings are available in multiples of $1,000. Interest is charged at 1.5% per month on the outstanding balance. When cash is available for making loan repayments, total interest owed will be paid prior to determining the amount of loan repayment to be made. The cash balance at May 31 is $12,000. Capital expenditures of $200,000 are planned in August and $300,000 in October.

Required

Prepare a cash budget for June through December.

PROBLEM SET B

23-B1. Sales and Production Budget. Pizzazz Pizzas, Inc., is preparing a master budget for the first quarter of 1986. Projected sales figures in units are as follows:

January	12,000	March	15,000
February	14,000	April	15,000

Approximately 20% of Pizzazz sales are for cash; of the remainder, 60% of the customers pay in the month following the sale, 30% pay in the second month following the sale, and 10% in the third month. Ending inventory of finished products each month should equal 25% of the following month's sales. On January 1, 1986, inventory is expected to total $11,375. A finished pizza sells for $5; the cost of finished goods in inventory is $4.55 per unit on December 31. FIFO is used to compute cost of goods sold.

Required

a. Prepare a quarterly sales budget.
b. Prepare a quarterly production budget.

23-B2. Production and Materials Purchases Budget. Pizzazz Pizza uses ingredients costing $.85 on an average product. (Refer to 23-B1 for additional information relevant to this problem.) Raw ingredients inventories are maintained at 40% of the following month's production needs. Raw ingredients inventory on January 1 is estimated to be adequate for producing 6,000 units; on April 1, 7,000 units. Three units of product can be prepared in two hours of direct labor. The average direct labor pay per hour of $4.00 will rise to $4.14 on March 1. Overhead is assigned according to direct labor activity at a rate of $1.60 per hour. This overhead charge includes depreciation of $3,500 each month. Selling and administrative services cost the firm an average of $15,000 per month, including depreciation of $1,200.

Required

a. Prepare the three-month raw ingredients purchase budget.
b. Prepare the direct labor budget.
c. Prepare the overhead budget.
d. Prepare the selling and administrative budget.

23-B3. Cash Budget. Refer to the information in 23-B1 and 23-B2. Additional information:

1. Raw ingredients invoices are paid in the following manner: 10% of current purchases are paid in the month of purchase; 65% are paid in the next month; and 25% are paid in the second month after purchase.
2. Raw ingredients totaling $12,500 and $11,500 were purchased in November 1985 and December 1985, respectively.
3. Direct labor is 75%, paid on a current basis; the remainder is paid the following month. Direct labor in December 1985 cost $35,000 for 8,720 hours.
4. Overhead and selling and administrative expenses are paid 50% in the current month and 50% in the following month. Overhead was applied at the rate of $1.55 per direct labor hour in December 1985; this figure includes a charge for depreciation of $3,200 a month. December 1985 selling and administrative expense was $11,500, of which $1,500 was depreciation.
5. Pizzazz will send cash payments for special equipment of $10,000 each in February, April, and June.
6. The projected cash balance for January 1, 1986, is $80,000. The cash balance is to be maintained at $75,000 during 1986's first half. Bank financing is available at 14% interest; loans are acquired in $1,000 increments as needed and paid back in $1,000 increments as the cash is available. Interest is paid at the time of repaying the principal.
7. October, November, and December, 1985, sales were $41,880, $70,000, and $92,500 respectively.

Required

a. Prepare an expected collections budget for the first quarter of 1986.
b. Develop the expected payments budget for the first quarter of 1986.
c. Develop the cash budget for the first quarter of 1986.

23-B4. Budgeted Income Statement. Prepare a budgeted income statement for Pizzazz Pizzas, based on the information in 23-B1 through 23-B3.

23-B5. Budgeted Statement of Financial Position. The projected statement of financial position for Pizzazz Pizzas is as follows:

Pizzazz Pizza, Inc.
Projected Statement of Financial Position
December 31, 1985

Assets			**Liabilities and Owners' Equity**		
Current assets			Liabilities		
Cash		$ 80,000	Accounts payable		
Accounts receivable		30,000	Ingredients	$ 13,475	
Inventories			Overhead	5,158	
Raw ingredients	$ 5,100		Selling and adm.	5,000	$ 23,633
Finished goods	11,375	16,475	Wages payable		8,750
Total current assets		$126,475	Total liabilities		$ 32,383
Property, plant, and equipment			Owners' equity		
Equipment	$350,000		Capital stock		419,460
Less: Depreciation	35,000	315,000	Retained earnings		45,757
Land		56,125	Total owners' equity		465,217
Total assets		$497,600	Total liabilities and owners' equity		$497,600

Required

Construct a budgeted statement of financial position as of March 31, 1986, using the above information and data in 23-B1 through 23-B4.

23-B6. Flexible Budgeting. The manager of Pizzazz is concerned about predicted operating losses. He has decided that the sales price per pizza must be raised to $6.50 but is concerned about the effect this might have on sales. He thinks that February's sales could be as low as 8,000 units. However, if an aggressive advertising campaign were run at a cost of $5,000, sales could beat the previous prediction by 20% for a record sales month of 16,800 units.

Required

Prepare a flexible budgeted income statement for February at 8,000, 11,000, 14,000, and 16,800 units using the new selling price.

23-B7. Production and Materials Budget. Harms Arms Inc. wishes to budget production and materials requirements for the first quarter of 1987. Expected unit sales are as follows:

January	10,000	March	9,000
February	12,000	April	10,000

The selling price per unit is $10. The ending inventory of finished goods on December 31, 1986, is 3,000 units. Management wants opening inventories of finished goods to be 20% of the month's expected sales. Each finished unit requires three units of raw material A @ $5 per unit and five units of raw material B @ $3 per unit.

Inventory of materials on December 31, 1986, is 6,000 units of raw material A and 16,000 units of raw material B. Purchases of raw material A should be enough for the month's production needs plus an inventory of 30% of the following month's production needs. Purchases of raw material B should be enough for the month's production needs plus an inventory of 60% of the following month's production needs. Ending inventories on March 31 are expected to be 9,000 units of raw material A and 30,000 units of raw material B.

Required

a. Prepare a production budget for the first quarter of 1987 (in units).
b. Prepare a raw materials purchase budget for the first quarter of 1987 (in units and dollars).

23-B8. Cash Budget. Due to its fast growth and the seasonal nature of its business, Blarney Stone Builders Inc. is preparing its first cash budget. Projected unit sales for 1986 are as follows:

1st qtr.	1,000	4th qtr., 1985	1,500
2nd qtr.	4,000		
3rd qtr.	9,000		
4th qtr.	2,000		

The unit selling price is $125, with 80% of sales for cash and 15% collected in the subsequent quarter. Approximately 5% of sales are never collected and are written off. The accounts receivable balance at the start of the year is $37,500.

Raw materials are 50% of sales, with 40% being paid in the month of purchase and 60% being paid in the following month. Accounts payable has a balance of $56,250 at the beginning of the year. Selling and administrative costs average 25% of sales and are paid in the quarter when incurred.

Extensive modernization of the existing facilities will be undertaken in the second quarter. This will cost $500,000 and will be paid for in the second quarter.

Cash on hand at December 31, 1985, is $67,000. The cash balance of $65,000 should be maintained throughout the year. Bank borrowings are in multiples of $1,000. Interest is 4% per quarter on the outstanding loan balance. Bank repayments are expected when the cash position allows. When cash is available for making loan repayments, total interest owed will be paid prior to determining the amount of loan repayment to be made.

Required:

Prepare a cash budget by quarters for fiscal year 1986.

COST-VOLUME-PROFIT ANALYSIS

CHAPTER OBJECTIVES
After studying Chapter 24, you should understand the following:

1. The basic uses of cost-volume-profit analysis.
2. The computational techniques of breakeven analysis, profit planning, and sensitivity analysis.
3. The graphic techniques of cost-volume-profit charts and profit-volume graphs.
4. The information needed for a cost-volume-profit analysis and the usefulness of variable costing techniques in providing this information.
5. The assumptions needed for a cost-volume-profit analysis.
6. The limitations of the cost-volume-profit analysis.

At a recent meeting of airline executives, one executive was overheard saying to another: "Since we have reduced our fares, passenger seat utilization has increased from 50 percent to 75 percent. We are now earning a satisfactory profit, whereas before we were just about breaking even." The two executives continued their conversation and finally concluded that the strategy of fare reduction was sound because they knew that any reduction in unit fares would be more than offset by an increase in the number of passengers traveling and that fixed costs would not significantly increase with increased volume.

The analysis the executives were using is an example of cost-volume-profit (CVP) analysis. The primary objective of such an analysis is to determine how profits are affected by changes in volume, selling prices, or costs. This chapter explains CVP analysis and illustrates its practical uses in decision making.

SIMPLE DEMONSTRATION OF CVP ANALYSIS

Assume that your business sells one steel press a year at $100,000 and that the press costs $95,000 to make. You are left with a profit of $5,000 per year. Now assume that you sell a different product—mousetraps—at one dollar each. The mousetraps cost 95 cents to make, leaving a profit of five cents on each mousetrap sold. Which would you rather be selling?

At first glance, you might prefer to sell the steel press. But what if you could sell 100,000 mousetraps and only one steel press in a year? You would end up with the same profit—$5,000. Now which would you prefer? Perhaps it would take less work to sell one steel press a year, but you might have a better chance of increasing sales on the dollar product. In a good year, you might be able to sell 200,000 mousetraps, at a profit of $10,000. Now which product would you rather sell? In sum, the volume of sales can affect how much money a firm makes. For example, oil companies use this principle, making only about three to five cents on each gallon of gas, although they sell a lot of gas.

COST-VOLUME-PROFIT ANALYSIS
An examination of how profits change with changes in volume.

In the preceding analysis, we assumed certain facts. First, we assumed the mousetrap had a unit selling price and a cost of $1.00 and $.95, respectively. We also assumed that these figures did not change regardless of the number of mousetraps produced and sold. Given this information, we could determine the amount of profits realized at any volume level. In essence, we performed a simple **cost-volume-profit analysis;** that is, we determined how profits would change with changes in volume.

USES OF CVP ANALYSIS

BREAKEVEN POINT
The point at which revenues and costs are equal.

CVP analysis has many practical uses in business. Our discussion focuses on three of them. Initially, we discuss how CVP analysis is used to do a breakeven analysis. Often companies want to know how much they must sell just to cover costs with no profits realized. This sales volume level is referred to as the **breakeven point.**

A second application of CVP analysis is for profit planning. Managers often have to determine how much sales must be realized to achieve a certain profit level. The CVP framework can assist managers in such determination and in the establishment of reasonable profit targets.

Finally, managers can do sensitivity analysis within the context of a CVP analysis. For example, a manager is thinking about automating a part of the production process. He knows that making such a decision will cause fixed costs to increase because of the additional depreciation on the new equipment. He also realizes that direct labor costs per unit—a variable expense—will be reduced. In doing a sensitivity analysis, he can calculate the impact of the decision on the breakeven point and determine how profits would be affected by the decision at different levels of volume.

Subsequent sections of this chapter describe and illustrate how CVP analysis is used to do breakeven and sensitivity analyses and profit planning. However, before we turn to this discussion, we need to describe what type of information is needed to do a CVP analysis.

NECESSARY INFORMATION

To do a CVP analysis, a manager must have an initial idea of fixed costs, contribution margin, or contribution margin ratio attributed to a product. Chapter 19 defined a fixed cost as any cost that remains constant over a relevant range of output. Theoretically, such a cost exists in the short run regardless of the level of production. In contrast, a variable cost was defined as any cost that remains constant on a unit basis but increases on a total cost basis in proportion to volume. For example, sales commissions are often considered to be a variable cost. If a salesperson were to earn one dollar on each unit sold and no units were sold, the salesperson would earn nothing. However, by selling 10,000 units, the individual would earn $10,000 in commissions.

A product's **contribution margin (CM)** is equal to the difference between the product's selling price per unit and the variable cost per unit. Thus, a product with a selling price of $5.00 and a variable cost of $3.00 has a contribution margin of $2.00. This contribution margin is used to cover fixed costs and to realize a profit. Another way to view a product's contribution margin is to calculate the **contribution margin ratio (CMR)** by dividing the contribution margin per unit by the selling price per unit. Using the preceding data, it's clear that our hypothetical product has a CMR of 40 percent ($2.00/$5.00). Thus, every dollar of sales will result in a "contribution" of $.40 (40% × $1.00) with which to cover fixed costs.

CONTRIBUTION MARGIN
The difference between a product's selling price and its variable cost per unit.

CONTRIBUTION MARGIN RATIO
Contribution margin per unit divided by selling price per unit.

FULL-ABSORPTION COSTING VERSUS VARIABLE COSTING

In management accounting, product cost has two approaches: full-absorption cost and variable (direct) cost. The primary difference is in the treatment of fixed manufacturing overhead.

Full-Absorption Costing

Under **full-absorption costing,** product cost comprises direct labor, direct materials, and variable and fixed manufacturing overhead. Fixed manufacturing overhead is a

FULL-ABSORPTION COSTING
A method of product costing that includes direct labor, direct materials, and both variable and fixed manufacturing overhead in product cost.

part of the inventoriable product cost. When following this approach, the income statement is prepared on a functional cost basis; that is, costs are classified based on the function performed (see Exhibit 24.1). Product costs are included in the cost of goods sold, and nonmanufacturing costs are part of the selling, general, and administrative expenses. The full-absorption approach is commonly used in practice, because it is required for external reporting and tax purposes. Note that this format does not provide any clear identity of fixed costs and variable costs. To make this distinction, the functional cost categories need to be analyzed with the fixed and variable costs for each category broken out separately. This is accomplished under variable (direct) costing.

Variable (Direct) Costing

VARIABLE (DIRECT) COSTING
A method of product costing that includes only variable manufacturing costs in product cost.

DIRECT COSTING
See Variable Costing

Under **variable (direct) costing,** product cost is equal to total variable manufacturing cost. This figure normally includes direct labor, direct materials, and variable manufacturing overhead. Fixed manufacturing overhead is treated as a period cost rather than as a product cost. Under direct costing, the income statement is prepared on a cost behavior basis; that is, costs are classified on the income statement based on whether they are fixed or variable. Exhibit 24.2 is an example of an income statement prepared on a direct cost basis. The income statement classifies costs based on cost behavior patterns and provides the necessary information required in a CVP analysis.

As stated earlier, the critical difference between full-absorption costing and variable costing is the treatment of fixed manufacturing overhead. Proponents of direct costing believe that fixed manufacturing overhead is incurred to provide a certain amount of productive capacity. Once the cost is incurred, it is sunk and therefore

EXHIBIT 24.1

JETCO Company
Income Statement (using a functional cost basis)
For the Year Ending 12/31/1986

Sales			$80,000
Cost of goods sold			
Beginning inventory		$10,000	
Cost of goods manufactured			
Raw materials used	$ 8,000		
Direct labor	12,000		
Factory overhead	30,000		
Total cost of goods manufactured		$50,000	
Goods available for sale		$60,000	
Ending inventory		10,000	
Cost of goods sold			$50,000
Gross profit			$30,000
Operating expenses			
Selling expense		$ 4,000	
Administrative expense		7,000	
Total operating expenses			$11,000
Profit before taxes			$19,000

EXHIBIT 24.2

JETCO Company
Income Statement (using a cost behavior basis)
For the Year Ending 12/31/1986

	$			%		
Sales			$80,000			100.0
Variable cost of goods sold						
Beginning inventory		6,000			7.5	
Cost of goods manufactured						
Raw materials used	8,000			10.0		
Direct labor	12,000			15.0		
Variable factory overhead	10,000	30,000		12.5	37.5	
Goods available for sale		36,000			45.0	
Ending inventory		6,000			7.5	
Variable cost of goods sold			$30,000			37.5
Contribution margin from manufacturing			$50,000			62.5
Variable operating expenses						
Variable selling expense		2,000			2.5	
Variable administrative expense		4,000	$ 6,000		5.0	7.5
Contribution margin (net)			$44,000			55.0
Fixed costs						
Fixed factory overhead		20,000			25.0	
Fixed selling expense		2,000			2.5	
Fixed administrative expense		3,000			3.8	
Total fixed costs			$25,000			31.3
Profit before taxes			$19,000			23.7

	Unit Data
Selling price	$ 8.00
Total variable costs	3.60
Contribution margin	$ 4.40

Fixed costs = $25,000 in total

(Note: This cost behavior format statement is used only for internal management purposes. The format is unacceptable for external reporting uses.)

should not be charged to individual units of production. The only costs directly chargeable to production are those manufacturing costs that vary in proportion to volume. In contrast to this position, full-absorption advocates firmly believe that because fixed manufacturing overhead is necessary to achieve any level of production, it should rightfully be charged to units produced. Fixed manufacturing overhead is therefore considered part of product cost.

Four basic implications of the differences between direct costing and full-absorption costing are:

1. The format of the income statement differs depending on the approach used. Direct costing is often recommended for internal purposes, because many accountants believe it supplies cost information in a form that facilitates decision making.
2. Product cost and net income will be different based on the method used. Because fixed manufacturing overhead is treated as a period cost under direct costing, product cost will always be lower under this method than under full-absorption costing.
3. Net income might be different between the methods depending on the relationship between sales volume and production. As Exhibit 24.3 indicates, net income will be the same for both methods when sales equals production. However, when production exceeds sales, net income will be higher under full-absorption costing, because a portion of the fixed manufacturing overhead will be in inventory—an asset—rather than charged as an expense against revenue as in direct costing. Following this same logic, if production is less than sales, net income will be higher under direct costing. The responsibility of the treatment of fixed overhead for this difference in income can be proven by reconciling the two income amounts: The difference in income between the two methods will always equal the product of the net unit change in inventory and the fixed manufacturing overhead application rate (see Exhibit 24.3).
4. Net income under direct costing is a function of sales volume; under full-absorption costing, it is affected by changes in inventory levels. Once again, operating managers believe that direct costing yields net income results that are more consistent with how the business is doing in reality.

Regardless of the controversy over which method is "correct," a manager with the information developed under variable costing techniques is prepared to do a CVP analysis. Let us examine how this would be done.

CVP ANALYSIS

As previously mentioned, CVP analysis has multiple uses, including breakeven analysis, profit planning, and sensitivity analysis. Using the data in Exhibit 24.3, we will first illustrate mathematical approaches to these methods and then discuss how some of the analyses could be performed graphically.

Breakeven Analysis

BREAKEVEN ANALYSIS
Analysis of the amount of sales required to cover all fixed and variable costs with no resulting profit.

Mathematical Approach. The primary objective of a **breakeven analysis** is to determine the amount of sales required to cover all fixed and variable costs with no resulting profit. This type of analysis can be most helpful in determining the feasibility

EXHIBIT 24.3

Variable (Direct) Versus Full-Absorption Costing
JETCO Company

Basic data

Cost to make one unit (product cost)

Direct materials	$1.30
Direct labor	1.50
Variable OH (application rate and actual)	.20
Fixed OH (application rate)	1.00
	$4.00

Additional information

Selling, general, and administrative expenses	$65,000 + 5% of sales
Selling price of product	$5.00 per unit

No materials or labor variances exist.

Under-applied overhead (excess of actual overhead beyond applied overhead) and over-applied overhead (excess of applied overhead beyond actual overhead) are charged off to cost of goods sold.

Situation I: Sales = Production (income the same under both methods)

Assume:	
Beginning inventory	10,000 units
Production	100,000 units
Sales	100,000 units
Ending inventory	10,000 units

	Variable Costing		Full-Absorption Costing
Sales	$500,000		$500,000
Cost of goods sold			
Beginning inventory	$ 30,000		$ 40,000
Current production	300,000		400,000
Ending inventory	(30,000)		(40,000)
Cost of goods sold	(300,000)		(400,000)
Contribution margin from manufacturing	$200,000	Under-applied overhead	(50,000)
Variable selling, general, and administrative expense	(25,000)		
Contribution margin, net	$175,000	Gross margin	$ 50,000
Fixed overhead	(150,000)	Selling, general, and administrative expense	(90,000)
Fixed selling, general, and administrative expense	(65,000)		
Loss	$ 40,000		$ 40,000

Difference = $0

Proof of difference in incomes

Ending inventory	10,000 units
Less beginning inventory	10,000 units
Net change	–0– units
Fixed overhead application rate	$1.00/unit
Excess of full-absorption costing income over variable costing income	$–0–

EXHIBIT 24.3
(continued)

Situation II: Sales > production (income higher under variable costing)

Assume:		
	Beginning inventory	10,000 units
	Production	100,000 units
	Sales	110,000 units
	Ending inventory	–0– units

	Variable Costing		Absorption Costing
Sales	$550,000		$550,000
Cost of goods sold			
Beginning inventory	$ 30,000		$ 40,000
Current production	300,000		400,000
Ending inventory	–0–		–0–
Cost of goods sold	(330,000)		(440,000)
Contribution margin from manufacturing	$220,000	Under-applied overhead	(50,000)
Variable selling, general, and administrative expense	(27,500)		
Contribution margin, net	$192,500	Gross margin	$ 60,000
Fixed overhead	(150,000)		
Fixed selling, general, and administrative expense	(65,000)	Selling, general, and administrative expense	(92,500)
Loss	$ (22,500)		$ (32,500)

Difference = $10,000,

Proof of difference in incomes

Ending inventory	–0– units
Less beginning inventory	10,000 units
Net change	(10,000) units
Fixed overhead application rate	$1.00/ unit
Excess of full-absorption costing income over variable costing income	$ (10,000)

EXHIBIT 24.3
(continued)

Situation III: Sales < Production (income higher under full-absorption costing)

Beginning inventory	10,000 units
Production	110,000 units
Sales	100,000 units
Ending inventory	20,000 units

	Variable Costing		Absorption Costing	
Sales		$500,000		$500,000
Cost of goods sold				
Beginning inventory		$ 30,000		$ 40,000
Current production		330,000		440,000
Ending inventory		(60,000)		(80,000)
Cost of goods sold		(300,000)		(400,000)
Contribution margin from manufacturing		$200,000	Under-applied overhead	(40,000)
Variable selling, general, and administrative expense		(25,000)		
Contribution margin, net		$175,000	Gross margin	$ 60,000
Fixed overhead		(150,000)		
Fixed selling, general, and administrative expense		(65,000)	Selling, general, and administrative expense	(90,000)
Loss		$ (40,000)		$ (30,000)

Difference = $10,000

Proof of difference in incomes

Ending inventory	20,000 units
Less beginning inventory	10,000 units
Net change	10,000 units
Fixed overhead application rate	$ 1.00/unit
Excess of full-absorption costing income over variable costing income	$10,000

of introducing a new product or expanding production facilities. For example, by comparing a product's breakeven point to expected sales, management can determine the riskiness of the new product.

The income statement in Exhibit 24.2 can be depicted in the following equation form:

$$\text{Profit} = \text{Revenue} - (\text{Variable costs} + \text{Fixed costs}) \tag{1}$$

The breakeven point would then be the volume of sales where

$$\text{Revenue} = \text{Variable costs} + \text{Fixed costs} \tag{2}$$

Total revenue is determined by multiplying the selling price per unit (SP) by the number of units sold (X), while the total variable costs equal the product of the variable cost per unit (vc) and the number of units sold. Given these relationships, it is possible to reformulate equation (2) into

$$SP(X) = vc(X) + \text{Fixed costs} \tag{3}$$

Rearranging the terms in equation (3), we can calculate the breakeven point in units as follows:

$$X = \frac{\text{Fixed costs}}{SP - vc \text{ (or contribution margin)}} \tag{4}$$

$$X = \frac{\$25{,}000}{\$8.00 - \$3.60} = 5{,}682 \text{ units}$$

As you can see, JETCO has a breakeven point of 5,682 units. As long as sales are above this level, the company will earn a profit. If, however, sales should fall below 5,682 units, a loss will result.

The more the actual sales exceed the breakeven point, the better off the company is. Many companies identify this distance by calculating a margin of safety (MOS). The **margin of safety (MOS),** expressed as a percentage, indicates how far sales at the breakeven point are from actual or expected sales as follows:

MARGIN OF SAFETY
The difference between sales at the breakeven point and actual or expected sales.

$$MOS = \frac{\text{Actual or expected sales} - \text{Sales at the breakeven point}}{\text{Actual or expected sales}} \tag{5}$$

If JETCO sells 10,000 units, its MOS is as follows:

$$MOS = \frac{10{,}000 - 5{,}682}{10{,}000} = 43\%$$

This calculation indicates that sales would have to decrease by more than 43 percent before a loss would be realized. Obviously, the higher the MOS percentage the better, because it indicates that the company is operating nowhere near the breakeven point and the likelihood of realizing a loss is therefore minimal.

In some firms, it is difficult to calculate the breakeven point in units, because different products are manufactured and sold. Typically, in the case of multiproduct companies, the breakeven point is calculated in terms of total sales dollars rather than units. Using the amounts in Exhibit 24.2, the breakeven point is calculated as follows:

$$\frac{\text{Fixed costs}}{(\text{Sales} - \text{Variable costs})/\text{Sales}} \tag{6}$$

$$\text{Breakeven point} = \$25{,}000/[(\$80{,}000 - \$36{,}000)/\$80{,}000] = \$45{,}455$$

To use equation (6) for a multiproduct firm, we must assume that the sales mix (i.e., the distribution of sales among the different products) is given in advance, since there can be different revenues and costs associated with each product.

Note that the denominator in equation (6) equals the contribution margin ratio. The MOS is calculated using the same formula as indicated in equation (5). However, it is necessary to use the appropriate dollar figure rather than units.

Graphic Approach. As an alternative to calculating breakeven points, one can prepare either a CVP graph as in Exhibit 24.4 or a PV (profit = volume) graph as in Exhibit 24.5. These graphs are relatively easy to prepare and are of great assistance to management in seeing how profit or loss varies with changes in volume.

CVP Chart. The most common graphic approach is to construct a **CVP chart** like the one in Exhibit 24.4 for the JETCO Company. The horizontal axis of such a chart represents volume, expressed in either units or sales dollars. The vertical axis represents total revenue or costs, depending on what figures are being plotted. Once the axes are properly labeled, the various cost and revenue curves can be drawn.

CVP CHART
A graphical approach to cost-volume-profit analysis that charts volume on the horizontal axis and total revenues or total costs on the vertical axis.

The first line to plot is the fixed-cost figure. This is represented by line A in the graph. This line is parallel to the volume axis, indicating that fixed costs remain constant regardless of the volume level. After the fixed-cost line is drawn, the variable cost line can be plotted. This line coincides with the fixed-cost line at a zero sales

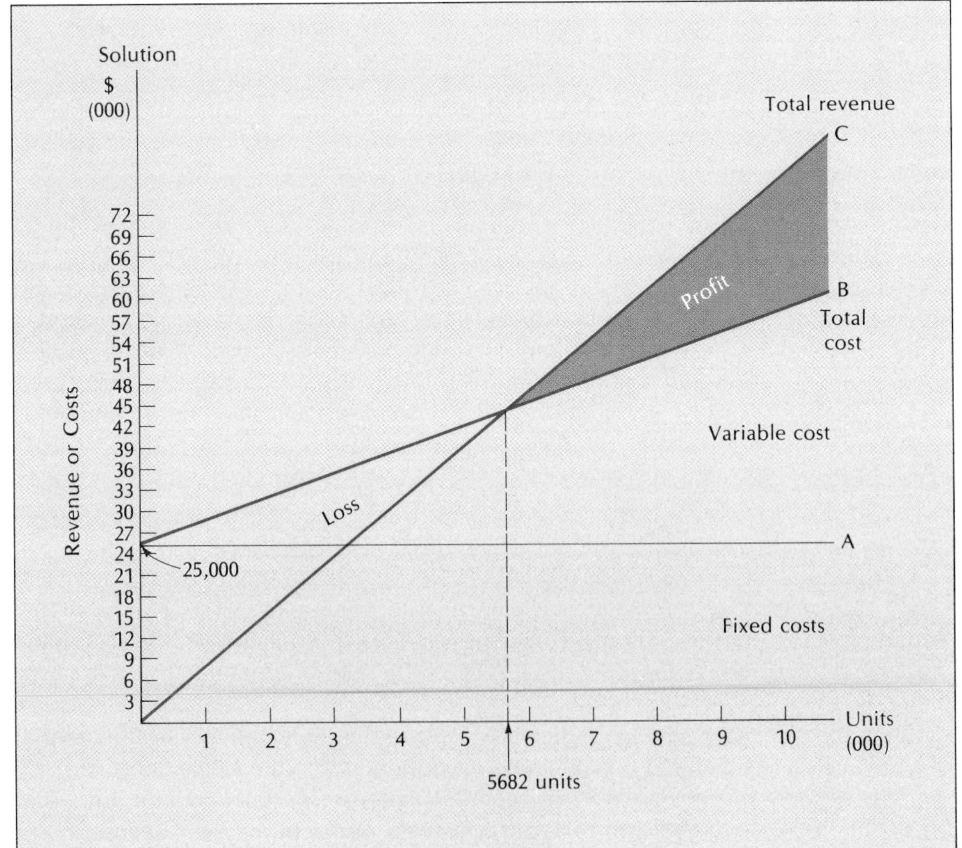

EXHIBIT 24.4

JETCO Company CVP Chart

level and thereafter increases in proportion to volume increases. For each additional unit sold, variable costs will increase by $3.60, which is equal to the variable cost per unit. Total variable costs are equal to the difference between the total cost line B and the fixed-cost line A. The slope of the total cost line is equal to the variable cost per unit.

Once all of the cost lines are drawn, the total revenue line (line C) is plotted. This line starts at the zero sales level point on the graph and increases with increases in volume. The slope of the revenue line is equal to the selling price per unit. The breakeven point can then be identified by drawing a vertical line from the point of intersection between the total revenue line and the total cost line to the volume axis and reading the number off this axis. In this case, the breakeven point is 5,682 units, which is equal to the number previously calculated for the JETCO Company using the formula approach. If the company is operating to the right of the breakeven point, it realizes a profit. The profit area is represented by the shaded region. Management can easily identify the profit or loss to be achieved at any particular sales level by calculating from the graph the dollar difference between the total revenue and total cost lines at that volume level.

PV GRAPH
A variation of a CVP chart where the horizontal axis represents sales and the vertical axis represents profits before taxes.

PV Graph. The **PV graph** in Exhibit 24.5 is a variation of the CVP graph. In this graph, the horizontal axis represents sales volume in units or dollars and the vertical axis represents profits before taxes. In essence, we are more clearly depicting in the PV graph the volume-profit/loss relationships indicated in the CVP chart. Thus, line A was determined by drawing a line between all the various possible volume-profit relationship points. For example, at a volume of 7,000 units, profit would be $5,800 [7,000 × ($4.40) − $25,000], while at a 4,000-unit volume level, a $7,400 loss [4,000 × ($4.40) − $25,000] would be realized. By constructing a PV chart, management can more readily determine the profit or loss to be realized at a particular sales level.

CASH BREAKEVEN POINT
(Fixed costs minus any noncash expenses) divided by contribution margin or contribution margin ratio.

Cash Breakeven Point. In practice, managers are often interested in determining how much volume is required to cover a company's fixed cash expenses. In the short run, the company must be able to cover at least these expenses to remain solvent. Unfortunately, the normal breakeven calculation misstates the breakeven point, because the fixed-cost category includes both cash and noncash expenses, such as depreciation and amortization. To the extent that noncash expenses exist and are included in fixed costs, the breakeven point is overstated. To eliminate this problem, managers usually calculate a **cash breakeven point** in addition to the normal breakeven point as follows:

$$\frac{\text{Fixed costs} - \text{Any noncash expenses}}{\text{Contribution margin or contribution margin ratio}} \qquad (7)$$

Assuming JETCO has $7,000 of depreciation included in fixed costs, the company has a cash breakeven point of $32,727. This is the sales amount necessary to cover the company's fixed cash expenses.

The cash breakeven point is particularly relevant in analyzing the profit potential of a new piece of machinery. When new machinery is acquired, fixed costs usually increase because of the increased depreciation expenses. In this situation, the usual breakeven analysis might distort the attractiveness of the purchase, because it will

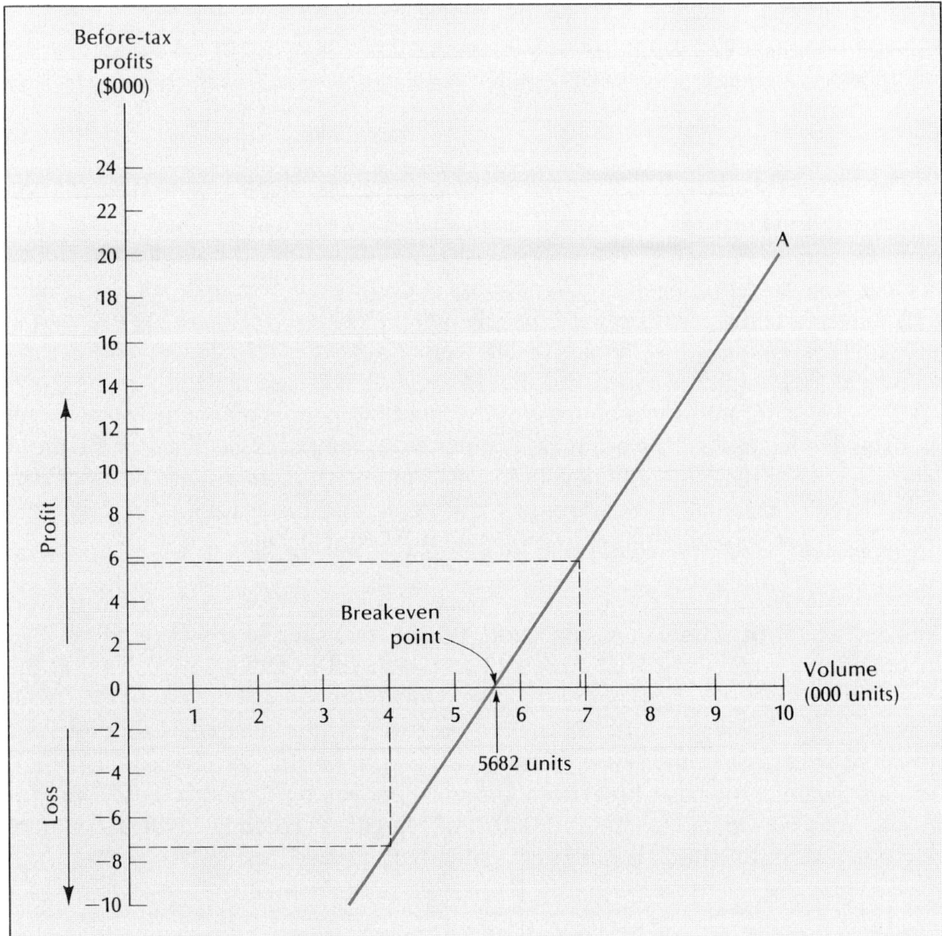

EXHIBIT 24.5

JETCO Company Profit-Volume Chart

overstate the machine's breakeven point when, in fact, the largest portion of the increased fixed costs involves no cash outlay. Thus, the cash breakeven analysis normally supplements any type of breakeven analysis.

Assumptions Underlying Breakeven Analysis. All of the preceding analyses made some basic assumptions about the information used. In practice, if we are to make proper use of this type of analysis, it is important to be aware of those assumptions:

1. The fixed costs, selling price per unit, and variable cost per unit remain the same throughout the relevant range.
2. Volume is the primary determinant of profit.
3. A linear relationship exists between costs and revenue.
4. Cost can be accurately classified into fixed and variable costs.
5. The number of units sold equals the number of units produced.

These assumptions do not seriously undermine the usefulness of breakeven analysis even though, on the surface, breakeven analysis appears to be a more static than dynamic approach to decision making. As we will see shortly, however, the CVP analysis can be made to be more dynamic by relaxing some of the preceding assumptions.

Profit Planning

PROFIT PLANNING
A modification of breakeven analysis used to examine the impact of changes in costs or revenues on profits.

If properly modified, the breakeven analysis framework can be used as a **profit-planning** tool to answer such questions as: How many units do we need to sell to achieve a given profit level? and What impact do income taxes have on our ability to achieve certain profits? Because management, as part of the planning process, is constantly examining the impact of alternative strategies to achieve profits, any analytical tool helpful in this cause should improve decision making.

We can best illustrate the usefulness of CVP analysis in profit planning by presenting an extended example. This example assumes management is given a specific profit target and must determine the level of sales required to meet the profit. Once this sales figure is calculated, management can determine the feasibility of achieving the sales target by comparing it to projected or historical sales.

Before-Tax Profit Target. Assume you are the manager of the department that manufactures and sells JETCO's product as described in Exhibit 24.2. During the planning process, the corporate vice president informs you that he expects your department to achieve a $10,000 before-tax profit in the next year. One of your initial tasks is to determine how many units need to be sold to achieve this target. You are aware of the basic breakeven formulas, but you must modify these formulas to take into consideration the $10,000 profit target. A recently hired accountant suggests that you treat the profit target similarly to a fixed cost:

$$\frac{\text{Fixed costs} + \text{Before-tax profit target}}{\text{Contribution margin or contribution margin ratio}} \tag{8}$$

$$\frac{\$25,000 + \$10,000}{\$4.40} = 7,955 \text{ units}$$

Check

Sales (7,955 @ $8.00)	$63,640
Variable costs (7,955 @ $3.60)	28,638
Contribution margin	$35,002
Fixed costs	25,000
Profits before taxes	$10,000 (rounding error)

Using this formula, you calculate the required sales level to be 7,955 units.

After you make this calculation and report it to the vice president, the vice president tells you that he actually wants you to achieve an *after*-tax profit of $10,000. Your new accountant tells you that before another determination of required sales can be made you must convert the after-tax profit target to a before-tax number to make it compatible with the fixed costs figure stated on a before-tax basis. To make this conversion, you must divide the after-tax profit target by one minus the company's tax rate, which is 40 percent:

Breakeven on Campus

The application of breakeven analysis is not restricted to business entities selling tangible products. Its use can be extended to firms selling intangible services as long as sales revenue and variable cost data on a per unit basis (or at least contribution margin ratio data) are available. For example, Dean Clark Olson of the School of Management at Eastern Land Grant University realized in the summer of 1984 that his school needed to earn $6.7 million in tuition in the next academic year just to break even.

Entering Olson's computations were charges allocated to the school by the university for such items as libraries ($328,000), plant services ($498,000), and computer usage ($218,000). In addition, salaries for administrative and clerical staff needed to support the faculty were estimated at $1,554,000. The total of all such costs was expected to exceed $8.7 million for the 1984–85 academic year. Since none of these costs were dependent upon enrollment, all $8.7 million was considered fixed costs.

On the revenue side, Olson expected to receive $382,000 in revenue from endowments, $344,000 in research contracts, and over $1.3 million in other grants and gifts. Thus, he estimated the school needed to realize $6.7 million in tuition revenue. With this information, Olson calculated that for the school to break even, enrollment must equal 781 full-time-equivalent students with an average contribution margin of $8,600.

Although this level of enrollment may have been well below the capacity of the school, Olson had still reaped the benefits of breakeven analysis: His "sales" goal had been stated in clear, objective terms with which he could compare actual performance and take action on any variances.

$$\frac{\text{Fixed costs} + \dfrac{\text{After-tax profit target}}{1 - \text{Tax rate}}}{\text{Contribution margin or contribution margin ratio}} \qquad (9)$$

$$\frac{\$25{,}000 + \dfrac{\$10{,}000}{1 - 0.40}}{\$4.40} = 9{,}470 \text{ units (or } \$75{,}760)$$

<u>Check</u>

Sales (9,470 @ $8.00)	$75,760
Variable costs (9,470 @ $3.60)	34,092
Contribution margin	$41,668
Fixed costs	25,000
Before-tax profit	$16,668
Taxes (@40%)	6,667
After-tax profit	$10,000 (rounding error)

Thus, to achieve this $10,000 after-tax profit, your department must sell 9,470 units.

After you give the vice president this new number, the vice president asks you to make one more calculation. Just recently, the company implemented an ROI system much like the one described in Chapter 22 in which investment centers are evaluated based on their returns on investment. Since return on investment equals the product of total asset turnover and profit margin, you, as a department head, will be responsible for setting the predetermined targets for total asset turnover and profit margin necessary to insure that the ROI goal will be reached. The vice president is thinking about setting your profit margin target at ten percent of sales on an after-tax basis and asks you to determine the required sales level. Unfortunately, you have no idea of how to make this calculation, so you ask the corporate controller for advice. She informs you that it involves a simple modification of the breakeven formula as follows:

$$\frac{\text{Fixed costs} + \dfrac{\text{After-tax profit margin objective} \times \text{Sales}}{1 - \text{Tax rate}}}{\text{Contribution margin percentage}} = \text{Sales} \qquad (10)$$

The sales variable is the only unknown in equation (10). Therefore, by plugging the known variables into the formula, you can determine the required sales figure. Note that the only difference between equations (9) and (10) is that the after-tax profit target is expressed as a percentage of sales rather than as a fixed amount.

$$\frac{\$25{,}000 + \dfrac{10\%\ \text{sales}}{1 - 0.40}}{0.55} = \text{Sales}$$

$$\$25{,}000 + 0.167\ \text{sales} = 0.55\ \text{sales}$$

$$\text{Sales} = \$65{,}274$$

Check

Sales	$65,274
Variable costs ($65,274 × .45)	29,373
Contribution margin	$35,901
Fixed costs	25,000
Before-tax profit	$10,901
Taxes at .40	4,360
After-tax profit	$ 6,541

Profit margin ($6,541/$65,274) = 10%

In this example, the required sales figure was calculated in dollars rather than units. Whenever the profit objective is stated as a sales percentage rather than as an absolute dollar amount, the contribution margin ratio must be used in the denominator of the CVP formula.

Using CVP analysis in profit planning gives management a powerful tool in decision making, allowing it to "back into" the sales targets required to meet different profit objectives. In this way, management can establish reasonable profit objectives and sales targets.

Sensitivity Analysis

One of the most powerful uses of CVP analysis is in "what if" analysis. Often managers are interested in answering such questions as What impact would a price reduction have on the product's breakeven point? Questions such as this require the manager to determine the impact of a change in one variable (or set of variables) on the final solution of a CVP analysis. In essence, the "what if" analysis is a form of **sensitivity analysis** where management determines how sensitive the final answer is to a change in key variables.

SENSITIVITY ANALYSIS A method of using cost-volume-profit analysis to determine the impact of a change in costs or prices on profits.

Three short examples of sensitivity analysis are included in Exhibit 24.6 for the JETCO Company. The first example examines the impact of a ten percent reduction in selling price. Such a change would increase the breakeven point by 22.2 percent. Therefore, the breakeven point is very sensitive to a change in product price. The more a particular change in a variable affects the final answer, the more critical the variable is to the analysis. Thus, one of the other benefits of a sensitivity analysis is that it allows management to systematically identify the key variables in a problem scenario.

The last two examples in Exhibit 24.6 show the impact of a five percent change in the variable cost per unit and an eight percent increase in fixed costs, respectively, on JETCO's breakeven point. In both instances, the impact on the breakeven point is approximately equal to the percentage change in the key variable, indicating that the breakeven point is not as sensitive to changes in these variables as it is to a change in product price.

SOME PROBLEMS IN USING CVP ANALYSIS

It would be unfair to end this chapter without at least mentioning some of the problems management might face in doing a CVP analysis. Most of the problems

EXHIBIT 24.6

JETCO Company
Example of Sensitivity Analysis

Change	Impact on Breakeven Point
10% reduction in price	$\dfrac{\$25{,}000}{\$7.20 - \$3.60} = 6{,}944$ units
	breakeven point increases by
	$\dfrac{6{,}944 - 5{,}682}{5{,}682} = 22.2\%$
5% reduction in variable cost per unit	$\dfrac{\$25{,}000}{\$8.00 - \$3.42} = 5{,}459$ units
	breakeven point decreases by
	$\dfrac{5{,}459 - 5{,}682}{5{,}682} = -4\%$
8% increase in fixed costs	$\dfrac{\$27{,}000}{\$4.40} = 6{,}136$
	breakeven point increases by
	$\dfrac{6{,}136 - 5{,}682}{5{,}682} = 8\%$

result from the assumptions underlying such an analysis as discussed earlier. However, a few of them require additional discussion.

Fixed and Variable Cost Identification

Probably the most difficult problem in doing such an analysis is to properly identify the fixed and variable costs. This problem has two aspects. The first relates to whether management uses historical, current, or projected costs. In actual application, most companies use current or projected costs, because the decision being made affects the future rather than the past.

■ CONCEPT SUMMARY 24.1

COST-VOLUME-PROFIT FORMULAS

	Definition	Formula
Breakeven point (BEP)	Level of sales at which revenues just cover fixed and variable expenses.	$BEP = \dfrac{\text{Fixed costs}}{\text{Contribution margin or ratio}}$
Cash breakeven point (CBEP)	Level of sales at which revenues just cover cash expenses.	$CBEP = \dfrac{\text{Fixed costs} - \text{Noncash fixed costs}}{\text{Contribution margin or ratio}}$
Margin of safety (MOS)	Percentage decline in actual sales allowed before creating a loss.	$MOS = \dfrac{\text{Actual sales} - \text{Breakeven point}}{\text{Actual sales}}$
Target point (TP)	Level of sales at which revenues achieve a given profit target.	
	For before-tax target:	$TP = \dfrac{\text{Fixed costs} + \text{Target profit}}{\text{Contribution margin or ratio}}$
	For after-tax target:	$TP = \dfrac{\text{Fixed costs} + \dfrac{(\text{Targeted profit})}{(1 - \text{Tax rate})}}{\text{Contribution margin or ratio}}$
	For after-tax profit margin:	$TP = \dfrac{\text{Fixed costs} + \dfrac{(\text{Targeted margin} \times TP)}{(1 - \text{Tax rate})}}{\text{Contribution margin or ratio}}$

(Note: When the contribution margin is used, the breakeven or target point will be in terms of units. When the contribution margin ratio is used, the breakeven or target point will be in terms of dollars.)

ANALYSIS OF ACCOUNTS METHOD
A method of projecting fixed and variable costs that relies on management's review and classification of accounts as either representing fixed or variable cost elements.

The second aspect of the problem relates to how management identifies fixed and variable costs. A host of techniques ranging in degree of sophistication are available to assist managers in this task. For example, the **analysis of accounts method** is a very useful informal technique that can be used in this process. This method simply requires management to review the expense accounts and, based on each manager's experience, classify each account as a variable or fixed expense. The managers would then observe the behavior pattern of these expenses over time and refine their classifications as appropriate.

Hi-Lo Method

For a more objective technique, the **hi-lo method** can be used, whereby management plots the total cost line using data from the highest and lowest recent production levels. The slope of this line can then be used as an estimate of variable costs per unit, and the intercept can be used as an estimate of total fixed costs (see Exhibit 24.7). This method is much simpler, less expensive, and faster, although less accurate, than the more sophisticated statistical techniques, such as multiple regression analysis, which can be used to properly classify costs. Such techniques, de-

HI-LO METHOD
A method of projecting fixed and variable costs from a line plotted from the costs of the highest and lowest levels of production.

EXHIBIT 24.7

Hi-Lo Method of Fixed Versus Variable Cost Classification

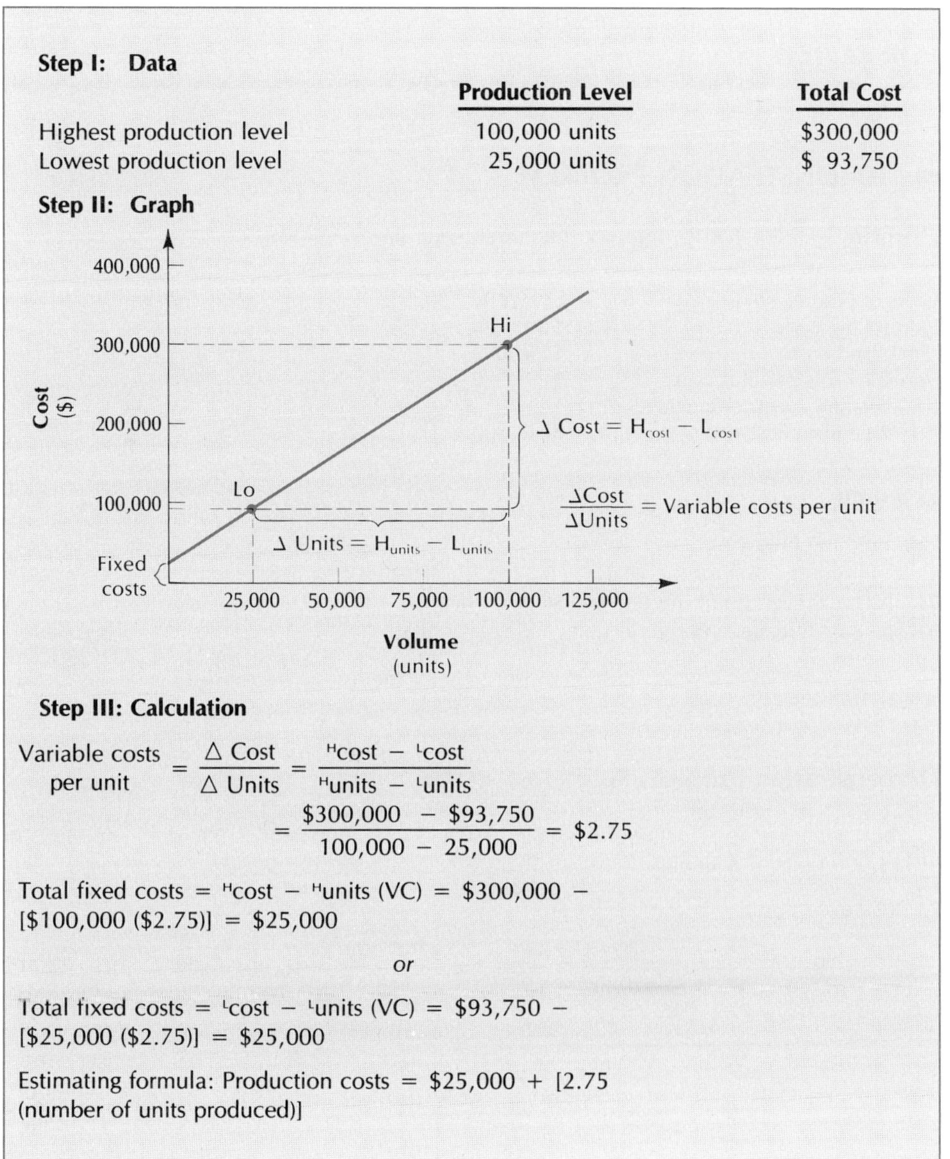

Step I: Data

	Production Level	Total Cost
Highest production level	100,000 units	\$300,000
Lowest production level	25,000 units	\$ 93,750

Step II: Graph

Step III: Calculation

$$\text{Variable costs per unit} = \frac{\Delta\ \text{Cost}}{\Delta\ \text{Units}} = \frac{{}^{H}\text{cost} - {}^{L}\text{cost}}{{}^{H}\text{units} - {}^{L}\text{units}}$$

$$= \frac{\$300{,}000 - \$93{,}750}{100{,}000 - 25{,}000} = \$2.75$$

Total fixed costs = ^{H}cost − ^{H}units (VC) = \$300,000 − [\$100,000 (\$2.75)] = \$25,000

or

Total fixed costs = ^{L}cost − ^{L}units (VC) = \$93,750 − [\$25,000 (\$2.75)] = \$25,000

Estimating formula: Production costs = \$25,000 + [2.75 (number of units produced)]

scribed in more advanced texts, are widely used in practice because of the accessibility of computers and advanced calculators capable of making such calculations.

Static Versus Dynamic Analysis

Finally, if not performed carefully and wisely, CVP analysis can become a static tool of analysis resulting in more harm than good. Fortunately, accounting researchers in recent years have significantly advanced our knowledge of this technique, making it more valuable. The CVP analysis has been extended and made more dynamic through computerization and modeling to the point where it has become a powerful management planning tool.

FOR REVIEW

DEMONSTRATION PROBLEM

Operating data for T.R.P., Inc., for the current year are as follows.

Units of product sold	15,000
Unit selling price	$ 20
Total fixed costs	$250,000
Variable costs per unit	$ 5
Depreciation expense (included in total fixed costs)	$ 40,000

Required

Compute the following:

1. Net income (loss) for the year.
2. The breakeven point in units and sales dollars.
3. The cash breakeven point in units and sales dollars.

Demonstration Problem Solution

1. The net income (loss) for the year is a $25,000 loss—(15,000 units × $20/unit) − $250,000 − (15,000 units × $5/unit)).

2. Breakeven point

$$\frac{\text{BEP}}{q} = \frac{\text{FC}}{\text{SP/u} - \text{VC/u}} = \frac{\$250{,}000 \text{ FC}}{\$20 \text{ SP} - \$5 \text{ VC}} = \frac{\$250{,}000}{\$15} = 16{,}667 \text{ units}$$

$$\frac{\text{BEP}}{\$} = \frac{\text{FC}}{\dfrac{\text{SP/u} - \text{VC/u}}{\text{SP/u}}} = \frac{\$250{,}000}{\dfrac{\$20 \text{ SP} - \$5 \text{ VC}}{\$20 \text{ SP}}} = \frac{\$250{,}000}{0.75} = \$333{,}333 \text{ sales}$$

3. Cash breakeven point

$$\frac{CBEP}{q} = \frac{FC - NC}{SP - VC} = \frac{\$250{,}000\ FC - \$40{,}000\ NC}{\$20\ SP - \$5\ VC} = \frac{\$210{,}000}{\$15} = 14{,}000 \text{ units}$$

$$\frac{CBEP}{\$} = \frac{FC - NC}{\frac{SP - VC}{SP}} = \frac{\$250{,}000\ FC - \$40{,}000\ NC}{\frac{\$20\ SP - \$5\ VC}{\$20\ SP}} = \frac{\$210{,}000}{0.75} = \$280{,}000 \text{ sales}$$

SUMMARY

- A cost-volume-profit analysis determines how profits are affected by changes in volume.
- Under full-absorption costing, product cost includes fixed manufacturing overhead; under variable costing, product costs include only variable manufacturing costs.
- Breakeven analysis is used to determine the amount of sales required to cover fixed and variable costs with no resulting profit. This amount is known as the breakeven point.
- Cash breakeven point often gives a truer picture of a firm's financial position than do regular reakeven computations, because noncash expenses included in total fixed costs are excluded om the analysis.
- The margin of safety is the difference between actual or expected sales of a company and the company's breakeven level of sales.
- Profit planning is a modified breakeven method that management uses in analyzing the impact on profits of alternative production strategies or for estimating the tax implications for the firm at various profit levels.
- Sensitivity analysis, or "what if" analysis, allows managers to explore the impact of changes in one variable or set of variables on the final solution of a CVP analysis.
- CVP is complicated by many of the assumptions needed to perform an analysis such as the identification of fixed and variable costs.

REVIEW QUESTIONS

24-1. What is the difference between full-absorption costing and direct costing?

24-2. Define the cash breakeven point and discuss the significance of this number.

24-3. What are the basic assumptions in breakeven analysis?

24-4. How would a change in the following items affect the breakeven point of the firm:
- **a.** Increase in fixed costs.
- **b.** Decrease in variable costs per unit.
- **c.** Increase in selling price per unit.

24-5. Explain the difference between a CVP chart and a PV chart.

24-6. Company A and Company B had the same sales, total of fixed and variable costs, and operating income for the current fiscal year. However, Company B had a lower breakeven point than did Company A. What would cause the difference in the breakeven point?

24-7. What is meant by contribution margin, and how does it differ from gross profit margin? If a product has a selling price of $50 and a variable cost of $35, what is its contribution margin?

24-8. How is the contribution margin ratio determined? What is the contribution margin ratio in 24-7? What does this figure tell us?

24-9. What formula is used to estimate required sales for a projected profit level on a before-tax and after-tax basis?

24-10. What is meant by margin of safety, and how can management use this information for decision-making purposes?

EXERCISES

24-E1. Company J has sales of $300,000 and a breakeven point of $250,000. What is its margin of safety? What does this figure tell us about Company J?

24-E2. Ajax Company has fixed costs of $40,000 and variable costs of $3.25 per unit. How many units would have to be sold at a price of $8.25 for Ajax to break even? How many units would have to be sold for the company to earn an after-tax profit of $60,000? Assume a tax rate of 40%.

24-E3. Beta Company manufactures a product that it sells for $4.00. It has variable costs per package of $2.75 and fixed costs of $32,500, which includes $7,500 of depreciation. Its closest competitor, Alpha Company, sells a similar product at the same price, has the same variable costs and fixed costs, but has no depreciation expense. Calculate the cash breakeven point for each company and explain the significance of the differences.

24-E4. Company Q has fixed costs of $600,000, variable costs of $240 per unit, and a sales price of $360 per unit. What would be the effect on the breakeven point if fixed costs were increased by 10%? If variable costs were reduced by 15%? If the sales price is reduced by 20%?

24-E5. Brous Company has fixed costs of $225,000 and variable costs equal to 25% of sales at the breakeven point. What is Brous Company's breakeven point?

24-E6. Using the information provided for Brous Company, what level of sales is required to realize an operating income of $30,000 before taxes? After taxes? Assume a tax rate of 20%.

24-E7. Novelty Toy Company has fixed costs of $6,000, variable costs per unit of $7, and a selling price of $10 per unit. What is the profit or loss at 600 units of sales? 1500 units of sales? 2200 units of sales? Use a PV graph to solve this exercise.

PROBLEM SET A

24-A1. **Breakeven Analysis.** The Travis Company sells dolls at a price of $18 per doll. The only variable costs to manufacture each doll are $3.10 for materials and $11.60 for labor. Fixed costs per month are $6,600.

Required

a. What is the monthly breakeven point in units sold and in sales dollars?
b. What is the total contribution margin at the breakeven point?
c. What is the monthly net income before taxes if 3,800 dolls are sold per month?
d. What sales level in units and in dollar sales is required to earn twice as much as the fixed costs per month before taxes?

24-A2. Breakeven Point—Impact of Changes. Plastic Stamping, Inc., feels that it can improve upon last year's results, from which the following data were selected, by decreasing the selling price 10%, increasing fixed costs by 50%, and decreasing variable costs per unit by 30%:

Total sales (units)	15,750
Selling price per unit	$ 15
Variable costs per unit	$ 10
Total fixed costs	$50,000

Required

a. Calculate the breakeven point (in both units and sales dollars) for the company existing before and after the proposed changes.
b. If sales volume increases 15% as management expects, based on the price reduction, what will Plastic Stamping's income before taxes be? What was Plastic Stamping's before-tax income last year?
c. Does it appear that the proposed changes will improve the company's performance?

24-A3. Comparative PV Charting. Wisco Company sells a single product with a selling price of $31.25. Variable costs per unit are $18.75, and total fixed costs are $125,000. Sales for the current year are $937,500. In an attempt to increase net earnings, the company is considering several alternatives.

Required

Prepare a CVP and PV chart for each situation and discuss the implications of each alternative on the company's breakeven point and net income.

a. Decrease the selling price to $25 per unit in an attempt to increase sales by 20%.
b. Increase the advertising budget by $37,500. If it chooses this alternative, sales are expected to increase by 15%.
c. Decrease the variable costs per unit by 10%.

24-A4. Profit and Cash Breakeven Points. Operating data for four selected companies are as follows:

	H Company	I Company	J Company	K Company
Sales	$140,000	?	?	$40,000
Variable costs	?	?	$ 60,000	?
Fixed costs	?	$90,000	$ 70,000	?
Net income (loss)	$ (4,000)	$36,000	$ 20,000	$ 5,000
Depreciation expense	$ 10,000	$ 0		$ 5,000
Breakeven point (units)	?	?	38,889	?
Cash breakeven point ($)	?	?	$104,167	?
Units sold	3,000	20,000	?	?
Unit contribution margin	$ 20.00	?	$ 1.80	$ 5.00
Contribution margin ratio	?	.70	?	.50

Required

Complete the information for each company.

24-A5. Breakeven and Margin of Safety. The following is the financial projection for 1986 for the Full Ton Company:

Full Ton Company
Financial Projection for Production USA
For Year Ending December 31, 1986

Sales (100 units at $100 a unit)		$10,000
Manufacturing cost of goods sold		
Direct labor	$1,500	
Direct materials used	1,400	
Variable factory overhead	1,000	
Fixed factory overhead	500	
Total manufacturing cost of goods sold		4,400
		$ 5,600
Gross profit		
Selling expenses		
Variable	600	
Fixed	1,000	
Administrative expenses		
Variable	500	
Fixed	1,000	
Total selling and administrative expenses		3,100
Operating income		$ 2,500

Required

a. How many units of the product would have to be sold to break even?
b. What would the operating income be if sales increase by 25%?
c. What would be the margin of safety if fixed factory overhead increases by $1,700?

24-A6. Impact of Changes and Sensitivity Analysis. The Marathon Shoe Company sells just one specialty jogging and running shoe. In 1986 it sold 21,000 pairs at $69 per pair. The variable costs for each pair are $41, of which $25 is manufacturing cost and $16 is a selling expense. The company incurred fixed costs of $520,800 during 1986 ($390,600 for manufacturing and $130,200 for selling and administrative).

Required

a. Determine the breakeven point in units and dollar sales.
b. What was the after-tax income in 1986 if the company's income tax rate was 40%?
c. Compute the approximate number of pairs of shoes that must be sold to break even if payroll costs are 60% of variable costs and 25% of fixed costs and wages and salaries are increased by 10%.
d. How sensitive is the breakeven point to the 10% wage and salary increase?
e. How many pairs of shoes would the company have to sell to maintain its after-tax profit of 1986 if the wage and salary increase of 10% were to go into effect?

24-A7. Decision Making with CVP Data. The Play Rite Company is a small manufacturer of sporting goods. Sales and cost data for last year are as follows:

Sales	$225,000
Variable costs	35% of sales
Fixed costs	$117,000

Required

a. Compute the sales level at which Play Rite will break even.
b. What margin of safety did the Play Rite Company operate at last year?
c. Last year the company had an offer from a discount retailer in Asia for the purchase of 600 tennis rackets at a price of $30 per racket. The sales manager refused the offer, because the same racket was sold to other U.S. retailers for $45 per unit. Given that the company had enough spare capacity to fill this order and the variable costs of manufacturing a racket are $24, should Play Rite have accepted the offer? Compute the net income before tax for last year for the offer's being rejected and for the offer's being accepted.

24-A8. Full-Absorption Costing Versus Direct Costing. A corporation finds it costs $2.50 in direct materials, $1.50 in direct labor, $.15 in variable overhead, and $.50 in fixed overhead (based on a normal volume of 200,000 units of output per month) to produce a single unit of finished product. Selling and administrative costs (all fixed) are $10,000 per month. The selling price of the product is $6.50 per unit.

Required

Assuming a beginning inventory of 20,000 units, production of 200,000 units, and sales of 180,000 units, prepare the corporation's income statement for the month under the full-absorption costing format and under the variable (direct) costing format.

PROBLEM SET B

24-B1. Breakeven Analysis. S.S.C. Corporation sells books at a price of $35 per volume. At a sales level of 1,000 books, total costs are $15,000; at a sales level of 5,000 books, total costs are $35,000.

Required

Calculate each of the following:
a. Total fixed costs (you can assume all fixed costs are cash expense items).
b. The variable costs per unit sold.
c. The contribution margin per unit.
d. The contribution margin ratio.
e. The breakeven point in terms of units.
f. The breakeven point in terms of sales dollars.
g. The monthly net income before taxes at the current sales volume of 5,600 books per month.

24-B2. Breakeven Point—Impact of Changes. The Upstar Corporation had a bad year and incurred a loss of $6,000 on sales of $120,000 as follows:

Sales, 7,500 units at $16/unit	$120,000
Less variable costs	90,000
Contribution margin	30,000
Less fixed costs (including depreciation)	36,000
Net loss	$ (6,000)

Required

a. Compute the company's breakeven point in both units and sales dollars.
b. The marketing manager believes that a 5% reduction in selling price coupled with a $4,000 increase in the advertising budget will increase unit sales by 80%. Compute the profit (loss) if this proposal is accepted.
c. The production manager proposes that new equipment be purchased that would reduce variable costs per unit by 10% but would increase depreciation expenses from $5,600 per year to $6,800 per year. How would income change if this plan were implemented?
d. Assuming that both proposals are reliable, what would your suggestion to Upstar's management be?
e. Refer to the original income statement. Ms. Newsome of Research and Development thinks that sales could be improved by repackaging the product. If repackaging will increase the cost by $0.20 per unit, how many units would have to be sold per year to break even?

24-B3. Comparative PV Charting. Fixit Manufacturing Company, whose plant is mostly manual, has a net income of $2,000 per month at maximum production capacity as follows:

Sales revenue	$20,000
Variable costs	(16,000)
Contribution margin	4,000
Fixed costs	(2,000)
Net income	$ 2,000

The vice president in charge of operations projects an increase of 50% in sales if production capacity is expanded. Management is considering a plan to double the present capacity by automating its production plant. If the plan is adopted, fixed costs would increase by $6,000 per month and the variable costs per unit would be reduced by 75%.

Required

Prepare a PV chart comparing the profit patterns under each method. What is your recommendation to Fixit management?

24-B4. Profit and Cash Breakeven Points. Operating data for four selected companies are as follows:

	W Company	X Company	Y Company	Z Company
Sales	$270,000	?	?	$160,000
Variable costs	?	?	$ 80,000	?
Fixed costs	?	$37,500	$ 70,000	?
Net income (loss)	$ 45,000	$22,500	$ 50,000	$ (30,000)
Depreciation expense	$ 15,000	$ 0	?	$ 12,000
Breakeven point (units)	?	?	7,000	?
Cash breakeven point ($)	?	?	$110,000	?
Units sold	30,000	5,000	?	?
Unit contribution margin	$ 3.00	?	$ 10.00	$ 7.20
Contribution margin ratio	?	.40	?	.45

Required

Complete the information for each company.

24-B5. Breakeven and Margin of Safety. In a recent period, Zero Company had the following experience:

	Fixed	Variable	
Sales (10,000 units @ $200/unit)			$2,000,000
Costs			
Direct materials		$ 200,000	
Direct labor		400,000	
Factory overhead	$160,000	600,000	
Administrative expenses	180,000	80,000	
Other expenses	200,000	120,000	
	$540,000	$1,400,000	1,940,000
			$ 60,000

Required

a. Calculate the breakeven point for Zero in terms of units and sales dollars.
b. What sales volume would be required to generate an after-tax profit of $96,000? Assume a 20% tax rate.
c. What is the margin of safety if management makes a decision that increases fixed costs by $18,000?

24-B6. Impact of Changes and Sensitivity Analysis. Courtland Company produced the following results during 1986:

Total sales	36,000 units
Selling price per unit	$36
Total fixed costs	$120,000
Total variable costs	$252,000

In 1987 the company plans to reduce the costs of raw materials, reduce the selling price, and engage in an extensive advertising campaign of one of its major products. The following changes are expected:

1. Selling price will be reduced to $29.85.
2. Variable costs per unit will amount to $19.50.
3. Fixed costs will increase by $30,000.

Required

a. What is the breakeven point for the company in terms of dollars before the proposed changes? After the changes?
b. What is the breakeven point in terms of units before the changes? After the changes?
c. Draw a CVP chart for present conditions and proposed conditions.

24-B7. Decision Making with CVP Data. Operating data for the Apex Corporation are sales, $400,000; fixed costs, $80,000; variable costs, $200,000; and net earnings, $120,000. Management is considering a plant expansion project that is estimated to increase sales by a maximum of $300,000. The plant has a useful life of 20 years and a $100,000 residual value. The original cost of the plant was one million dollars. The proposed addition will increase the company's fixed costs by $160,000 per year.

Required

As a consultant to Apex Corporation, would you recommend that the proposed expansion be undertaken? Support your answer with a PV chart and computations.

24-B8. Full-Absorption Costing Versus Direct Costing. A corporation finds it costs $5.00 in direct materials, $3.00 in direct labor, and $1.25 in variable overhead to produce a single unit of finished product. Selling and administrative costs (all fixed) are $15,500 per month. The selling price of the product is $14.50 per unit.

Assuming a beginning inventory of 10,000 units, production of 150,000 units (the normal volume), and sales of 155,000 units for the current month, the corporation's accountant has calculated that income under variable costing will be $10,000 greater than income under full-absorption costing.

Required

Calculate the following:

a. The fixed overhead costs per finished unit and the total budgeted amount of fixed overhead for the month.

b. Net income under full-absorption costing.

c. Net income under variable (direct) costing.

DECISION MAKING WITH A LOOK AT THE IMPACT OF TAXES

CHAPTER OBJECTIVES

After studying Chapter 25, you should understand the following:

1. How to recognize relevant costs.
2. How to examine the effect of taxation on cost decisions.

A common feature of managing is the need to make nonroutine, short-term decisions, frequently with the aid of cost-volume-profit (CVP) techniques. In such instances, the time factor is too brief for making major resolutions regarding existing equipment or the capacity of the factory. Short-term decisions often test management's ability to bring in the highest profit using the firm's current resources. Capital budgeting decisions, which generally require more extensive planning and a larger investment, are capable of affecting operations for many years; these decisions are examined in Chapter 26.

DECISION-MAKING CONCEPTS

DIFFERENTIAL ANALYSIS
An examination of the divergences in expected revenues and costs of two alternatives.

INCREMENTAL ANALYSIS
See differential analysis.

Differential, or **incremental, analysis** spotlights divergences in the expected revenues and costs of two alternatives. Differential revenue is the difference between the revenues of the two alternatives being considered; differential cost is the deviation between the costs of the two alternatives. These concepts can best be explained with the help of an illustration.

Suppose a company has the option of producing and selling one of two products: bicycles or tricycles. Yearly revenue from bicycles is expected to be $300,000; tricycles potentially will earn $180,000. Anticipated costs are $180,000 and $90,000, respectively. Which product should be produced?

	Bicycles	Tricycles	Difference
Projected revenue	$300,000	$180,000	$120,000
Projected costs	(180,000)	(90,000)	(90,000)
Net earnings	$120,000	$ 90,000	$ 30,000

The computations indicate that bicycles would be more profitable and should therefore be produced. Looking in this way at both products before deciding is called the total approach, since all the information about each product is compiled, even if doing so includes some of the same costs under each alternative.

On the other hand, the decision makers could view one of the two alternatives as an anchor point and compare the other to it. In this case, let us make bicycles the anchor product. Production of tricycles would reduce revenues from those predicted for bicycles by $120,000, but costs would drop by only $90,000. Thus, net earnings would be lower by $30,000. This computation can be observed in the last column, which concentrates only on the differences between the two products, and is called differential analysis or incremental analysis. In business decisions, only differential costs are relevant. Focusing on differential costs avoids involvement with items not affected by the outcome of this decision-making process and is especially valuable when the information needed under the total approach is incomplete.

Decision Situations

Qualitative or subjective factors certainly are important in decision making, but they are beyond the scope of this section. Because this discussion concentrates only on quantitative factors, when comparing the two alternatives, we will automatically recommend the path towards the greatest net earnings or smallest cost. In reality, however, management might rate other considerations highly and select a relatively unprofitable course that scores well on other accounts.

This discussion will analyze the following various decision situations:

1. Shutdown point determination.
2. Addition or elimination of a product line or a department.
3. Make-or-buy decisions.
4. Special orders and utilization of capacity.
5. Joint products.
6. Maximization of contribution margin from use of scarce resources.

Shutdown Point Determination. Sometimes the only viable options available to management are continuing production or closing the factory. Such a situation arises when a company cannot generate enough money to cover its fixed costs. The **shutdown point** is the level of activity at which the company becomes indifferent to either continuing operations or closing down. In other words, it is the point at which the same amount of money would be lost whether the factory is shut down or kept running. The following example illustrates this concept.

SHUTDOWN POINT
The level of activity at which the company becomes indifferent to either continuing operations or closing down.

A company sells 20,000 units per year at a selling price of $10 per unit. The variable cost per unit (including materials and labor) is $7, and the yearly fixed costs are $40,000. Of these fixed costs, $30,000 is directly attributable to production and is avoidable should no production occur. The remaining $10,000 is unavoidable and will be incurred whether or not the factory produces. These unavoidable costs are not differential and thus are not relevant to our decision.

The company's shutdown point can be found based on the preceding facts. Let X represent the number of units at the shutdown point. Then, using this formula relationship, the point of indifference can be calculated as the point where profit equals zero.

$$\begin{aligned} \text{Sales} - \text{Variable costs} - \text{Avoidable fixed costs} &= \text{Incremental profit/loss} \\ \$10X - \$7X - \$30{,}000 &= 0 \\ \$3X &= \$30{,}000 \\ X &= 10{,}000 \text{ units} \end{aligned}$$

If the firm can expect to sell more than 10,000 units yearly, running the production line would be preferred. Every unit above 10,000 will contribute $3 toward the $10,000 of unavoidable fixed costs. However, if sales are expected to be under 10,000 units, rational judgment would advise temporarily shutting down the factory to minimize the loss caused by not covering fixed costs. For example, if only 8,000 units were sold, the firm would generate a loss of $16,000 (sales of $80,000 less variable costs of $56,000 and fixed costs of $40,000), which is $6,000 more than the loss of $10,000 that would occur if production ceased.

Addition or Elimination of a Product Line or Department. Situations in which a product line is evaluated for adoption or discontinuation often differ only in size and complexity from decisions regarding opening or eliminating an entire branch or department. Let us look here at a relatively uncomplicated decision.

Assume that a company manufactures and sells wagons and wheelbarrows. The segmented earnings statement for the past year is as follows:

	Total		Wagon Division		Wheelbarrow Division	
s		$ 350,000		$ 200,000		$150,000
st of sales						
Direct materials and labor	$(120,000)		$(70,000)		$(50,000)	
Variable overhead	(45,000)		(30,000)		(15,000)	
Fixed overhead	(75,000)	(240,000)	(50,000)	(150,000)	(25,000)	(90,000)
Gross margin		$ 110,000		$ 50,000		$ 60,000
Operating expenses						
Variable	$(35,000)		$(20,000)		$(15,000)	
Fixed	(65,000)	(100,000)	(40,000)	(60,000)	(25,000)	(40,000)
Net earnings (loss)		$ 10,000		$ (10,000)		$ 20,000

On first glance at the earnings statement, the wagon division seems to be losing money and looks as if it should be discontinued. This line of reasoning presumes that with elimination of wagons the loss of $10,000 will vanish and result in an increase in the company's net earnings to $20,000 (representing the $20,000 earned by the wheelbarrow division). However, for the loss of $10,000 to disappear, all the revenues and costs relating to the wagon division would have to evaporate. Expecting revenues and variable costs to fade is reasonable, but all the fixed costs (allocated on the basis of an appropriate activity base) will not disappear. Only direct fixed costs can be eliminated.

To make a correct decision, the information must be recast into a segment margin statement, based on the principles of CVP analysis and direct costing. To continue our example, assume that $30,000 and $15,000 represent the direct elements of the fixed overhead costs for the wagon division and the wheelbarrow division, respectively. Now, should wagons be dropped?

	Total		Wagon Division		Wheelbarrow Division	
Sales		$ 350,000		$ 200,000		$150,000
Variable costs						
Materials and labor	$(120,000)		$(70,000)		$(50,000)	
Variable overhead	(45,000)		(30,000)		(15,000)	
Variable operating expenses	(35,000)	(200,000)	(20,000)	(120,000)	(15,000)	(80,000)
Contribution margin		$ 150,000		$ 80,000		$ 70,000
Direct fixed costs		(45,000)		(30,000)		(15,000)
Segment margin		$ 105,000		$ 50,000		$ 55,000
Indirect fixed costs						
Production	$(30,000)					
Operating expenses	(65,000)	(95,000)				
Net earnings		$ 10,000				

Of course, the total net earnings are the same under either method of presentation. However, the preceding statement shows segment contribution margins of $50,000 and $55,000. Such margins represent earnings that are direct to each product and that would disappear if the product line were discontinued. Utilizing direct costing principles, the indirect, or common, fixed costs have not been allocated but are considered a period cost to be borne by the company as a whole.

To conclude, the company would be unwise to discontinue production of wagons, because the segment margin of $50,000 would then be unrealized. As the following statement shows, without the wagon division a net loss of $40,000 would arise, since the segment margin from the wheelbarrow division would not cover the entire common fixed costs of $95,000.

Total earnings, without the wagon division

Sales		$ 150,000
Variable costs		
Materials	$(50,000)	
Variable overhead	(15,000)	
Variable operating expenses	(15,000)	(80,000)
Contribution margin		70,000
Fixed costs		
Direct	$(15,000)	
Indirect	(95,000)	(110,000)
Net earnings		$(40,000)

Actually, the wagon division's segment margin aids substantially in covering the common fixed costs. Note that even a segment margin of one dollar should encourage continuing production of wagons because one dollar is better than the segment margin if wagons should be discontinued.

Make-or-Buy Decisions. Normally a company is willing to purchase a component that it can also produce if the purchase price is less than the cost to manufacture. Qualitative factors such as the reliability of a new supplier or the danger of being too dependent on one supplier certainly are pertinent to the final decision. Such factors, however, must be analyzed on a single-decision basis. Therefore, we will illustrate here only the objective portion involved in a make-or-buy decision.

For example, a company manufactures 20,000 electrical components annually to use in the production of its end product. These components are manufactured in Factory West at a variable production cost of $7. The fixed cost of operating the factory is $200,000, of which $80,000 is fixed cost direct to the production of the components. No use for Factory West currently exists if electrical components are not produced there.

Now the company has received an outside offer to be supplied with 20,000 of these electrical components yearly at a purchase price of $12 each. Should the company make or purchase the components? Let's examine the alternatives.

Option—Make 20,000 components annually	
Variable production costs ($7 × 20,000 units)	$140,000
Fixed costs	200,000
Total cost	$340,000
Option—Purchase 20,000 components annually	
Purchase price ($12 × 20,000 units)	$240,000
Indirect fixed costs ($200,000 − $80,000)	120,000
Total cost	$360,000

Our results show that the make option is less expensive than the purchase option by $20,000 ($360,000 − $340,000). As illustrated, common fixed costs of $120,000 have been added to the purchase-option price because although Factory West would be closed, it would still incur these expenses. Hence, the purchase-option price would include a cost of $120,000, representing unavoidable common fixed costs.

Another way to view this decision is to compare the costs eliminated with a purchase decision to the costs of purchasing. In the preceding situation, by purchasing the components, direct costs totaling $220,000 ($7 × 20,000 units + $80,000) would be eliminated if $240,000 is spent. Such a decision seems unwise.

Special Orders and Utilization of Capacity. Since fixed costs do not vary within a relevant range of activity, concluding that management cannot control them in the short run is reasonable. Management's first hope is to produce as much as possible, to earn enough contribution margin to cover fixed costs, and, perhaps, to earn a profit. This maxim sums up why Japan, with its heavy fixed-cost burden of life-term employee contracts, must produce to capacity, exporting its surplus production.

Recognizing the importance of using existing capacity, all companies would like to operate at that level. However, production can be restricted by a number of factors, one of which is a limited demand for the product. Under such circumstances, the company should be willing to temporarily lease out, so to speak, its unused capacity by accepting special orders, subcontracts, and the like. Let's look closer at a special-order decision.

A company manufactures trophies in a factory having a yearly capacity of 50,000 units. The company currently produces 45,000 units each year to meet expected demand. The selling price per trophy is $10; the variable cost is $6. The company's fixed costs per year are expected to total $186,000. A new customer wishes to make a one-time purchase of 3,000 trophies at $7 and wants the units embossed in a particular manner. The mold for such embossing would cost $2,000 and would be discarded when the job is done. Should the special order be accepted?

If we solve the problem using the total approach, the options of rejecting the special order or accepting it must be considered in their entirety. The computations are as follows:

Option—Reject special order		
Sales (45,000 units × $10)		$450,000
Variable costs (45,000 units × $6)		(270,000)
Contribution margin		$180,000
Fixed costs		(186,000)
Net earnings/(loss)		$ (6,000)
Option—Accept special order		
Sales (45,000 units × $10)	$ 450,000	
(3,000 units × $7)	21,000	$471,000
Variable costs (48,000 units × $6)		(288,000)
Contribution margin		$183,000
Fixed costs	$(186,000)	
Cost of mold	(2,000)	(188,000)
Net earnings/(loss)		$ (5,000)

At first sight, the option of rejecting the special order and maintaining the present earnings situation is tempting. After all, the company is already losing $6,000 with the selling price at $10 per unit; additional sales at a price of $7 seem disadvantageous. However, the special order should be accepted, since it reduces the loss by $1,000 ($6,000 − $5,000). Let's examine the special order again using differential analysis.

Increase in revenue ($7 × 3,000 units)	$21,000
Increase in variable costs ($6 × 3,000 units)	(18,000)
Increase in contribution margin	$ 3,000
Increase in fixed costs	(2,000)
Increase in net earnings	$ 1,000

A special order usually should be accepted if the increase in revenue exceeds the additional variable and fixed costs, resulting in an increase in net earnings. Reasoning such as this is used by many companies that have idle time or facilities. For example, some companies use their excess capacity to manufacture items such as refrigerators or tents on specifications outlined by Sears and then sell the goods to Sears. Another example is popular magazines such as *Time* and *Newsweek,* which offer new subscriptions at half the newsstand prices. The magazine publishers can afford to do so, since the prices have to cover only the additional variable costs of producing and sending out a magazine. No additional cost is incurred to compile the subject matter of the magazine, since that cost is sunk and will not vary if one more copy is sold.

The special-order decision previously described concerned the use of excess capacity. The opportunity cost of this decision was zero and was correctly ignored. However, a situation might be encountered where the special order calls for a quantity that is greater than available capacity. To illustrate, we will modify the earlier problem by assuming that the special order is for 8,000 trophies at $9. An additional stipulation is that the special order should be accepted in its entirety or not at all. Should the special order be accepted under these conditions?

If the special order is not accepted, the company's net loss would remain at $6,000 as computed earlier. Accepting the order, however, would yield a net profit of $4,000 as follows:

Option—Accept special order		
Sales (42,000 units × $10)	$420,000	
(8,000 units × $9)	72,000	$ 492,000
Variable costs (50,000 units × $6)		(300,000)
Contribution margin		$ 192,000
Fixed costs	$(186,000)	
Additional cost of mold	(2,000)	(188,000)
Net earnings		$ 4,000

Note that only 42,000 trophies can be sold to regular customers; this figure is calculated by deducting the 8,000-unit special order from the 50,000-unit capacity. If the special order is accepted, the company will forfeit the opportunity to sell 3,000 trophies (45,000 − 42,000) to its regular customers. However, the special order is enticing; profits would increase by $10,000, from a $6,000 loss to a $4,000 profit. This increase can be probed further using differential analysis.

Increase in revenue (8,000 units × $9)	$ 72,000
Increase in variable costs (8,000 units × $6)	(48,000)
Increase in contribution margin	$ 24,000
Increase in fixed costs	(2,000)
Increase in net earnings from selling 8,000 units on special order	$ 22,000
Less: Opportunity cost, which equals the contribution margin lost on 3,000 units (3,000 units × $4)	(12,000)
Increase in net earnings	$ 10,000

The special order would draw $22,000 to the company. In terms of contribution margins, the $22,000 is the 8,000 trophies at $3 ($9 − $6) less the $2,000 direct fixed costs. However, to produce the special order, the company could provide only 42,000 units to its regular customers. This circumstance forces the company to reduce its planned sales by 3,000 units and to lose a contribution margin of $4 on each unit ($10 − $6), a total opportunity cost of $12,000. The difference between $22,000 coming in and the $12,000 sacrificed should cause management to accept the order.

Speculation can arise on the advisability of sacrificing sales to hard-earned and valued customers in favor of a one-time transaction. Various reasons might exist for such a move, one being management's expectation that a more permanent relationship will develop with the new client. On the other hand, a company might relinquish such a profit if its old customers are valued at a price above $10,000.

JOINT PRODUCTS
Different products that are the result of processing a single raw material.

SPLIT-OFF POINT
The point at which joint products reveal themselves as separate substances.

JOINT COSTS
All processing costs up to the split-off point.

Joint Products. When the processing of a raw material results in several distinct end products, the end products are called **joint products.** Examples of joint products are the different types of meat obtained from the slaughter of livestock and the various chemicals derived from crude oil. The point at which the joint products reveal themselves as separate substances is called the **split-off point,** and all processing costs up to then are called **joint costs.**

Although accountants attempt to allocate joint costs to the end products for financial statement purposes, management has little control over the cost of the process other than determining if it is economical. The joint products coming out of the processing must sell for more than production costs. Once the joint products have separated, management normally has two choices: to sell at the split-off point or to process further and sell later. Essentially, our next problem is concerned with such a decision—when to sell the products from a joint process.

Let us assume that three principal products—bread, doughnuts, and doughnut holes—result from a joint process. These products can be sold as frozen dough at split-off or processed and sold ready-to-eat. The relevant information regarding their selling prices and costs is as follows:

Product	Selling Price Per Case at Split-off	Variable Processing Cost Per Case After Split-off	Selling Price Per Case After Processing
Bread	$15	$ 8	$25
Doughnuts	12	10	20
Doughnut holes	3	8	9

The decision can be formed easily if the preceding information is tabulated as follows:

	Bread	Doughnuts	Doughnut Holes
Selling price per case after processing	$25	$20	$ 9
Selling price per case at split-off point	(15)	(12)	(3)
Increase in revenue after processing	10	8	6
Additional processing costs per case	(8)	(10)	(8)
Increase/(decrease) in contribution margin from additional processing	$ 2	$ (2)	$ (2)

Bread should be processed before selling, because incremental revenue per case ($10) exceeds the incremental costs ($8). On the other hand, management would prefer to sell both doughnuts and doughnut holes at the split-off point, since $2 is lost on each case by processing further.

In conclusion, processing should be completed only if the increase in revenue is greater than the additional processing costs. Additionally, such a decision should be reviewed periodically. Many joint products, such as crude oil wastes which at one time were thrown away, are now being processed for sale, since the revenues have climbed high enough to justify the cost of further processing.

Maximization of Contribution Margin from Use of Scarce Resources. This section relies on the reasoning used in the section on special orders but now within the context of limited production facilities. In the situations that we now examine, the scarce resources could be a material, such as oil, or labor, perhaps skilled computer technicians; and the company must try to maximize its earnings by using scarce resources in the most effective manner. An example should make the point.

The following information relates to three products—irons, toasters, and coffee makers—that can be produced in the company's factory:

	Irons	Toasters	Coffee Makers
Potential sales (units)	10,000	12,000	16,000
Selling price per unit	$17	$25	$26
Direct materials cost per unit	$ 6	$ 8	$ 7
Direct labor cost per unit	$ 5	$10	$10
Other variable costs per unit	$ 3	$ 5	$ 5
Expected direct labor hours needed per unit	1	2	2

The company's production is limited to 14,000 direct labor hours. Which products and how much of each should be produced?

First, the contribution margin per unit must be computed and converted into a measure of the contribution margin per unit of scarce resource—direct labor hours in this case. This computation can be shown as follows:

	Irons		Toasters		Coffee Makers	
Selling price per unit		$ 17		$ 25		$ 26
Variable costs per unit						
Direct materials	$(6)		$ (8)		$ (7)	
Direct labor	(5)		(10)		(10)	
Other	(3)	(14)	(5)	(23)	(5)	(22)
Contribution margin per unit		$ 3		$ 2		$ 4
Labor hours used		1		2		2
Contribution margin per labor hour		$ 3		$ 1		$ 2

Since the company's production is limited to the use of 14,000 direct labor hours, management should choose the most profitable option based on labor hours. Irons have the greatest contribution margin per labor hour, which means that utilization of one direct labor hour earns the company $3 on each unit, whereas toasters and coffee makers contribute only $1 and $2 per labor hour, respectively. The production schedule logically would be as follows:

Total direct labor hours available	14,000
Less: Production of irons	
(1 hour × 10,000 units)	(10,000)
Hours available	4,000
Less: Production of coffee makers	
(2 hours × 2,000 units)	(4,000)
Hours available	0

This schedule calls for a full output of 10,000 irons and uses the remaining 4,000 labor hours to manufacture the next most profitable product—coffee makers. The purpose of the analysis is to maximize the contribution margin when one or more of the production ingredients are in short supply. Note that if no scarcity of direct labor had hampered production, the company should have produced as many coffee makers as it could sell for full price. This strategy would realize up to $64,000 ($4 contribution margin × 16,000 units to be sold), whereas the full sales potential of irons would be limited to $30,000 ($3 contribution margin × 10,000 units to be sold).

CONCEPT SUMMARY 25.1 IMPACT OF VARIOUS COSTS ON DECISIONS

Type of Cost	Definition	Decision Impact
Direct	Cost that would not exist if cost center were eliminated.	Must be considered to determine cost center contribution margin.
Indirect (common)	Cost that cannot be assigned to a specific cost center.	Does not affect contribution margins of cost centers. Does not automatically disappear if cost center is eliminated.
Joint	Processing cost preceding the identification of separable products.	None. Processing costs after split-off are pertinent.
Opportunity	Cost of abandoning next best alternative.	Must be evaluated at every choice.
Sunk	Cost from which benefit is used up or to which firm is essentially committed.	None (other than subjective considerations).

EFFECT OF INCOME TAXES ON BUSINESS DECISIONS

Managerial decision making is impacted heavily by the effects of the federal income tax. Although income taxes were levied sporadically during the nineteenth century, they evolved into a regular feature of American life in 1913 when the Sixteenth Amendment gave Congress the power to levy income taxes. Initially, the tax rates were quite low: The maximum was seven percent. The main purpose of the tax was to raise enough money to run the government, an extremely small amount compared to the needs of modern bureaucracy. As the government took on additional responsibilities such as welfare and Medicare, more funds were needed. Therefore, taxes historically have increased—so much so that the maximum tax rate on income climbed to 70 percent during taxable years before 1982, when the maximum rate dropped to 50 percent.

Entities Subject to the Income Tax

Income taxes normally are payable by individuals, corporations, estates, and trusts. For our purposes here, we'll examine the first two types of taxpayers. An individual must pay income tax on his or her earnings, salary, profits from business, interest income, and like items based on the progressive rates prescribed by the government. Progressive rates require a taxpayer with a large income to pay a higher percentage of those earnings in taxes than a taxpayer with a small income. For a partner in a firm, the individual's share of the partnership profits, whether withdrawn from the business or not, is taxable as personal income. The partnership itself does not pay any income tax. Rates vary depending upon the status of the individual (see Exhibit 25.1).

EXHIBIT 25.1

Individuals—1985 Tax Rate Schedules

SCHEDULE X—Single Taxpayers

If taxable income is: Over—	but not over—	The tax is:	of the amount over—
$0	$2,390	—0—	
2,390	3,540	—— 11%	$2,390
3,540	4,580	$126.50 + 12%	3,540
4,580	6,760	251.30 + 14%	4,580
6,760	8,850	556.50 + 15%	6,760
8,850	11,240	870.00 + 16%	8,850
11,240	13,430	1,252.40 + 18%	11,240
13,430	15,610	1,646.60 + 20%	13,430
15,610	18,940	2,082.60 + 23%	15,610
18,940	24,460	2,848.50 + 26%	18,940
24,460	29,970	4,283.70 + 30%	24,460
29,970	35,490	5,936.70 + 34%	29,970
35,490	43,190	7,813.50 + 38%	35,490
43,190	57,550	10,739.50 + 42%	43,190
57,550	85,130	16,770.70 + 48%	57,550
85,130	——	30,009.10 + 50%	85,130

SCHEDULE Z—Heads of Household

If taxable income is: Over	but not over—	The tax is:	of the amount over—
$0	$2,390	—0—	
2,390	4,580	—— 11%	$2,390
4,580	6,760	$240.90 + 12%	4,580
6,760	9,050	502.50 + 14%	6,760
9,050	12,280	823.10 + 17%	9,050
12,280	15,610	1,372.20 + 18%	12,280
15,610	18,940	1,971.60 + 20%	15,610
18,940	24,460	2,637.60 + 24%	18,940
24,460	29,970	3,962.40 + 28%	24,460
29,970	35,490	5,505.20 + 32%	29,970
35,490	46,520	7,271.60 + 35%	35,490
46,520	63,070	11,132.10 + 42%	46,520
63,070	85,130	18,083.10 + 45%	63,070
85,130	112,720	28,010.10 + 48%	85,130
112,720	——	41,253.30 + 50%	112,720

(continued on next page)

EXHIBIT 25.1
Continued

SCHEDULE Y—Married Taxpayers and Qualifying Widows and Widowers

Married Filing Joint Returns and Qualifying Widows and Widowers				**Married Filing Separate Returns**			
If taxable income is:		**The tax is:**		**If taxable income is:**		**The tax is:**	
Over—	but not over—		of the amount over—	Over—	but not over—		of the amount over—
$0	$3,540	—0—		$0	$1,770	—0—	
3,540	5,720	—— 11%	$3,540	1,770	2,860	—— 11%	1,770
5,720	7,910	$239.80 + 12%	5,720	2,860	3,955	$119.90 + 12%	2,860
7,910	12,390	502.60 + 14%	7,910	3,955	6,195	251.30 + 14%	3,955
12,390	16,650	1,129.80 + 16%	12,390	6,195	8,325	564.90 + 16%	6,195
16,650	21,020	1,811.40 + 18%	16,650	8,325	10,510	905.70 + 18%	8,325
21,020	25,600	2,598.00 + 22%	21,020	10,510	12,800	1,299.00 + 22%	10,510
25,600	31,120	3,605.60 + 25%	25,600	12,800	15,560	1,802.80 + 25%	12,800
31,120	36,630	4,985.60 + 28%	31,120	15,560	18,315	2,492.80 + 28%	15,560
36,630	47,670	6,528.40 + 33%	36,630	18,315	23,835	3,264.20 + 33%	18,315
47,670	62,450	10,171.60 + 38%	47,670	23,835	31,225	5,085.80 + 38%	23,835
62,450	89,090	15,788.00 + 42%	62,450	31,225	44,545	7,894.00 + 42%	31,225
89,090	113,860	26,976.80 + 45%	89,090	44,545	56,930	13,488.40 + 45%	44,545
113,860	169,020	38,123.30 + 49%	113,860	56,930	84,510	19,061.65 + 49%	56,930
169,020	——	65,151.70 + 50%	169,020	84,510	——	32,575.85 + 50%	84,510

A corporation, unlike a partnership or a sole proprietorship, is considered a taxable entity. Tax is levied on its earned income with progressive rates as shown in Exhibit 25.2.

EXHIBIT 25.2

Taxable Income	Rate
Up to $ 25,000	15%
$25,001–$ 50,000	18%
$50,001–$ 75,000	30%
$75,001–$100,000	40%
Above $100,000	46%

The following example illustrates how the tax for corporations is computed. Assume that a corporation has a taxable income of $300,000. We must figure the tax payable using an incremental approach.

Income		Rate	Tax
On the first	$ 25,000	15%	$ 3,750
On the next	25,000	18%	4,500
On the next	25,000	30%	7,500
On the next	25,000	40%	10,000
On the balance	200,000	46%	92,000
Total	$300,000		$117,750

When discussing subsequent problems, we'll use only one tax rate, usually 46 percent. One reason is to simplify computations. Another is that most large corporations have taxable incomes well in excess of $100,000 per year. Any increase or decrease in taxable income will affect their taxes at the tax rate of 46 percent; that is, an increase in taxable income from $300,000 to $320,000 would increase taxes by $9,200 (46% of $20,000). The tax rate that is applied to the last dollar of taxable income earned is called the **marginal tax rate.** For a company whose taxable income is above $100,000, the marginal tax rate is 46 percent. If a firm's taxable income is only $23,000, the marginal tax rate is 15 percent.

MARGINAL TAX RATE
The tax rate that is applied to the last dollar of taxable income earned.

In addition to this tax levied on the corporation's income, individual shareholders must pay tax on dividends received from the corporation. Many investors criticize this system that taxes the same income twice, once in the hands of the corporation and again in the hands of the shareholders.

Computation of Taxable Income

Taxable income is an income figure computed in accordance with the provisions of the Internal Revenue Code. This web of law specifies what must be considered in the computation of taxable income and what can be ignored. Let us first examine the different accounting methods that can be used to compute taxable income and to consider the impact of taxation.

TAXABLE INCOME
Income computed in accordance with the provisions of the Internal Revenue Code.

Accounting Methods Used To Compute Taxable Income. The two commonly used methods of accounting for taxable income for corporations are the cash basis and the accrual basis (discussed earlier and briefly reviewed here).

1. **Cash basis of accounting.** Under this approach, revenue is considered earned when the related cash is received, and expenses are incurred when payment for them is made. This method is convenient for small businesses that do not have large amounts of receivables, payables, inventories, or fixed assets. The IRS permits use of the cash basis for tax purposes in many cases.

2. **Accrual basis of accounting.** The accrual method is considered more representative of the firm's earning process, because it does not depend on cash transactions. The IRS demands use of accrual accounting by businesses with substantial receivables, payables, or inventories.

Impact of Taxation. The impact of taxation on a corporation's income can best be illustrated by the following example. Assume that the following are summarized earnings statements of one firm with a relevant tax rate of 46 percent for three years.

($ in millions)	Year 1	Year 2	Year 3
Revenues	$100.00	$100.00	$101.00
Expenses, except tax	80.00	81.00	80.00
Net income before tax	$ 20.00	$ 19.00	$ 21.00
Tax at 46%	9.20	8.74	9.66
Net income after tax	$ 10.80	$ 10.26	$ 11.34

Comparing Years 1 and 2, revenue figures are identical, but in Year 2 expenses have increased by one million dollars. Accordingly, net income before tax has been

Apple Tries To Bite Into Taxes

Much discussion has stemmed from the 1982 proposal by Steven Jobs, co-founder of Apple Computers, Inc., to give an Apple to each of 83,000 schools in the United States. At first glance, the idea seems preposterous, but Jobs is a whiz at more than computers—he knows how to evaluate managerial problems, including the tax effects.

Some of the possible advantages of such a giveaway are as follows:

- Reportedly as much as $60 million in short-term tax advantages if Congress would pass a bill such as the Computer Contributions Bill of 1982, which would have allowed the donating firm to write off half the difference between the fair market value of the computer and the computer's actual manufacturing cost. (The cost is already deductible.)
- Increased revenues almost immediately from software, teacher training, and followup support.
- Increased revenues over the next five to ten years as Apple-trained students grow up and buy the machine with which they're already familiar.
- Advantageous locations for the old model Apple IIs as the new version is being placed in the warehouses for commercial shipment.
- A way to effectively freeze competitors from the school market—which is large—unless the competitors opt to give away computers, too.

Jobs' offer was made under the condition that the government give Apple the proposed tax break. Although the Computer Contributions Bill was passed by the House of Representatives by a huge majority in September of 1982, it was not passed by the Senate.

reduced by one million dollars, while net income after tax has been cut by only $540,000 ($10,800,000 − $10,260,000). In other words, an increase of one million dollars in expenses resulted in the reduction of income of only $540,000, since the government accepted a share (46 percent) of the additional expense—$460,000.

Similarly, looking at Years 1 and 3, we find that revenues vary by one million dollars, while expenses hold even. Results show a difference of $540,000 ($11,340,000 − $10,800,000) in net income after tax. The increase in revenue of one million dollars was shared, with $540,000 staying in the firm and the government claiming the additional $460,000 ($9,660,000 − $9,200,000).

Our conclusion must be that the government and the corporation share the corporation's profits and losses in the ratio of 46:54 when the tax rate is 46 percent. This tax effect is why the Reagan Administration wanted to make entertainment expenses (such as three-martini lunches) nondeductible (or at least partially so), as does the law in many other countries. For example, if $100 is spent on entertainment, a net cost of only $54 would be borne by the corporation if the expense were tax-deductible. Alternatively, the corporation would bear the entire cost of the $100 if the expense were not tax-deductible. As you can see, the company's desire to control costs will diminish as tax rates increase, because the government will acquire a larger proportion of each expense dollar. In other words, the actual reduction in net income caused by a one-dollar expense is $0.54 if the tax rate is 46 percent, but net income would be reduced by only $0.30 with a tax rate of 70 percent.

Tax Planning

Tax planning is a tool that seeks to minimize or defer the taxpayer's liability. To benefit from tax planning, a taxpayer arranges his or her finances to pay the least amount of tax. This procedure is called **tax avoidance.** The failure to report income earned or the inclusion of fictitious expenses or deductions when computing taxable income is called **tax evasion.** Tax avoidance is legal; tax evasion is not. In some situations, the tax effects have great importance and can influence the taxpayer's decision making. Tax planning is thus essential and some of its uses are discussed in the following paragraphs.

TAX PLANNING
A tool that seeks to minimize or defer a taxpayer's liability.

TAX AVOIDANCE
The process of arranging transactions so as to pay the least amount of tax.

TAX EVASION
Failure to report income earned or inclusion of fictitious expenses or deductions in determination of taxable income.

Form of Business Organization. When a taxpayer opens a business, he or she must determine if the business is to be a sole proprietorship, a partnership, or a corporation. Although many other factors do influence this decision, the tax treatment is especially pertinent. The following example will help our discussion.

Assume that you are starting a business that should produce an income in the range of $100,000 to $200,000. Taking $150,000 as an average amount of expected earnings, the tax that you as a single individual must pay on your business earnings differs depending upon whether the business is a sole proprietorship or a corporation, as shown in Exhibit 25.3. The tax computations for the analysis are based on the tax rate schedules found in Exhibits 25.1 and 25.2.

EXHIBIT 25.3

If organized as a sole proprietorship:	**Earnings**	**Rate**	**Tax**	**Total Tax**
Tax on	$ 85,130	from schedule	$30,009	
Tax on	64,870	at 50%	32,435	
Total	$150,000			$62,444
If organized as a corporation:				
A. Corporate tax				
Tax on first	$ 25,000	15%	$ 3,750	
Tax on next	25,000	18%	4,500	
Tax on next	25,000	30%	7,500	
Tax on next	25,000	40%	10,000	
Tax on last	50,000	46%	23,000	
Total	$150,000			$48,750
B. Individual tax on remaining profit of $101,250 ($150,000 − $48,750) distributed to owner as a dividend				
Tax on	$ 85,130	from schedule	$30,009	
Tax on	16,120	at 50%	8,060	
Total	$101,250			$38,069
Total tax if corporate organization				$86,819

The preceding computations indicate that running the business as a sole proprietorship has different tax implications from incorporating. By operating as a sole proprietor, you would get to keep $87,556 ($150,000 − 62,444). Alternatively, by incorporating, your business would have to pay $48,750 in corporate income tax. This would leave $101,250 ($150,000 − $48,750) available for distribution to the corporation shareholders. If you are the single shareholder and the entire balance of the earnings is distributed, you would owe a tax of $38,069. Barring other issues, if all earnings are distributed, operating as a sole proprietor would seem most attractive in this case.

Capital Expenditure Decisions. Taxes play a sizeable role in determining whether or not a certain asset should be purchased. This influence of taxes upon capital budgeting decisions is discussed in more detail in Chapter 26.

Debt Versus Equity. As previously explained, a company has two methods of raising funds—from outsiders (incurring liabilities) or from present or future shareholders (utilizing owners' equity). Obtaining funds from outsiders through the issuing of preferred stock or the incurring of debt provides the basis for leverage in capital financing. If the firm can obtain a higher rate of return than the rate at which it must pay interest or preferred dividends to its creditors, it has used financial leverage successfully. Although other factors also influence a debt-or-equity decision, taxes have an important impact. This point should be evident in the following example.

Assume that a company needs $2 million to finance a particularly desirable project. The finance manager has two alternatives: issuing ten-year, 15 percent bonds at par or selling 11 percent cumulative preferred stock at par. Let's assume the yearly return from the project will be $600,000 before interest and taxes and the marginal tax rate is 46 percent. We must advise the manager whether to sell stock or issue the new debt. The analysis is as follows:

	Bonds	**Preferred Stock**
Net income before interest and taxes	$600,000	$600,000
Less: Interest at 15% on $2,000,000	300,000	—
Taxable income	$300,000	$600,000
Less: Tax at 46%	138,000	276,000
Net income	$162,000	$324,000
Less: Preferred dividend at 11% on $2,000,000	—	220,000
Increase in retained earnings	$162,000	$104,000

Although the bonds carry a 15 percent interest rate and the preferred stock extends a lower 11 percent dividend commitment, the bond option benefits the firm with higher available earnings. This situation arises because the interest paid on bonds is deductible as an expense for tax purposes, and as explained earlier, the IRS picks up part of the cost of deductible expenses. On the other hand, a preferred stock dividend is a distribution of profits and is not deductible for tax purposes. Therefore, the annual interest expense would amount to an outflow of only $162,000, but the preferred dividend would draw the full $220,000 from the firm. Partly because of this tax effect, U.S. business depends heavily on debt and watches closely the escalation of interest rates.

DEMONSTRATION PROBLEM

A company has a choice of buying either of two machines for its manufacturing process. Machine A costs $100,000 and has a yearly capacity of 50,000 units. The useful life of machine A is five years, after which it will be sold for its salvage value of $20,000. Fixed costs attributable to using machine A are $200,000 a year, and variable costs are $4 per unit. Machine B costs $175,000 and has a yearly capacity of 60,000 units. Machine B is more efficient, and its variable costs are only $3.50 per unit. However, its fixed costs are $220,000 a year. Machine B has a useful life of five years and no salvage value. The unit selling price is $10, and the company can sell all it can produce. Ignore taxes and depreciation.

Required

1. Determine incremental cash flows for each machine over its useful life.
2. Determine shutdown points for each machine.
3. Why is the shutdown point higher for one machine than the other?

Demonstration Problem Solution

1.

Year 1	**Machine A**	**Machine B**
Revenues	$ 500,000	$ 600,000
Variable costs	(200,000)	(210,000)
Fixed costs	(200,000)	(220,000)
Purchase price	(100,000)	(175,000)
Cash flow	$ 0	$(5,000)
Years 2, 3, and 4	**Machine A**	**Machine B**
Revenues	$ 500,000	$ 600,000
Variable costs	(200,000)	(210,000)
Fixed costs	(200,000)	(220,000)
Cash flow each year	$ 100,000	$ 170,000
Year 5	**Machine A**	**Machine B**
Revenues	$ 500,000	$ 600,000
Variable costs	(200,000)	(210,000)
Fixed costs	(200,000)	(220,000)
Salvage value	20,000	0
Cash flow	$ 120,000	$ 170,000
Total cash flow	$ 420,000	$ 675,000

2. Machine A: $\$10X - \$4X = \$200,000$
$X = 33,333$ units

Machine B: $\$10X - \$3.5X = \$220,000$
$X = 33,846$ units

3. The shutdown point is higher for machine B, because the fixed costs are greater for that alternative.

■ SUMMARY

■ Analysis of nonroutine situations requires an understanding of differential (incremental) analysis.

■ Nonroutine situations that can be facilitated with differential analysis are shutting down a factory, dropping or adding a product, make-or-buy decisions, special orders, joint products, and the most profitable use of scarce resources.

■ Taxes normally are payable at progressive tax rates by individuals, corporations, estates, and trusts on income they earn.

■ Computation of taxable income is unlike computation of accounting income and is regulated by the Internal Revenue Code.

■ A taxpayer can legally reduce his or her taxable income and liability by tax planning. This process involves ascertaining the most favorable tax status and using the debt/equity tradeoff to advantage.

QUESTIONS

25-1. Does a partnership pay income tax? Explain.

25-2. When should a joint product be processed past the split-off point?

25-3. When is financing through debt more profitable than financing through equity?

25-4. When should a company shut down its factory?

25-5. Under what circumstances should special one-time orders be accepted?

25-6. What subjective considerations could override an objective solution to a make-or-buy decision?

25-7. Explain why corporate earnings are said to be double-taxed.

25-8. Give three examples of unavoidable fixed costs. Why would they be irrelevant to decisions regarding the future?

25-9. What is an opportunity cost? What do you estimate to be the opportunity cost you forfeit by attending college?

25-10. Why is differential analysis preferable to a decision-making approach that looks at total costs?

EXERCISES

25-E1. Using tax rates from this chapter, what is the tax liability for a single person with personal income in the following amounts? For a corporation's taxable income?

$ 20,000
$ 80,000
$135,000
$200,000

25-E2. Pipe Line Inc. processes crude oil into gasoline, motor oil, and a waste product that currently can be sold for $15 per barrel. With the increase in crude oil prices, Pipe Line Inc. believes that the waste product has become more valuable and is considering the possibility of processing it further rather than selling it as waste. Following are several products that can be made from the waste and the associated processing cost and sales price:

Product	Cost of Further Processing	Sales Price
Axle grease	$ 4 per barrel	$12 per barrel
Soap	$10 per barrel	$22 per barrel
Diesel fuel	$ 8 per barrel	$24 per barrel
Kerosene	$20 per barrel	$31 per barrel

Which products, if any, should Pipe Line begin to produce?

25-E3. A new corporation, Ramjet Robotics, needs to finance a $100,000 project. The firm is trying to decide whether to issue bonds paying 18% interest, to sell preferred stock paying an annual dividend of 12%, or to issue 1,000 shares of common stock. Prepare a schedule showing the leverage effects of these alternatives on earnings. Assume net income before interest and tax will be $25,000, the common dividend considered appropriate totals $10,000, and the tax rate is 20%.

25-E4. John American is just out of college with a degree in accounting. While attending school he was an athlete with excellent abilities and has been asked to play with a professional team for $100,000 per year. With his accounting degree, John has received an offer for a job starting at $25,000 per year. John's father, an insurance salesman, said John would be able to make up to $42,000 per year working for him.

Required

What is John's opportunity cost in the first year after graduation if he accepts the following:
a. a sports career
b. an accounting career
c. an insurance sales career

25-E5. A year ago, Universal Products installed a machine to produce widgets. The cost of the machine was $45,000; installation costs were an additional $2,500. The machine puts out 200 widgets a week at an average production cost of $12 (excluding depreciation) and is expected to be in use for a total of five years. The firm uses straight-line depreciation. Each widget sells for $20.

Recent developments in technology now make an improved widget-making machine available for $80,000. This machine, called the Beast, would produce 300 widgets per week at an average production cost of $10 per widget. The Beast has an expected life of four years. The sales department advises that the market can support this level of production at a selling price of $19 per widget. Assume production for 52 weeks per year. Should the Beast be installed at Universal? (Ignore tax considerations and depreciation.)

25-E6. Fisher Freezers sells an average of 10,000 units yearly for $600 each; the variable cost per unit is $350. The company's yearly fixed cost is $200,000, of which $40,000 is direct. What is Fisher's potential shutdown point?

25-E7. Kathy, Charlene, Pat, Marsha, and John drive together in a carpool each day to work in a town 30 miles from their homes. Each drives one day a week using his or her own car. The cost for the trip differs according to whose car is used. Estimated cost for each to drive one time roundtrip is as follows: Kathy, $4.25; Charlene, $5.00; Pat, $4.50; Marsha, $3.50;

John, $6.00. This cost is 60% for gas and oil and 40% for depreciation of car and tires. The carpool has been asked by a hometown dry cleaner to deliver some items to its branch in the other town every morning and to bring back some items every afternoon. Trunk room is ample for the deliveries, and both dry-cleaning branches are on the carpool's normal route. The dry cleaner will pay the carpool $2.00 a day to provide the delivery service. Which of the costs are relevant to the decision of whether or not to make the deliveries?

PROBLEM SET A

25-A1. Planning for Form of Organization. Phil Morris is trying to decide whether to incorporate his new business or to run it as a sole proprietorship. He expects the business to reap an annual income of $100,000 on the average. He also expects personal taxable income of $10,000 each year. Morris is married, but he files a separate tax return. If Morris incorporates, assume all earnings will be distributed to him as a dividend.

Required

How much will the savings be from one form of organization over the other? (Use the chapter's tax rates.)

25-A2. Evaluating Special Orders. Always Ready Battery Company produces and sells 300,000 batteries per year at a selling price of $20 per unit. Production costs of the batteries are $3 for direct materials; $7 for direct labor; and $1,500,000 of fixed costs, $900,000 of which is direct. The company has received an offer from a foreign retailer to purchase 25,000 units at $13 each. A special stamp would be required to engrave the name of the foreign retailer into each battery, would cost $35,000, and could be sold for $15,000 after it had been used. Always Ready Battery Company has determined that these foreign sales would not affect regular sales.

Required

Should Always Ready Battery Company accept the offer by the foreign retailer?

25-E3. Make-or-Buy Decision. Harley Company is planning to add a new line of snow removal equipment. This line, the HL-5000, will need to use a plow blade that is a different size from the blades Harley now manufactures for the currently produced HL-7500 line. Steelworks, Inc., has offered to supply the needed blades for $46.50 per blade. To produce the blades, Harley would have to retool several machines at a total cost of $2,500. Other costs that would be assigned to each blade produced would be as follows:

Direct labor	$10.00	
Raw materials	30.90	
Variable manufacturing overhead	5.20	
Fixed manufacturing overhead	3.90	($1 is direct)
Total cost per blade	$50.00	

If the blades are produced, Harley can manufacture them as needed. However, if Steelworks provides the blades, Harley must buy the entire anticipated inventory it needs of 10,000 blades and store the blades at an anticipated average cost of $30 per thousand.

Required

Should Harley buy or make the plow blades?

25-A4. Evaluating Product Lines. The joint processing done by Hippogriff Herbal Happenings produces two products: an ointment and a tea. Recently HHH has been contemplating a new product—body powder—using the same basic ingredient (known internally as the H herb). HHH also wants to reevaluate its current products in line with its current costs. Relevant information is as follows:

Product	Selling Price Per Oz. At Split-Off	Variable Processing Cost Per Oz.	Selling Price Per Oz. After Processing
Ointment	$4	$3	$10
Tea	$1	$1	$ 3
Powder	$1	$2	$ 4

The firm can produce as much of the H herb as management desires. Demand for the products is high.

Required

a. Which, if any, products should be sold at the split-off point?
b. Should the ointment and tea production continue?
c. Should production of the body powder be implemented?

25-A5. Planning for Production with Limited Resources. More-Tyme Company produces two different clock parts—faces and gears—each requiring precision work performed by machine. The one machine owned by More-Tyme is operated eight hours a day, 365 days a year. Gears require two hours of machining; faces require only one hour. Faces are made from raw materials costing $2.80 and can be sold for $5.30 each. Gears are made from raw materials costing $4 and can be sold for $10. Direct fixed costs for the firm are $2,000 per year. Due to electronics, the sales department has determined that only 800 gears can be sold this year, while a maximum of 2,000 faces can be marketed.

Required

Help More-Tyme decide what to produce this year.

25-A6. Shutdown Determination. Goes-Higher Kites can produce up to 900,000 kites per year but has recently been limited to 700,000 because of low demand. A kite requires $1 worth of raw materials and $.30 worth of direct labor and sells for $1.50. Annual fixed costs are $63,000, of which $18,000 is direct.

Required

a. If demand continues to decrease, at what point would Goes-Higher Kites be indifferent to shutting down?
b. If the sales price of the kites were reduced to $1.45 each, demand would rise to the full capacity of 900,000 kites. Would this reduction in price be beneficial to the firm?
c. An outside company offers to supply up to 900,000 kites per year at a cost of $1.39 each to Goes-Higher Kites. Should Goes-Higher accept the offer, and if so, should it sell each kite at $1.50 or $1.45?

25-A7. Machine Purchase Decision. The Ted-E-Bear Shop has been using a machine that produces 180,000 stuffed animals per year. The machine was purchased last year for $200,000 and has a current market value of $110,000. The sales department has determined that demand for stuffed animals is virtually unlimited. A new machine that costs $500,000 can produce the same kind of animals at a rate of 300,000 per year. Sales price per stuffed animal is $8.00. Costs are as follows for each machine:

	Old Machine	New Machine
Raw materials	$4.00/animal	$4.00/animal
Direct labor	$2.00/animal	$1.00/animal
Direct fixed costs	$118,000/year	$118,000/year
Indirect fixed costs	$ 60,000/year	$ 60,000/year

Required

Should the Ted-E-Bear Shop purchase the new machine?

25-A8. Tax Effect on a Decision. A taxpayer in the 46% bracket is trying to balance his investment portfolio.

Required

To assess the merits of the alternatives, the annual net earnings rate after taxes must be found for the following securities:
a. A municipal bond paying 10% annually (interest is nontaxable).
b. A $40 par preferred stock yielding $8 annually, market price $56 per share.
c. A common stock, par $20 and market $30 a share, whose average quarterly dividend is $.75 per share.
d. A federal treasury note bearing 8% interest rate (interest Is taxable).
e. A cumulative, 6% preferred stock.
f. A state bond paying 9% annually (interest is nontaxable).

PROBLEM SET B.

25-B1. Planning for Form of Organization. Mark Wood, a young entrepreneur, is about to commit his attention and resources to marketing his latest project, an energy recyclator. Wood has two major decisions still facing him—the volume of production and the form of business organization—and has asked your consulting firm for advice. Wood requests a presentation that will compare the tax consequences of incorporating to those of operating a sole proprietorship with earnings of (a) $30,000, (b) $70,000, and (c) $130,000. Wood is single and has no other income.

Required

Prepare a presentation for Mark Wood using the chapter's tax schedules.

25-B2. Evaluating Special Orders. Irish Woolens, Inc., has a productive capacity of 250,000 yards annually. Current production is limited by sales to 225,000 yards. Each yard of wool has a variable cost of $11.25 and a sales price of $15, and Irish Woolens' fixed costs are expected to total $450,000. Recently, the National Youth Organization has asked the company to produce a special one-time order of 40,000 yards for $525,000. Costs of setting up the special weave would be $5,000, and Irish Woolens would be barred from selling this design to anyone else.

Required

Should the company accept the order?

25-B3. Make-or-Buy Decision. For many years the production process of Charlemar, Inc., has used a homemade spool on which to wrap its product for shipment to retailers. The spools are manufactured at the Charlesville plant; the annual production of 200,000 spools is done at a per unit variable cost of $.78. Fixed costs of operating the plant in Charlesville amount to $115,000 annually, 40% of which is direct. The new purchasing agent of Charlemar has found a source to supply all the needed spools for $1.03 each.

Required

a. Should the spools be purchased if the factory has no alternate use?
b. If the factory can be converted to a use that draws a contribution margin of $60,000 with fixed costs remaining at $115,000, what is Charlemar's savings or cost from buying the spools?

25-B4. Evaluating Product Lines. A cosmetic firm is trying to decide how to make its profit picture look better by either adding a new line of products or eliminating some current lines. A proposed new line is makeup remover that sells for $15 per case and has a large demand. This product would require the purchase of a new machine costing $200,000. Sales and cost information on current products and on the new makeup remover are as follows:

	Blush	Lip Gloss	Eye Wear	Makeup Remover
Sales price/case	$25	$ 8	$19	$15
Direct materials/case	$ 8	$ 3	$11	$ 6
Direct labor/case	$ 5	$ 2	$ 3	$ 2
Total direct fixed costs	$20,000	$15,000	$29,000	$18,000
Case sales/year	1,900	4,200	5,800	2,600

Required

Should any product lines be dropped, and should the new line be accepted? (Ignore income taxes and depreciation.)

25-B5. Planning for Production with Limited Resources. Acme Products, Inc., manufactures three products, all of which utilize a thin wire element of a rare alloy. This wire must be specially produced for Acme, and Acme's supplier has warned that the supply during the next month will be limited to 200 feet. Acme also expects to have 75 feet available from current inventory, and management is reviewing production plans to see if changes should be made. Relevant information about the products is as follows:

	Product A	Product H	Product K
Potential sales per month	$18,000	$12,500	$15,750
Selling price per unit	$ 50	$ 125	$ 90
Direct materials cost per unit	$ 15	$ 45	$ 30
Direct labor cost per unit	$ 10	$ 15	$ 10
Other variable costs per unit	$ 10	$ 30	$ 25
Element wire used per unit	6″	12″	9″

(The cost of element wire is $16 per foot and is included in the direct materials cost.)

Required

What production schedule would be best for Acme?

25-B6. Shutdown Determination. A large retail chain has four stores located in different cities. Each store employs one manager and four clerks. At the end of every day, each manager forwards sales and labor information to the main headquarters at a separate location. A staff of four people at the headquarters receives a total of $135,000 per year. Rent and other fixed costs of the headquarters total $190,000. The fixed costs are allocated to each retail store on the basis of sales dollars. Following are the income statements prepared by the headquarters for each retail store:

	Total	Store #1	Store #2	Store #3	Store #4
Sales	$2,000,000	$ 600,000	$1,000,000	$ 300,000	$ 100,000
Direct variable costs	(1,250,000)	(384,000)	(630,000)	(195,000)	(41,000)
Direct fixed costs	(240,000)	(60,000)	(60,000)	(60,000)	(60,000)
Indirect fixed costs	(320,000)	(96,000)	(160,000)	(48,000)	(16,000)
Gross profit	$ 190,000	$ 60,000	$ 150,000	$ (3,000)	$ (17,000)
Taxes	(68,150)	(20,500)	(34,000)	(10,000)	(3,650)
Net income	$ 121,850	$ 39,500	$ 116,000	$ (13,000)	$ (20,650)

Required

Analyze the profitability of each retail store and state whether or not any stores should be closed.

25-B7. Machine Purchase Decision. The Dixie Company purchased a machine two years ago at a cost of $52,000. The machine is being depreciated on a straight-line basis and has an estimated life of seven years and a zero salvage value. A new machine has come onto the market that sells for $70,000 but is able to reduce operating costs by $18,000 per year. The machine would last five years and have a zero salvage value. The old machine can now be sold for only $16,000. An analysis by the president of the company follows:

Savings from new machine ($18,000 × 5 years)		$ 90,000
Cost of new machine		
Purchase price	$70,000	
Loss on old machine	36,000	106,000
Net cost of purchasing new machine		($16,000)

The president argues that the loss from the sale of the old machine wipes out any savings from the new machine.

Operating costs of the old machine are $40,000 per year. Sales and administrative expenses are $20,000 per year.

Required

a. Is the president's analysis correct? Explain.
b. Prepare an incremental analysis for the next five years to determine which alternative is least expensive?
c. Is it desirable to purchase the new machine?

25-B8. Tax Effect on a Decision. D & D Fabricators Inc. is a steel processor that has had a serious decline in business due to a slowdown in the automotive industry. Plant production has been cut back to 50% of capacity; the average production for the past ten years has been 75%. When orders began slowing down, the president of D & D secretly met with some of the company's largest customers to persuade them to buy all of their steel products from D & D Fabricators only. After a considerable number of meetings, it appeared that D & D would continue to operate at only 50% of capacity. In desperation, the president reviewed the average earnings associated with the two different volumes of production as follows:

	50% Capacity	75% Capacity
Sales	$ 800,000	$1,200,000
Direct materials	(200,000)	(300,000)
Direct labor	(300,000)	(450,000)
Variable overhead	(100,000)	(150,000)
Fixed overhead	(150,000)	(150,000)
Earnings before taxes	$ 50,000	$ 150,000

After close examination, the president returned to several customers and offered them bribes in return for a guaranteed sales level of 75% of capacity, which is considered normal. The president argued that since only $90,000 had been spent for an increase in earnings of $100,000, the money had been spent wisely.

Required

Discuss the incremental analysis explained by the president. Do you agree with his computations?

CAPITAL BUDGETING

CHAPTER OBJECTIVES

After studying Chapter 26, you should understand the following:

1. What capital expenditures are and why they are so important to a firm's financial position.
2. How the capital budgeting process is commonly implemented in most organizations.
3. The manner in which to identify the cash inflows and outflows relevant to a particular project.
4. How potential capital expenditures are evaluated using nondiscounted as well as discounted cash flow techniques.
5. How the risk of a project is incorporated into the capital expenditure evaluation techniques.

One of the most significant decisions managers often make is whether or not to invest in fixed assets. These decisions are particularly important because investments in fixed assets often require large amounts of money and commit an organization for long periods of time. The fixed asset decision, commonly referred to as the capital expenditure or **capital budgeting** decision, is the topic of this chapter. The chapter describes why such decisions are important to organizational success, how they are made, and the role of accounting information in the capital budgeting decision-making process.

CAPITAL BUDGETING
The process of comparing alternative capital expenditures and making decisions as to their desirability.

CAPITAL EXPENDITURES

Capital expenditures are investments that have a useful life of several years to a company—primarily expenditures for property, plant, and equipment, but also including such things as multiyear promotional campaigns or long-term programs of research and development.

CAPITAL EXPENDITURES
Investments that have a useful life to the company of several years—primarily expenditures for property, plant, and equipment.

Importance of Capital Expenditures

Capital expenditures can dramatically alter the financial position of a company for several reasons:

1. **Large amounts of dollars.** Capital expenditures normally involve large amounts of money, which might not be readily available. It takes careful planning to ensure the availability of adequate funds for a project without jeopardizing the financial stability of a company.

2. **Income-producing abilities.** Since the fixed assets of a company are normally the primary source of income, an ill-considered capital expenditure can affect the profits of the company for years.

3. **Long lives of assets.** Income-producing assets are generally used for many years. This is further reason to evaluate carefully an asset's potential productive capacity, useful life, and service record and the chances of the asset's becoming obsolete.

4. **Competitive position.** Most often, the purpose of purchasing new property or equipment is to enhance the competitive position of the company—that is, to get a "leg up" on the competition. Thus, a bad capital investment decision could seriously jeopardize a firm's ability to compete.

The evaluation of potential capital expenditures is an involved process. Basically, the decision involves determining the cost of the project (the amount the company will have to spend to acquire and maintain the needed property or equipment), the amount of money that will be earned as a result of acquiring the asset, and the relationship between costs and benefits. If the incremental benefits exceed the incremental costs, the investment should normally be made.

Capital budgeting is part of the company's normal budget process. In planning for the next one to five years, managers must determine what resources in terms of fixed assets are needed to satisfy the organization's goals and objectives. Management must divide priorities into categories, such as facilities to be expanded or remodeled, equipment to be replaced, and operations to be made more cost-effective. In thinking about these issues, management might decide to initiate a capital expenditure request

A Corporate Gamble

In the early days of American business, certain people are said to have literally risked all in business ventures. Some succeeded, some failed. Although we rarely hear of modern winner-take-all stories, the successful completion of the Alaskan oil pipeline might be an exception.

In the early 1970s, the Standard Oil Company of Ohio (SOHIO) was a medium-sized oil company, reasonably profitable with a bright future. Maintaining this corporate status quo would have been quite acceptable to investors. But top management saw a golden opportunity—the chance to develop the Alaskan oil fields and transport the oil to the lower 48 states.

There was nothing small or short-term about this project. Before the decision was made to proceed, a capital budgeting analysis was completed. On paper, it appeared that the project could provide the company with attractive returns. Unfortunately, the analysis also showed that the project involved an expenditure of millions of dollars over a period of 10 to 15 years on a project judged to be quite risky, but SOHIO's management took the risk and put SOHIO's financial future on the line.

The Alaskan pipeline was successful and catapulted SOHIO to the fifth largest oil-producing company in the nation within a decade.

with top management. In this request, it must describe what it wants and why it wants it and include an analysis of the project's incremental costs and benefits. Because top management will receive many more requests than it has funds available for, only the more profitable projects will be funded.

Necessity Projects

Capital expenditure projects normally fall into two broad classes: necessity projects and profit improvement projects. **Necessity projects** involve expenditures that cannot be justified in terms of profit improvement. Examples include expenditures for a new employee cafeteria, pollution and contamination prevention, and improved working conditions. The undertaking of such projects is necessary to maintain organizational success, but an evaluation criterion other than profit improvement is often used to justify the expenditure.

NECESSITY PROJECTS
Capital expenditure projects that involve expenditures that cannot be justified in terms of profit improvement.

Profit Improvement Projects

The second broad category of capital expenditures involves **profit improvement projects,** which can range from cost reduction projects involving equipment replacement to new product line introductions. Each project must be justified on the basis of cost-effectiveness, and normally those projects offering the highest return are accepted for funding.

PROFIT IMPROVEMENT PROJECTS
Capital expenditure projects that can be evaluated on the basis of future profit enhancements.

Not all capital expenditures require a formal request and analysis. If they did, management would probably spend an inordinate amount of time preparing and reviewing requests. Typically, management sets a minimum amount subject to formal request. For example, a limit of $5,000 might be set on the acquisition of tools, patterns, dies, and jigs. If the amount to be spent is less than $5,000, no formal request would be required.

Another way top management can control the number of formal requests requiring review is to establish approval limits for corporate officers at various levels of management. For example, in a decentralized company, the divisional manager might have authority to approve all capital expenditures below a certain level, for example, $100,000. If the dollar amount requested exceeds the manager's signing authority, it would then have to be approved by management at the next higher level.

Capital expenditure requests requiring formal approval are normally required to be justified on the basis of a formal financial analysis. Such a quantitative analysis (to be discussed later) is typically supplemented with a narrative justification. Requests originate at the lower management levels and proceed to higher levels of review.

The last element of an effective capital budgeting process is a post-audit of the acquisition. The objective of the post-audit is to determine the actual profitability of the capital expenditure in comparison to original estimates. This comparison should be helpful to management in refining its capital budgeting procedures and in evaluating the performance of managers initiating the capital requests.

ANALYZING CASH FLOWS

The evaluation of potential capital expenditures is an involved process requiring the estimation of the project's cash inflows and outflows and an analysis of these cash flows to determine the cost-benefit tradeoff.

Incremental Cash Flow Analysis

INCREMENTAL CASH FLOWS
Cash that is either received or spent as a result of making an investment decision.

It is important to note that rather than evaluate a project in terms of its profits, we will look at the project's **incremental cash flow,** that is, the cash either received or spent as a result of making an investment decision. When analyzing the attractiveness of a potential project, management is most interested in the project's cash flow potential. The focus on cash flow rather than profit results from the reality that a project's excess cash inflow can be immediately reinvested in other projects to generate additional cash inflows. In contrast, if a project realized an incremental profit, it would not necessarily imply that it could be reinvested in other projects because of the nature of the profit concept under the accrual basis of accounting.

To illustrate how a cash flow analysis might be conducted, review the data in Exhibit 26.1. Given this information, we need to determine the yearly cash flows of the new machine net of taxes. To do this, we need to analyze the relevancy of each piece of information to the investment decision. Such an analysis can be done by asking a series of questions about the information. A schematic of this inquiry approach is presented in Exhibit 26.2.

Initial Cash Outflows

Let's illustrate the inquiry process by determining the initial cost of the investment. The net result of our analysis is in Exhibit 26.3. The cost of the machinery is relevant

EXHIBIT 26.1

Basic Information

Palace, Inc., has examined its operations and has determined that one new machine will replace two machines presently being used in its production process. Careful analysis has related the following data:

1. New Machine
Cost is $70,000. Freight and installation charges are $5,000. Useful life is five years. Depreciation is straight-line. Estimated salvage value is $10,000.

2. Replaced Machine 1
Can be sold for $2,500. Book value is $1,800. When purchased eight years ago, the machine cost $5,000 and had an estimated salvage value of $1,000 and an estimated useful life of ten years. Depreciation has been computed on a straight-line basis.

3. Replaced Machine 2
Current sale value is $1,000. Book value is $2,000, which happens to equal the salvage value, since today is the end of the machine's estimated useful life.

4. Other Data
Because of the increased output of the new investment, the level of raw materials will have to be increased by an estimated $2,500, and it is assumed that the inventory level will be reduced at the end of the useful life of the project. Estimated savings is $26,000 per year for the next five years. The company is in the 40 percent tax bracket.

because it is an incremental cost and is therefore treated as a net outflow in the current period. Also added to this cost is the increased investment in inventory and the freight and installation charges necessary to put the machinery in working order. None of these incremental flows are impacted by taxes.

The sale of machine 1 has a twofold impact. First, the selling price of $2,500 generated a cash inflow in the current period that reduced the initial cash outflow of the project. Second, because there was a $700 gain on the sale of machine 1, the tax bill in the current period increased by $280 ($700 gain × tax rate of 40%).

EXHIBIT 26.2

Cash Flow Inquiry Scheme

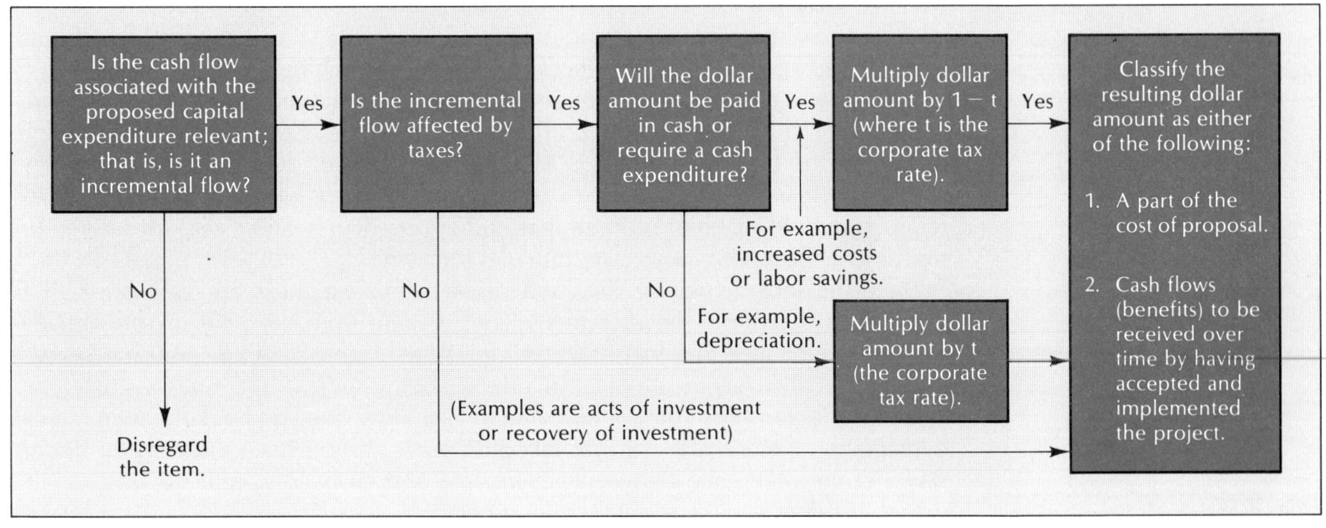

EXHIBIT 26.3

Initial Investment

Item	Amount
Purchase price	($70,000)
Freight and installation	(5,000)
Inventory investment	(2,500)
Sale of machine 1	2,500
Tax on gain on machine 1	(280)
Sale of machine 2	1,000
Tax savings on loss	400
Net cost of investment	($73,880)

Machine 1		Machine 2	
Sale price	$2,500	Sale price	$1,000
Book value	(1,800)	Book value	(2,000)
Gain on sale	$ 700	Loss on sale	($1,000)
Tax rate	.40	Tax rate	.40
Additional taxes to be paid	$ 280	Taxes saved	$ 400

The sale of machine 2 also has a twofold effect. A cash inflow of $1,000 is generated from the sale, and a tax savings of $400 is realized because the equipment was sold at a loss; that is, the machine's sale price was below book value [($1,000 − $2,000) × 40%]. The net effect of these cash flows results in an initial outlay of $73,880.

Yearly Cash Inflows

Once the initial investment is determined, an analyst would turn his or her attention to calculating the yearly cash inflows and outflows from the investment. The results of such an analysis, using the information in Exhibit 26.1, are in Exhibit 26.4.

The initial fact to consider is that the investment will result in an annual savings of $26,000. This savings results from the increased productivity of the new machine over the two old ones. Offsetting this savings is the increased depreciation associated with the new machine net of the depreciation expense the company would have had if it had kept the old machines. For example, machine 1 still had two years of useful life remaining. If the company had kept the machine, it would have depreciated it $400 in Years 1 and 2. Therefore, the incremental depreciation charge related to the new investment is $12,600 ($13,000 of depreciation on the new machine minus the depreciation expense the company would have had if it had retained the old machines). Note that no forgone depreciation was considered for machine 2, because it is already fully depreciated.

Once the incremental savings and depreciation expenses are calculated, it is possible to determine the incremental net income from the new investment. Exhibit 26.4 indicates that this is $8,040 for Years 1 and 2 and $7,800 for Years 3 through 5. However, incremental income is not the same as incremental cash flow. To make the transition from net income to cash flow, we add back the incremental depreciation expenses to the net income figures. If you have difficulty in understanding the difference between net income and cash flow, refer to Chapter 17, where this difference was initially described.

EXHIBIT 26.4

Yearly Cash Inflow Analysis

Item	Year 1	2	3	4	5
Savings resulting from purchase of new machine	$26,000	$26,000	$26,000	$26,000	$26,000
Depreciation on new machine*	(13,000)	(13,000)	(13,000)	(13,000)	(13,000)
Forgone depreciation on old machines					
Machine 1	400	400	–0–	–0–	–0–
Machine 2	–0–	–0–	–0–	–0–	–0–
Incremental profit before tax	$13,400	$13,400	$13,000	$13,000	$13,000
Taxes (.40)	5,360	5,360	5,200	5,200	5,200
Net income	$ 8,040	$ 8,040	$ 7,800	$ 7,800	$ 7,800
Add: Incremental depreciation resulting from investment	12,600	12,600	13,000	13,000	13,000
Lost salvage value on machine 1		(1,000)			
Salvage value of new machine					10,000
Reduction of inventory investment					2,500
Total cash inflow	$20,640	$19,640	$20,800	$20,800	$33,300

*Purchase price	$70,000	
Freight and installation	5,000	
Asset cost		$75,000
Salvage value		10,000
Depreciable base		$65,000
		÷
Useful life		5 years
Annual depreciation expense using straight-line method		$13,000

Sporadic Cash Flows

The last part of the cash flow analysis involves determining whether any other sporadic cash inflows or outflows occur during the life of the project. In our example, three occur. First, by selling machine 1, the company forgoes the opportunity to receive $1,000 at the end of Year 2, reducing the cash inflow of Year 2 by $1,000. The second factor we must consider is the $10,000 the company will receive for the new machine at the end of the machine's useful life. This is a cash inflow in Year 5, because the company will receive cash when the machine is sold. Finally, at the end of Year 5, the company will reduce its investment in inventory, resulting in a cash inflow of $2,500 that year.

Once these last cash inflows are considered, we can calculate the final annual cash flows associated with the project. This incremental cash flow analysis is a key component of the profitability analysis of new investment projects.

To summarize, a cash flow analysis involves determining a project's initial cash outlay, the annual cash inflows and outflows of the investment, and any other cash flows associated with the project. Exhibit 26.5 summarizes these steps for Palace, Inc. The timing of the flows—that is, the year in which the cash flows occur—is particularly important to the analysis. This point is discussed further in the section on discounted cash flow techniques.

EXHIBIT 26.5

Summary of Steps in Cash Flow Analysis

Determine Initial Cash Outlay

1. Cost of machinery.
2. Increased investment in inventory or other current assets.
3. Freight and installation charges.
4. Sale of old equipment (including impact of taxes).

Determine Annual Cash Inflows and Outflows

1. Annual savings from purchase of new machine.
2. Depreciation on new machine.
3. Forgone depreciation on old machines.
4. Salvage value of old machines.
5. Impact of taxes.

Determine Sporadic Cash Inflows/Outflows

1. Opportunity cost of selling old machine.
2. Salvage value of new machine.
3. Reduced investment in inventory.

FORMAL TOOLS OF INVESTMENT ANALYSIS

Generally, the techniques used to evaluate investment opportunities fall into one of two categories: those where the time value of money is ignored (nondiscounted cash flow techniques) and those where the time value of money is considered (discounted cash flow techniques).

Nondiscounted Cash Flow Techniques

PAYBACK METHOD
A method of evaluating alternative investment opportunities in terms of how quickly each project recoups its initial investment.

Payback Method. The **payback method** evaluates alternative investment opportunities in terms of how quickly each project recoups its initial investment. An illustration of this method is shown in Exhibit 26.6. Project A is the investment described in Exhibit 26.1, and Project B is an alternative project the company can decide to invest in. Project A has a payback period of approximately three and a half years, and project B has a payback period of two and a half years. Based on these data, project B appears to be a more attractive investment than project A. Management will view the project with the shortest payback period as the one with least risk, because it will get its money back sooner. Note, however, that the payback does not really measure the rate of return for each project. This method ignores the time value of money and the cash inflows realized after the payback period. For example, although project B returns the initial investment of $73,880 more quickly than does project A, it appears from Exhibit 26.6 that the total returns from project A are greater than the total returns from project B ($115,180 versus $100,000).

Despite its limitations, the payback method is commonly used. The method is simple and provides a practical way for management to assess the relative riskiness of alternative investment opportunities.

EXHIBIT 26.6

Payback Method

	Project A (refer to Exhibits 26.3 and 26.4)		Project B (numbers assumed)	
Initial investment outlay	$73,880		$73,880	
	Annual Cash Inflows	**Investment Balance**	**Annual Cash Inflows**	**Investment Balance**
Year 1	$ 20,640	$53,240	$ 10,000	$63,880
Year 2	19,640	33,600	50,000	13,880
Year 3	20,800	12,800	30,000	(16,120)
Year 4	20,800	(8,000)	5,000	(21,120)
Year 5	33,300	(41,300)	5,000	(26,120)
Total returns	$115,180		$100,000	

Average Accounting Rate of Return (ARR). The **average accounting rate of return** ranks investment proposals based on their average annual profit over the life of the project in relation to the project's average cost. A project's ARR is determined by dividing the average net income per year from the project by the average investment (initial outlay divided by two). As illustrated in Exhibit 26.7, project A has an ARR of 21.4 percent and project B's ARR is 18.5 percent. Thus, project A is more attractive than project B, because it has a higher ARR.

AVERAGE ACCOUNTING RATE OF RETURN
A technique that ranks investment proposals based on their average annual profit over the life of the project in relation to the project's average cost.

Unlike the payback period technique, averge rate of return considers the total income potential of an investment. The method also has the advantage of providing insight into the relative profitability of each project.

Offsetting these advantages are some serious deficiencies with the ARR method. First, the method uses profit rather than cash flow as a measure of attractiveness. As previously discussed, the incremental profit potential of a project does not really reflect how beneficial the project is to a firm. Second, the timing and relative size of the yearly incremental profits are ignored because of the averaging process. Therefore, under this method, two investment projects can have the same average profit but with different patterns of profit inflows. For example, assume the following profit patterns for projects X and Y:

Year	Project X	Project Y
1	—	400
2	—	400
3	1,200	400

EXHIBIT 26.7

Accounting Rate of Return

	Project A	Project B
	(refer to Exhibits 26.3 and 26.4)	(numbers assumed)
Initial investment outlay	$73,880	$80,000
Annual Net Income		
Year 1	$ 8,040	$ 6,000
Year 2	8,040	9,500
Year 3	7,800	4,000
Year 4	7,800	10,000
Year 5	7,800	7,500
Total	$39,480	$37,000
Average annual net income	$\frac{\$39,480}{5} = \$7,896$	$\frac{\$37,000}{5} = \$7,400$
Average accounting rate of return	$\frac{\$7,896}{(\$73,880/2)} = 21.4\%$	$\frac{\$7,400}{(\$80,000/2)} = 18.5\%$

Each project has an average profit pattern of $400. However, under normal circumstances, project Y would be preferable, because the firm gets part of its investment back sooner than with project X. Finally, the ARR measure uses average investment in the denominator, which may not be a realistic indicator of the firm's total investment in a project.

CONCEPT SUMMARY 26.1

FORMAL TOOLS OF FINANCIAL ANALYSIS—NONDISCOUNTED CASH FLOW TECHNIQUES

Technique	Formula	Acceptance Criterion	Advantages	Disadvantages
Payback period—the time required for the investment to return its initial cash outlay.	PBP = n, such that $\sum_{t=1}^{n} CFI_t = CFO$ where CFI_t is the net cash flow in, in year t, and CFO is the initial cash flow out.	PBP < maximum n—the payback period must be less than some subjective maximum time period.	Simple to use. Provides a practical way to assess the relative riskiness of projects (as projects with longer payback periods are deemed to be more risky).	Ignores the time value of money. Ignores cash inflows beyond the payback period.
Average rate of return—relationship of a project's average profit over the project's life to the average cost of the project.	$ARR = \frac{\text{Average annual net income of project}}{\left(\text{Initial investment outlay/2}\right)}$	ARR > minimum r—the average rate of return must exceed some subjective minimum rate of return.	Assesses total income potential. Considers relative profitability.	Uses profit figures rather than net cash inflows. Ignores timing and relative size of profit flows (i.e., ignores time value of money). Not a realistic indicator of the firm's total investment in the project.

Discounted Cash Flow (DCF) Techniques

All of the preceding techniques had two common problems: They ignored the timing of the cash flows, and they ignored the time value of money. To counter these problems, financial analysts use DCF techniques to evaluate the attractiveness of alternative investment opportunities. These techniques convert future dollars expended or received into today's dollars, thus taking into consideration the fact that a dollar received today is worth more than a dollar received tomorrow. Why? Because money received today can be invested to earn an additional return in the future. For example, if you could earn ten percent interest on your money, you would demand $1.10 a year from now in exchange for $1.00 today. Therefore, DCF techniques of capital budgeting make use of the present value concepts described in Appendix C following Chapter 15. Two of the more widely used DCF techniques are net present value and internal rate of return.

Net Present Value (NPV). The **net present value** of a project is the difference between the present value (today's dollars) of the cash inflows and of the cash outflows of the project. Assume a project has a present cost of $800 and will yield future returns totaling $2,000 with a present value of $1,400. The NPV of this project would be $600, calculated as follows:

NET PRESENT VALUE
The difference between the present value (today's dollars) of the cash inflows and the cash outflows of a project.

$$\text{NPV} = \text{Present value of returns} - \text{Present value of cost}$$
$$\$600 = \$1{,}400 - \$800$$

If an investment has an NPV greater than zero, it should be accepted, because it will generate more cash inflows in today's dollars than it will cash outlays.

Exhibit 26.8 is a more complex example of the NPV technique, once again using the data from Exhibit 26.1. The project has an initial cost of $73,880 and a useful life of five years. The company uses a discount rate of ten percent to determine the present value of the project's cash inflow stream. This ten percent rate is a target rate of return that the company believes it must earn on its investments to justify the use of capital. This target rate is often based on the firm's cost of capital. In essence, the **cost of capital** is the average cost of obtaining long-term funds from investors and creditors. As a general rule, a company interested in maximizing its market value will invest only in those projects promising a rate of return greater than the cost of capital.

COST OF CAPITAL
The average cost of obtaining long-term funds from investors and creditors.

In calculating the cost of capital, most firms use a weighted average approach; that is, the overall cost of capital is regarded as the sum of the weighted individual capital costs. For example, if a firm is wholly financed by long-term debt that carries an interest charge of ten percent and is in the 50 percent marginal tax bracket, its after-tax cost of debt is equal to five percent. If the debt represents the only source of funds to the firm, the firm's cost of capital is equal to five percent—the firm's cost of debt. This simplified example becomes more complex when additional sources of funds are introduced into the firm's capital structure. In this situation, determination of the cost of each capital source would first be necessary and then the individual capital costs would be combined into a weighted percentage figure, which would represent the firm's overall cost of capital.

Profitability Index Method. As Exhibit 26.8 shows, the project has a positive net present value of $11,611 and would therefore be acceptable for funding purposes. When comparing investment opportunities with differing investment sizes, it is some-

EXHIBIT 26.8

Net Present Value Technique

Assumptions

a. Initial investment of $73,880.
b. The company wants to earn at least ten percent on new investment projects.
c. Annual cash flows:

Year 1	$20,640
Year 2	$19,640
Year 3	$20,800
Year 4	$20,800
Year 5	$33,300

Steps

a. Calculate present value of initial cash outlay:

Outlay	$73,880	
Present value factor	× 1.00	(assumes outlay is made immediately)
Present value	$73,880	

b. Calculate present value of annual cash flows:

	Cash flow	×	Present value factor at 10%	=	Present value
Year 1	$20,640		.909		$18,762
Year 2	$19,640		.826		16,223
Year 3	$20,800		.751		15,621
Year 4	$20,800		.683		14,206
Year 5	$33,300		.621		20,679
Total present value of inflows					$85,491

c. Subtract the total present value of outflows from total inflows:

Inflows − Outflows = Net present value
$85,491 − $73,880 = $11,611

d. If the net present value (NPV) amount is positive, the project is acceptable.

PROFITABILITY INDEX METHOD
A method of analyzing capital expenditures in which the present value of the cash inflows are divided by the present value of the cash outflows.

times misleading to use the NPV technique, because the size of the project has an influence on the NPV. In such a situation, most analysts advocate using the **profitability index (PI) method,** whereby the present value of the cash inflows is divided by the present value of the cash outflows. For example, the project represented by the data in Exhibit 26.8 would have a PI of 1.16 ($85,491/$73,880), indicating that for every $1.00 of outflow it is getting $1.16 of inflow; thus, the project would be acceptable. Because the PI method controls for project size, it is a valuable measure in comparing alternative investment opportunities of differing sizes.

INTERNAL RATE OF RETURN
The discount rate that will equate the present value of a project's cash inflows with the present value of the cash outflows required by the project.

Internal Rate of Return (IRR). Under the NPV method, we used the firm's cost of capital to discount all flows. Because the project had a positive NPV, it implies that the project has a rate of return greater than the discount rate used in the NPV calculation. In some cases, the decision maker is trying to find the discount rate that will equate the present value of the returns with the present value of costs. This discount rate is known as the project's **internal rate of return.** For example, assume the cost of a project is $800 and at the end of a year you will receive $1,000.

Through a process of trial and error, unless you have a programmable calculator, you will find that the interest rate earned by the project is 25 percent ($800 × 1.25 = $1,000). The acceptability of a project is determined by comparing this IRR with the firm's cost of capital. If the IRR exceeds the cost of capital, it is acceptable for funding purposes.

A more elaborate example of the IRR method is illustrated in Exhibit 26.9, using the data provided in Exhibit 26.8. Our hypothetical project has an IRR of 15.6 percent, far in excess of the firm's cost of capital of ten percent.

CONCEPT SUMMARY 26.2

FORMAL TOOLS OF FINANCIAL ANALYSIS—DISCOUNTED CASH FLOW TECHNIQUES

Technique	Formula	Acceptance Criterion	Advantages	Disadvantages
Net present value—the excess of the present value of net cash inflows over the initial cash outflow.	$NPV = \sum_{t=1}^{n}(CFI_t)(PVIF_{t,k}) - CFO$ where $PVIF_{t,k}$ is the proper tabled value of the present value interest factor, using the cost of capital as the discount rate.	NPV > 0—the project must have a positive net present value, which means the present value of net cash inflows must exceed the initial cash outflow.	Explicitly considers the time value of money. Directly determines the effect of the project on the total present value of the firm and is therefore consistent with management's goal of maximizing shareholder wealth.	Does not scale the investment, i.e., does not show the return relative to the size of the project. Requires knowledge of the firm's cost of capital.
Profitability index—the ratio of the sum of the present values of the net cash inflows to the initial cash outflow.	$PI = \frac{\sum_{t=1}^{n}(CFI_t)(PVIF_{t,k})}{CFO}$	PI > 1—the project must have a profitability index greater than one, which means that the present value of the net cash inflows must exceed the initial cash ouflow.	Explicitly considers the time value of money. Scales the investment.	Requires knowledge of the firm's cost of capital.
Internal rate of return—the compounded annual rate of return that equates the net cash inflows with the initial cash outflow.	IRR = r, such that $\sum_{t=1}^{n}(CFI_t)(PVIF_{t,r}) = CFO$ where $PVIF_{t,r}$ is the proper tabled value of the present value interest factor, using the internal rate of return as the discount rate.	IRR > K—the project's internal rate of return must exceed the firm's cost of capital.	Explicitly considers the time value of money. Scales the investment. Allows IRR to be calculated without knowledge of the firm's cost of capital.	Requires the firm's cost of capital to be known to evaluate the project as acceptable or unacceptable. Assumes net cash inflows can be reinvested to earn the internal rate of return of the project. (NVP assumes only that net cash inflows need to be reinvested.)

EXHIBIT 26.9

IRR Illustration

Year	Cash Inflows (Outflows)	Present Value Factors and Amounts At 14%	$	15%	$	16%	$
0	($73,880)	1.000	(73,880)	1.000	(73,880)	1.000	(73,880)
1	$20,640	.877	18,101	.870	17,957	.862	17,792
2	$19,640	.770	15,123	.756	14,848	.743	14,593
3	$20,800	.675	14,040	.658	13,686	.641	13,333
4	$20,800	.592	12,314	.572	11,898	.552	11,482
5	$33,300	.519	17,283	.497	16,550	.476	15,851
NPV			$ 2,981		$ 1,059		($829)

—IRR greater than 15% but less than 16%

—IRR = 15% + [1059/(1059 + 829)](1%) =
15% + .56% = 15.56%

Summary of Decision Rules

Exhibit 26.10 summarizes the decision rules for investment under each method assuming independent and mutually exclusive projects. Mutually exclusive projects are defined as competing investment opportunities with the selection of one project automatically eliminating the other projects. It is important to note that under most situations, these evaluation techniques will yield the same "no-go" investment decision.

EXHIBIT 26.10

Decision Rules

Technique	Independent Projects	Mutually Exclusive
Payback period	Payback period lower than management's target	Project with shortest period
ARR	ARR greater than cost of capital	Highest ARR
NPV	Positive NPV	Highest NPV
PI	PI greater than 1.0	Highest PI
IRR	IRR greater than firm's cost of capital	Highest IRR

Certain situations exist in which methods might yield opposite rankings for two competing projects. For example, the rankings arising from NPV and IRR analyses might be in conflict because of the different assumptions regarding the reinvestment rates under each method. The NPV method assumes that subsequent years' cash flows are reinvested at the cost of capital rate, and the IRR method assumes that cash flows will be reinvested at a rate equal to the IRR. In addition, if the size or useful lives of projects are significantly different, the methods are likely to result in different rankings. Additional issues related to the conflicting ranking problem are covered in advanced financial and management accounting courses.

HOW TO DEAL WITH RISK

It would be inappropriate to leave this chapter without at least briefly discussing how risk or uncertainty should be handled in the capital budgeting process. All of our examples assumed that we could determine with certainty the variables required for the capital budgeting analysis. In reality, however, uncertainty would surround our cash flow estimates and profitability projections. Management can handle such a situation in any number of ways, ranging from the use of informal to formal methods of risk analysis.

Informal Basis

One way to handle risk is on an informal basis with no attempt made to quantify the risk component of a project. Under this approach, management simply makes a subjective evaluation of risk and adjusts for it in an informal manner. For example, in reviewing two projects—one involving a cost reduction and the other a profit improvement—management will probably conclude that the former project is less risky than the latter and would therefore not require as high a rate of return on the cost reduction project. The questions become, of course, How much risk is really associated with each project? and How much is the tradeoff between risk and reward?

Risk-Adjusted Discount Rate

Another more formal way management can handle risk is to use **risk-adjusted discount rates** rather than the firm's cost of capital. Risk-adjusted discount rates are discount rates that are adjusted away from the firm's cost of capital as an adjustment for the risk involved in undertaking a capital expenditure. For example, in the NPV model, the discount rate is the cost of capital; this is a minimum target return. If management perceived a project to be particularly risky, it could increase the hurdle rate accordingly, instead of using the minimum rate. In doing this, management can quantify the risk component of a project. Exhibit 26.11 illustrates the risk-adjusted

RISK-ADJUSTED DISCOUNT RATES Discount rates that are adjusted away from the firm's cost of capital as an adjustment for the risk involved in undertaking a capital expenditure.

EXHIBIT 26.11
Risk-Adjusted Discount Method

1. The risk-adjusted net present value is as follows:

	Year 1	Year 2	Year 3	Year 4	Year 5
CFI	$20,640	$19,640	$20,800	$20,800	$33,300
PV factor (20%)	.833	.694	.579	.482	.402
PV of cash inflows	$17,193	$13,630	$12,043	$10,026	$13,387
PV of cash inflows		66,279			
CFO (cost)		73,880			
Risk-adjusted NPV		($7,601)			

2. The risk-adjusted profitability index is as follows:

PV of CFI's/CFO = $66,279/$73,880 = 0.897

3. If the IRR is used as the decision criterion, the IRR (15.56%) is compared against the risk-adjusted rate (20%), which in this case would suggest a reject decision.

discount method. Of course, a practical issue still exists: What is the appropriate risk premium?

Expected Value Analysis

In place of risk-adjusted discount rates, managers can use expected value cash flows instead of single point estimates. For example, in a previous illustration we assumed the cost of a project to be $2,000. However, in reality, management feels there is a fifty-fifty chance the cost will be either $2,000 or $3,000. In this situation, the expected project cost is $2,500, calculated as follows:

(1) Value	(2) Expected Value Probability	(3) (1 × 2)
$2,000	.50	$1,000
$3,000	.50	$1,500
	Total expected value	$2,500

EXPECTED VALUE
The sum of the products of specific outcome possibilities and their associated probability of occurrence.

To do an expected value analysis, management must identify the possible outcomes and assign a probability to each. The sum of the probabilities must equal one, and the **expected value** is determined by summing the individual products of the specific outcomes and their associated probabilities. This expected value approach could be used to adjust the cash inflow side as well.

The preceding discussion simply illustrates some of the techniques management can use in considering risk in the capital budgeting decision. In this day and age of computers and increased quantitative models of financial analysis, the sophistication level of risk analysis has increased considerably. The main point, however, is that risk assessment is an important part of the capital budgeting decision and therefore cannot be ignored by management.

FOR REVIEW

DEMONSTRATION PROBLEM

A proposed investment requires an initial cash outlay of $100,000 for which it will return expected annual net cash inflows of $25,000 and annual profits of $28,000 for the next ten years. The investor's cost of capital is 15%.

Required

1. Determine each of the following for the investment:
   - **a.** Payback period.
   - **b.** Average accounting rate of return.
   - **c.** Net present value and profitability index.
   - **d.** Internal rate of return.
2. Is this a wise investment?

Demonstration Problem Solution

1a. Payback period

$$\text{Payback period} = \frac{\text{Total investment}}{\text{Annual profit}} = \frac{\$100{,}000}{\$25{,}000/\text{yr}} = 4 \text{ yrs.}$$

The payback period is four years.

1b. Average accounting rate of return

$$\text{Average accounting rate of return} = \frac{\text{Annual profit}}{\frac{\text{Total investment}}{2}} = \frac{\$28{,}000}{\frac{\$100{,}000}{2}} = 56\%$$

The average accounting rate of return is 56%.

1c. Net present value

Annual profit	$ 25,000
PVIFA 10 yrs, 15%	5.0188
Σ PV of annual inflows	$125,470
Initial cash outlay	100,000
Net present value	$ 25,470

Profitability index

$$PI = \frac{\Sigma \text{ PV of annual inflows}}{\text{Initial cash outlay}} = \frac{\$125{,}470}{\$100{,}000} = 1.255$$

The net present value is $25,470, and the profitability index is 1.255.

1d. Internal rate of return

$$IRR = I: \Sigma \text{ PV of CFI's} = CFO$$

	Rate	Σ PV of CFI's		
1%	21%	$101,351.95	$1,351.95	3,272.34
	IRR	CFO = $100,000		
	22%	98,079.61		

$$IRR = 21\% + X$$
$$IRR \approx 21\% + (\$1{,}351.95/\$3{,}272.34)\ (1\%)$$
$$IRR \approx 21\% + 0.41\%$$
$$IRR \approx 21.41\%$$

The internal rate of return is approximately 21.41%.

2. Since the investment's net present value is positive, its profitability index exceeds one, and its internal rate of return exceeds the cost of capital, the investment is a wise one.

SUMMARY

- Capital expenditures are investments in fixed assets that involve large amounts of money and are linked to a firm's income-producing abilities and competitive position.
- Incremental cash flows, both current and future, are particularly important in making capital expenditure decisions.
- Capital expenditure analysis can be done with nondiscounted cash flow techniques that ignore the time value of money or with discounted cash flow techniques that explicitly consider the time value of money.
- Payback and average accounting rate of return are the two most common nondiscounted cash flow analysis methods.
- The payback period is the time required for a project to return its initial cash outlay.
- The average accounting rate of return relates a project's average annual profit to the project's average cost.
- Net present value and internal rate of return are widely used discounted cash flow analysis methods.
- The present value of a project equals the excess of the present value of the project's net cash inflows (discounted at the firm's cost of capital) over the project's initial cash outflows.
- The internal rate of return of a project is the compound interest rate at which the project's initial cash outlay could be invested to earn future cash flows equal to those provided by the project.
- The profitability index relates the total present value of a project's net cash inflows to the project's initial cash outflows.
- The relative risk of alternative projects can be included in capital expenditure analysis by adjusting the discount rate used or by using expected value analysis in estimating future cash flows.

QUESTIONS

26-1. Discuss the ways that capital expenditures affect the financial position of a company.

26-2. Identify and define the two general categories of capital expenditures.

26-3. What are incremental cash flows?

26-4. How does depreciation affect cash flows?

26-5. The manager of the production department wants to buy a piece of capital equipment with an expected payback period of four years. Is this enough information to use when making an investment decision?

26-6. Becket Company uses the average accounting rate of return in evaluating capital investments. What advantages and disadvantages of the ARR method should Becket Company understand in analyzing its data?

26-7. Suppose you are the president of a company deciding whether or not to invest in a piece of machinery that cost $14,000. Future returns from this machinery total $18,500, with a present value of $13,000. Would your decision be to buy the equipment? Why or why not?

26-8. Why is the profitability index a good method for comparing possible capital investments?

26-9. Company B is considering investing in a project that will cost one million dollars. Cash inflows in each of the next five years from the project are expected to be $310,000. The company's cost of capital is 15%. Should Company B invest in the project?

26-10. Why is it important for companies to handle risk or uncertainty in evaluating possible capital investments? What methods can be used to aid companies in their analysis?

EXERCISES

26-E1. Rexway Company is considering the purchase of a new piece of equipment that costs $180,000. The costs of the present equipment and the proposed new equipment are as follows:

	Present Equipment	New Equipment
Labor	$37,650	$33,000
Depreciation	12,000	24,000
Repairs	9,000	2,250
Miscellaneous costs	6,000	2,400
	$64,650	$61,650

Compute the payback period for the new piece of equipment for Rexway Company.

26-E2. Milo Manufacturing Company is planning to purchase a machine in order to add a new product to its present line. The machine will cost $24,000, have a six-year life, be depreciated on a straight-line basis, and have no salvage value. Milo Manufacturing expects to sell 3,000 units per year of the new product. The projected income and expenses for each year are as follows:

Sales		$90,000
Costs		
Materials, labor, overhead	$48,000	
Depreciation on new machine	4,000	
Selling and administrative expenses	30,000	82,000
Income before taxes		$ 8,000
Income taxes		4,000
Net income		$ 4,000

Calculate the payback period and the average accounting rate of return.

26-E3. M Corporation is considering an investment that will cost $62,500. The cash inflows (after taxes) from the investment over the next four years are expected to be $20,000, $18,750, $20,000, and $18,750. The company uses a discount rate of 16%. On the basis of this information, what would you recommend to M Company regarding the investment?

26-E4. The Brown Company is evaluating two projects for investment. Top management requires a minimum rate of return of 18%. Using profitability index as a guide to investment decisions, which project is the more desirable investment for Brown Company?

	Project A	Project B
Initial cost	$24,000	$30,000
Inflows (after tax)		
Year 1	$15,000	$17,000
Year 2	$13,000	$16,000
Year 3	$10,000	$ 7,000
Year 4	–0–	$ 7,000

26-E5. Crane Chemical Corporation is considering the purchase of a new piece of capital equipment. The new equipment will cost $24,000. After-tax cash inflows from the purchase of this equipment are expected to be $8,000 each year over a four-year period. What is the IRR for this investment?

26-E6. XYZ Investment Company plans to invest in a project with a 40% probability that returns will equal $80,000, a 35% probability that returns will equal $85,000, and a 25% probability that returns will be $95,000. What is the total expected value of the returns on this project?

26-E7. Using the a) payback method, b) profitability index, c) net present value method, and d) internal rate of return, rank the following proposed projects. The minimum rate of return for this company is 16%.

	Initial Outlay	Expected Cash Inflows Per Year	Expected Life of Investment
Investment X	$21,000	$6,000	4 yrs.
Investment Y	$26,000	$4,375	10 yrs.
Investment Z	$42,000	$9,000	5 yrs.

PROBLEM SET A

26-A1. **Discounted Cash Flow Methods.** Johnston Company is considering two alternative investments, as follows:

Investment	Initial Cash Outlay	Expected Annual Net Cash Inflows	Expected Life	Risk Premium
A	$50,000	$6,000	20 yrs.	3%
B	$75,000	$9,000	15 yrs.	2%

Johnston's cost of capital is 5%.

Required

Calculate the net present value and internal rate of return for each project.

26-A2. **Nondiscounted Cash Flow Methods.** April Showers Plumbing, Inc., is considering the following four projects:

Investment	Initial Cash Outlay	Expected Annual Profit	Expected Annual Net Cash Inflows	Expected Life
A	$10,000	$6,000	$5,000	10 yrs.
B	$20,000	$8,000	$5,000	14 yrs.
C	$30,000	$4,000	$7,500	10 yrs.
D	$40,000	$1,000	$8,000	7 yrs.

April Showers' cost of capital is 10%. Ignore tax effects.

Required

a. Compute the payback period for each project and rank the projects from shortest payback to longest payback.
b. Compute the average accounting rate of return for each project and rank the projects from highest to lowest rate of return.

26-A3. Capital Budgeting Techniques. Mail Order Company is considering computerizing its operations. It estimates that the total cash outlay required to put the computer into operation will be $111,334. The computer is expected to contribute net cash inflow profits of $40,000 during each of its eight years of useful life, which amount will be taxed at the marginal rate of 40%. Mail Order's cost of capital is 9%.

Required

a. Compute the payback period for Mail Order's investment.
b. Determine the investment's average rate of return.
c. Calculate the investment's net present value and profitability index.
d. Calculate the internal rate of return.
e. Determine whether or not Mail Order Company should purchase the computer.

26-A4. NPV and IRR—Impact of Changes. Retail, Inc., is considering the purchase of a warehouse so that it can store larger shipments from wholesalers. A warehouse suitable to Retail's needs will require an initial outlay of $200,000 and will last 20 years. Retail expects that larger shipments will bring it quantity discounts on purchases and savings on ordering costs, with net (after-tax) savings of $20,000 per year. The cost of capital is 12%.

Required

a. Compute the net present value and internal rate of return for Retail, Inc.'s, warehouse purchase.
b. If the expected useful life of the warehouse were 30 years instead of 20 years, compute the new NPV and IRR.
c. If Retail's cost of capital were 15% rather than 12%, compute the new NPV and IRR.
d. Suppose that the annual savings were on a before-tax rather than after-tax basis, with Retail's marginal tax rate being 30%. Compute the new NPV and IRR.
e. Determine whether or not Retail, Inc., should purchase the warehouse.

26-A5. Selection Among Investment Alternatives. MFG Corporation has only four investments available. Following are some data relevant to these investments:

Project	Initial Cash Outlay	Expected Annual (After-Tax) Net Cash Inflows	Expected Life Of Investment
A	$ 50,000	$10,000	8 yrs.
B	$ 10,000	$ 3,000	10 yrs.
C	$100,000	$35,000	5 yrs.
D	$ 4,000	$ 1,200	15 yrs.

MFG's cost of capital is 10%.

Required

a. Rank MFG's investments by their net present values and internal rates of return.
b. If the investments are mutually exclusive, which should MFG Corporation accept?
c. If the investments are independent and MFG has $150,000 allotted for capital investments, which should MFG accept?

26-A6. Discounted Cash Flow Methods. The following data were selected from the capital budgeting worksheets of Smithson Corporation.

Investment	Initial Cash Outlay	Expected Life	Selection Criterion
X	$175,000	18 yrs.	NPV = $39,479
Y	$250,000	25 yrs.	IRR = 21.637%

Smithson's cost of capital is 15%.

Required

Calculate the expected annual net cash inflows for each investment. (Hint: Begin by finding the present values of the net cash flow streams.)

26-A7. Equipment Replacement Decision. Analyzer, Inc., is considering the replacement of two existing machines with one larger, technologically superior machine. Information relevant to each machine is as follows:

1. New Machine Purchase price is $250,000. Freight and installation costs are estimated to be $10,000. The machine is to be depreciated on a straight-line basis over a useful life of eight years with no salvage value.
2. Replaced Machine 1 Originally purchased three years ago at a price of $100,000, this machine was depreciated on a straight-line basis over its five-year useful life with $5,000 salvage value. Management estimates that the machine could be sold for $25,000.
3. Replaced Machine 2 Originally purchased last year at a cost of $200,000, this machine was to last for six years with $50,000 salvage value. Straight-line depreciation has been used. Management estimates that the machine could be sold for $150,000.
4. Other Data Due to the technological superiority of the new machine, management estimates that operating costs of $60,000 could be saved each year. Analyzer, Inc.'s, cost of capital is 12%, and its marginal tax rate is 40%.

Required

Analyze the preceding cash flows and determine, based on a net present value technique, whether or not Analyzer, Inc., should replace the machines currently employed.

26-A8. Decision Between Alternative Risky Equipment Replacements. Wholesaler Enterprises is considering two investments to improve the efficiency of its warehousing operations: a forklift to aid in receiving shipments and a conveyor belt to aid in assembling orders. Since its capital budget is limited, Wholesaler can afford to accept only one of the investments and so views the two investments as mutually exclusive. The following information is relevant to the two investments:

1. Forklift The forklift could be purchased for $100,000, including delivery, to replace the old forklift currently in use. The old forklift was purchased five years ago at a cost of $50,000 to last seven years, at the end of which it would be sold for its $1,000 salvage value. Consistent with this, management estimates the new forklift would last seven years and have a salvage value of $2,000. Management estimates that the new forklift could save $35,000 each year, but this is highly dependent upon the efficiency of the forklift's operator. Thus, management requires an 8% risk premium on the investment. Wholesaler has received an offer of $20,000 for the old forklift.
2. Conveyor belt The conveyor belt could be purchased for $90,000, including delivery and installation, and would free personnel from using a fleet of 50 hydraulic pushcarts. The pushcarts were purchased at a cost of $1,000 each when Wholesaler started in business ten years ago. Since that time, they have been fully depreciated without salvage value, but they

can now be sold for $100 each. Management believes the conveyor belt would last eight years without replacement or major overhaul. The benefit to be derived from the conveyor belt is directly dependent upon the speed at which it is run. While operating at low speed, the conveyor could save $18,000 per year. At medium speed, $23,000 per year could be saved; and at high speed, $27,000 per year could be saved. Management estimates that during the first two years, the belt will run on low speed 40% of the time, medium speed 50% of the time, and high speed 10% of the time. For the next four years, the belt would run 20% on low, 50% on medium, and 30% on high. In the final two years, the belt should run 40% on medium and 60% on high. Management believes this estimates the risk well and so does not impose a risk premium on this investment.

3. Other data Wholesaler Enterprises' cost of capital is 10%, and the company is in the 30% marginal tax bracket. Wholesaler uses straight-line depreciation for all of its capital assets.

Required

Analyze the preceding cash flows, taking risk into account as stated, and determine which investment Wholesaler Enterprises should make to maximize the firm's net present value.

PROBLEM SET B

26-B1. Discounted Cash Flow Methods. Charleson, Inc., keeps extensive records concerning its investment proposals. Certain records were destroyed in a recent office fire. Among the surviving data were the following:

Investment	Initial Cash Outlay	Expected Annual Net Cash Inflows	Expected Life	Selection Criterion
A	?	$15,000	20 yrs.	NPV = $65,700
B	?	$37,500	12 yrs.	IRR = 41%

Charleson's cost of capital is 11%.

Required

Calculate what the initial cash outlays of the investments must have been. (Hint: Find the present values of the net cash inflow streams first.)

26-B2. Nondiscounted Cash Flow Methods. Clipping Papermills, Inc., is considering four possible investments for its capital budget. The following data were selected from its analyses.

Investment	Initial Cash Outlay	Expected Annual Net Cash Inflows	Payback Period	Average Rate Of Return
A	$ 40,000	?	5.33 yrs.	?
B	$150,000	?	?	18.3%
C	?	$ 975	5.13 yrs.	?
D	?	$9,680	?	25.8%

Clipping's cost of capital is 17%. Tax effects were ignored in the analyses. Annual profits have equaled net cash inflows.

Required

Calculate the missing figures.

26-B3. Capital Budgeting Techniques. The Bharat Machine Tool Company is evaluating a proposal to acquire a 50-ton overhead crane. The crane costs $40,000 and would require an additional $4,000 to install and put into operation. The equipment is estimated to have a useful life of eight years with no salvage value and would be depreciated on a straight-line basis. The before-tax annual cash inflow from this investment is expected to be $11,000. The company is in the 40% tax bracket, and its cost of capital is 10%.

Required

a. Compute the after-tax payback period for this proposal.
b. Determine the after-tax average accounting rate of return on the investment.
c. Compute the net present value of the investment proposal and the internal rate of return.
d. Determine whether or not Bharat Machine Tool Company should acquire the overhead crane.

26-B4. NPV—Impact of Changes. Wholesaler Company is considering the purchase of a warehouse so that it can store larger shipments from manufacturers. A warehouse suitable to Wholesaler's needs will require an initial outlay of $500,000 and will last 20 years. Wholesaler expects that larger shipments will bring it quantity discounts on purchases and savings on ordering costs, with net (after-tax) savings of $60,000 per year. The cost of capital is 12%.

Required

a. What is the maximum amount that Wholesaler should be willing to pay for the warehouse, given the cash inflow stream? Compare this with the stated cost. Should Wholesaler buy the warehouse?
b. For how many years must the cash inflows continue (at the same level) for the warehouse to be an acceptable investment? Compare this with the stated life. Should Wholesaler buy the warehouse?
c. What maximum cost of capital will the investment support? Compare this with the stated cost of capital. Should Wholesaler make the investment?

(Hint: The minimum profitability of an acceptable investment is a net present value of zero.)

26-B5. Selection Among Investment Alternatives. Johanson Company is considering two mutually exclusive investment proposals. Relevant data are as follows:

			Return (Profit = Cash Inflow)		
Project	**Life**	**Cost**	**Year 1**	**Year 2**	**Year 3**
A	3 yrs.	$1,200	$ 100	$600	$1,100
B	3 yrs.	$1,200	$1,000	$500	$ 100

Johanson's cost of capital is 9%.

Required

a. For Project A, calculate the internal rate of return and average accounting rate of return. What is responsible for the difference between these measures?
b. Calculate the internal rate of return for Project B and compare it with the IRR of Project A. Which project should Johanson accept?
c. Compute the net present values for both projects. Based on the comparative NPVs, which project should Johanson accept?
d. Was the project selected by IRR (b) different from the project selected by NPV (c)? If so, what is responsible for the difference?

26-B6. Discounted Cash Flow Methods. Capital Corporation has only four investment alternatives. Following are some data relevant to the investments:

Project	Initial Cash Outlay	Expected Annual (After-Tax) Net Cash Inflows	Expected Life Of Investment
A	$100,000	$20,000	8 yrs.
B	$ 20,000	$13,000	10 yrs.
C	$150,000	$45,000	5 yrs.
D	$ 8,000	$ 6,200	15 yrs.

Capital Corporation's cost of capital is 10%.

Required

a. Calculate the internal rate of return for each of the investments.
b. What does the information in (a) suggest about the riskiness of each of the four investments?
c. Would the cost of capital be an appropriate standard for judging the value of each of the investments?

26-B7. Equipment Replacement Decision—Impact of Changes. Techno, Inc., is considering the replacement of two existing machines with one larger, technologically superior machine. Information relevant to each machine is as follows:

1. **New Machine** Purchase price is $450,000. Freight and installation costs are estimated to be $20,000. The machine is to be depreciated on a straight-line basis over a useful life of eight years with no salvage value.
2. **Replaced Machine 1** Originally purchased three years ago at a price of $150,000, this machine was depreciated on a straight-line basis over its five-year useful life with $5,000 salvage value. Management estimates that the machine could be sold for $30,000.
3. **Replaced Machine 2** Originally purchased last year at a cost of $150,000, this machine was to last for six years with $51,000 salvage value. Straight-line depreciation has been used. Management estimates that the machine could be sold but is unsure of minimum acceptable price.
4. **Other Data** Due to the technological superiority of the new machine, management estimates that operating costs of $90,000 could be saved each year. Techno, Inc.'s, cost of capital is 12%, and its marginal tax rate is 40%.

Required

Calculate the minimum sales price of machine 2 that Techno, Inc., must receive to make the investment acceptable. (Hint: First determine the present value of the net cash inflows and then find the sales price of machine 2 for which the initial cash outflow equals the present value of the net cash inflows.)

26-B8. Decision Between Alternative Risky Equipment Replacements—Impact of Changes. Entrepreneur Corporation is considering two investments to improve the efficiency of its warehousing operations: a forklift to aid in receiving shipments and a computer to maintain perpetual inventory records. Since its capital budget is limited, Entrepreneur can afford to accept only one of the investments and so views the two investments as mutually exclusive. Information relevant to the two investments is as follows:

1. **Forklift** The forklift could be purchased for $200,000, including delivery, to replace the old forklift currently in use. The old forklift was purchased five years ago at a cost of $50,000 to last seven years, at the end of which it would be sold for its $1,000 salvage value. Consistent with this, management estimates the new forklift would last seven years and have a salvage value of $4,000. Management estimates that the new forklift could save $55,000 each year,

but this is highly dependent upon the efficiency of the forklift's operator. Thus, management requires a risk premium on the investment. Entrepreneur has received an offer of $40,000 for the old forklift.

2. Computer system The computer system could be purchased for $90,000, including delivery and installation, and would free personnel from constantly updating the inventory sheets. Entrepreneur prints its own inventory sheets on ten printers purchased ten years ago at a cost of $1,000 each. Since that time, the printers have been fully depreciated without salvage value, but they can now be sold for $100 each. Management believes the computer system would last eight years without replacement or major overhaul. The benefit to be derived from the computer is directly dependent upon the speed with which personnel become accustomed to using it, rather than on the inventory sheets. An analyst has estimated that 25% of the personnel would learn to use the computer after two years of experience, 40% after four years, and 25% after six years, and that 10% will refuse to learn to use the computer. Management estimates that when used by unlearned personnel, the computer will save $20,000/year, instead of the $40,000/year savings provided with learned personnel. Mangement believes this estimates the risk well and so does not impose a risk premium on this investment.

3. Other data Entrepreneur Corporation's cost of capital is 10%, and the company is in the 30% marginal tax bracket. Entrepreneur uses straight-line depreciation for all of its capital assets.

Required

Calculate the risk premium that would need to be imposed on the forklift investment to make Entrepreneur Corporation indifferent between the two proposals. (Hint: Since two investments must have equal net present values for an investor to be indifferent between them, first calculate the net present value of the computer investment and then find the discount rate (i.e., cost of capital plus risk premium) for which the net present value of the forklift investment equals it.)

APPLICATION

Parker Hannifin Corporation

Introduction

In 1918, Arthur L. Parker, an engineer, inventor and entrepreneur, started the Parker Appliance Company in Cleveland, Ohio. In those days, the term appliance did not have a kitchen connotation. Rather, the main product was a new type of braking system for trucks and buses which used compressed air. To promote this concept and demonstrate the effectiveness of the braking system, Mr. Parker outfitted a truck to make a demonstration run between Akron, Ohio and Boston, Massachusetts over hilly and dangerous roads. Unfortunately, the truck went over the side of a mountain (though not through the fault of the braking system), and the entire capital of the fledgling company went with it.

Undaunted, Mr. Parker started the company over again in 1924 with Carl Klamm, his original first employee. In the meantime, new uses had been found for compressed air, and the technology became a powerful way to do many types of physical work. The company found additional markets than originally anticipated for its line of products, and the business prospered.

Parker Hannifin's history can be divided into several critical stages. In the late 1930's, Arthur Parker foresaw that there would be a major war between the United States and Nazi Germany, which would convert the country to a military-oriented economy. Parker held numerous patents on the hydraulic components and systems for military aircraft. When the production of aircraft exploded during World War II, the Parker Appliance Company became the largest producer of hydraulic connecting and metering devices in the world.

EXHIBIT 1

Parker Hannifin Corporation

Financial Summary* (Dollars in thousands, except per share amounts)	1985	1984	1983	1982	1981	1980	1979
Net sales	$1,459,518	$1,304,817	$1,086,046	$1,198,273	$1,156,503	$1,075,925	$ 935,339
Cost of sales	1,107,297	996,129	865,096	939,590	889,299	830,756	708,036
Selling, general and administrative expenses	191,490	173,842	155,360	153,256	146,313	127,629	116,743
Interest expense	15,872	16,097	18,185	22,045	24,823	22,003	13,858
Interest and other income, net	(4,019)	(5,447)	(1,880)	(3,403)	(1,679)	(1,722)	(1,034)
Gain on disposal of assets	—	—	(421)	(7,993)	(6,512)	—	(3,229)
Income taxes	64,743	52,697	18,269	35,493	41,314	38,666	46,117
Net income	84,135	71,499	31,437	59,285	62,945	58,593	54,848
Earnings per share:							
Primary	3.06	2.68	1.20	2.28	2.59	2.54	2.39
Fully diluted	$ 2.98	$ 2.59	$ 1.17	$ 2.22	$ 2.51	$ 2.45	$ 2.30
Average number of shares outstanding (thousands)	27,514	26,666	26,242	25,997	24,328	23,068	22,925
Cash dividends per share**	$ 1.10	$ 1.04	$ .98	$ .96	$ .88	$ .80	$ .75
Cash dividends paid**	$ 29,931	$ 26,903	$ 24,706	$ 24,006	$ 20,283	$ 17,249	$ 14,782
Net income as a percent of net sales	5.8%	5.5%	2.9%	4.9%	5.4%	5.4%	5.9%
Return on average assets	9.0%	8.3%	3.8%	7.2%	8.4%	8.9%	9.9%
Return on average equity	15.4%	14.4%	6.7%	13.1%	15.9%	17.5%	18.9%
Book value per share	$ 20.84	$ 19.33	$ 17.90	$ 17.93	$ 16.81	$ 15.45	$13.57
Current assets	558,567	552,093	492,805	517,094	506,873	454,366	416,907
Current liabilities	226,018	217,141	175,807	186,880	202,825	177,849	170,806
Working capital	332,549	$ 334,952	$316,998	$ 330,214	$ 304,048	$ 276,517	$ 246,101
Ratio of current assets to current liabilities	2.5	2.5	2.8	2.8	2.5	2.6	2.4
Plant and equipment, net	$ 391,743	$ 335,916	$ 304,068	$ 301,198	$ 276,638	$ 224,713	$ 191,303
Total assets	966,386	905,345	814,370	836,275	803,934	690,910	621,263
Long-term debt	129,127	145,669	145,983	166,298	153,016	144,928	128,408
Shareholders' equity	577,167	$ 518,321	$ 473,706	$ 467,766	$ 435,529	$ 357,306	$312,684
Debt to debt-equity percent	20.7%	23.5%	25.0%	29.7%	30.1%	35.3%	35.2%
Depreciation	$ 42,433	$ 37,421	$ 35,951	$ 33,587	$ 30,060	$ 25,060	$ 20,207
Capital expenditures	$ 91,818	$ 75,429	$ 45,421	$ 57,089	$ 49,779	$ 54,462	$ 50,163
Number of employees	23,064	22,167	19,059	20,036	23,144	21,056	22,272
Number of shareholders**	21,625	19,879	18,402	13,944	12,572	12,108	7,446
Number of shares outstanding at year-end (thousands)	27,689	26,808	26,469	26,083	25,907	23,123	23,040

*The year 1979 has not been restated for the effects of Statements of Financial Accounting Standards Nos. 43 and 52.

**Historical data not restated for poolings of interests.

EXHIBIT 2

Parker Hannifin Corporation Primary Measures of Divisional Performance (Note: These illustrations use 1984 financial data.)

1. Return on Sales

is the ratio of net earnings to net sales, expressed as a percentage.

Elements:

Net Sales	$1,304,817
Net Earnings (after tax)	71,499

Computation:

$$\frac{\text{Net Earnings}}{\text{Net Sales}} = \frac{\$71,499}{\$1,304,817} = 5.5\%$$

Memo:

1. This ratio depicts the percentage of each sales dollar remaining to the company for reinvestment or for paying dividends to shareholders. The ratio is commonly used to compare companies in similar businesses or to track profitability trends for a single business entity.
2. Parker's strategic goal for this ratio is 6.0%.

2. Gross Profit Margin

is the ratio of gross profit to net sales, expressed as a percentage. Gross profit is sales revenue less cost of sales, which is comprised of the costs of manufacturing products.

Elements:

Sales	$1,304,817
less: Cost of Sales	996,129
Gross Profit	$ 308,688

Computation:

$$\frac{\text{Gross Profit}}{\text{Net Sales}} = \frac{\$308,688}{\$1,304,817} = 23.7\%$$

Memo:

1. This ratio measures the percentage of each sales dollar remaining after deducting the cost of manufacturing the product.

3. Selling, General and Administrative (S. G. & A.) Expense to Sales

is the ratio of S. G. & A. expenses to sales, expressed as a percentage.

Elements:

Selling, General & Administrative Expense	$ 173,842
Net Sales	$1,304,817

Computation:

$$\frac{\text{S. G. \& A. Expenses}}{\text{Net Sales}} = \frac{\$173,842}{\$1,304,817} = 13.3\%$$

Memo:

1. Trends in individual expense items can be monitored over time by comparing their relationship to the movement in sales. This ratio is the percentage of each dollar of sales necessary to cover selling, general and administrative expenses.

4. Return on Cost Goal Assets

is an internal performance indicator which is used to determine incentive payout levels for certain salaried employees.

The return on cost goal assets is the ratio of cost goal earnings to cost goal assets. Cost goal earnings consist of divisional net earnings (D.N.E.) less the "standard requirement" plus tax credits and transfer credits. The standard requirement is an adjustment to an operating unit's D.N.E. to cover a portion of corporate general and administrative expenses. The standard requirement is adjusted by a "building equalization" factor which represents the difference between depreciation and rental expense forecasted by the division versus depreciation calculated by Corporate at a uniform rate per square foot. Tax credit adjustments relate to Federal taxes computed by Corporate while transfer credits arise from the transfer of inventory to another operating unit.

Cost goal assets are comprised of land and buildings, machinery and equipment, average net inventories, and average net trade receivables. The value of land and buildings is determined by taking all owned and leased floor space and applying square footage rates (which include an estimate for land value) established by Corporate. Machinery and equipment is valued at net book value at the beginning of each fiscal year and is not revalued during the year. Inventories and receivables are valued at a simple average of the net monthly balances of the previous twelve months ending May 31 of each year.

5. Months Supply

is the number of months of forecasted sales at standard cost invested in inventory.

Elements:

Inventory (at standard)	$54,900
Cost of Sales (at standard)	
November	19,000
December	17,000
January	16,300
February	13,000

EXHIBIT 2
continued

Computation:

		No. of Months' Cost of Sales Consumed
Inventory (at standard)	54,900	
Less: Cost of Sales (at standard)		
November	19,000	1
December	17,000	1
January	16,300	1
Remaining Inventory	2,600	
Proportion of final month's cost of sales required to liquidate inventory	= Remaining Inv. / Feb. Cost of Sales = 2,600 / 13,000 = .2	.2
Inventory Months Supply		3.2

Memo:

1. This ratio shows how many months of forecasted sales it takes to liquidate the current inventory balance.

6. Days Sales Outstanding (DSO)

is the number of days' sales which remain as a receivable at the end of a financial reporting period.

Elements:

Accounts Receivable	$199,108
Sales—June (30 days)	$122,840
May (31 days)	$120,084

Computation:

			No. of Days Consumed
Accounts Receivable	$199,108		
June Sales	$122,840		30
	$ 76,268		
May Average Daily Sales	$120,084 / 31	= $3,874	
Remaining Receivables / Average Daily Sales	$76,268 / $3,874	=	20
Days Sales Outstanding			50

Memo:

1. This ratio measures approximately how many days' worth of sales remain uncollected. If all customers are paying on time, the collection period should approximate the company's selling terms.

However, the death of Arthur Parker in January, 1945 preceded a critical period for the company. All of its production had been diverted to military purposes, and it had no other markets or major customers. With the end of the war, the company was faced with the prospect of no demand for its products, and no leader to get it through this crisis. S. Blackwell Taylor and Robert Cornell (both of whom later served as C.E.O.) took over the reins of the company and attempted to see what could be done with the products and the expertise that the company had developed during the war.

Fortunately, the late 1940's saw a growing demand for industrial hydraulic and pneumatic products. The company used this opportunity to provide precision devices which used fluid power components to meet the needs of industry. This led to solid and steady growth in the 1950's. The decade of the 60's saw a worldwide economic surge which led the company to quadruple its size and profitability. Even in the early 1970's, when the U.S. was in a period of recession, the company again doubled in size. The consistent strategy and management stability of Parker Hannifin has enabled it to respond to difficult times and to prosper when other companies might have collapsed.

Organizational Structure and Performance Measures

Today, Parker Hannifin is a worldwide corporation with 23,000 employees and sales of $1.45 billion. However, the basic philosophy of the company—to be the leading supplier of a total range of fluid power products—has not changed. Parker Hannifin is organized into three major business segments—industrial; automotive; and aviation, space and marine. These segments are, in turn, subdivided into 11 groups and 69 divisions which operate as profit centers, 133 manufacturing plants, 54 administrative and sales offices, and 72 product and distribution service centers around the world. Exhibit 1 contains a summary of financial data for the company for the past seven years.

The core operating units within Parker Hannifin are the divisions. These units are treated as profit centers and a divisional general manager is encouraged to operate his or her division as an independent, small company. Divisional performance is measured by several different indices as shown in Exhibit 2. Each year as part of the annual budget process goals are set for the corporation and its segments, groups and divisions. Throughout the year, performance is monitored by comparing actual attainment versus goals.

EXHIBIT 3

Parker Hannifin Corporation Financial Goals and Performance

	Goal	1985	1984	1983	1982	1981
Five-year compound sales growth (%)	10	6.3	6.9	7.3	13.1	16.8
Net income on sales (%)	6	5.8	5.5	2.9	4.9	5.4
Average assets/sales ($)	.60	.64	.66	.76	.68	.65
Return on average assets (%)	10	9.0	8.3	3.8	7.2	8.4
Return on average equity (%)	19	15.4	14.4	6.7	13.1	15.9
Five-year compound earnings per share growth (%)	12	3.8	2.3	(8.6)	7.3	15.3
Debt to debt-equity (%)	33–37	20.7	23.5	25.0	29.7	30.1
Dividend payout ratio (%)	33	35.6	37.6	78.6	40.5	32.2

Each year, the company publishes its financial goals and performance in the annual report, as shown in Exhibit 3.

Divisions are purposely kept small at Parker Hannifin—normally averaging $25 million in sales—so the company maintains its flexibility and entrepreneurial spirit. As the corporation has grown in size in the last decade additional levels of management and controls have been added to facilitate coordination and integration among business units. This need for greater control occasionally undermines the autonomy of divisional managers but does not eliminate the company's philosophy of decentralization through divisionalization.

Exercises

1. Evaluate the strengths and weaknesses of Parker Hannifin's system for evaluating divisional performance. What other factors do you feel are important in measuring the financial performance of these divisions?

2. Exhibit 4 is an excerpt from Parker Hannifin's 1985 annual report providing segment information by geographic area. What is the relative performance of the U.S. and European segments using the ROI and RI methods of evaluation. Assume the company has a cost of capital of 13%.

3. Assume you are a divisional manager with a divisional target return on cost goal assets of 32% (pre-tax). You are currently deciding whether to invest in a large piece of machinery with a return of 26%. What factors should you consider in making this decision?

4. Parker Hannifin's 1985 sales were approximately 12% higher than in 1984, yet income from operations increased by 19%. How did this happen?

EXHIBIT 4

Parker Hannifin Corporation Business Segment Information by Geographic Area

(Dollars in thousands)	1985	1984	1983
Net sales, including interarea sales:			
United States	$1,267,639	$1,118,362	$ 894,698
Europe	164,801	162,104	171,090
All Other	61,147	54,524	42,339
Interarea	(34,069)	(30,173)	(22,081)
	$1,459,518	$1,304,817	$1,086,046
Income from operations before corporate general and administrative expenses:			
United States	$ 165,749	$ 140,194	$ 71,665
Europe	13,511	9,241	7,768
All Other	8,058	7,328	4,726
	187,318	156,763	84,159
Corporate general and administrative	26,587	21,917	18,569
expenses	26,587	21,917	18,569
Income from operations	160,731	134,846	65,590
Other deductions	11,853	10,650	15,884
Income before income taxes	$ 148,878	$ 124,196	$ 49,706
Identifiable assets:			
United States	$ 744,598	$ 664,157	$ 571,665
Europe	159,915	155,129	169,193
All Other	38,530	34,150	30,981
	943,043	853,436	771,839
Corporate assets	23,343	51,909	42,531
	$ 966,386	$ 905,345	$ 814,370

Segment Information by Geographic Area (Fiscal Year 1985)

	Sales	Operating Income
United States	84.9%	88.5%
Europe	11.0%	7.2%
All Other	4.1%	4.3%

APPENDIX E
AN OVERVIEW OF INCOME TAXATION

Whether we like it or not, taxes are a part of life. At times it seems that we are bombarded with taxes—income taxes, sales taxes, property taxes, gift taxes—even death taxes. However, as April 15 nears each year, the tax with which most people are concerned is the income tax. Although many state and local governments require income taxes, the criteria for taxation often vary from state to state and municipality to municipality. The federal income tax, however, is common to all Americans. Because of its importance in personal and managerial planning, the federal income tax is the focus of this appendix.

Although the federal tax laws are extremely complex, the average individual needs a general understanding of the rules. The specifics of the regulations are not permanent, nor are they necessarily logical. A certain expense that might be deductible this year might not be deductible next year. This Appendix presents the federal tax code as it exists for 1985. Pending legislation is likely to change some of the tax law. Through a reform in tax legislation, the tax burden can shift from one taxpayer to another, such as from an individual taxpayer to a corporate taxpayer. Also, two similar transactions can be treated in different ways for tax purposes. For instance, alimony must be included in gross income, whereas child support is not taxable.

This appendix addresses only the fundamentals of the federal income tax, leaving a detailed examination of the intricacies to an income tax course. It is important, however, to recognize that the greater access an individual or corporation has to the interpretation of the federal tax laws—whether through direct knowledge or from advice of a tax expert—the better the chance of converting a tax consequence into a tax opportunity. Tax planning, thus, plays an integral part in the success of many corporations and individuals.

WHO PAYS TAXES?

Taxpayers are classified as individuals, corporations, estates, or trusts. We are concerned here only with individuals and corporations. Proprietorships and partnerships are classified as individual taxpayers. Proprietors report business income and deduct business expenses along with other personal income and deductions on individual tax returns. Partnerships are required to file a partnership tax return, on which net income is allocated proportionately to each partner.

INDIVIDUAL INCOME TAX

Filing Requirements

Individuals have a choice in claiming their status for income tax reporting purposes. The categories from which individuals can choose, as long as they are qualified, are single, head of household, married filing jointly, and married filing separately. The income tax liability will likely differ depending on which filing status is claimed.

A person who receives self-employment income of $400 or greater must file a tax return for the year. Any individual is required to file if adjusted gross income is in excess of the following amounts:

Single	$2,390	Head of household	$2,390
Married filing jointly	$3,540	Married filing separately	$1,770

The threshold filing amount for each category is referred to as the zero bracket amount and is discussed in the section on itemized deductions. An individual receiving less than the specified amount is not required to file but should do so if he or she is entitled to a refund in taxes that were withheld by an employer.

The form completed by the individual taxpayer is the 1040 form, the U.S. Individual Income Tax Return. The filing of income tax returns can be quite involved in cases where numerous supplemental tax forms and schedules need to be completed. The government allows calendar year taxpayers until April 15 of each year to file. Since most taxpayers operate on a fiscal year ending December 31, they have sufficient time to organize their records and complete their tax returns.

The Individual Income Tax Model

All taxpayers ideally seek to minimize total tax liability. Exhibit E.1 illustrates the individual income tax model. At each downward level, the model narrows, decreasing the potential tax liability. Tax planning is often a vital factor in reducing tax to the lowest extent possible. Each of the components of the individual tax model that pertain to the completion of the 1040 form is discussed in the following sections.

Gross Income. **Gross income** is defined in the Internal Revenue Code as "all income from whatever source derived." Thus, wages, tips, salaries, rents, royalties, interest, dividends, prizes, gains, and alimony are common elements of gross income. Unless a law exists that specifically excludes a particular type of income from gross income, the income must be included and is therefore taxable. The exceptions that the law allows to be omitted from gross income are called **exclusions.** Some examples of exclusions are life insurance proceeds, gifts, child support, interest on state and local bonds, limited Social Security payments, certain tuition scholarships, workers' compensation, and $100 of dividends ($200 for married individuals filing jointly, although each spouse must receive $100 of dividends to claim the full $200). Loans received are not gross income, because the money must be replaced by the taxpayer at some future date. However, if a debt is forgiven by the person or entity

GROSS INCOME
All income from whatever source derived.

EXCLUSIONS
Exceptions allowed by law to be omitted from gross income.

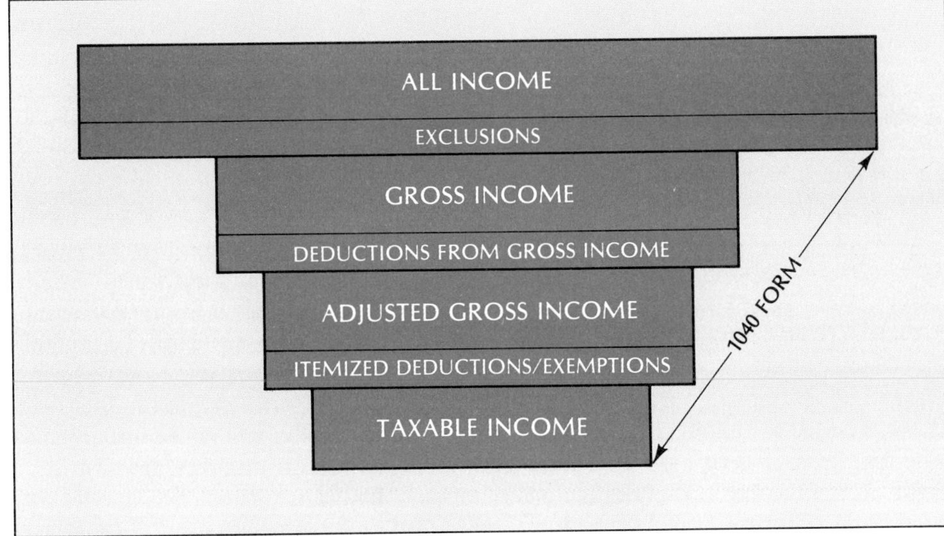

EXHIBIT E.1
The Individual Income Tax Model

who has granted the loan, the sum that was forgiven is then includible in gross income by the taxpayer.

DEDUCTIONS FROM GROSS INCOME
Deductions that are subtracted from gross income to arrive at adjusted gross income.

Deductions from Gross Income. The two types of deductions available to individual taxpayers are deductions from gross income and itemized deductions. Of the two, probably the more important are **deductions from gross income** (deductions subtracted from gross income to arrive at adjusted gross income). Typically, these deductions pertain to business or investment-related expenditures. The following paragraphs discuss some deductions from gross income.

Expenses Incurred in a Trade or Business. Since individuals who are involved in a trade or business must report all receipt of income in gross income, they are permitted a deduction for all expenses associated with the generation of that income. (This concept parallels sales less cost of goods sold in the arrival of net income before taxes on an income statement.) Ordinary and necessary expenses are deductible, along with business losses, such as uninsured casualty and theft losses.

Long-Term Capital Gain Deduction. As stated before, gains are includible in gross income. However, if a net gain for the year is classified as a long-term capital gain, the taxpayer is entitled to a 60 percent deduction on the gain. This process is discussed in detail in the Capital Gains and Losses section later in the appendix.

Employee Business Expenses. An employee is entitled to a deduction of most expenses incurred that directly pertain to employment and that have not been reimbursed by the employer. Expenses paid by an employee on a business trip are examples of deductible expenditures. The costs of traveling to and from work are not deductible.

Contributions to Health and Retirement Plans. The government currently allows a deduction for contributions to Individual Retirement Accounts (IRAs), health plans, and self-employment retirement plans, with certain limitations.

Other Deductions. Other deductions include losses from property held for investment purposes and alimony paid.

ADJUSTED GROSS INCOME
Gross income minus allowed deductions from gross income.

Adjusted Gross Income. **Adjusted gross income** is defined as gross income less allowed deductions from gross income. It is considerably advantageous to reduce adjusted gross income with deductions from gross income. One reason for this is that certain itemized deductions are based on adjusted gross income. For example, qualified medical expenses incurred are currently deductible in the amount paid that is in excess of five percent of adjusted gross income. Therefore, when adjusted gross income is decreased, the potential for claiming a greater amount of itemized deductions is increased.

ITEMIZED DEDUCTIONS
Specifically permitted items that can be subtracted from adjusted gross income to reduce an individual's taxable base.

ZERO BRACKET AMOUNT
A specific amount of deductions automatically granted to each taxpayer.

Itemized Deductions. **Itemized deductions** are specifically permitted items that can be subtracted from adjusted gross income to reduce an individual's taxable base. Itemized deductions relate to expenses that are usually personal in nature. They are often called excess itemized deductions, because it is only beneficial for individuals to itemize in excess of their zero bracket amounts. The **zero bracket amount** represents a specific amount of deductions automatically granted to each taxpayer. As stated before, the zero bracket amounts are $2,390 for single taxpayers, $2,390 for a head of household, $3,540 for married persons filing jointly, and $1,770 for a married person filing separately.

To illustrate how the zero bracket amount works, suppose that Mr. Jones, a single taxpayer, realized $3,000 of qualified itemized deductions during the year. Only the excess of the itemized deductions over the zero bracket amount can be claimed:

Total itemized deductions	$3,000
Zero bracket amount	2,390
Excess itemized deductions	$ 610

Mr. Jones would subtract $610 from his adjusted gross income. An individual who has accrued itemized deductions in an amount less than the zero bracket amount cannot use the itemized deductions. If Mr. Jones had acquired only $1,400 of itemized deductions during the year, he would not deduct them, because the $1,400 of deductions is less than his zero bracket amount of $2,390. He would claim zero itemized deductions, because the zero bracket amount deduction is automatically accounted for in the Tax Table. The first dollar of tax liability for a single taxpayer occurs at an income of $2,391. Therefore, each individual claiming single status is automatically granted $2,390 in deductions from income or, in other words, $2,390 of tax-free income.

Medical and dental expenses. As explained earlier, a restriction of five percent of adjusted gross income is applied to the total amount deductible. Doctor bills, dentist bills, hospital bills, insurance premiums, hearing aids, and eyeglasses are examples of qualified medical and dental expenses.

Taxes. Since taxes such as property taxes, sales taxes, and state and local income taxes are paid to state and local governments, the federal government currently allows a deduction for these amounts. These deductions, however, may be eliminated within the next few years.

Interest. Personal interest paid, such as home mortgage and credit card interest, is deductible.

Charitable contributions. The federal government allows a deduction for contributions to qualified charitable organizations, with certain limitations.

Other itemized deductions. Deductions for personal casualty and theft losses, union and professional dues, professional subscription fees, and fees for tax return preparation are allowed.

Exemptions. All individual taxpayers are permitted, in addition to itemized deductions, certain deductions from adjusted gross income. Each taxpayer is given one **personal exemption,** a deduction from adjusted gross income of $1,040. Married taxpayers filing jointly are allowed two personal exemptions. Any taxpayer who is at least 65 years old or blind is given an additional exemption. **Dependency exemptions** are deductions from adjusted gross income granted for all qualified dependents of a taxpayer. A dependent must fulfill the following requirements:

PERSONAL EXEMPTION
A deduction from adjusted gross income granted to individual taxpayers.

DEPENDENCY EXEMPTION
A deduction from adjusted gross income granted to taxpayers for each qualified dependent.

1. Be a relative of the taxpayer or a member of the taxpayer's household for most of the taxable year.
2. Have over one-half of his or her financial support provided by the taxpayer.
3. Receive less than $1,040 of income for the year, unless the person is the taxpayer's child who is under 19 or is a full-time student.
4. Be a U.S. citizen.
5. Not file a joint return with a spouse if married.

The taxpayer can claim an exemption of $1,040 for each dependent. A child who is the dependent of the taxpayer and who is under 19 or is a full-time student can also take a personal exemption if he or she is required to file a return, even if the parent claims the child as a dependent.

Taxable Income and Computation of Tax. After original gross income has been decreased through deductions and exemptions, the amount that remains is taxable income. To compute the tax, individuals with taxable income of $50,000 or less usually refer to the Tax Table, a portion of which is pictured in Exhibit E.2. In the left-hand column, the appropriate row is located that includes the corresponding taxable income amount. The tax is ascertained by moving across to the proper filing status on that row; this amount constitutes the tax liability for the year. Individuals accumulating over $50,000 and others who are not permitted to use the Tax Table must compute their tax from the Tax Rate Schedule. The 1985 Tax Rate Schedule

EXHIBIT E.2

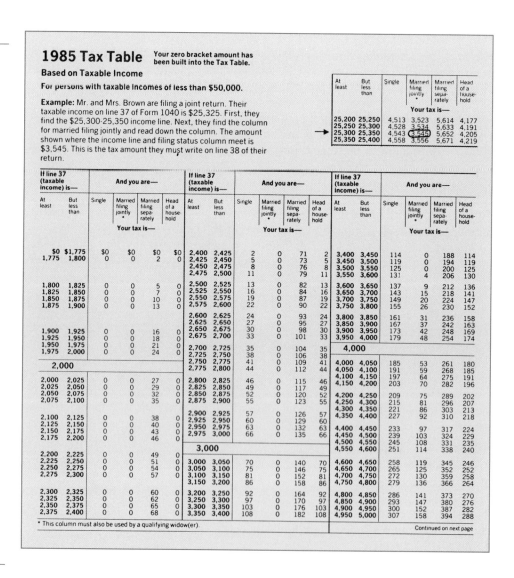

1985 Tax Table

Your zero bracket amount has been built into the Tax Table.

Based on Taxable Income

For persons with taxable incomes of less than $50,000.

Example: Mr. and Mrs. Brown are filing a joint return. Their taxable income on line 37 of Form 1040 is $25,325. First, they find the $25,300-25,350 income line. Next, they find the column for married filing jointly and read down the column. The amount shown where the income line and filing status column meet is $3,545. This is the tax amount they must write on line 38 of their return.

At least	But less than	Single	Married filing jointly *	Married filing separately	Head of a household
		Your tax is—			
25,200	25,250	4,513	3,523	5,614	4,177
25,250	25,300	4,528	3,534	5,633	4,191
→ 25,300	25,350	4,543	(3,545)	5,652	4,205
25,350	25,400	4,558	3,556	5,671	4,219

If line 37 (taxable income) is—		And you are—			
At least	But less than	Single	Married filing jointly *	Married filing separately	Head of a household
		Your tax is—			
$0	$1,775	$0	$0	$0	$0
1,775	1,800	0	0	2	0
1,800	1,825	0	0	5	0
1,825	1,850	0	0	7	0
1,850	1,875	0	0	10	0
1,875	1,900	0	0	13	0
1,900	1,925	0	0	16	0
1,925	1,950	0	0	18	0
1,950	1,975	0	0	21	0
1,975	2,000	0	0	24	0
2,000					
2,000	2,025	0	0	27	0
2,025	2,050	0	0	29	0
2,050	2,075	0	0	32	0
2,075	2,100	0	0	35	0
2,100	2,125	0	0	38	0
2,125	2,150	0	0	40	0
2,150	2,175	0	0	43	0
2,175	2,200	0	0	46	0
2,200	2,225	0	0	49	0
2,225	2,250	0	0	51	0
2,250	2,275	0	0	54	0
2,275	2,300	0	0	57	0
2,300	2,325	0	0	60	0
2,325	2,350	0	0	62	0
2,350	2,375	0	0	65	0
2,375	2,400	0	0	68	0

If line 37 (taxable income) is—		And you are—			
At least	But less than	Single	Married filing jointly *	Married filing separately	Head of a household
		Your tax is—			
2,400	2,425	2	0	71	2
2,425	2,450	5	0	73	5
2,450	2,475	8	0	76	8
2,475	2,500	11	0	79	11
2,500	2,525	13	0	82	13
2,525	2,550	16	0	84	16
2,550	2,575	19	0	87	19
2,575	2,600	22	0	90	22
2,600	2,625	24	0	93	24
2,625	2,650	27	0	95	27
2,650	2,675	30	0	98	30
2,675	2,700	33	0	101	33
2,700	2,725	35	0	104	35
2,725	2,750	38	0	106	38
2,750	2,775	41	0	109	41
2,775	2,800	44	0	112	44
2,800	2,825	46	0	115	46
2,825	2,850	49	0	117	49
2,850	2,875	52	0	120	52
2,875	2,900	55	0	123	55
2,900	2,925	57	0	126	57
2,925	2,950	60	0	129	60
2,950	2,975	63	0	132	63
2,975	3,000	66	0	135	66
3,000					
3,000	3,050	70	0	140	70
3,050	3,100	75	0	146	75
3,100	3,150	81	0	152	81
3,150	3,200	86	0	158	86
3,200	3,250	92	0	164	92
3,250	3,300	97	0	170	97
3,300	3,350	103	0	176	103
3,350	3,400	108	0	182	108

If line 37 (taxable income) is—		And you are—			
At least	But less than	Single	Married filing jointly *	Married filing separately	Head of a household
		Your tax is—			
3,400	3,450	114	0	188	114
3,450	3,500	119	0	194	119
3,500	3,550	125	0	200	125
3,550	3,600	131	4	206	130
3,600	3,650	137	9	212	136
3,650	3,700	143	15	218	141
3,700	3,750	149	20	224	147
3,750	3,800	155	26	230	152
3,800	3,850	161	31	236	158
3,850	3,900	167	37	242	163
3,900	3,950	173	42	248	169
3,950	4,000	179	48	254	174
4,000					
4,000	4,050	185	53	261	180
4,050	4,100	191	59	268	185
4,100	4,150	197	64	275	191
4,150	4,200	203	70	282	196
4,200	4,250	209	75	289	202
4,250	4,300	215	81	296	207
4,300	4,350	221	86	303	213
4,350	4,400	227	92	310	218
4,400	4,450	233	97	317	224
4,450	4,500	239	103	324	229
4,500	4,550	245	108	331	235
4,550	4,600	251	114	338	240
4,600	4,650	258	119	345	246
4,650	4,700	265	125	352	252
4,700	4,750	272	130	359	258
4,750	4,800	279	136	366	264
4,800	4,850	286	141	373	270
4,850	4,900	293	147	380	276
4,900	4,950	300	152	387	282
4,950	5,000	307	158	394	288

* This column must also be used by a qualifying widow(er).

Continued on next page

1985 Tax Table—*Continued*

If line 37 (taxable income) is—		And you are—				If line 37 (taxable income) is—		And you are—				If line 37 (taxable income) is—		And you are—			
At least	But less than	Single	Married filing jointly *	Married filing separately	Head of a household	At least	But less than	Single	Married filing jointly *	Married filing separately	Head of a household	At least	But less than	Single	Married filing jointly *	Married filing separately	Head of a household
		Your tax is—						Your tax is—						Your tax is—			
5,000						**8,000**						**11,000**					
5,000	5,050	314	163	401	294	8,000	8,050	746	519	858	680	11,000	11,050	1,218	939	1,412	1,159
5,050	5,100	321	169	408	300	8,050	8,100	754	526	866	687	11,050	11,100	1,226	946	1,423	1,167
5,100	5,150	328	174	415	306	8,100	8,150	761	533	874	694	11,100	11,150	1,234	953	1,434	1,176
5,150	5,200	335	180	422	312	8,150	8,200	769	540	882	701	11,150	11,200	1,242	960	1,445	1,184
5,200	5,250	342	185	429	318	8,200	8,250	776	547	890	708	11,200	11,250	1,250	967	1,456	1,193
5,250	5,300	349	191	436	324	8,250	8,300	784	554	898	715	11,250	11,300	1,259	974	1,467	1,201
5,300	5,350	356	196	443	330	8,300	8,350	791	561	906	722	11,300	11,350	1,268	981	1,478	1,210
5,350	5,400	363	202	450	336	8,350	8,400	799	568	915	729	11,350	11,400	1,277	988	1,489	1,218
5,400	5,450	370	207	457	342	8,400	8,450	806	575	924	736	11,400	11,450	1,286	995	1,500	1,227
5,450	5,500	377	213	464	348	8,450	8,500	814	582	933	743	11,450	11,500	1,295	1,002	1,511	1,235
5,500	5,550	384	218	471	354	8,500	8,550	821	589	942	750	11,500	11,550	1,304	1,009	1,522	1,244
5,550	5,600	391	224	478	360	8,550	8,600	829	596	951	757	11,550	11,600	1,313	1,016	1,533	1,252
5,600	5,650	398	229	485	366	8,600	8,650	836	603	960	764	11,600	11,650	1,322	1,023	1,544	1,261
5,650	5,700	405	235	492	372	8,650	8,700	844	610	969	771	11,650	11,700	1,331	1,030	1,555	1,269
5,700	5,750	412	240	499	378	8,700	8,750	851	617	978	778	11,700	11,750	1,340	1,037	1,566	1,278
5,750	5,800	419	246	506	384	8,750	8,800	859	624	987	785	11,750	11,800	1,349	1,044	1,577	1,286
5,800	5,850	426	252	513	390	8,800	8,850	866	631	996	792	11,800	11,850	1,358	1,051	1,588	1,295
5,850	5,900	433	258	520	396	8,850	8,900	874	638	1,005	799	11,850	11,900	1,367	1,058	1,599	1,303
5,900	5,950	440	264	527	402	8,900	8,950	882	645	1,014	806	11,900	11,950	1,376	1,065	1,610	1,312
5,950	6,000	447	270	534	408	8,950	9,000	890	652	1,023	813	11,950	12,000	1,385	1,072	1,621	1,320
6,000						**9,000**						**12,000**					
6,000	6,050	454	276	541	414	9,000	9,050	898	659	1,032	820	12,000	12,050	1,394	1,079	1,632	1,329
6,050	6,100	461	282	548	420	9,050	9,100	906	666	1,041	827	12,050	12,100	1,403	1,086	1,643	1,337
6,100	6,150	468	288	555	426	9,100	9,150	914	673	1,050	836	12,100	12,150	1,412	1,093	1,654	1,346
6,150	6,200	475	294	562	432	9,150	9,200	922	680	1,059	844	12,150	12,200	1,421	1,100	1,665	1,354
6,200	6,250	482	300	570	438	9,200	9,250	930	687	1,068	853	12,200	12,250	1,430	1,107	1,676	1,363
6,250	6,300	489	306	578	444	9,250	9,300	938	694	1,077	861	12,250	12,300	1,439	1,114	1,687	1,371
6,300	6,350	496	312	586	450	9,300	9,350	946	701	1,086	870	12,300	12,350	1,448	1,121	1,698	1,380
6,350	6,400	503	318	594	456	9,350	9,400	954	708	1,095	878	12,350	12,400	1,457	1,128	1,709	1,389
6,400	6,450	510	324	602	462	9,400	9,450	962	715	1,104	887	12,400	12,450	1,466	1,135	1,720	1,398
6,450	6,500	517	330	610	468	9,450	9,500	970	722	1,113	895	12,450	12,500	1,475	1,143	1,731	1,407
6,500	6,550	524	336	618	474	9,500	9,550	978	729	1,122	904	12,500	12,550	1,484	1,151	1,742	1,416
6,550	6,600	531	342	626	480	9,550	9,600	986	736	1,131	912	12,550	12,600	1,493	1,159	1,753	1,425
6,600	6,650	538	348	634	486	9,600	9,650	994	743	1,140	921	12,600	12,650	1,502	1,167	1,764	1,434
6,650	6,700	545	354	642	492	9,650	9,700	1,002	750	1,149	929	12,650	12,700	1,511	1,175	1,775	1,443
6,700	6,750	552	360	650	498	9,700	9,750	1,010	757	1,158	938	12,700	12,750	1,520	1,183	1,786	1,452
6,750	6,800	559	366	658	505	9,750	9,800	1,018	764	1,167	946	12,750	12,800	1,529	1,191	1,797	1,461
6,800	6,850	566	372	666	512	9,800	9,850	1,026	771	1,176	955	12,800	12,850	1,538	1,199	1,809	1,470
6,850	6,900	574	378	674	519	9,850	9,900	1,034	778	1,185	963	12,850	12,900	1,547	1,207	1,822	1,479
6,900	6,950	581	384	682	526	9,900	9,950	1,042	785	1,194	972	12,900	12,950	1,556	1,215	1,834	1,488
6,950	7,000	589	390	690	533	9,950	10,000	1,050	792	1,203	980	12,950	13,000	1,565	1,223	1,847	1,497
7,000						**10,000**						**13,000**					
7,000	7,050	596	396	698	540	10,000	10,050	1,058	799	1,212	989	13,000	13,050	1,574	1,231	1,859	1,506
7,050	7,100	604	402	706	547	10,050	10,100	1,066	806	1,221	997	13,050	13,100	1,583	1,239	1,872	1,515
7,100	7,150	611	408	714	554	10,100	10,150	1,074	813	1,230	1,006	13,100	13,150	1,592	1,247	1,884	1,524
7,150	7,200	619	414	722	561	10,150	10,200	1,082	820	1,239	1,014	13,150	13,200	1,601	1,255	1,897	1,533
7,200	7,250	626	420	730	568	10,200	10,250	1,090	827	1,248	1,023	13,200	13,250	1,610	1,263	1,909	1,542
7,250	7,300	634	426	738	575	10,250	10,300	1,098	834	1,257	1,031	13,250	13,300	1,619	1,271	1,922	1,551
7,300	7,350	641	432	746	582	10,300	10,350	1,106	841	1,266	1,040	13,300	13,350	1,628	1,279	1,934	1,560
7,350	7,400	649	438	754	589	10,350	10,400	1,114	848	1,275	1,048	13,350	13,400	1,637	1,287	1,947	1,569
7,400	7,450	656	444	762	596	10,400	10,450	1,122	855	1,284	1,057	13,400	13,450	1,646	1,295	1,959	1,578
7,450	7,500	664	450	770	603	10,450	10,500	1,130	862	1,293	1,065	13,450	13,500	1,656	1,303	1,972	1,587
7,500	7,550	671	456	778	610	10,500	10,550	1,138	869	1,302	1,074	13,500	13,550	1,666	1,311	1,984	1,596
7,550	7,600	679	462	786	617	10,550	10,600	1,146	876	1,313	1,082	13,550	13,600	1,676	1,319	1,997	1,605
7,600	7,650	686	468	794	624	10,600	10,650	1,154	883	1,324	1,091	13,600	13,650	1,686	1,327	2,009	1,614
7,650	7,700	694	474	802	631	10,650	10,700	1,162	890	1,335	1,099	13,650	13,700	1,696	1,335	2,022	1,623
7,700	7,750	701	480	810	638	10,700	10,750	1,170	897	1,346	1,108	13,700	13,750	1,706	1,343	2,034	1,632
7,750	7,800	709	486	818	645	10,750	10,800	1,178	904	1,357	1,116	13,750	13,800	1,716	1,351	2,047	1,641
7,800	7,850	716	492	826	652	10,800	10,850	1,186	911	1,368	1,125	13,800	13,850	1,726	1,359	2,059	1,650
7,850	7,900	724	498	834	659	10,850	10,900	1,194	918	1,379	1,133	13,850	13,900	1,736	1,367	2,072	1,659
7,900	7,950	731	505	842	666	10,900	10,950	1,202	925	1,390	1,142	13,900	13,950	1,746	1,375	2,084	1,668
7,950	8,000	739	512	850	673	10,950	11,000	1,210	932	1,401	1,150	13,950	14,000	1,756	1,383	2,097	1,677

* This column must also be used by a qualifying widow(er).

Continued on next page

is shown in Exhibit 25.1 in Chapter 25. Calculation of the tax on taxable income of $58,000 for the year to a single taxpayer is as follows:

Tax on $57,550	$16,771
Plus 48% of excess of $57,550	
($58,000 − $57,550) × .48	216
Total tax	$16,987

TAX CREDITS
Amounts subtracted from tax based on taxable income that serve to directly reduce the amount of tax paid.

When using the Tax Rate Schedule, the percentage rate that is applied to the excess amount represents the marginal tax rate. In the preceding example, 48 percent is the marginal tax rate, and the individual is referred to as being in the 48 percent marginal income tax bracket.

A taxpayer may be entitled to qualified **tax credits,** which are subtracted from the tax to reduce the tax itself. For example, an individual or business in 1985 is entitled to a ten percent investment tax credit on certain new investments. Other tax credits include the child care credit, residential energy credit, and political contributions credit.

An individual may be required to pay other taxes, such as the self-employment tax or the alternative minimum tax. (For a detailed discussion, refer to an income tax text.) Furthermore, a person most likely has had taxes withheld by an employer or has made quarterly payments of estimated tax to the government throughout the year. The sum of the amounts that have been withheld or paid is compared to the total tax figure. These adjustments could result in payment owed to the government or a refund due to the taxpayer at the end of the year.

Capital Gains and Losses. A taxpayer can reap the benefits of capital transactions only if the sale or exchange of a capital asset takes place. A sale constitutes the forfeiture of the asset for cash, and an exchange involves the receipt of other property in lieu of cash. A **capital asset** is described as any asset that is not one of the following:

CAPITAL ASSET
An asset that is not inventory, real estate or depreciable property used in trade or business, accounts receivable, some artistic works, or some government documents.

1. Inventory.
2. Real estate or depreciable property used in a trade or business.
3. Accounts receivable.
4. Some artistic works.
5. Some government documents.

Capital Gains. To receive capital gain treatment, the capital asset must be a long-term capital asset, which means the capital asset has been held by the taxpayer for at least six months before a sale or exchange takes place. If the holding period is less than six months, the capital asset is classified as short-term. To illustrate, assume Ms. Brown buys stock on January 1, 1986, at a cost of $5,000. On August 1, 1986, she sells the stock for $9,000. This is her only capital transaction for the year. Without the long-term capital gain provision, Ms. Brown would have to report the entire gain of $4,000 ($9,000 − $5,000) as ordinary income. (**Ordinary income** is any income that is included in gross income and taxable in full. If Ms. Brown is in the 48 percent marginal tax bracket, her tax on the gain would be $1,920 ($4,000 × .48). However, because the asset is a capital asset, the transaction resulted in a gain, and the holding period is long-term, Ms. Brown can exclude 60 percent of the gain from gross income. The effect of this process is illustrated as follows:

ORDINARY INCOME
Any income that is included in gross income and taxable in full.

Amount received from sale	$9,000
Cost to Ms. Brown	(5,000)
Gain (loss)	$4,000
Capital gain exclusion (.60 × $4,000)	(2,400)
Taxable income	$1,600
Tax rate	.48
Tax	$ 768

Ms. Brown can realize a tax savings of $1,152 ($1,920 − $768), because the gain is a long-term capital gain. If the stock had not been held for six months, the gain would be a short-term capital gain, and ordinary income would be recognized in the amount of $4,000.

Capital Losses. As important as it is to strive for long-term capital gains, it is also important to avoid long-term capital losses. Such losses are deductible from gross income at a rate of $1 for every $2 incurred, with a limit of $3,000 per year. Short-term capital losses are deductible dollar for dollar, although, again, at an amount of no more than $3,000 annually. An advantage to net capital losses for individuals is that such losses are deductible from, or can offset, ordinary income. Recall that ordinary losses (losses that do not involve capital transactions) do not have a restriction on total amount deductible. Unused capital losses for individuals can be carried forward and used to offset income in future years. Losses on property held for personal use and not for investment or business purposes are never deductible.

Net Gains and Losses. If an individual experiences more than one capital transaction in a taxable year, a net gain or loss will result. This process entails analyzing each transaction separately to determine the following:

1. Is the asset a capital asset?
2. Is the result a gain or loss?
3. Was there a short-term or long-term holding period upon disposition?

Long-term capital gains are netted with long-term capital losses, and short-term capital gains are netted with short-term capital losses. The long-term figure is then netted with the short-term amount to arrive at a final result. Study the netting procedure in Exhibit E.3; the net result is a long-term capital gain of $2,200. If both a long-term net loss and a short-term net loss are reached, or if both outcomes constitute net gains, netting is not applicable, and each long-term or short-term amount is treated separately.

Tax Planning for Individuals

IRA Contribution. Individuals should take advantage of the tax benefits available to them. A contribution to an IRA account (with limitations) is deductible from gross income. As stressed previously, deductions from gross income are especially desirable. No limit exists for deductions taken from gross income, whereas it is only beneficial to itemize in excess of the zero bracket amount. Thus, an individual who will probably not incur enough expenses to itemize can still deduct an IRA contribution from gross income.

Capital Transactions. Tax planning is vital in capital transactions. It is extremely advantageous to maximize long-term capital gains and short-term capital losses and

EXHIBIT E.3

Individual Transaction	Amount	Netting Procedure	Net Amount
Long-term capital gain	$ 6,000	$3,000	$2,200
Long-term capital loss	$(3,000)	Long-term capital gain	Long-term
Short-term capital gain	$ 1,200	$(800)	capital gain
Short-term capital loss	$(2,000)	Short-term capital loss	

to minimize short-term capital gains and long-term capital losses. If a capital asset can be sold at a gain, a taxpayer should make certain to hold the asset for at least six months, even if it involves postponing the sale. A tax expert should be consulted for areas that involve multiple capital transactions, because the difference in tax liability varies significantly depending on the character of the asset.

CORPORATE INCOME TAXES

Corporate income taxation is similar to individual taxation, though with some important differences.

Gross Income

Gross income for corporations includes all gross revenues, gains, dividends in excess of allowable exclusions, and interest. In fact, the concept of "all income from whatever source derived" also applies to corporations.

Deductions

All ordinary and necessary expenses, including salaries of owners if incurred by the corporation, and charitable contributions are deductible from gross income. Such deductions include certain expenditures that are not available to individual taxpayers, because they relate to business and not to personal purposes. For example, rental and lease payments are deductible by corporations but not by individuals. Some other deductions that are granted to corporations are depreciation or cost recovery allowances, organizational costs, and research and development expenditures. Only deductions from gross income are permitted in corporate taxation. Adjusted gross income does not apply to corporations, because itemized deductions, exemptions, and zero bracket amounts do not apply. Deductions are subtracted from gross income to determine taxable income.

Corporations are not entitled to the 60 percent long-term capital gain deduction. Alternatively, a tax rate of 28 percent is applied instead of the regular corporate tax rate to long-term capital gains. Unused capital losses can be carried back three years and forward five years and must offset only capital gains, not ordinary income. Capital losses are always categorized as short-term losses.

Corporations should aim for long-term capital gain treatment as long as the applicable tax rate is greater than the capital gain tax rate of 28 percent. Since capital losses are always short-term capital losses, tax planning as to what year to experience a loss can be an important factor in determining total after-tax income. It may be best to postpone a capital loss until a subsequent year, if possible, if a net long-term capital gain is recognized in the current year. In this way, the long-term capital gain will warrant preferential treatment without having been reduced, or offset, by the loss.

If a corporation invests in another corporation through stock ownership, 85 percent of the dividends received from the investment can be deducted by the investing corporation and 100 percent of the dividends can be deducted if either company owns at least 80 percent of the other.

Computation of corporate income tax is illustrated in Exhibit E.4, using the tax rates given in Exhibit 25.1 in Chapter 25.

EXHIBIT E.4

Corporate Tax Return Process

Gross receipt or sales	$900,000	
Less: Cost of goods sold	645,000	
Gross profit		$255,000
Capital gain (loss)		55,000
Dividends		35,000
Total income		$345,000
Less: Other expenses		175,000
Taxable income before special deductions		$170,000
Less: Charitable contributions	$ 3,000*	
Dividends (85% × $35,000)	29,750	32,750
Taxable income		$137,250
Less: Net long-term capital gain		55,000
Taxable income at conventional rate		$ 82,250
Tax ($3,750 + $4,500 + $7,500 + $2,900) =	$ 18,650	
Tax on long-term capital gains (28% × $55,000)	15,400	
Total tax		$ 34,050

*Corporations are limited to a charitable contribution deduction of 10% of taxable income before charitable contribution deduction, dividends received deduction, and capital or operating loss carryback.

Cash Versus Accrual Method of Accounting

When filing income tax returns, the following methods are permitted by the IRS: (1) cash method, (2) accrual method, or (3) a combination of methods 1 and 2. It is possible to use different methods for book and tax purposes, but to do so, the taxpayer must receive permission in advance from the IRS. All businesses that sell inventory as a main source of income must use the accrual method. However, taxpayers conducting more than one business can use a different method of accounting for each business.

The difference between cash and accrual for tax purposes rests with revenue recognition criteria, the same as for financial accounting. Revenue is recognized in the accrual method when income is earned. Therefore, a sale on account for an accrual basis taxpayer is included in gross income. A cash basis taxpayer includes in income only those receipts that provide an immediate cash claim. A paycheck received on December 31, 1985, by an individual reporting under the cash method represents income to the taxpayer even if the check is not cashed until January 3, 1986. The taxpayer had claim to the cash on December 31, even though the option to cash the check was not exercised on that day.

SUMMARY

- Taxpayers are classified as individuals, corporations, estates, or trusts. Proprietorships and partnerships are categorized as individual taxpayers.
- Gross income is defined as all income from whatever source derived. Exclusions from gross income must be specified by law.

- Deductions from gross income are available to individuals to reduce adjusted gross income and are usually business and investment-related in nature.

- Itemized deductions pertain to personal expenditures. Each person is automatically granted a zero bracket amount of deductions. It is only advantageous to itemize in excess of the zero bracket amount, which is why itemized deductions are referred to as excess itemized deductions when utilized.

- Taxpayers are given personal and dependency exemptions of $1,040 per qualified exemption.

- Individuals use the Tax Table or the Tax Rate Schedule to determine their tax. The highest rate applied in the Tax Rate Schedule is called the marginal tax rate. Tax credits reduce total tax.

- Sixty percent of long-term capital gains to individual taxpayers are excluded from gross income. Capital transactions should be planned because of the variations in treatment of gains and losses for tax purposes. Long-term capital gains are taxed at a rate of 28 percent to corporations.

- Corporations can deduct 85 percent of dividends received or 100 percent of dividends from another corporation if either company owns at least 80 percent of the other.

- Cash basis, accrual basis, and a combination of the two are valid accounting methods for the filing of federal income taxes.

EXERCISES

E-E1. Mrs. Lee, age 43, is single and has two children, Sally and John. Sally, who is 20, attends college full-time and earned $5,000 this year. Mrs. Lee contributed $4,000 to Sally's support. John is 23 years old, has no income, and lives at home. Mrs. Lee sent $4,000 during the year to her father, who is 65 years old and lives in another state. Her father received $3,000 a year from other sources. How many total exemptions can Mrs. Lee claim on her income tax return this year?

E-E2. Mr. King, an individual taxpayer, made the following transactions during 1986:

1. Purchased stock in Company A on February 3 at a cost of $10,000 and sold it on July 31 for $20,000.
2. Sold a car used for personal purposes at a loss of $2,300.
3. Incurred an uninsured casualty loss of $700 from a fire at the furniture business he operates from a large garage.
   a. For each transaction, state the amount, if any, that is deductible from gross income.
   b. As Mr. King's tax consultant, what advice would you have given him regarding the sale of the stock in transaction 1? What amount would be deductible from gross income in such a case?

E-E3. Joe Cunningham is a used car salesman. On December 1, 1985, he sold a car for $6,000 that he originally purchased for resale on March 1, 1985, for $4,000.

a. Is this a capital transaction? Why or why not?
b. Suppose that the car was Mr. Cunningham's personal use car. He purchased the vehicle on March 1, 1985, for $4,000 and sold it for $3,000 on December 1, 1985. Can Mr. Cunningham deduct this loss? Why or why not?

E-E4. A taxpayer receives total income (meaning no exclusions have been accounted for) of $75,000 as follows:

Dividends	$ 4,000
Long-term capital gain	7,000
Other income	64,000
Total income	$75,000

Calculate the tax (using the schedules in Exhibits 25.1 and 25.2 in Chapter 25 for the following:

a. The taxpayer is a single taxpayer, incurred $2,900 of qualified itemized deductions, and claimed one exemption.

b. The taxpayer is a married couple filing jointly, incurred $2,900 of qualified itemized deductions, and claimed two exemptions. (Each spouse received $2,000 of dividends.)

c. The taxpayer is a corporation and incurred $2,900 of other expenses. Other income above includes sales less cost of goods sold. (Refer to Exhibit E.4.)

E-E5. Mr. and Mrs. Miller own a proprietorship, which they are considering incorporating. The Millers withdrew $60,000 in 1985. Revenues totaled $300,000, and costs of goods sold amounted to $210,000. The Millers file a joint return, claim five exemptions, and have $5,500 of itemized deductions.

a. Illustrate the Millers' personal tax consequences (using the 1985 tax rates in Exhibits 25.1 and 25.2 in Chapter 25) if:

1. The Millers operate as a proprietorship.

2. The Millers operate as a corporation. (Withdrawals would be equal to salaries in this case.)

b. Assume the Millers incorporated and withdrew all of the after-tax profits as dividends. How would this affect their personal tax liability? (The only corporate expenses were for cost of goods sold and the $60,000 in salaries.)

APPENDIX F
INTERNATIONAL ACCOUNTING

RISING IMPORTANCE OF INTERNATIONAL ACCOUNTING

Historical Perspective

Throughout the world, local traditions in accounting have persisted to this day. LIFO, the inventory costing method so popular in the United States, is nearly unknown in other countries and is not even permitted in the United Kingdom. Inflation gone rampant in South America has led to price-level adjusted reports being issued as the continent's official communication, a practice rarely followed elsewhere. The United Kingdom and Australia have for some time tracked flyaway prices using current-cost accounting—a system that records an asset at its current price, not at the price paid upon acquisition. The United States provides more disclosure information to its shareholders than does any other country in the world—some say, too much. In other countries, business often flourishes behind closed doors.

For many years, these variations in accounting practices were of little consequence. Few companies were concerned with international dealings. Investors rarely placed their money at the disposal of foreign corporations. Transportation and travel moved slowly, and markets at home were not yet saturated. But time wrought changes, and technology has expanded the worlds of communication, transportation, and data processing. In addition, local natural resources are depleting, and broad foreign markets seem relatively untapped. Power no longer rests in the grips of just a few countries or with only the very largest of companies. Over the past ten years, interest in international accounting concerns has renewed, and we are currently witnessing the increased appearance of foreign business transactions, **multinational enterprises** (enterprises with holdings in more than one country), and foreign shareholders. Appendix F examines the progress in and difficulty of setting international standards and explores some of the international implications involved in accounting for foreign activities.

MULTINATIONAL ENTERPRISES
Enterprises with holdings in more than one country.

The Present Setting

The current international accounting scene is characterized by a concern for the accurate reflection of economic and environmental conditions in the financial statements. Many countries feel that their accounting practices present fair representations of reality. However, when someone from outside the local circle tries to utilize the financial statements as presented, difficulties become apparent. Comparability, lacking or hindered by nonuniform practices and limited disclosure, is a huge obstacle thrown in the path of many otherwise normal business decisions.

THE INTERNATIONAL ACCOUNTING STANDARDS COMMITTEE

Formed in June 1973, the **International Accounting Standards Committee (IASC)** is an international committee that seeks to set and secure compliance with international accounting standards and procedures. The founding members are Australia, Canada, France, Great Britain, Ireland, Japan, Mexico, the Netherlands, the United States, and West Germany. These members are entitled to vote, and two additional voting seats are rotated by election from the nonvoting membership ranks. Presently, nonvoting member countries total nearly 50. Although the IASC has no legal way to enforce compliance with its international standards, its members do pledge to seek general acceptance of IASC standards within their own countries.

INTERNATIONAL ACCOUNTING STANDARDS COMMITTEE
An international committee seeking to set and secure compliance with international accounting standards and procedures.

To arrive at a standard, the IASC operates similarly to our own Financial Accounting Standards Board. An accounting procedure is studied and outlined, drafted, presented to the public as an exposure draft for comment, and finally, when approved, issued as a standard. Since 1977, the IASC has defined 21 international standards and has several other projects under current study.

To date, the standards that the IASC has issued are those that the individual member nations will readily accept, and the standards are far from limiting in procedures allowed. No truly heated subject has been standardized as yet, but at least a start in the process of resolving international differences is under way.

Two additional characteristics of the IASC are worthy of mention. First, the role of the IASC in providing ready-made, market-tested standards for the developing third-world nations will be invaluable for those countries' rapid economic progress. The countries will be spared many of the difficult efforts of defining appropriate accounting methods. Second, the IASC is proceeding diplomatically with the other professional organizations, keeping the channels for communciation open and the dialogue flowing.

CORPORATE INTERNATIONAL ACCOUNTING

Accounting for Foreign Currency Transactions

Perhaps the most common way businesses enter the world of international accounting is by being party to a transaction based in a foreign currency. To examine the accounting treatment of such a transaction, let's assume that an American company, U.S. Popular Records (USPR), has arranged to purchase stereo records from a British distributor for 10,000 pounds on March 1, when the spot rate is $2.10. (The **spot rate** is the rate of exchange of one currency for another in effect at a given time. Thus, if you gave the exchange broker $2.10, you would receive one British pound in return.) Payment for the records must be made in 30 days. The following journal entry is required on USPR's books for March 1:

SPOT RATE
The rate of exchange of one currency for another that is in effect at any given time.

March 1	Purchases	21,000	
	Accounts payable (fc)		21,000
	(to record purchase of imported merchandise for 10,000 pounds at a spot rate of $2.10)		

Note the entry is recorded immediately in local currency (U.S. dollars in this case). The "(fc)" notation is helpful in indicating the part of the transaction that is denominated in currency of another country; USPR must remit pounds, not dollars, to satisfy the account payable. On the payment date, the spot rate has changed to $2.05, and USPR's entry is as follows:

March 31	Accounts payable (fc)	21,000	
	Cash		20,500
	Exchange gain		500
	(to record full payment of account; exchange gain is equal to 10,000 pounds times the spot rate change of $.05)		

Thus, simply because the dollar had strengthened against the pound, USPR was able to achieve a financial gain. Of course, the dollar has been known to weaken against foreign currencies, and foreign transactions can just as easily lead to losses.

HEDGING
The process of protecting transactions against future fluctuations in the market.

FORWARD EXCHANGE CONTRACT (FUTURE)
The purchase or sale of foreign currency for future delivery.

Specific and identifiable transactions can be protected against foreign exchange fluctuations in a process called **hedging.** Hedging opportunities can be created by the purchase of a **forward exchange contract** (also called a **future**) to buy or sell, as needed, foreign currency for future delivery. Let's take a closer look at hedging using a specific transaction to illustrate the concepts.

Suppose that USPR sold merchandise to Mexican Airwaves, Inc., on May 1 and the terms of the sale called for payment in the amount of 200,000 pesos in 30 days. The spot rate on May 1 is $.045, but USPR's management doubts that the rate will remain stable. Therefore, to hedge its potential loss, USPR enters into a forward exchange contract. Journal entries on the date of sale are as follows:

Date	Account	Debit	Credit
May 1	Accounts receivable (fc)	9,000	
	Sales		9,000
	(to record sale of exported merchandise payable in pesos at a spot rate of $.045)		
May 1	Due from exchange broker	8,900	
	Liability for exchange sold (fc)		8,900
	(to record the sale of 200,000 pesos, at a forward rate of $.0445; delivery to be made in 30 days)		

FORWARD RATE
The price quoted now for future purchase or sale of a foreign currency.

This second entry indicates that the company has contacted and entered into an agreement with an exchange broker. The broker will provide $8,900 in U.S. currency when USPR delivers 200,000 pesos to him in 30 days. The **forward rate,** a price quoted now for a future purchase or sale of foreign currency, does not necessarily coincide with the spot rate for immediate delivery. The contracted cash does not change hands at this time.

Entries in 30 days complete the illustration. The account called Foreign Exchange is used to account for the foreign currency separately from domestic cash. This first entry records the payment that was received from Mexican Airwaves.

Date	Account	Debit	Credit
May 31	Foreign exchange	8,800	
	Exchange gains and losses	200	
	Accounts receivable (fc)		9,000
	(to record the receipt of payment of 200,000 pesos from Mexican Airwaves; current spot rate is $.044)		

Next, payment of the promised 200,000 pesos is recorded. Note the gain that results from multiplying the number of pesos by the difference between the forward rate and the current spot rate [200,000 × ($.0445 − $.044)].

May 31	Liability for exchange sold	8,900	
	Foreign exchange		8,800
	Exchange gains and losses		100
	(to record delivery of the 200,000 pesos to the broker to cover forward contract)		

Finally, the broker's promised dollars are received and recorded.

May 31	Cash	8,860	
	Exchange gains and losses	40	
	Due from exchange broker		8,900
	(to record the receipt of cash from broker in settlement of the forward contract, less broker's fee of $40)		

The balance of exchange gains and losses from this type of transaction is included in income currently. In USPR's case, the net effect of the $140 exchange loss ($100 foreign exchange + $40 broker's fee) will be to reduce income by an equivalent amount.

Hedging is a practice sometimes used to cover other potential foreign currency risks as well. The required treatment in these other cases is beyond the scope of this book.

Financial Statement Translation

For growing companies, other nations can be more than the chance for an occasional transaction, and companies will expand into foreign areas by investing in stock, building a manufacturing plant, establishing a sales outlet, and so on. The financial holdings in the foreign division will have to be translated into the parent company's currency for reporting. Several major methods of translating the statement of financial position are in common use in various parts of the world. No one method has been accepted as theoretically and practically superior, and hybrid methods frequently are used.

CURRENT-NONCURRENT APPROACH
A method of translating financial statements from one currency to another in which all current items are translated at the exchange rate in effect on the statement date and all other items are translated at the exchange rate in effect when they were acquired.

CURRENT RATE
The term applied to the foreign exchange rate in effect on the date of financial statement preparation.

Common Approaches. One common approach operates on the theory that changes in the exchange rate affect only current items and that no gain or loss should arise from holding noncurrent accounts. When applied, this method, the **current-noncurrent approach** (CN), uses the foreign exchange rate in effect on the financial statement date (the **current rate**) to translate current assets and liabilities. Noncurrent items are translated into the parent's currency using the historical exchange rate prevailing at the time they were acquired. Revenues and expenses are translated at average exchange rates for the period. Depreciation and amortization accounts are adjusted by the same historical rate as the noncurrent account to which they relate.

In effect, the final translation gain or loss is based on the change in the subsidiary's net working capital (current assets less current liabilities).

A similar method applies particular exchange rates according to the account's classification as monetary or nonmonetary. Monetary items are assets and liabilities, such as cash, receivables, or payables, that are based on a set number of monetary units. Nonmonetary accounts are those that are not referring to a fixed sum of money but are using an amount to describe an aspect of the asset or liability. Examples of nonmonetary accounts are property, plant, and equipment, investments in common stocks, and inventories. Thus, the **monetary-nonmonetary approach** (MN) is one in which users translate monetary items using the exchange rate on the statement of financial position date and translate nonmonetary items using the historical rates. The most significant difference between the CN and the MN approaches is the treatment of inventories. Inventory is translated at the current exchange rate for the CN method but at the historical rate by the MN method.

MONETARY-NONMONETARY APPROACH
A method of translating statements from one currency to another in which all monetary items are translated at the rate in effect on the statement date and all nonmonetary items are translated at the historical rate in effect when the items were obtained.

The next method was developed in answer to critics of the monetary-nonmonetary method who held that the MN classification scheme was unrelated to measurement. The purpose of translating foreign statements is to provide measurement, not classification. Therefore, the **temporal approach** modifies the MN method primarily by treating assets at the current rate of exchange if the asset is carried at market. If the asset is still on the books at cost, the historical exchange rate is considered appropriate. Most significantly, inventory accounts often are lowered to market under the lower-of-cost-or-market rule. Revenues and expenses, if too large a volume for recording individually, are to be translated at average rates.

TEMPORAL APPROACH
A modification of the monetary-nonmonetary approach to translation of statements from one currency to another under which assets carried at market values are translated at current rates and other assets are translated at historical rates.

A popular method outside the United States, the **current rate approach,** translates all accounts at the current exchange rate on the financial statement date. Proponents of the method claim that only in this manner are the relationships between amounts on the statements unchanged by translation. Opponents feel that the historical cost principle has been adulterated by translating historical foreign currency costs by the current exchange rate.

CURRENT RATE APPROACH
A method of translating statements from one currency to another in which all accounts are translated at the exchange rate in effect on the statement date.

Exhibit F.1 contrasts the four methods. Under each method, a different figure is reached for the period's exchange gain or loss. Such differences would be material for many multinational companies. To compound the problem, no agreement exists as to the treatment of the gains and losses. Some companies show them on the income statement; others close them to an equity account. Each method results in different amounts of **exposure,** which is a measurement of those amounts subject to translation at current rates. Imagine an executive's difficulty when trying to decide how to protect a foreign net asset or liability position from risk due to exchange rate fluctuations. With all four methods in use throughout the world, comparability of multinational consolidated statements has grown complex. To narrow differing accounting treatments in our own country, FASB issued its relevant ruling in 1981.

EXPOSURE
A measurement of the amounts in a firm's accounts that are subject to financial statement translation at current rates.

FASB Statement 52. Entitled "Foreign Currency Translation," FASB Statement 52 aims to furnish information that is compatible with the actual economic effects that a rate change will bring upon an enterprise's cash flows and equity. It adopts the **functional currency approach,** whereby the overseas operation will report its operations in the currency of the primary economic environment in which it operates (the **functional currency**). If most transactions are based in the foreign currency, such currency is considered the functional currency. On the other hand, if the foreign operation primarily deals with the U.S. parent firm as an integral part of that firm, the functional currency is probably the dollar. For operations in highly inflationary

FUNCTIONAL CURRENCY APPROACH
An approach to accounting for foreign operations where the overseas operation reports its results in the currency used in its primary economic environment.

FUNCTIONAL CURRENCY
The currency in use in the primary economic environment of an overseas operation.

EXHIBIT F.1

Common Translation Methods Compared

Foreign subsidiary statement of financial position in foreign currency			Translated into U.S. Dollars[a]			
			Current-Noncurrent	**Monetary-Nonmonetary**	**Temporal**	**Current Rate**
Assets:	Cash	300	$ 225	$ 225	$ 225	$ 225
	Accounts receivable	300	225	225	225	225
	Inventories					
	Cost =	900	675	900		675
	Market = 1000				750[b]	
	Plant and equipment	600	600	600	600	450
	Total	2,100	$1,725	$1,950	$1,800	$1,575
Liabilities and Equity:	Accounts payable	400	$ 300	$ 300	$ 300	$ 300
	Long-term debt	800	800	600	600	600
	Owners' equity[c]	900	625	1,050	900	675
	Total	2,100	$1,725	$1,950	$1,800	$1,575
	Exchange gain (loss)[d]		(275)	150	0[e]	(225)
	Amount exposed[f] (in FC)		1,100	(600)	400	900

[a]Current rate: 1 FC = $.75
Historical rate applicable: 1 FC = $1.00

[b]Inventory in U.S. dollars: Cost = 900 FC × $1.00 = $900
Market = 1,000 FC × $ .75 = $750
Thus, under lower of cost or market, inventory is carried at $750.

[c]Owners' equity is a balancing figure except under current rate approach.

[d]Gain or loss equals the change in owners' equity in $ from the previous statement of financial position in $.

[e]This method does *not* always break even.

[f]Assets that would be translated at the current rate, measured in foreign currency, less liabilities exposed to current rate, measured in FC.

countries (where the cumulative three-year inflation rate is 100 percent or more), the functional currency is to be the more stable U.S. dollar.

If the U.S. dollar is not the functional currency, all asset and liability accounts are to be translated using the current rate method, except for owners' equity, which is translated using historical exchange rates. Using different rates will sometimes cause an imbalance on the statement of financial position. Any adjustment necessary due to translation should be made to shareholders' equity.

In case the functional currency is the U.S. dollar, the remeasurement process is achieved largely through the temporal method, and any translation adjustments in this case are made to income currently.

As an example of how the statement applies, assume that a U.S. parent is consolidating a subsidiary whose functional currency is the pound sterling. The subsidiary begins operations on January 1 with the statement of financial position (in pounds) as follows:

Statement of Financial Position (In Pounds)		
Assets		
Cash	70,000	
Inventory	65,000	
Total current assets		135,000
Fixed assets (10-year life)		200,000
Total current and fixed		335,000
Liabilities and Owners' Equity		
Short-term loans	60,000	
Total current liabilities		60,000
Long-term debt		175,000
Capital stock		100,000
Total liabilities and owners' equity		335,000

A review of exchange rate fluctuations reveals the following information:

Exchange rate at January 1	\$2.10/£
Exchange rate at December 31	\$2.40/£

The statement of financial position on December 31 (in pounds) and its translated statement (in dollars) are presented in Exhibit F.2.

As a special note, all expenses and other income statement items are translated at the exchange rate on the date when the transaction was recognized. As a practical consideration, however, weighted averages are used.

EXHIBIT F.2

Translation Under the Functional Approach

Statement of Financial Position (In Pounds)			Exchange Rate	Translated Equivalent	
Assets					
Cash	20,000		Current: 2.40	\$ 48,000	
Receivables	80,000		Current: 2.40	192,000	
Inventory	60,000		Current: 2.40	144,000	
Total current assets		160,000	Current: 2.40		\$384,000
Fixed assets	200,000				
Less depreciation	20,000	180,000	Current: 2.40		432,000
Total assets		340,000			\$816,000
Liabilities and Owners' Equity					
Short-term loans	10,000		Current: 2.40	\$ 24,000	
Payables	60,000		Current: 2.40	144,000	
Total current liabilities		70,000			\$168,000
Long-term debt		130,000	Current: 2.40		312,000
Capital stock		100,000	Historical: 2.10		210,000
Retained earnings		40,000	Current: 2.25*		90,000
Translation adjustment			Balancing figure		36,000
Total liabilities and owners' equity		340,000			\$816,000

Retained earnings translated at average rate for the year [(2.10 + 2.40)/2 = 2.25] because subsidiary started operations on January 1 of the current year and the historical rate is equal to the average for the first year of operations.

Transfer Pricing

Background. As you may recall, the pricing of goods transferred from one company division to another is commonly referred to as transfer pricing. Transfer pricing used to belong solely in the domain of internal management accounting. However, the issuance of FASB No. 14 in 1976, requiring segment reporting of large companies, also required showing segment revenues according to the transfer pricing policy and disclosure of the actual transfer pricing methods. Such policies are receiving more public attention now than in the past, and international complications are becoming more obvious.

The sheer volume of international intracompany trade is burdensome. Estimates place the proportion of world trade between related parties in the area of 40 to 50 percent. Add in the complexities of differing tax structures, tariffs, exchange rate risk, political threats, inflation variances, controls, competition, and nationalistic attitudes, and a company finds itself in a very different environment.

Arising from the need to balance all factors for optimal company benefit, the regular behavioral/motivational objectives of transfer pricing must be subordinated to new aims, such as the coordination of highly decentralized operations, the minimization of taxes, the circumvention of controls imposed by a host government, and the reduction of a variety of risks. The old objectives are not forgotten, but such global concerns can be too compelling to ignore. Many companies find that the remedy to meeting so many imperative objectives lies in dual record keeping, perhaps with one set of records tracking the prices according to management objectives and another set of records being used to form the company's segmental profit picture.

Environmental Considerations. The choice of a transfer pricing policy is definitely colored by environmental factors. A prime consideration of both the parent and the host companies is the income tax factor. Tax environments differ greatly, and an effective policy should operate to maximize overall company profits. For instance, high transfer prices could be set for goods shipped to divisions in high tax countries. Alternatively, low transfer prices for importing divisions in low tax countries would transfer much of the profit there. Either practice will subject the gross margin to taxation at the lower rates.

To further illustrate, suppose that a multinational company based in Great Britain has merchandising subsidiaries in Japan and Hong Kong. The parent would like to acquire some import goods from Japan, but both Great Britain and Japan have relatively high income taxes. The British parent could thus direct its subsidiary in Japan to purchase the goods at a cost of $5,000 and to resell the merchandise first to the Hong Kong subsidiary with a small markup—$5,500. Since Hong Kong's tax rates are substantially lower, the goods are then transferred to the parent for $10,000. Finally, the parent in Great Britain records a small margin and sells the goods to an unrelated party for $11,000. Total company gross margin adds to $6,000, but only $1,500 was subject to taxation in the higher-tax countries. The remaining $4,500 would be treated more favorably by Hong Kong's taxing regulations.

The practice of setting transfer prices to minimize taxes is not quite as easily done as the illustration suggests. Nowadays many countries are adopting an attitude similar to that of the Internal Revenue Service in the United States. Section 482 of the U.S. Tax Regulations states that the aim of the taxing authority is to make income between related parties comparable to the income that would have accrued had the parties been unrelated (sometimes called the arm's length concept). Should the IRS determine that reported income for the segments does not clearly reflect the true taxable income, it has the prerogative to disallow the company's transfer pricing system or to rearrange the figures. IRS reallocations are not to be desired, since they are final.

In many cases, the foreign country at the other end of a transfer might not allow adjustment of the foreign tax burden to compensate for additional U.S. taxes accruing. Rather than subject themselves to such arbitration, firms carefully consider the tax implications of their transfer pricing systems.

Another factor of the environment that can affect the transfer pricing decision is the competition in the subsidiary's local area. When a company initially goes into business in a foreign country, transfer prices on goods shipped to the subsidiary could be kept quite low and could thus increase the subsidiary's profits. When the branch can meet the competition without such help, the artificial pricing practice can be phased out. However, dangers arise: The competition could feel that the prices are unfair and sponsor an all-out campaign against the company, or the foreign host government might feel that an antitrust action is in order.

Other risks cannot be left unconsidered. Companies with branches in inflation-torn countries reduce the inflation risk by using high transfer prices on their subsidiary's imports from the parent in order to remove cash from the subsidiary. Similarly, low transfer prices can be attached to a subsidiary's exports in order to move the inventory out of an area where the threat of government confiscation looms. Again, side effects of such policies can be worse than the initial problems. Using high transfer prices to counter inflation could put all the profits into a high income tax country. Also, any transfer price not easily justifiable could come to the attention of the subsidiary's host government and seriously erode an important relationship for the company.

The objectives that can be achieved with transfer pricing policies are varied and are neither isolated one to a country nor stable. Companies operating in multiple locations must keep a global outlook and do what is best in the long run for the entire company. This balancing act is extremely difficult and does not promise to become easier in the near future.

OTHER CONCERNS

Foreign currency translation and transfer pricing are certainly not the only international problems confronting accounting today, nor are they necessarily the most compelling. Differences in the setting of accounting procedures, an utter lack of disclosure in many cases, and a world of differences in auditing conventions add to the difficulty of international business and foreign investing. As technology continues to allow global expansion, refinements in accounting practices will also be made.

SUMMARY

- International accounting is becoming increasingly important due to a rise in international business transactions, the growth of huge multinational firms, and a surge of investing in stocks of other countries.
- At the same time, international accounting has serious complexities: widely diverse, sometimes nonexistent, national accounting standards; foreign currency risk; financial reporting problems; increased nationalistic attitudes in some host countries.

- The International Accounting Standards Committee currently is setting worldwide standards and actively seeking their acceptance in order to make financial reports globally comprehensible.

- Foreign currency must be translated to local currency when dealing with foreign transactions or when reporting investments.

- Foreign transactions expose a company to gain or loss from a movement in the exchange rate.

- Foreign currency risk can be hedged; one method to do so is through the purchase of a forward exchange contract.

- No agreement exists regarding the best method for financial statement translation. Four approaches have been commonly found: current-noncurrent, monetary-nonmonetary, temporal, and current rate.

- FASB No. 52 has been recently introduced in the United States and advocates a hybrid method—the functional currency method.

- Transfer pricing is one managerial tool that has to be revamped for international purposes. A balance must be found between the varied objectives to be served by the system with their inherent advantages and disadvantages.

EXERCISES

F-E1. On April 20, Sam's Shoes, an American firm, purchased merchandise for resale from Caesar's Shoe Manufacturing, a Canadian business. The price was $1,500, to be paid in American dollars on May 1. The spot rate was $1.25 on April 20 and $1.15 on May 1. How much was Sam's exchange gain or loss upon payment on May 1? Would the gain or loss be different (and by how much) if the payment were to be made in Canadian dollars?

F-E2. U.S. Distributors purchased merchandise on August 1 from a Danish firm, where the local currency is the krone (DKr). The account is payable in the amount of 780,000 DKr on September 1. On August 1, the spot rate is $.187, and U.S. Distributors enters into a forward exchange contract with a broker to purchase the necessary currency. The forward rate is $.195. On September 1, when the spot rate is $.188, U.S. Distributors settles the forward exchange transaction and the account payable for merchandise. What are the necessary journal entries? (Ignore any brokerage fee.)

F-E3. Following are some common accounts found on a statement of financial position. Classify each as either monetary or nonmonetary.

a. Accounts Receivable
b. Buildings
c. Notes Payable
d. Paid-in Capital
e. Temporary Investments in Certificates of Deposit

F-E4. The following grid lists the real accounts of a foreign branch of a multinational firm. For each account, indicate what rate is appropriate for financial statement translation under the method listed at the top of the column. Note that the current rate method has been completed as an example. (Use CR to indicate current rate and HR for historical rate.) Explain any answers that might not be clear-cut.

		Translation Method		
Account	**Current Rate**	**Current-Noncurrent**	**Monetary-Nonmonetary**	**Temporal**
Cash	CR			
Accounts Receivable	CR			
Inventory, At Cost	CR			
Building, Net	CR			
Accounts Payable	CR			
Long-Term Note Payable	CR			
Owners' Equity	CR			

F-E5. The following statement of financial position is for the last period for the foreign branch of a U.S.-based firm. The amounts are Tanzanian shillings. The Tanzanian branch was organized at the start of this last period when the exchange rate was $.14; the exchange rate on the financial statement date is $.20. Translate this statement of financial position using the temporal approach.

Tanzanian Division
Statement of Financial Position
December 31, 1988
(In Shillings)

Assets	
Cash	5,000
Accounts receivable	4,000
Inventory	
Cost = 12,000	
Market = 10,000	10,000
Plant and equipment, net	40,000
Total assets	59,000
Liabilities and Owners' Equity	
Accounts payable	6,000
Note payable (long-term)	3,000
Owners' equity	50,000
Total liabilities and owners' equity	59,000

How much is the exchange gain or loss due to translation?

APPENDIX G

ACCOUNTING FOR NON-PROFIT ORGANIZATIONS

The primary objective of accounting for nonprofit organizations is basically the same as that for profit-oriented businesses: providing information useful to decision makers. However, several substantial differences do exist. In many nonprofit organizations, particularly governmental units, an emphasis on legal compliance with expenditure restrictions exists that is not present in profit-oriented businesses. The resource providers are not owners; they are taxpayers or donors and do not expect profits.

THE FUNDS CONCEPT

FUNDS
Independent accounting units within nonprofit organizations.

FUND BALANCE
The assets of a fund minus the fund's liabilities. Corresponds to owners' equity accounts of a corporation.

How do such differences manifest themselves in a system of accounting? One major difference is found in the concept of fund accounting. To assure compliance with restrictions on resource utilization, resources are segregated into independent accounting units (**funds**). Each fund is considered a self-contained accounting entity and includes the economic resources available (the fund's assets), the obligations (the fund's liabilities), and the net resources of the fund (the **fund balance**). The fund balance corresponds to the owners' equity accounts of a corporation.

TYPES OF FUNDS

Several general types of funds exist. The exact nature of the funds used depends on whether a governmental unit, a hospital, a college, a voluntary health and welfare organization, or some other nonprofit entity is being handled. As an example, we will describe the general kinds of funds used to account for a municipality, since these fund types are among the broadest and most common types found in a nonprofit environment.

GOVERNMENTAL FUNDS
The most widely used funds in accounting for a nonprofit entity.

Municipal funds can be grouped into three major categories: (1) governmental funds, (2) proprietary funds, and (3) fiduciary funds. In addition to these three types of funds, a group of accounts (not funds), called general fixed assets and general long-term debt, exists within the framework of the overall municipal accounting system. The first of our three fund types, **governmental funds,** is the most widely used in accounting for a nonprofit entity. We will describe governmental funds in some detail as an illustration of the application of accounting within nonprofit organizations.

GOVERNMENTAL FUNDS

GENERAL FUND
A fund that is used to account for all unrestricted financial resources that support the general operations of a nonprofit entity.

SPECIAL REVENUE FUNDS
Funds used to account for revenues legally restricted for a specific purpose in a nonprofit entity.

Five major subgroups of governmental funds can be identified:

1. **General fund**—Used to account for all unrestricted financial resources that support general operations.

2. **Special revenue funds**—Used to account for revenues that are legally restricted for a specific purpose. Several special funds can exist within any one municipal accounting system.

3. **Capital project funds**—Used to account for receipt and use of resources in specific support of capital facilities (fixed asset) construction. Several capital project funds can exist simultaneously—one for each active project.

4. **Debt service funds**—Used to account for the accumulation and use of resources for the payment of general obligation long-term debt, including both principal and interest.

5. **Special assessment funds**—Used to account for project construction costs and associated revenue collection and debt repayment where the charges for the project are levied specifically against the properties or persons benefited by the project.

CAPITAL PROJECT FUNDS
Funds used to account for the receipt and use of resources in specific support of capital facilities construction in a nonprofit entity.

DEBT SERVICE FUNDS
Funds that are used to account for the accumulation and use of resources for the payment of general obligation long-term debt, including both principal and interest for a nonprofit entity.

SPECIAL ASSESSMENT FUNDS
Funds used to account for project construction costs and associated revenue collection and debt repayment for a nonprofit entity where the charges for the project are levied specifically against the properties of the persons benefited by the project.

The General Fund

The operation of the general fund is representative of all five types of governmental funds and is examined in more detail in the following sections. Keep in mind that all of the concepts underlying journal entries and other bookkeeping techniques studied earlier apply to fund operations.

Modified Accrual Accounting

The recommended basis of accounting for the general fund is a system called **modified accrual accounting.** Under modifed accrual accounting, the definition of an asset becomes more restrictive than under normal accrual accounting. In addition to meeting the tests of control and future economic benefit, an item can be classified as an asset only if it will be available for future expenditure. Since fixed assets are not available for future expenditure, they are not recorded in the fund, and no depreciation is charged against operations. Likewise, inventory is not recorded, since the items contained therein will be used up, not spent. Fixed assets acquired by the expenditure of fund resources are recorded in the general fixed asset group of accounts for control purposes. Inventory items are treated as expenses when purchased. Also, long-term liabilities are not recorded within the fund but are recorded in the general long-term debt group of accounts.

MODIFIED ACCRUAL BASIS ACCOUNTING
The recommended basis of accounting for the general fund of a nonprofit entity.

Budgets and Control

Since profit is not relevant to nonprofit organizations, it is not available for control and performance evaluation. The focus of control in nonprofit organizations is shifted from profit to budgeting. Consequently, the preparation of a budget is of great importance. Because of the budget's importance and the need for legal compliance with the approved budget, the budget is formally recorded and becomes an integral part of the accounting system. As an example, if the City of Why anticipated one million dollars in revenues and passed a budget with $980,000 in appropriations, the following entry would be made to reflect adoption of the budget:

Estimated revenues	1,000,000	
Appropriations		980,000
Fund balance		20,000
(to record adoption of the budget)		

APPROPRIATIONS
The estimated obligations to be incurred and the legal authorization to expend resources in a nonprofit entity.

The debit to estimated revenues represents anticipated cash receipts for the period. The credit to **appropriations** is the estimated obligations to be incurred as well as the legal authorization to expend resources. The anticipated difference between receipts and appropriations is recorded as an adjustment to the fund balance.

Recording Commitments and Expenditures

ENCUMBRANCE
The commitment to expend funds recognized when an expenditure decision is made rather than when goods are actually purchased or received.

Because of the need to control expenditures, the recording of commitments to expend funds is done earlier than in a regular accrual accounting system. The commitment to expend funds is recorded as an **encumbrance** when an expenditure decision is made rather than when goods are actually purchased or received. If the exact amount of the expenditure is not known with certainty, an estimated amount is recorded when a purchase decision has been made. For example, a decision to purchase a typewriter at an estimated cost of $1,000 would be recorded as follows:

Encumbrances	1,000	
Reserve for encumbrances		1,000
(to record a purchase decision)		

When the typewriter is actually received at a cost of, say, $1,050, the following entry would be made:

Expenditure	1,050	
Accounts payable		1,050
(to record receipt of purchased item)		

The encumbrance would be eliminated as follows:

Reserve for encumbrances	1,000	
Encumbrances		1,000
(to remove encumbrance from books)		

The net balance in the fund account available for future expenditures is determined as follows:

Funds available = Appropriations − Expenditures − Encumbrances

Note that the expenditure of resources is recorded in essentially the same manner regardless of the nature of the item acquired. That is, the purchase of a new fire truck or the payment of a salary would be recorded as a debit to Expenditure and a credit to Cash or Accounts Payable. Of course, the fire truck would also be recorded in the general fixed asset group of accounts. Most municipal accounting systems would contain numerous subsidiary accounts for expendiutres and appropriations for detailed control purposes. In our illustration, we have used only the general control account titles.

Recording Revenue

Accounting for revenue received into the general fund also differs from regular accrual accounting, since receivables are not recorded unless collection is assured. All other expected collections are recorded only as cash is received. Sample entries for property taxes are as follows (property taxes are legally required to be paid and can therefore be recorded as a receivable):

Property taxes receivable	400,000	
Revenue		400,000
(to record property taxes receivable)		

When the property taxes are collected, the following entry would be made:

Cash	400,000	
Property taxes receivable		400,000
(to record collection of property taxes)		

A comparison of estimated revenues recorded when the budget was adopted with actual revenues recorded as cash is received is a useful control point for monitoring the progress of revenue collection.

Closing the Accounts

The revenue, expenditure, and encumbrance accounts are temporary and would be closed at the end of each accounting period. The estimated revenue and appropriation accounts (estimated expenditure and encumbrances) representing the original budget are likewise temporary and must also be closed at the end of each accounting period. All of the temporary accounts are closed to the fund balance (remember that the fund balance account in nonprofit agencies corresponds to the owners' equity accounts in a regular business accounting system).

If the estimated revenues in the original budget for an accounting period were one million dollars and the actual revenues turned out to be $990,000, the appropriate closing entry for revenue and estimated revenue would be as follows:

Revenue	990,000	
Fund balance	10,000	
Estimated revenue		1,000,000
(to close the revenue and estimated revenue accounts)		

Note that the difference between the estimated and actual revenue amounts becomes an adjustment to the fund balance.

If the authorized expenditures (appropriations) in the original budget for an accounting period totaled $980,000 and the actual expenditures were $910,000 with encumbrances of $50,000 in existence at the end of the period, the appropriate closing entry would be as follows:

Appropriations	980,000	
Expenditures		910,000
Encumbrances		50,000
Fund balance		20,000
(to close the appropriation, expenditure, and encumbrance accounts)		

Again, note that the difference between actual expenditures, outstanding commitments (encumbrances), and the initial budget appropriation is treated as an adjustment to the fund balance. In most cases it would be illegal for expenditures plus encumbrances to exceed original appropriations.

OTHER MUNICIPAL FUNDS

The operation of other municipal funds is similar to the general fund and is described without the bookkeeping detail presented in the previous discussion.

Proprietory Funds

PROPRIETARY FUNDS
Funds used to control governmental operations that are similar to private enterprises.

Proprietary funds are used to control governmental operations similar to private enterprises. Two primary groups of proprietary funds are found in practice:

1. Enterprise funds—used to account for businesslike organizations such as public utilities.
2. Internal service funds—used to account for goods and services provided by one municipal department to another for which a cost transfer is made.

Proprietary funds utilize regular accrual accounting: fixed assets, including depreciation, and long-term debt are recorded within the fund accounts.

Fiduciary Funds

FIDUCIARY FUNDS
Funds used to account for assets held by governmental units as a trustee or agent for someone else.

Fiduciary funds are used to account for assets held by governmental units as a trustee or agent for someone else. An example would be a governmental pension fund for the benefit of the municipal employees. Fiduciary funds can be used for both expendable and nonexpendable trust funds, pensions, and other agency funds. In most cases, fiduciary funds are maintained on an accrual basis.

FINANCIAL REPORTS

The financial reports prepared at the close of an accounting period are similar to those for a profit-oriented organization. A typical general fund statement of financial position would be as follows:

City of Why
General Fund
Statement of Financial Position
June 30, 1986

Assets		**Liabilities and Fund Equity**		
Cash	$40,000	Accounts payable		$30,000
Taxes receivable	20,000	Fund balance		
		Reserve for encumbrances	$14,000	
		Unencumbered	16,000	
		Total fund balance		30,000
Total assets	$60,000	Total liabilities and fund equity		$60,000

Since income is not a goal of nonprofit organizations, an income statement is not prepared. However, a statement of revenues and expenditures is often presented as follows:

City of Why
General Fund
Statement of Revenues and Expenditures
For the Year Ending June 30, 1986

	Budget	Actual	Variance
Revenues			
Property taxes	$ 900,000	$ 890,000	$ (10,000)
Income taxes	2,000,000	2,030,000	30,000
.	.	.	.
.	.	.	.
.	.	.	.
Miscellaneous collections	10,000	11,000	1,000
Total revenues	$10,000,000	$10,050,000	$ 50,000
Expenditures and encumbrances			
Police salaries	$ 400,000	$ 410,000	$ 10,000
Fire salaries	200,000	190,000	(10,000)
.	.	.	.
.	.	.	.
.	.	.	.
Miscellaneous expenses	5,000	6,000	1,000
Total expenditures and encumbrances	$ 9,980,000	$ 9,970,000	$ (10,000)
Excess of revenues over expenditures	$ 20,000	$ 80,000	$ 60,000

Note the emphasis on cash flow and budget control and the omission of depreciation on fixed assets and other noncash expenses.

SUMMARY

- The major difference between nonprofit organizations and profit-oriented businesses is the nonprofit organization's lack of an ownership group that expects a return on its investment in the form of profits.
- Depreciation is unnecessary for general government operations because matching revenues with specific utilization of fixed assets is without meaning.
- The concept of service provided is critical (usually measured by amount spent on the service), as is control over expenditures through the budgeting process.
- Accrual or modified accrual accounting is employed by nonprofit organizations with normal accounting for fixed assets and depreciation used only for those funds representing auxiliary operations of these organizations such as universities, hospitals, and voluntary health and welfare units.

EXERCISES

G-E1. The city government of Somewhere adopted the following budget for its 1986–87 fiscal year:

Estimated revenues	$15,000,000
Estimated expenditures	$14,950,000

Prepare the journal entry(s) necessary to record the budget estimates for the City of Somewhere.

G-E2. During the 1986–87 fiscal year, the city treasurer of Greenleaf purchased a new microcomputer for her office. The sequence of purchase commitments and decisions was as follows:

June 15 An order was placed for a new microcomputer system with Small Business Systems, Inc., at an estimated cost of $7,600.

July 10 The microcomputer was received by the treasurer along with a bill for the actual cost of $7,500.

July 20 A check for $7,500 was sent in payment by the City of Greenleaf to Small Business Systems.

Prepare any journal entries necessary to record the sequence of purchase commitments and decisions.

G-E3. On February 2, 1986, the City of Smalltown is notified that it should receive one million dollars in property taxes during its fiscal year ending January 31, 1987. During 1987, the City receives one million dollars in tax payments. Prepare any journal entries necessary to record the revenue estimate and its collection.

G-E4. During its fiscal year ending June 30, 1986, the following amounts were recorded by the city of Cando:

Estimated revenue	$7,500,000
Actual revenue	$7,400,000
Budgeted expenditures	$7,450,000
Actual expenditures	$7,300,000
Encumbrances, June 30, 1986	$ 50,000
Fund balance, June 30, 1985	$ 250,000

Prepare closing entries for the City of Cando for the fiscal year ending June 30, 1986.

G-E5. Identify how each of the following expenditures is handled in a general governmental fund under modified accrual accounting:

a. Purchase of a building
b. Purchase of supplies
c. Long-term borrowing
d. Receipt of cash

GLOSSARY

Accelerated Depreciation Method
A depreciation method that yields a greater expense in the early years of an asset's useful life than in the later years.

Account
A place to collect and record data arising from transactions.

Account Balance
The total amount in an account at a point in time.

Account Entry
The recording of data in an account.

Accounting Controls
Methods and procedures an organization uses to safeguard assets and to ensure the accuracy and reliability of its financial records.

Accounting Cycle
The sequence of events beginning with initial recognition of transactions and ending with financial statement preparation.

Accounting Entity
The organization that is being accounted for.

Accounting Equation
Assets = Liabilities + Owners' Equity. This equation is the basis of conventional accounting.

Accounting Worksheet
An informal document used by accountants to organize their work.

Accounts Payable
Future obligations to remit cash to suppliers for previous purchases.

Accounts Receivable
Amounts owed to an entity by customers from past credit sales.

Accounts Receivable Turnover
Credit sales divided by average net accounts receivable.

Accrual Basis
The method of accounting where transactions are recognized whenever cash is exchanged or the right to receive money or the obligation to pay money is established.

Accumulated Depreciation
The sum of all prior periods' depreciation expense.

Acid-Test Ratio
(Cash plus receivables plus marketable securities) divided by current liabilities.

Active Partners
Those partners actively involved in the day-to-day operations of a partnership.

Activity Ratios
See Turnover Ratios.

Actual Cost System
A cost system where only actual product cost data for labor, materials, and overhead are accumulated.

Adjusted Gross Income
Gross income minus allowed deductions from gross income.

Adjusted Trial Balance
A trial balance that combines original account balances with end-of-period adjustments.

Adjusting the Accounts
The periodic procedure by which accounting records are updated to reflect all transactions occurring up to a particular point in time.

Administrative Controls
Methods and procedures designed to monitor the efficiency of management's authorization procedures and the adherence of workers to those authorizations.

Administrative Costs
Those expenditures incurred for general administration of the company.

Aging of Accounts Receivable Method
A method of estimating bad debts expense where the estimate is based on past collection experience for accounts receivable.

All Financial Resources Concept
The preparation concept for the statement of changes in financial position where all significant changes are included whether or not cash or working capital is affected.

All-Inclusive Concept of Net Income
A method of determining net income where all unusual and nonrecurring items are included in the calculation of net income.

Allocation Base
The activity measurement used to allocate variable overhead costs to production.

Allowance Method
A bookkeeping procedure where estimates of bad debts are made in the same period in which the credit sales giving rise to the bad debts are made.

Amortization
The process of recognizing and measuring the periodic decline in future usefulness of intangible assets.

Analysis of Accounts Method
A method of projecting fixed and variable costs that relies on management's review and classification of accounts as either representing fixed or variable cost elements.

Annuity
A periodic series of equal payments.

Applications Controls
In a data processing environment, the methods and procedures designed to control some particular accounting task.

Appropriation of Retained Earnings
A restriction on the amount of assets represented by retained earnings that are available for dividends.

Appropriations
The estimated obligations to be incurred and the legal authorization to expend resources in a nonprofit entity.

Articles of Incorporation
The document that provides the legal framework for the operation of the corporation.

Asset
A resource controlled solely by an organization that is expected to provide future economic benefits.

Audit Trail
The forms and records that allow the accountant to trace an original transaction forward to a summarized total or to follow a summarized total back to the original transaction.

Authorized Shares
The number of shares of each category of stock that a corporation can issue.

Average Accounting Rate of Return
A technique that ranks investment proposals based on their average annual profit over the life of the project in relation to the project's average cost.

Bad Debt Expense
The estimated amount of uncollectible accounts for a given time period.

Balance Sheet
See Statement of Financial Position.

Bank Reconciliation
A report prepared to explain the differences between the balances in a firm's cash account and in the company's account as shown on the bank statement at a certain point in time.

Bank Statement
A summarization of transactions in a bank account issued by a bank to its customer.

Batch Processing
A method of processing data in which a large number of similar transactions are collected and then processed together.

Bearer Bond
See Coupon Bond.

Board of Directors
A body elected by the shareholders to strategically manage the company on their behalf.

Bond
A promise to pay a given sum of money at some future point and to pay periodic interest amounts for the use of the funds until loan repayment.

Bond Certificate
A document providing evidence of the issuer's debt to the investor.

Bond Indenture
The master agreement between the bond issuer and the bondholder.

Bond Issue
The total amount borrowed through one group of bonds.

Bondholder
A creditor who lends money by purchasing bonds.

Book Value
The amount at which an item is carried in the accounting records and reported in accounting statements.

Book Value Per Share
Common shareholders' equity divided by number of shares outstanding.

Borrower
One who borrows assets, usually cash.

Breakeven Analysis
Analysis of the amount of sales required to cover all fixed and variable costs with no resulting profit.

Breakeven Point
The point at which revenues and costs are equal.

Budgeted Income Statement
A projected income statement covering anticipated future transactions.

Budgeted Statement of Financial Position
A projected statement of financial position for anticipated future transactions.

Budgeting
A continuous process by which an organization attempts to anticipate the future and to see if the future, when it comes around, is as planned.

Bylaws
Rules established by the board of directors for operation of a corporation.

Call Premium on Bonds
The penalty payment required for the privilege of early repayment of callable bonds.

Call Premium on Stock
The difference between the par value of callable preferred stock and the amount that must be paid to the shareholders if a company decides to repurchase its callable preferred stock.

Callable Bond
A bond that provides for early repayment at the option of the issuer.

Callable Preferred Stock
Preferred stock that can be repurchased by the issuing corporation at its option.

Capital Account
An account that shows each partner's accumulated personal investment.

Capital Asset
An asset that is not inventory, real estate or depreciable property used in trade or business, accounts receivable, some artistic works, or some government documents.

Capital Budgeting
The process of comparing alternative capital expenditures and making decisions as to their desirability.

Capital Expenditures
Investments that have a useful life to the company of several years—primarily expenditures for property, plant, and equipment.

Capital Expenditures Budget
A plan that evaluates the desirability of incurring expenditures on plant, equipment, buildings, and so on, over a long time period.

Capital Lease
A lease that is, in substance, a sale of property from the lessor to the lessee.

Capital Project Funds
Funds used to account for the receipt and use of resources in specific support of capital facilities construction in a nonprofit entity.

Capital Stock
All of the firm's stock taken collectively.

Capitalized Expenditures
All expenditures that are added to an asset account rather than to an expense account.

Carrying Value
The amount at which an item is valued on an entity's books and reported on the financial statements.

Carrying Value of Bonds
Face amount of the bonds less any unamortized discount or plus any unamortized premium.

Cash Basis
The method of accounting where transaction recognition is restricted to those occasions when cash is exchanged.

Cash Breakeven Point
(Fixed costs minus any noncash expenses) divided by contribution margin or contribution margin ratio.

Cash Dividend
Dividends that are paid in cash.

Cell
A spot at the intersection of a row and column on a spreadsheet.

Central Processing Unit (CPU)
The heart of a computer consisting of an arithmetic-logic unit, a control unit, and primary memory.

Chart of Accounts
The total list of accounts of an organization.

Check
A written command to a bank from its customer (depositor) to pay a certain sum of money to a person or organization.

Classified Financial Statements
Financial statements where accounts are grouped by category for presentation within the statements.

Classified Statement of Financial Position
A statement of financial position that groups assets and sources of assets by type for presentation.

Closing the Accounts
The process of summarizing revenue and expense account totals into retained earnings.

Collection Period
365 divided by accounts receivable turnover.

Collusion
When two or more employees of an organization conspire to circumvent the company's system of internal control.

Common Stock
Stock that usually gives its holders voting rights and represents the residual owners' equity in the corporation.

Common-Size Statements
Statements in which each item is expressed as a percentage of some aggregate number in the statement.

Comparative Financial Statements
A company's statements presented for two or more accounting periods so that dollar and percentage changes can be analyzed.

Compound Interest
Interest calculations where the principal amount includes accumulated interest that has not been withdrawn or paid to the investor.

Conservatism Convention
The convention that accountants are prudent or cautious in their approach to financial reporting. It means that, in general, the accountant will select the alternative that has the least favorable impact on income.

Consigned Goods
Goods shipped from a supplier to a seller that remain the property of the supplier until sold.

Consistency Principle
The general requirement that accounting systems be operated and accounting reports be prepared in a similar manner from year to year.

Consolidated Financial Statements
Integrated financial statements that are the result of adding together the parent's and the subsidiary's separate statements.

Constant-Dollar Accounting
See General Price-Level Accounting.

Contingent Liabilities
Liabilities that arise from past activities where future outcomes and amounts owed are uncertain.

Contra-account
An account whose balance is offset against another account—the primary account—to determine the primary account's net book value.

Contribution Margin
The difference between a product's selling price and its variable cost per unit.

Contribution Margin Ratio
Contribution margin per unit divided by selling price per unit.

Control
Monitoring actual events to see if they turned out as planned.

Controlling
Making sure that plans are completed and goals are achieved.

Conversion Costs
Direct labor plus factory overhead costs.

Convertible Bond
A bond that can be traded for stock at the option of the bondholder.

Convertible Preferred Stock
Stock that can be exchanged for common stock or cash at the option of the holder, generally within a specified period of time.

Copyright
The right granted by the federal government to a writer or artist to control the use of his or her work.

Corporate Charter
The document that serves to create the corporation and grants it the right to do business.

Corporation
An artificial legal entity distinct from its owners and representatives.

Cost
The amount paid to acquire an asset or service.

Cost Center
A subunit in an organization that has primary responsibility for the incurrence of cost.

Cost Method
An accounting method for long-term investments in which the only income recognized by the investor is dividends and the long-term investment account is valued on the basis of the lower-of-cost-or-market rule.

Cost Method of Accounting for Treasury Stock
A bookkeeping method where the total cost of purchasing treasury stock is charged to the treasury stock account.

Cost Objective
The item or object for which a cost measurement is being made.

Cost of Capital
The average cost of obtaining long-term funds from investors and creditors.

Cost of Goods Sold
The amount paid to suppliers for merchandise sold to customers.

Cost-Volume-Profit Analysis
An examination of how profits change with changes in volume.

Coupon Bond
A bond that is issued with coupons attached covering interest payments over the life of the bond.

Coupons
Future-dated checks attached to a bond and payable on the date specified for the interest due on that date.

Credit
An accounting term meaning right side or increase in the right side of an account.

Credit Memorandum
A form issued by a bank when it makes deposits directly to a customer's account from a third party.

Creditor
Lender of assets to a business.

Cumulative Preferred Stock
A preferred stock issue where all dividends not paid in prior years must be paid along with the current year's dividends before the common stockholders can receive any dividends.

Current Assets
Assets that an entity expects to use or convert to cash within one year.

Current Liabilities
Obligations that must be repaid within one year.

Current Operating Method of Net Income
A method of determining net income where only items arising from normal operations are included in the calculation of net income. All unusual and nonrecurring events are reported directly in retained earnings.

Current Rate
The term applied to the foreign exchange rate in effect on the date of financial statement preparation.

Current Rate Approach
A method of translating statements from one currency to another in which all accounts are translated at the exchange rate in effect on the statement date.

Current Ratio
Current assets divided by current liabilities.

Current-Cost Accounting
An approach to accounting that ignores historical costs and restates accounts in terms of their current market values.

Current-Noncurrent Approach
A method of translating financial statements from one currency to another in which all current items are translated at the exchange rate in effect on the statement date and all other items are translated at the exchange rate in effect when they were acquired.

Current-Value Accounting
See Current-cost Accounting

CVP Chart
A graphical approach to cost-volume-profit analysis that charts volume on the horizontal axis and total revenues or total costs on the vertical axis.

Data Base
An integrated set of files that have logical interrelationships.

Debenture Bond
See Unsecured Bond.

Debit
An accounting term meaning left side or increase in the left side of an account.

Debit Memorandum
A form issued to indicate a charge against a customer's account.

Debt Ratio
Total debt divided by total assets.

Debt Service Funds
Funds that are used to account for the accumulation and use of resources for the payment of general obligation long-term debt including both principal and interest for a nonprofit entity.

Declining-Balance Method
A depreciation method that determines depreciation expense by multiplying a percentage (usually 150 or 200 percent of the straight-line rate) times an asset's book value at the beginning of each period.

Deductions From Gross Income
Deductions that are subtracted from gross income to arrive at adjusted gross income.

Default
Term applied when repayment of a debt is not made on or before the due date.

Deferred Income Taxes
The difference between income taxes actually paid in a period and tax expense computed on the basis of accounting income reported in that same period.

Deferred Revenue
Revenue received before completion of the earnings process.

Dependency Exemption
A deduction from adjusted gross income granted to taxpayers for each qualified dependent.

Depletion
The recognition that a naturally occurring asset has been reduced and some of the asset is now inventory.

Deposit in Transit
A deposit that a firm has recorded in its cash account but that the firm's bank has not yet recorded in its accounting records.

Deposit Slip
A listing of cash and checks to be deposited in a bank. Used to deposit currency and checks received by a business from its customers.

Depreciable Cost
Acquisition cost of an asset less the asset's residual value.

Depreciation
The accounting process by which the cost of a long-term asset is allocated to expense over the asset's useful life.

Differential Analysis
An examination of the divergences in expected revenues and costs of two alternatives.

Differential Costs
Those costs that are different between the alternatives and are relevant to a decision.

Direct Cost Method
A method of allocating costs from service departments to manufacturing departments.

Direct Costing
See Variable Costing.

Direct Costs
Those costs that can be physically traced to a cost objective.

Direct Labor
Total labor charges for those employees who work with direct materials to convert them into finished goods.

Direct Labor Rate Standard
The normal pay rate per hour of labor.

Direct Labor Rate Variance
The difference between actual direct labor cost per hour and the standard labor rate.

Direct Labor Usage (Efficiency) Standard
The expected amount of direct labor hours required to produce one unit of output.

Direct Labor Usage (Efficiency) Variance
The difference between the standard amount of labor required to produce a given amount of output and the actual amount of labor used.

Direct Materials
All of the important raw materials that can be traced directly to the manufacture of a product.

Direct Materials Price Standard
The expected cost per unit of direct materials.

Direct Materials Price Variance
The difference between actual materials price and standard materials price.

Direct Materials Usage Standard
The amount of direct materials expected to be used to produce one unit of output.

Direct Materials Usage Variance
The difference between the amount of direct materials used and the standard expectation.

Direct Write-off Method
A bookkeeping procedure where bad debt expense is not recognized until evidence of noncollectibility of customer accounts appears.

Discount on Bonds
The excess of the face amount of a bond over the actual cash provided by creditors when the bond is issued.

Discounted Note
See Noninterest-Bearing Note.

Discretionary Cost Center
A cost center that does not exhibit a direct relationship between input and output.

Dishonored Note
A note receivable that is not paid when due.

Disk Pack
Several magnetic disks mounted together on a central shaft.

Dividend
Distribution of assets from a corporation's prior earnings to the owners.

Dividend Payout
Dividends divided by net earnings.

Dividend Yield
Dividends per share divided by market value per share.

Dividends in Arrears
Dividends on cumulative preferred stock not paid out in prior years.

Dot-matrix Printers
Printers that form each character as a pattern of dots.

Double-Declining-Balance Method
A depreciation method that determines depreciation expense by multiplying 200 percent of the straight-line rate times an asset's book value at the beginning of the period.

Double-Entry System
A method of recording transactions whereby each transaction is recorded twice.

Drawee
An entity—usually a bank—required to pay the amount of a check.

Drawer
A person who fills out and signs a check.

Drawings
Amounts partners withdraw from a partnership for their personal use.

Drawing Account
An account used to record a partner's drawings; a contra-account to the partner's capital account.

Due Date
The specified time when repayment on a note is due.

Earnings Yield
Earnings per share available to common shareholders divided by market value per share.

Effective Rate of Interest
The actual rate of interest paid on debt.

Encumbrance
The commitment to expend funds recognized when an expenditure decision is made rather than when goods are actually purchased or received.

Engineered Cost Center
A cost center where there is a direct and observable relationship between the costs incurred in that unit and the output provided.

Equity Method
An accounting method for long-term investments where the investor includes its proportionate share of the income of the investee in its income whether or not any dividends are actually received.

Equivalent Units
The number of complete units that would have been produced if all work had been directed toward producing completed units, as if there had been no beginning or ending inventories of partially completed units worked on during the period.

Exclusions
Exceptions allowed by law to be omitted from gross income.

Expected Value
The sum of the products of specific outcome possibilities and their associated probability of occurrence.

Expenses
Assets consumed or traded to secure revenues.

Exposure
A measurement of the amounts in a firm's accounts that are subject to financial statement translation at current rates.

Extraordinary Items
Items that are both unusual in nature and infrequent in occurrence for a particular company.

F. O. B. Destination
A selling term that means ownership to goods does not change from the seller to the purchaser until the goods are delivered by the shipping company to the purchaser's place of business.

F. O. B. Shipping Point
A selling term that means ownership to goods changes from the seller to the purchaser when the goods are turned over to the shipping company.

Face Amount of the Bond Issue
The total amount specified in the bond issue.

Face Rate of Interest
The rate of interest agreed to in a debt instrument.

Face Value
The amount of money stated on a debt or investment instrument as the total owed or invested.

Federal Insurance Contributions Act (FICA)
The law regulating Social Security taxes and benefits.

Federal Unemployment Tax Act (FUTA)
The federal law regulating unemployment taxation at the federal level.

Fiduciary Funds
Funds used to account for assets held by governmental units as a trustee or agent for someone else.

Finished Goods Inventory
Inventory of completely finished but unsold units.

First-in, First-out (FIFO)
An inventory cost flow assumption by which the value of ending inventory is determined from the most recent purchase costs and the cost of goods sold is determined from the oldest purchase costs in goods available for sale.

Fixed Asset Turnover
Total sales divided by average fixed assets.

Fixed Assets
See Long-Lived Assets.

Fixed Cost
A cost that remains constant over a particular range of output.

Fixed Factory Overhead Budget Standard
The total expected spending for fixed overhead.

Fixed Factory Overhead Volume Standard
An estimate of the capacity needed for production.

Fixed Overhead Budget Variance
The difference between the amounts paid for items included in fixed overhead and the standard cost of the items.

Fixed Overhead Volume Variance
The dollar measurement of over or under utilization of plant capacity.

Flexible Budget
A budget that provides guidelines for different levels of activity.

Flexible Overhead Budget
An overhead budget that shows the budgeted amount of overhead at different levels of activity.

Footing
The process of adding up a column of figures.

Foreign Corrupt Practices Act
The 1977 law making internal accounting controls mandatory for many U. S. companies.

Forward Exchange Contract (Future)
The purchase or sale of foreign currency for future delivery.

Forward Rate
The price quoted now for future purchase or sale of a foreign currency.

Four-Way Analysis of Overhead Variances
A method of analyzing factory overhead that divides overhead into fixed and variable portions and further divides each portion into spending and usage variances.

Franchise
The right granted to sell specified products under a specified name in a specified geographic area.

Freight-in
Transportation charges paid by the purchaser.

Freight-out
Transportation charges paid by the seller.

Full-Absorption Costing
A method of product costing that includes direct labor, direct materials, and both variable and fixed manufacturing overhead in product cost.

Functional Currency
The currency in use in the primary economic environment of an overseas operation.

Functional Currency Approach
An approach to accounting for foreign operations where the overseas operation reports its results in the currency used in its primary economic environment.

Functional Pricing
A method of estimating replacement cost where the replacement cost is determined as a percentage of the cost of a newer, technologically superior asset.

Fund Balance
The assets of a fund minus the fund's liabilities. Corresponds to owners' equity accounts of a corporation.

Funds
Independent accounting units within nonprofit organizations.

Future Value
The value of an investment at a point in time subsequent to the date at which the investment is made.

Gain
The excess of assets received over those given up in a transaction not part of normal business operations.

General Controls
In a data processing environment, the methods and procedures relating to the overall control of all data processing activities.

General Fund
A fund that is used to account for all unrestricted financial resources that support the general operations of a nonprofit entity.

General Journal
A book of record used to record transactions in chronological order.

General Ledger
A book containing the complete set of accounts for an entity.

General Price-Level Accounting
An approach to accounting where adjustments are made to historical costs to account for the general effects of inflation.

General Price-Level Gains and Losses
Gains and losses that arise from holding monetary items during periods when price levels change.

Generally Accepted Accounting Principles
The assumptions, conventions, practices, and authoritarian pronouncements that form the basis for accounting practices.

Goal
Something you would like to accomplish within a particular time period.

Going Concern Assumption
The assumption that the accounting entity will continue to operate in the future.

Goods Available for Sale
The sum of beginning inventory and purchases.

Goodwill
Any factor that allows a firm to earn more than a normal return on assets for the type of business in which it is engaged.

Government Funds
The most widely used funds in accounting for a nonprofit entity.

Gross Earnings
All that a worker earns in a given time period. Generally equal to regular pay plus overtime pay, if any, plus, if applicable items such as holiday pay, bonuses, and meal allowances.

Gross Income
All income from whatever source derived.

Gross Margin
See Gross Profit.

Gross Margin Percentage
See Gross Profit Percentage.

Gross Method of Recording Purchases
The bookkeeping procedure where purchases are initially

recorded at total purchase price and purchase discounts are recorded separately if payment is made within the discount period.

Gross Method of Recording Sales
The bookkeeping procedure where sales are recorded at gross sales price and sales discounts are recorded only when taken by customers.

Gross Profit
Sales revenue minus cost of goods sold. Also known as gross margin.

Gross Profit Margin
(Sales minus cost of goods sold) divided by sales.

Gross Profit Method
A method of estimating ending inventory value by using the relationship among sales dollars, cost of goods sold, and gross profit.

Gross Profit Percentage
Total markup from purchase cost of goods sold expressed as a percentage of selling price. (sales price—purchase cost)/sales price.

Gross Selling Price
The initial price charged to customers for goods.

Hard Copy
Printed computer output.

Hedging
The process of protecting transactions against future fluctuations in the market.

Hi-Lo Method
A method of projecting fixed and variable costs from a line plotted from the costs of the highest and lowest levels of production.

Historical Cost
The accounting convention that measures the value of an item within the accounting system by reference to its original purchase price.

Holding Gains and Losses
Cost savings and dissavings that occur as a result of holding nonmonetary items.

Imprest System
A system that establishes an account or fund at a certain level and that requires periodic replenishment to that level.

Income
The excess of revenue and gains over expenses and losses for a given time period.

Income Statement
A statement presenting an entity's revenue, expense, gain, and loss information for a given time period.

Incremental Analysis
See Differential Analysis.

Incremental Cash Flows
Cash that is either received or spent as a result of making an investment decision.

Indirect Costs
Those costs that can not be physically traced to a cost objective but nonetheless are allocated to cost objectives on some basis.

Indirect Labor
All labor costs incurred in the manufacturing process that are not directly traceable to units produced.

Indirect Materials
Those material costs incurred in a manufacturing process that are not traced directly to production of given units or batches of products.

Input
Messages sent to a computer.

Input Controls
Methods and procedures designed to provide reasonable certainty that data received for processing has been properly authorized, converted into machine-sensible form, and identified.

Intangible Assets
Assets that do not possess physical characteristics.

Intercompany Analysis
Comparing a company's performance against similar companies or industry averages.

Interest
Fee charged for the use of money for a period of time.

Interest-Bearing Note
A note where interest is added to the face amount of the note to determine the total owed at the due date.

Internal Control
The plan of organization and all of the coordinate methods and measures adopted within a business to safeguard its assets, check the accuracy and reliability of its accounting data, and promote operational efficiency and adherence to management's policies.

Internal Rate of Return
The discount rate that will equate the present value of a project's cash inflows with the present value of the cash outflows required by the project.

International Accounting Standards Committee
An international committee seeking to set and secure compliance with international accounting standards and procedures.

Interperiod Tax Allocation
The term applied to accounting for the temporary differences between income tax expense shown on

accounting income statements and income taxes actually paid.

Intracompany Analysis
Evaluation of a company's financial performance against its own past performance or stated objective.

Intraperiod Tax Allocation
The distribution of the current year's tax expense among the components of net income responsible for the tax.

Inventory
Assets held by a company either for resale or for use in production.

Inventory Turnover
Cost of goods sold divided by average inventory.

Investment Center
A subunit in an organization where the manager is responsible for profits and the level of investment (asset base) of the subunit.

Investment in Bonds
The lending of money through bond acquisitions.

Issuance of Bonds
The act of borrowing money through long-term debt.

Issued at a Discount
The term applied when a bond is issued for less than its face amount.

Issued at a Premium
The term applied when a bond is issued for more than its face amount.

Issued at Par
The term applied when investors value a bond at its face amount when it is issued.

Issued Shares
Shares that have been issued at some time to the investing public.

Issuer of Bonds
The corporation borrowing money through the issuance of bonds.

Itemized deductions
Specifically permitted items that can be subtracted from adjusted gross income to reduce an individual's taxable base.

Job-Order Cost Sheet
A sheet that moves with the product as it is being produced and functions as a subsidiary ledger account for inventory.

Job-Order Costing
A method of cost accounting where direct labor, direct material costs, and factory overhead are physically traced to individual jobs or products.

Joint Costs
All processing costs up to the split-off point.

Joint Products
Different products that are the result of processing a single raw material.

Key Factor
See Limiting Factor.

Kilobyte (K)
A common measure of computer memory consisting of approximately one thousand bytes or characters.

Last-in, First-out (LIFO)
An inventory cost flow assumption by which the value of ending inventory is determined from the oldest purchase costs and cost of goods sold is determined from the most recent purchase costs in cost of goods available for sale.

Lease
A transfer of the right to use certain property for a specified time.

Leasehold Improvement
An improvement made by a lessee that becomes a permanent part of leased property.

Lender
One who lends resources, usually cash, to another.

Letter-quality Printers
Printers that produce documents that look as if they were produced on a typewriter.

Leverage
A term that refers to the amount of debt a company uses in its capital structure.

Leverage Ratios
Ratios that measure the extent to which a company uses debt and the impact of leverage on the company's ability to meet its interest payments.

Liabilities
The dollar amount representation of assets provided by creditors and claims of the creditors against the entity's assets.

Limiting Factor
In budgeting, the starting point for the budget process.

Liquidating Dividend
The term applied to a dividend distribution that reduces paid-in capital such as when the firm is permanently reducing its operations or going out of business.

Liquidation
A process whereby all assets are converted into cash, liabilities are satisfied and remaining cash is distributed to the owners.

Liquidity
A term that refers to how readily convertible a company's

assets are to cash—the more convertible the assets, the more liquid they are.

Liquidity Ratios
Ratios that provide insight into a firm's short-run solvency.

Long-Lived Assets
Assets expected to yield economic benefits to an organization for longer than one year or one operating cycle.

Long-term Assets
Assets that will be useful to an entity for more than one year.

Long-term Liabilities
Liabilities that will not be repaid within the next year.

Loss
The deficiency of assets received over those given up in a transaction not a part of normal business operations.

Lower of Cost or Market (LCM) Rule
A rule that assigns the lower of the historical purchase cost or current replacement value to an item for financial statement purposes.

Magnetic Disk
A metal or plastic platter coated with ferric oxide used as a secondary storage device within a computer system.

Magnetic Tape
A continuous plastic strip treated with an iron oxide coating used as a form of secondary storage in a computer system.

Mainframes
Large computers.

Maker of a Note Payable
A person who receives a loan of assets, usually cash, giving a promissory note in exchange.

Management Accounting
Accounting directed at individual's internal to an organization.

Management by Exception
The focusing of management's attention on areas that show deviations from standards.

Manufacturing Overhead
All manufacturing costs other than direct materials and direct labor.

Margin of Safety
The difference between sales at the breakeven point and actual or expected sales.

Marginal Tax Rate
The tax rate that is applied to the last dollar of taxable income earned.

Market Rate of Interest
See Effective Rate of Interest

Market Ratios
Ratios that provide information on the attractiveness of a stock investment.

Market Value Per Share
The price at which the sale of a share of stock is occurring at the stock exchange.

Marketable Debt Securities
Notes payable, certificates of deposit, or any other item that would eventually be repaid by a debtor.

Marketable Equity Securities
Capital stock of an outside entity.

Master Budget
A comprehensive picture of the results expected from a firm's future operations.

Matching Principle
The principle that requires all expenses to be recognized in the same time period as their associated revenues are recognized.

Materiality Convention
The convention that allows the accountant to overlook minor items not reported in conformity with generally accepted accounting principles.

Maturity Value
Total amount to be paid on a note. Includes both principle and interest.

Megabyte (M)
A common measure of computer memory consisting of approximately one million bytes or characters.

Microcomputers
Small computers.

Minority Interest
A separate class of owners on consolidated statements of financial position that have no rights with respect to the primary company around which the consolidation is built.

Mixed Costs
Costs that are neither exclusively fixed nor exclusively variable.

Modified Accrual Basis Accounting
The recommended basis of accounting for the general fund of a nonprofit entity.

Monetary Items
Accounts that represent the right to receive or the obligation to pay a fixed number of dollars.

Monetary-Nonmonetary Approach
A method of translating statements from one currency to another in which all monetary items are translated at the rate in effect on the statement date and all nonmonetary items are translated at the historical rates in effect when the items were obtained.

Money Measurement
Transformation of economic events into useful information in dollar terms.

Monitor
A TV-like screen used to communicate computer output.

Mortgage
A borrower's pledge of title to property made as security for a loan.

Mortgage Bond
See Secured Bond.

Multi-Stage Process Costing
A process cost system used when a product must pass through several different process steps before it is completed.

Multinational Enterprises
Enterprises with holdings in more than one country.

Mutual Agency
The characteristic of a partnership that each partner has the power to represent the firm.

Necessity Projects
Capital expenditure projects that involve expenditures that cannot be justified in terms of profit improvement.

Net Book Value
See Book Value.

Net Earnings
Gross pay less all deductions for a worker.

Net Income
Operating revenue minus operating expenses plus gains minus losses.

Net Method of Recording Purchases
The bookkeeping procedure where purchases are initially recorded net of permitted discounts and only those discounts not taken are recorded in the accounts.

Net Method of Recording Sales
The bookkeeping procedure where sales are recorded net of permitted discounts and sales discounts not taken by customers are recorded separately.

Net Present Value
The difference between the present value (today's dollars) of the cash inflows and the cash outflows of a project.

Net Purchase Cost
Gross price paid for merchandise plus any freight charges incurred less any price, quantity, or payment discounts granted and less any goods returned to the supplier.

Net Realizable Value
The amount of future cash inflows that an asset is expected to generate.

Net Sales
Gross selling price for goods minus sales discounts minus sales returns and allowances.

No Par Stock
Stock issued without an assigned par value.

Nominal Accounts
See Temporary Accounts.

Nominal Measures
Measures that use dollar valuations without concern for the possible inequalities of purchasing power.

Nominal Rate of Interest
See Face Rate of Interest.

Noncumulative Preferred Stock
A preferred stock that does not guarantee that its holders receive dividends in arrears before the common shareholders receive any dividends.

Noninterest-Bearing Note
Notes where the face value includes the interest. Maturity value of the note is equal to the face amount.

Nonmonetary Items
Accounts whose nominal market values are impacted by inflation.

Normal Cost System
A cost system where overhead is allocated to products on a predetermined basis rather than on an actual basis.

Note Payable
A liability represented by a written and signed promise to pay a stated amount of money at a stated time or upon demand, either without interest or with a stated interest rate.

Notes Receivable
Represent formal loans to other entities.

Objectivity Principle
The accounting principle that requires basing accounting reports on historical cost information obtained from written documents.

Operating Budget
A plan that describes the desired future operations in terms of expected revenues and costs.

Operating Income
Operating revenues minus operating expenses.

Operating Lease
A lease that transfers the right to use property but not the ownership of the property.

Opportunity Costs
The benefit foregone by using resources in one way as opposed to another.

Ordinary Income
Any income that is included in gross income and taxable in full.

Ordinary Note
See Interest Bearing Note

Out-of-pocket Costs
Costs that require the use of cash.

Output
Messages produced for users by a computer.

Output Controls
Methods and procedures designed to assure the accuracy and quality of data processing results and to guarantee that only authorized personnel receive the output.

Outstanding Check
A check that has been written and issued by a firm but has not been paid by the bank.

Outstanding Shares
The amount of stock that actually is in the hands of investors at a particular moment and on which a dividend could be paid.

Overhead Allocation Base
A base for assignment of overhead costs to production.

Owners' Equity
Representation of the total amount of assets provided by owners to a corporation through either investment or undistributed earnings of the business and the claims of the owners against an entity's assets.

Paid-in Capital
The term applied to the total amount of assets provided by owners in exchange for their original ownership interest in a corporation.

Par Value per Share
An artificial amount per share required by the laws of the state of incorporation.

Parent Company
A corporation that acquires over 50 percent of the voting stock of another corporation.

Participating Preferred Stock
A stock that offers its holders the right to receive additional dividends when the total dividends declared exceed the normal preferred amount.

Partnership
An association of two or more persons to carry on as co-owners of a business for profit.

Partnership Agreement
A contract between the partners specifying how the business is to be run.

Patent
The right granted by the federal government to an inventor to control a design or invention.

Payback Method
A method of evaluating alternative investment opportunities in terms of how quickly each project recoups its initial investment.

Payee
One who receives payment.

Payer
One who provides payment.

Payroll Register
A listing of the gross earnings, the deductions and withholdings, and the net earnings payable of each worker. Also known as a payroll journal.

Percentage of Sales Method
A method of estimating bad debt expense where the estimate is based on past credit sales experience.

Period Costs
Those costs considered an expense of the period in which they are incurred.

Periodic Inventory Method
The method of inventory record keeping where inventory levels are determined at the end of each accounting period, purchases are recorded as made in a separate purchases account, and cost of goods sold is determined by computation.

Permanent Accounts
Accounts whose balances are not closed to retained earnings at the end of each accounting period.

Perpetual Inventory Method
The method of inventory record keeping where each purchase of inventory is separately recorded in the inventory account and the cost of each item sold is entered into the cost of goods sold account at the time of sale.

Perquisites
Noncash benefits given to employees; for example, apartments, chauffeur-driven automobiles, and membership in country clubs.

Personal Exemption
A deduction from adjusted gross income granted to individual taxpayers.

Petty Cash
A special cash fund for paying small expenditures where actual cash is required such as cab fares and small C.O.D. packages.

Plan
A course of action developed by a manager.

Planning
The process of setting goals and developing strategies to accomplish those goals.

Pooling of Interests
A business combination in which the shareholders of the acquired corporation exchange their voting stock for that of the acquiring corporation and little or no cash is exchanged.

Post-closing Trial Balance
A listing of all account balances prepared following completion of the closing process.

Posting
The process of transferring data from the general journal to the general ledger.

Predetermined Overhead Rate
A predetermined amount of overhead charged to each unit produced regardless of actual overhead costs.

Preemptive Right
The right of existing stockholders to maintain their proportionate share of ownership by purchasing shares of stock from any new stock issue before the stock is offered to others.

Preferred Stock
Stock that generally confers some preferential rights to its holders over those of common shareholders but generally lacks voting privileges.

Premium on Bonds
The excess of cash received from investors over the face amount of a bond issue.

Prepaid Expense
Current assets that are paid for before their actual acquisition or use.

Present Value
The current value of amounts to be received or paid in the future discounted at some interest rate; the amount that must be invested today at some interest rate to accumulate to some specified future value.

Price Earnings Ratio
Market value per share divided by earnings per share available to common shareholders.

Primary Memory
The storage area contained inside the central processing unit of a computer.

Prime Costs
Direct materials plus direct labor costs.

Principal
The original amount of money borrowed or invested.

Prior-Period Adjustment
A rare item that is entered directly into retained earnings even under the all-inclusive concept of net income.

Process Costing
A method of cost accounting where material, labor, and overhead costs are accumulated for all units worked on in a department for a given period of time and all units produced are assigned the same average cost for that period.

Processing Controls
Methods and procedures designed to see that the processing has been performed as intended for the particular application.

Product Costs
Those costs associated with the production of inventory, usually inclusive of direct materials, direct labor, and manufacturing overhead.

Profit
See Income.

Profit Center
A subunit in an organization where the manager is responsible for both the generation of revenues and the incurrence of costs.

Profit Improvement Projects
Capital expenditure projects that can be evaluated on the basis of future profit enhancements.

Profit Planning
A modification of breakeven analysis used to analyze the impact of changes in costs or revenues on profits.

Profit-Sharing Ratio
The ratio that determines how profits and losses in a partnership are shared among the partners.

Profitability Index Method
A method of analyzing capital expenditures in which the present value of the cash inflows is divided by the present value of the cash outflows.

Profitability Ratios
Ratios that measure the overall effectiveness of management in operating the business.

Program
Instructions given to a computer to accomplish a given task.

Promissory Note
See Note Payable.

Property, Plant, and Equipment
Long-lived tangible assets used in the operation of a business that are not intended primarily for resale.

Proprietary Funds
Funds used to control governmental operations that are similar to private enterprises.

Purchase Discount
A discount from list price granted for prompt payment.

Purchase Returns and Allowances
The allowances granted by suppliers to purchasers for defective or returned goods.

Purchases
All inventory items acquired from suppliers during a particular time period.

Purchasing Power Gains and Losses
See General Price-Level Gains and Losses.

PV Graph
A variation of a CVP chart where the horizontal axis represents sales and the vertical axis represents profits before taxes.

Random-access Memory (RAM)
Computer storage area available to the user for instructions or data.

Ratio Analysis
An approach to financial statement analysis that examines key relationships by means of ratio comparisons.

Raw Materials
See Direct Materials

Raw Materials Inventory
Materials purchased for use in the production process.

Read-only Memory (ROM)
A memory area that can be read by a computer but the contents cannot be changed by the user's programs or data.

Real Accounts
See Permanent Accounts

Real Measures
Measures using dollar valuations adjusted to create equality of purchasing power.

Real Rate of Interest
See Effective Rate of Interest

Realized Gain/Loss
The difference between the original cost and the sales price of an investment.

Registered Bond
A bond where the issuer keeps a record of the name and address of each bondholder and sends each one an interest check on each interest payment date.

Relevant Range
The range of output for which fixed costs do not change.

Repair Expense
An expenditure for routine maintenance on a long-lived asset.

Replacement Cost
The cost that an organization would incur to replace its existing assets.

Residual Income
The difference between divisional profits and the divisional cost of capital.

Residual Value
See Salvage Value.

Responsibility Accounting
Accounting for responsibility centers.

Responsibility Center
A separate, identifiable segment of an organization that is managed by an individual.

Retail Inventory Method
A method of valuing inventory by which inventory records are maintained at selling prices and are reduced to historical cost by using the ratio of purchase cost to selling price of goods available for sale.

Retained Earnings
The account that represents the portion of the total assets held by a corporation that came from profitable operations.

Return on Equity (ROE)
Net earnings available to common shareholders divided by average common shareholders' equity.

Return on Investment (ROI)
Net earnings divided by average total assets.

Return on Sales
Earnings divided by total revenue (also known as profit margin).

Revenue Center
A subunit of an organization responsible for the generation of revenue.

Revenue Realization
The term applied to the point when the business entity acquires the right to receive payment from its customers.

Revenue Recognition
When revenues are recorded in the accounts. Generally, revenue recognition occurs in accrual accounting when services are rendered or when goods are delivered to customers.

Revenues
Inflows of assets from customers in exchange for goods provided or services rendered.

Risk-Adjusted Discount Rates
Discount rates that are adjusted away from the firm's cost of capital as an adjustment for the risk involved in undertaking a capital expenditure.

Running Balance Ledger Account
A form of ledger account where the account balance is determined and shown following each entry made to the account.

Sales Discounts
Discounts from sales price granted by sellers to buyers in return for prompt payment by the buyers.

Sales Returns and Allowances
The allowances made by sellers for damaged or returned goods.

Salvage Value
The value remaining when a fixed asset's useful life to an enterprise is at an end.

Secondary Storage
Additional memory that is not part of the CPU's primary memory.

Secured Bond
A bond that pledges specific assets to the creditors in the event the bond is not repaid when due.

Selling Costs
Those expenditures required to obtain and fill customer orders for finished goods.

Sensitivity Analysis
A method of using cost-volume-profit analysis to determine the impact of a change in costs or prices on profits.

Serial Bond
A bond issue where repayment occurs over a series of dates.

Shareholder
Part owner or investor in a corporation.

Shutdown Point
The level of activity at which the company becomes indifferent to either continuing operations or closing down.

Silent Partners
Those partners who, although they can participate in certain policy-making decisions, do not work actively in the business.

Simple Interest
Interest where the principal amount used in the computation is the original investment at the beginning of the time period.

Single-stage Process Costing
A process cost system applied when only one product is manufactured, and this product requires only one step in the manufacturing process.

Sinking Fund
Funds set aside each year for repaying a loan at maturity.

Soft Copy
Computer output displayed on a computer's monitor.

Source Documents
Documents used to collect data about a transaction.

Special Assessment Funds
Funds used to account for project construction costs and associated revenue collection and debt repayment for a nonprofit entity where the charges for the project are levied specifically against the properties of the persons benefited by the project.

Special Journal
A journal for keeping records of a specific type.

Special Revenue Funds
Funds used to account for revenues legally restricted for a specific purpose in a nonprofit entity.

Specific Identification Method
An inventory costing method by which the cost of goods sold and ending inventory amounts are determined by tracing the purchase cost of each inventory item as it moves through the business.

Split-Off Point
The point at which joint products reveal themselves as separate substances.

Spot Rate
The rate of exchange of one currency for another that is in effect at any given time.

Spreadsheet Software
An electronic version of the accounting worksheet.

Stable Monetary Unit Assumption
The assumption that the economic value of the dollar does not change over time.

Standard Cost System
A cost system where management collects and reports both actual and predetermined labor, materials, and overhead costs.

Standard Costs
Predetermined estimates of the amounts and costs of raw materials direct labor, and factory overhead.

Standard Overhead Rate
The expected overhead rate per unit of allocation base.

Standard Volume of Output
Selected activity level chosen by managers for product costing purposes.

Stated Value
An arbitrary assignment of value that has no significance in terms of shareholder liability and serves only to limit the amount that can be distributed as dividends.

Statement of Changes in Financial Position
A statement presenting a summary of all significant changes in a company's financial position occurring during a specified time period.

Statement of Cost of Goods Manufactured
An accounting statement that sets forth the details of the cost of goods produced in a given period.

Statement of Financial Position
A listing of the assets, liabilities, and owners' equity accounts at some specified point in time.

Static Budget
A budget process that focuses on one level of corporate activity.

Stock Dividend
A dividend that is paid in stock of the distributing corporation.

Stock Exchange
An organization where stocks are bought and sold.

Stock Split
The division of a company's stock into smaller shares while reducing the par or stated value per share proportionately.

Straight-line Depreciation
The depreciation method that allocates equal amounts of a long-term asset's cost to expense each period of the asset's useful life.

Subsidiary Company
A corporation where over 50 percent of the voting stock is owned by another corporation.

Subsidiary Ledger
A set of accounts that taken collectively equals an overall control account.

Sum-of-the-Years' Digits Method
A depreciation method that determines depreciation expense by multiplying an asset's depreciable cost by the remaining years of the asset's useful life at the beginning of the year divided by the sum-of-the-years' digits in the useful life.

Sunk Costs
Costs that have already been incurred and will not change regardless of the decision made.

T-Account
A simple form of an account shaped like a T.

Taking the Inventory
The process by which inventory items are counted, weighed, or otherwise physically examined.

Tangible Assets
Assets that have physical characteristics that can be seen or touched.

Tax Avoidance
The process of arranging transactions so as to pay the least amount of tax.

Tax Credits
Amounts subtracted from tax that serve to directly reduce the amount of tax paid.

Tax Evasion
Failure to report income earned or inclusion of fictitious expenses or deductions in determination of taxable income.

Tax Planning
A tool which seeks to minimize or defer a taxpayer's liability.

Taxable Income
Income computed in accordance with the provisions of the Internal Revenue Code.

Template
The form created with a spreadsheet that has a certain number of rows and columns with a specific amount of space allocated to each cell and names for the cells, rows, and columns.

Temporal Approach
A modification of the monetary-nonmonetary approach to translation of statements from one currency to another under which assets carried at market values are translated at current rates and other assets are translated at historical rates.

Temporary Accounts
Accounts that are closed to zero at the end of each accounting period with their balances being transferred to retained earnings.

Term Bond
A bond where repayment is made only at one specified future date for the total amount borrowed.

Term of a Note
The period of time between the date on which borrowing occurs and the repayment date.

Terminal
A common computer input device. Can be of many types but most often has a keyboard and a monitor.

Times Interest Earned
Earnings before interest and taxes divided by interest payments.

Timesharing
The term applied when several users are connected to and use the same central processing unit resources within a computer at same time.

Total Asset Turnover
Total sales divided by average total assets.

Trademark
A word, term, symbol, name, or design to identify a product or service.

Transaction
An identifiable economic event or activity that can be measured in money and recorded in the accounting system.

Transfer Price
The internal price paid by one division of a company to obtain goods from another.

Transferred-in Costs
Costs transferred in from earlier process departments to later ones.

Transportation-in
See Freight-in.

Transportation-out
See Freight-out.

Treasury Stock
Shares reacquired by the corporation that originally issued them for purposes other than share retirement.

Trend Percentages
Dollar figures stated as a percentage of some base-year figure.

Trial Balance
A listing of all of the accounts in the general ledger along with the balance in each.

Trustee
A person or organization that represents the interests of third parties.

Turnover Ratios
Ratios that indicate how efficiently management utilizes its assets.

Unearned Revenue
See Deferred Revenue.

Units-of-Production Method
A depreciation method that assigns equal amounts of depreciation expense to each unit of an asset's input or output.

Unrealized Loss
The difference between the original amount paid and the current market value for unsold investments.

Unsecured Bond
A bond that is not secured by the pledge of certain assets to the bondholders in the event of nonpayment by the bond issuer.

Variable (Direct) Costing
A method of product costing that includes only variable manufacturing costs in product cost.

Variable Costs
Costs that change in proportion to changes in output.

Variable Factory Overhead Efficiency Standard
The standard amount of variable factory overhead expected to produce one good unit of output.

Variable Factory Overhead Spending Standard
The expected purchase cost of variable overhead items per unit of allocation base.

Variable Overhead Efficiency Variance
The difference between the actual amounts of variable overhead items used and the standard usage expected for a given level of output.

Variable Overhead Spending Variance
The difference between the actual amounts spent on the variable overhead items used and the standard costs for the collective total.

Variances
Deviations of actual results from standard expectations.

Voucher
A special form prepared to provide control over and authorization for expenditures.

Weighted Average Costing Method
An inventory costing method by which all units sold during a period and all units remaining in physical inventory at the end of the period are assumed to have the same average cost per unit.

Window
A technique that allows a user to view parts of several items (e.g. pages of a large spreadsheet) on the monitor at the same time.

Work in Process
The inventory of products started but not yet finished at a given point in time.

Working Capital
The difference between current assets and current liabilities.

Zero Bracket Amount
A specific amount of deductions automatically granted to each taxpayer.

Zero-Based Budgeting
A method of budgeting that accepts no expenditure as reasonable unless the initiating department can substantiate the need for that recurring expenditure.

INDEX